Winner's Electoral College Vote %	Winner's Popular Vote %	Congress	House Majority Party	House Minority Party	Senate Majority Party	Senate Minority Party
**	No popular	1st	38 Admin†	26 Opp	17 Admin	9 Opp
	vote	2nd	37 Fed††	33 Dem-R	16 Fed	13 Dem-R
**	No popular	3rd	57 Dem-R	48 Fed	17 Fed	13 Dem-R
	vote	4th	54 Fed	52 Dem-R	19 Fed	13 Dem-R
**	No popular	5th	58 Fed	48 Dem-R	20 Fed	12 Dem-R
	vote	6th	64 Fed	42 Dem-R	19 Fed	13 Dem-R
HR**	No popular	7th	69 Dem-R	36 Fed	18 Dem-R	13 Fed
	vote	8th	402 Dem-R	39 Fed	25 Dem-R	9 Fed
92.0	No popular	9th	116 Dem-R	25 Fed	27 Dem-R	7 Fed
	vote	10th	118 Dem-R	24 Fed	28 Dem-R	6 Fed
69.7	No popular	11th	94 Dem-R	48 Fed	28 Dem-R	6 Fed
	vote	12th	108 Dem-R	36 Fed	30 Dem-R	6 Fed
59.0	No popular	13th	112 Dem-R	68 Fed	27 Dem-R	9 Fed
	vote	14th	117 Dem-R	65 Fed	25 Dem-R	11 Fed
84.3	No popular	15th	141 Dem-R	42 Fed	34 Dem-R	10 Fed
	vote	16th	156 Dem-R	27 Fed	35 Dem-R	7 Fed
99.5	No popular	17th	158 Dem-R	25 Fed	44 Dem-R	4 Fed
	vote	18th	187 Dem-R	26 Fed	44 Dem-R	4 Fed
HR	39.1†††	19th	105 Admin	97 Dem-J	26 Admin	20 Dem-J
		20th	119 Dem-J	94 Admin	28 Dem-J	20 Admin
68.2	56.0	21st	139 Dem	74 Nat R	26 Dem	22 Nat R
		22nd	141 Dem	58 Nat R	25 Dem	21 Nat R
76.6	54.5	23rd	147 Dem	53 AntiMas	20 Dem	20 Nat R
		24th	145 Dem	98 Whig	27 Dem	25 Whig
57.8	50.9	25th	108 Dem	107 Whig	30 Dem	18 Whig
		26th	124 Dem	118 Whig	28 Dem	22 Whig
79.6	52.9					
–	52.9	27th	133 Whig	102 Dem	28 Whig	22 Dem
		28th	142 Dem	79 Whig	28 Whig	25 Dem
61.8	49.6	29th	143 Dem	77 Whig	31 Dem	25 Whig
		30th	115 Whig	108 Dem	36 Dem	21 Whig
56.2	47.3	31st	112 Dem	109 Whig	35 Dem	25 Whig
–	–	32nd	140 Dem	88 Whig	35 Dem	24 Whig
85.8	50.9	33rd	159 Dem	71 Whig	38 Dem	22 Whig
		34th	108 Rep	83 Dem	40 Dem	15 Rep
58.8	45.6	35th	118 Dem	92 Rep	36 Dem	20 Rep
		36th	114 Rep	92 Dem	36 Dem	26 Rep
59.4	39.8	37th	105 Rep	43 Dem	31 Rep	10 Dem
		38th	102 Rep	75 Dem	36 Rep	9 Dem
91.0	55.2					
–	–	39th	149 Union	42 Dem	42 Union	10 Dem
		40th	143 Rep	49 Dem	42 Rep	11 Dem
72.8	52.7	41st	149 Rep	63 Dem	56 Rep	11 Dem
		42nd	134 Rep	104 Dem	52 Rep	17 Dem
81.9	55.6	43rd	194 Rep	92 Dem	49 Rep	19 Dem
		44th	169 Rep	109 Dem	45 Rep	29 Dem
50.1	47.9†††	45th	153 Dem	140 Rep	39 Rep	
		46th	149 Dem	130 Rep	42 D	
58.0	48.3	47th	147 Rep	135 Dem		
–	–	48th	197 Dem	118 Rep		
54.6	48.5	49th	183 Dem	140 Rep		
		50th	169 Dem	152 Rep		

D1469606

Source for election data: Svend Peterson, *A Statistical History of American Presidential Elections*. New York: Frederick Ungar Publishing, 1963. Updates: Richard Scammon, *America Votes* 19. Washington D.C.: Congressional Quarterly, 1991; *Congressional Quarterly Weekly Report*, Nov. 7, 1992, p. 3552.

Abbreviations:

Admin = Administration supporters
AntiMas = Anti-Masonic
Dem = Democratic
Dem-R = Democratic-Republican
Fed = Federalist

Dem-J = Jacksonian Democrats
Nat R = National Republican
Opp = Opponents of administration
Rep = Republican
Union = Unionist

— 13e —

Understanding American Government

Susan Welch
The Pennsylvania State University

John Gruhl
University of Nebraska–Lincoln

Susan M. Rigdon
University of Illinois at Urbana–Champaign

Sue Thomas
Pacific Institute for Research and Evaluation

 WADSWORTH
CENGAGE Learning

Australia • Brazil • Japan • Korea • Mexico • Singapore • Spain • United Kingdom • United States

WADSWORTH
CENGAGE Learning™

Understanding American Government,
13th Edition—No Separate Policy Chapters

Susan Welch, John Gruhl, Susan M. Rigdon, Sue Thomas

Publisher: Suzanne Jeans

Executive Editor: Carolyn Merrill

Development Manager: Jeffrey Greene

Associate Development Editor: Kate MacLean

Assistant Editor: Laura Ross

Editorial Assistant: Nina Wasserman

Media Editor: Laura Hildebrand

Marketing Manager: Lydia LeStar

Marketing Communications Manager:
  Heather Baxley

Marketing Assistant: Josh Hendrick

Content Project Manager: Cathy L. Brooks

Art Director: Linda Helcher

Print Buyer: Fola Orekoya

Production Service: Cadmus Communications

Text Designer: Stratton Design

Cover Designer: Rokusek Design

Cover Image: © Index Stock/Fotosearch

Compositor: Cadmus Communications

© 2012, 2010, 2008 Wadsworth, Cengage Learning

ALL RIGHTS RESERVED. No part of this work covered by the copyright herein may be reproduced, transmitted, stored, or used in any form or by any means graphic, electronic, or mechanical, including but not limited to photocopying, recording, scanning, digitizing, taping, Web distribution, information networks, or information storage and retrieval systems, except as permitted under Section 107 or 108 of the 1976 United States Copyright Act, without the prior written permission of the publisher.

For product information and technology assistance, contact us at
Cengage Learning Customer & Sales Support, 1-800-354-9706

For permission to use material from this text or product,
submit all requests online at **www.cengage.com/permissions.**
Further permissions questions can be emailed to
permissionrequest@cengage.com.

Library of Congress Control Number: 2010940702

ISBN-13: 978-1-111-34187-9
ISBN-10: 1-111-34187-7

Wadsworth
20 Channel Center Street
Boston, MA 02210
USA

Cengage Learning is a leading provider of customized learning solutions with office locations around the globe, including Singapore, the United Kingdom, Australia, Mexico, Brazil, and Japan. Locate your local office at **international.cengage.com/region**

Cengage Learning products are represented in Canada by Nelson Education, Ltd.

For your course and learning solutions, visit **www.cengage.com.**

Purchase any of our products at your local college store or at our preferred online store **www.cengagebrain.com.**

Printed in the United States of America
1 2 3 4 5 6 7 14 13 12 11 10

BRIEF CONTENTS

CONTENTS

The tears of joy shed by millions of people, black and white alike, on election night November 4, 2008, revealed that America had changed. Millions of whites joined with millions of blacks to elect the nation's first African American president.

Both high hopes and unrealistic expectations were part of that election night euphoria. Many observers thought that Obama could bring a less partisan environment. Others, uplifted by Obama's rhetoric, felt that with a solid majority in both houses of Congress, he could change the way Washington worked, turn the economy around, tackle climate change policy, and pass a health insurance bill, meanwhile digging out of the worst economic crisis since the Great Depression and fighting two wars.

President Obama could not possibly live up to all his supporters' expectations and hopes. The election of America's first black president could not eradicate the serious problems that our country faces or the divisions over the remedies. Obama's objectives would have been difficult to achieve in the best political environment.

Though Obama and the Democratic majorities in Congress were able to pass health care reform, stop the free fall of the economy, and put in place regulations for the financial industry, the hopes for national single-payer health insurance, climate change legislation, and a new way of doing business in Washington were dashed. Every day seemed to bring more antagonism and hostility between the parties and more public anger toward "Washington."

Politics changed in ugly as well as positive ways as debates over the country's direction became charged with fear and anger. Opponents of health care reform accused the president of acting like a "Hitler" or a "Stalin," or both. The more extreme opponents of the president charged that he was not an American citizen and therefore not eligible to be president. Racism lay not very far below the surface of charges that "he's not like us."

In Congress, the House Democratic leadership often refused to work with the Republican leadership. And in the Senate, the Republican minority used some old tactics in new ways to force Democrats to obtain 60 votes to pass major legislation, nearly bringing business to a standstill and frustrating solid majorities. In the media, even the craziest charges became magnified by 24-hour "news" coverage that was often not news at all and Internet sites where rumors could be magnified and transmitted.

This environment generated the "Tea Party" movement, a grassroots movement drawn largely from conservative Republicans and funded in large part by wealthy business interests who found a way to advance their antiregulatory policy objectives through citizens angry with government. The Tea Party supported very conservative candidates in the Republican primaries, many of whom challenged long-understood and agreed-upon government institutions and policies, such as Social Security. The Tea Party activists unseated a number of conservative Republican members of Congress who were not conservative enough for the activists. In the 2010 election, several Tea Party candidates were elected and immediately began to push other Republicans to adopt their agenda. Other Tea Party candidates were apparently perceived by the voters as too extreme and were not elected.

These conflicts over the size and role of government led us to focus in this edition on why government is the size and scope that it is. This question is central to understanding government and how it works. After all, government does not create itself; its growth in size and activity reflects the demands placed on it over the decades by citizens. The nature of those demands and why they occur are important to understanding the growth of government and the reactions against it.

In a democracy, we assume government is responsive to the citizens, primarily through elections. But some of the constitutional features of our government, the systems of checks and balances, make it, by design, less than responsive. The Tea Partiers would argue that the growth of government has not been responsive to the American people, while others would argue that over the years Americans have had plenty of opportunities to define the scope and size of government, and they have done so.

Despite the historic and unprecedented election, and the subsequent backlash against it, we hope students reading this book will come to understand that much about politics is predictable and rooted in the larger principles of government and political culture. The election of a black president was historic, but predictions of a Democratic victory in 2008 were based on well-known rules of politics—incumbents tend to be voted out when they are unpopular and in times of economic hardship. And though the level of subsequent popular anger may seem to make the 2010 election exceptional, historical trends would predict a 2010 midterm election swing to the Republicans even in the absence of that anger. These and other historical regularities of politics are important in interpreting the news of the day in the context of historical trends.

We want to convey to students, whether they are taking this course as an elective or a requirement, why it is important for every American to understand how our government functions. We hope they find that it is also an interesting and often exciting subject that has relevance to almost every aspect of their lives.

We believe an introductory course succeeds if most students develop an understanding of the major concepts of our form of government, an interest in learning more about politics, and an ability to analyze political issues and evaluate the news. Students should come out of an introductory course with a firm grounding in the essential "nuts and bolts" of American government, but it is also crucial that they understand the political environment in which government functions. We offer the essentials of American government, but we also want the student to understand why (and sometimes how) these important features have evolved, their impact on individual citizens' relationships with government, and why they are sometimes controversial and worth learning about. For example, we prefer that students leave the course remembering why government tries to regulate corporations, how it does so, and the political factors that lead to stronger or weaker regulations rather than memorizing specific regulatory acts. The latter will change or soon be forgotten, but understanding the "whys" will help the student understand the issues long after the course is over.

A particular emphasis throughout the book is on the *impact* of government: how individual features of government affect its responsiveness to different groups (in Lasswell's terms, "Who gets what and why?"). We realize that nothing in American politics is simple; rarely does one feature of government produce, by itself, a clear outcome. Nevertheless, we think that students will be more willing to learn about government if they see a relationship between how government operates and the impact it has on them as American citizens.

We hope a greater understanding of and appreciation for American government may encourage those not already engaged in civic and political activities to become more active citizens. Though students did vote at a higher rate in 2004 and 2008 than they have in decades, their turnout in 2010 plummeted. A 2006 survey by the National Constitution Center found that more teenagers could identify the Three Stooges (59 percent) than could name the three branches of government, six times as many knew the hometown of Bart Simpson than knew where Abraham Lincoln came from, and not even 2 percent could correctly identify James Madison.

THE ORGANIZATION AND CONTENTS OF THE BOOK

An important new feature of this edition is an introduction. The introduction sets the stage for a consideration of the size and role of government by looking at the Founders' conceptions of government, how and why government has grown in different historical periods, Americans' general ambivalence about government, and then why antigovernment opinions have taken root during the Obama years.

The organization of the book is straightforward. After the introduction and material on the American people and core political values, the Constitution, and federalism, the book covers linkages, including money and politics, and then institutions. Civil liberties and rights are treated after the chapter on the judiciary. The civil rights chapter (Chapter 15) integrates a thorough treatment of constitutional issues concerning minorities and women, a discussion of the civil rights and women's rights movements, and contemporary research on the political status of these groups. We include in this chapter the special legal problems of Hispanics and Native Americans.

The final section of the text includes chapters on economic, health, environmental, and foreign policies. This section includes two new chapters.

Chapter 17 on health policy takes a comprehensive look at health-related policies (research, prevention, and food and nutrition). We discuss the impact of health care spending on the economy and why health care is a growing part of public and personal spending. The chapter also describes the evolution of government's role in providing health care and health insurance. Of course, we also describe the recent health care reform legislation, including how it came about and reactions to it.

A new chapter on environmental policy (Chapter 18) focuses on climate change debates and reviews the passage and enforcement of environmental policy with emphasis on landmark legislation intended to improve the quality of water and air, protect us from toxic waste, and save endangered species. The multiple environmental challenges that we face now and in the future are featured throughout the chapter.

Additional substantive policy chapters also reinforce the emphasis on the impact of government action. The section on fiscal policy in the economic policy making chapter (Chapter 16) complements the section on budgeting found in the chapter on Congress. The description of basic economic problems that government is expected to address should help students better understand issues such as the deficit, inflation, and unemployment and should give them another perspective on the scope of government. Given the downward spiral of our economy, students may be more interested in these topics than before. The treatment of Democratic and Republican approaches to economic policy highlights the relationship between politics and the economy. This chapter also describes policy choices in the areas of tax reform, the deficit, income redistribution, and economic growth.

The chapter on foreign policy places current foreign policy issues in the context of the history of our foreign policy goals, especially since World War II, and features new issues arising from the post–9/11 world.

Some instructors will prefer not to use any of the policy chapters. The book stands as a whole without them because many policy examples are integrated into the rest of the text. Or different combinations of the policy chapters may be used because each chapter is independent.

But the book is flexible enough that instructors can modify the order of the chapters. Some instructors will prefer to cover institutions before process. Others may prefer to discuss civil liberties and rights when discussing the Constitution.

CHANGES IN THE THIRTEENTH EDITION

In addition to the new introduction highlighting issues around the size and scope of government, and the two new policy chapters, this edition includes full coverage of the historic 2008 presidential election and the first twenty-two months of the Obama presidency. We also discuss the growth of opposition to the Obama presidency and the 2010 congressional primaries and elections. These topics are integrated into a variety of chapters, including public opinion, the media, interest groups, political parties, elections, money and politics, and all the chapters on institutions and on policy.

Thus, the text of every chapter has been substantially revised. For example, in addition to the new chapters on health and environmental policies, in Chapter 9 we have a full treatment of the changes in campaign finance laws and their impact. Chapter 4, on public opinion, now features discussions of youth participation in the elections of 2008 and 2010, approval and disapproval levels of the job done by President Obama in 2009 and 2010, and public opinion about policy changes in the wars in Afghanistan and Iraq, the rights of lesbians and gays, and access to health care.

Throughout, we have also updated the photos and cartoons to complement the new material and to give students a chance to learn through graphic as well as textual material. As always, we have updated the judiciary, civil liberties, and civil rights chapters to incorporate new Supreme Court decisions.

SPECIAL FEATURES

Each chapter's opening section, called "**Talking Points**," includes anecdotes about a policy, policy makers, or political situations that lead students to consider a major feature of government. For example, in Chapter 14, Talking Points offers insights into the role of the Supreme Court in interpreting the Second Amendment to the Constitution, that pertaining to the right to bear arms in the context of "a well regulated militia." In Chapter 9, on money and politics, the focus is on Barack Obama's decision to reject public funding for his presidential campaign and the impact that has on our campaign finance regulatory system.

Behind the Scenes boxes focus on an aspect of politics that is not likely to be widely publicized but that has interest to students and importance to the institution or process discussed. For example, Chapter 8: *Elections* uses examples from the 2008 campaign to describe the rare spontaneous interchanges between candidates and their supporters on the rope lines following stump speeches and other campaign events. In Chapter 11, the box entitled "The Vice-President Who Wasn't" describes a man who probably was the first homosexual (though closeted) elected to that office. Anti-Semitism on the Supreme Court in the early twentieth century is the subject of a Behind the Scenes feature in the judiciary chapter (Chapter 13).

Constitution icons, ⭐, appear when the text of the Constitution is referred to, making it easy to reference the document in the appendix and to see how the Constitution deals with the topic at hand. The purpose is to call students' attention to how this founding document shapes our institutions and processes.

Democracy? questions ask students to consider how democratic a particular process or institution may be. This feature is intended to alert students to the fact that democracy is not a simple concept and that our Constitution and our practices include both democratic and undemocratic features.

In many chapters, **American Diversity** boxes illustrate the impact of the social and economic diversity of the American population on political life. These boxes help students understand how a variety of backgrounds and attitudes shape views of politics and positions on issues.

Key terms are boldfaced within the text and listed at the end of each chapter (with their page numbers) and in the glossary.

We are delighted to have the opportunity to write this thirteenth edition and to improve the text further in ways suggested by our students and readers. We have been extremely pleased by the reaction of instructors and students to our first twelve editions. We were especially gratified to have won three times the American Government Textbook Award from the Women's Caucus for Political Science of the American Political Science Association.

WHY IS *UNDERSTANDING AMERICAN GOVERNMENT* THE RIGHT BOOK FOR YOU?

It is the leader in DIVERSITY coverage:

- The book emphasizes the significance of our ethnic, religious, and economic diversity in the shaping and implementation of American government, as well as in our historic and future challenges. This important premise is first introduced as the framework for Chapter 1: *The American People* starting on page 18.

- The treatment of women, racial and ethnic minorities, and other marginalized groups is the best on the market. See, for example, the well-respected chapters on *Civil Liberties* starting on page 418 and *Civil Rights* starting on page 456.

- *Understanding American Government* is a three-time winner of the American Government Textbook Award for the Best Treatment of Women in Politics, by the Women's Caucus for Political Science.

- Lively *American Diversity* boxes illustrate the impact of the American population's social diversity on politics. See:
  - *Battle of the (Text) Books: Who Made America America?* p. 30
  - *Founding Mothers,* p. 42
  - *Political Culture and Federalism,* p. 72
  - *The Marriage Rights of Gays and Lesbians as a Moral Issue,* p. 98
  - *Media Habits of Men and Women,* p. 123
  - *The Origin of Gay and Lesbian Rights Groups,* p. 164
  - *Organizing Protest: The Montgomery Bus Boycott,* p. 176
  - *The Tea Party as a Third Party?* p. 186
  - *Blacks and Hispanics in Office,* p. 210
  - *Women in Office,* p. 214
  - *Men and Women Target Different Candidates,* p. 258
  - *Congress Is Not a Cross Section of America,* p. 286
  - *Presidential Candidates: The Pool Deepens but . . . ,* p. 327
  - *Do Women Judges Matter?* p. 399
  - *Anti-Semitism on the Bench,* p. 410
  - *Black Masters, Red Masters,* p. 460
  - *Pain of Recession Is Unevenly Spread,* p. 508
  - *Lack of Access to Medical Care Can Affect Life Outcome,* p. 549
  - *Environmental Justice,* p. 568
  - *Women in Combat,* p. 605

It has CURRENCY and uses respected SCHOLARSHIP:

- The text, citations, and photo program have been thoroughly updated to include current events through the 2010 election results, cutting-edge research, and the latest scholarship. See Chapter 8: *Elections* starting on page 206 as just one example.

- A unique chapter on *Money and Politics* focuses on laws that regulate how money can influence politics and the role and impact of money in elections; it also examines conflicts of interest on the part of decision makers in Congress and the executive branch. See Chapter 9 starting on page 250.

It encourages CRITICAL THINKING and gives an EVALUATIVE, NUANCED VIEW of American government:

- *Democracy?* questions appear periodically within the narrative and ask readers to consider whether a particular process or institution being discussed is democratic or not. Students become alert to the fact that democracy is not a simple concept and that our Constitution and our practices include both democratic and undemocratic features. See pages 96 and 219 for two examples.

Its ENGAGING writing and features spark students' interest and give them a BEHIND THE SCENES look at American government:

- *Behind the Scenes* boxes give readers a fascinating glimpse into interesting and important aspects of politics not widely publicized. See *An Accidental Classic* on page 70, *The Rope Line* on page 224, and *Military Spending and the Civilian Economy* on page 607 for a few examples.

It uses an ACCLAIMED PHOTOGRAPHY and ILLUSTRATIONS program:

- With over 370 carefully chosen photographs, cartoons, and figures—an average of 20 per chapter—the subject matter comes alive for students. Instructors praise the authors' use of candid, powerful images to reinforce important concepts, relay America's rich diversity, address difficult issues in our country's history and present political landscape, and maintain interest in the topic. Flip through the book, and the photo program will quickly draw you in.

SUPPLEMENTS FOR INSTRUCTORS

For details, please contact your Cengage representative or visit www.cengage.com/sso.

PowerLecture DVD with JoinIn™ and ExamView® for *Understanding American Government*

ISBN-10: 1111343888 / ISBN-13: 9781111343880

This DVD includes two sets of PowerPoint® slides (a book-specific and a media-enhanced set), a Test Bank in both

Microsoft® Word and ExamView formats, an Instructor's Manual, JoinInClickers, and a Resource Integration Guide.

Interactive book-specific PowerPoint lectures, a one-stop lecture and class preparation tool, makes it easy for you to assemble, edit, publish, and present book-specific lectures for your course. You will have access to a set of PowerPoints with outlines specific to each chapter of *Understanding American Government*, 13e, as well as photos, figures, and tables found in the book. The media-enhanced PowerPoints for each chapter can be used on their own or easily integrated with the book-specific PowerPoint outlines. Audio and video clips depict both historic and current events; NEW animated learning modules illustrate key concepts; tables, statistical charts, and graphs are included; and photos from the book as well as outside sources are provided at the appropriate places in the chapter. You can also add your own materials, using both types of PowerPoints and your own material to create a powerful, personalized classroom or online presentation.

A test bank in Microsoft Word and ExamView computerized testing offer an array of well-crafted multiple-choice and essay questions, along with answers and page references.

An Instructor's Manual includes learning objectives, chapter outlines, discussion questions, suggestions for stimulating class activities and projects, tips on integrating media into your class (including step-by-step instructions on how to create your own podcasts), suggested readings and Web resources, and a section specially designed to help teaching assistants and adjunct instructors.

JoinIn offers book-specific "clicker" questions that test and track student comprehension of key concepts. Political Polling questions simulate voting, engage students, foster dialogue on group behaviors and values, and add personal relevance; the results can be compared to national data, leading to lively discussions. Visual Literacy questions are tied to images from the book and add useful pedagogical tools and high-interest feedback during your lecture. By saving the data from students' responses all semester, you can track their progress and show them how political science works by incorporating this exciting new tool into your classroom. It is available for college and university adopters only.

The Resource Integration Guide outlines the rich collection of resources available to instructors and students within the chapter-by-chapter framework of the book, suggesting how and when each supplement can be used to optimize learning.

Political Theatre 2.0 DVD

ISBN-10: 0495793604 / ISBN-13: 9780495793601

Bring politics home to students with Political Theatre 2.0, up-to-date through the 2008 election season.

The second edition of this three-DVD series includes real video clips that show American political thought throughout the public sector. Clips include both classic and contemporary political advertisements, speeches, and interviews. Available to adopters of Cengage textbooks, version 2.0 provides added functionality with this updated edition.

Instructor Companion Website for *Understanding American Government*

ISBN-10: 1111343934 / ISBN-13: 9781111343934

The instructor companion site includes the Instructor's Manual; text-specific PowerPoints containing lecture outlines; photos and figures; and NewsNow PowerPoints, an additional set of multimedia-rich slides posted each week. You may use these slides to take a class poll or trigger a lively debate about the events that are shaping the world right now. And because this all-in-one presentation tool includes the text of the original newsfeed, along with videos, photos, and discussion questions, no Internet connection is required. You also have access to the Instructor's Guide to YouTube, which shows where you can find videos on the Internet that can be used as learning tools in class. Organized by fifteen topics, the guide follows the sequence of an American government course and includes a preface with tips on how to use Internet videos in class.

JoinIn on Turning Point® for Political Theatre

ISBN-10: 0495798290 / ISBN-13: 9780495798293

For even more interaction, combine Political Theatre with the innovative teaching tool of a classroom response system through JoinIn. Poll your students with questions created for you or create your own questions. Built within the Microsoft PowerPoint software, it's easy to integrate into your current lectures along with the "clicker" hardware of your choice.

The Wadsworth News Videos for American Government 2012 DVD

ISBN-10: 0495573094 / ISBN-13: 9780495573098

This collection of three- to six-minute video clips on relevant political issues serves as a great lecture or discussion launcher.

Great Speeches Collection

Throughout the ages, great orators have stepped up to the podium and used their communication skills to persuade, inform, and inspire their audiences. Studying these speeches can provide tremendous insight into historical, political, and cultural events. The Great Speeches Collection includes the full text of over sixty memorable orations for you to incorporate into your course. Speeches can be collated in a printed reader to supplement your existing course materials or bound into a core textbook.

ABC Video: Speeches by President Barack Obama

ISBN-10: 1439082472 / ISBN-13: 9781439082478

This DVD of nine famous speeches by President Barack Obama, from 2004 through his inauguration, includes his speech at the 2004 Democratic National Convention; his 2008 speech on race, "A More Perfect Union"; and his 2009 inaugural address. Speeches are divided into short video segments for easy, time-efficient viewing. This instructor supplement also features critical-thinking questions and answers for each speech, designed to spark classroom discussion.

Election 2010: An American Government Supplement

ISBN-10: 1111341788 / ISBN-13: 9781111341787

Written by John Clark and Brian Schaffner, this booklet addresses the 2010 congressional and gubernatorial races, with real-time analysis and references.

SUPPLEMENTS FOR INSTRUCTORS AND STUDENTS

CourseMate for *Understanding American Government*

ISBN-10: 1111571929 / ISBN-13: 9781111571924

The CourseMate for *Understanding American Government*, 13e, offers a variety of rich online learning resources designed to enhance the student experience. These resources include video activities, audio summaries, critical-thinking activities, simulations, animated learning modules, interactive timelines, primary source quizzes, flashcards, learning objectives, glossaries, and crossword puzzles. Chapter resources are correlated with key chapter learning concepts, and users can browse or search for content in a variety of ways.

NewsNow, a new asset available on CourseMate, is a combination of weekly news stories from the Associated Press, videos, and images that bring current events to life for the student. For instructors, NewsNow includes an additional set of multimedia-rich PowerPoint slides posted each week to the password-protected area of the text's Instructor companion website. Instructors may use these slides to take a class poll or trigger a lively debate about the events that are shaping the world right now. And because this all-in-one presentation tool includes the text of the original newsfeed, along with videos, photos, and discussion questions, no Internet connection is required.

How do you assess students' engagement in your course? How do you know your students have read the material or viewed the resources you've assigned? How can you tell if students are struggling with a concept? With CourseMate, you can use the Engagement Tracker to assess student preparation and engagement. Use the tracking tools to see progress for the class as a whole or for individual students. Identify students at risk early in the course. Uncover which concepts are most difficult for your class. Monitor time on task. Keep your students engaged.

CourseMate also features an interactive eBook that has highlighting and search capabilities along with links to simulations, animated PowerPoints, interactive timelines, video activities, primary source quizzes, tutorial quizzes, and flashcards.

Go to cengagebrain.com/shop/ISBN/0495910503 to access your Political Science CourseMate resources.

CourseMate

WebTutor™ on WebCT

ISBN-10: 1111479798 / ISBN-13: 9781111479794

Rich with content for your American government course, this Web-based teaching and learning tool includes course management, study/mastery, and communication tools. Use WebTutor to provide virtual office hours, post your syllabus, and track student progress with WebTutor's quizzing material. For students, WebTutor offers real-time access to interactive online tutorials and simulations, practice quizzes, primary source quizzes, and Web links—all correlated to *Understanding American Government*, 13e.

WebTutor™ on Blackboard

ISBN-10: 1111479763 / ISBN-13: 9781111479763

Rich with content for your American government course, this Web-based teaching and learning tool includes course management, study/mastery, and communication tools. Use WebTutor to provide virtual office hours, post your syllabus, and track student progress with WebTutor's quizzing material. For students, WebTutor offers real-time access to interactive online tutorials and simulations, practice quizzes, and Web links—all correlated to *Understanding American Government*.

CourseReader for American Government: Politics in Context

ISBN-10: 1111479984 / ISBN-13: 9781111479985

American Government CourseReader: Politics in Context will enable instructors to create a customized reader. Using a database of hundreds of documents, readings, and videos, instructors can search by various criteria or browse the collection to preview and then select a customized collection to assign their students. The sources will be edited to an appropriate length and include pedagogical support—a headnote describing the document and critical-thinking and multiple-choice questions to verify that the student has read and understood the selection. Students will be able to take notes and highlight and print content. The CourseReader allows the instructor to select exactly what students will be assigned with an easy-to-use interface and also provides an easily used assessment tool. The sources can be delivered online or in print format.

The Obama Presidency—Year One Supplement

ISBN-10: 0495908371 / ISBN-13:9780495908371

Much happens in the first year of a presidency, especially a historic one like that of Barack Obama. This full-color 16-page supplement by Kenneth Janda, Jeffrey Berry, and Jerry Goldman analyzes such issues as health care, the economy, and the stimulus package, changes in the U.S. Supreme Court, and the effect Obama policy has had on global affairs.

ACKNOWLEDGMENTS

We would like to thank the many people who have aided and sustained us during the lengthy course of this project.

We first want to thank Michael Steinman and John Comer, our original coauthors and original primary authors of Chapters 1, 11, and 12, and Chapters 4, 5, and 7, respectively, who helped plan this book and continued their coauthorship for several editions. The shape of the book still reflects their insights and efforts. Then, we thank Margery Ambrosius and Jan Vermeer for their intellectual contributions to this book through their coauthorship in previous editions. Our current and former University of Nebraska and Penn State colleagues have been most tolerant and helpful. We thank them all. In particular, we appreciate the assistance of Philip Dyer, David Forsythe, John Hibbing, Robert Miewald, John Peters, David Rapkin, and Beth Thiess-Morse, who provided us with data, bibliographic information, and other insights that we have used here. Susan Welch's Penn State colleagues Ron Filippelli and Ray Lombra have been a source of encouragement, support, and many interesting political insights.

We are also grateful to the many other readers of our manuscript and earlier editions of the book, as listed here. Without their assistance the book would have been less accurate, less complete, and less lively. And thanks, too, to those instructors who have used the book and relayed their comments and suggestions to us. Our students at the University of Nebraska have also provided invaluable reactions to previous editions.

Our editors at Cengage Publishing also deserve our thanks. Clark Baxter was a continual source of encouragement and optimism from the beginning of the first edition through the beginning of the ninth edition. Carolyn Merrill and Edwin Hill have been able replacements for this new edition.

REVIEWERS OF THE NEW EDITION

Russell Benjamin, *Northeastern Illinois University*

Michael D. Cobb, *North California State University*

Rebecca Deen, *University of Texas at Arlington*

Dennis Driggers, *California State University–Fresno*

Lois Duke-Whitaker, *Georgia Southern University*

Dennis Falcon, *Cerritos Community College*

Kenneth W. Moffett, *Southern Illinois University*

Peter Parker, *Truman State University*

Bernard Rowan, *Chicago State University*

Rorie Solberg, *Oregon State University*

Ronnie Tucker, *Shippensburg University*

Paul Vayer, *Brevard Community College–Cocoa*

REVIEWERS OF PREVIOUS EDITONS

Alan Abramowitz, *State University of New York at Stony Brook;* Larry Adams, *Baruch College–City University of New York;* Danny M. Adkison, *Oklahoma State University;* James Alt, *Harvard University;* Margery Marzahn Ambrosius, *Kansas State University;* Kevin Bailey, *North Harris Community College;* Bethany Barratt, *Roosevelt University;* Kennette M. Benedict, *Northwestern University;* James Benze, *Washington and Jefferson College;* Melinda K. Blade, *Academy of Our Lady of Peace;* Timothy Bledsoe, *Wayne State University;* Jon Bond, *Texas A&M University;* Paul R. Brace, *New York University;* Joseph V. Brogan, *La Salle University;* James R. Brown Jr., *Central Washington University;* Kent M. Brudney, *Cuesta Community College;* Chalmers Brumbaugh, *Elon College;* Alan D. Buckley, *Santa Monica College;* Richard G. Buckner Jr., *Santa Fe Community College;* Ronald Busch, *Cleveland State University;* Bert C. Buzan, *California State University–Fullerton;* Carl D. Cavalli, *Memphis State University;* Stefanie Chambers, *Trinity College;* Richard A. Champagne, *University of Wisconsin, Madison;* Mark A. Cichock, *University of Texas at Arlington;* Michael Connelly, *Southwestern Oklahoma State University;* Gary Copeland, *University of Oklahoma;* George H. Cox Jr., *Georgia Southern College;* Paige Cubbison, *Miami-Dade University;* Landon Curry, *Southwest Texas State University;* Jack DeSario, *Case Western Reserve University;* Robert E. DiClerico, *West Virginia University;* Ernest A. Dover Jr., *Midwestern State University;* Georgia Duerst-Lahti, *Beloit College;* David V. Edwards, *University of Texas at Austin;* Ann H. Elder, *Illinois State University;* Ghassan E. El-Eid, *Butler University;* C. Lawrence Evans, *College of William and Mary;* Rhodell J. Fields, *St. Petersburg College;* Robert Glen Findley, *Odessa College;* Murray Fischel, *Kent State University*; Bobbe Fitzhugh, *Eastern Wyoming College;* Jeff Fox, *Catawba College;* Stephen I. Frank, *St. Cloud State University;* Marianne Fraser, *University of Utah;* Jarvis Gamble, *Owens Community College;* Sonia R. Garcia, *St. Mary's University;* David Garrison, *Collin County Community College;* Phillip L. Gianos, *California State University–Fullerton;* Doris A. Graber, *University of Illinois–Chicago;* Michael Graham, *San Francisco State University;* Ruth M. Grubel, *University of Wisconsin–Whitewater;* Stefan D. Haag, *Austin Community College;* Larry M. Hall, *Belmont University;* Edward Hapham, *University of Texas–Dallas;* Peter O. Haslund, *Santa Barbara City College;* Richard P. Heil, *Fort Hays State University;* Peggy Heilig, *University of Illinois at Urbana;* Craig Hendricks, *Long Beach City College;* Marjorie Hershey, *Indiana University;* Kay Hofer, *Southwest Texas State University;* Samuel B. Hoff, *Delaware State College;* Robert D. Holsworth, *Virginia Commonwealth University;* Jesse C. Horton, *San Antonio College;* Gerald Houseman, *Indiana University;* Timothy Howard, *North Harris College;* Peter G. Howse, *American River College;* David W. Hunt, *Triton College;* Bernard-Thompson Ikegwuoha, *Green River Community College;* Pamela Imperato, *University of North Dakota;* Jerald Johnson, *University of Vermont;* Loch Johnson, *University* of Georgia; Terri Johnson, *University of Wisconsin–Green Bay;* Evan M. Jones, *St. Cloud State University;* Joseph F. Jozwiak Jr., *Texas A&M University–Kingsville;* Matt Kerbel, *Villanova University;* Marshall R. King, *Maryville College;* Orma Lindford, *Kansas State University;* Peter J. Longo, *University of Nebraska–Kearney;* Roger C. Lowery, *University of North Carolina–Wilmington;* H. R. Mahood, *Memphis State University;* Kenneth M. Mash, *East Stroudsburg University;* Alan C. Melchior, *Florida International University;* A. Nick Minton, *University of Massachusetts–Lowell;* Matthew Moen, *University of Maine;* Michael K. Moore, *University of Texas at Arlington;* Michael Nelson, *Vanderbilt University;* Bruce Nesmith, *Coe College;* Walter Noelke, *Angelo State University;* Thomas Payette, *Henry Ford Community College;* Theodore B. Pedeliski, *University of North Dakota;* Jerry Perkins, *Texas Tech University;* Toni Phillips, *University of Arkansas;* C. Herman Pritchett, *University of California–Santa Barbara;* Charles Prysby, *University of North Carolina–Greensboro;* Sandra L. Quinn-Musgrove, *Our Lady of the Lake University;* Donald R. Ranish, *Antelope Valley Community College;* Catherine C. Reese, *Arkansas State University;* Linda Richter, *Kansas State University;* Jerry Sandvick, *North Hennepin Community College;* James Richard Sauder, *University of New Mexico;* Eleanor A. Schwab, *South Dakota State University;* K. L. Scott, *University of Central Florida;* Earl Sheridan, *University of North Carolina–Wilmington;* Edward Sidlow, *Northwestern University;* Cynthia Slaughter, *Angelo State University;* John Squibb, *Lincolnland Community College;* Glen Sussman, *Old Dominion University;* M. H. Tajalli-Tehrani, *Southwest Texas State University;* Kristine A. Thompson, *Moorehead State University;* R. Mark Tiller, *Austin Community College;* Gordon J. Tolle, *South Dakota State University;* Susan Tolleson-Rinehart, *Texas Tech University;* Bernadyne Weatherford, *Rowan College of New Jersey;* Richard Unruh, *Fresno Pacific College;* Jay Van Bruggen, *Clarion University of Pennsylvania;* David Van Heemst, *Olivet Nazarene University;* Kenny Whitby, *University of South Carolina;* Donald C. Williams, *Western New England College;* James Matthew Wilson, *Southern Methodist University;* John H. Wilson Jr., *Itawamba Community College;* Clifford J. Wirth, *University of New Hampshire;* Ann Wynia, *North Hennepin Community College;* Alex H. Xiao, *Sacramento City College;* and Mary D. Young, *Southwestern Michigan College.*

Talking Points

In the scope of all human activity, "government plays a limited role," the historian Garry Wills reminds us. "It cannot be the family, the church, the local club, the private intellectual circle."[1] Few would disagree, but the lines between the responsibilities of government and private institutions are not as sharply drawn in law or practice as some think they are or should be.

Americans are acutely aware of these shifting lines because we have been in continuous debate over the appropriate role for government since 1787. At the convention where our Constitution was written, competing factions argued about the proper scope of government. Our political parties today are direct descendents of these factions and are organized around contrasting views about how big and active government should be.

It is unlikely that most Americans go about daily life thinking about how authority should be distributed across society, but there is no doubt that we do go through periods when some segment of the population becomes convinced that things are out of whack—government is intervening too much or too little in the market or in private life, either taking on functions that should be performed by the community or doing too little.

This is again a time where many Americans are debating the role of government. How big should government be? How active should it be? These perennial questions rose anew during the 2008 presidential campaign and since then have increasingly been a topic of debate, prompted by the severe recession of 2008–2009, by the campaign and election of the first black president, more liberal than any president since Lyndon Johnson, and by the efforts of the president and Congress to protect the economy and expand health care. Americans who feel left behind as our society and our economy have shifted have been among the most vocal, often in full-throated fury, in their opposition to the federal government, its officials, and its policies, insisting that the federal government should not be as big or as active as its current leaders and their policies call for it to be.

These debates over the role of government have a new focus but are as old as the republic. From the Whiskey Rebellion in 1786–1787 to the Tea (Taxed Enough Already) Party movement today, Americans periodically have rebelled against taxation and government curtailment of individual liberties. Even presidents have complained about big government. President Ronald Reagan never tired of talking about his dissatisfaction with big government and liked to say he preferred flying over Washington to being on the ground because, from the air, government looked smaller. The historian Garry Wills said it sometimes seems that tradition asks "us to love our country by hating our government."[2]

These developments provide the context in which today's politics occur. This Introduction will provide an overview of these developments before we plunge into the chapters that address our political institutions and processes.

WHY HAVE GOVERNMENT?

To govern, government has to have a measure of control over the people, and it usually has a monopoly on the use of military power. Although any government impinges on personal freedom, people decide to have government because, paradoxically, personal freedom is best protected in some sort of regulated society. The life of people within a society that has no effective government is, in the words of English philosopher Thomas Hobbes, "nasty, brutish, and short."[3] Today this may mean that civil war erupts or neighboring countries invade. Women and children are at the mercy of marauding bands of soldiers, some of them children themselves, who kill, rape, and plunder at will. There are no public services outside central cities, no educational structure, no health care, no clean drinking water, few good roads or effective means of transportation. Children die of infectious diseases that are easily cured in other societies. People fend for themselves or their extended family, and they die in what we consider their middle age.

In these societies, individuals are free from the usual constraints of government, but because there is no government to protect them, life is unpredictable and often painful and short. Contemporary examples include Somalia, where twenty years of civil war and marauding bands leave ordinary people as prey. The world also watched while the Haitian government was unable to provide even the most basic services after the devastating earthquake in 2010. Very few people argue that we need no government at all. Even those who call for minimalist government, like Libertarians such as Ron Paul, argue that we need a military to protect our nation and police forces to enforce our laws.

Of course, having a government with sufficient power to protect its citizens doesn't guarantee that it always will, as history has shown over and over again. Throughout the course of history, governments have chosen to persecute individuals and groups that were not in favor because of religious, ethnic, or policy differences, or differences over who should be the leader. In the United States, until the 1960s, government in many times and places did not choose to protect the rights of African Americans (see Chapter 15). And in 2007, when Hurricane Katrina hit New Orleans, neither federal, state, nor local government protected the life and property of New Orleans' residents.

At the other extreme from powerless or absent governments are dictatorships and totalitarian nations that try to regulate every aspect of life, including what people say and write, where they work, and even what they think. Nazi Germany and Stalinist Russia were modern examples of such governments. Although these two governments were quite different in their ideology and programs, they were similar in their near absolute power. Individuals could be imprisoned or executed for expressing opposition to the state or its leaders or even being suspected of being a dissident. There were no independent courts or police services, and groups could be singled out for persecution at the whims

Joel Pett Editorial Cartoon used with permission of Joel Pett and the Cartoonist Group. License 2010-233.

of the rulers. Nazi Germany slaughtered millions of Jews (and political and religious dissidents, Gypsies, homosexuals, and the mentally ill and enfeebled), while the communist Soviet Union slaughtered millions of landowners and middle-class citizens and other opponents of state policies.

Democracies fall between these extremes. They have enough power to govern effectively, but they do not control the lives and thoughts of their citizens.

Although the United States clearly has a big government, it is not as big, compared with the governments of modern democracies, as most Americans assume. Ours is in the middle in the number of government workers relative to all workers, and ours is lower than most European nations in tax levels and public spending.[4] Most other democracies tax more and spend more, and their social programs are more ambitious, often providing paid maternity leave, subsidized day care, comprehensive health care, longer unemployment benefits, more generous pension benefits (than our Social Security), and, in some countries, longer and paid vacations. Their governments own and operate major industries, such as telecommunications, transportation, and utilities, whereas ours restricts itself more to providing services the private sector finds unprofitable, such as Amtrak. Their bureaucracies regulate more stringently the businesses that remain in private hands.[5] Americans' antipathy toward government, and especially toward taxes, has prevented equally ambitious programs from being adopted in the United States.

How did the United States develop the size government that we have?

THE FOUNDERS' CONCEPTIONS

The Founders expected a limited government with limited input from its citizens.

Early Settlers

Early settlers came to America for multiple reasons, but two groups predominated. Many settlers came for religious reasons. Some had been persecuted by the authorities in their countries, so they sought religious freedom. Others had been tolerated in their communities, but they wanted to live among like-minded people and they hoped to establish religious enclaves where their religion would prevail.[6] Either way, the immigrants who came for religious reasons brought with them suspicion, if not hostility, toward government. They wanted to be left alone so they could practice their religions as they saw fit.

Many other settlers came for economic reasons. Some were impoverished and could afford passage to America only by agreeing to become indentured servants. Others were well off and could pay their own way. But whether poor or rich, these immigrants saw America as a land of opportunity. They saw it as a new continent where they could improve their economic standing, with the poor becoming rich and the rich becoming richer. They too brought with them wariness toward government, in particular, aversion to taxes and restrictions that might limit their economic climb.

Although some early settlers came as representatives of their governments back home, both of the early groups who predominated—those who came for religious reasons and those who came for economic reasons—were "runaways from authority."[7] And even though 20 percent of the colonists at the time of the Revolutionary War did not want to sever their ties with Britain,[8] those who did set the tone for American society, and they passed down these anti-authority views to their descendents, who in turn would pass down these views to *their* descendents. Eventually, these views would shape our Constitution and our country for generations to come.[9]

The Constitution

The Articles of Confederation, which governed the country after the Revolutionary War, were our first Constitution. Americans, who as colonists had chafed under rule by the English king and Parliament, wanted to avoid a government that was too strong. But the Articles created a government that was too weak to confront either foreign or domestic challenges. The government was unable to ensure either peace or prosperity. In frustration, the Founders called the Constitutional Convention and wrote a replacement for the Articles, a document we call "the Constitution" today.

The Constitution created a government that is stronger than the one under the Articles. However, the Founders, still wary of a strong government like the English government, wrote the Constitution to limit the power of the federal government. They fragmented governmental power by giving some to the federal government but reserving much for the state governments. They fragmented the power of the federal government further by dividing it into three branches—legislative, executive, and judicial—and then providing checks for each branch over the other branches. (Chapter 2 describes these provisions in more detail.) Founder James

Madison wrote at the time that the Founders first had to "enable the government to control the governed, and in the next place to oblige it to control itself."[10]

The Constitution gave authority over foreign affairs and some domestic matters, including regulation of interstate commerce, to the national government. But the Constitution gave authority over many other matters to the states. It gave authority to tax to both levels. The **Tenth Amendment**, which reflects the understanding of that time, says that the powers not delegated to the national government are reserved for the states. Although the Constitution's language is quite general and ambiguous, it's clear that the Founders thought they were creating a government that was limited in size and scope and therefore in power over states and individuals.

Yet, the Constitution states the purposes for establishing the United States of America in broad and positive terms, itemizing government's essential functions in its Preamble: to form a more perfect union, establish justice, ensure domestic tranquility, provide for the common defense, promote the general welfare, and secure the blessings of liberty to ourselves and our posterity. Moreover, the authority that the Constitution assigned to the various branches to carry out these functions has allowed the government to grow along with the nation. For example, Article I gives Congress the authority "To make all Laws which shall be necessary and proper for carrying into Execution the foregoing Powers [those enumerated], and all other Powers vested by this Constitution in the Government of the United States. . . ." (Article I, Section 8, clause 18). This **necessary and proper clause** is also called the "elastic clause" because it can stretch to authorize a wide variety of powers not specifically listed.

When states had to decide whether to ratify the Constitution, the people and the legislators discussed and debated how much authority government should have to carry out its specified functions. Just as there was disagreement then, so there are controversies now. The ambiguities in the Constitution, a result of disagreements over the size and scope of government at the time of the founding, continue to fuel debate.

The Role of the People

In creating the new government under the Constitution, the Founders believed that they should provide a way for the people to express their views and influence their officials. At the same time, the Founders worried that the people—the masses—could not be entrusted to have too direct an influence on national policy. They might be swayed by demagogues or be more concerned with narrow or local interests than the larger good. The Founders talked about "an excess of democracy" and feared "mob rule." Therefore, the Founders wrote the Constitution to allow citizens to vote for members of the House of Representatives, but not for members of the Senate (state legislatures would choose the senators from their states—until the Seventeenth Amendment, mandating popular election, was ratified in 1913) or for the president (electors in the Electoral College would choose the president—until political changes and state laws made the electors virtual rubber stamps of the voters in their state).

In summary, the Founders expected a limited role for the federal government but also a limited role for the people to influence that government. But they built in flexibility that allowed the Constitution to evolve to meet the changing needs of a growing nation.

REASONS FOR GOVERNMENT EXPANSION

Throughout history, Americans would confound the Founders' expectations by expanding the power of the government and also by expanding the power of the people to influence the government. Both the role of the government and the role of the people would become more robust than the Founders ever could have imagined.

Why Does Government Grow?

Some people have the impression that the government grows of its own accord. Usually government grows because citizens or interest groups want it to do more. As crises emerge or society changes, new problems surface and people ask the government to do more to respond to them. To do more, government has to grow, adding departments or agencies or expanding existing ones, thus hiring more workers and budgeting more money to pay the workers. In responding to the demand to do something about unemployment, for example, government has to spend money either by providing tax breaks to persuade businesses to hire more workers; or by building new roads, bridges, and other public works to create more jobs; or by giving unemployed workers more welfare (unemployment payments). Whatever the strategy, it has to issue new regulations to govern the expenditure of the money. It probably has to hire some people to disburse the money and others to make sure that the disbursement is done honestly.

To deal with their near financial collapse, some large financial firms asked the government to bail them out in 2008. Fearing a worldwide depression, government bailed them out and forced other financial firms to accept government bailouts too. And then, as two of the three major auto manufacturers in the United States, General Motors and Chrysler, teetered on the brink of bankruptcy, and economists and politicians feared the loss of tens of thousands of jobs in the auto industry, including the suppliers to the automakers, the federal government made massive loans to them too. Though there were some strings attached (the

As our country grew, our government grew, too. Washington sent soldiers, surveyors, road builders, and mail carriers to accommodate the needs of settlers. Here wagon trains head west in 1890.

CEO of General Motors had to step down and Chrysler had to accept a merger with another car manufacturer, Fiat), and the loans were to be repaid, again the government's role in the economy jumped, though perhaps temporarily.

Once government grows, it creates new clients for its services. These clients then make it difficult for government to cut back. This is true whether the clients are low-income individuals or huge corporations.

Sometimes government grows despite the ideological predilections of presidents. Thomas Jefferson called his election a revolution, abolished all internal taxes, and set about making government as small, simple, and informal as possible. He tried to keep the United States out of war in Europe and closed down ports and foreign trade, but he soon found he needed federal policing to enforce his policy.[11] And despite his support for small government, Jefferson bought the Louisiana territories from Spain (a transaction that would become known as the Louisiana Purchase). His expansionist vision instantly changed the country's destiny. From a compact coastal nation, it became a vast continental empire in which Jefferson's ideal of a small agrarian republic would no longer be possible.

Ronald Reagan wanted to cut the size of government. For example, he promised that he would eliminate the Department of Education. But his attempts to cut the department ran afoul of those who benefited from the existence of federal support for education, including tens of thousands of school districts across the nation. George W. Bush also wanted to cut the size of government, but he expanded it anyway when he saw the needs and opportunities.

Throughout history, the federal government has grown continuously, but it hasn't grown at a constant rate. When the country has experienced a massive crisis or major economic or social changes, the government has grown more because the people have demanded that it do more in response to the crisis or changes. Then it is very difficult to return government to its former size because the beneficiaries of government action become strong supporters of its programs. We'll briefly summarize these periods in which the government has grown the most.

Civil War

The first growth spurt occurred during the Civil War. The government expanded its army to fight the war. This expansion didn't result in growth all across the government, just growth in the parts of the government involved in the war effort. President Abraham Lincoln expanded the military and took bold steps marshalling governmental power. He denied states the right to secede from the Union and even arrested several Maryland state legislators who were going to vote for Maryland to join the Confederacy, a move that would have left Washington, D.C., surrounded by Confederate states. Lincoln also used his authority as a wartime commander to assume extraordinary powers over domestic policy. After the war, the federal government built homes for wounded and indigent Union veterans and paid for their medical care. This might be considered the first widespread social welfare program.

Industrial Revolution

The next spurt occurred in the decades following the Civil War, as the Industrial Revolution transformed our economy in the late nineteenth and early twentieth centuries. Factories sprung up in cities, drawing workers from small towns and rural areas. The factories revolutionized work and society, boosting the economy but creating new problems for workers and consumers. Adults and children often worked in sweatshops—factories where they worked long hours in unsafe conditions for low pay. To cite just one example, in canneries child labor was common, and the new canning machines and processes produced unsafe food, threatening consumers.

In response, Americans demanded reforms. Republican president Theodore Roosevelt used his office as a "bully pulpit" to advocate the improvement of working conditions, consumer protection, and environmental protection. These goals all required more regulation of big business. Roosevelt's concept of government as advocate for the average citizen expanded government and changed its purpose.

Great Depression

The largest spurt occurred during the **Great Depression**, which began when the stock market crashed in 1929 and continued until World War II. With the crash, many banks collapsed, and ordinary people lost their savings. Business activity declined, and many workers lost their jobs. Between one-third and one-fourth of the workforce were unemployed. Others toiled for sweatshop wages. In Brooklyn, girls worked for six cents an hour in a pants factory. After paying for carfare, lunch, and child care, one employee took home ten cents a week. In Birmingham, Alabama, 12,000 men applied for 750 jobs to dig a canal for twenty cents an hour.[12] Without their savings or jobs,

Child labor was common in the late 1800s and early 1900s. These boys toiled in a mine in Pittston, Pennsylvania. When Americans no longer tolerated child labor, government passed and enforced laws against the practice. To do so, it expanded the number of its workers, the size of its budget, and the scope of its authority.

Photo by Lewis W. Hine/George Eastman House/Getty Images

many Americans could no longer make payments on their house or farm.

On just one day in April 1932, one-fourth of the state of Mississippi—12 to 15 percent of property in towns and almost 40,000 farms—was auctioned off in sheriffs' sales, because the banks foreclosed on the property.[13] One-seventh of the farms in Iowa were auctioned off by 1932.[14] As the Depression worsened, many people became homeless. Encampments, called "Hoovervilles" (named for the president at the beginning of the Depression, Herbert Hoover), sprung up on vacant lots and under bridges. Many people also went without adequate food. The desperate walked up and down streets and knocked on doors each night to ask if there was any leftover food from dinner.[15] The really desperate haunted city garbage dumps.[16] Some malnourished men dropped dead in parks and froze to death in abandoned warehouses.[17] Increasing numbers of people were admitted to hospitals for malnutrition, some of whom were so far gone that they couldn't be saved; they literally starved to death.[18]

Unlike today, there was no systematic program of relief—no welfare, no food stamps, no unemployment compensation. Cities and states, which had provided some aid to the poor, were overwhelmed; they did not have the funds or organizations to cope with the increasing needs. Nor did private charities, including churches, which had provided some aid, have enough resources to assume the burden.

Americans turned to the government and the new president, Democrat Franklin Delano Roosevelt (1933–1945), who expanded government power at all levels to mitigate the effects of the Depression, the worst economic crisis the country had experienced. Roosevelt's predecessor, Republican Herbert Hoover, had taken a minimalist approach, and by the time FDR (as Roosevelt was universally known) came to office, the dislocation and suffering of millions of Americans threatened the political stability of the country.

Roosevelt immediately launched an ambitious program, which he called "a new deal for the American people," to stimulate the economy and reduce the suffering. Congress passed Roosevelt's proposals to regulate business and labor and also to establish a national welfare system. Although some people, especially business executives and corporations, resisted the changes strongly, most Americans embraced them.

These **New Deal** programs expanded the size of government more and at a faster rate than anything before or since. In the first six years of Roosevelt's administration, the number of federal employees in Washington, D.C., more than doubled,[19] the number of federal employees in the country almost doubled, and the size of the budget almost doubled as well.[20] Spending by states and localities also expanded greatly during this time. This expansion is considered to be the beginning of "big government" in the United States. These changes were so dramatic that one political scientist has said they created a "second American republic."[21] Compared with other Western countries, we got big government late, but in these years we got it fast.

President Franklin Delano Roosevelt used his unbridled confidence and the public's support for New Deal programs to greatly expand the role of the federal government.

Funds for these new programs came from new taxes levied on personal income, a power Congress acquired only after the **Sixteenth Amendment** to the Constitution was ratified in 1913. The power to tax individual income slowly expanded the reach of the federal government by providing fiscal support for many new activities. Some states also funded new programs by adopting new taxes or increasing existing taxes and finding other new revenue.[22]

Roosevelt's exuberance and experimentation had given people hope. As the country pulled out of the Depression, with help from the economic activity generated by World War II, people gave Roosevelt credit, electing him to an unprecedented four terms and returning Democrats to Congress to support him.

Overall, the New Deal brought a dramatic change in the relationship between the government and its citizens, making the government more prominent because of its greater involvement in daily life, its broader taxation activity, and also because of the more visible role for the president. People saw government's potential to make life better, and expectations were permanently changed.

World War II and the Cold War

World War II (1941–1945) further stimulated the growth of the national government, especially the military bureaucracy. As Lincoln did during the Civil War, Roosevelt assumed extraordinary powers to meet wartime emergencies, including price controls, rationing, and the suspension of some civil liberties (in fact, most civil liberties for most Japanese Americans). As soon as the war was over, the United States and the Soviet Union, no longer needing to cooperate as allies against Germany, resumed their hostilities in a Cold War. The nuclear arms race ensued, and the government expanded its military in anticipation that the Cold War would become a third world war.[23]

President Dwight Eisenhower, a Republican inclined toward small government, supported many new federal programs, ranging from the massive interstate highway system to college programs in science, engineering, and languages. Competition with the Soviet Union drove all of these initiatives.

Civil Rights Era

Government expanded again during the 1960s and 1970s as a result of pressure from African Americans for civil rights; women for equal rights; and environmentalists, consumers, and unions for greater regulation of business and for a healthier environment.

The presidency of Democrat Lyndon Baines Johnson coincided with the peak activism of the modern civil rights movement, whose struggle for political equality was brought into every home by television. As Americans watched protestors being beaten or attacked by police dogs, Johnson, like Eisenhower and John F. Kennedy before him, had to call up, or threaten to nationalize, state militia to force state and local officials to comply with federal law. At the same time, the mass media were making the country aware of the high levels of poverty and hunger in the United States. When the movement for greater economic justice joined forces with the civil rights movement, and when passive civil disobedience tactics were supplanted by riots, looting, and fires in some northern cities, there was concern that the United States might be approaching the dangerous levels of civil unrest that developed during the Great Depression.

Johnson responded to these problems by pushing through Congress civil rights legislation and a massive package of social welfare proposals that he said would promote "a great society." These **Great Society** proposals increased the scope of government and changed the nation-state relationship in two important ways. To implement Great Society programs, the federal government began funding work in domains that were formerly state and local preserves—law enforcement, fire protection, public education, and urban mass transit. With a tripling of aid to fund new programs, state and local governments became increasingly dependent on federal funding.[24]

And then, with federal civil rights guarantees in place, state governments no longer had the power to pass laws that overtly discriminated against African Americans in gaining access to public facilities and in voting or running for office. To administer, monitor, and enforce these civil rights reforms, as well as laws and regulations to protect consumers and the environment and to reduce discrimination against women that were adopted during the Nixon administration, the federal government created and staffed a host of new agencies and departments.

Backlash to Government Growth

None of these major expansions of the role and size of government occurred smoothly or without opposition. All along, some people fought against expansions of federal authority and charged that the government was acting precipitously and in disregard of individual liberties. Just as today, often citizens would refer to the Founders' expectations and quote the Founders' words, such as Thomas Jefferson's statement, "That government is best that governs least."

During the 1960s and 1970s, however, many people became disenchanted with government. In the 1960s, the civil rights movement, as well as the race riots in many big cities, alienated numerous people. The Vietnam War angered many Americans, both those who wanted leaders to escalate the war and achieve victory and those who thought we should never have been there in the first place and wanted leaders to pull out. Various lifestyle changes led to a generation gap, pitting the young against the old. In the 1970s, the economy slumped, and the Watergate scandal occurred.

The tumult over social issues and the turmoil throughout American society in the 1960s and 1970s produced a conservative backlash. By the mid-1970s, vocal critics began to call for a reduction in the size and scope of government. In 1980, the election of Ronald Reagan began a conservative era that would last into the 2000s. Reagan wanted to shrink government. Essentially, he campaigned on a platform against the federal government, vowing to make it smaller. He said, "Government is not the solution to our problems; government *is* the problem."

Reagan became a voice for Americans who wanted government to stop creating new programs and to begin downsizing. Reagan did try to cut spending for social welfare and enforcement of civil rights and environmental regulation, but he greatly increased military spending and the size of the defense-related bureaucracy. Reagan did persuade Congress to cut individual income taxes, especially for the wealthy. But when he left office, the government had a larger bureaucracy and budget, and it was running larger deficits than ever before. (Reagan and his successor, George H. W. Bush, doubled the national debt.)

Although the public, with its traditional distrust of big government, cheered when Reagan criticized the government, solid majorities opposed most of the cuts Reagan made (except welfare for the poor). Yet, in general, the public, because they agreed with Reagan's rhetoric criticizing the government, gave the president the support he needed to push through Congress the very cuts that many people opposed.

Rather than shrinking government, Reagan shifted the priorities of government, from social and nondefense programs to the military. Indeed, the battle between Republicans and Democrats since the Reagan years has largely been a war over priorities, not a war over the size of government. Republicans have wanted to deemphasize social and nondefense programs and spend more on the military and national security, while Democrats have wanted to reemphasize social and nondefense programs. The Republicans' goal of downsizing government has almost always been

AP Photo/Scott Stewart

President Ronald Reagan capitalized on the public's backlash against governmental growth and societal turmoil in the 1960s and 1970s to cut taxes and social programs in the 1980s.

expressed in terms of tax policy; the lower the taxes, the less money government will have to fund the social welfare programs that Republicans do not favor. This antitax stance has proven to be a more persuasive call to arms than a promise to shift priorities would have been. And Republican strategists realize that if government is shrunk, social and nondefense programs will be cut, because Americans will not tolerate a reduction of the military during a time of international tension.[25]

President Bill Clinton, like Reagan, had been a governor and believed in delegating powers to state and local governments. Presiding over a period of tremendous economic growth and job creation, the Clinton administration did manage to both decrease the size of the federal bureaucracy and balance the budget.

His successor, George W. Bush, was, like Reagan, unable to effect the government downsizing he had advocated when running for office, and he presided over two wars and a period of zero job growth. The federal bureaucracy grew during Bush's two terms, and by the time he left office he had more than doubled the national debt accumulated by all previous presidents. Bush also pushed through the largest expansion of federal support for health care since Medicare with a prescription drug subsidy for the elderly and the largest intervention in the public schools with his *No Child Left Behind* legislation. And near the end of his term, he authorized the more than $700 billion bailout of America's large financial institutions.

Although the public's focus, and this textbook's focus, is usually on the federal government, we should note that government in America also includes the states and their local governments, and they have grown much more since World War II than the federal government.[26] The federal government employs just under 3 million civil servants, less than twenty years ago, but the state and local levels employ almost 20 million, nearly a 60 percent growth in twenty years.[27] Some of the government actions that citizens rail against are administered and funded by state and local bureaucracies rather than by the federal government.

AMERICANS' AMBIVALENCE ABOUT GOVERNMENT

Americans are of two minds about government size and activity, as we can see from repeated public opinion polls.

Public Opinion about Government Spending

Often a majority of Americans say they want to cut government spending. At the same time, vast majorities say they want government to spend more on a variety of domestic matters, as Figure 1 shows, and often on the military too. (Government spending is a rough measure of both size and activity; government cannot grow in size or activity without, normally, more spending.)

Government growth during the first two years of the Obama administration was, in a general way, responsive to public sentiment about specific areas of government spending. The information in Figure 1 is drawn from a survey done in 2008. Americans do want government to help make life better, through retirement security, health care, police protection, environmental protection, and education. These numbers have been fairly stable for decades (though some

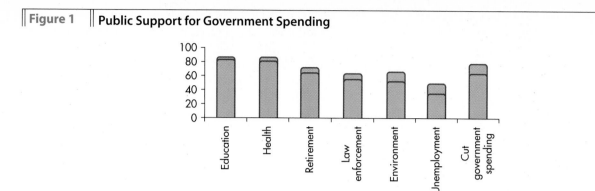

Figure 1 | **Public Support for Government Spending**

[Bar chart showing "Spend more" (red) and "Spend less" (blue) values on a 0–100 scale for the categories: Education, Health, Retirement, Law enforcement, Environment, Unemployment, and Cut government spending]

Spend more   Spend less

The public supports more government spending in numerous areas. At the same time, the public also supports cuts in government spending generally. The right hand column indicates (in red) those who favor cuts in spending and (in blue) those who oppose it.
SOURCE: *The General Social Surveys conducted by the National Opinion Research Center. These surveys, done every other year, poll national samples of adults. http://www.norc.org/GSS+Website/Data+Analysis/.*

areas rise and fall in reaction to government action). In other areas, such as foreign aid and welfare programs, majorities have consistently resisted public spending.[28]

But government growth, and the Obama policies, are not responsive to the public's general sense that government spending should be cut. Those general sentiments are also relatively consistent over time. For example, by the end of the Bush administration, 65 percent of the public favored cuts in public spending, while in mid-2009, after the government bailout of the big banks and car companies, 59 percent of the public thought that the Obama plans called for too much spending.[29] In other words, after the highly publicized expansion of public spending, only about the same (or maybe even fewer) numbers of Americans wanted to cut spending.

This contrast between support for specific areas of expanded spending and a general belief that government spends too much has been evidenced since survey research began to ask these questions nearly a half century ago. It is also broadly consistent with the growth of government during this time. Most Americans share the general sentiment that government should not be too big, yet they want government to act in ways that are important to them and act effectively in those areas.

In general, Republicans tend to be more skeptical of government actions than Democrats, though Republicans like big government in certain areas, including the military, law enforcement, and the regulation of personal behavior such as abortion and sexuality. Republicans are skeptical of government regulation of the economy or providing assistance to individuals, such as unemployment aid or medical care.

The Libertarian Party, founded in the early 1970s, is probably the most consistent current party in members' attitudes about big government. Libertarians oppose most government activity. In their vision, government would consist largely of a military and police force that would protect the lives and property of the citizens. Most everything else

would be run by private enterprise. Like most Democrats, they are opposed to government intervention in personal decisions like abortion and sexual orientation. But like most Republicans, they also oppose government's regulation of the economy. The Libertarians often run candidates for public office, including in 2008, when Ron Paul, a Republican member of Congress from Texas, ran for the Republican nomination for president. Although he did not receive many votes, his campaign won new publicity for the Libertarian cause. In 2010, his son Rand Paul was nominated for a Senate seat in Kentucky.

The Diversity of Antigovernment Groups

Some supporters of smaller government have done more than just express their displeasure in surveys. American history is dotted with movements that challenge government

"I hope this isn't another one of your experiments in limited government."

©Frank Cotham 2010/The New Yorker collection/www.cartoonbank.com

powers in peaceful or sometimes violent ways. Different movements challenge different aspects of government.

Some challenge governmental power to tax and regulate the market. The Whiskey Rebellion, a set of violent protests in 1791 against a tax on whiskey, was the first antitax protest after the Constitution was ratified. To suppress the farmer-based rebellion, George Washington himself led troops against the farmers and others mobilized to protest the tax. Ringleaders of the rebellion were arrested and convicted (but later pardoned). Since then, there have been many antitax movements, though none that required the military to put down.

A later manifestation of an antitax and antiregulation policy came about 140 years later in the vociferous opposition to Franklin Roosevelt and the New Deal. The American Liberty League was founded by conservative opponents of Roosevelt in his own Democratic Party and by conservative Republicans, and it was supported by leaders of major corporations, including U.S. Steel and General Motors. Stressing American values of individualism and rights to buy and keep one's property, they decried government action to diminish those rights by assisting the farmers, workers, and others who were facing economic ruin. Though most Americans then, as now, saw Roosevelt as a hero, he was hated by many who thought that he was undermining the American system. The League labeled Roosevelt's plan to rescue agriculture as "a trend toward Fascist control." Social Security was thought to be the end of democracy. The group pressed its claims that parts of the New Deal were unconstitutional, but the courts rejected those claims, and by World War II, the group had dissolved.[30] In the era before opinion polls, we do not know how many Americans supported the League, though its official membership was around 150,000. It presented itself as a popular movement, but its public supporters were largely the better off.

"States' rights," which is the refrain voiced in opposition to the federal government's domination of state governments, is yet another strain of antigovernment sentiment. States'-righters usually argue that the federal government is encroaching on the power of states, though often they are against state action too. In the middle of the nineteenth century, in an attempt to protect slavery, southern politicians led their states to secede from the Union. Secessionists argued that the federal government had no right to abolish slavery in new states and territories, assuming (probably correctly) that in an expanding nation this prohibition eventually would lead to the end of slavery. They believed that the states should have the right to decide if slavery would persist or not. More than 600,000 Americans, North and South, died in the ensuing Civil War. The secessionists lost, the Union was preserved, and slavery was abolished.

More recently, groups have used states' rights arguments to oppose government's attempts to reduce inequities in society or to create new opportunities for marginalized groups. In 1968, Alabama governor George Wallace, who had gained a national reputation opposing integration of the Alabama public schools, attacked civil rights leaders, antiwar dissents, and "pointy-headed bureaucrats" on his way to winning 13 percent of the vote and carrying five southern states while running for president as a third-party candidate. He gained millions of supporters, largely working class and mostly, but not exclusively, in the South, who sympathized with his attacks on the federal government's attempts to bring about racial equality and deny state governments their authority over such matters.

Antiwar movements are another manifestation of antigovernment activism. All U.S. wars have had vocal opponents. Probably the most successful was the the anti–Vietnam War movement, an amorphous movement of many groups, largely young people, who protested the Vietnam War and the growth and use of the American military. Antiwar movements often criticize the alliances between big business and government that allow business to make profits while young people are sent abroad to fight and sometimes die.

And, of course, some groups protest against big government in less specific ways. In the latter part of the nineteenth century, a variety of antigovernment groups (called anarchists) sprung up, affiliating with an international antigovernment philosophy. Some anarchists were affiliated with labor unions and sought to replace government with labor organizations. In 1886, anarchists staged a rally in Chicago's Haymarket Square. A bomb was thrown at police, and police opened fire on the crowd and, as it turned out, each other. Eleven people died.

In sum, individuals and groups protest against big government for many reasons and in different ways. Some people are consistently against government action in any arena, whereas most people favor government action in some areas but not in others.

OPINIONS ABOUT GOVERNMENT IN THE OBAMA YEARS

With an understanding of Americans' historical ambivalence about government, combining suspicion of government on the one hand but support for government action on the other, you can better understand today's contradictory currents. Although government has grown in some ways, with support from the 2008 electorate, there is also a very visible backlash against big government.

Impact of the Recession

The backdrop to today's backlash against big government is the severe recession of 2008–2009 and its lingering unemployment through 2010. Many Americans were laid off, and many others were unable to pay their mortgages. Countless people were afraid that they, too, would lose their jobs. Middle-class folks were worried that their children would face harder times and never achieve "the American dream." Polls showed widespread despair and loss of confidence.[31] Economic concerns underscored the events of the decade, which *Time* labeled "The Decade from Hell."[32]

Both the Bush and Obama administrations believed that it was necessary to bail out the huge companies—banks, insurers, and automakers—that were teetering on the brink of collapse. The companies were so big that their failures could cause our entire financial system to collapse. Economists feared that a second Great Depression could ensue.

The public's sour mood, however, prompted opposition to the bailouts, especially to the investment firms whose risky loans and investments caused the recession. No matter that most economists and most Republican and Democratic leaders considered the bailouts necessary. Many members of the public recoiled from the cost to taxpayers and from the activism of government that the bailouts symbolized. They wondered why the Wall Street bankers were being bailed out when the millions who lost their jobs weren't. And, the public wanted those responsible—the executives, who walked away with millions as employees lost their jobs and stockholders lost their retirement funds—held accountable. While the economists and politicians were thinking in pragmatic terms—What will keep this from getting worse?—many people were thinking in moralistic and political terms.

As the recession continued, the public questioned the value of the bailouts, which were seen as a gift to Wall Street but no help to Main Street. When people heard economists and politicians say that the huge corporations were "too big to fail," individuals who were struggling felt that they were "too small to notice."[33] These people included liberals as well as conservatives; average Americans across the board objected to the bailouts. They perceived "that one set of rules applies to one group of people—generally wealthy and well connected—and another set of rules applies to the rest. And worse, that the many are subsidizing the few, cleaning up the messes they made."[34] These feelings were rubbed raw when it became known that the executives of some failing banks were walking away with millions of dollars of bonuses.

Despite the opposition to the bailouts from many liberals and conservatives and many Democrats and Republicans, there are sharp differences between Americans who are liberal and Democratic and those who are conservative and Republican. Today, liberals and Democrats tend to favor more equal distribution of the nation's wealth, whereas conservatives and Republicans tend to favor lower taxes and smaller government. Conservatives and Republicans dominate the current antigovernment surge because many of them have also been spurred by their objections to President Obama and to Democratic policies.

Reaction to President Obama

Members of the public are more likely to accept far-reaching government actions when their party is in power or when they believe the president is acting in their interest. Thus, most Americans accepted the expansion of government immediately after 9/11 under President Bush because they trusted him and thought he was doing what was best for the country in that crisis. (Later, many people, mostly independents and Democrats, lost trust.)

But, even though President Obama also faced an emergency situation with the threat to the national economy, many people did not trust him. It was clear during the presidential campaign, when some voters admitted that they would never vote for a black man, that some Americans would never accept a black president if elected. He wasn't (and still isn't) even considered a real American by millions of our fellow Americans. These "birthers" claim that Obama was born in Kenya, where his father was from, rather than in Hawaii, where he was actually born.[35] If he was not born in the United States, he is not a citizen and not eligible to become the president. For the birthers, then, Obama isn't a legitimate president. The birthers are especially prevalent in the South. Almost a year into his presidency, a plurality of Arkansans still denied that Obama is a citizen.[36] Some people believe other ridiculous claims circulating on the Internet, that Obama's secret religion is Islam and that his educational records were fabricated, despite ample evidence to the contrary.

These questions might not have arisen if Obama were white. As historians have observed, race is often an

Although the Republican Bush administration and the Democratic Obama administration both considered government bailouts of Wall Street banks essential to protect the nation's economy, many Americans abhorred the policy.

underlying concern in eras where economic times are hard.[37] This, of course, does not mean that all or most opponents of Obama are racists or that all or most criticisms of Obama are motivated by racism. Yet it would be naïve to discount the role of racism in the views toward Obama.

Reaction to Democratic Policies

The election of Democratic majorities to the House of Representatives and Senate in 2006 and larger Democratic majorities and a Democratic president in 2008 brought expectations that the government would become more active in addressing intractable problems that had received scant attention in recent years. The Obama administration proposed an ambitious agenda, calling for health care reform, climate change measures, and education reform as well as stabilizing the economy, all in the president's first term. At the outset, Obama's chief of staff made a point of repeating a phrase that he said summarized the administration's approach: "A crisis is a terrible thing to waste." The press kept this phrase in the news, hammering home the point about the president's far-ranging goals.

Although Obama's agenda resonated with the public during the election campaign, once Obama was sworn in and the economic climate showed no signs of improving, the public's priorities became focused on creating new jobs rather than on these other issues. And the president, with his focus on stabilizing the financial system and addressing Wall Street's problems as well as passing health care reform, seemed to become disconnected from the public's extreme anxiety about the economy. Coupled with Americans' traditional distrust of big government, this anxiety led to a backlash against the Obama agenda, and his approval ratings fell from the mid-60s to about 50 percent.

Tea Partiers protest Obama health care plan.

AP Photo/Ed Andrieski

Health care reform also helped kindle vocal opposition to activist government. Conservative constituents flooded the town hall meetings held by members of Congress in 2009 when health care reform was under consideration. Some meetings became unruly forums as opponents of reform vented, calling their representatives, the president, and the entire federal government "socialist," "communist," or "fascist" (sometimes all of these simultaneously), and accusing them of acting like "Hitler" and "Nazis." (As one wag noted, students might be excused for wondering if we fought Germany in World War II because it provided too much health care.) Opponents could barely find language harsh enough to express their outrage. According to a woman who brought three busloads of protestors from Mississippi to Washington, "The consensus is that this is not a left-wing government, but that this is more of a Marxist [government]."[38] This rhetoric is similar to the anti–New Deal rhetoric of the 1930s, but with cable TV, blogs, and other ways to communicate instantly, the charges are multiplied and amplified.

Wild conspiracy theories promoted by Internet blogs, radio talk shows, and television commentators abounded. Rumors warned against "death panels" of government bureaucrats who would deny health care to deformed babies, the disabled, and the elderly. Rumors claimed that the administration would establish reeducation camps for the obese.[39] A woman at a town hall meeting in Virginia said, "I'm really afraid of this president. I mean, they're starting to talk about limits on family size, how many children you can have. In *our* America."[40] Another woman screamed, "Keep your government hands off my Medicare," apparently unaware that Medicare *is* a government program, in fact one of its biggest and most costly. These remarks spoke to the alienation from government that some Americans feel today. At a town hall meeting in Delaware, a woman wailed, "I want my country baaaaack!"[41]

The town hall meetings grew into the **Tea Party movement**, which represents many conservative voters.[42] Inspired by the Boston Tea Party of 1773 protesting taxation without representation (the colonists had no votes in Britain's Parliament, which levied taxes on them), the Tea Partiers complain that our modern government no longer reflects the Founders' expectations. These antigovernment protests around the country in 2009 and 2010 were promoted by Fox News and organized by a loose coalition of conservative populists who had formed small clubs connected through the Internet. The movement isn't a political party (at least as of this writing).

The Tea Partiers are disproportionately southern, white, male, and older than forty-five. They say they are conservative or very conservative.[43] They are also more likely than others to have a college education and less likely to be working class. A majority—nearly three times as many as other Americans—say they are "angry" about the way things are going in Washington.[44] About 70 percent of the

Talking Points

Barack Obama built a campaign strategy around a story of political identity, presenting himself, with a white mother from Kansas and black father from Kenya, as a kind of quintessential crossover, bridge-building, hyphenated American. His search was a journey millions of Americans have taken over the past thirty years as they studied family history and emerged with more clearly defined ethnic and racial identities and in some cases new political allegiances.

However, in the earliest days of our nation, it was taken for granted that creating a *nonhyphenated* American identity was essential for shaping a nation out of a loose confederation of competing states populated by immigrants from English-, German-, French-, and Spanish-speaking countries. At least one in five colonists had remained loyal to Britain during the Revolutionary War; although some were driven from the country, many remained. The founding generation of politicians believed that people would have to be carefully taught how to be American, learning a common language in public schools from books with common content and dictionaries whose vocabulary and spellings would be distinctly American. They saw a need for a new civic literature, including hagiographies of the Founders that would make them into something more than mortal men and thus focal points of a national identity.

By the late nineteenth century, in another peak period of immigration, leaders were still calling for the thorough "Americanization" of new arrivals. We "must see that the crucible turns our people out as Americans, of American nationality," Theodore Roosevelt argued, "and not as dwellers in a polyglot boarding house." The descendant of Dutch immigrants, Roosevelt did not believe in hyphenated identities, at least not for the purpose of political competition. He declared himself an "American-American."[1] An immigration-friendly politician, Roosevelt said the "hand of welcome" would be extended to all, but only if they threw off old ideas and became Americanized "in every way."[2] Any naturalized citizen who did throw off Old World habits and mores would then stand on level ground with any other American, including those descended from the Pilgrims. It was "a base outrage," Roosevelt said, for any voter "to oppose a man because of his religion or birthplace"; at the same time, he argued that no politician should ever compete for any vote by appeal to the voter's national origins.

When the poet Walt Whitman wrote, "Here is not merely a nation but a teeming Nation of nations," he said a lot about our country and its politics.[3] It is a cliché, yet true, that the United States is a land of immigrants, peopled by individuals from all over the world. Americans are a conglomeration of religions, races, ethnicities, cultural traditions, and socioeconomic groups—what one historian calls "a collision of histories."[4]

This chapter profiles the American people and explains why democracy, when practiced by people who are ethnically, economically, and religiously diverse and scattered across a vast and varied landscape, is destined to be characterized as much by competition and conflict as by cooperation and community. But it also identifies the political values we share, and describes how those values are expressed in our form of government. The final sections briefly describe how our diversity and political culture manifest themselves in our attitudes toward government and our participation in it.

A DEMOGRAPHIC PROFILE

Long before Europeans arrived, the population of North America was characterized by cultural diversity. Anthropologists are still debating the timing and points of origin of the first inhabitants, but many probably arrived by crossing a land bridge from Asia thousands of years ago, and others may have entered South America by sea and migrated north. Although sometimes characterized by a single term such as *Indians* or *Native Americans*, the first immigrants went on to found many different civilizations. Their nations were competitive and at times at war, and their differences were substantial enough to doom eighteenth-century efforts to form pan-Indian alliances against European colonization.[5] Today, the U.S. Census Bureau recognizes 564 different tribes, many fewer than there were 300 years ago, but still suggestive of the wide array of cultures that predated European settlement.

The umbrella term *European* is itself somewhat deceptive in that European settlers emigrated from countries that not only differed linguistically, religiously, and politically but also had often been at war with one another. Migrants carried some of these conflicts with them to America.

Immigration and Ethnic Diversity

Because the colonies were ruled from England, and its language and culture were dominant, we tend to think of early Americans as Anglos and Protestants. But the earliest European settlers of the southeastern and southwestern territories were more likely to be Roman Catholics from France and Spain than Anglo-Protestants. In fact, much of what is now Arizona, New Mexico, California, and Texas was populated by Mexican Catholics of mixed Spanish and Indian descent. Over time, Germany, a country linguistically and culturally distinct from Great Britain and one evenly

This Italian family arrives at Ellis Island in 1905.

Popperfoto/Getty Images

split between Catholics and Protestants, provided more immigrants to America than England.

By preference, or to avoid discrimination by earlier-arriving or more dominant settlers, immigrants often self-segregated into territories (Puritans in Massachusetts, Quakers in Pennsylvania and Rhode Island, Catholics in Maryland), which later became states. These different beliefs and traditions contributed to the rise of distinctive local cultures and to the varying character of state governments and politics.

Like Europeans, Africans, too, came from a huge continent that encompassed many languages, cultures, and religions. Even though the European slave trade was concentrated in coastal areas of West Africa, the men and women forcibly removed to the Americas did not share a common tradition. But their experience in the American colonies united most in a common condition as noncitizens lacking all political and economic rights.

After the Revolution and the formation of the United States, the new government began to articulate an immigration policy, removing it from the hands of state governments. Ever since, there have been disagreements over the standards for regulating admission. Congress began restricting immigration in 1798, when, through the Alien Act, it gave the president power to deport people he deemed "dangerous to the peace and safety" of the country. And the time

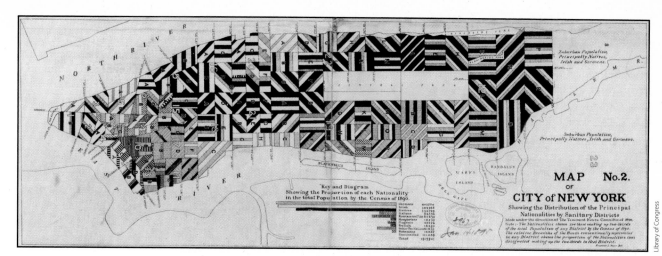

Library of Congress

This map of sanitary districts in New York City in 1895 shows the nationalities of immigrants' neighborhoods. Each pattern represents a different ethnicity.

behind the scenes

The Torch Passes

In 1882 a group of New Yorkers organized an art exhibit to raise money to pay for the erection of "Liberty Enlightening the World," the monumental sculpture France had given to the United States. One of the organizers asked a prominent New York writer to compose "some verses appropriate to the occasion."[1] Working only from photographs of the statue, which was yet to be shipped from France, Emma Lazarus wrote, "The New Colossus," which included these now famous words: ". . . give me your tired, your poor, your huddled masses yearning to breathe free, the wretched refuse of your teeming shore. Send these, the homeless, tempest tossed to me, I lift my lamp beside the golden door!"

Until Lazarus wrote those lines, neither the statue's donors nor its American recipients thought the Statue of Liberty had anything to do with immigration. Rather, it stood for the triumph of the republican form of government over monarchy. The woman with the torch symbolized the Enlightenment philosophy that had so influenced both American and French revolutionaries, and she served as a reminder of how the pursuit of enlightenment through reason and science could bring liberty to the world.

Why did Lazarus, whose family had been in America since at least the mid-1700s, who mingled with the families of America's literary aristocracy—Ralph Waldo Emerson, Nathaniel Hawthorn, James Russell Lowell, and Henry James— and who had shown no prior interest in immigration, want to redefine the statue's meaning? Lazarus was a secular Jew who just recently had been drawn into the cause of resettling Jewish immigrants fleeing persecution in Russia and eastern Europe. Her shock on learning about the conditions driving them from their home countries broadened her interest in all refugees entering the United States, and she believed that the erection of the statue in New York's harbor could be used to draw public attention to their plight.

Lazarus's poem *was* read at the fund-raiser despite the divergence of her views from those of the statue's benefactors and even though no one wanted to hear the lines about "wretched refuse." But it was then put aside and virtually forgotten. Lazarus died several years later, at thirty-eight, still a celebrated literary figure, although "The New Colossus" was little mentioned in obituaries. In 1903, in a service commemorating the twenty-fifth anniversary of her death, the poem was engraved on a plaque, deposited inside the statue's base, and then once again ignored.

But with the rise of fascism in Germany, Italy, and Spain in the 1930s, a new round of refugees began streaming toward America. The country began to celebrate itself as a land of immigrants, and "The New Colossus" plaque was moved nearer the statue's entrance. Alfred Hitchcock's wartime film, *Saboteur*, ended with the heroine reciting the Lazarus poem while standing in the statue's crown. By the postwar years, Americans were beginning to see the statue as Lazarus had: not as the symbol of liberty through reason, but as "The Mother of Exiles" lighting the way for all who were fleeing oppressive political or economic conditions. (That might have been little solace to Lazarus had she known that most European Jews had been denied entry before and during World War II.)

[1] This account is based on Esther Schor, *Emma Lazarus* (New York: Schocken Books, 2006), 189–256.

required for "free white citizens" to become naturalized citizens was extended from two, to five, and then to fourteen years. An 1807 law prohibited the migration or "importation" of people for purposes of slavery.

But the ethnic and racial composition of the American population broadened in the mid- to late-nineteenth century as new waves of settlers came from southern and eastern Europe, China, and Japan, as well as Ireland and Germany. They included large numbers of Roman, Eastern, and Russian Orthodox Catholics; Jews; and some Buddhists until the 1882 Exclusionary Act prohibited further immigration from China. A 1907 agreement with Japan restricted Japanese entries to the Hawaiian Islands. But immigration continued at high levels into the twentieth century before peaking in the decade 1905–1914, when more than 10 million immigrants entered the country. (See the "Behind the Scenes" box.)

This surge led to efforts to slow the number of admissions. Between the 1920s and 1960s, immigration was open mainly to the European countries represented in the American population at the time of the 1910 census, thereby favoring British, German, and northern Europeans and penalizing southern and eastern Europeans and those from other continents. Laws passed through the end of World War II added new categories of people prohibited entry, including anarchists and revolutionaries, members of communist parties, and others deemed undesirable.

Not all immigrants who came stayed. In addition to deportations, about 30 percent of those who arrived between 1900 and 1990 returned voluntarily to their home countries. For a few years during the Great Depression of the 1930s, more people left the United States than entered.[6]

In 1965 the civil rights movement led to the end of the nationality restrictions on immigration that had been in place since the 1920s. With the removal of the old quota system, the door opened to people of every race, religion, and nationality.

People in some political categories have been given preferential treatment. During the Cold War, for example, virtually everyone fleeing a communist country, including several million Cubans, Russians, eastern Europeans, Vietnamese, Cambodians, and Laotians, were allowed in. Thousands of Chinese students were granted permanent

american*diversity

Census and Sensibility

Every ten years, as mandated by Article I, Section 2 of the U.S. Constitution, the government must "enumerate" the American population "in a Manner as [Congress] shall by law direct." The main purpose of the **United States Census** is to determine the size and distribution of population within states for the purpose of apportioning the fixed number of seats in the House of Representatives. This task was assigned by Congress to a Census Bureau (now in the Department of Commerce).

Census taking should be a fairly straightforward statistical procedure, albeit expensive and ever more logistically difficult as the country grows. But how to count America's residents has become a very contentious political issue. This would be true if the census *only* determined the size of congressional delegations, but its findings have other important political and economic consequences. Of special significance are the figures that reflect the racial and ethnic breakdown of the population. These data have become essential for implementation of the Voting Rights Act and court rulings stemming from the modern civil rights movement, as well as for a smorgasbord of set-asides, entitlements, and affirmative-action programs worth hundreds of billions of dollars.[1]

The 2010 census was one of the most contested in recent decades. The battle began just a few years after the 2000 census had been completed. As Republicans gained control over both the White House and Congress, support grew for downsizing the scope of the census. Preparations for the next census were delayed, full funding for it was denied, and staff positions in the Census Bureau were left vacant or filled with political appointees. It was a manifestation of the battle between the two major parties for control of Congress, a battle whose outcome depends in part on how accurate a count is made of the population and how it breaks down along racial and ethnic lines. Democrats favor the fullest count possible because they believe that most of the uncounted are poor and minorities, who are more likely to vote Democratic than Republican, or that they are undocumented residents, who are highly likely to be Hispanic. Of course, undocumented residents cannot vote, but they are part of the population count that determines how many House seats a state will be allotted. By one estimate, if all Hispanics living in the country were counted, six states would gain an additional member of Congress, Arizona would gain two seats, and Texas perhaps four more.

Many Republicans have resisted funding for training of census staff in methodologies that could provide a more accurate count, and they have found allies among grassroots groups and media commentators who oppose the residency under an amnesty following the 1989 Tiananmen Square massacre in Beijing.

Rivaling the surge in legal immigration in the 1990s are the millions of people who have arrived without papers since 2000, most of whom entered the country by crossing the Mexican border into the southwestern United States. Another group of unauthorized residents entered the country on temporary visas and overstayed them. Although the government has no system for verifying that visitors leave when their visas expire, it estimates that several hundred thousand per year do not and that they now account for 40 percent of the nearly 11 million undocumented people living in the United States.[7] (See Figure 1.) Their numbers have fallen by a million or more because of the recession and the stepped-up border enforcement that began during the 2008 election season. But undocumented residents were about 4 percent of the total population and over 5 percent of the labor force in 2009.[8]

When permanent residents become citizens—and one-third of all Americans who are foreign-born *are* naturalized U.S. citizens—all immediate members of their families living outside the United States automatically qualify for residency visas. In 2008, for example, almost 65 percent of all permanent residency visas were granted to immediate relatives of new citizens or of legal permanent residents.[9] This preference system was put in place as part of the 1960s reforms, which gave priority to family reunification. However, the number of family-sponsored visas granted is limited by an annual quota on that category as well as by the admissions quotas assigned to each country.

The preference system also creates a second big category for immigrants with job skills that are in high demand, such as in science, engineering, mathematics, and medicine. People with special job skills accounted for 15 percent of all legal residency permits granted in 2008.[10] Proposals for immigration reform call for increasing the size of this preference category at the expense of family-sponsored admissions.

The two remaining preference categories are for diversity admissions—people applying from countries with historically low rates of legal immigration to the United States—and refugees and asylees, people who have been displaced by natural disasters and war, for example, or who

counting of noncitizens. Sen. David Vitter (R-La.), for example, tried to hold up funding for the Census Bureau until it agreed to include a question on the census form asking a person's citizenship. And during the taking of the 2010 census, he proposed a measure that would require the population tally to include only citizens. However, the census *must* by law count all residents, without respect to citizenship, just as was done in the first census (1790), when enslaved men and women who had no political rights were counted for the purpose of allotting House seats. To "enumerate" only citizens would require a constitutional amendment.

These disagreements date back many years, but in the taking of the 2010 census the politics of allocating House seats was compounded by grassroots movements questioning the size and role of government. These movements challenged the government's right to collect any information other than the number of residents at a given address. The basic census form consists of ten

"I'm just the census-taker—I don't have to read you your rights."

© Lee Lorenz/The New Yorker Collection/www.cartoonbank.com

questions sent to Congress for approval well in advance of the count. In addition to a household count, the questions cover the sex, age, race, and ethnicity of residents. The TV commentator Glenn Beck joined Rep. Michele Bachmann (R-Minn.) and some libertarians in urging Americans to engage in a "partial boycott" of the census by responding only to the household count question, arguing that it would be a strike for freedom, privacy, and responsible government to refuse to answer the questions of "nosy bureaucrats." But Republicans on the House subcommittee that oversees the census disassociated themselves, saying that a boycott was "illogical, illegal and not in the best interest of our country."[2] In the end, the completion rate for 2010 census forms was similar to previous rates.

[1] Lawrence Wright, "One Drop of Blood," *New Yorker,* July 25, 1994, 47.
[2] Kate Zernike and Jim Rutenberg, "Census Day is Near, Carrying a Weight Far beyond the Raw Numbers," *New York Times,* March 30, 2010, A12.

Figure 1 || **Immigration Reached an All-Time High in the 1990s**

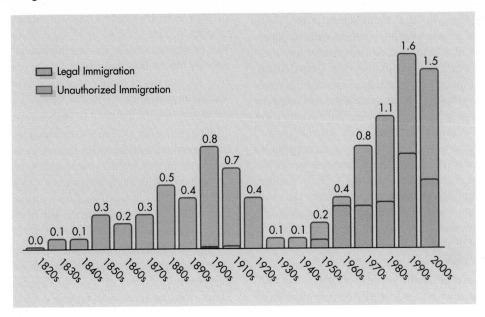

Note: *Figures for each decade are annual average number of immigrants in millions. Figures for legal immigration are arrivals only; figures for unauthorized immigration are estimates of net gain (arrivals minus departures).*
SOURCE: *Jeffrey Passel and D'Vera Cohn, U.S. Population Projections: 2005–2050 (Washington, D.C.: Pew Research Center, February 11, 2008), 85. pewhispanic.org/files/reports/85.pdf.*

are fleeing political or religious persecution. Diversity visas accounted for 3.5 percent of admissions in 2008 and refugees and asylees for 17 percent. There is no numerical limit on how many asylees can receive permanent residency each year, and both refugees and asylees are fast-tracked to citizenship after one year of legal residence.[11]

In 2008, 1.1 million people were granted legal residency. More were born in Mexico than in any other country, followed distantly by persons born in China, India, the Philippines, and Cuba.[12] The family preference system for granting residency ensures that current trends in the ethnic diversification of the American population will continue, and it also explains why Hispanics, who accounted for less than 7 percent of the population in the 1990 census and 14 percent in the 2000 census, are projected to be 29 percent of the population by 2050 if current trends persist.[13] (See Figure 2.)

Immigration and Political Cleavage

Antiforeign, or nativist, sentiments have been common throughout our history. Some native-born Americans have feared economic competition from newcomers or have perceived non-English-speaking people or anyone with different traditions and religious practices as cultural threats. A wave of Germans arriving in Pennsylvania in the 1750s had Benjamin Franklin complaining about the use of bilingual street signs in Philadelphia and warning that if German immigration were not stopped the German language would replace English, and "even our government will become precarious."[14]

Such anti-immigrant sentiments usually are most pronounced when immigration levels are high and economic times are bad, which is why strong nativist sentiments influenced the politics of the mid-1800s, 1920s, and 1990s, and why they are again a force today. Many more people responding to a 2009 poll saw conflict between native-born Americans and immigrants than between black and white Americans.[15] Some of the most intense political cleavages have arisen between older and newer immigrants. Over half of Hispanic Americans, for example, believe that the United States has too many immigrants from Latin America.[16]

The wave of immigration produced by Ireland's potato famine in the 1840s created a fever of anti-Irish and anti-Catholic sentiment, which found expression in the Know-Nothing Party. The 1849 California Gold Rush precipitated the first wave of immigration from China, which continued through the next several decades as construction of transcontinental railways attracted Chinese laborers. This period ended in physical assaults on and purges of Chinese from California cities and led to the Exclusion Law of 1882 restricting Chinese immigration.[17] On the East Coast the huge wave of immigration in the late 1800s and early 1900s prompted a reaction against big-city political machines, which were supported by Jewish, Italian, eastern European, and Irish immigrants.

Patriotic fervor during World War I produced hostility toward Americans of German ancestry, and the Russian Revolution led to the Red Scare of the 1920s and the deportation of many Russian and eastern European immigrants. During World War II, Japanese Americans were targeted as

| Figure 2 | Changes in the Race and Ethnicity of Americans |

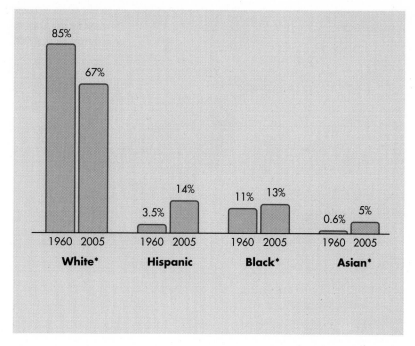

SOURCE: *Jeffrey Passel and D'Vera Cohn, U.S. Population Projections: 2005–2050 (Washington, D.C.: Pew Research Center, February 11, 2008), 85.*
pewhispanic.org/files/reports/85.pdf.

potential collaborators with Japan, had their property confiscated, and were imprisoned in camps under military guard.

Although each generation of immigrants has faced resentment from preceding generations, each has contributed to the building of America. Early European immigrants settled the eastern seaboard and pushed west to open the frontier. Africans' slave labor helped build the South's economy. Germans and Scandinavians developed the Midwest into an agricultural heartland, and free blacks and Irish, Italian, Polish, and Russian newcomers provided labor for America's industrial revolution and turned many cities into huge metropolises. Chinese immigrants helped build the transcontinental railroad linking East and West, and Japanese and Hispanics were instrumental in making California our top food producer. More recently, young Chinese and Indian immigrants have figured prominently in high-tech industries, and older Indian immigrants dominate the motel business in the United States. (See Table 1.)

Religious Diversity

We know that many of our earliest settlers—French Huguenots (Calvinists), German Anabaptists, British Methodists, Catholics, and Quakers—came here to escape religious intolerance in Europe. Nevertheless, few who emigrated to the Americas expected to live in a nonreligious state. Once here, many found it necessary to establish separate communities to ensure freedom for their form of religious practice. French Huguenots, who arrived in Florida fifty years before the Pilgrims set sail from England,

fled the Catholic-Protestant wars in France. But shortly after arriving in what was then a Spanish territory, the Huguenots found themselves targeted for burning and lynching by the king of Spain. Georgia eventually was established as a "buffer between the Protestant English colonies and the Spanish missions of Florida." Its charter banned Catholics.[18]

New Jersey, Pennsylvania, and Maryland were conceived and established as "plantations of religion" that gave state protection to specific religious groups.[19] Rhode Island was founded by the religious dissident Roger Williams, who, after being expelled from the Massachusetts Puritan society, which had executed several Quakers and banned Catholic priests, bought land from the Narragansett Indians and founded a colony for other religious outcasts.[20]

It was these experiences, not just religious intolerance in the Old World, that helped disabuse colonists of the idea that they could share both a government and a state religion. After independence, the Anglican Church in the United States gradually disassociated itself from the Church of England, which was, and is still today, headed by the monarch. Some at the Constitutional Convention wanted to name the newly independent Anglican, or Episcopalian, Church as the state religion, but most knew that a Constitution with such a provision would never be ratified. But six of the thirteen original states did establish an official religion, and some levied a religious tax, leaving it to individual taxpayers to designate which church would receive their tithes. Others set religious qualifications for state office, even though this was not allowed at the national level. State religions were not disestablished in Connecticut, Massachusetts, or New Jersey until

Table 1 — Relying on Immigrants

Percentage of American Workers Who Are Foreign Born*		Percentage of American Achievers and Innovators Who Are Foreign Born[†]	
1. Sewing operators	53%	Nobel winners (1990–2000)	26%
2. Drywall installers	51	International patent applicants	24
3. Farm workers	49	Venture company founders	24
4. Housekeepers	48	Tech company founders	25
5. Packers	45		
6. Gardeners	43		
7. Roofers	43		
8. Cab drivers	42		
9. Painters	41		
10. Masons	41		
14. General scientists	37		
20. Software developers	31		
21. Physicians	28		
28. Electrical engineers	26		

*The ranking of 187 professions ranges from the profession with the largest percentage of foreign-born workers to the one with the lowest percentage.

[†]The percentage of all Americans who are foreign born is just 13.

SOURCES: Census, "Higher Education, Innovation and Growth" by Giovanni Teri, 2007; "American Made: The Impact of Immigrant Entrepreneurs and Professionals on U.S. Competitiveness" by Stuart Anderson and Michaela Platzer, 2006; "The Ethnic Composition of U.S. Inventors" by William R. Kerr, 2006; "America's New Immigrant Entrepreneurs" by Vivek Wadhwa, et al., 2007, Kaufman Foundation; Foreign Labor Certification Data Center.

the nineteenth century, and even then, some courts considered Christian teachings an integral part of common law.[21]

Despite the diversity in religious practice, instruction and textbooks in public schools drew much of their content from the Protestant Bible. School officials maintained that instruction was "nonsectarian," but their reluctance to remove blatantly anti-Catholic material led to the creation of Catholic church-run schools, which remain today a major alternative to public schools. Occasionally, religious differences led to violence, as in Philadelphia's Bible riots of 1843, when Protestants burned down a Catholic school and thirteen people were killed.[22] The Philadelphia church burnings targeted only Irish Catholic churches, not those of the older American German Catholic population.

The Know-Nothing Party won popularity during this period by spreading fear of a Catholic takeover. Catholic-Protestant conflict lasted well into the twentieth century, could be intense, and sometimes trumped ethnicity. In the small farm community of Carroll, Iowa, for example, German and other Protestants joined forces against allied German and Irish Catholics, passing "puritan Sunday" laws that prohibited Catholic church dances, singing parties, and serving alcohol on the Sabbath.[23]

These anecdotes from the distant past are a reminder that being all white and all Christian did not spare communities from exclusionary or repressive assimilationist tactics or violence against those of a different ancestry or church

affiliation. Claims that our political unity is being undermined by ethnic and religious diversity are hardly new.

America's religious profile is changing along with its ethnic makeup. This is in part but not solely a function of immigration. The decennial census has not collected data on individual religious affiliations since 1950 because Congress refuses to authorize funding for it. Collecting the information is considered too personal and a possible disincentive to participate in the census, and it would add to the cost of census-taking as well. However, between 1850 and 1950 census takers did collect information on the number and type of religious organizations, and it showed a steady proliferation from 18 principal denominations in 1850 to 186 in 1906.[24]

Today, data on personal religious affiliations come from private surveys, and these show continued growth in types of affiliations and in religious mobility. A 2007 survey found that 28 percent of American adults had left the faith they were raised in and that 44 percent of all adults had made some shift in religious affiliation. Although 78 percent still identify as Christians, they are split among dozens of sects and denominations, and the once dominant Protestants are now barely half of the population. The Catholic Church has lost ground among native-borns but has held its share of the Christian population because of the high level of immigration from Catholic countries such as Mexico. Sixteen percent of Americans claim no religious affiliation,

When young people in downtown Chicago rallied for immigration overhaul, some publicly declared their illegal status.

AP Photo/M. Spencer Green

although the figure is higher (25 percent) for eighteen- to twenty-nine-year-olds. Most of the remaining 6 percent are adherents of other major religious traditions: Jews, Muslims, Hindus, and Buddhists.[25] (See Table 2.) To some observers, these figures represent the potential for social fragmentation; but as the great French philosopher Voltaire once wrote: a nation with one church will have oppression; with two, civil war; with a hundred, freedom.[26] In other words, a proliferation of religious affiliations may both bolster liberty and serve as its measure.[27]

Economic and Demographic Diversity

Diversity involves more than differences in national origin, race, and religious affiliation. Where people settle, what they do for a living, how much they earn, when they were born, and how long they have been here are all potential bases for political difference, and over time these factors are probably more important than religion or country of origin.

Although racial and ethnic cleavages have garnered much of the attention throughout our history, economic diversity is at least as important. In 2009 almost half of Americans believed that conflict between rich and poor was greater than that between blacks and whites.[28] We may think of America as a land of opportunity, but most people who are born poor in the United States stay poor. Opportunities knock harder and more often for those who are born into the upper and middle classes. And although our society is not as class conscious as many others, our personal economic situations play an important part in shaping our views toward politics and our role in the process. Most people who are poor, for example, do not vote, but those who do vote tend to vote Democratic. Most affluent Americans do vote, and they vote in larger numbers for Republicans than for Democrats. Economic inequality continues to grow as a flash point for political conflict as the gap between the lowest and highest income groups in America has grown from 35-fold to 75-fold over the past thirty years.[29]

Regional and residential differences can also be important, especially since they often intertwine with economic interests. Farmers in California and the Midwest, for example, are more likely than city dwellers to be supportive of farm subsidy legislation. City dwellers may be far more enthusiastic about federal laws that create national parks or wilderness areas than the Western ranchers who use the land to graze their livestock. And the concerns of citizens in poor southern states like Arkansas, Mississippi, and West Virginia may be very different from those in wealthy northeastern states like Connecticut and New Jersey, where annual per capita income is $25,000 to $30,000 higher.[30]

The classic and most costly example of regional conflict in our history was the division between South and North over the right of southern states to secede from the Union in order to maintain a regional economic system rooted in slavery. Although in that case economic and political disparities led to the bloodiest conflict in our history, regional diversity usually results in no more than political difference and economic competition. However, in the face of growing income inequality and the residential segregation of gated communities, there is the danger that residential separation will lead to the political indifference of the well-off to the needs of poor neighborhoods.

Age differences, too, can affect political orientation. The needs and interests of older citizens are substantially

Table 2	Religious Affiliations of Americans

Major Religious Traditions in the U.S. among All Adults . . . %*	
Christian	
Evangelical Protestant	26.3
Mainline Protestant	18.1
Historically black Protestant	6.9
Catholic	23.9
Orthodox Catholic (Russian and Greek Orthodox)	0.9
Mormon	1.7
Other World Religions	
Jewish	1.7
Buddhist	0.7
Muslim†	0.6
Hindu	0.4
Other faiths/world religions	1.5
Unaffiliated	16.1
Don't Know/Refused	0.8

*Due to rounding, figures do not add to 100.
†From *Muslim Americas: Middle Class and Mostly Mainstream* (Washington, D.C.: Pew Research Center, 2007).
SOURCE: 2007 U.S. Religious Landscape Study, Pew Forum on Religion & Public Life; (religions. pewforum.org/affiliations); Religion Among the Millenials, PEW poll, February 17, 2010 (pewresearch.org/Age/Religion-Among-the-Millenials.aspx).

different from those of young adults, especially in such basic policy areas as access to health care for the former and to educational and job opportunities for the latter. The United States, like Canada and western Europe, has an aging population; although mitigated by higher birthrates among newer immigrants, 13 percent of Americans were sixty-five or older in 2010, heading toward 20 percent by 2050.[31] Their interest groups are among the most powerful in the country, and in the 2010 midterm election they formed 23 percent of the electorate, compared to 11 percent for the under-thirties. This fact has made economic security and health care for senior citizens high-priority policy issues, even while the number of children living in poverty and job insecurity for college graduates are increasing.

Diversity and Identity Politics

Why, when the American population has always been so heterogeneous, does diversity seem to have so much more meaning in contemporary political life? One reason is that although society was diverse in the early decades of the Republic, the political spectrum was narrow, and the majority of citizens were excluded from participation. Those granted full rights of participation varied from state to state, but two groups—women and African American men, with the exception of a small number of free black men living in the North—were comprehensively shut out after the ratification of the Constitution. (So were some white men who did not own property or, for a brief time, did not belong to an established church).

Diversity's scope for expression has been greatly broadened through the slow expansion of the electorate and the opening up of the political system. The voting and politically active public has become steadily more heterogeneous since the 1920s. Later, the federal government's adoption of race, gender, and ethnic preference programs, beginning in the Nixon administration, and the wave of immigration from Asia and Latin America in the 1980s and 1990s, have also increased the importance of diversity in American politics.

As government adopted affirmative-action policies to compensate for historical discrimination (see Chapter 15), an individual's race, gender, or ethnicity took on added political importance. The use of such factors to influence the division of public resources has given rise to **identity politics**: the practice of organizing on the basis of one's ethnic or racial identity, sex, or sexual orientation to compete for public resources and to influence public policy.[32]

Paradoxically, identity politics has intensified during a period in which racial and ethnic boundaries are beginning to blur. DNA testing has shown how problematic the concept of race is when used as a category in the United States Census. The ways we group by ethnicity or cultural heritage are just as slippery.

American Indians have also felt the tug of identity politics in recent decades. Their once dwindling population is now

"Actually, I prefer the term Arctic-American."

© The New Yorker Collection 2007 Glen Le Lievre from cartoonbank.com. All rights reserved.

burgeoning. The numbers began increasing with the Indian rights movement in the 1960s, as more people with Indian ancestry felt new pride and reclaimed their heritage. The enactment of affirmative-action programs and the economic opportunities presented by the growth of the gambling industry on reservation land undoubtedly attracted others. According to the census, the population of Indians has more than quadrupled, to 4 million, since 1960, a population increase that cannot be explained by birth and death records.[33] This includes persons who have full Indian ancestry as well as those who have only partial, distant, or even imagined Indian ancestry, who had not chosen to identify themselves as Indians in earlier decades. Today some federally recognized tribes are authorized to issue a Certificate of Degree of Indian Blood, or "white card," certifying that the carrier has a specified Indian "blood quantum" in order to be eligible for certain benefits.[34]

Despite their common usage, many identity categories are simplistic. *Hispanic* is a census catch-all term for Mexicans, Puerto Ricans, Cubans, and others with national origins in Central and South America and the Caribbean. Some Americans of Spanish descent, especially those whose ancestors came directly from Spain, tend to reject the Hispanic label altogether as a means of self-identification, and more than 40 percent of Hispanics would choose a racial category other than what is offered on the census, most often identifying with their country of national origin.[35] These are culturally and linguistically distinct groups of people, very mixed racially, and with different legal status within the United States. For example, all people born in Puerto Rico, a U.S. commonwealth, are citizens by birth, and Cuban immigrants enter the country under rules that do not apply to other Hispanics seeking entry.

Hispanic residential patterns also vary by country of origin. Mexican Americans are heavily concentrated in California and the Southwest, though there are significant populations in Illinois and increasing numbers in other parts of the Midwest and South. Puerto Ricans tend to live in New York, New Jersey, Miami, Boston, and Chicago, while Cubans are heavily concentrated in south Florida and New Jersey.

The "African" census category could apply to an African American whose ancestors have been in the United States since the seventeenth century, or to first-generation Americans who emigrated after laws restricting immigration from Africa were lifted in the 1960s. Since that change, more Africans have come to the United States than were brought here against their will during all the years of slavery.[36] In metropolitan New York, for example, 40 percent of African Americans are either first- or second-generation Americans.[37] The arrival of people who share some African ancestry but who came from many different countries and cultures has complicated group identity by race. In 2007, 47 percent of African Americans either believed blacks were not a single race or were not sure.[38]

Asian Americans are also a heterogeneous group. Those who have been here longest include those from Japan, China, and the Philippines. Newer groups include Vietnamese and Cambodians from Southeast Asia, many of whom fled their countries after the Vietnam War; those from the Indian subcontinent; and many others with very different cultures and histories. The population of Asian Americans is found disproportionately on the West Coast, Hawaii, the larger cities of the East Coast, and Chicago.

Similar variance can be found in religious categories. No one today would suggest that "Christian," as an unmodified category, is a predictor of political views or voting behavior, but this is also true for "Muslim." American Muslims are one of the most diverse Islamic communities in the world. Twenty percent are native-born African Americans, one-quarter have Arab ancestry, 18 percent are South Asian, and the remainder have come from Iran, Europe, Africa, and other regions.[39]

The decidedly mixed ancestry of Americans is steadily becoming more complex through intermarriage. So much racial and ethnic mixing occurs that, by the 1990 census, 100 million Americans could name no specific ancestry, or they reported multiple ancestries.[40] At some point in our history at least forty states had laws preventing marriage between men and women of different races, but in 2008, 22 percent of all Americans said they had at least one relative in a mixed marriage.[41] By one estimate as many as a quarter of white Americans and nearly half of black Americans belong to a multiracial family.[42]

POLITICAL CULTURE

In recent years, *diversity* has become a political catchword and has been raised to the level of a civic virtue. Yet our national motto is *E Pluribus Unum* ("Out of Many, One"), referring to the union of many states and the molding of one people from many traditions. There is a popular saying that Americans are people of many cultures united by a single idea. But what is that single idea, and is it, however fundamental, sufficient to form a political culture? A **political culture** is a shared body of values and beliefs that shapes perception and attitudes toward politics and government and in turn influences political behavior.

The National Museum of the American Indian on the Washington Mall reflects identity politics. Native Americans lobbied for the museum, consulted on its design, and here participated in opening ceremonies.

The Significance of Political Culture

For their stability and vitality governments rely on the support of citizens: their identification with the country and its method of governing and their adoption of the political values and behavior necessary to sustain the system. Without this support, government is ineffective or placed in the position of attempting to gain obedience through force or coercion.

In a democracy, sharing a political culture does not mean that citizens must agree on specific issues or even on the government's role in dealing with the country's problems. Democracy embraces conflict and competition just as it requires cooperation and a sense of community. A basic function of government is to establish the rules under which interests can compete. Thus, the essence of political culture is agreement on fundamental principles and on a common perception of the *rights* and *obligations* of citizenship and the rules for participating in the political process. These shared values reduce the strains produced by our differences and allow us to compete intensely on some issues while cooperating on others.

Learning Political Culture

Whether the newly created United States of America came about by "design of Providence," was a "lucky accident," or was the result of the Founders' skill in shaping a workable Constitution, it faced a problem common to all political systems: how to create a national identity among the citizenry.[43] Although American society has often been characterized as a melting pot, it has been a slow melt, and it has not happened by luck or accident. The Founders spoke of a united country, a people with common ancestry, a shared language, the same religion, and a commitment to the same political principles. From what you have read earlier in this chapter, you know this view was in some part wishful thinking. One of the most significant challenges to establishing a national political culture was the division of Americans among sovereign states. It is easy to forget that not long ago, people's identity as Virginians or Pennsylvanians was much more important to them than being American. And it was not until the Civil War, under the influence of Abraham Lincoln's powerful reference at Gettysburg to the "unfinished work" of preserving the

american*diversity

Battle of the (Text) Books: Who Made America America?

"Founders Chic?" "White man's history?" This is how the historians Howard Zinn and Ray Rafael describe traditional accounts of the Founding. They maintain that by concentrating on the role of elites and great historical figures, these top-down accounts "marginalize the masses" and write the people out of the American story. Rhapsodizing about the role of the Founders and their collective genius as represented in the Constitution makes it seem that just a handful of key historical figures made America America. Such accounts omit or barely mention the role of women, African Americans, and other major players in the American story. Yet it was "real people, not paper heroes, [who] made and endured the American Revolution," Rafael writes.[1]

The growing influence of identity politics in the 1960s and 1970s awakened some scholars to the need to be more inclusive and influenced a shift in American studies from the top-down focus to the study of social history, popular culture, and the role of the people in the making of American history and political culture. The new movement politics also created an audience for a revisionist interpretation of the Founding and the evolution of American government.

The most famous of the books to come out of this period was Howard Zinn's *A People's History of the United States,* first published in 1980 with a printing of just 4,000 copies.[2] Zinn (1922–2010) removed what he called the "glow" from accounts of the Founders and other great men, reminding readers of Columbus's "genocidal" treatment of Native Americans, Theodore Roosevelt's "warmongering," and Lincoln's "racism." But Zinn's main purpose was to bring in the contributions of those he saw as the real principals in America's story—workers, farmers, women, abolitionists, and protesters of all varieties. "Shifting history's lens from the upper rungs to the lower, we are learning more than ever about the masses of people who did the work that made society tick."[3] Coinciding with the rise of inclusionist movements and post-Watergate iconoclasm, Zinn's book found a large audience and went on to sell (as of this writing) 2 million copies.

Zinn took all accounts of American history and government as reflections of their authors' views and saw no need for his own work to strive for impartiality. To scholars of the left, Zinn's book was "a step toward a coherent new version of American history." But to those in mainstream academia, Zinn was seen more as a popularizer whose partisan interpretations worked too hard at turning American icons into villains.[4] The success of Zinn's book led to other revisionist accounts that took

Union, that Americans began referring to the United States with the singular *is* rather than the plural *are*.[44]

Most of the Founders believed that an educated citizenry was essential to the survival of the new republic, and advocates of public education such as Daniel Webster argued that only educated citizens would be able to understand public issues, elect virtuous leaders, and "sustain the delicate balance between liberty and order in the new political system."[45] Jefferson put it much more ominously: "If a nation expects to be ignorant and free, in a state of civilization, it expects what never was and never will be." As the public school system emerged, increasing emphasis was placed on the "training of citizens in patriotism, political knowledge and public affairs."[46] Although schools were then (as they are now) under local control, there was some common content in civic education around the country. (See the box "Battle of the Textbooks.")

As the immigration rate exploded in the late nineteenth century, some officials began to worry that not enough was being done to assimilate new arrivals into American political culture. It was at this time that a concerted effort was made to establish the American flag as a national symbol.[47] Public schools started flying the flag in 1890, and the Pledge of Allegiance to the flag was adopted in 1892.[48] By the mid-twentieth century, most elementary school children were studying current events in their *Weekly Reader* and beginning each day by reciting the Pledge. Many states required high school students to pass an exam on the U.S. Constitution, and perhaps the state constitution as well, to graduate.

In the twentieth century the mass media emerged as another important agent of political acculturation (discussed in Chapters 4 and 5). Newspapers, magazines, radio, and television were important purveyors of information on the workings of government and the rules of the game. But today cable and online news services and blogs are much more diverse and fragmented in content than the old sources they are supplanting. They target specialized audiences, allowing each consumer of news to seek out those sources closest to his or her own views (sometimes collectively called the "Daily Me") rather than relying on several common sources shared by the great majority of the population,

the Founders down a peg or two while elevating the role of the common people. Among them was Rafael's popular book detailing how some of the best-known stories about the Founding had been written decades and even a century after the Revolutionary War.[5] We "cling" to these myths anyway, Rafael claims, because they are "good stories" and they help create a "collective identity."[6]

The adoption of Zinn's *People's History* as a high school social studies and college political science text fueled the controversy over whose version of America's Founding students should be reading. Among Zinn's fiercest academic critics were two historians, Larry Schweikart and Michael Allen, who wrote a countertext, *A Patriotic History of the United States*.[7] Wanting to restore the glow surrounding traditional accounts of the Founding and to resuscitate the concept of American exceptionalism, they emphasized the significance of the Reagan presidency and debunked heroes of American progressivism, such as Franklin D. Roosevelt, just as Zinn and his disciples tried to demythologize Columbus, the Founders, and Lincoln. Schweikart argued that America really "was a city set on a hill . . . founded by extremely devout people," and said that the idea that there is a separation of church and state in the United States "defies logic." No fan of people's movements such as those for consumer and environmental protection, he claimed that the Founders "would have been horrified by such intrusions on liberty, regardless

of the virtue of the cause."[8] The coauthors wrote that if "the story of America's past is told fairly, the result cannot be anything but a deepened patriotism."[9] Promoted by radio talk show host Rush Limbaugh, *A Patriotic History of the United States* joined Zinn's *People's History* on the *New York Times* bestseller list.

To read Zinn or Rafael on the one hand or Schweikart and Allen on the other, one observer wrote, "is to inhabit two utterly different Americas that have almost nothing to say to each other."[10] This battle of the textbooks is an indication of how seriously some people take the role of classroom reading in teaching political culture and in winning the hearts and minds of young people. But today, a historian of the American South says, "It is not regional or ethnic identity but ideological commitment that threatens to submerge larger "national myths."[11]

[1] Ray Rafael, *A People's History of the American Revolution: How Common People Shaped the Fight for Independence* (New York: The New Press, 2001), 1.

[2] Howard Zinn, *A People's History of the United States, 1492 -Present* (New York: HarperCollins, 2003), first published 1980.

[3] Howard Zinn, "Series Preface," in Rafael, *A People's History*.

[4] The historian Eric Foner quoted in Michael Powell, "Howard Zinn, Historian, Is Dead at 87," *New York Times*, January 29, 2010, B10.

[5] Ray Rafael, *The Founding Myths: Stories That Hide Our Patriotic Past* (New York: The New Press, 2004), 1.

[6] Ibid., 5.

[7] Larry Schweikart and Michael Allen, *A Patriotic History of the United States: From Columbus's Great Discovery to the War on Terror* (New York: Penguin, 2004).

[8] From an interview by Rush Limbaugh, March 2005, reprinted in the 2007 Sentinel edition of ibid., xi–xx.

[9] Introduction to the 2007 edition of Schweikart and Allen, *A Patriotic History*, xx1.

[10] Sam Tannenhaus, "Identity Politics Leans Right," *New York Times*, March 21, 2010, Wk2.

[11] The historian C. Vann Woodward, quoted in ibid.

as was the case when most Americans watched the network evening news or read a major newspaper.

A perennial issue in the debate over what is required to sustain a political culture is whether all citizens should speak a common language. But the Founders took it for granted that English would be the national language, and Noah Webster's 1783 textbook promoting "a new national language to be spelled and pronounced differently from British English" was one of the first attempts to create an American national identity.[49] Webster, a Connecticut schoolteacher, wanted British textbooks banned from the classroom, saying that the wiping out of Old World maxims had to begin in infancy: "Let the first word he lisps be Washington."[50] In 1828 Webster published the *Dictionary of American English*—a dictionary "suited to the needs of the American people"—because, he argued, Americans could never accept the British definitions of senate, congress, assembly, and courts.[51] Another objective was to standardize the multitude of dialects, some mutually unintelligible, spoken by Americans of the time.[52] Today the United States has fewer spoken dialects than any other of the world's largest countries, a considerable accomplishment given the diversity of our collective heritage and strong regional cultures.

Webster's belief that a single language was essential to developing a common political culture has been an abiding issue in American politics. But when new states were carved from French- and Spanish-speaking territories through the Louisiana Purchase and the Mexican-American War, there was official acceptance of bilingualism. It was not until after the Civil War, when new emphasis was placed on one nation rather than many states, that state laws and local policies embracing bilingualism were erased from the books. New assimilationist policies also attempted to stamp out dozens of Native American languages by enrolling Indian children in English-speaking schools. Fear of German-speaking

CAN YOU PASS THE TEST TO BECOME A CITIZEN?

The civics test required for those seeking to become naturalized citizens includes 100 questions. Here are 10. For the answers and the rest of the questions, see www.uscis.gov.

1. How many amendments does the Constitution have?
2. What stops **one** branch of government from becoming too powerful?
3. The House of Representatives has how many voting members?
4. There are four amendments to the Constitution about who can vote. Describe **one** of them.
5. What are **two** rights only for United States citizens?
6. The *Federalist Papers* supported the passage of the U.S. Constitution. Name **one** of the writers.
7. What territory did the United States buy from France in 1803?
8. Who was president during World War I?
9. Name **one** U.S. territory.
10. Why does the flag have thirteen stripes?

This woman from Yemen is sworn in as a new American citizen in Detroit.

immigrants in the early part of the twentieth century led Iowa to pass a law requiring all groups of two or more people to speak in English, even when using the telephone.[53] In the current era, when most immigration has come from non-English-speaking countries and some urban school districts teach in a hundred or more languages, thirty states and at least nineteen cities have passed laws establishing English as the official language. And proof of minimal competency in English is part of the civics test given to those applying for U.S. citizenship.

Today few schools require students to demonstrate proficiency in civics. Under the No Child Left Behind Act's mandatory testing for proficiency in math and English, the study of history and civics was neglected, something the 2010 education reforms sought to redress.[54] Based on data from surveys that test civic knowledge, it is safe to say that the majority of Americans would fail the test given to applicants for citizenship.[55] (See box "Can You Pass the Test to Become a Citizen?")

THE CORE VALUES

As described in this chapter, our "nation of nations" is crosscut with cultural, political, and economic cleavages, but despite our sometimes overwhelming diversity, most Americans do share some basic goals and values. The words Americans use to characterize their form of government are less likely to come from the Constitution than from the second paragraph of the Declaration of Independence: "We hold these Truths to be self-evident, that all Men are created equal, that they are endowed by the Creator with certain unalienable Rights, that among these are Life, Liberty, and the Pursuit of Happiness."

From these words we can infer the basic assumptions, or core beliefs, on which the American system was founded: universal truths that can be known and acted on, equality before the law, belief in a higher power that transcends human law, and rights that are entitlements at birth and therefore can be neither granted nor taken away by government. The fundamental concept is liberty, especially the freedom to pursue one's livelihood and other personal goals that lead to a "happy" life.

The Declaration was primarily a political argument for separation from Great Britain, so it was concerned with the basic principles and philosophy of government.[56] Later, the Constitution reinforced the Declaration's emphasis on equality while specifying other core principles of American democracy: majority rule exercised through elected representatives and minority rights (a reference to political and religious minorities, not to racial and ethnic minorities). The Declaration is all principle; the Constitution is, of necessity, founded on political compromise.

Here we look briefly at each of the core principles of our political culture. Chapter 2 provides a more detailed description of how they are expressed in the Constitution.

Individual Liberty

Our belief in individual liberty has roots in the Judeo-Christian belief that every individual is equal and has worth before God. It has also been shaped by the works of the English philosophers Thomas Hobbes and John Locke. Briefly, they wrote that individuals give up some of their rights to government in return for creation of a society governed by laws in which they would be protected from one another. Individuals then use their remaining liberties to pursue their individually defined visions of the good life. There was a difference between Hobbes and Locke on what price individuals paid for surrendering some of their liberty to government. Hobbes believed that the surrender of rights was nearly absolute once the people put themselves under government protection, and the curtailment of freedom was justified by the selfish, greedy nature of human beings.[57] Locke did not share this dark view of the need for unlimited government. He believed that in creating government individuals were entering into a voluntary covenant with one another (the "whole people"), that their surrender of rights was limited, and that the government created was subject to alteration or dissolution if it did not fulfill its purpose of protecting individual liberty.[58] He articulated the concept of **natural rights**, which are inherent, so they exist as soon as people are born; unalienable, so they cannot be taken away by rules; and self-evident, so they can be known to all.[59]

Hobbes's dark view of human nature was certainly shared to some degree by many Founders and is reflected in the institutional arrangements of our federal Constitution. But it was Locke's concept of limited government operating according to written law that had greatest sway over the writers of our state and federal constitutions.

Influenced by these ideas, and reflecting the long tradition of individual rights in British law, early Americans emphasized individual liberty over other goals of government, and later Americans have reinforced this emphasis. Thus liberty is clearly reflected in both the Bill of Rights adopted by the Founders and in court rulings articulated by later generations of judges.

Such individualistic values have molded popular expectations. Immigrants often came and still come to America to be their own bosses. Living in a society with a clear commitment to individual liberty can be exciting and liberating. The other side of this coin is that we are also at liberty to fail and accept the consequences. And people who are limited by prejudice or poverty are given less help by government in overcoming these problems than people are given in other developed democracies that put more emphasis on the community as a whole rather than on the individual.[60]

The commitment to liberty is not absolute, however. Some restrictions are imposed on individual rights for the good of the community. For example, local zoning laws may restrict the liberty of one person to build a gas station in a residential neighborhood out of consideration for the neighborhood's residents and the value of their property. But our emphasis on

Assimilation can take a while. These children of Asian immigrants—from Taiwan, India, the Philippines, Bangladesh, and Korea—have grown up in America but feel, one said, "like the hyphen" in *Asian-American*—that is, between Asian and American.

individual liberty means that for better or worse—actually, for better *and* worse—there are fewer restrictions than in other countries where different values prevail.

A lively debate in recent decades has been sparked by those who believe that individual liberty has been overemphasized at the expense of community interests. Advocates of this position believe that our fixation on individual rights has led to a declining sense of community and a general lack of civility. They advocate revitalizing the concept of citizenship, including the responsibilities to participate in public life and "the qualities of character that self-government requires."[61] They call their program *communitarianism* and claim that it is much closer to the Founders' republican conception of freedom than is the modern liberal celebration of the unencumbered individual.

At the same time, many other people think that individual rights are not given enough weight in our society, that there are too many limitations on people's rights to do what they choose. These feelings are expressed in groups such as the Libertarian Party or the Tea Party movement.

Political Equality

The Judeo-Christian belief that all people are equal in the eyes of God led logically to other types of equality, such as **political equality**. The ancient Greek emphasis on the opportunity and responsibility of all citizens to participate in ruling their city-states also contributed to our notion of political equality. But the Founders were also influenced by contemporary ideas, especially theories of capitalism that were sweeping across Great Britain and the European continent. For American government the most significant lesson from those writings on free or self-regulating markets was their inference about the political competence of each individual. The best known of these theorists, Adam Smith (author of the *Wealth of Nations*), saw every man as bent on self-improvement and believed that, whether farmer, artisan, or aristocrat, each would make economic calculations in more or less the same rationalistic way when operating in a free market. Then why, some reasoned, wouldn't each man make political judgments in the same rational way and the farmer be as politically competent as, and therefore the equal of, the aristocrat? This was the lesson taken by Thomas Jefferson, who was serving in Europe at the time; he saw the free market as "the blueprint for a society of economically progressive, socially equal, and politically competent citizens."[62]

When the Declaration of Independence proclaimed that "all Men are created equal," however, it did not mean that all people are born with equal talents or abilities. It meant, and still means, that all citizens are born with equal standing before government and are entitled to equal rights.

In the early years of our country, however, as in the ancient Greek city-states, full rights of citizenship were conferred only on those thought to have the intellectual and moral judgment to act in the public interest. In both Greece and the United States, such thinking denied political rights to slaves, who were believed incapable of independent judgment, and to women, whose knowledge was seen as limited to the private or domestic sphere. This left a deep tension between the religious view that sees each individual as equal before God and the secular concept of differential political rights. Over time, this conflict was resolved in favor of the inherent worth of every individual and hence

Jason Tanaka Blaney Photography

the political equality of all. The conscious closing of this gap was noted by Lyndon Johnson when signing the 1964 Civil Rights Act into law: "Those who are equal before God shall now also be equal in the polling places, in the classrooms, in the factories."[63]

Long before the Civil Rights Act was passed, most Americans considered themselves relatively equal politically and socially, if not economically. At minimum, Americans tend to believe that they are *inherently* equal, even when equality cannot be realized in the political arena. Alexis de Tocqueville, a perceptive Frenchman who traveled through the United States in the 1830s, observed that Americans felt more equal to one another than Europeans did. He attributed this feeling to the absence of a hereditary monarchy and aristocracy in this country. Americans did not look up to royalty and aristocrats as their "betters" the way Europeans did.[64]

Popular Sovereignty

A belief in political equality leads to **popular sovereignty**, or rule by the people. President Abraham Lincoln expressed this concept when he spoke of "government of the people, by the people, and for the people." If individuals are equal, no one person or small group has the right to rule others. Instead, the people collectively rule themselves.

Popular sovereignty, then, led to our form of government, a **democracy**. The word *democracy,* derived from the Greek, means "authority of the people." If all political authority resides in the people, then the people have the right to govern themselves. And this results in a government by the many rather than by the few (aristocracy or oligarchy or theocracy) or by one (monarchy or dictatorship).

Majority Rule

If political authority rests in the people collectively, and if all people are equal, then the majority should rule. That is, when there are disagreements over policies, majorities rather than minorities should decide. If individuals are equal, then policies should be determined according to the desires of the greater number. Otherwise, some individuals, the minority, would have more authority than others.

Majority rule helps provide the support necessary for a government. Those in the minority go along because they accept this principle and expect to be in the majority on other issues or at other times. (It helps if everyone wins some of the time.[65]) The minority also go along because they expect those in the majority to respect their basic rights. If these expectations are not fulfilled, the minority are less likely to accept majority rule and to tolerate majority decisions. Thus majority rule normally entails minority rights.

Minority Rights

The Founders were concerned about the rights of political and religious minorities. As a result of the expansion of individual rights in the twentieth century, Americans today are concerned about the rights of racial, ethnic, and sexual minorities as well.

Although **minority rights** are necessary to preserve majority rule in the long run, the two concepts clash with each other on a daily basis. For a democratic government, it's a delicate balance, and a constant struggle, to find an appropriate accommodation between majority rule and minority rights. Because the majority has more power, it tends to flex its muscles at the expense of the minority. The most egregious example has been the enslavement, segregation, and discrimination directed at African Americans, but other examples occur every day in our society. The idea that everyone loses when minority rights are trampled is a lesson that does not stay learned.

DEMOCRACY?

Throughout the text, we will be raising questions about democracy and about the compatibility of aspects of our government and our beliefs with it. Let's start with something basic: Why are minority rights and majority rule not mutually exclusive? Are there situations in a democratic republic when they might be?

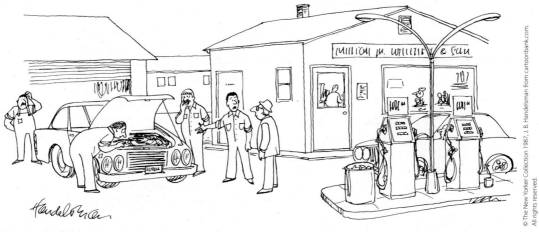

"We can't come to an agreement about how to fix your car, Mr. Simons. Sometimes that's the way things happen in a democracy."

© The New Yorker Collection 1987, J. B. Handelsman from cartoonbank.com. All rights reserved.

Economic Rights

The American Revolution was triggered by what the colonists saw as unfair taxation and other economic burdens placed on them by the British Parliament. To a certain extent, Americans fought the Revolution to be left alone to pursue their livelihoods and to ensure that they would not have to give up any part of their wealth without their consent.

Economic freedom, specifically the **right to own property**, is an adjunct to our concepts of individual liberty and natural rights. According to Locke, land rightly became the property of those who cleared and planted it, and with entitlement to all they produced through their own labor there was incentive to become more productive. Thus private property rights would lead to greater productivity for the economy as a whole.[66]

Just as tension exists between individual liberty and the public good, and between majority rule and minority rights, tension also exists between the political equality the Declaration of Independence avows and the property rights the Constitution protects (the latter will be discussed in Chapter 2). In reality, people who amass more wealth than others also exert more power over government.

Some Founders such as Thomas Jefferson and Charles Pinckney feared that democracy could not tolerate extremes of wealth and poverty. They thought that a wealthy minority, out of arrogance, and an impoverished minority, out of desperation, would seek their own improvement and disregard the public interest. Pinckney believed that at its founding the United States had less wealth inequality than any country on earth and thought it best that it stay that way to avoid the "dangerous influence" of rich men.[67] Most Founders worried less about this. They thought they could create a government that would protect individual diversity, including economic disparity, and still survive.

But the pursuit of political equality in a real world of great economic inequities has led government to a much greater role in regulating economic activity than the Founders anticipated. When we discuss antitrust laws and unfair business practices and when we discuss welfare, health care, and Social Security policies, we are implicitly debating whether government should reduce inequalities of wealth.

DEMOCRACY?

Can democracy function well when there are extreme differences in wealth and income? Why or why not?

We can see that democratic principles sometimes contradict each other. Americans have struggled for more than two centuries to reconcile practice with democratic aims and to perfect a system of government that was revolutionary for its time. We will see these contradictions many times in this book as we explore how government actually works.

THE AMERICAN CITIZEN

Supreme Court justice Louis Brandeis once said, "The most important office in a democracy is the office of citizen."[68] That democratic principles come alive only when people participate in government is a commonly held view. This raises two basic questions: how do rules for participation affect the level of participation, and how willing and prepared to participate is the average citizen?

One fundamental given that sets limits on citizen participation is that our form of government is an **indirect democracy**, also known as a **republic**. Citizens do not pass laws or make policy; they select policy makers to make decisions for them. It is members of Congress, not individual citizens, who vote most bills into law. These officials are

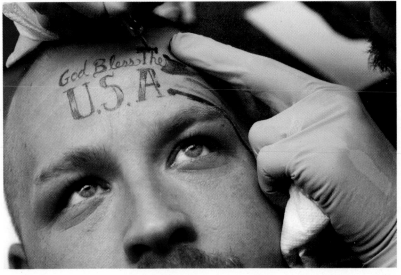

Americans are very patriotic, but many don't participate in our democracy.

AP Photo/St. Petersburg Times, Daniel Wallace

Talking Points

Some opponents of the health care reform passed in 2010 claim that the federal law is unconstitutional because the various regulations, mandates, taxes, and benefits usurp the powers of state governments under the Constitution. Some state attorneys general filed lawsuits to block the law, and some state legislatures considered legislation to prevent the law from taking effect in their states.

These opponents are called "**Tenthers**,"[1] because their argument is based on the **Tenth Amendment** to the Constitution, which declares, "The powers not delegated to the United States by the Constitution, nor prohibited by it to the States, are reserved to the States respectively, or to the people." Therefore, according to the Tenthers, any action taken by the federal government that isn't enumerated in the Constitution isn't constitutional. And providing for health care isn't enumerated. This argument rests on a very broad interpretation of the Tenth Amendment that is rejected by most constitutional scholars.[2]

Nevertheless, if accepted by the courts, this argument would have far-reaching consequences beyond health care legislation. The vast body of federal regulation of business,[3] which got the green light during the Great Depression, and social welfare programs such as Social Security, which was started during the Great Depression, would be invalid. Likewise, Medicare and Medicaid, which were adopted in the 1960s, may be invalid, according to Senator Jim DeMint (R-S.C.), a supporter of the Tenthers.[4]

Historians and political scientists have concluded that presidential initiatives, congressional laws, and Supreme Court rulings during the Great Depression expanded the role of the federal government and, in the process, modified our interpretation of the Constitution. However, the Tenthers argue that the expansion was illegitimate because it was an executive, legislative, and judicial coup, engineered by President Franklin Roosevelt during a public panic, against the "true" Constitution.

Some Tenthers go further, resurrecting John C. Calhoun's argument before the Civil War that states can nullify federal laws. In 2009, supporters of nullification rallied in Texas, and Governor Rick Perry even spoke, approvingly, of secession.

Thus these Tenthers not only reject the constitutional changes brought about during the Great Depression, but they also refuse to acknowledge, or perhaps to accept, the constitutional changes brought about by the Civil War.[5]

In this chapter, you'll see that there's real tension between the original Constitution (that is, the original interpretation of the Constitution), which was drafted by the Founders, and our current Constitution (that is, our current interpretation of the Constitution), which was reinterpreted by later generations, especially by those who lived during the Civil War and the Great Depression. The Tenthers cling to the original Constitution, while most Americans today accept our current Constitution.

Early settlers came to America for different reasons. Some came to escape religious persecution, others to establish their own religious orthodoxy. Some came to avoid debtors' prison, others to get rich. Some came to flee the closed society of the Old World, others to make money for their families or employers in that world. Some came as free persons, others as indentured servants or slaves. Few came to practice self-government. Yet the desire for self-government was evident from the beginning.[6] The settlers who arrived in Jamestown in 1607 established the first representative assembly in America. The Pilgrims, who reached Plymouth in 1620, drew up the Mayflower Compact in which they vowed to "solemnly & mutually in the presence of God, and one of another, covenant and combine our selves together into a civill body politick." They pledged to establish laws for "the generall good of the colonie" and in return promised "all due submission and obedience."[7]

During the next century and a half, the colonies adopted constitutions and elected representative assemblies. Of course, the colonies lived under British rule, so they had to accept the appointment of royal governors and the presence of British troops. But a vast ocean separated the two continents. At such distance, Britain could not wield the control it might at closer reach. It had to grant the colonies a measure of autonomy, which they used to practice the beginnings of self-government.

These early efforts toward self-government led to conflict with the mother government. In 1774, the colonies established the Continental Congress to coordinate their actions. Within months, the conflict reached flash point, and the Congress urged the colonies to form their own governments. In 1776, the Congress adopted the Declaration of Independence. (See box, "Founding Mothers.")

After six years of war, the Americans accepted the British surrender. At the time it seemed they had met their biggest test. Yet they would find fomenting a revolution easier than fashioning a government and drafting a declaration of independence easier than crafting a constitution.

This chapter will examine the Founders' efforts to craft a constitution, first the Articles of Confederation and then the Constitution itself. The chapter will also show how later generations modified the Constitution, especially as a result of the Civil War and the Great Depression.

american*diversity

Founding Mothers

Charles Francis Adams, a grandson of President John Adams and Abigail Adams, declared in 1840, "The heroism of the females of the Revolution has gone from memory with the generation that witnessed it, and nothing, absolutely nothing remains upon the ear of the young of the present day."[1] That statement remains true today; in the volumes written about the revolutionary and Constitution-making era, much is said of the "Founding Fathers" but little about the "Founding Mothers." Although no women were delegates to the Constitutional Convention, in various ways—besides birthing and rearing the children and maintaining the homes—women contributed significantly to the founding of the country. Many contributed directly to the political ferment of the time. Their role during the revolutionary and Constitution-making era was greater than it would be again for a century.

Before the Revolutionary War, women were active in encouraging opposition to British rule. Groups of women, some formed as the "Daughters of Liberty," organized resistance to British taxes by leading boycotts of British goods such as cloth and tea; they made their own cloth, hosting spinning bees, and their own drinks from native herbs and flowers.

A few women were political pamphleteers, helping increase public sentiment for independence. One of those pamphlet writers, Mercy Otis Warren, from Boston, was thought to be the first person to urge the Massachusetts delegates to the Continental Congress to vote for separation from Britain.[2] She also wrote poems advocating independence and plays satirizing British officials and sympathizers among the colonists (although the plays could only be read, not staged, because Puritan Boston forbade theater). Throughout the period before and after the Revolution, Warren shared her political ideas in personal correspondence with leading statesmen of the time, such as John Adams and Thomas Jefferson. Later, she wrote a three-volume history of the American Revolution.

When the Declaration of Independence was drafted, the printer—a publisher in Maryland named Mary Katherine Goddard—printed her own name at the bottom of the Declaration in support of the signers who were in hiding from the British.

Because the Continental Army lacked money to pay, feed, and clothe the troops, women raised funds by canvassing door to door and also made clothes for the

THE ARTICLES OF CONFEDERATION

Even before the war ended, the Continental Congress passed a constitution, and in 1781 the states ratified it. This first constitution, the **Articles of Confederation**, formed a "league of friendship" among the states that allowed each state to retain its "sovereignty" and "independence." That is, it made the states supreme over the national government.

This arrangement proved problematic, and American elites became dissatisfied with their governments. They disparaged the weakness of the national government and feared the democracy of the state governments.

National Government Weakness

The Articles of Confederation established a Congress, but they limited the powers that Congress could exercise, and they provided no executive or judicial branch. The Articles reflected the colonial experience under the British government. The leaders feared a central government with a powerful legislature or a powerful executive like a king, which could be too strong and too distant to guarantee individual liberty. In addition, the Articles reflected a lack of national identity. Most people did not view themselves as Americans. As Edmund Randolph remarked, "I am not really an American, I am a Virginian."[8] Consequently, the leaders established a very decentralized government that left most authority to the states.

The Articles satisfied many people. Most Americans worked small farms, and although many of them sank into debt during the depression that followed the war, they felt they could get their own state government to help them. They realized they could not influence a distant central government as readily.

But the Articles frustrated the bankers, merchants, manufacturers, and others in the upper classes who envisioned a great commercial empire replacing the agricultural society that existed in the late eighteenth century. More than local trade, they wanted national and even international trade. For this they needed uniform laws, stable money, sound credit, and enforceable debt collection. They needed a strong

soldiers. One group of women in Philadelphia made 2200 shirts.

During the Revolutionary War, many women followed their husbands into battle. As part of the American army, most filled traditional women's roles as cooks, seamstresses, and nurses, but there are reports of women swabbing cannons with water to cool them and firing cannons when their husbands were wounded. After Margaret Corbin's husband was killed, she manned his artillery piece and was wounded three times. Later she received pay as a disabled soldier, including the ration for rum or whiskey. (Many years later she was reburied at West Point.) Some women disguised themselves as men (this was before a military bureaucracy mandated preenlistment physicals) and fought in battle. One wrapped tight bandages around her breasts and served three years, surviving two wounds. Fellow soldiers thought she was a young man slow to grow a beard.[3] Still other women fought to defend their homes using hatchets, farm implements, and pots of boiling lye in addition to muskets.

Women also served as spies. When British soldiers commandeered one house for their quarters, the mother asked if she and her children could remain. One night she overheard the officers plotting a surprise attack on Washington's camp, and she sneaked out of town to warn the camp. A sixteen-year-old girl rode forty miles to warn a militia of another pending attack.[4] Women were so prominent in the war that British general Lord Cornwallis said, "We may destroy all the men in America, and we shall still have all we can do to defeat the women."[5] Following independence, a few women continued an active political role. Mercy Otis Warren campaigned against the proposed Constitution because she felt it was not democratic enough. Abigail Adams called for new laws that would provide some equality between husbands and wives, unlike English laws, which gave all power to husbands. She also called for formal education for girls.

Yet independence did not bring an improvement in the political rights of women. It would be another century before the rights of women would become a full-fledged part of our national political agenda.

[1] Quoted in Linda Grant De Pauw and Conover Hunt, *Remember the Ladies* (New York: Viking, 1976), 9. Also see Woody Holton, *Abigail Adams* (New York: Free Press, 2009).
[2] Alice Felt Tyler, *Freedom's Ferment* (New York: Harper & Row, 1962).
[3] Cokie Roberts, *Founding Mothers* (New York: HarperCollins, 2004), 79–82.
[4] Mrs. Betsey Loring also made a heroic contribution to the cause by keeping a British general so "lustily occupied" in Philadelphia that he failed to move his troops to Valley Forge, where he could have destroyed the Continental Army. Alas, her motive was not patriotism; she sought a position in the British army for her husband. Roberts, *Founding Mothers*, xviii.
[5] Ibid., xix.

© Bettmann/Corbis

Although the Articles of Confederation gave the national government authority to print money, the states circulated their own currencies as well.

a credible army or negotiate a binding treaty, the government could not get the British troops to leave American soil or the Spanish government to permit navigation on the Mississippi River.[9]

In addition to an inability to confront foreign threats, the Articles demonstrated an inability to cope with domestic crises. The country bore a heavy war debt that brought the government close to bankruptcy. Because Congress could not tax individuals directly, it could not shore up the shaky government. At the same time, the states competed with each other for commercial advantage, imposing tariffs on goods from other states. This practice slowed business growth.

In short, the government under the Articles of Confederation seemed too decentralized to ensure either peace or prosperity. The Articles, one leader concluded, gave Congress the privilege of asking for everything while reserving to each state the prerogative of granting nothing.[10] A similar situation exists today in the United Nations, which must rely on the goodwill of member countries to furnish troops for its peace-keeping forces and dues for its operating expenses.[11]

State Government Democracy

State constitutions adopted during the American Revolution made the state legislatures more representative than the colonial legislatures had been. Most state legislatures also began to hold elections every year. The result was heightened interest among candidates and turnover among legislators. In the eyes of national leaders, there was much pandering to voters and horse-trading by politicians as various factions vied for control. The process seemed up for grabs. According to the Vermont Council of Censors, laws were "altered—realtered—made better—made worse; and kept in such a fluctuating position that persons in civil commission scarce know what is law."[12] In short, state governments were experiencing more democracy than any other governments in the world at the time. National leaders, stunned by the changes in the few years since the Revolution, considered this development an "excess of democracy."

These leaders, most of whom were wealthy and many of whom were creditors, pointed to the laws passed in some states that relieved debtors of some of their obligations. The farmers in debt had pressed the legislatures for relief that would slow or shrink the payments owed to their creditors, and some legislatures had granted such relief.

These laws worried the leaders, and **Shays's Rebellion** in western Massachusetts in 1786 and 1787 frightened them. Boston merchants who had loaned Massachusetts money during the war insisted on being repaid in full so they could trade with foreign merchants. The state levied steep taxes that many farmers could not pay during the hard times. The law authorized foreclosure—sale of the farmers' property to recover unpaid taxes—and jail for the debtors,

central government that could protect them against debtors and against state governments sympathetic to debtors. The Articles provided neither the foreign security nor the domestic climate necessary to nourish these requisites of a commercial empire.

After the war, the army disbanded, leaving the country vulnerable to hostile forces surrounding it. Britain maintained outposts with troops in the Northwest Territory (the Midwest today), in violation of the peace treaty, and an army in Canada. Spain, which had occupied Florida and California for a long time and had claimed the Mississippi River valley as a result of a treaty before the war, posed a threat. Barbary pirates from North Africa seized American ships and sailors. (See box "The Black Flag on the High Seas.")

Congress could not raise an army, because it could not draft individuals directly, or finance an army, because it could not tax individuals directly. Instead, it had to ask the states for soldiers and money. The states, however, were not always sympathetic to the problems of the distant government. And although Congress could make treaties with foreign countries, the states made (and broke) treaties independently of Congress. Without the ability to establish

THE BLACK FLAG ON THE HIGH SEAS

Americans faced attacks from pirates as well as threats from foreign powers. As many as a hundred merchant ships sailed from American ports to Mediterranean cities each year, bringing salted fish, flour, sugar, and lumber and returning with figs, lemons, oranges, olive oil, and opium. Barbary pirates from North Africa—Algeria, Morocco, Tripoli (now Libya), and Tunis (Tunisia)—preyed upon ships in the Mediterranean Sea, seizing sailors, holding them for ransom or pressing them into slavery, and extorting money from shippers and governments.[1] Historians estimate that a million Europeans and Americans were kidnapped or enslaved by these pirates in the seventeenth and eighteenth centuries.

Although American ships were protected by the British navy (and by the British government's willingness to pay tribute) during colonial times, they were not shielded after independence. The weakness of the government under the Articles of Confederation left the ships' crews to fend for themselves.

The piracy was mostly over riches—the Barbary states used the raids to finance their governments—but it also reflected religious conflict. The Barbary states were Muslim, and although their societies would not be called fundamentalist or Islamist today—in fact, they treated their Jewish residents better than most European societies did at the time—their leaders told American officials that the Koran gave them the right to enslave infidels.[2]

The piracy would not cease until the new government under the Constitution created a strong navy and fought the Barbary Wars (1801–1805)—the first deployment of the American military overseas.[3]

[1] Other pirates patrolled the Caribbean, with some operating out of New Orleans.
[2] Previously, European states had held Muslim slaves.
[3] This led to the line in the Marines Corps anthem "to the shores of Tripoli."

SOURCES: Christopher Hitchens, "Black Flag," *New York Times Book Review*, August 21, 2005, 7–8; Max Boot, *The Savage Wars of Peace* (New York: Basic Books, 2002), 3–29.

essentially transferring wealth from the farmers to the merchants. The Massachusetts government wasn't as sympathetic to debtors as some other states were. The farmers protested the legislature's refusal to grant any relief from the law. Bands of farmers blocked entrances to courthouses where judges were scheduled to hear cases calling for foreclosure and jail. Led by Daniel Shays, some marched to the Springfield arsenal to seize weapons. Although they were defeated by the militia, their sympathizers were victorious in the next election.

Both the revolt and the legislature's change in policy scared the wealthy. To them it raised the specter of mob rule. Nathaniel Gorham, the president of the Continental Congress and a prominent merchant, wrote Prince Henry of Prussia, announcing "the failure of our free institutions" and asking whether the prince would agree to become king of America (the prince declined).[13]

To a significant extent, then, the debate at the time reflected a conflict between two competing visions of the future American political economy—agricultural or commercial.[14] Most leaders espoused the latter, and the combination of national problems and state problems prompted them to push for a new government.[15]

THE CONSTITUTION

Just months after Shays's Rebellion, Congress approved a convention for "the sole and express purpose of revising the Articles of Confederation."

The Constitutional Convention

The **Constitutional Convention** convened in Philadelphia, then the country's largest city, in 1787. State legislatures sent fifty-five delegates. They met at the Pennsylvania State House—now Independence Hall—in the same room where many of them had signed the Declaration of Independence eleven years earlier. Delegates came from every state except Rhode Island, whose farmers and debtors feared that the convention would weaken states' powers to relieve debtors of their debts.

The delegates were distinguished by their education, experience, and enlightenment. Benjamin Franklin, of Pennsylvania—printer, scientist, and diplomat—was the best-known American in the world. At eighty-one, he was the oldest delegate. George Washington, of Virginia, was the most respected American in the country. As the commander of the revolutionary army, he was a national hero. Washington was chosen to preside over the convention. The presence of men like Franklin and Washington gave the convention legitimacy.

The delegates quickly determined that the Articles of Confederation were beyond repair. Rather than revise them, as instructed by Congress, the delegates decided to draft a new constitution.[16]

The Predicament

The delegates came to the convention because they thought their government was too weak, yet the Americans had fought the Revolution because they chafed under a government that was too strong. "The nation lived in a nearly constant alternation of fears that it would cease being a nation altogether or become too much of one."[17] People feared both anarchy and tyranny. This predicament was made clear by the diversity of opinions among the leaders. At one extreme was Patrick Henry, of Virginia, who had been a firebrand of the Revolution. He feared that the government would become too strong, perhaps even become a monarchy, in reaction to the problems with the Articles. He said he "smelt a rat" and did not attend the convention. At the other extreme was Alexander Hamilton, of New York, who had been an aide to General Washington during the war and had seen the government's inability to supply and pay its own troops. Ever since, he had called for a stronger national government and had even suggested a monarchy. He did attend the convention but, finding little agreement with his proposals, participated infrequently.

In between was James Madison, of Virginia. The debate revolved around his plan. Throughout the convention, Madison was "up to his ears in politics, advising, persuading, softening the harsh word, playing down this difficulty and exaggerating that, engaging in debate, harsh controversy, polemics, and sly maneuver."[18] In the end, his views more than anyone else's would prevail, and he would become known as the Father of the Constitution.[19] (See box, "Small But Savvy.")

Consensus

Despite disagreements, the delegates did see eye to eye on the most fundamental issues. They agreed that the government should be a **republic**—a form of government that derives its power from the people and whose officials are accountable to the people. The term more specifically refers to an indirect democracy in which the people vote for at least some of the officials who represent them.[20]

They also agreed that the national government should be stronger than under the Articles and that it should have three separate branches—legislative, executive, and judicial—to exercise the three functions of government—making, administering, and judging the laws. They thought that both the legislative and executive branches should be strong.

When we refer to constitutional provisions, we'll call attention to them with this icon, and we'll also provide the location in the Constitution (unless the paragraph already indicates the location). The composition and authority of the legislative branch is addressed in Article I, that of the executive branch in Article II, and that of the judicial branch in Article III.

Conflict

Although there was considerable agreement over the fundamental principles and elemental structure of the new government, the delegates quarreled about the specific provisions concerning representation, slavery, trade, and taxation.

Representation   Sharp conflict was expressed between delegates from large states and those from small states over representation. Large states sought a strong government that they could control; small states feared a strong government that could control them.

When the convention began, the Virginia Plan, drafted by Madison, was introduced. According to this plan, the legislature would be divided into two houses, with representation based on population in each. But delegates from the small states calculated that the three largest states would have a majority of the representatives and could dominate the legislature.

---

behind the scenes

Small but Savvy

James Madison was described as "no bigger than half a piece of soap."[1] Although small and frail, timid and self-conscious as a speaker, he was nonetheless an intelligent and savvy politician.

He operated behind the scenes to organize the Constitutional Convention and to secure George Washington's attendance. Washington was in retirement at his plantation at Mount Vernon and had not planned to attend the convention. Because his presence would lend the convention more legitimacy, Madison notified other delegates that Washington would attend—without asking Washington first. After Madison created the expectation that he would attend, Washington reluctantly agreed to do so.[2]

Before the convention, Madison, who had studied other countries' governments, concluded that the Articles of Confederation should be replaced rather than reformed. He realized that he would have more influence if he had a plan to offer the delegates, who were disenchanted with the Articles but uncertain what to substitute. Madison secretly drafted a plan for a new constitution, a sharp departure from the Articles. Ultimately, his plan would set the agenda for the convention and lay the foundation for the Constitution.

[1] Quoted in Gary Wasserman, *Politics in Action* (Boston: Houghton Mifflin, 2006), 5.
[2] Fred Barbash, "James Madison: A Man for the '80s," *Washington Post National Weekly Edition*, March 30, 1987, 23.

These delegates countered with the New Jersey Plan. According to this plan, the legislature would consist of one house, with representation by states, which would have one vote each. This was exactly the same as the structure of Congress under the Articles, also designed to prevent the largest states from dominating the legislature.

James Wilson, of Pennsylvania, asked for whom they were forming a government—"for men, or for the imaginary beings called states?"[21] But delegates from the small states would not budge. Some threatened to leave the government and align themselves with a European country instead.[22]

The convention deadlocked, and some delegates left for home. George Washington wrote that he almost despaired of the likelihood of reaching any agreement. To ease tensions, Benjamin Franklin suggested that the delegates begin each day with a prayer, but they could not agree on this either; Alexander Hamilton insisted that they did not need "foreign aid."

Faced with the possibility that the convention would disband without a constitution, the delegates, after weeks of frustrating debate, compromised. Delegates from Connecticut and other states proposed a plan in which the legislature, Congress, would have two houses. In one, the **House of Representatives**, representation would be based on population, and members would be elected by voters. In the other, the **Senate**, representation would be by states, and members would be selected by state legislatures. Presumably, the large states would dominate the former, the small states the latter (see the box "Is the Senate Democratic?"). The delegates narrowly approved this Connecticut Compromise,[23] often called the **Great Compromise** because it not only resolved this critical issue but also paved the way for resolution of other issues.

This decision began a pattern that continues to this day. When officials face implacable differences, they try to compromise, but the process is not easy. It is an apt choice of words to say that officials "hammer out" a compromise; it is not a coincidence that we use *hammer* rather than a softer metaphor.[24]

Slavery In addition to conflict between large states and small states over representation, conflict emerged between northern states and southern states over slavery, trade, and taxation.

With representation in one house based on population, the delegates had to decide how to apportion the seats. They agreed that Indians would not count as part of the population but differed about slaves. Delegates from the South, where slaves made up one-third of the population, wanted slaves to count fully in order to boost the number of southern representatives. Although slaves had not been counted at all under the Articles or under any state constitution, southerners argued that their use of slaves produced wealth that benefited the entire nation. Delegates from the North, where most states had outlawed slavery or at least the slave trade after the Revolution, did not want slaves to count at

all. Gouverneur Morris, of Pennsylvania, said the southerners' position

> comes to this: that the inhabitant of Georgia and South Carolina who goes to the coast of Africa, and in defiance of the most sacred laws of humanity tears away his fellow creatures from their dearest connections and damns them to the most cruel bondages, shall have more votes in a government instituted for the protection of the rights of mankind than the citizen of Pennsylvania or New Jersey who views with a laudable horror so nefarious a practice.[25]

Others pointed out that slaves were not considered persons when it came to rights such as voting. Nevertheless, southerners asserted that they would not support the constitution if slaves were not counted at least partially. In the **Three-fifths Compromise,** the delegates agreed that three-fifths of the slaves would be counted in apportioning the seats.

Art. I, Sec. 2 This compromise expanded the political power of the people who were oppressing the slaves. The votes of southern whites became worth more than those of northerners in electing members to the House of Representatives and also in electing presidents (because the number of presidential electors for each state was based on the number of members in Congress from the state). By 1860, nine of the fifteen presidents, including all five who served two terms, were slave owners.[26] Ultimately, twelve presidents were slave owners.

Southerners pushed through two other provisions addressing slavery. One forbade Congress from banning the importation of slaves before 1808; another required free states to return escaped slaves to their owners in slave states. In these provisions, southerners won most of what they wanted; even the provision permitting Congress to ban the importation of slaves in 1808 would do little to limit slavery because by then planters would have enough slaves to fulfill their needs by natural population increases. In return, northerners, who represented shippers, got authority for Congress to regulate commerce by a simple majority rather than a two-thirds majority. Thus northerners conceded the provisions that reinforced slavery to benefit shippers.[27]

Art. I, Sec. 9 Yet the framers were embarrassed
Art. IV, Sec. 2 by the hypocrisy of claiming to
Art. I, Sec. 8 have been enslaved by the British while allowing enslavement of African Americans. Their embarrassment is reflected in their language. The three provisions reinforcing slavery never mention "slavery" or "slaves"; one gingerly refers to "free persons" and "other persons."

Slavery was the most divisive issue at the convention. As Madison noted, "The real difference of interests lay, not between the large and small, but between the northern and southern states. The institution of slavery and its consequences formed the line of discrimination."[28] The unwillingness to tackle the slavery issue more directly has been called the "Greatest Compromise" by one political scientist.[29] But

IS THE SENATE DEMOCRATIC?

After slavery was abolished and the right to vote was extended to racial minorities and women, the equal representation of states in the Senate is perhaps the most undemocratic aspect left in the Constitution.[1]

Because each state gets two senators regardless of its population, small or sparsely populated rural states enjoy disproportionate representation relative to their population. California, the most populous state, and Wyoming, the least populous state, have equal representation, although California has sixty-eight times more people. Therefore, voters in California have one-sixty-eighth as much representation, or power, in the Senate as voters in Wyoming have. (See Figure 1.)

At the time of the Founding, the disparities in state sizes weren't so large. Virginia, the largest state, had eleven times more people than Rhode Island, the smallest state.[2]

The equal representation of states in the Senate is not the result of some grand theory of government. As explained in the text, it was a major concession to the small states to maintain their allegiance to the country and to obtain their support for the Constitution. At that time, people identified more closely with their state than with the nation as a whole. Today, our mass society, mass media, and transportation networks weaken these ties and strengthen our sense of national identity.

Federalism, which splits power between the national government and the state governments, provides states with more authority than they would have in nonfederal systems. And the filibuster, which will be explained in Chapter 10, gives small states added leverage in the Senate. Do the people in small states have additional needs to protect than those already protected by federalism and the filibuster? And are these needs greater than the needs of other people who do not get extra representation, such as the people who have been the victims of widespread discrimination?

What if a similar rationale were applied to African Americans? If the 12 percent of Americans who are black had as many senators representing them as the 12 percent of Americans who live in our smallest states have representing them, the Senate would include forty-four black senators.

Yet even if most Americans decide that the equal representation in the Senate is unfair and undemocratic, it is unlikely they could change it. The Constitution stipulates, "No state, without its consent, shall be deprived of its equal suffrage in the Senate."[3] Furthermore, Article 5, which addresses amendments, limits amendments in two categories. The provision regarding the importation of slaves could not be amended until 1808, and the provision regarding the representation in the Senate cannot be amended ever.[4] Some constitutional scholars suggest that an amendment repealing this provision could be adopted first and an amendment altering the representation itself could be adopted next. Other scholars think the courts would not tolerate this obvious sabotage of the Founders' intentions.

Figure 1

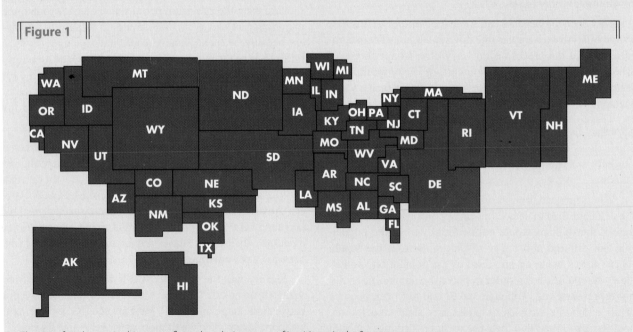

The size of each state in this map reflects the relative power of its citizens in the Senate.
SOURCE: *Michael Lind, "75 Stars," Mother Jones (January–February 1998), p. 130. Reprinted with permission.*

Regardless, it is a moot point, because amendment of the Constitution requires ratification by three-fourths of the states. Just thirteen states can block an amendment favored by the rest of the country. The thirteen smallest states, with only 5 percent of the nation's population, thus can thwart the wishes of the thirty-seven largest states, with 95 percent of the nation's people.

¹ Most information in this box is from Robert A. Dahl, *How Democratic Is the American Constitution?* (New Haven, Conn.: Yale University Press, 2001).
² Harold Meyerson, "Can Boxer and Feinstein Be Filibuster Busters?" *Los Angeles Times*, January 14, 2010, latimes.com/news/opinion/la-oe-meyerson14-2010jan14,0,5314241.story.
³ This provision is reinforced by Article 4, which stipulates that "no . . . state shall be formed by the junction of two or more states, or parts of states, without the consent of . . . the states concerned." Therefore, small states cannot be forced to combine as a way to reduce their representation.
⁴ J. W. Peltason, *Corwin and Peltason's Understanding the Constitution*, 9th ed. (New York: Holt, Rinehart and Winston, 1982), 113. For a creative alternative, see Michael Lind, "75 Stars," *Mother Jones* (January–February 1998), 44–49.

an attempt to abolish slavery would have caused the five southern states to refuse to ratify the Constitution.

Trade and Taxation

Art. I, Sec. 9 Slavery also underlay a compromise on trade and taxation. With a manufacturing economy, northerners sought protection for their businesses. In particular, they wanted a tax on manufactured products imported from Britain. Without a tax, British goods would be cheaper than northern products; with a tax, northern products would be more competitive—but prices for northern and southern consumers would be higher. With an agricultural economy, southerners sought free trade for their plantations. They wanted a guarantee that no tax would be levied on agricultural commodities exported to Britain. Such a tax would make their commodities less competitive and, they worried, amount to an indirect tax on slavery—the labor responsible for the crops. The delegates resolved these issues by allowing Congress to tax imported goods but not exported ones.

After seventeen weeks of debate, thirty-nine of the original fifty-five delegates signed the Constitution on September 17, 1787. Some delegates had left when they saw the direction the convention was taking, and three others refused to sign, feeling that the Constitution gave too much authority to the national government. Most of the rest were not entirely happy with the result (even Madison, who was most responsible for the content of the document, was despondent that his plan for a national legislature was compromised by having one house with representation by states), but they thought it was the best they could do.

Features of the Constitution

Years later, however, a British prime minister said the American Constitution was "the most wonderful work ever struck off at a given time by the brain and purpose of man."[30] To see why it was unique, we'll examine its major features.

A Republic

The Founders distinguished between a democracy and a republic. For them, a *democracy* meant a **direct democracy**, which permits citizens to vote on most issues, and a *republic* meant an **indirect democracy**, which allows citizens to vote for their representatives, who make governmental policies.

Although many small towns in New England used (and some still use) a direct democracy, the Founders opposed a direct democracy for the whole country. Some city-states of ancient Greece and medieval Europe had a direct democracy but could not sustain it. A large country would have less ability to do so because its people could not be brought together in one place to debate and vote. Moreover, the Founders believed that the people could not withstand the passions of the moment, so they would be swayed by a demagogue to take unwise action.

DEMOCRACY?

What are the implications—for our elections, officials, and laws—of having an indirect democracy rather than a direct democracy?

Art. I, Sec. 2 & 3
Art. II, Sec. 1 The Founders favored a republic because they believed that the government should be based on the consent of the people and that the people should have some voice in choosing their officials. So the Founders provided that the people would elect representatives to the House. They also provided that the state legislators, themselves elected by the people, would select their state's senators as well as their state's electors for the Electoral College, which chooses the president. In this way, the people would have a voice but one partially filtered through their presumably wiser representatives.

The Founders' views reflect their ambivalence about the people. Rationally, they believed in popular sovereignty, but emotionally, they feared the concept. New England clergyman Jeremy Belknap voiced their ambivalence when he declared, "Let it stand as a principle that government originates from the people; but let the people be taught . . . that they are not able to govern themselves."[31]

The Founders would have been aghast at the proliferation of such experiments in direct democracy as initiatives, referenda, and recall elections in many states. The **initiative** process allows citizens and interest groups to collect signatures on petitions and place a proposal on the ballot. If enough voters favor the proposal, it becomes law.[32] The **referendum** process allows the legislature to place a proposal on the ballot. **Recall elections** enable voters to remove officials from office before their terms expire.

The Founders considered a democracy radical and a republic only slightly less radical. Because they believed that the country could not maintain a democracy, they worried that it might not maintain a republic either. When the Constitutional Convention ended, Benjamin Franklin reportedly was approached by a woman who asked, "Well, Doctor, what have we got, a republic or a monarchy?" Franklin responded, "A republic, Madam, if you can keep it."

Fragmentation of Power

Other countries assumed that a government must have a concentration of power to be strong enough to govern. However, when the Founders made our national government more powerful than it had been under the Articles of Confederation, they feared that they also had made it more capable of oppression, so they fragmented its power.

The Founders believed that people are selfish, always coveting more property, and that leaders always lust after more power. They assumed that this aspect of human nature is unchangeable. Madison speculated, "If men were angels, no government would be necessary." "Alas," he added, "men are not angels." Therefore, "in framing a government which is to be administered by men over men, the great difficulty lies in this: you must first enable the government to control the governed; and in the next place oblige it to control itself."[33] The Founders decided that the way to oblige the government to control itself was to structure it so as to prevent any one leader, group of leaders, or factions of people from exercising power over more than a small part of it. Thus the Founders fragmented government's power. This is reflected in three concepts they built into the structure of government—federalism, separation of powers, and checks and balances. (The Founders' views are conveyed in the *Federalist Papers*, especially in Nos. 10 and 51, which are included in the Appendix of this text.)

Federalism   The first division of power was between the national government and the state governments. This division of power is called **federalism**.[34] The U.S. government under the Articles of Confederation had been confederal (as the Confederacy of southern states during the Civil War would be); that is, the state governments wielded most authority. The national government exercised only the powers given it by the state governments. At the other extreme, most foreign governments had been unitary; the central government wielded all authority.[35]

The Founders, who had had unhappy experiences with a confederal system (their own government under the Articles) and a unitary system (the British government during colonial times), wanted to avoid both types. They sought a strong, but not too strong, national government and strong state governments as well. So they invented a federal system as a compromise between the confederal and unitary systems.

Federalism was seen as a way to provide sufficient power for the government to function while checking excessive power that could lead to tyranny. The Founders worried about the **"mischiefs of factions"**—groups seeking something for themselves without regard for the rights of others or the well-being of all.[36] According to Madison, factions could be controlled through federalism.[37] A faction might dominate one state but would be less able to dominate many states.

We should note that federalism and democracy do not always go hand in hand. Federalism is not a necessary condition for having a democratic government. Some unitary governments, such as those of England and Sweden, are democratic. Likewise, federalism is not a sufficient condition for having a democratic government. The federalist government of the former Soviet Union was not democratic.

The Constitution delegates some powers to the national government and reserves other powers for the state governments. Authority over foreign affairs—to make treaties, repel attacks, and declare war—is given to the national government. Authority to print and coin money and to regulate interstate commerce was also given to the national government, and authority to tax was given to both levels.

Art. I, Sec. 8   These provisions ensured a stronger
Art. 6   national government in foreign and domestic matters than under the Articles.[38] In addition, the Constitution's **supremacy clause** declares that the Constitution is the supreme law of the land and that any laws and treaties made "in pursuance thereof" also are the supreme law of the land whenever they conflict with state laws or actions. But authority over many other matters, including broad authority to provide for the welfare of the people, was given to the state governments. The Tenth Amendment, which reflects the general understanding of the time, stipulates that the powers not delegated to the national government are reserved for the states. So this guarantee ensured reasonably strong state governments as well.[39]

Yet the Constitution's language is so general and so succinct that it is very ambiguous. This made the document acceptable both to advocates of a strong national government and supporters of strong state governments, but it also made the document flexible so it could be interpreted as later generations desired or critical challenges required. The language could support either nation-centered federalism, which underscores the power of the nation in the arrangement, or state-centered federalism, which emphasizes the power of the states. (These concepts will be explored further in Chapter 3.)

Separation of powers   The second division of power was within the national government. The power to make, administer, and judge the laws was split into three branches—legislative, executive, and judicial (see Figure 2). In the legislative branch, the power was split further into two houses. This **separation of powers** contrasts with the parliamentary systems in most developed democracies, in

Figure 2 | Separation of Powers

Branch:	Legislative *Congress*		Executive *Presidency*	Judicial *Federal Courts*
	House	Senate	President	Judges
Officials chosen by:	People	People (originally, state legislatures)	Electoral College, whose members are chosen by the people (originally, by state legislatures)	President, with advice and consent of Senate
For term of:	2 years	6 years	4 years	Life
To represent primarily:	Common people	Wealthy people	All people	Constitution
	Large states	Small states		

Separation of powers, as envisioned by the Founders, means not only that government functions are to be performed by different branches but also that officials of these branches are to be chosen by different people, for different terms, and to represent different constituencies.

which the legislature is supreme. In parliamentary systems, both executive and judicial officials are drawn from the legislature and are responsible to it. There is no separation of powers.

Art. II, Sec. 2
Art. III, Sec. 1 To reinforce the separation of powers, officials of the three branches were chosen by different means. Representatives were elected by the people (at that time mostly white men who owned property), senators were selected by the state legislatures, and the president was selected by the Electoral College, whose members were selected by the states. Only federal judges were chosen by officials in the other branches. They were nominated by the president and confirmed by the Senate. Once appointed, however, they were allowed to serve for "good behavior"—essentially for life—so they had much independence. (Since the Constitution was written, the Seventeenth Amendment has provided for election of senators by the people, and the state legislatures have provided for election of members of the Electoral College by the people.)

Officials of the branches were also chosen at different times. Representatives were given a two-year term, senators a six-year term (with one-third of them up for reelection every two years), and the president a four-year term. These staggered terms were designed so that temporary passions in society would not bring about a massive switch of officials or policies.

The Senate was intended to act as a conservative brake on the House, due to senators' selection by state legislatures and their longer terms. Upon his return, Thomas Jefferson, who was in France during the Constitutional Convention, met with George Washington over breakfast. Jefferson protested the establishment of a legislature with two houses. Washington supposedly asked, "Why did you pour that

coffee into your saucer?" "To cool it," Jefferson replied. Similarly, Washington explained, "We pour legislation into the senatorial saucer to cool it."[40]

Separation of powers creates the opportunity for **divided government**. Rather than one political party controlling both elected branches, one party might win the presidency while the other party wins a majority of seats in one or both houses of Congress. Divided government has been common throughout the nation's history. Since the emergence of the Democratic and Republican party system (1856), it has occurred as a result of two of every five elections.[41] Since World War II, it has been the dominant mode of government.[42] In this way, American voters have added another element to Madison's concept of separation of powers.

DEMOCRACY?

What implications from divided government would you expect? How might divided government affect the ability to pass laws? The need to foster compromise?

Checks and balances To further prevent concentration of power, the Founders built in **checks and balances** (see Figure 3). Madison suggested that "the great security against a gradual concentration of the several powers in the same department consists in giving those who administer each department the necessary constitutional means and personal motives to resist encroachments by the others. . . . *Ambition must be made to counteract ambition.*"[43] To that end, each branch was given some authority over the others. If one branch abuses its power, the others can use their checks to thwart it.

Art. I, Sec. 7 Thus, rather than a simple system of separation of powers, ours is a complex, even contradictory, system of both separation of

Figure 3   **Checks and Balances**

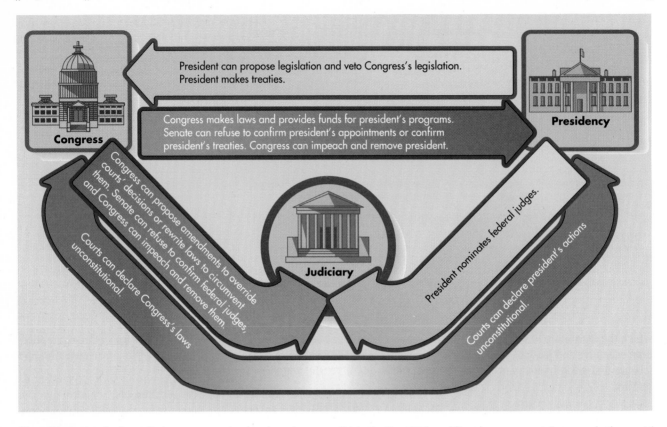

Most of the major checks and balances among the three branches are explicit in the Constitution, although some are not. For example, the courts' power to declare congressional laws or presidential actions unconstitutional—their power of "judicial review"—is not mentioned.

powers and checks and balances. The principle of separation of powers gives each branch its own sphere of authority, but the system of checks and balances allows each branch to intrude into the spheres of the other branches. For example, because there is separation of powers, 🔔 Congress makes the laws; but because there are checks and balances, the president can veto them and the courts can rule them unconstitutional. In these ways, all three branches are involved in legislating. One political scientist calls ours "a government of separated institutions competing for shared powers."[44]

With federalism, separation of powers, and checks and balances, the Founders expected conflict. They invited the several parts of government to struggle against each other and to limit any one part's ability to dominate the rest. The Founders hoped for "balanced government." The national and state governments would represent different interests, as would the branches within the national government. The House would represent the "common" people and the large states; the Senate, the wealthy people and the small states; the president, all the people; and the Supreme Court, the Constitution. Although each part would struggle for more power, it could not accumulate enough to dominate the others. Eventually, it would have to compromise and accept policies that would reflect the interest of all of the parts and their constituencies.

Undemocratic Features

The Founders left undemocratic features in the Constitution that later generations would have to deal with.[45] They denied some Americans the right to participate in their government and some Americans equal treatment by their government.

The Constitution did not forbid slavery, and it did not allow Congress to halt the slave trade for over two decades. The Three-fifths Compromise actually institutionalized slavery and increased the political power of slaveholders.

The Constitution also did not guarantee the right to vote, allowing states to exclude African Americans, Native Americans, other minorities, and women. For decades, states also excluded white men who didn't own property or those who weren't members of the established church from voting.

The Founders created the Electoral College to prevent the people from choosing the president. Even with the advent of popular election of the electors, the Electoral College still allows the election of a candidate who did not receive the most popular votes (as occurred in 2000). The Founders also allowed the state legislatures, not the people, to choose the senators. By giving each state two seats in the Senate, the Founders gave disproportionate power to the people who happen to live in small states (as explained in the box "Is the Senate Democratic?").

The Founders included these features partly because of their need to compromise and partly because of their view that the people could not be trusted. The people were seen as an unruly mob threatening stable, orderly government. As later history would show, however, the Founders exaggerated the dangers of popular majorities. When Americans became more egalitarian in the decades following the adoption of the Constitution, they demanded a greater role for the average person. One political scientist concluded that if the Constitution had been written in 1820 instead of 1787, it would have been a very different, and more democratic, document.[46]

Motives of the Founders

To understand the Constitution better, it is useful to consider the motives of the Founders. Were they selfless patriots, sharing their wisdom and experience? Or were they selfish property owners, protecting their interests? Let's consider the philosophical ideas, political experience, and economic interests that influenced the Founders.

Philosophical Ideas

The Founders were well-educated intellectuals who incorporated philosophical ideas into the Constitution. At a time when the average person did not dream of going to college, a majority of the Founders graduated from college. As learned men, they shared a common library of writers and philosophers.

The Founders reflected the ideals of the Enlightenment, also called the "Age of Reason," an intellectual force throughout Europe in the 1600s and 1700s. In this era, learned men emphasized the use of reason, rather than tradition or religion, to solve problems. So the Founders studied past governments to determine why the governments had failed in the hope that they could apply these lessons to their time. From all accounts, they engaged in a level of debate that was rare in politics, citing philosophers ranging from the ancient Greeks to the modern British and French.

The writings of John Locke, as explained in Chapter 1, underlay many of the ideas of the Founders. In addition to his views on natural rights and property rights, the Founders endorsed Locke's views about the relationship between the people and their government. Locke maintained that the people come together to form a government through a **social contract**—an implied agreement between the people and their government—that establishes a **limited government**, strong enough to protect their rights but not so strong as to threaten these rights. This government should not act without the consent of the governed.[47]

The views of Charles de Montesquieu, an eighteenth-century French philosopher, also influenced the debate at the convention and the provisions of the Constitution. Although others had suggested separation of powers before, Montesquieu refined the concept and added that of checks and balances. The Founders cited him more than any other thinker.[48] (Presumably, they cited him more than Locke because by

this time Locke's views had so permeated American society that the Founders considered them just "common sense."[49])

The principles of mechanics formulated by Isaac Newton, a late seventeenth- and early eighteenth-century English mathematician, also pervaded the provisions of the Constitution. Newton viewed nature as a machine, with different parts having different functions and balancing each other. Newton's principle of action and reaction is manifested in the Founders' system of checks and balances. Both the natural environment and the constitutional structure were viewed as self-regulating systems.[50]

Political Experience

Although the Founders were intellectuals, they were also experienced and practical politicians who had "to operate with great delicacy and skill in a political cosmos full of enemies."[51]

The Founders brought extensive experience to the convention. Eight had signed the Declaration of Independence, and thirty-nine had served in Congress. Seven had been governors, and many had held other state offices. Some had helped write their state constitutions. The framers drew on this experience. For example, although they cited Montesquieu in discussing separation of powers, they also referred to the experience of colonial and state governments that already had some separation of powers.[52]

As practical politicians, "no matter what their private dreams might be, they had to take home an acceptable package and defend it—and their own political futures—against predictable attack."[53] So, they compromised the difficult issues and ducked the stickiest ones. Ultimately, they pieced

© The New Yorker Collection 1974. Donald Reilly from cartoonbank.com. All rights reserved.

"Religious freedom is my immediate goal, but my long-range plan is to go into real estate."

together a document that allowed each delegate to return home and announce that his state had won something.

Economic Interests

At the same time, the Founders represented an elite that sought to protect its property from the masses. The delegates to the convention included prosperous planters, manufacturers, shippers, and lawyers. About one-third were slave owners. Most came from families of prominence and married into other families of prominence. Not all were wealthy, but most were at least well-to-do. Only one, a delegate from Georgia, was a yeoman farmer like most men in the country. In short, "this was a convention of the well-bred, the well-fed, the well-read, and the well-wed."[54]

The Founders championed the right to property. The promise of land and even riches had enticed many immigrants to come to America.[55] A desire for freedom from arbitrary taxes and trade restrictions had spurred some colonists to fight in the Revolution.[56] And the inability of the government under the Articles of Confederation to provide a healthy economy had prompted the Founders to convene the Constitutional Convention. They apparently agreed with Madison that "the first object of government" is to protect property.[57] They worried that a democratic government, responding to popular pressures, might appropriate their property or impose high taxes to help less wealthy people. They wanted a government that could resist such populism.

Yet the Founders' emphasis on property was not as elitist as it might seem. Land was plentiful, and with westward expansion, more would be available. Already most men were middle-class farmers who owned some property. Even those who owned no property could foresee the day when they would, so most wanted to protect property.

The Founders diverged from the farmers in their vision to create a national commercial economy in place of the small-scale agricultural economy. Toward this end, the Founders desired to protect other property, such as wealth and credit, in addition to land.[58] So the delegates included provisions to protect commerce, including imports and exports, contracts, and debts, and provisions to regulate currency, bankruptcy, and taxes.[59] (See Table 1.)

Political scientists and historians have debated which of these three influences on the Founders—philosophical, political, or economic—was most important. Actually, the influences are difficult to separate because they reinforce each other; the framers' ideas, political experience, and economic interests all point to the same sort of constitution.[60]

Ratification of the Constitution

Ratification was uncertain. Many people opposed the Constitution, and a lively campaign against it appeared in newspapers, pamphlets, and mass meetings.

Knowing that opponents would charge the framers with setting up a national government to dominate the state governments, those who supported the Constitution ingeniously adopted the name **Federalists** to emphasize a real division of power between the national and state governments. They dubbed their opponents **Anti-Federalists** to imply that their opponents did not want a division of power between the governments.

The Anti-Federalists faulted the Constitution for lacking a bill of rights. The framers had not included one because most states already had one in their constitutions. The framers also thought that fragmenting power would prevent any branch from becoming strong enough to deny individual rights. Yet critics demanded provisions protecting various rights, and the Federalists promised to propose amendments guaranteeing these rights as soon as the government began.

The Anti-Federalists also criticized the Constitution for other reasons. Localists at heart, they were wary of entrusting power to officials far away. They worried that the central government would accumulate too much power and the presidency would become a monarchy or Congress an aristocracy. One delegate to the Massachusetts convention blasted the Federalists:

> These lawyers, and men of learning and moneyed men, that talk so finely, and gloss over matters so smoothly, to make us poor illiterate people swallow down the pill, expect to get into Congress themselves; they expect to . . . get all the power and all the money into their own hands, and then they will swallow up all us little folks . . . just as the whale swallowed up Jonah![61]

But the Anti-Federalists had no alternative plan. They were divided, with some wanting to amend the Articles of Confederation and others wanting to reject both the Articles and the Constitution in favor of some yet undetermined form of government. Their lack of unity on an alternative was instrumental in their inability to win support.[62]

Within six months, nine states ratified the new Constitution, and the new government, with George Washington as president, began in 1788. Within one year, the four remaining states approved the Constitution.

Although this process might seem unremarkable today, this marked the first time that a nation had proposed a new government and then asked the people to approve or reject it. And the process occurred with little violence or coercion. As a constitutional historian observed, "The losers were not jailed, hanged, or politically disabled. They did not boycott, take up arms, or go into exile. They continued, as before, to be full and free citizens, but now living in a new republic."[63]

Changing the Constitution

The framers expected their document to last; Madison wrote, "We have framed a constitution that will probably be still around when there are 196 million people."[64] Yet,

© Tom Myer

because the framers realized it would need some changes, they drafted a Constitution that can be changed either formally by amendment or informally by judicial interpretation or political practice. In doing so, they left a legacy for later governments. "The example of changing a Constitution, by assembling the wise men of the state, instead of assembling armies," Jefferson noted, "will be worth as much to the world as the former examples we had given them."[65]

By Constitutional Amendment

That the Articles of Confederation could be amended only by a unanimous vote of the states posed an almost insurmountable barrier to any change at all. The framers of the Constitution made sure that this experience would not repeat itself. Yet the procedures, though not requiring unanimity, do require widespread agreement. More than nine thousand amendments have been proposed in Congress, but only twenty-seven (including the ten in the Bill of Rights) have been adopted.[66]

Procedures The procedures for amendment entail action by both the national government and the state governments. Amendments can be proposed either by a two-thirds vote of both houses of Congress or by a national convention called by Congress at the request of two-thirds of the state legislatures. Congress then specifies which way amendments must be ratified—either by three-fourths of the state legislatures or by ratifying conventions in three-fourths of the states. Among these avenues, the usual route has been proposal by Congress and ratification by state legislatures.

Art. V *Amendments* In the first Congress under the Constitution, the Federalists fulfilled their promise to support a bill of rights. Madison drafted twelve amendments, Congress proposed them, and the states ratified ten of them in 1791. This **Bill of Rights** includes freedom of conviction and expression—religion, speech, press, and assembly (First Amendment). It also includes numerous rights for those accused of crimes—protection against unreasonable searches and seizures (Fourth), protection against compulsory self-incrimination (Fifth), guarantee of due process of law (Fifth), the right to counsel and to a jury trial in criminal cases (Sixth), and protection against excessive bail and fines and against cruel and

Table 1	Constitutional Provisions Protecting Property

Numerous constitutional provisions, some obvious and others not, were designed to protect property:

Provision	Effect
For the House of Representatives, "the Electors [voters] in each State shall have the Qualifications requisite for Electors of the most numerous Branch of the State Legislature."	Allows states to set property qualifications to vote.
"The Congress shall have Power . . . To coin Money."	Centralizes currency.
"No State shall . . . emit bills of credit."	Prevents states from printing paper money.
"Congress shall have Power . . . To establish uniform Laws on the subject of Bankruptcies."	Prevents states from relieving debtors of the obligation to pay.
"The Congress shall have Power . . . To regulate Commerce . . . among the several States."	Centralizes commerce regulation and thereby establishes a national economy.
"No State shall . . . pass any . . . Law impairing the Obligation of Contracts."	Prevents states from relieving debtors of the obligation to pay and thereby establishes stable business arrangements.
"The United States shall guarantee to every State [protection] against domestic Violence."	Protects states from debtor uprisings.
"The Congress shall have Power . . . To provide for calling forth the Militia to execute the Laws of the Union, suppress insurrections."	Protects creditors from debtor uprisings.

unusual punishment (Eighth). (These will be covered fully in Chapter 14.) It also includes a right to a jury trial in civil cases (Seventh).

Two amendments in the Bill of Rights grew out of the colonial experience with Great Britain—the right to bear arms to form a militia (Second) and the right not to have soldiers quartered in homes during peacetime (Third). The Bill of Rights also includes two general amendments—a statement allowing for additional rights beyond the ones in the first eight amendments (Ninth) and a statement reserving powers to the states that are not given to the national government (Tenth).

Among the other seventeen amendments to the Constitution, the strongest theme is the expansion of citizenship rights:[67]

- Abolition of slavery (Thirteenth, 1865)
- Equal protection, due process of law (Fourteenth, 1868)
- Right of black men to vote (Fifteenth, 1870)
- Direct election of senators (Seventeenth, 1913)
- Right of women to vote (Nineteenth, 1920)
- Right of District of Columbia residents to vote in presidential elections (Twenty-third, 1960)
- Abolition of poll tax in federal elections (Twenty-fourth, 1964)
- Right of persons eighteen and older to vote (Twenty-sixth, 1971)

In recent decades, two amendments proposed by Congress were not ratified by the states. One would have provided equal rights for women (discussed in Chapter 15), and the other would have given congressional representation to the District of Columbia as though it were a state.

Although the Constitution expressly provides for change by amendment, its ambiguity about some subjects and silence about others virtually guarantees change by interpretation and practice as well.

By Judicial Interpretation

If there is disagreement about what the Constitution means, who is to interpret it? Although the Constitution does not say, the judicial branch has taken on this role. To decide disputes before them, the courts must determine what the relevant provisions of the Constitution mean. By saying that the provisions mean one thing rather than another, the courts can, in effect, change the Constitution. Woodrow Wilson called the Supreme Court "a constitutional convention in continuous session." The Court has interpreted the Constitution in ways that bring about the same results as new amendments would. (Chapters 13, 14, and 15 provide many examples.)

By Political Practice

Political practice has accounted for some very important changes. These include the rise of political parties and the demise of the Electoral College as an independent body. They also include the development of the cabinet to advise the president and the development of the committee system to operate the two houses of Congress. (Chapters 7, 8, and 10 explain these changes.)

Authorities empty barrels of beer after the Eighteenth Amendment, which prohibited alcohol, was adopted in 1919. The Twenty-first Amendment repealed the Eighteenth in 1933.

Library of Congress #LC-USZ62-123257

The Founders would be surprised to learn that only seventeen amendments, aside from the Bill of Rights, have been adopted in over two hundred years. In part this is due to their wisdom, but in part it is due to changes in judicial interpretation and political practice, which have combined to create a "living Constitution."

EVOLUTION OF THE CONSTITUTION

The Constitution has evolved since the Founding. This section will introduce the major conceptual changes, which have given us a quite different constitution than the one the Founders drafted.

Early Conflicts

The country faced secessionist threats almost immediately after its creation—by southern states when the Federalists (under John Adams) were in power and then by New England states when the Jeffersonians (under Thomas Jefferson) were in power. These threats were averted, but frequent conflicts between the nation and the states arose.

Supreme Court Rulings

The Supreme Court became the principal arbiter of the Constitution and soon faced questions about national supremacy. John Marshall, chief justice of the United States from 1801 to 1835, was a Federalist, a firm believer in a strong national government, and the decisions of his Court supported this view.

The Marshall Court established the legal bases for the supremacy of national authority over the states. Among the Marshall Court's most important rulings was **McCulloch v. Maryland** in 1819.[68] The case grew out of a dispute over the establishment of a national bank. The bank was unpopular because it competed with smaller banks operating under state laws and because some of its branches engaged in reckless and even fraudulent practices. When the government of Maryland levied a tax on the currency issued by the branch in Baltimore, the bank's constitutionality was called into question and a case was brought before the Court. The claim was that Congress, by establishing a national bank, infringed on the states' authority.

Marshall's ruling upheld the establishment of the bank and struck down the tax by the state. "[T]he power to tax involves the power to destroy," Marshall wrote, and the states shouldn't have the power to destroy the bank, because the bank was "necessary and proper" to carry out Congress's powers to collect taxes, borrow money, regulate commerce, and raise an army. Marshall maintained that if the goal of the legislation is legitimate, "all means which are appropriate, which are plainly adapted to that end, which are not prohibited, but consistent with the letter and spirit of the Constitution, are constitutional."

Art. I, 8 Marshall interpreted "necessary" quite loosely. The bank was not essential, but it was useful. This interpretation of the **necessary and proper clause** allowed Congress, and thus the national government, to wield much more authority than the Constitution appeared to grant. This interpretation recognized the existence of **implied powers**—ones implicit in the explicit powers specifically cited—for the national government. It meant that Congress can legislate in almost any area it wishes (including health care). Thus the Marshall Court embraced nation-centered federalism. By laying the foundation for a strong national government for our rapidly expanding nation, *McCulloch* would become one of the two most important rulings of the Marshall Court and indeed of the Supreme Court ever. (The other was *Marbury* v. *Madison*, which will be covered in Chapter 13.)

DEMOCRACY?

What might be the implications for democracy of a broad interpretation of the necessary and proper clause and a recognition of implied powers?

Conflicts between the nation and the states continued, and debates over slavery exacerbated them. These conflicts led to southern states' efforts to secede from the Union and to the Civil War.

The Civil War and Reconstruction

The Civil War, from 1861 through 1865, and Reconstruction, from the end of the war through 1876, constituted a "second American Revolution."[69] After the bloodletting and scorched earth, more than six hundred thousand soldiers lay in graves—one of every seven men between the ages of fifteen and thirty—and parts of the South lay in waste. The North's victory preserved the Union, but it did far more than this. It also altered the Constitution—in the minds of the people and in formal amendments to the document.

Although the North's leader, President Abraham Lincoln, a Republican, held views that would be considered racist today (he believed that black people were inherently inferior and that they should emigrate from the United States),[70] he despised slavery because it deprived persons of their unalienable rights to life, liberty, and the pursuit of happiness promised by the Declaration of Independence. But efforts to abolish slavery were constrained by the political climate, and Lincoln was a practical politician. Before the war, he was willing to allow slavery in the southern states as long as the Union was preserved. But one year into the war, he found this goal too limited.[71] Abolitionist sentiment was spreading in the North, giving Lincoln the opportunity to lead efforts to abolish slavery as well as preserve the Union.[72] In the process, he helped reinvent America.

The Emancipation Proclamation

The **Emancipation Proclamation** offered the promise of redefining the Constitution. President Lincoln announced the proclamation in September 1862 and ordered it to take effect in January 1863. The document proclaimed that the slaves "shall be . . . forever free" in the Confederate states where the Union army was not in control. Its language limited its sweep, for it exempted those parts of the Confederate states where the Union army was in control and also the slave states that remained loyal to the Union (Delaware, Kentucky, Maryland, and Missouri). And despite its language, it could not be enforced in the parts of the Confederate states where the Union army was not in control. Thus, as a legal document, the proclamation was problematic. However, as a symbolic measure, it was successful. The proclamation made clear that the war was no longer just to preserve the Union, but to abolish slavery as well. It captured people's imagination, and when slaves heard about it, many left their plantations and some joined the Union army. The desertion sowed confusion in the South and denied a reliable labor force to the region.

Two decades before the war, Lincoln had suffered from depression and considered suicide. He confided to a friend that he "had done nothing to make any human being remember" that he had lived. Years later, however, he remarked to the friend that the proclamation would justify his existence.[73]

The Gettysburg Address

President Lincoln's **Gettysburg Address** set the tone for new interpretations of the Constitution.[74] The battle at Gettysburg, Pennsylvania, in 1863 was a Union victory and the turning point in the Civil War. Lincoln was invited to deliver "a few appropriate remarks" during the dedication of the battlefield where many had fallen. Lincoln was not the main speaker, and his speech was not long. The main speaker took two hours, recounting the battle and reciting the names of the generals and even some of their soldiers; Lincoln took two minutes to give a 268-word speech. (He spoke so briefly that the photographer, with his clumsy equipment and its slow exposure, failed to get a single photograph.) Lincoln used the occasion to advance his ideal of equality.

He began: "Four score and seven [eighty-seven] years ago our fathers brought forth on this continent a new nation, conceived in liberty and dedicated to the proposition that all men are created equal." Here Lincoln referred not to the Constitution of 1787 but to the Declaration of Independence of 1776. For Lincoln, the Constitution had abandoned the principle of equality that the Declaration had promised. He sought to resurrect this principle. Lincoln did not mention slavery or the Emancipation Proclamation, which were

Library of Congress #LC-B811-3241

This view of the remains of Richmond, Virginia, conveys the destruction of the Civil War.

Slaves thank President Abraham Lincoln for issuing the Emancipation Proclamation. Although this image may seem demeaning to some people today, it reflected slaves' sentiments at the time. In fact, freed blacks raised funds for a statue with a similar scene in Washington, D.C.

divisive. A shrewd politician, he wanted people to focus on the Declaration, which was revered.

Lincoln concluded by addressing "the great task remaining before us . . . that we here highly resolve that these dead shall not have died in vain, that this nation, under God, shall have a new birth of freedom, and that government of the people, by the people, for the people shall not perish from the earth." This phrase, which Lincoln made famous, was borrowed from a speaker at an antislavery convention.[75] It depicted a government elected by all the people, to serve all the people.[76] Lincoln's conclusion reinforced his introduction—both emphasized equality.

Although his speech was brief, Lincoln used the word *nation* five times, including the phrase "a new nation." His purpose was not to encourage support for the Union, but to urge people to think of the nation as a whole, its identity now forged in a bloody war of brother against brother, rather than as simply a collection of individual states with their own interests.[77]

Thus the president essentially added the Declaration's promise of equality to the Constitution, and he substituted his vision of a unified nation for the Founders' precarious arrangement of a balance of power between the nation and the states. According to one historian, "He performed one of the most daring acts of open-air sleight-of-hand ever witnessed by the unsuspecting. . . . The crowd departed with a new thing in its ideological luggage, that new constitution Lincoln had substituted for the one they brought with them."[78]

The Gettysburg Address was heard by an audience of perhaps fifteen thousand, but its language was spread through word of mouth and newspapers and eventually by politicians and teachers. It was read, repeated, and sometimes memorized by generations of schoolchildren. Although some critics at the time perceived what Lincoln was attempting—the *Chicago Times* quoted the Constitution to the president and charged him with betraying the document he swore to uphold—most citizens came to accept Lincoln's addition. His speech, which has been called "the best political address" in the country's history, thus became "the secular prayer of the postbellum American Republic."[79] (The speech is reprinted in the Appendix.)

The Reconstruction Amendments

If the Gettysburg Address became the preamble of the new constitution, the **Reconstruction Amendments** became its body. These three amendments, adopted from 1865 through 1870, began to implement the promise of equality and the vision of a unified nation rather than a collection of individual states.

The Thirteenth Amendment abolished slavery, essentially constitutionalizing the Emancipation Proclamation.

The Fourteenth Amendment declared that all persons born or naturalized in the United States are citizens, overturning the Supreme Court's ruling before the Civil War that blacks, whether slave or free, could not be citizens.[80] The Fourteenth Amendment also included the equal protection clause, which requires states to treat persons equally, and the due process clause, which requires states to treat persons fairly. The equal protection clause would become the primary legal means to end discrimination, and the due process clause would become the primary legal means to give persons the full benefit of the Bill of Rights.[81] (This amendment and these clauses will be examined further in Chapters 14 and 15.) This amendment, one legal scholar observes, was "a revolutionary change. The states were no longer the autonomous sovereigns that they thought they were when they claimed the right of secession. They were now, in fact, servants of their people. [They] existed to guarantee due process and equal justice for all."[82]

The Fifteenth Amendment extended the right to vote to blacks. Because women could not vote at the time, the amendment essentially provided the right to vote to black men. (This amendment will be addressed further in Chapters 8 and 15.)

As important as the substantive content of these amendments was a procedural provision authorizing Congress to enforce them. ("Congress shall have power to enforce this article by appropriate legislation.") That is, the amendments gave Congress broad power, beyond that granted in the original Constitution, to pass new laws to implement the amendments. Consequently, the federal government would come to oversee and even intervene in the policies of state and local governments to make sure that these governments did not disregard the guarantees of the amendments. These amendments thus marked the start of a trend of federalizing the Constitution by increasing the power of Congress.[83] Five later amendments also would include this provision.

DEMOCRACY?

How does this provision have similar implications for democracy as the Supreme Court's interpretation of the necessary and proper clause in the *McCulloch* v. *Maryland* case?

During Reconstruction, the Union army occupied the South and enforced the amendments and congressional laws implementing them. But southern whites resisted, and eventually northern whites grew weary of the struggle. At the same time, there was a desire for healing between the two regions and lingering feelings for continuity with the past. In 1876, the two national political parties, the Democrats and the Republicans, struck a deal to withdraw the Union army and to allow the southern states to govern themselves again. The entrenched attitudes of southern whites prompted them to establish segregation and discrimination in place of slavery, thus preventing blacks from enjoying their new rights. As a result, the new constitution stressing equality and powers of the national government to enforce equality, as envisioned by Lincoln, would not really come into being until the 1950s and 1960s, when the civil rights movement, Supreme Court rulings, presidential initiatives, and congressional acts would converge to give effect to the ideal of racial equality. (These developments will be examined fully in Chapter 15.) In the meantime, the new constitution would lie, in our

DEMOCRACY?

Consider the vast implications for democracy of the Civil War, Emancipation Proclamation, Gettysburg Address, and Reconstruction amendments.

In the 1920s, the economy and stock market were booming. Herbert Hoover capitalized on the country's prosperity in the 1928 election.

The David J. and Janice L. Frent Collection

collective consciousness, as an unfulfilled promise, occasionally emerging to foster greater equality.[84]

During the industrialization and urbanization that followed the Civil War, the national government continued to extend its reach and expand its power, but more significant changes would occur during the Great Depression.

The Great Depression and the New Deal

In the 1928 election, Herbert Hoover, the Republican candidate who would become the next president, predicted, "We shall soon, with the help of God, be in sight of the day when poverty will be banished from this nation."[85] One year later the stock market crashed, and the Great Depression began. As explained in the Introduction to this text, millions of Americans lost their jobs and their savings, and many struggled to find enough food. Unlike today, there were no systematic welfare programs to relieve the suffering.

President Hoover, expecting the economy to right itself, resisted aggressive action and as a result lost his bid for reelection to Franklin Roosevelt, a Democrat, in 1932. President Roosevelt immediately initiated his **New Deal** program to stimulate the economy and ameliorate the suffering.

This era also altered the Constitution—not by formal amendments, but through judicial rulings and political practice. In the process, it changed the minds of the people.[86] As a result, we replaced our small, limited government, as envisioned by the Founders, with a big, activist government.

Judicial Rulings

In the late nineteenth and early twentieth centuries, a laissez-faire economic philosophy was popular in this country and was reflected in governmental policies. According

Talking Points

"Who is the sovereign, the state or the federal government?" That was the question put by a Republican member of the Utah legislature and leader of the Patrick Henry Caucus, formed to assert the "inviolable sovereignty of the State of Utah under the Tenth Amendment to the Constitution."[1]

States have been bucking the authority of the federal government since the earliest days of the Republic. Southern states threatened secession just a few years after John Adams was inaugurated, and northeastern states after Jefferson became president. In 1861, when secession became a reality, the Civil War led to more than 600,000 casualties, greater than the sum of all of America's other wars.

During President Obama's first year in office the "s" word surfaced again, notably when Texas governor Rick Perry said his state would assert its Tenth Amendment rights and leave the Union if Washington didn't stop thumbing its "nose at the American people."[2] A number of other Republican governors and legislators vowed publicly that they would not carry out this or that law, and a few joined Perry in suggesting that if law X were passed, their states too might consider secession. Some states approved resolutions or put on ballots measures saying their state had the right to opt out of federally mandated health insurance reform. Other measures claimed authority to override federal gun control laws and federal law enforcement, even on federal lands in their states. Governor Tim Pawlenty (R-Minn.) told delegates to a 2010 Tea Party convention to "take a 9-iron and smash the window out of big government in this country."

Not just conservative but also liberal-leaning states like Rhode Island, Vermont, and Wisconsin considered states' rights bills, such as authorizing, or requiring, governors to regain control of National Guard troops that had been put under federal authority and called up for active duty. "Something politically powerful is brewing under the statehouse domes," a states' rights advocate observed in 2010. "Everything we've tried to keep the federal government confined to rational limits has been a failure, an utter, unrelenting failure—so why not try something else?"[3]

A large majority of Americans were unhappy with the state of the country in 2010, but most (53 percent) said they were not "angry." And those who said government was doing too much appeared to be advocating that business and individuals should do more, not that state and local government should grow.[4] The anger state officials felt was easy to understand given how much they were being asked to do with diminished resources, but the problems the country was facing—recession, two wars, the worst environmental disaster in the nation's history—were too big for individuals, business, or any one state government. One hundred years ago President Woodrow Wilson warned that "it is no longer possible with the modern combinations of industry and transportation to discriminate the interests of the states as they once could be. . . . Interests once local and separate have become unified and national. They must be treated by the national government."

The victory of the Union over secessionist states in the Civil War (1861–1865) established that the Union was indivisible and that the states could not nullify federal law or the Constitution. The war settled little else about the federal relationship. Americans continue to disagree about just how big and how strong our national government should be. Nevertheless, because of the sheer size and complexity of our country, its role in world affairs, and our expanded expectations of government, we live in a nation with a strong central government. One indication of how dominant the national government has become in the public consciousness is the conflation of *federal* with *national*. It is a confusing but now common usage to say *federal government* when referring to the national government.

The Introduction described how in just over two hundred years, driven by war, economic crises, and the political agendas of presidents, the national government grew from a few hundred people with relatively limited impact on the residents of thirteen small states to a government employing several millions, affecting the daily lives of more than 300 million people in fifty states and billions of people beyond our borders. Chapter 2 explained much of the Founders' reasoning in choosing federalism, how they provided for it in the Constitution, and how the Marshall Court set the government on its course toward nation-centered federalism with its ruling in *McCulloch* v. *Maryland*. In this chapter, we look in greater detail at the politics behind the choice of federalism, how the distribution of power between Washington and the states has been changed over time by Supreme Court rulings, presidential management of federal relations, and the actions of Congress, state legislatures, and governors. In describing the everyday workings of federalism, we identify sources of cooperation and conflict in the division of powers. Finally, we look at the role of the people in the federal relationship.

FEDERAL AND UNITARY SYSTEMS

Except for a few loosely organized leagues of states, there were no federalist systems before the United States was created. Perhaps for that reason, there is a tendency to associate federalism with democracy and more centralized or unitary systems with monarchies or dictatorships. But this is a false distinction. In this section we explain the difference between federal and unitary governments.

Federal Systems

The term **federalism** describes a system in which power is constitutionally divided between a central government and subnational or local governments. In the United States, the subnational governments are the states. All federal systems are not alike: Germany, Belgium, Canada, India, Brazil, and Mexico, for example, vary greatly in their basic economic and political characteristics. They are similar only in that each has a written constitution allocating some powers to the national and some to the subnational governments.

In American federalism, both levels of government receive their grants of power from a higher authority, the will of the people (popular sovereignty) as expressed in the Constitution. In other words, federalism divides something—sovereignty—that is theoretically indivisible. This is the source of some of the conflict over jurisdiction that inevitably arises between levels of government. Making arrangements even more complex, the powers granted to each level are not necessarily exclusive. Both national and state governments have the power to tax, regulate, and provide benefits. And because each level of government is sovereign in its own right, neither can dissolve the other.

In contrast, in a **confederal system**, the central government has only those powers given to it by the subnational governments; it cannot act directly on citizens, and it can be dissolved by the states that created it. The first American government, established by the Articles of Confederation, was a confederal system in which all sovereignty was vested in the states. The national government was the creation of the states—not the people—and it existed only at the pleasure of the states. Like the first government of the United States, the United Nations is an example of a confederal system. The lack of central authority in such systems makes them basically unworkable as governmental arrangements for modern nations.

Unitary Systems

In contrast to federalism, the national government in a **unitary system** creates subnational governments and gives them only those powers it wants them to have. Thus the national government is supreme. In Britain, for example, the national government can give or take away any power previously delegated to the subnational governments, and it can even abolish them, as it did with some city governments in the 1980s. In unitary Sweden, the national parliament abolished 90 percent of its local governments between 1952 and 1975.

At least one delegate to the Constitutional Convention proposed abolishing the states to create a unitary system, but few took this option seriously.[5] However, each of the fifty states is unitary with respect to its local governments. Cities, counties, townships, and school districts can be altered or even eliminated by state governments. Yet every state is (and is required to be by the U.S. Constitution) a republic—that is, a representative democracy.

Unitary systems can be democratic or authoritarian. Some unitary systems are among the most democratic in the world (Britain and Sweden); others are authoritarian (Egypt and China). Likewise, federal systems can be democratic, such as Canada, Australia, Germany, or India, or authoritarian, like the Congo, the former Soviet Union, and the former Yugoslavia.

Whether or not a government is federal or unitary, all modern governments have to delegate some power because a central government, even in a unitary system, cannot run every local service or deal directly with every local problem. In Great Britain, for example, a good deal of local autonomy has devolved onto assemblies in Scotland, Wales, and Northern Ireland. And despite constitutional stipulations, the division of power in federal systems is not static. In the United States the competition among governmental units to shape and implement policy is never-ending and the balance of power is constantly shifting, often issue by issue.

Contemporary Federal Systems

By the 1960s, as much as half the world's territory was governed by federalism.[6] Some new nations created after World War II chose federalism because they, like the American colonies, were trying to unite diverse states or territories into a single country. Federal systems are often ethnically, linguistically, religiously, or racially diverse, though not always. In 2005, Iraqis wrote a constitution with a federal division of power among Arab Shia and Sunni Muslims and the mostly Muslim but non-Arab Kurds to get the bitterly divided factions to accept the new government. Agreeing to divide power among levels of government may be the only way to unite people who have strong motivation to live apart.

The power-sharing arrangements in federal governments often do not work, and many have failed. In the Iraq case, it remains to be seen if federal arrangements will work. In some cases, there are not enough shared values to hold a nation together. Muslims left predominantly Hindu India to create Pakistan, and the Bengali people split from Pakistan to create Bangladesh. After the fall of communism, the federal state of Yugoslavia, with a mixed Christian and Muslim population, spun apart into what are now seven separate nation-states. Federal systems that were not created by popular will are likely to fail when the authoritarian center collapses. Not only Yugoslavia, but also the Soviet Union, ceased to exist when communism fell, and its constituent republics became independent countries.

DEMOCRACY?

If the U.S. population becomes more geographically segregated along ethnic, religious, or racial lines as it continues to grow, will its survival as a federal republic be threatened?

Secession sometimes fails, or succeeds only after prolonged conflict. There have been failed secessionist movements in Nigeria, Canada, Mexico, the United States, and many other federalist nations. Unions have been kept together by military force, by political compromise, and by granting greater local autonomy. The ethnically French, Catholic population of Quebec (the Quebecois) tried unsuccessfully for fifty years to separate from British, Protestant-dominated Canada. In 2006 the prime minister proposed that the 7 million Quebecois be recognized as a nation within the Canadian union. This did not happen, but the province was given greater autonomy, and

Canada's prime minister must be bilingual. But the head of state is the British monarch and thus always a Protestant.

CHOOSING FEDERALISM: THE POLITICAL CONTEXT

As Chapter 2 made clear, the Founders of the United States did not choose federalism as an ideal form of government or as a principle in itself. The few historical examples suggested little to recommend it as a form appropriate to the American situation. The Founders had to write from scratch a document that would accommodate the political reality of their loose compact of states. But it was necessary to find a compromise that could satisfy those who thought only a strong central government could work and those who thought the Union could be preserved only if the individual state governments retained most of the authority they had under the Articles of Confederation. The Founders proposed a dual form of government, a hybrid to be created by mixing the *national* form with a strong central government favored by some delegates and the *confederal*, or league of states, form favored by others. In arguing for its ratification, James Madison defended the Constitution in just this way, saying it would create a government that was partly national and partly federal.[7] Although today we refer to the government in Washington as the "federal" government, the Founders referred to the government they created by the type of democracy it was—a republic. The word *federal* does not appear in the Constitution.

The Fear Factor

Given the tenuous ties that often exist between political entities agreeing to unite under a single government, one scholar argues that federal systems "more than any other kind of government benefit from written constitutions." Because they "originate in particular bargains struck at a particular time for a particular purpose, written constitutions are useful, even necessary records, of the terms of the bargain."[8]

In the public debates arguing for ratification of the Constitution and in those arguing just as vehemently against it, there was one dominant theme: fear.[9] The Federalists were afraid of another confederal arrangement and believed a new constitution had to create a central government strong enough to maintain the Union and protect it against external threats. The Anti-Federalists feared that, having just overthrown the British crown, they would be establishing another abusive central government if they ratified the Constitution. For them perhaps nothing raised the red flag higher than the Supremacy Clause, which they thought would emasculate state legislatures.

From every point on the political spectrum, people found something to fear in the proposed new government: some worried because there were no written guarantees for individual liberties, others because too much power was left with the state governments, and still others feared the opposite, that too many powers were invested in the national government—to tax, borrow money, keep a standing army, and make treaties. Each branch of government raised concerns: that the six-year term for senators would create a political class or aristocracy, that the executive would be too weakened by the power of impeachment, that an independent judiciary would have too much power, or that it would not have enough independence. And there were the people to fear as well: as described in Chapter 2, many of the Founders were wary of direct democracy and the "passionate tendencies" of the masses.

Federalism was the scarcely tried form of government chosen to assuage these fears, and those making the case for ratification had to convince the public that the Constitution was creating a national government that could and would do *only* what needed to be done at the center, leaving state sovereignty intact (see the Behind the Scenes box "An Accidental Classic"). Perhaps the benefit of the federal arrangement for the American colonies can be best understood by the adage "politics is the art of the possible." The division of powers made the Union possible. It allowed states their differences, ceded control over local affairs, and in the process protected against both an abusive central government and the tyranny of factions. But having reached agreement on

a division of powers with great difficulty, the Founders left vague the details of how the nation-state relationship would work. The Constitution did not specify the individual or institution that would resolve disputes over state and federal jurisdictions, but the federal courts assumed that role during the tenure of Chief Justice Marshall. (See Chapter 13.)

Dueling Federalisms

Once ratified, the Constitution was evidence of a bargain between Federalists and Anti-Federalists, but that was no guarantee that each side would interpret the terms of the document in the same way. It was immediately clear that they had not even resolved their disagreement over who had been the original parties to this social contract. Those who saw the Constitution as written by representatives of the people and ratified by the people were inclined to view the national government as the supreme power in the federal relationship. Alexander Hamilton clearly articulated this view of **nation-centered federalism** in the *Federalist Papers*. This interpretation acknowledges that the Constitution grants many powers to the states, recognizes that they existed before the Union, and agrees that states are sovereign in the sense that they cannot be dissolved by the national government. But the nation-centered view is that

behind the scenes

An Accidental Classic

Collected in a single volume as *The Federalist*, the eighty-five essays James Madison, Alexander Hamilton, and John Jay wrote in support of ratification of the Constitution have been described by contemporary scholars as "by far the greatest book on politics ever written in America."[1]

The "book," of course, was not a book in any conventional sense, but a collection of papers written by three men in a hurry, trying to hold together a tenuous union of thirteen states. In fact, the three men listed as coauthors were single authors working alone; they did not coordinate their work or collaborate to try to bring coherency to their arguments or writing style before publishing their essays. One authority on the papers says, "There is no evidence that one writer's work was ever revised on the advice of the others," even though the men's views—especially those of Madison and Hamilton, who between them wrote all but five of the essays—were known to conflict. Madison himself said that none of the authors could be expected to answer for the ideas of the other two.[2]

The *Federalist* essays were only one of the twenty-four series of articles written to argue for or against ratification, and it is not known how widely they were read or how many minds they swayed. Many scholars believe at best the essays may have influenced a few undecided voters in crucial ratification contests.[3] Yet they came to be regarded as one of the most "coherent Treaties on the basic principles of political theory" ever written. So many constitutional scholars have cited them as evidence of the intent of the Founders, and so many federal court rulings have referenced them that, as for the Bible and the works of Shakespeare, a concordance was developed.[4] Nevertheless, the divergent views of the authors are so apparent—John Adams said they read like "rival dissertations"—that the writings are said to suffer from a split personality.[5] In this sense, they are a true reflection of the competing arguments on how the Founders divided power among the nation, the states, and the people, and why, to this day, the country still suffers from a split personality.

[1] Bernard Bailyn, *The Federalist Papers* (Washington D.C.: Library of Congress, 1998).
[2] Ibid.
[3] Roy P. Fairfield, ed., *The Federalist Papers* (New York: Anchor Books, 1961), x–xi.
[4] Bailyn, *Federalist Papers*, 10–11.
[5] Ibid., 8.

James Madison

© The Art Gallery Collection/Alamy

the national government's sovereignty is supreme and its ultimate responsibility is to preserve the Union and ensure its indivisibility.[10] In support of their argument, the Federalists cited the **Supremacy Clause**, the very wording so feared by Anti-Federalists.

Art. VI, Sec. 1 The clause says that treaties, the Constitution, and "laws made in pursuance thereof" are to be the supreme law of the land whenever they come into conflict with state laws or state actions. It also stipulates that when there is a difference of opinion as to whether state actions are in conflict with the Constitution or federal law, the matter is to be decided at the national level.[11] (See the box "Immigration Enforcement: The States Step In.") Nation-centered federalism (also called centralized federalism) was the view used by northerners to justify a war to prevent the southern states from seceding in 1861.

Opponents of the Hamiltonian interpretation, including many from the South, argued that because the Constitution recognized the states' existence as sovereign entities before the creation of the Union, the form our system was to take was **state-centered federalism**, giving precedence to state sovereignty over that of the national government or the Union. They believed the Tenth Amendment limited congressional powers to those specifically mentioned in Article I and that this view was reinforced by Madison's words in *Federalist Paper* 45: "The powers delegated . . . to the federal government are few and defined. Those

which are to remain in the state governments are numerous and indefinite." In this view, any attempt by Congress to go beyond these explicitly listed powers violated state authority.

In justifying their secession from the Union, southerners held to the extreme version of state-centered federalism: that the Constitution had been written by representatives of the states, not the people. In their view, if the states had created the Union, they could dissolve it.

DEMOCRACY?

Would there be any implications for the democratic nature of our government if it was determined to be the creation of the states rather than the people?

The Constitution can also be interpreted as having created a government in which the division of power leaves neither level dominant over the other. In this view—**dual federalism**—the Constitution created a system in which the national government and the states each have separate grants of power, with each supreme in its own sphere. In this interpretation of the division of powers, sovereignty is not just divided but divided in such a way as to leave both levels of government essentially equal. The differences between levels derive from their separate jurisdictions, not from inequality of power. Madison's description in *Federalist Paper* 39 of the government created by the Constitution as a hybrid of national and federal forms provides one basis for this interpretation.

Over the years, the dominant interpretations of power sharing in our form of federalism have shifted among the nation-centered, state-centered, and dual views. Overall, there has been a general trend toward nation-centered federalism, but there have been significant short-term shifts in power back toward the states.

Describing our form of government as centralized federalism indicates where the preponderance of power lies; it does not suggest that at any time there is a national consensus on where it does or should lie. For decades after the Civil War, for example, the states that had remained in the Union were much more likely to accept the authority of the center to apply uniform rules to the states than were those states that had joined the Confederacy. (See Chapters 8 and 15.) State governments were able to refuse enforcement of basic constitutional guarantees on civil rights and liberties in large part because there was no national will to force compliance. But it was also recognition of the tenuous bargain struck by the Founders on the division of powers. Having fought our deadliest war over secession, the deal made in the postwar (Reconstruction) years restoring full powers to the secessionist states reflected that the primary concern continued to lie with keeping the Union intact. But the Union can also falter if too much value is placed on accommodation of state or regional preferences, especially if the differences among the states become more important than their commitment to common principles.

The constitutional provisions protecting the rights and individuality of the states were meant to accommodate what is sometimes called our "psychology of localism."[12] (See the American Diversity box "Political Culture and Federalism.") Although we are now a more mobile and a more nation-oriented people than we were in the eighteenth and nineteenth centuries, with communication and transportation links that bind us together, we retain enough local allegiance and commitment to individualism to tilt our federal system toward decentralization and fragmentation. Indeed, federalism creates separate power centers, and keeping them separate becomes an interest of those holding that power.[13] In part, federalism is *intended* to do this, but if taken too far, it can prevent coherence and unity. Even when there is need for national policy—whether on energy, the environment, health care, or defense spending—members of Congress may still base their votes primarily on local interests (see Chapter 10).

THE EVOLUTION OF FEDERALISM

The first fifty years under the new constitution were characterized by the growth of nation-centered federalism in legal doctrine, by small-scale state and national government in practice, and by the beginning of intergovernmental cooperation.

american*diversity

Political Culture and Federalism

When we refer to the Midwest, the Southwest, New England, or the Deep South, certain images still come to mind, not just of geographical areas but also of lifestyles, partisan preferences, ideology, and local economies. Our nicknames—such as the Corn, Sun, Bible, and Rust Belts—reflect this. Individual states have developed sufficiently different political styles and attitudes that campaign strategists would never design the same electoral strategy for a candidate in New York as they would for one in Idaho. For the same reason, candidates for national office change the points of emphasis in their stump speeches as they move from state to state.

States want to be different from one another because each is basically a political actor competing for a share of the nation's resources. Just as individuals organize around identity issues, states compete with one another on the basis of their distinctive profiles. Each has its own constitution, flag, song, motto, and symbols of state, not to mention its very own official state bird and flower. Illinois is not alone in having an official folk dance, insect, tree, soil, grass, fossil, fruit, animal, fish, amphibian, reptile, and snack food. Slogans (West Virginia: "Open for Business"; and Wisconsin: "Live Like You Mean It") advertise a defining characteristic that will make each state an attractive place to live and do business.

In Chapter 1, we defined political culture as a shared body of values and beliefs that shapes perceptions and attitudes toward politics and government and that influences behavior. For much of the twentieth century, the United States was said to have three geographically based political subcultures—three distinctive ways of looking at and participating in politics.[1] The tendency of people in New England and the upper Midwest to view politics as a way of improving life and to believe in their obligation to participate was labeled a *moralistic*

political culture. In the *individualistic* political culture, said to be typical of the industrial Midwest and the East, the ultimate objective of politics was not to create a better life for all, but to get benefits for oneself and one's group. In the *traditionalistic* political culture, associated with the states of the Deep South, politics was seen not as a way to further the public good but as a way to maintain the status quo, and little value was placed on participation. Today, traces of these patterns remain, but much has changed.

The Deep South, for example, having been the site of intense political mobilization during the modern civil rights movement, is now a center of significant grassroots activity, especially among religious conservatives. The out-migration of African Americans during the decades of segregation has been reversed, with a significant impact on electoral politics in the region.

The transformation of the United States from an industry- and agriculture-based economy to a high-tech and service economy also has had an inevitable impact on regional political cultures. Mass media, especially television and the Internet; franchises and chains bringing the same products to all parts of the country; and transportation systems that can carry us across the nation in a few hours have all had a leveling effect on some of our regional differences. This mobility makes it less likely that people will have political orientations as strongly rooted in a state or regional identity as in earlier decades. Until the recession and housing crisis of 2008 reduced mobility somewhat, about one in seven Americans were moving each year, one-quarter of those from one state to another. However, about 40 percent of Americans stay in their hometowns all their lives, and 57 percent never move outside the state where they were born. At the other extreme, only 14 percent of Nevadans were born in Nevada.[2]

In the administration of George Washington the federal government had only one thousand employees, and this number had increased to only thirty-three thousand by the presidency of James Buchanan seventy years later. Little revenue was raised by any level of government; most of the funding for the national government came from import-export and excise taxes (on alcohol, for example). State governments, too, were small and had limited functions. There were only a few federal-state cooperative activities. For example, the federal government gave land to the states to support education and participated in joint federal-state-private ventures, such as canal-building projects initiated by the states.

In this section we look at how federal court rulings have tilted the country toward state- or nation-centered federalism depending on the judicial philosophy of the justices. We also describe how presidential attitudes toward and management of the federal relationship and actions of Congress have shaped the division of powers.

The Courts and Federalism

Such was the gulf between those who thought they were creating an indivisible Union and those who thought they were writing a contract between states that the Constitution

---

Patterns of dispersion of African Americans, Hispanics, and Asians, and the clusters of immigrants settling by country of origin in a handful of states and big cities, contribute to the retention of regional differences and distinctive state profiles. In New Mexico, 45 percent of the population is of Hispanic origin, compared with just over 1 percent in Maine. In Mississippi, African Americans make up over 37 percent of the population; in Vermont, 0.6 percent. Minorities, collectively, now form the majority of the population in Texas, California, Hawaii, and New Mexico. In Florida, almost as many people are over age sixty-five (19.5 percent of the population) as are under eighteen (21 percent), but in Utah, young people outnumber senior citizens more than 3 to 1. In Mississippi, the poorest state, annual per capita income is only 52 percent of what it is in Connecticut, the highest-ranking state.[3]

These disparities make for different politics in the states. The priorities of older people (health care, for instance) are different from those of younger people (financial aid for education, for example). In states with larger numbers of Hispanics and African Americans, civil rights issues are more salient than in states with predominantly white populations. Southern Baptists, who comprise 11 percent of all American Christians, live predominantly in southern states and vote overwhelmingly Republican. Jewish Americans, who tend to be more liberal and vote Democratic, are concentrated in a handful of states, including New York, Florida, and California. Although state and regional differences have not been homogenized, the three old archetypes have morphed into the two more comprehensive categories now familiar to everyone as red states and blue states. Another scheme labels them retro (red) and metro (blue), but the basic distinction is between conservative and liberal policies and lifestyles.[4] The politically conservative/moralistic/red/retro label is now attached to the South, Plains states, lower Midwest, and near West. The liberal/nontraditional/blue/metro state label lumps together the Northeast, upper Midwest, northwestern coastal states, and California.

In fact, the division of states into such broad categories masks the diversity within the two groups and is misleading in suggesting a consonance of lifestyles and political orientation within them. The divorce rate in the Bible Belt states is 50 percent higher than the national average, whereas the nation's lowest divorce rate is in Massachusetts, the bluest of blue states.[5] The wealthiest states are all in the blue column and the poorest in the red column, which means that the citizens of conservative states who are most likely to oppose social welfare policies and government subsidy programs receive substantially more per capita in government benefits than they pay in taxes.[6]

State boundaries do still mean something beyond identifying the place where you register to vote. In policy areas as diverse as economic development, taxation, welfare, and regulation of personal morality, states vary widely. Nevada is the only state in the nation where prostitution is legal; Utah the only state where polygamy has been tolerated (even though illegal). South Dakota passed a law banning abortions that would never make it through the Massachusetts legislature, and Massachusetts, Iowa, and Vermont passed laws allowing same-sex marriages that would never have been passed in South Dakota or Montana. Federalism, even with a strong national government, provides sufficient autonomy for states to adopt and maintain policies consistent with their own political cultures.

[1] Daniel Elazar, *American Federalism: A View from the States*, 3rd ed. (New York: Harper & Row, 1984).

[2] Pew Research Center, "Who Moves Where," 12 (pewresearch.org), http://www.usatoday.com/news/nation/2007-11-29-Mobility_N.htm; Haya El Nasser and Paul Overberg, "Millions More Americans Move to Another State," *USA Today*, November 29, 2007.

[3] All figures in this paragraph from *Statistical Abstract of the United States, 2010*, tabs. 18, 19, and 665, pp. 24, 25; 437.

[4] John Sperling et al., *The Great Divide: Retro vs. Metro America* (Sausalito, Calif.: PoliPoint Press, 2004).

[5] Jim Holt, "States' Rights Left?" *New York Times Magazine*, November 21, 2004, 27; Naomi Cahn and June Carbone, *Red Families v. Blue Families* (New York: Oxford University Press, 2010), 1–15.

[6] Sperling, *The Great Divide*, 34.

might never have been ratified if it had contained specifics on the practice of federalism. Ultimately, it is the Supreme Court that decides where the lines are drawn between what is state and what is federal authority. There have been many Court rulings on the division of power between Washington and the states since the Marshall Court's ruling in *McCulloch* v. *Maryland* (Chapter 2), but like presidents, the federal courts swing between support for nation- and state-centered federalism, depending on the judicial philosophies of the justices.

Before the Civil War, in the years of small government, the Supreme Court overturned only two congressional and sixty state laws. Beginning in the 1880s, as Congress took a larger role in regulating business and the economy, a conservative Supreme Court used the dual federalism doctrine to rule unconstitutional many federal attempts to regulate. But this proved to be more of a pro-business bias than a dual federalist view. When state governments, spurred by the same revelations of unsafe and degrading conditions that led Congress to act, passed laws against child labor and to protect workers, the federal courts often ruled that they, too, had overstepped their powers. From 1874 to 1937, the Supreme Court found fifty federal and four hundred state laws unconstitutional, including some of FDR's key New Deal legislation.[14] After FDR was elected to a second term and had a chance to replace conservative justices, the Court looked on his legislative program more sympathetically.

The eventual Court decisions approving New Deal legislation were, in a sense, a return to the nation-centered federalism of John Marshall's day. But although the Supreme Court ultimately upheld much of the New Deal, it also approved more sweeping *state* regulations of business and labor than had the less activist pre–New Deal Court. Thus the change in Court philosophy did not enlarge the federal role at the expense of the powers of the states; *it enlarged the powers of both state and federal government.* In doing so, the Court was responding to the public's preference for government to play a larger role in helping people cope with the crises stemming from the Great Depression.

In the 1960s and early 1970s, during the height of the civil rights and women's movements, the courts struck down many state laws that restricted voting rights, criminal defendants' rights, and women's economic and educational opportunities, putting much greater enforcement power in the hands of the federal government. But since the 1990s, a federal court system dominated by Republican appointees has been reversing that trend by constricting Congress's power to overturn state laws.

In the past two decades, the rulings of the Supreme Court have shown a trend toward empowering the states at the expense of the national government. In 1992, the Court handed down the first of several key decisions that restrict Congress's ability to impose rules and regulations on state governments and prevent litigants from bypassing state courts to seek remedies in federal courts. In a 1995 decision, the Court ruled for the first time since the New Deal that

Race relations have often been a source of controversy between the federal government and southern state or local governments that resisted civil rights, claiming "states' rights" instead. Here police unleash dogs on peaceful civil rights demonstrators in Birmingham, Alabama, in 1963.

Congress had exceeded its authority to regulate interstate commerce, and in the following eight years it "overturned all or parts of thirty-three federal statutes, ten of them on the grounds that Congress had exceeded its authority either to regulate interstate commerce or to enforce the constitutional guarantees of due process and equal protection."[15]

Once it became clear that a majority on the Court were sympathetic to rolling back federal authority, dozens of federalism suits were filed by those who want to limit Congress's ability to extend federal laws to state jurisdictions. These suits have been successful in preventing some disabled people from suing their employers in state courts for alleged violations of their civil rights as guaranteed under the Americans with Disabilities Act. The limitation placed on such suits by the Court has been summarized as "rights without remedies," or one that permits Congress to confer rights on citizens but not to tell the states how to enforce them. The four dissenting justices in those rulings said that decisions giving states immunity from federal rules are the "result of a fundamentally flawed understanding of the role of the states within the federal system" and warned that they intend to go on dissenting in all cases where this principle of state immunity is applied by the Court's majority.[16] Two of that minority have since retired and been replaced by justices who appear likely to maintain the five-four division.

It should not be taken at face value that the leaning of recent Courts toward state-centered federalism has been based entirely on an originalist reading of the Constitution. The Court's decision to overrule the Florida courts and intervene in the 2000 presidential vote count (thus handing the election to George W. Bush) provides some evidence that at least some rulings may be inspired more by conservative politics than by the principle of dual federalism. Elections, whether for national, state, or local office, are the jurisdiction of the states, not the federal government (Article I, Section 4; Article 2, Section 1). Yet the Court's assertion of federal over state power came during a high tide of Court rulings in defense of states' rights.

Other exceptions to the Court's rulings in favor of states' rights also suggest that more than the principle of state-centered federalism is at play. The Court has been willing to allow Congress to overturn state laws when cases involved conservative values issues. For example, it has refused to uphold state or local laws on the medical use of marijuana and gun control laws that are stronger than those passed by Congress. In a departure from this trend, the Court did rule in 2006 that Congress could not use federal antidrug laws to overturn an Oregon "right to die" law that allows doctors to administer, at the request of terminally ill patients, lethal doses of drugs. However, in 2010 the Court effectively altered or struck down campaign finance laws in twenty-four states by ruling that limits on corporate and union campaign spending are unconstitutional restrictions on free speech.

Major tests of how the current Court will come down on the issue of state- versus nation-centered federalism will come in 2010 and 2011 as the Courts decide cases involving limits on Congress's ability to regulate interstate commerce (challenges to federal health insurance legislation) and a state's right to enforce federal law (challenges to immigration enforcement law).

Presidential Management of Federal Relations

Presidents come to office with some idea of how they will use the powers of office, but a president's theoretical view of the power of the federal government can be superseded by events. For example, the attacks of 9/11 changed George W. Bush's view of the powers of the federal government, and he expanded federal authority in areas related to civil liberties and war powers. Another significant way in which presidents influence how the federal relationship functions is through their appointments to the Supreme Court. But presidents also shape the federal relationship through their everyday management of government.

When most people think of the president, it is probably as a party, political, or foreign policy leader. But for much of their time in office, presidents are acting in the role of chief administrative officer, and in this capacity the amount of control they are willing to cede to the states in administering federal programs is an important indicator of their views on the division of powers. Presidents do differ in their views on how much, and what kind of, power should be shared with state governments.

A key element in power sharing is determining how, and on what, grants-in-aid are spent. **Grants-in-aid** are the tax revenues the federal government returns to states to help pay for essential services provided by state and local governments—mass transit, community development, social welfare, and unemployment compensation, for example. Some presidents are more interested in achieving administrative efficiency in the use of grants, some are more committed to achieving their policy or political goals, and still others may be more interested in the division of powers—with retaining maximum control over the states or in allowing states as much autonomy in implementing laws and programs as congressional legislation allows. We illustrate this with examples from six administrations from the modern era.

With his Great Society programs, Lyndon Johnson (1963–1969) was trying to transform society by securing the right to vote for African Americans, eliminating poverty, and providing health insurance for seniors and the poor. Johnson, a Texan, was steeped in the politics of states' rights and segregation, and he knew that when federal dollars went back to some states there would be great resistance in the state houses to using the money as the law intended. He also knew that rural-influenced state legislatures in the North would be less responsive to the needs of the inner cities. So he increased the number of grants that went directly to localities, bypassing as much as possible the state level of administration, because he believed the localities would be more likely to use the grants as intended by law. On doing this Johnson was not defending federal prerogatives so much as trying to ensure that his policy goals would not be subverted by local resistance.

When Republican Richard Nixon (1969–1974) came into office, he wanted to make government "more effective as well as more efficient." Nixon took a managerial approach to streamlining the cumbersome structure created by the profusion of Great Society programs. He saw a messy bureaucratic problem and an overconcentration of decision making at the federal level, and he tried to find a solution through more efficient management.[17] He did this by consolidating grants-in-aid into block grants, leaving it to the states and localities to determine how to fund programs in these functional areas. This loosening of central control gave local officials more opportunity to target projects to local needs, and it streamlined the process at the federal level.

In contrast to Nixon's managerial approach, the new federalism of Republican Ronald Reagan (1981–1989) had a more ideological purpose, which he made clear in his first inaugural address: "Government is not the solution to our problems," he said. "Government is the problem." Thus Reagan wanted to reduce the power and influence of Washington rather than to improve intergovernmental management. His new federalism was rooted not so much in state-centered or dual federalism as it was in his opposition to government in general.[18] This approach—cutting federal spending on local and state programs to downsize government at all levels—contrasts with Nixon's approach, in which making government more efficient and effective was an end in itself.

IMMIGRATION ENFORCEMENT: THE STATES STEP IN

The Constitution unequivocally puts the regulation and enforcement of immigration and rules for naturalization in the hands of the federal government.

Art. I, Sec. 8 But it is governors and local officials, not the president or Congress, who have to deal with the day-to-day problems of unregulated immigration. This is especially true for border states, where governors and mayors deal daily with rescue missions and the deaths of migrants who die from heat prostration and dehydration, with human smugglers (*coyotes*) and drug traffickers, with business owners who complain of labor shortages and who sometimes actively recruit undocumented workers, and with taxpayers who protest the additional costs of public services used by immigrants.

States and localities must obey federal rulings on immigration and find a way to pay for compliance, or for that portion of costs that federal grants do not cover. Federal law requires, for example, that children be educated and that hospital emergency rooms treat patients without respect to immigration status. These decisions are beyond the jurisdiction of governors, mayors, and state legislatures. Therefore, when the federal government fails to enforce immigration law or to reform it in ways that respond to both national and local needs, the states are left holding the bag. This puts great pressure on governors and local officials to act in lieu of the federal government, especially when economic times are hard and unemployment high.

Illegal Immigrants trek across the Arizona desert.

Vincent J. Musi/Aurora Photos

This was the case in 2010 in Arizona, the border state hardest hit by undocumented entries. After border enforcement was stepped up in California and New Mexico, the traffic moved east to Arizona, until by 2005 crossings along its 372-mile border with Mexico reached a half-million people per year. Local ranchers and some environmentalists were up in arms because of property, livestock, and environmental damage, while the Arizona Homeland Security department was worried that terrorists could be among the migrants. People entering the country with no papers, little money, and no transport caused a spike in car thefts and some other crimes. The Arizona Corrections system housed more than 4000 undocumented workers.[1] Border posses formed, and some local law enforcement officers, not empowered to enforce federal laws, looked for any kind of local statute, such as trespassing or loitering laws, to detain people who were in the state illegally.

Then Governor Janet Napolitano said her hand had been forced by federal inaction: "ranchers are at their wits' end . . . both federal governments [Mexico and the United States] let us down—there doesn't seem to be any sense of urgency." Governor Richardson also called the state of emergency he declared in New Mexico in 2006 "an act of desperation."[2] The vigilante action along the border and the millions protesting in the streets for legal status, Napolitano said, "was a cry from the country saying we want an immigration system that works and can be enforced."[3]

Governors across the nation shared this sense of urgency. State lawmakers introduced hundreds of immigration bills in the first half of 2006; Colorado empowered its attorney general to sue the federal government if it did not take action to enforce immigration laws.[4] And in faraway Hazelton, Pennsylvania, in what would become an emblematic test case, the city passed ordinances that would allow the suspension of business licenses of any employer who hired workers without residency papers and another making it illegal for a landlord to rent to an undocumented resident. The ordinances' constitutionality was immediately challenged in federal courts on the grounds that they preempted federal immigration law and as such were violations of the Supremacy Clause.

In 2007 Governor Napolitano asked President Bush to send the National Guard to patrol the border, which he eventually did, but in numbers too small to matter.[5] She also signed a bill giving local police more enforcement authority, and she billed the U.S. Department of Justice for $217 million to cover the costs of incarcerating illegal immigrants who had committed crimes.[6] Nothing worked.

By 2007, 9 percent of Arizona's residents were in the country illegally, and Arizona had supplanted Nevada as the fastest-growing state in the country. Arrests were running at over 1400 per day; and that year almost 200 died trying to cross the desert, with hundreds more in need of rescue. Arizona needed funds to build at least one new school each year to keep pace

with new enrollments. When the recession hit in 2008 and 2009, and unemployment rose as state revenues fell, the situation intensified. After a rancher was killed by men believed to be either *coyotes* or drug smugglers, the legislature passed and the new governor signed a law that made it a state crime to be in residence without federally issued entry papers. (Napolitano had resigned to become Obama's secretary of Homeland Security and was now an enforcer of federal rather than state law.) In other words, the legislature made it a state crime to be in violation of a federal law; when stopping someone for any infraction, police were empowered to ask for authorization papers from anyone who they had reason to suspect might be in the country illegally. The law required noncitizens to carry authorization papers and gave Arizonans the right to sue state and local agencies for noncompliance.

Of all the state and local laws adopted, Arizona's law drew the greatest national attention because of its potential for racial profiling. But another 1180 bills and resolutions dealing with immigration enforcement or demands on state resources were introduced in state legislatures during the first three months of 2010. Thirty-four states passed more than 200 of those measures, which were said to put in place "policies unique to their situations."[7] Some of these laws were supportive of migrants and none was as tough as Arizona's, but no other state was facing the same situation. The constitutionality of Arizona's statute was immediately challenged and in 2010 a lower court issued an injunction prohibiting the state from implementing those portions of the law that required noncitizens to carry proof of legal residency and police to inquire about a person's residency status when stopping them for another suspected offense. The state immediately appealed the ruling. The law's validity will ultimately depend on how the Supreme Court applies a 1976 Supreme Court ruling that says the states are not prohibited from passing immigration enforcement laws if they are consistent with federal law.

Typically nativist sentiment rises in bad economic times, so even though the number of undocumented residents was on the decline in the nation as a whole, opposition to illegal immigration hardened. Polls showed that more than two-thirds of Americans supported the Arizona law, including requiring aliens to carry documents and allowing the police to stop them for verification.[8] Prior to the lower court injunction against Arizona's law twenty other states were drafting similar bills. Congress and the president, even knowing the economic and law enforcement burden states and localities were carrying, and aware that new state and local legislation is creating a confusing patchwork of rules and may even be preempting federal law, failed to act before the 2008 presidential election year. They showed the same hesitancy before the 2010 midterms, paralyzed by partisanship in Congress and fear of a public reaction at the polls. Even President Obama's decision to send more National Guard troops to the border was delayed by the lack of trained personnel. Gridlock at the federal level has contributed heavily to the burst in state activism.

[1] Janet Napolitano, "Message of the Week," August 17, 2005, 1, http://azgovernor.gov/dms/.
[2] Ralph Blumenthal, "Citing Violence, 2 Border States Declare a Crisis," *New York Times*, August 17, 2005, A14.
[3] John M. Broder, "Governors of Border States Have Hope, and Questions," *New York Times*, May 17, 2006, 1.
[4] Katie Kelley, "A Deal in Colorado on Benefits for Illegal Immigrants," *New York Times*, July 12, 2006, 18. Data from the National Conference of State Legislators.
[5] Paul Davenport, "Napolitano Calls Summit on Immigration Law," June 8, 2005, www.azcentral.com.
[6] Napolitano, "Message of the Week," 1.
[7] National Conference of State Legislatures, "2010 Immigration-Related Bills and Resolutions in the States (January–March, 2010)," 1. (www.ncsl.org/default.aspx?Tabld=20244)
[8] Pew Research Center Publications, "Public Supports Arizona Immigration Law," May 12, 2010, 1. (pewreseach.org/)

Although Reagan had an ideological commitment to smaller government, he had no significant programmatic approach to achieve it. In fact, the size and expenditures of the federal government grew during his administration, and states gained few new powers.

Democrat Bill Clinton (1993–2001) came to office with an ex-governor's wary view of Washington and a commitment to working in partnership with the states. Reforming state-federal relations had been a special interest when, as governor, he chaired both the National Governors

Association and a reform group within the Democratic Party. A native of a southern state (Arkansas) where the states' rights tradition held sway, Clinton claimed to be a supporter of states' rights except in the area of civil rights policy. But he was not an advocate of state-centered federalism or smaller government for its own sake, as was Reagan. He was committed to the idea (earlier articulated by Justice Louis Brandeis) of the **"states as laboratories"**—that is, as places for policy experimentation. He used the phrase frequently, wrote it into executive orders, and eventually based his welfare, health care, and education policies around it.[19]

This reassignment of policy making or implementation powers from higher levels of government to lower levels is called **devolution**. From 1994 through the end of his Administration, Clinton and the Republican-controlled Congress supported devolution, until by the end of his second term the states had major responsibility for implementing federal environmental law as well as welfare programs. Clinton's federalism policies, like Nixon's, were primarily geared toward making government more efficient, whereas the Republican-controlled Congress favored devolution because most Republicans were ideologically opposed to central government authority over the states in domestic policy.

George W. Bush (2001–2009), like Clinton and Reagan, came to the presidency from the governorship of a southern state (Texas), but unlike Clinton, Bush openly advocated returning power to the states. Clinton had favored delegating rule implementation to state agencies, but he insisted on the right of federal agencies to set national standards, such as for clean air and water and consumer and worker safety, as well as to intervene in states to defend voting rights. Within months of taking office, Bush reversed Clinton-imposed regulatory standards for arsenic levels in water, pollutants in the air, and health and safety in the workplace. In addition, he issued a new order making it harder for federal officials

Marijuana use is prohibited under federal law, but its use for medical purposes is legal in fourteen states, including Colorado. Here a Boulder shop owner prepares a sample for sale at his dispensary. The Bush administration favored enforcing the federal prohibition and overturning state laws, but the Obama administration has avoided the issue, perhaps because states like California are beginning to crack down on exploitation of the medical exemption.

to overrule state decisions, including in the area of voting rights. The *rhetorical* position of the Bush administration on the nation-state division of power in domestic policy might be best summarized by a close adviser's description of an ideal government as one "cut 'down to the size where we can drown it in the bathtub.'"[20]

However, the Bush administration ended up sending mixed signals on state-centered federalism. Offsetting his advocacy of devolution in domestic policy making was an expansive view of presidential powers. His support for expanding the role of the states in making and implementing welfare policy was countered by his intervention in public education to impose mandatory national testing on local school systems. He resisted governors' demands that the distribution of electric power should be regulated at the state, not the national, level, and he butted heads with governors many times in the area of business and environmental regulation. When a dozen states tried to adopt stronger regulatory standards for fuel efficiency and clean air than those set by the federal government, his administration fought them in court, eventually losing. In contrast, Bush's two appointments to the Supreme Court strengthened the majority tendency toward state-centered federalism.

Barack Obama (2009–) went to the White House with no prior executive experience and only several years' service in a state legislature and the U.S. Senate. Because he was perceived as a liberal, the expectation was that he would be a strong advocate for nation-centered federalism. But in his first years he proved to be as much of a pragmatist as most of his predecessors, and he defined himself as such. In his first months he helped push through Congress a nearly $800 billion stimulus bill, much of it in aid to the states, with a strong focus on limiting job loss during the worst months of the recession. Although Obama received virtually no support from Republican members of Congress, almost all Republican governors did back his stimulus bill because they are obligated by law to balance their budgets, even during recessions. Obama gave states considerable leeway in how they would use the money, although set amounts were earmarked for education and saving teachers' jobs.

Like Clinton, Obama favors the states-as-laboratories approach and has endorsed the movement that activist governors and state attorneys general call "progressive federalism." Progressive federalism means that state governments take the initiative to regulate in key areas, such as consumer and environmental protection, where Congress and federal agencies have been dragging their feet. The very actions taken by states that the Bush administration went to court to stop—the setting of higher standards for clean air, for example—were encouraged by the Obama administration.

The optimism about new forms of federal-state cooperation faded in Obama's second year when some states began to push back against new federal mandates they believed were insupportable with declining tax revenues. Thirty-seven states challenged the constitutionality of one or more provisions in the 2010 health insurance bill. The resolution of these legal battles may have a longer-term impact on the division of powers than progressive federalism. Most presidents, Reagan excepted, cannot be easily pigeonholed in either the state-centered or nation-centered camp of federalism. Most tend to be instrumentalists, looking to whichever level is most likely to help achieve their policy goals.

Role of Congress

Only the president and vice president have a national constituency; the power of all other elected officials is based in the states and localities. Members of Congress are elected by their constituents in a particular geographic area, and it is their responsibility to represent them. And this is exactly what they do. Most members of the U.S. House and Senate spend far more time pursuing the interests of their districts and states than they do in defining and pursuing the national interest.

Congress varies in its leanings toward nation- and state-centered federalism, depending on the political composition of its members and the state of the nation at any given point in time. Congress supported the tremendous growth of government during Franklin Roosevelt's first three terms, but then many Republicans and southern Democrats wanted to swing the locus of power away from the center and back to the states. Southerners were particularly upset at the idea that federal laws could supersede state and local segregationist policies. Similarly, the growth in social welfare programs during the Johnson era eventually led to the Reagan-Republican smaller-government rebellion in the 1980s and 1990s and a reemphasis on states' rights.

Although willing to delegate authority to state governments for administration of the biggest, costliest social insurance programs, Congress often supersedes the states in rule making when state laws are in conflict with its will. Members typically sympathetic to states' rights have, paradoxically, pushed legislation to override state laws when states have passed legislation on issues such as late-term abortions, medical use of marijuana, and assisted suicides.[21]

Both Democrats and Republicans have repeatedly used congressional authority to regulate interstate commerce by preventing state governments from taxing e-commerce and other Internet activity, a prohibition that states claim has cost them billions in lost revenue.[22] Even after states negotiated interstate tax collection agreements and lobbied hard for lifting the ban, Congress continued to renew it, even during periods of huge budget deficits.

One member of Congress said of his colleagues that they "don't really believe in states' rights; they believe in deciding the issue at whatever level of government they think will do it their way. They want to be Thomas Jefferson on Monday, Wednesday, and Friday and Alexander Hamilton on Tuesday and Thursday and Saturday."[23]

The debate between state-centered and nation-centered federalism continues. In general, advocates of state-centered and dual federalism believe that with devolution Washington has only surrendered powers that by right belong to the states. Nonideological supporters of devolution see it as a practical measure to bring more efficiency to policy making and implementation.

 Amendments 13–15, 19, 24, and 26.

POWER SHARING IN AMERICAN FEDERALISM

Tension between the federal government and the states is endemic in a federal system. Few people argue that the states could do a better job than Washington providing for the national defense, but there is sharp disagreement over which level of government can make other policies more efficiently and effectively. States are not bureaucracy free. However, state officials are often more aware of how national problems like access to health care, climate change, and shortcomings in K–12 education affect local populations. States are also under more pressure to act to solve them. But, in turn, the governing units below the state level—counties, townships, cities, school and park districts, for example—often believe they are better equipped to legislate for local areas than state government.

The relations between Washington and the states and localities are a mixture of cooperation and conflict. One expert calls it "competitive federalism" because states and the federal government are competing for leadership of the nation's domestic policy.[24] But given the large number of governments in the United States (see Table 1), cooperation in carrying out the day-to-day work of government is essential. In this section, we look at the main points of cooperation and conflict in the everyday practice of federalism. Special attention is paid to the flow of tax revenues between Washington and the states and the conflict over fiscal issues.

Cooperative Federalism

The term **cooperative federalism** describes the day-to-day joint activities and continuing cooperation among federal, state, and local officials in carrying out the business of government: distributing payments to farmers, providing welfare and health care services, planning highways, organizing centers for the elderly, and carrying out all the functions that the national and state governments jointly fund and organize. It also refers to informal cooperation in law enforcement, tracking down the source of contagious diseases, and many other activities.

One example of informal but intensive cooperation is the Centers for Disease Control and Prevention in Atlanta, which helps state and local governments meet health emergencies and prevent the spread of contagious diseases, such as the H1N1 ("swine") flu virus. National and state police and other crime-fighting agencies share data on crimes and criminals. The federal government and the states also jointly regulate in many areas, including occupational safety and the environment. Today, state agencies are responsible for 90 percent of all environmental enforcement actions.[25] And since the 2001 terrorist attacks, there has been increased reliance on state resources to help with national defense, especially through training programs for first responders and use of state militia (National Guard) to supplement regular army troops in combat zones abroad.

The National Guard often figures in one of the best-known areas of state-federal cooperation—disaster relief. Destruction caused by a hurricane, flood, tornado, or earthquake may be so severe and widespread that the resources of the affected states and localities are overwhelmed. The governor can ask the president to declare the stricken counties a federal disaster area, or the president can declare a national emergency without a formal request for assistance from local officials.

The principal agency for coordinating relief efforts is the Federal Emergency Management Agency (FEMA). The agency was created in 1979 to cope with the effects of a nuclear attack or accident, but before 9/11 it was called on mainly to provide financial help, temporary shelters, and other emergency aid to areas struck by natural disasters. Created for one purpose and diverted to another, the agency got off to a rough start, and it has had a mixed record ever since. The collaboration of FEMA and other federal agencies with city and state offices after the September 11 attacks, with the help of nonprofits and volunteers from around the country, resulted in one of the most remarkable intergovernmental responses to disaster the country had ever seen. In the first nine months, federal, state, local, and nonprofit agencies cleared debris, repaired the damaged roads and sidewalks in the vicinity of the World Trade Center, and provided crisis counseling and a ferry service into Manhattan to replace the subway stations destroyed by the collapse of the towers. The Trade Center site was cleaned up six months ahead of schedule at one-tenth of the estimated cost.

But FEMA was not a priority of George W. Bush's administration, and it fell into disarray as Bush filled leadership positions with political cronies and left many positions unfilled. So, when Hurricane Katrina hit southern Mississippi and Louisiana in 2005, there was barely a hint of the federal-state cooperation that made the post-9/11 recovery so remarkable. Over a million people in Mississippi and Louisiana were left homeless; one hundred thousand New Orleaners were stranded in the city, most in the poorest neighborhoods; almost eighteen hundred died; and hundreds went missing. Bodies floated in the flooded streets with no one to recover them, and thousands were trapped in their homes or on rooftops for days waiting for rescue, without food, water, or electricity, and in some cases, medications. Half of its citizens still had not returned to New Orleans by 2008.

With a leadership vacuum at the national level, and first responders disabled or unable to communicate with one another, a profusion of public and private agencies responded on their own to Hurricane Katrina with little coordination of effort. It took several days just to assign the military responsibility for distribution of food and water. FEMA's successes and failures are lessons in the fundamental need for effective communication and clear chains of command among federal, state, and local agencies during emergencies.

Another important area of cooperation is in the management of federally owned land—military bases, weapons facilities, national parks, and wilderness areas. The federal government holds in trust for the American people almost 27 percent of all land within the United States, the majority of it in western states. In those states (Nevada, Idaho, Utah, Alaska, and Oregon) where half or more of the land is federally owned, state governments often do not have the control they would like to have over the state's natural resources, and cooperation can turn to competition and even conflict. Usually the friction is over economic exploitation of resources in park land, but sometimes states object to activities they believe put their populations at risk—such as radioactivity from weapons production or the testing and storage of nuclear waste. Nevada has been fighting the federal government in the courts for years to stop preparation of a national nuclear waste storage center at Yucca Flats just ninety miles from Las Vegas. One former governor even threatened to stand in front of any train carrying nuclear waste into the state. Presidents Clinton and Obama have supported Nevada's position against the wishes of federal agencies.

After his state's economy was deeply affected by a massive oil spill into the Gulf, Louisiana Governor Bobby Jindal scored political points by meeting with the press almost daily to criticize the federal government's response. But coordination of the federal, state, and local response was different than after a natural disaster because a private company, BP, caused the damage and was responsible for supervising and paying for most of the cleanup effort.

AP Photo/David Quinn

Money and Conflict in the Federal Relationship

Administration of federally mandated programs is shared, and it is marked by both cooperation and competition—competition because most states want as few strings as possible placed on how the money is spent, but also cooperation because states are dependent on federal largesse and the federal government relies on the states to implement a significant proportion of domestic policies. Moreover, over time, the performance standards and regulations attached to the grants have increased the professionalism of state and local bureaucrats.

| Figure 1 | What Does the Federal Government Give the States Money to Do? |

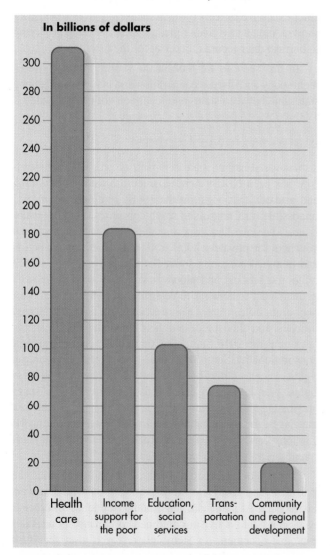

In billions of dollars

Ninety-five percent of the estimated $645 billion the federal government sends back to the states is for programs in these areas.
SOURCE: Budget of the United States, Fiscal Year 2010, "Analytical Perspectives" (Washington, D.C.: Government Printing Office, 2010), tab. 8.2, 44.

A substantial portion of state spending is paid for with tax dollars returned by Washington. (See Figure 1.) At the time of the 2008 recession, federal grants-in-aid accounted for just over 25 percent of state spending. Facing the sharpest decline in state revenues since the Great Depression, most states sought even more federal aid.[26] Because of their balanced budget requirements, states cannot deal with emergencies by spending beyond their revenues, most of which come from a variety of sales, property, income, and excise taxes. In a recession, those tax revenues fall as employment and property values fall. Thus, if federal aid is not increased to offset reduced tax receipts, legislatures must cut programs and services.

Much of the conflict between Washington and the states over finances does stem from the states' balanced budget requirements. The financial burdens on states from unfunded federal mandates are especially controversial. **Unfunded mandates** are provisions of legislation that impose a duty on state and local governments to take actions at the risk of losing some specific portion of federal funding. The states resent federal directives that tell them they must commit a certain amount of state or local funds to specific programs or risk losing federal matching funds or be subject to federal penalties.

Implementation of federal environmental regulations, for which the states now bear the greatest burden, imposes heavy costs. Other federal laws order states and localities to make alterations to public buildings, sidewalks, and transportation facilities to ensure that they are accessible to people with disabilities. States are required to educate the children of illegal immigrants and to pay a substantial portion of emergency health care for them, as well as to pay for increased law enforcement due to failure of federal authorities to control the border.

In the 1990s, the financial burden of unfunded mandates led state and local officials to join together to mount a national campaign to restrict their use. Congress passed a bill reforming procedures under which unfunded or underfunded mandates, especially regulatory mandates, are sent to the states, but it stopped short of prohibiting them. The federal government is required to provide information on the costs of implementing laws and rules before Congress or an executive branch agency, such as the Environmental Protection Agency, can adopt them. And federal agencies are required to consult with states and localities before imposing mandates and to adopt regulations that impose the smallest burden for implementation.[27] For more than a decade, the National Conference of State Legislatures has maintained a Mandate Monitor page at its website to track the costs federal laws are imposing on the states. According to the Monitor, between 2004 and 2009 Washington had shifted $131 billion in costs to the states, and that was before health insurance mandates and such antirecession measures as the extension of unemployment insurance.[28]

Unfunded mandates roll on under Democrats and Republicans alike: George W. Bush's "No Child Left Behind" program imposed a testing and reporting regime on states

Nurses at public hospitals in Minnesota strike to protest cuts in staffing. With increasing health care costs and federal requirements, states face huge budget pressures.

and local school districts, and new rules for state Homeland Security departments require spending on an array of new law enforcement and disaster preparation functions. States have also had to fund many of the secondary costs of having their state militia troops called up for national service. Since the first Gulf War, presidents have nationalized hundreds of thousands of state troops to serve abroad; Guard units from the fifty states have provided more than one-third of all troops who have served in the Iraq War. The federal government pays and equips them while they are under U.S. command, but the states have had to pay for social services and other assistance to the families of the wounded and dead. In addition, the states are left without the full complement of troops and equipment to deal with state emergencies such as forest fires and floods. A survey of the states' Homeland Security directors found that more than half of all states were less prepared for emergencies than before because of the demands being made on their National Guard troops by the federal government.[29]

Congress also mandated state involvement in the counterterrorism effort by passing the Real ID law in 2005. The law gave states two years to put in place standards for issuing drivers' licenses and other identity cards that will ensure that those in the country illegally cannot obtain legal means of identification. States claimed that their unreimbursed start-up and ongoing administrative costs would be too great, so they petitioned for time extensions, saying they may need up to ten years to implement the law. Several states have made no attempt to implement the law, and Montana legislators said they never will.[30]

GOVERNING IN THE STATES

State government is no small operation. Collectively, state and local governments account for over 87 percent of all civilian governmental employees, and their collective spending (excluding the recession years) accounts for just over 10 percent of GDP. Voters in the fifty states elect about

7400 representatives and senators to their state legislatures who, in turn, pass more than forty thousand laws each year that reflect the policy preferences of each state's citizens.[31] These laws, combined with those passed by local governments, affect many aspects of our daily life: the quality of public schools; tuition at public universities; maintenance of roads and bridges; terms for registering to vote or getting a driver's license; sales, property, municipal, and recycling tax rates and part of what you pay in income and excise taxes; conditions under which you can be married or divorced or gain child custody; police and fire protection; licensing of doctors and lawyers; choosing water and electricity suppliers; regulating cable; writing building codes and zoning laws; creating and maintaining parks and recreational facilities; and enforcing environmental and business regulations. In addition, state courts handle 95 percent of all litigation.

It is important to keep in mind that governors, as the chief executive officers of their states, like to run their own shows. And, at any given time, a number of them are trying to burnish their records for a run for the presidency.

In this section, we look at the scope of state government today and discuss cooperation and competition among states and between states and local units of government.

States as Power Centers

As discussed earlier, state activism, or progressive federalism, has been on the increase since the partisan infighting and gridlock that began in the 1990s continues to make it impossible for Congress to reach consensus on many major issues. The states have experimented with charter schools and vouchers for private schools, rolled back affirmative action and bilingual programs, looked at new ways to try to teach religion in schools, and adopted a variety of crime laws, such as mandatory sentencing, three-strike laws, and victims' compensation. Fifteen states have adopted term limits for elected officials, and almost half had their own campaign-financing laws until the 2010 Supreme Court ruling challenged their constitutionality. Some states have placed restrictions on gay rights, whereas others have passed laws strengthening those rights, granting health benefits to gay partners. Six states and the District of Columbia recognize the right to same-sex marriages. And since gaining control over welfare during the Clinton years, the states have experimented with many different job-training and work programs.[32]

Throughout the second Bush administration, while the president and Congress were preoccupied with the wars in Iraq and Afghanistan, huge budget deficits, and then a recession, state activism continued to expand. Four states established centers for stem cell research after the Bush administration refused to fund such work on religious grounds. As federal regulations were rolled back or went unenforced, the states began reregulating, especially in the areas of consumer and worker safety. While the federal government was negligent in regulating financial institutions, some state legislatures were outlawing predatory lending.[33]

Thirty-four states enacted some form of equal-pay legislation, and seventeen states raised the minimum wage above the national level. California led the way in adopting "clean car" air quality standards more stringent than those set by the EPA; eleven other states followed suit. While the Bush administration rejected the Kyoto protocols on climate change, the mayors of 132 cities in thirty-five states signed on to them. And unhappy with Washington's inaction on illegal immigration, local law enforcement officials around the country started using local ordinances (e.g., on trespassing, loitering) to detain illegal immigrants in their towns.

When Congress refused to deal with the crisis in health care, state legislatures began experimenting with their own health insurance programs. Massachusetts became the first state to adopt a mandatory universal coverage plan, and other states followed because health care consumes an increasing part of state budgets. And when Congress did finally pass a health insurance reform bill in 2010, it incorporated a plan similar to Massachusetts's, coupling mandates with private insurance providers.

Some scholars of federalism argue that the United States has become too large to govern from the center; they say that Madison's arguments about the advantages of size for protecting against the mischiefs of faction were made when the country had only 4 million people and no longer apply to a country of several hundred million. Now they say we should pay more attention to Madison's concern about the capacity of well-financed elites at the center of a large nation to capture a "widely dispersed population."[34]

Governors seem to be worried less about the power of big interest groups to sway local electorates than about Washington tying their hands at the very time it is unwilling to solve the problems that are debilitating state and local government. Governor Arnold Schwarzenegger (R-Calif.) made the case for his state's unwillingness to wait on Washington to come to grips with climate change or rising

heath care costs, saying California has the resources to solve its own problems: "We are the modern equivalent of the ancient city-states of Athens and Sparta. We have the economic strength . . . the population and the technological force of a nation-state."[35] But when the recession hit in 2008, California begged the federal government for a loan. Its independence depended on a strong economy.

Taking the initiative in regulation and other policy areas and just generally reasserting states' authority within the federal relationship makes sense to advocates of progressive federalism and to all state officials who are trying to find solutions to difficult problems with too little money. But state autonomy does not always sit well with the private businesses that have to navigate rule making by fifty bureaucracies. A U.S. Chamber of Commerce official complained that "free-for-all federalism" was bad for business and just leads to a "patchwork of laws."[36]

Interest groups sense a power shift away from Washington, and many have begun directing their lobbying efforts at the states. Some of the largest groups have lobbying operations in all fifty states. Both liberals and conservatives are focusing on the states. Liberals, believing they are unlikely to win on issues fought in federal courts that are now dominated by Republican appointees or to get legislation passed in a Congress paralyzed by partisanship, have redirected their efforts to the state level. Conservatives pursuing a Christian-values agenda, who find attempts to gain congressional passage of bills or constitutional amendments failing because of opposition from Democrats and moderate Republicans, have also turned to state legislatures and ballot initiatives. One lobbyist for Christian conservatives said, "It is on the state level where most family issues are decided."[37]

This continues the pattern of the past seventy years, with the fulcrum of change or reform shifting back and forth between Washington and the state capitals. When states could not or would not respond to calls for government action, Americans have turned to Washington. But when a consensus is reached that Washington is not responding to public or interest group demands, or not running programs effectively, people turn to the states. As one cynic has put it, for those times when "we have wrecked one level of government, the Founding Fathers had the foresight to provide a spare."[38]

States and localities are under enormous pressure to reform their public schools and improve student performance. Privately funded charter schools, such as Harlem Success Academy, give students an alternative to failing public schools, but thus far overall student performance at charter schools has been no better than at public schools.

Chris Hondros/Getty Images

States and Localities as Interest Groups

Lobbying is a crucial part of the relationship between the states and the federal government. The importance of federal money to state and local budgets, the imposition of unfunded mandates, conflict over federal administration of state lands, and the need for coordination between federal and state bureaucracies led to the creation of interstate organizations such as the National Conference of State Legislatures (NCSL), the National League of Cities, and the American Public Welfare Association. These groups lobby for favorable legislation for states and localities and

american*diversity

Learning Civics State by State

The Founders were aware of the need to establish public schools where a common history and the basis for a new political culture could be taught. But the Constitution does not mention schools because education was among the functions deferred to the states and localities. This means that states and localities set the curriculum and choose teaching materials.

At the K–12 level, because of local control there have always been some regional differences in the teaching of civics and American history. Students in states of the former Confederacy, for example, read a different version of Civil War history than students studying in northern schools. Students in Illinois learn a lot more about Abraham Lincoln than about Jefferson Davis, with the reverse true for Virginia's students. However, until the second half of the twentieth century, children in K–12 were taught, in broad terms, the same story about independence from Britain, the Founders' role, and the expansion of the country. This began to change in the 1960s as a result of scholarly research that shifted focus from top-down explanations of American history to an exploration from the bottom up, from the study of Founders and other elites to the study of social history, popular culture, and everyday life. This approach assigned much more significance to the role of the people in the making of American history.

The trend toward social history in academic scholarship reflected demands that arose from 1960s political identity movements. Each movement represented a group that saw itself as politically marginalized and written out of American history and politics—Black Power, feminist, Native American, and gay rights movements. A demand arose for new books and revised curricula that covered slavery, the treatment of American Indians, and the role of African Americans, women, and gays and lesbians in the country's history and politics. Other influential interest groups also wanted more balanced coverage of their role: unions, for example, protested the absence of working people in the American story and of government's collusion with business in busting labor unions. As the drive for inclusiveness expanded, reflecting changes in immigration policy that further diversified the population, many others came forward. Each group wanted its story told.

These revisions in the American story produced a backlash from both liberal and conservative defenders of the traditional canon. The liberal historian Arthur Schlesinger, for example, worried that the new courses and curricula that attacked "Eurocentrism" were being taught "not as disciplines but as therapies" to teach self-esteem.[1] The conservative opposition, however, was louder and more organized. The controversy has led to far greater interest in school board elections, as conservatives have tried to

---

work with federal agencies to ensure that new regulations are implemented in a way that is acceptable to the states. Most of these organizations have multimillion-dollar budgets and employ sizable staffs. Many individual states and cities have their own Washington lobbyists, some very successful. Between 2001 and 2006, one lobbyist representing forty-four state agencies and local governments in Florida persuaded Congress to earmark $173 million for projects sought by his clients. For every dollar Floridians paid the lobbyist, they got $18 in federal spending in return.[39]

But why should states form interest groups or hire lobbyists when they are all represented by their elected representatives in the House and Senate? One reason is that the members of a state's congressional delegation may belong to different parties than state leaders, or they may not agree with state leaders—as, for example, when Congress waived state sales taxes on e-commerce strongly favored by most state leaders. Or a state may have an urban majority, whereas its congressional delegation is closer in views to

rural and suburban residents. But mainly states hire lobbyists because there is a lot of money at stake.

The Assembly on Federal Issues, the group that coordinates the lobbying of the NCSL, monitors bills under consideration by every major committee in Congress. Their lobbying is largely to maintain maximum state control over legislative, regulatory, and taxing authority. The NCSL looks especially for any new provisions that would undercut state laws, have an impact on state revenue, or tie the hands of state officials in some policy area. For example, some states are concerned about the free-trade agreements Congress has approved. Many states are big exporters, and laws exempting foreign nations from paying import taxes could affect the competitiveness of a state's businesses and revenues. Most recently the overriding concern of the states has been with how new health insurance legislation will affect state budgets over the long term. Many governors ordered their attorneys general to go through the bill and challenge any provisions they believed unconstitutional.

gain control of boards or at least have a greater say in curricula and textbook selection for public schools. Conservatives, Christian conservatives especially, object to textbooks having no "through line" or "controlling narrative." They do not like texts in which "America is no longer portrayed as one thing, one people, but rather a hodgepodge of issues and minorities, forces and struggles."[2] Thus, in 2010 the governor of Arizona signed a bill ending ethnic studies in the public schools.

In Texas, a single commission, the State Board of Education, almost none of whose members are educators or scholars, rules on content for all textbooks used in the state's public schools. It determines what textbooks must include and what they must exclude if publishers want to sell their books to the Texas schools. Because Texas is one of the largest markets, choices made by the Texas Board may serve as a template for the content of tens of millions of K–12 texts used in as many as "46 or 47 states."[3]

The Board reviews content every five years, at which time interest groups can attend hearings and make a case for those people or events they believe school children should learn about, and they try to be as inclusive as possible while controlling the overall narrative of American history. In 2010, the Board's attempt to provide this "through line" included telling publishers that books must make the point that the Founders' intent was to establish a Christian nation. Thomas Jefferson was to be dropped from the list of Founders who influenced the content of the Constitution because of his passionate belief in the separation of church and state (and because he originated that phrase). Textbook publishers also were told that books used in Texas schools must define our form of government as a "constitutional republic" rather than as a democracy. The U.S. economy was to be called a "free-enterprise system" rather than "capitalist" because the majority of the Board believed the word *capitalism* has come to have negative connotations. They refused mention of hip-hop as a significant cultural movement and eliminated a requirement that sociology students learn about racism in contemporary America. They also denied a request from Hispanic groups for inclusion of a number of Hispanics, including those who fought at the Alamo with other Texans.[4]

The point of this exercise is that the Board wants Texas students to learn a common, positive story about the Founding and the development of the United States as essential elements in their political socialization. But it is a narrative that conforms to Board members' personal interpretation of America as a nation founded on Christianity and western European culture. Learning political culture is important, and K–12 textbooks are probably not the primary source. But in the battle for the hearts and minds of America's youth, should each state write its own version of American history?

[1] Arthur M. Schlensinger Jr., quoted in Sam Tannenhaus, "Identity Politics Leans Right," *New York Times*, March 21, 2010, Wk1.
[2] Russel Shorto, "Founding Father?" *New York Times Magazine*, February 14, 2010, 36.
[3] Ibid., 35.
[4] "Conservatives Carry Day for Curriculum in Texas," *Champaign-Urbana News-Gazette*, March 13, 2010, A4.

Stem cell research, such as that conducted at this University of Wisconsin research center, has been another area of conflict in the federal relationship. A number of states passed laws permitting stem cell research after Congress and the Bush administration prohibited federal funding for research that leads to the destruction of human embryos.

Darren Hauck/Getty Images

The National Governors Association (NGA) and regional governors' associations exist primarily to facilitate cooperation and exchange of information among state governments, but they also lobby Washington. In 2006, the NGA wrote President Bush stating its opposition to the Department of Defense's plans to redefine the role of the National Guard in national defense planning. All fifty governors signed the letter.[40] The Western Governors Association also has pressured the government to take action on illegal immigration and the price of gasoline.

Relations between the States

Dealing with Washington is not the only intergovernmental relations problem that the states face. State governments must also work with one another, and the measure of cooperation and conflict in these relations is similar to that between Washington and the states.

behind the scenes

Gambling for Revenue

Most states are required by their constitutions to have a balanced budget, so when they face budget shortfalls, as forty-seven states did in 2010, governors are left with little choice but to cut spending, find new sources of revenue, or use up the reserves in their rainy day funds.[1] Cuts in social spending are hard to justify at a time when higher unemployment combined with rising health care and fuel costs leave lower-income citizens in greater need than ever of government-supported programs.

Over the past two decades 42 states have turned to gambling as a reliable source of new revenue, especially to lotteries as a way to help fund public schools. Before the recession Americans were spending $64 billion a year on legal gambling, and many states have decided they would like to get an even bigger share of that money. By 2010, with gambling revenue in decline and desperate to fill budget gaps, twenty-five states had expanded or were considering expanding legalized gambling.

To win approval for legalizing new forms of gambling, industry lobbyists try to identify the programs or services—public schools, for example—that voters in each state believe need additional funding. Then they target that function as the recipient for new revenue from gambling in order to win public support. Often they are able to get schools and colleges that will benefit from additional revenue to support referenda or bills legalizing gambling operations, such as putting terminals for video poker and blackjack in bars and restaurants, or sports betting.

Casinos provide another source of state revenue; there are more than five hundred licensed casinos in 12 states. Using the opportunity of state budget crises, a number of Indian tribes are lobbying for authorization to build off-reservation casinos. Like state lotteries, some casinos are essentially state-sanctioned monopolies, and because they make huge profits, the states' cut can be substantial ($4.5 billion in 2009, compared to $14.5 billion from lotteries).[2] However, by relying on gambling to fill their budget gaps, states are trying to raise revenue from their poorest citizens. Lottery-ticket buyers especially are disproportionately low-income people. An estimated one-third or more of those profits are earned from the 2.4 percent of patrons who are problem or compulsive gamblers and whose lives are often ruined by their addiction.[3] And, overall, gamblers do not beat the house; if they did, casinos would not be such high-profit enterprises. This is why critics say encouraging gambling to increase revenue is trading short-term gains for long-term costs.

Nevertheless as gambling revenue has fallen off during the recession, states continue to search for new "sins" to tax—imposing levies on purchasers of pornography, strip club, and escort services; raising existing tobacco and alcohol taxes; and possibly legalizing and taxing marijuana sales.

[1] Elizabeth C. McNichol and Iris Lav, "29 States Face Total Budget Shortfall of at Least $48 Billion in 2009," Center for Budget and Policy Priorities, June 9, 2008, www.cbpp.org/1-15-08sfp.htm.
[2] Ian Urbina, "Drop in Gambling Revenues for the First Time," New York Times, September 10, 2009.
[3] Catherine Rampell, "Sin Is Sure Lucrative," New York Times, April 18, 2010, Wk5.

Art. IV, Sec. 1 The U.S. Constitution laid down some of the ground rules governing interstate relationships. One important provision is the **full faith and credit clause**, which requires states to recognize contracts made in other states. The Constitution also provides that if a fugitive from justice flees from one state to another, the suspect, once captured, will be extradited (sent back) to the state with jurisdiction.

Normally, meeting full faith and credit requirements is rather routine. However, politics varies from state to state, and occasionally for one state to honor the laws of another can be controversial. A historical example is the Fugitive Slave Act, which required the authorities in every state to return escaped slaves to their owners. Abolitionists (those favoring the abolition of slavery) living in free states were loath to return escaped slaves to their owners yet were bound to do so by the Constitution.

More recently, marriage contracts have become an issue. Some opponents to gay marriage have argued that under the full faith and credit rule, a gay marriage contracted in one state would have to be recognized by every state. When Vermont became the first state to register same-sex unions, it set off a controversy in other states worried about having to extend to gay partners the same legal status and rights (health, retirement, and inheritance benefits) as they do to married heterosexual couples. In response, Congress passed the Defense of Marriage Act, which gave every state the right not to recognize same-sex marriages conducted in other states. To resolve some of the interstate conflict, the Massachusetts Supreme Court, which does recognize same-sex marriages, ruled that out-of-state same-sex couples cannot be married in Massachusetts if their home states make such unions illegal. However, after gay rights activists challenged the constitutionality of the Defense of Marriage Act, on the grounds that by denying gays and lesbians the right to marriage it has created a second and inferior class of citizenship, Massachusetts also sought to overturn the law. The state argued that the federal government has no grounds for telling a state government what type of marriage it can recognize.

Cooperation between states is encouraged by the fact that all governors have to deal with a set of common problems, such as resource management, education, fostering economic growth, taxation, crime, and prison systems. In addition, they all have to manage a relationship with Washington. These common interests prompted the formation of the NGA and its regional counterparts.

Most state-to-state interaction is informal and voluntary; state officials consult with and borrow ideas from one another. But there are also formal channels for sharing ideas and policy initiatives. The NCSL has twelve standing committees whose members come from the various state legislatures; they meet at regular intervals to deal with state-to-state issues and to develop policy on federal-state relations.

Sometimes states enter into formal agreements, called *interstate compacts,* to deal with a shared problem—operating a port or allocating water from a river basin, for example. A common type of agreement between states is to exempt citizens from neighboring states who have taken up temporary residence from paying local income taxes. As energy demand and costs rose in 2006, fourteen states formed a new pact to cooperate in regulating electric power. And tired of waiting for Washington to act on greenhouse gases, a group of northeastern states has formed the Regional Greenhouse Gas Initiative to control carbon emissions.[41] The governors of Utah, California, and Montana even appeared in a nationally televised ad saying the governors were acting on climate change and now it was Congress's turn.[42]

Hard economic times have inspired new kinds of informal cooperation between state governments. With almost every state having trouble funding even the essentials, some neighboring states began bartering for goods and sharing services. Wisconsin and Minnesota have negotiated buying in bulk (police bullets, for example), sharing computer systems, and making license plates. Other states are sharing prison and juvenile detention centers.[43]

Along with the cooperation there has always been rivalry among the states, partly because of cultural, political, and regional differences and partly because they compete for private investment and for aid from the federal government. The same energy issues that have created alliances among states have also caused cleavages. States that get most of their energy from coal, for example, take a different position on federal legislation to limit carbon emissions than do those that get most of their energy from hydroelectric power or renewable sources. This so-called brown state–green state clash has led to their respective congressional delegations forming alliances to support or oppose federal legislation on climate change.[44]

Changing economic patterns and an overall loss of economic competitiveness by the United States in the world market have stimulated vigorous competition among the states to attract new businesses and jobs. Governors market their states to prospective new businesses by touting lower taxes, a better climate, a more skilled or better-educated workforce, and less government regulation than other states competing for the same business. Most states are willing to give tax subsidies and other financial incentives to companies willing to relocate. Critics believe that these offers erode a state's tax base and have little impact on most business relocation decisions, and there is some evidence to support that view.[45] Nevertheless, without offering tax breaks or deferments or other subsidies, most states feel at a competitive disadvantage in recruiting new businesses. The Obama administration is trying to discourage this kind of rivalry because it rachets up tax breaks (and therefore drives down revenues) as states and cities try to outbid one another to attract new business. Instead the administration is encouraging regional cooperation and offering financial rewards to states that team up on development projects that speed the economic recovery.

Success in competing for new investment requires states to pay close attention to their human capital as well. Although the recession has reduced mobility, almost 12 percent of the population is still on the move every year. States, especially those with aging populations, are trying to increase their populations with programs like Michigan's Cool Cities Initiative, aimed at keeping their own youth in the state and attracting young professionals. The competition between states for the "creative class" of "technically savvy" under-thirty-fives has been called a "hipness battle," as cities hype amenities (such as jazz and rock concerts, street cafes, and "greenness") to prove their "coolness."[46] Increasing the share of young professionals in its demographic makes a state more attractive to investors, and the new pool of young adults also means more children, schools, and growth in general.

Access to water is one of the most common areas of state cooperation and conflict. One certain prerequisite for business and population growth is an ample water supply. Maintaining or increasing water flow into and out of states is a high-priority issue, especially for states that do not have large bodies of water within their boundaries. How much water should New York State officials agree to take from upstate farmers for urban dwellers or for use in New Jersey and Connecticut? The waters of the upper Colorado River are shared by four states and those of the lower Colorado by three others. Rural residents of Colorado constantly struggle to keep ever-more water from being channeled from the Colorado River to meet the needs of fast-growing metropolitan areas in these other states. As drought crippled Atlanta in 2007, Georgia engaged Tennessee, Alabama, and Florida in disputes over boundaries and water rights. State officials continuously negotiate these issues.

As the federal government continues to devolve responsibilities to the states, and as federal aid has grown as a percentage of state spending, competition among states to get ever-larger shares of that aid has increased. Thirty-four states use "contingency fee" consultants whose job is to get as much money as possible from Washington to cover state Medicaid outlays. Because the consultants get a share of the money they bring in, they have every incentive to find any way within the law to claim additional payments to the states that employ them.[47]

States with high-ranking members in their congressional delegations usually fare better than others in the share of federal tax dollars returned to their home districts. And smaller states at times find common interest in voting as a bloc in the Senate to prevent the largest states from getting a share of aid in proportion to their population or need. An egregious case was the allocation of Homeland Security funding; when the more populous and higher-risk states such as New York attempted to win funding proportionate to their larger populations and greater chance of attack they were outvoted by smaller states.[48] It took several years of publicity about irrelevant equipment purchases by small rural states and municipalities to reallocate funding closer to security priorities.

When Sen. Ben Nelson (D-Neb.) talked committee members into adding a huge increase in federal money to cover Medicare costs in his state in exchange for a yea vote on the health insurance reform bill, he brought waves of protest from other states. In the end the "Cornhusker Kickback" was removed from the bill and an agreement was reached to increase the Medicare tax so that all states would receive more money to help pay for the new health mandates.

State-Local Relations

The relationship of states to their localities—counties, cities, and special districts—is another important feature of contemporary federalism. All but 51 of 87,476 government units in the United States are local governments (see Table 1). These relationships are defined by state constitutions; they are not dealt with in the federal Constitution. Although states cannot be altered or dissolved by the national government, localities can be eliminated or altered by their states. Yet some of the same problems that affect national-state relations also affect state-local relations. City and county officials often wish for more authority and fewer mandates from the state capital. Some state constitutions grant **home rule**

to local governments, giving them considerable autonomy in such matters as setting tax rates, regulating land use, and choosing their form of local government. Cities of different sizes may have different degrees of autonomy, depending on the state. And in some states, counties are given the power to create levels of government below them. In Illinois, for example, each county can decide whether to establish township governments or do without them.

Thirty-six states must also maintain working relationships with the tribal governments of Native Americans. Although local units of government may be altered or abolished by the state, tribal land is sovereign territory under treaty agreements with the U.S. government. States have no authority to govern these areas and must negotiate any conflict over taxes (such as those on casino gambling on reservations) and environmental issues and land or other resource use with tribal councils.[49]

THE PEOPLE IN THE FEDERAL RELATIONSHIP

One of the most important elements in the federal relationship is the people. In a system with power divided among levels of government and responsibilities divided among thousands of governmental units, where do the people fit? How do they elect and communicate with all these officials and get them to be responsive? There is also the matter of individual liberty and the constant struggle to keep government at all levels from encroaching on the rights guaranteed by the Bill of Rights, including those general rights reserved by the Tenth Amendment.

It is often claimed that people feel closer to their state than to the national government. At the state level, the argument goes, government and its decision makers are nearby and more accessible to the voters, more likely to have a sense of their public mood, and consequently more responsive to their specific preferences. This is important because economic conditions and political culture vary from state to state, resulting in different policy preferences. Moreover, local officials

Table 1		Number of Government Units in the United States					

Part of the reason that intergovernmental relations in the United States are so complex is that there are so many units of government. Though the number of school districts has decreased dramatically since World War II and the number of townships has declined slowly, the number of "special districts" created for a single purpose—such as parks, airports, or flood control management—continues to grow.

Year	States	Counties	Municipalities	Townships and Towns	School Districts	Special Districts*
1942	48	3,050	16,220	18,919	108,579	8,299
2007†	50	3,033	19,429	16,519	13,501	37,381

*Includes natural resource, fire protection, housing, and community development districts.
†The Census Bureau takes a count of governmental units every five years, in years ending in 2 and 7.
SOURCE: U.S. Census Bureau, http://www.census.gov/govs/cog/GovOrgTab03ss.html.

Figure 2   The Public Trusts Local Government Most, Though Trust Ebbs and Flows

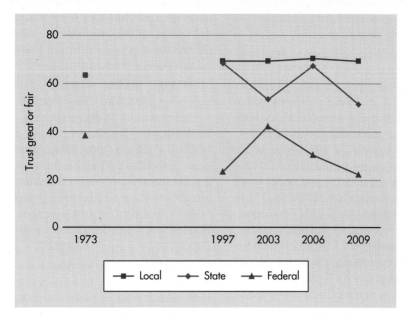

SOURCE: *Data are from state and local Gallup polls, September 2009, www.gallup.com/poll/122915/Trust-State-Governmnet-Sinks-New-Low.aspx. Federal government responses, except in 2010, from American National Election Study, www.npr.org/templates/stpry/story.php?storyId=126047343. 2010 data from Pew Foundation, pewresearch.org. Respondents on trust in state and local government were asked if they had a "great deal or fair amount" of trust in their state and local government. Respondents on trust in federal government were asked if they could trust it "all or most of the time." The latter question is probably a more stringent test of trust.*

may have a better grasp of local conditions and therefore be better situated to shape policy to fit these preferences.

Are state governments more responsive to the people? State governments are undeniably smaller than the national government. Yet, 42 percent of all Americans live in states with more than 10 million residents—hardly small units. At the other end of the spectrum, eight states have populations under a million. If the basic premise about size and distance were correct, then people would be even closer to local government than to state government. But smaller does not make for greater familiarity; the average person is not better informed about state and local government than national officials. Most local candidates and officeholders get far less media exposure than national candidates, partly because there are so many of them.

There are also layers of local government, some with taxing authority, such as townships, special districts, or planning agencies, that Americans know little about. New York has more than 10,000 governmental units below the state level, New Jersey has 566 municipalities, and Connecticut has 169 cities.[50] Given the administrative cost of maintaining so many units of government, some states are considering the merging of counties or of units below the county level to save money during these years of reduced revenue. Illinois state law, for example, allows counties to merge if a majority of voters in each of the counties involved approves the merger. This could test the degree of attachment people have to their local units of government.

Although most Americans know about school districts and city councils, voter turnout is much lower for these and other local elections than for other levels of government, and public knowledge about most local officials is also low. Local government may be "close to the people," but the people are only dimly aware of it. There is no national television, no bloggers or newspapers to shine a light on what goes on in localities, and in many localities there isn't even a daily paper to keep up with local political news. Given voter disinterest in, and lack of information about, local government, it is not surprising that the public gives local government higher ratings than either state or national government. (See Figure 2.)

Despite the public's relative confidence in local and state government, there is no evidence that state and local officials are more ethical than federal officials. In fact, it may be just the opposite. Lobbyists working in state capitals are at least as powerful as those working in Washington, work without public knowledge of what they are doing, and often have much more influence at the state than at the federal level. Conflict of interest and financial disclosure laws in many states are weaker than at the federal level, and state legislators in some states must rely more heavily on lobbyists for information than at the federal because they lack staff expertise. Twenty-eight percent of state legislators who filed financial disclosure statements in 2004 sat on committees that regulated one of the entities in which they had a financial interest; 18 percent had ties to organizations that lobbied their state government. In most states these ties are far more hidden that those between federal legislators and lobbyists because the press does not cover most state legislatures as intensely as the national press covers Congress.[51]

Despite their relative confidence in state and local government, voters in some states, mostly in the West, have tried to limit the power of state governments by approving **ballot initiatives.** This is a means for placing policy questions on state ballots and having them decided directly by voters. In the twenty-four states that permit initiatives, interest groups use them to bypass not only Congress but also state legislatures. Doing an end run around their state and local elected representatives, over the past fifteen years voters have approved initiatives that have killed state laws on affirmative action, sanctioned medical use of marijuana, imposed limits on campaign spending and contributions, expanded casino gambling, and given adopted children the right to know the names of their biological parents. About one-third of ballot initiatives in the 2006 elections became law, whereas only a tiny percentage of bills submitted to legislatures get passed into law.[52]

California remains the champion of legislating by ballot, putting so many measures before voters that one newspaper called it "government by referendum," and asked why California hadn't had a proposition against propositions.[53] Trying to legislate in this way can be both confusing and dangerous. One year, California's citizens had to wade through a 222-page pamphlet outlining ballot choices. In San Francisco, facing a ballot with more than one hundred items, voters passed one proposition for public financing of campaigns while simultaneously passing another measure outlawing it.[54]

Initiatives *can* achieve substantive change, however, and put power in the hands of the public. Thirty years ago, for example, Californians used a ballot initiative to create the California Coastal Commission, a twelve-member panel that monitors use of the state's 1100-mile coast by developers, local government, and private homeowners alike, with the power to kill construction and other projects. It has been called the single most powerful land-use authority in the United States.[55]

More recently Californians passed an initiative requiring a two-thirds vote for passage of any tax increase, thereby severely limiting the options of legislators who had to resolve the budget crisis brought on by the collapse of the housing market in 2008. This measure, along with a 2008 proposition (Prop 8) that overturned a California Supreme Court ruling upholding gay marriages, led one of the court's justices to say that the referendum process had rendered "state government dysfunctional." Noting that voters had approved a measure to regulate the caging of chickens on the same ballot they used to invalidate gay marriages, he said that "chickens gained valuable rights in California on the same day that gay men and lesbians lost them."[56] His point was that the use of ballot initiatives, by giving force of law to views intensely held at a particular point in time,

prempts a legislative process that is supposed to be based on fact checking and deliberation. (In 2010, a federal district court set aside California's Prop 8 saying there was no rational reason for the government to treat same sex marriages differently than those between a man and a woman. That ruling is under appeal.)

Whether binding or not, ballot initiatives continue to appear on everything from food safety and animal rights to prescription drug plans, tax cuts, and election reforms. In Washington and Oregon, voters have approved doctor-assisted suicide. In 2006, Maine voters were asked to exercise a "people's veto" and overturn civil rights protections for homosexuals passed by the legislature. In Michigan, voters prohibited the use of affirmative action in public institutions, while in South Dakota a measure failed that would have punished judges whose decisions the public did not approve of.

Initiatives are not a simple or clear reflection of local views, however. Big interests influence voting on ballot measures, with huge sums of money flowing into states from outside organizations to support or defeat them. They can use their money to hire signature-gatherers to collect the necessary number of voters' signatures to get a measure placed on the ballot, and some states even allow payment of a bounty for each signature gathered. In 2008, the Utah-based Church of Jesus Christ of Latter Day Saints, which has a very small membership in California, nevertheless underwrote the successful campaign to pass that state's Prop 8. That same year, interest groups for or against gay marriage, abortion, stem cell research, affirmative action, and physician- assisted suicide used state votes on these issues to force presidential candidates to take a stand. In the 2010 midterm election California voters rejected an initiative to legalize recreational marijuana, but about half of the citizen initiatives on state ballots that year did pass.

Some see the move toward more direct democracy as taking us nearer to the Founders' ideal of a government closer to the people. But the increasing use of grassroots initiatives is *not* a move toward the kind of government the Founders envisioned. The Founders established a system of checks on popular passions.[57] Indeed, the Founders feared policy making getting too close to the people and government being too responsive to popular demands. They saw the potential for overheating the political process through too much direct democracy, which is why they chose an indirect or republican form of democracy and a federal division of power.

The Founders did not foresee a national government that would surpass the states in power and scope of action in domestic policy. Yet one of the paradoxes of our system

DEMOCRACY?

What problems do the abilities of well-financed national campaigns to defeat or to pass state ballot initiatives present for Madison's explanation of federalism as the way to constrain the "mischiefs of faction" in a large country?

is that as the national government has gained extraordinary power, so have the states and localities. All levels of government are stronger than in the eighteenth century. Federal power *and* state power have grown hand in hand. It is also paradoxical that even as they supported the continuous growth and expansion of the country, many Americans clung to the belief that there is something more true or sacred about small and local government. But, as indicated by the frequent use of ballot initiatives to bypass both national and local legislators, there are always some Americans who believe that government at every level is not listening to the people.

In polls conducted in the months immediately following the 2001 terrorist attacks, Americans viewed government more favorably than in the months before the attacks, but by 2006 most Americans said that government is almost always wasteful and inefficient. Trust in the federal government had fallen to about half of what it was in 2001.[58] With the onset of a serious recession, trust continued to fall in the last year of George W. Bush's administration, reaching historic lows during Obama's first two years in office as the country experienced a slow, jobless economic recovery and huge budget deficits. This time public trust in all levels of government and all major private institutions was affected, and just when government was most needed to deal with failures in the private sector. While it is essential in our system that there be enough suspicion of government to prevent the abuse of power, there must be enough confidence in government for it to function and the Union to hold.

CONCLUSION: Federalism and the Role of Government

The role of the national government in federal systems varies widely throughout the world, with some (Russia, for example) having so much power concentrated at the center that in practice they look more like unitary governments. In other federal systems (Nigeria, for instance), the center is so weak that the country is constantly plagued with secessionist moves and political instability.

As federalism was designed and is practiced in the United States, the locus of power is never fixed. The sometimes clear, sometimes ambiguous, division of power has meant that the struggle between the center and the lower levels of government to change the balance is never ending. The competition is built into our form of government as a check on the overconcentration of power at any one level. Whenever events or presidential leadership tips the balance of power in the federal relationship too far toward Washington, there is movement to reset the balance.

After years of a big-government president such as Teddy Roosevelt, a party may nominate a string of small-government candidates (Taft, Harding, Coolidge, and Hoover). Conversely, if Washington is too slow to act when a federal response is needed, the people may elect an activist president (FDR) to replace a more passive one (Hoover). Currently we are going through a period when a majority appear to be dissatisfied in some way with the federal government—it is either doing too much or not doing enough for the average person; it is spending too much or spending for the wrong purposes. This has intensified the movement toward state activism or progressive federalism, in which states are legislating to deal with problems they believe Washington cannot fix or for which there is no one solution that will work for all states.

But public trust in state and local government has also taken a serious fall, and not everyone is satisfied with the current level of state activism. Washington does not want to see state legislatures preempting federal authority in areas of responsibility the Constitution assigned to it, even when the president and Congress are not fulfilling their responsibilities in those areas. And businesses involved in interstate commerce often find it more expensive, time-consuming, and confusing to comply with fifty different versions of a regulation than with a single federal rule.

Our history suggests that most people are pragmatic, favoring policies that work by whichever level of government can make them work. In the 1990s, when the public consensus was that Washington was not running welfare programs effectively, much of the responsibility was passed to the states; when state and local governments were judged to be failing at running public schools, Washington stepped in. In 2010, after the federal government passed health insurance reform, three dozen states legislated or sued to regain greater control over state spending on health care programs. And so it has gone for decades.

Today, across the United States, our belief in democracy, equality, and the rule of law binds us together. But to say that Alabama is more like New York than it used to be is certainly not to say that those two states are alike. Our federal system helps us accommodate regional differences by allowing both state and federal governments a role in policy making. In addition, it allows groups and individuals whose demands are rejected at one level of government to pursue them at another level. The federal system creates multiple points of access, each with power to satisfy political demands by making policy that was rejected at another level. The challenge is how to keep a balance in the division of power sufficient to prevent a tyranny of factions while maintaining a sense of national unity and purpose.

KEY TERMS

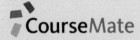 **CourseMate** Access an interactive eBook, chapter-specific interactive learning tools (including flashcards, quizzes, videos), and more at CourseMate for *Understanding American Government*. Log in at CengageBrain.com.

4 Public Opinion

A supporter of gay marriage (right) and an opponent face off in Albany, New York.

Talking Points

The 2008 election mobilized hundreds of thousands of new voters, including many young people who had not been interested in politics before but were inspired by one of the candidates, especially by Barack Obama. Pollsters estimated that the number of young voters in both the primaries or caucuses and the general election increased between 4 to 5 percentage points compared to 2004.[1] The youth vote throughout the electoral process went heavily for Obama.

This picture of an active and engaged young electorate contrasts sharply with the past behavior of young Americans. In general, young people have been the least informed and least involved segment of the electorate. A 2006 survey found that although 59 percent of teenagers could name the Three Stooges, only 41 percent could identify the three branches of the U.S. government. Seventy-four percent knew where Bart Simpson lives, but only 12 percent knew where Abraham Lincoln had lived. And only 2 percent knew that James Madison was the principal author of the U.S. Constitution and fourth president of the nation.[2]

At least for 2008, this pattern changed. Although there is no evidence that young people surpassed older ones in their political knowledge and sophistication—older adults also were galvanized by the 2008 election—the spurt in participation and information seeking by young adults was a positive sign for our political system.

Yet, one year after President Barack Obama was inaugurated, political participation among young people appears to have reverted to previous levels. Although it is not unusual for off-year elections to attract fewer voters than presidential elections, the youth vote in the 2009 gubernatorial elections in New Jersey and Virginia suggested that forecasts of a permanent increase in political participation among youth were somewhat optimistic. Less than 20 percent of adults from eighteen to twenty-nine turned out to vote in those elections. And in the January 2010 special election held in Massachusetts to fill the U.S. Senate seat formerly held by Democrat Ted Kennedy, despite the stakes for the Obama agenda in Congress, the youth vote was said to "collapse." Nearly half of young people voted in 2008; only 15 percent voted in the 2009 election. In contrast, 57 percent of those who were thirty years and older turned out to vote.[3] The drop in turnout among the young suggests that they were motivated more by Obama's persona than by a strong interest in the political process or fervent support for particular positions on the issues. The result of the 2010 midterm elections, in which the youth vote dropped by approximately half, from 18% to 9% participation, is consistent with that conclusion.

Public opinion is often contradictory. As was the case in 2010, citizens are often angry with political leaders for failing to respond to their needs. At the same time, they complain that leaders simply follow the latest polls rather than developing well-reasoned political positions. Additionally, many people do not trust government; they think it is too big and spends too much money. Yet they like the services it provides, and very few are willing to cut spending to eliminate services or programs that benefit them.

This chapter explores public opinion to better understand these contradictions. It describes how public opinion is formed and measured, assesses how informed and knowledgeable the public is with respect to public affairs, discusses the role of ideology in American politics, addresses divisions within the population over some important issues, and concludes with an assessment of the extent to which government is responsive to public opinion.

NATURE OF PUBLIC OPINION

Public opinion can be defined as the collection of individual opinions about issues, candidates, officeholders, and events of general interest—that is, those that concern a significant number of people. The direction of public opinion can be either positive or negative, that is, for or against something or someone.

DEMOCRACY?

In a democracy, should public officials be more responsive to a minority of citizens with very strong feelings about an issue or to the majority with less intense feelings?

Intensity reflects the strength of public opinion. The public may have weak feelings about something or feel strongly about it. Intense opinions often drive behavior. Many people now oppose the troop increase in Afghanistan, for example, but only the most intense communicate with their senators or representative or take to the streets to protest this decision. Public opinion is not very intense on most issues. A small minority may feel intensely about an issue or politician, but a majority rarely does.

Opinions also vary in stability. Some are constantly changing, whereas others never do. Stable opinions are often intense and grounded in a great deal of information—some of it accurate, some inaccurate. Feelings of attachment to political parties tend to be stable, whereas opinions about candidates and public officials, particularly high-profile ones like a president, fluctuate in response to changing events and circumstances. Former president George W. Bush began his presidency with a 60 percent job approval rating. This rose to 90 percent shortly after 9/11 and then dropped steadily to 30 percent in 2007 and remained at that level through the last year of his presidency. (See Figure 1.) President Obama's initial approval rating was 68 percent, the highest initial level since

President John F. Kennedy. But one year after his election, his approval rate stood at 53 percent, which is near the bottom of post–World War II presidents' first-year ratings. And by June of 2010, it had dropped to 46 percent.[4] The ongoing poor state of the economy, among other issues, is said to account for this drop.

FORMATION OF PUBLIC OPINION

People learn and develop opinions about government and politics through the process of **political socialization**. As in other spheres, individuals learn about politics by being exposed to new information supplied or filtered through parents, peers, schools, the media, political leaders, and communities. These **agents of political socialization** introduce each new generation to the rights and responsibilities of citizenship (see Chapter 1) as well as shape opinions and positions toward candidates, officeholders, and political issues. Individuals, particularly adults, also learn about politics and develop opinions through personal experiences.

Political learning begins at an early age and continues throughout life. In young children, learning is influenced by reasoning capacity and expectations.[5] The greater a child's intellect and the demands placed upon her, the more and faster she is likely to learn.

Preschoolers are unable to distinguish political from nonpolitical objects. Some are unable to separate political figures from cartoon characters, and some confuse religion with politics. A significant number of five- and six-year-olds report that the president takes orders from God.[6] By first grade, these confusions are resolved and children begin to see government as separate and unique.[7]

However, children's inability to understand abstract concepts or complex institutions means their conceptions of government are limited. Most identify government with the president.[8] Children at a very early age recognize him. In a 2002 study, 97 percent of a group of fourth graders were able to identify the president by name,[9] a proportion that has stayed constant for several decades.[10] Experiences with parents and other adults give children a basis for understanding their relationship with authority figures, like a president, with whom they have no contact.[11] Moreover, the feelings children have toward parents are likely to be generalized to presidents. Studies in the 1950s found children describing presidents as good and helpful;[12] many saw them as more powerful than they really are.[13] A more recent study notes that children are considerably less likely to evaluate a president as good.[14] At the same time, they are likely to describe a president as benevolent. The difference may reflect the greater capacity of children today to draw a distinction between the institutional presidency and the individual who occupies the office.

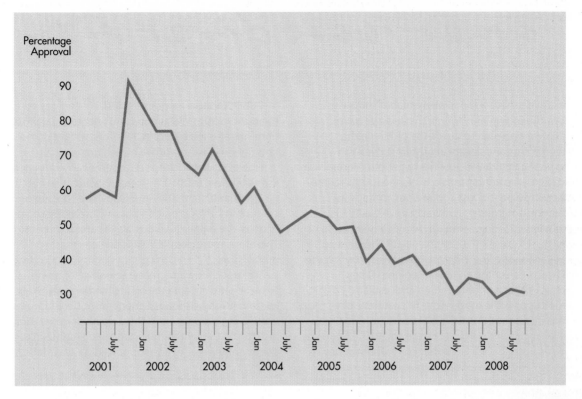

Figure 1 | **Public Opinion Can Fluctuate: President Bush's Approval Ratings**

President George W. Bush's approval ratings show how public opinion, especially toward political leaders, can fluctuate over time. Bush's ratings peaked after 9/11 and then declined sharply.
SOURCE: *From the Gallup polls, reported in http://www.gallup.com/poll/124085/One-Year-Election-Americans-Less-Sure-Obama.aspx; http://www.gallup.com/poll/113968/Obama-Initial-Approval-Ratings-Historical-Context.aspx.*

Older children are introduced to political ideas and political institutions in school and through the media. Their concept of government includes Congress, the act of voting, and ideas such as freedom and democracy. A positive view of government reflected in feelings toward the president gives way to more complex and realistic images. The process can be accelerated by political events and the reaction of others to them. Children were much less positive toward the president and government in the 1970s than in the 1960s. The Watergate scandal in 1973 lowered both adults' and children's evaluations of the president.[15] The Clinton sexual scandals and the impeachment proceedings of 1998, however, had no impact on adult evaluations of the president and government, and presumably none on children. The approval ratings of the president reached record levels, and confidence in the executive branch remained unchanged from the year before.[16] Even when scandal lowers children's evaluations of government, the effect may not last. Negative feelings of children during Watergate diminished as they aged.[17]

In adolescence, political understanding expands still further. Children discuss politics with family and friends. By the middle teens, positions on issues develop.[18] Some fifteen- and sixteen-year-olds develop opinions that resemble those of adults. Although they begin to recognize faults in the system, they tend to believe the United States is the best country in the world. Teenagers rate the country low in limiting violence and fostering political morality but high in providing educational opportunities, a good standard of living, and science and technology.[19] For most, the positive feelings toward government learned earlier are reinforced.

In adulthood, opinions about specific personalities and policies develop, and political activity deepens. Although most Americans respect the country and do not want to change the system, many tend to be cynical and distrustful of political leaders. Some of this negative feeling grows out of Americans' dislike of conflict and partisanship in politics.[20] Some of it, no doubt, flows from the perception that government is inefficient and can't deal effectively with the nation's problems. Some is influenced by media coverage, which not only highlights conflict but also often exaggerates it. Even so, the media remain fundamentally committed to and supportive of the American system itself.[21] And despite negative feelings about American institutions and politics on the part of some citizens, and the violent rhetoric of a minority, the system is stable. Except for the Civil War, criticism and even anger have never boiled over to the

american*diversity

The Marriage Rights of Gays and Lesbians as a Moral Issue

Any issue may have a moral element, but some issues are considered primarily moral. These issues have the greatest potential to divide the public. In the nineteenth century, slavery almost destroyed the nation. In the first decades of the twentieth century, prohibition—banning the sale of alcoholic beverages—was a controversial, if less contentious, moral issue.

Abortion emerged as a moral issue in the 1970s and remains so today. Although Americans are highly supportive of abortion when the health and safety of women are on the line, they are quite divided when the issue concerns ending an unwanted pregnancy.

In the 1990s, the rights of gays and lesbians emerged as a visible moral issue. At that time, gays and lesbians increasingly came out of the closet and organized for social and political change. In 2010, 63 percent of Americans said they knew someone who was gay or lesbian.[1] Higher levels of acceptance and extension of rights to lesbians and gays have accompanied more acquaintance and interaction with them. Now, a majority of the public endorses equal rights in the workplace and housing. And in 2010, 75 percent of Americans felt that gays and lesbians should be allowed to serve in the military whether or not they disclose their sexual orientation; 83 percent supported military service for gays and lesbians who did not disclose their orientation.[2]

Public support for granting lesbian and gay couples the right to form civil unions and related legal protections has also increased. In 2010, 66 percent of the population was supportive of civil unions.[3]

However, public support for same-sex marriages is much lower. In 2010, 47 percent were in favor of gay marriage.[4] To many Americans, the concept of civil unions reflects equal rights, whereas the concept of marriage entails religious beliefs and traditions. Therefore, more people view same-sex marriage as a moral issue.

The trends toward greater tolerance of homosexuality and acceptance of gay marriage are likely to continue because younger generations are more supportive of these positions than are older generations. In 2010, 65 percent of those who were eighteen to twenty-nine years of age supported gay marriage.[5]

[1] Washington Post/ABC News poll, http://www.washingtonpost.com/wp-srv/politics/polls/postpoll_021010.html (accessed February 12, 2010). This Washington Post/ABC News poll was conducted by telephone February 4–8, 2010, among a random national sample of 1,004 adults. The results from the full survey have a margin of sampling error of plus or minus three percentage points. Sampling, data collection, and tabulation by TNS of Horsham, Pa.
[2] Ibid.
[3] Ibid.
[4] Ibid.
[5] Ibid.; The Pew Forum on Religion and Public Life, "Majority Continues to Support Civil Unions," October 9, 2010, http://pewforum.org/docs/?DocID=481#1 (accessed February 10, 2010); Lynmari Morales, "Knowing Someone Gay/Lesbian Affects Views of Gay Issues," May 29, 2009, http://www.gallup.com/poll/118931/Knowing-Someone-Gay-Lesbian-Affects-Views-Gay-Issues.aspx (accessed February 12, 2010).

point of mass violence directed toward political institutions or leaders.

Critical comments about government and political leaders sharply declined after 9/11, but the drop was short-lived. Most Americans felt gratitude toward the brave people—many of whom lost their lives—who courageously rushed to aid those attacked. Yet, except for people who were called to serve in the armed forces or who were able to volunteer to help in the World Trade Center cleanup, Americans were not asked to translate these positive feelings into action. Though commentators on 9/11 and immediately afterward predicted that nothing would ever be the same, for most Americans life did return to normal quickly, and with it, the usual levels of skepticism toward government.

Agents of Political Socialization

Agents of political socialization—principally the family and schools—embrace the institutions and processes that are the foundations of American democracy, and thus help ensure that each new generation of Americans does too.

Family

Although recent research suggests that each of us may be born with a predilection toward political traits and points of view,[22] children's identification with a political party is strongly shaped by the family, particularly because of emotional ties of family and exclusive control during the early years.[23]

The family influences opinions in several ways. Parents share their opinions directly with children. They say or do things that children imitate. Children overhear parents' comments about the political parties and adopt them as their own. Children also transfer feelings toward parents to political objects. When children harbor negative feelings about their parents, they are more likely to be negative toward the president.[24]

The family also shapes the personality of the child. A child who is encouraged to speak up at home is likely to do so in public. Children also inherit their social and economic position from their parents, which influences not only how they view themselves but also how they view the world and how the world views them. For example, a child from a wealthy family begins with advantages and opportunities unshared by a child from a poor family.

Children are more likely to reflect their parents' views when these views are clearly communicated and important. Parents often convey how they feel about political parties during election campaigns, and children pick it up. Seventy percent of high school seniors, for example, were able to correctly identify their parents' political party, but no more than 36 percent could identify their parents' opinion on other issues.[25]

However, even where parental influence is strong, it is not immutable. As young adults leave their parents' circle, agreement declines between their opinions and party allegiances and those of their parents. New influences and experiences come into play.[26] Even among younger children, wider influences matter. Parents do not usually have exclusive control during a child's preschool years, and the number of households with two employed parents or with a single employed parent means that other caretakers and schools play a meaningful role in children's lives. Nevertheless, influence on children regarding political opinions and behaviors is about the same whether one is raised in a two-parent or a single-parent family.[27]

School

A child of our acquaintance who came to the United States at the age of five could not speak English and did not know the name of his new country. After a few months of kindergarten, he knew that George Washington and Abraham Lincoln were good presidents, he was able to recount stories of the Pilgrims, he could draw the flag, and he felt strongly that the United States was the best country in the world. This child illustrates the importance of the school in political socialization and how values and symbols of government are explicitly taught in American schools, as they are in schools in every nation.[28]

Although we do not understand exactly which aspects of formal schooling influence political opinions, there is little doubt that education and years of formal schooling make a difference via the skills and experiences they provide. People who have more education tend to be more interested in and knowledgeable about politics.[29] They are also more likely to participate in politics and to be politically tolerant.[30] Yet education does not necessarily lead to a greater appreciation of the workings of democracy, that is, a form of government where disagreements are typically resolved through bargaining and compromise.[31] Education does not always prepare citizens for how democracy works in practice, to recognize that disagreement is fundamental to democratic processes, or to build positive feelings toward these processes.

This boy, at a white supremacist rally, likely was socialized in these views by his parents.

How do the schools influence the political opinions of children? To begin with, schools promote patriotic rituals. Classrooms often begin each day with the Pledge of Allegiance, and schools include patriotic songs and programs in regular activities. In the lower grades, children celebrate national holidays such as Presidents' Day and Thanksgiving and learn the history and symbols associated with them. Involvement in such activities tends to foster respect for the country. In the upper grades, mock elections, conventions, and student government introduce students to the operation of government. School clubs operate with democratic procedures and reinforce the concepts of voting and majority rule. Illinois let the state's elementary school children vote to select the official state animal, fish, and tree, conveying the message that voting is the way issues are decided.

Textbooks also often foster commitment to stability by positively depicting government and the status quo. Those used in elementary grades emphasize compliance with authority and the need to be a "good" citizen. Even textbooks in secondary school present idealized versions of governmental processes and overemphasize the ease with which citizens can hold public officials accountable and shape public policy. At the same time, textbooks often fail to stress the importance of fully participating in politics and tolerating the views of others. Nor do many help students understand that conflicts and differences of opinion are inevitable in a large and diverse society and that because the role of politics is to address and resolve these disagreements, compromises and partial solutions are often necessary. Because schools themselves are not democratic institutions where students are encouraged to participate meaningfully, and school leaders are often averse to controversy, students' socialization is limited.

The number of civics courses taken in high school improves students' knowledge of government and politics and fosters the beliefs that government pays attention to people and that elections are important for holding government responsible. Courses during the senior year are particularly important. Because seniors are ready to make the transition to adulthood, government and politics may be more meaningful to them than during their early years.[32]

Reading habits and language skills are also important to democratic citizenship. Those who spend time reading are more likely to reflect attributes of democratic citizenship—including knowledge of public affairs, interest in politics, and tolerance—than those who do not.[33] Proficiency with language is important, too, as language is the mechanism for communicating and assessing information and evaluating new ideas and arguments.[34] Teachers as role models also contribute to proficiency in significant ways. Perceptions that school administrators and teachers are fair are linked with expressions of trust toward other people.[35]

DEMOCRACY?

Thomas Jefferson wrote: "What signify a few lives lost in a century or two? The tree of liberty must from time to time be refreshed with the blood of patriots and tyrants. It is its natural manure." Is this view more or less supportive of democracy than the alternative of socializing each generation to the existing political authority and routine ways of political participation?

In sum, the major impact of schooling from kindergarten through high school tends to be that it fosters "good" citizens—those who accept political authority and the institutions of our government and who focus their political activities on routine political tasks such as voting in elections. In this way, elementary and secondary education contributes to political stability and serves government and the status quo in ways that the dominant interests in society prefer. Schools may not be as effective, however, at fostering widespread political participation and commitment to a full range of democratic values. Nor do they do a good job of providing students with the skills to critically assess the social, political, and economic structures or policy approaches that are at the root of the nation's problems or strategies for dealing with injustice and effecting political change.[36] If the picture of politics portrayed by socialization in schools is idealized, perhaps it is not surprising that many adults are shocked by the rough and tumble of politics and the sharp disagreements of Americans about the nature of government.

The college experience often broadens students' perspectives and leads to greater understanding of the world around them. They often become more open and tolerant, less rigid and bound by tradition. Most students go to college to get a better job, make more money, prepare for a specific career, broaden their knowledge of the world, or learn about things that interest them. Some attend because their parents insist or because many or most of their peers are going. Few go to college seeking to become more tolerant, but this is often the result. College students are more open and tolerant than the population as a whole, and the longer they are in college, the more open and tolerant they become—seniors more so than freshmen, and graduate students more so than undergraduates.[37]

Some commentators argue that college professors indoctrinate students and suggest that state legislatures should investigate such "indoctrination."[38] Several states have even introduced legislation to prevent faculty from sharing their views on controversial issues. None of these proposals, however, has passed. It is true that college and university faculty have predominantly liberal orientations. One study reports that, from 1996 to 2008, 43 percent of professors identified themselves as liberal and 9 percent identified as conservative. (Liberalism and conservatism are discussed on pages 110–111.)[39] This research also concludes that professors tend to be liberal because the image in society of the college teaching profession is liberal and secular. So the people who are most attracted to the profession tend to be liberal.

But does this mean that college faculty are brainwashing their students? A 2006 study found that 48 percent of those between the ages of eighteen and twenty-five identified with the Democratic Party; 35 percent were Republican, the lowest number since 1987. Fifty-eight percent of those under twenty-six voted Democratic in the 2006 midterm elections. However, in the early 1990s, when college faculty were just as liberal, Republican identification in this age group was 55 percent.[40]

Other evidence also suggests it is unlikely that professors indoctrinate their students. At the height of the Vietnam War (1968–1971), students were more likely to identify themselves as liberal than students before or after the war.[41] During the same period, the outlook of college faculty changed very little, and while faculty strongly opposed air strikes in Afghanistan following 9/11, 79 percent of college students supported the war.[42] Although there is no doubt that college faculty have more liberal political orientations than the general public, it is doubtful that students adopt faculty views wholesale. At large universities, where the largest percentage of students attend, the environment is sufficiently diverse to reinforce many points of view. Arts and sciences faculty are generally liberal, but it is probable that engineering and business faculty are not. Moreover, college provides students with the self-confidence and independence that presumably equip them to think for themselves.[43] And, as discussed earlier, faculty members are only one of multiple competing influences on political socialization.

Evidence that university and college faculty political opinions are not proportionally shared by students comes from studies of college freshmen. Studies show that they look much like the population as a whole, liberal on some issues but conservative on others. They are liberal in that they want the government to do more to control the sale of handguns, provide national health care to cover everyone's medical costs, and guarantee homosexuals the right to marry, as well as in their belief that racial discrimination remains a problem. They are conservative in attitudes about crime: majorities wish to retain the death penalty and believe that the courts show too much concern for the rights of criminals. Small majorities are pro-choice and support taxing the rich more (see Table 1). Freshmen attending black colleges are more liberal than freshmen in general with respect to controlling handguns and national health care, but more conservative with respect to the legal rights of same-sex couples, laws prohibiting homosexual relations, and abortion. During the past several years, freshmen have become slightly more liberal in their opinions and are more likely to identify themselves as liberal; however, a plurality identify themselves as moderate or middle of the road.[44]

The level of interest in politics that college freshman report varies considerably over time and appears to be dependent on the circumstances they face. In 1968, during the Vietnam era when young men faced the draft, 60 percent of first-year college students reported talking frequently about politics, compared to 30 percent in 2007. In 2008, during the open-seat presidential race and the historically groundbreaking candidacies of Barack Obama, Hillary Rodham Clinton, and Sarah Palin, the rate was 35.6 percent. It dropped to 33.1 percent in 2009.[45,46]

Peers

In many instances, peers reinforce the opinions of the family or school. When there is a conflict between peer and parental socialization, peers sometimes win, but only on issues of special relevance to youth. Peers have the most influence when the peer group is attractive to individuals and when individuals spend time with the group. With growing numbers of single-parent families and employed parents, parental influence may be diminishing while the influence of friends and associates may be growing.

Mass Media

The primary effect of the media on children is to increase their information about politics. The primary effect on adults is to influence what they think about—that is, the issues, events, and personalities they pay attention to.[47] The media also influence opinions about issues and individuals. Research shows that changes in public opinion tend to follow sentiments expressed by television news commentators.[48] The impact of the media is explored in more detail in Chapter 5.

Adult Socialization

Not all political socialization occurs in the pre-adult years. Opinions develop and change throughout life as one

Table 1	Opinions of College Freshmen*	All Colleges (%)	Black Colleges (%)
The federal government should do more to control the sale of handguns.		76	84
A national health care plan is needed to cover everyone's medical costs.		75	84
Same-sex couples should have the right to legal marital status.		64	49
Wealthy people should pay a larger share of taxes than they do now.		58	59
Abortion should be legal.		57	52
There is too much concern in the courts for the rights of criminals.		56	44
Affirmative action in college admissions should be abolished.		48	29
Marijuana should be legalized.		38	38
Federal military spending should be increased.		31	32
The death penalty should be abolished.		35	46
It is important to have laws prohibiting homosexual relationships.		24	35
Racial discrimination is no longer a major problem in America.		20	12

*The percentages are those agreeing strongly or somewhat with the statement.
SOURCE: John H. Pryor, Sylvia Hurtado, Jessica Sharkness, and William Korn, *The American Freshman: National Norms for Fall 2007* (Los Angeles, Calif.: Higher Education Research Institute, 2007), 37–38

Televised images of the abuse of Iraqi prisoners by American jailers at the Abu Ghraib prison outside Baghdad influenced public opinion in the Middle East as well as in the United States.

experiences new and different things. Marriage, divorce, having children, unemployment, a new job, or a move to a new location can affect political opinions.[49]

Economic, political, and social events have the potential to change the way Americans think about politics. Many hard hit by the Great Depression were drawn to politics to seek help. For this reason, most of those voting for the first time in 1932 cast their ballots for FDR and the Democrats and continued to vote Democratic throughout their lives. World War II and the attack on Pearl Harbor shaped the opinions of a generation of Americans. The Vietnam War moved many college students to the streets in protest, whereas others moved to Canada to avoid the draft. In contrast, the terrorist attacks on the Pentagon and the World Trade Center pushed the public closer to government, although the impact soon dissipated (see the box "The Short-Term Impact of 9/11 on Public Opinion," p. 103).[50]

The ongoing wars in Iraq and Afghanistan and the 2007–2009 recession, which although officially over, continues to result in widespread economic dislocation, may shape young Americans in a more lasting way. Elections in 2006 and 2008 indicated a rise in Democratic Party affiliation among this age group, and that may be related, in part, to reactions against these challenges.

Impact of Political Socialization

Each new generation of Americans is socialized to a large extent by the one preceding it, and so in many ways each new generation will look and act much like its predecessor. In this sense, political socialization represents a stabilizing

and conserving influence. Typically, it leads to support for and compliance with government and the social order. Although many disagree with particular government policies, few question the basic structure of government.

MEASURING PUBLIC OPINION

Pollsters measure public opinion by asking people to answer questions in surveys or polls. Of course, other techniques are also used to measure opinion, and before scientific polls these techniques were all that were available. Elected officials consider the opinions of people who talk to them or write or e-mail them; journalists gauge public opinion by talking selectively to individuals; and letters written to newspaper editors, newspaper and newsmagazine editorials, and blogs are also indicators of public opinion. Protests and demonstrations reflect public opinion. All of these techniques provide an incomplete picture, however. Messages to public officials and newspapers are more likely to come from people with extreme or deeply held opinions[51] or from those with writing skills—that is, people with more education. Editorial opinion is even less likely to provide an accurate picture of public opinion because most newspaper publishers tend to be conservative, and this point of view is often reflected in their editorials. In most presidential elections in the twentieth century, newspapers favored the Republican candidate by about three to one.[52] In the new century, more newspapers endorsed John Kerry in 2004 over George W. Bush by a small margin, and, in 2008, 62 of the 100 largest-circulation newspapers endorsed Barack Obama compared to 25 for John McCain.[53]

Polls are the best measure of public opinion, but they are not perfect. Conducting a poll runs the risk of creating public sentiment rather than allowing public opinion to reveal itself. Rather than focus on what the public is concerned about, polls concentrate on what pollsters and their sponsors find most interesting. For this reason, many issues of public importance may never become the subjects of a poll. In spite of this and other problems, polling remains the only accurate way to assess what the nation as a whole thinks about specific political issues and public officials.

Early Polling Efforts

The first attempts to measure popular sentiments on a large scale were **straw polls** (or unscientific polls) developed by newspapers in the nineteenth century.[54] In 1824, the *Harrisburg Pennsylvanian*, in perhaps the first poll to assess preferences for candidates, sent reporters to check on support for the four presidential contenders that year. The paper reported that Andrew Jackson was the popular choice over John Quincy Adams, Henry Clay, and William H. Crawford.

Jackson did indeed receive the most popular votes, but John Quincy Adams was elected president after the contest was decided by the House of Representatives. Toward the end of the nineteenth century, the *New York Herald* regularly tried to forecast election outcomes in local, state, and national races. During presidential election years, the paper collected estimates from reporters and political leaders across the country and predicted the Electoral College vote by state.

Straw polls are still employed today. Some newspapers have interviewers ask adults at shopping malls and other locations about their voting preferences. Network and cable television run Internet polls about serious and trivial issues. CNN asks viewers of its early evening news show to register opinions on different issues and reports results before broadcasts end. Major events often trigger media polls. After each presidential debate, national media invite people to cast votes via the Web on who won. Straw polls are unscientific because there is no way to ensure that the sample of individuals giving opinions is representative of the larger population. If these polls are unrepresentative, they are unlikely to reflect public opinion accurately.

THE SHORT-TERM IMPACT OF 9/11 ON PUBLIC OPINION

Whereas the Great Depression had a long-lasting impact on American public opinion, and the Japanese attack on Pearl Harbor changed Americans' views of their role in the world, the traumatic attacks of 9/11 influenced public opinion intensely but only briefly.

Before the terrorist attacks, some Americans took government for granted and considered it unimportant or irrelevant to their lives. The booming economy and surging stock market during the 1990s contributed to complacency. At the same time, a steady stream of negative commentary about the government emanating from the media and politicians who found it useful to their careers or causes fed cynicism toward the government.

But the devastation and the flames of 9/11 had an immediate impact on Americans' attitudes. From the ashes of the World Trade Center and the Pentagon sprang feelings of patriotism, national unity, willingness to help others, and see the nation through a difficult crisis. Government became a positive force to many. More than 80 percent of people, compared with just 50 percent the year before, had a favorable view of the national government, and trust in government nearly doubled.[1] The public standing of the president and Congress similarly spiked. As someone remarked, "the only persons going up the stairs of the World Trade Center while everyone else was going down were government officials"—police officers, firefighters, and emergency personnel. "The events brought home the fact that the government does important work."[2]

Yet, these attitudes were short-lived. Perhaps they would have been longer lasting if the nation had been called upon to sacrifice as it had been in World War II, when gas, oil, and some foodstuffs were rationed and Americans were urged to plant "victory gardens" to feed their families. Instead, the president and Republicans in Congress used 9/11 to advance a partisan agenda including tax cuts for the rich, the Iraq war, and a substantial increase in presidential power. President Bush didn't urge the nation to use less energy to check our growing dependence on the foreign oil consumption that increased our vulnerability to instability in the Middle East. Nor did he call on the nation to support higher taxes to pay for the wars in Afghanistan and Iraq. President Bush's advice to Americans was, "Live your lives, hug your children."[3] When the president was asked how Americans could help, he suggested, "Go shopping" (to stimulate the economy). Thus the president called for no sacrifices and asked for no help. Even though millions of Americans were prepared to help, President Bush essentially told them to act as if nothing had happened. In doing so, he may have limited the impact of 9/11 on public opinion, as Americans turned back to their private lives.

[1] Alexander Stille, "Suddenly, Americans Trust Uncle Sam," *New York Times*, November 3, 2001, online article.
[2] "Public Opinion Six Months Later," Pew Research Center for the People and the Press, news release, March 7, 2002.
[3] Benjamin Wallace-Wells, "Mourning Has Broken," *Washington Monthly*, October 2003, 16–18.

The famed *Literary Digest* poll is a good example of an unrepresentative poll. The former magazine conducted polls of presidential preferences between 1916 and 1936. As many as 18 million ballots were mailed out to persons drawn from telephone directories and automobile registration lists. Although the purpose was less to measure public opinion than to boost subscriptions, the *Literary Digest* correctly predicted the winners in 1924, 1928, and 1932. In 1936, their luck ran out and, the magazine predicted that Republican Alfred Landon would win, but instead Democrat Franklin D. Roosevelt won by a landslide. This erroneous prediction ended the magazine's polling, and in 1938 the *Literary Digest* went out of business altogether.

Why did the *Literary Digest* miss in 1936? The sample was biased. Working-class and poor people who were those most likely to vote for Roosevelt did not own telephones and automobiles in the depths of the Great Depression.[55] Since the sample was drawn from telephone directories and auto registration lists, Roosevelt voters were significantly underrepresented. Today we know that unrepresentative samples lead to erroneous conclusions, but in spite of that, data from such samples are often accorded equal legitimacy by some media as representative samples. For example, a recent study reported a very high rate of drinking and unprotected sex engaged in by college women on spring break. Although the report claimed the data were from a random sample, it included only women who volunteered to answer questions. Moreover, 25 percent of the group never took a spring break trip.[56] Such a "sample" is hardly representative of college women in the United States.

Emergence of Scientific Polling

Scientific polling began after World War I, inspired by the then new field of marketing research. After the war, demand for consumer goods rose, and American businesses, no longer engaged in the production of war materials, turned to satisfying consumer demand. Businesses used marketing research to identify what consumers wanted and how products should be packaged to attract buyers. The American Tobacco Company, for example, changed from a green to a white package during World War II because it found that a white package was likely to attract women smokers.[57]

Applying mathematical principles of probability to business processes was also important to the development of scientific polling. To determine the frequency of defects in manufactured products, inspectors made estimates on the basis of a few randomly selected items, called a **sample**. It was a simple matter to extend the practice to individuals and draw conclusions regarding a large population based on findings from a smaller, randomly selected sample.

In the early 1930s, George Gallup and several others, using probability-based sampling techniques, began polling opinions on a wide scale. In 1936, Gallup predicted that the *Literary Digest* would be wrong and that Roosevelt would be reelected. Gallup's accurate prediction of the outcome lent credibility to probability-based polls, and in time, Gallup polls became a feature of American politics and probability-based polls the standard for tracking public opinion.

Consequently, government leaders increasingly came to rely on polling. In 1940, Roosevelt became the first president to use polls on a regular basis, employing a social scientist to measure trends in public opinion about the war in Europe.

Use of Polls

Many major American universities have units that perform survey research, and there are hundreds of commercial marketing research firms, private pollsters, and media polls. For politicians, polls have almost become what the Oracle of Delphi was to the ancient Greeks and Merlin was to King Arthur—a source of divine wisdom. During a budget debate between President Clinton and congressional Republicans, polls told Republicans that promising to "put the government on a diet" would be popular in the 1996 election. Polls led Clinton to counter by accusing the Republicans of trying to cut Medicare. When the media wanted to make sense of the debate, they conducted more polls.[58] In the 2006 midterm elections and the 2008 presidential elections, polls indicating the intense unpopularity of the Iraq War led the Democrats to promise to end the war in a speedy fashion. In both years, the Democrats' attention to that issue, among others, resonated with voters. They took back control of the House and Senate in 2006 and captured both the executive branch and both houses of Congress in 2008.

Use by Politicians

Beginning in the 1960s, presidents have regularly used polls to assess the public's thinking on issues.[59] President Clinton took their use to a new high. He spent more on polling than all previous administrations combined and tested every significant policy idea and the language with which to promote

Harry Truman exults in incorrect headlines, based on faulty polls and early returns, the morning after he won the 1948 election.

© Bettman/Corbis

it.[60] Weekly polls shaped his centrist message, leading to his reelection in 1996. If polls showed a position to be popular, Clinton was likely to adopt it. He embraced welfare reform, a Republican idea opposed by Democrats in Congress and liberals in his administration, in large part because it was popular.[61] A White House poll in 1997 suggested that Americans preferred using the budget surplus to bolster Social Security rather than administer a Republican-preferred tax cut. In his State of the Union address, therefore, Clinton called on Congress to "save Social Security first." Clinton even used polls to select a vacation spot.[62] Rather than vacation on Martha's Vineyard and play golf, Clinton went hiking in the Rockies because he was told by a consultant that golf was a Republican sport and that the voters he needed to win were campers.

Of course, Clinton did not always adopt positions because they were popular. He bucked public opinion and many leaders of his own party in his support for the North American Free Trade Agreement (NAFTA) and was again out of step with public opinion in his support for a multi-billion-dollar bailout of the peso during the 1994 Mexican economic crisis. President Clinton also defied public opinion in 1995 by sending troops to Bosnia for peace-keeping purposes. This decision came after the three-year Bosnian war, which was tied to instability following the collapse of the former Yugoslavia. To his surprise, his standing in the polls rose.[63]

President George W. Bush expressed disdain for the polling done by the Clinton White House. Yet, his administration also made extensive use of polls, but in a different way.[64] Along with its polling, the Bush administration mastered the use of **crafted talk**, which enabled him to cater to the views of the right-wing Republican base—while appearing to remain in the middle.[65] Thus, whereas Clinton relied on polls to identify policies with broad public support, Bush relied on them to package—some might say camouflage—policies favored by his conservative base.[66] For example, Bush proposed partial privatization of Social Security. But his pollsters learned that the word *privatization* scared the public by implying that the government would no longer guarantee a lifetime income, as Social Security does. Instead, the president opted to use such terms as *retirement security, personal accounts, choice,* and *opportunity*—without changing the substance of his proposal.

DEMOCRACY?

What are the implications for democracy if politicians rely heavily on public opinion to govern the nation?

President Bush also proposed the elimination of the inheritance tax, which is triggered when wealthy people die and leave their estates to their heirs. Traditionally this tax was called the "estate tax" because it was imposed on people with large estates. But the president and congressional Republicans renamed it the "death tax" to convey the notion that it was imposed on people when they die—that is, on everyone. In fact, it was imposed on only the wealthiest 1–2 percent of the population. Yet the phrase

This gimmick may have attracted customers, but it was not a scientific way to measure public opinion about President Clinton's impeachment.

death tax was a rhetorical success, persuading a majority of middle-class Americans to favor its elimination even though it would never affect them. Poll findings encouraged the administration to describe Bush's energy plan as "balanced" and "comprehensive" and as one that relied on "modern" methods to prevent environmental damage. The findings also prompted officials to call his proposal to give parents vouchers that would permit them to send their children to private schools "school choice" or "opportunity scholarships" rather than "school vouchers" or "aid to private schools."

In addition to polls, focus groups also help politicians find language to which the public reacts well. **Focus groups** are small groups of people brought together to share their reactions to candidates or policies. A focus group is not a scientific poll, and the participants may not be a cross-section of the population, but the process allows political consultants to explore participants' feelings in depth. Consultants search for the language, whether positive toward their side or negative toward the other side, that produces the desired effect on participants. This language can be used to discuss issues and can be incorporated in speeches or commercials. The same process is employed by market researchers to develop strategies to sell commercial products.

Many private pollsters work for one party or candidate. Although they undoubtedly wish to collect accurate data for their clients, their goal is to present their clients in the most favorable light.[67] They may sometimes manipulate the wording of questions to benefit clients. The results, when publicized, give the impression that the public think something that, in fact, it does not.

Push polls are an egregious example of misuse of polling. Suppose a pollster for Jones asks whether the person called supports Jane Jones or Mary Smith or is undecided in an upcoming election. If the answer is Smith or undecided, the voter is asked a hypothetical question that leaves a negative impression. "If you were told that Smith mistreats her staff and fudges on her expense reports, would it make a difference to your vote?" The voter is then asked her preference again. The pollster hopes the level of support for Smith falls. The goal is to see whether certain information or disinformation can "push" voters away from a candidate and toward the candidate favored by those doing the poll.[68]

Learning the weaknesses of the opposition has always been a part of politics, but push polls seek to manipulate opinion often by distorting facts, including candidates' records. In the 2008 Republican presidential contest in Iowa, a third-party group supporting Mike Huckabee used push polling techniques to attack Huckabee's opponents. If a voter said she supported McCain, for example, the pollster pointed out that McCain opposed a constitutional amendment to ban gay marriage; if the voter supported Rudy Giuliani, he was told that Giuliani was pro-abortion and in favor of civil unions for same-sex couples.[69]

A more vicious tactic is to pump thousands of calls into a district or state under the guise of conducting a poll but with the intent of spreading false information about a candidate. In the 2000 South Carolina primary, Sen. John McCain (R-Ariz.) accused the George W. Bush campaign of spreading false information in the guise of a poll when both were seeking the Republican presidential nomination. Rumors were spread that McCain had become mentally unstable as a result of his imprisonment by the North Vietnamese in the Vietnam War and had fathered an illegitimate black child (in fact, he and his wife had adopted a Bangladeshi child). This phony poll halted McCain's momentum, which had been surging until this primary. Both push polls and the phony polls are violations of polling ethics and corruptions of the political process.

Use by Media

Along with polling by candidates, polls by news organizations have also increased. **Tracking polls**, in which a small number of people are polled on successive evenings throughout a campaign to assess changes in levels of voter support, began in 1988 and exploded in 2000. Virtually every TV news outlet features daily tracking polls that monitor movement of candidates in presidential campaigns.[70] This "horse race" element makes a good story and attracts viewers. Polling on the horse race and related coverage during presidential campaigns have started earlier and earlier, in some cases before the nominees are decided. They are also regular features during presidential primaries.

The ease of conducting polls explains, in part, their increasing use. Pollsters can conduct a poll at a moment's notice and have results within hours. This ease often leads to sloppiness. On clearly defined issues where the people have thought about something carefully and hold views, such as the vote in an election taking place in a few days, a well-designed poll can provide an accurate picture of the public's views. However, polls taken well in advance of an election may indicate little about who will win because voters have

behind the scenes

Doubting the Holocaust?

A major problem for pollsters is designing questions that accurately measure opinions. Do you agree that it's not the case that a few words don't make a lot of difference in a poll question? You do, don't you? Because questions with a double negative are difficult to understand, results from such questions are unreliable. Poorly worded questions can confuse respondents and cause pollsters to draw the wrong conclusions. The point was illustrated in a poll to discover the proportion of Americans who doubt that the Holocaust happened. The survey asked the following question: "As you know, the term Holocaust usually refers to the killing of millions of Jews in Nazi death camps during World War II. Does it seem possible or does it seem impossible to you that the Nazi extermination of the Jews never happened?" The results: 22 percent said it was possible that the Holocaust never happened; another 12 percent were not sure. The conclusion: about one-third of the country either doubted that the Holocaust occurred or were uncertain.

Since no reputable historian denies that the Holocaust happened, this "finding" was shocking. Commentators reflected on how the public could be so ill-informed regarding a major event, not just of the twentieth century, but of recorded history.

But the wording of the question was the culprit. Another version asked, "Does it seem possible to you that the Nazi extermination of Jews never happened, or do you feel certain that it happened?" This time only 1 percent said it was possible that the Holocaust never happened. Eight percent were unsure, and 90 percent were certain that it happened.

Why the difference? A study of thirteen polls, with estimates of Holocaust doubters ranging from 1 to 46 percent, found that high estimates resulted from confusing language.

SOURCE: Richard Morin, "From Confusing Questions, Confusing Answers. From *The Washington Post*, July 18, 1994. Copyright © 1994 *The Washington Post*. All rights reserved. Used by permission and protected by the Copyright Laws of the United States. The printing, copying, redistribution, or retransmission of the Material without express written permission is prohibited.

not made up their minds. Early polls tend to measure how well the public know various candidates rather than specific opinions about them. Poll results reflecting support for candidates seeking office for the first time, or in primary elections, often fluctuate because voters do not know much about the candidates.

Even when issues are well defined and opinions are fairly stable, it is increasingly difficult to obtain samples that provide representative pictures of public opinion. Many respondents refuse to be interviewed,[71] either because they don't want to be bothered or because they fear they'll be asked to buy something or contribute money to a cause. Response rates for telephone surveys have also decreased because of extensive cell phone use and call-screening technologies that allow potential respondents to avoid calls altogether.[72]

Nonrespondents, those who refuse to be polled or cannot be reached, are an increasing proportion of those called and can be as high as 80 percent. Pollsters are concerned that those who do respond do not reflect the views of Americans as a whole.[73] However, research indicates that those who participate in these national polls differ little from those who do not, at least on issues that matter to pollsters.[74]

Other problems make it difficult for pollsters to get accurate readings of public opinion. For example, there is the tendency of some respondents to express an opinion when they don't have one. No one wants to appear uninformed. The problem is getting worse as pollsters probe topics on which the public has no opinion and on which there is little reason to believe it should. For example, pollsters asked citizens whether the levees in New Orleans were strong enough to hold back the surge of a major hurricane and whether the U.S. military had enough troops on the ground in Iraq to win the war. Without expert knowledge of levee construction or military strategy, the general public cannot be expected to provide sensible and useful answers.

Polls taken a few days before an election asking about vote choice, on the other hand, tend to be quite accurate. All eight of the election-eve polls in the 1996 presidential election predicted the winner, and the average error was very small.[75] In 2000, the Democratic and Republican candidates each received 48 percent of the vote, with Democrat Al Gore a half million votes ahead of Republican George W. Bush. The election proved too close to call, but all election-eve polls predicted the candidates' totals within each poll's margin of error. The polls taken the day before the 2004 election also were quite accurate, despite the closeness of the election. The average of fourteen major newspaper and network commercial polls had Democrat John Kerry at 47.4 percent and incumbent President Bush at 48.9 percent. The true vote was 48 percent to 51 percent.[76]

In the 1980s, some white voters were reluctant to indicate that they intended to vote against a black candidate and falsely reported their intention. This tendency was first identified in the 1982 California gubernatorial election where Democrat Tom Bradley, an African American candidate,

was defeated despite pre-election polls showing him leading the white candidate, Republican George Deukmejian. For that reason, this discrepancy is often called the **Bradley effect**. Later in the decade, Democrat Doug Wilder, another African American, was elected governor of Virginia, but by a much smaller margin than polls had predicted.[77]

Many analysts believe that the Bradley effect is no longer a factor in elections. In the 2008 primaries, for example, Obama's vote totals were close, sometimes larger and sometimes smaller, than the last pre-election polls. The one exception was in New Hampshire, where Obama had a significant lead but lost in a close race to Hillary Clinton. However, most pollsters think that the difference was mostly the result of a late surge by Clinton rather than a Bradley effect. Additionally, pollsters found that in the November general elections pre-election polls were highly accurate in predicting the national vote and the vote in crucial Electoral College states.[78] Although there might have been prejudice on the part of some voters in deciding for whom to vote, it was not evident in lower than expected votes for Obama based on polls.[79]

Election-day **exit polls** are ubiquitous and controversial features of media coverage. Before election day, the networks identify key precincts around the nation. On election day, as voters leave these precincts, pollsters ask them how they voted. Their responses, coupled with early returns and an analysis of how these precincts voted in past elections, are used to project the winner in the current election. When enough precincts in a state have been analyzed, the networks "call" the state for the winner. Since the 1960s, cable and network television outlets have used exit polls to project the winners before all of the votes have been counted. To reduce costs, the outlets jointly contract with one polling service, so they all receive the same data, and usually they all project the same winner about the same time. Because of fierce media competition, however, each news organization tries to beat the others, even if only by minutes.

Usually the exit polls have been accurate, but not always. At 7:50 p.m. on election night in 2000, the networks declared Democratic candidate Al Gore the winner over Republican George W. Bush in Florida. Because the election was very close and Florida had many electoral votes, it was already clear that whoever won this state probably would win the election. About 9:30 p.m., the polling service that conducted the exit polls notified the networks to pull back. Florida was "too close to call." At 2:15 a.m. the next morning, the networks declared George W. Bush the winner in Florida, and thus the next president of the United States, with 271 electoral votes, just 1 more than needed. They flashed their prepared graphics with a beaming Bush. But as more ballots were counted, Bush's lead in Florida eroded. About 3:30 a.m., the networks again pulled back. Florida again was "too close to call." Despite Dan Rather's assertion that if CBS called a state, "you can put it in the bank," the networks botched their calls twice in one night.

What happened? The election in Florida, as well as nationwide, was extremely close and the polling sample was too small to reveal the winner in such a close election. (The networks, which had been bought by corporations such as General Electric, for whom accurately predicting the election outcome was not a priority, slashed costs so much that the polling service couldn't sample enough precincts.[80]) Those polled were not representative of those who voted.[81]

In addition to the small sample, other problems compromised the exit poll results. Some absentee ballots cast before the election were not counted. In one large county, because of a confusing ballot layout, many voters thought they were voting for Gore but really had voted for a third-party candidate. Voters leaving the polls did not realize this and told pollsters they voted for Gore. Others simply refused to be interviewed. Conservative voters especially, those likely to vote for Bush, were less likely to grant an interview.[82]

The wrong calls were not merely an embarrassment to the networks. Because the networks initially called Florida for Gore ten minutes before polling places in the state's western panhandle closed, it is possible that some Republicans on their way to vote might have turned around and gone home. Because the networks later called Florida for Bush, proclaiming him the "forty-third president," it is likely that many people around the country considered Bush the legitimate winner even when the networks eventually decided that the election was too close to call. Once the election was over and the two sides struggled to make their case regarding who had been elected president, the fact that the networks declared Bush the winner made it appear that Gore was trying to take the presidency away from him.

Although the networks vowed to fix the polls for future elections, more problems arose during the 2004 election. Exit polls showed Democrat John Kerry beating Republican incumbent George W. Bush by a substantial margin. An aide took the president aside to tell him that he was going to lose. Of course, he did not. It is difficult to know just what happened. The pollsters may have accidentally oversampled Kerry voters or undersampled Bush voters. An alternative explanation is that the true votes may have been tampered with. Postelection investigations showed some fraud, though not enough to change any state's election results. However, the peculiar, and difficult-to-explain, finding is that the difference in the Democratic vote between the exit polls and the final tally was greatest in swing states, in areas with electronic voting machines, and in states with Republican governors.[83]

Even accurate and reliable polls can affect politics in a negative way. Poor standing in the polls may discourage otherwise viable candidates from entering a race, leaving the field to those who have less chance of winning or who lack the skills necessary to govern effectively. In 2000, several potential Republican candidates passed up the presidential race when early polls suggested that George W. Bush was the odds-on favorite to win the Republican nomination. And, in an unprecedented move, in 2002 Sen.

Robert Torricelli (D-N.J.) withdrew from his reelection race just thirty-six days before the election when polls showed that he could not win.

Additionally, polls can have a negative effect on political campaigns. Prior to polling, the purpose of campaigns was to reveal candidates' views on the issues and their solutions to the pressing problems of the day. Instead, polls find out what the voters want, and candidates adopt positions and develop images to suit the voters. Too often, candidates follow voters rather than lead them. They consider this strategy safer than trying to educate the public about complex problems or new solutions. Former senator Daniel Patrick Moynihan (D-N.Y.) decried politicians' addiction to poll results: "We've lost our sense of ideas that we stand by, principles that are important to us," he said.[84]

Poll results also influence fund-raising, and without money, a candidate cannot mount an effective campaign. Donors, especially large ones, give money to candidates who have a good chance to win. Candidates and would-be candidates with low poll numbers find it hard to raise the money that could give their candidacy visibility and raise their standing in the polls. Then Governor and present Agriculture Secretary Tom Vilsack (D-Iowa) entered the race for the 2008 presidential election and withdrew just two months later. Never getting more than a couple of percentage points in the polls, he was unable to raise the necessary funds to be competitive.

It is possible that the sheer number of polls may lead people to take them less seriously. Still, it is unlikely that ambitious politicians bent on winning will abandon something that may help them win.

In spite of problems and abuses, polls still provide a valuable service to the nation. If direct democracy, like the New England town meeting, is the ideal, the use of public opinion polls is about as close as the modern state is likely to get. Polls help interpret the meaning of elections. When voters cast their ballots for one candidate over another,

"Can you give him something to calm him down till the country gets straightened out?"

© Frank Cotham/The New Yorker Collection/www.cartoonbank.com

all anyone knows for sure is that a majority preferred one candidate. Polls can help reveal what elections mean in terms of policy preferences and thus help make the government more responsive to voters. For example, Republicans claimed that their victory in the 1994 congressional midterm elections was an indication that voters supported the party's Contract with America, a series of policies the party vowed to enact if it won a majority in the House. Polls showed that most Americans had never heard of it. Similarly, in the 2006 midterm elections, the Democrats sought to gain control of Congress with their "Six for 06" agenda, which included national security, jobs and wages, energy independence, affordable health care, retirement security, and college access for all. However, postelection polls indicated that the primary motivators of votes for Democratic candidates were the unpopularity of President Bush and opposition to the ongoing war in Iraq.

KNOWLEDGE AND INFORMATION

Asking citizens their opinions on matters of public policy, candidates for public office, and the operation and institutions of government presumes they possess sufficient knowledge and information to form opinions and that expressions of opinion reflect real preferences. But many Americans lack knowledge regarding many issues and aspects of government.

Nearly one-third of Americans do not know the name of the vice president, a proportion that has held constant for the past twenty years.[85] Only one-fourth can name their two senators,[86] and only one-third can name their U.S. representative.[87] However, whereas in most years few people can name the Speaker of the House, almost half can recognize the current Speaker, Nancy Pelosi (D-Calif.) most likely,[88] because of her status as the first woman in that position. In contrast, only 15 percent know Pelosi's counterpart, Harry Reid (D-Nev.), Majority Leader in the Senate.[89] Generally speaking, more people can identify sports and entertainment personalities than major political figures.[90]

Most of the public don't have a factual knowledge about policy. For example, two-thirds are unaware that the United States has a trade deficit, that more civilians than soldiers have died in Iraq, or that Sunni is the other Islamic branch besides Shia.[91] Only a small percentage can identify a single piece of legislation passed by Congress.[92]

Misperception regarding government policies is widespread. Although polls show that Americans favor reducing the size of the federal government, most have no idea whether government is growing or shrinking.[93] Most Americans feel that the country spends too much on foreign aid and think we should cut its amount, but one-half estimate foreign aid to be about fifteen times greater than it is. Asked what an appropriate spending level would be, the average answer is eight times more than the country spends.[94] In one poll, nearly half of the public had an opinion on a nonexistent law, the "Public Affairs Act." Fearing to admit that they had never heard of it, people gave an opinion anyway, just as they would for real policies they had never heard of.[95]

Although Americans respect the Constitution and see it as a blueprint for democracy, many do not know what it contains—and what it does not. One-third think it establishes English as the country's official language, and one-sixth think it establishes America as a Christian nation, neither of which is true. One-fourth can't name a single First Amendment right (freedom of religion, freedom of speech, freedom of the press, and freedom to assemble and petition government), and only 6 percent can name all four.[96] Perhaps more disturbing, although levels of education have increased significantly over the years, levels of knowledge regarding politics have not changed much since the 1940s.[97]

Despite this lack of basic knowledge, some argue that the general public knowswhat it needs to know to make sound political judgments.[98] Most citizens take an active interest in politics and pay attention when they have a personal stake. Eighty percent know that Congress has passed a law requiring employers to provide family leave following the birth of a child or in an emergency. When times are bad, voters tune in to government more. With the war in Iraq and a shaky economy, six in ten Americans reported giving the 2004 presidential election a lot of thought as early as February, much earlier than in 2000.[99] And, as more and more Americans grew concerned over the direction of the nation, turnout in the 2008 primaries and the general election soared, with many states setting new records and voters reporting greater interest in the campaign than before.

The general public may not know details of government, but most have strong opinions about whether things are going well or not.[100] At the same time, lack of knowledge is an impediment to holding government accountable and responsible to the people. Those who are less politically knowledgeable find it difficult to sort through the claims and counterclaims of politicians. Some support candidates and policies that work against some aspects of their self-interest. By their lack of information, citizens risk being manipulated.[101]

Politicians often contribute to citizen ignorance and misperception. They often avoid discussing issues, especially controversial ones, or worse, mislead by trumpeting suspect or false information. Even after no weapons of mass destruction were found in Iraq, eight out of ten Americans continued to believe Iraq had them.[102] Nearly one-half responded that Saddam Hussein was directly involved in carrying out the 9/11 attacks despite no evidence to support such a link.[103] The Bush administration encouraged these views and orchestrated officials' comments to assert explicitly that Iraq had weapons of mass destruction and to suggest implicitly that Iraq was linked to al-Qaeda. Even when the charges were shown to be false, the administration was reluctant to correct the record.[104]

DEMOCRACY?

Can a political system be a democracy when most citizens lack basic knowledge about what their government does?

It is hard work to stay informed. It takes time and energy. With work and family, many Americans have little time for politics. But failure to stay informed means that politicians can often ignore what the public wants.

IDEOLOGY

Americans hold opinions on many different issues. These opinions may be consistent with each other and reflect a broader framework or worldview, what scholars call an **ideology**, or they may be inconsistent and unrelated. One might, for example, express support for government assistance to farmers hit by hard times but oppose it for out-of-work steelworkers whose jobs have been outsourced to foreign countries.

Most Americans lack an ideological worldview; that is, they do not have consistent and coherent sets of opinions on political issues. Nor are they consistent in evaluations of candidates for public office or political parties. Yet the major contemporary ideologies, liberalism and conservatism, are

© Lee Lorenz/The New Yorker Collection/www.cartoonbank.com

useful in thinking about public opinion and understanding the institutions of American politics and political and social conflicts in society. Liberalism is sometimes identified by the label *left* or *left wing* and conservatism by the label *right* or *right wing*. These terms date from the French National Assembly of the early nineteenth century, when liberal parties occupied the left side of the chamber and conservative parties occupied the right.

Modern **liberalism**, used in the American political context, embodies the notion that government can be a positive and constructive force in society, responsible for assisting individuals, businesses, and communities with social and economic problems. Franklin Roosevelt and the Democrats' New Deal policies of the 1930s were enacted to relieve the economic hardships of the Great Depression and limit the harsh consequences of an unrestrained free-market economy through government regulation and control. Central to liberalism is the belief that government has a responsibility to make life better for citizens. A more recent manifestation of liberalism has been support for civil rights to promote equality of opportunity for racial minorities and women.

While liberalism endorses government action to bring about social equality and ease the hardships of economic distress, it opposes government intrusion into personal matters such as abortion and contraception, or **social issues**. Liberalism is also identified with opposition to government invasions of privacy, such as monitoring phone calls, reading material, and Internet activity.

Modern **conservatism** generally encompasses the notion that individuals and communities are better off without government assistance and that economic activity should be free from government interference. Central to conservatism is the belief that the free market should be allowed to function unencumbered by government rules and regulations, and individuals, rather than the government, are responsible for their own economic well-being. Short of harming others, individuals should be allowed to do as they please, succeeding or failing without government stepping in to hold them back or push them forward. Consistent with this view, the apparatus and role of government are necessarily small, and where there is a need for government, it is best if it is at the state or local rather than the more distant federal level. (See Figure 2.)

Although conservatives subscribe to the idea of an unfettered free-market economy, this principle has been abandoned in practice throughout the nation's history, as conservatives have promoted commercial and business interests and have favored certain occupational groups, such as farmers, with large subsidies and other government benefits. It has been observed that American liberals as well as conservatives are rhetorically conservative but "operationally" liberal. Americans talk about small government and low taxes, but they remain quite attached to the services that government provides, especially in economic downturns such as the recent recession.[105]

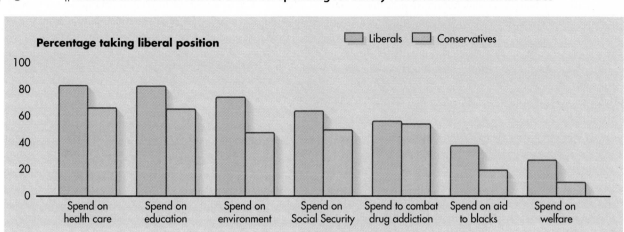

Figure 2 | Liberals and Conservatives Differ on Spending for Safety Net and Environmental Issues

The proportions are those who want to increase spending on each area.
SOURCE: *General Social Survey, 2002 (Ns = 602 to 1301). NORC, University of Chicago: http://www.norc.org/GSS/GSS+Resources.htm.*

As liberalism has its contradictions, so does conservatism. Opposed to government interference in most everything else, many conservatives endorse government intervention when it comes to sexual behavior and its consequences. Many conservatives favor severe restrictions on abortion, some favor limiting the availability of contraceptive devices, and most oppose giving lesbians and gays the right to marry or enter into civil unions. Some conservatives also favor government action in times of war to monitor personal phone calls, restrict political activity, and abolish some rights of defendants. After 9/11, the Bush administration and the Republican congressional majority enacted policies to monitor certain personal communications, to obtain information on individuals' book purchases and library checkouts, and to restrict the rights of those accused of sympathy toward terrorist organizations.

However, not all conservatives agree with these policies. Many traditional "small-government" conservatives oppose these invasions of privacy, whether political or sexual, and many oppose what they label George W. Bush's big-government conservatism.

These broad descriptions capture the core ideas of liberalism and conservatism, but individual politicians, the Democratic and Republican Parties, and most Americans reflect them imperfectly. Though liberalism and conservatism are not political parties, the Democratic Party has a much higher proportion of liberals than does the Republican Party, and the reverse is true for conservatives. There is, of course, a broad consensus between liberals and conservatives that government has some role in making people's lives better, but that consensus often breaks down when specifics are addressed.

Most Americans tend to be conservative on some matters and liberal on others. A little less than a third identify themselves as conservative, and a little more than a fourth identify themselves as liberal. However, more—approaching 40 percent—identify themselves as **moderate**, or middle of the road, neither liberal nor conservative.[106] Because moderates are the swing group, not only in voting but also in building support for policies, public officials will typically move to the middle or even incorporate ideas from those of different ideologies to garner majority support for their ideas. President Bill Clinton followed a typically conservative position when he endorsed a major overhaul of the nation's welfare program, limiting government assistance to families in need. President George W. Bush, while governing mostly from the right, confounded some conservatives by proposing an expansion of the Medicare program to include a drug benefit for seniors, usually considered a liberal position. President Barack Obama has angered some liberals by increasing troop levels in Afghanistan rather than winding down the war as many of them prefer. Many conservatives have praised him for this action.

PUBLIC OPINION IN RED STATES AND BLUE STATES

Liberalism and conservatism not only find expression in partisan differences but also reflect geographical differences. Ideological divisions have strong historical roots stemming from differences between northerners and southerners going back to the time of America's founding. The Civil War (1861–1865) was a stark manifestation of these divisions. After the Civil War and continuing to this day, more conservative agrarians in the Midwest have often found themselves in alliance with southern agrarians against the more liberal urbanites in the East and West.

In the parlance of today's media, the conflict is referred to as the **red states** versus the **blue states** (an updated version of the conflict between the "gray" and "blue" in the Civil War). Others have labeled the divide the "retro" states versus the "metro" ones. The red and blue labels stem from the maps employed on election night by the TV outlets, which present states that voted Republican in red and those that voted Democratic in blue. In the 2000 and 2004 elections, the blue states were in New England, the upper Midwest, and the West Coast, and the red ones were in the South, the Border and Plains states, and the Rocky Mountain West. The red states comprise most of the landmass of the United States but are more rural and sparsely populated than the blue states, which include many of the metropolitan centers. As Figures 3 and 4 illustrate, the pattern shifted a bit in 2008 when the Democrats won in more Mid-Atlantic states, some southern states, and more western states. Nevertheless, the divisions persist.

For journalists and pundits, red versus blue provides an interesting story line that reduces election outcomes to a simple and intriguing explanation. Conservative red America has been described as religious, moralistic, patriotic, white, masculine, and less educated. Liberal blue America has been depicted as secular, relativistic, internationalist, multicultural, feminine, and college educated. Reds are seen as supporting guns, the death penalty, and the Iraq War; blues as supporting abortion and the environment. According to the stereotypes, in red America Saturday's pastime is NASCAR; Sunday's is church. In blue America, Saturday is for the farmer's market, and Sunday is for reading the *New York Times*.[107]

Beyond stereotypes, there are differences between red states and blue states. Religion is one difference. The red states encompass the **Bible belt**, a broad area of the country where most people identify with a religion and evangelical Protestants are common. This area comprises most of the South and parts of Kansas and Missouri. In contrast, the West Coast and parts of the Southwest are much more secular. Forty-four percent of those living in red states identify themselves as born-again Christians; only 26 percent in blue states do. Many fewer people in the blue states identify with any religious organization. These religious differences are significant, because in recent national elections, born-again Christians and regular church attendees have been more likely to vote Republican. After the 2004 election, a map circulated on the Internet identifying the states that supported Kerry as one country—the "United States of Canada," as though they had seceded and joined

| Figure 3 || Election Results Reflect Geographic Pattern |

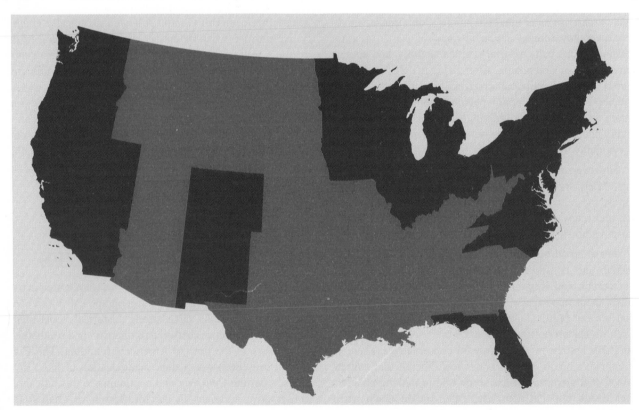

The states are colored red if a majority of voters cast their ballots for the Republican candidate, John McCain, in 2008; or blue if a majority voted for the Democratic candidate, Barack Obama. The map, with its large swath of red states, makes it appear that McCain won, but the red states are, on average, less populous than the blue states, so they have fewer electoral votes.
SOURCE: *http://www-personal.umich.edu/~mein/election/2008/.*

Canada—and the states that supported Bush as another country—"Jesusland."

Other differences also reflect more conservative values in the red states. For example, in red states, women are less active in politics, are less likely to hold political office, have lower incomes, and are less likely to be managers and professionals than in the blue states. Red states impose more restrictions on abortion and incorporate more abstinence education in sex education classes (see Table 2).

Red states are more hostile to labor unions, so they have adopted laws that enable many companies to avoid unionizing their workforce. Wal-Mart, which began in Arkansas and then spread through the nation, strongly discourages its workers from forming or joining unions. In contrast, blue states are more hospitable to labor unions. Cities such as New York, Chicago, and San Francisco are union bastions.[108]

For the 2004 election, the stereotypes were on full display. During the spring primaries, a conservative interest group ran a commercial opposing the candidacy of Howard Dean, then Vermont's governor, who was running for the Democratic nomination for president. In the commercial, average people advised Dean to "take his tax-hiking, government-expanding, latte-drinking, sushi-eating, Volvo-driving, *New York Times*–reading, body-piercing, Hollywood-loving, left-wing freak show back to Vermont, where it belongs." During the fall campaign, John Kerry, the Democratic nominee from "Taxachusetts," was derided for his ability to speak French. In the 2008 primary season, despite striking a chord in a 2004 Democratic convention speech that sought to move beyond stereotypes of red states and blue states, Barack Obama was widely criticized by conservatives as an elitist who condescended to ordinary Americans because of his campaign trail references to the price of arugula lettuce at Whole Foods Markets, and a remark that working-class Americans are bitter and cling to guns or religion out of frustration with their economic, social, and cultural circumstances.[109]

Based on such differences, in the aftermath of the 2004 election, one commentator declared that "the red states get redder, the blue states get bluer, and the political map of the United States takes on the coloration of the Civil War."[110] One adviser to President Bush commented, "You've got 80 percent to 90 percent of the country that look at each other like they are on separate planets."[111] Conservatives sneer at blue staters for being chardonnay-sipping elitists out of touch with average people, while liberals deride red staters

| Figure 4 | Most States Are Purple |

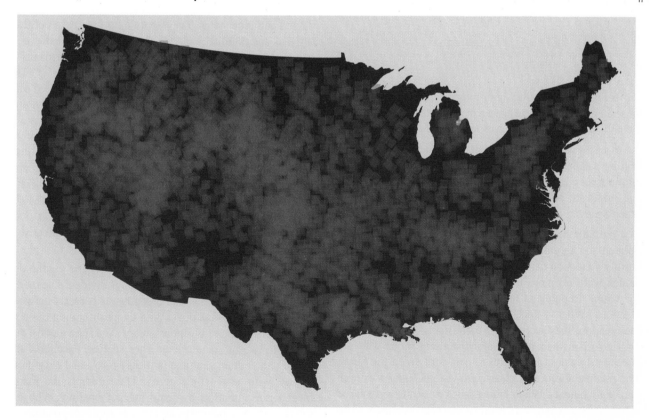

Despite all the talk about red states and blue states, most states are purple—a combination. This map shades each county according to the way its residents voted in the 2008 presidential election. If they voted heavily Republican, the county is brighter red; if they voted heavily Democratic, the county is deeper blue.

SOURCE: *www.-personal.umich.edu/~mejn/election/2008/.*

Table 2 | State Laws Affecting Reproductive and Homosexual Rights

An analysis of twenty-five categories of state laws affecting reproductive and homosexual rights, ranging from laws restricting contraception and abortion to laws recognizing same-sex partnerships, found sharp differences among the states. The states with the most restrictive laws were all red states, and the states with the most permissive laws were almost all blue states. (New Mexico was the exception, although it voted Democratic in 2000 and nearly did so again in 2004.)

Most Restrictive States	Most Permissive States
Ohio and South Dakota (tied for most restrictive)	New York and New Mexico (tied for most permissive)
Indiana	New Jersey
North Dakota	Washington
Oklahoma	California
Mississippi	Vermont
Kentucky	Massachusetts
Utah	New Hampshire
Nebraska	Connecticut
Missouri	Hawaii

SOURCE: Analysis conducted by the National Gay and Lesbian Task Force and two pro-choice groups—Ipas and the SisterSong Women of Color Reproductive Health Collective. David Crary, "In Gay, Reproductive Rights Rankings, S. Dakota, Ohio Last," *Lincoln Journal Star,* June 1, 2006, 4A.

© Bettman/Corbis

Long before the media coined the terms *red states* and *blue states,* differences in values and culture were evident between rural and urban America. One issue in the 1920s, as in the twenty-first century, was evolution. When Tennessee (and fourteen other states) banned teaching evolution or other theories challenging divine creation, John Scopes, a biology teacher, tested the law. Clarence Darrow, a Chicago lawyer, defended Scopes, while William Jennings Bryan, the Nebraska senator and Democratic presidential candidate, testified for the state of Tennessee against the idea of evolution. In this photo, Darrow is appropriately on the left and Bryan on the right.

for being beer-guzzling, gun-toting rednecks. However, these stereotypes are exaggerated; most states are purple—a combination of conservatives and liberals. (See Figure 4.)

In each state, there is a mix of values and opinions. Polling data show that there are sizable differences on hot-button issues such as abortion, homosexuality, gun control, and the death penalty, yet miniscule differences on many other issues.[112]

And although, based on exit polls, many in the media pointed to "moral values" as the reason for George W. Bush's victory in 2004, further analysis shows that moral values were no more likely to be mentioned as a reason for voting Republican than in either of the two previous elections. When voters identified their main concerns in the election, they were much more likely to mention war and terrorism than moral values. Among those who did cite moral values, one-fourth to one-third voted for Kerry. The relative absence of clear-cut divisions appears even in personal contexts. When unmarried Americans were asked whether they would be "open to marrying someone who held significantly different political views" from their own, 57 percent said they would.[113]

Like other simple story lines about politics, the characterizations of the states contain some truth but are exaggerated. They apply to a minority of the populations in the red and blue states. They apply most clearly to political activists and political junkies—the people who are the most involved and most interested in politics. These partisans in both parties are sharply divided, and increasingly so.[114] The characterizations also apply more and more to elected officials, who are also increasingly polarized.[115] Most are nominated in primaries, and only a minority of the public vote in primary elections, and these are the most partisan voters. (Primary turnout is typically about 15 percent, though the 2008 turnout exceeded that.) Republican candidates have to appease conservatives in their party, whereas Democratic candidates have to appease liberals in their party. Moreover, with little competition in most congressional districts, the more extreme and polarized views are not effectively challenged.

Because controversy attracts attention, the media also contribute to the sense that the nation is divided. The media frame issues as debates and elections as contests between two sharply opposing sides. With the proliferation of cable TV channels, talk radio shows, blogs, YouTube videos, and the rapid rise of social media sites such as Facebook and Twitter, the public can tune in those voices, and only those voices, with which they agree. This prompts the media to generate attention by featuring personalities who are extreme in their positions and hostile to the opposition. In contrast, in the early decades of television, there were only three national networks, which sought high ratings by not targeting their newscasts toward any one segment of the audience.

© Matthew Diffee/The New Yorker Collection/www.cartoonbank.com

DEMOCRACY?

What are the implications for democracy when citizens or elites are widely divided over the direction that public policy should take?

With political activists and public officials generally representing the more extreme views of their party, and the media usually emphasizing those views and characterizing opposing views as un-American, it is not surprising that our political debate has become more polarized despite the fact that people are not generally extreme in either direction.

PUBLIC OPINION TOWARD RACE

Public opinion has influenced, as well as responded to, the progress of the African American struggle for equality. Polls extending as far back as the 1940s show white America increasingly opposed to segregation and discrimination, at least in principle.[116] Whereas only one-third of whites accepted the idea of black and white children going to the same schools in 1942, in the 1980s more than 90 percent approved. Today nearly everyone approves. Over 80 percent respond that they have no objection to sending their children to schools where more than half of the students are black. Nearly two-thirds say they would not object to schools where most of the students are black. The percentage of people believing that whites have a right to keep African Americans out of their neighborhoods has been cut in half since 1963.[117] Thirty-eight percent of whites were against laws forbidding interracial marriage in 1963; 85 percent were opposed in 1996.[118] Before Barack Obama became a candidate, most Americans said that they would vote for a black candidate for president. His election

indicates that many racial barriers have fallen. And, it appears that Obama's campaign and election induced more positive white attitudes about race in general.[119]

Public opinion can change because individuals change or because older individuals with one set of opinions are replaced by a new generation with a different set of opinions. Changes in whites' racial opinions through the 1960s occurred for both reasons. Older whites with more stereotyped views of blacks were replaced by a younger generation whose members were more tolerant. At the same time, the civil rights movement prompted many Americans to reconsider their views on race.

Since the 1970s, most changes have occurred because of the replacement of older, more prejudiced whites with younger, less prejudiced ones. Differences in socialization between those born in the 1920s and 1930s and those born in the 1950s and 1960s have led to much greater support for racial integration. More change is likely as today's teens age and replace older Americans. But changes in white attitudes that appear to be influenced by the Obama election occurred in all age groups; older people still have more negative opinions toward African Americans than younger ones, but their positive change was greater than for any but the youngest voters.

Although white Americans accept integration, they have been much slower to accept government initiatives to achieve it. For example, racially segregated schools often are in poor central-city areas and offer inferior education, but busing to achieve racial balance in schools has never had much appeal for whites. Only about one-third support it.

Why is there a discrepancy between the increasing majorities of whites who support integration and the majorities who believe that government should not make special efforts to help minorities? In some cases, unwillingness on the part of whites to endorse government initiatives to end segregation reflects racist sentiments.[120] Although only few white Americans believe that differences in jobs, housing, and income between whites and blacks are the result of biological differences,[121] a plurality assert the racist belief that the cause of these differences is lack of motivation and will power on the part of blacks.[122] Thus a significant share of white Americans harbor some racist beliefs while also being willing to accept blacks, live in integrated neighborhoods, and have their children attend integrated schools.

However, some whites oppose government help for blacks on principle. They object to being told what to do by government or feel that government assistance for blacks is discrimination against whites. For some, government help violates their sense that individuals have a responsibility to provide for themselves.

Another reason that some white Americans are reluctant to accept government intervention on behalf of African Americans is that many do not see the need. African Americans and white Americans live in very different perceptual worlds. Anywhere from 40 to 60 percent of whites believe that the average African American is as well or better off than the average white American in schooling, job, income, and health care.[123] This is a direct contradiction to the reality that blacks lag behind whites on virtually every social and economic indicator. But misperceptions such as these lead many whites to reject any government effort to equalize the social and economic standing of the races. Whites who more accurately recognize the plight of black Americans are more likely to accept the government's role in providing equal education for black and white children and ensuring that blacks are treated equally by courts and police.[124]

Blacks see things differently. A majority view themselves trailing whites in education, income, jobs, and health care, and of course this is the reality.[125] A majority of black men see the economic system stacked against them, but a significant proportion also believe that the problems facing black men result partly from what they have failed to do rather than what white people have done to blacks.[126] Like whites, African Americans have become somewhat less supportive of government initiatives to improve their lots. Support for actions by the federal government to ensure blacks fair treatment in jobs and government assistance in school integration has declined since the early 1960s. Some blacks fear that government initiatives will only antagonize whites. Others fear that black children will suffer if they are in a climate where they are an unwanted minority. Still others believe government is ineffective in bringing about an end to discrimination.

The Obama election changed some attitudes of blacks. A poll taken one year after the 2008 election showed that blacks perceived that the state of black America improved more than at any time in the past twenty-five years. More than one-third of blacks said the "situation of black people in this county" is better than it was five years ago (compared to 20 percent in 2007); and increasing percentages also said that life for blacks in the future will be better than it is now. Yet, even with this progress, more than 80 percent of blacks said the country needs to make more changes to give blacks equal rights with whites.[127] And another poll, taken during the same period, noted that whereas 75 percent of blacks expected Obama's election to advance cross-racial ties, one year after inauguration, only 51 percent agreed that it had done so.[128]

The presidency of Barack Obama reflects both promise and problems in achieving equality in America. Obama's successes in primaries, caucuses, and the general election in 2008 suggest that Americans have come a long way. But the racism experienced by his campaign workers, the significant proportion of whites who said that race was a factor in their vote, and the fact that support for his presidency and his policies is lower among whites than blacks indicates that we have a distance to travel.

CONCLUSION: Public Opinion and the Role of Government

To what extent is the role of government to enact policies that reflect public opinion? On one hand, it makes sense that a representative democracy reflects the will of the people—and public opinion is a measure of that collective will. Yet, the Founders didn't want public opinion to always be translated into public policy. They knew that the course of action favored by a majority may not be the best course. That's why they established a federal system with separation of powers and checks and balances to ensure that, in the heat of the moment, the majority cannot work its will easily. So, even if it were always possible for government officials to know the people's will, we should not expect public opinion and policy to be in perfect agreement quickly or at all times.

The most direct way to assess how often and on what issues policy reflects public opinion is to compare changes in policy with changes in opinion. One study compared responses to policy questions in several hundred public opinion surveys conducted over forty-five years. On more than three hundred items, public opinion had changed. And when opinions changed, policies also changed more than two-thirds of the time. The policy changes matched the opinion changes especially when the opinion changes were large and stable (and when they moved in a liberal direction). The researchers concluded that the policy changes may have caused the opinion changes about half of the time. However, for the rest of the time, the opinion changes probably caused the policy changes or they both affected each other. On important issues, when changes in public opinion were clear-cut, policy usually became consistent with opinion.[129]

For many years, the public has supported more government action to help provide health insurance to those who could not afford it. In 2010, a law was passed to extend health insurance to many of the uninsured in the United States. But the vigorous Republican response to health care proposals of the president and the Democratic majority in Congress succeeded in turning a significant majority into a large minority. So, health care legislation has been responsive to a longer-term public opinion, but not to the opinion of the moment. Because the new law will not be fully implemented until 2014, public opinion about it will, no doubt, undergo some change.

Public officials also pay attention to the intensity of public opinion. Elected officials may support a minority opinion that is intensely held. President George W. Bush continued to push tax cuts when a majority of Americans preferred that their tax dollars be used to reduce the deficit or fund social programs.[130] The president was responding to his core constituency that strongly favored cuts. A minority with intense feelings is more likely to make financial contributions, provide campaign help, and ultimately vote for candidates who doewhat it wants (or against candidates who doe the opposite) than is a majority with weaker feelings.

Whether for good or ill, public policy isn't as consistent with opinion now as it used to be. Twenty-five years ago, congressional laws reflected public opinion polls about 60 percent of the time; more recently, the figure is 40 percent.[131] Both political and institutional changes may account for this pattern. For example, it may reflect the growing polarization among public officials and political activists. It may also be a result of gerrymandering of legislative districts, which provides most members of the House of Representatives with safe seats—either safely Republican and conservative or safely Democratic and liberal. Representatives from those districts don't have to cater to centrist opinion in their district as much as they did in the past.[132]

There are other reasons why public policy may not reflect public opinion. Interest groups, political parties, and public officials' own preferences influence policy, and they may not agree with public opinion. Before the 2006 election, for example, Republicans held solid majorities in both the House and Senate. After newly elected and reelected members were seated in January 2007, the Democrats controlled both houses. Polls showed that large majorities of the public voted for the Democrats because they thought that the United States should not be in Iraq. Though public opinion was heavily in favor when we invaded Iraq in 2003, by 2006 majorities blamed the Republicans for getting us into the war based on unsound judgments and then mismanaging it. Newly elected Democrats pledged to reflect their constituents' attitudes and get us out of the war, which had, at that point, become a quagmire. Yet, in January 2007, just a few weeks after the new Democratic Congress was sworn in, President Bush decided to escalate the war—in the administration parlance, to deploy a "surge" of troops. Though Democrats protested, there was little they could do, short of cutting off all funding. But, even when public officials make different decisions from the public, if the direction and intensity of public opinion persist, policy may eventually conform. In 2009, the Obama administration deescalated U.S. involvement in the war in Iraq by withdrawing troops from the country. The administration's longer-term goal is ending U.S. involvement in combat in Iraq.

Some observers worry that political activists and interest groups manipulate public opinion through the increasingly intrusive media, which distort the issues and blind the public to its self-interest. However, the fact that governmental policy usually reflects majority opinion, especially when that opinion is large and stable, does indicate that the government is generally carrying out its role in turning public opinion into public policy.

KEY TERMS

agents of political socialization	96
Bible belt	112
blue states	111
Bradley effect	107
conservatism, conservatives	110
crafted talk	105
exit polls	107
focus groups	105
ideology	110
liberalism, liberals	110
moderates	111
political socialization	96
public opinion	96
push polls	105
red states	111
sample	104
social issues	110
straw polls	103
tracking polls	106

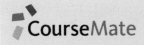
Access an interactive eBook, chapter-specific interactive learning tools (including flashcards, quizzes, videos), and more at CourseMate for *Understanding American Government*. Log in at CengageBrain.com.

5 chapter
News Media

○ Photographer Joe Raedle, embedded with the marines in Iraq, sends photos back to the United States.

Joe Raedle via Getty Images

Talking Points

J. Peter Freire, a young editor of *American Spectator,* a conservative magazine, had given an embarrassing interview on Fox News. Baited by the interviewer, he had called for a boycott of the *New York Times.* So he decided to attend "Pundit School"—actually, the Leadership Institute, a conservative organization that trains hundreds of would-be television pundits each year.[1]

At the school, Freire learned what color suit coat looks best on TV (charcoal), and he learned to use slogans and short phrases (such as "flip-flop"). He learned how to get his message across regardless of what he was asked (by interrupting and saying, "I think the real issue is . . ."). He gave a practice interview in a mock studio, with coaches critiquing his performance (look down occasionally, which suggests that you're thinking, rather than stare into space, which suggests that you're searching for an answer).

With the proliferation of cable TV channels and 24-hour newscasts, the cable networks need more talking heads to fill their airtime, and the print media and websites want more publicity for their reporters and writers. So the cable networks look for pundits, and the print media and websites supply them. With so much demand, it's no longer necessary for pundits to be established journalists with years of experience. Freire was just twenty-six at the time. Pundit school helped him transition from college dorm debates to prime-time TV.

This example illustrates multiple points about today's media that will become apparent as you read this chapter. The media are no longer dominated by a handful of prominent newspaper reporters and columnists and television newscasters and commentators. News organizations offer a variety of voices, whether expert or not.

A *medium* transmits something. The mass media—which include newspapers, magazines, books, radio, television, movies, records, and the Internet—transmit communications to masses of people.

Although the media don't constitute a branch of government or even an organization established to influence government, such as a political party or an interest group, they have an impact on government. In addition to providing entertainment, the media provide information about government and politics. This chapter focuses on the news media—those media that deliver the news about government and politics.

At the time of the Founding, "the media" included a number of small newspapers (and a handful of literary magazines). Although the newspapers occasionally influenced governmental officials, the Founders didn't expect the newspapers to play a major role in our political system. Yet the newspapers would flourish, and other media would arise and also flourish, combining to play a greater role than the Founders could have envisioned.

THE MEDIA STATE

The media have become "pervasive . . . and atmospheric, an element of the air we breathe."[2] Without exaggeration, another observer concluded, "Ancient Sparta was a military state. John Calvin's Geneva was a religious state. Mid–nineteenth-century England was Europe's first industrial state, and the contemporary United States is the world's first media state."[3]

Americans spend more time being exposed to the media than doing anything else. In a year, according to one calculation, the average full-time worker puts in 1824 hours on the job, 2737 hours in bed, and 3256 hours exposed to the media (almost 9 hours a day).[4] Ninety-eight percent of American homes have a radio, and the same percentage have a television. For years, more homes had a television than had a toilet.[5] Almost 20 percent of children younger than two have a television in their bedroom; more than 40 percent of children between four and six do; and almost 70 percent of older children do. A third of children younger than six live in homes where the television is left on all or most of the time.[6] The average child (from eight years old on) or adult watches television 3 hours a day.[7] By the time the average child graduates from high school, he or she has spent more time in front of the tube than in class.[8] By the time the average American dies, he or she has spent one-and-a-half years just watching television commercials.[9] With the development of digital technology, Americans spend even more time being exposed to the media.

Children and young adults, especially, expose themselves to multiple media simultaneously. One study found that eight- to eighteen-year-olds on average pack in 8½ hours of media in 6½ hours of time. A third of them pay attention to more than one medium "most of the time," usually music or television while using the computer.[10]

As Internet use has shot up, it has cut into family time more than anything else. Although the average Internet user spends 30 minutes less time watching television than before the Internet, he or she spends 70 minutes less time interacting with family members than before.[11]

The rest of this section will examine three continuing trends in journalism: the shifting dominance among various media, the increasing concentration of the media, and the increasing atomization of the media.

Shifting Dominance among the Media

American newspapers originated in colonial times, and political magazines appeared in the 1800s, but there were no "mass media" until the advent of broadcasting. Radio, which became popular in the 1920s, and television, which became popular in the 1950s, reached people who could not or would not read. Television became so central and influential in American life that one scholar speculated that the second half of the twentieth century will go down in history as "the age of television."[12] The Internet, which became popular in the 1990s, drew users away from the other media. The Internet likely will go down in history as an even more important medium than television has been.

When television became popular, newspapers waned. People didn't need their headlines anymore, and many didn't want their in-depth coverage either. Papers struggled

for readers and advertisers. Since 1970, the percentage of regular readers has declined, especially the percentage of young adult regular readers.[13] Only 19 percent of Americans between eighteen and thirty-four say they read a daily newspaper. The average age of regular readers is fifty-five.[14] As a result, more than three hundred daily newspapers have folded.[15] Ann Arbor, Michigan, a college town, became the first medium-size city left without a daily paper.[16] Journalists speculate which big city will become the first left without a daily paper.[17] Most surviving newspapers have shrunk, cutting reporters and reducing pages, to save money.[18] Some "daily" papers publish six days a week; Detroit's "daily" papers publish daily but deliver just two or three days a week now. So an editor of the *New York Times* says discussing the state of newspaper publishing is like being "a motivational speaker in a hospice."[19]

For several decades the evening newscasts of the major networks—ABC, CBS, and NBC—replaced newspapers as the dominant medium for coverage of politics. However, as cable television, talk radio, and the Internet became available, the audience for the networks' evening newscasts declined. Since the mid-1990s, the percentage of regular viewers dropped from 60 percent to 34 percent.[20] With so many sources of news at their fingertips, people don't need to tune in to the networks at a set time to hear a newscaster read the headlines. They can tune in to cable television or log onto the Internet at any time.

The Internet now is the third most popular news platform (ahead of newspapers and radio, and behind local television and national television). Sixty-one percent of Americans get news from the Internet; 33 percent of those who have cell phones access news from their phone.[21]

Most Americans get news from multiple platforms— local newspaper, national newspaper (for example, the *New York Times*), local radio, national radio, local television, national television, and the Internet. Almost half get news from four or more platforms on a typical day.[22]

Internet users aren't just consumers of information; they're also conduits, sending e-mails with links to stories and videos to their friends and the members of their social networking websites such as Facebook and MySpace. They're using the technology of the media as people traditionally have used word-of-mouth.[23] This technology is becoming an important political medium, because in addition to informing it facilitates organizing and mobilizing of like-minded citizens.

These trends will likely continue. Newspapers will lose more readers while television, especially the traditional networks, will lose its dominance and the Internet will gain new users (see Figure 1).[24]

Yet it's premature to conclude that newspapers are relics of the past. They provide most content for television news and online news.[25] In fact, newspapers' own websites are increasingly popular. Three-quarters of adults read a newspaper, whether in print or online, each week.[26] Thus most

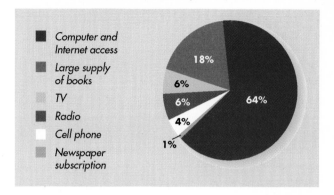

Figure 1 | If You Were Stranded on a Deserted Island . . .

- Computer and Internet access
- Large supply of books
- TV
- Radio
- Cell phone
- Newspaper subscription

64% 18% 6% 6% 4% 1%

and could take only one of the following with you, which would you take?
SOURCE: Asked of 1000 households with Internet access. IPSOS Insight U.S. Express Omnibus, August 2004, cited in "Primary Sources," *Atlantic Monthly*, January–February 2005, 54.

Americans get their news, either directly or indirectly, from newspapers, even as the print versions lose popularity.

The problem is that newspapers haven't figured out how to get online readers (or websites that link to their articles) to pay for the news they use. Although people are willing to pay for texting and pornography online, so far they are reluctant to pay for news online. Saying that "news wants to be free," as some do, ignores the fact that most news is generated by professional journalists working for news organizations, especially for newspapers. These organizations cannot continue to generate news for free (or for the limited revenue they get from advertising). In-demand newspapers, such as the *New York Times,* are experimenting with ways to charge online readers.

Today, different media appeal to different groups. Seniors read newspapers and watch the major networks' evening newscasts, whereas young adults surf the Web (see Table 1). The cable networks attract the least educated, and news magazines, political magazines, and the Internet attract the most educated. Conservatives tend to watch Fox News and listen to talk radio, whereas liberals tend to watch MSNBC and listen to National Public Radio (NPR).[27] Conservatives and liberals both scan the Web but favor different sites (see Table 2). Even men and women pay attention to different media and to different stories in the media (see box "Media Habits of Men and Women").

Concentration of the Media

Journalism is a big business, and it has become a bigger business in recent decades. First, small media organizations owned by local families or local companies were taken over by chains (owning multiple newspapers, radio stations, *or* television stations) or conglomerates (owning multiple newspapers, radio stations, *and* television stations). Then

Table 1	News Consumption by Age

Percentages who said they regularly learned something about the 2008 presidential campaign from . . .

	18–29 years	30–49 years	50 and more years	Gap between youngest and oldest
Local TV news	25%	39%	50%	−25%
Sunday network political shows	4	12	21	−17
Nightly network newscasts	24	28	40	−16
Daily newspaper	25	26	38	−13
Public TV newscasts	6	12	14	−8
Morning network shows	18	21	25	−7
Religious radio	5	8	12	−7
Cable network newscasts	35	36	41	−6
National Public Radio (NPR)	13	19	19	−6
Cable network talk shows	12	11	18	−6
News magazines	8	9	13	−5
Talk radio	12	16	17	−5
TV magazine shows	21	19	25	−4
C-SPAN	6	9	9	−3
"Lou Dobbs Tonight"	7	5	8	−1
Late night talk shows	10	8	9	+1
TV comedy shows	12	7	6	+6
Internet	42	26	15	+27

SOURCE: "Social Networking and Online Videos Take Off: Internet's Broader Role in Campaign 2008," January 11, 2008, Pew Research Center for the People & the Press, a project of the Pew Research Center.

large media organizations were taken over by chains or conglomerates. Finally, chains and conglomerates were bought out by larger chains and conglomerates.

A handful of huge companies—News Corporation, Time Warner, Viacom, and Walt Disney—form the top tier of media conglomerates. Time Warner, the largest, has over eighty thousand employees and $30 billion in annual revenues. It boasts 50 percent of the online business, 20 percent of the cable television business, 18 percent of the movie business, and 16 percent of the record business in the country. It also has 160 magazines, five publishing houses, and "Looney Tunes" cartoons.[28]

A proposed merger between NBC Universal and Comcast would add another huge company. NBC has in addition to its broadcast network 13 cable networks with 30 cable channels, 34 television stations, and Universal movie studio. Comcast is the largest cable system, with almost one-fourth of all cable subscribers in the country.[29]

The huge companies are linked to each other, owning parts of each other and engaging in ventures with each other. These arrangements reduce their competition, lower

Table 2	News Consumption by Democrats and Republicans

Percentages who use these media daily

	Democrats	Republicans
Local newspapers	48%	44%
Local television news	63	53
Nightly network news	43	25
Morning network news	35	24
Cable network news	35	37
Public television news	33	26
Public radio news	23	14
Radio talk shows	17	25
Internet websites	18	29

Results are based on interviews with 1010 adults, December 11–14, 2006, by the Gallup Poll. Reported in Lydia Saad, "Local TV Is No. 1 Source of News for Americans," Gallup News Service, January 5, 2007, and with additional data provided to the authors.

american*diversity

Media Habits of Men and Women

Men and women pay attention to different media. Women are more likely to turn on television news, whether a national network (ABC, CBS, or NBC) or a local station. They are more likely to watch both the morning and nightly newscasts. Men are more likely to switch on a cable network (CNN, Fox News, or MSNBC), and they are more likely to check the Internet for news or listen to radio talk shows for commentary and news.[1] Among men and women who watch the cable networks, men are more likely to watch the most strident programs (such as Sean Hannity's or Bill O'Reilly's on Fox News).[2]

Among more serious sources of news, men are more likely to read newspapers and newsmagazines (*Newsweek* or *Time*), though women are equally likely to follow the detailed newscasts of National Public Radio (NPR), which is the only "hard-news" source whose audience is about half female.[3]

Men and women also pay attention to different stories in the media. Men tend to favor sports stories and "hard news" examining government and politics. Women tend to prefer entertainment, lifestyle, health, safety, and religion stories. They like "soft news" that has a human interest angle.[4] They also follow crime news more closely.[5]

Men pay more attention to international affairs, while women pay more attention to the weather. Forty percent of men, compared with 27 percent of women, followed articles about the tension between the United States and Iran. During the same time, 40 percent of

women, compared with 25 percent of men, followed articles about devastating tornadoes within the United States.[6]

These media habits suggest that men are more interested in politics than women. Indeed, 42 percent of men, compared with 34 percent of women, told pollsters they are "very interested" in government and public affairs. Sixty percent of women, compared with 54 percent of men, said they are only "somewhat interested."[7]

Because men are more interested in politics, they are more likely to discuss politics than women are. According to one survey, 31 percent of men, compared with 20 percent of women, said they discussed national politics nearly every day; and 22 percent of men, compared with 16 percent of women, said they discussed local politics nearly every day.[8]

Social scientists are uncertain why this gender gap exists. Some believe it may be due to the small number of female governmental officials.[9]

[1] Lydia Saad, "Local TV Is No. 1 Source of News for Americans," The Gallup Poll, www.galluppoll.com/content/Default.aspx?ci=26053 &VERSION=p.
[2] Louis Menand, "Comment: Chin Music," *New Yorker*, Novbember 2, 2009, 39.
[3] Linda Hirshman, "16 Ways of Looking at a Female Voter," *New York Times Magazine*, February 3, 2008, 41.
[4] Ibid.; "Numbers," *Time*, February 25, 2008, 16.
[5] Hirshman, "16 Ways of Looking at a Female Voter," 41.
[6] "Numbers," *Time*, 16.
[7] Hirshman, "16 Ways of Looking at a Female Voter," 41.
[8] Sidney Verba, Nancy Burns, and Kay Lehman Schlozman, "Knowing and Caring about Politics: Gender and Political Engagement," *Journal of Politics* 59 (November 1997), 1051–1072.
[9] For examination of some explanations, see Verba et al. and Kira Sanbonmatsu, "Gender Related Political Knowledge and Descriptive Representation," *Political Behavior* 25 (December 2003), 367–388.

their risks, and at the same time erect high barriers for any upstarts that try to challenge their dominance.[30] Their goal is to control the information and entertainment markets of the future. Each conglomerate wants to offer the entire range of media—television stations, radio stations, newspapers, magazines, books, movies, records, and computer services. Each conglomerate seeks to become the sole source of your news and entertainment.

Already, an early expectation for the Internet—that it would provide unlimited diversity and offer an alternative to established media—is being dashed as powerful conglomerates are racing to swallow their competitors and influence the government to adopt policies that will lock in their advantage.[31] This trend toward concentration of the media is likely to continue. It will provide much more convenience, at somewhat more cost, for consumers.

This trend already makes some problems apparent. The news comes from fewer sources than it used to. Although there are tens of thousands of media entities in the United States, the numbers are misleading. Chains and conglomerates own the television stations with most of the viewers, the radio stations with most of the listeners, and the newspapers and magazines with most of the readers.[32] One media analyst, referring to these chains and conglomerates, observed, "Two dozen profit-driven companies, owned and managed by billionaires operating in barely competitive markets, account for nearly the entirety of the U.S. media culture."[33]

DEMOCRACY?

Consider the implications of this trend not for consumers, but for citizens in a democracy who rely on the media to inform them about their government and officials.

A newsstand in Brooklyn, New York, sells sixteen Russian-language newspapers to area immigrants.

Just ten companies publish the newspapers that reach 51 percent of the readers.[34] Six companies broadcast to 42 percent of the radio audience, and five companies broadcast to 75 percent of the television audience.[35] Six companies have more than 80 percent of the cable television market. Four companies sell almost 90 percent of all music recordings, and six companies earn more than 90 percent of all film revenues.[36]

Moreover, just one wire service—the Associated Press (AP)—supplies the international and national news for most newspapers. Five television networks—ABC, CBS, NBC, CNN, and Fox News—furnish the news for most television stations.

With fewer sources of news, there is a narrower range of views—less of a marketplace of ideas—than is healthy for a democracy. Instead, a small number of powerful people provide information and opinion—essentially, define reality—for the rest of the people.

These chains and conglomerates have begun to exercise their power through political activism and censorship. During the Iraq War, Clear Channel Communications, the largest radio chain, organized prowar rallies in seven cities.[37] Cumulus Media, the second-largest radio chain, halted airplay of Dixie Chicks songs on its country stations after a member of the band criticized President Bush.[38] Comcast, the largest cable system, and CNN, owned by Time Warner, rejected peace groups' attempts to buy time for antiwar ads.[39] Sinclair Broadcast Group, the largest television chain, forbade its ABC affiliates from airing *Nightline* the night it broadcast the names of military personnel killed in Iraq. The company said the show would "undermine" the war effort.[40] These instances, though relatively minor in themselves, are ominous signs for the future. It would be naive not to expect more attempts by media chains and conglomerates to flex their muscles.

In addition, the chains and conglomerates have exercised self-censorship when news coverage has threatened corporate interests. ABC killed a story that Disney, its owner, followed employment practices that allowed the hiring of convicted pedophiles at its parks.[41] NBC broadcast a report about defective bolts used in airplanes and bridges built by GE, at the time its owner, and by other companies, but the references to GE were removed. When the president of NBC News complained about the removal and corporate interference in their newscasts, the CEO of GE poked a finger in his chest and shouted, "You work for GE!"[42]

Another problem resulting from concentration of the media is financial pressure to reduce the quality of news coverage. News organizations are expected to match other divisions in their corporations and generate sizable profits each year. Corporate officers feel the heat from Wall Street analysts and major stockholders, who are more concerned with the value of the stock than the quality of the journalism. As a result, costs are cut—some reporters are let go, while others are shifted from time-consuming in-depth or investigative reporting to more superficial stories.[43] A reporter for a midsize newspaper in Illinois admitted, "If a story needs a real investment of time and money, we don't do it anymore." He asked, sarcastically, "Who the hell cares about corruption in city government, anyway?"[44]

A decline in local news is a common casualty of the media's concentration. A veteran reporter for the *Baltimore Sun* noted that the number of staffers on his paper was shrunk from 500 to 300, and "in a city where half the adult black males are unemployed, where the unions have been busted, and crime and poverty have overwhelmed one neighborhood after the next, the daily newspaper no longer maintains a poverty beat or a labor beat. The city courthouse went uncovered for almost a year. . . . The last time a reporter was assigned to monitor [the] burgeoning prison system, I was a kid working the night desk."[45] The executives of the company that runs the paper live in Chicago.

When a train derailed in Minot, North Dakota, and released over 200,000 gallons of ammonia, authorities tried to notify residents to avoid the area and to stay indoors. But when police called the six local commercial radio stations, nobody answered. The stations were all owned and programmed by Clear Channel, based in San Antonio, Texas.[46] By the next day, three hundred people had been hospitalized, and pets and livestock had been killed.[47]

Financial pressure squeezes the major news organizations too. In 2010, ABC News slashed 25 percent of its staff.

Atomization of the Media

Despite the increasing concentration of the media, a contrary trend—an atomization of the media—has also developed in recent decades. Whereas concentration has led to a national media, atomization has fragmented the influence of the national media. The major newspapers and broadcast networks have lost their dominance, and other media, some not even considered news organizations, have played a significant role in politics.

This trend is partly the result of technological changes, particularly the development of cable television and the Internet in the 1980s. Cable television, with an abundance of channels, can offer more specialization in programming. It can **narrowcast**—appeal to small segments of the audience—rather than having to **broadcast**—appeal to the overall audience—as the major networks do. For example, C-SPAN covers Congress on three channels and, unlike the major networks, lingers on members' speeches and committees' hearings.

Cable television can offer 24-hour news, as CNN, Fox News, and MSNBC do. Each network can carve out a niche in this market. After Fox fashioned itself as a conservative network, MSNBC, which had been searching for an identity, became, at least in the evenings, a liberal network. CNN, which pioneered 24-hour news to compete with the established networks, has tried to build a reputation as the least slanted cable news network.[48]

Narrowcasting also allows networks to gear programming to minorities and to speakers of languages other than English. National cable networks cater to blacks and Hispanics.[49] A cable system in Los Angeles and New York caters to Jews. A cable channel in California broadcasts (24 hours) in Chinese, one in Hawaii broadcasts in Japanese, and one in Connecticut and Massachusetts broadcasts in

Foreign-language media aren't new in America. Benjamin Franklin published a German-language newspaper to cater to the influx of German immigrants in his time.

Portuguese. Stations in New York also provide programs in Greek, Hindi, Korean, and Russian.

The Internet, which is a combination of a research library, a news source, and a debating forum as well as an entertainment medium, hosts numerous news sites. Print newspapers post their articles before delivering the papers themselves. Online "magazines" also address politics. Self-styled "journalists" hawk their news and views as well. Matt Drudge offers political gossip on his own website, the Drudge Report, which originated in his one-bedroom apartment.[50]

Even YouTube has become a factor in politics, especially in election campaigns, since its inception in 2005. The musician will.i.am. made a video, "Yes We Can," that celebrated Barack Obama's candidacy and became the site's most watched political video. Obama's pivotal speech on race, which was presented on a weekday morning to a small audience, was viewed 5 million times during the presidential campaign. YouTube offered a section of its site, YouChoose, which ran videos from the candidates. And, of course, the site ran gotcha moments and snide spoofs that also shaped voters' perceptions of the candidates.[51]

The trend toward atomization of the media, which was launched by cable television and the Internet, has also been driven by the populist backlash against government officials and established journalists, perceived as "Washington insiders," that has characterized American politics in recent decades. This populism is reflected in the popularity of radio talk shows. Many stations have such programs, and many people, especially conservative men, tune in.[52] Their numbers make talk radio a force in national politics.

The populism is also reflected in the attention paid to fringe media by the public. In the 1992 presidential campaign, the *Star*, a supermarket tabloid, published allegations by Gennifer Flowers, a former nightclub singer, that she had a twelve-year affair with Bill Clinton while he was governor of Arkansas. Then Flowers appeared on *A Current Affair*, a syndicated television show, rated Clinton as a lover on a scale from 1 to 10, and sang "Stand by Your Man." Thus Flowers did not need to take her story to the major media; she got the tabloid media to tell it (and pay her—$150,000 from the *Star* and $25,000 from *A Current Affair*),[53] and that got the major media to report it.

In the 2008 presidential campaign, the *National Enquirer* reported an affair between John Edwards, a Democratic presidential candidate and former senator, and a campaign staffer, and the tabloid revealed a baby from the affair. Despite the serious ramifications if Edwards had won the Democratic nomination, the mainstream media didn't touch the story until Edwards himself admitted the affair.

Because the public pays attention to the fringe media more than it used to, politicians have begun to use these media. Instead of announcing their candidacy at a press conference, as politicians traditionally have, some have announced their candidacy on television talk shows. In 2008, seven of the sixteen announced their candidacy on YouTube.[54] During the campaign, the candidates have appeared on various television shows. Bill Clinton played the saxophone on the *Arsenio Hall Show,* and George W. Bush kissed the host on the *Oprah Winfrey Show.* Hillary Clinton performed a skit on *Saturday Night Live,* and Barack and Michelle Obama cooked on *Rachel Ray.* Candidates swapped jokes with Jay Leno and David Letterman— and prayed they wouldn't look silly.

All this blurs the line between politics and entertainment. When Sen. Bill Bradley (D-N.J.), campaigning for the Democratic nomination for president, appeared at a Houston radio station, he expected to discuss his new book. Instead, the disc jockeys had two women disrobe from the waist up to report his reaction.[55]

Politicians have to be good sports, because people who pay little attention to political news do pay attention to these shows. Almost a third of adults say they get political information from late-night comedy shows; over a third of those under thirty say they get more information from these shows than from any other source.[56] So it may not be a joke when Letterman proclaims, "The road to the White House goes through me!" (though Letterman himself may be out of date, as young viewers pay more attention to Jon Stewart and Stephen Colbert than to Leno and Letterman).

Because of the expanding role of fringe media, mainstream journalists envision a shrinking role for themselves and their organizations. They no longer monopolize the market of political information; they no longer control the gates through which such information passes.

This trend toward atomization of the media has significant implications beyond its impact on the professional journalists and the established media. Although it makes the news more accessible to more people, it also makes the news less factual and less analytical.

The proliferation of news outlets and the availability of newscasts around the clock create intense competition for news stories. The media have more time or space to fill than information to fill it. So they feel pressure to find new stories or identify new angles of old stories. In addition, networks offer shows that blend news, opinion, rumor, and speculation, because such shows are cheap to produce and, if the hosts and guests are provocative, entertaining for their viewers. Thus the networks can fill airtime and attract an audience. But the result is a commingling of facts and falsehoods, and opinion and speculation. Then these facts and nonfacts are repeated by other organizations seeking to make sure that they are not left behind. In the rush to broadcast and publish, the media have less time for and put less emphasis on assessing the accuracy of the content they disseminate than they used to. The "great new sin," a veteran reporter observed, is not being inaccurate but being boring.[57]

Not only is the news less factual, but the newscasts are also more vile than they used to be. With the proliferation of media and the trend of narrowcasting, each organization finds its niche and caters to its audience. No longer constrained by the need of broadcasting to appeal to the great middle, each organization can now give vent to the beliefs and fears—and even paranoid delusions—of its audience. Personal attacks and wild claims flourish. Cable news, especially, has become "a sandbox" where "people throw things at one another."[58] MSNBC's Keith Olberman identifies, tongue in cheek, the "World's Worst Person" in the news that day. (The person is usually a conservative.)

Barack Obama's election and tenure as president have generated a virulent backlash from cable television commentators and talk radio hosts, who have demonized the president and promoted conspiracy theories.[59] Fox News's Glenn Beck expressed his fear that Obama has "a deep-seated hatred for white people."[60] Rush Limbaugh asserted, "In Obama's America, the white kids now get beat up, with the black kids cheering 'Right on! Right on!'"[61] Limbaugh called Obama's health care plan "Hitlerlike."[62] Numerous commentators claimed, falsely, that the plan included "death panels" of government bureaucrats who would deny health care to the elderly and the disabled. Talk radio hosts Alex Jones and Michael Savage peddled the notion that the Obama administration is creating internment camps— "reeducation camps"—for conservative teens.[63] Then the theory was applied to health care—that the administration is creating "reeducation camps" for the obese. None of this was based on facts.

Cable television and talk radio amplify the angry voices among us. The wild accusations crowd out the thoughtful discussions necessary to resolve the problems we face. They also polarize society and hamstring politicians when they try to negotiate and compromise with the other side.

The fringe media aggravate the problem. Because their goal is entertainment and their audience is politically unsophisticated, these media are less careful about the accuracy of the information they disseminate. Although the mainstream media are also commercial enterprises subject to the pressures of the marketplace, they have a tradition to uphold. Reporters at major newspapers and broadcast networks often speak of their responsibility to follow journalistic standards, whereas members of the fringe media sometimes reflect the views of radio personality Don Imus, who asserted, "The news isn't sacred to me. It's entertainment . . . designed to revel in the agony of others."[64]

The Internet also aggravates the problem. Any person with a computer and a phone line can create an independent web log—a **blog**—to convey his or her news or views worldwide. Blogs are an alternative to mainstream journalism, allowing citizen journalists to compete with media giants. Unlike "the sober, neutral drudges of the establishment press, the bloggers are class clowns and crusaders, satirists and scolds."[65] Some attract thousands or even hundreds of thousands of visitors per day. The most popular political blog—Daily Kos—has 600,000 readers each day, which is more than all but a handful of newspapers have.[66] Another popular blog—the Huffington Post—has more readers than the *Washington Post*.[67]

Some bloggers are "news aggregators," who offer a combination of mainstream news and (a healthy dose of) their opinions. About 40 percent of the content of the *Huffington Post*, for example, comes from other sources.[68]

About two hundred American soldiers in Iraq kept blogs (until the military cracked down), describing *their* war. "Sergeant Lizzie" described the result of a roadside bomb under her Humvee:

> I started to scream bloody murder, and one of the other females on the convoy came over, grabbed my hand and started to calm me down. She held onto me, allowing me to place my leg on her shoulder as it was hanging free. . . . I thought that my face had been blown off, so I made the remark that I wouldn't be pretty again LOL. Of course the medics all rushed with reassurance which was quite amusing as I know what I look like now and I don't even want to think about what I looked like then.[69]

One blogger began trading video clips of sexual pornography for soldiers' clips of "war porn"—attacks on enemy combatants and Afghani and Iraqi civilians. Before his site was shut down, he estimated that he had traded with 30,000 American troops.[70]

Blogs can function as "a lens, focusing attention on an issue until it catches fire."[71] Senate Majority Leader Trent Lott (R-Miss.), at a one-hundredth birthday party for Sen. Strom Thurmond (R-S.C.) in 2002, made a remark seeming to praise Thurmond's past advocacy of racial segregation. Although the mainstream media ignored the remark,

Army intelligence officer Rusten Currie blogged in preparation for his campaign for election to the House of Representatives.

the blogs kept it alive until other media addressed it. Two weeks later, Lott resigned his leadership position.

Yet some blogs push pure hoakum—for example, that the U.S. government, rather than al-Qaeda, destroyed the World Trade Center; that a cruise missile, rather than a hijacked jet, hit the Pentagon; and that United Flight 93 was shot down by an Air Force fighter, rather than forced down by its own passengers. And some bloggers are partisan operatives who have been trained to engage in "guerrilla Internet activism" while presenting themselves as average people.[72] Their fealty to the truth is far less than their passion for the cause.

Bloggers' persistent claims that Obama was born in Kenya rather than in Hawaii, and therefore ineligible to be president; that he was educated at an Islamist madrassah (an Islamic school that teaches fundamentalist religious doctrine) as a child in Indonesia; and that he is a secret Muslim rather than a Christian have dogged Obama through his campaign and into his tenure in office. Despite ample evidence that these accusations are false, the claims continue to ricochet through the blogosphere. Political sophisticates may roll their eyes when they hear such accusations, but many folks believe they are true or at least might be true. An elderly voter in a small town spoke for others when he said he didn't know which biography to believe—the one reported in the mainstream media or the one seen on the Internet and heard at his neighbor's house, at the grocery store, and at his son's auto shop.[73] In 2009, a poll still showed that 28 percent of Republicans believe Obama was not born in the United States and an additional 30 percent are "not sure."[74]

There's always a current, which one writer calls the "**undernews**"—stories sometimes true, often false, circulating in the blogs or tabloids—flowing under the news generated by the mainstream media. When this current gets large enough, the mainstream media, or perhaps the politicians who are the subjects of the stories, are forced to address them.[75] In Sarah Palin's campaign for vice

Tim Rue/Corbis

president, bloggers rumored that her four-month-old baby was actually her teenage daughter's baby—that Palin had faked her pregnancy to cover up her daughter's. The bloggers demanded the release of her obstetrical records. The mainstream media ignored the rumors. Eventually, however, Palin felt obligated to address them and debunk them.[76]

Professional journalists, who may have spent years observing and learning about the subjects of their stories, disdain the amateurs who blog. The journalists complain that the bloggers offer only opinions, not news, especially not in-depth reporting.[77] A *New York Times* editor said they just "recycle and chew on the news."[78] The journalists also point out that the bloggers don't have editors or fact checkers—the layers of "review, revision, and correction" that mainstream media have.[79] The bloggers counter that their readers serve as fact checkers, and thus the blogs have a way to correct themselves. Moreover, the mainstream media's own record, as evidenced by its coverage of the runup to the Iraq War, undermines its claims of accuracy and objectivity (as will be seen later in this chapter). Occasionally, the blogs have corrected inaccuracies in mainstream coverage. When CBS News displayed a letter about the National Guard service of President George W. Bush, bloggers with knowledge of old typewriters identified the letter as a fake.

DEMOCRACY?

What are the implications for a democracy when the media are dominated by professional journalists, with their fact checkers and editors? What are the implications when the media are more numerous, with fringe media and citizen journalists? Which situation do you think better enables citizens to distinguish the blarney from the gospel truth when candidates and officials speak?

In sum, two opposite trends—concentration of the media and atomization of the media—are occurring. The key question is how much control the media conglomerates will exercise and how much news and how many views will emerge through other outlets. Financial pressures are bearing down, and powerful corporations are competing to dominate the media business. At the same time, the Internet is wresting control from news organizations. Indeed, the Internet is transforming the relationship between news producers and news consumers. A participatory medium, the Internet allows consumers not only to forward news to friends but to produce "news" as well. An undergraduate at Temple University produced the "Obama Girl" music video that was downloaded and forwarded millions of times. Suggesting that Obama was young and exciting but also shallow, the video may have helped and hurt the candidate simultaneously. Regardless, it was created and circulated independent of Obama's campaign and of news organizations. It came from the bottom up rather than from the top down. In the future, then, the huge conglomerates may dominate more than they do now, while independent voices from the Internet will break through on matters that have a human interest angle.

RELATIONSHIP BETWEEN THE MEDIA AND POLITICIANS

"Politicians live—and sometimes die—by the press. The press lives by politicians," according to a former presidential aide. "This relationship is at the center of our national life."[80]

Although this relationship was not always so close—President Herbert Hoover once refused to tell a reporter whether he enjoyed a baseball game he attended[81]—politicians and journalists now realize that they need each other. Politicians need journalists to reach the public and to receive feedback from the public. They scan the major newspapers in the morning and the network newscasts in the evening. President Lyndon Johnson watched three network newscasts on three televisions simultaneously. (Presidents Ronald Reagan, who read mostly the comics, and George W. Bush, who read mostly the sports section, were exceptions to the rule.[82]) In turn, journalists need politicians to cover government. They seek a steady stream of fresh information to fill their news columns and newscasts.

The close relationship between the media and politicians is both a **symbiotic relationship**, meaning they use each other for their mutual advantage, and an **adversarial relationship**, meaning they fight each other.

Symbiotic Relationship

President Johnson told individual reporters, "You help me, and I'll help make you a big man in your profession." He gave exclusive interviews and, in return, expected favorable coverage.

Reporters get information from politicians in various ways. Some reporters are assigned to monitor beats. Washington beats include the White House, Congress, the Supreme Court, the State Department, the Defense Department, and some other departments and agencies. Other reporters are assigned to cover specialized subjects, such as economics, energy issues, and environmental problems, which are addressed by multiple departments or agencies.

The government has press secretaries and public information officers who provide reporters with ideas and information for stories. The number of these officials is significant; one year the Department of Defense employed almost fifteen hundred people just to handle press relations.[83] The Department of Defense and the Department of Homeland Security have an entertainment liaison office to provide information to help moviemakers and, at the same time, persuade moviemakers to portray government policies and employees positively.[84]

The government supplies reporters with a variety of news sources, including copies of speeches, summaries of committee meetings, news releases, and news briefings about current events. Officials also grant interviews, hold press conferences, and stage "media events." The vast majority of

Brown Brothers

Teddy Roosevelt called the presidency a "bully pulpit" from which he could persuade the public and Congress to support his programs. (In his time, "bully" was slang for "jolly good.") Modern presidents, however, have learned that there are real limits to this tactic.

reporters rely on these sources rather than engage in more difficult and time-consuming investigative reporting.

Interviews

Interviews show the symbiotic nature of the relationship between reporters and politicians. During the early months of the Reagan presidency, *Washington Post* writer William Greider had a series of eighteen off-the-record meetings with budget director David Stockman. Greider recounted:

> Stockman and I were participating in a fairly routine trans-action of Washington, a form of submerged communication which takes place regularly between selected members of the press and the highest officials of government. Our mutual motivation, despite our different interests, was crassly self-serving. It did not need to be spelled out between us. I would use him and he would use me. . . . I had established a valuable peephole on the inner policy debates of the new administra-tion. And the young budget director had established a valuable connection with an important newspaper. I would get a jump on the unfolding strategies and decisions. He would be able to prod and influence the focus of our coverage, to communicate his views and positions under the cover of our "off the record" arrangement, to make known harsh assessments that a public official would not dare to voice in the more formal setting of a press conference, speech, or "on the record" interview.[85]

Leaks

Interviews can result in **leaks**—disclosures of information that officials want to keep secret. Others in the administra-tion, the bureaucracy, or Congress use leaks for various reasons.

Officials in the administration might leak information about a potential policy—float a trial balloon—and then gauge the reaction to it before committing themselves to it. Officials might leak to prod the president or high-ranking official into taking some action[86] or to prevent the president or high-ranking official from taking some action. When President George W. Bush decided to appoint a Clinton administration attorney to be an antiterrorism adviser, Vice President Cheney's office leaked information to discredit the attorney and block her appointment.[87] (The attempt failed.) When President Obama was deciding whether to send additional troops to Afghanistan, he received a secret report, requesting 40,000 more troops, from his top gen-eral in Afghanistan. Before the president made his decision, Pentagon brass leaked the report to build a public case for the additional troops.

Officials might leak to force public debates on matters that would otherwise be addressed behind closed doors. After Congress investigated the intelligence failures leading up to the terrorist attacks on September 11, 2001, someone leaked the information that the National Security Agency (NSA)—the ultrasecret agency that engages in electronic surveillance around the world—had intercepted al-Qaeda messages on September 10 saying "Tomorrow is zero day" and "The match begins tomorrow" but had not translated the messages from Arabic until September 12.

Officials might leak to shift blame for mistakes. When the Iraqi insurgency cast doubt upon our presumed victory in the Iraq War, officials from the State Department leaked information suggesting that the Pentagon had rushed the country into war. Then officials from the Pentagon leaked information claiming that the CIA had exaggerated the intelligence about Iraq's nuclear weapons program. Then officials from the CIA leaked information indicating that the administration had distorted the intelligence about Iraq's weapons of mass destruction. Each group tried to absolve itself of the blame as the war turned sour.

Officials might leak to hurt an adversary. Diplomat Joseph Wilson (not the same Joe Wilson who as a member of Congress [R-S.C.] heckled President Obama) was sent to Niger, which exports uranium, to investigate the possibility that Iraq had sought a type of uranium used in nuclear weapons. Wilson found no evidence to support the claim. Yet President Bush included the claim as a fact in his next State of the Union address, and others in the administration repeated it to persuade the public to support a war against Iraq. Breaking his silence, Wilson wrote an article in the *New York Times* maintaining that the administration had "twisted" the intelligence to "exaggerate" the threat. In retaliation, officials in the administration leaked the identity of Wilson's wife, Valerie Plame, who had worked for the CIA as an undercover spy.[88] Unmasking Plame effectively ended her career as a spy and jeopardized the operations she had established and contacts she had made in foreign countries.[89]

Officials might leak embarrassing information to help an ally or protect themselves. By leaking this information at a particular time or in a particular way, they can minimize the damage it would otherwise cause. So, officials may leak embarrassing information during holidays or weekends, when the news receives less attention. They may leak to small- or medium-size newspapers rather than to the *New York Times* or the *Washington Post* because these influential papers dislike giving prominent play to stories broken by less prestigious papers.[90] After President George H. W. Bush nominated Clarence Thomas to the Supreme Court, an official in the Bush administration leaked the fact that Thomas had experimented with marijuana in college. The official's purpose was to inoculate Thomas from the greater controversy that could have occurred if the press had discovered and revealed this fact closer to the confirmation vote.[91]

Despite the lurking suspicion that leaks are from low-level bureaucrats in the opposite party, most are from high-ranking officials in the president's party. "The ship of state," one experienced reporter noted, "is the only kind of ship that leaks mainly from the top."[92] During the Vietnam War, President Johnson himself ordered an aide to leak the charge that steel companies were "profiteering" from the war. After an executive complained, Johnson assured him that "if I find out some damn fool aide did it, I'll fire the sonuvabitch!"[93]

Presidents as far back as George Washington have been enraged by leaks. Reagan said he was "up to my keister" in leaks, and Nixon established a "plumbers" unit to wiretap aides and, once it learned who was responsible, to plug leaks. George W. Bush, embarrassed about leaks revealing that the CIA operated secret prisons in foreign countries and the NSA wiretapped American citizens who made phone calls to foreign countries, launched the most extensive crackdown since Nixon. FBI investigations and CIA polygraph tests targeted government employees considered possible sources for the reports.[94]

President Johnson had a more effective response to leaks from officials in his administration. He reversed his decisions that had been leaked, which undermined the official who leaked them and embarrassed the media that publicized them.[95]

Leaks may serve the public by disclosing information that otherwise would not be available, but leaks would serve the public better if reporters explained the leakers' motives so the public could understand the bureaucratic or ideological conflicts behind the stories. Yet reporters are wary of antagonizing the leakers—their sources—for fear of not getting a story next time.

Leaks often enable reporters to break stories before their competitors can report them. Competition for these **scoops** is intense. During the 2004 presidential campaign, CBS displayed a letter about George W. Bush's National Guard service. In its zeal for a scoop, CBS aired the story before verifying the authenticity of the letter.[96] It turned out that the letter had been forged and the network had been snookered, which proved highly embarrassing to CBS and costly to Dan Rather, who lost his anchor position.

Press Conferences

Press conferences also show the symbiotic nature of the relationship between reporters and politicians. Theodore Roosevelt, who was the first president to cultivate close ties to correspondents, started **presidential press conferences** by answering questions from reporters while being shaved.[97] Franklin Roosevelt, who was detested by newspaper publishers, realized that press conferences could help him reach the public. He held frequent informal sessions around his desk and provided a steady stream of news, which newspaper editors felt obligated to publish. This news publicized his policies at the same time that the editors, under orders from the publishers, were writing editorials against them. John Kennedy saw that press conferences could help him reach the public more directly if he allowed the networks to televise the conferences live.[98] Then the editors couldn't filter his remarks.

Presidents and their aides eventually transformed the conferences into carefully orchestrated media shows. Now an administration schedules a conference when it wants to convey a message. Aides identify potential questions, and the president rehearses appropriate answers. (Former press secretaries brag that they predicted at least 90 percent of the questions asked—and often the reporters who asked them.[99]) During the conference, the president calls on the reporters he wants. Although he cannot ignore those from the major news organizations, he can call on others whom he expects will lob soft questions. The George W. Bush administration even gave press credentials to a Republican operative posing as a real reporter so he would ask the questions the president wanted to answer.[100]

Beaming the conference to the nation results in less news than having a casual exchange around the president's

"What do you want to know, boys?" President Franklin Roosevelt holds a casual press conference in 1935.

desk, which used to reveal his thinking about policies and decisions. Appearing in millions of homes, the president cannot be as open and cannot allow himself to make a gaffe in front of the huge audience.

This transformation of the conference frustrates reporters and prompts them to act as prosecutors. As one press secretary observed, they play a game of "I gotcha."[101] Still, reporters value the conferences. Editors consider the president's remarks news, so the conferences help reporters do their job, and the conferences also give them a chance to bask in the limelight.

Media Events

"Media events" also show the symbiotic nature of the relationship between reporters and politicians. Staged for television, these events usually pair a photo opportunity with a speech to convey a clear impression of a politician's position on an issue.

The **photo opportunity**, usually called a *photo op*, frames the politician against a backdrop that symbolizes the points the politician is trying to make. Photo ops for economic issues might use factories—bustling to represent

success or abandoned to represent failure. Presidential candidates in 2008 appeared at Google headquarters, which represents technological advancement, to identify themselves with the future. The strategy is the same as that for advertisements of merchandise: combine the product (the politician) with the symbols in the hope that the potential buyers (the voters) will link the two.[102]

Photo ops can be misleading. To persuade people that President Bush's tax cuts, which were designed primarily to benefit wealthy taxpayers, would help working Americans, the Speaker of the House, Dennis Hastert (R-Ill.), asked well-heeled lobbyists who favored the cuts to dress as construction workers and appear in photo ops featuring "a sea of hard hats" and signs proclaiming "Tax Relief for Everyone." The lobbyists were urged to participate: "WE DO NEED BODIES—they must be DRESSED DOWN, appear to be REAL WORKER types, etc."[103]

After Saddam Hussein's regime was overthrown during the Iraq War, his statue was pulled down by a crowd of joyous Iraqis in a spontaneous celebration. Or so it appeared. The incident convinced many Americans that the Iraqis were grateful for our presence. In reality, the incident was staged as a photo op by the American military. The statue,

© Brooks Kraft/Corbis

After the initial phase of the Iraq War in May 2003, President Bush used the opportunity for a dramatic photo op designed for his reelection campaign. Landing a navy jet on an aircraft carrier off the California coast, he swaggered across the deck, sporting a flight suit and backslapping the sailors. Standing under a banner that proclaimed "Mission Accomplished," he (prematurely) announced the end of major combat in Iraq.

which was attached to a cable, was pulled down by a tank, and the Iraqis, who were transported to the square for the cameras, numbered only thirty to forty. A video that was taken from a distance revealed a more accurate version than the close-up that was shown on television screens.[104]

The speech at a media event is not a classical oration or even a cogent address with a beginning, middle, and end. It is an informal talk that emphasizes a few key words or phrases or sentences—almost slogans, because television editors allot time only for a short **sound bite**. And the amount of time is less and less. In 1968, the average sound bite of a presidential contender on the evening news was about 42 seconds; by 1988 it was under 10 seconds, and since then it has dropped to less than 8 seconds.[105]

Speechwriters plan accordingly. "A lot of writers figure out how they are going to get the part they want onto television," a former presidential aide explained. "They think of a news lead and write around it. And if the television lights don't go on as the speaker is approaching that news lead, he skips a few paragraphs and waits until they are lit to read the key part."[106] This approach doesn't produce coherent speeches, but the people watching on television won't know, and the few watching in person don't matter because they are just props.

Perhaps more than any other source of news, media events illustrate the reliance of politicians on television and of television on politicians.

Adversarial Relationship

Although the relationship between the media and politicians is symbiotic in some ways, it is adversarial in others. Ever since George Washington's administration, when conflicts developed between Federalists and Jeffersonians, the media have attacked politicians and politicians have attacked the media. During John Adams's administration, Federalists passed the Sedition Act of 1798, which prohibited much criticism of the government. Federalist officials used the act to imprison Jeffersonian editors. Despite this history, once Jefferson himself was elected president, he called for "a union of opinion." Frustrated, he suggested that newspapers be divided into four sections—Truths, Probabilities, Possibilities, and Lies.[107] Later, President Andrew Jackson proposed a law to allow the government to shut down "incendiary" newspapers. Even now, a former press secretary commented, "there are very few politicians who do not cherish privately the notion that there should be some regulation of the news."[108]

Inevitably, politicians fall short of their goals, and many blame the media for their failures. When they do so, they confuse the message and the messenger, like Russian tsar Peter the Great, who, when notified in 1700 that his army had lost a battle, promptly ordered the messenger strangled. When President Kennedy became upset by the *New York Times*'s coverage of Vietnam, he asked the paper to transfer its correspondent from Vietnam. (The *Times* refused.) When President Nixon became angry at major newspapers and networks, he had Vice President Spiro Agnew lash out at them. He also ordered the Department of Justice to investigate some for possible antitrust violations and the Internal Revenue Service to audit some for possible income tax violations. When aides to President George W. Bush read a *Washington Post* article questioning the truthfulness of the president's statements, they suggested that the reporter be removed from the White House beat. (The *Post* refused.)[109]

After repeated salvos of harsh criticism from Fox News, President Obama retaliated by refusing to make administration officials available for interviews with Fox reporters. The administration claimed that Fox is an opinion organ rather than a news network. The move, however, was counterproductive. Other organizations, perhaps seeing themselves in Fox's position in the future, pressured the administration to end the freeze-out, and Fox's commentators used the fight to further enflame their viewers.[110]

Despite these examples, it would be incorrect to think that the relationship between the media and politicians is usually adversarial. Normally, it is symbiotic. Although journalists like to think of themselves as adversaries who

DEMOCRACY?

The head of CBS News said, "I'd like just once to have the courage to go on the air and say that such and such a candidate went to six cities today to stage six media events, none of which had anything to do with governing America."[1] Do you agree, or do you think that these media events are beneficial for the voters in a democracy?

[1] David Halberstam, "How Television Failed the American Voter," *Parade*, January 11, 1981, 8.

behind the scenes

Photo Ops and Racial Sensitivities

The most intriguing use of photos ops in the 2008 presidential campaign was the staging of the people who appeared behind Barack Obama when he made speeches. His team tried to downplay his race for fear of alienating white voters uncomfortable with the prospect of a black president. (Of course, Obama is half white and half black, but he is considered black by most people.) Although the crowds who attended Obama's speeches and many volunteers who knocked on people's doors in the South Carolina primary were disproportionately black, the cameras showed a "sea of white faces nodding approvingly or cheering wildly behind Obama." Campaign workers had ushered photogenic white families to seats on the speaker's platform in the cameras' eye and had ushered most black supporters to seats in the audience out of the cameras' eye.[1] In Pennsylvania, Obama campaigned heavily in the Philadelphia suburbs before adoring white supporters, but lightly in the city itself, where the crowds would have been mostly black. His team worried about the state's high number of blue-collar workers reluctant to vote for a black candidate. Showing Obama surrounded by enthusiastic whites would help defuse that concern; showing him surrounded by enthusiastic blacks would exacerbate it.

At one rally, Obama campaign workers also moved two Muslim women in headscarves out of camera range because of the Internet accusations that Obama is a secret Muslim.

[1] Jim Hoagland, "Candidates on Message," *Washington Post National Weekly Edition*, February 25–March 2, 2008, 5.

stand up to politicians, most of them rely on politicians most of the time.[111]

Yet the relationship has become more adversarial since the Vietnam War and the Watergate scandal fueled cynicism about government's performance and officials' honesty.[112] Many reporters, according to the editor of the *Des Moines Register*, "began to feel that no journalism is worth doing unless it unseats the mighty."[113] New reporters especially began to feel this way. Sen. Alan Simpson (R-Wyo.) asked

the daughter of old friends what she planned to do after graduating from journalism school. "I'm going to be one of the hunters," she replied. When he asked, "What are you going to hunt?" she answered, "People like you!"[114]

In response, politicians, fearing that they will say something that will be used against them, have restricted reporters' access. In turn, reporters, worrying that they will not get the information they need to do their job, have complained that politicians are not accessible. During George

Washington Post reporters Carl Bernstein (left) and Bob Woodward (right) uncovered the Watergate scandal.

W. Bush's presidency, one lamented, "The idea of a truly open press conference, an unscripted political debate, a leisurely and open . . . conversation between political leaders, or even a one-on-one interview between a member of the press and an undefended politician had become almost quaint in conception."[115]

At the same time, politicians have become more sophisticated in their efforts to **spin** the media—to portray themselves and their programs in the most favorable light, regardless of the facts, and to shade the truth. Politicians' spin prompts reporters to become more cynical. "They don't explicitly argue or analyze what they dislike in a political program but instead sound sneering and supercilious about the whole idea of politics."[116] Reporters' cynicism then prompts politicians to escalate their efforts to spin the media, which prompts reporters to escalate their comments that politicians are insincere or dishonest. And so the cycle continues.

After Vice President Al Gore announced his candidacy for president in 2000 from his family's farm in Carthage, Tennessee, ABC correspondent Diane Sawyer conducted an interview reflecting these dynamics. She began, "Are you really a country boy?" He replied, "I grew up in two places. I grew up in Washington, D.C. [as the son of a senator from Tennessee], and I grew up here. My summers were here. Christmas was here." Sawyer taunted Gore, "You mucked pigpens?" Gore answered, "I cleaned out the pigpens . . . and raised cattle and planted and plowed and harvested and took in hay." Sawyer, not satisfied, challenged Gore in an attempt to show that he was a hypocrite: "I have a test for you. Ready for a pop quiz? . . . How many plants of tobacco can you have per acre? . . . What is brucellosis? . . . What are cattle prices roughly now? . . . When a fence separates two farms, how can you tell which farm owns the fence?" By announcing from his family's farm, Gore was trying to convey his rural roots; by interviewing him in this manner, Sawyer was trying to question his sincerity.[117]

The increasingly adversarial relationship is also due to other factors mentioned earlier in the chapter. There are so many media, with so much space to fill, that they have a voracious appetite for news and a strong incentive to compete against each other for something "new." As a result, they often magnify trivial things. And because the fringe media now play a more prominent role, and because their stories eventually appear in the mainstream media, all media pay more attention to politicians' personal shortcomings with sex, drugs, and alcohol and raise more questions about politicians' "character" than they ever used to.[118] In 1977, one of every two hundred stories on network newscasts was about a purported scandal; by 1997 (*before* the Monica Lewinsky affair was revealed), one of every seven stories was.[119]

After 9/11, reporters were sensitive to, and even intimidated by, the public's fear and anger stemming from the terrorist attacks and its vocal support for the Iraq War. Consequently, reporters relaxed their stance. But they became more adversarial again when the American victory evaporated during the Iraqi insurgency.

Yet the apparent toughness usually is "a toughness of demeanor" rather than a toughness of substantive journalism.[120] Reporters exhibit tough attitudes rather than conduct thorough investigations and careful analyses. In fact, few engage in investigative journalism.[121] Even a decade years after 9/11, there has been remarkably little investigation of important questions: Why didn't the administration heed repeated warnings of the pending attack? If they discounted the warnings, why did top officials go to unusual lengths to protect themselves? After 9/11, why were al-Qaeda fighters airlifted out of Afghanistan? What arrangements—a deal?—were made with Pakistan?[122] Before Hurricane Katrina, reporters failed to notice that the Federal Emergency Management Administration (FEMA) was headed by political hacks rather than by officials experienced in disaster response. Nor did reporters question why a study found that employees' morale at FEMA was lower than that at any other federal agency.[123] And before the credit bubble burst, which led to the recession of 2008 and 2009, business reporters, who seemed enthralled by the power and glamour of financial CEOs, failed to notice the risky investments of the big banks or the lax regulation by the federal government.[124]

Courtesy of Franklin D. Roosevelt Library, 73-113:61

Because of polio, Franklin Roosevelt spent much of his life in a wheelchair, but journalists didn't photograph him in it. A friend snapped this rare picture. Journalists were reluctant to photograph or write about officials' afflictions or behaviors until the Watergate scandal ushered in a new era of more personal coverage.

Relationship between the Media and the President

Roosevelt Administration

Franklin Roosevelt created the model that most contemporary presidents use to communicate with the public. Newspaper publishers, who were conservative businessmen, opposed the president and his policies. In fact, a correspondent recalled, "The publishers didn't just disagree with the New Deal. They hated it."[125] They instructed their editors and reporters to criticize it. Recognizing that he wouldn't receive favorable coverage, Roosevelt realized that he would have to reach the public another way. He used press conferences to provide a steady stream of news about his policies. He also used radio talks, which he called **fireside chats**, to advocate his policies and reassure his listeners in the throes of the Depression. He had a fine voice and a superb ability to speak informally—he talked about his family, even his dog. He drew such an audience that he was offered as much airtime as he wanted (though he was shrewd enough to realize that too much would result in overexposure). This tactic enabled him to avoid the filters of editors and reporters and to take his case directly to the people.[126]

In addition, Roosevelt was the first president to seek systematic feedback from the people. He used public opinion polls to gauge people's views toward his policies. Thus for him, communication was a two-way process—to the people and from the people.

Reagan Administration

Ronald Reagan refined the model. As a young man, Reagan idolized Roosevelt, even developing an imitation with an accurate accent and a cigarette holder.[127] As president, Reagan duplicated Roosevelt's success in using the media. Although Reagan's command of the facts about his proposals and government programs was uncertain, his ability to convey his broad themes was uncanny. Reporters dubbed him the "Great Communicator."

As Roosevelt used radio, Reagan used television. By the time he reached the White House, after a career as an actor in theater, movies, and television, Reagan had mastered the art of speaking and performing in front of live audiences and on camera.[128] Tall, handsome, and poised, he knew exactly how to use an inflection, a gesture, or a tilt of his head to keep all eyes and ears focused on him. His speeches and even his casual comments were highly effective.

Reagan's aides knew how to make his appearances especially impressive. The administration realized that the media would cover the president extensively to fill their news columns and newscasts. An aide explained the strategy: "The media, while they won't admit it, are not in the news business; they're in entertainment. We tried to create the most entertaining, visually attractive scene to fill that box [the TV screen], so that the networks would have to use it."[129]

Aides sent advance agents days or weeks ahead of the president to prepare the "stage" for media events—the specific location, backdrops, lighting, and sound equipment. A trip to Korea was designed to show "the commander in chief on the front line against communism." An advance man went to the demilitarized zone separating North and South Korea and negotiated with the Army and Secret Service for the most photogenic setting. He demanded that the president be allowed to use the most exposed bunker, which meant that the army had to erect telephone poles and string thirty thousand yards of camouflage netting to hide Reagan from North Korean sharpshooters. The advance man also demanded that the army build camera platforms on a hill that remained exposed but offered the most dramatic angle to film Reagan surrounded by sandbags. Although the Secret Service wanted sandbags up to Reagan's neck, the advance man insisted that they be no more than four inches above his navel so viewers would get a clear picture of the president wearing his flak jacket and demonstrating "American strength and resolve."[130]

The Reagan administration also developed the technique of highlighting a single theme with a single message for every week and every day within the week to emphasize whatever proposal the president was pushing at the time. The administration then arranged the president's appearances and offered the media information that would reinforce the message. Aides strictly controlled the president. They determined "the line of the day" and instructed him what to say. They also instructed him not to answer reporters' questions about other matters. They didn't want other remarks to overshadow the message of the day. The strategy was to set the agenda rather than letting the media set it.[131]

By alternately using and avoiding the media, President Reagan's administration managed the news more than any previous administration.

News photo of President Reagan in Korea, staged to reflect "American strength and resolve."

Bush Administration

The George W. Bush administration emulated the Reagan administration in trying to manage the news by alternately using and avoiding the media.

Aides established a message for every day and e-mailed talking points to administration officials, instructing them to address these points. The president voiced the message at his appearances, where backdrops bearing the message printed as a slogan reinforced it. Administration officials who were contacted by the press repeated it. All were expected to "stay on message."

The president was made available for speeches to friendly audiences or for interviews with friendly reporters. Otherwise, access to the president was strictly limited. Press conferences were rarely scheduled. Bush held far fewer conferences than other modern presidents.[132] Reporters who displeased the administration were punished by losing their access.[133] When veteran reporter Helen Thomas of the Associated Press displeased the president, he refused to answer her questions at press conferences for three years.[134]

When the president attended a meeting in Ireland, an Irish reporter who had submitted questions in advance, as was required for interviews with Bush, was dissatisfied when the president answered in generalities. Interrupting, she pressed him for more specific answers. Her behavior was so unusual that it became a news story. Unlike American reporters, she didn't worry about future access to the White House.

The administration's communications strategy also entailed a very active and well-financed public relations machine. The administration contracted with public relations firms and advertising agencies to produce pseudo news reports, purporting to be actual news stories, that portrayed the administration as vigilant and compassionate.[135] These were distributed to television stations around the country, which integrated them into their newscasts. To viewers, they appeared to be news rather than propaganda.[136] The administration even paid some real reporters to say positive things about the administration's policies.

President Bush was not comfortable in front of television cameras. Initially, he shunned the role of "communicator in chief," and when aides scheduled public appearances, he bristled.[137] When he gave formal speeches or made informal remarks, he often looked awkward and sounded inarticulate. Reporters observed that he was "perhaps the least confident public performer of the modern presidency."[138] An aide to the previous president commented, "In the Clinton administration, we worried the president would open his zipper, and in the Bush administration, they worry the president will open his mouth."[139] As governor of Texas, Bush had worked behind the scenes and evidently expected to do the same as president.

The terrorist attacks thrust Bush into the public role he had avoided. Although he failed to return to the White House on September 11 to reassure Americans from the Oval Office,[140] later he visited the site of the World Trade Center and galvanized public support when he picked up a bullhorn and talked to the workers. Converting "grief to anger to action,"[141] he rallied the public behind the war on terrorism and the war in Afghanistan.

Bush's strength was to speak to moral clarity. The terrorist attacks allowed Bush to talk in these terms, but September 11 was "one of history's rare unnuanced days," a presidential adviser admitted.[142] On other issues, where there was less moral clarity, such as the clash between Israelis and Palestinians, Bush was less effective. His black-and-white view of the world and his "poverty of language"[143] made it difficult for him to convey any nuances in his comments. (He in fact told one senator, "I don't do nuance."[144])

Bush's speechwriters were quite effective in communicating with his supporters. The speeches incorporated religious language that appealed to evangelical Christians.[145] In addition to references to *evil* and *evildoers*, there were terms, such as *work of mercy* and *wonder-working power*, that were recognized by the devout. When the president announced the invasion of Afghanistan, his speech included allusions to Revelation, Isaiah, Job, Matthew, and Jeremiah.[146] (The president, however, did spur a backlash in the United States and abroad when he called the war on terrorism a *crusade*, thus linking it to the Crusades by European Christians against Eastern Muslims in the Middle Ages.)

Although his formal speeches were good, Bush tended to stumble when he spoke without a script. At times he forgot his train of thought, made up words, and left listeners bewildered.[147] But his lack of polish didn't seem to hurt him in the polls, at least until his policies became unpopular. He talked like many men, in his tone and simple words—even the belligerence in his voice—and thus related well to many voters. Sounding like a frontier sheriff in the Wild West, he declared that Osama bin Laden was "wanted, dead or alive." When Iraqi insurgents began to use roadside bombs against American soldiers, Bush threatened, "Bring 'em on." While some people were appalled by such comments, others liked the swagger in his delivery and the confidence in his gestures. One observer called Bush "a master of the American vernacular, that form of expression which eschews slickness and makes a virtue of the speaker's limitations."[148]

Obama Administration

Because of the rapid proliferation of new media and fringe media and their insatiable appetite for new information around the clock, the Obama administration has concluded that it's no longer possible for any president to control the agenda. Therefore, President Obama has been made available to more outlets more often. He's given more interviews and held more press conferences than his predecessors— more prime-time press conferences in six months than George W. Bush held in eight years.[149] He's appeared on Leno and Letterman, and he's picked his favorite teams for basketball's "March Madness" on ESPN. He's courted

Some critics believe that President Obama is in danger of overexposure, but the atomization of the media means that only those Americans who are news junkies will experience the president's image and words very often.

black and Hispanic media. The administration feeds content to blogs, Twitter, and Facebook, and uploads video clips to YouTube (whitehouse) and still photos to Flickr.[150] The danger of this strategy is overexposure. However, his aides believe that extensive exposure is necessary for the president to break through the constant din of the newscasts.

Obama is a gifted orator. He has relied on this talent to propel himself in politics—first to attract attention on the national scene, then to triumph in the primary campaign and in the election campaign for president, and now to overcome hurdles as president. He is also a careful speechwriter. His top aide, David Axelrod, a former journalist, said, "[O]ne of the great thrills is to watch him work on a speech. It's not just the content . . . but more than anyone I've ever worked with, he's focused on the rhythm of the words. Like, he'll invert words. He'll say, 'I need a one-beat word here.'"[151]

Obama chooses his words carefully for their meaning as well as the sound they convey. When describing his policies, he likes to use the word *pragmatic* to assure his listeners that the policies aren't too liberal or, as Bush's policies were considered, too ideological.[152] He tries to avoid the phrase *war on terror,* which is perceived as anti-Arab and anti-Islam in the Middle East and other Muslim countries. He substitutes *the enduring struggle against terrorism and extremism.* In this way, Obama is the reverse of Bush. As one English professor observed, "The Bush administration didn't set out deliberately to do things that were offensive, but they liked to do things that showed how strong they were, and to use language almost in an aggressive sense."[153] Choosing his words carefully, however, requires Obama to make frequent use of a teleprompter and, in impromptu comments, results in halting delivery.

Obama is the antithesis of a populist. Cool and calm—"No Drama Obama"—he offers rational answers to questions and rational solutions for problems. He disdains what he calls "the circus"—the cable brawls and the trivial interests of even mainstream reporters—for example, whether he bowed too deeply when he met the Japanese emperor.[154] Obama shuns what presidents from Reagan through George W. Bush thought was necessary to persuade the public—stagecraft, memorable phrases, and emotional appeals. But many people want a president "to emote and perform the proper theatrical gestures so they can see their emotions enacted on the public stage."[155] Especially in trying times, such as the recession of 2008 and 2009, fearful and angry people have a hunger for red-meat rhetoric, lambasting Wall Street, bank CEOs, and exorbitant bonuses. Obama doesn't offer such rhetoric and, unlike Reagan, doesn't have acting skills to project a concern for ordinary folks, so some people assume that he "doesn't get it" or, at least, doesn't feel it like they feel it. He doesn't connect with average Americans on a gut level.[156] One time Obama recognized the disconnect and tried to sound like a populist but gave "the impression of a dapper man trying on an ill-fitting suit."[157] The calm that served him so well in the campaign limits his ability to reach some citizens.

Obama's demeanor and tendency to recoil from irrational talk (along with his decision to let congressional Democrats work through competing health care proposals) also made him slow to respond to the accusations about his health care initiative. Critics' claims of "rationing," "death panels," and "government takeover" of the health care system planted a strong root in the public mind before the president began to push back. This slowness allowed opponents to trivialize and poison the national debate.[158] In today's hyperpartisan, 24-hour media environment, the president's desire to stay above "the circus" may be an unrealistic approach.

Relationship between the Media and Congress

Members of Congress also use the media but have less impact. They hire their own full-time press secretaries, who churn out press releases, distribute television tapes, and arrange interviews with reporters.[159] The Senate and House of Representatives provide recording studios for members and allow television cameras into committee rooms and C-SPAN into the chambers. Yet members still have trouble attracting the media's eye. One president can be the subject of the media's focus, but 535 members of Congress cannot. Only a handful of powerful (or, occasionally, colorful) members receive coverage from the national media. Other members get attention from their home-state or district media, but those from large urban areas with numerous representatives get little publicity or scrutiny even there.[160]

Members have resorted to stunts to get publicity. The chair of the House Appropriations Committee brought a machete to show his determination to cut spending. Another member brought a sledgehammer and smashed a Toshiba radio to protest the company's sale of technology to the former Soviet Union. A California representative who couldn't get a meeting with the Secretary of the Interior to discuss a massive fish kill on the Klamath River dumped 500 pounds

© David Burnett/Contact Press Images

On his blog, Lane Hudson posted amorous e-mails from Rep. Mark Foley (R-Fla.) to a male congressional page. The mainstream media picked up the story, and five days later Foley resigned from Congress. "My heart stopped," Hudson said. "I thought, 'Oh my God, what have I gotten myself into?'"

of dead fish outside the department's building. An Iowa senator who wanted to prove that ethanol was safe took a swig in front of the cameras.[161]

Congressional committees also use the media to influence public opinion. During the Whitewater hearings, President Clinton talked with a Republican senator on the investigating committee. "They were impugning Hillary," he recalled, "and I asked this guy, 'Do you really think my wife and I did anything wrong in this Whitewater thing?' He just started laughing. He said, 'Of course you didn't do anything wrong. That's not the point. The point of this is to make people *think* you did something wrong.'"[162]

Of course, members and committees don't simply use the media; they are restrained by the media as well. Scandals involving members are avidly reported. Congress can be restrained by the media even when its usual procedures are covered—and exposed. The Democratic health care reform proposals were covered extensively in 2009 and 2010. To attain a majority, Democratic leaders engaged in the negotiations, compromises, and trade-offs that often are necessary to pass controversial bills. But the spectacle was an eye-opener for many constituents, who were unfamiliar with congressional practices and enraged by them here. As a result of public anger, some members withdrew their support for the reform.

Relationship between the Media and the Supreme Court

Unlike presidents and members of Congress, justices of the Supreme Court shun the media. They rarely talk to reporters, and they also forbid their law clerks from talking to the press. They try to convey the impression that they aren't engaged in politics and therefore shouldn't answer reporters' questions or concern themselves with public opinion.

As a result, the media don't cover the Supreme Court nearly as much as the presidency or Congress. Few newspapers have a full-time Court reporter; no newsmagazines or television networks do. In one recent year, only twenty-seven reporters had Court press credentials, whereas an estimated seventeen hundred reporters had White House press credentials.[163]

When the media do cover the Supreme Court, they focus on the Court's rulings.[164] They seldom investigate or peer behind the Court's curtains. They often ignore even relevant concerns, such as questions about the justices' health. Most reporters on this beat, called "Washington's most deferential press corps,"[165] reject the role of watchdog. Consequently, the justices are shielded from both the legitimate investigation and the excessive scrutiny that officials in the other branches are subjected to.

Relationship between the Media and the Military

During wartime, the military has tried to control media coverage to avoid the negative reports and the disturbing photographs that typified the last years of the Vietnam War.[166] During the invasion of Grenada in 1983, the military excluded all journalists, even turning away at gunpoint those who reached the island on their own. During the invasion of Panama in 1989 and the Persian Gulf War in 1990, the military created press pools with a few journalists escorted to selected sites. These journalists provided the news for the organizations whose journalists weren't included in the pools.

For the Iraq War, the military tried a new approach, embedding the journalists into fighting units. Hundreds of journalists ate, slept, and traveled with the soldiers and were allowed to report live. But they were prohibited from revealing sensitive information and from having anonymous interviews, which would allow the soldiers to make critical comments. The military's goals were to appease the news organizations and at the same time use them to show the technological prowess of our military and the heroic exploits of our fighters. The news organizations would also report human interest stories about individual soldiers. According to an official, it was "important for the public to be invested in this emotionally and personally."[167] For this reason, any embedded photographers who had graphic photos published in their newspaper or posted on the Internet

Chris Hondros/Getty Images

When American soldiers killed the unarmed parents of this girl at an Iraq checkpoint, a photographer who was embedded with the unit snapped this photo. When the photo was published, the photographer was kicked out of the unit.

were kicked out of their unit; as a result, few photos of dead soldiers appeared.[168]

Studies show that the arrangement worked exactly as the military expected. The embedded reporters, compared with the less numerous independent reporters, covered the war from the military's perspective—the soldiers' viewpoint—focusing on threats to American troops rather than on casualties among Iraqi civilians or consequences for Iraqi society.[169]

The military was so anxious for uplifting coverage that when Pat Tillman, the Arizona Cardinals defensive back who patriotically volunteered for the army after 9/11, was killed by friendly fire, the army refused to reveal the cause of death to the public or even to his parents for over a month. Instead, it issued a false press release exaggerating his actions. As its most famous volunteer, Tillman was used as a heroic poster boy at a time when the Abu Ghraib scandal was emerging and soiling the army's reputation.[170] (Also see box "Influencing Hollywood.")

BIAS OF THE MEDIA

Every night, Walter Cronkite, former anchor for *CBS Evening News,* signed off, "And that's the way it is," implying that the network held a huge mirror to the world and returned a perfect reflection to its viewers, without selection or distortion. But the media do not hold a mirror. They hold a searchlight that seeks and illuminates some things instead of others.[171]

From all the events that occur in the world every day, the media can report only a handful as the news of the day. Even the fat *New York Times,* whose motto is "All the News That's Fit to Print," cannot include all the news. The media must decide what events are newsworthy. They must decide where to report these—on the front page or at the top of the

newscast, or in a less prominent position. Then they must decide how to report them.

When the Wright brothers invited reporters to Kitty Hawk, North Carolina, to observe the first airplane flight in 1903, none considered it newsworthy enough to cover. After the historic flight, only seven American newspapers reported the flight, and only two reported it on their front page.[172]

In making these decisions, it would be natural for journalists' attitudes to affect their coverage. As one reporter acknowledged, he writes "from what he hears and sees and how he filters it through the lens of his own experience. No reporter is a robot."[173]

Political Bias

Historically, the press was politically biased. The first papers, which were established by political parties, parroted the party line. Even the independent papers that succeeded them advocated one side or the other. The attitudes of publishers, editors, and reporters seeped—sometimes flooded—into their prose.

But the papers gradually abandoned their ardor for editorializing and adopted the **practice of objectivity** to attract and retain as many readers as possible. This means that in news stories (not in editorials or columns) they try to present the facts rather than their opinions. When the facts are in dispute, they try to present the positions of both sides. They are reluctant to evaluate these positions. Even when one side makes a false or misleading assertion, they are hesitant to notify their readers. Instead, they rely upon the other side to do so, hoping that their readers can discern which viewpoint is correct.

Although most mainstream media today follow the practice of objectivity, the public still thinks the press is biased. Many people think the press is "out to get" the groups they identify with. Executives believe the press is out to get businesses, and laborers believe it is out to get unions. Conservatives believe the press is biased against conservatives, and liberals believe it is biased against liberals. Republicans believe the press is biased against Republicans, and Democrats believe it is biased against Democrats.[174] For many people, the press is a scapegoat, "a secular devil for our times."[175]

Indeed, the public is more critical today, when most media at least attempt to be objective, than in the past, when the media did not even pretend to be. Back then, citizens could subscribe to whichever local paper reflected their own biases. Now, as local newspapers and television stations have given way to national newspapers and networks, and as independently owned newspapers and television stations have given way to large chains and conglomerates, people have less opportunity to follow only media that reflect their views. People with strong views are disappointed with today's more balanced coverage. So partisans on both sides criticize the same media for being biased—though in opposite directions.

behind the scenes

Influencing Hollywood

The U.S. Army has an office on Wilshire Boulevard in Los Angeles. The office helps decide which movies will get help from the military—access to bases and use of Humvees, tanks, ships, and planes. In exchange for access and use, the military demands to see the scripts and may request changes in them.

The Vietnam War spurred a cascade of acclaimed movies, such as *Apocalypse Now, Born on the Fourth of July, Deer Hunter, Full Metal Jacket,* and *Platoon,* but most portrayed the American involvement as doomed and the American soldier as deranged. According to the lieutenant colonel in charge of the army's office, "in the '80s and '90s, the Vietnam vet was 'the other'"; Hollywood had created "the crazy Nam vet" as a symbol of the lunacy of that war. From these movies, the American military learned a bitter lesson. Since then, it has tried to influence the next generation of filmmakers and shape the next crop of war movies.

The military helped to make *The Messengers* (2009), a sympathetic portrayal of soldiers during the Iraq War, but refused to aid *In the Valley of Elah* (2007), an examination of an actual incident suggesting that the army disregarded the mental health of its soldiers. The director of *Elah* said, "I did want to have a balanced and nuanced film. . . . I tried to be empathetic . . . not to make these kids into villains." After he received twenty-one pages of objections to his script, he proceeded without the military's help.

Pentagon officials deny that they censor movies. They claim that they request changes only when military policies or practices are misrepresented.

SOURCE: Julian E. Barnes, "The Iraq War Movie: Military Hopes to Shape Genre," *Los Angeles Times,* July 7, 2008, latimes.com/news/la-na-armyfilms7-2008jul07,0,5018814,print.story.

To assess the presence and the direction of **political bias**, it is necessary to examine the differences in coverage by the advocacy media and the mainstream media, the differences in coverage of elections and issues, and the differences in coverage of domestic policies and international policies.

Bias in the Advocacy Media

Some media don't try to be neutral. Advocacy media intentionally tilt one way or the other and seek an audience of people who share their views. Advocacy media can be found at both ends of the political spectrum, though far more are conservative than liberal.

Because conservatives perceived a liberal bias in the mainstream media, they established their own media in the 1980s and 1990s. This vocal complex includes newspapers, such as the *Washington Times,* the *New York Post,* and the *Wall Street Journal*'s editorial pages (not its news pages), various magazines, numerous radio and television talk shows, and Internet websites, plus a network of columnists, commentators, and think tanks. These conservative journalists see themselves as part of an ideological movement and members of the same team.

In contrast are the mainstream journalists who see themselves as objective reporters rather than as part of any ideological movement or members of any team. In fact, the mainstream journalists who are liberal have made a point of criticizing liberals and Democrats as a way of demonstrating their independence and impartiality. During the years in which conservatives established their own media, mainstream journalists offered relentless criticism of Bill Clinton and snide portrayals of Al Gore and John Kerry.[176] Today they offer regular criticism of Barack Obama.

The role of conservative journalists in talk radio has been especially powerful. The expansion of talk radio began in the 1980s, when the daytime television audience was mostly female and the daytime radio audience was mostly male, and a gender gap emerged in political preferences, with men becoming more conservative and women remaining more liberal. A backlash against feminism and affirmative action developed among middle-class and lower-middle-class whites, especially the men. During these years, a few large chains, with conservative owners, bought out many stations. To capture conservative male listeners and convey their own political views at the same time, they adopted a talk radio format with conservative hosts.[177]

Today, more than thirteen hundred talk stations fill the airwaves, and more than a fifth of American adults consider talk radio their primary source for news.[178] The vast majority of talk shows are hosted by conservative commentators,[179] such as Rush Limbaugh, Sean Hannity, Bill O'Reilly, G. Gordon Liddy,[180] Oliver North, and numerous others.[181] The Republican National Committee, in fact, has a Radio Services Department that provides talking points to these hosts every day so that they will reinforce the Republican message.[182] According to one analysis, 91 percent of the talk on the 257 news/talk stations owned by the top five chains was conservative; only 9 percent was liberal.[183]

The impact of talk radio was apparent concerning the immigration issue in 2007. President Bush and congressional Democrats agreed on a bill that had broad public support, but the compromise bill was denounced by talk show hosts because it wasn't punitive enough toward illegal immigrants. The hosts rallied their listeners, who pressured their representatives to kill the bill.[184]

The conservative advocacy media also include Fox News, the first major network to narrowcast rather than broadcast.[185] Owned by a conservative media mogul and operated by a former Republican consultant, Fox appeals to conservatives disenchanted with the mainstream media.[186] The network offers a combination of news and commentary. Sometimes the newscast is straight up (especially with Sheppard Smith); other times the newscast is laced with commentary. In addition, the network offers extensive commentary from Glenn Beck, Sean Hannity, and Bill O'Reilly. In its news and commentary, Fox follows the talking points from the Republican National Committee. In 2010, it hired three prominent Republicans as analysts, all of whom were expected to contend for the Republican nomination for president in 2012— Newt Gingrich, Mike Huckabee, and Sarah Palin.

Throughout its programming, the network blurs the distinction between news and commentary. For instance, when

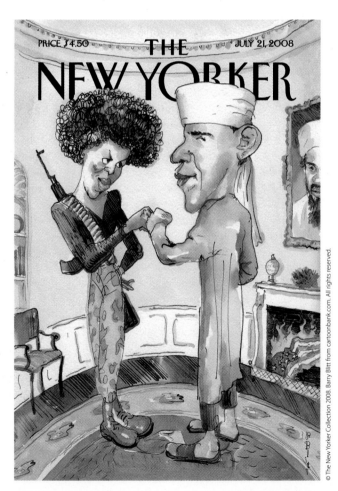

© The New Yorker Collection 2008 Barry Blitt from cartoonbank.com. All rights reserved.

After Internet sites and Fox News questioned Obama's Christianity and his patriotism, a cartoonist depicted Barack and Michelle Obama as radical Muslims bent on destroying America. Through exaggeration, the cartoonist lampooned the false accusations. Some Obama supporters, however, thought the cartoon reinforced the damning perceptions many Americans held.

reporting on a proposal by President Bush to cut taxes, the network ran a line along the bottom of the screen urging, "Cut 'em already."[187] When reporting on Swiss protesters against the Iraq War, an anchor referred to the demonstrators as "hundreds of knuckleheads." Another referred to France, which opposed the war, as a member of the "axis of weasels." The network then ran that phrase along the bottom of the screen when reporting about France. Fox aired relentlessly upbeat coverage of the Iraq War, urging its correspondents to downplay American casualties. (A memo from a senior executive instructed: "Do not fall into the easy trap of mourning the loss of U.S. lives.") They were also told to refer to Marine snipers as "sharpshooters," because the word *snipers* has a negative connotation. And all along, the network questioned the patriotism of liberals and critics of the war.[188] When apparent progress in the war deteriorated, Fox scaled back its coverage rather than report the failures of the war.[189] Not until numerous conservatives began to criticize the war did Fox air critical views.

During the presidential campaign in 2004, Fox repeatedly called for President Bush's reelection. In 2008, the network questioned Obama's patriotism and compared the candidate to Karl Marx—the communist theorist who called religion the "opiate" of the people.[190] Fox also compared Obama to Nazi leader Adolf Hitler, Soviet dictator Joseph Stalin, and Chinese chairman Mao Zedong, all leaders of authoritarian nations who murdered millions, as well as to Cuban leader Fidel Castro and to the Iraqi insurgents. When Barack and Michelle Obama bumped fists, Fox's E. D. Hill speculated that the gesture could be a "terrorist fist jab." During Obama's first year, the network's newscasters and commentators actively promoted—not simply reported—the Tea Party protests against the president and his policies.[191] The network's newscasts were consistently negative as well.[192]

A former Fox correspondent said it was common to hear producers remind them, "We have to feed the core"—that is, their conservative viewers.[193] Yet the network retains a veneer of neutrality, claiming to be "fair and balanced" and "spin free." The marketing strategy is to attract viewers by offering them conservative commentary but with the reassurance that this commentary is fact rather than opinion.[194]

MSNBC, which was competing with Fox News for conservative viewers, has decided to position itself, at least in the evenings, as the anti-Fox station to attract liberal viewers. It airs commentary from Chris Matthews and two outspoken liberals—Keith Olberman and Rachel Maddow—who chastise both conservatives and President Obama when he compromises or adopts a centrist position.

The conservative media also include Christian radio networks, television organizations, and more than thirteen hundred radio and television stations.[195] These media address political issues as well as spiritual matters.

Although liberals have as many magazines and Internet websites, the only advocacy media they dominate are documentary films.[196] For example, Michael Moore's films, such as *Fahrenheit 9/11* and *Sicko*, also offer a combination of facts, opinions, and speculation, though from the left rather than from the right.

Bias in the Mainstream Media

Although the advocacy media are far more slanted, allegations of bias are leveled against the mainstream media far more often. Conservative groups and commentators, especially, claim that these media are biased toward liberal candidates and policies.[197]

Journalists for the mainstream media are not very representative of the public. They are disproportionately college-educated white males from the upper middle class; disproportionately urban and secular, rather than rural and religious; and disproportionately Democrats or independents leaning to the Democrats, rather than Republicans or independents leaning to the Republicans. Likewise, they are disproportionately liberals rather than conservatives.[198]

Journalists who work for the most influential organizations—large newspapers, wire services, newsmagazines, and radio and television networks—are more likely to be Democrats and liberals than those who work for less prominent organizations—small newspapers and radio and television stations.[199] Journalists in the most influential organizations are more likely than the public to support the liberal position on issues. At the same time, they are not extremely liberal: they support capitalism and do not think that our institutions "need overhaul."[200]

Focusing on journalists' backgrounds and attitudes assumes that these traits color journalists' coverage. But several factors mitigate the effect of these traits. Most journalists chose their profession not because of a commitment to an ideology—according to veteran columnist David Broder, "There just isn't enough ideology in the average reporter to fill a thimble"[201]—but because of the opportunity to rub elbows with powerful people and be close to exciting events. "Each day brings new stories, new dramas in which journalists participate vicariously."[202] As a result, most journalists "care more about the politics of an issue than about the issue itself,"[203] so they are less likely to express their views about the issue. In addition, mainstream organizations pressure journalists to muffle their views because of a conviction that it is professional to do so and also a desire to avoid the headaches that could arise otherwise—debates among their staffers, complaints from their audience, perhaps even complaints from the White House or Congress.[204] Some organizations fear public perceptions of reporters' bias so much that they restrict reporters' private lives, forbidding any political activity, even outside the office and on their own time.[205] For these reasons, mainstream media don't exhibit nearly as much political bias toward candidates or policies as would be expected from journalists' backgrounds and attitudes.

To measure bias, researchers use a technique called content analysis. They scrutinize newspaper and television stories to determine whether there was an unequal amount of coverage, unequal use of favorable or unfavorable statements, or unequal use of a positive or negative tone. They also consider insinuating verbs ("he conceded" rather than "he said") and pejorative adjectives ("her weak response" rather than "her response"), and for television stories, they evaluate the announcers' nonverbal communication—voice inflection, eye movement, and body language.

Bias in Elections

Researchers have spent the most time examining media coverage of presidential campaigns. Their reports have found relatively little bias: the media typically have given the two major candidates equal attention, have usually avoided any favorable or unfavorable statements in their news stories, and have usually provided diverse views in editorials and columns, with some commentary slanting one way and other commentary slanting the opposite way. The authors of a study examining forty-six newspapers concluded that American newspapers are "fairly neutral."[206] Other studies have reached similar conclusions about various media.[207] An analysis of the data from fifty-nine studies found no significant bias in newspapers, a little (pro-Republican) bias in newsmagazines, and a little (pro-Democratic) bias on television networks.[208]

Media coverage of the 2008 presidential campaign was an exception to the rule, according to early studies. At least on television newscasts, Barack Obama received a boost. In the primary campaign, he garnered 75 percent positive (and 25 percent negative) comments, whereas Hillary Clinton got just 53 percent positive (and 47 percent negative) comments.[209] In the general campaign, Obama had a two-to-one ratio of positive to negative comments, whereas John McCain had the opposite—a two-to-one ratio of negative to positive comments.[210] Partly, though not completely, these differences were due to the fact that Obama ran an effective campaign, whereas McCain ran an inept one, and also due to McCain's choice of Sarah Palin as his running mate—a decision that was repeatedly questioned on the newscasts. (Obama's running mate, Joe Biden, received light but balanced coverage.) During his first year in office, however, Obama's coverage was evenly balanced on the major networks' newscasts and in the *New York Times, Newsweek,* and *Time.*[211]

Overall, there is less bias than the public believes or the candidates feel. When candidates complain, they are usually objecting to bad news or are trying to manipulate the media. The strategy is to put reporters on the defensive so that they will go easier on the candidate or harder on the opponent in the future, just as sports coaches "work the refs" over officiating calls.

Yet the way in which the media cover campaigns can have different implications for different candidates. The media report the facts that one candidate is leading while the other is trailing, that one campaign is surging while the other is slipping. "We all respond like Pavlov's dogs to polls," an experienced correspondent explained.[212] This coverage has positive implications for those who are leading or surging—swaying undecided voters, galvanizing campaign workers, and attracting financial contributions—and negative implications for those who are trailing or slipping. It does not benefit one party over the other party in election after election, but it can benefit one party's candidate over the other party's candidate in a particular election.[213] People who support the losers consider such reporting biased. Journalists, however, consider it simply a reflection of reality.

Another habitual practice has different implications for different candidates. The press pays more attention to minor things that are easy to report—and easy to ridicule—than to substantive issues that are difficult to explain.[214] Hence the voluminous coverage about President Clinton's sexual affairs. Although reporters are willing to criticize or even ridicule candidates about minor matters, they are usually reluctant to challenge them on substantive issues. Doing so would require more knowledge about substantive policies or more nerve to draw conclusions about these policies than most reporters have.

Likewise, when covering presidential debates, the press pays more attention to style and tactics than to substantive issues—more attention to how something was said than to what was said.[215] Reporters act more like theater critics than helpful guides to confused voters. These practices don't reflect bias by reporters as much as they reflect superficiality in reporting.

There are two exceptions to the generalization that overt political bias in elections is minimal. First, the media usually give short shrift to third-party candidates.[216] Ralph Nader, who first ran for president in 2000, was well known and held views partly shared by numerous voters, but he received scant coverage. When he held enthusiastic rallies on college campuses and in large coliseums, the national media virtually ignored them. Only when the election between Gore and Bush tightened and it appeared that Nader might be a spoiler did the national media pay attention. Then they focused on his potential as a spoiler rather than on his views that had attracted the crowds.[217]

Second, newspapers traditionally print editorials and columns that express opinions. In editorials before elections, papers endorse candidates. Most owners are Republican, and many influence the editorials. Since the first survey in 1932, more papers have endorsed the Republican presidential candidate, except in the elections of 1964, 1992, 2004, and 2008, when Obama received 287 and McCain only 159 endorsements.[218]

In columns, writers offer their own opinions. Although most newspapers provide a mix of columnists, the majority are conservative, according to a study of 96 percent of the country's English-language daily newspapers.[219] Sixty percent of the papers print more conservative than liberal columnists, while 20 percent print more liberal than conservative columnists, and 20 percent print an equal number.

Evidently the Republican owners want their paper's columns, like their paper's editorials, to reflect their conservative views.

Bias against All Candidates and Officials

Some critics charge that a general bias exists against all candidates and officials—a negative undercurrent in reporting about government, regardless of who or what is covered. President Nixon's first vice president, Spiro Agnew, called journalists "nattering nabobs of negativism." Critics believe that this bias increased after the Vietnam War and the Watergate scandal made reporters more cynical.

There is considerable validity to this charge. Analyses of newspapers, magazines, and television networks show that the overwhelming majority of stories about government and politicians are neutral.[220] However, the rest are more often negative than positive.[221]

Emphasizing the negative distorts what candidates say. In the 1996 presidential campaign, 85 percent of the candidates' comments made a positive case for the candidates, but 85 percent of the media's coverage dwelled on the negative attacks by the candidates.[222]

Emphasizing the negative also distorts what officials do. The *Washington Post* reported that Sen. Robert Byrd (D-W. Va.) got the National Park Service to fund a project for his state, including the renovation of a train station—for his "personal pork barrel." "Why did the National Park Service spend $2.5 million turning a railroad station into a visitor center for a town with a population of eight?" The compelling reason—Senator Robert C. Byrd, "who glides past on Amtrak's Cardinal Limited from time to time, heading to and from his home in Sophia, a few miles south." But Byrd did not ride that train, and that train did not go to that town.

"But, what if we're attacked in the press?"

© The New Yorker Collection 2004 Matthew Diffee from cartoonbank.com. All rights reserved.

Moreover, the Interior Department recommended the project; it was not "slipped" into other legislation "unwanted," as the article claimed. When the reporter was questioned, he replied with disgust, "Look, everyone knows that this is the way the world works in Washington. What's the big deal?" Indeed, this is the way things work in Washington sometimes, but apparently not this time. This article, which prompted editorials in newspapers across the country, reinforced readers' cynicism.[223]

Emphasizing the negative conveys the impression that the individuals involved are unworthy of the office they seek or the one they hold. It ultimately conveys the impression that the political process itself is contemptible.[224]

Bias toward Issues

The relative lack of bias in the coverage of elections (except for the negative tone against all candidates) doesn't necessarily mean there is the same lack of bias in the coverage of issues. Because elections are highly visible and candidates are very sensitive about the coverage, the media take more care to be neutral for elections than for issues.

Domestic issues   Empirical studies of the coverage of several domestic issues, including abortion, school busing, and nuclear power, indicate a tilt toward the liberal positions.[225] Anecdotal reports of the coverage of other domestic issues, such as gay rights, gun control, capital punishment, the environment, and homelessness, also suggest some bias toward the left.[226]

At the same time, the media exaggerate crimes, drugs, and other urban pathologies that stereotype African Americans and, to a lesser extent, Hispanics.[227] In this respect, they don't reflect a bias toward the left.

Popular television programs, movies, and records often promote social ideas or trends characterized as liberal, such as diversity, multiculturalism, acceptance of racial minorities, acceptance of casual sex, and disparagement of traditional religion. Conservative Christians, especially, feel that their beliefs are under daily attack by the "liberal media." (However, television programs and movies also glorify violence and guns—and since 9/11, torture of suspected terrorists[228]—which don't reflect liberal values. Moreover, television programs and movies rarely have their female characters choose an abortion when they face an unwanted pregnancy.[229]) These programs might have as much or even more effect on individuals' views than the news does. But this chapter focuses on the news media, not the entertainment media, which are beyond the scope of this text.

Although debates about bias revolve around liberalism and conservatism, perhaps the question actually should be reframed: does the coverage of domestic issues reflect class bias? An examination of the debate over the North American Free Trade Agreement (NAFTA), drafted to ease trade between American, Canadian, and Mexican companies, showed more emphasis on the benefits of free trade than on the loss of jobs from the treaty. Thus the media reflected the views of businesses over those of workers.[230]

Analysts now suggest that for domestic issues the most significant bias is not liberal or conservative but upper middle class over working class.[231] This bias usually favors the liberal positions on social issues and the conservative, or business, positions on economic issues.[232] It also closely reflects the suburban origins, college education, and social class of most journalists, who are "unlikely to have any idea what it means to go without health insurance, to be unable to locate affordable housing, to have their children in underfunded and dilapidated schools, to have relatives in prison or on the front lines of the military, [or] to face the threat of severe poverty."[233] Thus, "media bias in our country is not to the left or to the right, but to the top."[234]

Foreign issues   The bias in the coverage of foreign issues is quite different from that of domestic issues. The mainstream media toe the government line, at least until it becomes obvious that the official policy isn't working.[235] This is often the conservative position.[236]

During the Cold War, this meant harsh attacks on not only the Soviet Union but also on leftist Latin American regimes.[237] During the Persian Gulf War, this meant jingoistic coverage and unquestioning acceptance of administration claims.[238] Even during the Vietnam War, which is often cited as an example of harsh criticism of governmental policies, the media in fact offered blindly positive coverage for many years and then relatively restrained criticism near the end of the war.[239]

This bias, reflecting governmental policy, was apparent after the 2001 terrorist attacks. The media not only quoted the president and other officials extensively, as would be expected, but also adopted the mindset and language of administration officials. An analysis of the editorials of twenty metropolitan newspapers showed that they echoed the president's rhetoric, magnifying our feelings of fear and portraying a conflict between values decreed by God and evil perpetrated by the terrorists and their supporters. Like the president, the newspapers emphasized urgent action over debate and national unity over dissent.[240] The television networks also followed the administration, featuring patriotic logos and melodramatic music.

Some media went further. Two newspapers fired columnists who criticized the president's delayed return to the Capitol on September 11, and cable systems yanked *Politically Incorrect*, whose host Bill Maher questioned the president's use of the word *cowardly* to refer to the terrorists.[241] CNN's head warned the staff, "If you get on the wrong side of public opinion, you are going to get into trouble."[242] The patriotic fervor diminished media coverage and therefore public awareness of important matters, such as Arab opinion, the conflict between the Israelis and the Palestinians, and the disagreements among the countries fighting terrorism.[243]

This bias was also evident in coverage of the Iraq War. In the runup to the war, the sources cited in television news were overwhelmingly prowar—according to one study, 71 percent were prowar, whereas only 3 percent were antiwar[244]—and the pundits appearing on television talk shows were heavily prowar as well. Although there were snippets of doubt and clips of protests on television newscasts, there was no substantive debate.[245]

The media conveyed, without examination, officials' assertions that there was a link between Saddam Hussein and 9/11. They also conveyed, without examination, officials' assertions that Iraq possessed weapons of mass destruction—biological, chemical, and nuclear weapons. For many people, these became primary justifications for the war. (See the box "What You Watch Affects What You Believe.") Yet no evidence of either claim has been found (at least as of fall 2010).

During the war, the networks used special music, graphics, and promotions to dramatize American patriotism and evoke viewers' emotions. Fox and MSNBC used the administration's moniker for the war, "Operation Iraqi Freedom," and most networks used the administration's term *coalition*

forces, thus endorsing the administration's claim that there was a broad coalition. (In fact, the war was fought by troops from the United States, with some troops from Great Britain, fewer troops from South Korea, Italy, and Poland, and token representation from other countries.) CNN, with audiences around the globe, used two news teams to cover the war. One team, beamed to the United States, was overtly prowar; the other team, beamed to the rest of the world, was more neutral.[246]

Throughout the war, the American media, compared with European and Middle Eastern media, sanitized the combat. They were slow to report negative news[247] and reluctant to depict the blood and gore—the reality of war—in both words and pictures of both Americans and Iraqis.[248] When the behavior by American soldiers at Baghdad's Abu Ghraib prison was disclosed, the worst abuses weren't covered by many news organizations.[249] The media sanitized the coverage because "the dirty little secret of much war 'news' is that much of the audience wants to entrance itself into emotional surrender, and news officials want to elicit

WHAT YOU WATCH AFFECTS WHAT YOU BELIEVE

A majority of Americans have had serious misperceptions about important questions relating to the Iraq War, according to a study based on a series of polls. Respondents were asked whether world public opinion favored the United States going to war, whether there was clear evidence that Saddam Hussein was working with al-Qaeda, and whether weapons of mass destruction were found during the war. (Responses to the second and third questions are shown in Figure 2.) Respondents were asked what their primary source of news is and how often they watch, listen to, or read this source.

Respondents' misperceptions varied according to the media they followed. Those who watched Fox News had the most misperceptions, whereas those who watched public television or listened to public radio had the fewest.[1] The misperceptions were not due to people's paying little attention to the news. Just the opposite: those who watched Fox News more often had more misperceptions than those who watched it less often. Remarkably, as late as 2006, 50 percent of all Americans still believed that Iraq had weapons of mass destruction right before the war,[2] even though none have been found (as of fall 2010).

Not only do these results suggest biased or superficial coverage by some media more than others, but they also have policy implications. Respondents' misperceptions were related to their support for the war, and those with the most misperceptions expressed the most support. Without the public's misperceptions, the Bush administration may not have had enough political support to start or continue the war.

| Figure 2 | Misperceptions and Their Origins |

Primary news source for those who believe:

Since the war ended, the U.S. has found Iraqi weapons of mass destruction

Fox	33%
CBS	23%
NBC	20%
CNN	20%
ABC	19%
Print media	11%
PBS/NPR	17%

U.S. has found clear evidence that Saddam Hussein was working closely with the al-Qaeda terrorist group

Fox	67%
CBS	56%
NBC	49%
CNN	48%
ABC	45%
Print media	40%
PBS/NPR	16%

SOURCE: *Program on International Policy at the University of Maryland and Knowledge Networks. Poll of 3334 adults, conducted January–September 2003, with a margin of error of 1.7 percent (www.knowledgenetworks.com/ganp).*

[1] Researchers tried to control for the possibility that people presort themselves according to ideology by comparing the same demographic groups for each source and also by comparing similar political groups. For example, they compared people who planned to vote for Bush in 2004 and watched Fox News with people who planned to vote for Bush but followed other media.
[2] Charles J. Hanley, "Half of Americans Still Believe WMD Claims, Polls Show," *Lincoln Journal Star,* August 9, 2006, 1A.

precisely that surrender."[250] The media didn't offer grimmer reports and starker photographs until the insurgency and the lack of real security in Iraq became apparent.

For some time, the media were cowed by the power of the administration as well as by the demands of the public. Officials insinuated that any criticism, even questioning, by reporters was unpatriotic. Officials also issued veiled threats to reporters. The White House press secretary remarked, "People had better watch what they say."[251] Another official ominously warned a reporter that his name was on "a list," presumably of disloyal journalists who would be watched and, perhaps, dealt with.[252] The administration also threatened to deny access to reporters who displeased officials. This would mean no interviews, no tips or leaks, no invitations to special events, and no seats on the plane for presidential trips. Because access is all-important, this would make it difficult for reporters to do their jobs. The result was a chilling effect on reporters, editors, and executives.[253] So most media, including supposedly "liberal newspapers" such as the *New York Times* and the *Washington Post*, were little more than stenographers, writing down and passing on administration statements without serious questioning.[254] In the runup to the war, the *Post* had 140 front-page articles making the administration's case for the war and only a handful questioning the administration's claims.[255] Later, the *Post* acknowledged that its reporting before the war and early in the war was "strikingly one-sided at times."[256] (Ironically, Comedy Central's fake newscasts left a more accurate impression than the major networks' newscasts did.)[257]

As the aftermath of the invasion revealed serious flaws in U.S. policy, many media became more critical. The *Times* apologized for its lack of scrutiny and skepticism of administration claims.[258] Its apology prompted a letter to the editor that could have been sent to most American news organizations:

> I've followed all the stories and the "spin" to create a case for war from the beginning. . . . As a university student, I sat through it and asked questions as cabinet members made their case for war. In the sixteen months leading up to my activation to fight in Iraq as a tank platoon commander, I felt that this spin was an effort to find a magic button of support with the citizenry. . . .
>
> So off I went, to lead my men on this quest. We fought and died holding up the soldiers' end of the democratic bargain. I lived with many of the young men fighting and dying who had such blind faith in our system of government. They felt it was just right to do what we were doing, even though many of them could not explain or justify why.
>
> So on this Memorial Day weekend, as I sit and think about what I've done, the people who have been hurt, the future of this ongoing tragedy, I come to this conclusion: Shame on you.[259]

The mainstream media reflect the government line on foreign policy because they rely on government officials as their sources for most news.[260] They fear losing access to these officials. This means that their stories will bear officials' imprint. It also means that their stories will revolve around debates among officials—what "he said" versus what "she said." When there is little dissent within the government, as in the runup to the Iraq War, there is little coverage of opposing views by the media, even if there are alternative views in our society.[261] Journalists seem flummoxed when they can't frame an issue as a debate between opposing groups of officials.

Perceptions of Bias

We've seen that in the mainstream media there is minimal bias in favor of particular candidates or parties in elections, and there is some liberal bias in the coverage of social issues, some conservative bias in the coverage of economic issues, and often conservative bias in the coverage of foreign policy. Overall, however, there is far less political bias than many people believe. In particular, there is far less liberal bias than many conservatives believe.[262] Why do so many people perceive so much bias?

As noted earlier, there is some negative bias against all candidates and officials. People sense this bias against the candidates or officials on their side but don't see it against the candidates or officials on the other side. In addition, people hear aides to the candidates or officials complain about the media without realizing that the aides are simply "working the refs" rather than sincerely lodging a complaint.[263] Also, people hear the steady drumbeat from interest groups and talk shows that the media are biased against their side. Eventually, they come to believe it. They don't realize that the leaders of interest groups and hosts of talk shows are just trying to get people riled up so they will join the group, make a contribution, subscribe to a magazine, or listen to the show. One influential conservative downplayed liberal bias in an interview but at the same time was claiming liberal bias in subscription pitches for his magazine.[264] Karl Rove, President Bush's top aide, also dismissed the idea of liberal bias in the media.[265] Indeed, given the coverage of Clinton's presidency and the coverage of Bush's presidency after the terrorist attacks and during the runup to and the first years of the Iraq War, it's hard to insist that the mainstream media demonstrate a general liberal bias.[266]

Yet many conservatives assume the existence of a pervasive liberal bias by the mainstream media. Studies show that strong partisans with strong views perceive more bias than average people.[267] When strong partisans evaluate stories that are actually balanced, they perceive a bias against their side.[268] Certain that their side is correct, they consider balanced coverage to be biased coverage because it gives their opponents more credence than their opponents deserve.[269] When strong partisans evaluate stories that are clearly biased toward their side, they see no bias or less bias than average people do.[270] They consider this coverage fair, because in their eyes it reports the "truth."

Even if people's perceptions are inaccurate reflections of media coverage, their perceptions determine which newscasts they will watch. As a result of conservatives' criticism

The media frenzy over anthrax prompted some families, like this one in Chicago, to buy gas masks.

over the years, some mainstream media have become cowed. CNN has ordered producers to include more conservatives than liberals in their stories.[271] CBS canned its anchor, Dan Rather, to mollify conservative viewers.[272]

Commercial Bias

Although the public dwells on charges of political bias, **commercial bias** is far more pervasive and important in understanding media coverage of politics. As Ted Koppel, former anchor of ABC's *Nightline*, notes, "The accusation that [the] news has a political agenda misses the point. Right now, the main agenda is to give the people what they want. It is not partisanship but profitability that shapes what you see."[273]

Reasons for Commercial Bias

Traditionally, the mainstream media believed that they had a "public trust" to meet journalistic standards and provide important news. Newspapers made less money than other businesses, and television news divisions lost money every year. When *60 Minutes* first aired, the head of CBS told the creator of the show, "Make us proud."[274] The show became a hit and made so much profit—in its first decade, more than the Chrysler Corporation did during the same years[275]— that the executives started telling the producers, "Make us money!"[276] At the same time, television newscasts became more popular and even profitable. This transformation of the news from an economic backwater to a profit stream has had a huge impact on the major media.

As private businesses (except for public broadcasting), American media are run for a profit. The larger their audience, the more they can charge for their advertising. NBC's news division generates 40 to 50 percent of NBC's overall profit, with its entertainment and sports divisions dividing the rest.[277] Local stations' news programs also provide 40 to 50 percent of the stations' overall profit.[278]

With chains and conglomerates taking over most media, the pressure to make a large profit has escalated. In the 1970s, big-city newspapers expected to make a 7 or 8 percent profit; today, chains and conglomerates expect these papers to make a 20 to 30 percent profit.[279] Corporate executives worry that financial analysts will consider their companies a poor investment and mutual fund managers will refuse to buy or hold their stock if their earnings fall below those available "from investments anywhere else in the financial universe, from a shirt factory in Thailand to the latest Internet start-up."[280]

The pressure to make a profit and the need to attract an audience shape the media's presentation of the news and lead to commercial bias. Sometimes this means that the media deliberately print or broadcast what their advertisers want. CBS bowed to demands by Procter & Gamble that it drop episodes of *Family Law* dealing with gun ownership, capital punishment, interfaith marriage, and abortion.[281] Sometimes the media censor themselves. In 2004, VH1 and MTV pulled clips of, and refused to run ads for, the documentary *Super Size Me*, which shows what happened to a guy who ate every meal at McDonald's for a month. (It wasn't pretty.) They feared losing advertising from fast-food restaurants.[282]

Usually, though, commercial bias means that the media print or broadcast what the public wants, which is to say what the public finds entertaining. This creates a "conflict between being an honest reporter and being a member of show business," a network correspondent confessed, "and that conflict is with me every day."[283] When Dan Rather was asked why CBS devoted time to the demolition of O. J. Simpson's house two years after his trial, Rather answered, "Fear. . . . The fear that if we don't do it, somebody else will, and when they do it, they will get a few more readers, a few more listeners, a few more viewers than we do. The result is the 'Hollywoodization of the news.'"[284]

The dilemma is most marked for television. Many people who watch news on television are not interested in politics; a majority, in fact, say that newscasts devote too much time to politics.[285] Some watch newscasts because they were watching another program before the news, others because they were planning to watch another program after the news. Networks feel pressure "to hook them and keep them."[286] Therefore, networks try to make the everyday world of news seem as exciting as the make-believe world depicted in their entertainment programs. One network instructed its staff, "Every news story should, without any sacrifice of probity or responsibility, display the attributes of fiction, of drama. It should have structure and conflict, problem and denouement, rising action and falling action, a beginning, a middle, and an end."[287] As one executive says, television news is "**infotainment**."[288]

Consequences of Commercial Bias

The media's commercial bias has important consequences. One is to sensationalize the news. The anthrax infections that occurred after the terrorist attacks in 2001 deserved our full attention, but the media would not let up. Even after the initial flurry of reports, they ran one overwrought piece after another. *Time* magazine featured families who bought gas masks. The *Washington Post* wrote that America is "on the verge" of "public hysteria."[289] In fact, few people panicked. In polls, large majorities expressed concern but not fear. Yet the media realized that generating fear would force people to pay attention to the news.

Another consequence of commercial bias is to feature human interest over serious news. In 2005, the three main television networks devoted a total of 84 minutes to Michael Jackson's trial for child molesting but only 18 minutes to the massive genocide in Darfur, Sudan.[290] In 2006, *Time* magazine paid a reported $4 million for photos of Brad Pitt and Angelina Jolie's baby but let go two top-notch investigative reporters because the magazine couldn't afford them any longer.[291] In 2007, according to a search of news sources, 985 articles included the words *Britney* and *underwear*.[292]

The media's tendencies to sensationalize the news and to feature human interest over serious news lead to greater emphasis on scandal, sex, and crime. During President Clinton's terms, the media provided saturation coverage of the Whitewater scandal[293] and various other scandals, although a succession of special prosecutors could find nothing more damning than that the president had lied about having sexual relations with White House intern Monica Lewinsky.[294]

The media plunged into the affair with abandon.[295] The *Los Angeles Times* assigned twenty-six reporters to examine Lewinsky's life, interviewing babysitters and kindergarten classmates.[296] The networks interviewed a person who had eaten lunch with her three years earlier. The public was offered breathless reports about phone sex, the president's cigar as a sex toy, and the intern's dress with a semen stain. There was tittering about the "distinguishing characteristics" of the president's genitals—and speculation about how these would be proved or disproved in court.

Although the national media cover crime extensively, the local media cover it even more fully. Local television news is, in Ralph Nader's words, "something that jerks your head up every ten seconds, whether that is shootings, robberies, sports showdowns, or dramatic weather forecasts."[297] The saying "If it bleeds, it leads" expresses, tongue in cheek, many stations' programming philosophy. Thus crime coverage fills one-third of local newscasts.[298] A week before one presidential election, local stations in Columbus, Ohio, devoted more than twice as much time to various crimes than to the election, although the outcome in the state, and in the nation, was in doubt.[299] One station, however, did find time for an undercover investigation of a topless car wash.

A jaded reporter put it bluntly: "It doesn't matter what kind of swill you set in front of the public. As long as it's got enough sex and violence in it, they'll slurp it up."[300] (Even so, American stations don't go as far as the Bulgarian program *The Naked Truth*, which had women disrobe as they read the news.)

Another consequence of commercial bias is to highlight conflict. Stories about conflict provide drama. Reporters, one admits, are "fight promoters" rather than consensus builders.[301] So reporters frame issues as struggles between opposite camps. After the murderous rampage at Columbine High School in Littleton, Colorado, the media posed the question, Was the incident caused by the availability of guns in our society *or* by the glorification of violence in the media? In this moronic debate, the media prodded people to choose sides, as though the cause had to be one *or* the other rather than a combination of the two or something else entirely.

Sometimes this practice is taken to the extreme. Some stories about Holocaust survivors include bizarre statements by Holocaust deniers, claiming that the Nazis didn't have a plan to exterminate European Jews or that Hitler wasn't aware of it or even that the Germans didn't kill many Jews after all. The stories present these absurd statements as though they constitute an opposing opinion entitled to a public hearing.[302] With their fixation on controversy, the media allow themselves to be manipulated by ignorant or unscrupulous people. In the process, they promote confusion among those people who don't know any better. Most mainstream media gave short shrift to the "Birthers'" claims that Obama was born in Kenya rather than in Hawaii, but CNN allowed commentator Lou Dobbs to give full play, night after night, to the claims.

"Luckily, none of the people inside appear to be celebrities."

© Alex Gregory/The New Yorker Collection/www.cartoonbank.com.

The media's emphasis on conflict sometimes exacerbates the existing disagreements to the point where angry voices drown out rational debate. Never was this more apparent than at the town hall meetings held by members of Congress to discuss health care with their constituents. Charges fueled by cable television and websites, some false and some exaggerated, were shouted so loudly by riled constituents that the members and other attendees were unable to respond. Then media coverage focused on the conflict and on the charges, which were repeated over and over until they were believed by many people. Reform opponents who initially made these charges are media savvy, realizing that sensational charges would command center stage in the debate. Certainly Sarah Palin knew when she claimed that reform proposals would create "death panels," which would deny health care to her son with Down Syndrome, that the media would focus on the existence or nonexistence of "death panels" for months rather than on actual provisions in the bills.[303]

DEMOCRACY?

In highlighting conflict and framing issues as though they are debates between two polar opposites, the media polarize the public. What are the implications for a democracy? What are the consequences for the efforts by politicians and parties to find common ground? To forge compromises?

Commercial bias in the media leads to additional consequences for television specifically. One is to emphasize events, or those parts of events, that have visual interest. The networks have people whose job it is to evaluate all film for visual appeal. Producers seek the events that promise the most action, camera operators shoot the parts of the events with the most action, and editors select the portions of the film with the most action.[304] Television thus focuses on disasters and protests far more than their occurrence justifies, and it displays the interesting surface rather than the underlying substance of these events—for example, the protest rather than the cause of the anger.

Another consequence of commercial bias for television is to cover the news very briefly. A half-hour newscast has only 19 minutes without commercials. In that time, the networks broadcast only a third as many words as the *New York Times* prints on its front page alone. Although cable television has ample time, it follows this format, too, endlessly repeating the same stories without adding new information.[305]

Television stories are short—about 1 minute each—because the networks think viewers' attention spans are short. Indeed, a majority of eighteen- to thirty-four-year-olds with remote controls typically watch more than one show at one time.[306] Therefore, the networks don't allow leaders or experts to explain their thoughts about events or policies. Instead, the networks take sound bites to illustrate what was said. Although their correspondents try to explain the events or policies, they have little time to do so. A correspondent was asked what went through his mind when he signed off each night. "Good night, dear viewer," he said. "I only hope you read the *New York Times* in the morning."[307]

Game orientation   An important consequence of commercial bias, for both print and broadcast media, is to use a **game orientation** in reporting about competing candidates, officials, or parties.[308] The assumption is that politics is a game and politicians, whether candidates campaigning for election or officials performing in office, are the players. The corollary to the assumption is that the players are self-centered and self-interested. They are seeking victory for themselves and defeat for their opponents, and they are relatively unconcerned about the consequences of their proposals or of government's policies. With this orientation, reporters spotlight politicians' strategies and tactics, and they slight the substance and impact of politicians' proposals and policies.

The game orientation appeals to journalists because it generates human interest. It offers new story lines as new information comes to light, much like a board game where "chance" cards inject unexpected scenarios and alter the players' moves and the game's outcomes. This orientation also appeals to journalists because it is easy and relatively free from charges of partisan or ideological bias. (Stories emphasize which contestants are winning, not which ones should win or what consequences might result.) If journalists seriously examined policies and proposals instead of using the game orientation, they would be less able to offer human interest and would be more vulnerable to charges of bias.

The game orientation attracts an audience, but it breeds more cynicism. It creates the impression that politics is just a game, not an essential activity for a democratic society; that politicians are just the players, not our representatives;

that politicians act only in their self-interest, not in the public interest; and that politicians' goal is just to beat others, not to make good public policy.

For elections, the game orientation results in what is called **horse race coverage**, with "front-runners," "dark horses," and "also-rans." Although the race was a staple of journalism even in the nineteenth century,[309] the proportion of election coverage focusing on the race has increased in recent decades.[310]

Today, coverage of the horse race and the related subject of the candidates' strategy and tactics dominate election reporting. In the 2008 presidential campaign, the major networks devoted 55 percent of their coverage to these subjects. Due to the economic collapse, the networks devoted more time to policy debates than usual; even so, this was just 31 percent of their coverage.[311]

The quintessential feature of horse race coverage—reporting of candidates' poll standings—has increased greatly. Not only do the media report the results of polls taken by commercial organizations, but they also conduct polls themselves.[312] Nowadays, coverage of polls takes more space than coverage of candidates' speeches, and it usually appears as the lead or next-to-lead story.[313]

DEMOCRACY?

What are the consequences of the game orientation and horse race coverage for our elections? Do you think that these practices generate more interest and participation in the campaign? Or do you think that they leave the voters less informed and able to cast knowledgeable votes?

Even after elections, the game orientation continues. When President Clinton proposed a plan to overhaul the welfare system, all major newspapers focused on the political implications for his reelection; few even explained the plan, let alone its implications for welfare recipients.[314]

Overall, commercial bias in the media results in no coverage or superficial coverage of many important stories. This, more than any political bias, makes it difficult for citizens, particularly those who rely on television, to become well informed. During the year before the September 11 terrorist attacks, al-Qaeda was mentioned only once on the networks' evening newscasts.[315] However, during this time a report predicting a "catastrophic attack" was issued by a government commission, and a statement warning that Osama bin Laden's network was the "most immediate and serious threat" facing the country was made by the CIA director at a Senate hearing. These dire predictions generated little interest among the media. Following the terrorist attacks and during the first years of the Iraq War, the media did pay more attention to foreign affairs. In recent years, however, the media have scaled back their coverage of foreign affairs, despite two wars—in Iraq and in Afghanistan—the globalization of our economy, and our dependence on foreign oil. A survey of newspaper editors in 2008 found that almost two-thirds of their papers publish less international news than they did three years before.[316] The chief foreign correspondent for CBS, who finds it difficult to get her stories on the air, remarked, "If I were to watch the news that you hear . . . in the United States, I would just blow my brains out because it would drive me nuts."[317]

DEMOCRACY?

This chapter is premised on the assumption that it's important for citizens in a democracy, which entails self-government, to be informed about candidates and issues before voting. Is this assumption, which comes from classical democratic theory, correct in a mass society with different educational levels and individual interests? People aren't required to understand architecture before entering a building or technology before using a computer. Should they be expected to understand, say, the politics of the Middle East before casting a vote? Should they be informed? Why or why not?

CONCLUSION: What Role Do the Media Play?

The media aren't a consistent force for either a small, limited government or a large, activist government. The media's role in promoting one conception over the other varies according to the times and the aggressiveness of various media. By reflecting the novelty and excitement of Obama's candidacy in 2008, the mainstream media were a force for the larger, more active government that Obama champions. By reflecting public anxiety during the recession and conservative opposition to Obama's policies in 2009 and 2010, the conservative media were a force for the smaller, more limited government that conservatives favor.

Regardless of the role they think government should play in society, the media themselves have come to play an enormous role in politics and government. Although the Bill of Rights provides for freedom of the press, which will be covered in Chapter 14, the Founders did not anticipate the media playing a major role. At the time, the only media were newspapers. As the media expanded from newspapers to newsmagazines, to radio, to television, and to the Internet, the media became pervasive in American society and influential in American politics. They came to play a far greater role than the Founders could have imagined.

Sometimes the media are called the "Fourth Estate" or even the "Fourth Branch" of government, because they are powerful enough to check and balance the three branches of government. Today they provide extremely fast and relatively accurate reports of events. They also probe wrongdoing in government and by officials. Thus they serve as a check on government and officials in many situations. As a former government official noted, "Think how much chicanery dies on the drawing board when someone says, 'We'd better not do that; what if the press finds out?'"[318]

This role emerged as a tradition of serious journalism evolved in the nineteenth and twentieth centuries. The practice of objectivity emphasized the publication of facts over opinions, and the concept of editorial independence also took root. These concepts became, essentially, journalists' religion.[319] Newspapers saw themselves as independent of government and officials. The newsroom even came to see itself as independent of the business side of the organization, so reporters usually paid no attention to what the advertisers may have wanted, and independent of the organization's owners, so reporters usually paid no attention to what the owners may have preferred (except when the owners insisted on particular editorial positions or candidate endorsements). With objectivity and independence, journalists took on the jobs of educating the public and keeping the government honest. "This vision of a newspaper, one that prevailed at the highest levels of the craft for decades," according to a veteran reporter at the *Philadelphia Inquirer,* "ensured that the paper was not just a propaganda mill, the house organ of some rich man or political party, but a community of street-smart shoe-leather scholars who worked as the eyes, ears, and conscience of their city."[320]

This tradition was extended from major urban newspapers to small local newspapers all across the country. Then it was extended to major television and radio networks. At these mainstream media, the journalists saw themselves as representatives of the public as well as having responsibilities to the public. So, when officials or citizens got upset with news reports and pointedly asked, "Who elected you?" journalists replied that the people—their readers or listeners or viewers—"elected" them by paying attention to their news columns or newscasts.

But developments in recent decades have shaken the foundations of traditional journalism. The concentration of the media has resulted in the takeover of many news organizations by huge corporations with less respect for the standards of journalism than for the profits they hope to make. In addition, financial pressure is making it hard for news organizations to fulfill their responsibilities.

The atomization of the media—in particular, the development of cable television, the rise of talk radio, and the invention of the Internet—have challenged traditional media. These newer media have often rejected the standards established by the older media and in the process have pulled big chunks of the audience away from the older media.

Although these developments began in the 1980s,[321] they're still playing out. We're seeing a decline in newspapers—some observers already are speaking of "the post-newspaper era"[322]—and a decline in broadcast news. We're seeing a rise in niche media and a role, with huge potential, for Internet websites. Indeed, we're witnessing an information revolution on our doorstep. But we don't know what journalism will look like in the future. Comparing our times with Gutenberg's invention of movable type, one observer said, "We're collectively living through 1500, when it's easier to see what's broken than what will replace it."[323]

The decline of newspapers and the uncertainty about the future of journalism worry professional journalists, who believe that they have a public trust to perform serious journalism. They ask whether the American people who have flocked to the newer media and the fringe media, with their shouting and mudslinging, and their playing fast and loose with the facts, will want serious reporting. They ask whether a new business model will replace the old, shattered model. In particular, they wonder whether in-depth reporting and investigative reporting will continue to exist and whether the media will continue to play the essential role in our democratic government that they have played at least since the Civil War, when the tradition of independent reporting began.

They worry that the American people are paying less attention to the news. (The decreasing number of people who read newspapers is larger than the increasing number who check websites for news.) Although the public is better educated now than in the 1960s, it is less likely to follow the news and less able to answer questions about the government.[324] People under thirty-five especially reflect these trends. To retain their shrinking audience, many newspapers and newscasts have revamped their formats to replace hard news with soft features. If this process continues, it will have disturbing implications. Citizens who are not aware of the news or who do not understand it cannot fulfill their role in a democracy.

The problem is circular, as one political scientist points out:

> Because most members of the public know and care relatively little about government, they neither seek nor understand high-quality political reporting and analysis. With limited demand for first-rate journalism, most news organizations cannot afford to supply it, and because they do not supply it, most Americans have no practical source of the information necessary to become politically sophisticated.[325]

Ultimately, professional journalists fear that the American people may adopt the attitude of politicians such as Andrew Card, President George W. Bush's chief of staff, who rejected the role that the media have come to play. Card asserted that the journalists "don't represent the public any more than other people do" and that news organizations "don't . . . have a check-and-balance function."[326]

KEY TERMS

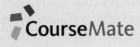 Access an interactive eBook, chapter-specific interactive learning tools (including flashcards, quizzes, videos), and more at CourseMate for *Understanding American Government*. Log in at CengageBrain.com.

6 Interest Groups

Environmental interest groups, objecting to the use of coal, are asking Congress to seek alternative forms of energy.

Barbara L. Salisbury/The Washington Times/Landov

Talking Points

The average American drinks about 530 cans—50 gallons—of sugared beverages a year. That's almost a can and a half per day and a gallon per week of soft drinks.[1] Scientists think this consumption of sugared drinks, new in human history, is partly responsible for the epidemic of childhood and adult obesity and, in turn, the growing rates of diabetes in children and adults. Adults who drink at least a soda (or, as a Midwesterner might say, a "pop") a day are 27 percent more likely than non–soda drinkers to be overweight.[2] Being overweight puts an individual at risk for a variety of serious health issues, including heart disease and strokes as well as diabetes.

For these reasons, many medical professionals, nutrition scientists, and interest groups promoting health and fitness have suggested a modest tax on soft drinks, perhaps a penny an ounce—twelve cents a can. Economists know that taxing a product results in fewer sales of that product. Thus taxing soft drinks would reduce consumption. Some estimates indicate that a tax of a penny an ounce would reduce consumption by about 23 percent. At the same time, it would raise billions of dollars.[3]

Health activists and some members of Congress thought this idea would be a winner in the discussions about health care reform. Not only would it reduce consumption of something detrimental to our health, but it would also produce new funding for preventive medicine initiatives called for in the reform bills. Thus a product that contributes to our health care costs would help pay for some of these costs.

But of course this idea was anathema to the beverage industry, those who manufacture, can, and deliver soft drinks. The decline in consumption foreseen by health advocates as a very good thing was, naturally, seen by soft drink producers as a very bad thing.

So beverage lobbyists got busy. They used several strategies to combat this incipient threat. They enlisted fast-food purveyors, such as McDonald's and Domino's

Pizza, who sell a lot of soda. They enlisted businesses that supply fast-food purveyors, such as paper producers, because these restaurants use huge quantities of paper for their cups of soda. Beverage lobbyists also argued that taxes on soda would lead to taxes on other foods. "It's us today; it's you tomorrow." This argument enabled them to enlist other food manufacturers to fight the tax. Even milk producers joined, fearful that chocolate milk might be taxed as well.

To legitimize their cause in the public eye, the beverage industry created a coalition with a public-spirited name, *Americans against Food Taxes.* And the coalition produced a series of television ads, one showing a woman with a grocery bag fretting, "Families around here are counting pennies to get through this economy. So when we hear about another tax it gets our attention. . . . They say it's only pennies. Well, those pennies add up when you're trying to feed a family."

In the end, the proposal for a beverage tax was dropped, despite the need—almost the desperation—of health care reformers to find ways to finance health care reform. The beverage lobby, with its coalition of other industries, was simply too strong. Members of Congress realized that they would be in trouble with multiple businesses in their district or state if they adopted the tax.

The tanning salon industry, however, isn't as large and powerful as the beverage industry and doesn't have as many allies. When the proposal for a soda tax was dropped, a tax on tanning sessions at tanning salons was suggested instead. Doctors have long criticized tanning salons, saying that the artificial rays in the tanning booths are likely more dangerous than the sun's rays as contributing factors to skin cancer.[4] To the surprise and consternation of the operators of tanning salons, this proposal passed, although it will generate only about $270,000,000 annually, far less than the $5 billion annually that a soda tax would have.

In the United States, everything from fruits to nuts is organized. From apple growers to filbert producers, nearly every interest has an organization to represent it. These organizations touch almost every aspect of our lives; members of the American College of Obstetrics and Gynecology bring us into the world, and members of the National Funeral Directors Association usher us out.

And all of us have lobbyists working for us in some capacity, no matter what our occupation or interest. This includes college students, faculty, and colleges and universities themselves, as well as the men and women who keep the campuses clean, organize athletic events, and build and manage new facilities. Organizations that try to achieve their goals with government assistance are **interest groups**. Fruit and nut growers want government subsidies and protection from imported products; doctors want a rational system for reimbursement of health care costs; funeral directors want limited government regulation and oversight; and, of course, students want low tuition and quality education.

The effort of an interest group to influence government decisions is called **lobbying**. Lobbying may involve direct contact between a **lobbyist**—or consultant or lawyer, as they prefer to be called—and a government official, or it may involve indirect action, such as attempts to sway public opinion, which in turn influences government officials.

People organize and lobby to promote their interests and enhance their influence. "The modern government," one lobbyist observed, "is huge, pervasive, intrusive into everybody's life. If you just let things take their course and don't get involved in the game, you get trampled on."[5] Of course, even if you do have a group working for you, you might get trampled on because not all groups are equally effective.

The Founders feared the harmful effects of interest groups, which they called "factions," but they didn't attempt to limit the opportunity of people to organize and speak out. When the Bill of Rights 🔔 was adopted, the First Amendment protected the right to speak, assemble, and petition the government. James Madison's answer to the **"mischiefs of faction"** was fragmenting government through federalism, separation of powers, and checks and balances (as explained in Chapters 2 and 3). These elements of the Constitution make it difficult for a single group or small part of society to dominate or constantly prevail.

However, Americans today complain about interest groups, calling them "special interests" and insisting that Washington caters to them while ignoring the interests of average men and women. Some analysts agree that the constitutional checks don't prevent "special interests" from manipulating government contrary to the interests of the majority or the society as a whole.[6]

Do interest groups undermine the interests of average men and women? Or, do they enhance their influence, making government more responsive to them by providing a way to participate in the political process? These questions are explored in this chapter.

FORMATION OF INTEREST GROUPS

America is a nation of joiners. As early as the 1830s, the Frenchman Alexis de Tocqueville, who traveled throughout the country, saw the tendency of Americans to form and join groups: "In no country in the world has the principle of association been more successfully used or applied to a greater multitude of objects than in America."[7] Even now, Americans are more likely than citizens of other countries to belong to groups.[8]

Why Interest Groups Form

Groups organize in the United States for a number of reasons. The freedom to speak, assemble, and petition government, guaranteed in the **First Amendment** 🔔, facilitates group formation. Without such freedom, only groups favored by government or those willing to risk punishment for speaking out against government would exist. The federal structure of government—with the national government, fifty state governments, and thousands of local governments—also facilitates group formation. All have significant authority, so groups develop at each level to influence them. Groups also organize because the United States, compared with most countries, is racially, ethnically,

The First Amendment protects interest group speech, even repulsive speech such as this message from a church in Topeka, Kansas, whose members believe that God is punishing Americans for tolerating homosexual behavior.

and religiously diverse. This diversity gives rise to varying interests and conflicting views on public issues and consequently to groups representing them.[9]

In addition to these features, which distinguish the United States from other countries, groups form here and elsewhere because of social changes, economic pressures, technological developments, and government action. When these disturb the status quo, groups form to cope with or benefit from the disturbances. These historical changes come in waves, so the formation of groups occurs in waves too, surging at some times, stable at other times.[10]

Social changes and economic pressures often lead to these surges. In the decades before the Civil War, debates over slavery led to the formation of abolitionist groups and, in response, to proslavery groups. In the decades after the Civil War, rapid industrialization led to the formation of trade unions and business associations. The greatest surge in group formation occurred between 1900 and 1920. Stimulated by the shocks of industrialization, urbanization, and immigration, the United States Chamber of Commerce, American Farm Bureau Federation, National Association for the Advancement of Colored People (NAACP), and countless others formed.[11]

Another great surge occurred in the 1960s and 1970s. The civil rights and antiwar movements created new groups, and their success spurred others representing racial minorities, women, consumers, the poor, the elderly, and the environment. Then the number of business groups surged in reaction to the success of consumer and environmental groups pushing government to regulate business.[12] In the two decades, the number of groups increased by 60 percent, and the number sending lobbyists to Washington doubled.[13]

Technological changes also accelerate group formation. In the 1960s and 1970s, computer-generated direct mail made it easier to recruit members and raise money. In the 1990s, the spread of personal computers and the growth of the Internet facilitated communication among people with an endless variety of narrow interests. The Internet is particularly useful for those wishing to organize citizen groups on a low budget.[14] It is also useful for groups outside the mainstream who wish to operate anonymously. These advantages became even greater in the 2000s when Facebook, YouTube, and other social media made it easy for individuals not just to receive information but also to interact with like-minded others.

Government action can also stimulate group formation. When Congress begins to pay attention to an issue area, interest groups start forming and coming to Washington.[15] When government passes a law, people who are adversely affected organize to get it changed,[16] while other groups spring up to defend it. In 1890, Yosemite National Park was established to preserve a spectacular stretch of the Sierra Nevada Mountains in California. Cattle ranchers, who wanted the land for grazing, proposed that the park be reduced by half. This prompted preservationists to form the **Sierra Club**, today a major

Library of Congress LC-US262-83799

Preservationists formed the Sierra Club to protect the new Yellowstone National Park, which cattle ranchers wanted to reduce by half.

environmental group, to block the ranchers' proposal, which it did. This pattern of action and reaction leads to a continuous expansion of the number of interest groups.

DEMOCRACY?

Should the rights of individuals to form or join interest groups be restricted in a democracy? Should the right of interest groups to lobby be restricted?

Why People Join

Although individuals can enhance their political influence by joining an interest group, many groups find it difficult to attract new members as well as keep the members they have. One reason is that some people lack a sense of **political efficacy**—the belief that they can make a difference. Instead, they feel that "I'm just one person. What can I do?" Even the people who possess a sense of political efficacy may not join because they're unwilling to bear the costs, such as the dues or their time and effort. They assume that the group will succeed without them, so they let others do the work. But they still expect to share the benefits if the group reaches its goal.[17] For example, if a group prods the government to reduce water pollution in a local river or lake, everyone who uses the river or lake, not just the members of the group, will share the benefits of cleaner water. This is called the **free-rider problem**.[18] Why should individuals join the group if they don't have to?

To overcome this natural human resistance, groups offer a variety of benefits—psychological, social, and economic—to attract members. One benefit is the psychological satisfaction that comes from doing good. So groups emphasize the worthiness of their cause and exaggerate the harm that will occur if their cause doesn't prevail. Groups also offer the social sense of belonging that comes from joining fellow citizens who share similar interests. They host meetings, dinners, and other activities to create feelings of solidarity among members. The National Rifle Association (NRA), which lobbies against gun control, provides safety and training classes for new shooters and sponsors competitions for the entire family. Groups also offer economic benefits. AARP, formerly the American Association of Retired Persons, provides discounted drugs; health, home, and auto insurance; a motor club; a travel service; investment counseling; and several magazines. These services lure members and generate millions for the organization.

Some people join groups because they are coerced. In a majority of states, lawyers are required to join the bar association, and employees in certain trades are required to join the labor union.

Which People Join

Although America is a nation of joiners, some are more inclined to do so than others. Those with more education and income are much more likely to belong. They are more interested in the news and government policies, they can afford membership dues, and they have the free time or flexible schedules that allow them to take part and the intellectual ability and social skills that enhance their participation. They also appear more attractive to many groups, and therefore are more apt to be recruited.

Men are somewhat more likely to join than women, and whites are somewhat more likely to join than blacks.[19] The elderly and middle-aged participate at higher rates than the young.

Have People Stopped Joining?

A widely publicized book, *Bowling Alone,* documents the decline in group membership in recent decades.[20] A variety of organizations, from labor unions to churches, PTAs, and bowling leagues, have experienced a decline.

One possible reason is that more families are headed by a single parent or by two parents who work outside the home. Women's lives especially have changed over the past generation, with most women now in the paid workforce while still carrying the largest share of household and child-raising activities. Women used to be the backbone of many local educational, religious, civic, and political groups, but they have far less time and energy to devote to these volunteer activities today than women did in the 1950s and 1960s. The entrance of women into the workforce also means that many men do more around the house and with their children than their fathers did. This too decreases the time and energy available for organized groups.

At the same time, technology, from television to computers, has enabled us to create little islands of our own at our homes; we don't need to join others in person for entertainment. Figuratively speaking, we still bowl, but we bowl alone or we bowl virtually.

However, at the same time that formal membership in interest groups has decreased, membership in issue advocacy groups is increasing.[21] These groups solicit "members" who "join" by donating money—writing an occasional check to support the organization's leaders and activities.[22] These **checkbook members** contribute to the cause but don't interact, face to face, as members of the group.

Individuals can also be virtual members of groups. They can learn about the activities of a group on the Web and offer their comments. Or they can be virtual participants in groups using social media, sharing their views in blogs or on Twitter, or joining a group on Facebook, for example. Facebook continually promotes the formation of new groups. After the BP oil spill in the Gulf, a "Boycott BP" group sprang up on Facebook and had over 800,000 "members" a few months later. But the life span of such groups is likely to be short.

Despite the ability of the Internet to help people find like-minded people all over the world, technology doesn't yet offer an effective way to reach workable compromises on difficult issues. Moreover, Web discussions can be abusive and divisive because anonymity loosens restraints on behavior. If you don't have to interact on a personal basis with others, you don't have the same incentive to compromise or even to agree to disagree.

DEMOCRACY?

What implications does the decline in traditional face-to-face groups have for democracy? Consider the roles that interest groups play in representing people, fostering discussions, fashioning compromises, and forging relationships and trust among citizens. Also consider the ways that interest groups conduct their meetings, elect their officers, and decide their positions on issues. How do these procedures reinforce democracy? Do virtual groups fulfill the same functions in a democracy?

TYPES OF INTEREST GROUPS

Interest groups come in various sizes and configurations. Some have large memberships, such as the American Federation of Labor–Congress of Industrial Organizations (AFL-CIO), a labor union with 9 million members. Others have small memberships, such as the Mushroom Growers Association with only fourteen members. Some have no members at all. Corporations, which act as interest groups when they lobby government,[23] have managers and stockholders but no members.

Some interest groups are formally organized, with elected or appointed leaders, dues-paying members, regular meetings, and established bylaws. Others are loose-knit, with no leaders and few rules.

Thus, interest groups can be distinguished according to their membership and their organizational structure. They can also be distinguished by their goals, as explained below.

Private Interest Groups

Private interest groups seek economic benefits for their members or clients. Examples include business, labor, and agriculture groups.

Business

Business organizations are the most numerous and, in the aggregate, the most powerful interest groups in Washington. Much of politics is essentially the interaction between business and government.[24] Businesses seek to maximize profit, whereas government, at least sometimes, works to protect workers and consumers from the unfettered effects of profit-seeking businesses through regulation of employees' wages and working conditions, product safety, environmental damage, and monopolistic practices. Thus business groups often oppose government regulation. (See Figure 1.)

Today, however, there is less confrontation between business and government than in the past. The Republican Party has long favored business, and since the 1990s the Democratic Party, anxious to compete for campaign contributions, has often favored business too.[25] In a capitalist economy, there are powerful incentives and pressures for politicians of all political persuasions to accede to, rather than antagonize, business, which is so important to the nation's economic success.[26] If the economy falters, politicians get blamed. So business usually does well regardless of which party occupies the White House or dominates Congress.

Lobbying by the pharmaceutical industry, one of the most powerful in Washington, illustrates the influence of business. Well financed, the industry spent $188 million in 2009 in lobbying activities and campaign contributions and employed more than 1000 lobbyists. During the first years of the twenty-first century, with Republican domination of the federal government, the industry supported Republican candidates and officeholders two to one.[27] In 2007, with a Democratic-controlled Congress, the industry split its contributions equally in an attempt to purchase the sympathy of, and access to, Democrats while maintaining the support of Republicans,[28] and since 2008, it has given a slight majority of its funding to Democrats. This pragmatic strategy is typical of big lobby groups, which typically give more to the majority party, though business always gives significant support to Republicans even when they are out of power.

The pharmaceutical industry had done very well during George W. Bush's presidency. A big victory came with passage of the Medicare prescription drug bill, which subsidizes prescription drugs for senior citizens.[29] The law not only guarantees huge sales for the companies, but it also includes restrictions that enhance their profits. It forbids the government from negotiating with drug companies for lower prices, and it forbids the reimporting of drugs manufactured in the United States but sold overseas for less than they are here. The prescription drug program provides billions in profits for the industry but costs the taxpayers more than it would without these restrictions.

We might expect Big Pharma (as it is sometimes called), representing corporate America, to be an opponent of government regulations and programs, and in the past the lobby had been an opponent of health care reform. But once Obama was elected, Big Pharma pursued a pragmatic course during the fight for health care reform, signing up early in support of Obama's reform plan while continuing to press its own interests. It spent millions of dollars for advertising to support health care reform, providing a significant boost for the administration but in exchange extracting important concessions.

By allying itself with the Obama administration in the health care reform fight, Big Pharma was able to protect the gains it had won in the prescription drug program during the Bush administration. The health care reform law continues to forbid government negotiation with drug companies for lower prices and and to forbid the reimportation of drugs. The lobby was also able to get twelve-year protection for new high-tech drugs so that these drugs would not have to compete with cheaper generic drugs. On the other hand, pharmaceutical companies will have to provide substantial discounts to Medicare patients and will pay additional taxes to support the reform plan. Overall, they were one of the winners in the health care law stakes. They will have millions of new customers, as those currently without health insurance will now be insured and able to buy prescription medicine as needed.

Given their political clout and pragmatic approach to politics, it is no surprise that the drug companies are the most profitable of the largest corporations in America, with about $200 billion in annual profits from "take-home" prescriptions (not even counting drugs administered in hospitals, doctors' offices, or nursing homes).[30]

The example of Big Pharma may convey the impression that large interest groups present a united front, but in fact many have internal battles. (See box "Groups Have Internal Battles Too.")

"You can't please all the people all the time, so you might as well please the pharmaceutical lobby."

© The New Yorker Collection 2006, Barbara Smaller from cartoonbank.com. All Rights Reserved.

Figure 1 Ideologically Aligned Industries

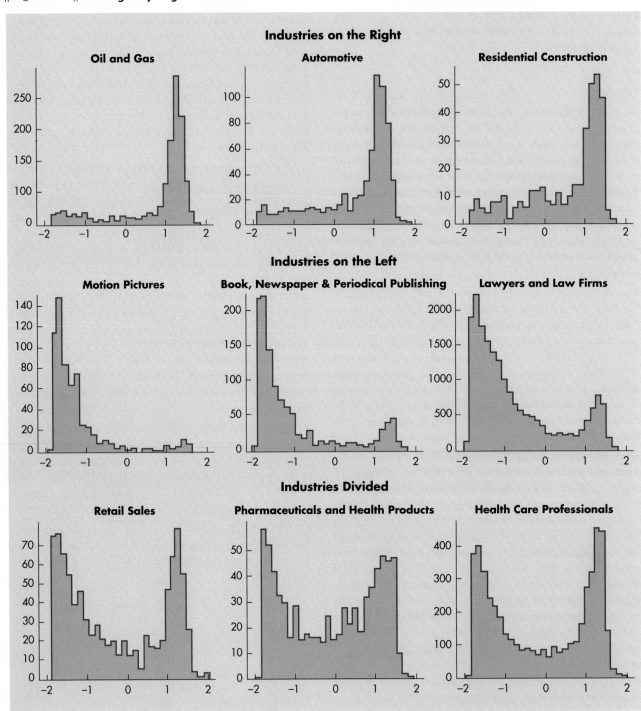

Although business, in general, tends to sit on the right end of the ideological spectrum, some industries are on the left and other industries are split. (The legal and health care professions aren't usually included in the "business" category but are included in this figure for comparison.)
SOURCE: *The graphs were derived from campaign contributions in the 2008 elections. Adam Bonica, "Ideologically Aligned and Ideologically Divided Industries," http://ideologicalcartography.com/2010/02/27/which-industries-are-polarized-and-which-are-just-polarizing/.*

Labor

Labor unions seek government policies that protect workers' jobs, wages, and benefits and ensure the safety of workplaces. They also have been part of a liberal coalition that has fought for civil rights, health care, and environmental protection in recent decades. Unions channel money to political candidates, chiefly Democrats, though far less than businesses funnel to Republicans. In addition to money, they rely on their membership to distribute campaign literature, man phone banks, and canvass door-to-door to get out the vote.

behind the scenes

Groups Have Internal Battles Too

Interest group leaders often have the challenge of keeping their membership together. Members might agree on the overarching goal of the organization but differ on strategies to accomplish the goal or on secondary goals. Most groups do not have democratic processes to make decisions about the positions the organization should take. Instead, the decisions are made by paid operatives in Washington, sometimes with input from a board of directors, but usually based on their knowledge of the organization. Most of the time, these decisions are supported by the membership, but sometimes such decisions backfire, bringing embarrassment to the organization.

The U.S. Chamber of Commerce, an important element in the business lobby that claims to represent 3 million businesses, recently had such a situation. With 300,000 actual dues-paying members, a $200 million lobbying budget, and a strong grassroots network, the Chamber is a significant voice for American business. And its big voice usually articulates the conservative perspective. The Chamber consistently fights labor law reform, consumer protection, financial regulation, and taxes. It also fought the health care reform bill.

With a group as large and diverse as the American business community, divisions are bound to emerge. A significant cleavage in the Chamber on some issues is the fact that, though most of its members are small businesses, many large corporations also belong, and their interests are not always the same. For example, although most owners of small businesses did not favor the Obama health care reform package (though we don't really know for sure the proportions who did and didn't), many large corporations did favor health care reform because the cost of providing health insurance to their workers was choking their profits. For example, on a per car basis, GM spent more on health insurance for its workers than on the steel to make the car. And other elements of the business community, such as big pharmaceutical manufacturers, also supported health care reform for their own reasons.

Another recent issue on which Chamber members disagree is climate policy. Conservatives have consistently opposed taxing carbon emissions (see Chapter 18), and so did the Chamber. But some major corporations have different views of climate change. In fact, several members of the Chamber's board of directors support the cap and trade plan that would allow companies to buy rights to emit noxious substances by paying a tax. But other members of the board, including executives of coal companies that would be hard hit by such a tax, adamantly oppose it. So the Chamber took a public position opposing cap and trade.

Failing to make their point within the Chamber, several corporate supporters of cap and trade, including Apple, Exelon, and Pacific Gas and Electric, withdrew from the Chamber in protest over its stance. Nike withdrew from its board of directors.[1]

The Chamber's spokesman accused these corporations of participating in a publicity stunt orchestrated by environmentalists. But in the aftermath of the defections, the Chamber lost some of its positive image. It was forced to admit that the 3 million businesses it claimed to represent were mostly members of local chambers, some of whom do not agree with the national Chamber.[2] And President Obama snubbed the Chamber by beginning discussions with the Business Roundtable, a smaller organization that represents many large corporations. Of course, the Chamber will survive and will be brought into discussions of other issues, but it may have to reevaluate its consistent antigovernment message.

[1] "The Financial Page: Exit through the Lobby," *New Yorker*, October, 19, 2009, 32.
[2] Steven Pearlstein, "Chamber Reaping the Whirlwind," *Lincoln Journal Star*, October 19, 2009, B4. Originally published in the *Washington Post*. See also Tom Hamburger and Alexander C. Hart, "White House Confronts the U.S. Chamber of Commerce," *Los Angeles Times*, October 25, 2009, latimes.com/news/nationworld/nation/la-na-chamber25-2009oct25,0,2759556.story.

Winning the right to unionize was a bitter struggle in the late 1800s and early 1900s. Before federal legislation gave workers the right to organize, companies often brought in strikebreakers—men and women willing to cross a picket line of striking workers and work for whatever the company would pay. Striking workers were often attacked by police or thugs hired by owners. Many large companies had a more potent arsenal than local police forces. In these confrontations, hundreds or thousands of workers were killed, but brutal incidents shocked the nation and led to the legislation that guaranteed the right to organize.

However, after unions boosted workers' standard of living in the 1950s and 1960s, they came to seem less important. And as manufacturing jobs, which had been the backbone of union strength, dwindled in the 1970s, union membership declined. From 35 percent of the workforce in 1955, their membership dropped to 20 percent in 1983 and to only 7 percent today (see Figure 2).[31] With the decline in membership came a decline in political clout.[32]

Because of strong antiunion sentiment in parts of the United States, particularly in the South and Southwest, 84 percent of union members are located in just twelve states.[33] This concentration limits their ability to influence the national government. Members of Congress generally reflect their constituents' opinions but are less sensitive to any groups located in other states.

Although unions have gained new members by organizing teachers and government workers, they have not had the political power to overcome the antiunion efforts of businesses, which have been tolerated by government. If a company negotiates in bad faith, it is simply told to negotiate in good faith. If a company illegally undermines unionizing campaigns by firing workers or shutting down facilities, or threatening to do so, it typically faces minimal penalties (for example, posting a notice promising not to do so in the future). If workers are fired illegally and win their case, they receive back pay but no other compensation to deter the companies in the future. As one observer said, businesses' strong-arm tactics to thwart unionization make elections that determine whether employees want a union often "as fair as elections in Cuba or China."[34] Thus business holds most of the power in the relationship, and conservative-dominated Congresses have not tried to redress this imbalance. The more recent Democratic-controlled congresses have introduced legislation to strengthen existing laws and increase the penalties for companies violating them, but the legislation has failed. In 2010 a bill passed the House but was filibustered to death in the Senate.[35]

Wal-Mart is an example. Unions have charged Wal-Mart with preventing its workers from organizing to boost their wages and improve their benefits. (Most Wal-Mart employees don't make minimum wage and don't have health insurance—until the health care reform law kicks in.) When meat cutters at a Wal-Mart in Texas organized, executives shut down the meat counters in the Wal-Marts throughout Texas and five neighboring states.[36] As the largest private employer in the United States, Wal-Mart sets the standard for other large retailers. To compete with Wal-Mart, they also keep workers' wages and benefits low and obstruct workers' right to unionize.[37] An exception is Costco, which pays its workers 70 percent more than Wal-Mart workers and makes up the difference by the lower turnover and lower levels of employee theft.[38] (In 2010, however, Wal-Mart did support health care reform requiring large employers to buy health insurance for their employees.)

Unions have also been hurt by global competition and government's unwillingness to protect American workers threatened by this competition. Fearful of losing their jobs or putting their employers at a disadvantage in a competitive market, workers are reluctant to strike. Without the threat of a strike, there is little reason to heed workers' demands.

Union workers make about 30 percent more money than nonunionized workers and are much more likely to have paid vacations, health insurance, and pensions.[39] The decline of unions has led to lowered wages—directly because strong unions gain higher wages for their workers and indirectly because higher wages for their workers pressure nonunion employers to pay higher wages to nonunion workers as well. The decline in unions has also blunted the liberal thrust of American politics because unions lobby not only for workers' rights but also for other progressive policies, such as government-funded health care.

Teachers' unions are one of the most successful unions and one of the most loyal constituencies of the Democratic Party. These unions comprise about one-fourth of all unions, and together they contribute more money, mostly to Democratic candidates, than any union representing another industry.[40] Yet President Obama disappointed many of these union members with his school reform proposals, including charter schools and merit-based pay, which teachers' unions opposed.

In an effort to expand membership in recent years, unions have reached out to low-wage service workers, such as hotel maids and nursing home employees, and to some non-blue-collar workers, such as computer specialists in Silicon Valley[41] (and even to graduate teaching assistants at some major universities—another group of low-wage service workers!).[42]

Nonetheless, labor still lags far behind business in ability to influence government.

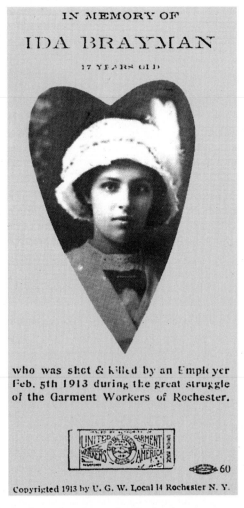

IN MEMORY OF

IDA BRAYMAN

17 YEARS OLD

who was shot & killed by an Employer Feb. 5th 1913 during the great struggle of the Garment Workers of Rochester.

60

Copyrigted 1913 by U. G. W. Local 14 Rochester N. Y.

This postcard commemorates the death of a seventeen-year-old woman murdered while striking for recognition of her union, an eight-hour day, and extra pay for overtime and holidays.

| Figure 2 | Union Membership in the United States |

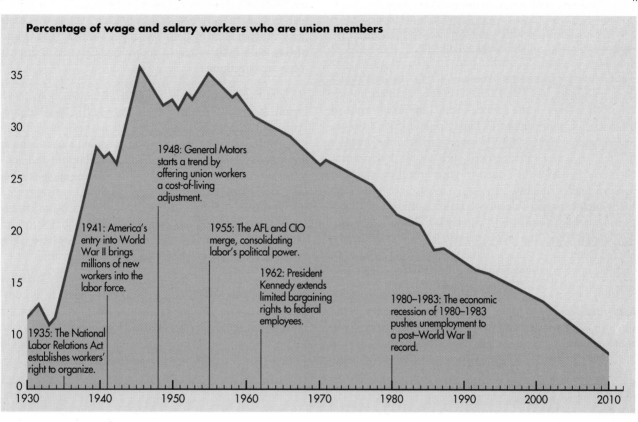

Percentage of wage and salary workers who are union members

1948: General Motors starts a trend by offering union workers a cost-of-living adjustment.

1941: America's entry into World War II brings millions of new workers into the labor force.

1955: The AFL and CIO merge, consolidating labor's political power.

1962: President Kennedy extends limited bargaining rights to federal employees.

1980–1983: The economic recession of 1980–1983 pushes unemployment to a post–World War II record.

1935: The National Labor Relations Act establishes workers' right to organize.

SOURCE: *U.S. Census Bureau, Statistical Abstract of the United States, online at www.census.gov/prod/www/statistical-abstract-02.html.*

Agriculture

Agricultural organizations are important in agricultural policy making. Large groups address general farm policy, and hundreds of commodity organizations, representing commodities such as cattle, milk, tobacco, cotton, and wool, promote particular products. Large agribusiness firms such as Cargill and Archer-Daniels-Midland also have influential lobbies in Washington.

Because American agriculture is dominated by agribusiness and large corporate farms, agriculture groups are dominated by these interests today. Although lobbyists invoke the small farmer and the family farm in their public appeals—they talk about the need to "save" the family farmer—they ask Congress for subsidies that go primarily to large corporate enterprises. Government spends more than $20 billion subsidizing crop production, or in some situations nonproduction, and most of this money goes to the largest and wealthiest—usually the corporate—farms.[43]

Public Interest Groups

While nearly all groups, even private groups that seek their own financial gain, think of themselves as pursuing the "public" interest, **public interest groups** are those that work for a cause that extends beyond the members of the

group. Amnesty International lobbies for the rights of political prisoners around the world even though its members aren't prisoners. The National Taxpayers Union lobbies for reduced taxes; although its members will receive lower taxes if it succeeds, other taxpayers will too.

The term *public interest* doesn't mean that a majority of the public favors the goals of these groups or that their goals are good for all or even most people. Both pro-choice and pro-life groups in the abortion debate are public interest groups, even though members of each side don't believe for a minute that members of the other are working in the public interest.

Public interest groups increased dramatically during the 1960s and 1970s.[44] The various groups founded by Ralph Nader and committed to the safety of consumer products reflect this trend. Today there are at least 2500 public interest groups with 40 million members.[45]

Multiple-Issue Groups

Public interest groups can be classified as multiple- or single-issue groups. Multiple-issue groups address a range of issues.

Racial and ethnic groups Organizations promoting the interests of racial and ethnic minorities are multiple-issue groups because they address a variety of issues of concern to racial and ethnic minorities. Chapter 15 discusses these organizations and their role in the civil rights movement.

Women's groups   Groups advocating women's equality range from large, mass-based organizations interested in a number of issues to smaller ones focused on a few. The National Organization for Women (NOW), the largest and most prominent, has 250,000 members and chapters in each state.[46] It lobbies at the national, state, and local levels in a number of policy areas, including reproductive freedom and economic rights. NOW's success spurred the creation of smaller, conservative groups such as the Independent Women's Forum, which opposes government programs to achieve gender equality.[47] By far the most successful group lobbying for women's election to national office is EMILY's List—*EMILY* stands for Early Money Is Like Yeast (it makes the "dough" rise). The group recruits, trains, and funds pro-choice Democratic women to run for public office. Pro-life and Republican groups promoting women candidates also exist, but none is nearly as successful.[48]

Gay and lesbian groups   Organizations promoting the interests of gays and lesbians fight for equal rights and more recently for same-sex marriage. The Lambda Defense Fund represents gay and lesbian students who have been discriminated against or harassed in school, and it educates teachers, administrators, and legislators about the challenges encountered by these students. (The box "The Origin of Gay and Lesbian Rights Groups" and Chapter 14 discuss these organizations.)

Religious groups   Many religious denominations have organizations representing their interests in Washington. Protestant groups are found on the left and right as well as in the middle and speak out on a wide range of issues. Catholic groups have long been active in the antiabortion and anti-nuclear movements and have recently become outspoken on the immigration issue. Jewish groups have long supported liberal causes and stressed Israel's security. Muslim groups lobby for Palestinian rights and favorable policies toward Muslim countries. In the aftermath of 9/11, they have taken up the cause of fair treatment for American Muslims.[49]

Evangelical Protestant denominations—the **Christian right** (sometimes called the "religious right" to encompass conservative Jewish groups as well)—have been the most potent religious force in American politics.[50] Until the 1960s, evangelical Protestants believed that they should

american diversity

The Origin of Gay and Lesbian Rights Groups

In the 1950s, homosexuals usually kept their sexual orientation private. When their orientation did receive public attention, homosexuals were characterized as deviates and subjected to humiliation. They were often fired (as they still can be in many places).

Consequently, gays and lesbians, especially those who hung out together, were vulnerable to blackmail and police harassment. Following a raid on a gay bar in 1954, a Miami newspaper headlined its story "Perverts Seized in Bar Raid." A decade later, New York's liquor authority declared that a meeting of three or more homosexuals in a bar was reason enough for the bar to lose its license.[1] Through the 1960s, police entrapment of homosexuals, with plainclothes officers patronizing gay bars and waiting for a proposition, was common.

The first national group organized to speak for homosexuals was the Mattachine Society, founded in 1950 to raise political consciousness among gays and to fight the persecution of gays that came with the anticommunist blacklisting in that decade.[2] But the Mattachine Society had branches in only a few cities, and the organization declined when it was revealed that some of its leaders were communists.

The modern gay rights movement began when police raided a seedy bar, the Stonewall, in New York's Greenwich Village, in 1969. Run by the Mafia, the bar operated without a liquor license and served as a dope hangout. It was a popular meeting place for a diverse group of gay men, "including drag queens, hippies, street people, and uptown boys slumming."[3] That summer the city's police were cracking down on illegal bars, especially those frequented by gay men, Latinos, and blacks. Several gay bars had already been raided without incident before the Stonewall, but each raid heightened the anger and desperation in the gay community.

A small police unit entered the Stonewall at 3 a.m. The employees were arrested for selling liquor without a license, and the customers were lined up and forced to show identification. The transvestites were separated for a "sex check." When a police van arrived to take away the arrested employees and transvestites, the crowd grew hostile and began to throw things—first coins, then cans and bottles, and even an uprooted parking meter. The police took refuge in the club, but the increasingly angry crowd pressed to break in, and the police drew their weapons. Soon lighter fluid and a match were thrown inside the building and a fire was not involve themselves in secular government. But in the late 1960s, they came together as a movement to protest the Internal Revenue Service's removal of tax-exempt status for Bob Jones University in North Carolina due to its racial discrimination.[51] After this foray into national politics, the Christian right became intensely involved in the hot-button issues of school prayer, abortion, and homosexuality and the related issues of divorce, birth control, and women's rights. The movement opposes the teaching of evolution and restrictions on religious symbols and practices in public schools and buildings. In general, it wants government's laws and policies to be based on Christian principles and to be acknowledged as such. It pushes its agenda through religious schools; religious media, including newspapers, magazines, radio, and television; and thousands of politically mobilized churches.[52]

The Christian Coalition, a prominent group within the Christian right, was established in the 1980s by television evangelist Pat Robertson, who sought the Republican presidential nomination in 1988.[53] The coalition is heavily involved in politics and closely linked to the Republican Party. In the early 1990s, its members were a majority in many Republican state and local party organizations.[54]

The Christian right urged the resignation or impeachment of President Clinton after his affair with Monica Lewinsky was revealed.[55] The movement also helped deliver the presidential nomination to George W. Bush in 2000 by mobilizing its followers against Bush's rival, Sen. John McCain (R-Ariz.). Then it helped deliver the presidential election to Bush in 2000 and again in 2004. With the election of Bush, the Christian right gained visibility and power in the highest reaches of government. Their leaders, emboldened by having conservative Republicans in control of all three branches of the federal government, flexed their muscles.

But the harder they pushed, the greater the backlash from moderate Americans.[56] Since the 2004 election, the power of the religious right has waned. Robertson and fellow television preacher Jerry Falwell, founder of the now defunct Moral Majority, didn't help their cause by making outrageous statements (for which they later apologized). Falwell proclaimed that AIDS reflected "the wrath of a just God against homosexuals"[57] and that the 9/11 attacks reflected God's judgment of "the pagans, and the abortionists, and the feminists, and the gays and lesbians."[58]

started, although casualties were averted when police reinforcements arrived. The crowd, feeling empowered by its attempt to fight back, moved down the street shouting "gay power" and celebrating newfound strength and solidarity.

After the unrest ended, gays' sense of injustice and pride from the protests were transformed into an organization, the Gay Liberation Front. Its founders were determined to use radical means to fight discrimination against homosexuals. Not long after, moderate gays and lesbians broke from the Gay Liberation Front to form the Gay Activist Alliance. Later, other groups evolved that used mainstream politics and legal challenges to support the cause. By the early 1970s, gay pride parades, usually held in late June to commemorate the anniversary of the Stonewall raid, were common in major cities.

"We're not doing anything for Gay Pride this year. We're here, we're queer, we're used to it."

© The New Yorker Collection 2001. William Haefeli from cartoonbank.com. All rights reserved.

Changes in the status of homosexuals soon followed. In 1973, the American Psychiatric Association removed homosexuality from its list of mental disorders. In the 1980s, the AIDS tragedy focused media attention on the gay community and brought public awareness to the discrimination issue. Entertainers and celebrities who acknowledged their homosexuality, including some who suffered from AIDS, raised public consciousness. As more homosexuals "came out of the closet," they received more support from straight people.

[1] Robert Amsel, "Back to Our Future? A Walk on the Wild Side of Stonewall," www.gayastrology.com/stonewall.shtml (excerpted from Advocate, September 19, 1987).
[2] The source for much of this discussion is Eric Marcus, Making History: The Struggle for Gay and Lesbian Equal Rights, 1945–1990 (New York: HarperCollins, 1992); see also Jeffrey Schmalz, "Gay Politics Goes Mainstream," New York Times Magazine, October 11, 1992, 18ff.
[3] Amsel, "Back to Our Future?"

The resistance was especially evident in 2005 after the strident attempts to use Terri Schiavo's case as a rallying cry. Schiavo, who was forty-one years old, had been kept alive by a feeding tube in a persistent vegetative state for fifteen years. Her husband petitioned to remove the tube, but her parents resisted. After nineteen Florida courts heard the case, and all three levels of the federal courts, including the Supreme Court, refused to intervene, the result was a court order to disconnect the tube. Conservative Christian groups, seeing a connection to their pro-life movement, made the case a cause célèbre, pressuring Florida officials and then Congress to intervene and overturn the court rulings. Congress urged federal courts to hear the case, and President Bush interrupted a break at his ranch to return to the capital to sign the bill. The courts, however, rejected the plea. So did 70 percent of the public.[59] In an effort to rally the movement, religious and Republican leaders alienated moderate Americans.

Some in the movement have become disillusioned because political activity has produced so little. Although their support has helped the Republicans control the presidency or Congress for much of the past quarter century, their electoral successes haven't led to many policy achievements. Gay marriage has been defeated at the ballot box in many states, but the idea of gay rights and a tolerance of gay lifestyles have become more accepted throughout the country. The movement hasn't succeeded in eliminating abortion, reinstating school prayers, or reshaping school curricula to teach creationism or intelligent design along with evolution. Some evangelical Christians, who constituted the majority of the religious right, feel used by the Republican Party—useful as loyal foot soldiers when it's time to march to the polls, but ignored when the GOP's bigwigs set the party's agenda and priorities.[60]

At the same time, some evangelicals have edged to the left on some issues. Now a majority express more interest in protecting the environment, alleviating poverty, tackling AIDS, and promoting human rights and less interest in addressing abortion and homosexuality than in the past. A third even say that Christian political activism has hurt Christianity.[61]

Moderate and liberal religious groups have also called for more attention to the plight of the poor.[62] These groups put greater weight on the Christian message of helping the less fortunate than on the social issues that have been so important to the religious right.[63]

Environmental groups   Earth Day 1970 marked the beginning of the environmental movement in the United States. Spurred by an oil spill in California, a "teach-in" on college campuses became a day of environmental awareness for millions of Americans nationwide. A minority movement in the 1970s, the environmental lobby today is large and active, and its values are supported by most Americans.[64]

Some environmental groups, such as the Sierra Club, National Audubon Society, and Natural Resources Defense Council, have permanent offices in Washington staffed with skilled professionals.[65] Other groups, such as Greenpeace, Earth First!, and Sea Shepherds, which seek a green cultural revolution, shun conventional lobbying in favor of confrontation. They are less willing to compromise with businesses and polluters.

Environmental groups were on the defensive during the administration of George W. Bush. Conservative Republicans often opposed environmental regulations, arguing that businesses should be allowed to regulate themselves. In response to the demands of its business allies, the administration rolled back environmental regulations adopted by the Clinton administration.[66] But heightened public concern about global climate change, the BP oil spill, and the rising price of oil have increased the salience of environmental issues, though it has not led to new, broad, public policies favored by environmentalists.

Single-Issue Groups

Public interest groups include single-issue groups as well as multiple-issue groups. **Single-issue groups** are distinguished by their intense concern for a single issue. Their zeal makes these groups reluctant to compromise.

The National Rifle Association (NRA) is an example. Its members are passionate in their opposition to gun control. They live in every congressional district, and they can be mobilized to contact their representatives in Congress. Although a majority of Americans have supported gun control for many years, the NRA has prevented Congress from passing most gun control proposals. And it has prevented the Treasury Department's Bureau of Alcohol, Tobacco, and Firearms from strictly enforcing the gun control laws that are on the books.[67]

The NRA campaigned for the election of George W. Bush, with a high-ranking official boasting that a Bush win would mean direct access to the Oval Office.[68] Indeed, the Bush administration was a close ally. Reversing sixty years of government policy, the administration adopted the position that the Second Amendment protects a right for individuals to keep and bear arms rather than the right of government to arm a militia to maintain domestic security.[69] (The Supreme Court, with Bush's appointees providing the votes to form a majority, agreed with the administration in 2008.[70]) The administration and congressional allies of the NRA also blocked the renewal of the ban on assault weapons and semiautomatic rifles.

The NRA has been so successful that some politicians, especially in "red" states, which are inclined to support gun control measures, have concluded that the risks to their election or reelection are so great and the probability of passing gun control measures is so small that it's prudent to go along with the NRA. It was an indication of the NRA's influence that after the Virginia Tech shootings in 2007 there were few calls in Congress for new gun control laws.

Yet the NRA may be shifting its focus. In recent years, the organization has become increasingly worried about the shrinking wildlife habitat available for hunting and fishing, as continued development near big cities has transformed fields

behind the scenes

The UFO Lobby

Not all lobbying efforts are visible to the public. Nor do all lobbyists represent well-financed corporations or interest groups. Individuals who believe that the government is hiding the facts about UFOs from the public have formed the Extraterrestrial Phenomena Political Action Committee (X-PPAC). The committee hired a professional lobbyist and is on the official list of groups who contribute funds to political campaigns. Even so, the group flies under the radar in Washington's lobbying universe.

Although the group has few dues-paying members or contributors, it actually represents more people than many lobbying groups do. About one-third of Americans believe that extraterrestrial beings have landed on earth, and a significant part of them believe that government is covering up its knowledge of extraterrestrial landings.

Despite this large potential constituency, the lobbyist for the group has a challenge that other lobbyists don't face. Most members of Congress are afraid to be seen with him, let alone speak publicly on the issue. So, his main strategy is to bombard members with alerts about extraterrestrial activity. The group's Facebook page has more than 1000 members, and his aim is to generate a million faxes to members of Congress.

The group's major objective is to get the government to disclose its files of purported UFO sightings and landings. The group's members believe, like every other group's members, that their objective is in the national interest. Their lobbyist has hope for the Obama administration, with its expressed philosophy of more open government.

Drawn from: Daniel Fromson, "Disclosed Encounters," *Washington Monthly*, January–February 2010, 24–25. X-PPAC's web page is www.x-ppac.org.

and streams and as the Bush administration's energy policies have opened more federal land for oil and gas drilling. Some members now consider the dwindling habitat a greater threat to hunting and fishing than gun control legislation, and they have pressured leaders to address this concern.[71] (For another single-issue group, see the box "The UFO Lobby.")

The **pro-life** and **pro-choice groups** in the abortion debate are other examples of single-issue groups. Pro-life groups, such as the National Right to Life Committee, want a constitutional amendment banning all abortions. Because this is unlikely, they have pushed for federal and state laws restricting the availability of abortions, such as laws requiring waiting periods and parental notification or consent for minors. In some states they have pushed for extra-stringent building codes or staffing requirements for clinics. The goal is to make abortions more difficult for the woman, the doctor, and the clinic.[72] Like the Christian right, from which it draws members, the pro-life movement is closely allied with the Republican Party. In 2004, it got the Republican-controlled Congress to forbid the late-term abortions ("intact dilation and extraction") called "partial birth abortions" by the movement and the media.

Pro-choice groups, such as the National Abortion Rights Action League (NARAL) and Planned Parenthood, want to maintain a woman's right to choose. (Often identified with abortion rights, Planned Parenthood also advocates for access to birth control, sex education in schools, and quality reproductive health care for women.) These groups are closely allied with the Democratic Party.

Single-issue groups have increased in recent decades, alarming some observers and many politicians. When groups form around highly emotional issues and refuse to

compromise, politicians can't deal with them as they deal with other groups, so the issues continue to boil,[73] consuming the time and energy of politicians at the expense of issues that many consider more important. On the other hand, single-issue groups have always been part of politics,[74] and they may represent interests that aren't represented by multiple-issue groups.

Fears about single-issue groups may result from a few of the groups' heavy media coverage, their exaggerated claims of influence, and their confrontational tactics.

DEMOCRACY?

Do either multiple-issue or single-issue groups pose a threat to democracy? Why or why not?

PACs and 527s

Political action committees (PACs), which raise and donate money to election campaigns, and **527 organizations**, which raise and spend money on political advertising (both explained further in Chapter 8), are specialized interest groups in modern American politics. Most large interest groups and corporations have a PAC, and an increasing number of groups have formed a 527 organization. Both PACs and 527s are authorized by federal law regulating the flow of money to political candidates and the use of money for political advertising. Both have leaders who articulate the group's views and decide how to spend the group's funds, as well as checkbook members who decide whether the group's views merit their donations.

PACs can be affiliated with private or public interest groups; 527s also can be private or public interest groups, though most are public interest groups.

© The New Yorker Collection 2002 Alex Gregory from cartoonbank.com. All rights reserved.

"If you still want to belong to an organization dedicated to killing Americans, there's always the tobacco lobby."

STRATEGIES OF INTEREST GROUPS

Interest groups use several strategies to influence public policy. These include initiating action, blocking action, and influencing key appointments.

Initiating Action

Interest groups initiate governmental action that will help them. They lobby Congress to pass new laws, and because the president is involved and influential in this process, they lobby the administration to push these bills. After the terrorist attacks and the anthrax scare, there was concern that terrorists might use smallpox in future attacks. The government decided to stockpile smallpox vaccine. The pharmaceutical industry lobbied Congress for a law that would grant drug companies immunity in case the vaccine, which can have serious side effects, caused illness or death.[75] As the bill worked its way through Congress, one drug company, Eli Lilly, got the bill's sponsors to sneak in a provision that would grant immunity for another drug made by the company that was unrelated either to the smallpox vaccine or to potential terrorist attacks. The provision was removed from the bill only when it was noticed by a few senators at the last minute.

Groups also lobby the administration to adopt new policies that don't require congressional action. When it was uncertain whether the United States would use economic sanctions or military attacks against Iraq in 1991, defense contractors lobbied the first Bush administration for war because they could sell more weapons to the government and see how the weapons performed on the battlefield. The National Wooden Pallet and Container Association, which represents companies that make pallets used to transport supplies, and the Composite Can and Tube Institute, which represents companies that make cardboard containers and the tubes around which toilet paper and paper towels are wrapped, also lobbied the administration for war, because the government would buy more pallets and cardboard containers, toilet paper, and paper towels.

Groups also lobby the White House to increase or decrease the enforcement of federal laws. As the head of the executive branch, the president is responsible for executing the laws. But in practice the president has discretion. Sometimes the laws are ambiguous, so they can be interpreted one way or another. Sometimes an agency lacks enough trained personnel to enforce all the laws it's responsible for, so it has to choose which ones to emphasize. In response to a group's pressure, the president may enhance or reduce an agency's capacity to enforce the laws through budgetary shifts or bureaucratic reorganizations.[76]

Groups also lobby the bureaucracy to adopt new rules. Congress passes relatively general laws, and it delegates authority to the bureaucratic agencies with expertise in the subject matter to adopt specific rules to implement the laws. These rules can be more important to the individuals or companies affected by them than the laws themselves. When the Federal Aviation Administration (FAA), which regulates air travel, banned firearms from airplanes in the 1960s, the NRA persuaded it to allow knives. This policy was still in effect on 9/11, when the hijackers used boxcutters to subdue the crews.

Thus bureaucrats, like members of Congress, are targets of lobbying. The new law passed in 2010 that tightens regulation of financial institutions passed is 2000 pages long. Like many congressional acts, it sets forth what was to be regulated but leaves the details to the agencies doing the regulating. For example, regulators have to decide how much money banks must set aside to protect themselves and their depositors against unforeseen losses. Immediately, bank lobbyists started making the case for a small amount. Consumer groups also geared up to make their case that the law is designed to protect the public from reckless financial institutions and that detailed regulations should do so. The debate over details that could gut or strengthen the bill will continue as regulations are drafted by numerous agencies, including the Federal Reserve, the Security and Exchange Commission, and the Federal Deposit Insurance Corporation. Said one consumer lobbyist, "It's out of the public eye, so a natural advantage that we benefit from—public outrage—we lose that a little. We know there's still a lot here left to do."[77]

Businesses also lobby government agencies to obtain **government contracts**—orders to purchase goods or services. Businesses are anxious to sell everything government wants to buy, whether big or small. Halliburton got lucrative no-bid contracts to supply services to troops in Iraq (so lucrative that the company was charging the government $100 for each 15-pound bag of laundry its workers put in washing machines and $45 for each case of soda);[78] other companies got contracts to provide private soldiers for security details in Iraq. Companies that make playing cards vie for government contracts for the decks that are distributed as souvenirs to people who fly on *Air Force One*—the president's plane. These prized cards are embossed with the presidential seal.

Blocking Action

Interest groups also work to block governmental action that will harm them, doing the reverse of what groups do to initiate action. They lobby Congress not to pass proposed bills and the administration not to push these bills, and they lobby the administration not to adopt new policies under consideration. They also lobby the administration not to increase or decrease the enforcement of federal laws that affect them. After 9/11, the FAA finally banned knives from airplanes, but airlines lobbied against the change, asking how first-class passengers could eat their steak without a knife. If these efforts fail, groups might file lawsuits either to delay the harmful action or to scuttle it altogether if the courts declare it illegal or unconstitutional.

Of the two strategies—initiating action or blocking action—interest groups resort to, and succeed with, the latter more often. In our system of federalism, separation of powers, and checks and balances, power is fragmented and government is decentralized. Initiating action may require a group to clear each level—federal and state. At the federal level alone, initiating action may require a group to clear each part of each branch—at the legislature, to win favorable decisions from multiple committees and both houses of Congress; at the executive, to win favorable decisions from the president and his advisers and from multiple agencies in the bureaucracy; and at the judiciary, to win favorable decisions from several levels of the courts. Groups that want to change a law or policy have to persuade officials at every step in the process. Groups that wish to maintain a law or policy only have to persuade officials at one point, any point, in the process. The American system, which was designed to prevent hasty action by individuals or groups, favors the status quo.

DEMOCRACY?

What are the implications for democracy of the bias toward the status quo in our governmental system?

Whether a group is interested in changing or preserving the status quo, the struggle to influence government can be ongoing. Congressional legislation called for efficiency standards for a variety of home appliances in order to conserve energy, but these standards have been contested and their implementation has been slow. The Clinton administration imposed more stringent efficiency standards for air conditioners, but air conditioner manufacturers got the Bush administration to scale back the standards to reduce manufacturing costs. (More stringent standards require more expensive technology.) Then a federal court ruled that the Bush administration violated the law by scaling back the standards. The Obama administration has issued new efficiency standards for other home appliances too, such as dishwashers and light bulbs,[79] but its new standards may not be the last word either.

Influencing Appointments

To shape government policy and accomplish their goals indirectly, interest groups also try to influence important appointments. The president nominates and the Senate confirms appointees to high positions in the executive branch and judges to the federal courts. Having a friend or ally in a key position can help secure a group's goals.

The auto industry opposed several of President Clinton's nominees to head the National Highway Traffic Safety Administration, fearing that they were more concerned with safety and consumers than they were with the auto manufacturers. Conservative groups criticized President Obama's choice to head the Centers for Medicare and Medicaid Services because he had made positive statements about the British Health Care Service (which, unlike our system, is run by the government). Conservative senators tried to block his appointment, so the president appointed him on an interim basis.[80]

Increasingly, interest groups have tried to influence presidential appointments of federal judges, as will be discussed in Chapter 13.

In pursuing these strategies—initiating action, blocking action, or influencing appointments—like-minded groups may join in a **coalition**. For example, amusement parks, lawn and garden centers, Kingsford Charcoal, and 7-Eleven stores joined the Daylight Saving Time Coalition to lobby Congress to extend daylight saving time. All wanted additional evening daylight hours for the users of their services and products: amusement parks so visitors have more time to play; lawn and garden centers so homeowners have more time to work in their yards; Kingsford so picnickers have more time for barbecues; and 7-Eleven so drivers have more time to stop for a snack while it is still daylight.

TACTICS OF INTEREST GROUPS

To implement their strategies, interest groups rely on a variety of tactics. Some try to influence policy makers directly, whereas others try to mold public opinion and influence policy makers indirectly.

Direct Lobbying Techniques

Direct lobbying entails individual contacts between lobbyists and officials. Thirty-two thousand lobbyists are registered in Washington, and there are a lot more who don't have to register because of various loopholes.[81] Some are salaried employees of the groups they represent; others are contract lobbyists—"hired guns" who represent any individual or group willing to pay for their service. Contract lobbyists include the numerous lawyers affiliated with the city's prestigious law firms.

Gaining access is the first and essential step in direct lobbying. As busy people, public officials are protected by their receptionists and aides, whose job is to shield them from those who would take their time.

Because former members of Congress, congressional staffers, White House aides, and federal bureaucrats already have contacts with current officials and knowledge about current policies, they are recruited as lobbyists once they leave public service. An official with the Securities and Exchange Commission (SEC), which regulates the stock market, hoped to capitalize on "Washington's revolving-door tradition whereby high-ranking federal officials move into high-paying private industry jobs." With his contacts and knowledge, he expected "to springboard to at least a $300,000 salary" with a lobbying firm when he left the SEC.[82] Rep. Billy Tauzin (R-La.), who steered the Bush administration's Medicare drug bill through the House, was rewarded by the pharmaceutical industry with a job as the head of the pharmaceutical lobby—at a salary of more than $4 million a year.[83] He then helped the pharmaceutical companies secure their financial interests in the fight for health care reform.

In addition to contacts and knowledge, former members of Congress have access to the House and Senate dining rooms and chambers, where no one but members and former members is allowed. Here they can buttonhole current members just before a vote. When they first came to Washington, most planned to return home after serving in Congress, but the longer they experienced the highly charged atmosphere of the most political city in the country, the harder it got to return home—and the more valuable they became to the myriad interests that lobby in Washington. So they decided to remain as lobbyists. Since 1998, more than 250 members of Congress and 275 aides to the president have registered as lobbyists.[84] When Bob Dole (R-Kan.) resigned from the Senate to run for president in 1996, he said he'd have no place to go but back to his hometown of Russell, Kansas, if he lost the election. Instead, he joined a lobbying firm as a "rainmaker," a prominent person who can attract clients who will bring millions of dollars to the firm.[85] (See box "From the Senate to a Lobbying Firm.")

Usually both Democrats and Republicans are recruited as lobbyists, so firms have access to both parties. This practice ensures that lobbying firms maintain access when control of government shifts from one party to the other.

When the Republicans controlled Congress in the 1990s, however, they pressured the firms to employ only

behind the scenes

From the Senate to a Lobbying Firm

Each "senator" cited in this cartoon is actually a former senator who became a lobbyist after losing reelection to, or retiring from, the Senate.

DOONESBURY © 2008 G. B. Trudeau. Reprinted with permission of Universal Press Syndicate. All rights reserved.

	Last Year in the Senate
Bob Torricelli (D-N.J.)	2002
Rod Grams (R-Minn.)	2000
Tom Daschle (D-S.D.)	2004
Slade Gorton (R-Wash.)	2000
Asa Hutchinson (R-Ark.)	2002
David Durenberger (R-Minn.)	1994
Bob Packwood (R-Ore.)	1995
Bennett Johnston (D-La.)	1996
Jake Garn (R-Ut.)	1992
Zell Miller (D-Ga.)	2003
John Breaux (D-La.)	2004
Al D'Amato (R-N.Y.)	1998
Dan Coats (R-Ind.)	1998
Jim Talent (R-Mo.)	2006

Republicans as their lobbyists. And then they pressured the lobbyists to make campaign contributions only to Republican officeholders and candidates. The goal was to deprive the Democratic Party of the funds necessary to remain competitive. The plan was dubbed the "K Street strategy" after the K Street corridor, home to lobbyists representing the nation's largest business corporations and trade associations.

House Republican leader Tom DeLay (R-Tex.) compiled a list of the four hundred largest contributors to the parties. Their lobbyists were summoned to his office, one by one, and told, "If you want to play in our revolution, you have to live by our rules." Friendly lobbyists were invited to help write legislation affecting their clients. So, chemical industry lobbyists helped decide hazardous waste regulations, oil company lobbyists helped determine energy policies, and defense contractors helped write weapons contracts.[86]

An old adage states, "Power corrupts and absolute power corrupts absolutely."[87] The Republicans' control of government and their aggressive efforts to maintain control led to corruption, forcing some members of Congress to resign and sending some lobbyists to prison. The spectacle contributed to the Democratic takeover of Congress in 2006. As a result of new Democratic majorities in Congress, the lobbying firms scurried to hire more Democratic lobbyists.[88]

Contacting Officials

Direct lobbying essentially means that lobbyists pay a visit or make a call to officials. They don't need to contact every legislator. Rather, they contact key legislators—party leaders and the members who sit on the committees with jurisdiction over the subject of the lobbyists' concern—and the professional staffers serving those committees.[89]

Successful lobbying is based on friendship. As a former chair of one House committee observed, "The most effective lobbyists here are the ones you don't think of as lobbyists." Referring to a prominent Washington lobbyist, he said, "I don't think of him as a lobbyist. He's almost a constituent, or a friend." Sen. Barbara Boxer (D-Cal.), referring to the same gentleman, described him as "a lovely, wonderful guy. In the whole time I've known him, he's never asked me to vote for anything." She joked that he's almost "a member of the family."[90]

Providing Expertise

When lobbyists contact officials, they might provide expertise that officials lack. Lobbyists make sure that they fully understand their client's business and the industry in which it operates. Consequently, they are an invaluable source of information for members of Congress and aides in the White House, who tend to be generalists rather than experts about policies. Thus officials rely on lobbyists to educate them. Former senator Ted Stevens (R-Alaska) chaired a committee whose jurisdiction included the Internet. His comments that the Internet "is not something that you just dump

something on. It's not a big truck. It's a series of tubes," led to many jokes but also to serious fears that the man in charge of congressional action in this area had no idea what he was talking about.

Lobbyists often draft legislation. A legislator may ask a lobbyist known to be an expert in an area to draft a bill, or a lobbyist may draft a bill and ask a legislator thought to be sympathetic to the cause to introduce the bill in Congress. (See box "Too Close Friendships?")

Giving Money

Lobbyists also give money, in the form of campaign contributions, to candidates for office and incumbents running for reelection. To give money, groups, including businesses and unions, set up PACs, which channel contributions to parties and candidates. Lobbyists give to those with whom they agree and those who are likely to be elected or reelected. The money greases the skids; it ensures access. A longtime financial backer of Ronald Reagan said that having a dialogue with a politician is fine, "but with a little money they hear you better."[91] A Democrat commented, "Who do members of Congress see? They'll certainly see the one who gives the money. It's hard to say no to someone who gives you $5,000."[92]

Consequently, interest groups often give to candidates they disagree with. Despite its liberal reputation, the entertainment industry donated more money to Republican candidates (59 percent) than to Democratic candidates (41 percent) in the 2006 congressional elections. Hollywood studios even donated to conservative Republicans who sat on committees with jurisdiction over issues, such as intellectual property rights, important to the industry.[93] With the Republicans in the majority at the time, Hollywood moguls were guided by their business interests rather than their ideological views.

So far, this discussion presumes that the groups freely decide whether to contribute their money. However, once the parties and candidates got used to receiving contributions, and as they faced escalating costs for television advertising, they began to pressure the groups to make contributions, as Republican leader Tom DeLay did when he told lobbyists they had "to pay to play"—that is, to contribute if they wanted to influence congressional bills or obtain government contracts.

Thus leverage is exercised in both directions. The groups give money to the parties and candidates as a way to influence current and future officials, and the parties and candidates demand money from the groups as a way to finance their campaigns. With only some exaggeration, one might say that the groups are practicing a legalized form of bribery and the parties and candidates are practicing a legalized form of extortion.

DEMOCRACY?

What are the implications of this pattern of legalized "bribery" and "extortion" for democracy?

behind the scenes

Too Close Friendships?

Friendships between members of Congress and lobbyists often develop because many lobbyists are former members of Congress. One-third of registered lobbyists have federal government experience.[1] Such lobbyists populate most big groups but are especially prevalent in corporate lobbies, which can offer lucrative positions to retired or defeated members of Congress. A spotlight was shone on this cozy relationship after the BP oil spill.

Eighteen former members of Congress represent oil and gas industries. Industry lobbyists also include two former directors of the Minerals Management Service—the prime federal regulatory agency—and "dozens" of presidential appointees (those who had high level federal jobs).[2] A spokesperson for a nonprofit group that tracks these crossover lobbyists points out, "With these numbers, you can see how the revolving door between the Hill and industry allowed problems in the [regulatory] agency to happen and not be addressed."[3]

BP itself employed thirty-one lobbyists with government experience, and the American Petroleum Institute, the leading lobby group for the industry, employed forty-eight more, including a former senator and two former representatives, all of whom played key roles in deregulation when in Congress.

It is logical to hire experts in the area to be lobbyists. In defense of this revolving door practice, the oil spokesman remarked, "If you want somebody to work on energy issues, you don't hire health care workers."[4] Yet the industry isn't likely to hire lobbyists who, in their congressional careers, fought for strict regulation of the industry. Thus any hope for a postcongressional job with a lobbying firm may impose a subtle, or perhaps not so subtle, pressure shaping the decisions of members of Congress.

By hiring former members of Congress, lobbies also have immediate access to current members who know the lobbyists and perhaps worked with them when they were in Congress. To the extent that former members were respected for their expertise while in Congress, they have increased legitimacy as lobbyists.

[1] These data were drawn from Dan Eggen and Kimberly Kindy, "Three of Every Four Oil and Gas Lobbyists Worked for Federal Government," *Washington Post*, July 22, 2010, www.washingtonpost.com/wp-dyn/content/article/2010/07/21/AR20100721060468.htm.
[2] Ibid.
[3] Ibid.
[4] Ibid.

Litigating in Court

Although interest groups do not lobby judges the way they do legislators and bureaucrats, some do use litigation to persuade courts to rule for their side in disputes over policies and laws. The groups may file a lawsuit, represent a defendant facing criminal prosecution, or submit a brief—written arguments—in favor of one side in a case.

Although most groups don't use litigation, some use it as their primary tactic, particularly those that lack influence with the legislative and executive branches. Litigation was a successful strategy for civil rights organizations. Throughout the first half of the twentieth century, when Congress and presidents were unsympathetic to the rights of black Americans, the National Association for the Advancement of Colored People (NAACP) fought segregation in the courts. Litigation has been the usual strategy of civil liberties groups, especially the American Civil Liberties Union (ACLU). (These groups' efforts are covered in Chapters 14 and 15.)

Environmental groups use litigation to challenge governmental policies. In local communities, environmental groups file lawsuits against new developments that threaten environmental damage. They hope to block the projects or, at least, delay the projects so that the costs will increase and the developers will have an incentive to make modifications. Then the developers may be more willing to make concessions in the future without the threat of a lawsuit.

With the current conservative and activist Supreme Court (see Chapter 13), conservative groups are aggressively using litigation as a strategy. After the passage of the health care reform bill, for example, many lawsuits were filed to prevent its implementation. Conservative groups hope that conservative justices on the Court will conclude that Congress has no authority to regulate this sphere of the American economy.

Indirect Lobbying Techniques: Going Public

Traditionally, lobbyists limited themselves to direct lobbying, but increasingly, they have turned to indirect lobbying, known as **going public**.[94] This technique includes mobilizing their supporters and molding public opinion. The goal is to get people to contact officials or to get them to vote in elections. By working through the public, groups lobby indirectly.

Lobbyists come in all shapes, sizes, and . . . species. This dolphin is trying to raise awareness of efforts to loosen restrictions on commercial fishing practices that entangle dolphins and whales in mammoth nets.

Mobilizing Supporters

Groups mobilize their members and supporters—called **grassroots lobbying**—through direct mail, e-mail, websites, texting, and other social media. To ensure response, they often exaggerate their opponents' views or strength or the dire consequences that could result if supporters don't heed the call. Such communications are "about scaring the hell out of people."[95]

The NRA is especially adept at mobilizing its members. It can generate thousands of letters, e-mails, or calls to members of Congress within days. The calls from irate members led one senator to remark, "I'd rather be a deer in hunting season than run afoul of the NRA crowd."[96] At rallies in 2000, NRA president Charlton Heston called the presidential election "the most important since the Civil War." If Gore won, he asserted, his Supreme Court will "hammer your gun rights into oblivion." Members turned out in droves, and that turnout was credited in moving West Virginia, a traditionally Democratic state, to the Republican column.

Messages don't always succeed, especially if they don't reflect a broad base. Sen. Tom Harkin (D-Iowa) received hundreds of letters opposing his antitobacco position, though from only one part of his state. Then he learned that all the letters came from employees of a Kraft food plant, owned by tobacco company RJ Reynolds.[97]

To be effective, the messages should appear spontaneous and sincere. Groups often provide sample letters to aid their members, but these aren't as convincing as those written in a member's own words. Postcards with preprinted messages aren't very convincing either. With the Internet, groups are using online petitions. Although these aren't as effective as individual communications, a huge number of signatures may have an impact. MoveOn.org, a liberal group with an e-mail list of nearly 2 million, can with the click of a mouse send hundreds of thousands of messages hurtling toward Washington.[98] (See box "MoveOn.Org.")

Messages can be sent through other means than old-fashioned or new media "mail." The Tea Party movement and its allies effectively mobilized supporters in 2009 when health care reform was pending. Conservative commentators and talk show hosts had claimed that the proposed bill would establish "death panels" that would decide whether elderly people would receive medical care. They also claimed that elderly people would lose their Medicare. Naturally, many people were irate over these fictional outrages. Interest groups representing insurance companies and other businesses seeking to block reform also ripped the bill. When members of Congress hosted open forum meetings—"town hall meetings"—for their constituents back home during the summer, Tea Party groups, some funded by the industries against the bill but others reflecting broader concerns about big government, decided to give their representative or senator an earful. With help from a website that provided the time and location of each meeting and local groups that offered transportation, the Tea Partiers filled the seats and dominated the meetings, interrupting the officials, shouting "You're lying!" and booing.

Because the bill was lengthy and complex, it was difficult for the officials to "prove" to their constituents that the charges were off base. And sometimes outspoken attendees were confused about other facts, urging government "to keep its hands off my Medicare" (a government program) or veterans' benefits (also a government program). Their anger and incivility fueled news reports for weeks. Although the protests did not stop health care reform from passing, they may have influenced the final bill, which did not contain a public option for health care insurance. The protests also drove down the approval ratings of President Obama and congressional Democrats, and they mobilized hundreds of thousands of individuals who found common ground and shifted their attention to conservative candidates in the 2010 elections.

Molding Public Opinion

Groups try to mold public opinion through commercials on television and radio and ads in newspapers and magazines. Groups also stage media events, including photo ops, to attract media coverage.

Framing an issue—causing people to view it one way rather than another—can be crucial in winning public support. Those opposing health care reform tried to frame the plan as "socialized medicine," painting the specter of

behind the scenes

MoveOn.org: Where Did They Come From, and What Are They Up to?

MoveOn.org burst upon the American political scene in 1998 when congressional Republicans launched the impeachment of President Clinton. Husband and wife Wes Boyd and Joan Blakes opposed the impeachment. Instead, they urged Congress to censure the president and then "move on." From their home in Berkeley, California, they started the website MoveOn.org. Their postings struck a responsive chord among liberal Democrats angered by the impeachment drive and the political circus surrounding it.

MoveOn surged during the presidency of George W. Bush, especially after the war in Iraq began. The organization vehemently opposed the war and sharply criticized President Bush and Vice President Cheney for initiating it, but it also targeted congressional Democrats for going along. And during the Obama administration, the organization opposed some of the president's policies, such as expansion of the war in Afghanistan and exclusion of the public option from health care reform, and provided a forum for mobilizing liberal Democrats against these policies. Throughout both administrations, the organization has reflected an insurgency against the Democratic Party's establishment, spurning conservative Democrats and liberal Democrats considered too timid.

Sites like MoveOn cater to people who are called the **"netroots"**—that is, the grass roots mobilized by political websites—citizens who are impatient with their party's organization and leaders. Netroots are also active on the Republican side.

MoveOn sends members e-mails about various affronts and outrages in the news, and it solicits donations for commercials to broadcast on television. It also offers interactive opportunities, such as contests for members to create political commercials. Then the organization asks its members to choose which commercials to air.

MoveOn boasts 3.3 million members ready to rally for a liberal cause. The membership includes twenty-somethings and middle-agers, with most in their forties and fifties. Contrary to expectations, they don't reside primarily in the liberal citadels on the East and West Coasts. Many live in the suburbs and rural areas of the Midwest. Through MoveOn, they find a connection to liberal causes they don't find in their communities. For liberals who live in "red" states where Democrats are few and far between and where the local and state Democratic Party is moribund, the MoveOn community is just a click away.

SOURCE: Matt Bai, "Profiting from Pummeling." From *The New York Times*, © September 23, 2007 *The New York Times*. All rights reserved. Used by permission and protected by the Copyright Laws of the United States. The printing, copying, redistribution, or retransmission of the Material without express written permission is prohibited.

government controlling personal health decisions. Those supporting reform stressed the heavy hand of insurance companies, their literal life-and-death power over middle- and low-income individuals who must have health insurance if they are socked with huge medical bills.

Business groups pushing "tort reform," which would limit the money that courts can award to individuals injured in auto accidents, air disasters, unsuccessful surgeries, and other mishaps, focus on notorious cases in which the victims have gotten huge awards relative to their injuries, such as the grandmother who spilled McDonald's coffee onto her lap and was awarded $2.9 million for her burns. (But, like many awards, this one was dramatically reduced by the judge, to $840,000, and then further reduced through secret negotiations between the litigants to avoid an appeal.) These groups hope to convince the public that "tort reform" is overdue and necessary to ensure that American businesses will remain competitive or, in malpractice cases, to ensure that American doctors will continue to practice medicine.[99] Lawyer groups that oppose "tort reform" instead focus on the poor victims seriously injured and left penniless by the careless behavior of big corporations or rich doctors.[100] These groups frame the debate as the little guy versus the big bully.

In their zeal to shape public opinion, groups occasionally fabricate information. Although there's a cardinal rule that lobbyists should not mislead officials because they would never be trusted again, there's no comparable rule against misleading the public. ExxonMobil, which opposes government efforts to reduce global warming, has tried to discredit the science of global warming. Although the scientific opinion on the existence of global warming is nearly unanimous, Exxon Mobil, according to one calculation, gave $16 million to forty-three groups between 1998 and 2005 to mislead the public into believing that the science is inconclusive and that the scientists are in disagreement.[101] The corporation assumed that it wasn't necessary to persuade people that there's no global warming; it was necessary only to convince them that the issue isn't resolved, so difficult steps to counter it don't have to be taken yet.[102]

Engaging in protest If groups are excluded from the political process or if they simply lack the money necessary to influence the process, they can turn to protest.

The civil rights movement is the best example of a successful protest in twentieth-century America. By demonstrating against legalized segregation, black and some white

Fred Blackwell

Students sit in at a segregated lunch counter in Jackson, Mississippi, during the civil rights era.

protestors called attention to the discrepancy between the American values of democracy and equality and the inferior status of blacks in the South. The protestors also called attention to the contrast between their own peaceful behavior and the police and vigilante brutality unleashed against them. In marches, sit-ins, and other demonstrations, the protestors practiced **civil disobedience**—intentionally but peacefully violating laws and getting arrested so they could challenge the laws in court. (See the box "Organizing Protest: The Montgomery Bus Boycott.")

Sometimes protest leads to hostility against, rather than sympathy for, the protesters. Antiwar demonstrations by college students in the 1960s and 1970s angered not only government officials, who targeted the leaders for harassment, but also ordinary citizens, including many who opposed the war. They were more antiprotest than antiwar.

Protest demands skill from the leaders and sacrifices from the followers. Continued participation, essential to real success, robs activists of a normal life. They can face jail, physical harm, or even death, and they need discipline to refrain from violence, even when they are targeted for violence.

Once protest groups find sympathetic officials willing to listen, they often shift to an inside strategy, working with those in power rather than against them. They switch from demonstrations to conventional lobbying techniques.

SUCCESS OF INTEREST GROUPS

Politics is not a game of chance in which luck determines the winners and losers. Some groups are more successful than others because of their resources and goals.

Resources

Money is important for success. Groups with money can establish and operate an organization, hire experienced lobbyists, and make campaign donations. They can also mold public opinion through television commercials and other actions. An economist called the system "survival of the fattest," because those with the biggest wallets have a significant advantage in our system.[103]

Size—number of members—might substitute for money, especially if members can be mobilized. AARP has 35 million members, senior citizens who focus on Social Security and health care and who vote in high numbers. (They pay dues, so AARP has a thick bankroll along with its huge membership.) The number of members relative to the number of potential members in a group can also be important. The American Medical Association (AMA) enrolled 70 percent or more of the nation's doctors for years, and it

american*diversity

Organizing Protest: The Montgomery Bus Boycott

The 1955 Montgomery, Alabama, bus boycott was the first successful civil rights protest, and it brought its twenty-six-year-old leader, Dr. Martin Luther King Jr., to national prominence.

Montgomery, like most southern cities, required blacks to sit in the back of public buses, reserving the seats in the front for whites. In Montgomery, blacks had to go to the front of the bus to pay their fare, then reboard through the back door (if the bus didn't take off before they got to the back). If a lot of whites were on board, blacks had to move further and further back; they couldn't even sit in the aisle across from a white person. One afternoon, Rosa Parks, a seamstress at a department store and a leader in the local NAACP, got on the bus to go home. The bus was crowded, and when a white man boarded, the driver called on the four blacks in "no-man's land" to move to the back. Three moved, but Parks, tired from a long day and tired of the racial injustice, refused. Under a law that gave him the authority to enforce segregation, the driver arrested her.

Parks was not the first black person in Montgomery to be arrested for not giving up her seat to whites. Two others had before her, but Parks was a better candidate for filing a legal complaint. Not only was she "above moral reproach (securely married, reasonably employed)," but she also possessed "a quiet fortitude as well as political savvy."

After consulting her mother and husband, Parks decided to file a lawsuit challenging the constitutionality of the law. That evening, a group of women professors at Alabama State College, a black college in Montgomery, led by Jo Ann Robinson, drafted a letter calling on their brothers and sisters to stay off the buses on Monday. Although fearful for their jobs and concerned that the state would cut funding to the college if it became known that they had used state facilities to produce the letter, they worked through the night, making thirty-five thousand copies of the letter to distribute to the city's black residents.

The following day, black leaders agreed to the boycott, and on Sunday, black ministers encouraged their members to support the boycott. On Monday, 90 percent of black workers walked, shared rides in private cars, or took black-owned taxis. The boycott inspired confidence and pride in the black community. Hundreds of blacks jammed the courthouse, as nervous police looked on, to make sure that Rosa Parks was safely released after being convicted.

At a mass rally later that evening, Martin Luther King Jr. cried out, "There comes a time when people get tired of being trampled over by the iron feet of oppression." Noting that the right to protest is the glory of American democracy, King appealed to the strong religious faith of the crowd: "If we are wrong, God Almighty is wrong. . . . If we are wrong, Jesus of Nazareth was merely a utopian dreamer. . . . If we are wrong, justice is a lie." These words established King as a charismatic leader of the civil rights movement.

Because of its initial success, the boycott was extended. Each successive day was a trial for the residents and their leaders. Thousands had to find a way to get to work, and

---

enjoyed a lot of clout. As its percentage of American doctors declined, its influence declined as well.

Cohesion and intensity might substitute for money and size. Public interest groups, especially single-issue groups such as pro-choice and pro-life groups, have cohesive and intense members who can be mobilized to contact officials, write letters to the editor, persuade their friends, and vote.

Groups that marshal the greatest resources are the most likely to influence government. They may even overcome the majority view, as reflected in public opinion polls. Supporters of gun control have long had public opinion on their side, but their main group, the National Council to Control Handguns, has less money, fewer members, and less cohesion and intensity among its members than the NRA can boast. As a result, the NRA has triumphed over public opinion for decades.

Goals

Groups that promote change, especially sweeping change, usually are less successful than groups that work to preserve the status quo. In our system of federalism, separation of powers, and checks and balances, groups promoting change must persuade numerous officials in multiple institutions; groups opposing change may have to persuade only one key official, or perhaps several important officials, in just a single institution. Thus it is more difficult to produce government action than to prevent such action.

leaders struggled to keep a massive carpool going. But each night's rally boosted morale for the next day's boycott. The rallies became prayer services, as the black community prayed for strength to keep on walking, for courage to remain nonviolent, and for divine guidance for their oppressors.

The city bus line was losing money. (Before the boycott, most riders on city buses were black people.) City leaders urged more whites to ride the buses to make up lost revenue, but few did. Black leaders, recognizing that the boycott could not continue forever, agreed to end it if the rules for "no-man's land" were relaxed. In response, city leaders concluded that they were on the verge of breaking the boycott, and they rejected the offer. Police officers began to harass carpoolers and issue bogus tickets for trumped-up violations.

City leaders then issued an ultimatum—settle or face arrest. A white grand jury indicted more than one hundred boycott leaders for the alleged crime of organizing the protest. In the spirit of nonviolence, the leaders, including King, surrendered.

The decision to arrest the leaders proved to be the turning point of the boycott. The white editor of the local paper said it was "the dumbest act that has ever been

AP Photo/Gene Herrick

Rosa Parks is fingerprinted in Montgomery, Alabama, after her arrest for refusing to give up her seat on the bus to a white man. Her refusal triggered a boycott of city buses that became the first successful civil disobedience in the civil rights movement and made Parks a hero to black and white Americans alike.

done in Montgomery." With the mass arrests, the boycott finally received national attention. Reporters from all over the world streamed into Montgomery to cover the story. The boycott became a national event, and its leader, Martin Luther King Jr., became a national figure.

A year later, the U.S. Supreme Court declared Alabama's local and state laws mandating segregation on buses unconstitutional. Only after the city complied with the Court's order did the boycott end.

When Rosa Parks died at the age of ninety-two in 2005, she was lauded as one of the key figures in the civil rights movement. Fifty thousand people filed through the U.S. Capitol Rotunda, where she lay in state, the first woman and second African American to be honored in this way. Thousands attended her funeral, and thousands more lined the streets to witness her casket pulled by a horse-drawn carriage to the cemetery. Parks had a modest view of her own role; as she said, "I did not get on the bus to get arrested; I got on the bus to get home."

SOURCES: Taylor Branch, *Parting the Waters: America in the King Years* (New York: Simon & Schuster, 1988), chs. 4 and 5; Juan Williams, *Eyes on the Prize* (New York: Viking, 1987).; quote about Parks is from Rita Dove, "Rosa Parks," *Time Magazine*, June 14, 1999, 168.

When President Bill Clinton proposed a major health care reform, medical, dental, hospital, and insurance associations and companies voiced their opposition. Different groups opposed different aspects of the proposal, and they came together to fight it. The plan became the most heavily lobbied initiative in history.[104] The plan's scope, along with the opponents' power, ensured the plan's defeat.

President Obama learned from the Clinton experience and made an effort to enlist some of the big interest groups in behalf of his reform plan even if he had to give up some things that he and fellow Democrats wanted. He was able to do this because the cost of health care spiraled between the time Clinton sought reform and Obama did. Many doctors and hospital administrators wanted change, and big

pharmaceuticals thought they could position themselves well when health reform passed.

Clinton's welfare reform, which was a major revision of an entrenched policy, was adopted without the controversies that the health reform spawned. It set work requirements for welfare recipients, who are the poorest and least politically active Americans. They don't have strong interest groups representing them, so they weren't able to block the requirements.

Groups that seek narrow benefits for themselves are usually more successful than those that seek broad policy changes for the entire society. If the proposals are complex, the media are less likely to call attention to them and the public is less likely to be aware of them. Virtually everyone is aware of hot-button issues such as abortion and capital punishment, but relatively few are aware of technical provisions that regulate or tax businesses. Most Americans paid little attention when Wall Street financial firms, such as Citibank and Goldman Sachs, lobbied hard to undo some regulations erected during the Great Depression to protect consumers and depositors from future economic crashes. These huge financial firms took advantage of the steady calls for deregulation during the conservative era of the 1980s, 1990s, and early 2000s, and they persuaded Congress and presidents to repeal existing regulations and allow the firms to engage in new and risky practices. When these big firms were on the brink of collapse in 2008 and 2009, they were deemed "too big to fail," because if they had failed, they would have taken the rest of the economy with them, plunging the nation into a deeper recession or even a depression. Thus they were bailed out with taxpayer money. Critics called the bailouts "welfare for the rich."

The tax code is riddled with exemptions for industries and corporations that have slipped through Congress without raising an eyebrow.[105] Some beneficiaries aren't identified by their name. One provision exempts Phillips Petroleum, identified in the law not by its name but as a "corporation incorporated on June 13, 1917, which has its principal place of business in Bartlesville, Oklahoma."[106] A member of Congress from a district with three national bakeries succeeded in inserting a provision into a tax bill that simply deleted "bakery drivers" from the list of occupations treated as employees.[107] The drivers, although hired by the bakeries, would be defined as self-employed rather than as bakery employees. This meant that the bakeries wouldn't have to pay Social Security, Medicare, or unemployment taxes on their drivers. Instead, their drivers would have to pay extra Social Security and Medicare taxes themselves. This rip-off was removed only when a congressional staffer noticed and publicized it.

DEMOCRACY?

Does it seem that interest groups enhance or detract from democracy?

Dominance in the Interest Group System

The interest group system is the combination of all the groups at work in Washington. Though many groups have unique interests, in general the system pits those who seek benefits for business and their allies against those who seek benefits for workers and consumers and their allies. This battle affects legislation that is passed and candidates who are elected as well, because interest groups devote substantial resources to helping their favored candidates. Thus elected officials are part of these coalitions.

In the last century, sometimes workers and consumers and their allies have been the dominant coalition. This was especially true in the 1930s, when new legislation was enacted to provide a safety net under the elderly (Social Security), the poor (welfare systems), and the unemployed (unemployment insurance), and to protect consumers and investors (banking regulations). Another era when workers and consumers and their allies were the dominant coalition was in the 1960s and 1970s, with the passage of legislation promoting civil rights, Medicare, workplace safety, product safety, and environmental protection.

With the 1980 election of Ronald Reagan, a conservative era began, and the protection of business interests took primacy over other interests. From 1980 through 2008, many regulations on business were relaxed or swept away, including those on financial firms. Other regulations were laxly enforced, such as environmental and consumer protections. Tax rates on the wealthy were significantly lowered. These trends persisted, with some exceptions, under the Clinton administration as well as under the Republican administrations that set the tone for the era. (During the Clinton administration, ironically, there was also a significant reduction of the deficits, a goal that has been a mainstay of conservative rhetoric but one that was never attained under these Republican administrations. In fact, due to tax cuts, the deficits grew under the Reagan and both Bush administrations.)

During the first years of the Obama presidency, the interests of workers, consumers, and environmentalists gained traction, with the passage of re-regulations on the financial industry and new regulations on the health care industry. As a consequence, business and its allies are fighting hard to paint the administration as antibusiness. The Chamber of Commerce, reflecting this position, accused the Obama administration of an "attack on our free enterprise system" with "government expansion, major tax increases, massive deficits, and job destroying regulations."[108] (In fact, the Chamber had supported the stimulus package, which was a big part of the 2009–2010 deficits.)

Nonetheless, American business is rightly seen as a driver of the U.S. economy, and its voices typically have great influence. It is weighing in to shape public opinion and to restore the primacy of its coalition.

CONCLUSION: Interest Groups and the Role of Government

In an indirect democracy, as in the United States, citizens elect representatives to pass laws and make policies for them. However, elections usually focus only on a few issues or on the candidates' personalities. They aren't referendums on all the issues that citizens want government to address. Furthermore, elections occur infrequently, and many citizens don't vote. So, elections don't reflect citizens' views on many issues. To supplement the ballot box in our political system, interest groups play an important role. They offer citizens the opportunity to join with others, and they monitor government action and make their views known to public officials.

By joining and paying dues or making contributions to a group, citizens essentially hire private representatives—the group's leaders—to act on their behalf much as they elect public officials to do so. Most citizens can't monitor the actions of the president, 535 members of Congress organized into almost 200 committees and subcommittees, and more than 100 bureaucratic agencies. And most citizens can't communicate their views to these officials, committees, and agencies. But interest groups can.

The theory that groups represent citizens and compete for the attention of and influence over government is called **pluralism**. There are thousands of groups representing the interests of millions of Americans. According to the theory, groups compete with each other for favorable treatment by the government, much as businesses compete with other businesses to sell their products and services. From this spirited competition in the political marketplace, policies are adopted that reflect the interests of the groups. Occasionally, some groups win while others lose, but usually the groups compromise, with each winning part of what it sought. Thus, according to the theory, our government is responsive to the people, because the people are represented by the groups in this competition.

However, although many people do join groups—more people than in other countries—some people don't, so these people aren't represented by groups, or at least by many groups or strong groups. People with the least education and the least income are the least likely to join groups. Much of the time, therefore, groups don't adequately represent the poor, the working class (except for those in unions), and the politically disinterested. Instead, they disproportionately represent the well-to-do and their businesses. A political scientist's observation from 1960 remains valid today: "The flaw in the pluralist heaven is that the angelic chorus sings with an upper class accent."[109]

The middle class can wield power, through its sheer numbers, when it is very aware of and interested in an issue. And sometimes middle-class concerns do benefit working-class people as well. For example, the middle-class members of AARP protect the interests of the elderly in all classes. And although those who promoted health care reform, including Big Pharma, weren't always thinking of the interests of the poor, the reform will provide significant benefits to poor people.

Interest groups make government responsive to their members. In fact, the country is so large and diverse that it is difficult to see how government could operate without groups. At the same time, the efforts of groups often prevent government from solving critical problems, even when a majority of citizens want government to address these problems. Ironically, as the groups are making government responsive to their members, they are rendering it unresponsive to the rest of society.

But not all of politics can be explained by powerful and well-funded interest groups. Consider the successes of Ralph Nader, the son of Lebanese immigrants and a crusader for average Americans against the giants of corporate America. Nader spearheaded an array of interest groups, including Public Citizen, that attracted young professionals (dubbed "Nader's Raiders") and fought for safer products and a healthier environment. More than any other person, Nader is responsible for seat belts, air bags, padded dashboards, steering columns that won't impale drivers, and fuel tanks that won't explode upon collision. Because of Nader, drinking water, baby food, and dental X-rays are all safer. Infant pajamas are less likely to catch fire. To a significant extent, Nader is also responsible for the creation of important government agencies—the Environmental Protection Agency (EPA); the Consumer Product Safety Commission (CPSC), which tries to ensure safe products; and the Occupational Safety and Health Administration (OSHA), which tries to ensure safe workplaces. Nader also deserves credit for the Freedom of Information Act, which exposes government actions and ensures greater accountability.[110] His work is a testament to how much concerned and active citizens, working through interest groups, can do, even when they are up against powerful opponents.

Consumer advocate Ralph Nader testifies against dangerous automobiles in 1968.

KEY TERMS

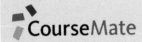

Access an interactive eBook, chapter-specific interactive learning tools (including flashcards, quizzes, videos), and more at CourseMate for *Understanding American Government*. Log in at CengageBrain.com.

7 Political Parties

○ Criticized by Republicans for being moderate, Pennsylvania Senator Arlen Specter feared losing to his conservative challenger in the Republican primary, so he switched parties.

Brooks Kraft

Talking Points

Arlen Specter entered politics in 1965 with the encouragement of moderate Republicans in his state of Pennsylvania.[1] He eventually was elected to the U.S. Senate, where he served five terms. Like most eastern Republicans, Specter was a moderate Republican and periodically defected from Republican orthodoxy. He was more supportive of taxes and labor unions than conservative Republicans were, and on abortion he was pro-choice. As a result, he garnered support from labor unions and independent voters. Increasingly, he found himself out of step with the Republican Party's march to the right. In 2009, he broke ranks and angered conservatives when he voted for President Obama's stimulus plan.

Specter knew he would be up for reelection in 2010, and a primary challenge from an antitax activist already was looming. Specter would have to win the Republican primary before he could become the party's nominee and run in the general election. His primary challenger—former representative Pat Toomey—was a conservative ideologue. Although he was the incumbent, Specter expected to lose the primary. Primary elections tend to favor more extreme candidates—staunch conservatives in the Republican Party and staunch liberals in the Democratic Party—because the voters in these elections, unlike in general elections, tend to be the parties' most ideological members. Specter also knew that 200,000 moderate Pennsylvanians had moved from the Republican Party to the Democratic Party during the 2008 campaign, so these voters—probably supporters—could no longer cast ballots in the Republican primary.[2]

Out of a combination of conviction and opportunism, then, Specter followed the 200,000 moderate Pennsylvanians and defected from the Republican Party in 2009. He was welcomed into the Democratic Party, where he provided (temporarily) its sixtieth vote in the Senate. Conservative bloggers and Rush Limbaugh (who had previously urged Colin Powell to leave the Republican Party) jeered him, and a Republican campaign committee used his defection to raise funds from conservative members. Its pitch was "GOOD RIDDANCE."[3]

Specter's defection and conservatives' response reflect the war within the Republican Party. As the party has shifted further and further to the right in recent decades, tension has escalated between the members committed to the party's expansion and other members committed to its ideological purity. The former advocate a "**big tent**," with diverse people and diverse views. This notion used to be commonplace in both parties but now is disdained by conservative Republicans, who believe that it muddles the coherence of the party's positions and image. Sen. Jim DeMint, a very conservative Republican from South Carolina, said, "I would rather have thirty Republicans in the Senate who really believe in principles of limited government, free markets, free people, than to have sixty that don't have a set of beliefs."[4] With this attitude, conservative Republicans often call moderate Republicans "RINOs"—Republicans in Name Only. So, the number of moderate Republicans has dwindled, and the battle to chart the course of the party into the future continues.

Although Specter avoided a primary battle in the Republican Party, he drew a primary challenge from one-term Rep. Joe Sestak, who campaigned as a real Democrat. Sestak ran commercials showing Specter, as a Republican, arm in arm with President Bush and Alaska governor Sarah Palin. At a campaign appearance before the Allegheny County Democratic Party, Specter absentmindedly thanked the "Allegheny County Republican Party" at both the beginning and the end of his speech. A survivor of heart surgery, brain surgery, and chemotherapy for cancer, Specter ultimately succumbed to an anti-incumbent mood and a primary challenge he didn't foresee would be so bruising—he lost to Sestak.

James Madison, the "Father of the Constitution," warned against the "mischief of factions," which today would include interest groups and political parties. George Washington, the "Father of the Country," cautioned against the "baneful" effects of parties and called them the people's worst enemies. Years later, however, a respected political scientist, E. E. Schattschneider, claimed that "political parties created democracy and that democracy was impossible without them."[5]

The public reflects these contradictory views. Americans, especially young adults, are cynical about parties, and many believe the country would be better off without them. People complain that politics is too **partisan**—that candidates and officeholders make decisions based on their party affiliation rather than on the country's needs. People say they're tired of "partisan bickering," as though the parties, like children, argue over nothing consequential. They believe that parties create conflict where none exists. Despite these views, however, most people identify with one of the parties, and many vote solely on the basis of party affiliation.

This chapter examines American political parties to see why they persist—indeed, why they are important—despite the criticism they face.

CHARACTERISTICS OF AMERICAN PARTIES

Political parties consist of three interrelated components: (1) citizens who consider themselves members of the party, (2) officeholders who are elected or appointed in the name of the party, and (3) professionals and activists who run the party organization at the national, state, and local levels (see Figure 1).[6]

The American party system is unusual among Western democracies, as we shall see when examining its distinguishing characteristics.

Two Major Parties

The American party system is a **two-party system**. Only two parties—the **Democratic Party** and the **Republican Party**—have a realistic chance to win the presidency or most seats in Congress. (Occasionally an independent wins a seat; today a socialist—Sen. Bernie Sanders (Vt.)—holds a seat.)

Two-party systems are rare. In Western Europe, **multiparty systems** are the rule. Italy has nine national

| Figure 1 | The Three Components of Political Parties |

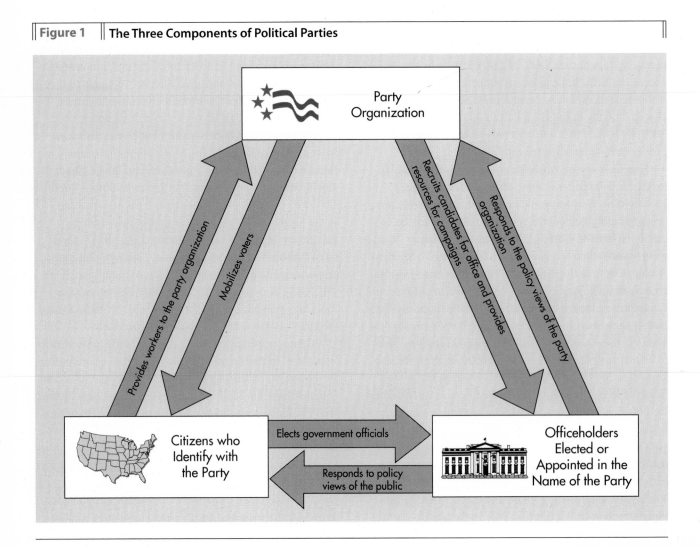

parties and several regional ones; Germany has five national parties. Great Britain, although predominantly a two-party system, has several significant minor parties. Multiparty systems are also found in Canada, which has three parties, and Israel, which has more than twenty.

Why two parties in the United States? The most common explanation is that American elections, with **single-member districts** and a **winner-take-all provision**, favor two parties.[7] These features mean that only one individual—the one who receives the most votes—is elected from a district. Although these features seem natural, even inevitable, to Americans, they contrast with **proportional representation** (PR), which is found in multiparty systems. PR elections employ multimember districts, where more than one individual is elected. In most, voters cast a ballot for a party slate, and each party receives the number of seats in the district equal to its percentage of votes in the district.[8] (There's no winner-take-all provision.) Consequently, representation in the national legislature is roughly proportional to the popular vote each party receives nationwide.

In single-member-district, winner-take-all elections, only the major parties are likely to win a legislative seat. In PR elections, even a modest showing—15 percent or possibly less—may win a legislative seat, enabling a small party to have a voice and a base to attract more supporters in the next election. This prospect encourages and sustains minor parties.

Minor Parties

Although American elections disadvantage minor parties, also called "third parties," such parties do exist. Most, including the Prohibition Party (since the 1860s), which opposes the sale of alcoholic beverages, and the Communist Party USA (since the 1920s), which proposes the adoption of communism, receive little notice and few votes. But some, such as the Progressive Party in the late 1800s and early 1900s, have had a major impact by proposing a new agenda that the major parties have felt pressured to address or even embrace.

Some minor parties, chiefly in the twentieth century, have been essentially an individual's organization. In 1968, Alabama's segregationist governor, George Wallace, split from the Democratic Party to run for president as the candidate of the American Independent Party. In 1992, Texas businessman Ross Perot decided to run for president. His willingness to use his personal fortune to fund an expensive campaign made him a viable alternative to the major-party candidates. He received 19 percent of the vote, an extraordinary showing for a minor-party candidate (but his candidacy didn't influence the outcome, as he siphoned votes from both major-party candidates). His campaign pushed the issue of the budget deficit to the top of the national agenda.

Consumer advocate Ralph Nader ran in 2000 and 2004. In 2000, he was the nominee of the Green Party, an offshoot of the antinuclear and environmental movements. He claimed that the major parties were simply pawns of corporate America, and he called for more checks on big business. In 2000, Nader received just 3 percent of the vote nationwide, but his total included 97,000 votes in Florida. Because most Nader voters preferred Al Gore over George W. Bush, many of their votes would have gone to Gore if Nader hadn't been on the ballot. In the tight election, Nader's votes were enough to deny Gore a victory in the state and, consequently, in the Electoral College.[9] (Of course, in such a close election, other factors affected the outcome as well.)

Despite Nader's impact as spoiler, third parties must overcome substantial barriers to have an impact. Most Americans feel long-standing loyalty to one of the major parties. They also realize that minor-party candidates can't win, so most don't want to "waste their vote" or, worse, help their least-preferred candidate, as Nader's Florida voters helped Bush. For these reasons, minor-party candidates can't raise the money or attract the media coverage they need.[10] Although many Americans—over half in various polls—tell pollsters that they want alternatives to the two major parties, few ever cast a vote for a minor-party candidate.

Historically, minor parties have done well only when the country has faced economic or social challenges that the major parties have failed to address. Then, once the minor parties have made an impact, the major parties have co-opted their ideas, and the minor parties, no longer needed, have faded into oblivion. After Perot focused the country's attention on the budget deficit, the incoming Clinton administration made the deficit its chief economic priority and thus eliminated the reason for supporting Perot.

Moderate Parties

The American party system encourages ideologically moderate political parties. In a two-party system, both parties typically are big tents with diverse members and views. To win, the parties have to attract many voters. Unlike in a multiparty system, where competing parties can gain legislative seats without winning a majority in any district, American parties can't focus their campaigns on just one or a few segments of the electorate. They must appeal to most of the electorate, which clusters in the middle rather than at the extremes (see Figure 2). This means that they usually choose pragmatism over ideology—put forth practical ideas that appeal to many voters over ideological ones that appeal only to their party's staunchest supporters. Therefore, the parties usually pitch their campaigns toward the middle, at least in nationwide contests.[11]

The Democrats tend to be a center-left party, and the Republicans tend to be a center-right party. For the presidency, the parties usually nominate moderate candidates. When the parties nominate more ideological or extreme candidates—a very liberal Democrat or a very conservative Republican—these candidates usually move to the center or at least obscure their positions during the campaign. In the 2000 election, George W. Bush called himself a "compassionate conservative" to signal moderate voters that he was

american*diversity

The Tea Party as a Third Party?

The *Tea Party movement* burst upon the American political scene in 2009 when it launched hundreds of protests claiming that our government is too big and our taxes are too high. As explained in the Introduction, the movement is disproportionately white, male, older (over forty-five), and middle class. Its conservative members rail against the Obama administration, which they claim has put the United States on a "socialist" path.

The movement has been a loose-knit coalition of grassroots clubs at the local level that have resisted becoming an organization with a structure. Instead, they have relied on television news and the Internet to spur attendance at rallies.

Tea Partiers helped elect Republican Scott Brown to a Senate seat from heavily Democratic Massachusetts in 2009, and they helped nominate insurgent candidates over establishment candidates in Republican primaries and conventions for House and Senate races in 2010. In seven states, they forced the Republican Party to nominate Tea Party candidates for the Senate over establishment candidates hand-picked by Republican officials.

Hoping to harness its energy to elect Republican candidates, the Republican Party has courted the Tea Party movement, and its consultants have helped it stage protests.[1] Two dozen Republican representatives have formed a Tea Party Caucus in the House. Yet movement leaders have resisted efforts by the GOP to take over, and this resistance and intensity have led many commentators to ask whether the movement might evolve into a third party.

The movement has been critical of both parties, including the Republicans for their associations with Wall Street, especially for their support under President George W. Bush of the bailouts to failing banks. Nevertheless, the movement has been far more critical of the Democratic Party. And most members—70 or more percent—are Republicans or independents who regularly vote for Republicans.

There is evidence that members see the movement as a way to pressure the Republican Party to do what they think it should do. Some complain that Republican leaders are actually liberals rather than true conservatives.[2] Thus the movement might simply reflect a war over ideological purity within the GOP (related to the war described in the opening vignette), pitting its Main Street component against its Wall Street and big business elements. Already Tea Partiers are running for precinct representatives within the GOP, hoping to take over that party one precinct at a time.[3]

Although Tea Partiers' frustration with Republican leaders makes some members yearn for a new party, a majority of the members say the country doesn't need a third party.[4] Moreover, the movement has no platform, unlike Ross Perot and his followers in the 1990s who targeted the deficits. Other than their heated rhetoric against government and taxes, and their opposition to reform of health care and bailouts for big companies, Tea Partiers don't voice support for any particular change in policy. (Despite their dislike of government spending and "socialist" policies, most want to keep their Social Security and Medicare.)[5] The movement has no platform partly because members' anger is amorphous, reflecting their unease with societal changes in recent years—especially the trend toward a multiracial, multiethnic, and multicultural society. Neither a third party nor the government can roll back these changes.

Members' anger is also directed, intensely, at the Democratic Party. Launching a third party would split the conservative vote and help the Democratic Party.

[1] Tim Rutten, "Crashing the 'Tea Party,'" *Los Angeles Times*, April 17, 2010, www.latimes.com/news/opinion/la-oe-rutten17-2010apr17,0,7423995.column.
[2] Megan Thee-Brenan and Marina Stefan, "'The System Is Broken': More from a Poll of Tea Party Backers," *New York Times*, April 18, 2010, A14.
[3] Kathleen Hennessey, "'Tea Party' Activists Filter into GOP at Ground Level," *Los Angeles Times*, latimes.com/news/la-na-tea-party15-2010feb15,0,1519774.story.
[4] Responses to this and other questions are available at "Polling the Tea Party," *New York Times*, April 14, 2010, www.nytimes.com/interactive/2010/04/14/us/politics/20100414-tea-party-poll-graph.
[5] Ibid.

actually a moderate (but couldn't say so without alienating conservative voters). However, once elected, he pursued very conservative policies that reflected his conservative base.

Although the parties aim for the center in national elections, both have members and supportive interest groups—left of center in the Democratic Party and right of center in the Republican Party—tugging them toward their extremes. In recent decades, this tendency has been stronger in the Republican Party, as conservatives have wrested control of the party's state and local organizations and the party's

congressional leadership from moderates (as noted in the opening vignette). In an effort to discredit President Clinton, Republican congressional leaders shut down the government over a budget dispute. However, public opinion supported Clinton, and he won reelection. In his second term, Republican congressional leaders impeached the president. Again, public opinion supported Clinton and he survived.

Following the 2000 election, President Bush's chief political aide, Karl Rove, and his vice president, Dick Cheney, tried to mold the Republican Party into a highly disciplined and ideologically uniform party of the right. A conservative agenda for both foreign and domestic policies was set, and all congressional Republicans, including the remaining moderates, were pressured to follow. The goal was to mobilize the party's base of conservative Republicans. Although the agenda seemed out of step with Americans' views toward domestic policies, the strategy seemed to work after the 9/11 attacks, as Americans' fear of terrorism led to support of Republican policies against terrorism and ultimately to Republican congressional victories in 2002 and President Bush's reelection in 2004. But the problems inherent in the strategy surfaced when the terrorist threats appeared to recede. Independents felt that the party had moved too far to the right, and voters elected Democratic majorities to Congress in 2006 and a Democratic president and larger majorities to Congress in 2008.

In 2010, the Republican Party moved further to the right in response to Tea Party groups and candidates who challenged, and defeated, numerous establishment candidates who had been endorsed by Republican officials in the primary elections. After these elections, Republican officials embraced the Tea Party candidates as a way to tap into the Tea Party groups' anger toward President Obama and the Democratic Congress. Despite its lurch to the right, the Republican Party won the majority of the races in 2010 because the economy had not recovered from the recession and many voters rejected the policies of the Democratic president and Congress.

Fragmented Parties

The American party system also features fragmented political parties, meaning that their power is dispersed among their components. Party voters throughout the country; party officeholders at the national, state, and local levels; and officials in the national, state, and local party organizations are not unified through either a tight structure or a common program. Instead, reflecting the nature of American government itself, which disperses power through federalism, separation of powers, and checks and balances, party elements are relatively independent of one another.

Fragmentation makes it difficult for party leaders to fashion a coherent and consistent program and persuade their officeholders to accept it. Although presidents usually get support from their party members in Congress,[12] some party members go their own way. To get reelected, they need only the votes of their constituents—not the approval of the president or party leaders. When President Clinton proposed an increase in gas taxes to reduce the deficit, Sen. Herbert Kohl (D-Wisc.) told him the increase could be no more than 4.3 cents per gallon. Clinton had to accept Kohl's figure because the bill's outcome was in doubt and the senator's vote was essential. When President Bush proposed immigration reform, conservative Republicans rebelled and refused to pass the bill.

Figure 2 **Where the Voters Are**

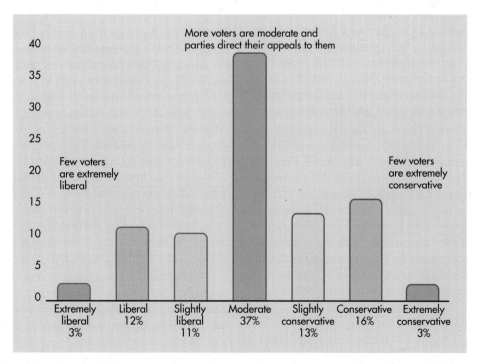

The figures indicate how the voters characterize themselves today. In recent years, more have characterized themselves as conservative than as liberal, but most have characterized themselves as moderate. Thus the parties usually aim their campaigns at the middle.
SOURCE: *Data from General Social Survey, 2008.*

Toles copyright © 2009. Universal Press Syndicate. Reprinted by permission.

Party Organization

Party organization—the professionals and activists who staff the party apparatus at each level—reflects the fragmentation of the parties. The organization isn't a hierarchical, top-down structure like the military, in which the higher-ups issue commands and the underlings follow them. The national party organization doesn't dictate policies to the state and local levels or impose penalties on these levels. Party organization is layered, with each layer linked to, but independent of, the others.

National party organizations   The national party organization, called the **national committee**, is headed by the **national party chair**, who is appointed by the president or, for the opposition party, by its national committee. The chair raises money and speaks out on behalf of the party. The national committees rarely meet, although they do choose the site of the party's national convention and determine the formula for calculating each state's number of delegates.

Both parties also have House and Senate campaign committees, which raise money, recruit candidates, and develop strategy for upcoming campaigns.[13] Rep. Rahm Emanuel (D-Ill.), now chief of staff for President Obama, headed the Democratic Congressional Campaign Committee in 2006 and was charged with producing a Democratic majority in the House for the first time in twelve years. Hyperactive and ruthless—he was nicknamed "Rahmbo"—Emanuel recruited centrist candidates for conservative districts, such as retired NFL quarterback Heath Shuler of North Carolina. Shuler resisted Emanuel's pleas to run, insisting that he wanted to spend time with his family, but Emanuel persisted, calling him five times a day.[14] Reported Shuler, "He calls one morning: 'Heath, I'm taking my kids to school,' then he just hangs up. At 11:30, he calls and says, 'I'm leaving my office to eat lunch with my kids.' Then, 'Heath, it's 3:30, and I'm walking into school.'"[15] Shuler finally relented—and won his election—and Emanuel delivered a majority for the Democrats.

State and local party organizations   State and local party organizations have committees and chairs to direct party activities at these levels. Some communities have strong party organizations made up of volunteers who recruit candidates to run and citizens to work the precincts and man the telephones. In other communities, the parties are so weak that they have little organization at all. In most communities, any citizen who wants to become active in the party needs only to show up at party meetings and be prepared to work.

Now we'll turn to history to see how the parties originated and developed and to see what roles they've played in the American political system.

THE RISE OF AMERICAN PARTIES

The Founders dreaded the prospect of political parties, fearing that rival parties, seeking to win favors for themselves at the expense of the common good, would undermine the new nation and its fledgling government.[16] They hoped, unrealistically, to govern by consensus.

Because of the Founders' misgivings, the Constitution doesn't mention political parties. Nevertheless, the Constitution created a government in which parties, or something like them, were inevitable. With popular election as the mechanism for selecting political leaders, an agency for organizing and mobilizing the supporters of competing candidates became necessary.

Birth of Parties

With George Washington's unanimous election to the presidency in 1788, it appeared that the nation could be governed by consensus. But conflicts soon emerged. Alexander Hamilton, Washington's secretary of the treasury, favored a strong national government. He and his supporters in Congress, who called themselves **Federalists**, were opposed by Thomas Jefferson, Washington's secretary of state, who feared a strong central government. This disagreement led Jefferson to challenge John Adams, a Federalist, for the presidency in 1796. Jefferson lost, but his defeat showed him the value of organization. He recruited political operatives in each state who established newspapers to publicize his views, thus creating the first American political party—the **Jeffersonians**. Backed by his new party, Jefferson won the presidency in 1800. (See the box "Alexander Hamilton, Party Tactician.")

Before Jefferson left office, most members of Congress—more than 90 percent—were either Jeffersonians (later called Jeffersonian Republicans) or Federalists and consistently voted in support of their party's positions.[17]

Development of Mass Parties

Andrew Jackson introduced the idea of a political party with a large following among rank-and-file voters. Running for president in 1828, he reached out to the masses, and his appeals

behind the scenes

Alexander Hamilton, Party Tactician

Alexander Hamilton, who as secretary of the treasury laid the foundation for American capitalism, also was responsible for the first religious attacks on political opponents in election campaigns.[1]

Hamilton was an unlikely advocate of religion. A libertine, he was involved with his sister-in-law and with a woman described as a "grifter" (a swindler).[2] He was not a practicing Christian until the dueling death of his oldest son, just three years before his own dueling death.

Although Hamilton supported separation of church and state, he was a practical politician, and an opportunistic one. Realizing that appealing to the religious sentiments and prejudices of the people was "an important means of influencing opinion,"[3] he urged fellow leaders not to be "overscrupulous" about manipulating the masses.[4]

As the leader of the Federalists, Hamilton opposed the Jeffersonians. In the election of 1800, he launched a smear campaign to portray Thomas Jefferson as a godless and amoral man who, if elected president, would bring depravity to the nation's capital. Hamilton hoped to discourage Christians from supporting Jefferson, who was inspired by philosophy and science more than by religion and who rejected Christian dogma and criticized its clergy.

Hamilton's efforts backfired, as the voters recognized the strategy behind the charges. Nonetheless, his efforts showed savvy politicians how religious issues might be used to manipulate public opinion in the future.

[1] This box is drawn from Brooke Allen, *Moral Minority: Our Skeptical Founding Fathers* (Chicago: Ivan R. Dee, 2006), ch. 6.
[2] Ibid., 123.
[3] Ibid., 130.
[4] Ibid., 131.

drew five times more voters to the polls than in 1824. Jackson's opponents deplored his approach, calling him a "barbarian" and his campaign "the howl of raving democracy."[18]

Like Jefferson, Jackson saw the strength of American democracy in the common person. Because his administration encouraged participation in government, property ownership as a qualification for voting was lifted in most states where it still existed,[19] extending the franchise to almost all white men. Members of the Electoral College were elected by the people rather than selected by state legislatures. National party conventions, with representatives from every state and locality, were established to nominate presidential candidates.[20] These reforms encouraged political participation by average people. Historians would refer to this era's emphasis on the common person as **Jacksonian democracy**.

With the enhanced participation fostered by these reforms, the idea of a political party with a mass following took root in American politics. As population increased, the electorate continued to expand, doubling by 1840.[21]

Golden Age of Mass Parties

Parties reached their high point in the late nineteenth and early twentieth centuries, when party leaders controlled nominations for public offices and mobilized voters during election campaigns. Voting rates reached their highest levels ever during this period.

Political Machines

Much of the power of local parties was concentrated in **political machines,** powerful organizations that could deliver the votes. Also known as "urban machines" because they were prevalent in big cities, they flourished during this period, with some lasting until the middle of the twentieth century.

Unlike today's parties, political machines were hierarchical organizations. A city was divided into small neighborhoods called precincts, and the precincts were grouped into larger neighborhoods called wards. Party operatives were designated as "precinct captains" and "ward heelers." Their job was to know their constituents, tend to their needs, and then get their votes for the party's candidates in the next election. The head of the machine was a boss, who often served as mayor and who directed the organization and ran city government to maintain control for his party. (See the box "A Day in the Life of a Machine Politician.")

The machines relied on the votes of the poor and working class, many of whom had recently immigrated from Europe. Although most accounts of machine politics are negative, dwelling on corruption, the machines provided valuable services for their constituents.

Providing welfare Political machines served as an informal welfare system for poor people before government established a formal welfare system. Party workers were an early "Welcome Wagon" for new immigrants, meeting them on the dock as they came off the ship and helping them settle into their new community in this strange country. The party provided food, clothing, or housing for people in need.

Longtime Rep. Tip O'Neill (D-Mass.) told the story of Boston mayor James Curley, a leader of the city's Democratic organization in the early twentieth century. As winter approached, Curley called Filene's, a local department store, and told the owner he needed five thousand sweaters. When the owner balked, Curley reminded him that it was

In 1828, opponents of Andrew Jackson called him a jackass. Political cartoonists and journalists began to use the donkey to symbolize Jackson and the Democratic Party (left). In the 1870s, cartoonist Thomas Nast popularized the donkey as a symbol of the party and originated the elephant as a symbol of the Republican Party. His 1874 cartoon (right) showed the Democratic donkey dressed as a lion frightening the other animals of the jungle, including the Republican elephant.

time to reassess Filene's property for tax purposes, a none-too-subtle threat that its taxes would go up if the sweaters weren't delivered. So, the sweaters were delivered and then distributed to poor people in the city.[22]

Of course, party leaders were not motivated by altruism but rather by self-interest. They granted favors to get favors in return (votes). As New York City's boss George Washington Plunkitt said, "If a family is burned out, I don't ask whether they are Republicans or Democrats. . . . I just get quarters for them, buy clothes for them if their clothes were burned up and fix them up 'til they get things runnin' again. It's philanthropy, but it's politics too—mighty good politics. Who can tell me how many votes one of these fires brings me?"[23]

Providing jobs   Because they controlled government jobs, the machines also served as an informal employment agency. Under their **patronage system**,[24] virtually all government jobs, from the mayor's top aide to street sweepers, went to political appointees. When one party captured control of city government, city workers who supported the losing party were fired and new workers who supported the winning party were hired in their place. "To the victor belong the spoils," the saying went. So the patronage system came to be known as the **spoils system**. The practice began with the presidency of Andrew Jackson, who wanted common people to get a share of government jobs and so gave jobs to western frontiersmen rather than eastern businessmen.

In adopting this practice, the machines provided jobs to some middle-class people and to many poor people and new immigrants. By 1900, New York City's machine controlled 60,000 city jobs. In the 1960s and 1970s, Chicago's mayor, Richard Daley, one of the last of the big-city bosses, controlled 35,000 city jobs and, indirectly through public contracts, 10,000 private ones.[25]

When the parties provided welfare and jobs, the recipients were not only grateful but also indebted to the party. Fearful of losing their jobs, they formed an army of campaign workers, going door-to-door and when necessary taking residents to the polls to cast their votes for the party.

Turnout in elections was sky-high in the era of machine politics. In the 1896 presidential election, party workers got 90 percent of eligible voters (outside the South) to the polls, an astonishing number when many voters lived in isolated rural areas and used horses and buggies for transportation.[26]

Engaging in corruption   Although the machines provided undeniable benefits, they also engaged in undeniable corruption (as the story about the sweaters illustrates). Bribes and kickbacks were common, and payoffs were necessary for businesses to get government contracts. Widespread corruption eventually produced a backlash against the machines, and the middle class, which was less dependent on the machines, pressured legislators to enact reforms that led to their demise.

DEMOCRACY?

Does it seem that the parties in this era made government more democratic or less democratic than the parties of today do?

Functions of Parties

When political parties were at the height of their power, they performed important functions for society. (When we speak of institutions or organizations performing "functions," we mean that institutions or organizations do things that society finds useful. These things become their "functions" for social scientists.) The parties' primary function, then as now, was to get their candidates elected, but to accomplish

A Day in the Life of a Machine Politician

George Washington Plunkitt was a ward leader in the infamous Tammany Hall machine, the Democratic Party organization that governed New York City for seven decades in the late nineteenth and early twentieth centuries. Although Plunkitt was on the city payroll, he did not have a free ride. The demands of his job were exhausting. But providing social services to his constituents created opportunities to build support for his party.

Entries from Plunkitt's diary illustrate the typical tasks he faced each day.

- 2:00 A.M. Aroused from sleep by a bartender who asked me to go to the police station and bail out a saloon keeper who had been arrested for violating the excise law. Furnished bail and returned to bed at three o'clock.
- 6:00 A.M. Awakened by fire engines. Hastened to the scene of the fire . . . found several tenants who had been burned out, took them to a hotel, supplied them with clothes, fed them, and arranged temporary quarters for them.
- 8:30 A.M. Went to the police court to secure the discharge of six "drunks," my constituents, by a timely word to the judge. Paid the fines of two.
- 9:00 A.M. Appeared in the municipal district court to direct one of my district captains to act as counsel for a widow about to be dispossessed. . . . Paid the rent of a poor family and gave them a dollar for food.
- 11:00 A.M. At home again. "Fixed" the troubles of four men waiting for me: one discharged by the Metropolitan Railway for neglect of duty; another wanted a job on the road; the third on the subway; and the fourth was looking for work with a gas company.
- 3:00 P.M. Attended the funeral of an Italian. Hurried back for the funeral of a Hebrew constituent. Went conspicuously to the front both in the Catholic church and the synagogue.
- 7:00 P.M. Went to district headquarters to preside over a meeting of election district captains, submitted lists of all the voters in their districts and told who were in need, who were in trouble, who might be won over [to Tammany] and how.
- 8:00 P.M. Went to a church fair. Took chances on everything, bought ice cream for the young girls and the children, kissed the little ones, flattered their mothers, and took the fathers out for something down at the corner.
- 9:00 P.M. At the clubhouse again. Spent $10 for a church excursion. Bought tickets for a baseball game. Listened to the complaints of a dozen pushcart peddlers who said they were being persecuted by the police. Promised to go to police headquarters in the morning and see about it.
- 10:30 P.M. Attended a Hebrew wedding reception and dance. Had previously sent a handsome wedding present to the bride.
- 12:00 A.M. In bed.

Alistair Cooke, Alistair Cooke's America (New York: Knopf, 1973), 290–291; adapted from William L. Riordon, Plunkitt of Tammany Hall (New York Dutton, 1963), 91–93.

George Washington Plunkitt holds forth in his unofficial office, a bootblack stand at the New York County Court House.

SOURCE: Alistair Cooke, *Alistair Cooke's America* (New York: Knopf, 1973), 290–291; adapted from William L. Riordon, *Plunkitt of Tammany Hall* (New York Dutton, 1963), 91–93.

this goal they had to perform other functions that gained the allegiance of voters.

We've already seen that the parties provided welfare and jobs to many people. They also provided information about politics through party newspapers. Though one-sided, the newspapers helped party supporters learn about politics and government and recognize their stake in upcoming elections.[27] After gaining the allegiance of many people, the parties were in position to mobilize their supporters on election day.

Candidates for public office were recruited from party workers who had moved up the ladder from low-level jobs to more responsible jobs. (The boss of New York City's machine began by delivering coal to poor people in the winter.) Once the workers had proven themselves, party leaders would consider them for elective office. The party controlled nominations at the local level (city council and mayor), state level (state legislature and governor), and national level (Congress and the president). These nominations weren't open contests in which any aspiring citizen could compete; they were awarded to those who had proven themselves and demonstrated their loyalty. Without the party's blessing, no candidate could secure the nomination or hope to win the election. The parties also ran campaigns for their candidates, mapping strategy, raising funds, and recruiting workers. In the 1896 election, Republican workers brought 750,000 persons from all over the United States to the Ohio home of their candidate, William McKinley, who greeted the visitors from his front porch.[28]

If successful in gaining peoples' allegiance and winning their votes on election day, a party could control the government. Thus the value of political parties in a democracy was to give average people political power. As individuals, ordinary people were powerless; they acquired power only as members of a political party. Collectively, they could wield power that only corporations or wealthy individuals could exercise.

In the late nineteenth century and early twentieth century, parties benefited society and in the process strengthened themselves by performing functions that made them indispensable to society. What, however, would happen if parties could no longer perform these functions? We will return to this question shortly.

THE DECLINE OF AMERICAN PARTIES

Although many Americans think that political parties are too powerful today, they are in fact far less powerful than they were in the late nineteenth and early twentieth centuries.

Progressive Reforms

American political parties began to lose power with the advent of the **Progressive movement**, which morphed into a third party, the Progressive Party, in the early 1900s. Middle-class Americans concerned with the corruption of big-city machines fueled the movement, which sought to wrest control from the machines and from the immigrants and poor people served by the machines. The movement championed numerous reforms that reduced corruption but also weakened the power of political parties and consequently reduced the power of poor and working-class voters.

Election reforms, including voter registration, the secret ballot, and primary elections, brought the golden age of political parties to an end. **Voter registration**, which required voters to register their name and address before an election, made it difficult for parties to stuff ballot boxes with fraudulent votes. The parties could no longer urge their workers to "vote early and vote often." The **secret ballot** prevented party workers stationed at the polls from knowing how any citizens voted—in particular, how their (assumed) supporters voted. The parties could no longer reward their supporters for their votes. These reforms reduced the corruption fostered by the machines, but primary elections undermined the parties' control of nominations, which was devastating to the parties' power. **Primary elections**, held several weeks

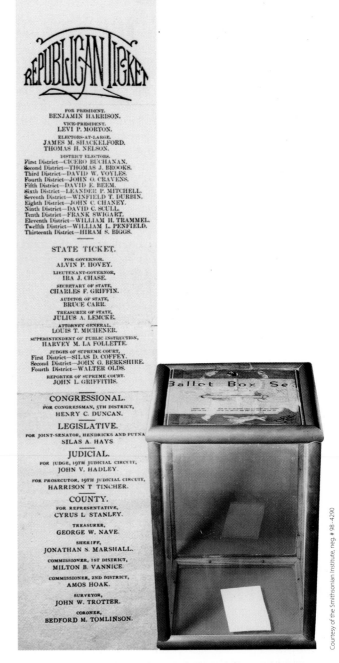

Until the 1890s, there was no pretense of secrecy in voting. Each party's ballot was a different color. Voters chose their party's ballot, like this Republican ballot for the 1888 election in Indiana, and placed it in a clear, glass-sided ballot box.

Courtesy of the Smithsonian Institute, neg. # 98-4290

or months before the general election, allowed the party's voters rather than the party's leaders to decide who would be the party's nominees in the general election. The party's leaders could no longer reward the most effective and most loyal workers with nominations. And, after the election, the leaders could no longer demand the officials to remain faithful to the party and its policies. Instead, the officials only had to remain popular with the voters.

Another Progressive reform, the **merit system**, allocated government jobs on the basis of competence rather than affiliation with a party. Once established, merit systems were expanded to cover more and more jobs. Eventually, the merit systems at the local, state, and national levels replaced the patronage systems for all but a small number of jobs—the top aides to the president, governor, and mayor.

Although the Progressive Party never captured the presidency, it became the most influential third party in American history. Its ideas were enacted into law throughout the country.

Welfare Programs

During the Great Depression, which started in 1929, the federal government established welfare programs for the needy and the elderly—basic welfare, now known as Temporary Assistance, and Social Security. In later decades, it added food stamps, Medicaid (health care for poor people), and Medicare (health care for the elderly and others on Social Security). In addition, it provided unemployment compensation to those temporarily out of work. Thus the government substituted systematic welfare programs for the hit-or-miss efforts of the party machines.

Because these benefits come from the government, people don't have to seek them from the parties. Therefore, government welfare programs, along with government merit systems, severed the links between many people and political parties. No longer the source of welfare and jobs, the parties had less hold on the allegiance—and the votes—of lower- and middle-class Americans.

For the most part, the changes during the Progressive era and the Great Depression were desirable. Political corruption was reduced; government jobs went to those individuals competent to perform them, rather than to political hacks; and welfare programs reached everyone in need, not just the supporters of the party in power. But the changes did curtail the parties' power and hence their ability to represent and fight for average people.

Independent Media

The parties also lost their monopoly over political information. In the 1800s independent newspapers replaced party newspapers,[29] and in the 1920s and 1950s radio and television emerged and gained mass audiences. Although many newspapers and radio and television stations expressed political preferences, they were independent of either party. With exposure to multiple news sources, people could, and did, decide for themselves how to vote.

Diminution of Campaign Roles

Today the parties don't even perform their core functions of nominating candidates and running campaigns as they used to.

Party voters in primary elections choose the nominees. The parties still hold their conventions, but the conventions

Party officials no longer determine their nominee for president; party voters in primary elections do. In 1976, Democratic officials were reluctant to endorse Jimmy Carter, who was relatively inexperienced, but Democratic voters in the primaries liked his decency. Carter received enough support from them that the party had to nominate him. Although he won the general election (thus vindicating the voters in the primaries), he was unable to govern effectively (thus vindicating party officials). Consequently, in 1980 he lost his reelection bid.

merely ratify the choices of the voters and rally public support for the ticket.

Nor are parties the driving force behind campaigns. Although candidates receive money, advice, and workers from local, state, and national party organizations, most rely on their own campaign teams. Modern media elections require extensive expertise: specialists in polling, fundraising, and advertising, including experts to design and produce the ads, others to buy television time and newspaper space for the ads, and others to generate direct mail. Now candidates also need specialists to design and maintain web pages and blogs. They need campaign managers and speechwriters. Some use speech and drama coaches to help them speak, gesture, and move effectively.

This talent is expensive. The 2008 presidential primary candidates spent, collectively, nearly $1 billion. The parties help pay the bills but can't afford the majority of the costs, so the candidates turn to wealthy individuals and interest groups for the rest. Once elected, the officials may feel more beholden to their contributors than to their party.

Thus interest groups play a big role in funding modern campaigns. As the parties have lost power, interest groups have gained it. Picture a teeter-totter with political parties on one end and interest groups on the other. As the power of political parties has gone down, the power of interest groups has gone up.

For these reasons, elected officials are more independent of their party, and less obligated to follow its platform, than they used to be. Therefore, the parties aren't able to control the government as they used to do.

Erosion of Popular Support?

Because parties don't perform the same functions or don't perform them to the same degree as they used to, people aren't as attached to parties as they once were. **Dealignment** is the term for this lessening of citizens' attachment.[30]

Political scientists pointed to two trends after the 1960s that reflected dealignment. The percentage of voters who declared themselves independent, rather than a member of either party, increased. And the percentage of voters who split their ticket—voting for both Democrats and Republicans in an election—increased. (See Figure 3.)

Because of these trends, political scientists in the 1970s and subsequent decades speculated that American parties would continue to decline and perhaps even disappear. But this speculation was premature. Despite some dealignment, there remains considerable support for the parties.

Independents

The proportion of voters calling themselves **independents** rose from less than 15 percent in 1960 to almost 40 percent today.[31] The proportion may have peaked in the 1970s and slightly reversed since then.[32] Yet young Americans are more likely than older Americans to consider themselves independents.

Even so, these numbers are misleading. Some independents are "conflicted centrists," who are closer to the Democrats on social issues but closer to the Republicans in their skepticism of big government.[33] They vacillate from party to party. But they may number no more than 10 percent of the electorate.[34] Most "independents" actually feel some attachment to one party and usually vote for the candidates of that party. They are "closet partisans."[35] Perhaps they like to consider themselves independent because the media and many people decry partisanship and glorify independence. Thus the "increase" in independents is more apparent than real.

Split-Ticket Voting

Split-ticket voting occurs when a voter casts a ballot for a candidate from one party for one office and a candidate from another party for another office—for example, a Republican presidential candidate and a Democratic House or Senate candidate, or a Republican House candidate and a Democratic Senate candidate. Split-ticket voting reflects less attachment to either party than straight-ticket voting. These voters are motivated by the personalities of the candidates or the issues in the campaign rather than by party affiliation.

Split-ticket voting increased after 1960, but it has fluctuated since then. There has been no clear pattern. Although it was over 30 percent in 1980 and 2004, it was less than 20 percent in 1996 (at least for votes for Congress) and 2008. (See Figure 3.) Thus the frequency of

| Figure 3 | Support for Parties |

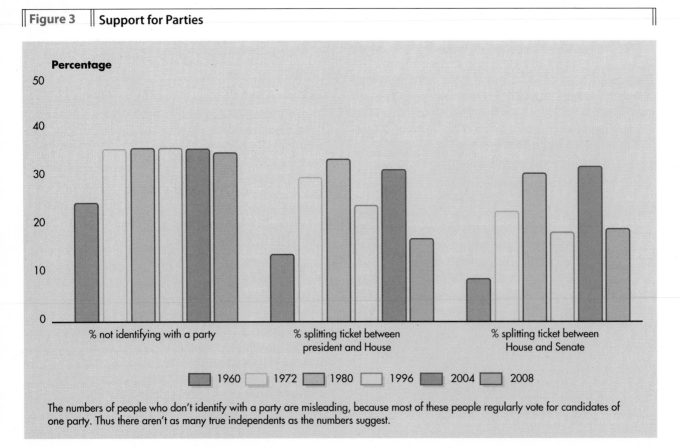

The numbers of people who don't identify with a party are misleading, because most of these people regularly vote for candidates of one party. Thus there aren't as many true independents as the numbers suggest.

SOURCE: American Election Study, Center for Political Studies, University of Michigan, 1960–2008, www.umich.edu/nes.

split-ticket voting shows significant dealignment from the parties in some years but considerable support for the parties in other years.

THE RESURGENCE OF AMERICAN PARTIES

The parties have recognized their decline and fought to revitalize themselves. They have adjusted to the changing political landscape by raising substantial amounts of money and bolstering their organizations with professional and specialized staffers and linking with political consultants. In recent decades they have also benefited from the polarization and heightened partisanship of American society, media, and government.[36] They have been resilient. Although they are weaker today than a century ago, they still play important roles in American politics.

Informing

Parties continue to provide information to supporters, now through direct mail, radio and television advertising, and the Internet. During election campaigns, party supporters may receive flyers, e-mails, and phone calls from national, state, and local party organizations and congressional campaign committees extolling the merits of the party's candidates and soliciting contributions for them.

Nominating and Campaigning

Although the parties no longer control the nominations, they do continue to recruit candidates and to provide them with campaign services and financial support. They also host workshops on topics such as raising money and talking to reporters, and they sometimes offer the services of specialized consultants.

Governing

Political parties continue to dominate Congress. The majority party in each house organizes and runs its chamber. It selects the presiding officers, who set the agenda, deciding which issues are debated and which are voted upon. The majority also designates the chairs of the committees and subcommittees and controls the committees and subcommittees.

Members of Congress usually vote with other members of their party, and members of the president's party usually follow his lead. Partisan voting in Congress has increased dramatically since the 1970s.[37] During the Bush presidency, House Republicans voted together 90 percent of the time, and the Democrats voted together about 85 percent of the time (on issues over which the parties opposed each other). (See Figure 4.)

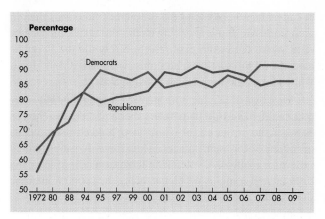

Figure 4 | **Party Unity in the House**

Party unity in the House of Representatives increased as the two parties became more ideological.
SOURCE: *CQ Weekly.*

Before the 1980s, congressional Democrats included many southern moderates and conservatives, who sometimes voted with the Republicans, and congressional Republicans included some northern moderates and liberals, who sometimes voted with the Democrats. Thus party voting was less prevalent. Since then, southern conservatives have gravitated to the Republican Party, and northern liberals have moved to the Democratic Party (as we'll explain in the next section). Thus both parties in Congress have become more ideologically consistent.[38]

Party voting in the past two decades also reflects the election of conservative Republican members of Congress during the Clinton administration and the election of George W. Bush in 2000 and 2004. Determined to capitalize on their control of Congress and the White House and later on the swell of public support for the president following 9/11, Republican leaders in Congress pushed a very conservative agenda. With the aid of talk radio, Fox News, and conservative interest groups, they pressured the remaining moderate Republicans to go along. As mentioned in the opening vignette, those who appeared reluctant were dubbed "RINOs" (Republicans in Name Only).[39] Facing intense heat, the moderates wilted, rationalizing their capitulation by saying that the voters needed to see that the party could govern the country.[40] In response, Democrats, who traditionally have been less united than Republicans, came together in an attempt to check the very conservative policies of Republicans. These dynamics led to more partisan voting in Congress.

Party-line voting is likely to remain high as long as each party has a distinct vision of where it wants to take the country. However, a president committed to building bridges across party lines and a minority party willing to work with him might lessen party voting. President Obama has made overtures toward bipartisanship, but congressional

Democrats have been less willing, and congressional Republicans have been very resistant, seeing more political advantage in blocking the president's proposals than in compromising and influencing them. As a result, the Democrats wrote the health care reform bill while the Republicans sat on the sidelines, and most Democrats voted for it while all but one Republican voted against it.

Most Americans deplore partisan wrangling, but clear partisan divisions do help voters recognize the differences between the parties and also help them hold elected officials accountable for their policies. Thus these divisions, which reflect the reality that voters don't agree on how to solve the difficult and complex problems facing the country, increase the likelihood of popular control of government.

Despite the increase in partisan voting, the American party system falls short of what political scientists call **responsible party government**. Under this model, political parties would take clear and opposing positions on major issues, voters would understand these differences and vote on this basis, and officeholders would enact the party's positions into law. Some European democracies, which have much stronger parties, come close to this ideal. Citizens vote for a party, with its positions on the issues, rather than for a candidate. They assume that the party is cohesive enough to enact its positions if it wins the election. Once elected, legislators do vote with their party on major issues. If they defect—a rare occurrence—they risk expulsion from the party and loss of their seat. Even if they abstain, they risk punishment.[41]

In recent congresses, our system has come closer to this model than it typically has in the past. Democrats and Republicans have taken opposing stands on controversial issues, and they have made concerted efforts to enact their party's positions into law. Of course, American citizens vote for individual candidates rather than for a party, and American officials retain more independence than European officials do. Nevertheless, there is mounting pressure on Democratic officials to accept Democratic positions and, especially, on Republican officials to accept Republican positions. Conservative interest groups have tried to purge moderate Republicans, and even conservative Republicans who cooperate with the Democrats in bipartisan efforts, from national office by pressuring the officials and by recruiting and funding more conservative candidates to challenge the officials in primary elections.[42] In these hyperpartisan times, voters may support this strategy.

Yet it is unlikely that we will adopt the responsible party government model for the long term. In contrast to Europeans, Americans hold individualistic rather than communitarian values. Constituents tolerate, even expect, representatives to deviate from their party at times. They praise representatives who are "independent," and representatives claim to be "independent" of their party and its leaders. To get elected and reelected, of course, representatives need to appease their constituents rather than their party.

Moreover, our separation of powers makes responsible party government unlikely. One party may control the presidency while the other controls one or both houses of Congress. Divided government diffuses and obscures responsibility rather than pinpoints it. With divided responsibility, the voters are unable to determine which party to praise or blame for government policies.

PARTY REALIGNMENTS

Although we have two competitive parties, at any given time the two parties may not be evenly matched. Usually one is dominant, winning the presidency and Congress in election after election. Eventually, some major event, such as a war or a depression, destabilizes voters' party allegiance and triggers a massive movement of voters from one party to the other party, which then becomes the dominant party. The process by which one party loses many supporters to the other party is referred to as a **realignment**.[43]

These upheavals—revolutions without bloodshed—have occurred about every thirty to forty years. Since the party system was established, there have been three major realignments—during the Civil War in the 1860s, the depression in the 1890s,[44] and the Great Depression in the 1930s.[45] There have also been minor realignments limited to certain geographical regions or demographic groups. (See Figure 5.)

Major Realignment in the 1930s

The realignment of the 1930s set the stage for the politics of recent decades. The Republicans had dominated since the realignment of the 1890s. When the Great Depression rocked the country, those hit hardest, such as the poor, working men and women, recent immigrants, and black Americans, who had favored Abraham Lincoln's party since the Civil War, turned to the Democrats, electing Franklin D. Roosevelt as president and Democratic majorities to Congress. The 1932 election started a major realignment, from Republicans to Democrats, and marked a new era. Most new voters and some Republican supporters in previous elections became Democratic supporters. Democrats would control the presidency for the next twenty years, electing FDR to an unprecedented four terms, and would control at least one house of Congress until 1954.

Roosevelt's **New Deal coalition**, composed of city dwellers, blue-collar workers, Catholic and Jewish immigrants, blacks, and southerners, was a potent political force, but it was an uneasy alliance—conservative, rural, white southerners committed to racial segregation and liberal, urban, black and white northerners. After FDR's death in 1945, the coalition began to fray. The party's support for civil rights, which began in 1948 and accelerated in the 1960s, alienated white southerners, and U.S. involvement in the Vietnam War split the party in 1968. The coalition continued to erode. Even though the party would dominate Congress until 1994, it would win the presidency only three more times during the twentieth century.[46]

Figure 5 ‖ Evolution of the Political Parties in the United States

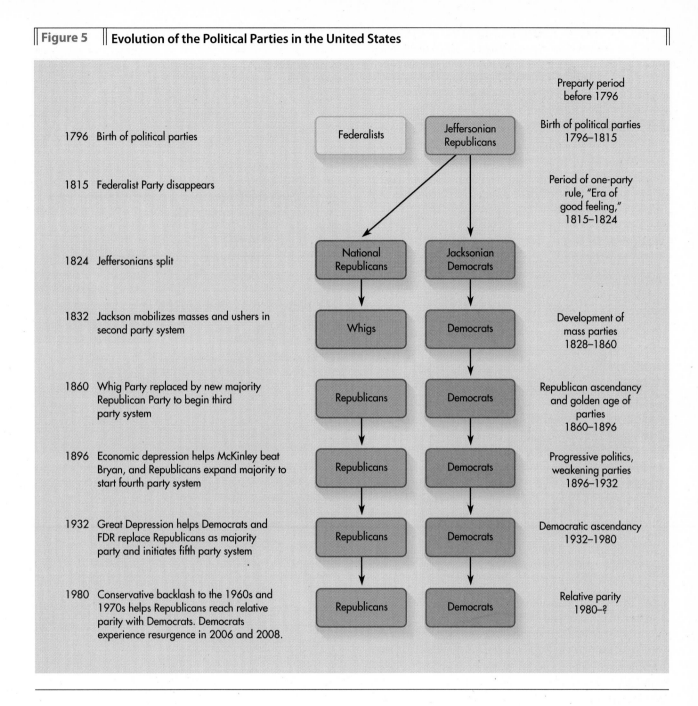

Remember the historical pattern—a new realignment about every thirty to forty years. If the pattern continued, there should have been another realignment during the 1960s or 1970s. With the Democratic Party in disarray in 1968 and 1972, Republican Richard Nixon was elected. His landslide victory in 1972 seemed to confirm a new realignment toward the Republican Party, but his Watergate scandal, forcing him to resign halfway through his second term, tarnished the Republicans' reputation and may have diminished the anticipated realignment. The Democrats continued to control Congress, and Democrat Jimmy Carter won the presidency in 1976.

Minor Realignment in Recent Decades

But a conservative backlash to the liberalism and turmoil of the 1960s and 1970s was brewing. Republican Ronald Reagan was elected president (over Carter) in 1980 and reelected in a landslide in 1984. His vice president, George H. W. Bush, was elected president in 1988. Although Democrat Bill Clinton was elected president in 1992 and 1996, Republicans gained control of both houses of Congress in 1994, the first time in four decades.

Clearly, the Democrats were no longer the dominant party, but neither were the Republicans. There had been enough realignment to dethrone the Democrats but not enough to enthrone the Republicans. A minor realignment, limited to certain geographic regions and demographic groups, had occurred and had fostered rough parity between the parties. Some blocs of voters had shifted to the Republicans, while others had shifted to the Democrats, with a net gain for the Republicans.

This minor realignment involved southern whites, northern blue-collar workers, white-collar professionals, and regular churchgoers. This realignment was a slow realignment, spanning at least four decades, unlike previous realignments that transpired more suddenly.[47] And this realignment revolved around social cleavages in society, unlike the realignment in the 1930s that revolved around economic cleavages.

Southern Whites

In the 1960s, the combination of the civil rights movement and the federal government's efforts to eliminate racial segregation caused many southern whites to leave their longtime home in the Democratic Party. Their move to the Republican Party was the most significant switch in this minor realignment.

Southern whites' disaffection with the Democratic Party began after World War II, when Democratic president Harry Truman, who took office upon Roosevelt's death, integrated the Armed Forces. In 1948, the president and the Democrats included a civil rights plank in the party's platform. The move prompted Strom Thurmond, Democratic governor of South Carolina, to form a breakaway party, the States' Rights Party, commonly called the Dixiecrats. Thurmond ran for president against Truman and carried four southern states. Although the Dixiecrats returned to the fold, southern discomfort with the party grew in the 1950s when northern Democrats again proposed civil rights legislation.

The exodus gained momentum when Democratic president Lyndon Johnson pushed, and the Democratic Congress passed, the landmark Civil Rights Act of 1964. The legislation, also supported by many Republicans, gave African Americans the right to patronize private businesses open to the public, such as restaurants, hotels, and theaters. The bill was strenuously opposed by southern whites, including southern Democrats in Congress, because it undermined traditional white supremacy. Upon signing the bill, Johnson commented that it would deliver the South to the Republicans for "the next fifty years."[48]

It didn't take long for his prediction to come true. Barry Goldwater, the Republican presidential nominee running against Johnson in 1964, denounced the act as an affront to **"states' rights."** Although Goldwater himself seemed not to have a racial motive—he believed in states' rights in other areas as well—Republicans used his opposition to appeal to southern segregationists.[49] With a wink and a nod, "states' rights" became code for letting the South maintain segregation. Goldwater carried five states in the Deep South, more than any Republican since the New Deal.

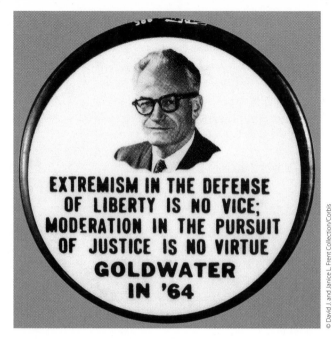

Arizona senator Barry Goldwater captured the Republican nomination for president in 1964. His acceptance speech, quoted on this campaign pin, reflected the new dominance of conservatives over moderates in the party.

In his bid for the presidency in 1968, Richard Nixon consciously pursued a **southern strategy** to lure disaffected southern whites from the Democratic Party. He promised "to change the direction" of the Supreme Court, which had ordered desegregation of the public schools and other public facilities, and to appoint southern judges to the Court. Appealing to white voters, he used racial code words such as "states' rights," "law and order," and "welfare" to send a clear message that the states should be allowed to handle racial matters; control black demonstrators, rioters, and criminals; and crack down on welfare cheats (who were assumed to be African American), all as the states preferred to rather than as federal laws or court decisions told them to. After taping a campaign commercial stressing "law and order in the schools," he said to his aides, "Yep, this hits it right on the nose. . . . It's all about law and order and the damn Negro–Puerto Rican groups out there."[50]

In 1980, Ronald Reagan followed Nixon's lead. He opened his presidential campaign in Philadelphia, Mississippi, where three civil rights workers had been brutally murdered by local citizens with assistance from law enforcement officers, one of the most notorious crimes of the civil rights era (see Chapter 15). In his campaign, Reagan talked about "states' rights" and "welfare queens," a thinly veiled reference to black women who were assumed to be living the high life on welfare.

In 1988, George H. W. Bush, campaigning against Democratic nominee Michael Dukakis, ran a television commercial featuring a black felon, Willie Horton, who had received a weekend furlough from Dukakis, who as Massachusetts's governor had followed the state's policy. On furlough,

Horton raped a white woman. Bush's commercial deliberately linked black criminals and Democratic candidates. The commercial was so powerful that when people were asked after the election what they recalled about the campaign, they mentioned "Bush, Dukakis, and Willie Horton."[51]

Although hardly concealed, the racial strategy of the Republican Party was implemented carefully and cautiously, with code words that stated one thing but meant something else. Candidates and party officials rarely, if ever, praised segregation or used racial epithets, as politicians of both parties had in earlier generations. Whenever confronted about their strategy, Republicans denied that their statements were racist or intended to appeal to racists.

However, in an unguarded moment celebrating the 100th birthday in 2002 of Strom Thurmond, who formed the Dixiecrats and later joined fellow southerners switching to the Republican Party, Trent Lott, a Mississippi Republican and Senate majority leader, disregarded these norms. After declaring that his state was proud to have voted for Thurmond in 1948, he added, "And if the rest of the country had followed our lead, we wouldn't have had all these problems over the years either." For his lapse, Lott apologized, but the public condemnation, including a rebuke by President Bush, forced him to resign his position as majority leader.

The shift of southern whites to the Republican Party doesn't mean that all or even most are racist. What is clear, however, is that since 1964 the Republicans have used a conservative and sometimes implicitly racist approach to race-related issues to build their dominance in the region, just as the Democrats did for generations before them.[52]

Although racial attitudes were the original factor driving the movement of southern whites, their conservative views on other issues, ranging from foreign policy to gun control to religious matters, also made the Republican Party a congenial home for southern whites.

The southern strategy proved highly successful for the Republican Party. The South went from a solidly Democratic region to a reliably Republican one. Since 1968, the Republicans have carried the South in every presidential election except 1976, when the Democrats nominated former Georgia governor Jimmy Carter. Even then, a majority of southern whites voted for the Republican, Gerald Ford. Since 1994, the Republicans have garnered a majority of southern whites' votes for their congressional, state, and local candidates as well. Meanwhile, southern blacks have become the backbone of the southern Democratic Party.[53]

The shift of conservative southern whites to the Republican Party not only makes the South more Republican, but it also makes the Republican Party more conservative and the party system more ideological. The southern Republican members of Congress are more conservative than the southern Democratic members they replaced, and they are more conservative than many northern Republican members. They push their party further to the right. At the same time, their departure from the Democratic Party makes that party more liberal. Thus the transformation of the South has made the parties more ideological, which has made them more polarized and less cooperative than before the shift.

Northern Blue-Collar Workers

Blue-collar workers who were the second- and third-generation sons and daughters of European immigrants, especially from Catholic countries such as Ireland and Italy, were at the heart of the New Deal coalition.[54] But when southern whites left the Democratic Party, some northern blue-collar workers did too.[55]

With the New Deal's success and the 1950s' and 1960s' booming economy, blue-collar workers enjoyed the economic security that allowed them to consider other issues. As the Democratic Party turned from bread-and-butter issues to civil rights, the Vietnam War, and women's equality—issues that motivated the upper middle class more than the lower middle class—some blue-collar workers abandoned the party. Although liberal on economic issues, they were conservative on social issues and on foreign policies. Many were drawn to the Republicans' emphasis on "traditional" values.

Reagan captured a majority of these voters, but when the economy has slumped, some have returned to their partisan roots. In the 2000s, a small majority—no longer a large majority—has supported the Democrats.

White-Collar Professionals

From the Depression through the 1980s, more affluent, better-educated, white-collar workers voted Republican. However, as some blue-collar workers drifted from the Democratic

Strom Thurmond broke with the Democratic Party to run for president in 1948 on the Dixiecrat segregation ticket. Later he became a Republican. In 2002, President Bush and Senate leader Trent Lott (R-Miss.) congratulated him on his 100th birthday.

Stephen Jaffe/AFP/Getty Images

The Republican Party has tried to pull blue-collar workers away from their traditional home in the Democratic Party. President Reagan was especially effective in luring these voters.

Party, some white-collar professionals, especially teachers, lawyers, doctors, and scientists, gravitated to it. (Most business executives remained in the Republican Party.)

White-collar professionals reject the uncompromising and intolerant approach of the Republican core on social issues. They tend to support abortion rights and have a "live and let live" mindset, rather than a traditional values mindset, toward homosexuality,[56] and they tend to favor civil rights, women's equality, and environmental protection, which turned off many blue-collar workers. White-collar professionals also have more liberal attitudes toward foreign policies than blue-collar workers have. (In the 1960s, this split surfaced as student demonstrators with draft deferments—many of whom would eventually become professionals—infuriated the "hard hats" by protesting the Vietnam War.) In recent elections, the Democrats have fared very well in affluent communities populated by white-collar professionals.[57]

Regular Churchgoers

Catholic and Jewish immigrants were also a part of the New Deal coalition. Since the Depression, Catholics and Jews tended to be Democrats because they were largely from the blue-collar immigrant groups helped by the political machines in the big cities. Protestants tended to be Republicans because they were likely to be better off financially and to live in small towns and on farms. As economic issues gave way to social issues, this religious cleavage has

declined and a new cleavage has emerged—between those who are very religious and those who are less religious or nonreligious.

Church attendance now is more correlated with party affiliation than either income or education is.[58] Weekly churchgoers congregate in the Republican Party, and less religious or nonreligious people connect with the Democratic Party. Because there are more weekly churchgoers than irregular churchgoers or non-churchgoers, the shift has benefited the Republicans. But the nonreligious group is growing faster. (Among people eighteen to twenty-five years old, 20 percent report no religious affiliation, up from 11 percent in the late 1980s.[59])

The Supreme Court's school prayer rulings in the 1960s and, especially, the abortion ruling in 1973 were catalysts prompting conservative Christians, who deplored the sexual revolution and the secular drift of modern America, to become politically active. They formed pro-life groups that coalesced into the Christian right. Eventually, the Christian right became one of the strongest forces in the Republican Party. Former senator John Danforth (R-Mo.), himself a minister, observed that his party has been transformed "into the political arm of conservative Christians."[60]

Republicans have allied themselves with conservative Christians, especially churchgoing Protestant Evangelicals. President Bush spoke their language.

The Net Result

In this minor realignment, the net result has been a gain for the GOP, because the southern whites, northern blue-collar workers, and regular churchgoers who left the Democratic Party far outnumber the white-collar professionals who left the Republican Party. This minor realignment has created a rough parity between the two parties.

A major realignment has not occurred. With the patriotic fervor following the 9/11 attacks, and with the election of Republican majorities in Congress and the reelection of President Bush, the Republican Party had an opportunity to solidify its gains. Karl Rove, the president's chief political adviser, worked to produce a major realignment. But the administration and congressional Republicans overreached, adopting policies to benefit Republican constituencies rather than broaden their appeal to Democrats and independents as well. Tax cuts were doled out mostly to the wealthy. Energy, environmental, and consumer regulations were rolled back for big business. Heated rhetoric about gay marriage and abortion was offered for religious conservatives. Most damaging, an aggressive foreign policy was pursued, with the "war on terrorism" used to justify a preemptive attack on Iraq. As the war dragged on and the deficits from tax cuts, war spending, and new entitlements soared, the popularity of the president and the party plummeted.

The Democrats won control of both houses of Congress by small margins in 2006 and larger margins in 2008, and they captured the White House in 2008. New voters, especially young voters, flocked to Democratic candidates. So far, "millenials"—the generation born between 1982 and 2003—are registering overwhelmingly as Democrats.[61]Although the 2008 election results and the youth registration figures suggest the possibility of some realignment toward the Democrats, the country remains sharply split.

The 2010 congressional elections brought Republican gains in both houses. Some gains were expected, as the president's party usually loses seats in years when there is no presidential election. Moreover, economic problems stemming from the severe recession of 2008 and 2009 and lingering through the election year of 2010 turned some independents who had supported the Democrats in 2008 against the party this year. Given the impact of the economy on the election, it is difficult to know whether the results of the election signal a future upturn for the Republicans or only a temporary setback for the Democrats.

In the future, there may be further realignments, although they are likely to be minor realignments rather than major realignments, and they are likely to be ongoing rather than occurring in a fixed pattern, especially if the dealignment trend continues.[62]

PARTY IDENTIFICATION

Party identification is the psychological link that individuals feel toward a party. Unlike European parties, which have official members who pay dues and sign pledges accepting party principles, American parties have no formal members. You are a Democrat or a Republican if you consider yourself one.[63]

Almost two-thirds of Americans identify with a party. In 2010, about 33 percent of Americans identified themselves as Democrats, 27 percent as Republicans, and the largest proportion—37 percent—as independents.[64] These percentages are somewhat misleading, however, as most independents who lean toward one party regularly vote for candidates of that party. (See Figure 6.)

We like to think that we're rational individuals exercising free will when we adopt a party, but that isn't the case for

---

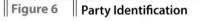 **Figure 6** | **Party Identification**

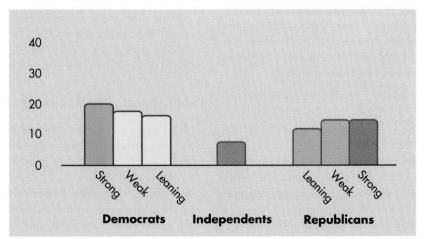

People are asked what party they identify with. If respondents indicate the Democratic or Republican Party, they are asked whether they consider themselves to be a strong member or not a strong member. If respondents say they are independent, they are asked whether they usually vote for the candidates of one party. If so, they are categorized as independents leaning toward that party.
SOURCE: *American Election Study, Center for Political Studies, University of Michigan, 2008, www.umich.edu/nes.*

most people. Party identification typically is determined by our parents' party affiliation; our sexual, racial, ethnic, and religious characteristics; and various geographic factors.

The previous section of the chapter has explained the party identification of some groups that have realigned, but we'll recapitulate those groups and address other groups here so you'll have a complete picture of party identification today.

Parents' Party Affiliation

Party identification usually develops through the process of political socialization, explained in Chapter 4. Parents pass down political views, including party identification, to their children. If both parents identify with the same party, their children probably will as well. If the parents identify with different parties, their children receive mixed signals and may identify with either party or be independent. If both parents are uninterested in politics, their children may ignore both parties.

The party identification of one's parents is the most important determinant of one's own party identification, but other characteristics and factors also come into play.

Sexual, Racial, Ethnic, and Religious Characteristics

The two genders and some racial groups, ethnic groups, and religious groups favor a particular party, so if you belong to one of these groups, it's likely that you'll favor the same party.

For generations, men and women voted similarly. After women got the right to vote, most wives followed their husband's lead. In the 1980s, however, a **gender gap** emerged. During this conservative era, more men moved to the right than women did. Men liked Reagan's anticommunist foreign policies and his pro-business views.[65] Women preferred the Democrats' social policies, which used government to cushion life's hardships and to regulate business's impact on its employees and on the environment. Women also rejected aggressive foreign policies, including military action and military spending. (The gap isn't due to abortion views. Men's and women's views on that issue are similar.)

Today the gender gap persists. It is most marked for working women and unmarried women, who are more likely to be Democrats. Men and stay-at-home moms are more likely to be Republicans.[66]

Homosexuals are presumed to be Democrats. They are difficult to poll because many feel vulnerable and are reluctant to acknowledge their sexual orientation even in a confidential survey. But the tolerance of alternative lifestyles by the Democratic Party and the opposition to same-sex marriage, civil unions, and antidiscrimination laws by the Republican Party undoubtedly have driven most gays and lesbians into the Democratic camp.

Racial minorities tend to be Democrats. African Americans cast a higher percentage of their votes for Democratic candidates than any other group does. They have never left the New Deal coalition because the Democratic Party has championed civil rights and economic policies favorable to working people.

Latinos are not a monolithic group, so their political preferences vary according to the country they or their parents came from. Cuban Americans in south Florida have been staunch Republicans, although generational differences are beginning to emerge. Mexican, Puerto Rican, and other Latin Americans tend to be Democrats, though to a lesser extent than African Americans are. Even so, in 2008 Latino voters enabled Obama to carry Colorado, Florida, Indiana, and Nevada—states that Republicans usually won.[67] In recent elections, Asian Americans have also supported Democratic candidates.[68]

Although some Latinos and Asians have lived in the United States for generations—Latinos in the Southwest predated the arrival of Anglos in the East—many are immigrants or from families of recent immigrants. As relative newcomers, their party identification isn't as fixed as other Americans' identification is. Both parties are vying for their allegiance, especially for Latinos' allegiance, because their population is the fastest-growing in the United States. As the percentage of (non-Hispanic) white births, relative to all births in the United States, declines—in 2008 it was 52 percent; soon it will be less than 50 percent[69]—Republicans fear that they can't remain competitive if they can't convert significant numbers of Latino voters. The Bush administration made a concerted effort to woo them. The president gave his weekly radio address in Spanish, appointed a Hispanic as White House counsel and then attorney general, and proposed immigration reform that would allow illegal immigrants in the United States for a long time to work toward citizenship rather than be deported. His proposal, however, was rejected by congressional Republicans. The apprehension—sometimes the hostility—toward Spanish-speaking immigrants by its conservative base is a stumbling block for the party's efforts to woo Latino voters.

Most Jews remain Democrats, but Catholics waver between the parties. Among Catholics and Protestants, regular churchgoers are very strong Republicans, and the less religious and nonreligious are almost as strong Democrats.

Socioeconomic Characteristics

Individuals' education, occupation, and income, which indicate their social class, also influence their party identification. Historically, the parties split clearly along class lines, with the upper classes being Republicans and the lower classes being Democrats. However, the pattern has blurred in recent decades because of the emergence of social issues such as abortion, gay rights, and gun control. The upper class itself still prefers the Republicans, and the lower class itself still prefers the Democrats, but educational and occupational characteristics have created exceptions to the pattern, especially for the upper middle class.

Individuals with graduate degrees (beyond undergraduate school) have gravitated to the Democrats. They are part of the minor realignment that has occurred in recent decades. In addition, white-collar workers in the public sector—government and education—are mostly Democrats. On the other hand, white-collar workers in the private sector remain disproportionately Republicans.

Geographic Factors

Individuals' region of the country and type of community—urban, suburban, exurban, or rural—also influence their party identification.

The Great Plains and the Rocky Mountain West traditionally have been Republican bastions, although the Democrats have made inroads in the latter. The South, in the minor realignment of recent decades, has become another Republican region. The Northeast and the West Coast are mostly Democratic regions. These patterns give rise to red and blue states, discussed in Chapter 4.

Big cities are strong Democratic locales, and small towns and rural areas are strong Republican locales. Suburbs lie in between. Some, which resemble the stereotype with posh homes owned by business executives, are mostly Republican. Others, which lie on the fringe of the city itself, are mostly Democratic. Exurbs, which are the rapidly growing areas just beyond the suburbs, are heavily Republican.

Now consider the last three categories addressed—sexual, racial, ethnic, and religious characteristics; socioeconomic characteristics; and geographic factors. These characteristics and the factors themselves don't make people Democrats or Republicans. Residing on the coast doesn't make one a Democrat any more than residing in the heartland makes one a Republican. The process is more subtle. Each of these characteristics represents a set of experiences or a network of family, friends, and neighbors at home or of colleagues at work that surrounds an individual with other persons who are like-minded. The other persons reinforce the tendency of the individual to identify with one party rather than the other. Black Americans' history of pervasive discrimination and economic hardship prompts most of them to become Democrats. White rural residents' very different set of experiences and network of people prompt most of them to become Republicans.

Changes in Party Identification

Individuals who come into the electorate are influenced by the environment of the time. Most individuals who first voted in the 1930s supported Roosevelt and became Democrats (and most of them still are Democrats). Many individuals who first voted in 1980 supported Reagan and became Republicans (and most of them still are Republicans). Voters who came of age during the Clinton and George W. Bush administrations increasingly became Democrats. For a glimpse of partisan differences from one generation to the next, see Figure 7.

| Figure 7 | Party Affiliation by Generation |

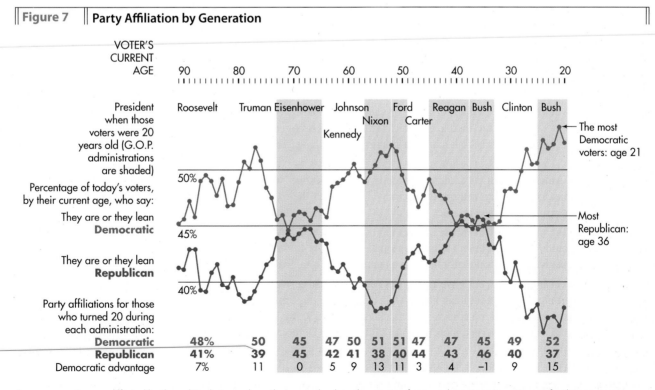

Some new voters are affected by the political atmosphere that prevails when they come of age, and most continue to vote for the same party as they grow older. Those who came of age during the Depression, World War II, the Vietnam War, or the Watergate scandal were very likely to become Democrats. Those who came of age during the Eisenhower or Reagan years were less likely to do so. Those casting their first votes in recent years have been the most Democratic, and least Republican, voters of any generation.

Party identification usually remains constant through an individual's life. However, it can change if the country experiences a major economic, political, or social upheaval. The Great Depression was a catalyst for some people, prompting numerous Republicans to become Democrats. The civil rights movement and the Vietnam War were catalysts for other people, prompting numerous Democrats to become Republicans and some Republicans to become Democrats.

Party identification can also change if one's social status changes—for example, if one gets a college degree, especially a graduate degree; pursues a professional career; or moves to a different place. Such changes provide new experiences and more exposure to different people, which can lead to new political views and party identification.

In the next chapter, we'll see that party identification is one factor—a very important factor, but not the only factor—that determines how people vote.

DEMOCRACY?

In what ways do parties make American government more democratic?

CONCLUSION: Political Parties and the Role of Government

Although the Founders initially opposed the idea of political parties, some eventually turned to parties when they realized that there was no consensus to govern the country. There were sharp differences among the people. To prevail, the leaders recognized that they needed a following of loyal supporters to elect the candidates and adopt the policies they favored. Thus parties arose as vehicles to organize people to win elections, and they continue for this reason.

But parties also serve the needs of citizens. The party labels next to the candidates' names on the ballot provide cues for voters. Some voters pay little attention to election campaigns and have little knowledge about the candidates or issues. Other voters who do pay attention can be confused, because some campaigns do not illuminate the differences between the candidates or their stands on complex issues. Indeed, campaigns may obscure them. So voters can simply check the party labels and vote for their party's candidate. Because the parties and their candidates have a history of taking positions and casting votes on issues, knowing a candidate's party provides a general understanding of the candidate's positions. Thus parties ease the tasks of citizens and increase the probability of citizens making decisions that serve their interests.

By attracting and aggregating millions of people, the parties help average Americans influence government officials and policies. The parties give ordinary people political power they would not have otherwise. Without the parties, only wealthy people or celebrities would have the money or prominence to wield any clout. Thus the major contribution of parties to democracy is to make government more responsive to citizens.

The parties also provide a counterweight to interest groups. Although interest groups represent people, and large interest groups represent many people, they represent a narrower range of people—those with a particular interest—than parties do. Each of the parties tries to attract a majority of the people. When the parties succeed, they can check the influence of special interests.

American citizens, especially young adults, are cynical toward parties. Yet parties serve important functions. Without parties, voters would face a bewildering array of candidates. They would be at the mercy of campaign consultants, big donors, special interests, and the media. Without parties, conflicts over how to use the nation's limited resources—what politics is about—would still exist, but narrower interests would have greater influence, and average men and women would have less.

The dean of American political scientists recently concluded that "we can be pretty sure that a country wholly without competitive parties is a country without democracy."[70] Although the existence of competitive parties is no guarantee that average men and women will prevail, they would most assuredly fail without parties.

By marshalling millions of members, parties can wield power. They can force government to become larger and more active, or they could force government to become smaller and more limited. Usually they have forced government to become larger and more active, but occasionally they have restrained it from growing any further.

Since the Great Depression, our government has been large and active. The Democratic Party, especially, has favored this role for the government. The Republican Party, while accepting a large and active government, has been less enthusiastic and less willing to expand it. With the conservative backlash in the 1980s, 1990s, and 2000s to the liberal period of the 1960s and 1970s, the parties have diverged more sharply. Although the Democrats still want to use government to address societal problems and improve peoples' lives, the Republicans, especially the conservatives who dominate the party now, want to shrink government and remove it as much as possible from economic life.

During President Obama's term, the Democrats have advocated the most aggressive measures to restore the economy battered by the recession. The Democrats also have pushed financial industry reform, health care reform, and climate change measures. The Republicans have opposed each of these,[71] arguing that the reforms will make the government too large and active—even make our government "European" or "socialist."

The conflict between Democrats and Republicans reflects the ambivalent views among Americans. Today, as through history, citizens want government to address problems in society, but at the same time most citizens don't like the idea of big government and many citizens are skeptical of the ability of big government to solve the problems. This ambivalence leads to apparently contradictory responses in public opinion polls. For example, in 2010 most Americans said they wanted health care reform, and large majorities said they favored the major provisions of the Democratic bill. Yet a small majority said they opposed this very bill.

Despite the general pattern outlined here, there are inconsistencies in the parties' attitudes toward an active role for government. Regarding sexual matters, the Democrats want government to be relatively inactive—to take a hands-off approach—so people can use birth control and abortion and schools can teach sex education as they see fit. The Republicans want government to be very active—to foster morality, as they view it—so people are discouraged or prevented from using some forms of birth control and any forms of abortion and schools are encouraged to promote sexual abstinence. Regarding religious matters, the parties reflect a similar pattern. The Democrats want government to accept the concept of separation of church and state and avoid involvement with religion. The Republicans want government to downplay the concept of separation of church and state, instead embracing religion and promoting it in the public sphere and among the citizenry. (These issues are addressed further in Chapter 14.)

Whether the parties want a more active or less active role for government, each tries to attract as many supporters as possible to implement its own view of the appropriate role for government.

KEY TERMS

big tent	183	political machines	189
dealignment	194	political parties	184
Democratic Party	184	primary elections	192
Federalists	188	Progressive movement	192
gender gap	202	proportional representation	185
independents	194	realignment	196
Jacksonian democracy	189	Republican Party	184
Jeffersonians	188	responsible party government	196
merit system	192	secret ballot	192
multiparty systems	184	single-member districts	185
national committee	188	southern strategy	198
national party chair	188	split-ticket voting	194
New Deal coalition	196	spoils system	190
partisan	184	"states' rights"	198
party identification	201	two-party system	184
patronage system	190	voter registration	192
		winner-take-all provision	185

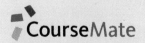 CourseMate   Access an interactive eBook, chapter-specific interactive learning tools (including flashcards, quizzes, videos), and more at CourseMate for *Understanding American Government*. Log in at CengageBrain.com.

8 Elections

○ Barack Obama's election stimulated artists, such as Billi Kid, who creates collages from stickers.

Billi Kid Obama Combo Slaps. Made from stickers collected from all over the world and featuring a poster from Zoltron. Used with permission.

Talking Points

The 2008 election was filled with invective tossed at the candidates. Opponents charged that Obama was a secret Muslim (he's really a Christian), foreign born (he was born in Hawaii), or even an anti-Christ. Sarah Palin accused Obama of "palling around with terrorists," because of his community ties with a man who, in the 1960s, was part of the Weather Underground (a violent, communist antiwar group) but who became a distinguished professor of education at the University of Illinois Chicago.

McCain was a target too. Some charged him with being brainwashed during his years as prisoner of the North Vietnamese. An official Obama ad poked fun of McCain's computer skills, stating he was out of touch, but also implying that he was too old to be president. (McCain's aides say that his war wounds make prolonged typing painful.)

Did the 2008 election reach a new low in mud throwing? Maybe, but American history has been filled with slanderous charges against presidential candidates almost from the beginning. In 1796, a Federalist editorial, supporting John Adams, prophesied that if Thomas Jefferson were elected, "murder, robbery, rape, adultery and incest will be openly taught and practiced."[1] These two founding fathers continued their very low standard in 1800.

John Adams accused Jefferson of being an atheistic coward who wanted to "rip Bibles from the homes of God-fearing Americans."[2] Allegedly some people were so frightened by this that they buried their Bibles to hide them from Jefferson's imaginary search. Jefferson called the portly Adams "his rotundity" and accused him of tyrannical tendencies.[3]

Twenty-eight years later, when Andrew Jackson ran for president, his mother was called a prostitute, his father a mulatto (someone of mixed races, black and white), his wife a profligate woman, and himself a bigamist.[4] Jackson's wife was so stressed by these charges that she had a heart attack and died before Jackson was inaugurated. Jackson, in turn, called John Quincy Adams, his opponent, a "pimp" and accused him of procuring women for the Russian czar when he served as the American ambassador to Russia.[5]

It appears, then, that campaign nastiness is as American as apple pie. Even our national icons slung mud. A British observer of American elections in 1888 described them as a "tempest of invective and calumny . . . imagine all the accusations brought against all the candidates for the 670 seats in the English Parliament concentrated on one man, and read . . . daily for three months."[6] And now, of course, the campaign is far longer than three months and cable TV brings us the mud fight 24/7.

Americans have fought and died in wars to preserve the rights of citizens to choose their leaders through democratic elections. Some have even died here at home trying to exercise these rights. Despite this, most Americans take these important rights for granted; about half do not bother to vote even in presidential elections, and fewer still participate in other ways.

Moreover, the process by which we choose our leaders, especially the president, has been sharply criticized in recent years. Critics charge that election campaigns are meaningless and offer little information to the voters, that candidates pander to the most ill-informed and mean-spirited citizens, and that public relations and campaign spending, not positions on issues or strength of character, determine the winners. And in some recent elections, some voters' votes were not counted, largely because of defects in the election process itself.

In this chapter, we analyze why voting is important to a democracy and why, despite its importance, so few do it. Then we examine political campaigns and elections to see how they affect the kinds of leaders and policies we have. We will see that the lack of participation by many reinforces the government's responsiveness to those who do participate, especially those who are well organized.

THE AMERICAN ELECTORATE

During the more than two centuries since the Constitution was written, two important developments have altered the right to vote, termed **suffrage**. First, suffrage gradually was extended to include almost all citizens aged eighteen or over. This expansion occurred largely through federal action: constitutional amendments, congressional acts, and Supreme Court decisions. Second, in recent years serious issues of lack of access to the ballot have arisen. These limitations are largely being imposed by several states under the guise of ensuring that only eligible voters vote.

Early Limits on Voting Rights

Although the Declaration of Independence states that "all men are created equal," at the time of the Constitution and shortly thereafter the central political right of voting was denied to most Americans. States decided who would be granted suffrage. In some, only an estimated 10 percent of the white males could vote, whereas in others 80 percent could.[7] And these were just white males. In the first presidential election, only about 6 percent of all Americans were eligible to vote.[8]

Controversial property qualifications for voting existed in many states. Some argued that only those with an economic stake in society should have a say in political life. But critics of the property requirement repeated a story of Tom Paine's:

You require that a man shall have $60 worth of property, or he shall not vote. Very well . . . here is a man who today owns a jackass, and the jackass is worth $60.

Today the man is a voter and he goes to the polls and deposits his vote. Tomorrow the jackass dies. The next day the man comes to vote without his jackass and he cannot vote at all. Now tell me, which was the voter, the man or the jackass?[9]

Because the Constitution gave states the power to regulate suffrage, 🔔 the elimination of property requirements was a gradual process. By the 1820s, most were gone, although some lingered to midcentury.

In some states, religious tests also were applied. A voter had to be a member of the "established" church or could not be a member of certain religions (such as Roman Catholicism or Judaism). However, religious tests disappeared even more quickly than property qualifications.

By the time of the Civil War, state action had expanded the rights of white men. However, slaves, Indians, and free southern blacks could not vote, although northern blacks could in a few states.[10] Women's voting rights were confined to local elections in a few states.[11]

Blacks and the Right to Vote

The Civil War began the long, slow, and often violent process of expanding the rights of blacks to full citizenship. Between 1865 and 1870, three amendments were passed to give political rights to former slaves and other blacks. One, the Fifteenth Amendment, 🔔 prohibited the denial of voting rights on the basis of race and thus gave the right to vote to black men.

For a short time following the ratification of this amendment, a northern military presence in the South and close monitoring of southern politics enabled blacks to vote and hold office in the South, where 90 percent of all blacks lived. During this **Reconstruction** period, two southern blacks were elected to the Senate and fourteen were elected to the House of Representatives between 1869 and 1876. One state, South Carolina, even had a black majority in its legislature. And in Mississippi, historians have discovered that, during Reconstruction, 226 black officials served in a variety of offices, from local to national.[12] In most places, however, blacks did not dominate politics or even receive a proportional share of offices; whites saw blacks' political activities as a threat to their own dominance anyway. White southerners began to prevent blacks from voting through intimidation that ranged from mob violence and lynchings to economic sanctions against blacks who attempted to vote.

Northerners soon tolerated these methods, both violent and nonviolent. The northern public and political leaders lost interest in the fate of blacks or simply grew tired of the struggle, and in 1876, a compromise ended Reconstruction. In the wake of the disputed 1876 presidential election, southern Democrats agreed to support Republican Rutherford B. Hayes for president in return for an end to

Blacks comprised a majority of the population in South Carolina in 1866 and elected a black majority to the state legislature. The black legislators worked for civil rights, black male suffrage, and state constitutional reform. *Radical* was the name given to Republicans at that time.

grandfather clause exempted those whose grandfathers had the right to vote before 1867—that is, before blacks could legally vote in the South.

The **poll tax** also deprived blacks of voting rights. The tax, though only a couple of dollars, was often a sizable portion of working people's monthly income. In some states, individuals had to pay not only for the present election but also for every past election in which they were eligible to vote but did not.

In the **white primary**, where party nominees were chosen, blacks were barred from voting. Because the Democrats always won the general elections, the real contests were in the Democratic primaries. The states justified excluding blacks on the grounds that political parties were private rather than government organizations and thus could discriminate just as private clubs or individuals could.

Less formal means were also used to exclude blacks from voting. Registrars often closed their offices when blacks tried to register, or whites threatened blacks with the loss of jobs or housing if they tried to vote. Polling places were sometimes located far from black neighborhoods or were moved at the last minute without notifying potential voters. If these means failed, whites threatened or practiced violence. In one election in Mobile, Alabama, whites wheeled a cannon to a polling place and aimed it at about 1000 blacks lined up to vote.

The treatment of blacks by the southern establishment was summarized on the floor of the Senate by South Carolina Senator Benjamin ("Pitchfork Ben") Tillman, who served from 1895 to 1918. As he put it, "We took the government away. We stuffed ballot boxes. We shot them. We are not ashamed of it."[13]

Over time, the Supreme Court and Congress outlawed the "legal" barriers to black voting in the South. The Court invalidated the grandfather clause in 1915 and the white primary in 1944. Through the Twenty-fourth Amendment, Congress abolished the poll tax for federal elections in 1964, and the Court invalidated the tax for state elections in 1966.[14] But threats of physical violence and economic reprisals still kept most southern blacks from voting. Although many blacks in the urban areas of the Rim South (such as Florida, North Carolina, Tennessee, and Texas) could and did vote, those in the rural South and most in the Deep South could not; in 1960, black voter registration ranged from 5 to 40 percent in southern states.[15] (See the box "Blacks and Hispanics in Office.")

The Voting Rights Act and Redistricting

Despite our shameful history of depriving African Americans the right to vote, today black voting rates approach those of whites. In the Deep South, much of this dramatic change was brought about by the 1965 passage of the **Voting Rights Act (VRA)**, which made it illegal to interfere with

the northern military presence in the South and a hands-off policy toward activities there. By the end of the nineteenth century, blacks were effectively disfranchised in all of the South. The last southern black member of Congress served to 1901. Another would not be elected until 1972.

Southern constitutions and laws legitimized the loss of black voting rights. **Literacy tests** were often required, supposedly to make sure voters could read and write and thus evaluate political information. Most blacks, who had been denied education, were illiterate. Although many whites also were illiterate, fewer were barred from voting. Local election registrars exercised nearly complete discretion in deciding who had to take the test and how to administer and evaluate it. Educated blacks often were asked for legal interpretations of obscure constitutional provisions, which few could provide.

Some laws had exemptions that whites were allowed to take advantage of. An "understanding clause" exempted those who could not read and write but who could explain sections of the federal or state constitution to the satisfaction of the examiner, and a "good moral character clause" exempted those with such character. Again, local election registrars exercised discretion in deciding who understood the Constitution and who had good character. Finally, the

american*diversity

Blacks and Hispanics in Office

Before the Voting Rights Act (VRA) in 1965, few African Americans held major public office. Only a handful were members of Congress, and few were state legislators, mayors of major cities, or other important political officers. Following the VRA, southern blacks began to have the political clout to elect members of their own race to office for the first time, and northern blacks began to increase their influence, winning races in districts where blacks were not always majorities. Progress, though slow, has occurred; in 1970, there were only 179 blacks holding state and national legislative seats; by 2001, the number had more than tripled, to 633. Only two African Americans have won a governor's seat in modern times, Virginia's Douglas Wilder and, in 2006, Massachusetts's Deval Patrick. Barack Obama's Senate victory in 2004 made him only the third black person to hold a Senate seat in the modern era.

Richard Hatcher, who became mayor of Gary, Indiana, in 1968, was the first African American mayor of a major U.S. city. By 2010, more than 600 African Americans were serving as mayors, nearly 50 of them in cities of 50,000 and more, and many in communities where blacks are far less than half the population.[1]

Nationally, the number of black officeholders increased from an estimated 1200 in 1969 to more than 9400 in 2002. Although this is far from proportional representation, it is a dramatic increase. (Data gathering on black elected officials has lagged, so it is difficult to know exactly what has happened in the 2000s.)

Hispanics, too, have improved their representation in political office. From a total of little more than 3000 Hispanic public officials in 1985, their numbers by 2008 had grown to more than 5200, including 280 elected to state and national office.[2] Hispanic officials are more geographically concentrated than African American officials, with nearly two-thirds in California or Texas.

In sum, though progress is slow, African Americans and Hispanics, like other ethnic groups, are achieving political power through elections. The election of Barack Obama as the president is, of course, the most visible manifestation of that success.

[1] Data from the Joint Center for Political and Economic Studies and the National Conference of Black Mayors, http://ncbm.org/category/about/.
[2] Data from the website of the National Association of Latino Elected Officials.

SOURCE: *Statistical Abstract of the United States 2010* (Washington, D.C.: Government Printing Office, 2010), tabs. 404 and 405.

---

anyone's right to vote. The act abolished the use of literacy tests, and, most important, it sent federal voter registrars into counties where less than 50 percent of the voting-age population (black and white) was registered. The premise of this requirement was that if so few had registered, there must be serious barriers to registration. Registrars were sent to all of Alabama, Mississippi, South Carolina, and Louisiana, substantial parts of North Carolina, and scattered counties in six other states.[16] Any changes in election procedures had to be approved by the Department of Justice or the U.S. District Court for the District of Columbia. States or counties had to show a clean record of not discriminating for ten years before they could escape this supervision. Those who sought to deter blacks from voting through intimidation now had to face the force of the federal government.

Though black registration had been increasing in the Rim South due to voter registration and education projects, the impact of the VRA in the Deep South was dramatic.[17] Within a year after federal registrars were sent, hundreds of thousands of southern blacks were registered, radically changing the nature of southern politics. In the most extreme case, Mississippi registration of blacks zoomed from 7 to 41 percent. In Alabama, the black electorate doubled in four

years. Because of these increases, not only have dozens of blacks been elected, but white politicians must now court black voters to get elected. Even the late George Wallace, the segregationist Alabama governor who had opposed the civil rights movement in the 1960s, eagerly sought black votes in the 1970s and 1980s.

The VRA was renewed and expanded in 1970, 1975, 1982, and again in 2006, despite some grumbling by white Republican conservatives about the continuing federal scrutiny of voting rights in the South. It now covers more states and other minorities, such as Hispanics, Asians, Native Americans, and Inuits (called Eskimos in the past), and thus serves as a basic protection for minority voting rights. For example, states must provide bilingual ballots in counties where 5 percent or more of the population does not speak English.

The VRA dramatically changed the face of the electorate in the South and then later in other parts of the nation. Given the success of the VRA and faced with an expanded black electorate, some white officials in areas of large black populations used new means to diminish the political clout of African Americans. Their technique was *gerrymandering*, discussed more later in the chapter. Through devices

Blacks line up to vote in Peachtree, Alabama, after enactment of the Voting Rights Act of 1965.

that political scientists call "**cracking, stacking, and packing**," districts were drawn to minimize black representation, depending on the size and configuration of the black and white populations. *Cracking* divides significant, concentrated black populations into two or more districts so that none will have a black majority; *stacking* combines a large black population with an even greater white population; and *packing* puts a huge black population into one district rather than two, where blacks might otherwise approach a majority in each.

Initially, the Supreme Court was reluctant to find these practices illegal without specific proof that their intent was to discriminate against black voters.[18] But in 1982, congressional revision of the VRA required states with large minority populations to draw boundaries in ways to increase the probabilities that minorities would win seats. The focus of the voting rights legislation then turned from protecting the right of suffrage to trying to ensure that voting rights would result in the election of African American and other minority officeholders. With this new statute as an indication of congressional intent, the Court then did strike down districting in North Carolina as inappropriately diluting black voting power.[19]

After the 1990 census, eleven new **majority-minority districts** were created for blacks and six for Hispanics. Partly as a result of this redistricting, blacks and Hispanics dramatically increased their congressional representation. Blacks were elected to Congress for the first time since Reconstruction in Alabama, Florida, North Carolina, South Carolina, and Virginia. Hispanics were elected for the first time ever in Illinois and New Jersey.[20] However, after this

post-1990 redistricting, which used extensive gerrymandering to create the majority-minority districts, some white voters challenged their legality. In a series of cases, the Supreme Court then ruled that racial gerrymandering, the drawing of district lines specifically to concentrate racial minorities to try to ensure the election of minority representatives, is as constitutionally suspect as the drawing of district lines to diffuse minority electoral strength.[21] Despite the consequent redrawing of several majority-minority districts after the 1994 election, the African American incumbents were still able to win reelection in 1996 and after.

Creating majority-minority districts affected the partisan composition of some southern states. Black voters were redistricted from solid Democratic districts to create new majority black districts. This left their old districts with Republican majorities and helped Republicans get their first victories in eighteen congressional districts in the 1994 elections.

Women and the Right to Vote

When property ownership defined the right to vote, women property owners could vote in some places. When property requirements were removed, suffrage came to be seen as a male right only. Women's right to vote was reintroduced in the 1820s in Tennessee school board elections.[22] From that time on, women had the vote in some places, but usually only at the local level or for particular kinds of elections.

The national movement for women's suffrage did not gain momentum until after the Civil War. Before and during

Women's contributions to the war effort during World War I helped lead to the ratification of the women's suffrage amendment in 1920. Here Broadway chorus women train as Home Guards during the war.

that war, many women helped lead the campaign to abolish slavery and establish full political rights for blacks. When black men got the right to vote after the Civil War, some women saw the paradox in their working to enfranchise these men when they themselves lacked the right to vote. Led by Susan B. Anthony, Elizabeth Cady Stanton, and others, they lobbied Congress and the state legislatures for voting rights for women.

The first suffrage bill was introduced in Congress in 1868 and each year thereafter until 1893. Most members were strong in their condemnation of women as potential voters. One senator claimed that if women could hold political views different from their husbands, it would make "every home a hell on earth."[23]

When Wyoming applied to join the Union in 1889, it had already granted women the right to vote. Congress initially tried to bar Wyoming from the Union for that reason, but then relented when the Wyoming territorial legislature declared, "We will remain out of the Union one hundred years rather than come in without the women." Still, by 1910, women had complete suffrage rights in only four western states.

Powerful interests opposed suffrage for women. Liquor interests feared that women voters would press for prohibition because many women had been active in the temperance (antiliquor) movement. Other businesses feared that suffrage would lead to reforms to improve working conditions for women and children. Southern whites feared that it would lead to voting by black women and then by black men. Political bosses feared that women would favor

political reform. The Catholic Church opposed it as contrary to the proper role of women. According to some people, suffrage was a revolt against nature. Pregnant women might lose their babies, nursing mothers might lose their milk, and women might grow beards or be raped at the polls (then frequently located in saloons or barber shops).[24] Others argued less hysterically that women should be protected from the unsavory practices of politics and should confine themselves to their traditional duties.

About 1910, however, the women's suffrage movement was reenergized, in part by ideas and tactics borrowed from the British women's suffrage movement. A new generation of leaders, including Alice Paul and Carrie Chapman Catt, began to lobby more vigorously, reach out to the working class, and engage in protest marches and picketing, all new features of American politics. Eight more western and prairie states granted suffrage to women between 1911 and 1917, and others had granted the right to vote in presidential elections.[25]

In 1917, the National Women's Party organized around-the-clock picketing of the White House; their arrest and subsequent torture through beatings and forced feedings embarrassed the administration and won the movement some support. These incidents, plus contributions by women to the war effort during World War I, led to the adoption in 1920 of the Nineteenth Amendment guaranteeing women the right to vote. Although only 37 percent of eligible women voted in the 1920 presidential election, as the habit of voting spread, women's voting rates equaled those of men. (See the box "Women in Office.")

Young People and the Right to Vote

Federal constitutional and legislative changes extended the franchise to young adults. Before 1971, almost all states required a voting age of nineteen or more. The service of eighteen-year-olds in the Vietnam War brought protests that if these men were old enough to die for their country, they were old enough to vote. Yielding to these arguments and to the general recognition that young people were better educated than in the past, Congress adopted and the states ratified the Twenty-sixth Amendment giving eighteen-year-olds the right to vote. As we will see, however, young people are a lot less likely to vote than other groups.

Felons and the Right to Vote

The restriction of voting rights for felons—those convicted of serious crimes—is an exception to the general liberalization of the right to vote. Most states bar convicted felons from voting while in prison or on probation, but four states, including Florida and three other southern states with large black populations,[26] bar felons from voting forever. In some states, these laws stem from Reconstruction-era policies targeted to reduce the voting power of blacks. Since 2004, three states have reinstituted voting rights to felons after they serve their time.

Nationally, more than 5 million people are prevented from voting by felony convictions, including one in seven black men (in Alabama, one in three black men are barred).[27] Nationally, 40 percent of those barred from voting are black.[28] Analyses of these laws suggest that they have had a significant effect in putting conservative Republicans in office in states with large black populations.[29]

Some might argue that we should not worry about the voting rights of felons. Loss of voting rights might be seen as part of their punishment. However, most felons barred from voting have served their time and returned to society. Many times they were convicted as young people and have been law-abiding citizens for years or even decades since. Moreover, this particular punishment does not really seem to fit the crime.

In sum, today only convicted felons, the mentally incapable, noncitizens, and those not meeting minimal residence requirements are legally barred from voting. Except for felons, voting has become an essential right of citizenship rather than a privilege for only those qualified by birth or property.

Electoral Reform and New Threats to Voting Rights

Despite these advances, recent elections have uncovered new threats to voting rights, especially for African Americans. The most widely publicized problems were in the 2000 and 2004 elections. Months after the 2000 presidential election that saw Al Gore win the popular vote but George W. Bush win the electoral vote and the presidency,

half of the electorate thought that the outcome was unfair or downright crooked. (See the section titled "The 2000 Election: A Perfect Storm.") Many African Americans, who believed they were systematically disfranchised by the way the election was run in Florida, were especially outraged. Hundreds or thousands (no one knows for sure) had been purged from the rolls before the election.[30] And one of ten votes in largely African American precincts in Florida was thrown out as invalid, compared with one of thirty-seven in white precincts, significantly reducing the Democratic vote and changing the outcome of the presidential election.[31]

Voter Reform Legislation

The 2000 election also revealed a number of problems with our electoral system. (The problems had existed for a long time, but in a close election they become more crucial.) Many areas had voting equipment that did not work well, resulting in many votes not being counted. Many states also had unclear laws governing procedures for recounts and challenges to voter eligibility.

To deal with some of these issues, in 2002 Congress passed electoral reform legislation that offered states funding to buy new, modern voting equipment; mandated state-wide registration lists; and required states to train poll workers, post a list of voters' rights in each polling place, keep up-to-date computerized lists of voters, and allow voters whose names do not appear on the precinct lists to cast a provisional ballot, which can be accepted or challenged later. This legislation did bring about some positive changes. Though most of the money to purchase the machines was not provided by the federal government, many areas did buy new electronic machines that work like ATMs, responding to touches on the screen.[32] And many states enacted new standards for counts and recounts. However, these changes brought new problems. Most technical experts, and many others, are fearful that some of the new electronic machines are open to fraud. One information-security expert argues

Election campaigns in the nineteenth century featured more hoopla, which spurred tremendous turnout. This illustration shows the 1840 Whig gimmick—party members rolled a huge ball from town to town—that prompted the phrase "keep the ball rolling."

Courtesy of the Smithsonian Institute

american*diversity

Women in Office

As secretary of state and former senator, Hillary Clinton is probably the most highly visible woman officeholder in the United States, and former Speaker of the House Nancy Pelosi (D-Calif.) is the most highly visible elected officeholder, but even before women were given the right to vote nationally, they held political office. Women officeholders in colonial America were rare but not unknown. In 1715, for example, the Pennsylvania Assembly appointed a woman as tax collector.[1]

Elizabeth Cady Stanton, probably the first woman candidate for Congress, received twenty-four votes when she ran in 1866.[2] It was not until 1916 that the first woman member of Congress, Jeannette Rankin (R-Mont.), was actually elected. In 1872, Victoria Claflin Woodhull ran for president on the Equal Rights Party ticket, teamed with abolitionist Frederick Douglass for vice president.

More than 100,000 women now hold elective office, but many of these offices are minor. Inroads by women into major national offices have been slow. Geraldine Ferraro's 1984 vice-presidential candidacy was historic but not victorious. Similarly, though vice-presidential candidate Sarah Palin galvanized the 2008 Republican campaign and millions of conservative Republicans, she lost.

In recent years, women have slowly increased their membership in Congress. After 2008, they numbered about 17 percent of both the House and Senate. More than three-quarters of the women in each house are Democrats.[3] Pelosi, as the first woman (and Italian American) Speaker of the House, is now third in the line of presidential succession. That is, if both the president and vice president were to die or become incapacitated, the Speaker of the House becomes president. In 2010, Republican women ran in unprecedented numbers, encouraged by Sarah Palin's example and in many cases by her support: "Look out Washington! There's a whole stampede of pink elephants crossing the line."[4] Continuing the animal analogies, Palin often refers to these women as "mama grizzlies," implying that they are tough. Most are very conservative.

In achieving state and local offices, women have made real progress. They hold six governorships, equally divided between Republicans and Democrats, 18 percent of the lieutenant governorships, and 18 percent of the mayorships of medium and large cities.

In 1969, only 4 percent of the state legislators were women; today, nearly 25 percent are. However, the rates of increase have slowed in recent years, with only a 2 percent growth in the past decade.[5] The proportion ranges widely, from 10 percent in South Carolina to 37 percent and more in Colorado, New Hampshire, and Vermont, and to more than 30 percent in seven more states.[6]

Do women officeholders make a difference in policy? Behavioral studies of women members of Congress and other legislative bodies indicate that they are, on the whole, more liberal than men.[7] Women tend to give issues

---

that one particular system was "so deficient in security it could be compromised by a bright teenager intent on hacking an election."[33] The reason is that in many of the new machines there is no paper backup. Your vote for X could be counted as a vote for Y and you would never know it. Various studies have shown that machines can be tampered with in only a minute, and in some machines tampering can be done wirelessly. To deal with this potential for fraud, thirty-two states have now required paper backup for all electronic machines. Nearly one-third of the states have also required mandatory random audits of the paper records.[34]

The requirement to have computerized, up-to-date lists of voters has also had some negative effects. In most states, elections are controlled by the office of the secretary of state or some similar statewide office with an elected head. Some of these state offices, which are charged with keeping accurate records, have "updated" lists by reducing the number of voters of the party not in control of the state's election machinery. States have a legitimate interest in making sure that voter lists reflect current voters and their addresses, but sometimes purging goes far beyond this to be used to disfranchise lower-income and minority voters or to reduce the other party's voters.[35] Sometimes private companies are hired to purge voter lists and are paid according to how many they purge. Florida, in trying to update its voter lists, purged 22,000 black voters (largely Democratic) from the voter registration lists, but only 61 Hispanics (who, in Florida, are more likely than blacks to be Republicans). Florida officials claimed this partisan purge was accidental, though others disagreed.[36]

VOTER TURNOUT

Paradoxically, as the *right* to vote has expanded, the proportion of eligible citizens *actually* voting has contracted.

relating to women, children, and the family higher priority than do male legislators.[8] Across numerous industrialized democracies, legislatures with more women have been more likely to adopt family leave legislation.[9] Women are also less likely to be involved in corrupt activities.

As more and more women are getting graduate and professional education and working outside the home, and as the public increases its support for women in politics, the trend toward more women in public office will continue. In general, women candidates are elected at the same rate as male ones. Even so, sometimes women still face sexism in their quest for office. This was most obvious at the highest levels. As Hillary Clinton's campaign unfolded, so too did evidence of sexism; it was public and needed no code words. John McCain was asked by a supporter how he was going to beat "the bitch," and he did not bother to correct her. Several white male cable newscasters seemed to have little compunction about offering a variety of sexist comments showing their contempt for a woman candidate, such as MSNBC's Tucker Carlson's comment that "when [Clinton] comes on television, I involuntarily cross my legs." While Chris Matthews of MSNBC was chastised by his network and made to apologize for his comments that "Clinton was a front-runner because her husband messed around" (presumably he meant that she mostly was getting sympathy votes), most of the other statements were apparently made without criticism from the newsman's bosses.

The Internet advertises all sorts of campaign-related offensive material slurring candidates, but a shop on Chicago's Michigan Avenue (a high-end shopping street) prominently displayed a shirt with the motto "Better a

Bro than a Ho." The Clinton "Nutcracker" was advertised widely in mainstream outlets that presumably would not have advertised racially offensive items (Amazon. com would not likely sell an Obama jockey doorstop or minstrel figure).

Recently Republican women have also been the subject of sexism. *Harpers* titled an article "Is Sarah Palin Porn?"[10] (even though the article was a more general one about image politics). Palin walks a fine line in encouraging sexualized comments, however. "She showed off major leg in a racy spread with *Runner's World*, wearing a pair of tight, short shorts. . . . In other pictures, she wears skintight leggings and assumes saucy 'warm-up' positions."[11] Nikki Haley, a candidate for the gubernatorial position in South Carolina, was accused by two men of having inappropriate physical contact. Further investigation revealed that one was working for a primary opponent, and the other was likely gay. Voters ignored the charges and nominated her in the primary.

[1] Joseph J. Kelley, *Pennsylvania: The Colonial Years* (Garden City, N.Y.: Doubleday, 1980), 143.
[2] Elisabeth Griffin, *In Her Own Right* (New York: Oxford University Press, 1983).
[3] Data are from the Center for American Women and Politics, National information Bank on Women in Public Office, Rutgers University, www.rci.rutgers.edu/cawp/pdf/elective.pdf.
[4] Malcolm Gay, "Mama Bear," *Washington Monthly*, August 5, 2010, www.washingtonmonthly.com/features/2010/1007.tms.html.
[5] Kira Sanbonmatsu, *Democrats, Republicans, and the Politics of Women's Place* (Ann Arbor: University of Michigan Press, 2002).
[6] Data are from the Center for American Women and Politics, Rutgers University, 2010, www.cawp.rutgers.edu/Facts.html#leg.
[7] Susan Welch, "Are Women More Liberal than Men in the U.S. Congress?" *Legislative Studies Quarterly* 10 (1985), 125–134.
[8] Sue Thomas and Susan Welch, "The Impact of Gender on Activities and Priorities of State Legislators," *Western Political Quarterly* 44 (1991), 445– 456; Miki Caul Kittilson, "Representing Women: The Adoption of Family Leave in Comparative Perspective," *Journal of Politics* 70 (April 2008), 323–334.
[9] Kittilson, "Representing Women."
[10] Jack Hitt, www.harpers.org/archive/2010/06/0082976.
[11] Greg Mitchell, "Palin's Porn," http://www.thenation.com/blog/palin-porn.

Political Activism in the Nineteenth Century

In 1896, an estimated 750,000 people—5 percent of all voters—took train excursions to visit presidential candidate William McKinley at his Ohio home during the campaign.[37] This amazing figure is but one indication of the high level of intense political interest and activity in the late nineteenth century.

In those days, politics was an active, not a spectator, sport. People voted at high rates, as much as 80 percent in the 1840 presidential election,[38] and they were very partisan. They thought independents were corrupt and ready to sell their votes to the highest bidder. In colonial America, voters usually voted by voice, but by the mid-nineteenth century, most states used paper ballots that were distributed by elaborate and well-organized parties. After being coached by

party leaders, voters simply dropped their party's ballot into the box. **Split-ticket voting**—that is, voting for candidates from different parties for different offices—and secrecy in making one's choice were impossible.[39]

Progressive Reforms

The **Progressive reforms** of the late nineteenth and early twentieth centuries brought radical changes to election politics. Progressive reformers, largely professional and upper middle class, sought to eliminate corruption from politics and voting, but they also meant to eliminate the influence of the lower classes, many of them recent immigrants. These two goals went hand in hand because the lower classes were seen as the cause of corruption in politics.

The Progressive movement was responsible for several reforms: primary elections, voter registration laws, secret

Modern campaigns have their own ephemera, but the products, such as these 2008 condoms, are usually generated by private businesses rather than by political parties.

ballots, nonpartisan ballots (without party labels), and the denial of voting rights for aliens, which removed a major constituency of the urban party machines. The movement also introduced the merit system for public employment to reduce favoritism and payoffs in hiring.

The reforms, adopted by some states at the end of the nineteenth century and by others much later, were largely effective in cleaning up politics. But the reformers also achieved, to a very large extent, their goal of eliminating the lower classes from politics. Taking away most of the reason for the existence of political parties—choosing candidates and printing and distributing ballots—caused the party organization to decline, which, in turn, produced a decline in political interest and activity on the part of the electorate. Without strong parties to mobilize voters, only the most interested and motivated participated. Moreover, the new restrictions on voting meant that voters had to invest more time, energy, and thought in voting; they had to think about the election months in advance and travel to city hall to register. As a consequence, voting declined and politics began to be a spectator activity. Turnout figures from the nineteenth century are not entirely reliable and not exactly comparable with today's figures. In the days before voter registration, many aliens could vote, and some people voted twice. In some instances, more people voted in a state election than lived there! Nevertheless, it is generally agreed that turnout was very high in the nineteenth century and then diminished substantially, dropping from more than 77 percent in 1840–1896 to 54 percent in 1920–1932, when the Progressive reforms were largely in place. During the New Deal era, when the Democratic Party mobilized new groups of voters, turnout rose again, but it has never achieved the same levels as in the nineteenth century.

Recent Turnout

Voting rates were above 60 percent in the 1950s and 1960s, then slowly declined to barely 50 percent in 2000. However, in 2004 that proportion increased significantly, to 58 percent, and remained there in 2008.[40] These data take into account all the adult population in the United States. However, we know that, in recent years, millions of people have not been eligible to vote, including more than 3 million felons and nearly 20 million noncitizens in 2008. Looking only at the population *eligible* to vote, turnout is slightly higher, over 60 percent, and about the same as in the 1950s. (See Figure 1.)

In 2008, turnout in the primaries was higher than normal, however. In state after state, the turnout far exceeded recent previous turnouts. More than 3 million new voters registered and voted in the primaries,[41] with the increase particularly notable in the Democratic primaries. Senator Barack Obama sparked the enthusiasm of hundreds of thousands of new voters, many of them young, and they registered and voted in huge numbers. Voters under the age of thirty increased from 9 percent of Democratic primary voters in 2004 to nearly 15 percent in 2008. But many older citizens turned out too. Hillary Clinton energized tens of thousands of working-class voters, especially women, to register and vote. And tens of thousands of African American voters, especially young people, registered and voted for the first time, excited by the candidacy of Barack Obama. The turnouts in many primary states moved into the 30 to 40 percent range—hardly numbers to brag about, but far exceeding the usual dismal primary turnout.[42]

Although nations count their turnouts differently, it is clear that Americans vote at a lower rate than citizens of

| Figure 1 | Voting Rates Plummeted in the 1970s and 1980s, but Have Risen in Last Three Elections |

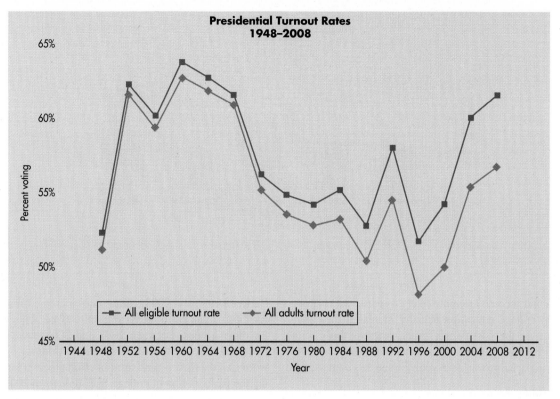

This figure illustrates the decline and then the increase in voting rates along with the difference between voting proportions of all eligible citizens and those of all adults. As explained in the text, millions of adults are not eligible because they are felons or non-citizens. Turnout rates appear higher when only those who are eligible to vote are analyzed.
SOURCE: *Michael McDonald, "United States Election Project," http://elections.gmu.edu/voter_turnout.htm.*

other Western democracies. Only Switzerland, which has allowed women to vote only since 1971, approximates our low turnout levels. Within the United States, turnout varies greatly among the states. In the 2008 presidential election, for example, 73 percent of Minnesota's citizens voted, but only 45 percent of Hawaii's did.[43] Turnout tends to be lower in the South and higher in the northern Plains, New England, and Mountain states.[44]

Not only do relatively few people vote, but even fewer participate actively in political campaigns. For example, in a recent year, about one-quarter of the population said that they worked for a party or candidate. About an equal proportion claimed that they contributed money to a party or a candidate. Smaller proportions attended political meetings or actually belonged to a political club. However, these rates of campaign participation reflect increases, even while voting rates were declining in the 1970s and 1980s. More people give money to candidates and parties than they used to, probably because, unlike thirty years ago, candidates and parties now use mass mailings and the Internet to solicit funds from supporters.[45] Hundreds of thousands of potential donors can be reached in a very short time. The candidates are getting very good at using the Internet to raise funds, and in 2008 Obama was a pathbreaker. We will discuss this further in the next chapter.

Who Votes?

There are vast differences in voting habits among different groups of people, especially on the basis of to socioeconomic class and age.

Socioeconomic Class

Voting is related to education, income, and occupation—that is, to socioeconomic class. Those who are more educated, have more money, and have higher-status jobs vote more often. If you are a college graduate, the chances are almost 75 percent that you will vote; if you have less than a high school education, the chances are only one-third that.[46] Differences between higher- and lower-income people are also quite large and growing. (See Figure 2.)

Differences between voting rates of the middle and upper classes are much greater in the United States than elsewhere and greater today than in nineteenth-century America.[47] Something unique about the contemporary American political system inhibits voting participation of all citizens, but particularly those whose income and educational levels are below the average. Just as there is a strong class basis to voting, there is also a strong class basis for participation in campaign activities.[48] Those with more

Figure 2 | **Class Differences in Voting Are Striking, and Growing**

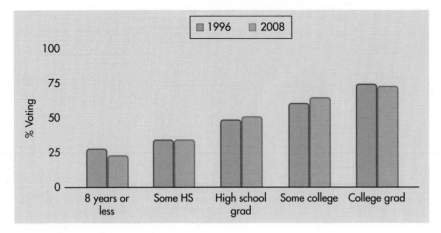

SOURCE: Statistical Abstract of the United States 2010, tab. 406. Turnout rates are those in the presidential election. Class is represented by education.

---

education and income are more likely to participate. Those with some college education actually increased their participation over the past twenty years, whereas those with less than a high school education decreased theirs. Thus, the class bias in participation, as in voting alone, has increased.[49]

Age

Voting is also much more common among older people than younger people. Young people are volunteering in their communities in record numbers,[50] so why the low voting rates? Young people's initial tendency to vote or not vote is influenced by their parents' education and political engagement and by their own high school experiences and that of going on to college. This tendency usually stays the same through the life stages of getting married, establishing a stable residence, and becoming active in the community.[51] Thus, low turnouts may reflect many who grew up in homes where there was a low interest in government and the news; they did not learn that politics is important.[52] Then, too, like many of their elders, some young people cannot discern significant differences between the two major political parties, or they believe that candidates do not address issues of primary concern to young people. Low voter turnout is also a product of mobility: young adults change their residences frequently and do not have time or do not take time to figure out how and where to register. Finally, many young people are preoccupied with major life changes—leaving home, going to college, beginning their first full-time job, getting married, and starting a family.

The 2008 campaign generated tremendous political interest and enthusiasm among many young voters who had never been engaged in politics before. When asked whether they were paying attention to the campaign, fully 74 percent of those under thirty said "yes," compared with only 42 percent in 2004 and a meager 13 percent in 2000.[53] Still, the turnout of young people was much lower than that of their elders.

Between 1996 and 2008, voting rates increased significantly for those eighteen to thirty-four and stayed about the same for older groups. Between 2004 and 2008, though, voting increased only for those twenty-one to thirty-four. In other words, all the rhetoric and turnout efforts focused on increasing the participation of college-age students in 2008 seemed to have no impact at all on overall rates. (See Figure 3.)

Participation in Other Activities

In other kinds of political participation, even taking education into account, men usually participate slightly more than women, whites somewhat more than blacks, older people more than younger people, and southerners more than northerners. But these differences change over time. Young people participated more than their elders, and blacks more than whites, during the late 1960s and early 1970s.[54] The civil rights and anti–Vietnam War movements drew many young and black people into political activity.

Obama's candidacy prompted a spike in the turnout of African Americans and young voters.

Figure 3 | **Age Differences in Turnout**

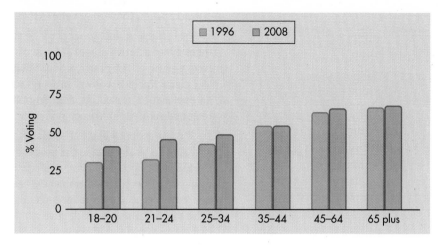

SOURCE: Statistical Abstract of the United States 2010, *tab. 406. Turnout rates are those in the presidential election.*

Why Turnout Is Low

In addition to class and age, there are other personal and institutional reasons why more Americans, especially low-income and young Americans, do not vote. Of course, one reason that turnout is lower than in other nations is that millions of American residents are not eligible to vote. However, the rest of this section focuses on reasons why those who *are* eligible do not vote. These reasons include

DEMOCRACY?

Is our system democratic when the voting rate of those with less income and education is only a fraction of the rate of those higher on the socioeconomic ladder? Should we try to increase the voting rates of those in the lower socioeconomic brackets?

citizens' attitudes, lack of social rootedness, failures of political parties to mobilize voters, lack of strong labor unions, state barriers to registration and voting, partisan efforts to deter voting, and in the case of legislative elections, noncompetitive districts.

Attitudinal Explanations

Voters' attitudes explain some nonvoting.

Voter satisfaction? For example, one reason sometimes given for low rates of voter turnout is that nonvoters are satisfied; failing to vote is a passive form of consent to what government is doing.[55] This argument falls flat. Over the past half century, voter turnout has not fluctuated with public trust in government (Figure 4). Moreover, if staying at home on election day were an indication of satisfaction, one would expect turnout to be lower among the well-off, not among the working class and the poor.

Negative attitudes toward politics Significant proportions of nonvoters, when asked why they did not vote, say they

are disgusted with politics.[56] In explaining low turnout, analysts often point to the hateful advertising, attacks on other candidates, candidates who do not tell the truth about their positions, incessant polling, and lack of thoughtful media coverage.[57]

These analyses would seem to contain some grains of truth, but they don't explain much.[58] People who are most likely to pay attention to the media, watch the ads, hear about the polls, and follow the campaigns are the most likely to vote, not the least likely. Turnout is inversely related to media spending; the more the candidates spend, the lower the turnout. But negative advertising does not affect turnout much, if at all,[59] and negative advertising and other media attention cannot explain the class bias in nonvoting.

In addition to the *quality* of the campaigns, some people think turnout is lower than it should be because our elections are so frequent, campaigns last so long, and so many offices are contested that the public becomes bored, confused, or cynical.[60] At the presidential level, the sheer quantity of coverage, much of it focused repetitively on "who's winning," may simply bore people. At the local level, voters elect so many officeholders, all the way down to weed and mosquito control commissioners, that many have no idea for whom or what they are voting. This proliferation of elective offices, thought by some to promote democracy and popular control, may promote only voter confusion and alienation. The problem is compounded because elections for different offices are held at different times. For example, most states have decided to hold elections for governor in nonpresidential election years because they think this will focus more attention on the governor's race. However, in fact, this decision reduces both turnout in the presidential election and even more significantly reduces the turnout in these gubernatorial elections.[61] Primary elections also affect turnout. One estimate is that holding primary campaigns diminishes the general election turnout by 5 percent.[62]

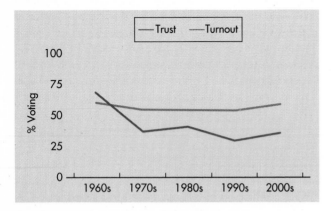

| Figure 4 | Turnout Little Related to Trust in Government |

SOURCE: *Data on turnout from Michael McDonald, http://elections. gmu.edu/voter_turnout.htm. Data on trust from people-press.org/ reports/images/606-5.gif; trust is the proportion of people saying that they trust the government in Washington all the time or most of the time.*

By contrast, in Britain the time between calling an election (by the current government) and the actual election is only a month. On April 6, 2010, Prime Minister Gordon Brown asked the Queen to dissolve Parliament, and the election was called for one month later, on May 6, 2010. All campaigning was done during that time. There were no primaries. Moreover, as in most other parliamentary democracies, British citizens vote only for their representative in Parliament and (at one other time) for their local representative. Voters are not faced with choices for a myriad offices they barely recognize.

Voting as a rational calculation of costs and benefits A more general attitudinal explanation for nonvoting is that it may also be the result of a rational calculation of the costs and benefits of voting. When 35 percent of Americans think voting on *American Idol* is more important than voting for the president, obviously many voters do not think that the stakes in elections are great.[63]

Economist Anthony Downs argued that people vote when they believe the perceived benefits of voting are greater than the costs.[64] If a voter sees a difference between the parties or candidates and favors one party's position over the other, that voter has a reason to vote and can expect some benefit from doing so. For that reason, people who are highly partisan vote more than those less attached to a party, and people with a strong sense of political efficacy, the belief they can influence government, vote more than others.

Voters who see no difference between the candidates or parties, however, may believe that voting is not worth the effort it takes and that it is more rational to abstain. In fact, 21 percent of nonvoters in 2000 gave only the excuse that they were "too busy" and another 12 percent that they were "not interested," suggesting a large degree of apathy.[65]

Others think that their vote does not matter. Perhaps misled by the continual public opinion polling and the widely publicized results, some may believe they don't need to vote.

Nevertheless, many people will vote even if they think there is no difference between the candidates because they have a sense of civic duty, a belief that their responsibilities as citizens include voting. In fact, more voters give this as an explanation for voting than any other reason, including the opportunity to influence policy.[66]

Downs assumes that the costs of voting are minimal, but, in reality, for many people the time, expense of time off from work or transportation costs, and possible embarrassment of trying to register are greater than the perceived benefits of voting. This is especially true for lower-income people who perceive that neither party is attentive to their interests. Moreover, they are especially vulnerable to a climate where voters are being challenged at the polls over their right to vote. Finally, the frequency, length, and media orientation of campaigns may lower the perceived benefits of voting for people of all incomes by trivializing the election and emphasizing the negative.

Lack of Social Rootedness

Turnout is lower among those who lack "social rootedness."[67] Middle age, marriage, and residential stability lead to rootedness in one's community. But Americans move around, marry late, and get divorced more than those in other nations. Mobility alone may reduce voting by as much as 9 percent.

Americans living abroad, whether in the armed forces or for private reasons, have special barriers to registering and voting. In a bizarre development, in 2004 the Pentagon discouraged citizens living abroad from voting by shutting down a state-of-the-art website designed to make it easy for those citizens to register and obtain ballots.[68]

Failures of Parties to Mobilize Voters

Voter turnout in the United States may not increase substantially until one of the political parties works to mobilize the traditional nonvoters through policies that appeal to them. For example, Roosevelt's New Deal mobilized thousands of new voters. If voters believe they have a reason to vote, then their calculation of the benefits of voting increases relative to the costs.

Traditionally, political parties did mobilize voters to turn out. In the 1980s and 1990s, however, the parties spent more time raising funds than mobilizing voters.[69] The failure of parties to mobilize voters is an especially important reason for low turnout among the working class and poor. Because of their low income, a majority of nonvoters are Democrats. If mobilized, they would probably vote for Democrats, but not to the degree many Republicans fear. In many elections, the preferences of nonvoters have simply reflected the preferences of voters.[70]

In 2004 and 2008, parties and candidates returned to their traditional mobilization function, and, consequently, voting increased. The parties—and, in the 2008 primaries, the candidates—emphasized registering voters and getting them to the polls. Both parties used increasingly sophisticated technology to link information about each party supporter with neighborhood information. Each party communicated with its core supporters via e-mail and frequently urged them to register and vote.

Both parties have also developed sophisticated databases recording individuals' residential location, gender, education, race, homeowner status, and many other variables. They gather data not just from public sources such as voter registration rolls and driver's license registrations but also from consumer data from stores ranging from book vendors to auto dealerships. So, for example, we know that Republicans are more likely to drink bourbon and Democrats gin, and Democrats buy Volvos while Republicans buy Fords and Chevys.[71] Parties increasingly use sophisticated polls to develop profiles of voters who are likely to support them. Then they can use census and other neighborhood data to target areas on which to focus their get-out-the-vote drives. Because Republicans have done a better job mobilizing their own supporters, they are more likely to oppose legislation that makes it easier for the general electorate to vote.[72] States with the highest turnout tend to have active and liberal Democratic parties, giving voters a choice and thus a motive to vote.

Decline of Strong Labor Unions

Working-class citizens are much less likely to vote than white-collar and professional workers. Yet, among working people, union members are much more likely to vote than are others. Unions inform their members about the stakes of the election and then work to get their members and their families to the polls. Just as parties can increase the perceived benefits of voting by educating voters about the consequences of election choices, unions do the same with their membership. Consequently, as labor union strength has declined, voting turnout has decreased.[73] Although labor strength has declined in other nations as well, most other democracies have much stronger labor unions than the United States and consequently higher rates of turnout among blue-collar workers.

State Barriers to Registration and Voting

States can raise or lower the costs of voting by making it easy or hard to register and to vote.

Barriers to registration Most people who register to vote do vote in the general election for president. But many people never register. In most other democracies, either the state or parties are responsible for registering voters. Voter registrars go door-to-door to register voters, or voters are registered automatically when they pay taxes or receive public services. Usually, these registrar offices are nonpartisan and consider it their duty to register voters. Consequently, almost everyone is registered to vote.

The United States is unique in putting the responsibility for registering on the individual citizen. Moreover, registration is handled at the state level, usually by agencies controlled by one or another party. These conditions are a major impediment to voting, with the result that only about 70 percent of U.S. citizens are registered.[74] Difficult registration procedures have a special impact on low-income Americans, who are 17 percent less likely to vote in states with difficult registration procedures than in other states.[75]

Given that states are laboratories—some things are tried in one state, other approaches in another—we know that some registration procedures encourage people to register and vote and others do not. One estimate is that voter turnout would be 9 percent higher if all states used procedures similar to those used by states that try to facilitate voter registration.[76] Voter registration increases when registration periods last up to election day (most states require registration at least twenty-five days before the election),[77] registration offices are located in neighborhoods rather than just one central county office, registration is by mail, registration offices are open at convenient hours, and voters who vote irregularly are not purged from the registration lists.

In other jurisdictions, voter registrars do not provide these options, and some actually try to hinder groups working to increase registration. Some states do not allow volunteers to register voters outside the registration office.[78] Florida tried to impose fines of $250 for every voter registration form filed more than ten days after it was collected, even if a hurricane passed through in the meantime, and a fine of $5000 for every form that was not submitted. The law was declared unconstitutional, and a modified, less draconian, version was implemented.[79]

To increase registration, a national law—the **motor voter law**—allows people to register at public offices, such as the Department of Motor Vehicles and welfare offices.[80] The law, passed in the early 1990s, led to the greatest expansion of voter registration in American history: 5 million new voters registered.[81] It did not immediately increase turnout in the 1990s,[82] but it may have facilitated turnout after 2000.

Barriers to voting Some states work to facilitate voting turnout of those already registered, while others do not. For example, some states do not provide sample ballots or publicize where voters should go to vote, whereas other states mail sample ballots and information about where to vote to registered voters. Some states have limited polling hours; others open the polls very early and keep them open until 9 p.m. or later so that voters can vote before or after work. About half the states, including most of those west of the Mississippi, allow voters to vote with absentee ballots, even if they are not planning to be absent from their homes on election day. Absentee balloting makes voting something that can be done at the voter's convenience. One observer remarked, "The concept of Election Day is history. Now it's just the final day to vote."[83] Though this is clearly an overstatement, 30 percent of the voters voted before election day in 2008; in Oregon, all of them did.[84] In nine other states, more than 50 percent voted early.[85] To reach these early voters, parties must begin television advertising and flyer mailing much earlier. Providing information, extended polling hours, or using absentee ballots has a positive impact on voting rates, particularly for the young and less educated.[86]

Other states make it harder to vote. The states with the highest barriers to voting tend to be states with the largest minority populations. Some estimates are that one out of four Ohio voters in 2004 experienced problems on voting day, including having to go to more than one polling place, having to wait more than twenty minutes to vote, or leaving the polls before voting. Nearly half of Ohio's African American population experienced one of those problems.[87] African Americans were also more likely to be asked for identification and to feel intimidated at the polls.

Many states are considering requiring identification at the polls, a change that could result in even fewer low-income people voting.

Partisan Efforts to Discourage Voting

Sometimes, political parties try to raise the costs of voting for the other party's likely voters. In the 2004 election, there were many instances of partisan attempts to deter registration and voting; fewer such instances were reported in 2008.[88]

Noncompetitive Districts

In most states, legislatures draw the boundaries for congressional districts and state legislative districts, so districts are normally drawn to benefit the party in control of the legislature. A district whose boundaries are devised to maximize the political advantage of a party or a racial or ethnic group is known as a **gerrymander** (for more on gerrymanders, see Chapter 10). A gerrymander aims to ensure that one party dominates in a particular district.

One side effect of gerrymanders is that they reduce voter turnout. With the candidate from the dominant party sure to win, the benefits of voting are greatly diminished and so fewer have an incentive to vote. Consequently, accountability to voters is decreased. In 2006 congressional races, voter turnout in districts won by a landslide (defined as 80 percent or more) was only 60 percent that of races where the margin was 20 percent or less. Millions more might vote in off-year elections if they were more competitive. The best way to ensure competitiveness is to take redistricting out of the hands of the legislature and put it in the hands of a nonpartisan or bipartisan group, which has been done successfully in Iowa and Washington.[89]

PRESIDENTIAL NOMINATING CAMPAIGNS

In the early days of our nation, it was thought unseemly to "run" for office. John Quincy Adams, our sixth president,

Obama's candidacy generated excitement among young voters, who volunteered to work in campaign offices such as this one in Ohio.

refused to campaign for the job. He thought that seeking the voters' approval was "beneath the dignity of the office" and believed that men—and, of course, all candidates at that time were men—who openly wanted the office didn't deserve it.[90]

Today, things are much different. Individuals declare their candidacy and run hard for the office. But not all have an equal chance of winning. Many Americans believe in the Horatio Alger myth: that with hard work anyone can achieve great success. This myth has its parallel in politics, where it is sometimes said that any child can grow up to be president. In fact, only a few run for that office, and even fewer are elected. Most people have little chance of being president: they are unknown to the public; they do not have the financial resources or contacts to raise the money needed for a national campaign; they are the wrong race or gender; they have jobs they could not leave to run a serious campaign; and their friends would probably ridicule them for even thinking of such a thing.[91]

Who Runs for President and Why?

Most candidates for president are senators or governors.[92] In recent decades, governors (George W. Bush, Bill Clinton, Ronald Reagan, and Jimmy Carter) have been more successful than senators (George McGovern, Robert Dole, and John Kerry), but the 2008 election returned a senator to the White House, the first since Richard Nixon. Vice presidents also frequently run, but George H. W. Bush was the only successful candidate during the twentieth century (though Richard Nixon had been a vice president, he was a private citizen when he ran successfully in 1968).

Why do candidates run? An obvious reason is to gain the power and prestige of the presidency. But they may have other goals as well, such as to gain support for a particular policy or set of ideas. Ronald Reagan, for example, clearly wanted to be president in part to spread his conservative ideology. Ron Paul (R-Tex.) ran in 2008 to promote his libertarian ideas (libertarians combine a conservative disdain for government regulation of the economy with liberal

Chris Hondros/Getty Images

distain of big government regulation of personal behavior; the result is an ideology that favors very little government action at all). Sometimes candidates run for the presidency to be considered for the vice presidency, probably viewing it as an eventual stepping-stone to the presidency. But only occasionally—as when John Kerry picked John Edwards or Barack Obama chose Joe Biden—do presidential candidates choose one of their defeated opponents to run as a vice-presidential candidate.

How a Candidate Wins the Nomination

The nominating process is crucial in deciding who eventually gets elected. Boss Tweed once said, "I don't care who does the electing, so long as I get to do the nominating."[93] American presidential candidates are nominated through a process that includes the general public, the financial supporters of each party, and other party leaders.

Over time, voters and fundraisers have gained more power at the expense of party leaders. Presidential candidates try to win a majority of delegates at their party's national nominating convention, which takes place in the summer preceding the November election. Delegates to those conventions are elected in state caucuses, conventions, and primaries. Candidates must campaign to win the support of primary voters and those who attend caucuses and conventions.

Normally, candidates formally announce their candidacies in the year preceding the presidential election year. Their aim is to persist and survive the long primary and caucus season that begins in January of election year and continues until only one candidate is left. To maximize their chances of survival, candidates carefully choose the primaries and caucuses where they will devote their resources. They must be successful in enough primaries so that they are seen as national, not regional, candidates, but they cannot possibly devote time and resources to every primary or caucus. Especially important are the early events—the Iowa caucus and the New Hampshire primary—and the larger state primaries.

Caucus and primary strategies played a big role in the 2008 elections. On the Republican side, former New York City mayor Rudolph (Rudy) Giuliani decided that since he probably wouldn't win the early primaries and caucuses in rural states, he would save his money and focus on the Florida primary, held three weeks and six primary and caucus events after the Iowa caucus. (Florida Republicans include many former New Yorkers.) He failed to foresee that by not campaigning in those first six states, he would get very little media attention while the frontrunners were building name recognition and a track record of success. Consequently, when the Florida primary was held, he finished third, and a few days later he quit the race.

Fred Thompson, another Republican and an actor who had starred in *Law and Order*, also misjudged the dynamics of the primary and caucus season. Commentators and party activists were thrilled by the idea that he might run; some saw him as the new Reagan. But rather than getting organized, he apparently relished the positive attention he was getting without campaigning and delayed his formal announcement and active campaign until September 2007. Although this date was well before the Iowa caucus in early January, the other Republican candidates had been campaigning and building name recognition during most of 2007. By September, they had already held nine televised debates. Observers joked that Thompson's campaign peaked the day before he announced. He fizzled when actual primary and caucus voting occurred and withdrew after the first few events in January.

On the Democratic side, Senator Hillary Clinton and her campaign made a huge strategic error by not paying much attention to the caucus states. In those contests, most of them early in the primary season, victory goes to the best organized, and the Obama organization focused early on organizing in the caucus states. Obama won all but one of them, many by lopsided margins. Even though the caucuses have tiny turnouts (typically 1 to 5 percent of registered voters, though Iowa with 16 percent was an exception), their electoral votes added up and gave Obama a small lead by the end of February that was impossible for Clinton to overcome, even though she won most of the large state primaries and had a string of other successes in March, April, and May.

Candidates attempt to raise substantial amounts of money early. A large war chest can mark a candidate as unbeatable. George W. Bush started strong in the 2000 primaries because he had raised millions more than all his opponents combined. Barack Obama's fundraising success gave him a large advantage in the 2008 primary campaign.

Candidates also try to find the position, slogan, or idea that will appeal to the most voters. In 1984, Ronald Reagan presented himself as the candidate embodying traditional America. As one of his staff aides wrote in a campaign memo, "Paint RR as the personification of all that is right with, or heroized by, America."[94] Barack Obama was the candidate for "change," rallying his supporters around the slogan "it's our time" to change the country. John McCain's campaign did not have a simple slogan, but he capitalized on his reputation as an independent "maverick" and on his war hero credentials. Hillary Clinton took too long to find a theme that resonated. Her early emphasis on experience sent a mixed message because much of the public was fed up with Washington and many people already had strong feelings about her from her days as first lady. Later in the campaign she combined the "ready on day 1" theme with a strong populist message of fighting for the underdogs, a message that especially resonated with many women and blue-collar workers.

To compete successfully, candidates also need considerable media coverage. They must convince reporters that they are serious candidates with a real chance of winning. Journalists and candidates establish expectations for how well each candidate should do based on poll results, the quality of a candidate's campaign organization, the amount of money and time spent in the campaign, and the political

behind the scenes

The Rope Line

Though presidential campaigns are conducted primarily through the media, candidates do make personal appearances in towns and cities across the United States. And usually, after a speech or event, the candidate will stay for a few minutes—or longer—to shake hands and speak briefly with some of those who came to see him or her. This ritual takes place at "the rope line," now usually a metal barrier separating the candidate and the surging crowd.

At the rope line, a member of the public might shake a candidate's hand, give her a memento (a coin, rabbit's foot, book, photograph, or any number of other odd items), ask to have a photo taken with the candidate (usually with a cell phone

Hillary Clinton was very effective working the "rope line" at her campaign stops.

camera), get an autograph, give the candidate advice about a policy or even about getting enough sleep, or tell the candidate of a personal problem—all in a few seconds. Sometimes these brief encounters are reflected in later speeches, where the candidate will mention a person, sometimes by name, who told of a harrowing personal story that could be alleviated or avoided with better government policies or procedures.

The rope line offers a relatively spontaneous moment in what are usually very tightly controlled appearances. "I got to smell him, and it was awesome," said one Obama fan, caught between him and another woman trying to hug him. "I can't believe she picked me out of a crowd," said a Clinton supporter, after she gave him a bottle of water and signed a photograph for him. (The reporter noted that the man had fainted in front of her, so he was easy to pick out.)

Observers reported that Obama is not much of a hugger or handshaker and does "about 20 voter touches per 30 seconds." He rarely signs autographs on the spot. By contrast, Hillary Clinton is "a rope lining dynamo," charging into the crowd, spending more time with supporters, signing autographs on everything from T-shirts to Krispy Kreme boxes, and, like her husband, seeming to enjoy the experience. On the other hand, John McCain, reported an observer, "invites respectful distance." His war injuries make it difficult for him to reach out with his arms. "His approach is dutiful, like a Boy Scout mowing a lawn."

Of course, the secret service does not like rope lines because they are unpredictable as people press in on the candidate. One man on a Hillary Clinton rope line reported that he was asked to take off his respirator mask but was "allowed to keep his goggles and blue rubber gloves on." (He wanted to talk about the chemical industry.)

SOURCE: Mark Leibovich, "Where to Catch the Sights, Sound and Smell of a Campaign," *New York Times*, May 24, 2008, www.nytimes.com/2008/05/24/us/politics/24rope.html.

---

complexion of the state. (Sometimes these journalists and campaign pros are jokingly called "the expectorate."[95]) If a candidate performs below expectations, this may be seen by the press as a weakness. Even if a candidate wins, the victory may be interpreted as a loss if it's by a narrower margin than anticipated. On the other hand, a strong showing when expectations are low can give a boost to a candidate's campaign. Consequently, candidates try to lower media expectations. Bill Clinton finished second in the New Hampshire primary in 1992, but because the top vote getter (Paul E. Tsongas) was from neighboring Massachusetts, Clinton's

second-place finish was considered a victory. Coming from far behind, he pronounced himself "the comeback kid," a designation that became the story of the primary.

In 2008, McCain was counted out before the primaries even started because his campaign was disorganized and he lagged far behind his rivals in raising funds. And he finished fourth in the Iowa caucuses. Yet a personal style that went over well in town meeting settings, his national visibility, and the deficits of his opponents led to victories in early primaries. His major opponent, Mitt Romney, withdrew in early February.

On the Democratic side, after being the dominant front-runner before the first caucus and primary, Hillary Clinton finished below expectations in the Iowa caucus, finishing third. She then turned around and surprised the "expectorate" by winning the following week in New Hampshire, thus setting the stage for the long, back-and-forth Democratic primary. Nonetheless, when she continued to run behind because of her poor caucus showing, the press and Obama operatives increasingly called on her to leave the race, implicitly challenging her right to continue to compete.

In sum, the primary season is a game among the media, the candidates, and the voters, with the candidates trying to raise voter enthusiasm and lower media expectations simultaneously.

The common wisdom about presidential primaries is that the key ingredient is "momentum." That is, a candidate needs to win early, or at least do better than expected, to gain momentum, and then keep winning to maintain momentum. The "expectorate" needs to pronounce him a winner. In 1976, Jimmy Carter, then an unknown governor from Georgia, won the Iowa caucuses; this performance attracted tremendous media attention, which, in turn, led to further primary wins and eventually the nomination. John Kerry, by winning Iowa and then New Hampshire in the 2004 Democratic primaries, gained so much momentum that he knocked the other candidates out of the race very quickly, in what was originally billed as a tightly contested race. In 2008, however, on both the Republican and Democratic sides, the momentum seemed to shift back and forth.

Candidates must avoid making a big mistake or, worse yet, being caught covering up a mistake or untruth. Gary Hart's 1988 candidacy collapsed when the media discovered that his marriage did not prevent him from having affairs with other women. He compounded the damage by lying, thereby raising questions about his character and honesty. In contrast, during the primary campaign, Clinton admitted that his marriage was not perfect. (The Monica Lewinsky scandal occurred after he was in the White House and was already a popular president.)

Incumbent presidents seeking renomination do not have the same problems as their challengers. Incumbents usually have token or no opposition in the primaries. No incumbent who sought renomination was denied it in the twentieth century.

In addition to these general strategies, candidates must deal specifically with the particular demands of caucuses, conventions, and primaries.

Presidential Caucuses and Conventions

Some states employ caucuses and conventions to select delegates to attend presidential nominating conventions. A caucus is a neighborhood meeting of party members who discuss the candidates and then vote for their preference. These results are then added across the state. A convention, on the other hand, is usually a statewide event. Delegates to the convention are elected at the local level by party voters.

The Iowa caucuses, except for their timing and newsworthiness, are similar to those in other states. Iowa, as the first state to hold its caucuses, normally gets the most attention. Thousands of representatives of the media cover these caucuses, which have gained importance beyond what one would normally expect for a small state. Although only a handful of delegates to the national convention are at stake, a win with the nation's political pros watching can establish a candidate as a serious contender and attract further media attention and the financial donations necessary to continue the campaign.

Presidential Primaries

Delegates to presidential nominating conventions are also selected in direct primaries, sometimes called **presidential preference primaries**. In these elections, governed by state laws and national party rules, voters indicate a preference for a presidential candidate, or they vote for the delegates committed to a candidate, or both. (In states where voters merely indicate their preference, the delegates are actually selected in conventions or caucuses and the primaries are called "beauty contests" because they are meaningless in terms of winning delegates, though they can be important in showing popular support.) Like other primaries, presidential primaries can be open (to all voters) or closed (to nonparty members).

Through the 1960s, presidential preference primaries usually played an insignificant role in presidential nominations because only a handful of states employed primaries to select delegates. Thus Vice President Hubert Humphrey gained the Democratic Party's nomination in 1968 without winning a single primary. A majority of the delegates to the Democratic convention were selected through party caucuses and state conventions, where party leaders supportive of Humphrey had considerable influence. Humphrey's nomination severely divided the Democratic Party. Many constituencies within the party, particularly those opposed to the Vietnam War, charged that the nomination was controlled by party elites out of touch with rank-and-file Democrats.

Delegate Selection Reform

In response, the Democratic Party changed delegate selection procedures to make delegates more representative of Democratic voters. One change established quotas for blacks, women, and young people to reflect the groups' percentages in each state's population. These reforms significantly increased minority and female convention representation and, quite unexpectedly, made the primary the preferred method of nomination. Criteria of openness and representativeness could be more easily satisfied through primary selection. In recent years, more than 70 percent of the Democratic delegates have been chosen in primaries. Although the Democrats have replaced quotas for minorities with guidelines urging minority involvement in party affairs, the quota for women remains: half the delegates must be women.

Shepard Sherbell/Corbis

Republicans keep looking for the next Ronald Reagan who can unify the party and win over the voters.

The Republican Party has not felt as much pressure to reform its delegate selection procedures, but Republicans have tried to eliminate discrimination and increase participation in the selection process.

Reforming the Nomination Process

Each election year political observers discuss changing the presidential nomination process. They correctly complain that primaries weaken political parties by removing the decision from party officials and that primaries have very low, unrepresentative turnouts. But while caucuses empower the party elite, they are a barrier to broad participation and even more unrepresentative than primaries.

The Caucuses

The caucus system came under attack in 2008, especially by Clinton supporters. Although Clinton's campaign did not pay close enough attention to the rules that gave caucuses significant power, it is also true that, as they alleged, caucuses favor individuals who have a good deal of flexible time, such as independent professionals. They do not empower working-class people because participation in a caucus requires several hours. Thus, those who have child care responsibilities, are out of town, are ill or disabled, or have inflexible work schedules are disfranchised.

Moreover, the small number of participants means that caucuses can be very unrepresentative of the overall primary electorate. In 2008, in the four states that had both primaries and caucuses, Obama won the caucuses by margins 5 to 34 percent greater than the popular vote and thus piled up huge delegate margins. (In three of the four states, the primaries were only "beauty contests"; the vote didn't count in the delegate selection.) On the Republican side, McCain did very poorly in the caucuses because of his organizational problems yet was able to win most of the big primaries, which, because of the Republican's method of delegate allocation, he converted into large numbers of delegates.

The Primaries

The primary electorate, often in the 25 to 35 percent turnout range, is much larger than the number of caucus participants but significantly smaller than the number of voters in the general election. Primary voters include the citizens who are most interested in politics and tend to hold more extreme views than other people. Thus Democratic primaries have a disproportionate number of liberals, and Republican primaries have a disproportionate number of conservatives. These primary voters pull the Democratic candidates further to the left and the Republican candidates further to the right than the candidates might choose to position themselves or than the electorate as a whole might want the candidates to position themselves.

Moreover, until 2008, the system gave disproportionate influence to two small states, Iowa and New Hampshire, that come first in the process. Voters in most other states did not get to see most candidates; they had already been weeded out by the time the April, May, and June primaries occurred. There are some advantages to having the small states go first,[96] particularly the fact that campaigns in small states can be personal and relatively inexpensive compared to the costs of the big media markets in large states. But in 2008, the system changed. Legislators in the larger states moved to get their states into the early action. The Iowa caucus and then the New Hampshire primary remained first, but a month later twenty-two states, including many large states, held primaries. This new lineup put a much bigger premium on having money and gaining support early, since only media buys allowed candidates to be visible in so many large states simultaneously.

Rearranging the schedule does not address the central problem: that primaries remove power from political parties. Many people are glad that we no longer have the "smoke-filled rooms" where party bosses chose the nominees. Nevertheless, the primary system has weakened political parties, and the small primary electorate is unrepresentative of the general public, though it is more representative than the caucuses. It is possible that primary voters are even less representative of the public than the party bosses who met in smoke-filled rooms. Certainly they know less about the nominees than the party bosses did. But the days when party leaders could anoint the nominees are probably gone forever.

Another issue with primaries is how the votes are counted. In 2008 the Republicans operated with a winner-take-all system; that is, the candidate winning the most votes won all the delegates in the state. This is analogous to the Electoral College system for determining the general election winner. The Democrats, on the other hand, split each state's delegates according to the proportion of votes they received in the primary or caucus. Thus, a 51 percent victory for John McCain gave him all the state's delegates; a similar victory for Barack Obama gave him only 51 percent. Several commentators have pointed out that had the Democrats operated under the Republican rules, Hillary Clinton would have been the Democratic nominee.

DEMOCRACY?

Can we know whether caucuses or primaries are more representative of the party? Of the general electorate? Which are more democratic, primaries or caucuses?

The National Conventions

Once selected, delegates attend their party's national nominating convention in the summer before the November election. Changes in party rules have reduced the convention's role from an arena where powerful party leaders came together and determined the party's nominee to a body that ratifies a choice based on the outcome of the primaries and caucuses. In other words, the conventions now routinely nominate whichever candidate wins the most primaries.

In the "old" days, often many ballots were necessary before a winner emerged. In 1924, it took the Democrats 103 ballots to nominate John W. Davis. Now nominees are selected on the first ballot. Sometimes commentators predict a close nomination race, which would force the decision to be made at the convention, but this hasn't happened since the primaries have been used extensively. Instead, the national party conventions served other purposes: to endorse the nominee and his choice for vice president, to construct a party platform, to whip up enthusiasm for the ticket among party loyalists, and to present the party favorably to the national viewing audience. Thus even without choosing the nominee, the national conventions give meaning to the notion of a national party.

After the reforms of 1972, convention delegates have become a more diverse group, especially on the Democratic side. In 2004, 50 percent of the Democratic and 43 percent of the Republican delegates were women; 18 percent of the Democratic and 6 percent of the Republican delegates were black. (Only 2 percent of Republican voters are black, compared with 28 percent of Democratic voters.) Similarly, Democratic delegates are much more likely to be Latino and very slightly more likely to be Asian than are Republican delegates.[97] Compared to the population, delegates to national party conventions are well educated and financially well-off. Delegates also tend to be more ideologically extreme than each party's rank and file. Democratic delegates are more liberal and Republican delegates more conservative than their party's supporters and the public in general. (See Figure 5.)

The Activities of the Convention

National party conventions are full of color and portray at least a semblance of excitement. They are a montage of balloons, placards, and demonstrations. Candidates and their lieutenants scurry around in search of uncommitted delegates, while behind-the-scenes negotiators try to work out differences among factions of the party. Journalists are everywhere, covering the trivial and occasionally the momentous. The keynote address reviews the party's glorious past, speaks to a promising future, and levels attacks, usually relatively gentle, at the opposition. Each candidate is placed in nomination by a party notable who reviews the candidate's background and experience. The roll call of the states ratifies the party's choice, and on the last night delegates cheer the acceptance speeches of the presidential and vice-presidential nominees. Those who contested the nomination often join the nominees on the platform at the end in a display of party unity.

During the convention, each party endorses a platform, a statement of what it plans to do dressed up in flowery language about how it is the only possible choice for patriotic Americans. Although platforms are filled with platitudes, they do have some substance. Most of the platforms contain pledges of proposed future actions, and most of those pledges are fulfilled.[98] Platforms do provide observant voters with information about what the party will do if elected.

| Figure 5 | National Convention Delegates Are More Ideologically Extreme than Rank-and-File Members |

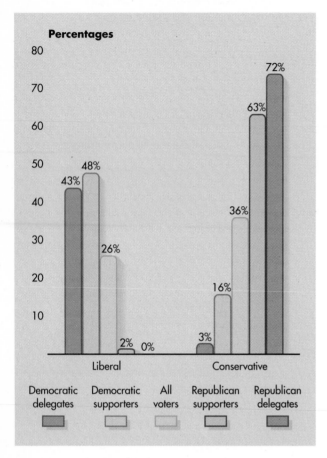

The numbers represent the percents of those who identify themselves as "Liberal" on the left hand set of bars or "Conservative" on the right hand set. In other words, of Democratic delegates 43% consider themselves liberal and 3% conservative. (Others are middle of the road).
SOURCE: Data from 2008 delegate and public surveys reported in the New York Times, September 1, 2008, graphics8.nytimes.com/packages/pdf/politics/20080901-poll.pdf?scp=5&sq=delegate%20survey&st=cse.

many media representatives as delegates at the conventions.[100] The parties try to put on a show they hope will attract voters to their candidates, controlling who speaks and when. Polls usually show the party's candidate doing better during and after the party's convention, called the "convention bounce," though the effect does not last long.

When there are deep divisions in the party, it may be impossible to prevent them from surfacing at the convention during prime time. This has not happened since the 1968 Democratic convention, which was filled with conflict, both inside the convention between the supporters of Hubert Humphrey and opponents of the Johnson policies on the Vietnam War, and outside the convention on the streets of Chicago between antiwar demonstrators and the Chicago police. Television covered both events, associating the division in the convention with the turmoil outside and dimming Humphrey's chances of winning the election.

Because subsequent conventions have been predictable, with few controversial issues, the major networks are no longer showing them "gavel to gavel," leaving that coverage to public television or specialty cable networks such as CNN and C-SPAN. The major networks showed only a few prime-time events of each 2008 national convention: the keynote speech and an occasional speech by a party luminary, such as the ailing Ted Kennedy at the Democratic convention and several of the defeated presidential candidates at the Republican one. The vice-presidential and presidential nominees' acceptance speeches are also given extensive coverage. In 2008, coverage of the Democratic convention focused on whether Clinton supporters would rally around Obama, and the media gave extensive coverage to speeches by Hillary Clinton and Bill Clinton. At the Republican convention the focus was on the controversies swirling around John McCain's surprise pick of Sarah Palin, governor of Alaska, as his vice-presidential nominee. This limited coverage is the logical outcome of the successful attempt of party leaders to control the conventions. Still, even if there's no controversy, the media's talking heads will work hard to create conflict and excitement.

Selecting a Vice-Presidential Nominee

In modern times, the vice-presidential candidate is selected by the party's presidential nominee and then merely ratified at the convention, although in 1956, Democratic presidential nominee Adlai Stevenson broke with tradition and left the decision to the convention. In earlier years, party bosses chose the running mate. When Rutherford B. Hayes (1877–1881) first got word that William Wheeler was to be his running mate, Hayes responded, "I'm ashamed to say: Who is Wheeler?"[101]

Presidential candidates usually select a vice-presidential nominee who can balance the ticket. What exactly does "balance" mean? A careful analysis of vice-presidential choices of both parties since 1940 revealed that presidential candidates tend to balance the ticket in terms of

Finally, the conventions close with the acceptance speeches of the presidential and vice-presidential nominees, which are the highlights for most viewers. Overall, the function of the conventions might best be summarized by the comment "Conventions are now like bar mitzvahs. They are rites of passage. But rites of passage are very important in society. The guy is changing from a politician and a candidate to one of the two people who are going to be president for sure; it gives them a certain majesty."[99]

The Media and the Convention

With the beginning of radio coverage in 1924 and television coverage in 1940, the conventions have become media events. In recent years, there have been several times as

The intense primary contest between Clinton and Obama lasted until early summer, when Clinton conceded defeat.

age—choosing a running mate from a different age cohort, as John McCain did with Sarah Palin.[102] Those with little Washington experience usually balance the ticket by choosing a Washington insider as a running mate (as, in 2008, relative outsider Obama did by choosing Joe Biden and as, in 2000, outsider George W. Bush did by choosing Dick Cheney). Although common wisdom also suggests that presidential candidates balance the ticket in terms of region (for example, John F. Kennedy from Massachusetts chose

Texan Lyndon Johnson in 1960) or ideology (for example, the more liberal Michael Dukakis chose the more conservative Lloyd Bentsen in 1988), this happens only occasionally.[103] In 2008, both presidential candidates had running mates whose ideologies were similar to their own.

Gender traditionally was not part of a ticket-balancing effort, but since Walter Mondale's historic choice of Geraldine Ferraro in 1984, women are sometimes among those given consideration. Much discussion of both parties' tickets in 2008 swirled around the issue of whether a woman would be asked to join the ticket. Though Barack Obama passed over Hillary Clinton as his choice in favor of Sen. Joe Biden (Del.), John McCain did choose Sarah Palin. Though his primary aim may have been to woo disaffected Clinton supporters (an attempt that failed), the major impact was to rally the religious right to his ticket. Palin, a conservative Republican, energized the Republican base and gave the ticket new excitement.

Pundits often opine that choosing a vice-presidential candidate from a large state will help win that state in the November election. [104] In fact, this is not true; the added advantage of a vice-presidential candidate in his or her home state is less than 1 percent, and the bigger the state, the less the advantage.[105] About one-third of the vice-presidential candidates since 1960, including John Edwards, did not even carry their home state.[106] Bush and Kerry in 2004 and Obama and McCain in 2008 ignored the large-state potential in choosing their running mates. In fact, Dick Cheney, Sarah Palin, and Joe Biden came from the nation's smallest states, with three Electoral College votes each.

Do vice-presidential choices affect the election outcome? In most cases, no, although Kennedy's selection of Johnson probably enabled him to carry the state of Texas in the tight 1960 race. Without Texas, Kennedy would have lost. In recent years, presidential candidates have been more attentive to the possible contributions a vice president would make after being elected. Other than that, as one commentator quipped, "picking a running mate is . . . like picking a pet. How much time are you planning to spend with the little fellow? How much exercise will he be getting on an average day? On the one extreme, you have the William Wheeler model [Rutherford B. Hayes's vice president].There's the living room, go find a corner and sleep in it. On the other end, there's the Cheney version in which the pet takes over the checkbook, diversifies the family investment portfolio and starts strafing the neighbor's cat."[107]

Independent and Third-Party Nominees

Independent and third-party candidates are part of every presidential campaign. Most of the candidates are invisible to all except the most avid political devotee. It's not easy for independents to get on the ballot; state laws control access to the ballot, and state lawmakers are Republicans or Democrats. But in recent elections, strong independents have emerged with some frequency, including Ross

In the 1950s, at the dawn of the television age, Democratic Party leaders instruct their delegates how to behave on camera.

John McCain's last-minute choice of Sarah Palin as his vice-presidential running mate surprised and energized the Republican Party and its conservative base.

Perot in 1992 and 1996 and Ralph Nader in 2000. The Nader candidacy probably cost Al Gore the election by taking some liberal votes away from him in closely fought states.

THE GENERAL ELECTION CAMPAIGN

We take it for granted that the election campaign is what determines who wins, and it does have a modest effect.[108] But consider this: only twice since 1952 has the candidate who was ahead in the polls in July, before the national conventions, lost the election. Those years were 1988, when Dukakis led, and 2000, when Al Gore led (and since Gore won the popular vote, perhaps his case is only a partial exception to the rule).[109] This suggests that although campaigns can make a difference, a lot of other factors determine who is elected.

Campaign Organization

Staffing the campaign organization is crucial, not only hiring talented people but also getting those with considerable national campaign experience and a variety of perspectives. The candidate's own personal organization is only one part of the overall campaign organization. The national party organization and state parties also have some responsibilities, including the very important functions of registering potential party voters and getting them to the polls, as well as trying to make sure that the presidential candidate's local appearances will help the party's congressional and state

candidates. Party organizations are also crucial in raising funds after the conventions, when direct fundraising by candidates is no longer legal if the candidate accepts public funding.

Campaign Strategies

In developing a strategy, candidates primarily seek to do two things: mobilize those who are already loyal to them and their party and persuade independent voters that they are the best candidate. At the national level, given entrenched party loyalties, little effort is spent to try to convert the opposition. Democrats have to work harder at mobilizing their voters than do Republicans because Democratic voters often do not vote.

Most partisans vote for their party's candidate, so the job there is to mobilize them. Both parties must try to persuade independent voters, who are swing voters and can determine the outcome, even though true independents are only about 10 percent of the electorate. (Most of those who say they are independent lean strongly to one party or another; for example, in 2004, among white voters, 88 percent of those who claimed to be independent but "leaning Democratic" voted for Kerry, and 87 percent of their Republican-leaning independent counterparts voted for Bush.)

The crucial strategic question is where to allocate resources of time and money: where to campaign, where to buy media time and how much to buy, and where to spend money helping local organizations. Skill in raising money is, of course, also one of the keys to a successful political campaign. We will discuss this much more fully in the next chapter.

Allocating Resources among States

Candidates know that they have to win a majority of the Electoral College vote (see "The Electoral College" section later in this chapter). The most populous states, with the largest number of electoral votes, are vital. However, compared to thirty years ago, more states are now "safe" (see the box "America the Sorted"). So candidates focus their resources on a decreasing number of so-called **battleground states (or swing states)**, where the results are in doubt. That includes not just the large states of Ohio, Pennsylvania, and Florida, but also medium-sized states such as Wisconsin and Iowa and even smaller states such as New Mexico, with its five electoral votes, and New Hampshire with its four.

Thus in the 2008 presidential campaign, there was little advertising or activity in several of the largest states—California, New York, and Texas—because the first two were considered sure Obama states and the last a sure McCain state. Meanwhile, the swing states received massive attention. Obama and McCain totaled twenty-seven visits to Pennsylvania and twenty-nine to Ohio, while California and New York received less than half that. Smaller swing states, including Missouri, Colorado, Virginia, and Florida, had presidential candidate visits more frequently than New York and California, even though they had many fewer electoral votes.[110] And Texas, safely in the Republican column,

received only two visits. In 2004 the same dynamics were at work: "More money was spent on television advertising in Florida . . . than in 45 states and the District of Columbia combined. More than half of all campaign resources were dedicated to just three states—Florida, Ohio, and Pennsylvania."[111]

In focusing on swing states, candidates are attempting to expand their existing bases of support. Most of the Rocky Mountain states have been solidly Republican in their presidential loyalties. Republicans must build on this base and their strength in the South by carrying some of the large eastern or midwestern industrial states.

Democrats have a strategic problem stemming from the fact that Republicans locked up most of the Rocky Mountain and southern states in the 1970s and 1990s. Between the end of Reconstruction (in 1877) and 1948, the South was solidly Democratic. Since 1976, the Democrats have consistently lost the South, as we discussed in Chapter 6. President Clinton, himself a southerner, proved that Democrats could win without most of the South, although he did win three southern states in each election. (This strategy was also used successfully by the Republicans between the 1870s and the 1920s, when they were able to capture the White House regularly without ever winning a southern state.) Obama won North Carolina and Virginia, giving hope to the Democrats that the Republicans' lock on the

When Bill Clinton selected Al Gore as his running mate in 1992, he chose someone who was from the same generation and region and who had the same ideology (moderate liberal). Although Gore, unlike Clinton, was a Washington insider, observers were surprised that there wasn't more effort to balance the ticket. Yet the two couples (including Hillary Clinton and Tipper Gore) developed a bond that energized their campaign.

Photo by Cynthia Johnson/Liaison/Getty Images

behind the scenes

America the Sorted

Because of the geographic mobility and economic circumstances that allow most Americans to move around more than previously, Americans are much more likely than in previous generations to live among others of similar economic statuses and cultural beliefs. For example, whereas in 1970 people with college degrees were fairly evenly spread across cities, today college graduates are leaving some areas and congregating in others. Those areas are booming, while other areas are declining.

Because cultural differences influence political choices, this **Big Sort** has had dramatic political consequences. As the author of the book by that name illustrates, before 1980, only about a third of voters lived in counties where one or the other presidential candidate won by a landslide (at least 20 points). In 2004, nearly half of the voters did.

That sorting, in turn, has consequences for democracy. Communities of like-minded individuals can become homogeneous and even extreme in their political attitudes because there is little diversity of opinions generated by individuals of widely different circumstances. Central cities are overwhelmingly Democratic, while many suburbs and small towns are overwhelmingly Republican.

Each community can act boldly based on its relatively homogeneous constituency. For example, some communities pass end-the-war resolutions while others pass those supporting the president, and the representatives they send to Congress are also more extreme than if the communities were moderate and diverse. Unfortunately, as communities thus become more homogeneous and active, Congress becomes more polarized and dysfunctional.

SOURCE: Bill Bishop, *The Big Sort* (Boston: Houghton Mifflin, 2008).

South has been broken, but he lost all the rest of the southern states.

The Republicans' strategic problem is that the party has become heavily reliant on the thirteen states of the old Confederacy. Those states have provided more than half of the Republicans' electoral votes in every election since 1992 (as well as almost half of the Republicans' congressional representation).[112] As the South becomes more multicultural and diverse in other ways, Republicans' grip on parts of the South may be slipping.

Obama also won Nevada and Colorado, solidly Republican in the Bush years, and New Mexico, which had voted Republican in 2004, putting another crack in a Republican stronghold.[113]

Creating Images

Largely through the media, candidates try to create a favorable image and portray the opponent in an unfavorable way. In 2000, George W. Bush used his warm personality to establish a positive image despite the concerns many voters had about his abilities. Voters were comfortable with Gore's abilities but had reservations about his personality, which in public was sometimes wooden and overly earnest. In 2004, Bush defined himself as a resolute war leader and defined Kerry as a "flip-flopper" with no principled positions. In 2008, McCain portrayed Obama as different, radical, and out of touch with ordinary people, while Obama challenged McCain's ability to relate to ordinary people given his tremendous wealth and his age, and he

described McCain's positions as "more of the same" failed Bush policies. Obama also attempted to paint McCain as an out-of-touch, erratic decision maker who would appoint an unqualified person to take up the vice presidency for his own political benefit.

Issues can also be the basis for an appeal to voters. Democrats traditionally have used "pocketbook" issues, arguing that economic times are better with Democratic presidents. They did the same in the 2008 election. Given the problematic state of the economy, high gas prices, and the slumping housing market, the Democrats fought the 2008 campaign on economic issues. McCain tried to gain advantage on foreign policy and war issues, arguing that Obama was an untried leader and that Obama would rather win an election than the war. As a war hero himself and an experienced senator, McCain had some advantage on these issues. Republican surrogates even cast doubt on Obama's patriotism, while far-right ideologues tried to make an issue out of Obama's middle name, Hussein. But, even with two ongoing wars, economic issues touched people the most, and Obama and the Democrats were seen by the electorate as better on those issues.

Issue appeals are usually general, and often candidates do not offer a clear-cut choice even on the most important controversies of the time. For example, the 1968 presidential election offered voters little choice on Vietnam policy because the positions of candidates Nixon and Humphrey appeared very similar.[114] Voters who wanted to end the war by withdrawing and voters who wanted to escalate the war had no real choice between the candidates. In 2008, it was hard to see any differences between McCain and Obama on the war in Afghanistan, but, on Iraq, Obama pushed for a timetable for withdrawal, while McCain argued for staying until the United States achieved "victory."

Ideally, the major campaign themes and strategies have been put into place by the end of the summer, but these themes and strategies are revised and updated on a daily, sometimes hourly, basis as the campaign progresses. Decisions are made not only by the candidate and the campaign manager but also by a staff of key advisers that includes media experts and pollsters. Campaigns use sophisticated polling techniques to produce daily reports on shifts in public opinion across the nation and in particular regions. Campaign trips are modified or scratched as the candidate's organization sees new opportunities. And media events can be planned to complement the paid advertising the candidate runs.

Campaign Communication

Candidates use multiple ways of communicating with their supporters and with the millions of swing voters who might vote either way. Campaign advertising, appearances on television, candidate debates, mass mailings, and many forms of electronic communication are all part of campaign communication. They inform, they help set the campaign agenda, and they help persuade voters.[115]

Media Advertising

Paid advertisements allow candidates to focus on points most favorable to their cause or to portray their opponents in the most negative light. Most of the cost of campaigns is in advertising, and in that category in 2008, Obama outspent McCain by $83 million.[116] (Recall that McCain's entire publicly funded presidential campaign budget was $84 million.)[117] Obama's campaign had so much money that it even ran ads on evangelical radio stations "just to hold down the McCain margin."[118] It was, as his campaign manager noted, "like fantasy camp for political operatives."[119]

Most advertising is done through television, increasingly on cable channels, although radio and the Internet also reach significant audiences.[120] Television ads were first used in the 1952 campaign. One, linking the Democratic Truman administration to the unpopular Korean War, showed two soldiers in combat talking about the futility of war. Then one of the soldiers is hit and dies. The other one exposes himself to the enemy and is also killed. The announcer's voice says, "Vote Republican."[121] Today's ads are shorter and less melodramatic but still appeal to emotions. The 1984 Reagan commercials hearkened back to an idyllic past before the turmoil of the 1960s and 1970s and proclaimed American greatness again. Their cheerful tag line was "It's morning in America."[122] (Many historic ads are available for viewing online at www.movingimage.us, under "The Living Room Candidate.")

Targeting advertisements There is both an art and a science to campaign ads. Most political ads are quite short, thirty or sixty seconds in length. Campaigns are sophisticated in placing ads, targeting them to demographic groups they hope will be sympathetic to their candidates. This technique, called "**narrowcasting**," is possible today because of the many cable TV and local radio stations in existence. BET attracts blacks, Univision appeals to Hispanics, ESPN to men, Lifetime to women, Fox to conservatives, and MSNBC to liberals. Although these are generalizations, if your target audience is moderates and liberals, for example, you won't advertise on Fox. Radio stations also have particular demographics. Conservative talk radio shows, pop stations, and NPR have different demographics, as well as a local audience.

The Obama campaign used narrowcasting quite effectively. Initially concerned about the possible erosion of women's support with Sarah Palin on the Republican ticket, the campaign launched a targeted radio campaign to reach moderate women in suburban areas of swing states. The focus was to convince them that McCain was pro-life (which he was) and against stem cell research (which he wasn't) in order to paint McCain as out of the mainstream and not supportive of women. The campaign was quite successful; by the end of the campaign, middle-of-the-road women were more likely to identify McCain as pro-life.[123] This narrowcasting was effective because it reached a select audience without getting national media attention that might have, in this case, reinforced McCain support among pro-life voters and pointed out the misleading part of the Obama ads.

Both campaigns focused on the battleground states and wasted little of their advertising budget on states already thought to be sure for one candidate.[124] But within the battleground states, Republicans generally focus more on rural and exurban (outer suburban) areas than do Democrats.

Negative or positive campaigning Campaigns also have to decide what combination to run of positive ads that introduce the candidates, their ideas, and their programs; negative ads that attack their opponents; and response ads that respond to opponents' charges.

We described at the beginning of the chapter how negative advertising is nothing new in American politics. Even the Founders engaged in it. In the more immediate past, negative ads were prominent in both 2004 and 2008 elections. In 2004, the Bush campaign ran far more negative ads than the Kerry campaign.[125] This high level of negativity is unusual for an incumbent but probably reflected Bush's low approval ratings, since strong frontrunners tend to stay positive.[126] This pattern was true in 2008. Negative ads were the staple of the McCain campaign, while the Obama campaign had a greater balance of positive and negative. The Obama campaign could do this, not only because it was the frontrunner throughout the campaign, but also because it outspent McCain on advertising by a substantial margin,

american*diversity

Racism in the 2008 Campaign

With the election of Barack Obama, the racial barrier to the presidency fell. Some other barriers had fallen in earlier decades. In 1960, only 71 percent of all voters said they would vote for a Catholic for president, and some doubted whether a Catholic could ever be elected.[1] But in 1960, John F. Kennedy was elected, and that barrier was broken. Twenty years later Ronald Reagan became the first divorced person to be elected. Race, however, is a much more distinctive barrier than even religion.

In some ways, the 2008 election seemed light-years away from earlier eras, when the idea of a woman of any color or an African American man running for president would have seemed ludicrous. Both Hillary Clinton and Barack Obama had millions of campaign supporters who included men, women, blacks, and whites (and, of course, Americans of other ethnicities too), and both their campaigns broke fundraising records. In these ways, their campaigns were much different than Jesse Jackson's 1984 campaign, which appealed mostly, though certainly not entirely, to black Americans, or earlier bids for the presidency by Shirley Chisholm in 1972, who never had a chance to become a mainstream candidate.

Racism in the campaign was alive and well, though more subtle than the sexism that Hillary Clinton faced. Few, if any, mainstream commentators made blatantly racist comments. Yet race was injected into the campaign in many different ways. A minority of voters, but a significant one, stated in preelection and exit polls that race was a factor in their vote. While some of these were African American voters positively inclined toward Obama, others were white voters stating they would not vote for a black person. Although Obama was very successful in caucuses in overwhelmingly white states, his support in the larger states with racially diverse populations was more mixed. Obama did well among white voters in many states, but in the later primaries Clinton won large margins among working-class white men and women in states such as Pennsylvania, Ohio, and West Virginia.

Several Clinton supporters made comments that cast, or seemed to cast, aspersions on Obama as an African American candidate. Geraldine Ferraro, the party's vice-presidential candidate in 1984 and the only woman to run as a major party candidate for that position, claimed that Obama would not be the leading candidate if he were white. Obama decried these comments as "divisive," and Clinton removed Ferraro from her fundraising team. Bill Clinton, who during his terms was a strong supporter of African American interests, and they of him, made several statements demeaning Obama in ways that were seen as offensive. Commenting on Obama's South Carolina primary victory, he stated: "Jesse Jackson won South Carolina in '84 and '88. Jackson ran a good campaign. And Obama ran a good campaign here." Neither of these statements was obviously racist, but both comments were seen by Obama supporters as demeaning. Obama was trying to run a campaign not focused on race, and Bill Clinton turned the focus to race.

Race became more salient in the general election. McCain accused Obama of playing the race card when Obama declared that McCain was trying to portray him as "the other," not like other presidents you see on dollar bills. In fact, Obama generally did not bring race into the election, and McCain was racializing the campaign himself. He had been articulating a frequent Republican campaign theme to portray Obama as different, even when race was not mentioned. Republican rallies often called attention to Obama's middle name, Hussein. On the Internet, questioning of his American ancestry continued (and continues into his presidency). These were not direct, old-fashioned racial slurs, but attempts to make salient that Obama was not "one of us."[2]

The election results showed that enough Americans cast aside their doubts about a relatively inexperienced African American candidate to elect him by a large margin. In fact, the campaign itself seemed to bring about a modest change in whites' attitudes about blacks.[3] Though Obama did not win a majority of white votes, he won a higher proportion than any Democrat since Jimmy Carter. Even many voters who admitted prejudice against an African American candidate voted for him because they thought he would better protect their economic interests or they doubted whether the McCain-Palin team was up to the job.

[1] Barry Sussman, "A Black or Woman Does Better Today than a Catholic in '60," *Washington Post National Weekly Edition*, November 21, 1983; 42.
[2] Shankar Vedantam, "Why Those Rumors Stick," *Washington Post National Weekly Edition*, October 20–26, 2008, 37.
[3] Lee Sigelman and Susan Welch, "The 'Obama Effect' and White Racial Attitudes," forthcoming in the *Annals of the American Academy of Political and Social Science*, 2010.

SOURCE: www.cbsnews.com/htdocs/pdf/ 020306woman.pdf; Gallup poll data from www.atheists.org/flash.line/atheism9.htm.

so it could do both positive and negative advertising. With a more limited budget, the McCain campaign decided that negative ads were more effective.[127] Many of the most negative ads are run not by the candidates and their campaigns but by independent groups supporting them (we will discuss independent groups in the next chapter).

Because negative ads do provide some helpful information about issues, they supplement media news coverage, which focuses heavily on personalities, conflicts, and the "horse race" aspect of campaigns.[128] Many, though not all, negative ads contain a grain of truth. Obama *was* more supportive of government spending than McCain, and McCain *was* more hawkish on the Iraq War than Obama.

However, some negative ads are simply false. Among the most discussed negative ads in 2004 were those of the Swift Boat Veterans for Truth, who attacked Kerry's war record. (Kerry, as a young naval lieutenant, commanded a "swift boat" in the Vietnam War and won medals for heroism as well as for his wounds.) The Swift Boat Veterans did not serve with Kerry, and several were angry with him for opposing the war after returning from Vietnam. The Kerry campaign was slow to respond to these August ads and lost ground in the polls during this period, despite the fact that independent reexaminations of the record found nothing to substantiate the Swift Boat Veterans' ad claims. The Swift Boat ads were so effective that reporters coined a new verb—"to swift-boat"—meaning to produce a commercial that is dishonest but plausible to viewers.

Negative ads, whether true or false, tend to reinforce viewers' previous beliefs. So, if you believed that Kerry wouldn't be a strong leader or that Democrats wouldn't stand up to foreign threats, you would be more likely to believe the Swift Boat ads that questioned Kerry's Vietnam service and implicitly draw those damning conclusions. Campaign advisers think that negative ads are very effective, even though most people say they do not like them.[129] One adviser said, "People won't pay any attention [to positive ads]. Better to knock your opponent's head off."[130] Polls do show that negative ads can have a dramatic short-term effect on a candidate's standing. The Swift Boat commercials suggest that negative ads, even if false, can have a long-term effect as well.

Some observers speculate that negative ads increase voter cynicism and thus depress turnout, but there is little evidence of this effect. In fact, negative ads may activate the supporters of the attacker while depressing the turnout of the person being attacked.[131] However, there is evidence that Republicans and independents find negative ads more believable than Democrats do, perhaps because Republicans and independents are more cynical about politics and government to begin with.

Some checks do exist on negative campaigns.[132] One check is the press, which could point out errors of fact. In recent campaigns, the press has tried to do this. In 2004 and again in 2008, fact checkers were more active, and many papers ran critiques of the truthfulness of ads (and the statements in debates). In the process, however, the press often simply gave more attention to the negative messages.[133] Another check is the voters, who might become outraged. But although the voters complain, campaign research shows that negative ads often influence them, perhaps even the same ones who complain.

E-Campaigning

Increasing numbers of people are using the Internet as a source of news. In fact, during the 2008 election, nearly half of Americans said they looked online for news about the campaign or got e-mails about it. Seventeen percent claimed to look for campaign news online on a daily basis.

Not surprisingly, then, candidates are increasingly relying on electronic communication to keep supporters informed about the campaign and the issues, to raise money, and to solicit volunteer activity. Their tools include websites, e-mail, blogs, YouTube, text messaging, and social networking sites like MySpace, Facebook, and Friendster.

Use of e-mail and texting is a particular form of narrowcasting, sometimes called **microtargeting**, that uses electronic messages to communicate with hundreds of thousands of people, making them feel like insiders and encouraging their continued support, allegiance, and activity. These e-mail messages supplement the use of direct postal mailings, which are more expensive and less responsive to breaking events. An e-mail can be prepared and sent in a few hours and can be linked to a website or streamed video.

Barack Obama led, by far, in using the Internet to attract supporters and keep them engaged. "Our e-mail list had reached 13 million people. We essentially created our own television network, only better, because we communicated directly with no filter to what would amount to about 20 percent of the total number of votes we would need to win,"

"Now, that was an attack ad!"

© Mick Stevens 2010. Reprinted from *Time Magazine.*

claimed his campaign director.[134] The Obama campaign sent more than 1 billion e-mails and included 1 million people in its texting program.[135]

Whether as a cause or effect of this aggressive program, Democrats favoring Obama were the most likely group to be online. More than 80 percent were regular online users, compared to more than 70 percent of Clinton's supporters. Though McCain's supporters were about as likely as those of Obama to use the Internet, they were much less likely to use it to get political news or to promote their views (such as by signing an online petition or forwarding a link to someone else).

Obama's Internet activity also fit well with the overall demographics of Internet users. Younger people, the core of Obama's support, are more likely to use the Internet as a news source: half of those under fifty look online for news, compared to only 15 percent of those over sixty-five. Similarly, less educated and lower-income people are less likely, by a considerable margin, to go online. However, there are few racial differences in using the Internet for political news.[136]

As another example of Obama's Internet presence, his Facebook site showed more than 1.2 million supporters, and his website linked to Flickr, Twitter, Black Planet, AsianAve, Faithbase, EONs, Glee, MiGente, MyBatanga,

LinkedIn, and DNC PartyBuilder, social networking sites for African Americans, Asian Americans, religious believers, baby boomers, gays and lesbians, Latinos, business professionals, and Democrats. Estimates are that individuals, collectively, spent "more than 14 million hours watching over 1800 Obama-related videos on YouTube that garnered more than 50 million views."[137]

The Republican candidates, with the exception of Ron Paul, were not as effective in using the networking capacities of the Internet. For example, even in summer 2008, the McCain website offered places for supporters to sign up and keep in contact but did not offer links to networking sites. Thus, it is not surprising that the McCain Facebook address had less than 200,000 supporters.

YouTube is increasingly used as a campaign tool. Of course, it can be a negative, because a candidate's dumb statements or actions, if captured on camera, live on forever in cyberspace and are easily retrievable. George Allen (R-Va.), during his campaign for reelection to the Senate in 2006, called an Indian American "macacca" (considered a racial slur). This exchange was videotaped by someone in the crowd and posted on YouTube. There it was replayed to another 100,000 people and picked up by the major media and replayed on television. This no doubt contributed to his narrow defeat for reelection.[138] In 2008, Obama came under

behind the scenes

Blogs and the Big Sort

Political blogs are an increasingly common way to keep track of politics. About one-third of individuals claim to read blogs, and of those about half read political blogs. One survey identified 476 political blogs, though that probably only scratches the surface.

Most blogs are read by only a few people, perhaps friends and acquaintances of the blogger. On the other hand, blogs such as the Huffington Post and Daily Kos (both on the left) and the Drudge report (on the right) are read by millions. Some nonpartisan blogs are widely read too, such as RealClearPolitics, which posts articles and information from many ideological perspectives.

As we would expect, blog readers are more likely to be educated and highly interested in politics (not just marginally interested). They are likely to be strong Democrats and individuals who consider themselves liberal or very liberal rather than moderate or conservative, though very conservative individuals also read blogs more than those with more moderate positions. Thus, though fewer Republicans than Democrats are bloggers, those that do blog are disproportionately very conservative. Consistent with the "Big Sort" models of the American electorate, blog readers tend to read the blogs that are consistent with their political views. More than 94 percent of blog readers read only blogs from one side of the spectrum, and only 6 percent read blogs from both sides. With few exceptions, only liberals read the Daily Kos and only conservatives the Drudge report, for example.

Television news also has a polarized viewership, but blog reader polarization is much more extreme. Even though Fox viewers are mostly conservative, they have some moderate and liberal viewers. And the network newscasts, MSNBC, and CNN have many moderate viewers and a few conservatives. Readers of right-wing blogs are considerably to the right of Fox News viewers, and those readers of left-wing blogs are to the left of the rest of the media.

Blogs are another way that individuals can interact with people like themselves. That's true for self-help groups and also true of politics. Rather than widening individuals' perspectives, they largely provide a way to reinforce them.

SOURCE: Henry Farrell, Eric Lawrence, and John Sides, "Self Segregation or Deliberation? Blog Readership, Participation, and Polarization in American Politics," paper presented at the Midwest Political Science Association, Chicago, Illinois, April 2008, and linked to the blogsite *Monkey Cage*, a political but nonpartisan blog: www.monkeycage.com.

attack when a video of a sermon by his preacher, including the phrase "God damn America," was posted on the Internet, was played millions of times, and became the subject of intense journalistic and blogosphere discussion. His momentum was slowed, and, eventually, he repudiated the minister and left that church.

Blogs also have become a campaign tool. Candidates and their supporters can air their views and attack opponents through blogs; a few prominent ones are read by millions.[139] Although talk radio is dominated by conservative Republicans, the most popular political blogs are those on the liberal side.

Of course, the Internet spreads lies as well as truth. Those receiving e-mail in the last part of the 2008 campaign were more likely than others to believe Obama was a Muslim, for example, and that he "palled around with terrorists."[140] And the Internet has other limitations too. Obama intended to use his powerful Internet presence to generate support after he was elected, but this plan has fallen short. It is easier to mobilize people for a short time around the rhetoric of change than it is to rally them for a prolonged period around the nitty gritty business of compromise and governing.

Television Appearances and Media Events

As we described, mass media buys are the biggest part of a campaign's expenses. It is still true that "for the large majority of voters, the campaign has little reality apart from the media version."[141] Media exposure includes paid advertisements focused on selected states and areas. Given the increasing sophistication of the campaigns, most television and radio ads never appear in states that are solid for one candidate or another. Although voters in battleground states might consider it a blessing not to have to face an onslaught of campaign ads, voters in other states may feel less connected to the campaign.

But some media exposure is free. One way to garner media attention is to appear as a guest on various television shows. Before the 1990s, presidential candidates appeared only on "serious" shows, such as the Sunday morning talk shows, where candidates would be interviewed by one or more members of the press. Now it is common for candidates to appear in more informal, sometimes humorous, settings, such as late-night talk shows, daytime shows targeted to women, or comedy shows. The candidates hope to use these settings to show voters that they are approachable and down-to-earth. They also give candidates a chance to poke fun at their own foibles and thus possibly defuse opponents' attacks. Candidates' appearances on such shows often become major stories themselves, prolonging the impact of the appearance. (And, then, in 2008 there were Tina Fey's impersonations of Sarah Palin on *Saturday Night Live* that poked fun at her lack of preparation for major interviews, and *those* shows also became news stories even though Palin was not actually there.)

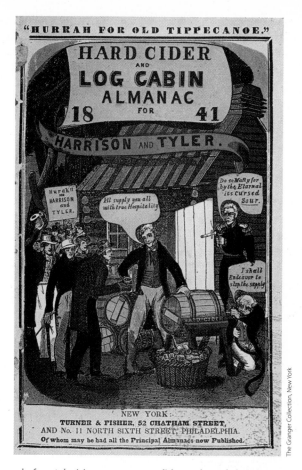

Long before television cameras, candidates shaped their image. In 1840, William Henry Harrison campaigned as the log cabin and hard cider candidate—a common man—even though his father was a wealthy planter, a Virginia governor, and a signer of the Declaration of Independence. To underscore his purported origins, Harrison gave Indian war whoops at rallies.

The candidates also vie for media attention at the local level. In fact, candidates spend most of their time going from media market to media market, hoping to get both national and local coverage.[142] Vice-presidential candidates often appear in the smaller media markets, while the presidential contenders hit the major metro areas. They stage media events with photo opportunities in front of enthusiastic crowds and patriotic or other positive symbols.

Televised Debates

A third form of free media exposure is the televised debate. In 1960, Kennedy challenged Nixon to debate during their presidential campaigns. Nixon did not want to debate because as vice president he was already known and ahead in the polls. He remembered his first election to the House of Representatives when he challenged the incumbent to debate and, on the basis of his performance, won the election. Afterward he said the incumbent was a "damn fool" to debate. Nevertheless, Nixon did agree to debate, and when the two contenders squared off, presidential debates were televised to millions of homes across the country for the first time.

Courtesy of the Smithsonian Institute

Before television, candidates made personal appearances. But for many years, personal appearances and speeches were considered beneath the dignity of the presidential office. William Jennings Bryan was the first presidential candidate to break this tradition. In 1896, he traveled more than 18,000 miles and gave more than 600 speeches. One observer complained that he was "begging for the presidency as a tramp might beg for a pie." Although Bryan lost the election to William McKinley, his approach became the standard. This photo illustrates how the term *stump speech*, used to refer to candidates' boilerplate campaign speeches, may have developed.

Nixon dutifully answered reporters' questions and rebutted Kennedy's assertions. But Kennedy, to compensate for his youth and inexperience, projected an image of vigor. He also sought to contrast his attractive appearance and personality with Nixon's. So he quickly answered reporters' specific questions and then directly addressed viewers about his general goals. Kennedy's strategy worked. He appealed to people and convinced them that his youth and inexperience would not pose problems. While Kennedy remained calm, Nixon became nervous, smiling at inappropriate moments, with his eyes darting back and forth and beads of sweat rolling down his face, which had a five-o'clock shadow that projected a somewhat sinister look.

According to public opinion polls, people who saw the debates thought that Kennedy performed better in three of the four. (The only debate in which they thought Nixon performed better was the one in which the candidates were not in the same studio side-by-side. They were in separate cities, and with this arrangement Nixon was less nervous.) Yet people who heard the debates on radio did not think Kennedy performed as well. They were not influenced by the visual contrast between the candidates or the Kennedy strategy of looking directly into the camera. Clearly, television made the difference.

No more presidential debates were held for sixteen years. The candidates who were ahead did not want to risk

their lead. But in 1976, President Ford decided to debate Carter, and in 1980, President Carter decided to debate Reagan. Both incumbents were in trouble, and they thought they needed to debate to win. Although President Reagan was far ahead in 1984, he decided to debate Mondale because he did not want to seem afraid. By agreeing to debate, he solidified the precedent begun anew in 1976.

In 2000, the media's low expectations for Bush's performance, coupled with his congenial, personal style, helped him hold his own or even win the debates in the view of many, even though the debates revealed his limited grasp of issues and misstatements of facts. Gore's mannerisms seemed stiff and overbearing. And the press, which is far more inclined to evaluate the debates as theater performances than as policy discussions, addressed Gore's body language more than Bush's grasp of issues and misstatements of facts.

Because candidates have different strengths, each campaign wants a debate format that builds on its candidate's strengths. The "debate about debates" has become as predictable a part of campaigns as the debates themselves. Representatives of candidates debate the number of debates, the formats, the topics to be covered, the size of the audience, even the size and shape of the podia. The 2004 debates were governed by a thirty-two-page set of rules agreed to by the candidates' representatives.

In 2004, those negotiating for Bush argued that the first debate should be about foreign policy, ostensibly Bush's strength. He thought he could easily show Kerry to have an uncertain grasp and a vacillating policy. Instead, Kerry looked assured and confident and attacked Bush's foreign policy mistakes throughout the debate. When cameras focused on Bush listening to Kerry, he looked surly and angry at being attacked. And when Bush responded, he wasn't able to offer a coherent defense of his policies. Consequently, although Kerry had been trailing in the polls before the debate, his performance in this debate narrowed the gap. The president prepared more for the second and third debates and looked more confident and pleasant.[143]

In 2008, the first and second debate came in the middle of a free fall in the economy, with the Dow stock market index losing more than 2500 points between the first and last debate and one of Wall Street's largest investment firms, Lehman Brothers, collapsing. McCain was quoted as saying the economic fundamentals were strong, a view held by almost no one else and that played into the hands of the Obama campaign, which had been arguing that McCain was out of touch.

This economic context favored Obama, who pounded home the point that the economic disaster was a result of failed Bush policies that McCain would continue.[144] Moreover, Obama, who had not done well in the primary debates against Clinton, prepared thoroughly for the debates. McCain hated to prepare.[145] "Not today" was a frequent response to the suggestion that he practice. As a result,

Families all across the country gathered in front of their TVs to watch the first televised presidential debates in 1960, featuring Senator John F. Kennedy and Vice President Richard Nixon.

whereas Obama came over as assured and knowledgeable, McCain came over as grumpy and dismissive of Obama. Said one commentator afterwards, "Do people want to put up with four years of that? Of [him] sitting there, angrily, grumpily, like a codger?"[146]

McCain did better in the third debate when he attacked Obama on the grounds that he would likely raise taxes. McCain's poll numbers started increasing modestly afterwards and his charge that Obama would raise taxes began to stick, but the change was not great enough to affect the outcome of the election.[147] Overall, then, the debates of 2008 served largely to solidify Obama's lead, while reinforcing both his point that McCain was out of touch, and then, at the last, McCain's point that Obama was likely to raise taxes.

A newer feature of debates is that, in recent primary campaigns, various groups have sponsored debates among primary candidates. The results of these debates tend to be minimal, especially when, as in the 2008 race, there are a lot of candidates. A debate among seven or ten candidates allows for even less direct exchange than a debate between two candidates. However, these debates are a way for the people who are paying attention to the election to learn more about the candidates. And, in 2008, after winnowing took place, the debates did allow a direct comparison of Clinton and Obama. Though Clinton was widely thought to have bested Obama in the debates, the strategic mistake her campaign made to overlook the caucuses had dug too deep a hole for her candidacy.

The Electoral College

In the United States, we do not have a direct election of the president. All planning for the campaign has to take into account the peculiar American institution of the **Electoral College**, described by one wit as "the exploding cigar of American politics."[148] Most of the time it works fine as "little more than a question on the citizenship test and a subject for political thriller novels." Then, every so often, "it blows up in our faces, throwing whole elections in doubt and making a mockery of the popular will."[149]

The last time it blew up in our faces was in 2000, when although Al Gore had over 500,000 more votes than George W. Bush, he lost the election. The Electoral College is another feature of the American constitutional system that limits democracy.[150]

The Way the System Works

What counts is the popular vote in each state, because that vote determines which candidate will receive the state's electoral votes. Each state has as many electors as its total representation in Congress (House plus Senate). The smallest states (and the District of Columbia) have three, whereas the largest state—California—has fifty-five. Voters choose electors of the Electoral College when they vote for president. Technically, they vote for the electors pledged to the candidate and whose names are on file with the state government. The outcome is not official until these electors gather in each state capital in December after the presidential election to cast their votes for president and vice president.

With the exception of Maine and Nebraska, which divide some of their Electoral College votes according to who wins in each congressional district, all of each state's electoral votes go to the candidate winning the most votes in that state. If one candidate wins a majority (270) of the electors voting across the United States, then the election is decided. If the electoral vote is tied, or if no candidate wins a majority, then the election is decided in the House of Representatives, where each state has one vote and a majority is necessary to win. This has not happened since 1824, when John Quincy Adams was chosen. But it nearly happened in 1976 with the shift of a few thousand votes in Delaware and Ohio. If voting in the Electoral College for the vice president does not yield a majority, the Senate chooses the vice president, with each senator having one vote. If it should get to that stage, the largest and smallest states would have equal weight, a very undemocratic procedure.

Strategic Implications

The campaign strategies that candidates use are shaped in part by the Electoral College system. In general, candidates have incentives to spend more time in the large states where the majority of the electoral votes are. A one-vote margin in Pennsylvania, for example, yields twenty-one votes for the winning candidate compared to only three votes in North Dakota. Thus it is more important to get that extra vote in Pennsylvania. Given the need to focus on a small number of swing states, more time is consequently spent in the larger ones than the smaller ones.

However, as we described earlier, only some large states get attention. So, in 2008, we expected political activists from California not to spend much time there, but rather head for Colorado or New Mexico or Oregon, where there was competition. The Electoral College system, then, favors "states" over "people." As one observer pointed out, gun owners or women, for example, live all over the country, but only those in swing states get wooed.[151]

Smaller states tend to favor the Electoral College system because their Electoral College votes give them a larger influence on the Electoral College than their population proportion would. But unless they are swing states, they are ignored as well. The safe Republican states in the prairies, the South, and the Great Plains are largely ignored by the candidates.

Rationale and Outcomes of the Electoral College

The Founders neither wanted nor envisioned a popular election of the president; selection of the president was placed in the hands of state elites, the electors. The Founders also agreed to enshrine the influence of small states (at that time, disproportionately southern, slaveholding states) in the fundamental framework of the Constitution, and the Electoral College was one way to do that.[152]

The Founders assumed that the Electoral College would have considerable power, with each elector exercising independent judgment and choosing from among a large number of candidates. They did not foresee the development of political parties or of a political climate in which the popular vote was considered the source of legitimacy for a candidate. In practice, as state parties developed, the electors became part of the party process, pledged to party candidates. Therefore, electors usually rubber-stamp the choice of voters in each state rather than exercise their own judgment.

A discrepancy between the Electoral College and the popular vote outcome occurred three times in the nineteenth century (1824, 1876, and 1888). However, after more than a century of presidential elections whose outcome was known once the popular vote was tallied, and since the principle of "one person, one vote" has become enshrined in law and political culture, the American public has become used to thinking of elections as an expression of the will of the people.

When the 2000 election yielded an Electoral College winner who had not won the popular vote, there were immediate calls for the elimination or reform of the Electoral College system. However, these calls went nowhere, and the Electoral College remains (see Figure 6).

Possible Reforms

The Electoral College was designed both to temper the influence of voters by establishing an intermediate body of electors who actually choose the president and to make sure that the South had a disproportionate influence on the choice of the president.[153] It is a distinctly undemocratic mechanism that institutionalizes in the presidential election process part of the excess weight given to smaller states in the U.S. Senate (because the number of electors for each state is based on the number of senators and representatives in each state).

Over the years, several proposed reforms have been considered. One reform would be to abolish the Electoral College altogether and leave the choice of president to the popular vote because direct election is a more understandable system. This change would require a constitutional amendment (which requires a two-thirds approval by members of Congress and three-quarters of the states), which is very difficult because the small states that think they benefit from the current system and the swing states that do benefit from the existing system will block it.

Another target of reform is the constitutional requirement that if the electoral vote is tied, the presidential choice is to be thrown to the House of Representatives. There is no expectation that each state's House delegation would vote for the presidential candidate that its state's voters chose; rather, states would reflect the majority party in their House delegation. Moreover, each state would have an equal vote: Alaska would carry the same clout as California. This would be a very undemocratic feature and would probably cause

Figure 6 | The Electoral College Vote

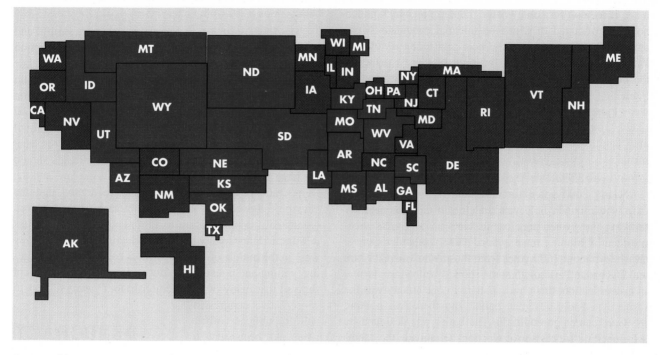

Because of the overrepresentation of small states in the Senate, and the fact that the Electoral College vote for each state equals their representation in the House plus the Senate, the votes of voters in small states have more power than in large states. This map is drawn so that each state is drawn in proportion to the relative power of their average voter. For example, California has nearly 12% of the U.S. population, but only 10% of the Electoral College votes, whereas Wyoming has .17% of the population but has .5% of the Electoral College vote. So the average vote in Wyoming is worth more than the average one in California.
Note: In Nebraska, one electoral college vote went to Obama, four to McCain.

a crisis if actually used to elect a candidate with a minority of the popular vote.

Another undemocratic feature of the Electoral College is that not all states require their electors to cast their votes for the candidates who won the state vote. The **faithless elector** is one who casts his or her vote for a personal choice, even someone who was not on the ballot. Even though the intent of the Founders was to allow electors to cast their votes any way they desired, modern reformers have proposed that, in our more democratic era, electors should be bound by the wishes of the voters in their states. It is true that no faithless elector has ever made a difference in the outcome of an election, but in the 2000 election, as few as three faithless electors could have made a difference.

A current reform proposal is the National Popular Vote, a movement gaining some ground. The idea, supported by a group of electoral reform advocates, is that each state would pass a law entering into an agreement to award all its electoral votes to the candidate who receives the most popular votes nationally. The proposal, then, could take effect when states whose total electoral votes equal 270, the Electoral College majority, have entered the agreement. Maryland, New Jersey, and Illinois

DEMOCRACY?

Why do Americans tolerate the undemocratic features of the electoral college?

have signed on, and other states are considering it. This proposal would make the presidential choice a popular vote choice without having to amend the Constitution.

The 2000 Election: A Perfect Storm

The election of 2000 demonstrates the antidemocratic nature of the Electoral College. It was won by George W. Bush, who got fewer votes than his rival, Al Gore. In another antidemocratic twist, the election was decided by the U.S. Supreme Court, when, by a 5–4 vote, it stopped the recount of votes ordered by the Florida Supreme Court. The division in the Electoral College was very close, and the decision rested on the outcome in Florida, where election mismanagement, partisan politics, and unavoidable human error came together to create chaos in a closely divided race.

Election day exit polls of Florida voters showed Gore winning by a small margin. But after first declaring Gore the winner, the television networks declared Bush the winner, and then in the early morning hours decided it was too close to call. The election hung in the balance. Bush had a tiny lead of several hundred ballots.

Confusion reigned in the days afterward. The press and election observers reported several problems, some of them serious. Thousands of Gore votes were lost because of the strange "butterfly ballot" configuration in Palm Beach

County, a heavily Democratic liberal county. The odd format, designed by the supervisor of elections in the county, made it difficult for some voters to determine which punch hole corresponded to which presidential candidate. More than 3000 voters punched the hole registering a vote for Patrick Buchanan, listed to the right of Gore's name on the ballot. This is particularly ironic because the areas of Palm Beach County casting the most votes for Buchanan were those inhabited by mostly Jewish voters, the least likely group to support Buchanan, who is thought to be anti-Semitic. As one elderly Jewish woman exclaimed after mistakenly voting for Buchanan, "I would rather have had a colonoscopy than vote for that son-of-a-bitch Buchanan."[154]

Nearly 3000 voted for Gore and the socialist candidate whose punch hole was underneath Gore, apparently thinking they voted for Joseph Lieberman, Gore's vice-presidential running mate, whose name was under Gore's. (Bush lost about 1600 votes from those who voted for him and Buchanan.) Although some spoiled ballots are normal in every election, this erratic pattern in one county was the result of a badly designed ballot. But there was nothing the Gore campaign could do. The ballot was designed by a Democratic supervisor of elections who made the candidates' names larger so elderly voters could read them better and without an intention to deceive any voters.

There was also a problem with overseas ballots. Americans overseas have the right to vote. They must ask for a ballot before the election and mail it by the day of the election, but the ballot need not be received by local officials until ten days after the election, to allow for mail delays. There are strict rules about how these ballots are to be certified to avoid vote fraud, but hundreds of these ballots came in lacking postmarks (or having U.S. postmarks) or lacking a witness and from voters who were not registered. Many military personnel whose home state was Florida must have decided to vote after the election when the outcome appeared uncertain, and some may have been persuaded to do so by partisan groups. Under law, these ballots shouldn't have been counted, but the Bush campaign, assuming the ballots were mostly Republican, claimed that it would be unpatriotic not to count them. The Gore campaign was put in the unenviable position of choosing either to accept the illegal Republican ballots or to appear to deny our overseas military personnel their right to vote.

After the election, Gore pursued a conservative strategy to deal with these problems that likely cost him the election. He did not call for a complete recount, and he did not challenge the likely fraudulent overseas ballots. Nothing could be done about the butterfly ballot problem save a revote.[155] Finally, when the Florida Supreme Court mandated a recount in every county, so much time had elapsed that the U.S. Supreme Court threw up its hands and gave the election to Bush.

Gore's biggest mistake was to refrain from challenging the overseas votes, even the hundreds that were patently illegal under Florida laws. As a consequence of the illegal military ballots alone, Gore lost Florida by 537 votes when his election day margin—that is, the margin given him by people who voted on election day rather than by mail ballot—was a 202-vote victory.[156]

The Bush postelection campaign was more skillful and more aggressive. Republican representatives urged election officials in Democratic-majority counties to follow the law in handling overseas ballots, so that illegal ballots would not be counted; in Republican counties, they urged election officials to disregard the law, so that illegal ballots would be counted.[157] (There is nothing illegal or even immoral about Republican supporters doing this, that is, they had the legal right to challenge ballots. But the election officials should not have given in and should have upheld the law, and the Democratic representatives should have argued that the laws be followed.) At one point the Bush campaign even organized a demonstration to intimidate election officials in Miami-Dade County to stop conducting the recount they were in the middle of. Demonstrators barged into the building, yelling and pounding on doors. Photos from that event showed that many of the "demonstrators" were staffers in conservative congressional Republican offices who had been sent to Florida to do this, though at the time the election officials recounting the ballot did not know that. The demonstration succeeded in getting the officials to halt the recount.

DEMOCRACY

How democratic is it to attempt to intimidate election officials? Is that just a normal part of political activity, or does it go beyond what we would expect in a democracy?

In addition, the Bush campaign had strong political allies in Florida who held the levers of power. Bush's brother, the governor, and the secretary of state, who oversees the election system, were cochairs of Bush's Florida campaign. At every opportunity the secretary of state ruled in favor of the Bush campaign and forced the Gore campaign to go to court to obtain recounts and redress. Time also worked in favor of the Bush campaign, because it held a narrow lead throughout the post–election day period and because it knew that the deadline for certifying Florida's electors would put pressure on the courts to stop the recount. Thus the Bush campaign used delaying tactics to slow and stop the recounts.

The outcome of this election will long be argued. It is likely that a bare majority of Florida voters, in fact, favored Gore.[158] Systematic analyses have proven that the Buchanan vote was inflated by at least 2500 votes intended for Gore in Palm Beach County.[159] As one commentator noted, "No election analyst will say with a straight face that the butterfly design didn't cost Al Gore the presidency."[160]

Of course, the overseas ballots contributed, too, by an unknown amount. That is, we know how many ballots were illegal, but we don't know for sure their distribution between Bush and Gore. Nearly two-thirds of the 2400 overseas ballots counted after November 7 were for Bush. Presumably the illegal overseas ballots also broke for Bush. Two independent scholars argue that the probability is about

99 percent that Gore would have won if the invalid overseas ballots had been handled properly and a statewide recount had been allowed under any reasonable standard.[161]

The confusion surrounding the 2000 election outcome highlights an important aspect of our electoral process: state law and local policies determine the mechanics of presidential elections. The election brought into stark relief the problems that shoddy election procedures can create. Former president and Nobel Peace Prize winner Jimmy Carter, who, through his Carter Center, now works for peace and social justice around the world, is often invited to monitor elections in Asia and Africa and to attest to their fairness. He remarked, "I was really taken aback and embarrassed by what happened in Florida. If we were invited to go into a foreign country to monitor the election, and they had similar standards and procedures, we would refuse to participate at all."[162]

VOTING BEHAVIOR

Voting behavior is shaped by party identification, candidate evaluations, and positions on the issues.

Party Identification

Party identification is crucial in predicting how a person votes. Because we discussed this extensively in Chapter 7, we will not revisit it here. Keep in mind that overwhelming proportions of individuals with party identifications vote for candidates of their party. In the 2008 election, around 90 percent of members of each party did so.

Candidate Evaluations

Candidates' personalities and styles have had more impact since television has become voters' major source of information about elections. Bush's popularity in 2000 is an example of the influence of a candidate and his personality. The perceived competence and integrity of candidates are other facets of candidate evaluation. Voters are less likely to support candidates who do not seem capable of handling the job, regardless of their issue positions. Jimmy Carter suffered in 1980 because of negative evaluations of his competence and leadership among voters.

behind the scenes

Are Independents Really Independent?

"The independent voter" is a popular topic in the press. Since most party loyalists vote for their party's candidate, the movement of the independents can, supposedly, swing the election. But how many independents are there?

Newspaper accounts often peg the number of independent voters as around 30 percent or even more. However, political scientists who study elections have a quite different viewpoint. They have discovered that most independents actually support one party most of the time. Perhaps they like to think of themselves as independent or perhaps they say they're independent because they don't want to reveal their preferences to pollsters. If pressed, they will then say they are closer to one party or the other. In fact, only about 7 to 10 percent of the "independents" are really independent. Most vote like those who claim to be party supporters.

An examination of the vote of independents in the 2008 election illustrates what political scientists have found:[1]

Percentage Vote for Obama	
Strong Democrats	92
Weak Democrats	83
Independents "leaning Democratic"	88
Independent independents	50
Independents "leaning Republican"	17
Weak Republicans	10
Strong Republicans	2

In sum, there are few truly independent "independents." The rest tend to vote like party loyalists. Thus, when, for example, a media commentator on the Tea Party movements states that they are mostly independents but most will vote Republican, the translation is most likely that most are Republican-leaning independents.

[1] Data for the 2008 election from Paul Abramson, John Aldrich, and David Rohde, *Change and Continuity in the 2008 Election* (Washington, D.C.: CQ Press, 2009), xx. "Three Myths about Political Independents," http://www.themonkeycage.org/2009/12/three_myths_about_political_in.html.
SOURCE: Mark Blumenthal, "How Independent Are the Independents?" *National Journal.com*, February 22, 2010, http://www.nationaljournal.com/njonline/mp_20100219_9614.php; John Sides,

"I want to vote my fears this year, but they'll only let me vote once."

© The New Yorker Collection 2009, Barsotti from cartoonbank.com. All rights reserved.

Clinton's popularity puzzled some observers. Many voters did not like his evasions and his adulterous behavior, but they voted for him anyway. During the impeachment debates, many journalists expressed amazement that Clinton's popularity remained high. The public, more than journalists, seemed to be able to separate his public and private roles. They continued to support him because they felt he was doing a good job as president, not because they admired him personally.

Personality was important in the 2004 campaign. John Kerry seemed unable to connect with people and uncomfortable on the campaign trail. Kerry could not shake his image as an effete, somewhat snobbish, Boston patrician who was out of touch with average Americans. George Bush, on the other hand, seemed more at ease, comfortable working the crowd. In 2008, the tables were turned. McCain often seemed out of touch with the average person, while Obama had a kind of star quality that drew people to him.

Issues

Issues are a third factor influencing the vote. Although Americans are probably more likely to vote on issues now than they were in the 1950s, issues influence only some of the voters some of the time. In 2000 and 2004, voters saw themselves as much closer to the Democratic candidates than to Bush.[163]

To cast an **issue vote**, voters obviously must have a position on an issue. In recent elections, more than 80 percent of the public had a position on issues such as government spending, military spending, and women's rights.[164] An issue vote also requires the candidates to differ with respect to their issue positions and for the voters to recognize this difference. A substantial minority of voters are able to detect some differences among the issue positions of presidential candidates.[165] Lastly, voters must cast their vote for the candidate who reflects their position on the issue or at least is the one closest to that position.

In every election since 1972, more than 70 percent of voters who met these conditions cast issue votes.[166] The highest proportion of issue voting was on those issues that typically divided Republicans and Democrats, such as government spending, military spending, and government aid to the unemployed and minorities. In 2008, issue voting on health care was also high, with most voters identifying different Obama and McCain positions. More than 70 percent who agreed with Obama on health insurance voted for him, compared to less than 30 percent whose position on universal health insurance was closer to that of McCain.[167] However, because many in the electorate were unable to define both their own and the candidates' positions on each issue, the proportion of the total electorate that can be said to cast an "issue vote" is usually less than 40 percent, and for some issues it is much less.[168]

Because abortion is a salient issue for many, it attracts issue-related votes. In 2008, for example, about 70 percent of the voters cast issue-related votes on abortion, similar to previous years. Of those voters (who had a position and also knew the candidates' position), 16 percent of those who opposed abortion under any conditions voted for Obama, a supporter of abortion rights, compared with 79 percent of those who believed that abortion should be a matter of personal choice.[169]

Issue voting may be mostly an evaluation of the current incumbents. If voters like the way incumbents or their party has handled the job in general or in certain areas—the economy or foreign policy, for example—they will vote accordingly, even without much knowledge about the specifics of the issues.

Voting on the basis of past performance is called **retrospective voting**. There is good evidence that many people do this, especially according to economic conditions.[170] Voters support incumbents if national income is growing in the months preceding the election. Since World War II, the incumbent party has won a presidential election only once when the growth rate was less than 3 percent (Eisenhower in 1956) and lost only twice when it was more than 3 percent (Ford in 1976 and Gore in 2000).[171] For example, in 2008, 89 percent of voters who strongly approved of Bush's handling of the economy voted for McCain, and only 11 percent voted for Obama. However, only 30 percent of the public approved of Bush's handling of the economy by 2008, and those who disapproved gave Obama 67 percent of their votes.[172]

Parties, Candidates, and Issues

All three factors—parties, candidates, and issues—clearly matter. Party loyalties are especially important because they help shape our views about issues and candidates. However, if issues and candidates did not matter, the Democrats would have won every presidential election between 1932 and 2000 because the plurality of voters were Democrats. Republican victories suggest that they often have had more attractive candidates (as in 1952, 1956, 1980, and 1984) or issue positions (in 1972 and, in some respects, in 1980). However, the Democrats' partisan advantage shrank throughout the 1980s. Although there are still more registered Democrats than Republicans in the United States, the margin is slight, and the number of independents is large enough to tilt the outcome.

Party loyalty, candidate evaluations, and issues are important factors in congressional elections just as in presidential ones. Chapter 10 discusses voting in congressional elections.

Voting Patterns in the 2008 Election

The 2008 election, as historic as it was, in many ways followed the traditional script. Obama held 89 percent of those identifying as Democrats and lost 90 percent of those identifying as Republicans. Independents broke his way by a much smaller margin (52 percent to McCain's 44 percent). Obama's winning coalition included majorities of several groups that have been loyal to the Democratic Party for decades: urbanites, Jews, Catholics, blacks, and women.[173]

What about race? Typically African Americans vote overwhelmingly for Democrats, and they did so in 2008, with a majority of 95 percent. Obama also captured two-thirds of all Hispanic voters and nearly as large a proportion of Asians. Whites gave a solid majority (55 percent) to McCain, though whites under thirty voted for Obama. However, the proportion of white votes for Obama was slightly higher than for John Kerry, the Democratic candidate in 2004. We might have expected them to be even higher given that 2008 was a Democratic year and Obama ran a better campaign than Kerry. The proportions he won among blacks was higher too than the vote they gave Kerry.

The fact that Obama was black did have an impact in some parts of the Deep South, however. The white vote for Obama decreased in three states with the largest black populations: Louisiana, Alabama, and Mississippi—in the former two, significantly.[174] These states have traditionally been the most resistant to breaking down the old barriers of segregation and inequality. In some parts of the Rim South, Obama did much better than Kerry. But the idea that whites, in general, were less likely to support Obama than other recent Democratic candidates is not true.

In a new development, young people voted Democratic in astounding proportions. Fully 66 percent of voters between eighteen and twenty-nine voted for Obama. He also won a majority of those aged thirty to forty-four and tied McCain in the forty-five- to fifty-nine-year-old group. McCain won only the vote of those sixty and over, and then only because of a sizable majority in the South.

These age-related voting patterns suggest difficulty for Republicans in the years ahead if these patterns hold, because individuals usually retain their initial voting allegiances. For example, a majority of those who came of voting age during the New Deal remained Democrats throughout their lives, and a majority who first voted during the Reagan years held on to their Republican loyalties.[175]

Damon Winter/The New York Times/Redux

Many blue-collar workers, such as these steelworkers in Pennsylvania waiting to hear Barack Obama, were skeptical about his candidacy. In the end, Obama won 60 percent of voters in families making less than $50,000, including 47 percent among whites in that category.

As in past elections, Democrats won large majorities of the vote of the unmarried and of gay, lesbians, and bisexuals. They also picked up a majority among those with children, also a new development. Republicans won large majorities of those currently married, white Protestants, those who attend church often, and those who are born-again or evangelical Christians. McCain also bested Obama in small towns and rural areas. Voters in suburbs, traditionally a Republican stronghold, gave a tiny majority to the Democrats, and Democrats won a sizable majority in towns of 50,000 to 500,000.

The Republicans did well in the Great Plains, the non-coastal West, and the South, though they lost Virginia and North Carolina.

Issue voting was evident. Generally, economic issues are highly salient to voters, especially in hard times. In this election, more than 70 percent of those who felt their family's financial situation was worse voted for Obama; 60 percent who thought it was better voted for McCain. Those who thought their financial situation was about the same as it had been split more evenly but gave the edge to McCain.

In general, the Republican vote was strongest in the oldest, least educated, and slowest-growing part of the American population. But the increasing diversity of Americans will pose a challenge, even in Republicans' traditional strongholds of the South and Plains. For example, the party must find a way to win Hispanic and Asian votes. This is not to say that the Republicans are doomed to become a minority party. With new issues, and changing voter concerns, they may return to the dominance they showed in the first part of the millennium.

THE PERMANENT CAMPAIGN

The **permanent campaign** is a term coined by political scientists to describe the current state of American electoral politics.[176] During each election cycle, the time between the completion of one election and the beginning of the next gets shorter and shorter. No longer does the election campaign start in the election year; now it is nearly a four-year process, as candidates hire consultants and fundraisers, assemble field operations, and commission polls.

Several factors are responsible for this change, some political and some technological. The political process has changed a great deal during the past thirty years. Primaries have become the chief means by which candidates get nominated, and parties have shrunk in importance in the nominating process. The necessity to win primaries in different regions of the nation means that potential candidates must start early to become known to key political figures, and ultimately to the voting public, in these states. In the "old days," candidates had to woo only party leaders, a process that, though not easy, was much less public and much less expensive than campaigning for primary victories.

Technology has also contributed to the permanent campaign. Certainly, in comparison to the turn of the twentieth century, transportation and communications technology have revolutionized campaigns. Then travel was by rail, ship, or horse, and candidates could not dart about the country spending the morning in New York City and the afternoon in Seattle. Telephone communication was primitive, and there were no radios or televisions. The idea of potential candidates spending four years publicly campaigning for office under these conditions would have been ludicrous.

But even in comparison with only thirty years ago, the media and information technology have revolutionized campaigning and thus have contributed to the permanent campaign. Modern computer and telephone technology enables the media and private organizations to take the pulse of the public through opinion polls almost continually. As polls have become more common, they have become a source of fascination to the media (and as pollsters have discovered that the media's appetite for polls is nearly insatiable, polls have proliferated). Whereas in the 1950s polls were rarely done and poll results were rarely discussed in media coverage of elections, by the 1980s hundreds of stories about each election campaign focused on poll results. Indeed, much of the media coverage of the campaign focuses on exactly that. In 2008, there was almost daily polling from the beginning of the primaries. Polls are easily accessible at websites such as Rasmussen Polls, Real Clear Politics, fivethirtyeight.com, and many other sites. Candidates and potential donors and campaign operatives pay considerable attention to these polls, so candidates must begin campaigning early to earn name recognition from the public.

And, more generally, the fact that campaigns have become media events means that candidates must begin early to establish themselves as worthy of media attention. Until candidates have organizations, fundraisers, and pollsters, the media do not take them seriously. Nor would it be very rational to do otherwise, because a modern campaign cannot succeed without these things. The same is true of the

We hold these truths to be self-evident, that all men are created equal.

Ratified November 4, 2008

Toles Copyright © 2008, Universal Press Syndicate. Reprinted by permission.

blogosphere. Political bloggers begin to track candidates, their activities, and their poll results from the beginning of their campaign. To develop momentum, to be discussed, a candidate must be doing or saying something.

All of these factors—the decline of the party organizations and the increased importance of primaries, the growth of polling, the ubiquity of Internet news and commentary, and the overwhelming role the media now play in campaigns—have contributed to the perpetual motion that modern elections have become. These trends seem irreversible. Only eliminating the primary system would seem to make much difference, and that change is nearly impossible.

CONCLUSION: Elections and the Role of Government

Do elections contribute to the growth of government and to what government does? Unequivocably yes! Government grows primarily because the electorate wants it to do more. Candidates promise to do things, usually to provide more and better services or to stimulate the economy. When they are elected, they usually try to carry out their promises. It is a brave and rare candidate who promises to cut a popular program (candidates often talk about cutting the deficit or slashing waste—but that's easy talk). Even in 2010, when concerns were being expressed about the size of the deficit, the public was far more concerned about jobs and what government could do to help create them.

Even though elections are the mechanism by which the public decides what it wants from government, in fact, it is hard to interpret what voters want. In the popular press, we hear a lot about "mandates." A president with a **mandate** is one who is clearly directed by the voters to take some particular course of action—such as reduce taxes or begin arms control talks. Barack Obama won by a comfortable majority in 2008. Did he have a mandate? If so, what for? The largest proportion of the public, 63 percent, was concerned about the economy and jobs issues.[177] Most of those people voted for Obama, but some voted for McCain. More than 70 percent of those who felt their family's financial situation was worse voted for Obama; 60 percent who thought it better voted for McCain. Those who thought their financial situation was about the same as it had been split more evenly but gave the edge to McCain. A majority wanted the government to do something about the economic crisis, but a majority did not favor the bailout of the financial system engineered by the Bush administration (with Democratic support).[178] So it is difficult to detect just what the mandate on this issue was, even when a clear majority of the voters believed that economic issues were important.

In the context of several decades of public opinion indicating approval for the government to do more about health care, Obama campaigned partly on a pledge to reform health care and provide health insurance for everyone. When he was elected, he set out to do that. But Republican leaders charged him with going against the best interests of the public, again indicating the difficulty of agreeing on what an election mandate is. (Extreme opponents of health care reform called him a Hitler and a Stalin, for the most part betraying their ignorance of what Hitler and Stalin did.)

Mandates are also difficult to describe with foreign policy. Most of those who said the Iraqi War was the most salient issue voted for Obama, and those who said that terrorism was most important voted for McCain. So did Obama have a mandate in foreign policy?

Because voters' issue positions influence their party loyalties and their candidate evaluations, it is primarily political parties that translate the mix of various issues into government action. Over time, a rough agreement usually develops between public attitudes and policies.[179] A vote for the candidate of one's own party is usually a reflection of agreement on at least some important issues. Once in office, the party in government helps sort out the issues for which there is a broad public mandate from those for which there is not.

In close elections, few would argue that there is a mandate. In 2000, voters favored the Democratic policy positions and did so in a time of peace and prosperity. A plurality gave their votes to Gore. Yet Bush became president and acted as though his narrow Electoral College victory was a mandate in support of his foreign policies and conservative domestic policies.

On the other hand, elections that appear to be clear mandates can become "mandates for disaster." More than one observer has pointed out that every twentieth-century president who won the election by 60 percent or more of the popular vote soon encountered serious political trouble. After his landslide in 1920, Warren Harding had his Teapot Dome scandal involving government corruption. Emboldened by his 1936 triumph, Franklin D. Roosevelt tried to pack the Supreme Court and was rebuffed on that issue. Lyndon Johnson won by a landslide in 1964 and was soon mired in Vietnam. Richard Nixon smashed George McGovern in 1972 but then had to resign because of Watergate. Ronald Reagan's resounding victory in 1984 (a shade less than 60 percent) was followed by the blunders of the Iran-Contra affair. Of these presidents, only Roosevelt was able to recover fully from his political misfortune. Reagan regained his personal popularity but seemed to have little influence on policy after Iran-Contra. One recent observer has argued that these disasters come because "the euphoria induced by overwhelming support at the polls evidently loosens the president's grip on reality."[180]

Elections can point out new directions for government and allow citizens to make it responsive to their needs, but the fact that many individuals do not vote means that the new directions may not reflect either the needs or wishes of the public. If election turnout falls too far, the legitimacy of elections may be threatened. People may come to believe that election results do not reflect the wishes of the majority. For this reason, the increase in turnout since 2004 should hearten all of us. If elections promote government responsiveness to those who participate in them, higher turnouts help increase responsiveness. Those dissatisfied Americans who want to "take back our country" are saying, presumably, that they want to change the majority vote in the next election.

On the other hand, if we believe in democracy, we should be concerned about the declining competitiveness of congressional elections. Essentially, in most states, state legislative majorities have had the capacity to determine election outcomes, including their own seats, for a decade. While the power to redistrict has always been in state legislative hands, the power and precision of new technology makes this power even greater. This is a significant challenge to responsiveness.

KEY TERMS

battleground states (swing states)	231
Big Sort	232
cracking, stacking, and packing	211
Electoral College	239
faithless elector	241
gerrymander	222
grandfather clause	209
issue vote	244
literacy tests	209
majority-minority districts	211
mandate	247
microtargeting	235
motor voter law	221
narrowcasting	233
permanent campaign	245
poll tax	209
presidential preference primaries	225
Progressive reforms	215
Reconstruction	208
retrospective voting	244
split-ticket voting	215
suffrage	208
Voting Rights Act (VRA)	209
white primary	209

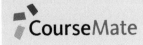

CourseMate Access an interactive eBook, chapter-specific interactive learning tools (including flashcards, quizzes, videos), and more at CourseMate for *Understanding American Government*. Log in at CengageBrain.com.

9 Money and Politics

Barack Obama used his popularity to solicit campaign contributions from millions of supporters, such as these citizens in Portland, Oregon.

Talking Points

Since 1976, presidential candidates have received public funds for their campaigns. These funds are donated by millions of taxpayers who can simply check a box on their tax form and have $3 of their tax go to fund the presidential campaigns. In the primary elections, candidates can receive public funds matched to their own fundraising, but in the general election, according to the law, the candidates who receive public funds cannot raise additional funds. They must run their campaign on the public funds, although these are substantial. In 2008, they amounted to more than $84 million apiece for the two major party candidates.

Candidates do not have to accept the public funds. In 2004, for the first time, some decided not to accept the public funds for their primary campaigns. But until 2008, all candidates relied on public funding for their general election campaign.

In 2007, candidate Barack Obama indicated that he would accept public funding in the general election if his Republican opponent did, adding, "If I am the Democratic nominee, I will aggressively pursue an agreement with the Republican nominee to preserve a publicly financed general election."[1] Then Senator Obama shocked even the most informed political professionals with his ability to raise his own funds during his primary campaign. Energizing hundreds of thousands of voters, he raked in funds from smaller donors through Internet appeals and from financial fat cats through his political networks. About 90 percent of his donors gave less than $100, but a majority of his funds came from those who gave more than $200.[2]

By the end of the primary season, Obama had raised $300 million, by far the most ever raised by a primary candidate. (In contrast, in 2004, George Bush raised $258 million.) Obama's chief primary opponent, Hillary Clinton, raised $230 million, and John McCain was far behind in his successful quest for the Republican nomination, raising $110 million.

After receiving the nomination, however, Senator Obama announced that he would not be accepting public funding, the first general election candidate to take this position. Arguing that the system was broken and that Senator McCain's allies would smear him through independent spending, he portrayed his refusal to participate as a reform position because a lot of his support came from the grassroots. (As we will describe later in the chapter, "independent spending" is spending, usually for television commercials that attack one candidate, by interest groups nominally unattached to any candidate but who in fact are working to elect the other candidate.)

Both Republicans and supporters of campaign finance reform, not surprisingly, had quite a different interpretation. They accused him of hypocrisy and of undermining the part of the system that did allow the average person, not lobbyists, to fund campaigns by contributing $3. There is nothing more grassroots than that. Opponents of Obama pointed out that the likely reason for Senator Obama's position is that he was confident he could raise far more than $84 million and far more than Senator McCain.

Although these criticisms of Obama's flip-flopping on this issue circulated widely, Obama and his campaign staff obviously believed that these charges would be outweighed by his ability to raise money and vastly outdo Senator McCain. And they were right. Obama became the most prolific fundraiser ever, raising more than $750 million from more than 3 million voters.[3]

ormer Speaker of the House of Representatives Tip O'Neill (D-Mass.) once said, "There are four parts to any campaign. The candidate, the issues . . . , the campaign organization, and the money. Without money you can forget the other three."[4] Conventional wisdom holds that "money is the mother's milk of politics." But we are not sure whether that milk is tainted or pure. On the one hand, without money, candidates or people with new political ideas would find it hard to become known in our massive and complex society. Television spreads names and ideas almost instantaneously, so having money to buy television time means that your ideas will be heard. In that sense, money contributes to open political debate.

On the other hand, money can be a corrupting influence on politics. At the least, it can buy access to decision makers. At the worst, it can buy decisions. Money allows some points of view to be trumpeted while others are forced to whisper. Some candidates or groups can afford to spend hundreds of thousands of dollars for each prime-time minute of national television or for prestigious Washington law firms to lobby; others can afford only web pages and letters. Money increases inequities in political life.

Although, in most cases, we see nothing wrong when individuals of great wealth are able to buy goods and services that others cannot afford, many people feel uneasy when high-income individuals or well-bankrolled groups are able to buy political favors. We feel so uneasy that we have outlawed certain kinds of buying of political favors, such as politicians paying voters for their votes or interest groups paying politicians and bureaucrats for their support.

But we are also uneasy about placing other limits on the influence of money. Many people feel that individuals or groups should be allowed to contribute as much money to candidates as they want and that candidates should be permitted to buy as much media time as they can afford to get their point of view across. This view holds that contributing money and buying media time are forms of constitutionally guaranteed freedom of speech.

These issues are growing more important as the cost of political campaigns increases. In 2004, presidential candidates spent slightly over $1 billion, less than half from public funds, an increase of nearly 50 percent from 2000.[5] And various independent groups spent another $1 billion. Costs of congressional and state races are also increasing. So it is not surprising that political candidates scramble for money.

Americans have struggled with these contradictions about money and politics. Periodically, after a series of outrages relating to the impact of money on legislation, regulation, or elections, we pass laws seeking to reduce the impact of money in political life; but then, everyone finds ways around all the rules and a new cycle of outrage and legislation starts again.

In this chapter, we first focus on the development of laws that regulate how money can influence politics, then turn to the role and impact of money in elections, and finally briefly examine conflicts of interest on the part of decision makers in Congress and the executive branch.

MONEY AND POLITICS IN AMERICA'S PAST

Concern about the illegitimate influence of money on politics is older than the Republic. In 1699, after asking how campaign money could be regulated, the Virginia House of Burgesses (the colony's legislature) voted to prohibit the bribing of voters.[6] In his campaign for the Virginia House of Burgesses in 1757, George Washington was accused of vote

The influence of money was evident as the railroads pushed their way across America, pressuring and bribing the federal and state governments to provide free land for their tracks and additional land along the tracks to make their enterprise "profitable." Here workers toast the completion of the transcontinental railroad line at Promontory Point, Utah, in 1869.

buying. He had given out twenty-eight gallons of rum, fifty gallons of rum punch, thirty-four gallons of wine, forty-six gallons of beer, and two gallons of cider. Because there were only 391 voters in his district, he had provided more than a quart and a half of beverages per voter![7]

Obviously, Washington survived these charges, and his constituents probably survived the effects of the rum and cider. But most discussions of the impact of money on politics were more sober. In his well-known analysis of controlling factions, James Madison, in *Federalist Paper* 10, recognized that "the most common and durable source of factions has been the various and unequal distribution of property." Madison went on to say that although ideally no one should be allowed to make decisions affecting his or her own self-interest, almost any subject of legislation—taxes, tariffs, debts—involves self-interest. For those making laws, "every shilling with which they overburden the inferior number is a shilling saved to their own pockets."

Madison hoped that the design of the new nation, with the power of the government divided among the branches of government and between the nation and the states, would mean that no one interest or faction would overwhelm the others. The interest of one person or group would check the interest of another. This view of counterbalancing interests is an optimistic one and has not always worked. Over the decades, Americans have found it necessary to make additional rules to restrict the ways that people or groups with money can try to influence policy makers.

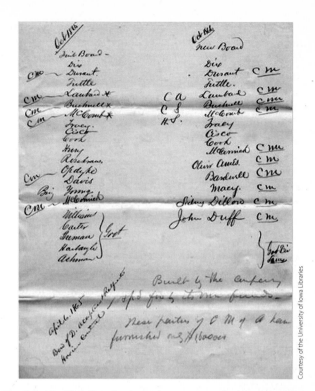

Courtesy of the University of Iowa Libraries

The Union Pacific Railroad organized a company, called Credit Mobilier, to lay the track for the transcontinental railroad line. Although Credit Mobilier was basically the Union Pacific Railroad, with many of the same members on its board of directors, that fact was kept secret. Credit Mobilier distributed stock to influential members of Congress so they could enrich themselves and would favor the railroad as the line was built. The photo shows a list of members of the Board of Directors of Union Pacific. Those marked "CM" were also directors of Credit Mobilier.

Money in Nineteenth-Century American Politics

The influence of money on politics has shaped several epochs of American history. For example, from the earliest westward expansion of the nation, charges of graft and corruption surrounded the government's sale and giveaway of land. Indeed, the West was developed by giving land to speculators and railroads, sometimes in exchange for bribes. When Congress was debating whether to give federal land to the railroads, the lobbyists "camped in brigades around the Capitol building."[8]

The impact of money on political life probably reached its peak in the late nineteenth century, during the so-called Gilded Age after the Civil War. During that time, the United States grew from a small agrarian society to a large industrialized one. This industrialization produced great wealth in such fields as oil exploration and refining, the steel industry, and the railroad companies that were spanning the nation. Major components of the economy came to be controlled by companies that owned most of the country's resources in a particular area, such as steel, oil, and rubber. John D. Rockefeller's Standard Oil sold more than 80 percent of all oil products sold in the United States.[9] This was the era of "robber barons," when the owners of these giant corporations (called *trusts*) amassed huge wealth and openly bought political favors.

Business contributions to campaigns and to politicians were routine. One railroad president justified the bribing of political officials by noting, "If you have to pay money to have the right thing done, it is only just and fair to do so."[10] Mark Hanna, a Republican fundraiser in the presidential election of 1896, assessed banks at a fixed percentage of their capital and also collected substantial sums from most insurance companies and large corporations.[11] However, Cornelius Vanderbilt, one of the wealthiest men of his time, refused to contribute to election campaigns, believing that it was cheaper to buy legislators after they were elected!

Not only did lobbyists bribe politicians, but politicians bribed reporters. In the 1872 presidential campaign, the Republican Party gave money to about three hundred reporters in return for favorable coverage.[12]

As we saw in Chapter 7, urban machines used money to cement a complex network of businesses, voters, and party organizations. Business payoffs to government and party officials for licenses and contracts and party payoffs to voters for their support were the norm. Graft was tolerated and even expected. Born in 1842, George Washington Plunkitt, a famous leader of the New York City machine known as Tammany Hall, began life as a butcher's helper and ended up a millionaire through deals made in his role as a party leader and public official. He held a number of state and local public offices; at one point, he held four at the same time and drew a salary for three of them simultaneously. (See the box "Honest Graft.")

U.S. senators bought their own seats (this was before senators were elected by the public) by bribing state legislators to select them. When one member proposed that all of those who had bribed their way into the Senate be expelled, another member observed that "we might lose a quorum" if that were done.[13]

Early Reforms

Around the turn of the twentieth century, the Progressive reformers and their allies in the press, called **muckrakers**, began to attack this overt corruption. They wanted to break up the trusts and break the financial link between business and politicians. In 1907, a law prohibited corporations and banks from making contributions to political campaigns, and a few years later, Congress mandated public reporting of campaign expenditures and set limits on campaign donations. Prohibitions against corporate giving to political campaigns were broadened over time to forbid utilities and labor unions from giving as well.

When Republican Theodore Roosevelt became president after the assassination of William McKinley, he fought the trusts, forced them to open their books, and filed suits to break them up. Although he accepted campaign contributions from big corporations when he ran for the presidency in 1904, he would not show them any favor. This prompted a major contributor to his campaign to complain, "We bought the son of a bitch, but he did not stay bought."[14]

The 1920s was another era of financial scandal as stock markets rose and banks sold worthless stocks and bonds. The **Teapot Dome scandal** of 1921 stimulated further attempts to limit the influence of money on electoral politics. The secretary of the interior in the Warren Harding administration received almost $400,000 from two corporations that then were allowed to lease oil reserves in California and Wyoming (one of them was called the Teapot Dome). This led to the Federal Corrupt Practices Act (1925), which required the reporting of campaign contributions and expenditures.

Because none of these laws were enforced, each had only a momentary effect. Nevertheless, the reforms did seem to make open graft and bribery less acceptable and less common. Instead of outright bribes, political interests now sought to influence politicians through campaign contributions.

Reforms of the 1970s

A significant period of reform occurred in the early 1970s. Prompted by the increasing use of television in campaigns and the rising cost of buying television time, Congress passed a law regulating spending on advertising in 1971. The law limited the amount that candidates could donate to their own campaigns and required candidates to disclose the names and addresses of donors of more than $100. In the course of the Watergate investigations, it became clear that corporations were not abiding by these restrictions, as several corporations had secretly funded President Richard Nixon's reelection campaign. For example, Nixon's Justice Department negotiated a settlement favorable to the ITT Corporation in a pending legal dispute soon after an

"HONEST GRAFT"

Plunkitt's view of graft illustrates the casual attitude about the influence of money on politics common among many of his time (and perhaps today too):

There's all the difference in the world between [honest graft and dishonest graft]. There's an honest graft, and I'm an example of how it works. I might sum up the whole thing by sayin': "I seen my opportunities and I took 'em."

Just let me explain. . . . My party's in power in the city, and it's goin' to undertake a lot of public improvements. Well, I'm tipped off, say, that they're going to lay out a new park at a certain place. I see my opportunity and take it. I go to that place and I buy up all the land I can in the neighborhood. Then the board of this or that makes its plan public, and there is a rush to get my land, which nobody cared particular for before. Ain't it perfectly honest to charge a good price and make a profit on my investment and foresight? Of course, it is. Well, that's honest graft.

Tammany was beat in 1901 because the people were deceived into believin' that it worked dishonest graft. . . . [They supposed that] Tammany men were robbin' the city treasury or levyin' blackmail on disorderly houses, or workin' in with the gamblers and law-breakers. . . . Why should the Tammany leaders go into such dirty business when there is so much honest graft lyin' around?

. . . I don't own a dishonest dollar. If my worst enemy was given the job of writin' my epitaph . . . he couldn't do more than write: George W. Plunkitt. He Seen His Opportunities, and He Took 'Em.

SOURCE: William L. Riordon, *Plunkitt of Tammany Hall* (1905; repr., New York: Dutton, 1963), 3–6.

Warren G. Harding, one of our least successful presidents, couldn't say "no" to his friends. This failure led to the Teapot Dome scandal in 1921.

ITT subsidiary gave the Republican National Committee $400,000.[15] Altogether, twenty-one individuals and fourteen corporations were indicted for illegal campaign contributions, mostly but not entirely to the Nixon reelection campaign.

In response to these scandals, Congress again attempted to regulate campaign financing in 1974. The objectives of the 1974 law were to limit campaign spending, to make the campaign finance system more open by disclosing the names of donors, and to force candidates to be less reliant on a few big donors. The act also established the bipartisan **Federal Election Commission (FEC)** to enforce the law. However, within a decade, candidates and parties discovered ways to get around this law, and the Supreme Court had declared parts of it unconstitutional.

REGULATING MONEY IN MODERN CAMPAIGNS

As the 1974 legislation became ever less effective, new calls for campaign finance reform became more insistent.

The McCain-Feingold Act and Its Aftermath

In 2002, Congress passed the **McCain-Feingold Act**. The chief aim of this legislation was to limit the amount that corporations and unions could give to so-called independent groups (groups not directly connected to a candidate or party) for advertising. The act also tried to regulate **soft money** donations (funds given to and spent by national parties). However, by 2004, lawyers and political operatives had found loopholes in this law too. And in 2010, the Supreme

Court put another nail in the coffin when it declared, by a 5–4 vote, that corporations and unions can spend as much as they like supporting or opposing candidates as long as they are not officially part of a candidate's campaign.

This ruling by the Roberts Court disregarded the Supreme Court's precedents stretching back sixty years. Because spending to advertise enables candidates to get their message out, the Court concluded that giving money is an indirect form of expression protected by the First Amendment. The decision, which struck down laws in twenty-two states as well as federal law, declared that "government may not suppress political speech on the basis of the speaker's corporate identity." Thus, the Court declared that free speech provisions in the First Amendment protect corporations in addition to persons.[16]

Reaction to the decision was predictably mixed. The president of Democracy 21, a group trying to limit the influence of money on elections, declared, "This is the most radical and destructive campaign-finance decision in the history of the Supreme Court."[17] President Obama called it a "major victory for big oil, Wall Street banks, health insurance companies and other powerful interests that marshal their power every day in Washington to drown out the voices of everyday Americans."[18] Many Republicans praised the decision. Sen. John Cornyn (R-Tex.) commented, "These are the bedrock principles that underpin our system of governance and strengthen our democracy."[19]

Later, a federal appeals court used the decision to strike down barriers limiting individual contributions to independent groups working for or against candidates.

DEMOCRACY?

Is it more democratic to let individuals and corporations spend as much as they want to influence elections, or is it more democratic to limit spending? Why?

But neither the Supreme Court nor the appellate court struck down requirements that groups working for or against candidates must disclose the names of their donors.[20]

John McCain has said, "Money is like water: it finds cracks in the wall."[21] In a democracy, it is hard to find ways to restrict the flow of private resources into political campaigns. Because of loopholes, enforcement problems, and judicial action, our campaign finance regulatory system is largely one where disclosure is mandated, giving directly to candidates and parties is limited, but most everything else is unlimited.

Four Elements of Campaign Finance Regulation

We will discuss four aspects of campaign finance regulation.

1. **Public disclosure**: requiring that the names of donors be on the public record
2. Public financing of elections
3. **Contribution limits** on the overall amount of money that individuals and groups give to candidates
4. Spending limits: limitations on candidate spending in political campaigns, including so-called **independent spending**, and spending by other groups in support or opposition to candidates

Disclosure

Federal law requires candidates and independent groups working to support or oppose candidates to disclose the source of their contributions. The Federal Election Commission provides public reports on who has given money to whom. Through this part of the law, journalists and the public can see what private interests are contributing and who the beneficiaries of their contributions are. In fact, you can find on the Web who in your community has given to what

candidates, campaign committees, or PACS (www.fecinfo. com/cgi-win/x_stateguide.exe?DoFn=&sYR=2006).   This is one aspect of regulatory legislation that, up to now, has been relatively effective and uncontroversial. However, the conservative activism of the current Court gives hope to those who do not want to disclose names of individual or corporate donors, so these provisions certainly will be challenged.

Public Funding

Since 1974, presidential candidates have been eligible for public funding for the primary and general elections. The amount increases each year to take account of inflation. The funds come from a voluntary checkoff of $3 that individuals can make on their tax returns. If a candidate accepts public funding, he or she must adhere to certain spending limits. Candidates who do not accept public funding can spend as much as they can raise, as we described at the beginning of this chapter.

Candidates in primaries can receive a significant amount of public funding matched to their own fundraising by demonstrating their abilities to raise money in at least twenty states (maximum amounts are adjusted each election for inflation).

Once candidates receive their party's nomination, public funding amounts to about $84 million for the general election campaign if the candidate chooses to accept it. Candidates can accept several million more from their party's national committee. At this point, fundraising is supposed to be officially over for the candidates if the public funding is accepted.

Accepting public funding does not limit other groups, not under control of the candidate and party, from raising and spending money to sway public opinion and thereby help their favored candidate. If the candidate refuses public funding, he can continue private fundraising under the restrictions described below.

The public financing system is close to death. In 2004, several major candidates, including incumbent George W. Bush, did not accept public money for their primary elections. Both Bush and John Kerry, his Democratic opponent, accepted public funding for the general election, perhaps because each thought he could not raise significantly more money than his opponent (and unless you can do that, it makes sense to avoid the pain and the time involved in fundraising).

In 2008, several major candidates, including John McCain, Barack Obama, and Hillary Clinton, did not accept funding for the primaries. And, as we saw, Barack Obama set a precedent by spurning public funding for the general election campaign, knowing that he could raise more money than the $84 million he would receive in public funds. Because of his fundraising success, he had a huge advantage over McCain in campaign spending, both for television ads and for on-the-ground organizations.

The 2008 campaign was the most expensive in history, at $1.6 billion, twice as expensive as the 2004 campaign and three times as much as the 2000 campaign.[22] In fact, Obama alone raised enough money (more than $750 million) to cover the payroll of the New York Yankees, the baseball team with the largest payroll, for nearly four seasons.[23]

DEMOCRACY?

Would public funding make elections more democratic or less?

Contribution Limits

Although limits on giving to "independent" groups working on behalf of candidates or causes have been struck down by the Court, federal law does regulate the amount that individuals and groups can give to candidates and their official campaigns. Those limits have not been struck down. For example, individuals can now give $2400 per candidate per election, up to a total of $69,900 per year to all candidates and party committees. PAC giving to candidates and parties is also regulated, though with slightly different limits. The law also regulates donations to national party committees and to state or local committees.

Because of these legal restrictions on direct donations to candidates and campaigns, and because of new technology, some candidates have put a lot of effort into raising money through the Internet from people who are not big donors. Howard Dean, the Democratic front-runner in the early 2004 primary season, first realized the potential of the Internet to link his supporters with the campaign and with each other.[24]

In 2008, Barack Obama took the lead in using the Web to raise funds. He mobilized hundreds of thousands of supporters and reaped millions in small contributions, reportedly from 1,500,000 donors. His major primary rival, Hillary Clinton, after an early reliance on bigger donors, also turned to small donors connecting to the Internet, and mention of www.hillaryclinton.com was a staple in her election night speeches. However, both Obama and Clinton raised most of their money from bigger donors.

Republican candidates were less reliant on small donors and more on bigger traditional ones, and normally they raise more money than the Democratic candidates. However, in 2008, McCain and the other leading Republican candidates lagged far behind both Obama and Clinton in their fundraising ability. This relatively weak fundraising effort was probably partly a function of the candidates themselves and partly the fact that many Republicans were discouraged by the actions and unpopularity of the Bush administration.

Spending Limits

Attempts to limit campaign spending have been ineffective. The Supreme Court knocked huge holes in campaign funding legislation when it struck down spending limits except in publicly funded presidential elections.[25] The argument was the same as that used in striking down limits on corporate donations to independent groups: because money often goes to buy advertising, the Court said that spending restrictions violated the First Amendment right of free speech. (The ruling does not apply to spending limits in presidential races when the candidates accept public funding because they agree to the limits as a condition of accepting the funding.) Consequently, spending limits apply only in presidential races when candidates accept public funds.

Federal law classifies nonparty and candidate spending in different ways that open loopholes in the legislation. We will discuss political action committees (PACs), independent spending, and soft money.

Political action committees (PACs) Although the main purpose of **political action committees (PACs)** is to disperse money to candidates and their campaigns, they are limited in what they can give to individual candidates to $5000 in each election, or $10,000 combined in a primary and a general election. They can also give $15,000 a year to national parties and $5000 a year to another PAC. And, of course, they can give to multiple candidates, parties, and PACs. Consequently, they are a prominent feature of the campaign funding scene (see Figure 1).

PACs are different from the independent groups we discussed above because PACs give money directly to candidates, whereas independent groups are not officially connected with candidates even though they might spend millions on advertisements for and against candidates.

PACs are funded from dues and "voluntary" contributions from members of labor unions, "voluntary" contributions from employees of businesses, and voluntary contributions from industry groups or public interest groups. PACs are one way that individuals can channel more money to their favorite candidates. Individuals can give a limited amount directly to candidates and then give more money to each of several PACs, which in turn give it to candidates.[26] About 400 of the 4000 or so PACs give more than $100,000

american*diversity

Men and Women Target Different Candidates

Hillary Clinton was not the first woman candidate for president, but she was the first who had a realistic chance of winning. Though she did not at first target her candidacy to women, such appeals became a larger part of her campaign as the primaries went on. In most states, women favored her by margins ranging from slim to huge. And women campaign donors gave disproportionately to her too.

Near-final tallies of primary campaign donations show that women provided about half of the funds that Clinton raised and were 55 percent of all donors to her campaign. Clinton's campaign fundraising was greatly aided by EMILY'S List, a political action group that raises money for pro-choice Democratic women candidates (EMILY stands for Early Money Is Like Yeast). By bundling individual donations, EMILY'S List raised more than $500,000 for Clinton.

Among the other major contenders, Barack Obama was next in support from women. He raised 42 percent of his funds from women, and they were about 44 percent of his donors. Female financial support for John McCain and his chief rival, Mitt Romney, trailed far behind. Romney raised 32 percent and McCain only 23 percent of his funds from women.

Women's Financial Support for Major Primary Candidates

	As % of total funds raised by the candidate	As % of total donors to the candidate
Clinton	50%	55%
Obama	42	44
Romney	32	30
McCain	23	27

SOURCE: Center for Responsive Politics on its website, Open Secrets: opensecrets.org/pres08/index.php?cycle52008.

Hillary Clinton, as a senator (D-N.Y.), speaks at a conference sponsored by EMILY's List, which raises money for female candidates.

Figure 1 | Types of PACs Reflect Dominance of Business in American Politics

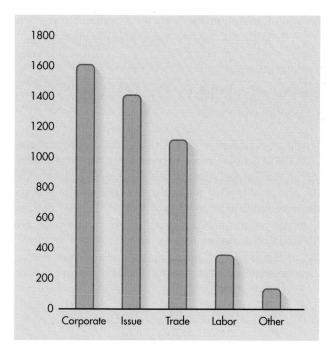

SOURCE: *The data are numbers of PACs of each type. U.S. Census Bureau, Statistical Abstract of the United States, 2010 (Washington, D.C.: Government Printing Office, 2010), tab. 410. Data from 2009.*

in total. These wealthy PACs represent corporate interests, trade interests (groups of professionals or industries, such as the National Pork Producers Council), or issue coalitions.

Although PACs differ in the targets of their donations, they show a distinct preference for Republicans in the presidential races and for incumbents—Republicans or Democrats—in congressional races (see Figure 2). This preference is especially noticeable when Republicans control Congress. PACs usually want to give to the candidate they believe will win, normally the incumbents, so that they will have access to a policy maker. They also give money to members in districts where they have a substantial interest, such as a large number of union members for a union PAC or a large factory for a corporate PAC.[27] PACs also target contributions to members of key congressional committees. For example, those organized by defense contractors give disproportionately to members who serve on the Armed Services Committees, which have a big role in deciding what weapons to purchase.[28]

Women's PACs, including EMILY's List (see Chapter 6), are unusual in focusing most of their money on nonincumbents. Their goal is to get more women elected, which often means supporting nonincumbents with strong chances of winning.

Independent spending Independent groups can be a wealthy individual or a corporation that gives itself a public-spirited-sounding name. Or they can be a group of people who want to promote or oppose an issue or candidate. Such groups can spend an unlimited amount of money as long as they are not officially linked to a candidate or party through contributions, formal organization, or endorsements.[29]

The Courts have knocked down almost all barriers to independent spending, even though the organizers of groups might be important party activists and donors. The assumption is that this spending is truly independent, but it often isn't.

Two examples illustrate how tenuous these definitions are. The Media Fund, headed by a former Clinton White House adviser, ran television ads throughout the 2004 primary campaign. One featured a shot of a factory with the voice pointing out that "it's true that George W. Bush has created more jobs. Unfortunately, ..." The camera then revealed that the factory was in China, and the voice announced that most of the new jobs were in places like China.[30] Although the ad did not endorse Kerry, it clearly worked in his interest. On the other side, the Swift Boat Veterans for Truth was financed largely by Bush supporters and advised by an attorney who was an official in the Bush campaign (and who resigned when this tie was revealed). Technically, however, the group was "independent" of the Bush campaign.

Soft money Some campaign donations are so-called soft money. Soft money is supposed to be used for such "party-building" activities as national party conventions, voter registration drives, direct mailings, polling, issue ads, and advertisements for nonfederal party candidates. Donors who want to give more than their legal federal maximum can give soft money to national party committees. Soft money was exempted from limitations of federal legislation because, in theory, it was not to be used for campaigns. In reality, most soft money is spent by independent groups for national television advertisements for the parties' candidates.[31]

Overall, then, federal laws regulating campaign finance have been successful in requiring disclosure; fairly successful in regulating donations to formal candidates, parties, and PACs; but remarkably unsuccessful in limiting the flow of money into the campaign process through soft money and independent groups. Fat cats can, in fact, give as much as they want on behalf of their candidates, just not directly to the candidate or the party.

Honest Graft? The Impact of Our Campaign Finance System

Our campaign finance system has a number of important effects. In general, the perception that big money buys influence and access, if not actual votes, has a corrosive impact on public trust in government. Indeed, much of the public believes that most individuals in government are out to feather their own nests and that many are crooks. Some of the reasons for this distrust have nothing to do with money. But public trust was certainly affected by the Watergate

Figure 2 | Incumbents Received Most Political Action Committee Donations

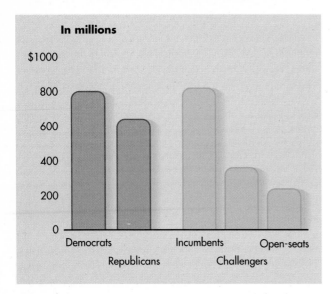

In millions

PACs give overwhelmingly to incumbents. The donations charted above were to House and Senate candidates. Open seats are those races without incumbents.
SOURCE: U.S. Census Bureau, Statistical Abstract of the United States, 2010 (Washington, D.C.: Government Printing Office, 2010), tab. 414. Data from the 2007–2008 election cycle.

scandal in the 1970s and the ethical scandals in the early 2000s, and it is likely that continuous revelations about big-money lobbying activity since then reinforce public cynicism and distrust.

American elections are funded, for the most part, by private money. It is therefore not surprising that candidates turn to people who have money to help with that funding. It is also not surprising that the current system alienates voters. Even if we believe that no votes are actually bought, the appearance of conflicts of interest that permeate the existing system and clearly disturb the public should give pause to those interested in the health of our political system.

Walter Lippmann, a respected journalist, once said that American attitudes about corruption alternate between "fits and starts of unsuspecting complacency and violent suspicion."[32] We think nothing is wrong, and then we think everything is wrong. So it is with our views of campaign money. For several years after major post-Watergate campaign finance reforms in 1974, we thought things were going along pretty well. More recently, many people have become convinced that the nation is in terrible jeopardy because of the influence of money. This fear is compounded because money from corporations subject to regulation has flowed generously into the system at a time when regulations were dropped or laxly enforced, with the consequent failures of the economy, the housing industry, and environmental safety. The big-money link between business and government has eroded confidence in both.

We might view our current campaign finance system as the modern version of George Washington Plunkett's "honest graft." Unless there is a direct payment for a vote, it is perfectly legal to provide funds for a member's campaign, but to many people, the outcome is a lot like graft.

FUNDRAISING IN TODAY'S CAMPAIGNS

Waging a campaign is expensive. Fundraising for national elections is done by the party committees, candidates themselves, and private groups that support candidates. And because most funding for such campaigns is private, candidates for office must continually look for funding sources. Potential presidential candidates appear on television and fly around the country to woo potential donors and fundraisers and to attend fundraising functions. Without money, even the best candidates with the best ideas will go nowhere.

The President as Chief Fundraiser

The chief fundraiser in national politics is likely to be the president. This certainly creates awkwardness and can diminish the president's stature. To raise soft money for the Democratic National Committee and thus for his campaign, President Bill Clinton invited big donors to the White House to have coffee with him and, in some cases, to stay overnight. These and other revelations about fundraising practices prompted cries of outrage from Republicans. Said candidate George W. Bush, "Will we use the White House . . . as a fundraising mechanism—in other words, you give money and you get to sleep in the Lincoln Bedroom? The answer is no."[33]

But once in office, the Bush administration just as blatantly exploited his office for partisan fundraising, as the president invited big donors to dine with diplomats at an embassy and meet with cabinet officials.[34] Indeed, Bush and his organization were by far the biggest fundraisers ever among political candidates. They used their close connections to industry to raise staggering amounts from corporate executives eager to have high-level access to the president and his team.

Large donors were given perks, such as photos with the president or the first lady, Laura Bush. After 9/11, capitalizing on the tragedy, Republican donors were given photos of George W. Bush calling Vice President Cheney on September 11, 2001.[35] Some elite donors were offered a chance to "dine with diplomats and embassy officials and discuss international affairs at one of Washington's famous embassies."[36]

More substantively, after the 2000 elections, 104 of Bush's top fundraisers received government jobs. Four were named cabinet secretaries—Tom Ridge, Don Evans, Elaine Chao, and Alphonso Jackson—and twenty-two received

behind the scenes

To Swift-Boat: A Verb?

Sometimes political observers remark that a group has "swift-boated" a candidate. Aside from being bad grammar, this term means that an attack is untruthful or unfair. The term grew from an ad run by an independent group, Swift Boat Veterans for Truth, in the 2004 presidential election against Democratic candidate John Kerry.

Kerry, a Vietnam veteran wounded and decorated for valor—he won three Purple Hearts for wounds and both a Silver and Bronze Star for valor—commanded a swift boat, a small patrol boat used by the navy on Vietnamese rivers during the war. He probably could have dodged the draft, like his opponent George W. Bush and many others of his cohort. (Bush spent the war doing occasional training exercises for the Texas National Guard. In those days, the National Guard was never called to active duty in a war.) But Kerry didn't.

In election campaigns, Republicans often accused Democrats of not being patriotic, so Kerry decided to use his war experience to inoculate himself from such charges. And, Kerry thought, who better than an actual combat veteran to make decisions about the two wars—Afghanistan and Iraq—America was involved in?

But after Kerry left the service, and while the Vietnam War dragged on, he testified in a Senate hearing that the war was wrong and the United States should withdraw. The next day, at an antiwar rally with 1000 other Vietnam veterans, he threw his medals away in protest. Some conservative veterans never forgave him.

In 2004, a group of conservative veterans who supported George W. Bush organized as an independent group called the Swift Boat Veterans for Truth (some of them had also served on swift boats but not with Kerry). The group put together a commercial alleging that Kerry had been a coward and his wounds had been trivial, and that he was lying about his experience. The allegations circulated on blogs and then were picked up by conservative talk radio hosts and by Fox News, the largely Republican television channel. Happy with the stir that the charges were making, some major Bush contributors donated more funds so that the ad could run nationally and frequently.

Once it ran nationally, the mainstream media reported the story and, in the process, publicized the allegations but also started to check the facts in the ad. The allegations were simply false. Navy records and the testimonies of veterans who had served with him supported Kerry's reports of his service, his wounds, and the actions that led to his Bronze and Silver Stars.

However, it was too late for the facts. Kerry was not a nimble candidate, and he did not challenge the ad soon enough. By the time he realized the damage that had been done to his reputation and his standing in the polls, many Americans believed that the misnamed "Swift Boat Veterans for Truth" were telling the truth and that Kerry was lying. Thus Kerry's war experience was transformed from an asset into a liability. His campaign never recovered.

The ad was so influential that it spawned a new verb, "to swift-boat," that journalists have used in subsequent elections.

ambassadorships, including one found guilty of swindling his business partners out of $1 million.[37]

For many, access is more important than jobs. Many large donors and fundraisers are heads of companies and lobbyists.[38] Access to top policy makers is worth paying for. In Bush's campaigns, executives and lobbyists for the financial and real estate world, energy, construction, and transportation were well represented in this elite group.

Did the Bush administration deregulate specifically because it received campaign funds from big construction and other regulated industries? Probably not; conservative Republicans prefer to let business regulate itself and would favor deregulation independent of contributions. Did construction executives give money to the Bush campaign specifically to thank the administration for relaxing regulations and allowing them to make even more money? We do not know. Did they give the funds in the hope and expectation of future policies loosening regulations? Again, no one knows for sure, but that is a reasonable expectation.

In the 2008 campaign, Obama claimed that he did not take money from lobbyists. And this is true, if one has a very narrow definition of lobbyists, those who list their occupation as lobbyist. But he took millions (as did Hillary Clinton and John McCain) from lawyers in Washington who represent large corporate interests and from corporate executives who have many pending legislative interests.[39] Apparently Obama recognized that the public does not want favors or access to be purchased with campaign contributions, but he was less than honest in his declarations. And of course, large donors and fundraisers for Obama received plum jobs just as they always do, though perhaps in fewer numbers.

It is difficult to point out the exact cause and effect of these close ties between donors and public officials. Even if all that is being bought and sold is access, access is worth something. If access did not influence policy, most people would not be trying to buy it. Even if no favors were exchanged for money and nothing illegal transpired, many Americans find these activities unethical and unbecoming a president. Indeed, the most troubling activities are the ones that are apparently legal. Unless voters elect members of Congress who agree, campaign finance activities will continue to provide material for cartoonists and comedians, embarrassment for public officials, and ultimately loss of public trust in both business and politics.

Members of Congress as Fundraisers

Members of Congress are aggressive in soliciting for donations. They fear defeat in the next election and think that raising a lot of money can protect them. Senators, for example, must raise more than $20,000 each week during all six years of their term to fund an average winning reelection campaign, which in 2008 cost $6.5 million. A senator from a populous, high-cost state or in a hotly contested election needs to raise much more.[40] In 2008, Al Franken (D) defeated incumbent Norm Coleman (R) in a tightly contested Minnesota race where the two together spent $35 million. Many incumbents raise millions even when they face little-known opponents.

In the House, an average winning race costs just over $1 million. That means the average House member has to raise about $10,000 a week over the course of a two-year term.

Until the 1960s, most fundraising by members of Congress was done in their home districts because members did not want their constituents to think they were influenced by Washington lobbyists. In contrast, today members of Congress are heavily supported by PACs, and the majority of PAC funds are raised in Washington.[41] Members of Congress continually hold fundraisers to which dozens of lobbyists for PACs are invited. Well-known lobbyists get hundreds of invitations to congressional fundraisers every year.[42] Indeed, the number of these events is so large that a private company sells a special monthly newsletter listing all of them.

Raising money for congressional campaigns is becoming nationalized in other ways too. Individual donors from across the country pour money into districts that are considered competitive or otherwise important. Interest groups and political parties may raise the call to their checkbook donors to send contributions to key targeted districts. In 2010, in the high-profile California Senate race between Democrat Barbara Boxer and Republican Carly Fiorina, money flooded in from all over the nation, more than $30 million by midsummer 2010. These trends tend to strengthen parties and give members of Congress reasons to weigh national interests, as seen by those parties, alongside their local interests.

REFORMING CAMPAIGN FINANCE

Campaign finance reform is a perennially vexing topic to both supporters and opponents. It's like weather—everyone talks about it, but few people are in a position to do anything

about it. Most Americans find the campaign finance system distasteful and accurately believe that big interests with big money have special access. However, there is no agreement, even among the turned-off public, on what the right solutions are.

Elected officials appear to be more afraid of being without campaign donations than they are that the campaign finance system will further erode confidence in the whole political system. Ideologically, Democrats are more sympathetic to limiting the influence of big money, but practically, Democratic incumbents are heavily dependent on their PAC "fixes." Thus, neither party has much incentive to support campaign finance reform, despite the fact that the public is repelled by the existing system.

At least some of those who give money see donations as an opportunity for access and influence, and at least some officeholders see nothing wrong with rewarding large donors with political favors or favorable policy decisions. It is these relationships that prompt continuing calls for campaign finance reform. Yet, as soon as laws are passed, loopholes are opened by the FEC, which is responsible for overseeing the campaign finance laws, and by candidates themselves, who are very creative in finding ways to get around the limits. And currently, the Roberts Court takes a dim view of attempts to regulate campaign donations, except directly to the candidates, and spending.

Opposition to Reform

There is a strong constituency who oppose campaign reform. Some individuals, on both sides of the liberal-conservative divide, think that prohibitions on private giving are a violation of free speech. Some emphasize that individuals should have the right to spend as much as they wish on the candidate of their choice. Others believe that private groups should be able to run as many advertisements as they want in support of their views.[43] These are the arguments by which the Roberts Court struck down parts of the McCain-Feingold legislation. Still others oppose reform because they dislike government regulation in general.

Some people think that campaign reform is impossible to implement if we want to allow people to give to campaigns. They argue that campaign finance reform simply leads to ever more sophisticated searches for loopholes without accomplishing much.[44]

Most elected officials are not big fans of campaign finance reform either. As incumbents, they have an advantage in fundraising. They do not want to tie their own hands by limiting their abilities to raise funds from friendly interest groups. After all, when one party starts spending money in a close race, the impulse is for the other party to match or exceed it, a kind of campaign finance arms race. In a close contest, both sides want to do everything possible to win, and a few extra hundreds of thousands of dollars might indeed make the difference.

behind the scenes

Where the Money Goes

On what do candidates spend their money? The media often expose inappropriate personal expenditures, such as the $400 haircuts that 2008 Democratic candidate John Edwards received or the $150,000 clothes-shopping spree of vice-presidential candidate Sarah Palin that was paid for by the Republican National Committee.

But most spending is more mundane, even if the sums are staggering. During the 2008 primaries, the candidates spent around $1 billion. The best-funded candidates, Barack Obama and Hillary Clinton, spent more than $1 million a day. The beneficiaries of campaign spending are not just the staff who run and work for the campaigns, but also a variety of private firms, consultants, media contacts, telemarketers, pollsters, event planners, and even credit card companies.

Media and consulting constitute more than one-third of all spending. A number of private firms benefit from this, most particularly, in recent elections, the consulting and media acquisition firms (firms that plan and execute media buys for the candidates) employed by Obama and Clinton, and to a lesser extent (because they had less money to spend), Mitt Romney, John McCain, and John Edwards.

Salaries and benefits (such as insurance and tax contributions) have been the next largest spending category. Although campaigns are largely staffed by volunteers, the top managers and campaign strategists who set the overall directions for the campaign, as well as local operatives who organize the volunteers, are on the payroll.

During the 2008 campaign, direct mail and telemarketing firms together received nearly $150 million of business from the candidates. Travel is another big item, and collectively the candidates spent more than $100 million. In addition to flying the candidate and the staff around the country, the campaigns must also provide for the press. When money is flush, the press may be able to ride on comfortable large planes. When money is tight, they may be riding a bus and staying in cheap motels. The chief beneficiary in recent years was one air charter company that both Obama and Clinton used, but one commercial airline also got significant business from a variety of candidates.

Candidates also use event planners to stage rallies, election night celebrations, and other events and to make bumper stickers and banners. In 2008 they collectively spent more than $50 million in this category.

The residual spending is for things like running local offices, renting space and furniture, obtaining phone service, and paying credit card fees. Obama alone spent $8 million in credit card fees. The Clinton campaign was widely criticized because early on it assumed that the primaries would be over after "Super Tuesday" in early February 2008. Thus, campaign staff stayed at expensive hotels and their election day parties were catered expensively. Even the Dunkin' Donuts bill during one month was $1200. As the primaries moved along, their campaign stretched their dollars much further.

SOURCE: Michael Luo, J. Becker, and Patrick Healy, "Donors Worried by Clinton Spending," *New York Times*, February 22, 2008, www.nytimes.com/2008/02/22/us/politics/22clinton.html?ref-opinion.

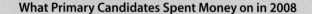

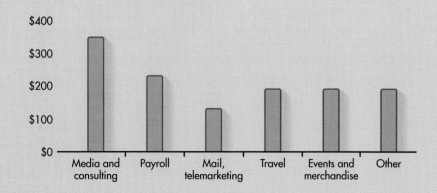

What Primary Candidates Spent Money on in 2008

Data are for primaries only.

Oliphant Copyright © 1990. Universal Press Syndicate. Reprinted by permission.

Powerful interest groups with money to spend also resist reform. Though reform would save them money in the short run, many big interests believe that their clout with key elected officials in getting favorable legislation is worth what they donate and much more. Major areas of business—including "pharmaceuticals, mining, oil and gas, defense, commercial banking and accounting—have basically made a decision to back the GOP."[45] Democrats, in turn, have the strong support of unions, the entertainment industry, and trial lawyers. These divisions reflect the ideological divisions of the parties,[46] and these groups are not eager to upset the status quo of campaign finance.

Ideas for Reform

Still, the unappetizing spectacle of wealthy donors, both individuals and corporations, receiving political favors from those they supported keeps the idea of reform alive even though specifics on campaign reform are not high on voters' lists of priorities.[47] Several ideas have been floated to level the playing field: free media, more public financing, more distance between officeholders and donors, a constitutional amendment, immediate disclosure, and stricter enforcement.

Free Media

One proposal might avoid the pitfalls of the attempts to limit soft money by mandating that radio and TV stations grant free time to the candidates. This proposal focuses on reducing the cost of campaigns and hence the need to have so many private donors.

Why should the media be asked to donate time? There may be several good reasons. Radio and television stations have free use of the public airwaves and make billions from it. Former presidential candidate and senator Bob Dole (R-Kans.) called it "a giant corporate welfare program."[48]

Nearly 10 percent of TV profit is earned through political ads, which are stations' third-largest advertising category, bigger than, for example, fast-food or movie ads.[49] A New York television station sales manager, contemplating the media ads from the 2000 Hillary Clinton–Rudy Giuliani Senate race, exulted, "It's like Santa Claus came."[50] And nearly two-thirds of modern democracies do offer free access to the media.[51]

Moreover, a large part of the cost of campaigns is buying media ads. Advertising, most of it for television, comprises about 30 percent of all presidential election campaign costs and probably about the same in congressional races. That would mean that candidates for federal office spend $800 million in media costs. Independent spending totals hundreds of million more.[52]

The National Association of Broadcasters (NAB) lobbies hard against such ideas, even a proposal to donate five minutes of time a day or to offer candidates their least expensive advertising rates. This latter proposal passed the Senate but was killed in the House. We can expect other proposals dealing with media costs to be on the reform agenda because it is unlikely that we can stem the flow of money into campaigns without curbing the costs of the campaigns themselves.

Free or reduced-price media would dramatically reduce the costs of campaigns. Unless it was combined with public financing, however, it would not eliminate private gifts or affect the role that outside groups play in campaigns.

More Public Financing

A second idea is more public financing. Public funding seeks to limit the overall cost of the campaign and eliminate the need for private donations and the special access that comes with them. Currently, the presidential campaigns have such financing, but it does not begin to cover campaign costs. As noted earlier, the presidential candidates together receive $168 million for the general election, if they choose to accept it, and several million more goes to primary candidates who agree not to raise private funds. However, this is a small fraction of the costs of presidential campaigns.

The public generally favors public funding. A 2008 poll showed that 40 percent supported the system of public funding we have now, and another 32 percent favored a tighter system mandating that all presidential candidates take public funding. Only 19 percent opposed public funding (the rest had no opinion).[53]

Some people have proposed extending public financing to congressional elections. About half the states have some public financing for their own state legislative or judicial candidates, several in conjunction with spending limits. But it seems unlikely that a major expansion of public funding for national candidates will be adopted anytime soon.[54] Opposition to government spending, public dissatisfaction with political campaigns, and the uncertainty that such a plan would really limit private money in politics all militate against it. And public funding does not solve the problem, if it is a problem, of independent organizations' collecting funds and promoting candidates.

Putting Distance between Officeholders and Donors

Many ways to separate officeholder and donors have also been suggested. One is to allow unlimited giving but keep the identity of the givers secret from the recipients. This proposal focuses on the unsavory relationship between money given and favors sought. Thus people would give as much as they want, but it would be channeled to candidates through an organization that would keep the donations anonymous. Some people, who give out of ideological and partisan conviction, would still give, but others might not give if they could not use the fact of their giving as leverage. Of course, anyone could tell a candidate that he or she gave, but the candidate would have no way of knowing who did and who did not.

Constitutional Amendment

Another suggestion for reform is to amend the Constitution, allowing Congress to limit free speech in the area of campaign finance. Proponents of this idea argue that although prohibiting donations might limit "speech" in some respects, the cost to democracy of allowing big money to dictate public policy is much greater. However, this idea seems both impractical, given the difficulty of passing a constitutional amendment, and a threat to traditional free speech values.

Public financing, media donation of time, and separating donors from public officials all may have some merit, but none of the reforms address the fundamental issue of spending by groups who have opinions about candidates and issues. And a constitutional amendment that tried to clamp down on political discussion by independent groups would surely be further than most Americans would want to go.

Immediate Disclosure

Another idea for reform is to make disclosure of donors more immediate. Currently, while all donations must be disclosed, the process takes weeks until quarterly reports are due. Then, more days elapse while the reports are prepared for public distribution. Donations made in the last half of an election year may not be public until after the election. Some reformers have suggested that moving to a system in which donations must immediately be reported and placed on the Web would make the system more accountable.

Enforce Existing Laws

Police have learned that the best way to clean up bad neighborhoods and reduce serious crime is to stringently punish minor violations. Such a policy reassures the public, who are less likely to be confronted with street graffiti, vandalism, and turnstile jumpers and who come to believe that the neighborhood has not been left to criminals. It also deters potential criminals because they come to believe that their crimes will be reported and punished.

Some observers have argued, not wholly in jest, that many ethical issues surrounding Congress could be ameliorated with stricter enforcement of the laws that do exist, just as on city streets. Such stricter enforcement might involve not only taking serious complaints to the Ethics Committee and the FEC but also having FEC investigators actually hanging around congressional offices and lobbyists' offices (often dubbed K Street for the street most of them are on), looking for tips about smelly deals. It might also involve higher penalties for those caught violating the rules. Those convicted of bribery might be sent away for very long terms as an example to others who might be tempted.

Of course, citizens have to demand that laws be enforced, just as they do in neighborhoods being threatened. But although they say they do want change, 98 percent of House members are typically re-elected, so perhaps the public really doesn't want it. As one criminologist noted, local police often are tougher on streetwalkers than on call girls, who commit similar offenses out of the public eye. "Congress is like the call girls," said one observer, "people don't feel the impact directly."[55]

Whatever the problems with the current system, we should be careful not to contrast it with an idealized version of the past. After all, over one hundred years ago, Mark Twain observed, "It could probably be shown by facts and figures that there is no distinctly native American criminal class except Congress."[56] Big interests have always had influence and access in Washington. The ways in which they exercise that influence are different now. In some ways, this influence is more open because the campaign finance reforms have made public the organizations working for special interests and the money they spend doing it. Forty years ago, we would not have known how much each member of Congress received from each lobbying group; today we do.

THE IMPACT OF CAMPAIGN MONEY

We have discussed several aspects of money in elections: how much there is, who contributes it, and how they do so. Now we turn to the question of what difference campaign money makes. An obvious question is whether money influences the outcomes of elections. But we will also focus on three other kinds of potential effects of money and the way it is raised: the recruitment of good candidates, the policy decisions of elected leaders, and the cynicism of the public.

Campaign Finance and Candidate Recruitment

When John Glenn, an unsuccessful Democratic candidate in 1984, was asked whether running for president had been worthwhile despite his defeat, Glenn replied, "My family was humiliated. I got myself whipped. I gained 16 pounds. And I'm more than $2.5 million in debt. Except for that, it was wonderful."[57] In 1998, nearing the end of his career, Glenn remarked in a similar vein, "I'd rather wrestle a gorilla than ask anyone for another 50 cents."[58]

Potential candidates often bow out early, overwhelmed by the magnitude of necessary fundraising. In 2000, George W. Bush's huge campaign war chest deterred several potential candidates from entering the race. Bush raised more than twice as much as his next-best-financed competitor, John McCain. In 2008, the fundraising abilities of Barack Obama and Hillary Clinton made it difficult for other Democratic candidates to get much traction, and one by one they dropped out. On the Republican side, Mitt Romney outraised other candidates, but John McCain, better known to voters because of his 2000 run, was able to hang in by holding town hall meetings and getting free publicity. That helped him win New Hampshire, and that win loosened the pockets of Republican donors.

The necessity of raising a lot of money deters congressional candidates, too. As one leading congressional scholar noted, "Raising money is, by consensus, the most unpleasant part of a campaign. Many candidates find it demeaning to ask people for money and are uncomfortable with the implications of accepting it."[59] This sentiment was echoed by a former senator who commented that, after a day of fundraising calls, "I always left that room feeling like a cheap prostitute who'd had a busy day."[60] And once elected, many new members of Congress are surprised and chagrined to find that they must begin raising funds for their next campaign almost before they are sworn into office. The campaign finance system allows national party committees to recruit candidates with the promise that they will help them raise funds and provide them with significant assistance. In that sense, the system can help recruit candidates. Still, the bulk of the work raising money falls on the individual candidates.

Campaign Finance and Election Outcomes

Money helps win elections. It's not the only factor, of course. Many candidates have tried and failed to "buy" elections with their own money. But money certainly aids in getting the candidate's message out.

Fundraising in Presidential Elections

Looking first at presidential elections, the evidence is mixed as to the impact of money on winning presidential primaries. Primaries are the crucial elections that lead to each party's nomination. Some candidates are never considered serious contenders because they do not have sufficient money to mount a large campaign. In that sense, money is crucial.

In primaries, candidates of each party run against others of their party to achieve the nomination. Most primary candidates start out with little name recognition. Moreover, candidates cannot count on party loyalty to win votes. In primaries, voters choose among candidates of their own party; that is, Republican voters have to choose among Republicans rather than between a Republican and a Democrat. For both those reasons, money is crucial to increase candidate visibility.

Primary candidates who appear to be doing well generally attract money.[61] "Doing well" includes getting favorable media coverage that suggests the candidate is gaining popularity and momentum. Actual success in early primaries also stimulates giving. Money, in turn, allows further purchases of media ads to become known in the next primaries.

Other things being equal, spending does influence voting in primaries. Money appears to be a necessary condition for primary victory, although it is not sufficient by itself. Money is most important in multicandidate races, as is often typical early in the primary season when candidates are seeking to distinguish themselves from other little-known contenders.[62] Money is less important in two-candidate primary contests, often the situation late in the primary season when one candidate has emerged as a front-runner.

The 2008 primaries did not follow the common wisdom perfectly. On the Republican side, Rudy Giuliani, former mayor of New York City, and Mitt Romney, former governor of Massachusetts, outraised John McCain. Giuliani's fundraising success did not, however, translate into votes. He made the strategic mistake of ignoring the early primaries and caucuses, thinking their few votes wouldn't matter. He staked everything on Florida, whose election was a few weeks after Iowa and New Hampshire.

By the time attention turned to Florida, Romney and McCain had notched victories and received significant media attention. Giuliani became an "also-ran" before he even got started.

Romney had excellent fundraising success. But questions about what he really stood for dogged him throughout the race. He had been a centrist governor of a liberal state, even going along with gay marriages. But because the Republican primary electorate is conservative, he veered to the right in his primary campaign, opening himself to attacks from both right and center. Some of the Christian Right also found his Mormon religion to be a drawback.

Hillary Clinton was outspent by Obama by margins of three and four in most of the states she won after January. However, Clinton's name recognition gave her some advantages that other candidates would not have. Even so, she was not able to mount as expansive a campaign as Obama did in some states because of her more limited resources. John McCain was also outspent by his rivals early in the primary season, but he survived and racked up enough successes that the money started to flow in.

By the time presidential candidates are nominated, they have already spent a great deal of money. The name recognition achieved during the primaries and at the national conventions carries into the general election campaign. Presidential candidates receive extensive free media coverage in news stories. The amount that they spend after the convention is less likely to be as crucial. This is just as well for the health of the two-party system, because if money determined elections, the Republicans would have won every presidential election since World War II. However, of the presidential elections lost by the Democrats during that time, probably only the election of 1968 between Richard Nixon and Hubert Humphrey and possibly the Gore-Bush 2000 election were close enough that they might have turned out differently had the Democrats been able to spend more.[63] When the elections are close, as in 1968, the Republicans definitely have the advantage by having more money.[64] However, the Democrats are catching up. In 2008, the Democrats were far ahead in fundraising, setting new records. Anger at the Bush administration coupled with genuine enthusiasm for several Democratic candidates, especially Obama and Clinton, spurred Democrats to give record amounts in donations small and large. It is this margin that led Obama to spurn public funding and opt to raise funds from private donors.

Fundraising in Congressional Races

In congressional races, incumbents usually start with a huge advantage. Some analysts estimate that their advantage is about 5 percent of the vote just by virtue of being incumbents.[65] Their name is recognized by many, if not most, of their constituents, and as incumbents, they are able to raise money early to finance their campaigns. In many cases, the incumbents' huge war chests deter potentially strong challengers from even entering the race.[66] Challengers know that they must raise considerable money to fund media ads even to be competitive. Thus the ability of challengers to raise and spend money is crucial to any chance of success in the election. In 2006, the average amount spent by those running against incumbents was less than $100,000, while incumbents spent about nine times that much.

But incumbent fundraising and spending are also important. Fundraising is important early in the campaign to deter potential opponents. And campaign spending is important, especially for relatively new members of Congress. That is because those who have served only a few terms are less well known than more senior incumbents and thus are considered vulnerable.[67] Of course, incumbents tend to spend the most when they have the toughest opponent. In general, as challengers spend more, so do incumbents.[68]

Most of the time, the person who spends the most to win a congressional seat wins. That was particularly true in 2008, when about 93 percent of the House and Senate candidates spending the most money won.[69] Most of these winners are incumbents, and the link between spending and victory is also a link between incumbency and victory.

Sometimes the biggest spender loses, but the relative rarity of this occurrence only highlights the general link between spending and victory. In 2008, Democratic challenger Kay Hagan was outspent by almost $10 million in a North Carolina Senate race but was still able to defeat incumbent Elizabeth Dole. She was one of only two outspent Senate candidates to win, however.[70]

Buying Influence

As we have seen, donors are not a random cross section of the public. Money usually buys access, and that access is by the wealthiest segment of the population, whose views on public issues, especially economic issues, are more conservative than those of the larger population.

Buying Access

In recent years, corporate interests have pushed hard to deregulate and to lower taxes and have used substantial gifts to help gain access to rule makers. The accounting industry, for example, in the early 1990s helped fund more than three hundred congressional races, including both Democratic and Republican, and spent $2 million for lobbyists. This clout led to Congress passing a law erasing liability for accountants and lawyers aiding and abetting securities fraud. Although President Clinton vetoed the law, his veto was overridden.[71] The law provided a disincentive for auditors to uphold strict accounting standards and removed a tool by which stockholders could hold companies accountable.

After the huge Enron company went bankrupt, enriching its executives and leaving its stockholders with nothing, investigations showed that Enron had given, during a dozen years, nearly $6 million to parties and candidates, three-fourths of it to Republicans.[72] According to the *Wall Street Journal,* "No company in America did more to help George W. Bush get elected president than Enron."[73] Its funds also helped elect friendly members of Congress, mostly Republicans but also many Democrats; gain access at the highest levels; and buy loosened regulation and favorable tax policies. Enron made billions of dollars and benefited greatly from government deregulation of the energy industry. Enron executives who had advance knowledge of the impending collapse sold their stock before the announcement that earnings were inflated, and they made millions (Kenneth Lay, the CEO, had made $103 million in the year before the bankruptcy; and the top one hundred executives collectively

AP Photo/Michael Stravato

Enron CEO Kenneth Lay is led away in handcuffs. While awaiting sentencing for his financial crimes, he died of a heart attack.

made $300 million). Lower-level Enron employees, many of whose pension plans were invested heavily in Enron, collectively lost millions, many of them their life savings. Ordinary investors also found their stock worthless.

Buying Votes

If money buys access, does it also buy votes? Both anecdotal and systematic evidence suggest that money does buy votes, although only under some conditions.

Money is not likely to buy votes on issues that are highly publicized, because legislators' constituents usually have strong views on these issues and legislators feel pressured to follow them.[74] For the same reason, money is less likely to buy roll-call votes on the floor of each house than votes in committees. The former are public and recorded; the latter are not as visible to the public. Compared to their activity on the floor, when they are in committees, legislators with PAC support are more active in speaking and negotiating on behalf of the PAC's positions and offering amendments that reflect these positions.[75]

Money is also not likely to buy votes on moral issues, because legislators themselves often have firm views on these issues. These sorts of issues (abortion, gay rights, and school prayer, for example) also tend to be publicized.

But most matters that come to a vote are neither highly publicized nor moral issues. Most are relatively technical matters that constituents and legislators do not care as strongly about as PACs do. For these, members are susceptible. The deregulation of the energy industry was done when the public had no interest. "You can't buy a Congressman for $50,000. But you can buy his vote," a member admitted. "It's done on a regular basis."[76]

One survey of members found that about one-fifth admit that political contributions have affected their votes on occasion, and another one-third are not sure.[77] Analysis of voting has revealed that contributions from the AFL-CIO affected voting on the minimum wage legislation, and contributions from the trucking interests led senators to vote against deregulation of trucking.

Senators facing reelection the year in which the vote was taken were most susceptible.[78] Voting is also related to donations in such disparate areas as minimum wage legislation, gun control, and billboard regulation.[79]

One classic, well-studied example concerns used-car legislation. Auto dealers spent $675,000 in the 1980 congressional elections. This investment seemed to pay off in 1982 when Congress voted against a rule requiring dealers to inform prospective buyers of any known defects in used cars. The senators who opposed the measure received twice as much money from the auto dealers' PAC as those who voted for it. In the House, those who opposed the measure received on average five times as much money as those who voted for it. Almost 85 percent of the representatives opposing the legislation had received PAC money.[80] The relationship between PAC money and votes still existed even when the party and ideology of the members were taken into account. For conservatives, who might have voted against requiring auto dealers to list defects anyway, PAC contributions made only a marginal difference in their voting; but for liberals, PAC money substantially raised the probability that they would vote with the used-car dealers. "'Of course it was money,' one House member said. . . . 'Why else would they vote for used-car dealers?'"[81]

The relationship between PAC contributions and voting should not be exaggerated, however.[82] Even on these low-visibility votes, a member's party and ideology are important. The constituency interests of members are also key factors explaining votes. For example, members with many union workers in their districts are going to vote for those interests regardless of how much or little they get in PAC contributions.[83] Members without these constituents, though, may be more swayed by PAC contributions.

More recent ties between donors and legislators concern the "buying" of special earmarks in omnibus legislation, legislation that is thousands of pages and contains hundreds of special favors for pet projects of legislators and lobbyists. We discussed earmarking in Chapter 5 and will have more to say about it in Chapter 10.

Buying Influence in the Executive Branch

Money can also buy influence with the executive branch. Presidential candidates tend to have widely publicized views, and their actions as president are subject to intense scrutiny and publicity. Once in office, presidents need donors less than donors need them, thus making the leverage of a campaign donation uncertain. Contributors are sometimes disappointed, as we saw with President Teddy Roosevelt earlier. However, on actions not widely visible to the public, donors can help shape policy.

The Bush fundraising success was partly based on support from the oil and gas industries, which were rewarded with deregulation of both accounting and financial requirements and environmental standards. In fact, Ken Lay, the CEO of Enron, was even allowed to interview a candidate for the top job at the agency that regulated Enron.[84] The Enron scandal was only the tip of the iceberg. Contractors who received billions of dollars worth of contracts in Iraq and Afghanistan had donated generously to the Bush campaign. The director of the Center for Public Integrity commented that there is a "stench of political favoritism and cronyism surrounding the contracting process in both Iraq and Afghanistan."[85]

Analyses of large donors to and fundraisers for the 1992 George H. Bush campaign reveal that many were given special favors or benefits from the federal government. The Department of Labor reduced a proposed fine by nearly 90 percent against a large sugar farmer who gave $200,000 to the campaign.[86] President Clinton created a furor when, on his last day in office, he pardoned the fugitive ex-husband of a major campaign donor, Denise Rich. Rich had contributed generously to the Democratic Party and later to the Clinton presidential library.[87] (As of this writing, no similar scandals have been reported for the Obama administration.)

Large contributions to presidential campaigns often lead to appointments to public office, especially ambassadorships to countries that are desirable vacation locales. No political appointee has ever been ambassador to Chad or Bulgaria; and few career foreign service officers ever get to be ambassador to Great Britain, Ireland, and other countries in western Europe (see Table 1).[88] The **spoils system**, the practice of rewarding jobs to supporters, has been with us since at least the time of Andrew Jackson, so it cannot be blamed on modern PACs and soft money.

Although it is impossible to prove a cause-and-effect relationship in these cases, clearly large donors who expect favorable treatment have plenty of precedents to lead them to that conclusion. As the leader of a watchdog group noted, "The point is, we're not just electing politicians. . . . We're also electing their patrons and their priorities."[89]

Table 1	Ambassadorships in Desirable Locations More Often Go to Political Appointees

Area	% political appointees
Caribbean	73
Western Europe	72
Australia, New Zealand*	49
North and Central America	42
South Asia	28
East Asia	25
Eastern Europe	22
South America	22
Africa	15
Middle East	14
Central Asia	0

*And elsewhere in Oceana, including Micronesia, Samoa, and Fiji.
NOTE: Data are from 1960 to October 2010. Many of the political appointees were big donors to presidential campaigns. The appointees evidently prefer the Caribbean and western Europe for their service.
SOURCE: http://www.afsa.org/ambassadorcontinents.cfm.

behind the scenes

America's Petro-State

Economists have long noticed that the countries with great oil and mineral wealth tend to be the countries with low growth rates, low living standards, and serious economic inequality. Venezuela, Nigeria, and the Middle Eastern countries are examples of these "petro-states."[1] Because they have oil revenue, these countries do not invest in the non-oil-producing economy. When oil prices are high, they use that revenue to import what they need rather than invest in domestic companies. Meanwhile, revenues from oil leases to corporations tend to go into the pockets of public officials and other elites, leaving average people doubly poor: they have access neither to oil revenues nor to other productive work in the private sector. The major public issue then becomes the question of who controls the oil revenues. This tug of war leads to weakening of political institutions as well as to corruption. In Venezuela, after seven years of unprecedented high oil prices, the number of poor people had increased, the government had grown significantly, and the rich had become richer.[2]

In the United States, our petro-state is Louisiana. Since the beginning of the twentieth century, when oil was discovered in Louisiana, the state has produced 17 trillion gallons of oil, equal to the output of the rest of the United States (and it has produced 159 trillion cubic feet of natural gas too). As in petro-states abroad, oil in Louisiana, instead of producing prosperity, has left the state one of America's poorest, one of its most corrupt, and with one of its most despoiled environments.

It is hard to quantify corruption (however, see graph) but observations of corruption in Louisiana are legion. One former member of Congress from the state claimed that his constituents "don't want good government, they want good

Reporters' Views of Most Corrupt States	
Most corrupt	Rhode Island
2	Louisiana
3	New Mexico
4	Oklahoma
4 (tie)	Delaware
6	Alabama
7	Kentucky
8	Arizona
8 (tie)	West Virginia
10	Illinois
11	Ohio

This survey reflects the observations of local reporters who follow state politics. They were asked to rate the degree of corruption among state officials in their state on a scale of 1 to 7, with 7 the most corrupt. The states shown were the eleven perceived to be most corrupt. Overall, the scores ranged from 5.5 on average in Rhode Island, perceived to be the most corrupt state, to 1.5 in South Dakota, North Dakota, and Colorado, the least corrupt. Massachusetts, New Hampshire, and New Jersey were not included in the study, because their reporters didn't respond. In the number of convicted officials per capita, Louisiana also ranks high.
SOURCE: *http://www.nytimes.com/2008/12/14/weekinreview/14marsh.html.*

Campaign Finance and Income Inequality

The influence of big money in presidential campaigns probably makes both parties more conservative. The biggest contributors to the Republicans in the last few presidential elections have been some of the most conservative people in that party. The big-money contributors to the Democrats are, on the whole, less liberal than the mainstream of the party.

Some Democratic House leaders were surprised when members said they could not vote against a capital gains tax cut (which would benefit the wealthy) because it would anger their business contributors. Said one member, "I get elected by voters. I get financed by contributors. Voters don't care about this; contributors do."[90] A former aide to a prominent Democratic senator remarked that he had to remind the senator that a fundraising event was not a focus group, that is, that those who attend fundraisers are not representative of all voters. He went on to remark that "it's the rare politician whose perspective is not affected by his or her constant exposure to the wealthy people whose money [politicians] need to get elected."[91]

Beyond the specific policies and appointments that reflect the influence of big money, we can step back and look at the bigger picture. Public policy helps shape the distribution of income in our society through taxation, the regulation of corporations and unions, and many other ways.

entertainment."[3] Thus it's not surprising that years later another cracked that "half of Louisiana is under water and the other half is under indictment."[4]

Among the states, Louisiana ranks forty-ninth in life expectancy and forty-sixth in the number of adults with college degrees. It ranks second in rates of infant mortality and the percentages of people below the poverty line, and third in the rates of violent crime.[5]

Oil companies have built a network of roads and canals through the marshes and wetlands that border the Gulf of Mexico. They have built thousands of wells within three miles of the coast, many of which are abandoned and leaking. The BP oil spill of 2010 further damaged a coastal environment that was already far from pristine. As one Louisiana economic expert noted, "We've always been a plantation state. What oil and gas did is replace the agricultural plantation with an oil and gas plantation culture."[6]

Oil and gas interests dominate the political process and wield significant influence in both political parties. Wealthy and powerful individuals in Louisiana typically have invested in stock holdings in the oil and gas industries. Even judges have. When cases challenging oil interests come to the courts, many judges recuse (disqualify) themselves because of their energy interests. In an important global warming case, half the judges on the sixteen-member Fifth Circuit U.S. Court of Appeals in New Orleans recused themselves.[7] Four more did not recuse themselves but should have. Thus only four of the sixteen on the court had no conflict of interest. In another case, a federal district court judge who suspended President Obama's moratorium on offshore drilling had interests in oil companies. (He did rush to sell his ExxonMobil stock so he could hear the case.[8]) When the case was appealed to the appellate court, two judges hearing the case had represented oil companies before becoming judges, and two others still held stock in oil companies. They supported the district court judge's decision.

Oil influence is even more pronounced in the legislature, where legislators are not required or expected to recuse themselves for conflicts of interest. In exchange for industry jobs, the state has provided a lucrative climate for oil and gas industries with little regulation of them and low taxes on them. This close relationship was illustrated in 2010 when oil industry supporters blocked a bill that would have allowed the state to hire a private attorney to help in the state's case against BP for the spill.[9] Oil industry supporters also tried to halt state funding for Tulane's environmental law clinic after it filed suit against oil companies and coal plants (and won). The sponsor of that bill, which did not pass, was himself the owner of a gas company.

State officials were eager to resume drilling after the BP spill because stopping drilling would cost thousands of Louisianans their jobs. Environmental risk was relegated to a far-distant second priority. And so were the company's negligence and the regulatory failures that led to the death of the nine BP workers on the rig that exploded.

[1] Terry Lynn Karl, *The Paradox of Plenty: Oil Booms and Petro-States* (Berkeley: University of California Press, 1997).

[2] Ibid; http://www.econlib.org/library/Columns/y2005/Martinezpetro.html.

[3] Jacob Weisberg, "Political Corruption Smackdown," *Slate*, December 13, 2008, http://www.slate.com/id/2206523/.

[4] Bret Schulte, "A Troubling Bayou Tradition: Louisiana's History of Corruption Bodes Ill for the Relief Money Headed Its Way," *U.S. News and World Report*, October 2, 2005, http://www.usnews.com/usnews/news/articles/051010/10louisiana.htm.

[5] These U.S. Census data are reported in Steven Mufson, "Oil Spills. Poverty. Corruption. Why Louisiana Is America's Petro-State," *Washington Post*, July 18, 2010, B01.

[6] Ibid.

[7] A majority of judges is required for a quorum on federal courts of appeals. Therefore, if the court sat *en banc* (as the entire court, rather than in panels of three—see Chapter 13), it would need at least nine judges. See Douglas A. Henderson, "Global Warming Appeal Dismissed by Fifth Circuit Because No En Banc Quorum," *Emerging Issues Law Blog*, June 4, 2010, www.lexisnexis.com/Community/emergingissues/blogs/emergingissueslawblog/archive/2010/06/04.

[8] Ibid.; John Broder, "Court Rejects Moratorium on Drilling in the Gulf," *New York Times*, July 8, 2010, http://www.nytimes.com/2010/07/09/us/09drill.html?_r=1&scp=1&sq=Obama%20moratorium%20drilling%20federal%20courts&st=cse.

[9] Mufson, "Oil Spills."

During the past quarter-century, the rich have gotten a lot richer, and almost everyone else has struggled to maintain what he or she has. The wealthiest 1 percent of Americans now own 47.3 percent of all the country's wealth. In 1980, the richest 5 percent of Americans had 14.6 percent of all income; by 2001, they had 21 percent. The rest of the top 20 percent of wealthiest Americans also gained, but everyone else lost.[92] Turning from shares of income to income that we actually spend, Table 2 provides an eye-opening look. Between 1970 and 2000, before the Bush administration, the average income of the bottom 90 percent of Americans fell by $25 in real terms (that is, adjusted for inflation), whereas the average income of the top 10 percent grew by tens of thousands, and the top

1 percent by hundreds of thousands. These trends of a growing gap between the wealthiest and poorest continued at least through 2007, with the Bush tax cuts that benefited the wealthiest the most.[93] After the 2010 census data are released, we will know specifically how income inequality changed as a result of the recession that began in 2008.[94]

We can look at income and wealth data in different ways, using different years of comparison, but each supports the same general conclusion that the income gap is increasing. In addition, during the past twenty-five years, regulation of corporations has been weakened, health insurance has decreased for millions of Americans, and other holes in our social safety net have been enlarged.

| Table 2 | The Rich Are Getting Richer | | | | | | |

Year	Bottom 90%	90–95%	95–99%	99–99.5%	99.5–99.9%	99.9–99.99	Top 13,400 Households
1970	$27,060	$ 80,148	$115,472	$202,792	$317,582	$ 722,480	$ 3,641,285
2000	$27,035	$103,860	$178,067	$384,192	$777,450	$3,049,226	$23,969,767
Percentage Change	–0.1%	29.6%	54.2%	89.5%	144.8%	322.0%	558.3%

NOTE: Figures are mean individual income in 2000 dollars.
SOURCE: David Cay Johnston, *Perfectly Legal* (New York: Portfolio, 2003). Data from Thomas Piketty and Emmanuel Saez.

It would be inaccurate to charge the campaign finance system with all of these rising inequities. Technological change, advanced education for some, sending jobs overseas, and immigration all have played a part.[95] However, it would be shocking if the tens of millions of dollars flowing to the campaign coffers of our elected officials and the consequent increased access and influence of the wealthiest and most powerful interests in society did not have an impact on public policy, shrinking opportunities for working-class Americans and widening them for wealthy ones. The Obama administration's different legislative agenda, including health care insurance for everyone, college loan policies that provide more for students and less for banks, and regulation of the financial sector, generated significant public anger, partly as a backlash to these changing priorities.

corporate interests an open quid pro quo: they give, and they get to help develop Republican strategy and interests and shape legislation that Republican leaders will support.[97]

Not all of the fundraisers are for campaign contributions, but all involve putting the arm on lobbyists. As one example, before Sen. Ted Stevens (R-Alaska) was killed in an airplane crash, a fundraiser titled "Salute to the President Pro Tempore" was designed to "honor [his] career and public service." The funds were to go to Stevens's foundation to benefit Alaska and thus were both tax exempt (campaign contributions are taxable) and not subject to the limitations of campaign finance laws. But Alaskans at the fundraiser were in short supply. The invitation list included most Washington lobbyists who were concerned about the legislation their groups had pending

Campaign Finance and the Culture of Extortion

It is also important to understand that PAC, corporation, and union contributions to campaigns are products of mutual need. Special interests need access to and the votes of members of Congress and the president, and elected officials usually need large sums of money to win elections. Thus donations are useful to both officials and donors.

Although special interests try to buy access and sometimes votes, members of Congress are not simply victims of greedy PACs and corporations. Indeed, as one observer remarked, "There may be no question that the money flowing into campaign coffers is a crime. But there is a question whether the crime is bribery of public officials or extortion of private interests."[96]

Pressure on corporations and unions is unrelenting. Some members keep lists of PACs that have given to them on their desks as an implicit indication that it is those groups that will have access. Others play one PAC off against another. Tom DeLay (R-Tex.), then the majority leader in the House, was quite open in soliciting funds and promising returns, as we saw in Chapter 6 in the discussion of the "K Street strategy." He offered lobbyists and

In the 1990s, House majority leader Tom DeLay (R-Tex.) told lobbyists that they had "to pay to play."

behind the scenes

The Strings Attached

Since the 1980s, conservatives and corporations have pushed for deregulation of various industries, from airlines to trucking. In the 1990s and early 2000s, they pushed for deregulation of Wall Street financial firms. Although deregulation was driven largely by the Republican agenda, many Democrats also were swept up in the push. One was Charles Schumer, senator from New York and an influential leader within the Senate Democratic caucus. Throughout his career, Schumer had courted Wall Street, and the firms had reciprocated, contributing to his campaigns. When he became chair of the Democratic Senatorial Campaign Committee and responsible for success of the Democratic Senate candidates, he raised more money from Wall Street. His fundraising, coupled with his recruitment of viable candidates and his strategic thinking during the campaign, helped transform the Democrats from a minority to a majority party in the Senate.[1]

Senator Charles Schumer

Over the years, Schumer worked hard to deregulate Wall Street. Like oil in Louisiana, tourism in Florida, and wheat in North Dakota, Wall Street is an important part of New York's economy and a key element of New York City's identity. So Schumer did what senators are expected to do—represent his constituents—and what nearly all senators do—represent his powerful constituents in particular. As a member of the Senate Finance and Banking Committees, he was in a good position to do so.

Of financial deregulation, Schumer said, "I am obsessed with it."[2] He wanted to keep Wall Street the financial capital of the world, rather than seeing the financial firms flee to London or elsewhere. In his view, that meant reducing regulation—for example, restrictions on new forms of financial transactions and requirements for extensive reporting to government watchdogs—and it meant raising barriers to lawsuits against the firms. He also led the effort to limit Security and Exchange Commission (SEC) regulation of credit-rating companies like Standard & Poor's and Moody's, which evaluate the health of corporations and the quality of their stocks. (The credit-rating companies, which were paid by the corporations they were evaluating, ultimately touted the stocks of these corporations as good buys even when the evidence suggested the opposite.)

As long as the economy boomed and Wall Street earned billions for its workers and investors, deregulation seemed like a good idea. But when the economy crashed and a severe worldwide recession ensued in 2008, most analysts blamed financial deregulation for the collapse and pointed their finger at Wall Street as the culprit.[3] In this climate, being out in front as a deregulator was an unpopular position for any official courting middle-class voters or representing the Democratic Party.

Schumer had become a spokesperson for Senate Democrats, and even in a body whose members crave publicity, he had been known for his efforts to be seen and heard on key issues. A senator quipped that "the most dangerous place in Washington is between Charles Schumer and a television camera."[4] Unlike most elected officials, Schumer holds Sunday press conferences. Because Sunday is a slow news day, his words are more likely to get on the air than they would on other days. A colleague called him "the schmoozemeister of the world."[5]

But the voluble Schumer was quiet after the financial collapse and the mounting anger of middle-class voters. Accepting contributions from Wall Street and advocating deregulation of financial firms constrained his actions and his advocacy. As the Democrats put together a financial reform package to rein in financial firms' gambles with their stockholders' money, Schumer was not the point man. Such are the constraints of campaign contributions.

Yet, as a canny politician, Schumer was able to pivot. He began to argue that strong financial regulation is necessary to restore investors' confidence in American markets and maintain New York City's standing as the world's financial capital.[6] Behind the scenes, he worked on the financial reform package with fellow Democrats, and eventually he helped the Democrats break a Republican filibuster blocking the bill.

[1] For background on Schumer and his positions, see Jeffrfey Toobin, "The Senator and the Street," *New Yorker*, August 2, 2010, 51–57.
[2] Ibid., 57.
[3] Ibid., 51.
[4] There were, of course, plenty of other culprits, but as the most prominent financial center, and one that had become untethered from government control, it took the blame.
[5] Sen. Bob Dole (R-Kans.).
[6] Toobin, "The Senator and the Street," 57.

AP Photo/Charles Dharapak

before the Senate Appropriations Committee, of which Stevens was the chair.

In recent years, some corporations, including General Motors, Ameritech, and Monsanto, have said that they do not intend to give more political contributions. Companies such as this should favor campaign finance regulation, which could provide a defense against fundraising pressure.[98]

Campaign Finance and Public Cynicism?

We have seen repeatedly that public confidence and trust in government have diminished greatly over time. Indeed, most of the public believes that most individuals in government are out to feather their own nests (see Table 3) and that many are crooks. Some of the reasons for this low trust have nothing to do with money. But public trust was certainly affected by the Watergate scandal in the 1970s, and it is likely that revelations about big-money lobbying activity reinforce public cynicism and lack of confidence.

American elections are funded, for the most part, by private money. It is therefore not surprising that candidates turn to people who have money to help with that funding. It is also not surprising that the current system alienates voters. Even if we believe that no votes are actually bought, the appearance of conflicts of interest that permeates the existing system and clearly disturbs the public should give pause to those interested in the health of our political system.

For several years after the 1974 reforms, many Americans thought things were going along pretty well. More recently, many people have become convinced that the nation is in terrible jeopardy because of the influence of money. This fear is compounded because money has helped bring about regulatory lapses, which in turn have been partly responsible for failures to check dishonesty in several key industries, including large investment banks and energy companies. So beyond leading Americans to grow cynical about government, which they certainly have, the campaign finance system has indirectly helped lead to a loss of confidence in business, too.

Of course, elected officials appear to be more afraid of being without campaign donations than they are that the campaign finance system will further erode confidence in the whole political system. Ideologically, Democrats are more sympathetic to limiting the influence of big money, but practically, Democratic incumbents are heavily dependent on their PAC "fixes." Thus neither party has much incentive to support campaign finance reform, despite the fact that the public is repelled by the existing system. The Supreme Court's invalidation of much legislation regulating independent groups is also a disincentive to change.

However, a culture of greed cannot sustain itself forever. The two clearest examples of previous eras of rampant corruption in the American political and business systems suggest that they end unhappily. In both cases, at the end of the Gilded Age and the Roaring Twenties, they ended with the failure of thousands of banks and companies and with unemployment and despair. Our own era of corruption has led, so far, to the severest economic decline since the Great Depression.

Table 3	Public Opinion Is Cynical about Government

Percentage of people agreeing that they have a great deal of confidence in . . .	
The military	36%
The church	26%
The presidency	23%
Congress	11%
Big business	7%
Percentage of people who believe . . .	
Government is run by a few big interests	64%
Government is run for the benefit of all the people	28%

NOTE: 2% had no opinion on the first poll and 8% were unsure on the second poll.
SOURCES: Gallup poll of 1002 adults nationwide, margin of error = 3%, May 21–23, 2004; and CBS News and *New York Times* poll of 955 adults nationwide; margin of error = 3%, July 11–15, 2004; both polls online at www.pollingreport.com/institut.htm.

CONFLICTS OF INTEREST

In addition to money's influence on political campaigns and policy making, it also leads to **conflicts of interest**, situations in which officials face decisions that may directly affect their own personal livelihood or interest. The campaign contribution system we have just described, the "honest graft" of the twenty-first century, presents a huge conflict of interest. Presidents and members of Congress make decisions about policies affecting people who give them campaign money. But conflicts of interest are not confined to decisions involving campaign money. As James Madison noted, almost every decision involves potential conflicts of interest. Decisions made by presidents, bureaucrats, and members of Congress can affect their personal financial interests (including stocks, bonds, and other investments).

It is sometimes difficult to untangle the effects of personal financial interests, constituency interests, and party loyalties. For example, most people on the Agriculture Committee have agribusiness interests and represent districts with large agricultural interests. If those members vote in favor of agricultural interests, they are voting both for their own interests and those of their constituents. And they are likely to think that they are advancing the national interest at the same time. It appears that the impact of these personal interests on voting is fairly small once constituency interests are taken into account.[99]

Most members of Congress own stocks, which sometimes seems to present a conflict of interest with legislation. For example, many lawmakers who had key committee positions in the debate over reforming health care held stock in drug companies, home health care, nursing homes, and other corporations with health care interests. Some held millions, some a few thousand.[100] One member had holdings in thirty different health care companies, but these $3–7 million holdings were a small fraction of her overall wealth.[101]

Congress deals with these conflicts by requiring disclosure of financial holdings, including those of spouses. In general, the requirements Congress imposes on itself are less than those imposed on other branches of government and on corporate insiders (officers and members of boards), though Congress does require annual reporting.[102]

Despite periodic attempts to limit conflicts of interest, violations of ethics codes still occur in Congress and in the executive branch. One of the more colorful was in 1981, when six House members and one senator were convicted in an FBI undercover operation. Five were even videotaped accepting cash bribes. In 2006, Rep. William Jefferson (D-La.) was also taped accepting a bribe, and police found a freezer full of bills in his office refrigerator. He was convicted of bribery and sentenced to thirteen years in prison. Another recent former member now residing in prison is Randy "Duke" Cunningham (R-Calif.), who resigned after being sentenced to federal prison for accepting more than $2 million in bribes. Cunningham even went so far as to develop a "menu" of his prices (bribes) for giving corporations the contracts they wanted. For example, he would help a business with a federal contract worth $16 million in exchange for a $140,000 gift.[103] Incidents of blatant bribery such as this are rare, but conflicts of interests are very common.

Despite rules against accepting gifts from lobbyists, lawmakers collectively accept millions of dollars worth of gifts, often in the form of free trips to luxury resorts and other vacation areas. A 2006 report found that, over a five-year period, members of Congress had accepted $50 million for 23,000 free trips. A significant number of trips cost more than $5000 each, and some much more. The report concluded that "while some of these trips might qualify as legitimate fact-finding missions, the purpose of others was less clear."[104] Probably in the latter category were the 200 trips to Paris, 150 to Hawaii, and 140 to Italy. Congressional travelers "pondered welfare reform in Scottsdale, Arizona and the future of Social Security at a Colorado ski resort."[105]

The Abramoff Scandal and Concierge Politics

In 2005 to 2006, investigators uncovered one of the largest conflict-of-interest schemes and other misdeeds in recent memory. Jack Abramoff, the former national chairman of the College Republicans and close associate of Tom DeLay, the majority leader of the House of Representatives, was convicted of several felonies and implicated a wide variety of public officials, staffers, and lobbyists in his schemes.[106] A lobbyist who originally represented clients ranging from the apartheid regime in South Africa to Russian energy companies, Abramoff decided he could make money faster through less orthodox means. As one observer remarked, he decided that "the traditional lobbying practice—charging, like law firms, by the hour—was for chumps. Instead he demanded huge commissions that represented a cut of the enormous sums a big government could provide his clients."[107] Abramoff received funds from clients, such as the Indian tribes fighting to prevent casinos from being legalized on non-Indian property, and promised his clients access to the powerful people in Washington, including the White House. He then distributed the money to favored groups and associates in return for access, or to curry favor with powerful officials and old cronies, or as income to be kicked back to himself. Later some of the Indian tribes sued Abramoff and his associates, accusing them of a "blatant, calculated scheme to defraud a client . . . in a series of kickbacks, misappropriated funds, and unauthorized charges."[108]

Abramoff's dealings, and ultimately crimes, can be viewed in the context of the culture that has developed in Washington. Significant conflicts of interests have always existed, but Tom DeLay's "K Street strategy"—to make it clear to lobbyists that they pay to play (that is, donate money to Republican candidates in exchange for influencing legislation)—has made influence buying more open (see Chapter 6 for more on the K Street strategy). One scholar, a fellow in a conservative think tank, describes the K Street project as a "Tammany Hall operation."[109] Money is kicked into the machine, and favors emerge. Big lobbying firms are expected to hire only Republicans at the top jobs that pay as much as $1 million a year. Once hired, "everyone is expected to contribute some of that money back into Republican campaigns."

Some former colleagues termed DeLay's role as akin to a hotel concierge, calling on favors from these wealthy donors and "arranging corporate jets, private cars, fishing trips and other expense-paid trips during congressional breaks, key votes, and party conventions, all financed by wealthy donors with interests before Congress."[110] Members getting the favors were then expected to come through with appropriate votes on pending legislation.

Abramoff, an early supporter of DeLay's bid for congressional leadership, used the close ties he had developed with DeLay and his key staffers to raise millions of dollars. Potential clients knew that he could use his clout with

DeLay to get things done. After all, DeLay had publicly called him one of his "closest and dearest friends."[111]

Only a little of Abramoff's money went to the White House, as when he charged the Indian tribes $25,000 to gain access for two of their representatives to the president.[112] Most went elsewhere. For example, $2.5 million went to the U.S. Family Network, ostensibly a grassroots organization dedicated to moral improvement, but mostly a front organization to pay the organizer of the group, a former DeLay chief of staff, who in turn hired Tom DeLay's wife at $3200 a month for a job involving little work. Millions more went to Americans for Tax Reform, founded by Abramoff's old colleague Grover Norquist, who then funneled some of those funds to other operatives. The National Center for Public Policy Research, another Abramoff organization, provided funds to take the House majority leader, Tom Delay, and other officials to Scotland. Yet another organization, Capitol Campaign Strategies, run by another DeLay former staffer, received funds from the Indian tribes and kicked back significant amounts to Abramoff. And the American International Center, supposedly a "think tank," was in reality a house in Rehoboth Beach owned by the same former DeLay staffer. This front organization moved money to Abramoff and also to Ralph Reed. Another front organization, the Capital Athletic Foundation, even funneled funds to a sniper school in Israel and an orthodox Jewish school founded by Abramoff.

As of this writing, several people have gone to jail for this scheme, including Abramoff, two former DeLay aides, a member of Congress, and an executive branch employee, the former chief of staff at the General Services Agency (the chief purchasing agency of the government) and then the White House's chief procurement officer. Investigations continue, and others may be charged; Abramoff himself, from prison, cooperated in the investigation. Of course, members of Congress and the Bush White House hurried to disassociate themselves from Abramoff.

Regulating Ethical Behavior

Congress does have an ethics committee in each house, and there are provisions for registering lobbyists. But the ethics committees were nonfunctional until recently and even now are cautious committees. When in 2004 the House Ethics Committee reprimanded Tom DeLay (R-Tex.) three times, the Speaker of the House, Dennis Hastert (R-Ill.), replaced the chair of the committee and several other Republicans with those less interested in an activist committee and more responsive to the Republican leadership.[113] The Senate committee has not investigated any of the recent scandals.

Although, in light of the Abramoff and other 2005 scandals, some members pledged to put new rules in place regulating such travel, nothing was done. In fact, John Boehner (R-Ohio) was elected House majority leader, in part because he opposed any new regulation of such gifts, calling such regulation "childish."[114] Boehner himself took two hundred free trips, worth $157,000,[115] during this five-year period.[116] And he passed out checks from tobacco lobbyists to Republican representatives on the floor of the House.[117] However, perceived widespread congressional corruption and influence peddling were motivating factors for voters in the 2006 election, and the Republicans lost control of Congress.[118]

Although Democrats pledged to raise the ethical standards of Congress, with Speaker Nancy Pelosi (D-Calif.) promising to "drain the swamp" of Washington corruption, they have been embarrassed by some high-profile cases, such as Charles Rangel (D-N.Y.) and Maxine Waters (D-Calif.), both prominent members of the party and the

High-powered lobbyist Jack Abramoff leaves court during his trial for fraud, conspiracy, and tax evasion.

Tom Williams/Roll Call/Polaris

Black Caucus. These cases will go to the House Ethics Committee for adjudication. Rangel has been accused of failing to report income in his disclosure statements to the House; Waters is charged with using her influence to try to get federal aid for a bank where her husband has a significant financial interest. These cases will test whether the Democrats can be effective in carrying out Pelosi's promise.

In the executive branch, decision makers operate under much less direct public and media scrutiny. Yet they, too, may be acting on matters that affect their personal economic position. Since the Carter administration, all high-level administrative officials have been required to file public financial disclosure statements to allow the public to see when they are making decisions that benefit their own financial interests. But the rules do not require officials to step aside on matters that would affect them financially.

It is also a conflict of interest to use one's government position to line up a job following a public service career. The term for using access to powerful people to make money is called **influence peddling**. Former high government officials can and do use their access to former colleagues to win jobs representing clients in business or labor and then use that access to lobby for favorable policies and contracts for their new firms.[119]

The Ethics in Government Act of 1978 tries to regulate this. The act bars former public servants from lobbying their former agencies for a year and, on matters in which they "personally and substantially" participated as public officials, for life. In 2007, the one-year prohibition was extended to two. However, members can still be employed by big lobbying firms, but in positions as "special adviser," until the two years pass. Current employees also are prohibited from participating in decisions affecting interests with which they are negotiating about future employment. But the act is not very stringently enforced.

Because many companies that regularly deal with government think experience in government is an asset, especially experience in the agency that regulates the company's activities, many officials take well-paying jobs in the industry they came to know while in government. Critics call this the "revolving door," referring to the movement of people from government service to the private sector and sometimes back again. Most of the top executives of the Department of Homeland Security, led by Tom Ridge, its first director, have left government service to become executives, lobbyists, or board members for firms now contracting with the Homeland Security agency.[120]

DEMOCRATIC AND REPUBLICAN CORRUPTION

Conflicts of interest and influence peddling are bipartisan phenomena. Most of our examples have pinpointed Republicans because they controlled both branches of government

"Still, you've got to applaud the transparency."

© The New Yorker Collection 2009, Robert Mankoff from cartoonbank.com. All rights reserved.

from 2001 to 2007, and only since 2007, when they won a majority of both the House and Senate, have Democrats been in control of one branch. When the Republicans controlled both branches, those who wanted to buy influence had to buy it from them. But conflict-of-interest accusations also swirled around the Clinton White House. Although no high official was convicted of illegal acts in office, both President Clinton and First Lady Hillary Clinton were accused of conflicts of interest in the long-running investigation of the Whitewater affair (an investment scheme in which they had participated years earlier). They were never found guilty of anything, but a number of Clinton administration members, including a cabinet secretary, left office under an ethical cloud relating to conflicts of interest and influence peddling.

George W. Bush came to Washington saying that the ethical standards of his administration would be higher than those of the Clinton White House, but influence peddling seemed to escalate to a whole new level during his administration. In some cases, corporate interests became part of secret policy-making processes inside the White House in ways never seen before. Halliburton, which Cheney headed from 1995 to 2000, was given advance notice to plan for the postwar period in Iraq and received billions of dollars' worth of contracts without competitive bidding. In 2004, an audit revealed that Halliburton had billed the government for $4.3 billion in reimbursement for work that had cost the company only $1.8 billion (Halliburton's response was that conditions in Iraq made keeping up with paperwork difficult).

Conflicts of interest can never be completely eradicated from government, but presidents can make their expectations clear. George W. Bush's administration seemed less concerned about conflicts of interest than those of his predecessors, Bill Clinton and George H. W. Bush. His administration was intent on privatizing many parts of government, including military support operations, and was unembarrassed about awarding lucrative contracts to top supporters without benefit of competitive bidding.

Some observers have pointed out that although both Democrats and Republicans have ethical lapses, the kinds of ethics problems they have are quite different. Corrupt Democrats steal. They accept bribes and improper campaign donations, divert public funds to their own pocket, and seek personal financial aggrandizement. This style of corruption is reminiscent of the "honest graft" of the big-city political machines (see the box "Honest Graft" earlier in the chapter). Although some Republicans also steal—for example, Abramoff and Cunningham; former vice president Spiro Agnew, who pleaded no contest to charges of kickbacks, bribery, and extortion; and former representative Joseph McDade (R-Pa.), who was convicted of bribery and racketeering—most of these sorts of scandals have involved Democrats. Examples include Daniel Rostenkowski (D-Ill.), former chair of the House Ways and Means Committee, convicted of corrupt acts involving mail fraud, and Robert Torricelli (D-N.J.), censured by his Senate colleagues for accepting gifts from lobbyists.

Republican ethical failings tend to be related to the use of government for improper means. President Nixon's Watergate scandal involved trying to use the powers of government to punish his personal enemies and then lying about it. He also ordered Cambodia to be bombed and tried to keep it a secret. President Reagan tried to subvert the constitutional powers of Congress by secretly selling arms to Iran and supplying weapons to rebels in Nicaragua, both expressly against the law. The Republicans' K Street strategy was basically an attempt to get lobbyists to buy influence over government policies and to buy government contracts in a rather overt way.

Although Democratic presidents have also been guilty of misuse of government power (for example, President Johnson lied about alleged attacks by the North Vietnamese on an American ship to justify getting the United States more deeply involved in the Vietnam War, and President Kennedy ordered the FBI to wiretap Martin Luther King Jr.), subverting government seems more a Republican style of corruption.

Why do these differences exist? They could be coincidental, of course. But one Democrat argued that these differences were tied to the class basis of the parties: "The lower classes steal; the upper classes defraud." A prominent Republican had a different view: "Most Republicans are contemptuous of government; few Democrats are." Whatever the reason, these examples suggest that partisanship extends to more than presidential preferences.

CONCLUSION: Does the Influence of Money Affect the Role of Government

The influence of money in American politics is a perennial source of concern to those who want to live up to the democratic ideals of political equality and popular sovereignty. Our democratic values tell us that government should represent all, the poor as well as the rich, and that everyone should have an equal chance to influence government. We know that, in the real world, things do not work this way. We tolerate much inequality in access because that seems to be the way the world works in the private as well as in the public sphere, because everyone is not equally interested in influencing government, and because for most people the effort of changing this pattern would be greater than the benefits gained.

Nevertheless, our reaction to the influence of money seems to be cyclical. We tolerate it; then, when stories of inside deals, influence peddling, and buying access and even votes become too frequent, we act to do something about it. But that happens rarely, and then we slip back into apathy until the next cycle comes along.[121]

In the recent history of using money to buy access, the historical low points were probably during the Watergate scandals associated with the 1972 election and then again with the scandals swirling around Jack Abramoff in 2005. After 1972, we reacted strongly by passing new laws and cleaning up our campaign finance system. But as the years went by, we found ways to get around the laws until they became nearly meaningless, with the important exception that we know how much money is being given to candidates. In response to the Abramoff scandals, voters apparently decided that the culture of corruption had gone too far and put the Democrats in control of Congress. (And Abramoff and several of his colleagues went to jail.) The controversies over the role of lobbyists in the McCain and Obama campaigns also reflect that we continue to be in an era of substantial concern over ethical standards in government.

We should, of course, put the amount of political money into a larger perspective. After all, it is useful to remember that the more than $1 billion spent by the primary candidates in 2008 is about what Americans spend on chocolate each month.[122] Americans spend $5 billion a year on laundry detergent, car companies spend $1 billion a month to sell their wares, and the federal government spends $1 billion every few hours.[123] But it is not the amount of money in politics as much as its possible effects that concern us.

Neither should we think of our times as the low point in government morality. In political campaigns, big money is certainly less influential than it was a century ago. Campaign funding disclosure legislation means that the public can at least know who is buying influence.

Nor should we conclude that ethical standards are lower in government than in the private sector. After all, some public officials are selling favors, but it is members of the private sector who are buying them. Conflicts of interest and influence peddling in government reflect the ethical standards of the larger society. A good part of the news for the last thirty years has focused on stories of Wall Street bankers who bought and sold illegal insider tips, savings and loan officers who looted their institutions of millions of dollars, military contractors who cheated government, and corporate leaders who falsified corporate income and plundered corporate funds for personal gain while shareholders lost their investments. One businessman lamented, "We are all embarrassed by events that make the *Wall Street Journal* read more like the *Police Gazette*,"[124] and several years later another remarked, "In my lifetime, American business has never been under such scrutiny, and to be blunt, much of it deserved. You pick up the paper, and you want to cry."[125]

But the effects of money are hard to pin down. It is difficult to measure exactly the influence of money on political outcomes. Money sometimes influences votes and policies, campaign contributions have some impact on voting in Congress, and money seems to have moved both parties toward more conservative policies. Money in politics is no doubt responsible for the increased inequality between the rich and poor. But sometimes, especially when the public is paying attention, money appears to have little impact.

We do not know exactly how presidential candidates might be influenced by huge campaign donations or whether bureaucrats are using promises of future jobs as trade-offs for current favors. We think that good candidates are hindered or deterred from running by a shortage of money or even just by the knowledge that they need to raise big money, but it is difficult to measure exactly how many. Even though money is very tangible, its influence sometimes is quite intangible.

To the extent that money has an impact, it limits the responsiveness of government to the average citizen. It causes some policy makers to be more responsive to the big interests than to the average person. This does not mean, though, that those with the most money always win. Organization and a sense of the public interest can sometimes defeat even big money.

It also seems that the campaign finance system contributes both to big government and to big deficits. Most people want low taxes and good government services for themselves and their group. These desires are magnified by interest groups and the campaign finance system. Those carrying these messages have inside access and the power to hurt legislators who do not go along by withholding campaign donations. Very few lobbyists are lobbying for smaller government; most want things from government, and they reinforce that demand by campaign contributions.

In designing laws to regulate the use of money in political life, perhaps the best that reformers can reasonably hope for is a system in which public officials who want to be honest will not feel under pressure to be influenced by money. Certainly, there will always be a few "bad apples," and no political system can protect us completely from them. It should be enough to design rules and structures that ensure that people of average honesty who serve in public office are rewarded for putting the public interest, rather than their private interests, first. Our current laws, especially our congressional campaign finance laws, do not always do that. The penalties we suffer are less in politicians stealing from the public till (relatively little of this occurs, certainly in comparison with the stealing that has been revealed in corporate America). They are more in the loss of public trust, an increasing alienation from government, and anger at politicians who seem to be putting their interests before the public interest. Perhaps, then, even a largely symbolic effort by our legislators to limit the influence of money on the political process is important, because it sends the signal that they are aware of and accountable to public concerns.

Any discussion of campaign finance should include a mention of the role of citizens. Perhaps it is the voters who need a lower tolerance for corruption, higher expectations for the performance of elected officials, and a sense of realism about the complexities of reaching compromises in legislation that affect this vast and complex nation.

KEY TERMS

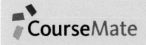 Access an interactive eBook, chapter-specific interactive learning tools (including flashcards, quizzes, videos), and more at CourseMate for *Understanding American Government*. Log in at CengageBrain.com.

10 Congress

○ Responding to the poor economy and vocal opposition to Democratic policies, voters defeated numerous Democratic incumbents and elected a Republican majority to the House of Representatives in 2010.

Talking Points

The Democrats won the 2008 election by running on the promise of change, especially a change in the way things were done in Washington. They widened their margin of control in both the House and the Senate and, by winning the White House as well, ended divided government. It was a time for action.

Eighteen months later, Congress had turned out major legislation with potential for bringing big change, but the governmental process itself appeared no different than before the election. The hyperpartisanship of the Bush years was, if anything, even more hyper.

Almost 80 percent of Americans thought the country was headed in the wrong direction; the same percentage disapproved of the job Congress was doing, and, far more unusual, 60 percent did not think their own representative deserved reelection. Word began to spread long before the 2010 midterm election: it was going to be an anti-incumbent year.

It was nothing new, a political reporter observed. "Americans have been cursing their incumbents—and periodically rising up to eject them from office—since angry Bostonians took a bucket of tar and some feathers to their customs commissioner in 1774"[1] And with a whiff of hot tar in the air again, many of the incumbents seeking reelection began treating 2010 as a time for evasive, not decisive, action.

It was a year for insiders to present themselves as outsiders and to attack broken government. It was a time to distance oneself from the center of power even while standing in the circle. Even the president was talking about how Washington did not work, appearing to mean Congress rather than the branch he headed. But in 2010 everyone was a critic: "My gosh, these people in Washington are running the country right into the ground."[2] The speaker? Sen. Orrin G. Hatch (R-Utah), a thirty-four-year veteran of the House and Senate.

The Founders clearly intended Congress to be the dominant branch of government. The description of Congress and its powers in Article I of the Constitution ⚲ comprises almost half the document. Through its formal powers, Madison believed, Congress would dominate the presidency because it alone had "access to the pockets of the people." But Congress has not always been first in the hearts of the people, nor the most respected or trusted branch of government.

In this chapter, we look at the composition of Congress and how its members get elected, and we offer a few measures for evaluating how representative it is. We describe how Congress is organized and how it carries out its constitutional responsibilities, then look at how individual members carry out their duties in Washington and their districts and explain why such a high percentage get reelected. Finally, we look at Congress's relationship to the other branches of government and to the public.

MEMBERS AND CONSTITUENCIES

In this section we describe who can run for Congress, the terms of service, and the compensation and perks of the jobs. We also explain what is meant by "constituency," the areas and people that members of Congress represent.

Members

Alexis de Tocqueville was not impressed with the status of members of Congress, noting that they were "almost all obscure individuals, village lawyers, men in trades, or even persons belonging to the lower class." His view was shared by another European visitor, Charles Dickens, who was shocked in 1842 to find Congress full of tobacco spitters who committed "cowardly attacks upon opponents" and seemed to be guilty of "aiding and abetting every bad inclination in the popular mind."[3] However one views their behavior, members of Congress were not then, and are not now, a cross section of the American public. But they are a more diverse group than the members of Congresses in the eighteenth and nineteenth centuries ever were or thought they should be.

Who Can Serve?

The Constitution places few formal restrictions on membership in Congress. One must be twenty-five years old to serve in the House and thirty in the Senate. One must have been a citizen for at least seven years to be elected to the House and nine years to be elected to the Senate. Members must reside in the states from which they were elected, but House members need not reside in their own districts. As a practical matter, however, it is highly unlikely that voters will elect a person to represent their district who is not from the district or who does not maintain a residence there. ⚲ Art. I, Sec. 2

Local identity is not as significant a factor in Senate races; national figures such as Robert Kennedy and Hillary Rodham Clinton, who established in-state residency within weeks or months of the election, both ran successful campaigns in New York. It is, however, difficult to imagine that happening in every state or with relatively unknown transplanted candidates.

Length of Service

Every member of the House stands for election every two years, and senators serve six-year terms, with one-third of the membership standing for election every two years. Although the Articles of Confederation did set a limit on the number of terms a representative could serve, the Constitution placed no cap on how many times an individual can be elected to the House or Senate. Perhaps the Founders thought that no one would want to serve more than a few terms. In the late eighteenth and early nineteenth centuries, leaving one's home to serve in Congress was considered a great sacrifice. Washington was a muddy swamp, with debris-filled streets, farm animals running loose, and transportation so poor that almost no one got home during a session. In fact, during Congress's first forty years, 41 percent of House members, on average, dropped out every two years, and in the early 1900s the median length of service for a representative was still only five years.[4]

But as Washington became a power center and a much more livable and accessible city, members were more receptive to longer periods of service. In the 1910s and 1920s, power in the House became less centralized, and individuals were able to build personal power bases. And as seats went uncontested in the one-party South, more legislators became career politicians, spending thirty and even forty years in Congress. These long-serving members began to dominate committee work and to control the legislative agenda. Although they did not comprise a majority of Congress, they were probably foremost in the minds of those Americans who began to see government as increasingly unresponsive to the public.

Term Limits

During the height of public anger with government in the 1990s, there was a nationwide move to limit the number of terms that state and national legislators could serve, and most Americans claimed to favor such limitations in mid-1990s surveys.[5] Although Congress narrowly defeated term-limit legislation, in twenty-three of twenty-four states that allow ballot initiatives, voters adopted term limits for their members of Congress and state legislatures.

Some supporters of term limits believed that by not having to worry constantly about getting reelected, legislators would be free to consider the "public interest" and would have no desire to build personal empires. Others also saw

In its early years, Washington, D.C., was described as "a miserable little swamp." When this photo was taken in 1892, it still retained the look and feel of a small town.

term limits as a way to weaken the power of government, by always having inexperienced legislators. Because legislators would be relative novices, opponents of term limits thought they would weaken Congress at the expense of the special interests and the federal bureaucracy and president.

This debate subsided when in 1995, in a 5–4 vote, the Supreme Court held term limits for members of Congress unconstitutional. The majority argued that permitting individual states to have diverse qualifications for Congress would "result in a patchwork of state qualifications, undermining the uniformity and national character that the framers envisioned and sought to ensure."[6] By adding to the criteria spelled out in the Constitution (age and citizenship), the Court ruled that states were in effect "amending" the Constitution. By definition, then, such laws would be unconstitutional because the Constitution can be amended only through the processes of adoption and ratification it specifies, not by state or congressional laws or ballot initiatives.

By the late 1990s, enthusiasm for term limits in the *state legislatures* had also waned; courts eventually overturned them in four states, and in two others the state legislatures repealed them.[7] By 2010, only fifteen states still had legislative term limits, although the governors of almost all states, like the U.S. president, are term-limited.[8]

Constituencies

The district a member of Congress represents is called a **constituency**. The term is used to refer to both the area within the electoral boundaries and its residents. There are two senators from each state, so each senator's constituency is the entire state and all its residents. Most states have multiple House districts, though seven states (Alaska, Delaware, Montana, North Dakota, South Dakota, Vermont, and Wyoming) have populations so small that they are allotted only a single seat in the House of Representatives. For these "at-large districts," the constituency for the House member is also the entire state. Except for those seven states, every House district must have (in accordance with the one-person, one-vote rule) roughly the same number of residents, so the number of districts in each state depends on its total population.

Except in the single-district states, the geographic size of a constituency is determined by the distribution of the population within the state. In states with large urban populations, several districts may exist within a single city. The logistics of campaigning are thus very different for a representative from New York City, whose district may be as small as 12 square miles, and one from Montana, who must cover the entire state (147,042 square miles).

Reapportionment

Initially, the House of Representatives had fifty-nine members, but as the nation grew and more states joined the Union, the size of the House increased too. Since 1910, it has had 435 voting members, except when seats were added temporarily (while awaiting the 1960 reapportionment) for newly admitted states Alaska and Hawaii. Every ten years, in a process called **reapportionment**, the 435 seats are allocated among the states based on the latest U.S. census. **Art. I, Sec. 2** Since the first Congress, the number of constituents each House member represents has grown from 30,000 to more than 900,000 in the largest district, with the average size being 650,000.

Within a constant 435-seat House, states with fast-growing populations gain seats, whereas those with slow-growing or declining populations lose seats. Since World War II, population movement in the United States has been toward the South, West, and Southwest and away from the Midwest and Northeast. This change has been reflected in the allocation of House seats. For example, from 1950 through 2000, California gained twenty-three seats and New York lost fourteen. Illinois, Wisconsin, Pennsylvania, and Ohio lost House seats after the 2000 census, whereas Arizona, California, Colorado, Florida, Georgia, Nevada, and Texas gained seats. Eastern and midwestern states are on track to continue losing and Southern, Western, and Southwestern states to continue gaining seats after 2010, although, because of a recession-related decline in both legal and illegal immigration, population growth in the southwestern border states has slowed. The census counts all residents, irrespective of legal residency or citizenship, and several of the seat-gaining states are home to millions of undocumented residents. California, for example, has been experiencing a net loss of its native-born population each year and would have shown population loss after the last census if not for the number of undocumented immigrants living in the state.

DEMOCRACY?

Is it democratic to count undocumented residents who are not eligible to vote in determining the number of House seats a state is entitled to? What is the significance for the principle of one person, one vote?

Redistricting

States that gain or lose seats and states whose population shifts within the state (rural to urban or urban to suburban, for example) must redraw their district boundaries, a process called **redistricting**. This is always a hot political issue because the precise boundaries of a district determine the election prospects of candidates and parties. In most states, the state legislature controls the redistricting process, so districts are normally drawn to benefit the party in control of the legislature. A district whose boundaries are devised to maximize the political advantage of a party or a racial or ethnic group is known as a **gerrymander** (see also Chapter 8). This boundary manipulation can result in bizarrely shaped districts, but it also secures political advantage for majority parties in state legislatures. At the same time, boundaries must comply with the Supreme Court ruling that all congressional districts be approximately equal in population.

Before 1960, states were often reluctant to redistrict their state legislative and congressional boundaries to conform to population changes within the state for fear that doing so would endanger incumbents and threaten rural areas whose populations were declining. After decades without reapportioning, some legislative districts in urban areas had nineteen times as many residents as rural districts. When state legislatures, many of which were still dominated by rural representatives, refused to reapportion themselves, the Supreme Court, in *Baker* v. *Carr* (1962), issued the first in a series of rulings forcing states to reapportion their legislative districts.[9] Two years later, the Court required congressional districts to be approximately equal in population, thus mandating the principle of *one person, one vote*.[10] As a result, during the 1960s, most states had to redraw district lines, some more than once. The decisions provoked strong opposition, and a constitutional amendment was proposed to overturn them. But over time the principle of one person, one vote has come to be widely accepted.

Because of the important role state legislatures play in the redistricting process, and increasing technological sophistication, relatively few congressional districts are competitive. Software now available can measure voting patterns down to the block level. This allows legislators, using voter registration records that record party preferences, to draw district lines to create "safe" (noncompetitive) legislative districts for either the Republican or Democratic candidate. After the 1990 state legislative elections, which gave Republicans control of the majority of states, many states drew boundaries favoring Republicans, a factor in the Republicans' victories in 1994. A lack of competitive seats is a serious problem for democratic accountability because fair and competitive elections are the primary way the public exercises authority over government.

Because of the number of open seats in the 2008 election and widespread public dissatisfaction with the direction of the country, there were more competitive races than in recent years, but only about 13 percent of the House seats were seriously contested even then.[11] In 2010, again there were a number of open seats and, because it was an anti-incumbent year, as many as one hundred House seats were considered in play, but the majority of incumbent losses were in marginal, that is, non-safe districts.

After the results of the 2010 census are known, redistricting will begin again; how district lines are redrawn in each state then will depend on which party controls its legislature, and in 2011 the advantage will again be with the Republicans. If one party controls both the legislature and the governorship, it will try to create as many safe seats for its candidates as possible. Redistricting has become such a political battleground that there is growing support in a number of states to take responsibility away from the legislature and put it in the hands of bipartisan commissions, which would be freer of partisan incentives. In 2008 Gov. Arnold Schwarzenegger convinced California voters to pass an initiative doing just that so redistricting is no longer under the control of that state's legislature. An attempt to rollback this reform was defeated on a 2010 ballot initiative, and in two other states voters either passed redistricting powers

Figure 1 | House Incumbents Have Had Secure Jobs in Recent Years

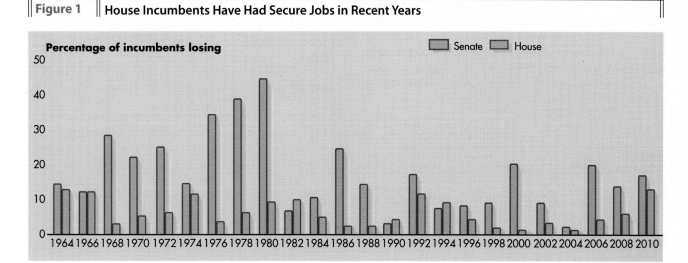

In the 1980s and 1990s, more House incumbents lost in the reapportionment years (1982 and 1991); in the 1970s, most lost in 1974, the Watergate year. In the 1960s, reapportionment occurred both before the 1964 and 1966 election. Senate results do not reflect this cycle because, of course, there is no redistricting of the Senate constituencies. Each senator represents the whole state.
SOURCE: Statistical Abstract of the United States 2004: Center for Responsive Politics (opensecrets.org/bigpicture/reelect.php?cycle=2006). CQ Weekly, November 8, 2010, 2547.

DEMOCRACY?

If gerrymandering is used to make the majority of House seats safe for one party or another, what is the potential for increasing voter apathy and decreasing voter turnout, and how does that affect democracy?

to an independent commission or set standards for the legislature to use when redistricting. The belief is that through such reform voters in more districts would have a choice between candidates, each of whom would have a decent chance of winning, rather than having the district outcome largely predetermined.

Tenure

As congressional seats became ever more safe, congressional tenures became ever longer.[12] The typical member of the House serves about a decade, and in the Senate about thirteen years. In noncompetitive districts, members are almost certain to be reelected (see Figure 1). Whereas in the years just after World War II, each new Congress averaged about seventy-eight new members; there were only fifty-seven freshmen in 2009 as a result of the 2008 elections. Only 6 percent of House members and 14 percent of senators seeking reelection were defeated in primaries or the general election.[13] However, the 112th Congress will have the largest freshman class in two decades (16 in the Senate and at least 93 in the House).

Congress as a Representative Body

To take the measure of how representative Congress is, we first have to establish what *representation* means. During the Revolutionary War, John Adams said that the legislature to be created under the new government "should be an exact

portrait, in miniature, of the people at large, as it should think, feel, reason, and act like them."[14] Benjamin Franklin said simply that Congress should be a mirror of the people. These statements leave unresolved what has priority in representation. Is it more important, for example, for Congress to look like a demographic cross section of the public or to reflect constituents' issue preferences in the policies it advances? And in what situations can elected representatives use their delegated authority to act as their conscience dictates to do what they believe is right or in the national interest, even if not supported by a majority of their constituents?

What Does Representative Mean?

A Congress that reflects the demographic mix of the country is one where descriptive representation is high. This kind of representation is not rooted in what legislators *do* but rather on their personal characteristics—what they *are,* or *are like.*[15] The rise of identity politics has increased demands for a Congress that better reflects the country's demographic profile, and so today it is more likely than ever that a predominantly Hispanic, white, or African American congressional district will be represented by a member of the corresponding ethnicity or race. But Congress is still far from representative in this sense (see the box "Congress Is Not a Cross Section of America").

For the first century of the Republic, the possibility of having citizen-legislators who were a cross section of the general public was just a romantic notion. Only certain landed, business, or professional white men could even think about running for Congress. It was not until 1920 (with ratification of the Nineteenth Amendment, granting women the right to vote) that a majority of Americans could vote, and most of them, realistically, could not stand for office.

Although federal barriers to African American male suffrage had been removed after the Civil War, state laws in the South prevented most from voting until the 1960s. Today, even though adults in all economic categories can meet the minimum requirements needed to stand for office, the demands of the nomination and selection process, especially campaign costs, limit the number of people who are able to run.

"Acting for" Representation

If Congress still has a way to go to *look* like the American public, does it "think, feel, reason, and act" like them? Part of the reason why there has been interest in having Congress look like America is that there is a relationship between a person's sex, race, ethnicity, income, and religious views and that person's position on issues. That is, individuals are

american*diversity

Congress Is Not a Cross Section of America

Congress is not now, and never has been, a cross section of the American population. The citizens who serve in Congress are still disproportionately white and male: white non-Hispanic males, who make up about one-third of the total population, held about 64 percent of the seats in the House of Representatives and 79 percent of the seats in the Senate in 2010. Women, who make up 51 percent of the nation's population, are the most underrepresented demographic group. They were just 18 percent of the House membership and 17 percent of the Senate's in the 111th Congress (see Table 1). Three states (Delaware, Iowa, and Mississippi) have never elected a woman to Congress.[1] Most states do send at least one female representative, however, and California's delegation had twenty-one women in 2010, including both of its senators. Almost one-quarter of all the women in the House were elected by Californians.

Hispanic, Asian, and African Americans are also below parity with their numbers in the population. But thirty-seven of the forty-one congressional districts whose populations are one-third or more African American have elected an African American to represent them.[2]

Congress is also not representative of the range of religious views among the general public. Seventeen percent of the population claims "other" or no religious affiliation, but just 1 percent of congressional members claim no affiliation and only 2 percent adhere to religions other than Christianity and Judaism.[3] However, two Buddhists and the first Muslim were elected to the House in 2006, and a second Muslim was elected in 2008.

Members are much better off financially than the average householder; 172 of 535 members of the 111th Congress were millionaires, and a number were

Table 1	Members of the 111th Congress: Not a Cross Section of the Public (2009–2010)		
	Population (%)	House* (%)	Senate (%)
Women	51	18	17
African American	12	9	1
Hispanic	15	6	3[†]
Asian Pacific	4	2	2
American Indian	1	0.2	0
Lawyer	0.3	38	57
College grad	28	94	99
Millionaires	7[‡]	27	55
Foreign born	14	3[§]	1[§]
Average age	37	57	63.7

*Does not include nonvoting members from Puerto Rico, Guam, American Samoa, the U.S. Virgin Islands, the Mariana Islands, or the District of Columbia.
† Two Hispanic senators resigned during the first session.
‡ The figure is inexact but thought to be between 6 and 7 percent.
§ Does not include those born abroad of American parents, such as John McCain.

SOURCE: Mildred Amer, "Membership of the 111th Congress: A Profile," Congressional Research Service, Report R40086, December 31, 2008, 1–6.

not just interested in having someone look like them, but also want representatives "acting for" them.

Women, African Americans, Hispanics, and Asian Americans are seen as *national* constituencies with distinct issue priorities. House members now organize around these identities so as to represent national constituencies as well as their home districts (see "Making Alliances" later in this chapter). But do women, for example, really represent their constituents differently from their male colleagues? There is no guarantee that any one woman (or African American or Mexican American) will represent women (or blacks or Hispanics) collectively better than, say, a white man; there is no rule that a millionaire will not look out for the interests of blue-collar workers or that a Christian or Jew will not care about the civil rights of a Muslim.

multimillionaires. The 10 wealthiest had net worths in the hundreds of millions.[4] Members also tend to rank well above average in education; nearly all have college degrees, and more than 400 have graduate or professional degrees. Although blue-collar workers constitute nearly one-quarter of the working population, only 17 members of Congress claim blue-collar backgrounds.

The most common occupational background of members has been the law. But this pattern is changing, especially in the House, as legislative careers have become more demanding. Today it is difficult for an attorney to maintain a law practice and also serve as a legislator. Ethics laws requiring financial disclosure and information about client relations have also discouraged practicing attorneys from running for congressional office. Although 57 percent of senators name law as their primary occupation, there are now more House members with backgrounds in public service and business than in law. Twenty-five members, including 16 MDs, have backgrounds in health and medicine, but only 11 were trained in science and engineering.

Increasingly, Congress is drawing its members from professional politicians; in 2009, over half of all House members and 40 percent of senators had served in their state legislatures. Others have been mayors, judges, governors, cabinet officials, ambassadors, and law enforcement officials, and 125 had experience as congressional or White House staffers. Another dent in the citizen-legislator ideal has been the presence of "dynasty" families (the Adamses, Harrisons, Lodges, Kennedys, and Bushes; the 112th Congress will be the first without a Kennedy in fifty years). There were four pairs of siblings (three of them Hispanic) and a father and son in the 110th. The Udall cousins, who represented House districts in Colorado and Arizona and whose fathers served in the House and the Kennedy and Johnson cabinets, both won Senate seats in the 111th.

Members of the Senate are even less a cross section of the American population than the House, but the Senate was established to represent the interests of the states, not to be a mirror of the people. Representation in the Senate is based on a one-state, two-vote standard, not one person, one vote. This structure allows for the overrepresentation of the interests of low-population states and the underrepresentation of the interests of the larger, more urban, and more ethnically and racially diverse states. Senators must define

Representatives Linda Sánchez (left) and Loretta Sanchez, both Democrats from Southern California, are the first sisters in Congress. Linda was also the first unmarried pregnant member of Congress.

and represent state interests in the aggregate, not just those of a specific group or district. This is less complicated for senators from low-population states that are more socially and economically homogeneous, such as Nebraska and Wyoming, than for senators from much larger and more diverse populations and economies such as New York and California. Personal profiles for all members of the 112th Congress, which convenes in January 2011, were not available at the time of writing, but it will be younger, have a higher percentage of whites and Protestants, fewer women and minorities, and more veterans and medical professionals.

[1] A list of all women who have served in the House can be found at www.loc/gov/thomas; those who have served in the Senate can be found at www.senate.gov/artandhistory/history/common/briefing/women_senators.htm.
[2] Unless otherwise indicated, data on members of the 110th Congress are taken from Mildred Amer, "Membership of the 111th Congress: A Profile," Congressional Research Service, Report R40086, December 31, 2008, 1–6.
[3] Estimates of how many Americans have no religious affiliation are from a Pew Research Center survey published June 24, 2008, pewresearch.org. Congressional affiliations are from Amer, "Membership of the 111th Congress," 5.
[4] These are estimates drawn from members' financial disclosure statements; a complete list is posted at opensecrets.org. Members must file statements in May of every year but need only report income and assets within a broad dollar range; so, for example, the net worth of one of the wealthiest members of the House can only be estimated at somewhere between $112 and $377 million.

There is some evidence that our overly broad categories do not capture similarities of interests. For example, first- and second-generation immigrants are not necessarily supportive of those recently arrived or of illegal immigrants. Japanese American, Christian senators from Hawaii are not likely to have the same perspective on the world as newly arrived immigrants from China and India or as Muslim Indonesians or Pakistanis. Rep. John Salazar (D-Colo.), a man whose family emigrated from Spain and helped found Santa Fe in the 1500s (before the Mayflower arrived), does not share many of the same experiences as those who organize today as Hispanic Americans.

There is reason to believe, however, that as women, blacks, Hispanics, and Asians increase their presence in Congress, the likelihood that the issues of greatest concern to them will be heard will also increase. Imagine a Congress made up not of wealthy males but of blue-collar females. It is hard to imagine that the legislation coming out of that Congress would be the same as it is today. Of course, we cannot test that speculation; but as the proportion of women in Congress has increased, so have the number of bills of special importance to them.[16] This suggests that there is a relationship between *descriptive* and *"acting for" representation* and that as the Congress begins to look more like a cross section of the population, legislation may become more representative of the wishes of the broadest segment of the electorate.

One simple measure of "acting for" representation is party identification. About 90 percent of the population either identify in surveys with one of the parties or regularly vote for one or another party. In Congress, Republicans and Democrats hold more than 99 percent of the seats (there are only two independents in the House and two in the Senate, and both Senate independents caucus with the Democrats).[17] (See Figure 2.)

Another measure of "acting for" representation is a legislator's voting record. By casting hundreds of votes each year, members try to represent the interests of their constituencies, bring benefits to the district, and in the

process win support for reelection. Members must consider what benefits their districts as a whole as well as the needs of subgroups within the district, such as party voters, socioeconomic groups, and personal supporters.[18] Overall, if districts are filled with farmers, the members must represent farmers, whether or not they know anything about farming. Representatives of districts with large universities must be sensitive to the reactions of students and professors even if they personally think academics have pointed heads.

To keep in touch with their home districts so that they can pursue policies their constituents favor and vote as they would on issues, most members do spend about half of each year in their districts. On the whole, the member's issue positions are usually not far from those of his or her party or the majority of the constituency *that votes*. But members are more likely to share the issue position of constituents when the issue is important to constituents and when their opinions are strongly held. Since constituents are often uninformed, divided, or apathetic, and most votes in Congress are on bills the electorate knows little about, members can vote their personal issue preferences, with their party, or with those constituents or donors who most forcibly make their positions known.

Voters can send confusing signals, however. At the state level, for example, Iowa, a racially homogenous, conservative agricultural state, sends one Republican and one Democrat to the Senate, where their voting records show an almost 70-point differential on liberal versus conservative positions. Which, if either, is representing the Iowa constituency? Massachusetts voters, who had reelected the liberal John Kerry two years earlier, surprised everyone in 2010 by sending Tea Party favorite Scott Brown to the Senate to replace the late Edward Kennedy, a seat that had not been held by a Republican for sixty years. Sometimes even senators from the same party vary considerably in their policy positions: Arizona

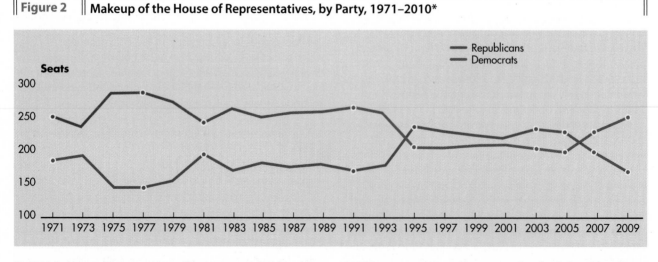

Figure 2 | **Makeup of the House of Representatives, by Party, 1971–2010***

*In 2011 the House of Representatives will be composed of 242 Republicans and 192 Democrats, with one House race still undecided as of this printing.

Senator Charles Grassley faces his constituents in Afton, Iowa. The Republican had been negotiating health care reform with Senate Democrats and President Obama until he felt his constituents' anger in town hall meetings. After a few such meetings he announced his opposition to the reform.

Republican John McCain received a 57 composite conservative score for votes cast in the Senate in 2006 compared to his colleague Jon Kyl's 91.[19]

Constituents are becoming more active in communicating with their legislators, flooding them with phone calls and e-mails, often at the encouragement of radio or television talk shows or interest groups mobilizing their memberships, and now friending them on Facebook as well. These communicative individuals, however, are often not representative of the majority in a member's constituency and tend to hold their positions with greater intensity than the average voter.

Over the past thirty years Congress has become more extreme in its views than the public in general, although there were signs in 2010 that the public was also moving away from the center. Since the mid-1980s the percentage of Americans who identify as centrists, or at the ideological midpoint, has declined from 41 to 28 percent, although this is more pronounced among Republicans than Democrats.[20] At the same time, only small numbers identify as very conservative (6 to 9 percent) or very liberal (4 to 5 percent).[21]

ELECTING MEMBERS OF CONGRESS

Elections determine who gets to represent the rest of us. Because reelection is an important objective for almost all members of Congress and *the* most important objective for many, members work at being reelected throughout their terms.[22] Most are successful, though senators are not as secure as members of the House.

Campaigns

In the nineteenth century, political parties organized congressional and presidential campaigns, and the candidates had relatively little to do. Today, however, congressional as well as presidential campaigns are candidate centered.

Congressional candidates usually hire the staff, raise the money, and organize their own campaigns. They may recruit campaign workers from local political parties, interest groups they belong to, unions, or church, civic, or other voluntary organizations; or they may simply turn to friends and acquaintances.[23]

Political parties do have a significant role, however. National and local parties work hard to recruit potential candidates. Presidents make personal appeals to fellow party members who they think can run strong races, and national campaign committees also recruit aggressively. Said one Democratic congressional campaign chair, "I'm not looking for liberals or conservatives. . . . I'm looking for winners."[24]

Parties redouble their efforts when, as in recent elections, control of Congress is at stake. In 2006, the Democrats, led by campaign chair Rahm Emanuel, worked hard to recruit candidates who would be seen as tough on national security. Thus they made a special effort to recruit those who had served in the military, such as Democrat Jim Webb, who upset incumbent Republican George Allen in Virginia, or who had moderate records, such as Democrat Bob Casey, who defeated conservative Republican Rick Santorum in Pennsylvania. But by looking for the likeliest winners, that is, candidates who can appeal to the broadest segment of the electorate, parties risk ending up with caucus members who are not fully committed to the national party's agenda.

Recognizing the need to make candidates beholden to the party, national campaign organizations have increasingly provided services to congressional candidates—helping them manage their campaigns, develop issues, advertise, raise money, and conduct opinion polls. National party organizations give substantial sums of money to congressional candidates. These developments have pushed our political parties closer to British-style **party government**, a system in which the central party leaders recruit those who run for office and attempt to get all candidates and elected officials to speak with a similar voice and vote along party lines in Parliament.

Congressional Media Campaigns

To wage a serious campaign, the challenger or a contender for an open seat must wage a media campaign. Candidates hire media consultants and specialists in polling, advertising, and fund-raising. Old-style politicians who might have been effective in small groups but who cannot appear poised and articulate on television have given way to those who can project an attractive television image and not embarrass themselves on YouTube. Candidates are elected on the basis of their media skills, which may not be the same skills as those needed to be a good lawmaker.

The Democratic Party recruited moderate, rather than liberal, candidates to run in conservative states. Jim Webb, with his wife, celebrates his election to the Senate from Virginia in 2006. Webb criticized the Iraq War but had a military background, and during the campaign he wore the combat boots of his son, a marine serving in the war.

Campaign Money

An old adage says, "Half the money spent on campaigns is wasted. The trouble is, we don't know which half." This bromide helps explain why congressional campaigns are expensive. There is a kind of "campaign arms race" as each candidate tries to do what the other candidate does and a little more, escalating costs year by year. We examined congressional fund-raising in the previous chapter on money.

The Advantages of Incumbency

Most members are reelected even if they have not done that much for their home districts.[25] In most election years, reelection is almost certain unless the member has been accused of corruption or is involved in a sex scandal. Indeed, one Republican member remarked, "Let's face it, you have to be a bozo to lose this job."[26]

Incumbents believe the best way to ensure victory is to be so good at serving the home district, so successful in getting money for their districts, and so well known to the voters that no serious rival will want to run. Incumbents hope potential rivals will bide their time and wait for a better year or run for some other office.[27]

Given the advantages of office that incumbents have in name recognition and in favors they can do their constituents, you may wonder why they worry about losing. But worry they do. One political scientist proclaimed that members feel "unsafe at any margin."[28] No matter how big their last victory, they worry that their next campaign will bring defeat. And despite the high reelection rate of incumbents, some do lose. This fear prompts members to spend even more of their energies preparing for the next campaign. By some estimates, members spend fully half of their time fund-raising.

For the most part, this fear is misplaced. Turnover in Congress comes primarily from those who decide not to run. Even in the anti-incumbent election of 2010, when nineteen House members and ten senators retired, of those who sought reelection, about 83 percent of senators and 87 percent of House members were re-elected. However, only four of the eleven House members who ran for the Senate were successful.

Unless there is some major mood change in the country at large, House members really do have to offend their constituencies to lose. Most senators are also reelected, but the probabilities of defeat are higher than for the House. In the late 1970s and early 1980s, it was not uncommon for a third of the senators running to be defeated, but by 2008 it was down to 11 percent before rising again to 17 percent in 2010. Still, the electoral benefit of incumbency continues for the great majority of candidates who choose to run for reelection. Voters do have a general impression of the voting habits of their representatives. In fact, voters are more likely to vote for representatives whose votes on major issues reflect their own preferences. In this sense, there is accountability in congressional elections. However,

AP Photo/Ron Edmonds

it usually takes more than voting behavior to drive voters away from well-entrenched incumbents.[29]

Before they even take the oath of office, newly elected representatives are given an introduction to the advantages of incumbency. At meetings arranged by the Democratic and Republican leadership and by the House Administrative Committee, new members learn about free mailing privileges, computers and software to help them target letters to specialized groups of constituents, facilities to make videotapes and audiotapes to send to hometown media, and other "perks" designed to keep members in touch with their constituencies and, not coincidentally, to help win reelection (see the box "Pay and Perks of Office").

Incumbents win because they are better known than nonincumbents. Voters have seen their representatives and senators on television or received mail from them, and they can give a general rating of their performance.[30] Although most voters can correctly identify their representatives and senators as liberal or conservative, only a small minority know how these legislators voted on any issue. Therefore, incumbents have the advantage of name recognition without the disadvantage of having voters know how they actually cast their votes on most pieces of legislation.

Incumbents' high level of public recognition is not so surprising given that members of Congress spend much of their time and energy looking for and using opportunities to make themselves known to their constituents. Members spend half or more of their days in their district, making an average of thirty-five trips home a year—at taxpayers' expense.[31] Congress is recessed during major holidays, part of the summer, and prior to elections—the House and Senate often do not meet at all in August, a month designated as a "District [or State] Work Period."

What are the specific advantages that members have as incumbents?

Casework

Arguably the main advantage of incumbency is the opportunity that being in office gives representatives to perform services and do favors for their constituents. Members send constituents calendars, U.S. flags that have flown over the Capitol, and publications of the federal government. This is one of the best ways members of Congress have to make themselves known in their districts and to create a kind of patron-client relationship. You will not read about this in the Constitution, where the duties of Congress are defined. But in practice, electoral politics has meant that members must spend a great deal of their time serving the specific interests of their districts, which are not necessarily synonymous with the interests of the nation as a whole. Members take this aspect of their representational responsibilities very seriously because it is their own constituents who will reelect them—or not.

In the decade between 1997 and 2007, the amount of mail received by the House and Senate jumped from just over 30 million pieces per year to more than 490 million pieces, most of it e-mail. Looked at another way, the average member gets nearly 1 million pieces of mail a year! The work of answering questions and doing personal favors for constituents who write or call for help is called **constituency service** or **casework**. More than 30 percent of senators' staffs and almost half of all representatives' staffs are located in their home state or district offices to better serve constituents.[32]

Congressional staff function as red-tape cutters for everyone from elderly citizens having difficulties with Social Security to small-town mayors trying to get federal grants for new sewer systems. They provide information to students working on term papers, people looking for federal jobs, citizens puzzled about which federal agency to ask for assistance, or residents trying to get information about a relative in the military. Typically, responsibility for mediating with federal agencies is divided among the casework staffers by issue area, allowing them to specialize and resolve constituents' problems—passports, immigration, Social Security payments, and the like—more efficiently.

Of course, not all casework is directed toward winning reelection. Some members say they enjoy their casework more than their policy roles, perhaps because the results of casework are more immediate and tangible. Individually, they may have limited power in trying to get important legislation passed, but in dealing with a constituent's problems, their power is much greater because of their clout with bureaucrats. A phone call or letter to a federal agency will bring attention to the constituent's problem. And casework does allow members to build nonpartisan and seemingly nonpolitical ties with their constituents.

Mailing Privileges

For the 112th Congress, taxpayers will provide more than a half billion dollars for office and franking expenses (mailing costs).[33] The franking privilege is a great asset of incumbency because it allows members to write their constituents without paying for postage out of pocket or using campaign funds. (The frank is a facsimile of the member's signature, and it works like metered mail, with the frank appearing where the stamp would be.) It is not free; Congress pays the postal bill at the end of each year. How much each House member is allowed is determined by the number of residential addresses in his or her district, but the value of the frank has been estimated as equivalent to $350,000 in campaign contributions.

The frank helps each member increase name recognition (and newly elected members can begin using the frank immediately, even before they are sworn in). Much of the time, the frank is used to send constituents material they have requested, such as government forms or publications, and this too increases a member's name recognition. But members can also send out newsletters that inform constituents of their work for the district or to survey constituents'

PAY AND PERKS OF OFFICE

The first members of Congress made $6 a day, which paid for boardinghouse accommodations, firewood, candles, their meals, and a mileage allowance for travel to and from the capital.[1] Today members receive a handsome salary, generous benefits, and money for office, staff, mailing, and travel.

Personal Benefits

Salary

Congress has indexed members' pay to inflation so that members no longer have to vote directly each session on increases unless they want to refuse them. Congress did elect to freeze its pay for 2010 and 2011, when salaries stood at $174,000. The Speaker gets an additional $49,500 and the Majority and Minority Leaders in both chambers another $19,400 over the base pay. On retirement a Speaker is entitled to more than $800,000 in expenses annually (for such things as office and staff, cell phone, Internet and satellite television services, and car leasing) for up to five years.

Health Care

For a modest monthly premium (about one-third of its cost), members can opt for one of several first-class private health care plans and can seek free outpatient care at one of two military hospitals. Taxpayers spend millions more each year to keep five doctors and fourteen nurses on site at the Capitol's Wellness Center, which also houses a pool and gymnasium, in nearby congressional office buildings.

Pensions

Members of Congress have four pension plans to choose from and can begin collecting them as early as age fifty if they have served at least twenty years. An average congressional pensioner in recent years would collect about $61,000.[2]

Should members find themselves under criminal investigation, they can be reassured that only certain felony convictions will prevent them from receiving benefits. The law was tightened in 2007 to deny benefits to those convicted of perjury, bribery, or fraud, but as many as twenty members with felony convictions before 2007 have been able to collect retirement benefits, some while in prison.

Benefits That Help Reelection Chances

Office and Clerical Support

Representatives are authorized to hire up to eighteen staff members out of their member's representational allowance (MRA), about $1.5 million on average per year. Salaries take up almost two-thirds of the MRA; the remainder is for mailing, travel, and office expenses. (Members keep one or more offices in their districts.) Senators' annual allowances vary with the population of their states and range from $3 to almost $5 million, including staff, mailing, travel, and office expenses. Senators from more populous states might have as many as thirty clerical and administrative workers on staff, but no senator can hire more than three legislative aides.[3] However, members who serve as committee chairs or in leadership positions are allowed additional staff and more for expenses.

Other Perks

Members of Congress enjoy many other perquisites, including subsidized travel abroad, subsidized meals in the Senate and House dining rooms, free parking in Washington and at airports, free car washes, and a child care center.

A Final Benefit

Taxpayers fund life insurance policies and a death benefit equal to a year's salary for each member of Congress. (In 2011 a death benefit of $174,000 will be paid to the widow of Sen. Edward Kennedy.) And if a legislator so desires, the sergeant-at-arms will arrange for an undertaker to plan the member's final journey.

[1] Per diem and travel allowances for the first members were verified in 2002 when Senate custodial staff found an eighteenth-century ledger with payment accounts.
[2] Patrick J. Purcell, "Retirement Benefits for Members of Congress," Congressional Research Service, Report RL30631, February 9, 2007, 1–13.
[3] Ida A. Brudnick, "Congressional Salaries and Allowances," Congressional Research Service, Report RL30064, October 28, 2009, 1–3.

issue positions. These mass mailings cannot be sent out within sixty days of elections, however. Nor can the frank be used to send personal correspondence to constituents or to ask them for their vote or a campaign contribution.

The overall use of the frank has declined by about two-thirds over the past twenty years. Partly this reflects tighter regulation of its use, and partly it reflects a massive increase in various forms of electronic communication. But its use remains

Media and Technology Advantages

Matching the increasingly sophisticated means that members have for communicating with constituents are the production equipment and technology available to them to make television and radio shows to send home. Constituents may see or hear stories about their representatives on local television and radio news programs produced in congressional studios by the representatives' own staff and paid for out of campaign or party funds. Members like to tape themselves at committee meetings asking questions or being referred to as "Mr. (or Madam) Chairman" (many members chair at least a subcommittee). The tape then is edited to a thirty-second sound bite and sent to local television stations. Often stations run these productions as news features without telling their viewers that they are essentially self-promotion pieces prepared by the members. Congressional staffers also write press releases about the accomplishments of their bosses and fax them to local newspapers, which often print them as written.

Every member of Congress has an official website. Though it focuses on congressional business and cannot be used to solicit funds or do campaigning, it provides voluminous information about the member. Typical websites allow constituents to ask for help or order American flags that have flown over the Capitol, and they have a section for press releases, information about the member's policy positions, and perhaps headlines about what the member has done for her district or state lately.

Fund-raising

As we have discussed in the previous chapter, incumbents have advantages in fund-raising. Committee assignments are also extremely important in fund-raising. If a member wins a seat on one of the powerful "juice" committees—one that considers legislation important to big-money interests or that appropriates money—the chances of attracting large campaign donations are greatly increased.

Pork-barrel Funding

Incumbents can gain the attention of or curry favor with constituents by obtaining funds for special projects, new programs, buildings, or other public works that bring jobs, benefits, and business to their districts or states. Such benefits are widely known as **pork-barrel projects**. A pork feature of virtually every annual budget is money for yet another bomber, fighter plane, weapon, or military construction project the Pentagon has not requested. Universities are also perennial winners in the pork sweepstakes, receiving several billion dollars for campus projects.

Because members consider pork-barrel projects crucial to their reelection chances, there is little support in Congress for eliminating projects most know to be unwise or wasteful. David Stockman, director of the Office of Management and Budget during the Reagan administration, observed, "There's no such thing as a fiscal conservative when it comes to his district."[34] Liberals and conservatives, Democrats and Republicans, protect these kinds of projects. (For more on pork-barrel projects, see "Budget Making.")

Voting for Congress

In Chapter 8, we reviewed the impact of parties, issues, and candidates on voting choices. The same factors influence voting choices in congressional races.

Party loyalty, candidate evaluations, and issues are important factors in congressional elections just as in presidential ones.[35] Party loyalty is even more important for congressional than for presidential elections because congressional elections are less visible, so more people base their vote on party identification. Incumbency is also much more important than in presidential races. The result is that increasingly, since about 1960, voters have split their tickets in voting for presidential and congressional candidates. In 2010, with the public unhappy with government in general and Congress in particular, 60 percent of Americans said they preferred a **divided government**, that is, one in which one party controls the White House and another controls one or both houses of Congress.[36] This has been the case in many recent Congresses; Bill Clinton had to deal with a Republican majority in both houses during most of his presidency, George W. Bush had to work with a Democratic majority in each house after the 2006 midterm elections, and Barack Obama will have to work with a Republican House in the second half of his first term.

HOW CONGRESS IS ORGANIZED

An institution with 535 voting members that must make thousands of policy decisions every year without benefit of a unified leadership is not likely to work quickly or efficiently.[37] Like all organizations, legislatures need some structure to be able to accomplish their purposes. Congress does have both a leadership system and a committee structure, but each is organized along party lines. Alongside this partisan organization exist many other groups—special interest caucuses, coalitions, work and study groups, and task forces—whose membership cuts across party lines or reflects the division of interests within party caucuses. Some of this micro-organizing is a means of bypassing the

"There's nothing wrong with you, Steve—it's just you're the incumbent."

Sen. Blanche Lincoln (D-Ark.) celebrates her narrow victory in the primary election in 2010. Lincoln defeated a Democrat running to her left in the primary, but she lost to a Republican running well to her right in the general election.

committee system that dominates Congress's legislative and oversight functions.

The Evolution of Congressional Organization

The Constitution calls for the members of the House of Representatives to select a **Speaker of the House** to act as its presiding officer and for the vice president of the United States to serve as president (or presiding officer) of the Senate. Art. I, Sec. 2 & 3 But the Constitution does not say anything about the powers of these officials, nor does it require any further internal organization. So little about the Speaker is specified in the Constitution that there is no requirement that the position even be held by a member of the House.

The first House, meeting in New York in 1789, had slow and cumbersome procedures. For its first several sessions, Congress's legislative work was accomplished by appointing ad hoc committees. By the Third Congress, there were about 350 committees, and the system had become too unwieldy. Soon permanent committees were created, each with continuing responsibilities in one area, such as taxes or trade.[38]

As parties developed, the selection of the Speaker became a partisan matter, and the Speaker became as much a party leader as a legislative manager. The seventh Speaker, Henry Clay (Whig-Ky.), who served ten of the years between 1811 and 1825, transformed the Speakership from a ceremonial office to one of real leadership. To maintain party loyalty and discipline, he used his powers to appoint committee members and chairs. Under Clay's leadership, the House was the dominant branch, but its influence declined when it, like the rest of government, could not cope with the divisiveness of the slavery issue. At the time it was said that "the only people in Congress who are not carrying a revolver are those carrying two revolvers."[39] By 1856, it took 133 ballots to elect a Speaker. Many physical fights broke out on the House floor; duels were held outside.[40]

The Senate, a smaller body than the House, was less tangled in procedures, less rule-bound, and more effective in its operation. Its influence rose as visitors packed the Senate gallery to hear the great debates over slavery waged by Daniel Webster (Mass.), John C. Calhoun (S.C.), and Clay (who had moved from the House). During this era, senators were elected by state legislatures, not directly by the people. Art. I, Sec. 3 Thus they had strong local party ties and often used their influence to get presidential appointments for home-state party members. But the Senate, too, became ineffective as the nation moved toward civil war. Senators carried arms to protect themselves as debates over slavery turned to violence.

After the Civil War, with the presidency weakened by the impeachment of Andrew Johnson, strong party leadership reemerged in the House, and a period of congressional government began. Speaker Thomas Reed (R-Maine), nicknamed "The Czar" by his colleagues, assumed the authority to name members and chairs of committees and to chair the **Rules Committee**, which decided which bills were to come to the floor for debate. A major consequence of the Speaker's extensive powers was greater party discipline. Members who voted against their party might be punished by a loss of committee assignments or chairmanships.

At the same time, both the House and the Senate became more professional. The emergence of "national" problems and a proactive Congress made a congressional career more prestigious. Prior to the Civil War, membership turnover was high; members of the House served an average of only one term; senators, only four years. After the war, the strengthening of parties and the growth of the one-party South, where Democrats controlled virtually all elective offices, made reelection easier, thus offering the possibility of a congressional career.

This desire for permanent careers in the House produced an interest in reform. Members wanted a chance at choice committee seats and did not want to be controlled by the Speaker. Resistance against the dictatorial practices of Reed and his successor, Joseph Cannon (R-Ill.), grew. Cannon, more conservative than many of his fellow Republicans, used his powers to block legislation he disliked, to punish those who opposed him, and even to refuse to recognize members who wished to speak. In 1910, there was a revolt against "Cannonism," which had become a synonym for the arbitrary wielding of the Speaker's powers.

The membership voted to remove the Speaker from the Rules Committee and to strip him of his authority to appoint committees and their chairs. The revolt weakened party influence because discipline could no longer be maintained by the Speaker's punishment of members through loss of committee assignments. And it gave committees and their chairs a great deal of independence from leadership influence.

The Senate also was undergoing a major reform. As part of the Progressive movement, pressure began to build for the direct popular election of senators. The election of senators by state legislatures had made many senators pawns of special interests—the big monopolistic corporations (called trusts) and railroads. In a day when millionaires were not as common as now, the Senate was referred to as the "Millionaires' Club" because that is whose interests senators were thought to represent.

Not surprisingly, the Senate first refused to consider a constitutional amendment providing for its direct election, although in some states popular balloting on senatorial candidates took place anyway. Finally, under the threat of a call for a constitutional convention, which many members of Congress feared might lead to other changes in the Constitution, a direct-election amendment was passed in the House and Senate in 1912 and ratified by the states a year later. 🔑 **Seventeenth Amendment** These reforms of the early twentieth century dispersed power in both the House and the Senate and weakened leadership. House members no longer feared the kind of retribution levied by Speaker Cannon on members who deviated from party positions. In the Senate, popular elections made senators responsive to the diverse interests of the electorate rather than to party leaders.

Contemporary Leadership Positions

The Speaker of the House is the only leadership position specified in the Constitution. Other leadership positions came into being with political parties, and the Founders did not anticipate institutionalized national political parties.

House Leadership Positions

The leaders of each party are selected by their respective members sitting in caucus—meeting as a group to conduct party business. **Party caucus** refers both to party meetings and to the party members collectively (alternatively known as the party conference). The House Republican caucus (or conference), for example, consists of all Republicans serving in the House, and the Democratic caucus (or conference) consists of all Democratic members. When independents or third-party members are elected to the House, they can ask to caucus with one of the major parties.

The full House must elect the Speaker of the House, as specified in the Constitution, but it is a straight party-line vote, so the real selection is made in the majority party's caucus. Once elected, the Speaker becomes second in line to succeed to the presidency, after the vice president (provided the Speaker is not foreign-born). The Speaker's institutional task is to act as presiding officer and to see that legislation moves through the House.

Party leadership positions in the House, which have evolved through practice, include a majority leader, a minority leader, and majority and minority whips. The **majority leader** is second in command to the Speaker and is officially in charge of the party's legislative agenda (since the Speaker is technically an officer of the House, not of her party). The majority leader, working with the Speaker, also schedules votes on bills. The **minority leader** is, as the name suggests, the leader of the minority party. **Whips** originated in the British House of Commons, where they were named after the "whipper in," the rider who keeps the hounds together in a fox hunt. This aptly describes the whips' role in Congress. Party whips try to maintain contact with party members, determine which way they are leaning on votes,

Vitriolic exchanges are not a new phenomenon in Congress. Here is a fight in the House in 1798. After Rep. Matthew Lyon (Vt.) spit on Rep. Roger Griswold (Conn.) and the House refused to expel Lyon, Griswold attacked Lyon with a cane. Lyon defended himself with fire tongs as other members looked on—with some amusement, it seems.

Library of Congress

and attempt to gain their support. Assisting the majority and minority whips are a number of deputy and assistant whips who keep tabs on their assigned state delegations.

Party organization in the House also includes committees that assign party members to standing committees, work out the party's stance on major policy issues, plan legislative and campaign strategies, and allocate funds to party members running for reelection.

Because the Speaker has become more a party than an institutional leader, he or she is expected to use the Speakership to maximize partisan advantage in committee and staff appointments and to secure the passage of measures put forward by the party or the president, if the majority party also controls the White House. For this reason, the person selected usually has been someone who has served in the House a long time and is a skilled parliamentarian who can negotiate compromises and put together legislative majorities.

Trying to win partisan support is often difficult, but the Speaker has some rewards and punishments to dispense for loyalty and disloyalty. Speakers have a say in who gets to sit on which committees, which committees will be given jurisdiction over complex bills, what bills will come to the House floor for a vote and under what rules they will be considered, and how their party's congressional campaign funds are allocated. The Speaker also decides who will be recognized to speak on the floor of the House and whether motions are relevant. She has the authority to appoint members to conference and select committees and to control some material benefits, such as the assignment of extra office space. Speakers also have the power to name the chair of the Rules Committee and all of their party's members on the committee. Despite these formal powers, the Speaker must be persuasive to be effective and also attentive to the reelection needs of members of the party caucus. As one veteran legislator has described the Speaker's role, "It's all about your caucus. Never, ever, use your power to twist the results. . . . The Speaker must be empowered at all times to make the call. But you must be sure that your decisions don't cost you and your membership the majority."[41]

In modern times, the only Speaker to attempt the level of control achieved by such strong predecessors as Reed and Cannon was Newt Gingrich (R-Ga.). Before his election in 1995, Gingrich had been the intellectual and tactical leader of conservative House Republicans. Like other Speakers who were too controlling, Gingrich met with rebellion in his own party, had to fight back a challenge to his leadership in his third year, and resigned his House seat after his fourth year as Speaker. Gingrich's demands for party discipline in support of a national legislative program (Contract with America) undercut the power of committee chairs and also left many members with too little flexibility to respond to their constituencies, which risked their chances for reelection. This is one reason why an ideological moderate with a conciliatory manner is often sought for the Speaker's position.

When Nancy Pelosi (D-Calif.) became Speaker in 2006, she promised to be a leader of the House, not of her party: to push for ethics reform and open up the legislative process. But Pelosi was born into a political family and had been a party fund-raiser and organizer long before she ran for Congress. She almost immediately was seen as a party rather than an institutional leader, though her technique has been quite different from Gingrich's rigid ideological approach and insistence on party unity. Pelosi took on a high-profile role as party spokesperson in the two years before the Democrats won the White House. But as chief head counter she was, unlike Gingrich, willing to bend to the issue needs of more conservative caucus members, especially new members, in order to get as many reelected as possible. As one of the more conservative members of her caucus said, "She's a very practical, tough strategist who knows what people can and what they can't do."[42] Or, as a House ally said, "she's recognized from Day One that you have to find the center of gravity in your caucus."[43] Giving maneuvering room to Democrats from more conservative or closely contested districts on hot-button issues like gun control, abortion rights, and the Iraq War was made easier for Pelosi in 2009 when she was handed a seventy-nine-seat advantage over the Republicans (59 percent of the House). When conservative Democrats had to break ranks to vote with the Republicans, Pelosi could still corral the simple majority needed to pass bills from within her own caucus. Her successor as Speaker will have about a fifty-vote margin to work with in organizing a caucus with issue differences similar to those Pelosi had to manage.

By being attentive to the district needs of all caucus members, Pelosi built loyalty and increased the chances of achieving consensus on party votes. She used this to shepherd through the House almost every major piece of legislation backed by the Obama administration, including a health insurance bill that neither she nor the majority in her district favored. (They preferred the "public option," a government-run insurance program.) These successes were mostly lost on the public because most of a Speaker's work is done behind closed doors and because many of the bills that passed the House never made it through the Senate. It illustrates why the Speakership is fundamentally an institutional position and why effectiveness in the role is judged internally. "The complexity and minutiae of legislation have never been widely understood or celebrated," a House member said in explaining Pelosi's low public approval ratings. In her fourth year as Speaker, Pelosi was being ranked among the great floor leaders, some saying she had become the most powerful Speaker since Cannon in 1911.[44] Even after the huge House losses in 2010 Pelosi was retained as Democratic leader, (thus becoming the House Minority Leader in 2011), an indication of how effective her legislative leadership was regarded within her own caucus.

Senate Leadership

The Senate has no leader comparable to the Speaker of the House. The vice president of the United States is formally the presiding officer and could attend and preside any time he chooses; part of his expense allowance is designated for Senate work. In reality, the vice president attends infrequently and has relatively little power. However, when sitting as Senate president, he is allowed to cast the tie-breaking vote in those rare instances when the Senate is evenly split. **Art. I, Sec. 3** Therefore, whenever a head count predicts the chance of a deadlocked vote on an important bill, the vice president shows up to preside, as Joe Biden did when the Senate voted on the controversial health insurance reform bill in 2010. Consistent with the Bush administration's hands-on legislative strategy, Richard Cheney was an active presence on Capitol Hill during his tenure as vice president, making regular trips to his office just off the Senate floor and holding weekly lunches with Republican senators.

The Senate has an elected president pro tempore, by tradition the senior member of the majority party. It is an honorific post with few duties except to preside over the Senate in the absence of the vice president. In practice, during the conduct of routine day-to-day business, presiding duties are divided among junior senators. This releases the senior member from boring work while giving the Senate's newest members a chance to learn the rules and procedures.

As in the House, both parties also elect assistant floor leaders and whips to help maintain party discipline. These are important, if not essential, positions for working one's way into the top leadership in both the House and the Senate.

The position of Senate majority leader was not created until 1911 and has often been held by individuals of no particular distinction in their parties. The office has none

of the Speakership's potential for control of chamber proceedings. A congressional watcher once said the majority leader "is often more a coat-check attendant than a maitre d' or chef."[45] The instances of powerful majority leaders are few, the most notable being Lyndon Johnson (D-Tex.). He assumed office at a time when the Democrats had a slim hold on the Senate, giving him an opportunity to exercise his extraordinary powers of personal persuasion to keep party members in line on key votes. Johnson's reputation was made through a combination of his forceful personality and mastery of the legislative process (he had been a staff aide to the House Speaker and then served in the House before election to the Senate). He made it his business to know everything about his colleagues—"what they drank, where their wives wanted to go on junkets, whether they had a mistress" or were "happy with their parking space [and] what the interests and needs of their constituents were." Acquiring this information and being "ruthless" in using it made him, by one estimation, the "greatest vote counter ever in Congress."[46] There is nothing inherent in the office to give a majority leader the power Johnson had, and no one has had it since.

The Senate majority leader is a spokesperson for his (no woman has ever held the position) party's legislative agenda and is supposed to help line up members' votes on key issues. But procedurally, the Senate is a free-for-all compared to the House, with "every man and woman for him- or herself."[47] At least two former majority leaders, Howard Baker (R-Tenn.) and Trent Lott (R-Miss.), described the job as "herding cats"; Lott even wrote a book with that title about his time in the Senate.

© George Tames/The New York Times/Redux

As Senate majority leader, Lyndon Johnson (D-Tex.), shown *(left)* with Sen. Theodore Green (D-R.I.), "used physical persuasion in addition to intellectual and moral appeals. He was hard on other peoples' coat lapels." If the man he was trying to persuade was shorter, Johnson would "move up close and lean over." If the man was taller, Johnson would "come at him from below, somewhat like a badger." Quotes are from Eugene McCarthy, *Up 'til Now* (New York: Harcourt, 1987).

One observer attributes the chamber's resistance to modernization and reform to "its anti-majoritarian and unbounded quality, its free play of antique egos, its cluttered toolbox of little-used procedures."[48] Unlike the Speaker of the House, the Senate majority leader cannot control the terms under which a bill is considered on the floor; instead, rules are assigned by unanimous consent agreements after negotiations with other senators and a bill's floor managers.

The majority leader also has little power to stop a filibuster—a procedural maneuver that allows a minority to block a bill from coming to the floor by monopolizing the session with nonstop speeches. This means that a majority leader needs to do much more than keep his own party in line to keep legislation moving through the Senate. He can influence the general atmosphere of deliberation in the Senate by adopting an approach to working with the minority party that is either conciliatory or partisan. But whether he chooses a more traditional conciliatory and clubby approach or a more aggressively partisan approach, the majority leader must be less strident than a Speaker like Gingrich because that would never be accepted in the more egalitarian atmosphere of the Senate. As former senator Arlen Specter said, "Senators don't get here to be pushed around."[49] If senators see themselves as less subject to central discipline, it is in part because there are only one hundred of them, and at any given time, a number of them aspire to or are actively running for the presidency.

The Senate minority leader's job is similar to that of the majority leader in that its effectiveness depends on a limited package of incentives and procedural ploys to enforce party discipline. Historically, the Senate's majority and minority leaders have worked closely together to conduct Senate business. But if either or both are seen as overly partisan, or more interested in personal political ambitions than in running the Senate, it can weaken the collegial relationship and slow the legislative process. One more sign of the deterioration of cross-party cooperation in the Senate is that majority and minority leaders have gone out on the campaign trail to defeat their counterparts in their reelection bids, something unheard of under old rules of collegiality.[50]

Both the majority and minority leaders must articulate their parties' issue positions and try to win support for bills supported by their parties. Fulfilling this duty is tricky if either leader has presidential aspirations because he must carve out issue positions that distinguish him from other senators in his party who are also seeking the nomination.

In representing the party, Senate leaders also may undercut their political viability at home if their constituents are more conservative or liberal than the leadership of the national parties. In 2004, minority leader Tom Daschle (D-S.D.), a high-profile spokesman for party positions that were more liberal than those held by his constituents, became the first Senate party leader in fifty-two years to lose a bid for reelection.

Harry Reid (D-Nev.), who succeeded Daschle as minority leader and who became Senate majority leader in 2007, had to

Senate majority leader Harry Reid (D-Nev.) and Senate minority leader Mitch McConnell (R-Ky.) usually went in opposite directions. Reid tried to pass legislation proposed by President Obama and Democratic colleagues, while McConnell tried to block virtually all of the proposals.

walk the same fine line. Also a Democrat from a Republican state, Reid was more conservative (an opponent of abortion rights, for example) than the mainstream of his party. As the spokesman for the more liberal Senate Democratic caucus, he risked his own reelection. This contrasts with the situation faced by his counterpart in the House: Speaker Pelosi frequently has to defend Democratic caucus positions that are more conservative than her own or those of her very liberal San Francisco district. The difference is that Pelosi has a safe seat, one she typically wins with 60 to 70 percent majorities. In 2010, despite approval ratings in the low thirties, Senator Reid won reelection to his Nevada seat, thanks to a Tea Party opponent who ran to the right of most Nevada Republicans.

Committees

Much of the work of Congress is done in committees. Observers of American politics take this for granted, yet the power of legislative committees is rare among Western democracies. In Britain, for example, committees cannot offer amendments that change the substance of a bill. In our Congress, the substance of a bill can be changed in committee *even after its passage* by both chambers.

The division of labor provided by committees and subcommittees enables Congress to consider a vast number of bills each year. If every member had to review every measure in detail, it would be impossible to deal with the current workload. Instead, most bills are killed in committee, leaving many fewer for each member to evaluate before a floor vote. Committees also help members develop specializations. Members who remain on the same committee for some time gain expertise and are less dependent on professional staff and executive agencies for background information.

Standing Committees

In the 111th Congress there were twenty **standing committees** in the House and sixteen in the Senate. Each deals with a different subject matter, such as finance or education or agriculture. Each has a number of subcommittees, totaling more than one hundred in the House and about seventy-five in the Senate.[51] The number of committees and subcommittees fluctuates, declining during years of reform and cost-cutting and increasing during years of government growth. During the George W. Bush administration, as government grew, with a new cabinet department and two new intelligence agencies, so did the number of congressional committees.

The number of seats on any committee also can change from one session to another as party caucuses try to satisfy as many of their members' preferences as possible. Standing committees vary in size from ten to seventy-five members in the House and from six to twenty-nine in the Senate. Party ratios—the number of Democrats relative to Republicans on each committee—are determined by the majority party in the House and negotiated by the leadership of both parties in the Senate. The ratios are generally set in rough proportion to party membership in the particular chamber, but the majority party gives itself a disproportionate number of seats on several key committees to ensure control.

Will Rogers, the homespun philosopher popular during the Great Depression, said he never met a man he didn't like. Members of the Tea Party movement in Nevada were less charitable about Sen. Harry Reid, whom they saw as too liberal and targeted for defeat in 2010. Reid survived the challenge in large part because his Tea Party–backed Republican opponent's policy positions were seen as too radical.

Committee membership Committees are essential not only to the legislative process but also for building a power base within Congress, attracting campaign donors, gaining the influence and name recognition needed for reelection, and perhaps even winning a higher office. New members and members seeking committee changes express their preferences to their party's selection committee. The party tries to accommodate members' requests for assignments that will be most beneficial to their constituencies, but there is some self-selection by seniority.

Historically, junior members did not ask for the most prestigious posts, but this tradition has broken down as freshmen have become bolder in their requests and even receive instruction in how to get the assignments they want. And if there are freshmen members whose reelection races are likely to be tough or who the party leadership believes have the potential to be future leaders, those members will likely be given helpful committee assignments. For example, Barack Obama was given a position on the influential Foreign Relations Committee in his freshman year, just as Hillary Clinton had been given her first choice in 2001, a seat on the important Armed Services Committee, to burnish her credentials for a possible future role as commander in chief.

The committees dealing with appropriations, taxes, and finance are always sought after because having a say in the allocation of money and how the tax burden falls on individuals and businesses gives members power and enhances their ability to help their home districts. These are sometime called "juice committees" because of the advantage they give members in squeezing interested parties for campaign contributions. Most members also want committee assignments that let them tell constituents they are working on problems of the district. Members from rural districts, for example, seek seats on committees that deal with agricultural and trade issues.

Media coverage is another criterion important in deciding committee preference. The work of some committees is more likely to be covered by television. Committees scrambled to hold attention-getting hearings on corporate fraud in 2002 and on 9/11 failures and the reorganization of intelligence agencies in 2004. In 2008, the attention-grabbing issue was the investigation of subprime mortgage lenders, and in 2010 it was hearings on the causes and consequences of BP's massive oil spill into the Gulf of Mexico. Getting on the right committee is important to those who want to become nationally known. When a journalist once asked then senator Joseph Biden (D-Del.) why he was so newsworthy, Biden replied, "It's the committees, of course." Biden served on the three committees with the greatest media exposure, sufficient to make him a credible potential candidate for the presidency in every Democratic primary season for twenty-five years and finally a vice-presidential candidate who could convincingly balance Barack Obama's lack of foreign policy experience.

The practice of filling each committee with representatives whose districts have an especially strong economic interest in its work encourages committees to be rather parochial in their outlook. It also leads to costly and wasteful legislation; if committee members' constituents benefit from programs under their jurisdiction, the members have no incentive to eliminate them or pare them back. This is one of the biggest weaknesses in the committee system.[52]

Committees are also often filled with members who have financial interests in the businesses they make policies for. Most members who sit on the banking committees own bank stock, many on agriculture committees own agribusiness stock, and those on the armed services committees hold stock in defense industries.[53] The farm subsidies illustrate these conflicts well. For example, Charles Grassley (R-Iowa) and his family own a farm and for over a decade received more than $200,000 in farm subsidies. On the other side of the aisle, Jon Tester (D-Mont.) and his wife received about the same amount.[54] In another of many examples, Ron Paul (R-Tex.), who owns shares in gold-mining companies worth about $1.5 million, serves as ranking minority member of the subcommittee that oversees monetary policy, mints, and gold, and he advocates for a United States return to the gold standard.[55] Jane Harmon (D-Calif.) chairs a subcommittee on technology, intelligence, and homeland security while owning more than $1 million in shares of companies who contract with the government in these areas.[56]

Committee chairs   The chair is usually the most influential member of a committee. Chairs have the authority to call meetings, set agendas, and control committee staff and funds. In addition, chairs usually have strong substantive knowledge of the matters that come before their committees, and this, too, is a source of influence.

Historically, the member of the majority party with the longest service on a committee became its chair by the so-called **seniority rule**. The rule was adopted to protect committee members from powerful Speakers of the House, who often used their authority to award committee chairs to friends and allies. But it allowed members who might be senile, alcoholic, or personally disliked by every member of the committee to become chairs if they were the most senior committee member of the majority party. It also led to chairs who were dictatorial and out of step with the rest of their party. In response to those complaints, in the early 1970s both parties agreed that the seniority rule no longer had to be followed.

Since then, Steering and Policy Committees in the Republican and Democratic caucuses have recommended chairs and voted on committee assignments. However, in the House, the Speaker has power to name members to the Rules Committee and to appoint or recommend the chairs of the most powerful committees. Recent Speakers have used this power to build support for their agendas and to curb independent action by committee chairs. In her first year, Speaker Pelosi allowed the seniority system to work in choosing most chairs, but she did use her powers to award

the chairs of a few important committees to more junior members from whom she could expect less independence. Pelosi also used her influence over appointments to ensure that women (22 percent of the Democrats) and minority members (28 percent) would hold a percentage of chairs equal to their proportion in the Democratic caucus.[57]

Some members prefer the Speaker appointment system because they believe it can prevent potentially damaging intraparty fights over who will chair important committees, just as the seniority principle did, but without producing the autocratic chairs who were common under the pure exercise of seniority. Before 1975, committee chairs were less supportive of their party than other party members in roll-call votes.[58] They could go their own way with impunity because their powerful positions were guaranteed. Since 1975, committee chairs in the House have had to be party loyalists if they wanted to keep their jobs. In that sense, the reforms have strengthened party influence in Congress, especially in the House, where they have led to a greater concentration of power, away from committees and to the leadership.

To further limit the use of standing committees as individual power bases, the Republicans, when they gained control of the House in 1995, established a three-term limit on service as a committee chair. Opponents argued that term limits punished experience and weakened oversight because chairs were forced out just when they were becoming fully familiar with the operations of the agencies they oversaw.[59] In 2009 the Democrats did away with the term limits rule. Nevertheless, committee chairs have not regained the independence and power of old, and the tendency toward party government and centralization of power in the leadership of the two party caucuses continues.

Subcommittees   Each standing committee is divided into subcommittees with jurisdiction over part of the committee's area of responsibility. The House Foreign Affairs Committee, for example, has seven subcommittees—Africa and Global Health; Asia, the Pacific, and the Global Environment; the Western Hemisphere; the Middle East and South Asia; Europe; International Organizations, Human Rights, and Oversight; and Terrorism, Nonproliferation, and Trade. These roughly parallel the seven subcommittees of the Senate's Foreign Relations Committee.

In the days of strict seniority rule, standing committee chairs chose the subcommittee chairs and controlled subcommittees' jurisdiction, budget, and staff. For the past three decades, each House and Senate subcommittee operates semi-independently of the parent committee.

These reforms, sometimes called the "subcommittee bill of rights," allowed more members, especially newer members, to share in important decisions. In this way, they made Congress more democratic. But by diffusing power, they also made it less efficient because the very number of subcommittees contributed to government gridlock. Complex legislation might be sent to several subcommittees, each with its own interests and jurisdiction.

In general, there is a tendency toward committee creep, with periods of committee reduction followed by periods of growth, resulting in many overlapping jurisdictions. When President George W. Bush proposed establishing the cabinet-level Department of Homeland Security, for example, twelve House committees were involved in reviewing the bill. Today there are eighty-eight committees and subcommittees that can claim oversight authority for some aspect of the department's work, an expansion some lawmakers defend as "purposeful redundancy."[60]

Select, Special, Joint, and Conference Committees

There are a few other types of congressional committees. *Select* or *special committees* are typically organized on a temporary basis to investigate a specific problem or to hold hearings and issue a report on special problems that arise, such as the impeachment of a federal official or an investigation into a policy failure such as the government response to Hurricane Katrina. Speaker Pelosi appointed a select committee as a way to move legislation on which the permanent standing committee on energy and commerce had been unwilling to act. (See the box "The Seniority System: The Speaker Looks Away.") Select and special committees are usually disbanded when their work is completed. The exceptions are the House and the Senate Select Committees on Intelligence and the Senate Select Committee on Ethics, which are in effect permanent committees.

Four *joint committees* include members from both houses, with the chair alternating between a House and Senate member. *Conference committees,* appointed whenever the Senate and the House pass different versions of the same bill, also have joint membership. Members from the committees that managed the bill in their respective chambers work out a single version for the full membership to vote on. Conference committees are dissolved after the compromise version is agreed on. Their work is discussed in greater detail in the section on lawmaking.

Task Forces

The traffic jams and turf wars around much committee work have led members of Congress with strong interests in particular policy areas to look for ways to bypass the committee structure. Task forces and ad hoc committees have existed in the House for decades, used by Democratic and Republican leaders alike, to study major issues and draft legislation, sometimes to speed action on a bill when a committee is dragging its feet or producing an outcome not in accord with what the leadership wants.[61] Speaker Pelosi, for example, bypassed the standing committee on official conduct and named a bipartisan House task force to write the 2007 ethics reform bill. The Senate makes less use of task forces but there are a number of cross-chamber study groups, most devoted to health issues like AIDs and smoking, in which both representatives and senators participate.

Staff and Support Agencies

The legislative branch encompasses not only elected representatives but also a staff of more than 30,000, about 17,000 of whom work directly for the House and Senate.[62] The 1947 authorization for House and Senate members to hire personal staff was a reaction to the gravitation of power and expertise to the Roosevelt White House during the Great Depression and World War II. As FDR recruited some of the country's greatest talent to work for him, Congress came to understand that it could not serve its proper role as a check on the executive branch if it did not have its own information base. To this end, members began hiring not only personal staff but also specialists to support the work of congressional committees.

Today thousands more employees staff the legislative branch's support agencies and carry out various research functions. The Government Accountability Office (GAO) checks on the efficiency and effectiveness of executive agencies, the Office of Technology Assessment provides long-range analyses of the effects of new and existing technology, and the Congressional Budget Office provides the expertise and support for Congress's budgeting job. To research complex problems, members can call on the seven hundred full-time staff members of the Congressional Research Service (CRS) in the Library of Congress. These researchers have issue specializations and contacts with experts in the academic world, in all the federal agencies, and with the interest groups that lobby on behalf of these issues. No member of Congress would have the time to develop this kind of expertise, yet without it, effective legislation could not be written, and Congress would not have the background it needs to challenge facts and figures presented in communications from the executive branch. The cost of funding the legislative branch as a whole in 2011 will be more than $5 billion.[63]

WHAT CONGRESS DOES

The importance of Congress is reflected in the major, explicit constitutional powers the Founders gave it: to lay and collect taxes, coin money, declare war and raise and support a military, and regulate commerce with foreign governments and among the states. 🔑 **Art. I, Sec. 7 & 8** Most of the named powers that the Constitution invests in the national government—including "All legislative Powers herein granted"—were given to Congress. 🔑 **Art. I, Sec. 1** These and other powers specifically mentioned in the Constitution are called the *enumerated powers* of Congress.

Congress also has *implied powers;* that is, it is permitted to make all the laws "necessary and proper" to carry out its enumerated powers. Although the Founders did not necessarily foresee it, this tremendous grant of power covers almost every area of human activity.

behind the scenes

The Seniority System: The Speaker Looks Away

When party leaders want to pass legislation that is not supported by the chair of the committee responsible for its review and markup, they may look for a way to bypass the committee. Establishing a task force or select committee, as discussed in the text, is one way; replacing a chair is another, but much less preferred, route because it is more of a challenge to the normal order of business in Congress.

Speaker Nancy Pelosi found her herself in this situation after the Democrats gained control of the House in 2007. An ardent supporter of new regulatory policies on energy and the environment, she knew that the chair of the Energy and Commerce Committee, John Dingell (D-Mich.), would put up roadblocks. Michigan's economy is deeply tied to the auto industry, so Dingell has district interests to protect, especially the jobs the auto companies have been providing Michigan workers for decades. He has never been sympathetic to legislation that places new restrictions on automakers, and, with his state's economy bottoming out, he was less sympathetic than ever. Dingell had even helped write a bill that would have prevented a dozen states, including California, from setting higher standards for auto emissions than those set by the federal government because he believed compliance with those rules would drive up costs for both automakers and buyers.

Pelosi had different priorities, both as the person responsible for getting the party's agenda translated into legislation and passed through the House and as a representative from California, a state that gets far more of its energy from renewable sources than do the industrial states of the Midwest like Michigan. Knowing that Dingell was not about to pass out of committee a bill with provisions favored by the party leadership, Pelosi first tried the select committee route for drafting new energy legislation. She and others also tried to get Dingell to step down from the chairmanship, but he refused. He was, after all, the "dean of the House" with fifty-seven years of service, responsible for some of the Democrats' landmark legislation, and he had been chair or ranking member of Energy and Commerce for thirty years.

Then, in 2009, with control of both the White House and Congress, the Democrats saw a golden opportunity to finally pass energy legislation. Dingell again refused to give up his chair, but this time he was challenged by another senior member, Henry Waxman, a Pelosi ally on energy and a fellow Californian who did not like Dingell's attempts to make California roll back its fuel emissions standards. As Waxman began quietly gathering votes in the Democratic caucus to win the chair from Dingell, Pelosi remained publicly neutral, although one member noted that she had "sent some top dogs into the race."[1] By not backing Dingell, Pelosi was looking past the seniority system, basically signaling that she thought progress on energy and environmental issues was more important than House traditions.

In cultivating support among younger and newly elected members (a number of whom had received money from his PAC), Waxman said he was running on a platform of change and warned that House Democrats were at a "unique moment" for writing transformative legislation. Dingell prepared for a fight and began lining up his supporters, especially fiscal conservatives and members of the black and Hispanic caucuses, strong supporters of the seniority system, one of whom flatly told Waxman, "I don't want change!"[2] A Pelosi ally described the contest as "Zeus and Thor . . . hurling lightning bolts at each other. You just wanted to duck and get out of the way."[3]

Waxman tried to keep the contest behind closed doors, doing nothing that smacked of lack of respect for Dingell. In the end the issues beat tradition, as the caucus bought Waxman's argument that the Democrats could not pass up a once-in-a-generation opportunity to remake energy policy. To smooth things over, Waxman bestowed the title of "chair emeritus" on Dingell, who remained on the committee. But one of Dingell's supporters said, referring to the seniority system, "in the long run we are going to pay for what we did. . . . It's not good for the order of things."[4]

[1] Coral Davenport, "Waxman Claims a Premier Gavel," *CQ Weekly*, November 24, 2008, 3148.
[2] Rep. Charles Rangel (D-N.Y.), then chair of the powerful Ways and Means Committee, quoted in ibid, 3150.
[3] Rep. George Miller (D-Calif.), quoted in ibid, 3148.
[4] Rep. John Lewis (D-Ga.), quoted in ibid.

Lawmaking

In each congressional session, thousands of bills and resolutions are introduced, but most die in committee (Figure 3). Of those passed, many are noncontroversial, including the so-called sense of the chamber measures, such as resolutions congratulating the winners of the Super Bowl, or very specific bills such as for the naming of a federal courthouse. In recent years, however, even these conventionally nonpolitical resolutions have become victims of partisanship. Former Republican Senate majority leader Bill Frist refused to allow a vote on a congratulatory

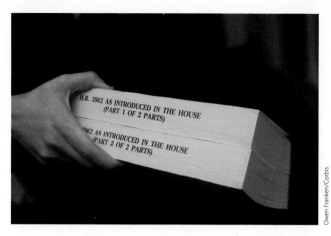

Proposed bills often are long and complex, in part because of references to provisions of past legislation that they are required to include.

resolution offered by New Jersey's two Democratic senators on behalf of their constituent, Bruce Springsteen, celebrating the thirtieth anniversary of his "Born to Run" album.

How does Congress decide which of the thousands of bills introduced each year it will pass? As we have noted, the Constitution says virtually nothing about the legislative process itself. The way bills work their way through the House and Senate today evolved with the development of party caucuses and the committee system. The procedures can be very arcane, and every several years, or as often as significant procedural changes require, the parliamentarian of the House of Representatives issues a new version of the pamphlet *How Our Laws Are Made* (http://thomas.loc.gov/home/lawsmade.toc.html), now in its twenty-third edition. The Senate publishes its own online description of the legislative process, which it describes, realistically, as "one way" a bill can become a law. We will reduce the complexities by focusing on some general steps in the process: bill introduction and referral, subcommittee hearings and markup, full committee hearing and markup, calendar and rule assignment by leadership, floor debate, vote, resolution of differences in House and Senate versions, president's signature or veto, and vote to override veto when applicable. The formal steps by which a bill becomes a law are important but do not reveal the bargaining and trade-offs at every step in the process.

A number of the bills passed each year are private; they resolve an issue an individual or private party has with the government, such as citizenship status or a monetary claim. Our concern is with public bills, those that become laws affecting the general public.

In 2009, out of more than 9,000 bills and resolutions introduced in the House and Senate, only 125 public laws were enacted.[64] This is in part because turning a bill into a law is like running an obstacle course. Opponents have an advantage because it is easier to defeat a bill than to pass one. Will Rogers's observation in the 1930s still reflects the difficulty of passing legislation today: "Congress is so strange. A man gets up to speak and says nothing. Nobody listens—and then everyone disagrees."[65]

Because of the need to win a majority at each stage, the end result is always a compromise. That does not mean a compromise of all interests, only of the strongest interests that played a role in shaping the bill. In defending the compromises that Nancy Pelosi made to get the health care reforms through the House, one observer explained, "[T]he real world has limits, and one of them is that there will never be a major bill to emerge from the House of Representatives that doesn't have something regrettable in it."[66]

Submission and Referral

Bills may be introduced in either the House or the Senate, except for tax measures (which, according to the Constitution, must be initiated in the House) 🔔 **Art. I, Sec. 7** and appropriations bills (which by tradition are introduced in the House). This reflects the Founders' belief that the chamber directly elected by the people should control the purse strings.

Although the White House initiates much of the legislation Congress enacts, only members can introduce bills for consideration. The president, like interest groups or constituents who initiate legislation, must find congressional sponsors for each bill in his legislative agenda. After a bill's introduction, it is referred to a standing committee by the Speaker of the House or the presiding officer in the Senate. The content of the bill largely determines where it will go, although the Speaker has some discretion, particularly over complex bills that cover more than one subject area. Many such bills are referred to more than one committee simultaneously.

Committee Action

Once the bill reaches a committee, it is assigned to the subcommittee that covers the appropriate subject area. One of the main functions of the subcommittees is to screen bills with little chance of passage. (If a committee kills a bill, there are procedures that members can use to try to get the bill to the floor, but these are used infrequently.) If a subcommittee decides to take up a proposed piece of legislation, it may call hearings. Unless otherwise specified, hearings are open to the public, although few people know about them or would have the time or opportunity to sit in. Consequently, lobbyists fill most of the hearing rooms. For critical meetings, lobbyists will hire messengers to stand in line for them, sometimes all night, and then pack the hearing room. Members who receive financial or other support from groups affected by the legislation often face intense and direct pressure to vote a particular way in committee. Sometimes lobbyists mob members as they leave the hearing room.

After the hearings, House subcommittees hold **markup** sessions using the testimony from the hearings and staff research to rewrite a bill or add amendments. Subcommittee markup is more unusual in the Senate, where more work is done outside the committee structure. Following markup

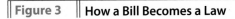

Figure 3 ‖ **How a Bill Becomes a Law**

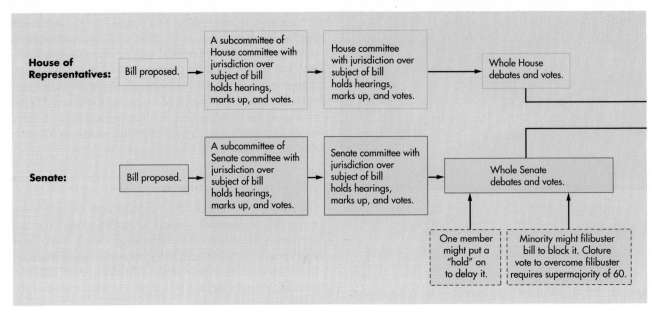

Of the 9000 or more bills introduced in Congress each year, only about 125–400 become law. This diagram highlights the key steps in the process. (See the chapter for an explanation and elaboration of the process. At every step, bills are subjected to political pressures that can't be conveyed in a diagram.) Bills can be killed at any step. Most are killed in the subcommittee of the committee. If they pass the committee, they usually pass the whole chamber. Although the process looks similar for the two chambers, House leaders have more power to influence the process than Senate leaders do. And the use of holds and filibusters allows the minority in the Senate to delay and block bills. Allowing filibusters is especially significant, because doing so requires a supermajority of sixty votes to get a bill to the floor for an up or down vote.

in the subcommittee, if the bill is approved, it is sent to the full committee along with a report explaining the subcommittee's action and reasoning. The standing committee may hold additional hearings and markup sessions.

Scheduling and Rules

Once a House committee approves a bill, it is placed on one of five "calendars," depending on the subject matter of the bill. The Senate has just two calendars: one for private and public bills and another for treaties and nominations. Bills from each calendar are generally considered in the order in which they are reported from committee. In the House, the Rules Committee sets the terms of the debate over the bill by issuing a rule on it. The rule either limits or does not limit debate and determines whether amendments will be permitted. A rule forbidding amendments means that members have to vote yes or no on the bill; there is no chance to change it. If the committee refuses to issue a rule, the bill dies.

In earlier years, the Rules Committee was controlled by a coalition of conservative Democrats and Republicans who used their power to block liberal legislative proposals, including, for decades, meaningful civil rights proposals. Under Republican control from 1995 to 2006 the committee was dominated by the Speaker and the majority leadership rather than by coalitions supporting or opposing specific bills. Speaker Pelosi followed this practice, so that in this era the Rules Committee "has become unambiguously, a

tool of the leadership, with its members taking orders from above and hardly ever shaping policy directly."[67]

The powers inherent in the Speakership allow the majority leadership to use or bend rules to force measures to the floor, where only a simple majority is necessary for passage. House members have few tactical options against a Speaker who uses full powers to set the rules. Pelosi's predecessor, Speaker Dennis Hastert (R-Ill.), was also willing to use the rules to prevent amendments and other changes in the wording of bills that the leadership had agreed on. When Democrats assumed control, they vowed that bills would "come to the floor under a procedure that allows open, full and fair debate" and promised an amendment process that would allow "the minority the right to offer its alternatives." But the Democrats used the closed rules that permit no debate on floor amendments about as often as the Republicans did, claiming that Republicans were using the amendment process not to change, but to kill, bills.[68]

Because the Senate is a smaller body, it can operate with fewer rules and formal procedures. It does not have a Rules Committee. A lot of work is accomplished through the use of privately negotiated unanimous consent agreements, which allow the Senate to dispense with standard rules and define terms for debating and amending a specific bill. As the Senate's workload has increased and its sense of collegiality has decreased, it has become more difficult to get opponents to accept a unanimous consent agreement. A single senator can use parliamentary

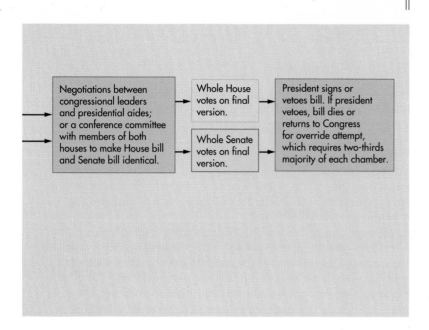

| Negotiations between congressional leaders and presidential aides; or a conference committee with members of both houses to make House bill and Senate bill identical. | Whole House votes on final version. | President signs or vetoes bill. If president vetoes, bill dies or returns to Congress for override attempt, which requires two-thirds majority of each chamber. |
| Whole Senate votes on final version. | | |

tactics to freeze the agenda. A senator once held up an antibusing bill for eight months with 604 amendments.

Debate

Debate on a bill is controlled by the bill managers, usually senior members of the committee that sent the bill to the full chamber. The opposition, too, has its managers, who schedule opposition speeches. "Debates" are not a series of fiery speeches of point and counterpoint. They are often boring recitations delivered to a handful of members, some of whom may be reading, conversing, or walking around the floor. In the House, after the time allotted (typically five minutes per speaker) for debate is over, often no more than a day, the bill is reported for final action. And if a bill is brought to the floor under a rule allowing no amendments, even a day's debate can lead to no more than an up or down vote on the bill as presented.

In the Senate, the lack of fixed rules on debate and the majority leader's inability unilaterally to set them have made unrestricted debate a principal method of defeating or delaying consideration of a bill. The major mechanism for doing this is the **filibuster**, a continuous speech made by

President Obama meets with Sen. Susan Collins (R-Maine), one of the few remaining moderate Republicans in the Senate. The president has tried to negotiate the content of proposed legislation with moderate Republicans to win their votes.

behind the scenes

Hold That Nomination

Fifteen months into his presidency, Barack Obama was still waiting on the Senate to confirm ninety-six of his appointees. For a time during those months, Obama's party held sixty of the Senate's one hundred seats; only a simple majority is needed for confirmation, but the president couldn't get it done.

Senate rules encourage this kind of gridlock by allowing a single member to place a hold on any nomination (or bill), anonymously, for any reason, thus preventing an up or down vote. A senator who places a hold must identify himself or herself six days after a vote has been called for and also state the reasons for the hold. However, if, before the sixth day, the senator withdraws the hold and gets a colleague to place it anew, the originator can remain anonymous. And by passing a hold from one senator to another within the six-day limit, all can remain anonymous. By mid-2010, secret holds had stalled nominations for an average of 106 days.[1]

The hold originated as a courtesy in the days when senators had to travel by horse; holding a vote allowed members time to reach the capital and read a bill or consider a nominee before voting.[2] Today the hold is used occasionally to stall a nomination for political or policy reasons, such as appointments to the Federal Elections Commission, but most holds have little to do with policy, qualifications, or personalities, and certainly not with travel delays. They are more often used by senators as a bargaining chip to get something they want. Sen. Jim Bunning (R-Ky., ret. 2011) blocked a confirmation vote on Obama's nominee to be deputy U.S. trade representative for six months because he was trying to force the government to challenge Canada's ban on flavored tobacco (tobacco is one of Kentucky's primary crops). Richard Shelby (R-Ala.) placed a blanket hold on seventy nominees because he wanted assurances that the work on a new tanker for the Pentagon would be done in his state and also that a planned new FBI facility would be located in Huntsville.[3] This quid pro quo leveraging of a vote is why the hold has been described as the "bare-knuckled politics of obstruction."[4]

Sen. Claire McCaskill (D-Mo.), having once tried seventy-six times in one day to win unanimous consent for bringing Obama's nominees to a vote, introduced a bill to ban all secret holds, saying, "if you're gonna stall and block, let's see who you are." She was seconded by Sen. Charles Grassley (R-Iowa), who challenged his colleagues to "have the guts to go public."[5] But McCaskill was not expected to succeed because, as Sen. Ron Wyden (D-Ore.), sponsor of a more limited reform, said, a hold is "one of the most powerful tools a member of the Senate has today to influence policy."[6]

[1] Jim Abrams, "No Holds Barred as Senators Block Confirmation Votes," *Champaign-Urbana News-Gazette*, May 9, 2010, A5.
[2] George Packer, "The Empty Chamber," *The New Yorker*, August 8, 2010, 47.
[3] Gail Collins, "No Holds Barred," *New York Times*, February 6, 2010, A19.
[4] Sen Sheldon Whitehouse (D-R.I.) quoted in Abrams, "No Holds Barred."
[5] "Pssst, Over to You" (Editorial), *New York Times*, May 12, 2010, A30.
[6] Abrams, "No Holds Barred."

---

one or more members to prevent a piece of legislation from being brought to the floor for a vote.

When the first Congress met, the rulebooks of the House and Senate were basically the same, and both allowed for debate to be cut off by a simple majority. But in 1805 Vice President Aaron Burr, acting as Senate president, encouraged the streamlining of the Senate rulebook and the elimination of duplicate rules. During this process the rule allowing for a simple majority to end debate was eliminated "by accident."[69] The rule's removal, which made easy the use of the filibuster, was not intended as a means for protecting the minority or allowing for extended debate, as now claimed by champions of the 60-vote rule for stopping or preventing a filibuster.

The use of the filibuster as a legislative tactic did not begin in earnest until 1837, after which time it was used periodically to block election reform, nominations, and civil rights legislation.[70] Up into the early twentieth century, Senate leaders tried many times to reinstate the original simple majority rule. Failing, they developed rules such as unanimous consent to avoid the possibility of filibusters.

In 1917, under pressure from President Wilson, citing wartime needs, the Senate adopted the **cloture** rule, which allowed debate to be cut off by two-thirds of those present and voting. In 1975 the rules were changed again to allow three-fifths of the membership (sixty senators if there are no vacancies) to end debate. A successful cloture vote is called invoking cloture, or closing debate; once cloture is invoked, debate must end within thirty hours and the measure brought to a vote.

The public became aware of the use of the filibuster to block legislation during the 1960s civil rights movement, when it took a cloture vote to end fifty-four days of debate and get the 1964 Civil Rights Act to the floor for a vote. It was not widely used again until the 1990s.

During Bill Clinton's first year in office, Republicans frequently used the filibuster to block proposals from the Democratic Senate majority. At the time the Senate was so evenly divided that the majority party would not have been able to muster sixty votes to override a filibuster if it did occur, so, after a while, only the threat of a filibuster was necessary to block action. Democrats used the same tactic when they were in the minority for most of George W. Bush's presidency, and the practice continued with even greater frequency with Republicans again in minority after the 2008 election. These days, actual filibusters rarely occur because the threat of one is now sufficient to stop action on a bill or other piece of Senate business. In effect, this has meant that a **supermajority** of 60 votes is often necessary to pass a bill in the Senate—well beyond a simple majority of 51. More precisely stated, it means that it takes 60 votes to bring some bills to the floor for a vote. Once a bill makes it to the floor, only a simple majority is required for passage, unless it is being considered under special rules. In the past two Congresses, more than 30 percent of the roll-call votes in the Senate have required 60 votes for success, a historic high.[71]

In 2009, when for a brief time the Democrats held sixty Senate seats, there was talk of a filibuster-proof majority. But because it is difficult to hold all members of a party in line, a filibuster-proof majority usually requires a party to have more than sixty seats. Democrats especially have strong intraparty differences on fiscal and some social issues, which makes lining up a unanimous vote very difficult.

Senator Strom Thurmond, at the time a Democrat from South Carolina, is congratulated by his wife for setting a record for the longest filibuster. He talked for twenty-four hours and eighteen minutes to prevent a civil rights bill from being voted on in 1957. His effort was in vain, as the bill was adopted.

The filibuster is of importance beyond voting on bills or nominations; the threat of one can also be used by the minority to stop routine procedural motions and essentially bring Senate business to a halt. Senate minority leader Mitch McConnell (R-Ky.) has boasted of his success in leveraging Senate rules to stop the majority from acting. He said he learned fairly early "that it is pretty important and certainly useful to learn as much about procedure as you can, because frequently procedure is policy."[72]

DEMOCRACY?

Minority rights are a foundational element in our form of democracy, but how far does this principle extend to the legislative process? Should a minority be able to consistently block bills that are supported by a majority of elected officials?

The filibuster impedes the majority's (including a bipartisan majority's) right to legislate and contributes to gridlock, but it also can prevent precipitous action or total domination by the majority party. Some scholars argue that by dragging out the deliberative process the filibuster rule contributes to producing bills that are better thought through and more acceptable to a broader range of the membership and the public. Others are more inclined to see the routine use of the filibuster as one of the negative consequences of "an ideologically polarized Senate."[73]

At any given time some senators are working to reimpose the simple majority rule for ending debate, and, of course, the majority party can call the bluff of those who threaten to filibuster, forcing the minority to hold the floor with a nonstop debate until cloture can be invoked.

With the breakdown of the deliberative process, the threat of filibusters, the use of holds, and the proposing of dozens of amendments all continue to be effective ways for the minority party, or even an individual senator, to influence or block legislation. Whereas the 1,600-page "Senate Procedures: Precedents and Practices" was rarely read by any but the most avid student of legislative tactics, in recent years it has been "ransacked for every conceivable way to delay a debate and vote." Republican members have even been sent memos on how to use stalling tactics.[74]

The Senate was created to make sure that Congress did not rush to pass ill-considered legislation, or as Sen. Lamar Alexander (R-Tenn.) says, it was not created to be efficient, but rather inefficient.[75] George Washington is alleged to have made this point when he compared the Senate with a saucer: you pour your hot coffee (the more populist measures passed by the House) into a saucer to cool it. But carried to extreme, this deliberate gridlock of the Senate legislative process has created bad feelings in the House, where, with its simple majority rule, legislation continued to move in the first years of the Obama administration. The inaction of the Senate also contributes to the accurate public perception

that Congress is ineffectual in dealing with many issues. Since the Democrats regained control of both chambers in 2006, the Senate has refused to take up more than 400 bills passed by the House.[76] A senior Democrat remarked that "senators are so proud of being the saucer" that "the Senate no longer has the ability to answer the problems of this nation in real time."[77]

The Vote

When and if a bill ever makes it to an up-or-down floor vote, the vote may be taken in several different ways—by voice, a standing count, or recording of individual votes—depending on the level of support and the importance of the legislation. At the time members finally cast their votes on major public bills, they are usually voting on the general aim of the bill without knowing its exact provisions. Rarely does any member read such a bill in full. Republicans complained that the 2010 health care reform bill was long and complicated and was being "rushed" through. At more than 2000 pages, it was indeed long, but not out of line with laws passed by Republican Congresses such as the No Child Left Behind Act, the first PATRIOT Act, and the prescription drug benefit for seniors, which ran from 800 to more than 1000 pages. The USA PATRIOT Act, which had serious implications for civil liberties, was rushed through Congress in just a few weeks with virtually no member having read it, a far shorter deliberative period than the months it took for Congress to negotiate health care reform.

When a measure passes, it is sent to the other chamber for action.

Conference Committee

The House and Senate must agree on an identical version of a bill before it can become law, and since this rarely happens, the two versions must be reconciled. Sometimes the chamber that passed the bill last will simply send it to the other chamber for minor modifications. But if the differences between the two versions are not minor, a **conference committee** is set up to try to resolve them. The presiding officers of each chamber, in consultation with the chairs of the standing committees that considered the bill, choose the members of the committee. Both parties are represented, but there is neither a set number of conferees nor a rule requiring an equal number of seats for each chamber.

If the leaders of both parties are strongly committed to passing a version of a bill, they may negotiate the compromise themselves and essentially impose it on the committee. They may even negotiate the final version with the president to avoid a veto. These negotiations can also be planned by the White House with the intent of limiting the wiggle room party leaders have to negotiate compromises.

Conference committees, or the individuals in control of them, have tremendous latitude in how they resolve the differences between the House and Senate versions of a bill. Officially, nothing can be added to the bill that is not germane to it, and no part of a bill can be amended that had not been amended prior to passage. But sometimes a bill is substantially rewritten, and occasionally a bill is killed. Or, as President Reagan once said, "an apple and an orange could go into a conference committee and come out a pear."[78] A White House aide described these committees as "no-man's land" because there are so few formal rules governing how they operate.[79] The power of conference committees to alter bills after their passage is why they are sometimes called the "Third House" of Congress.[80]

Once the conference committee reaches an agreement, the bill goes back to each chamber, where its approval requires a majority vote. It cannot be amended at that point, so it is presented to the membership on a take-it-or-leave-it basis. In the Senate, however, any individual member can challenge a provision added in conference that was not related to the original bill. In practice, both House and Senate accept most conference reports because members of both parties in each chamber have participated in working out the compromise version. Clearly, conference committees can be very influential in determining the final provisions in major legislation, yet the work they do happens almost completely out of public view.

Knowing how to win a seat on a conference committee, that is, to participate in rewriting an important piece of legislation, is an essential skill for any legislator who wants to wield influence. However, in the years of **unified government**—periods when one party has controlled the White House and both houses of Congress (the first two years of the Clinton administration, most of George W. Bush's terms, and the first years of Obama's presidency, for example)—the White House and congressional leaders have preempted much of the conference process by working out final wording of bills among themselves. Minority parties often felt so blocked out of the negotiations that determined the final wording of a bill that they refused to sign on to conference committee reports. Rank-and-file members of both parties who are appointed to conference committees also feel left out of the process when the White House and congressional leaders have already reached agreement on the major changes before the committee ever sits. In the last years of the Bush presidency, only 2 percent of public bills were passed through conference committees, compared to 25 percent in the early 1970s.[81]

Presidential Action and Congressional Response

The president may sign a bill, in which case it becomes law. Or the president may veto it, in which case it returns to Congress with the president's objections. The president also may do nothing, and the bill will then become law after ten days unless Congress adjourns during that period. ♜ **Art. I, Sec. 7**

Most presidents have not used the veto lightly, but when they do veto a bill, Congress rarely overrides them. A two-thirds vote in each house is required to override a presidential veto. Congress voted to override only nine of former President Reagan's seventy-eight vetoes, only one of President George H. Bush's forty-six, only two of Clinton's thirty-four, and two of George W. Bush's ten. President Obama used the veto only once in his first eighteen months in office, and it stood.

After the bill becomes a law, it is assigned a number (which always begins with the session of Congress that passed it), published, and entered in the United States Code.

Oversight

As part of the checks-and-balances principle, it is Congress's responsibility to make sure that the bureaucracy is administering federal programs as Congress intended. This monitoring function, called **oversight**, has become more important as Congress continues to delegate authority to the executive branch. For a variety of reasons, Congress is not especially well equipped, motivated, or organized to carry out its oversight function. Nevertheless, it does have several tools for this purpose.

One tool is the Government Accountability Office (GAO), created in 1921 and known as the General Accounting Office until 2004. The GAO functions as Congress's watchdog in oversight and is primarily concerned with making sure that money is used properly. GAO reports have produced most of the information the public has about waste and fraud in government spending, such as in military contracts awarded to private firms for logistical support in the Iraq War and fraud on the part of some providers of Medicare services.

Committee hearings are another method of oversight, albeit not always an effective one. They give members an opportunity to query executive branch staff on the operation of their agencies, but the level of cooperation and frankness varies with the problem being investigated, and at times with instructions from the White House limiting

cooperation. Nevertheless, officials in agencies view hearings as a possible source of embarrassment for their agency and usually spend a great deal of time preparing for them. This is especially true when Congress decides, often for political reasons, to seek maximum media coverage for hearings.

This attempt at publicity points to one of the problems with the use of televised proceedings to carry out the oversight function: hearings are often held after oversight has failed and Congress wants to convince the public that it is doing something to correct a problem. This was painfully clear after the corporate collapses of 2002—of Enron, Global Crossing, and WorldCom, for example—when four Senate and three House committees held hearings in succession, all vying for media time. Prominent members of oversight committees, such as Joseph Lieberman (I-Conn.) and Christopher Dodd (D-Conn., ret. 2011), who represent a state where some of the failed businesses were headquartered and who had received large campaign contributions from them, actively worked to prevent new regulations from being adopted. Then they are seen on an oversight panel questioning regulatory officials and corporate executives about why the crises occurred. But if Congress had exercised oversight and had not weakened the regulatory clout of the Securities and Exchange Commission, these scandals might not have occurred and some of the enormous costs to employees and investors might have been prevented. Occurring after the failures, the hearings were more aftersight than oversight, but they were also a means for Congress to consider remedial measures.

We saw a repeat of this in 2008 when, after the financial crisis caused by lax regulation of mortgages and financial institutions that led to the near collapse of federal mortgage insurers Fannie Mae and Freddie Mac, members of Congress rushed to hold hearings. During this "competitive rush for headlines," the barn door was wide open and the horses were loose, but members were eager to exercise "aftersight."[82] Congress also exercises oversight when it holds hearings on the president's nominees for top positions in regulatory agencies and cabinet departments. By questioning the experience, training, and perspectives of the nominees, congressional committees are also focusing on what they believe the needs and issues confronting the agencies are.

The incentive of committee members to place constituent protection and the interests of big campaign donors above rule enforcement is one weakness of oversight. The fragmentation of oversight responsibility is also a problem. There were at least seven Senate committees and six House committees with some oversight responsibility for the accounting and financial practices that led to so many industry bankruptcies in 2002. And many more committees were responsible for oversight of the defense and intelligence agencies whose failures were so widely publicized after 9/11.

Congress can also exercise its oversight function through informal means.[83] One way of doing this is to request reports on topics of interest to members or committees. In a given year, the executive branch might prepare 5000 reports for Congress.[84] Moreover, the chair and staff of the committee or subcommittee relevant to the agency's mission are consulted regularly by the agency. But it is hard to find any serious informal oversight. There are few electoral or other incentives for members to become involved in the drudgery of wading through thousands of pages of reports or for doing a really thorough job in any area of oversight, at least until a crisis arises or public confidence in the economy or government institutions is threatened.

The primary means for congressional oversight is its control over the federal budget. Congress can cut or add to agencies' budgets and thereby punish or reward them for their performance. Members with authority over an agency's budget can use that power to get benefits for their constituents, and by going along with the members' wishes, agencies may stand a better chance of having their budget requests approved. There is an incentive in this relationship for congressional committees to exercise oversight, but increasingly they have failed to do so. Congress has allowed authorizing legislation to expire for agencies as important as the Consumer Product Safety Commission, the U.S. Commission on Civil Rights, the Corporation for Public Broadcasting, and the Federal Election and Trade commissions, among others. The agencies continue to function because Congress waives budget rules to provide annual funding for them without oversight by authorization committees.[85]

If Congress has received low marks for gridlock in legislating, it was absent without leave in carrying out much of its oversight function during most of the Bush administration, when compliant Republicans did not want to investigate anything that made the administration look bad.

Many members of Congress were critical of their institution's laxity, especially with respect to oversight of intelligence operations, defense policy and appropriations, and the financial industry. In the wake of 9/11, the Bush administration encouraged Congress to neglect oversight in these areas by arguing that the president needed a free hand to wage the war on terrorism.

Former senator Rick Santorum (R-Pa.) explained the weakening of oversight in the Republican-controlled Congress as a party preference: "Republicans don't enjoy oversight—not nearly as much as Democrats—and so . . . we don't do as much."[86] However, as Rep. Henry Waxman (D-Calif.) pointed out, House Republicans took "more than 140 hours of testimony to investigate whether the Clinton White House misused its holiday card database but less than 5 hours of testimony regarding how the Bush administration treated Iraqi detainees."[87] In fact, during the years when Republicans had majorities in Congress (1995–2006), 99 percent of the 1015 subpoenas issued by congressional committees to provide testimony or documents for congressional hearings were for investigations of actions by the Clinton administration, and 1 percent for actions of the Bush administration. Not surprisingly, after the Democrats took control of Congress in 2007 and there was no longer unified government, the number of oversight hearings doubled and four new oversight committees were created.

In other words, members of Congress would rather exercise oversight on presidents from opposing parties. Members from the president's party fear that negative publicity might weaken not just the president but also their party. However, in most eras, institutional pride in congressional prerogatives and Congress as an equal branch partially

The CEOs of financial firms prepare to testify before a congressional commission investigating the financial collapse of 2008, which was driven by the risky practices of the huge firms. Congressional committees hold hearings as part of their oversight of federal agencies.

overcomes the reluctance to investigate the administration. The Obama administration has not differed much from its predecessor on oversight of intelligence agencies, but it has supported passage of legislation to increase oversight of the banking and the financial sectors as well as over environmental watchdog agencies.

Budget Making

The topic of budget making may be dull, but without money government cannot function. Real priorities are reflected not in rhetoric but in the budget. An increasingly large part of the job of Congress is to pass a budget. The Constitution gave Congress the power to appropriate money and to account for its expenditure, ♟ Art. I, Sec. 9 but in the 1920s, Congress delegated its authority to prepare the annual budget to the president (through the Office of Management and Budget, or OMB). In years when the president's party does not control Congress, the congressional majority also produces its own budget, with priorities distinctly different from the president's.

The House and Senate have subcommittee-free budget committees whose membership includes representatives from the leadership of both parties. The budget committees have existed only since 1974 and were created to work with the Congressional Budget Office (CBO) on big-picture issues such as economic forecasting and fiscal planning, including deficit management and control of overall spending. The House Budget Committee prepares a budget proposal that sets out spending goals in the context of projected federal revenues. The House and Senate's budget committees are not as powerful as their appropriations committees, and neither can enforce the spending limits they recommend. During the budgetary process, the budget committees hold hearings, but these have become a sideshow to the main event.

Congress is aided in budget review by the CBO, which provides expertise to Congress on matters related to both the budget and the economy. Before the establishment of the CBO, members of Congress felt they were junior partners in budget making because they had to depend on information provided by the president, his budget advisers, and the OMB. Because the CBO is responsible to both parties in Congress, it provides a less politically biased set of forecasts about the budget than the administration or the leadership of either party would.

Characteristics of Budgeting

Historically, congressional budgeting has had two basic characteristics. First, the process is usually incremental; that is, budgets for the next year are usually slightly more than budgets for the current year. Normally, Congress does not radically reallocate money from one year to the next; members assume that agencies should get about what they received the previous year. This simplifies the work of all concerned. Agencies do not have to defend, or

members scrutinize, all aspects of the budget. Second, Congress tends to spend more in election years and in times of unemployment.

There are exceptions to these general rules, such as times of war or domestic crisis. The first budget submitted after 9/11, for example, requested a huge increase in defense spending. Thereafter the increases were far larger than the annual budgets show because most of the money for the wars in Afghanistan and Iraq was requested in "supplementals," special appropriations bills that authorize spending not included in the fiscal year budget. There are also instances of ideological budgeting. President Reagan's domestic budget cuts and increased military spending in 1981 were clearly an exception to incrementalism.

Authorizations and Appropriations

Each year, Congress passes a budget resolution that sets a dollar amount of spending for the fiscal year, but money is not appropriated in a single piece of legislation. Since the 1970s, the budget has been divided and reviewed as separate bills, each of which focuses on a different area of expenditure, such as defense. All budget legislation goes through a process similar to but more complicated than other bills.

To grasp the complexity of this process, it is necessary to understand the distinction between budget authorizations and budget appropriations. **Authorizations** are acts that enable agencies and departments to operate, either by creating them or by authorizing their continuance. They also establish the guidelines under which the agencies operate. Although authorization bills might specify funding levels, they do not actually provide the funding. **Appropriations** are acts that give federal agencies the authority to spend the money allocated to them. Both authorization and appropriations bills must pass each house, and differences must be resolved in conference.

Typically, authorizations precede appropriations, although this is not always the case. Budgetary procedures are not defined in the Constitution but are determined by House and Senate rules, which can be, and often have been, changed. The standing committees that oversee the work of the agency or program being funded usually work out the authorizations. The House Interior and Insular Affairs Committee and the Senate Energy and National Resources Committee, for example, review the authorization of the Park Service in the Department of the Interior, and the agricultural committees write authorizations for the Department of Agriculture. Close ties often exist between the agency being reviewed and the authorizing committee, which can cause proposed funding levels to be set without consideration of the overall demand on federal revenues. So the real power to limit spending rests with the House and Senate Appropriations Committees.

The Appropriations Committee within each house has subcommittees corresponding to the functional areas into which budget allocations are divided. The chair of the two Appropriations Committees and the ranking minority member (and the ranking majority member in the Senate as well) can sit as members of any or all of the subcommittees, adding to their power. The Appropriations Committee assigns a spending limit for each area, and the relevant subcommittee then decides how to apportion it among the agencies in its jurisdiction. The power of those who chair appropriations subcommittees is suggested by their nickname, "The Cardinals." In reviewing an agency's proposed budget, the subcommittee is not bound to fund it at the level requested in the president's budget proposal or in the authorization bill. Nor do a subcommittee's funding proposals have to be accepted by the whole committee.

Although appropriations subcommittees may develop close ties with the agencies they review, the committee as a whole does not, and it may not be as generous as its subcommittees. In the bills it sends to the floor for a vote, the Appropriations Committee can increase or cut the previous year's funding levels, or it can recommend the elimination of an agency altogether.

Problems with the Budget Process

Almost everyone is critical of congressional budget making. One reason is that members simply cannot agree on spending for any fiscal year; it has become common for the new fiscal year to begin before Congress has passed all the necessary appropriations bills. Then, under time pressure, they sometimes lump spending into several omnibus bills in order to keep government operating. These cumbersome bills are difficult to decipher and make oversight by scrutiny of agency budgets very difficult.

Another problem is that Congress does not honor its own budget resolutions that establish the amount of total spending for each fiscal year. Congress has frequently outspent the dollar limit that it set.[88] As emergencies or unforeseen needs arise, Congress passes supplemental spending bills such as for Iraq and Afghanistan or to deal with a natural disaster like Hurricane Katrina.

Congress also now consistently violates the **pay-as-you-go (paygo)** rule, which requires all new spending to be offset by a revenue source or spending cuts elsewhere. The paygo rule, established at the end of the first Bush administration and observed throughout Clinton's presidency, was one of several key factors that made it possible to balance the budget in 2000. When George W. Bush took office, the budget was in surplus, and both he and the Congress abandoned paygo. There have been attempts to restore paygo since 2009, but spending on the financial crisis and the recession, plus the cost of two wars, has made it difficult to reach agreement on new taxes or how to cut existing programs to offset the new spending.

The budgeting process also suffers from the dynamics of committee government. By developing expertise in a few areas, House members are often more responsive to narrow interests and constituencies and less responsive to national priorities when deciding how to spend money. Over time, members of congressional subcommittees develop close relationships both with lobbyists for interest groups whose goals are affected by committee decisions and with the staff in executive branch agencies the subcommittee oversees. Over the years, these three groups—legislators, lobbyists, and bureaucrats, sometimes called an "iron triangle"—get to know one another, often come to like and respect one another and seek to accommodate one another's interests. The lobbyists are likely to be among the legislators' campaign contributors. These personal relationships can result in favorable treatment of special interest groups or reluctance of committee members to decrease funding levels for an agency.

A major problem with budgeting, in fact and in public perception, is the lack of transparency. Few people can imagine what $3 trillion means, and keeping track of how it is spent and how revenues are raised to cover those expenditures is impossible for the average citizen, even though the annual budget is published and available to everyone online (see www.whitehouse.omb.gov). The lack of transparency is due in part to the sheer size and complexity of the budget and to what we might call creative accounting techniques, such as paying for wars off budget. Certain aspects of the process are deliberately hidden from view, for example, how money is spent gathering intelligence; others, such as the real cost of the wars in Iraq and Afghanistan, are camouflaged . Paradoxically, the attention paid to lack of transparency has focused on earmarks, which account for 2 percent or less of public spending.

An **earmark** is a specific amount of money designated, or set aside, at the request of a member, almost always for a project in his or her district or state. Bringing money and jobs ("pork") home to the district is nothing new for members of Congress, but the earmark method of doing it dates to around 1970. Not surprisingly, the most successful earmarkers have always been the most senior and most powerful members of appropriations and authorization committees, but today all members have the opportunity to include earmarks in the budgets of agencies they oversee. However, it is not a level playing field; women and minority members are less successful in winning their earmark requests. The fact that some African American members represent districts gerrymandered to create safe seats has hurt their chances of getting their earmark requests. The corollary is that newer members in highly competitive seats tend to do well because the leadership wants to boost their reelection chances by sending money to their districts.[89]

Although presidents often rail against Congress for members' special funding requests, it should not be forgotten that the White House typically includes hundreds of its own earmarks in the budget proposals it sends to Congress. The argument against earmarking is based primarily on its being a corruption of the budgetary process. Members' requests are put into appropriations bills or reports to agencies directing them on how to spend their appropriations without any consideration of the merits of the project or program. The requests are often entered unattributed and are seen as violations of what should be an open or transparent process. The public is entitled to know who requests money for these projects. Some also argue that earmarks are a kind

Luke Sharrett/The New York Times

Sen. Jack Reed (D-R.I.) shows signs of the tedium and frustration of the legislative process, here marking up the bill to regulate the financial industry.

of pay-for-play arrangement in which members can attract contributions for reelection campaigns by getting funding for a project that will benefit one of the potential donors.

Earmarking is a beloved bipartisan tradition. It has continued in peacetime and wartime, when the budget is balanced and when it is in deep deficit. The practice is so common and such a necessary legislative skill that a Washington, D.C., firm offers a training seminar in how to get an earmark.[90] Members say they are the people best informed on special problems in their districts and are obligated to get money to deal with them. Earmarks can mean building a road, museum, park, or research center that may mean a great deal to a locality. One member said that taking a share of tax dollars back to the district was his "constitutional obligation."[91] It has been suggested that the huge budget deficits accruing during this recessionary period will turn voters against the tradition of winning tax dollars for the home district. In the unlikely event this happens it would constitute a radical change in how most members campaign for, and retain, their seats.[92]

"Not all earmarks are equal," one House leader argued. A secret earmark for a lobbyist's corporate client is not the same as earmarking money for a project that will benefit a member's district. He pointed out that one of his earmarks was for repair of a dangerously unsafe city bridge that was on the exit route designated by Homeland Security for emergency evacuations.[93] It is also important to keep in mind that members' constituents are enablers of this behavior. Although collectively we talk as if we want an ethical, high-minded Congress whose members are always responsive first to the national interest, when fragmented into individual constituents, the public often responds quite differently. The average voter does expect his or her representative to deliver for the district.

Although Senator John McCain attributed much of the deficit problem to earmarks during his 2008 campaign for the presidency, the cost of earmarks that year would not have paid for two months of the Iraq War. One pundit said that trying to balance the budget by eliminating earmarks was like trying to solve global warming by banning bathroom night lights.[94]

When Democrats took control of Congress, they vowed to reform earmarks but not to eliminate them. The number of earmarks, and their cost, did decline in 2007, but in 2008, an election year, they rose again. The Democrats also put through rules that outlawed earmarks for any private business or corporation. However, corporations, sometimes with help from their members of Congress, immediately adapted by establishing nonprofit foundations, or universities, to front for them as recipients of the earmarks. One of the first appropriations bills signed by President Obama contained almost 8000 earmarks, but their $5.5 billion cost was a tiny fraction of the total budget. So far, the main reform in the earmarking process has been to force every member to publicly identify the projects and amounts they request.

Many members are more troubled by the fact that for decades Congress has been slowly ceding budget-setting power to the executive branch. White House staff typically get involved in negotiating final dollar amounts with congressional leaders, but both the Bush and Clinton administrations superseded the conventional congressional bargaining process by working out final versions of appropriations bills with the congressional leadership before conference committees ever met. The real budget decisions are made in these kinds of private negotiations among congressional leaders, their staff, administration aides, individual members, and the president. The rest of Congress is often left with a take-it-or-leave-it budget package laid out in separate bills for each of twelve functional areas or in several omnibus bills.

Executive branch agencies as well are often left high and dry by this method of budgeting. They have to plan and carry out daily business on continuing resolutions, not knowing how much money will actually be appropriated for their agency in any fiscal year. They may not receive an appropriation until four or five months into the year and then be expected to spend it (or lose it) within the remaining months of the year. This is one significant way in which the legislative branch can hinder the work of the executive branch and contribute to the federal bureaucracy functioning less efficiently and effectively.[95]

MEMBERS ON THE JOB

This section examines how members of Congress go about the day-to-day business of legislating, budget making, oversight, and constituency service, as well as carrying out party caucus- and campaign-related activities.

Negotiating the Informal System

To be successful, representatives and senators must not only serve their constituents and get reelected but must also know how to work with their colleagues and how to maneuver within the intricate system of parliamentary rules, customs, and traditions that govern the House and Senate.

Informal Norms

First among the many lessons every new member must learn are the customary ways of interacting with colleagues both on and off the floor of Congress.[96] These **informal norms** help keep the institution running smoothly by attempting to minimize friction and allowing competition to occur within an atmosphere of civility. In recent years, the norms of Congress have changed to become less collegial.

The Founders' velveteen breeches, frock coats, and white wigs symbolized the drawing room gentility of their circle and helped to mask bitter rivalries. It was Thomas Jefferson, the best known of the gentlemen farmers, who in 1801 wrote the foundational rules for in-chamber conduct in an effort to contain the inevitable conflict between Federalist and Anti-Federalist, abolitionist and slave owner. His notes laid the groundwork for Congress's system of informal norms.

Throughout much of the twentieth century, the most important norm was institutional loyalty, the expectation that members would respect their fellow members and Congress itself, especially their own chamber. Personal criticism of one's colleagues was to be avoided, and mutual respect was fostered by such conventions as referring to colleagues by title, such as "the distinguished senator from New York," rather than by name.

Although it is still the norm in Great Britain's House of Commons to hear members refer to one another as the "right honorable member" or "my right honorable colleague," never using personal names, today one is apt to hear much more informal and not particularly polite language when members of our Congress talk to and about one another and the institution. And even in the House of Commons, the formal terms of address are a veneer, as Labour and Conservative members sit on opposite sides of a narrow chamber floor hooting and shouting epithets at their fellow honorables. However, this is a long and well-loved tradition in the House of Commons and not a modern manifestation of increased hostility.

Melina Mara/*The Washington Post*/Getty Images

When President Obama gave his State of the Union speech to Congress, he asserted that his proposal did not cover illegal aliens. Representative Joe Wilson (R-S.C.) interrupted and yelled, "You lie!" (Obama's proposal in fact did not cover illegal aliens.) The outburst reflected the incivility that pervades Congress now.

In recent years, hostility among members of Congress seems as sharp as among those delegates to the First Congress, but scholars differ on the origins of this decline in civility. Some say it dates back decades to the time Democrats had a lock on both chambers, leaving Republicans permanently aggrieved. Some say it began with Watergate—that Nixon's enemies list and Congress's impeachment hearings poisoned the atmosphere. Others tie it to the hearings on the nominations of Robert Bork and Clarence Thomas to the Supreme Court, which were notorious for their overheated exchanges and character bashing. Still others trace the decline to Newt Gingrich's strategy as a minority tactician in the 1980s. He attacked not only the Democratic leaders but also Congress as an institution, calling it "sick," a severe departure from the institutional loyalty norm, in an attempt to sour the public on Congress so that voters would be inclined to defeat incumbent Democrats. Once the Republicans captured control of the House and Gingrich became their leader, he encouraged an aggressive, combative style on the floor of the House.

Figure 4 shows the proportion of all votes in which majorities of one party oppose the majority of the other. If we use this as a definition of partisanship, this information gives little support to the idea that it was a strong Democratic majority or Watergate that caused the upturn in partisan voting. The proportion of votes cast along party lines stayed about the same from the 1950s through the 1970s. Then the proportion of these votes began to increase and did so steadily through 2009 (the last measurement we have at the time of this writing). The only exception was a dip right after 9/11, but during the last four years of the Bush administration, the proportion returned to the Clinton era levels.

Another way to think of partisanship in congressional voting is what proportion of each party goes along with its majority on party votes. That increase is also vivid. In the 1950s through the 1970s, between 63 and 70 percent of party members voted with their party. This proportion rose in the Reagan years but the increase was dramatic in the Clinton and Bush years. Now, on party majority votes, nearly 90 percent of all members in both the House and Senate vote with their party. Thus party unity voting has increased between 20 and 30 percentage points in the House and Senate since the peak years of Democratic dominance in the 1950s through 1970s.[97]

The voting data give more support to the Bork, Thomas, and especially the Gingrich explanations, since there was some increase in partisanship in 1987, at the time of the Bork hearing; in 1992 and 1993, after the Thomas hearings; and dramatically in 1995, after Gingrich became majority leader.

It was in this climate that Republicans launched the impeachment hearings against President Clinton, leaving many Democrats wanting revenge for what they felt was an outrageous diversion of time and energy from crucial business. Under former Speaker Hastert's leadership, it seemed at first that there would be a trend toward more conciliation and civility in the conduct of House business. But in 2003, the Republican leadership, reinvigorated by gains in the midterm elections and determined to tighten procedural control over the House, called in the Capitol Police to break up a meeting of Democratic members. Several months later, Hastert broke House rules by holding a vote open for three hours while he rounded up the support needed to pass a Bush administration bill.

The strengthening of party leadership and unity voting has continued under Democratic control, and the long

---

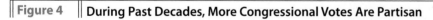

| **Figure 4** | **During Past Decades, More Congressional Votes Are Partisan** |

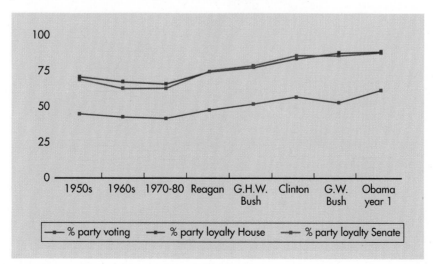

Note: "% party voting" are the percentage of votes where a majority of one party opposes a majority of the other; "% party loyalty" are the proportions of each party who support their party when party voting occurs.
SOURCE: *CQ Weekly, January 11, 2010, 124.*

history of centrist collaboration across party lines that continued, albeit somewhat diminished, into the early 1990s has not returned. A veteran congressional scholar has described the conduct of business in recent years as "the demise of regular order . . . a situation in which producing the party program trumps any institutional concerns. There is no one tending to the institutional maintenance of Congress."[98]

The only reassuring aspect of the intense degree of partisanship is that it is neither new nor destined to last. Congress passes through cycles of greater and lesser civility. Although they may be name-calling now, and having the occasional shoving match, they are not beating up or shooting at one another as members were in the years leading up to the Civil War. And Jefferson's ears were hardly virgin; a frequent target of gossip and character attacks, he could dish with the best and used paid agents to spread slander about his Federalist opponents.

Formal Standards of Conduct

In addition to the informal rules, members of Congress are expected to conform to the ethical standards of conduct they have set for themselves. The Constitution gives each chamber the power to establish rules, pass judgment on conduct, and, by a two-thirds vote, expel a member. 🗲 **Art. I, Sec. 5** Each chamber has a select committee to hear ethics complaints; it is the only committee where membership is equally split between the parties rather than in proportion to the number of seats they hold. In the House a separate subcommittee is established for each new investigation. Unethical behavior includes such action as using one's position for personal enrichment, using it for financial gain of a family member or campaign contributor, misusing campaign funds, violating codes of conduct toward other members, or being found guilty of criminal conduct.

The 109th Congress (2005–2006) was one of the most scandal-ridden in decades, with members of both parties and hundreds of staff members accused of ethics violations for acceptance of gifts, free travel, and questionable campaign contributions from powerful lobbyists. (Refer to Chapter 9 for more on these scandals.)

At the beginning of the 110th Congress, no fewer than eleven members were under federal investigation, and several others were being investigated by ethics committees. (Of Alaska's three-member congressional delegation, two were being investigated by federal authorities and the third was the subject of an ethics complaint.[99]) Corruption was one of the issues voters cited as extremely important in how they voted in the 2006 elections, and the Democrats promised to make ethical reform an issue if they won control of either or both houses. The 2007 Honest Leadership and Open Government Act authorized a new Office of Congressional Ethics, which is to be staffed by six nonpartisan outsiders, three chosen by the Speaker and three by the minority leader. The main goal of the reform was to reduce the influence of lobbyists by restricting their ability to make gifts to members and do favors for them.[100]

Despite the issuance of new ethics manuals, there is no sign that the reform will actually change the way members and lobbyists interact. Both members and lobbyists immediately saw ways to evade the law by passing money previously spent on meals and gifts indirectly to members through their campaign committees. Also, the reforms were mainly a reaction to the lobbying scandals that were in the public eye. Less well known to the public is that many members of the House and Senate, including the Senate majority leader Reid, have close

Cross-aisle collaboration is not as common in the Senate as it used to be, but *(from left)* Democrat John Kerry (Mass.), Republican Lindsey Graham (S.C.), and independent Joe Lieberman (Conn.) coauthored a bill on energy reform and climate change. But after a disagreement with Senate Majority Leader Reid about scheduling of the bill, Sen. Graham dropped his sponsorship and the bill never came to a vote.

relatives who lobby Congress. And some members employ family with campaign funds or use their positions in other ways to financially benefit relatives. As evidence of how little has changed, nineteen House members and three senators were believed to be under investigation during 2009–2010.[101]

Specialization

By specializing, a member can become an expert, and possibly influential, in a few policy areas. Given the scope of Congress's legislative authority, members cannot be knowledgeable in all areas, so House members especially specialize in subject areas important to their home districts or related to their committees. The leader of one freshman class of legislators advised his new colleagues, "If you've got twenty things you want to do, see where everything is. You'll find that maybe ten of those are already being worked on by people and that while you may be supportive in that role, you don't need to carry the ball. . . . If you try to take the lead on everything, you'll be wasting your time and re-creating the work that's already going on."[102]

The Senate's smaller membership cannot support this degree of specialization. In addition, each senator represents an entire state with interests in a much broader range of issues than those of a single House district. For those senators considering a run for the presidency, there is also a need to be well versed on a variety of issues.

Reciprocity

Tied to specialization is the norm of reciprocity. Reciprocity, or "logrolling," is summarized in the statement "You support my bill, and I'll support yours." The term *logrolling* dates to the 1780s, when an Ohio Federalist said that he did not really understand the terminology but he thought it meant "bargaining with each other for the little loaves and fishes of the State."[103]

Reciprocity helps each member get the votes needed to pass legislation favored in his or her district. The traditional way in which reciprocity worked was described by the late Sam Ervin, Democratic senator from tobacco-growing North Carolina: "I got to know Milt Young [then a senator from North Dakota] very well. And I told Milt, 'Milt, I would just like you to tell me how to vote about wheat and sugar beets and things like that, if you just help me out on tobacco.'"[104]

Reciprocity is another informal norm that is disappearing. Open meetings, media scrutiny, stronger party leadership, and more partisan voting have made it more difficult for members to "go along" on bills unpopular in their constituency or with the party leadership. However, it is still important for winning acceptance of earmark requests (don't oppose the new museum for my district and I won't oppose the road work in your district) and for passing the big Christmas tree bills, such as farm subsidies. Former senator Henry Jackson (D-Wash.) explained how he put together enough votes to pass a complex bill this way: "Maggie said

he talked to Russell, and Tom promised this if I would back him on Ed's amendment, and Mike owes me one for last year's help on Pete's bill."[105]

Making Alliances

Any member who wants to get legislation passed, move into the party leadership, or run for higher office needs to develop a network of allies among colleagues. Members of the more egalitarian House may be able to move faster on this than their colleagues in the Senate, but all newcomers have to be sensitive to the prerogatives of the senior members and committee chairs. Former senator Alan Simpson (R-Wyo.) described his first two or three years as "really tough . . . you just try to look like you're smart. I just tried to dress well and show up and hope they'd think I was smart."[106]

Crossing ideological lines to find sponsors or votes for a bill is not uncommon. One of the most unusual alliances of recent years was between former senators. Hillary Clinton (D-N.Y.) and the Christian conservative Sam Brownback (R-Kans.) joined forces to promote new measures to stop human trafficking, especially the selling of women and children into prostitution.

An increasingly common venue for cooperation among members, especially in the House, is the **special interest caucus.** Caucuses are organized by members who share partisan, ideological, issue, regional, or identity interests to pool their strength in promoting shared interests and gaining passage of related legislation. Caucus size ranges from a handful to more than a hundred; almost every member belongs to at least one. The House and Senate have 250 caucuses, some organized cross-chamber. Some caucuses have a narrow focus, such as those promoting bikes, ball bearings, boating, the wine industry, or wireless technology. Some are rooted in personal experience, such as the caucuses of Vietnam veterans and cancer survivors.[107]

Among the most significant of the caucuses are those designed to pool the strength of women and minorities. These caucuses develop policy in key issue areas and serve national constituencies. The Caucus for Women's Issues, working across party, racial, and ethnic lines, has managed to recruit almost all women members and many male colleagues as well. With a Republican and a Democrat serving as cochairs, the caucus is regarded as one of the most bipartisan in Congress. Its legislative agenda includes supportive measures for women-owned businesses, pay equity, and women in the military.

Hispanics, East Asians, Native Americans, Asian Indians, and African Americans also have special interest caucuses. The Black Caucus was organized in 1970 by thirteen House members determined to gain some clout, and in the 111th Congress, all forty African Americans in the House were members. Because there were no African American

Rep. Earl Blumenauer (D-Ore.) chairs the House Bicycle Caucus, which promotes the bicycle as a green alternative to the car.

conservative Senator Orrin Hatch (R-Utah). Sometimes the chair of a committee develops both a close working relationship and personal friendship with the ranking minority member, as happened, for example, between Senators Richard Lugar (R-Ind.) and Joseph Biden (D-Del.) of Foreign Relations, before Biden became vice president. In both houses, much of the work gets hammered out in personal conversations and exchanges away from official venues.

Political Action Committees

The most influential members of Congress now have their own PACs for raising campaign funds to disperse to colleagues. When Hillary Rodham Clinton was just a junior senator, she was able to use her celebrity and connections to raise millions of dollars for her PAC, Friends of Hillary. She used the funds to support the reelection campaigns of colleagues, building a network of supporters. She could then cash in these favors when looking for a committee chair or a leadership position and later during her run for the presidency. Nancy Pelosi was able to beat out rivals for the minority leader position in 2001 largely because of her phenomenal ability to get campaign donations for colleagues. By the time she announced that she wanted the position, dozens of fellow House members were in her political debt. Tom DeLay, the very powerful former House Republican majority leader, also built his clout by dispensing funds. Today the use of personal PACs to dole out money to the reelection committees of colleagues is standard practice for any member with ambitions within Congress or beyond.

Republicans in Congress, the Black Caucus declined in influence under the Republican majority. Although there will be two African Americans among the Republicans who take control of the House in 2011, only one has said he will join the Black Caucus.

Personal Friendships

In some cases, caucuses are the source of a House member's closest political allies. But with the exception of its Centrist Coalition, caucuses are not as important in the much smaller Senate. There, personal friendships might count for more than committee or caucus membership. "Acquire a friend" by helping someone when he needs it, "and you'll never regret it," is the advice of former senator Bob Kerrey (D-Neb.) to those new to the Senate.[108]

Strong relationships of trust sometimes develop across party lines. John Kerry (D-Mass.) and John McCain (R-Ariz.), two decorated Vietnam War veterans, became friends while working together on veterans' issues. A more unusual example was the close friendship between the very liberal Senator Edward Kennedy (d. 2010) and the very

Using the Media

Forty years ago, the workday routine in both House and Senate for resolving most issues involved bargaining with other members, lobbyists, and White House aides. Working privately, one on one in small groups, or in committees, members and staff discussed and debated issues, exchanged information, and planned strategies. Even though many issues are still resolved through these private channels, much has changed in the way Congress operates.

For today's members to further their goals, it is often as important to "go public," to reach beyond colleagues and to appeal directly to the larger public, as it is to engage in private negotiation.[109] **Going public** means taking an issue debate to the public through both the "old" media, as Congress does when it televises floor debates and important hearings, and the new media on the Web. The most media-oriented members of Congress are experts in providing short and interesting comments for the nightly network news, writing articles for major newspapers, appearing on talk shows and as commentators on news programs, and using their websites to publicize their priorities and opinions.

No member of Congress today has to wait for the press to come to her. All members have websites, which they use to facilitate casework and publicize their own actions. Every district visit, town meeting, and photo-op is put up on the website immediately. Members who are more technologically savvy (or have a staff member who is) post their speeches on YouTube, linked to their website, have a Facebook site, and link to Twitter, Flickr, and other social websites. Some with larger political ambitions maintain their own blogs. Tweets and Facebook postings are used not only to keep constituents abreast of policy positions and the minutiae of members' daily lives but also to alert voters to other opportunities to see or hear them—such as radio and TV interviews and scheduled stops in the district. House minority leader John Boehner (R-Ohio) reported more than 100,000 Facebook friends in 2010, and John McCain (R-Ariz.) led the Senate and placed second only to Oprah Winfrey in number of Twitter followers.[110]

Despite members' growing reliance on computers and electronic communication, the ban on the use of laptops on the floor of the House and Senate remains in place, and neither senators nor their staff are allowed to use their PDAs in chamber. The House does allow members to use their PDAs to receive and send e-mails from the House floor, but cell phones are banned.[111]

Of course, television remains important in publicizing activities of members. In the early days of television, networks broadcast only important congressional proceedings, such as the McCarthy hearings and testimony on investigations into the Watergate scandal and the Iran-Contra affair. In 1979, after considerable controversy and anxiety, the House began televising its proceedings on the new Cable Satellite Public Affairs Network, or C-SPAN, created and funded by cable companies as a public service. Fearful of being overshadowed by the House, in 1986 the Senate followed suit. C-SPAN broadcasts 24 hours a day, and two of its three advertisement-free channels are available with almost all basic cable services. They reach 100 million households and have about 40 million regular viewers. Although viewership is small compared with that of commercial networks, the C-SPAN audience has a higher educational level and is better informed and more interested in both local and national government than the general public. Viewers are equally divided among liberals and conservatives, and nine out of ten viewers voted in the 2008 election.[112]

Local television listings provide times for daily coverage of House and Senate floor proceedings as well as for committee hearings and other official business. In addition, C-SPAN covers members of Congress on the campaign trail, attending fund-raisers, giving stump speeches, and chatting with constituents. Besides its unbroken coverage of events, what sets C-SPAN apart from commercial network coverage of Congress is that there is no intermediary between the viewers and the events and people they are watching. C-SPAN does not use reporters, so televised events are free of commentary and on-the-spot analysis. This may be why C-SPAN is only one of three television news sources to be named as "most trusted" by Republicans, Democrats, and independents alike.

The congressional leadership goes public, too. Leaders of both parties regularly call producers of television talk shows to suggest guests. They meet with the press and often have prepared statements. Before important congressional votes on key issues, the leadership plans letters to the editors of important newspapers and floor speeches designed for maximum television coverage.

Balancing the Work

Multiple committee assignments, in combination with party caucus work, fund-raising, and visits to the district, mean that members have impossible schedules. At times, committees cannot obtain quorums because members are tied up with other obligations. Members attend meetings with legislative staff in tow to take notes and to consult with during hearings. If they cannot attend or have to leave for floor business or another meeting, a staffer is there to take notes and brief the member later.

Use of Staff

We have already noted the huge staff available to members. Members of the majority party are at an advantage here because they control two-thirds of the money budgeted for committees and therefore can hire two-thirds of committee staff. Staffers do most of the background work on the complex foreign and domestic issues that cross the members' desks every day, aided when deep expertise is needed by the CRS staff. The Senate Appropriations Committee alone has 150 staff members, each of whom specializes in some arcane aspect of the budget, in the process gaining a good deal of power through the mastery of information crucial to funding the government. In the Senate, where staff are often better versed on an issue than the member, cultivating colleagues' chief aides may be essential to winning support for legislation. "You can get the senator on your side, and that works nine times out of ten, but if you don't have the staffer on your side too, it is very, very difficult."[113]

Through their service, staffers gain a great deal of experience and the opportunity to create a network of contacts who can help them should they decide to run for Congress, so it is not surprising that 125 members of a recent Congress were former congressional staffers.[114]

CONGRESS AND THE PUBLIC

As we have noted, one of the most frustrating things about Congress for the average citizen is the "messiness" of the legislative process. Not only is the process of crafting laws

DOONESBURY © 2007 G. B. Trudeau. Reprinted with permission of Universal Press Syndicate. All rights reserved.

incredibly complex, but it also provides many places along the way where individual legislators and interest groups, often for seemingly (or truly) selfish motives, can exact concessions from the people who want to pass the bill. Add to that the partisan bickering, with Democrats picking a proposal apart simply because a Republican introduced it or vice versa, and casual observers throw up their hands in exasperation.

It seems that the more media exposure Congress gets, with the processes of democracy exposed for all to see, the less supportive the public is of its work. The conflict and gridlock, if not admirable, are not surprising either, given our complex constituencies with competing interests and worldviews. But members contribute to the poor image by belittling colleagues and the institution itself when they seek reelection by running against "Washington."

Now as never before, every step—or misstep—that members of Congress take is carried to every part of the nation. Or, as one observer commented, "A member's every twitch is blared to the world, thanks to C-SPAN, open meetings laws, financial-disclosure reports, and every misstep is logged in a database for the use of some future office seeker."[115] And that was more than a decade ago; today we must add all manner of mobile phones, YouTube, social network sites, and blogs. Members must keep in mind that every public utterance is almost certainly being monitored by someone and that if it is the least bit newsworthy, it will soon appear in a blog or—worse—YouTube. Of course, now members have round-the-clock electronic access to their constituents and therefore the means to get out their own versions of a story.

Media attention is valuable, because we prize open government in a democracy. But too much is not so good, because in a heterogeneous society we rely on compromise to achieve our public goals, and under the harsh glare of media, there are fewer opportunities to compromise and deliberate without fear of losing votes back home. But the public has little patience for extended partisan debates even when they reflect real policy differences among the people.

Of the three branches of government, the public has been least supportive of Congress and generally gives its highest level of support to the Supreme Court, the institution that is most isolated from the public. Unlike legislative debates, little of the disagreement, negotiation, and compromise of the Court has taken place in public view. Confidence in the presidency and approval ratings for individual presidents can fluctuate wildly, as both Bushes discovered when their approval ratings fell from near 90 percent to the high 20s. A president's support can soar when acting as a national leader (chief of state), especially in wartime, and then suffer huge losses as a political leader (head of government) when his policies fail.

But the public's attitudes about Congress are also conflicted (see Figure 5). In recent decades people's approval of their own representative was 20 or more points higher than approval for Congress as a whole. Members benefit from local media coverage that is overwhelmingly positive, in part because many of these stories are prepared by the members themselves. But local press stories on Congress as a whole are also far more positive than those written by the national press corps.[116] Occasionally the public gets so down on Congress that it affects constituents' attitudes toward their own representatives. This was true prior to the 2006 midterm election, when Congress's approval ratings stood at a historic low of 23 percent and the Democrats took control of both Houses from the Republicans.[117] It was true again before the

| Figure 5 | Public Opinion toward Congress |

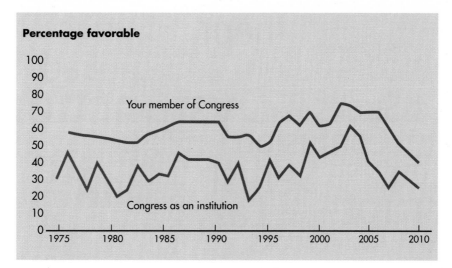

People were asked whether they approve of the way Congress is handling its job and whether they approve of the way the representative from their congressional district is handling his or her job. People consistently voice more approval of their member than of Congress itself. In 2008, according to Rasmussen polls, congressional approval fell into the single digits.

SOURCE: Combined responses from similar surveys by the Gallup Organization and the Harris Survey. Roger H. Davidson, Walter J. Oleszek, and Frances E. Lee, Congress and Its Members, 11th ed. (Washington, D.C.: CQ Press, 2008), 490.

2010 midterms, when some polls showed congressional approval ratings below 20 percent.

A major factor in Congress's low approval ratings is the public's perception that most members care more about power than about the best interests of the nation and more about pleasing lobbyists who can feed their campaign coffers than serving the interests of the district. The public is not mistaken in its impression of a cozy relationship between Congress and special interest lobbies (see Figure 6). What is less clear is the overall impact that has.

One of the factors contributing to low public confidence in government before the 2008 election was the subprime mortgage crisis. Many in the public realize that antipathy to regulation in both the White House and Congress played some role in the collapse of the financial industry, and that the reluctance to regulate may have had something to do with the large campaign contributions members had received from those firms. It was also not far from the public mind that some members responsible for legislation to deal with the crisis had ties to the industries under investigation.

Despite all this, the idea of Congress as a constitutionally mandated "people's house" is esteemed by the public. It is the people in Congress and the way Congress works that the public dislikes. Just over half of all voters turn out for congressional elections (less in years when the president is not being elected), and most of the public is poorly informed about what Congress does and how it works. For example, about half of Americans polled thought the Senate should

change the filibuster rule, but a survey of civic knowledge showed that only 26 percent of Americans actually know that it takes 60 votes to stop a filibuster.[118]

This pattern persists even with C-SPAN coverage and even though many local papers each week print a congressional scorecard with the voting records of local legislators. Constituents are much more likely to know about the ethics violations and sexual improprieties of members of Congress than they are about the legislation passed in any session.

The public evaluation of Congress as accomplishing "not much" or "nothing at all" stems in part from the public's lack of awareness of what Congress has actually done. However, in 2006 very little actually was done because members were waiting to see what the balance of power would be after the 2006 midterm elections. This happened again before the 2010 midterms, when Republicans believed they had a chance of retaking control of one and perhaps both chambers of Congress. It was in their interests to try to block every Democratic bill that might help Democrats at the polls, even extension of unemployment compensation for the long-term jobless. Even so, the Senate did pass several pieces of major legislation, including health care reform and financial reform. It was more difficult for Republicans to block House action because of House rules and the Democrats' large majority. But because of the 60-vote rule in the Senate, coupled with the powers given to individual senators, it is easy in the Senate to prevent most House-passed bills from becoming law.

Figure 6	The Public Had Few Good Words for Congress in 2009

Wordles are created at a website that provides a visual representation of the frequency that words are used in a text or list. This wordle was created from a list of words that individuals used to describe Congress in a survey done in March 2009, after months of congressional wrangling over health care and before the bill was passed.
SOURCE: *http://pewresearch.org/pubs/1533/congress-in-a-word-cloud-dysfunctional-corrupt-selfish.*

CONCLUSION: Congress's Role in Government

James Madison could not have stated it more clearly than he did in *Federalist Paper* 51: "In republican government, the legislative authority necessarily predominates." That does not mean the other two branches always accept a leading role for Congress. In fact, Senate historian Richard Baker says the Constitution is "a virtual invitation to struggle" between the branches of government. However, no one quarrels with the premise that Congress's constitutional mandate is to legislate and to raise and appropriate money to pay for government.

In addition to its responsibility for cooperating with and acting as a check on the other two branches, Congress's main problem in governing is how to balance the obligation to represent its various local and state constituencies against its responsibility to work for the national interest, which is something more than the sum of its parts. The pressures of elections, especially fund-raising, and of constituency service seem at times to undermine Congress's ability to focus on making policy that serves the national interest. Pressure to be in the home district meeting constituents competes with legislators' desires to do a good job at lawmaking and to work more efficiently. This is the perennial dilemma of representatives and senators: how to meet the demands of the district or state—that is, to do the job members are sent to do—in order to get reelected and at the same time serve the national interest. The public is part of the problem because citizens in each state and district want their senators and representatives to take care of local needs and interests, even while looking down on the institution for its pork-barrel politics and big spending.

Pressure to raise money for reelection campaigns incurs obligations to interest groups that may not be consistent with either the members' or the constituents' views. Indeed, congressional leaders from both parties have problems articulating a clear vision in part because so many of them have become dependent on the contributions of PACs for their campaign funding. This puts them in the position of having to support some interests that are not consistent with voters' views or interests.

The procedures and organization of Congress give individuals and small groups opportunities to block or redirect action, and the fragmented committee and subcommittee structure in both houses also offers many venues in which bills can be killed.

The increasing partisanship in Congress has been one of the biggest changes since the mid-1990s. In the past decade, partisan voting has hit record highs in both parties as the legislative process has become party-dominated.[119] Under Republican control, the Democrats were shut out of many important stages of the process, including the drafting of final versions of legislation in conference committees, and back in the majority, the Democrats returned the favor. This behavior heightens partisan divisions and makes the output of Congress less a product of compromise and thus less responsive to the broader public.

Hyperpartisanship also affects the relationship of Congress to the other branches and to governance as a whole when it allows the legislative process to become hostage to party conflict. The use of holds to stall action on nominations to the executive branch or the judiciary, the threat of filibusters to block legislation, and the political wrangling over appropriations that impairs the work of the federal bureaucracy put the will of individual members or the party above the constitutional obligation to govern the nation. For those who believe that government is best that governs least, the use of tactics that prevent government from acting may be seen as positive. But that was not the intent of the Founders in making Congress the most important branch. Congress is the branch most accountable to the people through direct elections, and it is Congress that appropriates the money without which the federal bureaucracy cannot do its work or the government even exist. It is Congress that raises armies and provides for national defense; it is Congress that established the federal judiciary below the Supreme Court level and the Senate that must confirm its justices; and it is Congress that stands as the greatest check on abuse of presidential power.

KEY TERMS

appropriations	311	minority leader	295
authorizations	311	oversight	309
casework	291	party caucus	295
cloture	306	party government	290
conference committee	308	pay-as-you-go (paygo)	312
constituency	283	pork-barrel projects	293
constituency service	291	Seventeenth Amendment	295
divided government	293	reapportionment	283
earmark	312	redistricting	284
filibuster	305	Rules Committee	294
gerrymander	284	seniority rule	300
going public	318	Speaker of the House	294
informal norms	314	special interest caucus	317
majority leader	295	standing committees	299
markup	303	supermajority	307
		unified government	308
		whips	295

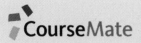

Access an interactive eBook, chapter-specific interactive learning tools (including flashcards, quizzes, videos), and more at CourseMate for *Understanding American Government*. Log in at CengageBrain.com.

Public expectations for President Obama were sky-high and unrealistic.

Talking Points

In 1967 Lyndon Johnson was facing every president's dilemma— the hard truth that governing is all about making choices. Johnson was a legendary legislator who had become one of the most ambitious—some say overreaching—presidents of the twentieth century. He was the principal backer of, and legislative strategist for, much of our social safety net, including Medicare and Medicaid and greater income support for the poor, programs collectively known as the Great Society. Johnson also saw through Congress the major civil rights legislation of the modern era, all the while backing the expansion of American military power and the war in Vietnam.

Presiding over a thriving economy in a time of increasing political equality and social justice, Johnson was nevertheless pushing himself toward political self-immolation by refusing to accept that his administration would not be able to do everything he hoped for. He told presidential historian Doris Kearns Goodwin (his former aide), "If I left the woman I really loved—the Great Society—in order to get involved with that bitch of a war on the other side of the world, then I would lose everything at home. All my programs. . . . All my dreams. . . ."[1]

Presidents have to set priorities and make the hard choices forced on them by the finiteness of resources, including public support, and the limitations of presidential power. But Johnson said, "I was determined to be a leader of war *and* a leader of peace. I refused to let my critics push me into choosing one or the other."[2] Even as he came to see that the Vietnam War was not winnable and that it was costing him the public support and revenue necessary to achieve his highest priority—the domestic program— Johnson was unable to scale back his goals.[3]

When historians rank Johnson among American presidents, his Vietnam policy often overshadows the domestic successes. "He did more for racial justice than any president since Abraham Lincoln. He built more social protections than anyone since Franklin Roosevelt. He was probably the greatest legislative politician in American history," but he was also "largely responsible for one of the greatest disasters in American history"—the Vietnam War, which he inherited but sharply escalated.[4]

The lesson for any ambitious president worried about his legacy is the necessity of accepting the fact that to govern well is to choose wisely.

© Chris Britt 2009

Pharaohs, consuls, kings, queens, emperors, tsars, prime ministers, and councils of varied sizes served as executives in other governments before 1789. But no national government had a president, an elected executive with authority equal to and independent of a national legislature, until George Washington was elected president of the United States.

At its inception, the presidency was a not very powerful office in a fledgling country that had few international ties and virtually no standing army. The office's first occupants were drawn from among the Founders, and a few of them, Washington and Thomas Jefferson especially, served with some reluctance. Jefferson in fact called the office a "splendid misery," and one of his successors, John Quincy Adams (1825–1829), said, "No man who ever held the office would congratulate another on attaining it." Throughout the nineteenth century, except during the Civil War, the real power at the national level resided in Congress, so much so that Woodrow Wilson, who was a political scientist before becoming president, characterized our national government as a "congressional government."[5] Consequently, between Andrew Jackson in the 1830s and Franklin Roosevelt in the 1930s, most men who sought the presidency were "ordinary people, with very ordinary reputations."[6] There were powerful exceptions—such as Abraham Lincoln, Theodore Roosevelt, and Woodrow Wilson—and a few with exceptional achievements before their presidencies—such as Ulysses Grant (1869–1877) and Herbert Hoover (1929–1233)—who fared badly in the White House.

Today, the president of the United States is among the most powerful people in the world. When he enters a room, everyone stands. When he appears at ceremonial functions, the band plays "Hail to the Chief." Wherever he goes, a military aide carries the nuclear "suitcase" containing descriptions of options, protocols, and authentication codes in case he has to launch a nuclear attack. Under presidents who stretched their powers to the outer limits—Johnson, Nixon, and George W. Bush—the office became so powerful that some scholars and commentators spoke of the "**imperial presidency**."

Nevertheless, all presidents become frustrated with the limits on their power. At times, they feel that they're saddled with an "impossible" or "imperiled" presidency.[7]

Consider the past two presidents. Bill Clinton saw his agenda, aside from economic policy and welfare reform, sidetracked by one congressional investigation after another and found himself impeached for lying about a sexual affair. But George W. Bush, with a boost from public support after 9/11 and an acquiescent Republican-majority Congress, started two wars, adopted numerous policies restricting civil liberties, and pushed through major tax cuts. The Clinton terms suggested an impossible presidency, whereas the Bush years sparked renewed talk about an imperial presidency.

In this chapter, we'll consider the paradox of presidential power and presidential weakness. We look first at the terms of office, then at the formal duties that reflect the Founders' ideas of the president's role in a federal republic. Next we describe the additional roles presidents took on as political parties were established, government grew, and the people began looking to presidents as political advocates and problem solvers. We describe the organizational structure of the presidency, the role of staff and of the first lady and vice president, and the president's relationship with Congress. Finally, we discuss the ebb and flow of presidential power.

TERMS OF SERVICE

The Constitution specifies only three conditions to be eligible for the presidency: one must be a "natural-born citizen," be at least thirty-five years old, and have resided in the United States for at least fourteen years before taking office. Art. II, Sec. 1

Historically, it has helped to be a white male with roots in small-town America; a Protestant with ancestry from England, Germany, or Scandinavia; a resident of a populous state; and a "good family man." In recent decades, this profile has broadened considerably as society has become more inclusive, the electorate more diverse, and social norms more tolerant of divorce, but sexual, racial, and religious barriers remain. (See the box "Presidential Candidates: The Pool Deepens, but . . . .")

In addition to the religious, gender, and race issues noted in the box, class (education, income, and social standing) also poses constraints on electability. Our early presidents were clearly from among the elite, but at least since the election of Andrew Jackson in 1828, most candidates have felt the need to evoke the image of the common man. In 1840, William Henry Harrison used a log cabin as his campaign symbol even though he grew up on a Virginia plantation.[8] Probably no one did more to reinforce the image of the common man as a wise and great leader than Abraham Lincoln, who really did grow up in a log cabin. But Harry Truman, who, like Lincoln, actually had been a plowman,

american*diversity

Presidential Candidates: The Pool Deepens, but . . .

John Kennedy was the first Roman Catholic elected to the White House (1960) and Ronald Reagan the first divorced man (1980). But no non-Christian has broken the religion barrier. In 2008, Mitt Romney, a Mormon (a member of the Church of Jesus Christ of Latter Day Saints, which identifies itself as a Christian denomination), found his religion a major issue in the race for the Republican nomination, especially among those who do not accept Mormons as Christian. (See Figure 1.)

Although the number of religiously unaffiliated Americans is growing, it is improbable that a nonbeliever could get elected to the White House. It is also unlikely that an openly gay or lesbian candidate could get elected, even though several have broken through that barrier by winning seats in Congress. But to date Americans have only once elected a never-married man to the presidency.

In 1972 Rep. Shirley Chisholm (D-N.Y.), the first black woman to seek a major party nomination for president, said that she met more discrimination as a woman than as an African American (see Chapter 8). The 2008 primaries revived the debate over whether sexism or racism is the greater barrier to winning the White House. Poll respondents thought Hillary Clinton had more experience and was more prepared to be commander in chief than Obama, but she was unable to escape her identity as the wife of an ex-president. Campaign literature against her candidacy employed virtually every known form of antifeminist stereotyping. And while Obama won the Democratic nomination, he lost the white working-class vote in the primaries and constantly had to fight attacks on his patriotism and religious convictions because his father was a nonpracticing Muslim from Kenya. Once elected, he was a frequent target of racial slurs and caricatures and challenges to his native-born American citizenship, even while much of the rest of the country was congratulating itself on being postracial.

Figure 1 **Voters' Perceptions of Mitt Romney**

During the presidential primaries in 2008, voters were asked, "What are the first three words that come to mind when you think about [name of candidate]?" These words were assembled in a "tag cloud" according to the frequency with which they were mentioned. The words in largest print were the ones respondents cited most often. Although Republican candidate Mitt Romney had been governor of Massachusetts, his religion was cited far more often than his experience or any other characteristic.
SOURCE: Washington Post *poll of a national sample of 1007 adults, November 28–December 2, 2007.*

---

was the only twentieth-century president who profited from playing off that image.

Yet the public continues to expect that candidates should not be too detached from everyday experience. So even though nine of the ten presidential nominees from the major parties since 1988 have had a degree from Harvard or Yale, they have tried to prove they were not far removed from those who live in the heart of the country.[9] George W. Bush played up his Texas rather than his wealthy Maine and Connecticut roots, and John Kerry, another multimillionaire Yale graduate, took the press corps on a hunting photo-op. (Today, when log cabins are no longer in people's memory, nothing says common man like guns and hunting.)

Barack Obama was not born into an elite family—he was abandoned by his father and raised by his mother and, at times, by his grandparents—but he emphasized his work as a community organizer rather than his degrees from Columbia University and Harvard Law School. He spoke of his Kansas "roots," although he never lived there (his mother had, but he grew up in Hawaii and Indonesia), and of his ties to Chicago's tough South Side, although he taught at the elite University of Chicago and lived in an upper-middle-class neighborhood. John McCain balanced his background of privilege and wealth by choosing as a running mate a woman from the middle class who hunted and fished and was married to a blue-collar worker and union member.

While the candidates for the presidency and vice presidency are being drawn from a more diverse pool of Americans, these candidates still spend a great of time explaining why they are not all that different from the average Joe and Jane.

Experience

In addition to having the "right stuff" in terms of gender, race, religion, sexual orientation, and a common touch, does it matter if a candidate has experience, and if so, what kind of experience? Evidence suggests there is no neat correlation between experience in government or in the armed services and performance in the White House, or even that experience is helpful in winning votes. In 2008, the man with least experience among the major candidates won the election. Abraham Lincoln had little experience compared to his predecessor James Buchanan or his successor Andrew

Johnson, but he was an incomparably greater president. Neither of the very highly experienced Adamses, John or John Quincy, fared that well in the White House, and neither was reelected.

Former White House chief of staff and cabinet veteran James A. Baker claims that "there's no such thing as presidential experience outside of the office itself."[10] Even if this is true, presidents who get reelected usually fare worse in their second term than in their first term. There is little evidence that experience gained in office builds in a way that makes a president increasingly effective over time.

Pay and Perks

The Constitution authorizes Congress to award the president "a Compensation," which can be neither increased nor decreased during a president's term of office. This was $25,000 a year for our first seventeen presidents; then it jumped in increments to $200,000, where it stayed for many years. It did not reach its current level of $400,000 until 2001. In real dollars, President Obama makes less than George Washington, despite the vast increase in responsibilities and scope of the job. (See Figure 2.)

In addition, there are substantial fringe benefits. Most are obvious—the White House, the rural Camp David retreat, the best health care money can buy, and fleets of cars and aircraft. The president receives $50,000 for expenses. After leaving office, the president is entitled to a generous pension (about $186,000 per year in 2009), as well as money

| Figure 2 | Presidential Pay Has Declined |

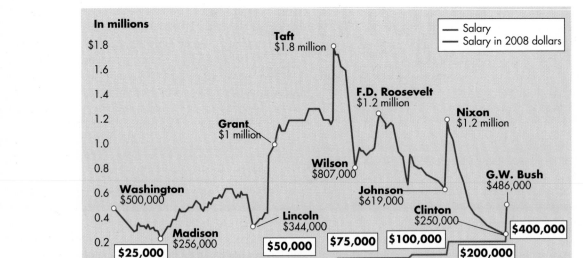

In real dollars (that is, dollars adjusted for inflation over the years), William Howard Taft was the best-paid president, with a salary of $1.8 million in today's dollars, and Bill Clinton the worst, with pay of $250,000 in today's dollars.
SOURCE: *"POTUS Pay Scale," CQ Weekly, February 2, 2009.*

for travel, an office and staff, and ten years of Secret Service protection.

Tenure and Succession

Presidents serve four-year terms. The Twenty-second Amendment 🔔 limits them to serving two terms (or ten years if they complete the term of an incumbent who dies or resigns). Four presidents died in office from illness (Harrison, Taylor, Harding, and Franklin Roosevelt), and four were assassinated (Garfield, McKinley, Lincoln, and Kennedy).

Presidents can be removed from office by impeachment and conviction. The House has the power of **impeachment**, that is, the authority to bring formal charges against a president (similar to an indictment in criminal proceedings) for "Treason, Bribery, or other high Crimes and Misdemeanors." 🔔 **Art. II, Sec. 4** In an impeachment inquiry, the House holds hearings to determine whether there is sufficient evidence to impeach, and if a majority votes yes, the president is impeached and the process moves to the Senate, where a trial is held with the chief justice of the United States presiding. Conviction requires a two-thirds vote of members present in the Senate and results in removal from the presidency.

The Founders established the impeachment option as part of the system of checks and balances, a final weapon against executive abuse of power. They borrowed it from British law as a means to remove a president who had abused his power—for example, violated the Constitution—or committed serious crimes, not as a means for unseating a president for partisan reasons. Thus James Madison objected to the inclusion of the phrase "and other high crimes and misdemeanors" because he thought it was so vague that it *could* be used for political purposes.[11] The phrase was retained, but it was precisely to guard against its partisan use that the Founders divided indictment and removal powers between the House and the Senate. 🔔 **Art. I, Sec. 2 & 3** If trying the charges were left to the popularly elected House, Hamilton wrote in *Federalist Paper* 65, "there will always be the greatest danger that the decision will be regulated more by the comparative strength of parties, than by the real demonstrations of innocence or guilt."

The procedure is cumbersome and meant to be; the Founders did not intend for the president, as head of state and the only nationally elected official in government, to be removed from office easily. Only three presidents have been targets of full impeachment proceedings.[12] Andrew Johnson, who came to office on Lincoln's assassination, was a southerner who was unpopular in his own party; he was impeached by the House in a dispute over Reconstruction policies in the post–Civil War South. By a single-vote margin, the Senate failed to convict. A century later, the House Judiciary Committee voted to impeach Richard Nixon on obstruction of justice and other charges stemming from the Watergate scandal, whereupon Nixon resigned as president,

President Richard Nixon, under threat of impeachment, was forced to resign from office.

knowing he would lose the vote if it were brought to the full House. Once out of office, he avoided indictment on criminal charges through a full pardon granted by his successor, Gerald Ford, a move that aroused a storm of controversy at the time. In 1998, Bill Clinton became the third target of the process when the House voted to open an unrestricted inquiry into possible grounds for his impeachment. The House brought two charges against him for obstruction of justice stemming from lies he told about a sexual relationship with a White House intern, but the Senate refused to convict.

Should a president be removed, die, resign, or become incapacitated, his replacement is provided for by the Constitution and supplemental laws. 🔔 **Art. II, Sec. 1** At the time the Constitution was written, it was assumed that the vice presidency would be occupied by the man who had been the runner-up in the presidential election, and the wording simply said that presidential powers "shall devolve on the Vice President." It was left to Congress to make provisions for filling the vacated vice presidency and dealing with a situation in which both the presidency and the vice presidency were vacated. When Lincoln was assassinated, there still were no provisions for replacing Vice President Andrew Johnson when he succeeded to the presidency. Had Johnson been convicted in his impeachment trial, the presidency would have gone to the president pro tempore of the Senate, who was next in the line of succession according to rules in effect at the time.

Not until 1947, two years after the death of Franklin Roosevelt had put the virtually unknown Harry Truman in the White House, did Congress pass the Presidential Succession Act, which established the order of succession of federal officeholders should both the president and the vice president be unable to serve. The list begins with the Speaker of the House, followed by the president pro tempore of the Senate, and then proceeds through the secretaries of the cabinet departments in the order in which the departments were created. However, if a cabinet member is foreign-born, which is not unusual, he or she is skipped in the line of succession.

The Succession Act has never been used because we have always had a vice president when something has happened to the president. To ensure that this is always the case, the Constitution was amended in 1967. The Twenty-fifth Amendment directs the president to name a vice president acceptable to majorities in the House and Senate if the vice presidency falls vacant. These provisions have been used twice. Nixon chose Gerald Ford to replace Spiro Agnew, who resigned after pleading no contest to charges of taking bribes when he was a public official in Maryland. After Nixon resigned and Ford became president, Ford named Nelson Rockefeller, the former governor of New York, as his vice president.

The Twenty-fifth Amendment also charges the vice president and a majority of the cabinet—or some other body named by Congress—to determine, in instances where there is doubt, whether the president is mentally or physically incapable of carrying out his duties. This provision was meant to provide for situations in which it is unclear who is or should be acting as president, such as when James Garfield was shot in July 1881. He did not die until mid-September, and during this period he was unable to fulfill any of his duties. In 1919, Woodrow Wilson had a nervous collapse in the summer and a stroke in the fall and was partially incapacitated for seven months. No one was sure about his condition, however, because his wife restricted access to him.

Under the amendment's provisions, the vice president becomes "acting president" if the president is found mentally or physically unfit to fulfill his duties. As the title suggests, the conferral of power is temporary; the president can resume office by giving Congress written notice of his recovery. If the vice president and other officials who determined the president unfit do not concur in his judgment that he has recovered, they can challenge his return to office by notifying Congress in writing. Then it falls to Congress to decide whether the president is capable of resuming his duties.

Reagan and then George W. Bush followed the spirit of this section. When they were undergoing surgery, they sent their respective vice presidents letters authorizing them to act as president while they were unconscious.

The issue of succession arose again after the terrorist attacks of 2001 when the Bush administration, just hours after the attack, activated an emergency plan established during the Eisenhower administration to provide for continuity of government in case of a nuclear attack. A shadow government of from 75 to 100 senior executive branch officials (serving in a rotation system) were removed to a secret fortified location outside the capital where they lived and worked underground twenty-four hours a day. In the immediate months after the 9/11 attacks, then Vice President Dick Cheney spent much of his time at undisclosed locations that the press referred to collectively as "the Bunker."

PRESIDENTIAL POWERS

Presidents derive their official authority from four sources: explicit powers, which are stated in the Constitution—chief executive, head of state, and commander in chief of the armed forces—implicit powers, which are implied by, or can be inferred from, the explicit powers; inherent powers, which are not in the Constitution, explicitly or implicitly, but are considered to be a national executive's prerogatives; and delegated powers, such as budget-making, which are granted to Congress by the Constitution but given to the president by various statutes. Collectively, they represent a towering set of responsibilities. In this section we look at the explicit powers and the implied and inherent powers derived from them. Art. II, Sec. 2 & 3

Chief Executive

Article II of the Constitution stipulates, "The executive power shall be vested in a president," and it charges him to "take care that the laws be faithfully executed." Sec. 1 & 3 The Founders expected Congress to pass laws and the president to implement them and manage the executive branch. Thus the president is the **chief executive**. According to the *Federalist Papers*, with respect to lawmaking, the president's responsibilities would be "mere execution" and "executive details."[13]

The Constitution has few specific provisions describing the president's administrative duties, but it does invest the president with the authority to demand written reports from his "principal officers," assigns him significant appointment and administrative powers, and implies others.

Appointment and Removal Powers

Most of the executive branch is staffed with civil service hires, but the president nominates about 4000 people to civilian positions in the departments and agencies and to boards and advisory commissions, and he also must approve (or reject) approximately 65,000 military appointments and promotions. All require Senate confirmation, but it is routinely given to about 99 percent of the presidents' appointments. Only 450 or so of the most important policy-making jobs—heads of regulatory agencies, boards and commissions, cabinet secretaries and ambassadors, and federal judges, for example—receive careful review.[14] For the highest-profile positions, such as the secretaries of state and defense, televised hearings are held prior to a confirmation vote in the Senate.

For decades, it was customary for the Senate, no matter which party controlled it, to approve the president's nominations to policy-making positions on the grounds that, having won the election, he was entitled to surround himself with people who could help put his policies in place. But the highly partisan context of the Senate in the last several decades has weakened this tradition somewhat. Nevertheless, it is expected that the president will appoint people to

After his election in 2008, Barack Obama asked President Bush to organize a meeting of past presidents so that he could solicit their advice. From left, George H. W. Bush (1989–1993), Obama, George W. Bush (2001–2009), Bill Clinton (1993–2001), and Jimmy Carter (1977–1981).

policy-making positions who, in addition to being qualified, are in agreement with his policy goals.

It also has been customary to give preference in some appointments to people with politically useful backgrounds, such as by naming a westerner secretary of the interior, a person with union ties to be labor secretary, or a close associate of the president to be attorney general. These considerations were never confining and have become less important with time. However, Barack Obama observed them in his picks to head the Interior, Labor, and Justice Departments.

The power to remove appointees is not in the Constitution, but presidents have it. Their power to name people they trust implies a power to remove those they find wanting, but because the power is not explicit, Congress has not always recognized it. The battle over removal powers was fought and largely won by Grover Cleveland, who on entering office in 1885 insisted on replacing many policy-making officials with his own appointees. He was challenged by the Senate, but he persevered. His persistence is credited with helping revitalize a presidency weakened by Andrew Johnson's impeachment.

In 1935, the Supreme Court refined this removal power by saying that presidents can remove appointees from purely administrative jobs but not from those with quasi-legislative and judicial responsibilities. This ruling protects many appointees, but distinguishing quasi-legislative and judicial positions from those with no policy-making authority can be subjective.[15]

Presidents cannot remove officials appointed to policy-making positions with fixed terms, such as those on regulatory boards and the Federal Reserve Board. Nor can the president remove federal judges, who serve for life.

Of course, presidents can appoint and remove political aides and advisers on their White House staff at will; none of these appointments require Senate approval. Presidents also have wide latitude in replacing cabinet heads and some agency directors—even though these positions do require Senate confirmation—because they are seen as agents of presidential policy. This does not keep the Senate from trying at times to badger a president into firing one of his appointees, as it did repeatedly and unsuccessfully with Clinton's attorney general, Janet Reno. More widespread pressure was placed on George W. Bush to remove Donald Rumsfeld as his secretary of defense for his conduct of the Iraq War, and Alberto Gonzalez as his attorney general for his perceived lack of political independence. A president may give in for political reasons, as Bush eventually did, but he cannot be compelled to do so. However, Congress does have the power of removal through impeachment and conviction of all "civil Officers of the United States." 🔔 **Art. II, Sec. 4**

Reorganizing Agencies

When the president enters office, a huge bureaucracy is already in place. Each new president has to be able to reorganize offices and agencies to fit his administrative and working style and to be consistent with the issue priorities he has set.[16] This can mean reassigning responsibilities, merging or abolishing offices, or creating new ones.

Within the White House Office itself, the president has a fairly free hand to reshuffle staff and offices. But any major reorganization of government departments and agencies requires congressional approval, such as George W. Bush's creation of a new cabinet-level Department of Homeland Security, which led to the reorganization of dozens of executive branch agencies and the reassignment of more than 200,000 federal employees. Congress had to approve new spending authority and the transfer of funds from one agency to another. This precipitated a classic turf battle, both within the bureaucracy and between the White House and Congress (and eight years later, investigations found the new agency to be hopelessly mired in duplication, secrecy, and bureaucracy).[17]

Inherent Executive Powers

Because the Constitution charges the president with ensuring that "the laws be faithfully executed," the courts have ruled that the president has inherent power to take actions and issue orders to fulfill that duty.

Executive orders   One of the president's inherent powers is the authority to issue directives or proclamations, called **executive orders**, that have the force of law as long as they do not violate the Constitution. Thus executive orders are a form of legislative power for the executive branch.

The rationale for executive orders is that Congress often lacks the expertise and ability to act quickly when technological or other developments require fast action and flexibility.[18] Because the numbering and recording of the orders did not start until 1907, it is unclear how many have been issued. But since 1946, Congress has required all executive orders, except those dealing with classified national security issues, to be published in the *Federal Register*.[19]

Many of these executive orders have had a significant impact. Truman, for example, used an executive order to integrate the armed forces, Kennedy to end racial discrimination in public housing, and Lyndon Johnson to require affirmative-action hiring by firms with federal contracts. George W. Bush made heavy use of executive orders in responding to problems created by the 9/11 attacks. Presidents more commonly use executive orders to deal with organizational problems and internal procedures, but presidents also use them to implement the provisions of treaties and legislative statutes that are ambiguously stated (perhaps deliberately) by Congress.

In fact, presidents have used executive orders to make policies opposed by congressional majorities. Reagan and both Bushes used this power to ban abortion counseling in federally financed clinics and financial aid to United Nations–sponsored family planning programs. Another significant use of executive orders is to manage the controversial system for classifying government documents and withholding information from the public (see Chapter 12).

Through the exercise of this inherent power of office, the presidency has acquired significant legislative authority. But executive orders are much more easily overridden than congressional acts; a president can rescind or countermand some orders issued by a predecessor, as Clinton did with foreign aid restrictions on family planning and George W. Bush did with several of Clinton's environmental protection orders. When Barack Obama took office, he rescinded some of the restrictions Bush had placed on environmental regulation, and so it goes. Furthermore, the legality of executive orders can be challenged in federal court. Early in his presidency, George W. Bush ordered the posting of signs in union shops informing workers that they were not required to allow union dues to be withheld from their paychecks. A federal court ruled that this was a misuse of an executive order.

DEMOCRACY?

The first sentence of the Constitution assigns "all legislative Powers" to Congress. Is it significant that, in a government by the people, the president can, on his own authority, issue directives that have the force of law?

Executive privilege   To ensure that they receive the full and frank advice of their aides and advisers or of any visitors to the White House, presidents also have **executive privilege**, the right to refuse to make public some internal documents and private conversations.

Presidents since George Washington have asserted executive privilege, usually when Congress has requested information. Since the 1970s, federal court rulings have argued that without such a privilege a president cannot fulfill his administrative duties because he would not be able to get full and frank advice from his aides. The courts have also ruled that the power is limited in scope rather than absolute, but they have not defined its limits, deferring that task to Congress. Congress has also refused to specify the limits of executive privilege, leaving it to the courts to resolve each invocation of privilege that the president and Congress cannot resolve.

In the landmark ruling **United States v. Nixon**,[20] ordering President Nixon to turn over tape recordings of Oval Office conversations to the Watergate special prosecutor, the Supreme Court did establish that executive privilege cannot be invoked to withhold evidence material to an investigation of criminal wrongdoing. President Nixon had installed a taping device in the Oval Office, which had secretly recorded conversations between the president and everyone he talked to there. The conversations could confirm or refute the charges of White House complicity in the break-in at the national office of the Democratic Party (in the Watergate Hotel), the attempt to place wiretaps on its phones, and then the cover-up of these actions. The special prosecutor demanded the tapes. When the president, citing executive privilege, refused to hand them over, the special

BILLY WASN'T TOO EXCITED ABOUT HIS NEW ACTION FIGURE

HE JUST CALMLY ANALYZES THE SITUATION.

Mike Smith, Las Vegas Sun, King Features Syndicate

prosecutor filed suit and the justices ruled unanimously that the privilege didn't apply in this situation. After twelve days of weighing his options, Nixon decided to comply with the ruling. Just seventeen days after the ruling, when it became clear that Congress would impeach and remove him, Nixon resigned. Although the tapes didn't indicate that he participated in planning the break-in, they did show that he participated in covering it up. (Years later, however, one aide claimed that the president himself had ordered the break-in.)[21]

Similarly, the Supreme Court ruled against President Clinton when he invoked the privilege to prevent an aide from testifying before a grand jury about possible criminal wrongdoing. However, the courts upheld Clinton's extension of executive privilege to his conversations about political strategy with his aides and to those between his aides and the first lady, who served as his political adviser and whom the courts had already recognized as serving in a quasi-official role.

The George W. Bush administration, which made the strongest case for presidential power of any administration since Nixon's, claimed executive privilege many times. In 2002, Congress subpoenaed records of Vice President Cheney's meetings with executives from energy industries. The White House, claiming that executive privilege extended to the vice president, refused to turn over most of the documents, even after being ordered to do so by a federal court. Bush also used executive privilege to order active and former aides, including Karl Rove, not to testify before Congress, even when subpoenaed to do so, and even though some of the actions under investigation, such as the alleged Justice Department firing of U.S. attorneys for political reasons, could have involved criminal wrongdoing. The matter was in litigation until after Bush had left office, when improprieties were found but no basis for criminal charges.

There is no definitive ruling on what information or documents a president can choose to withhold from the public or Congress, but the courts continue to give strong support to claims of executive privilege. This authority extends even to former presidents, a precedent set by Harry Truman. When a congressional committee subpoenaed him a year after he left office, Truman answered, "If the doctrine of separation of powers and the independence of the presidency is to have any validity at all, [executive privilege] must be equally applicable to a president after his term of office has expired."[22] The committee backed down, and ex-presidents have gone on to claim the privilege.

Signing statements. When presidents sign a bill into law, they may attach comments when they believe it contains vague language that may hamper implementation or constitutionally ambiguous provisions that may later be contested in federal court. Known as **signing statements**, these written comments are deposited with new laws and recorded in the *Federal Register.*

Historically, signing statements have been seen as an administrative act, not as a presidential power. Presidents have used them primarily to clarify their understanding of vague language in a bill in case those provisions would be contested in the courts, or they might state outright their belief that one or more provisions in a bill are unconstitutional. The use of signing statements increased under Reagan, who issued 71, and continued under Clinton, who attached 105.[23]

In his attempt to exert executive authority over the legislative branch, George W. Bush interpreted this power very broadly. Bush set a record in his two terms by attaching signing statements that challenged 1200 sections of bills.[24] The legislation covered a wide policy range, including foreign and military policy but also "affirmative action, immigration, whistleblower protections, and safeguards against political interference in federally funded research."[25]

More important than the number of statements was their scope. In some, Bush exempted himself from a president's constitutional obligation to provide information to congressional oversight committees. In others, he exempted himself from a president's constitutional obligation to "faithfully execute" the laws passed by Congress. By use of the signing statement, Bush, for example, signed into law a bill forbidding the use of torture while at the same time attaching a statement—one that no one in the public would read—saying he had no intention of enforcing the legislation when he thought it interfered with his powers as commander in chief.

These and other statements were a de facto declaration of Bush's intention not to enforce, in whole or in part, the laws he was signing, on the grounds that the chief executive has complete authority to instruct executive branch agencies how to implement the laws. For a president to say that he's not obligated to "faithfully execute" the laws passed by Congress was a rare, if not to say bizarre, interpretation of the president's constitutional duties. His directives also implied that the president has authority to pass judgment on the constitutionality of a law, but that power lies solely with the federal courts.

The veto is the only constitutional power a president has to block congressional legislation. (See the section "The

President and Congress.") But vetoes attract publicity and can be overridden. Signing statements escape public notice and provide no opportunity for congressional challenge. And they mislead the public about which laws the president supports and which he opposes.

President Obama has continued the practice of issuing signing statements, although thus far more in the tradition of noting ambiguous language or provisions whose constitutionality may be challenged. And he ordered executive branch officials to check with the attorney general before following any directions given in signing statements written by previous presidents.[26]

Head of State

The **head of state** is the official representative of a country and its people. He or she symbolizes the identity and the unity of the nation. In the United States, the president is the head of state and as such performs various nonpolitical functions, especially on ceremonial occasions, such as lighting the White House Christmas tree; opening the baseball season; greeting foreign visitors to this country; or attending the swearing in, coronation, or funeral of foreign dignitaries. The president's role as unifier of the nation was acted out by Bill Clinton in leading the national mourning for victims of the bombing of the federal building in Oklahoma City and by George W. Bush in participating in a memorial service at Washington's National Cathedral for the victims of 9/11. (See box, "If They Can't Get Back from the Moon . . . .")

The president is also the **head of government**. In this capacity, he is the leader of a political party with a partisan agenda. For these dual roles to be combined in one person is unusual. In most other Western democracies, the state and government are separate entities headed by different people. The government is presided over by politicians and elected officials with partisan interests. The state is the embodiment of the nation itself, the people and their history and traditions, and in most other nations, its representative (a king or queen or elder statesman) is assumed to be above partisan politics. In Great Britain, for example, the queen is the head of state and the prime minister is the head of government.

In the United States, the fusion of the two offices gives the president a political advantage that leaders of other Western governments do not have. Members of Congress, the press, or the public who may attack him freely in his partisan role as head of government usually show more—some say too much—deference when thepresident is acting in his capacity as head of state. When he stands in public behind the Great Seal of the United States of America, he is not just a party leader who was elected to govern, but a nonpartisan representative of all the people, entrusted with the symbols, emblems, and traditions of the country.

behind the scenes

If They Can't Get Back from the Moon...

When a tragedy strikes, the president is expected to be the "mourner in chief." In the days before American astronauts were sent to the moon in 1969, government officials feared that a malfunction might leave them stranded on the moon, unable to return to earth. According to documents that surfaced at the National Archives years later, the Nixon administration had prepared for this contingency. A speechwriter penned a speech for President Nixon to give in the event the astronauts were still alive but had no hope of returning:

Fate has ordained that the men who went to the moon to explore in peace will stay on the moon to rest in peace.

These brave men . . . know that there is no hope for their recovery. But they also know that there is hope for mankind in their sacrifice.

These . . . men are laying down their lives in mankind's most noble goal: the search for truth and understanding.

In ancient days, men looked at stars and saw their heroes in the constellations. In modern times, we do much the same, but our heroes are epic men of flesh and blood.

Others will follow, and surely find their way home. Man's search will not be denied. But these men were the first, and they will remain the foremost in our hearts.

Before giving the speech, the president would contact the "widows-to-be." After giving the speech, he would instruct NASA to cut off all further communications with the astronauts to cut short the public agony over their deaths. Then a clergyman would follow the protocol used for a burial at sea and conclude with "The Lord's Prayer."

Of course, the president didn't have to implement these plans, as the astronauts, after twenty-one hours on the moon, returned home safely.

SOURCE: "Nixon Had Words Ready for Moon Disaster," *Lincoln Journal Star*, July 10, 1999.

Addressing the Nation

As head of state, the president is required by the Constitution to report to Congress "from time to time" about the "State of the Union." 🏛 **Art. II, Sec. 3** There is no required form for these reports, and Jefferson's practice of submitting it in writing—because in his view a personal address to Congress too closely resembled the monarch's speech that opens each session of the British Parliament—lasted for a hundred years. When Woodrow Wilson revived the practice of reporting in person, one senator labeled it a "cheap and tawdry imitation of English royalty."[27]

Today these addresses are televised and delivered in the House of Representatives before a joint session of Congress within several weeks of the opening of each congressional session. The president notes the successes of the past year, addresses problems, and outlines his policy agenda for the coming year. Part of the report deals with the mood of the country and identifies goals for maintaining or increasing national unity. These addresses are usually written from boilerplate and are rarely memorable; the "state of the union" is pronounced "strong," and Americans are reassured that they live in a great nation. An analysis of all State of the Union addresses concluded that it is impossible for speechwriters to overuse *freedom* or references to the United States as "great" and "good."[28]

Even when presidents are mired in political controversy—Nixon during the Watergate investigation or Clinton delivering the 1998 State of the Union address just weeks after the revelation of personal misconduct—congressional leaders usually remind the membership that the president is speaking in his constitutional role as head of state and they must show respect for the office.

Pardon Power

As head of state, the president is authorized to grant pardons. Through the **pardon power**, the president can erase the guilt and restore the rights of anyone convicted of a federal crime, except an impeached president. 🏛 **Art. II, Sec. 2** Short of issuing a pardon, he can grant clemency by commuting a felon's sentence without erasing the conviction.

One of Lincoln's last acts, signed the day he was assassinated, was to pardon a Union Army deserter. Blanket pardons have been issued to Confederate Army veterans and Vietnam draft evaders, but most presidents have used the power to clear the names of offenders who have served their sentences. This is consistent with Chief Justice Marshall's definition of a pardon as "a private, though official act of grace."[29]

Each year hundreds of people petition the president for pardons, the overwhelming majority of which are vetted by the Office of the United States Pardon Attorney in the Department of Justice and recommended for denial. Presidents usually follow the lawyers' advice, but they not required to do so, or even to consult government lawyers before granting pardons. In *Federalist* 74 Alexander

Hamilton argued that the "benign prerogative of pardoning should be as little as possible fettered or embarrassed." Nevertheless, pardons do occasionally embarrass or come back to haunt a president.

Using pardon power to absolve government officials or persons convicted of crimes with political overtones can evoke strong public reactions. George H. W. Bush discovered this when he pardoned Reagan's secretary of defense and five other officials charged with or convicted of crimes related to the Iran-Contra scandal. So did Clinton, with his last-minute pardon of a fugitive commodities trader whose ex-wife was a large donor to the Democratic Party. Perhaps this is why George W. Bush was very cautious, granting only 189 pardons, fewer than any president since World War II, and only to felons who had served their full terms.[30] He did grant clemency eleven times, including to Cheney aide and administration loyalist Lewis "Scooter" Libby, thus wiping out the two-and-a-half-year prison sentence he had received for lying and obstructing justice during the investigation into the leak of the identity of CIA agent Valerie Plame. The other ten to whom Bush granted clemency had been convicted of drug trafficking.[31]

Chief Diplomat

The Constitution established the president as the nation's chief diplomat by authorizing him to negotiate treaties with foreign countries, appoint ambassadors, and receive foreign ambassadors. 🏛 **Art. II, Sec. 2** However, the president's treaty-making powers are constrained by the requirement that two-thirds of the Senate must approve them before they can take effect. Just as it is difficult to obtain two-thirds majorities to override a veto, it is also difficult to obtain a two-thirds majority to approve a treaty. That means that the Senate has leverage to bargain with the president. After Jimmy Carter (1977–1981) negotiated a treaty to give the Panama Canal to Panama and put the Canal Zone under its authority, the Senate demanded, as a condition of ratification, partial renegotiation of treaty terms to ensure that the United States retained the right to intervene militarily against any threats to the canal and that its ships receive priority passage during wartime.

The president evidently can terminate treaties without any involvement by the Senate. The Supreme Court allowed Carter to terminate the 1903 treaty with Panama to make way for the new one.[32] A more striking example of unilateral termination (because no substitution for it was under negotiation) came in 2001 when George W. Bush withdrew the United States from the ABM (anti-ballistic missile) treaty not long after taking office.[33]

The president frequently conducts diplomacy directly with other world leaders, such as at summit conferences, where they gather to discuss economic, trade, environmental, or arms issues. In his negotiations with other heads of government, the president may reach executive agreements or trade agreements below the treaty level. These are not mentioned in the Constitution but are considered implicit in the president's diplomatic authority. Although similar to treaties, most do not require Senate approval to be formalized.[34]

The president appoints, with Senate approval, ambassadors to represent the United States abroad and also "receives" foreign ambassadors, who must present their credentials upon arriving in this country to begin their postings. This ceremonial duty has inherent policy-making power because accepting the credentials of foreign ambassadors constitutes recognition of their governments. When a government has come to power by revolution, coup, or fraudulent elections, the United States may choose not to recognize its legitimacy. The United States didn't recognize the government of the Soviet Union until sixteen years after the Bolshevik Revolution or the communist government of China until twenty-five years after it took power.

From the country's earliest days, officials referred to the president as the "nation's organ for foreign affairs."[35] In 1936, the Supreme Court revised this characterization, calling the president the "sole organ" for foreign affairs, reflecting the growth of presidential power.[36] This interpretation remains controversial because the Constitution also grants Congress confirmation and budgetary powers over foreign affairs, and it gives Congress the sole power to declare war. Nonetheless, the statement accurately conveys the fact that the president dominates foreign policy making.

To underscore the importance of speaking with one voice in foreign affairs, Congress passed the Logan Act in 1799, prohibiting unauthorized citizens from negotiating with foreign governments. There is no record of prosecutions for violating the act, although prosecutions were threatened during the Vietnam War when peace advocates traveled to North Vietnam and again when Jesse Jackson went to Cuba in violation of U.S. policy.

Commander in Chief

The Constitution designates the president "**Commander in Chief** of the Army and Navy . . . and of the Militia of the Several States, when called into the Actual service of the United States." **Art. II, Sec. 2** In doing so, the Founders were designating the president "first general" and "first admiral," as Hamilton wrote in *Federalist Paper* 69. The Founders realized that use of the military is sometimes necessary in the conduct of foreign policy. By making the president the "first general," they made it clear that civilian authority has primacy over military authority; the president can countermand the order of any officer.

Being "first general" and "first admiral" allows the president to determine military strategy if he chooses to do so. The army could not have dropped hydrogen bombs on Hiroshima and Nagasaki unless it had been authorized to do so by President Truman. The decisions to wage limited wars in Korea and Vietnam and not to use tactical nuclear weapons were based on presidential beliefs that victories over North Korea and North Vietnam were not worth risking a nuclear holocaust.

As commander in chief, the president appoints military officers. During the Civil War, President Lincoln couldn't understand why the Union Army hadn't pressed its advantage over the Confederate Army. When he visited the Antietam battlefield, he discovered that his top general, George McClellan, was both pro-Union and proslavery. Hoping for a stalemate in the war, McClellan tried to block Confederate advances but refused to rout Confederate troops. Lincoln replaced him.

President Obama salutes soldiers returning from war in caskets. He called the ceremony "a sobering reminder" of the sacrifices made by our troops. President Bush didn't want to be linked in peoples' minds with war casualties, so he didn't meet the caskets or allow any photographs of them.

During the Korean War, when General Douglas MacArthur tried to expand the conflict into a full-scale war with China against the express orders of President Truman, Truman replaced him, effectively ending his military career. Truman also went against the wishes of the military command by issuing an executive order ending racial segregation in the armed forces. Truman had been an infantry officer during World World I and appeared confident in exercising civilian authority over the military, but sometimes a president with no military experience is less willing to go against military brass. President Clinton, for example, could have used the same authority to end discrimination against gays in the military, but he declined to do so.

However, in 2002, prior to the invasion of Iraq, President Bush and his secretary of defense forced the retirement of the chairman of the Joints Chiefs of Staff (later named Veterans' Affairs secretary by Obama) when he testified before Congress that the war would require far more troops than the civilian leadership was recommending. And President Obama effectively ended the career of General Stanley McChrystal by removing him as commander of U.S. troops in Afghanistan in 2010 after McChrystal and his aides belittled the policies of the president, the defense secretary, and State Department personnel in *Rolling Stone* magazine.

War and Presidential Powers

The Founders did not give the president the sole power to make war. In the words of one delegate, they believed "the Executive should be able to repel and not to commence war." The Founders, fearing that presidents, like the British kings from whom they had recently freed themselves, would be too eager to go to war, gave Congress the power to declare war.[37] James Madison expressed the view of several of the Founders when he argued that "the executive is the branch of power most interested in war and most prone to it. [The Constitution] has, accordingly, with studied care, vested the question of war in the legislature."[38]

The Founders therefore set up a system of checks and balances in military affairs; the president commands the troops, but Congress has the power to declare war and to decide whether to authorize funds to pay for it. Thomas Jefferson thought this arrangement would be an "effectual check to the dog of war, by transferring the power of letting him loose from the executive to the legislative body, from those who are to spend to those who are to pay."[39]

By explicitly naming the president as commander in chief of the "Army and Navy," the Constitution leaves no doubt that this role is limited to a relationship with the military. The president is *not* the commander in chief of the nation. His role as chief presiding officer of the government is subject to all the checks and balances enumerated in the Constitution. Yet some presidents have claimed that their commander in chief role gave them the authority to impose domestic policies they judged crucial to achieving their national security goals.

Historically, these powers have been exercised most extensively during wars that have endangered national survival. Lincoln assumed extraordinary powers during the Civil War, believing the survival of the Union was at stake. Because many in Congress agreed with him, he was able to do what he thought necessary and in some cases receive retroactive congressional approval. Acting under his expansive definition of commander in chief, Franklin Roosevelt put 100,000 Americans of Japanese descent into camps during World War II. He also had the government seize and operate more than sixty industries important to the war effort and vulnerable to union strikes. In addition, he created special agencies to control the consumption and price of gasoline, meat, shoes, and other goods.

Wars that do not threaten our national survival tend not to generate high levels of support for executive actions. When Truman had his secretary of commerce seize most of the nation's steel mills during the Korean War to keep them operating in the face of a possible labor strike, one of the steel companies took him to court. In 1952, the Supreme Court sided with the company by ruling that Truman had not exhausted other, legal remedies to the problem.[40]

The historian Garry Wills argues that it was the acquisition of nuclear weapons during World War II that led to a redefinition of the commander in chief's role and to the subsequent expansion of executive power. Without amending Article II and without the consent of Congress, presidents have been able to use their control over the nuclear arsenal, or "bomb power" as Wills calls it, to alter our history "down to its deepest constitutional roots." It has made it possible for a president to argue that if he "has the sole authority to launch nation-destroying weapons, he has license to use every other power at his disposal that might safeguard that supreme necessity." While strongly disagreeing that this expansion of the commander in chief's role has been constitutional, Wills says that since World War II "every executive encroachment or abuse was liable to justification from this one supreme power."[41]

No president ever made more extraordinary claims for the unbounded nature of the commander in chief role than did George W. Bush. The national emergency precipitated by the 9/11 attacks gave his administration opportunities to claim more latitude for unilateral action as a "wartime" president. In planning a response immediately after the attacks, Vice President Cheney argued that if there was even a 1 percent chance that a person or a situation was a threat, the government had to act, a position later labeled "The One Percent Doctrine."[42]

Following Cheney's lead, Bush demanded the power to take any action he deemed necessary to protect the American people. He claimed that as commander in chief he had unilateral war-making powers that allowed him, on his own authority, to declare any persons he chose enemy combatants, hold them for any length of time without bringing charges or allowing access to lawyers or courts, have them interrogated under rules he set independently of international laws and treaties the United States has signed, and establish tribunals outside the military justice system to try detainees. And because the Pentagon and all intelligence agencies are in the executive branch, the president was said to have the power to collect any kind of intelligence, open mail and e-mail, look at bank accounts, seize library records, and wiretap phone calls as he saw fit. He claimed the same right to exercise these powers inside the United States as well as outside its borders. The president could do this, his legal advisers argued, in a written opinion requested by the president, without court or congressional oversight—except when the president chose to brief members of Congress on whatever aspects of a program he chose to reveal.[43] If these powers were practiced by presidents, as Bush's lawyers said they were entitled to, our government would be closer to a dictatorship than a constitutional democracy.[44] We will discuss these issues further in Chapter 14.

Historically, when presidents have used war or other national crises to justify expansion of their powers, the separation of powers has reasserted itself when the crises eased. But the powers that Bush claimed for his office presented a greater threat to maintaining three coequal branches than those made by presidents in earlier wars because the "war on terrorism," as Bush defined it, would last into the indefinite future.

A Justice Department review of the interpretation of Article II powers made by Bush's legal advisers found their constitutional arguments flawed and the lawyers guilty of professional misconduct. Even before he came to office, President Obama promised to curtail the executive powers Bush had claimed as a wartime commander in chief, but it is not yet clear just how much of that authority he has renounced.

Together the roles of chief diplomat and commander in chief enable the president to exercise tremendous power over foreign affairs, greater power than over domestic matters.

THE POLITICAL BASES FOR PRESIDENTIAL LEADERSHIP

The Founders didn't anticipate that one day the president would be the leader of a national party with a political agenda and accountable to the people. They envisioned a president chosen by the Electoral College and removed from the public, and our earliest presidents in fact did have little direct public contact. George Washington and Thomas Jefferson averaged only three speeches a year to the public; John Adams averaged one. Adams spent eight months of his presidency at home in Massachusetts, avoiding Congress and procrastinating on a decision whether to get involved in a war between England and France.[45] Abraham Lincoln thought it prudent to make few speeches. He told people gathered at Gettysburg the night before his famous address, "I have no speech to make. In my position it is somewhat important that I should not say foolish things. It very often happens that the only way to help it is to say nothing at all."[46]

This is not an option for a president who is dependent on a national electorate and who runs for office as the head of a party and on the promise of what he will do for the people. Whether packaged as the Square Deal (Theodore Roosevelt), the New Deal (Franklin Roosevelt), the Fair Deal (Truman), the New Frontier (Kennedy), or the Great Society (Johnson), or with no snappy title at all, most presidents come to office with a legislative agenda. As the main salespeople of their party's legislative program and the only national spokespersons for the government in Washington, presidents now stay in constant touch with the public. These two extragovernmental factors—the growth of political parties and the spread of mass communications—have added immeasurably to their ability to expand on their constitutional role.

The Personal President

As the president's legislative role grew and as the media became more pervasive, the once distant administrator and diplomat became the voice of the people and the most visible figure in government. Teddy Roosevelt's bully pulpit presidency became Harry Truman's "lobbyist for all the people" presidency, and the people came to feel that they had a personal relationship with their president.[47] The holder of those austere titles—chief executive, head of state, and commander in chief—morphed into a **personal president** whom people were willing to entrust with greater power. In the words of one presidential scholar, "The great powers of the American people have been invested" in this one office, "making it the most powerful office in the world . . . precisely because it is truly the people's power."[48]

In return the people expect presidents to produce. "Everybody now expects the man inside the White House to do something about everything."[49] It is as if the people have an unwritten contract with the president.[50]

When President Franklin Roosevelt died, most Americans, reflecting the personal presidency, felt a personal loss. Chief Petty Officer Graham Jackson plays "Nearer My God to Thee" as the president's body is carried to the train that returned him to Washington for burial.

The president who is credited with (some would say blamed for) doing most to develop and institutionalize this one-to-one relationship with the public, and greatly expanding the powers of the presidency in the process, was Franklin Roosevelt. His radio addresses, or fireside chats, were the first attempt to use the media to speak directly and regularly to the people in their homes. The talks made the president the focal point and public face of the government. In a personalized style and conversational tone, FDR began, "My friends," and even talked about his dog. People gathered around their radios whenever he was on, and many felt as though he was talking directly to them. One listener said the reach of FDR's radio chats was so pervasive that on a summer day, with windows open, one could walk down the street and never miss a word of the talk because the radio in every home was tuned in. Roosevelt also pioneered the use of public opinion polls to gauge the public's views. Thus he created a communications loop—to the people and from the people—that helped him sell his policies.

Whereas his predecessor Herbert Hoover (1929–1933) had received an average of 40 letters a day, Roosevelt, after initiating his chats, received 4000 a day.[51] He even received some addressed not to himself, by name or position, but simply to "My Friend, Washington, D.C." Hoover needed only one clerk to handle his mail but Roosevelt needed fifty. By 2010 President Obama was receiving 40,000 letters a day.

The personal presidency has both advantages and disadvantages for the country. The relationship enables presidents to marshal public support for important goals and thus overcome the inertia of a system with fragmented power. On the other hand, it fosters unrealistic assumptions about what presidents can achieve. It encourages the tendency to see presidents as all-powerful and to assign them too much blame when things go wrong and too much credit when things go right, such as when the economy sags or surges.

Because they have unrealistic expectations, citizens encourage, actually pressure, candidates for president to make unrealistic promises. The candidates oblige in order to garner more contributions for their campaign or votes for their election. Jimmy Carter, who was one of our most honest presidents, nonetheless told campaign audiences, "If you ever have any questions or advice for me, please write. . . . I open every letter myself, and read them all."[52] George H. W. Bush promised to send astronauts to Mars, be the "education president," the "environmental president," and do many other things while cutting the budget deficit yet promising "no new taxes." Barack Obama promised health care to every American, reform of the educational system, victory in Afghanistan, and the restoration of America's image abroad.

Most presidents at least try to deliver on a majority of their promises.[53] Inevitably they must neglect some and Congress will block others, which can prompt presidents to seek more power. They get caught in a cycle in which they try to grasp more power to honor past promises and then make new promises for which they need even more power. Thus the rise of the personal presidency fed the expansion of the office.

The Media President

FDR also set a standard for use of the media to maximize the political reach of the presidency. Today, of course, all presidents must have a media strategy if they want to get their policies enacted.

Presidents try to persuade the public directly, and also indirectly by persuading opinion leaders, such as the executives, reporters, columnists, and commentators of the media and the leaders and lobbyists of interest groups, including the executives of big businesses. These people have the ability to influence the public (and interest groups have the money to provide campaign contributions). The strategy of appealing to the people to gain cooperation from Congress and Washington power brokers is known as **going public**.[54] It entails giving television and radio addresses, holding press conferences, making speeches at various events around the country, and giving interviews, through satellite technology, to local media, big conventions, or other audiences.

Today, when a president is not heard from frequently, the media complain because they count on presidential communications to fill their newscasts and news columns. Ronald Reagan, often called the "Great Communicator," spoke in public an average of 200 times a year. When he spoke, he didn't discuss the details of his proposals. Rather, he dwelled on anecdotes about people he knew earlier in life or people who had written letters to the White House. Like FDR, he personalized his speeches. As Roosevelt was the most effective president on radio, Reagan was the most effective on television. Bill Clinton spoke in public an amazing 550 times a year.[55] Perhaps the most effective extemporaneous speaker ever to serve in the White House, Clinton also partially wrote or revised his formal speeches, sometimes in the back of the limousine on the way to the event.

Today presidents have a large communications staff, led by a media adviser and a press secretary, to get their message out. Following Reagan's practice, they determine a message for every day and every week, and they direct everyone in the administration to stay "on message"—to repeat the message and to avoid other topics that could deflect attention from the message. Inevitably, other topics will pop up, prompting the administration to regain control of the agenda.

The George W. Bush administration was very disciplined in staying on message, especially during the first four years. On any day, viewers of newscasts or listeners of talk radio heard administration officials delivering the same message in virtually the same words. Running such an operation is a high-pressure job, and press secretaries usually do not last long. When Bush's first press secretary resigned after two years, he said he wanted to do "something more relaxing, like dismantling live nuclear weapons."[56] After Bush's second press secretary resigned, he wrote a book describing how the White House staff manipulated intelligence information to convince the public that an invasion of Iraq was necessary.[57] It is an example of how the White House can dominate both the topics covered in the news and how they are covered.

President Kennedy cultivated a persona of youthful vigor and cool elegance.

John F. Kennedy Library/Zumapress

Presidents try to control how the public sees as well as hears them. Teddy Roosevelt was able to do this even in the days before presidents had a huge communication apparatus. He cast himself as a manly man—a big-game hunter and a Rough Rider who led a charge in the Spanish-American War. The observation that "politics is theater" is intended as ridicule, but image does matter in a president's drive for popular support. To project an image that conveys the kind of character and style they want the people to see in them, presidents are willing to "make fully realized dramatic characters out of themselves. . . . The character has to bear some relation to the real person . . . but it is still a genuine act of creation."[58]

Although television became popular in the 1950s, not all politicians immediately recognized its potential. Dwight Eisenhower shunned televised speeches because, he said, "I can think of nothing more boring, for the American public, than to have to sit in their living rooms for a whole half hour looking at my face on their television screens."[59] But the young medium became a powerful political tool in the 1960s. John Kennedy was the first president to recognize its utility for presidential spectacles. To overcome public concerns about his youth and inexperience, he initiated live television coverage of presidential press conferences. The idea was to court the viewers rather than the reporters asking the questions. He would demonstrate his intelligence and command of the issues and, in the process, leaven it with his wit.

In other ways, Kennedy tried to make a virtue of his youth and inexperience by conveying a sense of athleticism, with photo-ops of sailing and playing touch football and by exhorting Americans to take long hikes. And always Kennedy promised "vigor," which became his signature word. In fact, Kennedy had been ill for most of his life, with many hospitalizations and daily drug treatment for Addison's disease, a fact he kept from the public.

Another image of his administration, largely created by his wife after his death, was modeled on the mythical "Camelot," with the royal couple bringing glamour and sophistication to the White House and, like King Arthur's "Knights of the Round Table," carrying social justice and democratic ideals to the world. The administration left a lasting image of a tuxedoed president and his beautiful wife hosting galas for classical musicians and great intellects. Although the first lady may have favored these activities, the president himself preferred listening to Frank Sinatra and reading Ian Fleming's James Bond books.

Ronald Reagan and George W. Bush portrayed themselves as dramatic characters who evoked masculine toughness. A Reagan aide proposed that the president reflect "America's idealized image of itself."[60] An actor, Reagan had little difficulty projecting himself as a rugged individualist, riding horses and clearing brush at his California ranch, although he grew up in Illinois and had spent much of his life in Hollywood's studio system or as a spokesman for corporations. George W. Bush's persona as a Texas

The public didn't always agree with President Reagan's views or policies, but he remained popular partly because of his image as a rugged individualist.

Bush that was also the disadvantage. He had announced the end of the war in Iraq far too soon, and the photo-op came back to haunt him.

If a president fails to manage his image, the press or his opponents will do it for him—and in ways he won't like. Bill Clinton intended to convey an image of a knowledgeable leader whose gaze was directed toward the future but who, with his own humble origins, understood the problems of average people and knew how to deal with them. Instead, his image for many people became that of a womanizer who hung out with Hollywood celebrities and paid for a $200 haircut. Although he was one of our most knowledgeable presidents, he allowed his intellect to be overshadowed by his personal indiscretions.

President Obama established his persona in a memoir written well before he was a public figure, although almost certainly with the possibility in mind of some day running for office. So he entered his presidential campaign already having laid down the template for his presidential image as a cosmopolitan, multiracial man with roots in the rural Midwest, who could serve as the face of twenty-first-century America. His aides also arranged a number of spectacle events abroad with Obama speaking in huge arenas before hundreds of thousands of people to shape the image of a man who in fact had little foreign policy experience as a world leader.

Obama is the first president to have begun his political career in the era of electronic communications and the first to be fully conversant with its political potential. His is the first presidency Americans have been able to follow on Facebook and YouTube and through daily updates from his Twitter account, in addition to the 24/7 cable news coverage. It will be a test of whether the use of media has gone as far as it can go in strengthening the presidency's direct connection to the people and expanding the personal presidency.

Despite presidents' constant concerns about their image and their public support, as measured by their approval ratings, there's no strong correlation between presidents' popularity and their clout in Congress.[62] High approval ratings don't guarantee passage of their legislative proposals, because most constituents never learn whether their representative or senators voted for a president's proposals.

cowboy—he wore cowboy boots to his inaugural and made sure the press photographed him wearing them—was mostly invented. His packaging as a war leader was even more intentional. The staging of the flight-suited commander in chief landing by fighter jet on an aircraft carrier and speaking in front of a *MISSION ACCOMPLISHED* banner was one of the most dramatic image-creating photo opportunities in the history of the presidency. It is a good example of a symbolic spectacle, a gesture designed to shape public perceptions and gain public support, and the frequent use of such staged events has created what some political scientists call the "spectacle presidency."[61] The advantage of such bold efforts is that the visual image lingers. But for

ORGANIZATION OF THE PRESIDENCY

To perform all of the above functions, modern presidents have a large staff, especially compared to their early predecessors. George Washington paid a nephew out of his own pocket to be his only full-time aide, and Jefferson had only four cabinet officers to advise him. Congress did not appropriate funds for a presidential clerk until 1857, and even then, Lincoln, with a staff of four, opened and answered much of the daily mail himself. The telephone was introduced in the White House in 1879, and in the 1880s Grover Cleveland was still answering it himself. Even in the early twentieth century, Woodrow Wilson typed many of his own speeches.[63]

As the work of the president has expanded, staff size has exploded. Today, as presiding officer of the executive branch, the president heads, in addition to the military, a civilian bureaucracy of fifteen cabinet departments and 2.7 million civil servants (their work is described in Chapter 12). To carry out the day-to-day duties of this office, the president has a large staff of policy specialists and liaisons to Congress and federal agencies.

Executive Office of the President

The bureaucracy that surrounds the modern president had its origins in the administration of Franklin Roosevelt. Because his small staff was overwhelmed by the workload of administering New Deal agencies and programs, FDR called in a team of public administration experts to help restructure his office. In 1939 Congress finally passed the statute creating the **Executive Office of the President (EOP)**, and with it the White House Office.[64]

The EOP is essentially the president's personal bureaucracy, sitting atop the executive branch and monitoring the work done in cabinet departments and agencies to see that

George W. Bush cultivated an image as a tough cowboy. This image proved popular with many Americans. However, as his administration's foreign policy failures mounted, the image became a liability.

Christopher Morris/VII

the president's policies are carried out. Many EOP staffers are career civil servants, but the president appoints those who fill the top policy-making positions. Since FDR's administration, the EOP has been reorganized many times to reflect changing national problems and the issue priorities of individual presidents. It is not a single office but a group of offices, councils, and boards devoted to specific functional or issue areas such as national security, trade, the budget, drug abuse, the economy, and the environment.

The EOP continued to grow in size from the 1930s to more than 2000 people today. The powerful OMB (Office of Management and Budget) accounts for a large part of the growth. The influence of other EOP heads varies with the president's issue priorities, but the head of OMB is almost always influential.[65]

White House Office

The EOP also includes the White House Office, which employs the president's closest advisers, as well as the office of the first lady. Members of the White House staff have greater influence than most advisers because the president appoints all of them, works daily with them, and tends to trust them more than others. They are often people who helped him get elected or worked for him when he held other offices. Many presidents have counted their wives among their closest advisers, and every first lady has her own office and staff within the Office of the White House. (See the box "The First Lady: A Twofer?")

Jimmy Carter and Bill Clinton are notable among recent presidents for their degree of reliance on their wives and other longtime associates. Unlike Kennedy, Nixon, Johnson, and the first George Bush, neither Carter nor Clinton had experience in Washington, and they filled their top staff positions with old friends and political operatives from their respective home states, Georgia and Arkansas. George H. W. Bush was a consummate Washington insider but relied heavily on his fellow Texan and longtime friend James Baker to serve on the White House staff, in the cabinet, and as his campaign manager. Of recent presidents, Ronald Reagan, who had no close personal friends in politics, was the only one not to fill his top staff positions with longtime friends and close associates.

George W. Bush's initial appointments were notable for their insider backgrounds; three-quarters had previous Washington experience, and nearly half had served in his father's administration. His closest advisers, Karl Rove and Karen Hughes, had worked for him in Texas, and his first chief of staff, Andrew Card, and national security adviser, Condoleezza Rice, had worked in his father's administration.[66] Barack Obama, who had settled in Chicago, his wife's hometown, developed a tight circle of Chicago-based friends and advisers who ran his Senate and presidential campaigns. He appointed most to top White House staff positions, and he named another Chicagoan, Rep. Rahm Emanuel, as his chief of staff.

President Johnson worked continuously. When he awoke, he read newspapers, ate breakfast, and met with his staff—all before getting out of bed.

Management of the White House staff varies with the president's personal style. Franklin Roosevelt and John Kennedy cared little for rigid lines of responsibility. More concerned with who could serve the president best, they gave staffers different jobs over time and fostered a competitive spirit. Lyndon Johnson's style was the archetype of aggressive, hands-on management. Known for his commitment to using all resources at his disposal to find government solutions to virtually every problem, Johnson was often accused of overworking and bullying his staff.[67]

Richard Nixon valued formal lines of authority. Nixon's chief of staff, H. R. Haldeman, saw his job this way: "Every president needs a son of a bitch, and I'm Nixon's. I'm his buffer and his bastard. I get done what he wants done and I take the heat instead of him."[68] Part of Nixon's approach was to be reclusive and keep his cards close to his vest. He demanded at least two days a week when he would see no one so he could work in seclusion; even his closest staff often did not know what he was working on.[69]

The Watergate scandal led Presidents Ford and Carter to avoid the appearance of strong staff chiefs. But Reagan prided himself on delegating authority to the best people and letting them do their work without interference.[70] Serious problems developed, however, because no one had authority to make final decisions on more important matters, and Reagan was too removed from daily affairs to do so. This detached management style had its costs, most noticeably the Iran-Contra scandal.[71] After that, he appointed a series of strong staff chiefs whose coordination of White House operations helped restore his image.

Clinton's appointment of many staffers with little Washington experience and diverse policy positions showed his determination to immerse himself in policy details and to be the final arbiter of many competing views. He directed his first staff chief to channel all paperwork to him. However, running the White House this way made it difficult for Clinton to keep his and the nation's focus on important issues. He got so bogged down in details that his wife complained that he had become the "mechanic-in-chief."[72]

Clinton also rejected a hierarchical organizational structure. In fact, White House meetings resembled college bull sessions. A young, unruly staff and Clinton's penchant for sitting up all night with them talking issues and policy without fixed agendas were taken by some as symptoms of a chaotic and disorganized management style.[73] Under Clinton's second and third staff chiefs, lines of authority and communication were tightened.

George W. Bush employed a near-opposite approach to management. With experience as an enforcer of political loyalties on his father's staff, and as the only president to hold an MBA, Bush set out to run his White House along corporate lines. He tried to delegate work along crisp lines of authority, kept to a tight schedule, and demanded complete team loyalty with no public dissent from administration policy.[74] But the deeper Bush got into his term, he found what most presidents find: that it is impossible to keep rivalries and dissident policy positions from emerging, even among close advisers. The most noted negative relationship among Bush's appointees was that between his secretary of defense Donald Rumsfeld and his first secretary of state Colin Powell, who had disagreements over the use of intelligence and the conduct of the war in Iraq.

But this top-down style, though efficient, insulated the president, preventing him from receiving essential information. Aides were discouraged from correcting his misconceptions or challenging his policy ideas. "The first time I told him he was wrong," a young aide said, "he started yelling at me. Then I showed him where he was wrong, and he said, 'All right, I understand. Good job.' He patted me on the shoulder. I went and had dry heaves in the bathroom."[75] Stifling dissent discourages aides from challenging common wisdom and bringing new facts and perspectives to the discussion. Perhaps consequently, Bush's first secretary of the treasury said that, in cabinet and private meetings, he seemed disengaged and uninformed on issues.[76]

During his first years in office, Barack Obama was similar to Bill Clinton in wanting to listen to all views on an issue before sifting through them to reach his own conclusions. But he was different from Clinton in running a much tighter ship and in being more aloof in the final decision making.

Office of the First Lady

There is no mention of a presidential spouse in the Constitution, and she has no official duties and no salary, but she does have her own office and staff within the White House Office and plays an important role in the functioning of the presidency. Concern over the influence and public impact of presidential spouses is as old as the Republic, and George Washington expected his wife "to set a tone both dignified and democratic."

In addition to an intense schedule of state social functions, the first lady must oversee the White House domestic staff. (Whether a first husband would do this remains to be seen.) She is expected to serve as what Martha Washington called "the hostess of the nation."[77] And it has become the custom for first ladies to identify causes, usually nonpartisan, on which they will focus special effort. Jacqueline Kennedy devoted herself to historic preservation, Claudia (Lady Bird) Johnson to environmental issues, Barbara and Laura Bush to literacy, Hillary Rodham Clinton to child welfare, and Michelle Obama to childhood obesity and healthy eating.

In recognition of the role that the first ladies play, in 1978 Congress made formal budgetary provisions for the Office of the First Lady as an official unit within the EOP's White House Office.[78] Although still without salary, the first lady is entitled to a small annual pension.

With the parallel power base established by his vice president (see the next section) and Rove's reputation as the key political strategist, Bush sometimes appeared to be a secondary figure in his own administration. Bush's press staff had to work hard to convince the public that the president was in charge of the White House, and the president himself frequently reminded the press corps that he was "the decider."

Rahm Emanuel, President Obama's former chief of staff, lobbied members of Congress, such as Sen. Max Baucus (D-Mont.), during negotiations for the health care reform bill.

Dennis Brack-Pool/Getty Images

Office of the Vice President

The EOP also includes the Office of the Vice President. The vice president has his own budget for office and staff (housed adjacent to the White House), an official airplane (*Air Force Two*), and his own white mansion (the former home of the chief of naval operations).[79]

The vice president has few formal duties—to preside over the Senate, which he rarely does (junior senators are assigned this usually thankless task to help them learn rules and procedure); cast tie-breaking votes, which he rarely needs to do; and succeed to the presidency if necessary. That vice presidents have succeeded to office unexpectedly nine times (following eight presidential deaths and one resignation) may be responsible for the growing importance of the office.

Benjamin Franklin suggested that the vice president should be addressed as "His Superfluous Excellency" because he had so little to do. "Standby equipment" is how Nelson Rockefeller described the job. Franklin Roosevelt's first vice president, John Nance Garner, was less elegant in observing that his job was not worth a "pitcher of warm piss."

Historically, presidents gave their vice presidents little information and few opportunities to prepare for succession. They were usually chosen to balance the ticket geographically or ideologically, not because they were men whom presidents wanted to work with. In 1960, the youthful New Englander, John Kennedy, chose the experienced Texan, Lyndon Johnson. The two had a chilly relationship. Kennedy was wary of the less polished Johnson, and the self-made Johnson bristled at the privileged background and Harvard degrees of the Kennedy clan.

Sometimes presidents have been reluctant to delegate important responsibilities to their vice presidents because the vice presidents are planning their own runs for the office and working to build an independent political base. This may make them more loyal to their own ambitions than to the president's agenda. Historically, vice presidents were assigned ceremonial duties or partisan activities (such as being the attack dog during the campaign, leaving his or her running mate free to appear more presidential).

How much work and authority vice presidents are given depends on the personal relationship with the president, how needy the president is for assistance, or how generous he is about sharing power. Jimmy Carter was the first president to delegate to his vice president responsibilities for day-to-day White House operations. Vice President Walter Mondale, who had the Washington experience Carter lacked, was included in all important meetings.[80] Carter said he spent as much as four to five hours a day with Mondale.[81] Ronald Reagan, Bill Clinton, and both George Bushes added to this new tradition.

Prior to the Bush-Cheney administration, the closest working relationship between a president and vice president was undoubtedly that between Bill Clinton and Al Gore.

THE FIRST LADY: A TWOFER?

Long before there were cameras, radio, or television, first ladies were involved in promoting their husbands' careers.[1] They walk a fine line between being supportive of their husbands and not looking as though they are politically out in front of them. The savvy Martha Washington chose to wear a homespun gown on her first visit to the capital in keeping with the plain brown suit her husband wore to his inauguration.[2] Louisa Adams, wife of John Quincy Adams, felt hemmed in by the limits of acceptable behavior and titled her autobiography *The Adventures of a Nobody.*[3]

The visibility of the first lady increased enormously after the arrival of photography in the mid-nineteenth century and later mass-circulation newspapers and magazines provided new means for satisfying public curiosity about the president's private life. Early in the twentieth century, first ladies began accompanying their husbands at official functions, and with the advent of television the candidates' wives began to figure much more prominently in campaign strategy. Even first ladies not interested in electoral politics were used to great effect in getting votes. For example, Dwight Eisenhower considered his wife a better campaigner than he was, and Jacqueline Kennedy attained a level of popularity and celebrity that surpassed her husband's. Laura Bush's approval ratings were at least double her husband's during his second term, and Michelle Obama's are well above her husband's.

Every first lady chooses one or two issues as her special interest. Michelle Obama chose to focus on nutrition, childhood obesity, and organic gardening. Here she is in the demonstration organic garden she had planted on the White House grounds with some of the schoolchildren she regularly invites to learn by doing.

First ladies have been loved (Dolley Madison), feared (Abigail Adams, Edith Wilson), and both loved and feared (Eleanor Roosevelt). When John Adams's opponents referred to his wife, Abigail, as "Mrs. President," they meant something more than her marital status. Abigail Adams was an accomplished writer with strong views on women's rights (for example, that women would "foment a Rebellion" if made subject to laws without representation) and other issues. During her long and happy marriage to John Adams, she was his principal adviser, leading both supporters and opponents of the president to believe she had "undue" influence on policy decisions. During a seven-month period when Woodrow Wilson was disabled by a stroke, Edith Wilson served what she called a "stewardship" (but what others called "bedside government").[4] She decoded classified diplomatic and military messages, encoded presidential responses, controlled access to her husband, and kept information about his condition from the public.

Although many first ladies have been political advisers to their husbands, no one did it quite so publicly, or from such an independent platform, as Eleanor Roosevelt. She held press conferences for women journalists shut out of the president's briefings and wrote a syndicated newspaper column read by millions. She also made regular radio broadcasts and was the first person from the administration to address the country after the Japanese attack on Pearl Harbor.[5] She discussed policy with her husband, peppered him with memos, and brought supporters of the causes she advocated into the White House. (It was reportedly common for FDR, at cabinet meetings, to begin sentences with "My Missus tells me."[6]) She served on countless committees and traveled around the world promoting racial equality, women's and social justice issues, and the war effort. After her husband's death, she served as a delegate to the United Nations, where her efforts in support of human rights and international cooperation earned her the title "First Lady of the World."

Mrs. Roosevelt's stature was attained under the exceptional circumstances of her husband's long tenure in the White House during a prolonged period of national crisis. Although some thought her too powerful, Mrs. Roosevelt always deferred to her husband in joint appearances, saying it was the job of a wife to offer no personal opinions, limit her appearances, and "lean back in an open car so voters always see *him.*"[7]

Most first ladies have not been traditional wives, and since the 1960s, strong-willed women have been the norm. Lady Bird Johnson, whose husband pronounced her "the brains and money of this family," is said to have greeted him in the evenings with the query "Well, what did you do for women today?" Although she exercised her influence mainly out of public view, her stamp was said to have been on each of the two hundred environmental laws passed during her husband's administration.[8]

In defiance of her husband's party's position, Betty Ford was an outspoken supporter of the Equal Rights Amendment and abortion rights, and she argued for a salary for her successors as first lady. Her popularity often surpassed that of her husband. Nancy Reagan, most often seen in public gazing adoringly at her husband, controlled access to the Oval Office and weighed in on the hiring and firing of key advisers.

The term *co-president* was revived for Hillary Clinton, a lawyer and lobbyist for child welfare causes, who was one of her husband's closest advisers and strategists throughout his career in elective office while also serving as the family's principal wage earner. Shortly after her husband's inauguration, she moved the first lady's office into the West Wing to be among the policy makers. She prompted greater opposition to first-lady activism than anyone since Eleanor Roosevelt.[9] Nevertheless, in 2000 Mrs. Clinton became the first presidential wife to run for and win elective office. However, in her failed run for the presidential nomination in 2008 it became apparent that the career-for-two she had shared with her husband for so many years made it difficult for her to move out of his shadow—or for him to lean back in the car so that people could see her.

Michelle Obama, a former corporate lawyer with young children, said after her husband's election that she intended to be "Chief Mom" and had no interest in a policy role or being co-president. Her concentration on nutrition, organic gardening, and fighting childhood obesity earned her the highest approval ratings of any recent first lady.

When wives have played active roles in getting their husbands nominated and elected, it is likely that their advice will be sought after the election. And in most long and close marriages, it is natural for husbands and wives to become confidants and to rely on one another's judgment. The first lady is not subject to congressional approval, but neither are the members of the White House staff or the president's close advisers outside government. Yet worry persists that the special nature of a marital relationship provides opportunities for influence—of the kind Betty Ford called "pillow talk"—unavailable to others. We frequently refer to lobbyists as "getting into bed" with politicians, but wives do not have to pay to get there, and if they are successful in changing their husband's views, it is not likely that money will have had anything to do with it.

[1] Much of the material in this box is drawn from Carol Chandler Waldrop, *Presidents' Wives: The Lives of 44 American Women of Strength* (Jefferson, N.C.: McFarland, 1989); Lewis L. Gould, ed., *American First Ladies* (New York: Garland, 1996); and Kati Marton, *Hidden Power: The Impact of Presidential Marriages on Our Recent History* (New York: Pantheon, 2001).
[2] Cokie Roberts, *Founding Mothers* (New York: William Morrow, 2004), 230–231.
[3] Edith P. Mayo, *The Smithsonian Book of First Ladies* (Washington, D.C.: Smithsonian Institution, 1996), 11, 43.
[4] Phyllis Lee Levin, *Edith and Woodrow* (New York: Scribner, 2001).
[5] You can listen to Mrs. Roosevelt's Pearl Harbor broadcast by going to www.c-span.org/PresidentialLibraries and linking to the Franklin D. Roosevelt Library.
[6] Jonathan Alter, *The Defining Moment* (New York: Simon & Schuster, 2006), 261.
[7] Carl Sferrazza Anthony, "The First Ladies: They've Come a Long Way, Martha," *Smithsonian*, October 1992, 150.
[8] Lawrence Wright, "Lady Bird's Lost Legacy," *New York Times*, July 20, 2007; and Lady Bird Johnson, *A White House Diary* (New York: Holt, Rinehart and Winston, 1970), 518. Mrs. Johnson kept a daily record—an estimated 1 million words—during her years in the White House. This book is drawn from that diary and is an excellent account of what the first lady's job looks like from the inside.
[9] Henry Louis Gates Jr., "Hating Hillary," *New Yorker*, February 26, 1996, 121.

Gore became so influential in the Clinton White House that he was referred to as a "shadow president" and his staff as a "shadow cabinet." Divisions did not surface until Gore was running his own presidential campaign and trying to distance himself in order to establish his own identity.

Richard Cheney, George W. Bush's vice president, was already well known to Bush from his service in George H. W. Bush's administration, and he had far more administrative and Washington experience than the new president. Cheney ran Bush's transition team and chose many members of the White House staff. He came to office with the goal of "merging" the vice president's office with the president's to create a "single Executive Office" in which the vice president would serve as the president's "executive and implementer."[82] He headed the most important policy-making groups in the White House and was the author of its energy policy. He also created his own national security staff, placed his own people in key defense and state department offices, and worked closely on military policy with his old friend Donald Rumsfeld, secretary of defense (a position Cheney had once held).

Cheney had unprecedented access to the Oval Office, meeting the president every morning and sometimes several times more during the day. He was also deeply involved in the president's legislative strategy, went to Capitol Hill at least once a week to meet with the Republican caucus, and

Library of Congress #LC-USZ62-85212

Vice President John Nance Garner, here in retirement, complained to President Franklin Roosevelt that he didn't have much to do.

behind the scenes

The Vice President Who Wasn't

The vice presidency of William Rufus DeVane King, the running mate of Franklin Pierce in 1852, was one of the most exceptional in American history—exceptional because he was the only vice president ever to be sworn into office on foreign soil and because behind the scenes, for years prior to his nomination, he had been the target of rumors that he was homosexual.

King, a long-time aspirant to the vice-presidency, was a man of substantial political experience. He had served in his state legislature and the U.S. House and almost thirty years in the Senate, where he became president pro tem. In between terms, he had been an envoy to several European countries. He was regarded as "courtly," generous, and a fastidious dresser.[1] His refinement contrasted with the heavy-drinking Pierce, who was said to be "the hero of many a well-fought bottle."[2] Pierce also brought inexperience and no particular reputation or policy positions to the top of the ticket, except that, like King, he was committed to the Union, which the Democratic party valued at a time when all the major players were lining up for and against slavery and turning the capital into a battleground. On the surface, it was a conventional ticket, with King, a southerner, balancing Pierce, the northerner (campaign slogan: "We Polked you in 1844, we shall Pierce you in 1852").

While drink was the subject of gossip about Pierce, it was King's friendship with James Buchanan that inspired the rumormongers. Buchanan, our only never-married president, was both friend and political ally to King and for some years the two men shared a Washington apartment. Some of the catty remarks about their relationship were undoubtedly inspired by political rivalry within the party. President Polk's law partner called King "Mrs. Buchanan" and referred to him with the feminine pronoun. The former president and warrior militant Andrew Jackson (1829–1837) called King "Miss Nancy."[3] This did not stop Buchanan and King from being favored for a short time to head the Democratic ticket in 1844.[4] Instead, King was named U.S. ambassador to France, from where he wrote letters to Buchanan about the pain of being parted from him.[5]

The country never got a chance to see how Vice President King would have fared presiding over the Senate as the Civil War approached. He was so ill in the last months of the 1852 campaign that after his election victory he sailed for Cuba seeking a warm-climate cure for his tuberculosis. It took an act of Congress to allow him to take the oath as vice president on foreign soil. Soon after, he was taken home to Alabama, where he died the month after the inauguration, never making it to Washington. His friend James Buchanan went on to win the White House in 1856.

[1] L. Edward Purcell, *The Vice-Presidents: A Biographical Dictionary* (New Haven: Facts on File, 1998), 124.
[2] Diana Dixon Healy, *America's Vice-Presidents* (New York: Atheneum, 1984), 71.
[3] Ibid., 74; Purcell, *The Vice-Presidents*, 124–125.
[4] Purcell, *The Vice-Presidents*, 125.
[5] Ibid.

kept an office in the House of Representatives (the only vice president ever to do so). Bush told members, "When you're talking to Dick Cheney, you're talking to me."[83] At the end of Bush's first term, one political scientist said Cheney had accrued so much power that it was an "insult" to call him "vice" president. "He's got this weird combination of roles and responsibilities that make him a . . . legitimizer, mentor, grim reaper, tutor, and grandfather."[84] Well into Bush's second term, many observers continued to believe that the far more experienced and policy-savvy Cheney was running a large part of the White House operation and it was consistent with Bush's preference for delegating work. A White House lawyer said that Bush "thinks that the Reagan style of leadership is best—guiding the ship of state from high up on the mast. . . . the vice president is more willing to get down in the wheelhouse below the decks."[85]

By virtually everyone's judgment, Cheney was the most powerful vice president in U.S. history. But outperforming the president, setting policy directions, and serving as attack dog had consequences for the vice president's political standing. Midway into Bush's second term, Cheney's approval ratings stood at 18 percent.[86] The Bush-Cheney administration was an exceptional situation of a much more experienced man in the second rather than the top spot, with both men believing deeply in the expansion of executive over legislative power. Few people who reach the White House are as willing as Bush was to gamble their professional reputations on their second in command.

The Obama-Biden relationship reinforces the conclusion that Cheney's taking the vice presidency to an entirely new level was not precedent setting. Joe Biden's broad legislative and foreign policy experience brought experience to the administration that Obama lacked. He has a deep

Larry Downing/Reuters/Landov

Vice President Dick Cheney was the driving force behind many Bush administration policies.

knowledge of how Congress, especially the Senate, works and a history of sunny collegial relationships on both sides of the aisle. Biden meets regularly with the president, sits in on any meeting of his choosing, and has been an important adviser on foreign and security policies and relations between the White House and Congress. But he has none of Cheney's skill in behind-the-scenes bureaucratic maneuvering, nor has Obama given him that charge. He also did not ask for any independent spheres of operation or responsibility for policy initiatives as Cheney did, but rather was said to aspire to Cheney's role as most influential adviser, or "the last voice in the room."[87]

THE PRESIDENT AND CONGRESS

In the modern era, presidential power has increased relative to congressional power because the presidency has inherent advantages over Congress. The president is one person, whereas Congress includes 535 members who are divided into two houses, hundreds of committees and subcommittees, and dozens of leaders. These leaders struggle to develop and articulate policy goals acceptable to their party and their members, and then to keep the members committed to these goals. While the members of Congress talk and negotiate, the president can decide and act. The president can also attract the attention of the media, which focus on the single president rather than the multiple members of Congress. Hence the White House has a bigger megaphone.

In addition, the president has more information, collected by the huge bureaucracy of the executive branch. In foreign affairs, the president has a monopoly, or near monopoly, of information from the intelligence agencies. The president can keep this information secret, revealing as much as necessary to persuade the members of Congress and the public. Or he can falsely claim the existence of classified information to make his case.

But the presidency has also grown through powers delegated by law or voluntarily ceded by Congress (preparing the budget, dominating security policy during the Cold War and again in the war against terrorism) or assumed by default through congressional inaction. In this section we discuss Congress's contributions to the expansion of presidential power, the areas of greatest conflict and cooperation between the president and Congress, and the president's role as an election ally and foe of members of the House and Senate.

Passing Laws

Congress, of course, was expected to dominate the legislative process, but the president has come to play an important role. Presidents designate their legislative priorities, but members of Congress have their own preferences and initiate their own bills. Even when they take up a president's proposal, they amend it. Virtually all bills emerge from Congress in very different form from the original proposals. But if a president is an effective salesman, he can have great influence over which bills are given priority in any session of Congress and considerable influence over the final shape of legislation.

Negotiating with Congress

When asked how a president should deal with Congress, Lyndon Johnson replied: "continuously, incessantly, and without interruption."[88] Not every president has Johnson's stamina or zest for the job, but effectiveness does depend on how active a role the president wants to take and how involved he is in policy detail, as well as his knowledge of congressional operations and personal powers of persuasion. Presidents must discuss, cajole, negotiate, bargain, and then, at the right moment, compromise to get as much as they can.

As the party's leader, presidents have various favors and penalties to dispense to enhance their persuasiveness. They might direct government projects to the district or state of the legislator. Or presidents might call in their "chits," reminding the legislator about the time they backed a bill, appointed an official or judge pushed by the legislator, or campaigned for the legislator back home. The message? "Now it's your turn to help me." They might also observe the custom of **senatorial courtesy** and appoint a legislator's

Stephen Crowley/The New York Times

President Obama has continued the recent practice of assigning significant duties to the vice president. Here Joe Biden leads a meeting of cabinet officials.

first choice for federal marshal or prosecutor or to the bench of a federal court serving his or her home state. By tradition, senators from the president's party have had a virtual veto over these appointments, but there is no legal requirement that a president honor their choices.

Social invitations, such as to receptions or dinners at the White House, are prized, as are personal calls from the president. Former Speaker of the House Tip O'Neill (D-Mass.) remarked, "The men and women in Congress love nothing better than to hear from the head guy, so they can go back to their districts and say, 'I was talking to the president the other day.' The constituents love it too."[89] After a call from President Reagan, a Democrat exclaimed, "I was so thrilled, I thought I was talking to the pope."[90]

Presidents also use the trappings of their office, offering rides in the presidential limousine or on *Air Force One*. Depending on how impressionable or how jaded the lawmakers, the experience they get from the ride and the story they can tell about it can make them more favorably disposed to a president's request.

Presidents can also threaten retaliation if a legislator refuses to heed a request. For example, they might block a bill sponsored by the legislator or refuse to appoint an official or judge recommended by the legislator. They can play hardball, vowing to reduce the party's funding for the legislator in the next election or, as a last resort, threatening to campaign for the legislator's opponent in the primary election. But despite the numerous means at their disposal, they can't use all of them or even many of them on a single issue, because these tactics, when multiplied by many members

of Congress, take considerable time and lose their effect if used too often.

No president was more effective in persuading members of Congress than Lyndon Johnson. Having been in both houses of Congress and majority leader in the Senate, he knew how the institution worked and what made its members tick. He knew their views, their favorite programs and least favorite programs, their strengths and weaknesses, their health, their quirks—which ones had "a nagging wife" and which ones liked a 5 o'clock scotch. A congressional leader said LBJ "could talk a bone away from a dog." But Johnson did not rely on sweet talk; he knew how to cut a deal. One senator remembered, "You needed a bridge built on some highway, and, by God, he got your vote or you didn't get the bridge."[91] Johnson also knew where the skeletons were buried. When necessary, he quoted FBI reports about a member having a mistress or IRS reports about a member submitting inaccurate tax returns. His unspoken threat was that he would leak the incriminating information to the media or ask the IRS to conduct an audit.

Although Johnson was often accused of the raw use of power in getting legislators to support him, he said that few understood just how much work went into preparing for those bargaining sessions.[92] It must also be noted that Johnson served in Congress and the White House in a very different era. When he was Senate majority leader, Johnson said that it was the "solemn responsibility" of Congress to work with the president and that it was "the politician's task to pass legislation, not to sit around saying principled things."[93]

As a result of Johnson's tremendous drive and consummate skills working with Congress, he left a legacy of legislative accomplishments. In contrast, George W. Bush was not an effective persuader, especially during the period of divided government. Although he had strong support after 9/11, enabling him to get much of what he wanted from Congress, he lost support as the Iraq War dragged on and Congress changed hands. He was unable to get his domestic legislative agenda passed, in part because he lacked the skills and the interest in the legislative process that many of his predecessors had.

Bush also did not have close relationships with members of Congress and did not engage in "Washington schmoozing."[94] He demonstrated "thinly veiled contempt" for Congress, even when Republicans controlled both chambers.[95] When he met with lawmakers about funding for Iraq, he simply demanded their support. When one senator tried to ask a question, the president interrupted him, saying, "I'm not here to debate you."[96] In rating presidents on their ability to work with Congress, a presidential and congressional scholar concluded, "If you had to evaluate presidents, 1 to 10, and Johnson is a 10, this president [Bush] is a 1."[97]

Of course, the major work of negotiating with Congress is not done by the president personally but by his staff. Every president has assistants whose sole purpose is to serve as liaisons with Congress, and in addition almost every president appoints one or more congressional veterans to top staff positions or chooses one as a running mate. President Carter said that having Senate veteran Walter Mondale as

his vice president was worth ten votes on any crucial issue. Presidents Clinton and Obama both chose highly regarded senators as their running mates, and Obama named as his chief of staff a member of the House Democratic leadership.

Measuring Legislative Effectiveness

How often Congress passes legislation that the president publicly supports is one of the important indicators of his effectiveness. Most presidents have their greatest success during their first year in office. This was true for Reagan, who got Congress to approve a major tax cut and increase military spending during his first year. Then a recession and 11 percent unemployment led to a drop in his effectiveness, and even after the economy recovered and he had won easy reelection, his success with Congress never returned to its earlier level. Congressional support for George H. W. Bush was weak throughout his term. He had fewer congressional Republicans to work with than any GOP president in the twentieth century, and he had low support even among them.

Clinton tried to emulate Reagan's successful first-year strategy of asking Congress to vote on a few high-priority bills. With both houses of Congress controlled by Democratic majorities at the outset of his administration, Clinton did not have to deal with a divided government. Despite substantial disagreements among congressional Democrats, he succeeded in getting majority support for most of his early economic proposals. His early legislative record was

Opposition to President Obama's policies and to the president himself has been fierce. In Mason City, Iowa, a Tea Party group, reflecting the over-the-top anger and irrationality common today, erected this billboard comparing Obama to the Nazi Adolf Hitler and the communist Vladimir Lenin.

impressive, but it did not give him a reputation for effectiveness. It was overshadowed by the scandals that followed him into his second term and by his failure to articulate larger goals in a way that let the American people know where he wanted to lead them.

George W. Bush's first-year success rate of 87 percent was nearly identical to that of Clinton's first year, partly because Bush took fewer positions and usually took a public stand only after Congress had drafted a bill in a form likely to pass.[98] With this low-risk strategy, Bush equaled Clinton's early success rate. His success rate remained high until his seventh year in office, when it fell to the same level as Clinton's during his seventh year (38 percent).

Barack Obama entered office with larger congressional majorities than any president since Lyndon Johnson had had. Working with a much more partisan Congress than Johnson had to deal with, Obama set a record high of 97 percent for congressional success in his first year. There was nowhere to

go but down and with a divided congress in the second half of his term, his success rate will surely fall. (See Figure 3.)

Veto Power

If Congress will not pass legislation the president supports, he has little recourse. But if it passes bills he opposes, he can exercise his **veto power** (Latin for "I forbid"), his principal constitutional power in the legislative process. The veto power is not listed among the president's formal powers in Article II, but rather is included in Article I as a check on Congress's power to legislate. **Art. I, Sec. 7**

When the president receives a bill passed by Congress, he has three options: he can sign it into law; he can veto it by sending it back to Congress, along with his objections, unsigned; or he can take no action, in which case the bill becomes a law after ten congressional working days. A bill returned by the president unsigned can be passed into law if two-thirds of both houses vote to override the veto. But if Congress adjourns within ten working days after sending legislation to the White House and the president chooses to pocket the bill—that is, not to act on it—the legislation dies. This option, called a **pocket veto**, is a means by which the president can kill a bill without facing an override attempt in Congress.

The veto, and the ever-present threat of a veto, help presidents influence legislation. Given the presence of White House supporters in Congress and the president's ability to go public, mobilizing two-thirds majorities in both houses to override a veto is usually very hard. As a result, presidents can try to influence the content of bills by threatening to veto them if they do not conform to presidential wishes.

George Washington, not surprisingly, cast the first veto, but it was the only veto he cast in his first term. In his second term, he cast one more. In both cases he believed the

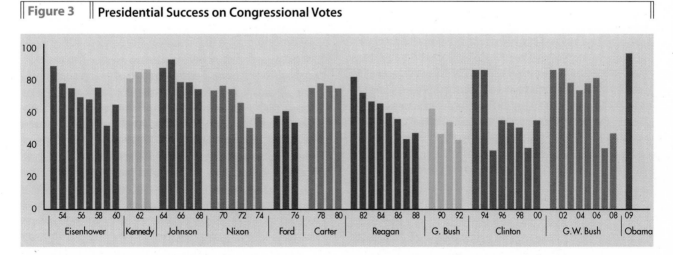

| Figure 3 | Presidential Success on Congressional Votes |

This graph indicates the percentage of time in which the president got Congress to support his position in roll-call votes. Presidents usually have the most success with Congress early in their first term. Barack Obama set a record for success in his first year.
SOURCE: *CQ Weekly, January 11, 2010, 113.*

bills contained provisions that were unconstitutional. He was acting as one who had to execute the law, not as one trying to write law. Congress rewrote those provisions rather than trying to override.[99]

Franklin Roosevelt, the longest-serving president, holds the record with 635 vetoes in fourteen years, but the great majority were private bills, not public laws. Only 9 were overridden. Only seven presidents never vetoed a bill (both Adamses, Jefferson, Harrison, Taylor, Filmore, and Garfield).[100] George W. Bush didn't use the veto until his sixth year, but then used it nine more times in his last eighteen months in office. President Obama used his veto power only once in his first two years in office. Presidents who use the veto too often may appear isolated or uncooperative or may seem to be exercising negative leadership. But the fact that presidents are rarely overridden is a reminder of their power when they decide that they really want something.

Failing to get Congress to sustain his veto, the president can try to block implementation of laws he disagrees with, either by directions to the bureaucracy issued in signing statements, as discussed above, or by appointing people to head executive branch agencies who will not implement laws or portions of laws the president disagrees with. (This is discussed in Chapter 12.) These routes violate the presidential oath to "faithfully execute" the laws passed by Congress unless a federal court agrees with the president's interpretation and rules the provisions unconstitutional.

Budget-making

The president's budget-writing power is one of the greatest sources of friction in relations between the executive and legislative branches. Little is possible without funding, so the stakes in the budget process are high.

For many years, the president had a negligible role in managing the federal budgets because the Founders gave the House of Representatives the power to originate taxing and spending bills and the Senate the power to concur, dissent, or amend. The president's authority was limited to the same signing or vetoing power he has over other legislation. **Art. I, Sec. 7** Federal agencies sent their budget requests directly to the House, unreviewed and unchanged by the White House. But by the end of World War I, a general awareness had developed that a larger government required better management. In the Budget and Accounting Act of 1921, Congress delegated important priority-setting and managerial responsibilities that have given presidents who are so inclined the opportunity to dominate budgetary politics.

Having the Office of Management and Budget (OMB) within the Executive Office of the President gives the president an edge in dealing with Congress on budget issues because the OMB's hundreds of experts work only for the president. They write the president's annual budget message, which contains recommendations for how much money Congress should appropriate for every program funded by the national government. Preparing the message requires the White House to examine all agency budget requests and to decide which to support or reject.

Congress's nonpartisan budget office, the Congressional Budget Office (CBO), prepares budget reports that are regarded as substantially more reliable than those of the OMB, but the policy initiative lies with the OMB and the White House because they prepare the first budget draft.

Presidents who are little interested in the details of domestic policy, such as Reagan and both Bushes, do not get maximum political leverage out of the budgetary powers Congress has delegated to them. But a president whose strength lies in the mastery of detail may be able to use those powers, as Clinton did, to dominate budgetary politics and the debate over deficit reduction.

The delegation of budget authority to the president is partly responsible for the growth of presidential power and the engorgement of the Executive Office of the President (EOP). The OMB alone occupies an eight-story building near the White House. But budget authority also carries political liabilities. Although no money can be spent unless authorized by Congress, the president as budget initiator is held just as responsible for bad fiscal policy and budget deficits as Congress, if not more so. Nevertheless, some members of Congress believe that passing this political hot potato to the executive branch was a mistake and an evasion of their constitutional duty.

War-making

Along with budget making, the decision to commit U.S. troops to battle is the policy area that creates the most conflict between the executive and legislative branches. Although the Constitution empowers Congress to declare war, it has done so only five times. Using their power as commander in chief, presidents have committed troops to battle far more often without prior congressional approval than with it.

The extent to which Presidents Johnson and Nixon exercised their war-making power during the undeclared war in Vietnam led Congress to place limits on the power of the president to take unilateral military action. In 1973, over Nixon's veto, Congress passed the **War Powers Resolution** to limit the president's ability to commit troops to combat. It says that the president can use troops abroad under three conditions: when Congress has declared war, when Congress has given the president specific authority to do so, or when an attack on the United States or its military creates a national crisis. If a president commits troops under the third condition, he is supposed to consult with Congress beforehand, if possible, and notify it within forty-eight hours afterward. Unless Congress approves the use of troops, the president must withdraw them within sixty days, or ninety days if he needs more time to protect them. Congress can pass a concurrent resolution (not subject to presidential

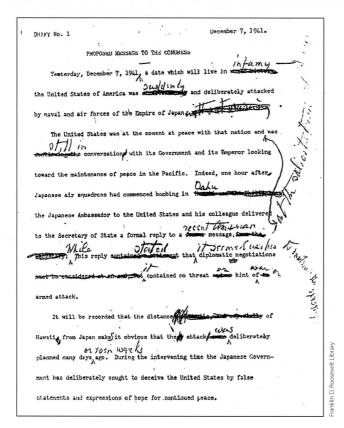

President Franklin Roosevelt edited his speech to Congress about the Japanese attack on Pearl Harbor. The word *infamy*, which made memorable the phrase "a date which will live in infamy," was one of his corrections.

veto) at any time ordering the president to end the use of military force.

Every president since Nixon has believed the resolution violated his constitutional authority to protect the nation from military threats. Although presidents have not questioned Congress's constitutional authority to declare war, all have fought congressional involvement in the use of troops. As a result, enforcement of the act has proved difficult.

For example, when George H. W. Bush sent troops to invade Panama in 1989, he did not even refer to the War Powers Resolution in the two-page letter he sent to Congress, sixty hours *after* the invasion began, justifying the invasion. He also ordered 250,000 troops to the Persian Gulf between August and November 1990 on his own authority and delayed announcing his decision to double this number until after the November elections. This kept the decision that changed the mission from defense (Operation Desert Shield) to offense (Operation Desert Storm) from coming to Congress until Bush had mobilized U.S. and world opinion and gained United Nations support. By the time Congress authorized using force in January 1991, the question of whether it should be used was, practically speaking, already decided. The same can be said for George W. Bush's decision to invade Iraq in 2003. He reluctantly went to Congress for authorization, but the decision to invade had effectively been taken well before Congress consented.

The War Powers Resolution is ineffective because when troops are deployed into combat areas, Congress hesitates to oppose the president, fearing that doing so may be seen as disloyalty to the troops and by other nations as a sign of American weakness or lack of resolve. There is almost always a "rally 'round the flag" effect on the public when the president commits troops to combat. Thus any vote, such as against an increase in military expenditures, that can be painted as a lack of support for troops in combat can be used against the members of Congress by their political opponents in the next election. However, the presidential advantage can be short-lived, as both George Bushes discovered, and as President Obama may be realizing about his decision to expand the war in Afghanistan. Presidents who take military action without a broad consensus need to accomplish their goals quickly or face loss of public support.

The open-ended nature of the Iraq War, its poor execution, and its use to expand presidential powers into the domestic sphere virtually unchecked by Congress led a bipartisan group of constitutional experts and former government officials to conclude, after a year-long study, that the resolution was "ineffective at best and unconstitutional at worst." Former Republican secretary of state James A. Baker said it was not good for the rule of law to have a statute on such a critical issue be routinely ignored. "No president has complied with it and reports to Congress under it just collect dust. People in Congress say it's just a charade."[101]

Party Leader

As party leader, the president is an electoral adversary of members of the House and Senate who do not belong to his party, and he can use his reputation and the weight of his office to try to unseat those who oppose them.

To improve the electoral chances of their party, presidents try to help recruit good candidates for House and Senate races. They send their political aides to help boost the campaigns of fellow partisans, and sometimes even go themselves. Because seeing a president in person is an exciting and rare event, even unpopular presidents can draw large crowds and media attention. In addition, presidents help their congressional candidates raise money by being the headliner at fundraising events and by staying on good terms with major contributors and inviting them to the White House. But the president usually tries to camouflage his role as party leader when trying to persuade people to support him or to vote for his party's candidates, because people are more likely to listen to a president when they see him as head of state.

Playing an active party role has a purpose: the more members of a president's party who sit in Congress, the more support he gets for his policies. However, a president's support, when he chooses to give it, is no guarantee of electoral success for congressional candidates, especially in off-year elections (see Table 1).

Franklin D. Roosevelt Library

Table 1	The President's Tattered Coattails: Congressional Gains and Losses for the President's Party in Off-Year Elections

Seats Gained or Lost by the President's Party			
Year	President	House	Senate
1934	Roosevelt (D)	+9	+10
1938	Roosevelt (D)	−71	−6
1942	Roosevelt (D)	−45	−9
1946	Truman (D)	−55	−12
1950	Truman (D)	−29	−6
1954	Eisenhower (R)	−18	−1
1958	Eisenhower (R)	−47	−13
1962	Kennedy (D)	−4	+3
1966	Johnson (D)	−47	−4
1970	Nixon (R)	−12	+2
1974	Ford (R)	−48	−4
1978	Carter (D)	−15	−3
1982	Reagan (R)	−26	+1
1986	Reagan (R)	−5	−8
1990	G. H. Bush (R)	−8	−1
1994	Clinton (D)	−54	−8
1998	Clinton (D)	+5	0
2002	G. W. Bush (R)	+6	+2
2006	G. W. Bush (R)	−31	−6
2010	Obama (D)	−63	−6
Average, all off-year elections		−28	−3.5
Average, all presidential election years		+20	+3

SOURCES: *CQ Weekly*, November 8, 2010, 2524; Roger H. Davidson, Walter J. Oleszek, and Frances E. Lee, *Congress and Its Members*, 11th ed. (Washington, D.C.: CQ Press, 2007), 107.

Since 1934, the president's party has lost an average of twenty-eight House and between three and four Senate seats in off-year elections.

However, in recent years, while the president's party has lost seats in these off-year elections, it typically loses fewer than the historical average. (Clinton's losses in 1994 and Bush's in 2006 were throwbacks to the old pattern.) The blunting of the off-year election pattern is due to the number of safe seats. District lines are drawn to protect incumbents, almost all of whom run for reelection with a tremendous fundraising advantage. In recent years, these factors have helped make candidates safe even when their presidential candidate loses or is unpopular at midterm. The

1998 election was the first off-year election since 1934 in which the president's party had a net gain, and that feat was duplicated in 2002. In the 2006 and 2010 midterm elections, the traditional pattern returned with the president's party losing seats in both chambers. Such losses do not inevitably weaken the president in his dealings with Congress, but there is a good chance they will diminish his overall reputation for effectiveness.

THE EBB AND FLOW OF PRESIDENTIAL POWER AND REPUTATION

Every president comes to office with a somewhat different view of the office and its reach and, depending on personality, talents, education, experience, and ideology, varying predispositions to exercise established powers or to expand them. Political scientists have extensively studied presidential character and personality as a way to explain presidential actions and successes or failures.[102] In this final section we explain why the evaluation of a president's performance fluctuates over the years, and why the powers of the office ebb and expand with the times and with the person holding office.

Rating Presidential Performance

How can presidential performance be measured? Presidential scholar Richard Neustadt called the presidency a "choice-making machine," and presidents who can act decisively are often well regarded. Truman epitomized the decisive style and has probably benefited from the contrast with the more waffling approaches of recent presidents, who are often seen as driven by polls and focus groups. "The Buck Stops Here" plaque that Truman kept on his desk illustrated both his sense of accountability and his no-nonsense rhetoric. In historical perspective, his leadership skills have looked more impressive than they did while he was in office, and this view has helped move him to the ranks of near-great presidents.

Any concept of presidential effectiveness inevitably involves vision. A president will likely be seen as effective only if he has a clear idea of where he wants to take the country. The nineteenth-century historian Henry Adams compared the job to being the commander of a ship at sea. He must have a helm to grasp, a course to steer, a port to seek.[103] That is, the incumbent must have a goal, a destination toward which he is leading the nation; he must have programs and a course of action to enable the nation to get there; and he must be willing and able to use the instruments of his office to reach that goal.

This is why Reagan is regarded by much of the public as a more effective president than George H. W. Bush, a man consistently described as lacking in vision. To rank with the greats, however, vision must be coupled with the

behind the scenes

Trading Favors

In 1962, President John Kennedy received a call from Senate minority leader Everett Dirksen (R-Ill.) requesting a favor. An aide to former president Dwight Eisenhower was under investigation for income tax evasion and expected to be formally charged the next day. Eisenhower's wife, Mamie, was a close friend of the aide's wife, who worried that the aide might commit suicide if indicted. Eisenhower did not know Kennedy, so he asked his fellow Republican, Dirksen, to approach the president and ask, "as a personal favor to me, to put the . . . indictment in the deep freeze. . . . [A]dvise him he'll have a blank check in my bank if he will grant me this favor."

Kennedy had no knowledge of the matter but said he would do what Eisenhower asked. He called his brother Robert, the attorney general, and told him not to sign the indictment. His brother objected on the grounds that granting a special favor to a tax evader would be politically disastrous. But the president told him to do it or submit his resignation.

Weeks later, the nuclear test ban treaty with the Soviet Union was pending in the Senate, where ratification required a two-thirds vote. This was especially difficult to obtain at the height of the Cold War. Americans didn't trust the Soviets, and conservatives claimed a treaty banning the testing of nuclear weapons would give the Soviets the upper hand. A head count showed the treaty falling short of a two-thirds majority. Kennedy rang Dirksen and called in his chits. He asked the senator to change his vote and to get Ike to endorse the treaty too, saying the treaty was important to him, the country, and all mankind. If both men lent their support, Kennedy would consider his favor repaid. With public support from the minority leader and the popular former president, enough Republicans joined the Democrats to ratify the treaty.

SOURCE: The account of this deal appeared in Bobby Baker (with Larry L. King), *Wheeling and Dealing: Confessions of a Capitol Hill Operator* (New York: W. W. Norton, 1978), 97–99.

political and administrative skills necessary to achieve it. In the scholarly consensus, Bush was willing and able to grab the helm but was steering to no port in particular; Reagan had a fixed destination but no firm hand on the helm and insufficient knowledge or interest to steer the ship. Like Bush, Reagan had a mediocre legislative record and an abysmal fiscal record, but in the public eye, Reagan had a clear vision of what he wanted for the country. In contrast, Clinton had all the political and communication skills to steer the ship but was perceived as someone who kept changing his destination. He was unsuccessful in projecting to the public a clear and consistent vision of where the country should be headed.

In the early years of his presidency, George W. Bush gave a clearer idea of what he wanted to do with the office of president than he did about where he wanted to lead the country. Early assessments were based almost entirely on how he handled the aftermath of the 9/11 attacks—how both his policy response and his personal demeanor projected the national will. The public took his aggressive military posture as a sign of character and strong leadership and gave him high approval ratings, until disillusionment with the Iraq War set in. Up to that point Bush was very successful in turning the war against terrorism into a permanent crisis that allowed him to greatly expand the powers of office.

Almost all rankings of presidents list Washington, Lincoln, and Franklin Roosevelt among the greats. But it is not always immediately clear how deep an impact a president's tenure has had on the direction of the country, and assessments of presidential performance do change over time. Truman exemplifies a president who was unpopular during his tenure and in the immediate years afterward but who left a legacy of directness, personal integrity, and decisiveness on key decisions during an extremely difficult time (the national trauma of FDR's death while we were engaged in World War II).

Scholarly assessment of Eisenhower's administration has also changed significantly. Shortly after he left office, he was judged an average president, a good and honest man with strong administrative skills but one who took few chances and lacked an overall vision for the country. In retrospect, analysts regard as levelheaded and prescient both his leadership during an extremely volatile period in the nuclear arms race and his warnings about the dangers the military-industrial complex would present to the economy and our sense of national purpose.

Former presidents sometimes get a bounce in poll ratings: Truman, Eisenhower, Carter, and Reagan, for example, received much higher favorable ratings in retirement than they had at the end of their terms. But higher approval does not necessarily lead to a higher performance ranking; Clinton finished his term with strong approval ratings and in the 2009 C-SPAN poll was ranked in the top three on economic management and the top four in pursuit of social justice, but he finished fifteenth overall. In contrast, Lyndon Johnson, who left office with little popular support, is outranked only by FDR in his handling of congressional relations and only by Lincoln for his pursuit of social justice, and he finished eleventh overall in the 2009 survey (see box "Rating the Presidents").

The Fluctuating Powers of Office

Despite its advantages, presidential power should not be exaggerated. Most presidents since World War II have seemed at times almost powerless to shape events affecting the national interest. The immensely popular war hero Dwight Eisenhower (1953–1961) was unable to buck Cold War sentiment and prevent the buildup of the military-industrial complex. John Kennedy (1961–1963), who enjoyed an extraordinary success rate in a conservative Congress, was stymied in getting civil rights legislation accepted. The domestic goals of Lyndon Johnson (1963–1968), along with his chances for reelection, were derailed by a war that took Richard Nixon (1969–1974) years to end. And Nixon, for whom the "imperial presidency" phrase was coined, was forced from office on obstruction of justice charges for covering up criminal activity in the Watergate scandal. Three of their four successors could not get reelected.

Reaction against the arrogant use of presidential powers led to the modest presidencies of Gerald Ford (1974–1977) and Jimmy Carter (1977–1981). Both men came across as more humble than Johnson or Nixon and less interested in power for its own sake. Ford, who became president when Nixon resigned, was a kind of accidental president and could not get reelected. Nor could Carter; he had ambitious programs, especially in energy and conservation, but his

ascetic, if not dour, demeanor and demands for American sacrifice put him at a disadvantage against the sunny disposition of his election opponent and successor, Ronald Reagan. But Reagan, one of our most popular recent presidents, was so frustrated when Congress thwarted his foreign policy initiatives that he condoned illegal activities, producing the Iran-Contra scandal and tarnishing his personal reputation. Reagan, George H. W. Bush, and Bill Clinton all had ambitious agendas, although Reagan's and Bush's were directed more toward foreign than domestic policy.

Under Clinton, the presidency seemed to be imploding as the personal presidency reached a new level. A former employee of Arkansas state government sued him, and the Supreme Court ruled that he had no immunity while in office because the conduct occurred before he took office.[104] The judges, in a colossal misjudgment, doubted that the case would take much of his time and attention. In fact, it not only took his time but also diverted the attention away from his domestic agenda. Then came the impeachment.

The continuous investigations of Clinton by Congress, special prosecutors, and conservative groups looking for dirt resulted in media saturation of the most private and intimate details of a president's life ever revealed. "It is entirely possible," one reporter observed, "that the Clinton era will be remembered by historians primarily as the moment when the distance between the President and the public evaporated forever."[105]

As the people experience one personal presidency after another, they can become disillusioned. Their unrealistic

George Tames/The New York Times

This photo of President Kennedy in the Oval office has been used to build the mystique of the presidency, especially the weight and loneliness of the office. In fact Kennedy was not alone with his thoughts but leaning over the *New York Times* and cussing out its best-known columnist to one or more aides who stood behind him out of shot.

Rating the Presidents

In 2009, at C-SPAN's request, fifty-eight presidential historians rated the presidents on ten personal and professional qualities: economic management, moral authority, crisis leadership, public persuasion, relations with Congress, international relations, administrative skills, vision and agenda setting, pursuit of equal justice, and performance in context of the time. Their overall ranking of the top and bottom ten was derived from averaging those scores.

Table 2	Presidential Rating Survey

Top Ten (in rank order)	Bottom Ten (in rank order)
1. Abraham Lincoln	33. Rutherford Hayes
2. George Washington	34. Herbert Hoover
3. Franklin D. Roosevelt	35. John Tyler
4. Theodore Roosevelt	36. George W. Bush
5. Harry S. Truman	37. Millard Fillmore
6. John Kennedy	38. Warren G. Harding
7. Thomas Jefferson	39. W. H. Harrison
8. Dwight Eisenhower	40. Franklin Pierce
9. Woodrow Wilson	41. Andrew Johnson
10. Ronald Reagan	42. James Buchanan

SOURCE: C-SPAN survey, 2009.
Full results at www.c-span.org/PresidentialSurvey/presidential-leadership-survey.aspx.

assumptions about presidential power, which prod the presidential candidates to make unrealistic promises, set the presidents up for failure in the eyes of the people. When the presidents can't deliver, the people lose faith. And, all along, the media exposure and scrutiny take a toll. Presidents' novelty wears off and their flaws appear. Few presidents can withstand the media microscope without losing their public esteem. Most presidents suffer a decline in popularity as they continue in office. (See Figure 4.)

Some historians speculated that Clinton's impeachment would leave a legacy similar to Andrew Johnson's, which weakened the presidency for the next half-century.[106] But when George W. Bush came to office in 2001, he brought with him a retinue of Washington professionals and set out to restore the presidency to its former preeminence. Despite many strong actions and the successes of his first term, Bush also fell prey to the ills that beset second-term presidents. He watched his popularity plummet to historic lows as his once popular wars dragged on at an increasing cost and as the economy fell into recession.

Wars and crisis situations are always temptations for a president who believes his office is not as strong as he wants it to be or believes it needs to be to meet a crisis. This tendency has been strengthened by the evolution of a personal presidency and the likelihood that the public will look first to the president to act in a crisis. The ability of the president to command the stage in these situations may in turn tempt Congress to abdicate its constitutional obligations, especially in a unified government. But the Bush administration's interpretation , according to one Republican legal adviser, "staked out powers that [were] a universe beyond any other administration."[107] In the political climate created by the 2001 direct attack on the country and the significant loss of lives, the Republican leadership in Congress was reluctant to exercise its oversight of executive branch actions, and it was just as reluctant five years later. Frustrated critics in Congress charged that Bush acted as if the system of checks and balances did not exist.

There is no doubt that the public, after the spectacle of the Clinton impeachment, wanted to see dignity returned to the White House and Congress get back to the real business of governing. But there is no reason to believe that the public was looking for more power to gravitate to the presidency or for Congress and the courts to abandon their responsibility to act as checks on executive power. In other words, the move to expand presidential powers was not necessarily government responding to the people, but rather government officials trying to institutionalize their personal vision of the presidency.

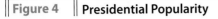

Figure 4 ‖ **Presidential Popularity**

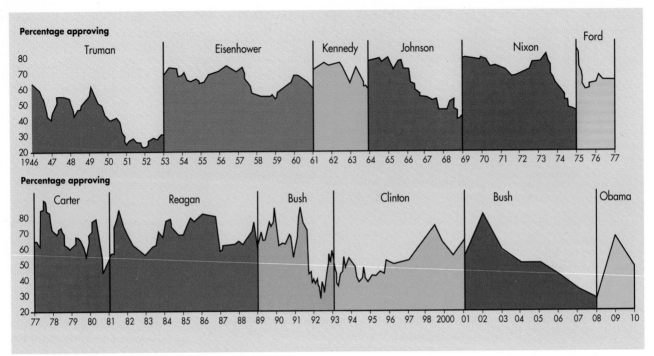

Since the end of World War II, presidential popularity has usually declined over time. Only three presidents—Eisenhower, Reagan, and Clinton—left office with ratings at a level comparable to that when they entered.
SOURCE: *Gallup polls, reported in* Public Opinion *and updated at www.presidency/ucsb.edu/data/popularity.php.*

Eventually the Bush-Cheney reach for imperial powers led to the same kind of rebuff experienced by other presidents with long arms. Cheney's approval ratings fell to single digits, Bush's to the high twenties, and in 2007 *Time* magazine did not even list the president among the world's most influential people.[108] With a divided government in his last two years, Bush's congressional success rate fell to 38 percent and he began to exercise his previously unused veto power. In his last year in office, *The Daily Show* began referring to him as "Still" President Bush.

This "diminished presidency" was matched by a weak Congress, with approval ratings even lower than the president's.[109] The powerful executive-driven government Bush and Cheney tried to put in place led instead to a stalemated government in which no branch was carrying out its role. These developments seemed to illustrate that those presidents who overreach in trying to make a lasting imprint on the office can do serious harm to their own legacies while the office itself gets reshaped by its next occupant.

Barack Obama rode into office on a wave of public adulation and with high expectations that he would smite partisanship and bring a new way of governing to Washington. But despite his remarkable first-year success with Congress and a host of new legislation, partisanship was worse than ever. Whereas in his first term Bush successfully used the "rally round the flag" effect to dampen Democratic opposition, congressional Republicans showed little deference to Obama's huge electoral victory. Most Democrats had supported Bush's No Child Left Behind school reform as well as his foreign policy. Some even helped pass his other major goal—tax cuts for the highest earners. Obama, on the other hand, was unable to win more than a few Republican votes for any of his top legislative priorities. Obama's early successes with Congress would have been impossible if he had not had, in his first two years, the largest congressional majorities of any Democrat since Lyndon Johnson. Furthermore, some Republican members of Congress showed a lack of respect for the office of president itself, one House member even shouting, "You lie!" at the president as he delivered the State of the Union speech to the nation. During his first eighteen months in office, Obama saw his approval ratings drop by twenty points but those for Congress stood as much as thirty points lower.

Nevertheless, it is too soon to conclude that what we have now is a diminished presidency. Scholars and journalists sometimes overreact to short-term events, and these changing perceptions of the presidency illustrate that, as conditions change, so do the ways in which presidents exercise their authority. One of the most interesting aspects of this unusual office is its resilience and elasticity. The Constitution does not give the presidency the dominant role in government, and the office can be stretched and shrunk from one administration to another or even within a single administration. Each occupant is likely to make something quite different of it than his predecessor, either by the attitude and skills he brings to it or because the times force him to do so.

CONCLUSION: The President's Role in Government

The presidency has become the most consistently visible office in government as well as one of the most personalized and responsive. Americans expect leadership from the president even in times of "less" government because whoever holds that office has an almost direct relationship with the public. Using the media, a skillful president can tell us what he wants and attempt to shape our opinion. Through public opinion polls and the ballot box, we tell the president what we think.

The Founders did not intend the president to have this close relationship to the people. After all, the president was to be chosen by an Electoral College, not a popular constituency. But as the president became the head of a political party with a political agenda, and as the Electoral College evolved to embrace voters' participation, the president became more politically powerful and the role of the presidency in government became more dominant. Congressional government gave way to presidential government.

There is a danger in this personal presidency. To remain popular, a president may concentrate too much on the election cycle and do what is most popular while seeking only short-term solutions to the nation's problems., Catering to public opinion can siphon off the attention and resources the president should be devoting to the country's long-term needs.

Most recent presidents gradually came to understand the limits of presidential power, sometimes the hard way. Indeed, the moral of the personal presidency suggests that presidents who become popular by making exaggerated promises have trouble keeping both the promises and their popularity in this system of fragmented power. The Clinton years illustrated another danger of exercising the personal presidency in the age of tabloid media: the risk of diminishing the office when scrutiny of the occupant's private life overtakes evaluation of his public role. And the media are much more pervasive now than they were then.

The balance of power swings like a pendulum, depending upon major events at the time, the personality of the president, and the composition of Congress. Sometimes the presidency is dominant, sometimes Congress is dominant, and other times the two are more evenly matched.[110] The important lesson, as one presidential scholar reminds us, is that "the Presidency is not the government. Ours is not a presidential system."[111] Rather, "the most outstanding feature of the American system is the separation of powers."[112]

KEY TERMS

chief executive	330	impeachment	329
commander in chief	336	imperial presidency	326
Executive Office of the President (EOP)	342	pardon power	335
		personal presidency	338
executive orders	332	pocket veto	351
executive privilege	332	senatorial courtesy	348
going public	339	signing statements	333
head of government	334	*United States* v. *Nixon*	332
head of state	334	veto power	351
		War Powers Resolution	352

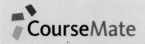

Access an interactive eBook, chapter-specific interactive learning tools (including flashcards, quizzes, videos), and more at CourseMate for *Understanding American Government*. Log in at CengageBrain.com.

12 The Bureaucracy

In an effort to reduce the paper bureaucracy, the IRS has stopped mailing 1040 forms directly to taxpayers, encouraging all to file online.

Roger Ressmeyer/Corbis

Talking Points

One of the constants in the federal bureaucracy is the battle between political appointees and career civil servants. Although only 0.17 percent of federal civilian employees are political appointees, they sometimes try to impose their will on career bureaucrats, most of whom were hired on the basis of merit and demonstrated competence. Take the case of Jim Hansen, an expert on climate change and the longtime head of NASA's Goddard Institute for Space Studies, who, in 2006, complained that the Bush administration had ordered him to stop giving speeches on global warming and not to talk about how his findings differed from administration policy.[1] One of his research reports was edited by a twenty-four-year-old political appointee—previously a public relations aide in the presidential campaign—to make Hansen's conclusions appear nearer the president's position. He had been sent to NASA with no scientific training and in fact no college degree.[2]

Hansen's case was the most publicized but far from the only attempt of Bush appointees to put policy preferences above the scientific findings of career civil servants and even of scientists and professionals appointed by Bush himself. Bush's surgeon general, for example, was told to rewrite a report to downplay the dangers of secondhand smoke and not to discuss the medical implications of global warming, stem cell research, or emergency contraception.[3] Bush appointees were ordered to edit even those scientific papers with no immediate policy implications. A scientific analysis of the Big Bang explanation of the origins of the universe was altered to magnify its uncertainty, presumably to leave room for a biblical interpretation. In another paper a reference by NASA scientists to the death of the sun in the far distant future was expunged. A spokeswoman for the agency said, "NASA is not in the habit of frightening the public with doom and gloom scenarios."[4]

It is of course easier for political appointees to accept presidential policy directives than it is for career professionals because appointees hold their positions precisely because they were hired to implement the president's policies. A NASA public affairs officer—a political appointee—said his job was "to make the president look good." However, his counterpart at the Goddard Institute said it was not *her* job nor that of the Institute's. "I'm a career civil servant and Jim Hansen is a scientist."[5] And that is exactly why we have a permanent civil service selected through merit hiring—to help formulate and implement policy in a competent and politically neutral manner.

When George Wallace ran as a third-party candidate for president in 1968, he campaigned against "pointy-headed bureaucrats" in Washington making decisions that regulated good people's lives. Bureaucrats, according to Wallace, were out of touch with everyday citizens and their concerns. Wallace did not invent bureaucracy bashing, but he helped make it popular among candidates for federal office. And ever since, some candidates have found they can score points with the electorate by bashing the government and its bureaucracy. When most politicians refer to "Washington," they mean big government using too much money to do unnecessary things. Government critics imply that bureaucrats are not like ordinary citizens. Rather, they are busybodies committed to expanding government's size, spending taxpayers' money, and designing regulations to make life more difficult for individuals and businesses.

Bureaucratic decision making is involved in so much of our lives because government has come to serve many different purposes and interests. The federal government employs butchers, truck drivers, engineers, mathematicians, physicists, chemists, and accountants. These civil servants do crop research and soil analysis, run hospitals and utilities, fight drug trafficking, check manufacturers' claims about their products, inspect mines, develop high-tech weapons systems, send out Social Security checks, authorize Medicare payments, administer student loan programs, and regulate air traffic, to mention only a few responsibilities.

In all, the federal bureaucracy had about 2 million full-time civilian workers in 2010, but that does not count those in the Postal Service, the 7.6 million hired on federal contracts, or those on federal grants. (For more on contract workers, see the section "Privatizing Government Work.") The armed forces put another 2.3 million on the federal payroll. According to one of the leading experts on the federal bureaucracy, the "true size of government," arrived at by counting everyone employed with federal money, is close to 14 million.[6] To some people, the federal bureaucracy has become the symbol of big government and the embodiment of everything they dislike about it. It is seen as equivalent to a fourth branch of government—powerful, uncontrollable, and with a life of its own. In fact, the federal bureaucracy has no *independent* legislative authority, only that delegated by Congress, and it has no budgetary powers. The bureaucracy's official role is to implement and enforce policies made by elected officials—that is, by Congress and the president. In doing this, bureaucrats do, in some instances, make new law. But departments and agencies exist at the pleasure of Congress, which can eliminate them or trim their budgets if it does not approve of their behavior. If an agency within the bureaucracy consistently supersedes its authority, it is because Congress is intentionally letting it do so or is failing to fulfill its oversight duties.

As we shall see, government bureaucrats are a lot like everyone else. They are ordinary citizens with attitudes that mirror those of their fellow citizens. Very few of these civil servants, about 15 percent, work in the Washington, D.C., metropolitan area. It may not fit your image of people pushing paper in buildings the size of the Pentagon, but the great majority of federal bureaucrats serve in offices near you; check the U.S. government listing in your telephone book and see how many branch offices of federal agencies are located in or near your community.

In this chapter, we look at the evolution of the federal bureaucracy—its growth in size, function, and lawmaking powers. We describe the people who staff the bureaucracy, how they are recruited, what rules govern their work, and how Congress and the president set guidelines for the executive branch and oversee its activities. Finally, we describe ways in which the public can join in the work of monitoring the bureaucracy and have a say in the rules it makes.

THE NATURE OF BUREAUCRACIES

Many people automatically associate the word *bureaucracy* with the federal government. They may visualize rows of cubicles with nameless clerical workers doing monotonous work very inefficiently. Trying to cash in on this stereotype, a Virginia company once sold a "Bureaucrat" doll as "a product of no redeeming social value. Place the Bureaucrat on a stack of papers on your desk, and he will just sit on them."[7] The problem with this joke is that the parodied traits are no more common among government bureaucrats than among workers in other large bureaucracies. All organizations except the very smallest have bureaucracies: your college or university has one, as did your local school district; every corporation, most religious denominations, and large philanthropic foundations have them, too, not to mention the Olympics, your favorite sports league, and the unions that represent the players in that league.

All these bureaucracies, public and private, share some common features. For example, all have hierarchies of authority; that is, everyone in a bureaucracy has a place in a pyramidal network of jobs, with fewer near the top and more near the bottom. Almost everyone in a bureaucracy has a boss, and, except for those in the bottom tier, most have some subordinates. People advance up the hierarchy on the basis of performance or seniority, so those with more authority tend to be those with more experience and expertise.

Because of the hierarchical structure, bureaucratic behavior is not always consistent with democratic principles. Most bureaucrats are not elected, and, as in any hierarchical organization, higher-level authorities can restrict the opportunity of someone lower in the pyramid to express an opinion or share expertise in the decision-making process. In their relative lack of openness, bureaucracies have the potential to restrict consumer and client access to information about their products and services and how they operate. Thus, they can limit citizens' access to information about their own government. In effect, organizational tendencies, if unrestrained in a government bureaucracy, could transform "citizens" into "subordinates."[8] But our constitutional system provides checks on the power of federal bureaucrats and ways for the public to participate in decision making that few people know about or take advantage of.

Not only are government bureaucracies structurally similar to private ones, but they also do the same types of work. Employees in both private and public bureaucracies perform a lot of routine tasks. Auditing expense vouchers, managing employee travel, and creating personnel systems, for example, are as routine in business firms as in public agencies. And both also have workers who are productive, honest, and efficient and others who are not. But there are some distinctions between private and public bureaucracies. Here we look at several.[9]

Goals

Businesses are supposed to make a profit; if they do not, they fail. Public agencies are supposed to promote the "public interest"; if they do not, they fail to serve the people who pay their salaries. Although people disagree over what the public interest is, it is not the same thing as making a profit, just as a government is not a business. This is why we have different words for these two kinds of organizations: they exist for completely different reasons.

The goals of a public bureaucracy are defined by elected officials, who collectively determine what is in the public interest. They are sometimes accused of setting goals as if they were in a private bureaucracy—that is, making policies that will help them at the polls rather than policies that best serve the public. But in general, the goals set by these officials are supposed to accomplish tasks and provide services

that private bureaucracies cannot. In some cases, such as providing for national security during wartime, they must do so irrespective of cost.

Some part of the public's varying perception of how well the bureaucracy does its job stems from a lack of agreement on the work it is given to do. One person's lazy, red-tape-ridden, uncaring bureaucracy is another's responsive agency. But even when unhappy with its performance, Americans still expect government to provide a vast array of services costing billions of dollars annually, from highways that accommodate high-speed cars to Social Security payments that arrive on time, from clean tap water to safe neighborhoods, from protection from foreign enemies to a cure for cancer.

Performance Standards

It is relatively easy to judge if a private organization is meeting its goals (ignoring for the moment fraudulent accounting) by asking if it is profitable. We might dislike the chocolate-covered raisins that a candy company produces but would still consider the company successful if it made a profit selling them. We would not typically denigrate the company because it makes something we do not approve of.

When a private company reaches bankruptcy, we can be fairly certain that something in its bureaucratic structure was not working. General Motors, for example, once the model American corporation, reached this point in 2009 when it would have collapsed had it not been for a taxpayer bailout. Its huge bureaucracy had produced a culture so "slow-moving" that layers of executives had to approve a very new idea—such as plans for hybrid cars—leaving it incapable of responding as quickly as its competition to changes in consumer demand.[10]

Federal regulations mandate setting standards and testing autos for safety. These dummies allow simulations of the impact of crashes.

We rightly use a different standard than profitability in judging government. But what is the appropriate standard for evaluating the performance of government if making a profit is not the goal?

One obvious method is to determine whether a public agency is efficient and cost-effective. That sounds logical, but any method of assigning dollar values to bureaucratic output must be partly subjective. It is usually easier to place a value on a commodity than on a government service. We can estimate what price to place on a chair or a house by computing the cost of constructing it. But placing a dollar value on such public goals as education or consumer safety is much harder. How many children have to die from swallowing pills and medications before government requires pharmaceutical manufacturers to use childproof caps on bottles? How many lives saved makes it worthwhile for government to require auto manufacturers to install air bags? How much was the life of each person killed in the World Trade Center on 9/11 worth (a calculation made in order to provide compensation to their families)? Over 5000 people were killed in workplace accidents in 2008 and millions more injured; how much should the Occupational Safety and Health Administration (OSHA) spend inspecting worksites to reduce these numbers?[11]

These are questions bureaucrats must answer. To determine whether it is cost-effective to adopt a safety rule, for example, bureaucrats in regulatory agencies put a dollar value on human life by calculating how productive an individual will be during his or her lifetime. Then they estimate the cost of putting the policy in place, as well as of monitoring and enforcing it.

Private bureaucracies ask the same questions before their leaders decide whether it is profitable to install safer fuel tanks in cars or to remove a low-risk flaw from a child's toy. Although the federal bureaucrat, too, is always weighing costs against benefits, many people believe that the government should not use cost as the primary standard when lives are at risk.

Another way to evaluate performance is to measure waste that stems from inefficiency and corruption. It is not particularly difficult to calculate how much more an agency paid out because it failed to get competitive bids for equipment and supplies, hired more employees than necessary to do a job, contracted consultants to do imaginary work, or erred in calculating welfare payments or farm subsidies. One spectacular case of waste in government spending resulted from the Department of Homeland Security's (DHS's) mismanagement of rescue and recovery after Hurricane Katrina. Millions in housing support was paid out to ineligible applicants and millions more wasted in purchases made on no-bid contracts.

Some kinds of government waste are harder to measure because no matter how well a program may be run, part of the public will always be opposed to its goals. Perhaps the program is providing services a taxpayer thinks inappropriate for government, or maybe it serves relatively few people at a large cost. These were the criteria many Americans used to evaluate welfare programs. Accusations of waste and fraud were common, but as a percentage of overall expenditures, there was little client fraud in the welfare program. Most criticism stemmed from opposition to the program itself and services provided at great cost to a small clientele without appropriate results.

Similar criticism comes from opponents of government health care and social insurance programs; some argue that private health insurance and pension programs are by definition more efficiently run because private businesses exist to make a profit. But in fact the administrative costs of Medicare are well below those of private health care insurers, and many private pension programs have been catastrophically underfunded and either terminated or placed in government receivership.

In a less publicized example, a government commission called it wasteful to keep open hundreds of very small post offices that served rural communities. The commission was not alleging fraud or mismanagement, but it believed that the post offices cost too much for the small number of people served. To the residents of these communities, however, their post offices were a good return on their tax dollars, and paying to keep them open was more efficient than having to drive miles to a distant office.

Citizens have rarely applied this standard of waste to corporate behavior, at least not prior to our more environmentally conscious era. Historically, private corporations have been able to waste more than a government agency of comparable size without the public ever taking notice. If a business or industry makes a profit, most people think it is a job well done, without asking whether the product or service offered is in itself wasteful. Marketing a hundred different kinds of breakfast cereal in packaging twice the size of the contents may not be an efficient use of resources, but if they sell, consumers are inclined to say, "Why not?" We may not like lime-green sofas with pink stripes, but we do not consider their manufacturer wasteful for making them as long as the product is profitable. In 2001, when senior managers in the federal bureaucracy got bonuses averaging $11,000, it prompted public scrutiny of their agencies' performances.[12] But when CEOs of corporations that lost billions got multimillion-dollar bonuses in 2002, much of the public simply said, "Whatever the market will allow." This thinking changed in 2008 when the economy crashed, and the following year when CEOs of banks and brokerages got billions in bonuses after a government bailout, the public was enraged.

We see government expenditures as *our* money (it is!), and we feel entitled to complain, especially since payment of that money (taxes) is not voluntary. Public attention to how private bureaucracies manage investors' money is much lower, perhaps, because only recently has such a large percentage of the public held stock in private companies. Sometimes private investments are made through public bureaucracies, such as a university's or a school district's pension fund, and when losses occur because of corruption or poor performance by the corporate bureaucracy, it may still be the public bureaucracy that takes much of the heat.

Openness

The openness of public bureaucracy is another feature distinguishing it from a private bureaucracy. Private firms operate with much more secrecy than public agencies do, even when private actions have a significant impact on the public. For example, tobacco companies' lack of openness—long assumed to be their right—cost the lives of many people. The courts ordered tobacco companies to open their files only after much scientific evidence on the dangers of tobacco had accumulated.

In contrast, the greater visibility, or openness, of public agencies helps make them more responsive. Only by having knowledge of both the process and the content of public decisions can interested groups and individuals express their preferences effectively. No one articulated this better than James Madison when he wrote, "A popular Government without popular information or the means of acquiring it, is but a Prologue to a Farce or a Tragedy or perhaps both. Knowledge will forever govern ignorance, and a people who mean to be their own Governors, must arm themselves with the power knowledge gives."[13]

To this end, Congress in 1813 established the federal depository library program "to guarantee public access to government information by making it available free of charge" in local libraries around the country. Today there are 1250 depository libraries. But as government grew and agencies and paper proliferated, it became harder for the public to keep track of what government was doing. In 1934, Congress passed the Federal Register Act, requiring that all government rules, regulations, and laws be published in the *Federal Register* and that all rules in their final version appear in the *Code of Federal Regulations*. (Today both are available online at www.gpoaccess.gov/fr/index.html.)

Congress went further in 1946 by passing the **Administrative Procedure Act (APA)**, which provides for public participation in the rule-making process. All federal agencies must disclose their rule-making procedures and publish all regulations at least thirty days in advance of their effective date to allow time for public comment. Today citizens can often post comments on proposed rules at an agency's website, but it is common for public hearings to be held on controversial rules or those with wide impact. Environmental rules frequently provoke citizen reactions, with comments sometimes numbering in the tens of thousands.

Congress increased public access to the bureaucracy in another way by passing the Freedom of Information Act in 1966. As amended in 1974, **FOIA** (pronounced "foy-ya") lets any person (corporate or individual) apply to an agency for access to unclassified documents in its archives. The act has been amended several times since, including in 1996 to provide for access to electronic records.[14]

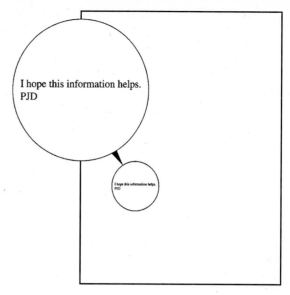

FOIA requires the release of documents, but sometimes the government will censor information within them. This comment was all that remained of an e-mail that the Bush administration censored before releasing.

FOIA requests must be made according to a formal procedure, and they must cite specific documents. The government puts out a handbook telling how to take advantage of access rights, and every government website is required to have a link to its FOIA office. Agencies are not obligated to give "information," only to provide copies of the documents requested, if they have them and if they are not in an exempt category. Intelligence agencies cannot make any record available to a foreign government, and FOIA cannot be used to gain access to trade secrets, internal records such as personnel files, or sensitive documents on a living person.[15] (But it can be used to get your FBI file, should you have one, or the file of a person no longer living.) A "deliberative process" exemption allows the withholding of records describing behind-the-scenes decision making and is one of the most frequently used exemptions by government agencies; "Exemption 3" covers all information Congress has, by law, specifically shielded from disclosure.

Federal agencies receive hundreds of thousands of FOIA requests annually, and each agency is required to make public the number of requests it receives.[16] Efforts to make government agencies more open often run up against a desire to limit the distribution of critical or embarrassing information. It is the rare public or private bureaucracy that wants to reveal its failures. Thus an evaluation of FOIA found that agencies used many tactics to discourage people from seeking information, such as delaying responses to requests, charging high fees for copies of records, and requiring detailed descriptions of documents requested.[17] The FBI is one agency that has developed a reputation for finding ways not to comply with requests. According to the National Security Archive, only one-third of FOIA requests to the FBI are successful, a failure rate five times higher than for any other federal agency.

As the chief executive, a president's views on the openness of agencies are also important. The president's policy on FOIA implementation is communicated to federal agencies by the attorney general at the beginning of each administration. Under Presidents Reagan and Bush Sr., federal agencies adopted a narrow reading of the act, making it more difficult to get information.[18] In contrast, President Carter banned classification of documents unless they were clearly related to national security, and President Clinton issued an executive order authorizing the declassification of most documents twenty-five years old or older. A FOIA request was to be met unless there was "foreseeable harm" in the document's release, a phrase based on the "reasonable danger" standard established by a 1953 Supreme Court ruling.[19] Clinton also put a ten-year limit on the classified status of new documents unless a review had determined that they must remain secret.[20]

George W. Bush, virtually upon taking office, began tightening access to government documents as part of his broader goals of strengthening the presidency and reducing both congressional and public oversight of the executive branch.[21] For the same reasons, Vice President Cheney had been a long-standing opponent of FOIA.[22] By executive order, Bush immediately established new rules for access to presidential papers, including his father's, which were due to be opened to the public. He also extended the right to review and withhold sensitive papers to the vice president and to presidents' heirs and descendants. (The American Political Science Association was among the plaintiffs who sued to reverse the order.)[23]

Under the Bush standard, any FOIA request denied by an agency on any "sound legal basis" could expect Justice Department backing. The administration ordered thousands of scientific and technical documents removed from public release after 9/11, some from libraries and many from government websites, such as an Environmental Protection Agency (EPA) database on chemicals used at industrial sites.[24] But it also had removed from public view documents on World War II, the Korean War, relations with China, and other foreign policy papers that had been declassified decades ago.

By executive order, Bush also reversed a Clinton policy that had prohibited thousands of department and agency heads from stamping documents "secret" on their own authority. Whereas during Clinton's presidency four times as much material had been declassified as in the previous fifteen years, during Bush's first term the number of classified documents doubled and declassification dwindled to about 10 percent of what it had been at the end of the nineties.[25] By 2004, the Bush administration was classifying an historic high of 125 documents per minute, in large part by creating vague new security classifications—at an estimated cost of $7.2 billion.[26]

The increasing reliance on electronic communications has complicated the enforcement of openness standards.

The first George Bush took his aides' e-mail tapes with him when he left office and argued that they were not public property. But a 1996 FOIA amendment expanded public access to many electronic records, and a federal appeals court ruled that Bush administration tapes *were* public records and must be preserved. The court applied the same ruling to Clinton administration requests for exemption.

Because of these rulings, George W. Bush was very cautious about exchanges of views by e-mail and restricted its use on government servers. Bush himself stopped sending personal e-mails from White House computers. In Bush's second term a congressional investigation into alleged political firings of U.S. attorneys demanded access to e-mails between Bush aides relevant to the investigation, only to find that 22 million had "gone missing"; they were not recovered until a year after he had left office. Many others had apparently been sent on Republican Party e-mail accounts rather than from the government accounts that are public property.

Bush's narrow definition of public access rights and his penchant for secrecy drew criticism from both conservatives and liberals. In 2007–2008, many new laws were introduced in Congress to expedite FOIA requests, keep costs reasonable, and open federal contracts (such as with military contractors in Iraq) to public scrutiny.[27] Congress also empowered the National Archives to require that the White House and related agencies preserve all electronic records.

Barack Obama came to office with new promises of transparency in government, pledging to make accessible electronic records from the government's estimated 10,000 major internal information systems. Data.gov is his administration's attempt at creating "a one-stop shop for free access to data generated across all federal agencies."[28] Obama also promised to post all legislation Congress sent him at least five days before signing it to allow for public comment, and, in response to complaints about backroom deals, he had a website created where the public could track how and where money from the 2009 stimulus bill was being spent. To clear up the confusion in how to declassify documents, he also established a National Declassification Center and ordered all agencies to revise the guides they use to determine what had to be protected and what could be declassified. (There were more than 2000 different manuals in use at the time.)[29]

In practice Obama, like most of his predecessors, has delivered less transparency than promised, citing the national security and deliberative process exemptions as reasons for not releasing photos taken at the Abu Ghraib prison in Iraq and for not making available completed logs of White House visitors. His administration also cited technical problems for not posting legislation sufficiently in advance of signings to allow for public comments, as was pledged in the campaign. And it has had to defend numerous FOIA lawsuits, many unsuccessfully, that have been filed by newspapers or press agencies trying to get access to the decision-making process on key decisions such as the bank bailouts.[30] Referring to the generality of Obama's statements on openness, a legal analyst said that it was "clear he wants to change the background tone of government but also that he recognizes the limits of transparency."[31]

As an indication of this new tone, the White House maintains an "open government" blog on its website. Despite the limitations placed on FOIA, it has enabled individuals and groups to gain important and useful information. Citizens have used it to gather injury and fatality information on defective cars, to assess dangerous infant formulas, to reveal a link between aspirin and a disease known as Reye's syndrome, to learn that J. Edgar Hoover authorized the FBI to carry out a four-year investigation of women's rights groups, and to force the Internal Revenue Service (IRS) to release a 40,000-page manual on its auditing procedures.[32] Scholars have used FOIA to retrieve thousands of documents on Cold War diplomacy, to get records of medical experiments on the effect of radioactivity conducted on unwitting subjects, and to retrieve the FBI files of anthropologists kept under surveillance during the Cold War and the McCarthy era. In 2009 a FOIA lawsuit forced the FBI to release its "Domestic Investigations and Operations Guide," giving the public a better understanding of how far the law allows the agency to go in spying on American citizens with little or no judicial oversight.[33]

Another significant law mandating openness in government is the aptly named **Sunshine Act**. Adopted in 1976, it requires that most government meetings be conducted in public and that notice of such meetings must be posted in advance. Regulatory agencies, for example, must give notice of the date, time, place, and agenda of their meetings and follow certain rules to prevent unwarranted secrecy. State governments have adopted their own sunshine laws, and today it is difficult for any public body—city council or planning commission or any of their subgroups—to meet in secret to conduct official business. Results of meetings conducted in closed, unannounced sessions are open to citizen challenge.

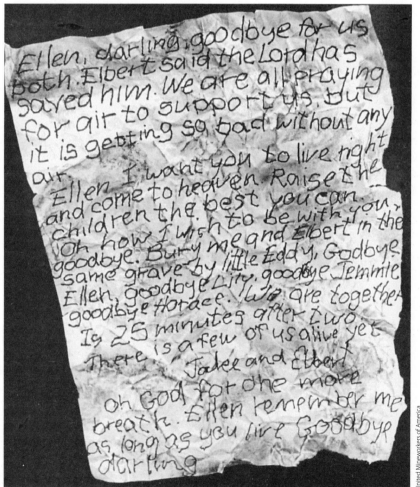

United Mineworkers of America

Jacob Vowell wrote this letter shortly before suffocating after a mine collapse in Fraterville, Tennessee, in 1902. Such disasters prompted government regulation of mining, which has since saved many lives. However, mining companies resist some regulations, and occasional disasters still occur.

SIZE OF THE FEDERAL BUREAUCRACY

Readers will note almost no Constitution icons in this chapter. That is because the Founders made few formal provisions for the federal "bureaucracy." Of course, they recognized the need for administrators and clerical workers to carry out laws and programs passed by Congress, and in Article II they refer to "executive Departments" and "Heads of Departments." 🔔 **Art. II, Sec. 2** By authorizing the raising of an army and navy, levying of taxes, and creation of a diplomatic corps and a judiciary, they anticipated all of the early growth of the bureaucracy, if not how the growing size and complexity of the country would engorge it.

George Washington's first cabinet included only three departments and the offices of attorney general and postmaster general, and all combined employed just a few hundred people. More people worked at Mount Vernon, Washington's plantation, than in the executive branch in the 1790s.[34] The Department of State had just nine employees. By 1800, the bureaucracy was still small, with only 3000 civil servants. Only the Treasury Department had much to do, collecting import and excise taxes and purchasing military supplies for an army of a few thousand. From then until 1990, the bureaucracy grew continuously, though at an uneven rate.

Why the Bureaucracy Has Grown

As we saw in the Introduction, government, over time, responded to public wishes by creating federal agencies to assist and promote the emerging economic interests of business, agriculture, and labor and more recently to provide health and economic protections for workers, consumers, retirees, and other groups.[35] One scholar explained the bureaucracy's growth by pointing to Americans' discovery that "government can protect and assist as well as punish and repress."[36]

The numerous programs created during the Great Depression to put the unemployed to work and pull the country out of the hard times nearly doubled the size of the bureaucracy during the 1930s.

World War II created additional demands for health care and other services for veterans. The Administrative Procedure Act was passed in 1946 partly because the bureaucracy had grown so much in size and power during the Depression and World War II that Congress believed it needed to increase its oversight.[37] But after the Cold War, when thoughts turned to downsizing the Defense Department, supporters of military spending found new justifications for government expansion in the threat of global terrorism. Decades later, in 2001, forty-five days after 9/11, Congress rushed to pass the USA PATRIOT Act (officially, the Uniting and Strengthening America by Providing Appropriate Tools Required to Intercept and Obstruct Terrorism Act), which increased both the power and the size of the federal bureaucracy. Implementation of government's extraordinary new power to wiretap, search e-mail, and gain access to library borrowing records and many business records, both paper and electronic, required more personnel and increased spending.

Bureaucrats cannot produce growth on their own. Every agency, and its budget, must be authorized and approved by Congress and the president. It can continue to exist only if it is valuable to enough people with enough influence to sustain it. Sometimes government grows because the president and Congress want it to be more accountable. This often results in hiring more managers, which produces

Lewis W. Hine/The Granger Collection, New York

Early in the twentieth century, many young children worked twelve-hour days in unhealthy conditions, such as in this vegetable cannery. Eventually, public demands to stop this practice led to government regulations on child labor and to the creation of bureaucratic agencies to enforce the regulations.

greater inefficiency, and, ironically, more difficulty in holding agencies accountable.[38]

The growth of the bureaucracy should be seen in the perspective of the overall growth of our economy and population. Between 1988 and 2008 the ratio of federal employees fell from 110 for every resident to 1 for every 155 residents.[39] Given how many people are employed in the private sector with federal money, that figure is a little deceptive, but public sector employment is still "heavily skewed toward the state and local level."[40]

Controlling Growth

When new bureaucracies are created, the intent is to hold them to their original size, but most grow over time because once they are in place, additional responsibilities are assigned to them. Consolidation or elimination is rare. More commonly, departments become so large that they must subdivide (for example, the Department of Commerce and Labor was divided into separate departments of Labor and Commerce) or offices and agencies become so big or their work so important that they are made into cabinet departments (Veterans Affairs, DHS), where they become even larger.

Almost every president since Lyndon Johnson (1963–1968) has tried to streamline or downsize the bureaucracy on the general assumption that size and performance are linked. Presidents often think they can establish more efficient management plans and then cut personnel. Richard Nixon tried to merge seven departments into four but could not gain approval, and despite many attempts to ax the Department of Education, it is stronger than it ever has been. Jimmy Carter (1977–1981) was a committed deregulator and a micromanager who oversaw the elimination of thousands of rules and some regulators.

For all Ronald Reagan's (1981–1989) talk against big government, it grew by over 200,000 employees during his administration. Although many agencies lost personnel (the biggest loser was the Department of Housing and Urban Development), others, such as Defense, Justice, and the Treasury, gained. In addition, Reagan created a new cabinet office, the Department of Veterans Affairs, from what had been an independent agency. He had entered office with a plan to wage a "war on waste," but he left office with the country another trillion dollars in debt and the Defense Department buying $600 toilet seats.

Bill Clinton's administration (1993–2001) had its "reinventing government" initiative, a brainchild of Vice President Al Gore to downsize government. Hand in hand with budget retrenchment, federal employment fell by 20 percent during their years in office.[41]

George W. Bush (2001–2009) had a "Management Agenda" and Program Assessment Rating Tools to cut ineffective programs. But despite stated admiration for smaller, more efficient government, the federal bureaucracy grew by 5 percent just during his first three years in office, and it added another 100,000 jobs during his last year.[42] Some of the early growth was due to the war on terrorism—adding a new cabinet department and increasing defense appointments. But there was also some padding—or thickening—of the bureaucracy through the creation of new senior positions in cabinet departments that have nothing to do with national security.[43] The number of people at the highest pay level more than tripled during Bush's first three years. Layers of administration were added to cabinet departments at a time when the efficient upward and downward flow of information within the bureaucracy had become a major issue, even a life-and-death issue, as it was in the intelligence bureaucracy in 2001. Within two years after its creation, the new Department of Homeland Security (DHS) had developed twenty-one layers of administration and had 146 senior administrative positions.[44]

When Barack Obama entered office, he had 64 discrete titles to oversee just at the top layer of government.[45] He promised in his inaugural speech that he would not ask "whether government is too big or too small, but whether it works." If a program helped "families find jobs at a decent wage, care they can afford, a retirement that is dignified," then it would be retained, and if not it would be cut. He kept Bush's overall management plan with its rating tools for evaluating programs by performance and shortly after taking office appointed a Chief Performance Officer.[46] He also directed departments and agencies to identify $100 million in cuts within ninety days. Conservative budget cutters immediately issued a press statement ridiculing "Obama's 0.0025 percent budget cut."[47] In any case, responding to a severe recession, Obama soon requested large spending increases and in his first two years added another 100,000 employees to the federal payroll.[48]

Career civil servants are skeptical about the attempt of every administration to take on the bureaucracy and cut it down to size. One explanation of the perception gap is that there is a "natural antipathy" between presidents and career civil servants because the president is elected on his ability to articulate basic human values, whereas "civil service is about enforcing rules and procedures and treating all citizens and issues equally." Bureaucrats are not about *values* in the sense that politicians use that term.[49]

Reform is made difficult when presidents fill political leadership positions in agencies with individuals who do not stay around long enough to learn their jobs and have little chance of really reshaping their agencies. Presidents and their appointees find that reality does not always match political slogans. And presidents find that reforming the bureaucracy is much tougher than they anticipated and soon turn to other activities with more immediate payoffs. Thus, in the view of a former Office of Management and Budget (OMB) official, reform is mostly "three yards and a cloud of dust."[50]

Privatizing Government Work

An alternative to reforming the bureaucracy is **privatizing** or outsourcing the work of government to private industry;

behind the scenes

Battling Acronyms: Turf Wars in the Federal Bureaucracy

Some may think of the federal bureaucracy as an impenetrable monolith implacably devoted to frustrating individual and public will, but it is actually hundreds of agencies, each devoted to serving its own constituency and preserving its mission. Positions and projects are often jealously guarded from both budget cutters and other agencies suspected of territorial encroachment. In other words, at any given time there are number of turf wars within the federal bureaucracy.

When the 9/11 Commission was investigating the breaches in security that allowed the terrorists to be successful, it was told that the State Department had maintained a list of 61,000 known or suspected terrorists whose travel should be restricted. But when the commission asked Federal Aviation Administration (FAA) officials how many of those names were on *their* "no fly" registry, the FAA said none, and in fact it did not even know the State Department kept such a list. The FAA said it did have its own list of 12 names, but it included none of the 9/11 hijackers, even though 2 of the 12 were being sought by the FBI.[1]

While the FAA was paying little attention to State, it was often actively opposing the NTSB, the National Transportation Safety Board. The NTSB's main mission is passenger safety; the FAA's is aviation regulation, but it is more often seen as a friend of the airline industry. For years one agency, the NTSB, has been proposing safety rules, and the other, the FAA, resisting them because it believes the cost of implementing the regulations would hurt the industry.[2]

After 9/11 the whole country was made aware of the inability of intelligence agencies to share information because of inadequate or incompatible communications systems but also because not every agency is willing to hand over *its* information to another agency with a separate mission. The establishment of a new Directorate of National Intelligence (DNI) was supposed to end the rivalries and redundancies and get all intelligence agencies working together, but that was a pipe dream. Every time a threat is exposed, or a terrorist attempt prevented, each agency wants to investigate, much as congressional committees rush to hold hearings on any headline-grabbing event. The classified nature of intelligence gathering enables senior officials reluctant to share information to use secrecy "to cut out rivals," and even to "undermine the normal chain of command."[3] And with so many agencies, it is not always easy to know what the chain of command is. Turnover among the DNI directors has been rapid. In 2010, President Obama appointed the fourth DNI director in five years, a sign of the continuing competition among intelligence agencies.

Meanwhile, the CIA was having its own little war with the Department of Justice (DOJ). With a change in administrations, the DOJ finally gave in to public pressure and appointed a prosecutor to investigate possible CIA involvement in detainee abuse in Iraqi prisons. The CIA director was livid and sent the agency's top lawyer to the DOJ to persuade the attorney general to back down. He refused. Both men were Obama appointees and responsible for carrying out his policies, but each advocated vigorously for his agency's viewpoint.[4]

The economic crisis of 2008 shone a light on another set of agency rivalries. After regulatory agencies engaged in a heavy round of mutual finger pointing about which was more responsible for enabling the financial meltdown of 2008, they began to compete for the new authority Congress was about to assign to re-regulate the banks. As agencies fought to retain their existing responsibilities and to gain new powers, officials from the Federal Reserve Bank (the Fed), the Federal Deposit Insurance Corporation (FDIC), and the Office of the Comptroller of the Currency (OCC) lobbied Congress and the public. The dispute was so heated that the secretary of the treasury said if the administration's reforms failed it would be because of the turf warfare between agencies.[5] These three agencies were joined in the fight by two others—the Securities and Exchange Commission (SEC) and the Commodity Futures Trading Commission (CFTC)—over which was best suited to regulate the trade in derivatives. And all of the existing financial regulatory agencies appeared to be fighting to keep consumer advocate Elizabeth Warren from being named the head of a new consumer protection agency, even though the idea for the agency was hers. Obama sidestepped the fight by naming Warren to a temporary position on the White House staff with responsibility for setting up the new consumer agency.

[1] Thomas H. Kean and John Farmer Jr., "How 12/25 Was like 9/11," *New York Times*, January 6, 2010, A23. The authors were the cochair and chief counsel of the 9/11 Commission.
[2] Al Baker, "Collision Bares Longtime Rift over Air Safety," *New York Times*, August 14, 2009.
[3] Ibid., A9.
[4] Peter Baker, David Johnston, and Mark Mazzetti, "Abuse Issue Puts the C.I.A. and Justice Dept. at Odds," *New York Times*, August 28, 2009.
[5] Stephen Labaton, "Geithner Takes Regulators to Task on Turf Battle," *New York Times*, August 6, 2009; Stephen Labaton and Edmund L. Andrews, "As U.S. Overhauls the Banking System, 2 Top Regulators Feud," *New York Times*, June 14, 2009.

these are jobs that would otherwise be done by civil servants or military personnel. The federal government has been steadily privatizing jobs for at least thirty years as successive presidents have been convinced that turning over public sector work to private employers is one route to downsizing the civilian bureaucracy and the armed forces and to making government more efficient and less costly. The number of people working for private businesses on contract to the government now dwarfs the federal bureaucracy. In this section we raise three questions about the trend toward privatization: Does it save taxpayers money? Is there an effective way to oversee this work, that is, to hold contractors accountable to the government? and Can contractors be trusted to put the public interest first when there is a conflict of interest and a corporation's responsibility to make a profit?

The most publicized aspect of privatization has been in the military: in the first Gulf war, about 10 percent of the personnel worked as private contractors, and the same was true of the Clinton-ordered military involvement in Bosnia in the 1990s. But at points during the wars in Iraq and Afghanistan there were more private contractors than military personnel.[51] At the peak there were 190,000 contractors in Iraq, and, according to the Congressional Research Service, in 2009 contractors still accounted for 48 percent of the Department of Defense's workforce there and 57 percent in Afghanistan (see Figure 1).

One of the less noticed areas of outsourcing has been in intelligence gathering and analysis (see the box "The Privatization of Intelligence Gathering"). The attacks of 9/11 led many in government to believe that the United States was not prepared for a war against terrorists and that shoring up intelligence work had to be expedited. To that end the Bush administration made it easier for intelligence agencies to outsource work to private contractors because it was much faster than the process of hiring civil servants. Today almost 30 percent of

Sheila Bair, the Bush-appointed head of the FDIC, found herself in frequent turf battles with another Bush appointee, Ben Bernanke, director of the Federal Reserve Bank, over which agency should oversee the re-regulation of banks.

intelligence work is done by employees of private businesses, and there are as many private contractors working for the Department of Homeland Security as there are civil servants.

Health care is another area where a substantial portion of the administrative work has been privatized. Nearly one-quarter of the 45 million seniors on Medicare get all their medical benefits through private health plans; in some states this figure is as high as 30 percent. The federal government pays the bills, but the patient deals only with the middleman: the private insurance company.[52] This is one reason why a number of seniors angry about the 2010 health care legislation were under the impression that Medicare was a private program.

The use of private contractors does make the government's permanent work force look smaller but they have cost taxpayers more, not less, than civil servants. Private health providers for Medicare produce no savings for taxpayers; in fact, payments for medical care under these private plans are about 15 percent higher than those for seniors enrolled in traditional Medicare. And the private contractors who make up less than a third of the intelligence workforce account for 49 percent of the personnel budget.[53] As more and more security work was outsourced, corporations raided government intelligence agencies for personnel to fill their new positions. The opportunity to make substantially more money as a contractor led some of the most experienced people to follow the money. The CIA in particular lost some of its most senior people. So taxpayers ended up paying more for the same work from the same people, while corporations, acting as the middlemen, raised their profit margins at taxpayers' expense.

It is not just higher salaries that have driven up the cost of intelligence gathering. Each agency wants to have the top-of-the-line equipment, accoutrements, and perks of office that other intelligence agencies have—the "bling" of national security work. This means security details, Mercedes, and buildings especially constructed for top-secret work. "You can't be a big boy unless you're a three-letter agency" and have a special top security facility, said the

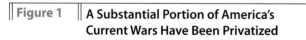

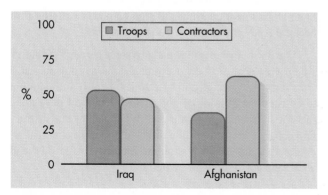

Figure 1 | **A Substantial Portion of America's Current Wars Have Been Privatized**

The numbers are the proportion of the total American force that were contractors and troops in December 2009. For example, in Iraq there were 111,000 troops and 100,000 contractors.
SOURCE: *CQ Weekly, April 12, 2010, 889.*

During the Depression, government agencies hired the unemployed for numerous projects. Out-of-work artists were paid to paint murals in government buildings, post offices, and public monuments such as Coit Tower in San Francisco.

© David R. Frazier/The Image Works

head of a firm that constructs the buildings.[54] By 2010 there were 4000 corporate offices in Washington that handled classified material, and the construction of top-security buildings was still under way. The fact that six of the ten wealthiest counties in America are now in the Washington, D.C., metropolitan area is attributed in part to the growth of private businesses involved in intelligence work.[55]

Government contractors not only cost more, but they are also held to lower standards of accountability than are federal agencies. More than $102 billion in contracts were awarded for work in Iraq and Afghanistan in the first six years after the wars began. Most of the early contracts were no-bid, with contractors essentially naming their own price. Contractors have been paid for work done well or badly or not done at all.[56] KBR, the former Halliburton subsidiary, had received $24 billion in military contracts by 2007, but attempts to audit its accounts were stymied because the military felt it was too dependent on KBR's services. Faulty electrical work by KBR caused almost three hundred fires that damaged or destroyed military facilities and that led to at least eighteen deaths and to many other soldiers being severely shocked while taking showers.[57] Yet when the Pentagon's contract manager, a career civil servant, tried to hold up payments and threaten KBR with penalties, he was fired and an outside auditor (nongovernmental) was brought in to

approve the payments. And despite paying out $4 billion to private contractors in 2007, the State Department still had only seventeen contract compliance officers.[58]

Private contractors such as Blackwater, which provides bodyguards and other security services to the State and Defense Departments, are not supposed to perform any operational functions, but Blackwater employees have been indicted on murder charges in Iraq and reportedly have been involved in CIA missions in Afghanistan. But the State Department continues to sign contracts with the firm because it says there are no good alternatives.

The line between public and private becomes very blurry when what seem to be government jobs are outsourced.[59] Outsourcing, especially in war zones, is also an invitation to corruption. Billions of dollars in foreign aid have gone missing in Iraq and Afghanistan. "When money and instructions change hands multiple times in a foreign country," as one analyst remarked, the public interest can get lost and abuse and corruption get invited in.[60]

Despite the enthusiasm of Congress and successive presidents, outsourcing has not brought greater efficiencies or overall cost savings for taxpayers. There is also the question of whose priorities are being served when a private health insurer's commitment is to company profits rather than to cost savings for taxpayers, or when an intelligence agent's boss is a corporation rather than the government. This was at the root of CIA director Leon Panetta's concern that private contractors now form such a large part of intelligence agencies' workforce. Their responsibility is to the shareholders, and that's "an inherent conflict," he pointed out.[61]

TYPES OF FEDERAL AGENCIES

The Constitution says little about the organization of the executive branch other than indicating a need for the president to have a cabinet. As government's role expanded, it became clear that a single type of organization would not be appropriate for every task assigned to the bureaucracy. Cabinet departments, for example, are headed by people who serve at the president's pleasure and who are there to help carry out his policies. But other agencies must implement law without reference to an individual president's preferences. These agencies require protection from political interference, as do those established to carry out highly technical work. In this section, we review the major types of agencies in the executive branch.

Departments

Departments are organizations within the executive branch that form the president's cabinet. Their heads, called secretaries (except for the head of the Justice Department, who is called the attorney general), are appointed by the president with the consent of the Senate, and they are directly

---

behind the scenes

The Privatization of Intelligence Gathering

When people complain about the federal bureaucracy and government waste, they often have in mind an IRS agent, a social worker in a welfare office, the red tape associated with collecting some government benefit such as food stamps, agricultural subsidies, and Medicare or Social Security payment. But since 9/11 the great engorgement of the bureaucracy has been in the departments that deal with national security and counterterrorism—the Department of Defense (DoD), the Department of Homeland Security (DHS), and sixteen intelligence agencies, including the CIA.

Even before 9/11, some scholars referred to our immense defense and intelligence bureaucracies as a kind of shadow government—the National Security State—but since 9/11 the growth in personnel has been staggering. A two-year *Washington Post* investigation found that "1,271 government organizations and 1,931 private companies work on programs related to counterterrorism, homeland security and intelligence in some 10,000 locations across the United States." Of the 854,000 people (1½ times the population of Washington, D.C.) who have top-secret security clearances, 265,000 work on contract.[1]

The work has grown so fast that it has been called a "jobs program," and the proliferation of agencies so great that no one is sure who is in charge or if anyone is capable of coordinating the work. The former undersecretary of defense for intelligence (now director of the Office of National Intelligence) said that God was the only "entity in the entire universe" that had a view of all the ultra-secret projects known as SAPs (special access programs). The Pentagon's list of code names for these projects runs over three hundred pages, and there are hundreds more in other agencies and thousands of subprojects under them.[2]

"The complexity of the system defies description," said a former Iraq troop commander who was assigned to track DoD's top-secret programs. "I'm not aware of any agency with authority, responsibility or a process in place to coordinate all these interagency and commercial activities."[3]

The Obama administration has been trying to reduce outsourcing, but intelligence agencies are now completely dependent on private contractors to maintain essential operations. All sixteen agencies rely on corporations to set up their computer networks and their systems of communications with other agencies, as well as on private contractors to serve as translators and linguists. The ultra-secret National Reconnaissance Office (NRO) "cannot produce, launch or maintain its large satellite surveillance systems . . . without the four major contractors it works with."[4]

The sheer volume of contracts has also made it difficult to identify positions to cut. The DoD alone has eighteen commands and agencies handling information operations.[5] When DoD secretary Robert Gates set a goal of cutting contractors back to their pre-9/11 level, he said he had to make a "terrible confession": he was unable to "get a number on how many contractors" worked for his own office.[6]

[1] Dana Priest and William M. Arkin, "A Modern World, Growing beyond Control," *Washington Post*, July 19, 2010, A1. The text, graphics, and supplemental material from the *Post*'s investigation are at TopSecretAmerica.com.
[2] Ibid., A9.
[3] Lt. Gen. John R. Vines, quoted in ibid., A6.
[4] Michael D. Shear, "National Security, Inc.," *Washington Post*, July 20, 2010, A9.
[5] Priest and Arkin, "A Modern World, Growing beyond Control," A8.
[6] Shear, "National Security, Inc.," A8.

Figure 2 | The Development and Relative Size of Cabinet Departments

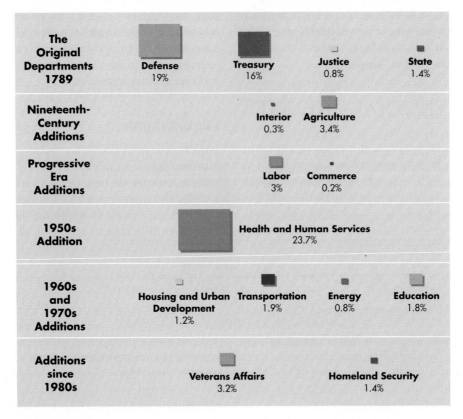

Percentages are each department's estimated share of the budget authority for Fiscal 2011. The figures add to less than 100 percent because they do not include budget allocations to the many other executive branch agencies (such as the EPA) and to the legislative and judicial branches. The relatively large square for HHS includes mandatory spending on Social Security and Medicare, and for the Treasury mandatory spending on the financial bailout (much of which will be repaid) and interest on the debt, which will continue to grow. In contrast, the size of the DoD square is almost all due to nonmandatory (discretionary) spending, money that Congress appropriates annually as it sees fit.
SOURCE: United States Budget for Fiscal Year 2011 *(Washington, D.C.: Government Printing Office, 2010).*

responsible to the president. There are fifteen departments; the newest is DHS (see Figure 2). These departments constitute the lion's share of the federal bureaucracy; the largest employer is the Defense Department, with close to 30 percent of all civil servants.

Cabinet departments exist to carry out the president's policy in specific functional areas: national security, federal law enforcement, fiscal policy, health and welfare, foreign relations, and so forth. They are staffed by career civil servants, but all top policy-making positions in each division of a department are held by presidential appointees. The fifteen cabinet departments have more than 350 such positions. Permanent staff believe that the increase in the number of appointive senior positions makes their work more difficult.

Independent Agencies

Independent agencies differ from departments in that they are usually smaller; and their heads do not sit in the cabinet. Agency heads are, however, appointed by and responsible to the president. And occasionally a president does extend

cabinet status to the head of an independent agency, most notably the director of the EPA. Some agencies, such as the EPA, the CIA, the Social Security Administration, the Peace Corps, and the National Aeronautics and Space Administration (NASA), are well known to the public. Others, such as the Office of Government Ethics, are relatively unknown.

Some independent agencies are responsible for highly specialized areas of policy, such as space exploration (NASA) or law enforcement (FBI). The people appointed to head them usually have an appropriate professional background, not just a political profile acceptable to the president. However, if the agency deals with policy that has widespread impact, as the EPA and CIA do, political credentials are likely to be among the president's first consideration in naming a director.

Independent Regulatory Boards and Commissions

Although unfamiliar to most Americans, independent regulatory boards and commissions affect almost every aspect of our daily lives—the air we breathe, the water we drink, the interest on a bank loan, the fee at an ATM, the terms under which we buy or sell stock, labeling on food and manufactured goods and conditions in the plants where they were made, phone and mail service, and the construction of every car, train, plane, or bus we ride on.

Each independent regulatory board and commission regulates a specific area of business or the economy. Examples include the Federal Communications Commission (FCC), which regulates the electronic media; the Securities and Exchange Commission (SEC), which makes and enforces rules regarding stocks, bonds, and securities; and the Federal Reserve System (the Fed), which sets prime interest rates and controls the amount of money in circulation. These and other regulatory agencies are designated "independent" because the work they do is supposed to be removed from politics as much as possible. Congress created the first such commission, the Interstate Commerce Commission, in 1887 to decide such things as interstate freight rates, railroad ticket prices, routes, and conditions of service.

Each of these independent regulatory boards and commissions is directed by five to ten presidential appointees. By law, each board and commission must be balanced with members of both major political parties. Appointees serve staggered terms and cannot be removed by presidents who dislike their decisions. Because of the technical knowledge needed for decision making, appointments are supposed to be based on expertise rather than partisan considerations. Of course, it is almost impossible for politics, in the sense of an individual's values, not to have some impact on decision making. Presidents who want less government regulation appoint commissioners who share that value. Commissioners, in turn, can make it difficult for the professionals in the agency to carry out their regulatory mission. However, the goal of having these independent commissions is to make politics secondary to professional expertise.

Government Corporations

Government corporations are businesses run by government to provide services the public needs but that no private company will provide because they are not profitable—or were not profitable at the time government began providing the service. The first government corporation, the Tennessee Valley Authority (TVA), was created during the Franklin Roosevelt administration when no utility company was willing to invest in the infrastructure necessary to bring electricity to what was then a very poor, undeveloped region of the country. The TVA still supplies electricity to its part of the country.

The United States Postal Service, which was originally a cabinet department, was converted to a business operation in 1971. Formerly a government monopoly, it now has competition from companies like UPS and FedEx for some of the services it provides. In the 1960s, when railroads were no longer willing to provide passenger service, the government created the National Railroad Passenger

Corporation (Amtrak). And because no private insurance company would ever bear the risk of insuring private bank deposits, the government established a corporation to protect your savings account (the Federal Deposit Insurance Corporation).

Similarly, the government is now the main purveyor of terrorism insurance. After 9/11, private firms were no longer willing to assume the risk, just as after Hurricane Katrina, private insurers wanted government to take even greater responsibility for insuring homeowners in coastal areas against flood damage.

Government corporations charge for their services or products but their primary objective is to provide a needed service, not to make a profit. Of course, the government is quite happy if they do or if they at least break even. When a government corporation does become profitable, its assets may be sold to private businesses and the corporation closed. This is what happened with CONRAIL, the government corporation that took over rail freight, turned it back into a profitable enterprise, and then sold it back to private investors. The U.S. Postal Service, after decades of needing government subsidies to balance its budget, had a brief period of solvency before electronic mail took away much of its business and left it with a $7 billion deficit in 2010. Opponents of government corporations would like to see both the Postal Service and the unprofitable Amtrak completely privatized. But the services provided are so important to the national economy that without the certainty that private businesses would guarantee their continuation, government would have difficulty justifying the sale of their assets.

WHAT BUREAUCRATS DO

After elected officials make a law, someone must implement it. **Policy implementation** is the primary job of the bureaucracy. Bureaucrats convert laws passed by Congress and signed by the president into rules and actions that make it possible to realize the intent of the law. The general process of policy implementation has two major components: administering policies and making them.

But before looking at the specifics of administering and making policies, it is important to remember that the bureaucracy provides continuity in governing. Presidents and members of Congress come and go, and political appointees in the bureaucracy stay an average of two years; many barely learn their jobs by the time they leave. Career civil servants have a much deeper knowledge of their agencies' work, which makes them better at it and more productive than short-term political appointees. They keep government agencies functioning day in and day out so that all essential work continues even as elected and appointed officials come and go from office.

We now look in greater detail at the sources of the bureaucracy's authority and the policy-administering and policy-making responsibilities assigned to it.

american diversity

Women and Minorities in the Civil Service

Americans expect their public bureaucracies to be open and responsive. Andrew Jackson recognized this when he opened the civil service to people of "common" origins. By putting his frontier supporters in office, he hoped to make the bureaucracy more responsive by making it more representative. In the twentieth century, the expectation that public agencies should be open to all qualified applicants gave some groups, such as Irish, Jewish, and African Americans, more job opportunities than were open to them in the private sector because of segregation and quotas.

In the past two decades, significant progress has been made in making the federal bureaucracy more reflective of American diversity. Minorities comprise 31 percent of American population and are currently about 34 percent of the civilian federal workforce. African Americans are particularly well represented, being a substantially larger portion of the federal workforce (18 percent) than of the general population (13 percent). American Indians and Asian Americans have a percentage of federal jobs close to their population share, whereas Hispanics remain significantly underrepresented in the federal workforce, despite an aggressive Hispanic recruitment program. However, the census does not distinguish between legal and illegal residency, and millions of Hispanics included in the population count would not be eligible for federal jobs. Women are 44 percent of the federal workforce, slightly less than their representation in the private labor force (46 percent) and considerably below parity with their 51 percent share of the population.

The relatively good news about the overall profile of the bureaucracy fades at the top of the pay scale. Women and minority men have not yet broken completely through the "glass ceiling" that has kept them out of top management positions. There is progress, however. Women's proportion of these senior-grade pay positions has increased, and in 2009, women filled just over 30 percent of them (about one-fifth of the women were minorities). This is more than twice the share women held in 1990. And, collectively, minorities held about 15 percent of all senior positions, a number that has also grown. Federal court rulings and out-of-court settlements in discrimination cases, as well as changing generations in leadership positions, account for some of the improvement in upward mobility.

SOURCE: All percentages cited are from U.S. Office of Personnel Management, Federal Equal Opportunity Recruitment Program report to Congress for fiscal year 2009, 4–38. Diversity statistics in hiring by agency can also be found at www.data.gov.

African Americans Are Overrepresented and Hispanics Underrepresented in the Federal Workforce Compared to the Overall Civilian Workforce

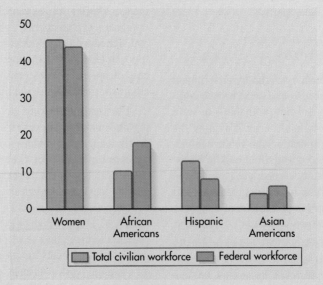

SOURCE: All percentages cited are from U.S. Office of Personnel Management, Federal Equal Opportunity Recruitment Program report to Congress for fiscal year 2009, 4–38. Diversity statistics in hiring by agency can also be found at www.data.gov.

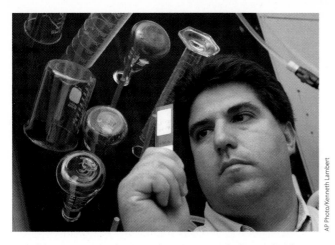

Not all bureaucrats push paper. This scientist with the Food and Drug Administration (FDA) examines breast cancer protein in his lab in Bethesda, Maryland.

Policy Administration

Public bureaucracy's oldest job is to administer the law. To "administer" is to execute, enforce, and apply the rules that have been made either by Congress or the bureaucracy itself. Thus if policy makers decide to go to war, they must empower agencies to acquire weapons, recruit and train soldiers, and devise a winning strategy. Policy making without administration is tantamount to no policy at all.

Administration includes thousands of different kinds of activities. It involves writing checks to farmers who receive payments for growing—or not growing—crops, providing direct services to the public, evaluating how well programs are working, prosecuting those who try to defraud the government, and maintaining buildings and offices. For forest rangers, administration involves helping backpackers in the Grand Canyon or putting out a forest fire in northern Minnesota.

Policy Making

Responsibility for administering policy inevitably confers lawmaking powers on the bureaucracy. This can be illustrated with the example of the Americans with Disabilities Act (ADA). The ADA directs employers to make a "reasonable accommodation" for a competent worker with a disability that "substantially limits" a major life activity such as seeing or walking, except when this causes "undue hardship."[62]

This seemingly straightforward law is in fact extremely complex and its impact far-reaching. Although the act went into effect in 1992, the Equal Employment Opportunity Commission (EEOC), which has responsibility for its implementation, was still clarifying what specific provisions in the act meant when Congress revised and strengthened it in 2008. Some of the ambiguities in wording that the EEOC had to help clarify were what Congress meant by a "reasonable accommodation" and an "undue hardship." When voters want local governments to spend less, is the $2 million

that Des Plaines, Illinois, had to shell out for sidewalks and curb cuts an "undue hardship" or not?[63] Would colleges and universities be allowed to make only some classrooms and offices accessible to students and staff in wheelchairs, or would they have to make every classroom and faculty office accessible to people with disabilities? When do the costs of such changes become unsustainable?

Answering such questions and formulating rules to implement them is *de facto* policy making. Implementation requires disseminating the rules and negotiating interpretations with the parties who have to put them in place and enforce them. State and local counterparts of the EEOC and their clients must be informed of the rules, assisted in their attempts to use the rules, and monitored in their progress. Bills must be paid, disputes resolved, and information collected as to how successful the program is. If affected parties reject the EEOC's interpretation or the officials' implementation, the rules can be challenged in federal court. This is where almost all disputed provisions of the ADA are being decided. Bureaucrats very often do not have the last word in determining how a policy is implemented.

The passage of thousands of complex bills like the ADA accounts for the growth in policy-making functions of public bureaucracies. Industrialization, population growth, urbanization, and profound changes in science, transportation, and communications have put problems of a more complex nature on government's agenda. The large number and technical nature of these problems—think about writing environmental protection rules, for example—as well as policy differences among its members, have often limited Congress's ability to draft specific policy responses.

Congress often responds to this situation by enacting a general statement of goals and identifying actions that would help achieve them. Congress then delegates the power to an agency with the relevant expertise to draft specific rules that will achieve these goals. This **delegated legislative authority** empowers executive branch agencies to draft, as well as execute, specific policies. Just as the ADA left rule making to the EEOC, any tax-reform legislation requires thousands of rules to be written by the IRS and the Treasury Department. Agency-made policy is just as binding as acts of Congress because agencies *make it at the direction of Congress*. In strictly numerical terms, agencies make much more policy than Congress because agencies issue many new rules and regulations for the implementation of each new law Congress passes.

Many political scientists believe that Congress abdicates its authority and acts in an irresponsible manner by refusing, because of political pressures and its heavy workload, to develop specific guidelines for agencies.[64] This leaves agencies to implement policies without much guidance from Congress beyond the wording of each bill. Sometimes, however, agency complaints about the ambiguities or lack of specificity in legislation are just excuses not to implement disliked policies. Differences in interpretation

The Transportation Security Laboratory in Atlantic City, New Jersey, tests bomb-detection equipment by making bombs with various explosives (left), and planting them in abandoned luggage purchased by the government.

can lead to partisan conflicts, especially over regulatory policy. Congress can send more detailed directives to agencies, but this does not prevent the political appointees who head executive branch agencies from resisting congressional directives they dislike on the grounds that they are too complex or unrealistic to follow.

In effect, the competition between the White House and Congress was extended to the bureaucracy when Congress delegated legislative authority to agencies. This competition can intensify or subside, depending on whether the president is of the same party as congressional majorities. However, the competition has continued even under unified governments.

Sometimes agencies are in the difficult position of having to satisfy competing demands. To figure out what Congress, the president, and others want, agency officials read congressional debates and testimony and talk to members of Congress, committee staffers, White House aides, lobbyists, and others. Although agencies also try to determine what the public wants, they are more likely to respond to well-organized and well-funded groups that closely monitor their actions. As a result, agency-made policy is often less responsive to the general public than to particular interests.

An excellent example of these competing interests surfaced in 2010 as Congress wrote legislation to re-regulate the financial industry. Lobbyists were paid a reported $1 billion to argue the industry's case to influential members of congressional committees.[65] The lobbyists' goal was to get Congress to exclude rules not favored by the industry and to make the law's language sufficiently specific that regulators would not be able to write rules the industry did not favor. On the consumer side, activists lobbied for their choice to head the new regulatory agencies because, as one said, "A lot of us are terrified about what happens in rule-making."[66] They wanted people heading the agencies who, in implementing the new law, would write rules that looked first to consumer protection.

Regulation

A special kind of policy making called **regulation** produces rules, standards, or guidelines conferring benefits and imposing restrictions on business conduct and economic activity. Regulations have the force of law and are made by agencies whose directors and board members are appointed by the president and whose operating procedures are generally governed by the Administrative Procedure Act. An estimated quarter million federal workers are paid to write and enforce regulations and their work has become one of the most contested areas of the bureaucracy's role in government.

Regulatory agencies include not only independent regulatory boards and commissions but also some independent agencies, such as the EPA, and some agencies within cabinet departments, such as the Food and Drug Administration (FDA) in Health and Human Services and the Office of Safety and Health Administration (OSHA) in the Labor Department. Regulatory actions include two steps: making rules and adjudicating their enforcement. Rule making is the establishment of standards that apply to a class of individuals or businesses. Adjudication is the process of trying individuals or firms charged with violating standards, and makes use of procedures that are very similar to those used by courts.

Most regulations derive from laws passed by Congress that direct agencies to take actions to accomplish the goals established in the legislation. Environmental legislation, for example, requires regulatory agencies to set standards for clean air, safe disposal of toxic wastes, or safe workplaces that businesses must meet. Businesses are often allowed some flexibility in the methods used to meet the standard, but failure to comply can result in fines or other legal penalties.

Consumer protection legislation directs federal regulators to set quality or safety standards for certain types of

DEMOCRACY?

In practice, bureaucracies make policy. What features of our constitutional system make this consistent with democracy? Under what circumstances can it be undemocratic?

Photographs by Librado Romero, The New York Times/Redux

products, such as cars, toys, food, and medical equipment. This is why there are seat belts, air bags, and shatterproof windows in cars and why materials used to make children's toys or clothing cannot be flammable or toxic. Regulations may also require businesses to provide information through labeling, such as the cancer warnings on cigarette packages and lists of ingredients noting transfats, sugar, salt, and vitamin content on packaged food.

Another form of regulation is licensing the right to own or use public properties. For example, the FCC licenses the publicly owned airwaves to people who own and operate radio and television stations.

Data Collection and Analysis

In the course of policy making and administration, the bureaucracy performs other functions. It collects data, as in the decennial census, and it makes information available to the public. Much of what we know about ourselves as a people comes from the government's collection of data on births and deaths, occupations and income, housing and health, crime, and many other things. A cursory glance at the annual *Statistical Abstract of the United States* shows that the government reports on everything from basic facts on births, deaths, and population to specialized information relevant to particular policy makers, lobbyists, and the public, such as the incidence of abortions, the export of zinc, how much celery we eat, the partisan composition of Congress, and how many DVDs we own.

Bureaucracy also keeps us informed about what government is doing, and the Internet is a valuable tool to assist in this function. Every federal agency has a website with information about its policies and programs and an e-mail link for feedback from the public. If we want to know the

---

behind the scenes

Project Medea: The CIA and Climate Change

The government's Project Medea has nothing to do with Euripides' classic play about a woman so full of revenge she murders her children. It is just another government acronym, in this case for Measurements of Earth Data for Environmental Analysis, a scientific group established in 1992 to advise the government on environmental surveillance. The group's main purpose is to see if any of the data collected by intelligence agencies, as a byproduct of their search for other kinds of information, could help scientists reach a better understanding of the "hidden complexities of environmental change." The scientists look for images of clouds, glaciers, deserts, and tropical forests picked up by "spy satellites and other classified sensors" that would help them determine, for example, why and how fast glaciers are melting.

Medea is run by the CIA, which arranges for scientists to have access to highly classified data collected by the National Reconnaissance Office (NRO) that would otherwise be unavailable to climate researchers. All sixty participating scientists, most from academia, have security clearances and work under the guidance of the National Academy of Sciences, which advises the government.

One climate scientist said the data sharing was vital to their research because academic researchers "have no way to send out 500 people" to the Arctic to collect data that are the equal of what the government's reconnaissance satellites and other highly sophisticated imaging and detection equipment can gather. Their analysis can in turn have significant economic implications for any industries, such as shipping and fisheries, that utilize the Arctic waters, or for oil companies looking for new places to drill. The scientists' predictions on ice floes and what they may mean for the navigation in the Arctic Sea and the possible opening of new sea lanes also have military implications, matters of great interest to the CIA.

Despite the promising applications of the data collected, Project Medea was shut down in 2001 after George W. Bush took office. Bush did not like the idea of America's top spies sharing information with some of America's top scientists, even less those studying climate change. But in 2009 after a plea from former vice president Al Gore to the Senate Intelligence Committee, the project was reinstated. It has received tacit backing from the Obama administration and especially from CIA director Leon Panetta, who believes "it is crucial to examine the potential national security implications of phenomena such as desertification, rising sea levels, and population shifts."

Despite official backing, little is said publicly about the collaboration. For security reasons, images captured by satellites that have been declassified are made less sharp to avoid revealing satellite capabilities to enemies. (Some of these images can be seen at the National Academy of Science's website.) But the sharing of classified data with environmental scientists is still politically controversial. One senator said the agency should be using its sophisticated equipment to fight terrorists, "not spying on sea lions."

SOURCE: William J. Broad, "C.I.A. Is Sharing Data with Climate Scientists," *New York Times*, January 5, 2010, A1. The final quote was by Sen. John Barrasso (R-Wyo.).

rules governing camping in national parks or how to book a reservation in one of its lodges, we can call the National Park Service or go to its website. If we want to know the fate of a bill in Congress or how our representatives voted on it, we can find it posted on the Internet.

The bureaucracy engages in research, too. A prime example is the Department of Agriculture, which for nearly 150 years has conducted research on how to grow bigger and better crops, raise healthier animals, and transport and market products more effectively. Government researchers, such as those at the National Institutes of Health and the Centers for Disease Control and Prevention, do much of the country's medical research, especially research related to mental health and epidemiology. Many vaccines and prescription drugs are also developed in government labs, and the Internet was invented by military bureaucrats. Every cabinet department has career civil servants—geologists, chemists, physicists, engineers, social scientists—carrying out research relevant to its area of policy making, be it rocketry, soil erosion, climate change, space travel, weapons development, high-tech communications and surveillance, or housing issues.

POLITICS AND PROFESSIONAL STANDARDS

As the part of government that implements policies made by elected officials, the bureaucracy cannot escape politics and so is subject to constant lobbying. That does not mean that civil servants have the green light to implement policy in a partisan manner. Today's civil servants are governed by laws that give priority to professional competence over political loyalty. Most Americans want fair, apolitical performance so that the quantity and quality of any government service they receive are not dependent on whether the civil servants performing the service belong to the same party as the president or their member of Congress. And most of us would prefer to have a civil engineer rather than a political crony in charge of building the dam near our town. The chances that the engineer will get the job over the crony

A recruitment poster for federal agencies seeking new hires for high-security intelligence jobs.

have improved significantly since patronage was outlawed in the federal bureaucracy.

The Merit System

For decades, American public bureaucracies were staffed under the **patronage** system, which allowed elected officials to fill administrative jobs on the basis of political loyalty rather than merit. By providing their supporters with jobs, elected officials could strengthen their political base, and many people regarded this as simply a means for government agencies to provide employment to citizens. Patronage hiring was usually referred to as the spoils system because it operated in rough accordance with the principle "to the victor belong the spoils," as the newly elected filled jobs with their own supporters.

At the federal level, Andrew Jackson's presidential election in 1828 was a watershed in using the patronage system. Jackson believed that any white male citizen of average intelligence and goodwill could do a government job well. So he reversed the existing practice of naming mostly well-off people from the East Coast by appointing less-well-off supporters from frontier areas.

The most obvious problem with staffing the bureaucracy with political supporters rather than by competitive recruitment is that jobs will go to people who are not competent to perform their duties. This became a major problem as government work became more technical and specialized. Furthermore, patronage could and frequently did lead to corruption, in particular to deal making between candidates and voters or individuals who controlled blocs of voters. Voters supported candidates who promised them jobs or other favors. Such corruption increasingly sullied city councils, state legislatures, and Congress during the 1800s.

Although patronage was affecting government performance, the influence wielded by the political machines that had grown powerful through its use kept Congress from acting until an unsuccessful federal job seeker assassinated President James Garfield in 1881. The Pendleton Act of 1883 established the **Civil Service Commission** to fill designated positions within the bureaucracy with people who had proved their competence in competitive examinations. Jobs under the commission's jurisdiction were part of the **merit system**. The new law also protected people holding merit positions from pressure to support or oppose particular candidates and from dismissal for political reasons.

Neutral Competence

The merit system established **neutral competence** as the professional standard for civil service employees. It requires that individuals filling merit positions be chosen for their expertise in executing policy and that they carry out their work in a nonpartisan or neutral manner. This standard assumes that there is no Republican or Democratic way

Carmona testifies before a Senate committee that the Bush administration pressured him not to address the medical implications of global warming, stem cell research, or emergency contraception, because the scientific findings in these areas conflicted with the administration's policies.

to build a sewer, collect customs duties, or fight a war. In effect, it says that partisan politics has no place in bureaucracy. It also implies that bureaucrats should not profit personally from the decisions they make.

Theodore Roosevelt (1901–1909) is considered the "father" of the modern civil service for his championing of merit hiring and neutral competence. "The government is us," he said. "Government jobs belong to the American people, not to politicians, and should be filled only with regard to public service."[67]

Woodrow Wilson (1913–1921), another strong advocate of neutral competence, believed that bureaucrats could learn to execute policy both expertly and responsively.[68] He saw government jobs as either political or administrative in nature and felt that by knowing which was which, we could create a bureaucracy that elected officials could control. Most current observers are less sanguine about the possibility of completely separating politics from administration.[69]

The Pendleton Act authorized the president to extend merit system coverage to additional federal jobs by executive order. In 1884, the merit system covered about 10 percent of the jobs in the federal bureaucracy, and by the middle of the twentieth century the figure rose to 90 percent. This created a rather rigid system of job classifications, pay, and rank known as the *general schedule*. It limited the president's appointment powers and also made it difficult to remove people for cause.

Improving the Merit System

Reforming the system was a central issue in Jimmy Carter's 1976 run for the presidency. The Civil Service Reform Act of 1978 was an attempt to modernize the personnel system and make it more competitive with the private sector. It was also a response to complaints from interest groups such as

Ralph Nader's Public Interest that the Civil Service Commission was concentrating on management at the expense of merit hiring, equal opportunity, and regulation.

The act got rid of the Civil Service Commission and divided its functions among several agencies. The Office of Personnel Management (OPM) today is responsible for managing a merit system for all federal employees nationwide and for working with the president to ensure that appointments to positions in exempt categories also adhere to basic standards of merit and political neutrality. Grievances and discrimination complaints are now handled by separate agencies—the Merit Systems Protection Board and the Equal Employment Opportunity Commission. The act also created a Whistleblowers Protection Agency (WBA) and an Office of Special Counsel to defend whistleblowers against retaliatory action by their agencies.

The act gave managers more opportunity to fire incompetent subordinates, and it established a more flexible classification of civil service positions. It also created the Senior Executive Service (SES) to fill the top management positions in the executive branch in the civil service. Those in the SES may be career civil servants or political appointees; they are not locked into a position but can move from agency to agency, carrying rank with them. They are also paid on the basis of performance and may receive bonuses. A number of other alternate personnel systems have been created, such as the State Department's Foreign Service and the personnel systems for the Pentagon and DHS.

At least one-quarter of all positions in the federal bureaucracy are now in categories exempt from the hiring and compensation rules that govern the general schedule of civil service appointments, although all are supposed to be governed by the basic rules of merit and neutral competence. In fact, although still a tiny portion of the whole workforce, there are many more political appointments in the upper levels of bureaucracy today than there were thirty years ago.

Even within the regular civil service, merit is not all that counts. The system favors veterans by adding a 5-point bonus to their test scores (disabled veterans get 10 points). And positioning counts as well: people already in the system are favored because they know about job openings first and may have skills identical to those in the job listing. As in the private sector, sometimes job descriptions are written to fit particular individuals.

Civil Service Employees and Political Activity

Banning patronage from federal hiring did not end partisan political activity by federal employees, so Congress passed another law expressly defining the limits on such activities. The **Hatch Act** of 1939 prohibited federal employees from active participation in partisan campaigns, even at the state and local levels. Political activities were restricted to voting, attending rallies, and having private conversations. Under the 1939 act, federal employees were not allowed to participate in party-sponsored voter registration drives, endorse party candidates, or work for or against them in any way.[70] These prohibitions also applied to employees of state and local government who were supported by federal funds.

The Hatch Act was controversial from the beginning. Supporters argued that it protected the neutral competence of civil servants from partisan influences. Critics said it made civil servants second-class citizens by denying them the First Amendment guarantees of freedom of speech and association. In 1993, Congress changed the law to allow most federal employees to hold office within a political party, to participate in political campaigns, and to raise funds for political action committees when they are not on duty. However, all employees of law enforcement and national security agencies remain under the earlier, more stringent prohibitions.

Politicizing the Merit System

No president has challenged the basic principles of merit hiring or neutral competence in theory or rhetoric, but some have challenged them in practice. White House and Justice Department staff in the George W. Bush administration were charged with multiple violations of both principles. Bush's chief aide, Karl Rove, organized White House liaisons to cabinet agencies into an "asset deployment team" that tried to coordinate the travel of cabinet secretaries and the awarding of grants and policy decisions by federal agencies with the needs of White House–backed candidates in the 2004 election campaign. During Bush's first seven years in office, Rove held more then one hundred political briefings for political appointees in executive branch agencies

to offer advice on how the agencies' assets could be used to make Republican candidates more competitive in battle-ground states. Rove claimed such briefings were within the law because they were directed only at political appointees, not the permanent bureaucracy. But federal agency decisions on the use of public money and other assets cannot be made on the basis of the political needs of election campaigns, and the Office of Special Counsel found at least one of the briefings in violation of the Hatch Act.[71] Congressional oversight committees launched investigations into other actions of Rove's asset deployment teams.

Bush appointees were also found guilty of multiple violations of merit hiring standards. A 2005 directive from the White House to its executive branch liaisons recommended that Internet searches be conducted on applicants for federal jobs to look for evidence of their political views and activities and their attitudes toward the president. Novice Justice Department lawyer Monica M. Goodling took this to heart, searching the Internet for applicant views on "guns, god + gays" and asking interviewees, "Why are you a Republican?"[72] The Department of Justice's inspector general found that the department had broken the law and violated departmental practices in using political criteria for the hiring of federal prosecutors, immigration judges, and other nonpolitical offices. Goodling admitted to a congressional committee she had "crossed the line."[73]

Science is another area where neutral competence often conflicts with political agendas. The thousands of government scientists, mathematicians, engineers, investigators, and data analyzers who provide the information that informs policy making and implementation were hired specifically for their professional expertise, and it is their mandate as civil servants to provide that information with neutral competence. It is up to elected officials whether they choose to act on the information provided.

All administrations vet scientific reports, and on many issues there is no clear consensus in the findings. There are many examples, such as whether it is the right or wrong time to raise taxes or cut taxes, to raise the prime interest rate or hold it steady, or whether there is enough evidence to approve or ban a new medical procedure. Even when there is consensus among experts, presidents are not obligated to act on it and may even cherry-pick reports for the evidence that supports their own policy preferences. Government researchers whose findings are not followed may not be happy with the policy results, but if they are not pressured to change their data or their conclusions, their neutral competence has not been challenged.

For example, President Reagan did not try to alter scientific findings about HIV/AIDS, but he did refuse to act on them. However, C. Everett Koop, his surgeon general, undertook a mass education campaign on AIDS against administration wishes but in accordance with his own understanding of his public responsibility. The mailing of information to every American household helped reduce panic and fear about the disease and change behavior, and it undoubtedly

© Fred R. Conrad, The New York Times/Redux

Scientist Jim Hansen, a government expert on climate change, was ordered by the Bush administration to stop giving speeches about global warming, as mentioned in the Talking Points earlier in the chapter.

contributed to saving many lives. And, even going against the man who appointed him, Koop managed to keep his job.

The threat to neutral competence comes when a president or his political appointees in federal agencies suppress data or actually edit the content of research reports to fit policy. These attempts are most egregious when there is a consensus among experts.

Falsifying or suppressing scientific research in the interest of political goals can work in the short run. In the long run, however, it undermines the public's faith in government and in science, too, and it can delay government action on issues crucial to public welfare and national security. As the chair of the House Committee on Science remarked on his retirement, "This is a town where everyone says they are for science-based decision making—until the science leads to a politically inconvenient conclusion."[74]

Ethics

The neutral competence standard prohibits bureaucrats from gaining materially from their decisions. Civil servants are supposed to make decisions based on their professional judgment and not to advance the cause of something in which they have a financial stake. For example, bureaucrats who are stockholders in chemical companies are not supposed to be making policy about chemical waste. Even if it were possible for policy makers to put self-interest aside, holding stakes in firms they regulate automatically takes on the appearance of a conflict of interest. This in turn would allow critics of a decision to challenge the regulation in court. Furthermore, the appearance of a conflict of interest undermines public confidence in government.

To better define what constitutes a conflict of interest, Congress passed the Ethics in Government Act in 1978 to prevent former public officials with inside information from using it and their contacts to give their new employers an unfair competitive advantage. The act barred former public servants from lobbying their agencies for one year and prohibited for life lobbying on matters in which they "personally and substantially" participated as public officials. In 1989, news that former Reagan administration officials had used their government service for substantial financial gain led to the passage of a law designed to strengthen the 1978 act. These new rules had little more impact than the old ones.

President Clinton issued an executive order requiring many of his political appointees to sign a pledge that they would not lobby the agencies in which they worked for five years after leaving government and would never lobby for foreign political parties and governments. But in 2002, four of Clinton's former cabinet members and other high-level political appointees, including his trade representative and the heads of the FCC and the SEC, each held multiple seats on corporate boards. It is not unthinkable that they were hired for their government contacts, although holding such positions in itself does not violate any ethics rule.

George W. Bush appointed more corporate executives to head government agencies than any other president, and some were responsible for regulating industries whose payrolls they had just left or in which they had held stock.

Sometimes the range within which bureaucrats can exercise neutral competence is severely restricted by their superiors. Agencies and department heads are political, not merit, appointees, and many are specifically charged with carrying out the programs of the president who appointed them. In addition, some of the policy that bureaucrats are implementing was made by presidential directive or executive order. EPA bureaucrats gearing up to implement Clinton's executive orders on clean water and clean air in December 2000 were required to write very different rules several months later when Bush rescinded Clinton's orders and substituted radically different policies. When Obama took office he rescinded, by executive order, most of the Bush rules. When an agency appears to be partisan in the way it implements, or fails to implement, congressional acts, it may simply be acting on such changes in presidential directives or on orders issued by the short-term political appointee temporarily heading the agency.

OVERSEEING THE BUREAUCRACY

The principal overseers of the bureaucracy are, of course, the president, who heads it and appoints its top policy makers; the Senate, which holds confirmation powers; Congress as a whole, which has authority to create, monitor, and fund agencies; and the federal courts, which often have to interpret the meaning of regulations or rule on their constitutionality. Congress has also given the public a significant, if vastly underused, role through legislation that mandates openness in government.

President

The president, constitutionally the chief executive, has primary responsibility for directing executive branch agencies and monitoring their responsiveness. He has several significant means for providing executive leadership, including budgeting, appointment and removal powers, the authority to initiate executive branch reorganizations, an office within the White House specifically for oversight, and, of course, his power to issue executive orders.

Congress decidedly enhanced the president's administrative powers in 1921 by delegating its authority to write the annual budget. In 1937, when Congress approved Franklin Roosevelt's executive branch reorganization, it moved the Bureau of the Budget (BOB) into the new Executive Office of the President (EOP) to help the president manage the bureaucracy. During Nixon's reorganization of the EOP, the newly created Office of Management and Budget

(OMB) absorbed BOB and was given specific responsibility for overseeing executive agency performance. (It reports its findings to the public as well as the president by posting them on its website.) This constant monitoring of agencies from within the EOP gives the president more administrative control than does budget writing itself. Presidents can try to cut agency appropriations to limit agencies' range of actions or they can tie conditions to appropriations to make them take specific actions, but Congress does not have to approve White House requests. And because it has power to approve appropriations, Congress has more opportunity than the president to attach strings to funding.

Reagan established the practice of using the OMB's Office of Information and Regulatory Affairs (OIRA) to review all regulations proposed by executive branch agencies, giving the White House the opportunity to reject or modify them, using cost-benefit analysis, before the rules were issued. Both Reagan and Clinton used this process to reduce the number of new rules and the cost to businesses of enforcing them. The Bush administration, which continued the practice with a stronger ideological focus, tried to eliminate regulations opposed by industry, especially environmental regulations. Many of the new rules rejected were based on findings of government scientists, leading to additional charges of politically charged decision making in what is supposed to be a neutrally competent bureaucracy.

A president's best chance to direct the work of an agency is to put a surrogate in charge of it, that is, to appoint someone who shares his views. This is true of OIRA itself. Reagan and both Bushes appointed men predisposed to reject proposed regulations. President Obama appointed a well-known professor of constitutional law who is committed to using cost-benefit analysis, not to reject regulations, but to write rules that would address such politically controversial problems as climate change while doing little or no damage to economic growth in the short run.[75]

It is easiest for a president to direct oversight of an agency if it is one whose head is a political appointee, such as with the EPA, OMB, and OIRA, and cabinet departments, because it is accepted that a president is entitled to appoint politically like-minded people to his own cabinet and White House staff. Thus, Reagan and both Bushes filled health care–related positions in the Department of Health and Human Services with people who were against keeping abortion legal, whereas Clinton filled them with people who were pro-choice. Appointments to independent and regulatory agencies receive more scrutiny because neutral competence plays a greater role, but presidents do get most of their choices confirmed. Republican presidents tend to appoint people who favor business, and Democratic presidents appoint those who lean toward the interests of consumers and organized labor. Reagan chose heads for regulatory agencies such as OSHA, the Consumer Product Safety Commission, and the EPA who agreed with his goal of reducing government regulation, whereas Clinton named a lifelong environmental activist to head the EPA.

Of course, sometimes presidential appointees, despite being screened for issue positions, may end up, especially if they stay in a position long enough, representing long-standing agency policies and norms rather than the president's interests. Most appointees have less expertise and experience in agency operations than career civil servants, and some come to rely on career officials for information about agency history, procedures, and policy questions. But much depends on the president's leadership, how much he pushes for change in an agency, and how closely he monitors a particular agency's activities and directives.

Administrative reform is a third means by which a president can increase his control over the bureaucracy. Generally, the more sweeping a president's recommendation for change, the more he must anticipate congressional and interest group resistance. For example, Reagan wanted to abolish the Departments of Education and Energy and merge the Commerce and Labor Departments, but Congress would not support him. When George W. Bush reorganized twenty-two executive branch agencies with 220,000 employees to create the new cabinet-level Department of Homeland Security (DHS), he found Congress resistant to his request that it cede substantial budgetary and oversight powers over the agency to the White House. After the DHS's organizational problems led to its disastrous response to Hurricane Katrina, Congress reorganized the chain of command, giving FEMA primary responsibility for responding to such natural disasters. The secretary of DHS, presumably with the president's approval, immediately tried to override this congressional directive by reclaiming for his own office the responsibility Congress had just given FEMA.

The White House can also try to influence independent agencies and commissions by lobbying and mobilizing public opinion. Attempts by presidents of both parties to influence Federal Reserve Board decisions on interest rates, for example, are legion.

Despite these powers, there are many limits on the president's executive leadership. Given the size and complexity of the federal bureaucracy, the president cannot possibly influence every important decision. Moreover, as the civil service expanded, presidents found it increasingly difficult to lead an executive branch with 90 percent of its positions filled by merit system employees deliberately insulated from presidential control. The creation of the SES and alternative personnel systems allows for short-term and emergency appointments and easier movement within the bureaucracy. In addition, the 1978 law gave managers more opportunity to fire incompetent subordinates, and it authorized bonuses and a new pay scale for managers to encourage better performance.

Despite the changes, presidents often still feel thwarted by the constraints on removing civil servants for poor performance or because they will not do a president's bidding. Although job security is not meant to shield public servants who do poor work, it does make firing incompetent workers difficult and time-consuming. Thus the organization of public employees into unions makes firing them more difficult but at the same time unions protect workers from being dismissed without grounds. The government's rate of discharging people for inefficiency, 0.01 percent a year, did not increase after the 1978 reforms, though no doubt some employees left after being threatened with dismissal or demotion. As one public employee said, "We're all like headless nails down here—once you get us in you can't get us out."[76] This attitude captures what some say is the civil service's built-in bias toward job survival rather than innovation.[77]

Agencies that have strong allies in Congress, in powerful interest groups, or in the public provide another limit to presidential leadership. Presidents have more success controlling agencies that lack strong congressional allies and domestic clientele groups, such as the Treasury and State departments, than agencies that have such allies, such as the Social Security Administration and the Agriculture and Health and Human Services departments. However, the increasing number of political appointees in senior positions gives the president many more opportunities to exercise his influence over agency operations, even in agencies like the EPA, which has strong bipartisan support in Congress and powerful interest groups monitoring its work.

Not all presidents have the same interest in exercising executive leadership over the bureaucracy. Some are preoccupied with foreign policy, some are not interested in administration, and most realize that a president's ability to manipulate bureaucratic decision making will run up against the constraints of civil service law. Although all want to appoint people to policy-making positions who are committed to a similar set of goals, the will to pressure these individuals after they have been appointed varies. George W. Bush arguably interpreted the president's role as chief executive more absolutely than any of his predecessors. He maintained that a president's powers as chief executive as stated in Article II are exclusive and that as a **unitary executive** his orders to executive branch agencies trump any directions from Congress or the courts. Bush asked his appointees in the Justice Department to write a legal justification of his claim for the president's absolute control over the executive branch (a claim whose legal basis is rejected by most constitutional scholars). He argued that a unitary executive was empowered to staff even positions in the permanent bureaucracy, which are subject to the neutral competence standard of performance, using political criteria, and to override congressional mandates to executive branch agencies as well.

At the end of his tenure Bush transformed a number of his political appointees into civil servants. This practice, known as "burrowing," was used by many of his predecessors as a way to reward loyal underlings with tenured positions in the federal bureaucracy. However, it is also a way of planting one's political allies in agencies in the expectation they will try to carry forward an administration's policies after it is gone. Bush named a "package" of six managers,

known opponents of environmental regulations, to positions within the Interior Department.[78]

Congress

Although the president has the edge in leadership through his appointment powers, Congress has greater scope for oversight and control. Much of the bureaucracy's power is delegated authority from Congress, and much of its work is implementing laws passed by Congress. Congress has the power to create, reorganize, or eliminate agencies and the ultimate instrument of control—the power of the purse strings.

Congress not only has the power to increase or decrease the amount of money the president requests to fund an agency, but it can also tell an agency how it has to spend the money it allocates. Often, a congressional committee tells an agency that it must spend x number of dollars from its budget to pay for a project earmarked by one or more members of Congress, even when the project was not named in the budget and even when the president opposes the spending or the project itself.

Congress also has dozens of committees (supported by a staff of thousands) to which executive agencies must report. But just as an agency's outside allies can work to thwart presidential control, they can also limit congressional oversight. Agencies frequently work closely with certain congressional committees and interest groups for mutual support and outcomes favorable to all. (These relationships are sometimes called "iron triangles" or issue networks.) Agencies may adjust their actions to suit the preferences of the congressional committees that authorize their programs and appropriate their funds. For example, decisions by members of independent regulatory commissions are sensitive to the views of members of their congressional oversight committees. When the membership of the committees becomes more liberal or more conservative, so do the decisions regulators make.[79]

Iron triangles can make oversight look less like monitoring the bureaucracy and more like collusion. Two of the most extreme examples of incestuous relationships between agency officials and businesses they were supposed to regulate surfaced after the West Virginia coal mine disaster and the massive BP oil spill in the Gulf of Mexico in 2010. Employees of the agencies that were supposed to be regulating for mine safety and overseeing government-licensed oil drilling were found to have accepted gifts (including meals and tickets to sporting events) from companies they regulated, conducted inspections under the influence of drugs, and, in the case of mining oversight, used drugs and had sexual relationships with the very people whose economic activities they were supposed to be overseeing. The Minerals Management Service, which oversaw oil leases, was said by the Department of Interior's inspector general to have allowed drilling without the necessary permits and to have developed a "culture of lax oversight and cozy ties to industry."[80] President Obama used his executive authority to split up the agency, rename it, and appoint a new director.

Constituent service, by contrast, provides a motive for members of Congress to try to shape bureaucratic decision making. Members often try to influence agencies to take some action on behalf of constituents or in the interest of their districts. In fact, congressional staff who do casework often have their duties assigned according to the agencies they are responsible for contacting about constituent complaints. This can lead members to pressure bureaucrats to help satisfy constituent demands rather than using neutral competence as their standard of decision making. When Secretary of Defense Robert Gates announced closure of military installations in Virginia as part of his cost-cutting campaign, members of that state's congressional delegation immediately went public, protesting the loss of money and jobs and trying to pressure Gates to revoke his decision. It is this kind of pressure that keeps military bases open years beyond their usefulness, simply because they are good for the economy of a member's district.

Courts

Federal courts act as another check on the bureaucracy. Judicial decisions shape agency actions by directing agencies to follow legally correct procedures. Of course, the courts cannot intercede in an agency's decision making unless some aggrieved person or corporation files a suit against the agency. Nevertheless, in almost any controversial agency action, there will be aggrieved parties and possibly some with sufficient resources to bring a court action.

The courts interpret lawmakers' intentions by deciding what congressional majorities and the president had in mind

"Nice little touch of humility!"

when they made a law. This can be difficult. Sometimes, in their haste, lawmakers fail to specify crucial elements of a law, or they may be unable to reach agreement on a provision and leave it ambiguous in order to get the bill passed. Lawmakers may also write a certain amount of vagueness into a law so that agencies will be able to adapt it to unknown future conditions. How the courts read a law may augment or reduce the ability of Congress and the president to influence its implementation. In the current Supreme Court, the conservative majority has increasingly used its authority to interpret the intent of congressional acts in ways that expand the Court's own powers. We discuss these issues in Chapter 13.

Regulators and other agency policy makers appear to be quite sensitive to federal court decisions. For example, when the courts overturn the National Labor Relations Board's decisions in a pro-labor direction, the board's decisions soon become more pro-labor. Similarly, decisions drift the other way when courts overturn agency decisions in a pro-business direction.[81]

Interest Groups and Individuals

The public has numerous opportunities to oversee and to influence bureaucratic decision making. Most of these rights stem from laws designed to ensure openness in government.

Openness laws also extend to media access and thus provide another important check on bureaucratic abuses. But the media can also make the bureaucracy's work more difficult. Reporters like to cover conflict and bad news and are therefore usually on the lookout for stories about internal policy disputes. Newspapers and other media outlets make frequent use of FOIA to obtain documents from government agencies.

Businesses and interest groups also use FOIA to gain access to agency information or government data that help them develop strategies to better influence future agency decisions that will affect them. Businesses want information that will help them avoid new regulations. Interest groups want to make sure bureaucracies adopt rules and enforcement practices they favor. An environmental group cannot rest on its laurels just because Congress has passed a law placing new safeguards on toxic waste disposal. The group's job is not over until it makes sure the EPA writes strict rules to enforce the law. Consequently, the group must lobby the regulators as well as Congress.

Interest groups and their lobbyists are also part of the public. Lobbyists tend to take much greater advantage of their rights of access than the general public does, and they are the source of many of the public comments on proposed rules received by agencies. But it is not unusual for the EPA or other regulatory agencies to get thousands of responses when they post new rules on their websites for public comment.

© Frank Cotham/The New Yorker Collection/www.cartoonbank.com

If an agency seems to be sabotaging the intent of Congress, interest groups can work with friendly congressional committees to put pressure on the agency to mend its ways. And interest groups can also try to rally public opinion to their side to pressure Congress or the president to do something about the agency. Environmental groups are especially skilled at this. Sometimes interest groups pressure an agency so effectively that the agency is said to be "captured."[82] This term is used most frequently for regulatory agencies thought to be controlled by the groups they are supposed to be regulating.

We know that interest groups can influence the bureaucracy, but can individual citizens affect policy too? It is difficult for an individual to influence public agencies when acting alone, but that does not mean there are no opportunities to do so. Perhaps one person posting a comment on a website will not change agency policy, but if all residents opposed to a decision on cleaning up a hazardous waste site in their neighborhood file comments, it can make a difference. Rules have been reversed or amended. Some observers of the lobbying process have suggested that citizen comment has become so important that iron triangles have now become quadrangles. When citizens weigh in by the thousands, as does happen with some rules posted for comment at agency websites, they can influence the content of the rule, but rarely do citizens have the opportunity to interact directly with the rule makers as lobbyists do.

An individual who uses FOIA to retrieve documents that expose agency corruption or abuse can also make a difference by going public with the story. And members of the general public are increasingly taking advantage of openness laws, though the process is not easy for those who try. A lot of paperwork is involved, some costs, and often a long wait, even though government agencies employ over 5000 administrators to process the requests.

Ordinary citizens could have a greater impact if they used all the tools that Congress has given them to oversee and to influence the bureaucracy. They can even be whistleblowers by suing companies with government contracts that defraud the government (and if successful, share in the money recovered).[83] But individual **whistleblowers** within the bureaucracy often have the best opportunity to monitor agency practices. Some whistleblowing is unsuccessful, but some makes a real difference. One of the most famous whistleblowers was Pentagon employee Daniel Ellsberg, who in 1968 leaked thousands of documents on the conduct of the Vietnam War to the *New York Times*. Henry Kissinger claimed that Ellsberg was the most dangerous man in the world, but Ellsberg's acts helped the public understand that the Johnson and Nixon administrations' private rationale for fighting the war was not the same as the reasons they stated in public.

Bunny Greenhouse, chief contracting officer in the United States Army Corps of Engineers, blew the whistle on a no-bid, five-year, $7 billion offer to Halliburton and its subsidiaries to get Iraqi oilfields running. (Vice President Cheney was CEO of Halliburton before becoming vice president.) After being pressured by superiors to approve that and other contracts that would allow the company essentially to set costs and add a service fee, and without competitive bidding or appropriate controls, Greenhouse signed the contracts because of the needs of those trying to get Iraq stabilized, but with a note saying she was doing it under pressure and in spite of irregularities. A FOIA request uncovered the documents and her comments. At a 2005 forum organized by the Democrats looking into charges of overbilling and fraud in Iraq War contracts (the Republican-dominated Congress refused to hold such hearings), Greenhouse testified that these agreements were "the worst activity in contracting that I'd ever seen in all my contracting career."[84] Three weeks later, she was demoted to a lower civil service grade, despite years of exemplary reviews. Although she asked for a full investigation, she was never able to return to her job.

Disclosure of bureaucratic failures increased after 9/11 because many individuals saw that neglected shortcomings could have serious consequences. But retaliation continued. In recent years, airport baggage screeners, border patrol agents, and the chief of the United States Park Police were disciplined or fired for reporting problems in their agencies. The most publicized case was that of Medicare's chief actuary, who was threatened with dismissal by the political appointee who headed his agency if he provided Congress with accurate numbers on the cost of the Bush administration's proposed prescription drug benefit for seniors.

In 2004, Congress responded by writing a new law with stronger protections for whistleblowers, including freedom from reprisal for those, like the Medicare actuary, who provide information to Congress. But the bill was strongly opposed by the Bush administration, which contended that it "unconstitutionally interferes with the president's ability to control and manage the government."[85] Protections for whistleblowers hit a new low in 2008 when the Office of Special Counsel, which is charged with providing legal protection to whistleblowers, was raided by the FBI. The director of the office had been under investigation for three years for abuse of office, retaliating against whistleblowers in his own office, and destroying evidence on his office computer.[86]

Despite the legal protections, it is the rare person who will set aside cordial relations with colleagues and ambition for promotion in order to challenge the status quo. Most people, whether working in the private or the public sector, find it difficult to expose their employer's dirty laundry. And even if the law does protect their jobs, their careers may be effectively ruined. About half of all whistleblowers lose their jobs, half of those lose their homes, and half of those lose their families.[87]

CONCLUSION: The Bureaucracy's Role in Government

Without a bureaucracy, none of the laws passed or programs established by Congress could be implemented. But has the bureaucracy become an impenetrable forest or an uncontrollable fourth branch of government, as some portray it? The turf wars, miscommunication, and fragmented authority that surfaced after 9/11 and continue today certainly indicate that at least part of the federal bureaucracy is an impenetrable forest. It is not surprising that most of the agencies that failed so badly at that time (for example, the CIA and the FBI) were among the least open to citizens or the media and even to congressional oversight. Nine years after 9/11, the problems of interagency information sharing have still not been resolved and may have been worsened by the rapid growth and privatization of work that most agree is rightfully a job for government. However, how large government's role in intelligence gathering can become without infringing on another of its essential functions—protecting individual liberty—is highly controversial.

And in another part of the forest—the health care and social services bureaucracies—there continue to be significant disagreements about whether health care and income support for the poor and seniors are appropriate roles for government. But the bureaucracy as a whole is not an errant fourth branch of government. Most of the bureaucracy is subject to presidential and congressional control, providing they are willing to exercise their powers. Indeed, one of the by-products of the Bush administration's attempt to increase presidential control of executive branch agencies at the expense of Congress was that it did reawaken Congress to its oversight lapses.

Nothing brought the lapses in oversight and regulation more sharply to public attention than the subprime mortgage crisis of 2008. Had regulatory agencies been doing their jobs and Congress monitoring them to see that they were doing their jobs, the risky and sometimes fraudulent lending practices that led to the crisis may have been terminated before they became pervasive. But civil servants cannot do their job or exercise neutral competence if their political minders will not let them do so. As investigations subsequent to 9/11 revealed, part of the reason for the failures of intelligence agencies was that their experts were overridden by their politically appointed superiors and not allowed to exercise neutral competence.

Our fragmented political system means that our public agencies operate in an environment of uncertainty and competition. Bureaucrats have many bosses: a president, his appointees, Congress and its many committees and subcommittees, and the federal courts. In addition, numerous interest groups try to influence the work of federal agencies. The often contradictory demands for responsiveness and neutral competence contribute to an uncertainty of expectations. As a result, agencies try to protect themselves by cultivating the support of congressional committees and interest groups. Even presidents can have trouble influencing agencies because of these alliances.

There is a vaguely defined but frequently articulated public suspicion that any bureaucracy is destined to be intransigent and inefficient. We have tried to show that some of that attitude stems from lack of consensus on what the work of government should be. If you do not like the work that Congress and the president have assigned to the bureaucracy, there is not much chance you will view the bureaucracy as functioning within its constitutional role. If the dissatisfaction is more over how the bureaucracy does its work, there is hope that at least some areas of performance will meet with your approval. The public does have tools to influence how bureaucrats do their work, but it has many more ways to lobby Congress and the president to change the work they give the bureaucracy to do.

Despite people's negative feelings about the bureaucracy, the mail is delivered, Social Security paid, and passports issued. The bureaucracy usually does what it is supposed to do. Some public agencies, such as Social Security and Medicare, operate far more efficiently than their private counterparts. When government fails badly, such as before 9/11, in the response to Hurricane Katrina, in the refusal to regulate financial markets, or in not enforcing the most basic standards for bidding, auditing, and accountability in awarding military contracts for work in Iraq, the human cost can be enormous. But these failures are not caused by the public's view of or trust in government. These failures are most likely to happen when those in charge of overseeing the bureaucracy have a negative view of government, particularly of the bureaucracy, and refuse to let it function according to professional standards.

Today there is a more serious concern for and greater awareness of the costs of poorly functioning government agencies. The head of one government watchdog group summarized the feeling this way: "Before September 11 there was a bit of a blasé attitude of 'OK, the government screwed up again.' Now people see the consequences on their lives and see the necessity of government functioning well."[88]

KEY TERMS

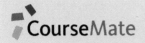

Access an interactive eBook, chapter-specific interactive learning tools (including flashcards, quizzes, videos), and more at CourseMate for *Understanding American Government.* Log in at CengageBrain.com.

13

The Judiciary

○ Lilly Ledbetter lobbies Congress to overturn the Supreme Court ruling limiting pay discrimination lawsuits.

Fanny Carrier/AFP/Getty Images

that. As a lawyer in the Reagan administration, he wrote that "the Constitution does not protect a right to an abortion."[32] He argued for more presidential power than courts allow and less congressional power than Congress exercises. He maintained, for example, that Congress didn't have the power to pass the Truth in Mileage Act, which forbids car dealers from misleading the buyers by turning back the odometers in used cars. Yet at his confirmation hearings, he resisted all attempts to engage in a dialogue. "He was like a chauffeur who speaks only when spoken to, and doesn't presume to converse."[33] When asked about his past statements, he soft-pedaled them, saying that he was an advocate in the Reagan administration. As a justice, he insisted, he would have no political agenda. (Once on the bench, however, he has revealed a political agenda.)[34] After Alito's confirmation, the chair of the Judiciary Committee observed, "The hearings are really . . . a subtle minuet, with the nominee answering as many questions as he thinks necessary in order to be confirmed."[35]

DEMOCRACY?

What are the implications for our democracy when judicial nominees refuse to reveal their views on legal controversies, yet senators confirm them anyway? Consider the implications for presidential power and congressional power, and the implications for the role of the people in this process. Are the American people entitled to know the nominees' views so the people can register their approval or disapproval before the Senate confirms the nominees for lifetime appointments? Or are the American people entitled to know the views only of the candidates for president and Congress?

Role of the Senate

Although the Senate played a vigorous role in the appointment process in the nineteenth century, rejecting twenty-two of eighty-one presidential nominations to the Supreme Court between 1789 and 1894, it routinely accepted the president's nominations in the first half of the twentieth century, rejecting only one nomination until 1968.[36] Then it rejected two by President Johnson, two by President Nixon, and two by President Reagan.[37]

Of these six nominees, most were qualified in an objective sense.[38] Although some were accused of ethical lapses, most were rejected for ideological reasons.[39] Johnson's were deemed too liberal, while Nixon's and Reagan's were deemed too conservative.

Nominations to the Supreme Court have been contentious since the 1960s partly because of the Court's activism at that time—both liberals and conservatives saw what the Court can do—and partly because of the divisions that have characterized our government and our society since that time. Often one party has dominated the presidency while the other party has dominated Congress, so they have fought over the judiciary to tip the balance. Even in the 2000s, when one party often has controlled both branches, the two parties have been matched evenly enough that they have fought over the judiciary. Nominations have also become contentious because of the culture wars between reformers and traditionalists that began in the 1960s and the corresponding rise of interest groups on the left and the right that scrutinize the appointments, pressuring presidents and senators on their side to nominate and vote their way.

Even nominations to the lower courts, especially to the courts of appeals, which serve as "farm teams" for future justices, have become contentious in recent decades.[40] This trend reflects the polarization of American politics and the role of interest groups today. "You go out on the streets of Raleigh," former Sen. Jesse Helms of North Carolina said, "and ask one hundred people: 'Do you give a damn who is on the Fourth Circuit Court of Appeals?' They'll say: 'What's that?'"[41] But political activists representing interest groups on the left and the right do know and do care, deeply, because they see the connection between the lower court judges and the interest groups' goals. In elections, these political activists mobilize their party's base of voters. Thus they have influence on their party, which needs their help. They can persuade, sometimes demand, that their party's senators fight a nomination by the other party's president.[42]

Strategy of the Opposite Party

Even when the senators in the opposite party don't consider a nominee too extreme to confirm, they might pick a fight over the nomination. Based on the available evidence, both of President Obama's nominees to the Supreme Court were mainstream candidates considered moderately, but not very, liberal. Sonia Sotomayor had a moderate record as an appellate judge. As a former prosecutor, she was less supportive of criminal defendants' rights than many liberals are. Elena Kagan, as a former dean of Harvard's law school, hired several conservative professors to diversify the liberal faculty that dominates the school. Yet both nominees faced formidable opposition from Republican senators. In fact, there was considerable opposition before either nominee was named. The opposition revealed multiple strategies.

Republican senators opposed Sotomayor and Kagan as a way to energize the party's conservative base and enflame Tea Partiers' populist anger toward President Obama. Although the nominees had no responsibility for Obama's policies, criticism of the nominees would validate conservatives' and populists' anger and reinforce their opposition to the president and his policies.[43]

Republican senators also opposed the nominees as a way to lure more voters to the Republican Party. They capitalized on a remark by Sotomayor in a speech to Latino law students: "I would hope that a wise Latina woman with the richness of her experiences would more often than not reach a better conclusion than a white male who hasn't lived that life."[44] The speech was intended simply as an inspirational pep talk to the students, yet it was cited by opponents as evidence that Sotomayor was a "racist."[45] They also capitalized

© 2010 Chan Lowe

on a decision she had joined while on the court of appeals. That ruling followed a Supreme Court precedent involving racial discrimination in the workplace. The result, however, meant that some minority firefighters in New Haven, Connecticut, had a better chance of promotion and some white firefighters had a lower chance of promotion than they would have if the ruling had gone the opposite way. (When the ruling was appealed, the Supreme Court narrowed its own precedent and ruled for the white firefighters.)[46] Republican senators called the firefighter who initiated the lawsuit to testify, and he claimed that Sotomayor had discriminated against him because he is white. The goal was to pull white men, especially blue-collar workers who believed that they had lost ground due to affirmative action, away from the Democratic Party.[47]

Similarly, Republican senators capitalized on a position Kagan took as dean of Harvard's law school. She criticized the federal "don't ask, don't tell" policy, which prohibited homosexuals from serving openly in the military (explained in Chapter 14). She said that this policy conflicted with the school's non-discrimination policy to deny help in recruiting to any employer (in this case, the military) who discriminates in hiring. Although Kagan followed the law in this dispute, Republican senators characterized her as anti-military.[48]

Republican senators also picked the fights to help the party and its supporting interest groups raise money. As long as the nominations were pending, the groups could mail out solicitations condemning the nominations and many conservatives would send in donations for the groups to finance their fights and maintain their "vigilance" in the future.[49]

Results of Selection

Judges are drawn from large law firms or the federal government, and higher court judges are often drawn from the lower courts. Because these established legal circles are dominated by white men, most judges have been white men. Although recent presidents have appointed more minorities and women, the bench's composition changes slowly because of judges' life tenure. (See the box "Do Women Judges Matter?")

Despite the efforts to provide geographic, religious, racial, and sexual diversity, no effort has been made to reflect socioeconomic diversity. Throughout history, judges have come from a narrow, elite slice of society. Most have come from upper-middle-class or upper-class families with prestige and connections as well as expectations for achievement.[50]

No Supreme Court justice since Warren Burger in 1969 has attended a public university or graduate school. Every justice since then has had a degree from one of four prestigious, private schools—Chicago, Harvard, Stanford, or Yale.[51] Every justice on the Court now has attended Harvard or Yale law school.

Many justices—at least five on the current Court—have been millionaires.[52] Most justices have extensive stock holdings. Federal judges must disqualify themselves if they own stock in companies that are litigants in cases before their court. In a recent term, the Supreme Court could not hear one case because it could not assemble a quorum of six justices. Too many had a conflict of interest.[53] Many lower court judges have been millionaires, too. Forty percent of Clinton's appointees and 58 percent of Bush's appointees were millionaires.[54]

Despite her Ivy League education, Sonia Sotomayor is an exception to the norm in various ways. She's the only justice whose first language wasn't English and the only one whose childhood was spent in a public housing project where drugs and crimes were common. She was raised by a single mother after her father, a welder who had a third-grade education, died when she was nine. As an adult, she has struggled to pay her mortgage and credit card bills.

With the power to nominate judges, presidents have a tremendous opportunity to shape the courts and their decisions (see Figure 2).

DEMOCRACY?

What implications might the class background, prestigious education, and wealth of most Supreme Court justices and many lower court judges have on court decisions? On judicial interpretations of the Constitution?

Tenure of Judges

Once appointed, judges can serve for "good behavior" **Art. III, Sec. 1.**, which means for life, unless they commit "high crimes and misdemeanors." These are not defined in the Constitution but are considered to be serious crimes or, possibly, political abuses. Congress can impeach and remove judges as it can presidents, but it has impeached only fifteen and removed only eight. The standard of guilt—"high crimes and misdemeanors"—is vague, the punishment drastic, and the process time-consuming, so Congress has been reluctant to impeach judges.[55]

american diversity

Do Women Judges Matter?

Some people believe that there should be more women judges because women are entitled to their "fair share" of all governmental offices, including judgeships. Others believe that there should be more so women will feel that the courts represent them too. Still others believe that there should be more because women hold different views than men and therefore would make different decisions.

A study of Justice Sandra Day O'Connor, the first woman on the Supreme Court, shows that although she generally voted as a conservative, she usually voted as a liberal in sex discrimination cases. Moreover, her presence on the Court apparently sensitized her male colleagues to gender issues. Most of them voted against sex discrimination more frequently after she joined the Court.[1] A study of federal courts of appeals judges found the same pattern among female judges and male colleagues.[2]

Some studies found similar results for women justices on state supreme courts. Even women justices from opposite political parties supported a broad array of women's rights in cases ranging from sex discrimination to child support and property settlement.[3] But studies that compare voting patterns on issues less directly related to gender have less clear findings. Women judges appear more liberal than men in cases involving employment discrimination and racial discrimination. Perhaps the treatment they have experienced as women has made them more sympathetic to the discrimination others have faced. They're also more liberal than men in cases involving asylum for immigrants.[4] On the other hand, women judges don't appear more liberal or conservative than men in cases involving obscenity, criminal rights, or other areas of the law.[5]

Studies that compare the sentencing of criminal defendants in state courts find scant differences between men and women judges.[6] However, women judges do tend to sentence convicted defendants somewhat more harshly.[7] Women judges in Harris County, Texas, which includes Houston, have applied the death penalty with "greater ferocity" than their male predecessors. This *county*, a majority of whose judges are female, has given the death penalty to more defendants than all other *states* but one.[8]

But the studies comparing men and women judges find more similarities than differences. This should not be surprising, because the two sexes were subject to the same training in law school and the same socialization in the legal profession, and they became judges in the same ways as others in their jurisdiction.

Perhaps the greatest difference women judges have made is to protect the credibility of women lawyers and witnesses. In court, some men judges and lawyers have made disparaging remarks about women lawyers, suggesting that they should not be in the profession—for example, calling them "lawyerettes." Many male judges and lawyers have made paternalistic or personal remarks to female lawyers and witnesses, referring to them by their first name or by such terms as "young lady," "sweetie," or "honey." Sometimes, in the midst of the proceedings, men have commented about their perfume, clothing, or appearance. "How does an attorney," one asked, "establish her authority when the judge has just described her to the entire courtroom as 'a pretty little thing'?"[9] Even if the men considered their remarks harmless compliments rather than intentional tactics, their effect was to undermine the credibility of women lawyers and witnesses in the eyes of jurors. Women judges have squelched such remarks.

[1] Karen O'Connor and Jeffrey A. Segal, "Justice Sandra Day O'Connor and the Supreme Court's Reaction to Its First Female Member," in *Women, Politics, and the Constitution*, ed. Naomi B. Lynn (New York: Haworth Press, 1990), 95–104.
[2] Christina L. Boyd and Lee Epstein, "All Else Being Equal, Choose a Woman," *Washington Post National Weekly Edition*, May 11–17, 2009, 26.
[3] David W. Allen and Diane E. Wall, "Role Orientations and Women State Supreme Court Justices," *Judicature* 77 (1993), 156–165.
[4] Julia Preston, "Big Disparities in Judging of Asylum Cases," *New York Times*, May 31, 2007.
[5] Sue Davis, Susan Haire, and Donald R. Songer, "Voting Behavior and Gender on the U.S. Courts of Appeals," *Judicature* 77 (1993), 129–133; Thomas G. Walker and Deborah J. Barrow, "The Diversification of the Federal Bench," *Journal of Politics* 47 (1985), 596–617; Boyd and Epstein, "All Else Being Equal."
[6] John Gruhl, Cassia Spohn, and Susan Welch, "Women as Policymakers: The Case of Trial Judges," *American Journal of Political Science* 25 (1981), 308–322.
[7] Darrell Steffensmeier and Chris Hebert, "Women and Men Policymakers: Does the Judge's Gender Affect the Sentencing of Criminal Defendants?" *Social Forces* 77 (1999), 1163–1196.
[8] Jeffrey Toobin, "Women in Black," *New Yorker*, October 30, 2000, 48.
[9] William Eich, "Gender Bias in the Courtroom: Some Participants Are More Equal than Others," *Judicature* 69 (1986), 339–343.

Qualifications of Judges

Given the use of political criteria in selecting judges, are judges well qualified?

Political scientists who study the judiciary consider federal judges generally well qualified. This is especially true of Supreme Court justices. Presidents realize that they will be held responsible for their appointees. Moreover, presidents have so few vacancies to fill that they can confine themselves to persons of their party and political views and even to persons of a particular region, religion, race, and sex and still locate good candidates. This is less true of lower court judges. Presidents and senators (through senatorial courtesy) jointly appoint them,

so both can avoid taking responsibility for them. These judges are also less visible, so a lack of merit is not as noticeable.

Presidents do appoint some losers. President Truman put a longtime supporter on a court of appeals who was "drunk half the time" and "no damn good." When asked why he appointed the man, Truman candidly replied, "I . . . felt I owed him a favor; that's why, and I thought as a judge he couldn't do too much harm, and he didn't."[56]

Sometimes presidents appoint qualified persons who later become incompetent. After serving for many years, they incur the illnesses and infirmities of old age, and perhaps one-tenth become unable to perform their job well.[57] Yet they hang on because they are allowed to serve for "good behavior," and they prevent other lawyers from filling their seats on the bench.

This problem has prompted proposals for a constitutional amendment setting a term limit of eighteen years[58] or a mandatory retirement age of seventy. Either of these changes would have a substantial impact because over one-third of all Supreme Court justices have served longer than twenty years and past seventy-five years old. But constitutional amendments are difficult to pass, and mandatory retirement ages are out of favor now. Furthermore, some of the best judges have done some of their finest work late in their career. Recently, however, some observers of appointment battles have argued that having fixed terms might lessen the stakes, and therefore the fights, over the appointments.

Figure 2 | **Percentage of Liberal Decisions Handed Down by District Court Appointees of Presidents Woodrow Wilson through George W. Bush**

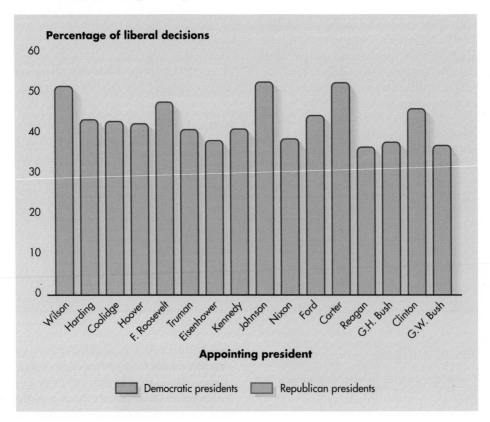

Appointees of Democratic and Republican presidents tend to decide cases somewhat differently.
SOURCE: *Robert A. Carp, Ronald Stidham, and Kenneth L. Manning,* Judicial Process in America, *6th ed. (Washington, D.C.: CQ Press, 2004), fig. 7-1.*

Independence of Judges

Given the use of political criteria in selecting judges, can judges be independent on the bench? Can they decide cases as they think the law requires? Or do they feel pressure to decide cases as presidents or senators want them to?

Because judges are not dependent on presidents for renomination or senators for reconfirmation, they can be independent to a great extent. When President Nixon claimed executive privilege to keep the Watergate tapes secret, three of his appointees joined the other justices in ruling against him.[59] When President Clinton asserted presidential immunity from Paula Jones's lawsuit charging sexual harassment, both of his appointees joined the Republican justices in deciding against him.[60]

After surveying the Warren and Burger Court decisions involving desegregation, obscenity, abortion, and criminal defendants' rights, one scholar observed, "Few American politicians even today would care to run on a platform of desegregation, pornography, abortion, and the 'coddling' of criminals"[61] (as the Courts' decisions were characterized by critics).

Presidents have scoffed at the notion that their appointees become their pawns. A study concluded that one-fourth of the justices deviated from their president's expectations.[62] Theodore Roosevelt placed Oliver Wendell Holmes on the Court, believing that Holmes shared his views on trusts. But Holmes voted against Roosevelt's position in an antitrust case, prompting Roosevelt to declare, "I could carve out of a banana a judge with more backbone than that!"[63] Holmes had ample backbone; he just didn't agree with Roosevelt's position in this case. Likewise, President Eisenhower placed Earl Warren on the Court, assuming that Warren was a moderate. But Warren turned out to be a liberal. Later Eisenhower said his appointment of Warren was "the biggest damn fool thing I ever did"[64] (although many legal scholars rank Warren as a great justice). President Truman concluded that "packing the Supreme Court simply can't be done. . . . I've tried it and it won't work. . . . Whenever you put a man on the Supreme Court he ceases to be your friend."[65]

Truman exaggerated, although some presidents have had trouble "packing" the courts. They have not been able to foresee the issues their appointees would face or the ways their appointees would change on the bench. (During Harry Blackmun's confirmation hearings, no senators asked about his views on abortion law, yet within six months *Roe* v. *Wade* would reach the Court, and Blackmun would author the controversial opinion.[66]) Nevertheless, presidents who have made a serious effort to find candidates with similar views usually have been able to.[67]

ACCESS TO THE COURTS

In our litigation-prone society, many individuals and groups want courts to resolve their disputes. Whether these individuals and groups get their "day in court" depends on their case, their wealth, and the court involved.

Courts hear two kinds of cases. **Criminal cases** are those in which governments prosecute persons for violating laws. **Civil cases** are those in which persons sue others for denying their rights and causing them harm. Criminal defendants, of course, must appear in court. Potential civil litigants, however, often cannot get access to court.

Wealth Discrimination in Access

Although the courts are supposed to be open to all, most individuals don't have enough money to hire an attorney and pay the costs necessary to pursue a case. Only corporations, wealthy individuals, or seriously injured victims suing corporations or wealthy individuals do. (Seriously injured victims with a strong case can obtain an attorney by agreeing to pay the attorney a sizable portion of what they win.) In addition, a small number of poor people supported by legal aid programs can pursue a case.

The primary expense is paying an attorney. New lawyers in law firms charge approximately $100 an hour; established partners may charge several times that.[68] Other expenses include various fees for filing the case, summoning the jurors, paying the witnesses, and also lost income from missed work due to numerous meetings with the attorney and hearings in court.

Even if individuals have enough money to initiate a suit, the disparity continues in court. Those with more money can develop a full case, whereas others must proceed with a skeletal case that is far less likely to persuade judges or jurors. Our legal system, according to one judge, "is divided into two separate and unequal systems of justice: one for the rich, in which the courts take limitless time to examine, ponder, consider, and deliberate over hundreds of thousands of bits of evidence and days of testimony, and hear elaborate, endless appeals and write countless learned opinions," and one for the nonrich, in which the courts provide "turnstile justice."[69] (During the week that one judge spent conducting the preliminary hearing to determine whether there was sufficient evidence to require O. J. Simpson to stand trial for murdering his ex-wife and her friend, other judges in Los Angeles disposed of 474 preliminary hearings for less wealthy defendants.) Consequently, many individuals are discouraged from pursuing a case in the first place.

Interest Group Help in Access

Interest groups, with greater resources than most individuals, help some individuals gain access to the courts by sponsoring and financing their cases. Of course, the groups don't act out of altruism; they choose the cases that will advance their goals. An attorney for the **American Civil Liberties Union (ACLU)**, which takes criminal cases to prod judges to protect constitutional rights, admitted that the defendants the ACLU represents "sometimes are pretty scurvy little

The newest justice, Elena Kagan, had never been a judge before, although she was the solicitor general—the government's lawyer at the Supreme Court—and before that the dean of Harvard's law school.

creatures, but what they are doesn't matter a whole hell of a lot. It's the principle that we're going to be able to use these people for that's important."[70]

Some liberal groups—especially civil liberties organizations such as the ACLU, civil rights organizations such as the National Association for the Advancement of Colored People (NAACP), environmental groups such as the Sierra Club, and consumer and safety groups such as Ralph Nader's organizations—use litigation as a primary tactic. Other groups use it as an occasional tactic. In the 1980s and 1990s, some conservative groups began to use litigation as aggressively as these liberal groups. The Rutherford Institute arose to help persons who claimed that their religious rights were infringed upon, representing children who were forbidden from reading the Bible on the school bus or praying in the school cafeteria. Today, the Alliance Defense Fund, which sponsors eighty to one hundred cases at a time, prods the courts to reflect conservative Christian values in disputes involving education, homosexuality, and embryonic stem cell research.[71]

Interest groups have become ubiquitous in the judicial process. About half of all Supreme Court cases involve a liberal or conservative interest group,[72] and many lower court cases do as well. Even so, interest groups can help only a handful of the individuals who lack the resources to finance their cases.

Proceeding through the Courts

Cases normally start in a district court. Individuals who lose have a right to have their case decided by one higher court to determine whether there was a miscarriage of justice. They normally appeal to a court of appeals. Individuals who lose at this level have no further right to have their case decided by another court, but they can appeal to the Supreme Court. However, the Court can exercise almost unlimited discretion

in choosing cases to review. No matter how important or urgent an issue seems, the Court doesn't have to hear it.

When the husband of Terri Schiavo, who was brain dead but physically alive in a persistent vegetative state, sought to have her feeding tube removed, her parents, with the help of pro-life groups, sued to take custody from her husband, then to maintain the feeding tube, and, once taken out, to reinsert it. They appealed to the Supreme Court six times. Although congressional leaders, thundering about federal judges, made her situation a political cause, the Supreme Court refused to hear the case each time it was appealed. Sen. Tom Coburn (R-Okla.) responded, "I don't want to impeach judges; I want to impale them."[73] Still, the Court refused to hear the case.

Litigants who appeal to the Supreme Court normally file a petition for a **writ of *certiorari*** ("made more certain" in Latin). The Court grants the writ—agrees to hear the case—if four of the nine justices vote to do so. The rationale for this "rule of four" is that a substantial number, though not necessarily a majority, of the justices should deem the case important enough to review. Generally, the Court agrees to review a case when the justices think an issue hasn't been resolved satisfactorily or consistently by the lower courts.

From eight to ten thousand petitions each year, the Court selects eighty or fewer to hear, thus exercising considerable discretion.[74] The oft-spoken threat "We're going to appeal all the way to the Supreme Court" is usually just bluster. Likewise, the notion that the Court is "the court of last resort" is misleading. Most cases never get beyond the district courts or courts of appeals.

That the Supreme Court grants so few writs means that the Court has tremendous power to determine which policies to review. It also means that the lower courts have considerable power because they serve as the court of last resort for most cases.

DECIDING CASES

In deciding cases, judges need to interpret statutes and the Constitution and determine whether to follow precedents. In the process, they exercise discretion and make law.

Interpreting Statutes

In deciding cases, judges start with **statutes**—laws passed by legislatures. Because these statutes are often ambiguous, judges need to interpret them in order to apply them, as you saw for the Lilly Ledbetter case.

For another example, Congress passed the **Americans with Disabilities Act** to protect people from discrimination in employment and public accommodations (businesses open to the public, such as stores, restaurants, hotels, and health care facilities). The act applies to people who have a "physical impairment" that "substantially limits" any of their "major life activities." The statute does not define these terms. Thus the courts have to do so, and in the process they determine the scope of the act.

When a dentist refused to fill a cavity for a woman with HIV, she sued, claiming discrimination under this act. The Supreme Court agreed by a 5–4 vote.[75] The majority concluded that HIV was a "physical impairment," although the woman was in the early stages and the disease didn't prevent her from performing any activity yet. The majority acknowledged that HIV would limit the "major life activity" of reproduction, because the disease could infect her fetus if she got pregnant. (Of course, HIV would also affect other important life activities as well.) The dissenters interpreted the statute to mean repetitive activities that are essential for daily existence rather than important activities that rarely occur in a person's life. Therefore, they denied that reproduction is a "major life activity." (None of this relates to dentistry, but the justices were defining the scope of the statute for future cases involving HIV as well as for this case.)

When a woman developed carpal tunnel syndrome on the assembly line at a manufacturing plant, she sued, claiming that the company didn't make the reasonable accommodation—give her a different job that didn't require repetitive manual labor—that was required under the act. She said her condition limited her "major life activities" of performing manual tasks at work and at home, including lifting, sweeping, and gardening; playing with her children; and driving long distances. The Court ruled that these aren't "major life activities,"[76] because they aren't of central importance to daily life, as seeing, hearing, and walking are.

Thus the Court had discretion. It interpreted the act broadly when it covered persons with HIV but narrowly when it refused to cover workers with less serious ailments.

Interpreting the Constitution

After interpreting statutes, judges determine whether the statutes are constitutional. Or if the cases involve actions of government officials rather than statutes, judges determine whether the actions are constitutional. For either, they need to interpret the Constitution.

Compared to constitutions of other countries, our Constitution is short and therefore ambiguous. It speaks in broad principles rather than in narrow details. The Fifth Amendment states that persons shall not be "deprived of life, liberty, or property without due process of law." The Fourteenth Amendment states that persons shall not be denied "the equal protection of the laws." What is "due process of law"? "Equal protection of the laws"? Generally, the former means that people should be treated fairly and the latter means that they should be treated equally. But what is fairly? Equally? These are broad principles that need to be interpreted in specific cases.

Sometimes the Constitution uses relative terms. The Fourth Amendment provides that persons shall be "secure . . . against unreasonable searches and seizures." What are "unreasonable" searches and seizures? Other times, the Constitution uses absolute terms, which appear more clear-cut but aren't. 🔔 The First Amendment provides that there shall be "no law . . . abridging the freedom of speech." Does "no law" mean literally no law? Then what about a law that punishes someone for falsely shouting "Fire!" in a crowded theater and causing a stampede that injures some patrons? Whether relative or absolute, the language needs to be interpreted in specific cases.

Occasionally, politicians, following the lead of Richard Nixon, assert that judges ought to be "strict constructionists," that they ought to interpret the Constitution "strictly." This is nonsense. Judges can't interpret ambiguous language strictly. When politicians or commentators use this phrase, they're trying to persuade voters that judges from the other party are deciding cases incorrectly, as though they are departing from some clear and fixed standard.

When judges interpret the Constitution, they exercise discretion. As former Chief Justice Charles Evans Hughes candidly acknowledged, "We are under a constitution, but the Constitution is what the Supreme Court says it is."[77]

The Fourth Amendment prohibits "unreasonable" searches and seizures, but the courts have to define which ones are reasonable and which ones are unreasonable. The Supreme Court has established guidelines for stops and searches of drivers and cars.

Restraint and Activism

All judges exercise discretion, but not all engage in policy making to the same extent. Some, classified as restrained, are less willing to declare laws or actions of government officials unconstitutional, whereas others, classified as activist, are more willing to do so.

Restrained judges believe that the judiciary is the least democratic branch because federal judges are appointed for life rather than elected and reelected. Consequently, they should defer to the other branches, whose officials are elected. That is, they should accept the laws or actions of the other branches rather than substitute their own views. They should be wary of "government by judiciary." They should recognize, Justice Harlan Stone said, that "courts are not the only agency of government that must be presumed

behind the scenes

Do Personal Preferences Matter?

The Supreme Court ruled that Michigan and New York can't prohibit out-of-state wineries from shipping wine to customers in their states while allowing in-state wineries to ship wine to residents in their states.[1] That is, the states can't discriminate against out-of-state wineries, which these states did to boost the business of their in-state wineries. The ruling means that wine connoisseurs can order fine wine from wineries throughout the United States.

The question was whether the commerce clause (Art. I, Sec. 8), which prohibits states from interfering with interstate commerce, or the Twenty-first Amendment, which repealed Prohibition and which allows states to regulate liquor, should prevail. A plausible argument could be made either way.

The majority emphasized the commerce clause, which opened the states to shipments from more wineries, rather than the Twenty-first Amendment. One insider observed that the five justices in the majority (Breyer, Ginsburg, Kennedy, Scalia, and Souter) happened to be the wine aficionados on the Court. Justice Breyer called the majority "the rosy-cheeked caucus."[2]

[1] *Granholm v. Heald*, 161 L.Ed.2d 796 (2005).
[2] Jeffrey Toobin, *The Nine: Inside the Secret World of the Supreme Court* (New York: Doubleday, 2007), 306.

to have the capacity to govern. For the removal of unwise laws from the statute books, appeal lies not to the courts, but to the ballot and the processes of democratic government."[78]

Restrained judges also maintain that the power to declare laws unconstitutional is more effective if it is used sparingly. Justice Louis Brandeis concluded that "the most important thing we do is not doing."[79] That is, the most important thing judges do is declare laws constitutional and thereby build up political capital for the occasional times that they declare laws unconstitutional.

Ultimately, restrained judges contend that showing appropriate deference and following proper procedures are more important than reaching desired results. When a friend taking leave of Justice Oliver Wendell Holmes one morning said, "Well, Mr. Justice, I hope you do justice today," Holmes replied, "My job is not to do justice but to follow the law."[80] Justice Harry Blackmun reflected this view in a capital punishment case:

> I yield to no one in the depth of my distaste, antipathy, and, indeed, abhorrence for the death penalty, with all its aspects of physical distress and fear and of moral judgment exercised by finite minds. That distaste is buttressed by a belief that capital punishment serves no useful purpose that can be demonstrated. For me, it violates childhood's training and life's experiences, and is not compatible with the philosophical convictions I have been able to develop. It is antagonistic to any sense of "reverence for life." Were I a legislator, I would vote against the death penalty.

But as a judge, he voted for it in 1972.[81]

Activist judges are less concerned with showing appropriate deference and following proper procedures. Some are more concerned with the results; others are more outraged at injustice. Chief Justice Earl Warren said that the

courts' responsibility was "to see if justice truly has been done." He asked lawyers who emphasized technical procedures during oral arguments, "Yes, yes, yes, but is it right? Is it good?"[82]

Activist judges don't believe that the judiciary is the least democratic branch. Warren, who had served as governor of California, saw that the legislators, though elected, were often the captives of special interests. As a result of these attitudes, activist judges have a flexible view of separation of powers. District court judge Frank Johnson, who issued sweeping orders for Alabama's prisons and mental hospitals, replied to critics, "I didn't ask for any of these cases. In an ideal society, all of these . . . decisions should be made by those to whom we have entrusted these responsibilities. But when governmental institutions fail to make these . . . decisions in a manner which comports with the Constitution, the federal courts have a duty to remedy the violation."[83]

Activist judges don't believe that the power to declare laws unconstitutional is more effective if it is used sparingly. Rather, they claim that the power is enhanced if it is used frequently—essentially, they urge their colleagues to "use it or lose it"—because the public gets accustomed to it.

Thus judicial restraint and judicial activism are belief systems and role concepts that people think judges should follow when they decide cases. Some judges tend to be restrained, whereas others tend to be activist; most fall somewhere in between.

Both conservatives and liberals have practiced both restraint and activism depending on the political climate at the time. In the late nineteenth and early twentieth centuries, the Court was conservative and activist, striking down regulations on business. After its switch in the 1930s, the Court was liberal and restrained, upholding regulations on business. Then in the 1950s and 1960s, the Court was liberal and activist, striking down restrictions on individual rights. Today the Court tends to be conservative and activist. (See the box "Who Are the Activists?")

Although restraint and activism are useful concepts, we shouldn't make too much of them. It's usually more important to know whether a judge is conservative or liberal than whether the judge purports to be restrained or activist. Political science research shows that justices' votes reflect their ideology: conservative justices vote for the conservative position, and liberal justices vote for the liberal position in most cases. When justices claim to be restrained, their decision, allowing a particular law or policy to continue, produces the conservative or liberal outcome they prefer.[84] Thus some political scientists conclude that "judicial restraint" is little more than "a cloak for the justices' policy preferences."[85] It enables them to proclaim their "restraint" while actually voting on the basis of their ideology—without ever admitting this to the public.

We should be skeptical when we hear judges or politicians using these terms, whether touting their "restraint" to pacify the public or deriding opponents' "activism" to inflame the public.

Following Precedents

In interpreting statutes and the Constitution, judges are expected to follow precedents established by their court or higher courts in previous cases. This is the rule of *stare decisis* ("stand by what has been decided" in Latin).

WHO ARE THE ACTIVISTS?

Ever since the 1950s and 1960s, when the Supreme Court under Chief Justice Earl Warren was a liberal court and an activist court, many people have assumed that liberals are activist judges and conservatives are restrained judges. This is not necessarily true. Liberals may be activist or restrained, just as conservatives may be restrained or activist.

A study of the last eleven terms, from 1994 through 2005, of the Supreme Court under Chief Justice William Rehnquist confirms this conclusion.[1] The study shows that the conservative justices (Thomas, Kennedy, Scalia, Rehnquist, and O'Connor) voted to declare congressional statutes unconstitutional far more often than the liberal justices (Breyer, Stevens, Ginsburg, and Souter) did.[2] Thus the conservative justices were the most activist toward federal laws. But the liberal justices were the most activist toward state laws. The liberal justices voted to declare state statutes unconstitutional far more often than the conservative justices did. The study also incorporates votes to overturn precedents as a measure of judicial activism. Examining these votes shows that the conservatives were more activist than the liberals were.

When all three measures are totaled, the study reveals that Justice Thomas—the most conservative member of this Court—was the most activist justice. Other conservatives (Kennedy, Scalia, and O'Connor) were among the most activist justices. The liberals (Souter, Stevens, Breyer, and Ginsburg) were among the most restrained justices. Only Chief Justice Rehnquist, who was both conservative and restrained, fit the (inaccurate) stereotype that most people hold.

Justice	Votes to Declare a Congressional Statute Unconstitutional	Votes to Declare a State Statute Unconstitutional	Votes to Overturn a Precedent	Total
Thomas	34	27	23	84
Kennedy	31	36	16	83
Scalia	30	27	19	76
O'Connor	24	39	12	75
Souter	21	45	7	73
Stevens	17	46	9	72
Breyer	14	44	10	68
Ginsburg	17	41	8	66
Rehnquist	25	21	12	58

[1] The membership of the Court during these years remained unchanged, so these justices heard the same cases.
[2] This group of conservatives includes justices who are moderately conservative and others who are very conservative. This group of "liberals" includes justices who are more liberal than the conservatives but who are considered moderate or moderately liberal.
SOURCE: Lori A. Ringhand, "Judicial Activism: an Empirical Examination of Voting Behavior on the Rehnquist Natural Court," *Constitutional Commentary,* 24 (2007), 43–67.

Justice Clarence Thomas shares a laugh with his clerks in his chambers.

Stare decisis provides stability in the law. If different judges decided similar cases in different ways, the law would be unpredictable, even chaotic. "*Stare decisis*," Justice Brandeis said, "is usually the wise policy; because in most matters it is more important that the applicable rule of law be settled than that it be settled right."[86] *Stare decisis* also promotes equality in the law. If different judges decided similar cases in different ways, the courts would appear discriminatory toward some litigants.

In 1962, the Supreme Court held unconstitutional a New York law requiring public school students to recite a nondenominational prayer every day. This ruling became a precedent.[87] The following year, the Court held unconstitutional a Baltimore school policy requiring students to recite Bible verses.[88] The Court followed the precedent it had set the year before. In 1980, the Court held unconstitutional a Tennessee law forcing public schools to post the Ten Commandments in all classrooms.[89] Although this law differed from the previous ones in that it did not require recitation, the majority concluded that it reflected the same goal—to use the public schools to promote the Christian religion—so it violated the same principle—separation of church and state. In 1992, the Court ruled that clergy cannot offer prayers at graduation ceremonies for public schools.[90] Although this situation, too, differed from the previous ones in that it did not occur every day at school, the majority reasoned that it, too, reflected the same goal and violated the same principle. Finally, in 2000, the Court ruled that schools cannot use, or allow clergy or students to use, the public address system to offer prayers before high school football games.[91] For almost four decades, the Court followed the precedent it originally set when it initially addressed this issue.

Stare decisis is considered so important that judges sometimes follow precedents that they wouldn't have agreed to establish originally, even precedents that they don't agree with still. In *Roe* v. *Wade* in 1973, the Supreme Court established a right to abortion.[92] After five straight Republican appointments to the Court since the ruling, it appeared that a majority on the Court might be willing to reverse the ruling. Pennsylvania passed a law denying a right to abortion—essentially inviting the justices to reverse the ruling. In 1992, the law reached the Court. A bare majority overturned the state law and upheld the Court's precedent.[93] Three justices in the majority said they disagreed with the precedent but felt obligated to follow it. One of these, Justice Souter, wrote,

For two decades of economic and social developments, people have organized intimate relationships and made choices . . . in reliance on the availability of abortion in the event that contraception should fail. The ability of women to participate equally in the economic and social life of the nation has been facilitated by their ability to control their reproductive lives. . . . [O]nly the most convincing justification . . . could suffice to demonstrate that a later decision overruling the first was anything but a surrender to political pressure. . . . So to overrule under fire in the absence of the most compelling reason to re-examine a watershed decision would subvert the Court's legitimacy beyond any serious question.

Thus the right to abortion remained only because three justices who disagreed with it decided to follow the precedent rather than their preference. (Of course, not all justices feel equally obligated to follow precedents, as shown in the box "Who Are the Activists?")

Making Law

Many judges deny that they make law. They say that it is already there, that they merely "find" it or, with their education and experience, "interpret" it. They imply that they use a mechanical process. Justice Owen Roberts wrote for the majority that struck down a New Deal act in 1936:

> It is sometimes said that the Court assumes a power to over-rule . . . the people's representatives. This is a misconception. The Constitution is the supreme law of the land. . . . All legislation must conform to the principles it lays down. When an act of Congress is appropriately challenged in the courts as not conforming to the constitutional mandate, the judicial branch of government has only one duty—to lay . . . the Constitution . . . beside the statute . . . and to decide whether the latter squares with the former.[94]

In other words, the Constitution itself dictates the decision.

However, by now it should be apparent that judges do not use a mechanical process. They *do* exercise discretion, and they *do* make law—when they interpret statutes, when they interpret the Constitution, and when they determine which precedents to follow or disregard.[95] In doing so, they reflect their own political preferences. As Justice Benjamin Cardozo said, "We may try to see things as objectively as we please. Nonetheless, we can never see them with any eyes except our own."[96] They do not shed their attitudes, even their prejudices, when they don their robes.

But to say that judges make law is not to say that they make law as legislators do. Judges make law less directly, in the process of resolving disputes brought to them. They usually make it by telling governments what they cannot do, rather than what they must do and how they must do it. And judges make law less freely. They start not with clean slates, but with established principles embodied in statutes, the Constitution, and precedents. They are expected to follow these principles. If they deviate from them, they are expected to explain their reasons, and they are subjected to scrutiny by the legal profession.

DEMOCRACY?

Once we realize that judges make law as they decide cases, do we have to alter our conception of democratic government?

Deciding Cases at the Supreme Court

The Supreme Court's term runs from October through June. Early in the term, the justices decide which cases to hear, and by the end of the term, they decide how to resolve those cases.

After the Court agrees to hear a case, litigants submit written arguments. These "briefs" identify the issues and marshal the evidence—statutes, constitutional provisions, and precedents—for their side. (The word *briefs* is a misnomer, as some run to more than one hundred pages.)

Often interest groups and governments, whether federal, state, or local, submit briefs to support one side. These **friend of the court briefs** present additional evidence or perspectives not included in the litigants' briefs. Major cases can prompt many briefs. A pair of affirmative-action cases from the University of Michigan in 2003 had a record 102 briefs.[97]

Several weeks after receiving the briefs, the Court holds oral arguments. The justices gather in the robing room, put on their black robes, and file into the courtroom, taking their places at the half-hexagon bench. The chief justice sits in the center, with the associate justices extending out in order of seniority. The crier gavels the courtroom to attention and announces:

> The Honorable, the Chief Justice and Associate Justices of the Supreme Court of the United States! Oyez, oyez, oyez! [Give ear, give ear, give ear!] All persons having business before the Honorable, the Supreme Court of the United States are admonished to draw near and give attention, for the Court is now sitting. God save the United States and this Honorable Court.

The chief justice calls the case. The lawyers present their arguments, although the justices interrupt with questions whenever they want. When Thurgood Marshall, as chief counsel for the NAACP before becoming a justice, argued one school desegregation case, he was interrupted 127 times. The justices ask about the facts of the case: "What happened when the defendant . . . ?" They ask about relevant precedents that appear to support or rebut the lawyers' arguments: "Can you distinguish this case from . . . ?" They ask about hypothetical scenarios: "What if the police officer . . . ?" These questions help the justices determine what is at stake, how a ruling would relate to existing doctrine, and how a ruling might govern future situations. They are experienced at pinning lawyers down. Chief Justice Rehnquist, who was affable toward his colleagues, was tough on the lawyers appearing before him. When asked whether the lawyers were nervous, he replied, "I assume they're all nervous—they should be."[98] Occasionally, one faints on the spot.

In the process of questioning the lawyers, the justices are also trying to persuade each other. Their questions, while directed at the lawyers, are designed to reveal the weakness of the position they oppose and to convey this weakness to their colleagues.[99]

On the current Court, Justice Antonin Scalia is an aggressive interrogator; Justice Thomas, on the other hand, rarely asks any question. In her first term, Justice Sotomayor was the "most exuberant rookie interrogator" since Scalia's first term. "Like a transfer student who picks a fight on the first day of school, Sotomayor seemed to be showing that she was not to be taken—as she variously had been, in the months leading up to her debut—for a pushover, a token, or a slouch. She would not be cowed by the pomp of the setting—the velvet draperies, the spittoons—nor would she be inhibited by the Court's finicky codes of seniority and decorum."[100]

The chief justice allots a half hour per side. When time expires, a red light flashes on the lectern, and the chief

Justice Sonya Sotomayor, appointed by President Obama, is the first Latino on the Supreme Court.

justice halts any lawyer who continues. Rehnquist, who valued efficiency and punctuality, cut lawyers off in mid-sentence when their time was up.

The oral arguments identify and clarify the major points of the case for any justices who did not read the briefs, and they assess the potential impact of the possible rulings. The oral arguments also serve as a symbol: they give the litigants a chance to be heard in open court, which encourages the litigants to feel that the eventual ruling is legitimate. However, the oral arguments rarely sway the justices, except occasionally when a lawyer for one side is especially effective or ineffective.

As a lawyer before becoming chief justice, John Roberts argued thirty-nine cases at the Court. He was considered especially effective.[101]

After the lawyers have presented the case, the Court holds Friday conferences to make tentative decisions and assign the opinions. The decision affirms or reverses the lower court's decision. The opinion explains why. It expresses principles of law and establishes precedents for the future, thus telling lower courts how to resolve similar cases.

A portrait of Chief Justice John Marshall presides over the conference. To ensure secrecy, no one is present but the justices. They begin with handshakes. (During his tenure, Chief Justice Marshall suggested that they begin with a drink whenever it was rainy. But even when it was sunny, Marshall sometimes announced, "Our jurisdiction extends over so large a territory that the doctrine of chances makes it certain that it must be raining somewhere."[102] Perhaps this accounts for his extraordinary success in persuading his colleagues to adopt his views.) Then the justices get down to business. The chief justice initiates the discussion of the case. He indicates what the issues are and how they ought to be decided, and he casts a vote. The associate justices follow in order of seniority. Although the conference traditionally featured give-and-take among the justices, discussion became perfunctory under Rehnquist, and the conference became a series of quick votes.[103]

The Court reaches a tentative decision based on these votes. If the chief justice is in the majority, he assigns the writing of the opinion to himself or another justice. If he is not in the majority, the most senior associate justice in the majority assigns it. This custom reveals the chief justice's power. Although his vote counts the same as each associate justice's vote, his authority to assign the opinion can determine what the opinion says. He knows that certain colleagues will use strong language and lay down broad principles, whereas others will use guarded language and hew closely to specific facts in the case.

Before Marshall became chief justice, each justice wrote his own opinion. But Marshall realized that one opinion from the Court would carry more weight. He often convinced the other justices to forsake their opinions for his. As a result, he wrote almost half of the more than eleven hundred opinions the Court handed down during his thirty-four years. Recent chief justices have assigned most opinions—82 to 86 percent—but have written just slightly more than their share—12 to 14 percent.[104]

After the conference, the Court produces the opinion. This is the most time-consuming stage in the process. After Justice Brandeis died, researchers found in his files the thirty-seventh draft of an opinion he had written but still had not been satisfied with.

Because the justices are free to change their vote anytime until the decision is announced, the justice assigned the opinion tries to write it to command support of the justices in the original majority and possibly even some in the original minority. The writer circulates the draft among the others, who suggest revisions. The writer circulates more drafts. These go back and forth as the justices attempt to persuade or nudge their colleagues toward their position.

Unlike legislators, however, the justices don't engage in horse-trading—if you join me on this, I'll join you on that. According to one justice, there's "[n]one of that, zero. The coalitions float. Each . . . case is a new day."[105]

Sometimes the outcome changes between the tentative vote in the conference and the final vote in the decision. According to Justice Blackmun's notes, eleven times during his last three years on the Rehnquist Court, one or more justices switched sides to fashion a new majority from the original minority. In the case involving graduation prayers, Justice Anthony Kennedy was writing the **majority opinion** to allow such prayers, but he was unable to persuade himself. He abandoned the majority and joined the minority, thus making it the eventual majority.[106]

These inner workings underscore the politicking among the justices. Justice William Brennan, a liberal activist on the Warren and Burger Courts, was a gregarious and charming Irish American who was well liked by his colleagues. After drafting an opinion, he sent his clerks to other justices' clerks to learn whether their justices had any objections. Then he tried to redraft it to satisfy them. If they still had qualms, he went to their offices and tried to persuade them. If necessary, he compromised. He didn't want "to be 100 percent principled and lose by one vote," a law professor observed.[107] Brennan was so adept at persuasion that some scholars consider him "the best coalition builder ever to sit on the Supreme Court."[108] In fact, some say the Warren and Burger Courts should have been called the Brennan Court.

Justice Scalia, a conservative activist on the Rehnquist and Roberts Courts, is a brilliant and gregarious Italian American who, when appointed by President Reagan, was expected to dominate his colleagues and become the leader of the Court. Yet he has not fulfilled this expectation. He has been brash and imprudent, appearing to take more pleasure in insulting his colleagues than in persuading them.[109] In a case in which Justice O'Connor, who also was conservative but more cautious, did not want to go as far in limiting abortion rights as he did, Scalia wrote that her arguments "cannot be taken seriously."[110] In another case in which Chief Justice Rehnquist, who usually voted with Scalia, voted opposite him, Scalia wrote that his arguments were "implausible" and suggested that any lawyer who advised his client as Rehnquist urged should be "disbarred."[111] As a result, Scalia has not been as effective in luring moderates as Brennan was or in forging a consensus among conservatives as Brennan was among liberals.

Leadership, by someone, is necessary with nine strong-willed individuals, each of whom has risen to the top of the legal profession and each of whom is essentially operating

Ruth Bader Ginsburg, appointed by President Clinton, was the second female justice. Although she tied for first place in her graduating class from Columbia Law School in 1959, she was turned down for a clerkship by Justice Felix Frankfurter and for law jobs with New York City firms. As a Jew, a woman, and a mother with young children, she had three liabilities at that time. Instead, she taught law and served as an attorney with the ACLU. In the 1970s, she argued six sex discrimination cases before the Supreme Court, winning five.

a one-person law firm. (See the box "Anti-Semitism on the Bench.") Sometimes the chief justice becomes the informal leader. Marshall set the standard; Warren and Rehnquist were also effective leaders. Burger, however, possessed neither the interpersonal skills nor the intellectual firepower to earn the respect of his colleagues. Some observers think Roberts has the potential to become an effective leader.

If the opinion does not command the support of some justices in the original majority, they write a **concurring opinion**, which indicates that they agree with the decision but not the reasons for it. Meanwhile, the justices in the minority write a **dissenting opinion**, which indicates that they do not agree even with the decision. Both concurring and dissenting opinions weaken the force of the majority opinion. They question its validity, and they suggest that at a different time with different justices, there might be a different ruling. Chief Justice Hughes used to say that a dissenting opinion is "an appeal to the brooding spirit of the law, to the intelligence of a future day."[112]

Unlike the high courts of many other countries, which don't report any dissents, the Supreme Court of the United States routinely does, and the American people usually accept the existence of such disagreements.[113] In recent terms, about 60 percent of the Court's cases have had dissents.[114] But too many dissents indicate a fractious Court. One-third of the Rehnquist Court's cases were decided by a 5–4 vote in 2001, possibly the highest proportion ever.[115]

Finally, the print shop in the Court's basement prints the opinions, thus preventing the leaks that might occur if the opinions were printed elsewhere, and the Court announces its decisions and distributes the opinions in public session.

EXERCISING POWER

The Founders expected the judiciary to be the weakest branch of government. In the *Federalist Papers,* Alexander Hamilton wrote that Congress would have power to pass the laws and appropriate the money; the president would have power to execute the laws; but the courts would have "merely judgment"—that is, only power to resolve disputes in cases brought to them. In doing so, they would exercise "neither force nor will." They would not have any means to enforce decisions, and they would not use their own values to decide cases. They would simply apply the Constitution and laws as written. Consequently, the judiciary would be the "least dangerous" branch.[116]

This prediction was accurate for the early years of the Republic. The federal courts seemed inconsequential. The Supreme Court was held in such low esteem that some distinguished men refused to accept appointment to it; others accepted appointment but refused to attend sessions. The first chief justice thought the Court was "inauspicious,"[117] without enough "weight and dignity" to play an important

american*diversity

Anti-Semitism on the Bench

President Woodrow Wilson admired James McReynolds's zeal as a trust-busting attorney, so Wilson chose McReynolds as his attorney general. But after brief service in this post, McReynolds'"violent temper and abusive nature" made Wilson anxious to get rid of him, so Wilson appointed him to the Supreme Court in 1914,[1] where McReynolds exercised his violent temper and abusive nature for twenty-seven years. He was called "the rudest man in Washington."[2]

The product of a severe upbringing along the Kentucky-Tennessee border, McReynolds was especially prejudiced toward Jews. When Louis Brandeis, the first Jew on the Supreme Court, was appointed, McReynolds refused to speak to him for three years. And for the annual photograph of the justices one year, McReynolds refused to sit next to Brandeis, where he was assigned according to seniority, and the chief justice was forced to cancel the photo shoot. McReynolds also refused to join the other justices at a ceremonial event in Philadelphia because, he wrote the chief justice, "I am not always to be found when there is a Hebrew abroad." For the same reason, the chief justice had to divide the justices into two groups when he invited them to dinner. Years later, when Benjamin Cardozo, the second Jew, was sworn in, McReynolds conspicuously read a newspaper while muttering, "another one." When Felix Frankfurter, the third Jew, was appointed, McReynolds exclaimed, "My God, another Jew on the Court!" and refused to attend Frankfurter's robing ceremony.[3]

McReynolds didn't want any Jews to visit his Washington apartment, and he didn't even want his aides to fraternize with the aides of the Jewish justices.[4] He was so cantankerous and intemperate that Justice William Douglas named a card game after him, called "Son of a Bitch."[5]

It wasn't only McReynolds' sour personality that dismayed Washingtonians, but also his evident shift from a progressive attorney for the government to a reactionary member of the Court. McReynolds became one of the "Four Horsemen" who, when they were able to obtain the vote of another justice, struck down government regulations on businesses and stymied President Franklin Roosevelt's New Deal program for years.[6]

Yet, after McReynolds retired from the Court, European newspapers reported that this lifelong bachelor was financially supporting thirty-three English children left homeless by the German blitz during World War II. And when he died, he willed most of his estate to charities for needy children.

Nonetheless, based on his jurisprudence and his personality, McReynolds has gone down in history as perhaps the worst justice ever to sit on the Supreme Court.[7]

[1] Henry J. Abraham, *Justices and Presidents: A Political History of Appointments to the Supreme Court*, 2nd ed. (New York: Oxford University, 1985), 175.
[2] Dennis J. Hutchinson and David J. Garrow, eds., *The Forgotten Memoir of John Knox: A Year in the Life of a Supreme Court Clerk in FDR's Washington* (Chicago: University of Chicago, 2002), xix.
[3] Abraham, *Justices and Presidents*, 176.
[4] Hutchinson and Garrow, *Forgotten Memoir*, 36–37.
[5] Ibid., 177.
[6] The other three "Horsemen" were Justices Butler, Sutherland, and Van Devanter.
[7] Abraham, *Justices and Presidents*, 178, 377–379.

---

role.[118] So he resigned to be governor of New York. The second chief justice resigned to be envoy to France.

When the nation's capital was moved to Washington, D.C., in 1801, new homes were built for Congress and the president but not for the Supreme Court. Planners considered the Court too insignificant for more than a small room in the Capitol. But the Court couldn't even keep this room. For decades, it would be shunted from one location to another, from the marshal's office to the clerk's office, from the clerk's home to the Capitol's cellar—a dark and damp chamber in which visitors joked that Lady Justice wouldn't need to wear a blindfold because she couldn't see anyway—and from one committee room to another.[119] It wouldn't get its own building until 1935.

However, the status of the Court began to change after the appointment of the fourth chief justice, John Marshall. Under his leadership, the Court began to develop "weight and dignity" and to play an important role in government. The use of judicial review by the courts and the exercise of political checks against the courts show the extent of their power.

Use of Judicial Review

We'll examine two eras—the Founding era and the modern era—to see how the Court has used judicial review.

The Founding Era

In the Founding era, the **Marshall Court** established judicial review and national supremacy.

Establishing judicial review The authority to declare laws or actions of government officials unconstitutional is called **judicial review**. The Constitution doesn't mention judicial review. Although the idea was proposed at

Chief Justice John Marshall *(right)* swears in President Andrew Jackson in 1829. Although Marshall's party, the Federalists, had dissolved, Marshall remained as chief justice, serving for thirty-four years.

the Constitutional Convention, it was strongly opposed by some delegates who feared that it would strengthen the federal courts too much and, ultimately, weaken the state governments. The delegates who favored judicial review didn't press for its inclusion because they worried that doing so might jeopardize the Constitution's ratification.[120]

Nevertheless, the Supreme Court claimed the authority of judicial review in the case of **Marbury v. Madison** in 1803.[121] The dispute originated in 1800, when the Federalist president, John Adams, was defeated in his bid for reelection by Thomas Jefferson and many Federalist members of Congress were defeated by Jeffersonians. With both the presidency and Congress lost, the Federalists tried to maintain control of the judiciary. The lame-duck president and lame-duck Congress added more judgeships, most of which were unnecessary. (Forty-two were for justices of the peace for the District of Columbia, which was a sparsely populated swamp.) They hoped to fill these positions with loyal Federalists before the new president and new Congress took over.

In addition, Adams named his secretary of state, John Marshall, to be chief justice. At the time, Marshall was still secretary of state and responsible for delivering the commissions to the new appointees. But he ran out of time, failing to deliver four commissions for District of Columbia justices of the peace. He assumed that his successor would deliver them. But Jefferson, angry at the Federalists' efforts to pack the judiciary, told his secretary of state, James Madison, not to deliver the commissions.[122] Without the signed commissions, the appointees could not prove that they had in fact been appointed.[123]

William Marbury and the three other appointees petitioned the Supreme Court for a writ of *mandamus*

("we command" in Latin), an order that forces government officials to do something they have a duty to do. In this case, it would force Madison to deliver the commissions.

As chief justice, Marshall was in a position to rule on his administration's efforts to appoint these judges. Today this would be considered a conflict of interest, and he would be expected to disqualify himself. But at the time, people were not as troubled by such conflicts.

Marshall could issue the writ, but Jefferson would tell Madison to disobey it, and the Court would be powerless to enforce it. Or Marshall could decline to issue the writ, and the Court would appear powerless to issue it. Either way, the Court would reflect weakness rather than project strength.

Marshall shrewdly found a way out of the dilemma. He interpreted a provision of a congressional statute in a questionable way and then a provision of the Constitution in a questionable way as well.[124] As a result, he could claim that the statute violated the Constitution. Therefore, the statute was unconstitutional, and the Court couldn't order the administration to give the commissions. Thus Marshall exercised judicial review. He wrote, in a statement that would be repeated by courts for years to come, "It is emphatically the province and duty of the judicial department to say what the law is."

Marshall sacrificed the commissions—he couldn't have gotten them anyway—and established the power of judicial review instead. In doing so, with one hand he gave the

This portrait of William Marbury is the only portrait of a litigant owned by the Supreme Court Historical Society, testifying to the importance of the case of *Marbury v. Madison*.

Jeffersonians what they wanted—permission not to deliver the commissions—while with the other he gave the Federalists something much greater—judicial review. And all along he claimed he did what the Constitution required him to do.

Jefferson saw through this. He said the Constitution, in Marshall's hands, was "a thing of putty,"[125] adding that Marshall's arguments were "twistifications." But the decision didn't require Jefferson to do anything, so he couldn't do anything but protest. Most of Jefferson's followers were satisfied with the result. They weren't upset that the Court had invalidated a Federalist law, even though it had established judicial review to do so.

Of course, they were shortsighted because this decision laid the cornerstone for a strong judiciary. A case that began as a "trivial squabble over a few petty political plums"[126] became perhaps the most important case the Court has ever decided.

Establishing national supremacy   After *Marbury,* the Marshall Court declared numerous state laws unconstitutional.[127] These decisions solidified the authority of judicial review and symbolized the supremacy of the national government over the state governments.

The Court also advanced the supremacy of the national government by broadly construing congressional power. In ***McCulloch* v. *Maryland***, discussed in Chapter 2, the Court interpreted the **necessary and proper clause** to allow Congress to legislate in many matters not mentioned in the Constitution and not anticipated by the Founders.[128]

In the Founding era, the Court laid the foundation for judicial review and national supremacy. Of course, it would take the Civil War to resolve the conflict between the nation and the states and to enable the Court to build upon this foundation.

Now let's leap forward to the modern era, where we'll see how the Court has used judicial review and national supremacy to grant civil liberties and civil rights.

The Modern Era

The modern era for the Supreme Court began when President Dwight Eisenhower, fulfilling a campaign pledge to a presidential rival, Earl Warren, appointed him chief justice. In the 1950s and 1960s, the **Warren Court** decided many cases involving civil liberties and civil rights that pitted individuals against the government. Often they pitted minority individuals—whether a racial minority, a political minority, or a religious minority—against the majority of the public, whose views were reflected in government policy.

Historically, the courts had paid little attention to civil liberties and civil rights, allowing the government to ignore these constitutional rights. But the Warren Court reversed this lax attitude. It completely replaced traditional legal doctrine involving racial segregation, legislative reapportionment, criminal defendants' rights, libel, obscenity, and religion. It also modified traditional legal doctrine involving political speech. In the process, it held many laws, especially state laws, unconstitutional. The Warren Court was more activist in civil liberties and civil rights cases than any Supreme Court had ever been (see Figure 3).

The Warren Court sympathized with powerless groups and unpopular individuals when they challenged government policies. Thus the most elite institution in our government used its power to benefit many nonelites in our society. In its sympathies, the Warren Court differed sharply from previous Courts, which typically favored the haves over the have-nots and the efforts to preserve the status quo over the struggles to change it.[129]

The Warren Court's decisions brought about a conservative backlash.[130] President Richard Nixon vowed to change the Court's direction, and after Earl Warren retired Nixon appointed Warren Burger to be chief justice. Then Nixon and his former vice president, President Gerald Ford, appointed four more justices as vacancies occurred, seeking to slow, halt, or even reverse the Court's liberal doctrine. They expected the **Burger Court** to bring about a "constitutional counterrevolution."

But the Burger Court in the 1970s and 1980s did not. Although it eroded some liberal doctrine,[131] it left most intact. And it initiated new liberal doctrine in two areas where the Warren Court had been silent—sexual discrimination and abortion. Although it was not as committed to civil liberties and civil rights as the Warren Court, the Burger Court was more committed to them than any earlier Court.

President Ronald Reagan and his former vice president, George H. W. Bush, also sought to reverse the Court's liberal doctrine. When Burger retired, Reagan elevated

Chief Justice Earl Warren, flanked by Justices Hugo Black *(left)* and William O. Douglas.

© Dennis Brack/Black Star

Figure 3 | Laws Regulating Economic Activity and Restricting Civil Liberties and Rights Declared Unconstitutional by the Supreme Court since 1900

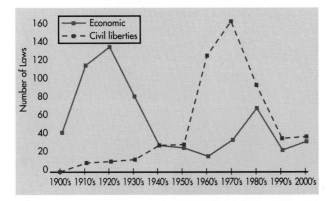

The Supreme Court was nearly as activist in striking down laws in the 1910s, 1920s, and 1930s as it was in the 1950s, 1960s, and 1970s. But in the former years, it was activist in economic cases (usually those involving government regulation of business), whereas in the latter years, it was activist in civil liberties and civil rights cases.
SOURCE: *Lawrence Baum,* The Supreme Court, *9th ed. (Washington, D.C.: CQ Press, 2007), 176.*

William Rehnquist, the most conservative associate justice, to be chief justice. Then Reagan and Bush appointed five more conservatives as vacancies occurred. By this time, Republican presidents had named ten justices in a row.

President Bill Clinton's election led to the first Democratic justices since 1967. Although these two moderate liberals (Breyer and Ginsburg) slowed any further swing to the right, the conservative justices controlled the **Rehnquist Court** in the 1980s, 1990s, and early 2000s. But conflicts among the conservatives splintered their bloc. Some were bold, eager to sweep away liberal precedents and substitute conservative principles. Others were cautious, willing to uphold liberal precedents they would not have agreed to set in the first place and inclined to decide cases on narrow bases rather than on broad principles. In some terms, the former group dominated, but in other terms the latter group dominated.[132] Overall, the Rehnquist Court, though markedly more conservative than the Burger Court,[133] did not bring about a "constitutional counterrevolution" either.

The Rehnquist Court also practiced judicial activism, though from the right rather than from the left. For example, it struck down laws implementing gun registration, affirmative action, legislative districts that help racial minorities elect their candidates, and governmental policies that help religious minorities practice their religion. It also invalidated a series of congressional laws regulating the states. In eight of the last years of the Rehnquist Court, the justices invalidated thirty-three federal laws, the highest annual average ever.[134]

In ***Bush v. Gore***, which arose from the disputed presidential election of 2000, the conservative majority deliberately intervened—essentially, picked the president—even though the Constitution gives Congress, not the courts, primary authority to choose the president in electoral deadlocks.[135] The Court's ruling was pure judicial activism.

President George W. Bush, like recent Republican presidents, tried to fashion a more conservative Court. When William Rehnquist died in 2005, Bush appointed John Roberts to be chief justice. He then appointed another conservative, Samuel Alito. The **Roberts Court** is emerging as an even more conservative court than the Rehnquist Court. It, too, has practiced judicial activism, overturning precedents while striking down campaign finance laws and gun control laws and limiting affirmative-action policies. The five justices who form the conservative majority on the Roberts Court all were either appointed by President Reagan or worked as lawyers in the Reagan administration.[136]

Since the Warren Court, there has been a steady trend toward more conservative justices. Justice John Paul Stevens, who was appointed by President Ford in 1975, observed that every justice, except one, appointed between 1971 and 2009 has been more conservative than the justice he or she replaced. Stevens was a moderate Republican, but as the Court shifted to the right, he wound up on the left—the most liberal justice on the Rehnquist and Roberts Courts.[137] A study confirmed his impression, concluding that four of the five most conservative justices since 1937 are on the Roberts Court now. (The fifth was Rehnquist.)[138]

In the modern era, the Court has used judicial review to be a policy maker. In general, the Warren Court was a liberal policy maker, the Burger Court a moderate policy maker, and the Rehnquist Court a conservative policy maker. All three courts were activist rather than restrained. For the time periods of these Courts, see Table 1.

The Role of Judicial Review

Judicial review is the most powerful tool courts use to wield power. When the courts declare a law or action unconstitutional, they not only void that law or action but also might put the issue on the public agenda, and they might speed up or slow down the pace of change in the government's policy.

When the Supreme Court declared Texas's abortion law unconstitutional in *Roe* v. *Wade* in 1973, the Court put the abortion issue on the public agenda. Abortion hadn't been a raging controversy before the Court's ruling.

The Court also used judicial review as a catalyst to speed up change in the desegregation cases in the 1950s. At the time, President Eisenhower wasn't inclined to act, and Congress wasn't able to act because both houses were dominated by senior southerners who, as committee chairs, blocked civil rights legislation. The Court broke the logjam.

In the first third of the twentieth century, the Court used judicial review as a brake to slow down change in business cases. After the Industrial Revolution swept the United States, powerful corporations abused their employees, their customers, and their competitors. Although Congress and state legislatures passed laws to regulate these abuses, the

Stephen Voss/WPN

President George W. Bush pushed the Supreme Court further to the right when he appointed Chief Justice John Roberts *(right)* and Justice Samuel Alito.

Court, dominated by justices who had been lawyers for corporations, often struck down the laws. The Court delayed some policies for several decades.

Judicial review, an American contribution to government, was for years unique to this country. It is now used in numerous other countries, but not as extensively or as effectively as in the United States.

The Supreme Court alone has struck down over 150 provisions of federal laws and over 1200 provisions of state and local laws.[139] The number of laws struck down, however, isn't a true measure of the importance of judicial review. Instead, the ever-present threat of review has prevented the legislatures from enacting many laws they feared would be struck down.

By using judicial review to play a strong role in government, the Court has contradicted the Founders' expectation that the judiciary would always be the weakest branch. Usually it has been the weakest branch, but occasionally it has been stronger. Arguably, these times include some years during the early nineteenth century, when the Court established national supremacy; the late nineteenth century and early twentieth century, when the Court thwarted efforts to regulate business; and the 1950s and 1960s, when the Court extended civil liberties and civil rights.

Table 1	Modern Supreme Courts	
Warren Court		1953–1969
Burger Court		1969–1986
Rehnquist Court		1986–2005
Roberts Court		2005–present

Nevertheless, the extent to which the Court has played a strong role in government shouldn't be exaggerated. At any given time, the Court has focused on one broad area of the law—in the modern era, civil liberties and civil rights—and has paid little attention to other areas. Moreover, this area has always involved domestic policy. Traditionally, the Court has been reluctant to intervene in foreign policy.[140]

Use of Political Checks against the Courts

The courts have exercised judicial review cautiously because they're subject to various political checks by the other branches.

Checks by the Executive

Presidents can impose the most effective check. If they dislike courts' rulings, they can appoint new judges when vacancies occur. Many appointees remain on the bench two decades after their president has left the White House.[141] President Nixon resigned in disgrace in 1974, but his appointee William Rehnquist stayed on the Court until he died in 2005.

Presidents and state and local executives, such as governors and mayors and even school officials and police officers, can refuse to enforce courts' rulings. School officials have disobeyed decisions requiring desegregation and invalidating class prayers. Police officers have ignored decisions invalidating some kinds of searches and interrogations. Yet executives who refuse to enforce courts' rulings risk losing public support, unless the public also opposes the rulings. Even President Nixon complied when the Court ordered him to turn over the incriminating Watergate tapes.

Checks by the Legislature

Congress and state legislatures can overturn courts' rulings by adopting constitutional amendments. They have done so four times (with the Eleventh, Fourteenth, Sixteenth, and Twenty-sixth Amendments).[142]

They can also overturn courts' rulings by passing new statutes. When courts base decisions on their interpretations of statutes, or when they make decisions in the absence of statutes, legislatures can pass new statutes, with clear language, that negate the decisions. From 1967 through 1990, Congress passed statutes to negate 121 Supreme Court rulings.[143] In 1986, the Court ruled that the Air Force didn't have to allow an ordained rabbi to wear his yarmulke with his uniform.[144] The next year, Congress passed a statute permitting military personnel to wear some religious apparel while in uniform. And, as you saw at the beginning of the chapter, Congress passed a statute overturning the pro-corporation ruling in the Lilly Ledbetter case.

Legislatures can refuse to implement courts' rulings, especially when money is necessary to implement them. The legislators simply don't appropriate the money.

Although these checks are the most common, Congress has invoked others, though only rarely. It can alter the structure of the lower federal courts, it can limit the appellate jurisdiction of the Supreme Court, and it can impeach and remove judges.

It can also limit the use of *habeas corpus* if there's a rebellion or an invasion of the country. After prodding by the Bush administration, Congress twice tried to eliminate the use of *habeas corpus* by alien detainees at Guantanamo Bay, Cuba. This would have prevented the detainees from challenging their detention in any court. However, the Supreme Court invalidated the congressional acts, ruling that the constitutional provisions for suspending the writ must be interpreted narrowly because the writ serves as a check on the legislative and executive branches.[145]

As a result of occasional checks or threatened checks, the courts have developed a strong sense of self-restraint to ensure self-preservation. This caution, more than the checks themselves, limits their use of judicial review.

Used by permission, Utah State Historical Society, all rights reserved

Although many children worked long days in unsafe conditions, for years the Supreme Court interpreted the Constitution to bar laws prohibiting child labor. This boy worked in the coal mines in the early 1900s.

DEMOCRACY?

Is judicial review compatible or incompatible with democratic government? In what ways is it compatible? Incompatible? Does the existence of political checks against the courts make judicial review more compatible with democratic government than it would be without them?

CONCLUSION: The Courts and the Role of Government

The courts tend to reflect the views of the public. Studies comparing 185 Supreme Court rulings from the mid-1930s through the mid-1990s with public opinion polls on the same issues found that the rulings mirrored the polls in approximately 60 percent of the cases.[146] The justices reflected the views of the public about as often as elected officials did. Thus the justices either responded to the public or, having been appointed by political officials chosen by the public, simply reflected the views of the public as political officials did.

Research shows that citizens know almost nothing about the judges; more adults can identify the character names of the Three Stooges than a single justice on the Supreme Court.[147] They also know little about the cases, but they do remember controversial decisions and they do recognize broad trends.[148] If they dislike these decisions or trends, their opinions pressure presidents and members of Congress to appoint justices with different views.

Although the courts are directly or indirectly responsive to the public, the Founders did not intend for them to be very responsive. The Founders gave judges life tenure so the courts would be relatively independent of both officials and the public. Indeed, the courts are more independent of political pressures than the other branches are. This enables them, in the words of appellate court judge Learned Hand, to stand as a bulwark against the "pressure of public panic." They can provide a "sober second thought."[149]

The courts can even protect the rights of various minorities—racial minorities, religious minorities, political dissidents, and criminal defendants—against the demands and the wrath of the majority. Chapters 14 and 15 will show how the courts extended civil liberties and civil rights to unpopular groups and individuals who lacked clout with the other branches and support from the public. Yet protecting the rights of these groups and individuals has historically been the exception rather than the rule. It was typical of the Warren Court and to some extent the Burger Court, but it was not typical of Supreme Courts before and has not been typical of Supreme Courts since.

In short, the courts are part of the political process and are sensitive to others in the process, especially to the president and Congress, but ultimately to the public, which makes its wishes known to, and through, these branches. Although the courts enjoy relative independence, they aren't immune to political pressure. They have therefore "learned to be a political institution and to behave accordingly" and have "seldom lagged far behind or forged far ahead" of public opinion.[150]

Because the courts tend to defer to the president and Congress, they usually allow government to expand its role in society if that is what these branches, in response to public opinion, attempt to do. Because the courts have some independence, however, they may counter efforts by the president and Congress to expand the role of government at least for a while, as the Supreme Court did in the first third of the twentieth century. Ultimately, however, they will be pressured to go along, as the Court was in the 1930s. Some observers foresee the possibility that a similar scenario may be developing today, as a reform-minded president and Congress pass legislation that expands government's role in various areas, such as the economy, health care, and the environment, at the same time that a conservative majority on the Supreme Court is increasingly asserting its will.[151]

KEY TERMS

activist judges	404
American Civil Liberties Union (ACLU)	401
Americans with Disabilities Act	402
Burger Court	412
Bush v. *Gore*	413
civil cases	401
concurring opinion	409
criminal cases	401
dissenting opinion	409
federal courts of appeals	392
federal district courts	392
friend of the court briefs	407
habeas corpus	393
judicial review	410
jurisdiction	392
majority opinion	408
Marbury v. *Madison*	411
Marshall Court	410
McCulloch v. *Maryland*	412
necessary and proper clause	412
Rehnquist Court	413
restrained judges	403
Roberts Court	413
Senate Judiciary Committee	395

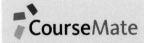 Access an interactive eBook, chapter-specific interactive learning tools (including flashcards, quizzes, videos), and more at CourseMate for *Understanding American Government*. Log in at CengageBrain.com.

14 Civil Liberties

The Roberts Court has ruled that the Second Amendment gives individuals a right to possess guns. When President Obama spoke in Arizona, which allows individuals to carry guns openly, a dozen men displayed weapons as an implied threat to the president and his policies.

Jack Kurtz/The Arizona Republic

Talking Points

The **Second Amendment** states, "A well regulated militia being necessary to the security of a free state, the right of the people to keep and bear arms shall not be infringed." When the amendment was adopted, there was no standing army to protect people from foreign invasions, Indian uprisings, or mob riots. The amendment was intended to protect people from these threats. The language implies that the right belongs to a local or state militia.[1] At the Founding, the militias were the ragtag bands of civilians in each community; today they would be the National Guard of each state. However, the National Rifle Association (NRA), in statements to its members and to the public over the years, has routinely deleted the first half of the amendment and only quoted the second half to emphasize its view that the amendment provides an *individual* right rather than a *collective* right for each community or state.

For years, the courts rejected the NRA's view.[2] Conservative chief justice Warren Burger criticized the NRA for misleading the American public in its efforts to thwart gun control legislation. Burger said that the amendment "has been the subject of one of the greatest pieces of fraud—I repeat the word 'fraud'—on the American public by special interest groups that I have ever seen in my lifetime."[3] The courts' interpretation meant that the Second Amendment was a useless anachronism. It merely allowed the National Guard to have weapons, which was never doubted. But the NRA's advocacy and the public's predisposition to believe it undermined the courts'

interpretation.[4] Conservative politicians, and sometimes judicial nominees, were expected to offer an enthusiastic endorsement of the NRA's view.

In 2008, a case challenging the District of Columbia's thirty-one-year-old ban on handguns gave the Roberts Court an opportunity to address the issue. In *District of Columbia* v. *Heller*,[5] the divided Court ruled 5–4 that the Second Amendment does provide an individual right after all. The five most conservative justices banded together to challenge settled precedents and overturn the law.

The case shows that the justices need to interpret constitutional provisions, and the ruling shows that their interpretation may reflect their ideology. The ruling also demonstrates that conservative justices can be activists, as they were here in disregarding the precedents and invalidating the law. Ultimately, of course, the ruling shows how the law—even the Constitution—can change as the membership of the Court changes.

However, the ruling doesn't mean that most gun control laws will be struck down. The amendment refers to a "well regulated militia," meaning that the new right is not an absolute right. It can be limited because guns are dangerous. Certain weapons, such as assault rifles, and any weapons for felons and mentally ill people may still be banned. Carrying weapons into schools and other government buildings may still be forbidden. Various restrictions on the sale of arms may still be enacted. Other limits on the right may also be allowed.[6]

Americans value their "rights." Eighteenth-century Americans believed that people had "**natural rights**" by virtue of being human. Given by God, not by government, the rights could not be taken away by government. Contemporary Americans do not normally use this term, but they do think about their rights much as their forebears did.

Yet Americans have a split personality when assessing their rights. Most people tell pollsters they believe in constitutional rights, but many don't accept these rights in concrete situations. During the Cold War, for example, most people said they believed in free speech, but many also said that communists, socialists, or atheists shouldn't be allowed to speak in public or teach in schools.

Surveys show that Americans remain divided over their support for civil liberties. Many would ban expression that might upset others.[7] In one survey, one-third said they wouldn't allow a rally that might offend community members. Two-thirds said they wouldn't allow people to say things in public that might offend racial groups, and over one-half said they wouldn't allow people to say things in public that might offend religious groups. One-fifth said they wouldn't allow newspapers to publish without government approval of the articles.[8]

Conflicts over civil liberties and rights have dominated the courts since the 1950s. This chapter, covering civil liberties, and the next, covering civil rights, explain how the courts have interpreted these rights and tried to resolve these conflicts. The chapters show how judges have acted as referees between the litigants, brokers among competing groups, and policy makers in the process of deciding these cases.

THE CONSTITUTION AND THE BILL OF RIGHTS

The term **civil liberties** refers to individual rights in the Constitution. Some rights are identified in the body of the Constitution, and more rights are listed in the Bill of Rights.

Individual Rights in the Constitution

The Constitution bans religious qualifications for federal office. 🔔 **Art. VI** (England had required its citizens who sought public office to profess their allegiance to the Church of England, which kept Catholics and religious dissenters on the sidelines.) The Constitution also guarantees jury trials in federal criminal cases. 🔔 **Art. III, Sec. 2** It bans bills of attainder, which are legislative acts rather than judicial trials pronouncing specific persons guilty of crimes, and *ex post facto* ("after the fact") laws, which are legislative acts making some behavior illegal that wasn't illegal when it was done. 🔔 **Art. I, Sec. 9 & 10** The Constitution also prohibits suspension of the writ of *habeas corpus,* except during rebellion or invasion of the country. 🔔 **Art. I, Sec. 9**

The Bill of Rights

The civil liberties people usually think of are listed in the Bill of Rights.

Origin and Meaning

The Constitution originally didn't include a bill of rights; the Founders didn't think traditional liberties needed specific protections because federalism, separation of powers, and checks and balances would prevent the national government from becoming too powerful. But to win support for ratification, the Founders promised to adopt constitutional amendments to provide such rights. James Madison proposed twelve, Congress passed them, and in 1791 the states ratified ten of them, which came to be known as the **Bill of Rights**.[9]

The first eight grant specific rights. (See the box "Civil Liberties in the Bill of Rights.") The Ninth Amendment says that the listing of these rights does not mean they are the only ones the people have, and the Tenth says that any powers not granted to the federal government are reserved for the state governments.

The Bill of Rights provides rights against the government. According to Justice Hugo Black, it is a list of "Thou shalt nots" directed at the government.[10] In practice, it provides rights for political, religious, or racial minorities against the majority, because government policy toward civil liberties tends to reflect the views of the majority.

As explained in Chapter 2, the Founders set up a government to protect property rights for the well-to-do minority against a jealous majority. The Constitution's fragmentation of power and some specific provisions (see Table 1 in Chapter 2 titled "Constitutional Provisions Protecting Property") were designed to prevent the masses from curtailing the rights of the elites. However, as Americans became more egalitarian and as the masses gained more opportunity to participate in politics in the nineteenth and twentieth centuries, the relative importance of property rights declined while the relative importance of political rights increased. Thus the Bill of Rights became the means to protect the fundamental rights of political, religious, and racial minorities and of criminal defendants—people who are out of the mainstream and often unpopular and powerless—when they come in conflict with the majority.

Responsibility for interpreting the Bill of Rights lies with the federal courts. Because federal judges are appointed for life, they are more independent of majority pressure than elected officials are.

DEMOCRACY?

Does the emphasis upon minority rights in the Bill of Rights contradict democracy or enhance democracy? What implications does this emphasis have for a conception of democracy that is based on majority rule?

Application

For many years, the Supreme Court applied the Bill of Rights only to the federal government, not to the state governments

CIVIL LIBERTIES IN THE BILL OF RIGHTS

- First Amendment grants freedom of religion; freedom of speech, assembly, and association; freedom of the press.
- Second Amendment grants right to keep and bear arms.
- Third Amendment forbids quartering soldiers in houses during peacetime.
- Fourth Amendment forbids unreasonable searches and seizures.
- Fifth Amendment grants right to a grand jury in criminal cases and right to due process.
- Fifth Amendment forbids double jeopardy (more than one trial for the same offense), compulsory self-incrimination, taking private property without just compensation.
- Sixth Amendment grants right to speedy trial, right to public trial, right to jury trial in criminal cases, right to cross-examine adverse witnesses, right to present favorable witnesses, right to counsel.
- Seventh Amendment grants right to jury trial in civil cases.
- Eighth Amendment forbids excessive bail and fines and cruel and unusual punishment.

(or to the local governments, which are under the authority of the state governments). That is, the Bill of Rights restricted the actions only of the federal government.[11]

In ruling this way, the Court followed the intentions of the Founders, who assumed that the states, with their capitals closer to their people, would be less likely to violate the liberties of their people.[12] The Founders didn't realize that the states would in fact be more likely to violate the liberties of their people. Because the state governments represent smaller, more homogeneous populations, they tend to reflect majority sentiment more closely than the federal government, so they often ignored—and sometimes obliterated—the rights of political, religious, or racial minorities or of criminal defendants.

However, in the twentieth century there was a growing sense that individual rights are important and that the state governments as well as the federal government should protect them. Starting in 1925[13] and continuing through 1972,[14] the Supreme Court gradually applied most provisions of the Bill of Rights to the states.[15] In addition, the Court established some rights not in the Bill of Rights, and it applied these to the states, too—presumption of innocence in criminal cases, right to travel within the country, and right to privacy. Thus most provisions in the Bill of Rights, and even

some not in it, now restrict the actions of both the federal and the state governments.

By forcing the states to grant national constitutional rights, the Supreme Court strengthened national governmental authority. This development was one factor that contributed to the evolution from the state-centered federalism favored by some Founders to the nation-centered federalism evident today. (Recall the discussion of these concepts in Chapter 3.)

To see how the Court has interpreted these provisions, we'll look at four major areas—freedom of expression, freedom of religion, rights of criminal defendants, and right to privacy. We'll put the major rulings of the Supreme Court in italics because the Court's doctrine is complex.

FREEDOM OF EXPRESSION

The **First Amendment** guarantees freedom of expression, which includes freedom of speech, assembly, and association, and freedom of the press.[16] The amendment also guarantees freedom of religion, which will be addressed in the next section. (Take note, in case you're asked. Americans can name more members of *The Simpsons* cartoon family and more judges on *American Idol* than they can rights in the First Amendment.)[17]

The amendment states that "Congress shall make no law" abridging these liberties. The language is absolute, but no justices interpret it literally.[18] They cite the example of the person who falsely shouts "Fire!" in a crowded theater and causes a stampede that injures someone. Surely, they say, the amendment doesn't protect this expression. So the Court needs to draw a line between expression the amendment protects and that which it doesn't.

Freedom of Speech

Freedom of speech, Justice Black asserted, is "the heart of our government."[19] There are important theoretical justifications for freedom of speech. By creating an open atmosphere, it promotes individual autonomy and self-fulfillment. By encouraging a wide variety of opinions, it furthers the advancement of knowledge and the discovery of truth. The English philosopher John Stuart Mill, who championed freedom of speech, observed that individuals decide what is correct by comparing different views. Unpopular opinions might be true or partly true. Even if completely false, they might prompt a reevaluation of accepted opinions. By permitting citizens to form opinions and express them to others, freedom of speech helps them participate in government. It especially helps them check inefficient or corrupt government. Finally, by channeling conflict toward persuasion, freedom of speech promotes a stable society.

DEMOCRACY?

Why would philosopher John Dewey say that "democracy begins in conversation"?[21]

Governments that deny freedom of speech become inflexible. Eventually, their inflexibility fosters rebellion among their people. [20]

Because of our tradition and constitutional guarantee, almost all speech is allowed. However, there are some restrictions on the content of speech—what is said—and other restrictions on the manner of speech—how it is said. We'll first examine the restrictions on the content of speech, focusing on seditious speech, offensive speech, hate speech, and sexual speech. We'll then examine the restrictions on the manner of speech.

Seditious Speech

Seditious speech is speech that encourages opposition to or rebellion against the government.[22] The public becomes most hostile to seditious speech, and the government becomes most likely to prosecute people for such speech, during or shortly after war, when society is most sensitive about patriotism and loyalty. Criminal prosecution for seditious speech strikes at the heart of our principle of freedom of speech, which is supposed to protect individuals and groups who criticize the government and its officials.

World War I era Numerous prosecutions came with World War I and the Russian Revolution, which brought the communists to power in the Soviet Union in 1917. The Russian Revolution prompted the **Red Scare**, in which people feared conspiracies to overthrow the U.S. government. Congress passed laws that prohibited "disloyal, profane, scurrilous, or abusive language about the form of government, Constitution, soldiers and sailors, flag or uniform of the armed forces."[23] State legislatures passed similar laws.

The federal government prosecuted almost two thousand and convicted almost nine hundred persons under these acts, and the state governments prosecuted and convicted many others. They prosecuted individuals for saying that war is contrary to the teachings of Jesus, that World War I should not have been declared until after a referendum was held, and that the draft was unconstitutional. Officials even prosecuted an individual for remarking to women knitting clothes for the troops, "No soldier ever sees those socks."[24]

These cases gave the Supreme Court numerous opportunities to rule on seditious speech. In six major cases, the Court upheld the governments' laws and affirmed the defendants' convictions.[25] The Court concluded that *these defendants' speech constituted a "clear and present danger"* to the government. Justice Edward Sanford wrote, "A single revolutionary spark may kindle a fire that, smoldering for a time, may burst into a sweeping and destructive conflagration."[26] In reality, there was nothing clear or present about the danger; the defendants' speech had little effect. The Court, reflecting our society at the time, was simply intolerant of dissent.

When a Harvard Law professor criticized the Court's rulings, the university's administration, prompted by the Justice Department, charged him "unfit" to be a professor. He was narrowly acquitted.[27]

Cold War era More prosecutions came after World War II, as the uneasy alliance between the United States and the Soviet Union during the war gave way to the Cold War between the two countries in the 1950s. Politicians, especially Sen. Joseph McCarthy (R-Wisc.), exploited the tensions, claiming that many government officials were communists. He said he had a list of 205 "known communists" in the State Department alone. He had little evidence—and provided no list.[28] Other Republicans also accused the Democratic Truman administration of covering for communists in government and goaded it into prosecuting communists outside government so it would not appear "soft on communism."

In 1940, Congress had passed an act that prohibited advocating overthrow of the government by force and organizing or joining individuals who advocated overthrow.[29] The government used the act against the communists. The Court upheld the act and affirmed the convictions of eleven upper-echelon leaders of the American Communist Party.[30] Although these leaders organized the party and the party advocated overthrowing the government by force, the leaders had not attempted to overthrow the government. (If they had, they clearly would have been guilty of crimes.) Even so, the Court concluded that *they were a clear and present danger.* After the Court's decision, the government prosecuted and convicted almost one hundred lower-level communists as well.

The public's fear was so consuming that the government's actions extended beyond criminal prosecutions to other measures, and beyond active communists to former

At congressional hearings, Sen. Joseph McCarthy identified the supposed locations of alleged communists and "fellow travelers."

During the Cold War, Americans feared communism so much that some built bomb shelters in their yards, believing that taking refuge would protect their family in a nuclear attack.

Loomis Dean/Time & Life Pictures/Getty Images

alleged subversives from public jobs such as teaching or private jobs such as practicing law or serving as union officers. Federal and state legislative committees held hearings to expose and humiliate them. These actions cost an estimated ten thousand Americans their jobs.

Eventually, the Cold War thawed somewhat, and the Senate condemned McCarthy after he tried to bully the army. His method was likened to witch hunts, and the tactic of making political accusations or name-calling based on little or no evidence came to be known as **McCarthyism**. (However, McCarthyism began before and continued after McCarthy's tenure in the 1950s, as other politicians and the Senate's Internal Security Committee and the House's Un-American Activities Committee used similar tactics.)[31]

Although McCarthy and others were bullies who hurt many innocent or harmless people, there actually were communist spies in the federal government, from the atomic labs at Los Alamos, New Mexico, to the State Department and the White House, according to records revealed after the collapse of the Soviet Union. Apparently most spies were discovered before the 1950s, but some were never uncovered.[32]

In the meantime, two new members, including Chief Justice Earl Warren, joined the Supreme Court. In a series of cases in the mid- to late 1950s and early 1960s, the **Warren Court** made it more difficult to convict the communists.[33] (See box "The President Summons the Chief Justice.")

Ultimately, the Warren Court created a new doctrine for seditious speech.[34] The justices drew a distinction between advocacy and incitement. *People can advocate, enthusiastically, even heatedly, as long as they don't incite illegal action—that is, urge immediate action to violate any laws.* This doctrine protects most criticism of the government, whether at a rally, from a pulpit, or through the media, and it remains in effect today.

Thus after many years and many cases, the Court concluded that the First Amendment protects seditious speech as much as other speech. Justice William Douglas noted that "the threats were often loud but always puny."[35] Even

communists—some Americans had dabbled with communism during the Great Depression in the 1930s—and even to individuals who had never been communists but who were lumped together as "commie dupes" or "comsymps" (communist sympathizers).

In the midst of this fear, the federal government and some state governments required government employees to take "loyalty oaths" and then fired those who refused, even on principle, and those who (purportedly) lied. Some state governments banned communists, former communists, and

---

behind the scenes

The President Summons the Chief Justice

When the Supreme Court made it more difficult to convict American communists in the 1950s and 1960s, the justices incurred the wrath of the public, Congress, and President Dwight Eisenhower, who summoned Chief Justice Warren to the White House. In a private conversation, the president criticized the rulings. Warren asked Eisenhower what he thought the Court should have done with the communists. Eisenhower replied, "I would kill the SOBs."[1] Warren ignored the remark.

[1] Earl Warren, *The Memoirs of Earl Warren* (Garden City, N.Y.: Doubleday, 1977), 6.

the attorney general who prosecuted the major communist cases later admitted that the cases were "squeezed oranges. I didn't think there was much to them."[36] Nevertheless, the Court had permitted public fear to overwhelm the First Amendment for a long time.

The Vietnam War didn't prompt the same concerns as did the Red Scare during World War I or the Cold War following World War II, and Congress didn't pass any comparable laws. Nonetheless, the federal government took some actions against individuals and groups. Antiwar groups were harassed by federal grand juries, and their leaders were spied on by the U.S. Army. Some prominent opponents were prosecuted for conspiring against the draft.[37] However, opposition to this war was so widespread that the government's actions didn't silence the protesters' speech.

Although the collapse of the Soviet Union and the demise of the Cold War made communism less threatening, the seditious speech doctrine remains important. After the Oklahoma City bombing in 1995, government surveillance of right-wing militia groups increased, but prosecution of the members, under terrorism laws, was limited because most of the evidence was fiery rhetoric, which is protected speech (unless it urges immediate action to violate any laws).

After the terrorist attacks in 2001, pressure to conform—to temper criticism and to support the government's policies—mounted. In an effort to prod the schools to discipline and restrain their professors, one organization identified forty college professors with "un-American" agendas. (Negative reaction prompted the organization to remove the names from its website.)[38] A tenured professor at the University of New Mexico who cracked, "Anyone who can blow up the Pentagon gets my vote," was reprimanded, and a lawsuit demanding his termination was filed.[39] During the Iraq War, pressure to conform was linked to support for our troops. Critics were branded as "unpatriotic" and "disloyal" by conservative commentators who stoked their listeners' anger.[40] Pressure to conform was muted only when the

initial victory unraveled in the invasion's aftermath and the public's criticism of the war increased.

The state and federal governments have also limited offensive speech, hate speech, and sexual speech, which we will turn to now.

Offensive Speech

Arrests for swearing, especially at police officers or in the presence of police officers, were numerous for many years. In the District of Columbia, for example, about ten thousand people per year were arrested for swearing (and charged with "disorderly conduct").[41] As swearing became more common in the 1960s and 1970s, and as it became a clear manifestation of the poor relations between inner-city residents and the officers who patrolled their neighborhoods, the justices decided that *swearing in many situations is protected speech* (though not on radio or television, as we'll see). They expect police, who are trained to face emotionally charged situations, to tolerate swearing.[42]

During the Vietnam War, a man on his way to observe a trial walked through the corridors of the Los Angeles County courthouse wearing a jacket with the words "Fuck the Draft" emblazoned on the back. A cop arrested him, and a judge convicted him. The Supreme Court reversed the young man's conviction, as seventy-two-year-old Justice John Harlan remarked that "one man's vulgarity is another's lyric."[43] Harlan recognized that "much linguistic expression serves a dual communicative function: it conveys not only ideas capable of relatively precise, detached explication, but otherwise inexpressible emotions as well. In fact, words are often chosen as much for their emotive as their cognitive force. . . . [The former] may often be the more important element of the overall message."

Hate Speech

Hate speech is derogatory speech—racial, ethnic, sexual, or religious slurs—usually aimed at a group rather than at an individual. When aimed at an individual, the speech impugns a characteristic the individual shares with the group. Hate speech demeans people for characteristics that are innate, such as race, ethnicity, or sexuality, or perhaps for religious faith. Such speech can cause emotional or psychological harm.

Even so, it can be difficult to distinguish hate speech from other speech. What one person considers hate speech another may consider a simple observation or a valid criticism. And because of the First Amendment, *hate speech normally can't be prohibited by governments.*[44]

In 1978, lower federal courts required the Chicago suburb of Skokie to permit the American Nazi Party to demonstrate.[45] The Nazis intentionally chose Skokie as the site for their demonstration because many Jews lived there—forty thousand of the seventy thousand residents. Hundreds were survivors of German concentration camps during World

Opposition to the Vietnam War was so widespread that there were few prosecutions for seditious speech.

© Paul Conklin/PhotoEdit

for attachment than any other it is the principle of free thought—not free thought for those who agree with us but freedom for the thought we hate."[46]

Cross-burning by the Ku Klux Klan presents a more difficult question. In the Klan's heyday, a cross-burning was a clear threat to the black families it was directed toward, and even today it might be used this way. But in other circumstances, a cross-burning *might* be intended only as a rallying symbol to the Klan's members. The Supreme Court ruled that persons who burn a cross to intimidate or to threaten—for example, to frighten their black neighbors—can be prosecuted, but those who burn a cross at a KKK rally in a private field hidden from other people and passing cars cannot be prosecuted.[47]

Despite the First Amendment, many colleges and universities adopted hate speech codes in the 1980s and 1990s because they worried that such speech created a hostile and intimidating environment for the victims.[48] A student who was jeered nightly by taunts of "Faggot!" said, "When you are told you are not worth anything, it is difficult to function."[49] Some students were disciplined under the codes. But colleges and universities, more than other institutions in our society, have traditionally fostered free expression and debate. And the codes, which were inherently difficult to write, were often too broad or too vague. Some were struck down by lower courts, and others were abandoned by the schools. Some were rewritten to focus on harassment and threats, which can be prohibited, and to apply to computers using university networks. George Mason University forbade students from using computers "to harass, threaten, or abuse others." Virginia Tech disciplined a student for posting a message on the home page of a gay men's group calling for gays to be castrated and to "die a slow death."[50]

The First Amendment prevents governments—not businesses—from restricting your speech. When Lorrie Heasley boarded a Southwest Airlines plane, she wore a T-shirt featuring President Bush, Vice President Cheney, Secretary of State Rice, and the title of the movie *Meet the Fockers*—except an expletive was substituted. The flight crew removed her from the plane. Although the government could not restrict this expression, the airline could.

© Melanie Conner/The New York Times/Redux

War II, and thousands were relatives of people who had died in the camps. The city, in anticipation of the demonstration, passed ordinances that prohibited wearing "military-style" uniforms and distributing material that "promotes and incites hatred against persons by reason of their race, national origin, or religion." These ordinances were an attempt to bar the demonstration, and the courts threw them out. One court quoted Justice Oliver Wendell Holmes's statement that "if there is any principle of the Constitution that more imperatively calls

DEMOCRACY?

Does the outcome of this case suggest another theoretical justification for freedom of speech? Does freedom of speech make people more tolerant, because they can't silence those they disagree with? Tolerance is essential in a multiracial, multiethnic, multicultural nation like the United States. If we can tolerate the Nazis' venomous speech, we should be able to tolerate the less hateful speech of other groups.

Sargent © Austin-American Statesman. Reprinted with permission of Universal Press Syndicate. All rights reserved.

In 2010, Ireland banned "blasphemy," which was defined as speaking critically of anything sacred to any religion.[52] Islamic countries have campaigned for an international treaty banning blasphemy in an attempt to protect religious symbols, personalities, and dogmas from criticism or ridicule. The proposed treaty, of course, would limit freedom of speech, and the United States has announced that it will not join any such treaty.

Sexual Speech

In some contexts, sexual speech—that is, language or situations that fall short of obscenity—has been prohibited. (Obscenity, whether in print or film or on radio or television, is never allowed. But its legal definition and judicial doctrine are complex and beyond the scope of this text.)

Governments can forbid nude dancing,[53] even though it may qualify as expression. Through zoning, *governments can restrict pornographic theaters or sex shops* from most (though not all) parts of their cities.[54]

The Federal Communications Commission (FCC) can forbid radio and television stations from broadcasting some sexual language and situations. A California radio station broadcast a monologue by comedian George Carlin. Titled "Filthy Words," it lampooned society's sensitivity to seven words that "you couldn't say on the public airwaves . . . the ones you definitely wouldn't say, ever." The seven words, according to the FCC report, included "a four-letter word for excrement" repeated seventy times in twelve minutes. A majority of the Court ruled that although the monologue was part of a serious program on contemporary attitudes toward language, it was not protected under the First Amendment because people, including children, who were tuning in the radio could be subjected to the language in their homes.[55] The Court also ruled that the FCC can ban even "fleeting profanities"—single spontaneous expletives voiced in a nonsexual context.[56] Now the FCC forbids indecent material on radio and noncable television between 6 a.m. and 10 p.m. and fines any media that violate the ban. (Large fines were levied on the *Howard Stern Show,* before it moved to satellite radio, and on a New York City radio station that broadcast a tape of a couple having sex in Saint Patrick's Cathedral.)[57] Yet the Court struck down a Utah law restricting indecent material on cable television. By subscribing to and paying for cable television, its customers are accepting exposure to its programming.[58]

In each of these areas we have covered—seditious speech, offensive speech, hate speech, and sexual speech—courts allow more freedom for individuals today because the Supreme Court broadened its interpretation of the First Amendment during the second half of the twentieth century.

We'll now examine the restrictions on the manner of speech, focusing on demonstrations and symbolic speech.

Some conservative Christian students object to school policies promoting tolerance of homosexuals. This student heads a campus group called S.T.R.A.I.G.H.T.—Students Reinforcing Adherence in General Heterosexual Tradition. The presence and activities of such groups pit the guarantee of free speech against the goal of social tolerance.

AP Images/Centre Daily Times, Pat Little

Some conservative Christians, funded by evangelical ministries and interest groups, have launched an attack on tolerance policies toward gays and lesbians. They demand that schools and workplaces revoke their policies, including speech codes and, in lower grades, dress codes prohibiting antigay T-shirts. A Georgia Tech student who was reprimanded for sending a letter that berated students who came out as gay filed suit, claiming that her faith compelled her to speak out against homosexuality.[51]

These disputes highlight the fine line between harassment and free speech. So far, the Supreme Court hasn't addressed college and university speech codes or school tolerance policies.

In contrast to the United States, most Western countries, including Canada, England, France, and Germany, and other countries such as India and South Africa, ban hate speech and make it a crime to provoke racial or religious hatred. French actress Brigitte Bardot, an animal rights activist, was fined $23,000 by the French government for criticizing a Muslim ceremony that entails a sheep slaughter.

Demonstrations

Protesters want people to see or hear their demonstrations, so they seek locations where people congregate and provide an audience. Although some people won't like their message or their use of public places to disseminate the message, protesters have a right to demonstrate.

Individuals are allowed to use public places, such as streets, sidewalks, parks, theaters,[59] and the grounds around public buildings,[60] *to express their views on public issues.* These places constitute the **public forum** and serve as "the poor person's printing press."

Private property is not part of the public forum, so *individuals have no right to demonstrate on private property* without the owner's permission.[61] Shopping malls usually forbid demonstrations. During the runup to the Iraq War, a sixty-year-old man wore a T-shirt with the slogan "Give Peace a Chance" at a mall in Albany, New York. Security guards ordered him to take off the shirt or leave the mall. When he refused, he was arrested.[62] Although his shirt was not what we think of as a demonstration, it did express his views, and the mall could forbid such expression.

Even in the public forum, individuals can't demonstrate whenever or however they want. The streets, sidewalks, parks, and theaters in the public forum are used for purposes other than demonstrations—especially for transportation and recreation—so individuals can't disrupt these activities. They can't, Justice Arthur Goldberg remarked, hold "a street meeting in the middle of Times Square at the rush hour."[63]

Therefore, abortion protesters can demonstrate on public streets and public sidewalks near abortion clinics, and they can approach staffers and patients who come and go. But *protesters cannot block access* (and to ensure this, judges can order them not to come within a certain distance—for example, fifteen feet—of driveways and doorways).[64] Moreover, they cannot demonstrate at the doctor's house even if they stand on a public sidewalk. After protesters repeatedly picketed at a doctor's residence in a Milwaukee suburb, the town passed an ordinance forbidding such picketing. The Court ruled that protesters can march through residential neighborhoods but *cannot focus on particular houses,* because such picketing interferes with the privacy of the home.[65]

To ensure that potential demonstrations don't disrupt the normal activities of the places in the public forum, *governments can require groups to obtain a permit, which can specify the place, time, and manner of the demonstration. Officials can establish restrictions to avoid disruptions. However, officials cannot use these restrictions to censor speech.* They cannot allow one group to demonstrate but forbid another, no matter how much they dislike the group or its message. They cannot forbid the group even if they say they fear violence (unless the group actually threatens violence).

Symbolic Speech

Some demonstrations feature **symbolic speech**, which is the use of symbols rather than words to convey ideas. Sometimes symbolic speech has been prohibited when

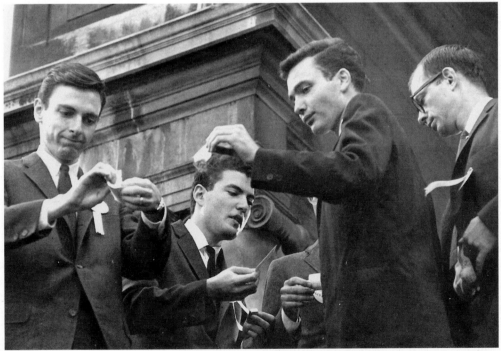

When young men illegally burned their draft cards to protest the Vietnam War, the Supreme Court refused to protect their action as symbolic speech.

© Hiroji Kubota/Magnum Photos

actual speech, with the same message, would have been permitted.

During the Vietnam War, some young men burned their draft cards to protest the war and the draft. Their action was powerful expression—symbolic speech was a novelty in the 1960s—and Congress tried to stifle it by passing a law prohibiting the destruction of draft cards. The justices upheld the law and expressed their discomfort with the concept of symbolic speech.[66]

But the Court came to accept symbolic speech in the late 1960s and early 1970s.[67] To protest the war, a Massachusetts man wore a flag patch on the seat of his pants and was arrested and sentenced to six months in jail. A Washington student taped a peace symbol on a flag and then hung the flag upside down outside his apartment. The Court reversed both convictions.[68]

When a member of the Revolutionary Communist Youth Brigade burned an American flag outside the Republican convention in 1984, the justices faced the issue of *flag desecration*—the ultimate symbolic speech. A bare majority of the **Rehnquist Court** *permitted* this symbolic speech.[69] Justice William Brennan wrote that the First Amendment can't be limited just because this expression offends most people. "We do not consecrate the flag by punishing its desecration, for in doing so we dilute the freedom that this cherished emblem represents." The ruling invalidated the laws of forty-eight states and the federal government.

In a dissent, Chief Justice William Rehnquist emotionally criticized the decision. He said the First Amendment shouldn't apply because the flag is a unique national symbol. He recounted the history of "The Star-Spangled Banner" and the music of John Philip Sousa's "Stars and Stripes Forever," he quoted poems by Ralph Waldo Emerson and John Greenleaf Whittier that refer to the flag, and he discussed the role of the Pledge of Allegiance.

Civil liberties advocates praised the decision, but veterans' groups were outraged and many Americans were upset. Congress passed a statute prohibiting flag desecration. Yet the justices, dividing the same way, declared the new statute unconstitutional for the same reasons they reversed the prior conviction.[70]

European countries are less willing to accept symbolic speech. As they struggle with high numbers of Muslim immigrants and the reluctance of these immigrants to assimilate, some prohibit Muslim symbols. France banned the hijab (headscarf), worn by some young Muslim women, in public schools and the burqa (full veil), worn by some older Muslim women, in public places. In another backlash against Muslim immigrants, Swiss voters adopted a constitutional provision banning minarets—the towers on some mosques.[71]

In this chapter so far, we've focused on adult speech. Now we'll turn to student speech. Students below the college level are considered children rather than adults, so they aren't afforded full First Amendment rights.

Student Speech

During the Vietnam War, junior and senior high school students in Des Moines, Iowa, wore black armbands to protest the war. When they were suspended, their families sued school officials. The Warren Court ruled that the schools must allow the students freedom of speech as long as the students don't disrupt the schools.[72] Public schools, Justice Abe Fortas said, "may not be enclaves of totalitarianism."

However, this case, which involved political speech, has proven to be the exception to the rule. According to the **Burger Court** and the Rehnquist Court, *administrators in public or private schools can restrict student speech for educational*

---

behind the scenes

The Internet and Free Speech in China

China doesn't grant free speech to its citizens, but many people have predicted that the Internet will force the regime to open up and allow more freedom. Yet American computer companies, in an effort to land lucrative business deals in the communist country, have been complicit in the government's crackdown on dissidents and censorship of speech. Cisco Systems provided the hardware China uses to monitor and censor Internet communications among its people. Google, Microsoft, and Yahoo, at the behest of the government, censor Internet searches in the country. Microsoft shut down a blogger who antagonized Chinese officials. Yahoo identified two journalists who disseminated prodemocracy writings. This information led to their arrest and conviction and their sentence of ten years in prison.

Although top executives at these companies speak about the Internet's liberating power, their drive for profits may exceed their commitment to free speech and transparent government. However, the companies respond that they must follow the laws of the countries where they operate and that a censored Internet is better than no Internet.

SOURCE: Editorial, "Yahoo Betrays Free Speech," *New York Times*, December 2, 2007, WK9.

© Clay Good/ZUMA Press

Student speech that celebrates or condones drug use can be prohibited by school administrators.

purposes. They can restrict speech or clothing that is lewd or vulgar[73] or that promotes sex, drugs, or violence.

When the Olympic Torch Relay passed through Juneau, Alaska, for the 2002 Winter Games, high school students were released early to watch.[74] As the relay approached and television cameras filmed the scene, some students unfurled a banner that said, "BONG HiTS 4 JESUS." The principal was not amused and suspended the student who initiated the prank. (When the student quoted Thomas Jefferson on free speech, the principal doubled his suspension.) Although the student said the phrase was "meaningless and funny, in order to get on television," the **Roberts Court**, by a 5–4 vote, upheld the suspension because the phrase might have been understood to celebrate or condone drug use.[75]

Administrators restrict hate speech as well. Conflicts over hate speech arise in public schools because many administrators and teachers believe they should encourage tolerance. Disputes over antigay speech have been especially controversial, but the Supreme Court hasn't ruled on this issue.

Administrators can also censor student publications, even serious articles that don't promote sex, drugs, or violence or contain hate speech. The Rehnquist Court allowed censorship of student newspaper articles about the impact of pregnancy and of parents' divorce on teenagers.[76]

After the ruling, a Colorado principal blocked an editorial criticizing his study hall policy while allowing another editorial praising it. A Texas principal banned an article about the class valedictorian who succeeded despite the death of her mother, the desertion of her father, and her

own pregnancy. North Carolina administrators shut down a high school newspaper and fired its adviser because of three articles, including a satirical story about the "death" of the writer after eating a cheeseburger from the school cafeteria.

Some principals have tried to restrict their students from using the Internet to criticize school officials or policies. But like the underground newspapers of the 1960s and 1970s, web pages created off campus (rather than in class) can't be censored and their creators can't be disciplined by administrators, unless the pages urge illegal action or make terrorist threats. A Georgia student was arrested for suggesting that the principal be shot, his daughter kidnapped, his car keyed, and its locks clogged with Superglue. (Also see the box "The Internet and Free Speech in China.")

Freedom of Association

Although the First Amendment does not mention *association,* the Supreme Court has interpreted the right to speak, assemble, and petition the government for a redress of grievances, all of which the amendment does list, to encompass a **freedom of association** for individuals to join with others to do these things.

The right is strongest when the organization forms for "expressive association"—that is, when it speaks, assembles, and petitions the government for a redress of grievances. The right is also strong when the organization forms for "intimate association"—that is, when it is relatively personal, selective, and small, such as a social club or a country club.

This freedom implicitly entails a right not to associate as well. Therefore, *organizations formed for expressive or intimate association can exclude others.* The Supreme Court allowed organizers of Boston's Saint Patrick's Day parade to exclude a group of gays, lesbians, and bisexuals.[77] Because the organizers were private individuals—the parade wasn't sponsored by the city—and because a parade is an expressive activity, the organizers didn't have to allow any views contrary to their views. The Supreme Court also allowed the Boy Scouts of America to expel an assistant scoutmaster who was openly gay.[78] The Court concluded that the Boy Scouts is an expressive organization, which espouses various values, including an opposition to homosexuality.

The right is weakest when the organization forms for "commercial association"—that is, when it is designed to enhance the business interests of its members and is relatively large, unselective, and impersonal. *Organizations formed for commercial association, such as civic clubs, can't exclude others* (in states or cities that adopt nondiscrimination laws). Their right to associate can be overridden by the individual's right to be free from discrimination.[79] Therefore, the Jaycees (the Junior Chamber of Commerce), which was a business organization of young men, and the Rotary Club, which was a civic organization of men, can't discriminate against women in states that have laws forbidding sex discrimination.[80]

Freedom of the Press

Freedom of the press is measured by freedom from prior restraint and from restrictions on gathering news.

Prior Restraint

The core of **freedom of the press** is freedom from prior restraint—censorship. If the press violates laws prohibiting, for example, libelous or obscene material, it can be punished after publishing such materials. But freedom from prior restraint means the press can disseminate the information it considers appropriate and the public can see this information.

Yet freedom from prior restraint isn't absolute. During the Vietnam War, the secretary of defense in the Johnson administration, Robert McNamara, ordered a thorough study of our engagement. The study, known as the **Pentagon Papers**, laid bare the reasons the country was embroiled—reasons not as honorable as ones the officials had fed the public—and it questioned the effectiveness of military policy. The study was so revealing that McNamara confided to a friend, "They could hang people for what's in there."[81] He classified the papers "top secret" so few persons could see them. One of the authors, Daniel Ellsberg, who was a planner in the war, originally supported the war but later turned against it. Haunted by his involvement, he photocopied the

papers and passed them to the *New York Times* and *Washington Post* in the hope that their publication would sway public opinion and force the government to halt the war. (He also passed them to the television networks—ABC, CBS, and NBC—but they were afraid to use them.)[82]

The newspapers began to publish excerpts of the papers. Although the information implicated the Kennedy and Johnson administrations, the Nixon administration, which was still fighting the war, sought injunctions to restrain the newspapers from publishing more excerpts. In the *Pentagon Papers Case*, the Supreme Court refused to grant the injunctions.[83] Most justices said they would grant the injunctions if publishing the papers clearly jeopardized national security. But the information in the papers was historical; its disclosure didn't hinder the current war effort.[84] Thus *the rule—no prior restraint—remained, but some exceptions could be made.* (See box "The Road to Watergate.")

One exception occurred in 1979 when *The Progressive,* a monthly political magazine, planned to publish technical material about the design of hydrogen bombs. The article, "The H-Bomb Secret: How We Got It, Why We're Telling It," argued against secret classification of this material. Although the article wasn't a "do-it-yourself guide," it might have helped a medium-size nation develop a bomb sooner than the nation could otherwise. At the government's request, a federal judge granted an injunction prohibiting the magazine from publishing the article.[85]

The press in the United States is freer than that in Great Britain, where freedom from prior restraint began. Britain, which has no constitutional provision comparable to the First Amendment, tolerates more secrecy. The government banned radio and television interviews with all members of the outlawed Irish Republican Army and its political party,

The press chief of the *Washington Post* hails the Court's decision allowing publication of the Pentagon Papers.

behind the scenes

The Road to Watergate

When the *New York Times* and *Washington Post* began to publish excerpts of the Pentagon Papers, President Richard Nixon was furious. He hated the press, especially the eastern press, and he feared the liberal groups who were criticizing—undermining, he believed—his Vietnam policies and his entire administration as well. He barred *New York Times* reporters from the White House and *Air Force One,* and he ordered his staff members to have no dealings with "any of those Jews." He ordered his attorney general to prosecute "those bastards."[1] But Nixon still wasn't satisfied. He summoned his chief of staff and his national security adviser and demanded:

> I have a project I want somebody to take. . . . This takes eighteen hours a day. It takes devotion and loyalty and diligence such as you've never seen. . . . I really need a son of a bitch . . . who will work his butt off and do it dishonorably. . . . And I'll direct him myself. I know how to play this game and we're going to start playing it. . . . I want somebody just as tough as I am for a change. . . . We're up against an enemy, a conspiracy. They're using any means. We're going to use any means.[2]

This tirade set in motion the developments that would culminate in the Watergate scandal. The president and his underlings initiated a series of actions challenging the rule of law. Among these actions was a directive to party operatives to break in and steal Daniel Ellsberg's records from his psychiatrist's office and then leak the records to the press in an effort to tarnish his reputation.

[1] Quoted in Garry Wills, *Bomb Power: The Modern Presidency and the National Security State* (New York: Penguin, 2010), 171.
[2] Erwin N. Griswold, "No Harm Was Done," *New York Times,* June 30, 1991, E15.

including its sole representative in Parliament.[86] The French government banned the sale of a song critical of the West during the Persian Gulf War, and it blocked the broadcasting of anti-Semitic programming by an Arab channel in 2005. The German government, which has prohibited the display of the Nazi swastika since World War II, banned the sale of music by skinhead groups after neo-Nazi violence in recent years. The Austrian government imprisoned a British historian for publicizing his book denying the Holocaust.

Restrictions on Gathering News

Although prior restraint is an obvious limitation on freedom of the press, restrictions on gathering news are less obvious but no less serious. They also keep the news from the public.

The Burger Court *denied reporters the right to keep the names of their sources confidential.* In investigative reporting, reporters frequently rely on sources who demand anonymity in exchange for information. The sources might have sensitive positions in government or relations with criminals that would place them in jeopardy if their names were publicized. A Louisville reporter was allowed to watch persons make hashish from marijuana if he kept their names confidential. But after publication of his story, a grand jury demanded their names. When the reporter refused to reveal them, he was cited for contempt of court, and his conviction was upheld by the Supreme Court.[87] The majority said reporters' need for confidentiality isn't as great as courts' need for information about crimes. So reporters face a difficult choice: either do not guarantee anonymity to a potential source, which means they might not obtain information

for an important story; or do guarantee anonymity, which means, if the courts demand their source, they might be cited for contempt and jailed for months. Grand juries have demanded reporters' sources increasingly in recent years.[88]

Invasion of Privacy

Freedom of the press can result in an invasion of privacy when the press publishes personal information. In these conflicts, the Supreme Court has favored freedom of the press.

The Court has *permitted the press to publish factual information.* For example, although Georgia law prohibited the press from releasing the names of crime victims, to spare them embarrassment, an Atlanta television station announced the name of a high school girl who was raped by six classmates and left unconscious on the lawn to die. When her father sued the station, the Court said the press needs freedom to publish factual information from the public record so that citizens can scrutinize the workings of the judicial system.[89]

When a man in a crowd watching President Gerald Ford noticed a woman, close by, pull out a gun, he grabbed the gun and prevented an assassination. Reporters wrote stories about this hero, including the fact that he was a homosexual. This coverage caused him considerable embarrassment and practical problems as well, so he sued. The courts sided with the press again. The man's good deed made him newsworthy, whether he wanted to be or not.[90] Persons who become newsworthy are granted little privacy. Justice Brennan said this is a necessary evil "in a society which places a primary value on freedom of speech and of press."[91]

However, the Court has prohibited the press from sending reporters and photographers with law enforcement officers when they conduct a search or make an arrest at someone's home.[92] The Court decided that the police department's desire for good publicity and the local media's desire for interesting stories don't justify the invasion of a resident's privacy.

When freedom of the press and invasion of privacy conflict, European countries are far more sensitive to invasion of privacy. They consider privacy a fundamental human right. Perhaps because of their bitter experience with the Nazis' Gestapo and East Germany's Stasi (secret police), they recoil from the public exposure of individuals' private lives. In 2010, an Italian court convicted three Google executives for not blocking a video posted on YouTube that showed an autistic boy being bullied by his schoolmates. The video was up for two months before a complaint led to its removal. The court ruled that Google should have a process in place for blocking such videos.[93] These rulings have serious implications not only for Internet companies but also for the flow of information across borders.

DEMOCRACY?

Recall the assertion earlier in the chapter that freedom of speech is "the heart of our government." Some commentators claim that freedom of the press is just as important, or more important, for a democracy in modern society. Why would they claim this?

Libel

Libel consists of printed or broadcast statements that are false and that tarnish someone's reputation. Victims are entitled to sue for money to compensate them for the harm done.

Historically, the justices considered libelous material irrelevant to the exposition of ideas and search for truth envisioned by the framers of the First Amendment. The minimal benefit such material might have had was outweighed by the greater need to protect persons' reputations. For many years, the Court allowed the states to adopt libel laws as they saw fit.

However, the Warren Court recognized that state libel laws could be used to stifle legitimate political criticism; they could be used to thwart freedom of the press. The justices forced radical changes in these laws in the landmark case *New York Times* v. *Sullivan* in 1964.[94]

The *Times* ran an ad by black clergymen criticizing Montgomery, Alabama, officials for their response to racial protests. The ad contained trivial inaccuracies. Although it didn't name any officials, the commissioner of police claimed that it implicitly referred to him, and he sued. A local jury ordered the *Times* to pay him a half-million dollars. Meanwhile, another local jury ordered the *Times* to pay another commissioner another half-million dollars for the same ad. It was apparent that traditional libel laws could be used to wreak vengeance on a critical press—in this case, on a detested northern newspaper for its coverage of controversial civil rights protests.

The Court, ruling against the commissioner, made it more difficult for public officials to win libel suits. It held that *officials must show not only that the statements made about them were false, but also that the statements were made with "reckless disregard for the truth."* This standard gives the press some leeway to make mistakes—to print inaccurate statements—as long as the press is not careless to the point of recklessness.

This protection for the press is necessary, according to Justice Brennan, because the "central meaning of the First Amendment" is that citizens should have the right to criticize officials. This statement prompted one legal scholar to herald the decision as "an occasion for dancing in the streets."[95]

In later cases, the Court *extended this ruling to public figures*—other persons who have public prominence or who thrust themselves into public controversies. These include candidates for public office[96] and activists for various causes.[97] The Court reasoned that it should be more difficult for public figures, as for public officials, to win libel suits because they also influence public policy and also are newsworthy enough to get media attention to rebut false accusations against them.[98]

In sum, the Warren Court's doctrine shifted the emphasis from protection of personal reputation to protection of press freedom. This shift in emphasis has helped the press report the news—and helped the public learn about the government—during a time when media coverage of controversial events has angered many people. Since the 1960s, individuals and groups have sued the press not primarily to gain compensation for damage to their reputation, but to punish the press for its coverage. For example, a lawyer for a conservative organization that sued CBS for its depiction of the army general who commanded the U.S. military in Vietnam admitted that the organization sought the "dismantling" of the network through libel suits.[99]

FREEDOM OF RELIGION

Some people came to America for religious liberty, but once they arrived, many didn't want to grant this liberty to others. Some communities became as intolerant as those in the Old World from which the people had fled.[100] But the colonists came with so many religious views that the diversity gradually led to grudging tolerance. By the time the Constitution and the Bill of Rights were adopted, support for religious liberty was fairly widespread.

Both the diversity and the tolerance are reflected in the two documents. Unlike the Declaration of Independence, the Constitution is a secular document. It doesn't mention "God," "Creator," "Providence," or "divine."[101] It doesn't claim to be a compact between the people and God (or, like some monarchies, between the rulers and God); rather, it's a compact among the people, as the Preamble underscores— "We the people . . . ."

The Bill of Rights grants freedom of religion in the First Amendment, which states, "Congress shall make no law respecting an establishment of religion, or prohibiting the free exercise thereof." These two clauses—the establishment clause and the free exercise clause—were intended to work in tandem to provide freedom for people's religions and, by implication, freedom from others' religions.

The Founders recoiled from Europeans' experience of continuous conflict and long wars fought over religious schisms. Consequently, Thomas Jefferson explained, the clauses were designed to build "a wall of separation between church and state."[102] Each would stay on its own side of the wall and not interfere or even interact with the other. **Separation of church and state** was a novel idea; according to one historian, although the phrase isn't in the Constitution, it's the "most revolutionary" aspect of the Constitution.[103]

When the District of Columbia was designed, a triangular configuration popular at the time was adopted. In one corner was the Capitol building for Congress, and in another was the White House for the president. In the third corner in many other nations, a large church representing the state religion reflected the spiritual power. Because of separation of church and state, however, the Founders didn't want a church in that corner. (They could have put the Supreme Court there, but the Court wasn't considered important then and wouldn't get its own building until 1935.) Instead, they located the Patent Office in that corner to represent the spirit of innovation. They anticipated many inventions.[104] (Now the building houses the National Portrait Gallery and the Museum of American Art.)

Today some deeply religious people scorn the idea of separation of church and state, thinking it devalues the importance of religion. But the Founders saw it as a means to preserve the peace that had eluded European states. In addition, they saw it as a way to protect religion itself. Without interference by government officials, whether to hinder or to help, churches would be free to determine their dogma and establish their practices as they saw fit. They would be free to flourish. Indeed, religion is stronger in the United States than in western Europe, where the churches endorsed and supported by the government sit mostly empty and most people are not believers. Some scholars think that religion is stronger in the United States *because of* separation of church and state.[105]

Despite the Founders' intention to separate church and state, as society became more complex and government became more pervasive, church and state came to interact, sometimes to interfere, with each other. Inevitably, the wall began to crumble, and the courts had to devise new doctrine to keep church and state as separate as possible while still accommodating the needs of each, as we'll see.

Free Exercise of Religion

The **free exercise clause** allows individuals to practice their religion without government coercion.

© Tom Defoe, 1965, Des Moines Register and Tribune Co.

Amish children head for the cornfields to avoid school officials in Iowa.

Direct Restrictions

Government has occasionally restricted free exercise of religion directly. Early in the country's history, some states prohibited Catholics, Quakers, or Jews from voting or holding office, and as late as 1961, Maryland prohibited nonbelievers from holding office.[106] In the 1920s, Oregon prohibited students from attending parochial schools.[107] More recently, prisons in Illinois and Texas prohibited Black Muslims and Buddhists from receiving religious publications and using prison chapels.[108] The Supreme Court *invalidated each of these restrictions.*

A suburb of Miami tried to ban the Santeria religion in 1987. Santeria blends ancient African rites and Roman Catholic rituals, but its distinguishing feature is animal sacrifice. Adherents believe that animal sacrifice is necessary to win the favor of the gods, and they practice it at initiations of new members and at births, marriages, and deaths. They kill chickens, ducks, doves, pigeons, sheep, goats, and turtles. When adherents, who had practiced their religion underground since refugees from Cuba brought it to Florida in the 1950s and 1960s, announced plans to construct a church building, cultural center, museum, and school, the city passed ordinances against ritualistic animal sacrifice, essentially forbidding adherents from practicing their religion. The Court struck down the ordinances.[109] "Although the practice of animal sacrifice may seem abhorrent to some," Justice Anthony Kennedy wrote, "religious beliefs need not be acceptable, logical, consistent, or comprehensible to others in order to merit First Amendment protection."

Indirect Restrictions

Government has also restricted free exercise of religion indirectly. As society has become more complex, some laws have interfered with religion, even when not designed to do so. The laws have usually interfered with minority religions, which don't have many members who serve as legislators and look out for their interests.

At first the Court distinguished between belief and action: individuals could believe what they wanted, but they could not act accordingly if such action was against the law. In 1878, male Mormons who believed their religion required polygamy could not marry more than one woman.[110] The Court rhetorically asked, "Suppose one believed that human sacrifices were a necessary part of religious worship?" Of course, belief without action gave little protection and scant satisfaction to the individuals involved.

In the 1960s, the Warren Court recognized this problem and broadened the protection by *granting exemptions to laws.* A Seventh-Day Adventist who worked in a textile mill in South Carolina quit when the mill shifted from a five-day to a six-day workweek that included Saturday—her Sabbath. Unable to find another job, she applied for unemployment benefits, but the state refused to provide them. To receive them, she had to be "available" for work, but the state said she wasn't available because she wouldn't accept any jobs that required Saturday work. The Court ordered the state to grant an exemption to its law.[111] The Burger Court, which followed the Warren Court's doctrine, ruled that employers need to make a reasonable effort to accommodate employees' requests to fit work schedules around their Sabbath.[112]

Congress, too, has granted some exemptions. It excused the Amish from participating in the Social Security program because the Amish support their own elderly. And in every draft law, it excused conscientious objectors from participating in war.

The Court has been most reluctant to exempt individuals from paying taxes. It didn't excuse either the Amish[113] or the Quakers, who as pacifists tried to withhold the portion of their income taxes that funded the military.[114] The Court worried that many other persons would try to avoid paying taxes, too.

The Rehnquist Court, which was less sensitive to minority rights, *refused to grant such exemptions.*[115] The Native American church uses peyote, a hallucinogen derived from a cactus, in worship ceremonies. Church members believe that the plant embodies their deity and that ingesting the plant is an act of communion. Although peyote is a

Alfred Smith, fired for using peyote in religious ceremonies, challenged Oregon's law prohibiting use of the drug.

controlled substance, Congress has authorized its use on Indian reservations, and many states have authorized its use off the reservations by church members. But when two members in Oregon, a state that didn't allow its use off the reservations, were fired from their jobs and denied unemployment benefits for using the drug, the Court refused to grant an exemption.[116] A five-justice majority rejected the doctrine and precedents of the Warren and Burger Courts. Justice Antonin Scalia, a Catholic, admitted that denying such exemptions will put minority religions at a disadvantage but insisted that this is an "unavoidable consequence of democratic government." (See box "Accommodating and Balancing.")

As a result of the decision, some adherents of minority religions weren't allowed to practice the tenets of their religions. Families of deceased Jews and Laotians, whose religions reject autopsies, were overruled. Muslim prisoners, whose religion forbids them to eat pork, were denied other meat as a substitute. Sikh construction workers, whose religion requires them to wear turbans, had been exempted from the law mandating hard hats at construction sites; after the decision, this exemption was rescinded.[117]

Even mainstream churches worried about the ruling's implications, and a coalition of religious groups lobbied Congress to overturn it. Congress passed an act reversing the ruling and substituting the previous doctrine from the Warren and Burger Courts. But the Rehnquist Court invalidated the act because it challenged the justices' authority and altered their interpretation of the First Amendment without going through the process required to amend the Constitution.[118]

Establishment of Religion

Two competing traditions reflecting the role of government toward religion have led to intense conflict over the **establishment clause**. Many settlers were Christians who

DEMOCRACY?

Compare the implications for democracy of (a) the Warren and Burger Courts' doctrine granting exemptions to religious minorities with (b) the Rehnquist Court's doctrine denying exemptions to these groups. Is one more democratic? Or do they emphasize different facets of democracy? What would be the consequences if the Rehnquist Court's doctrine were extended to other provisions of the Bill of Rights?

---

american diversity

Accommodating and Balancing

The annual Sun Dance is the Northern Arapaho Indians' most important religious ceremony. Winslow Friday, who lives on the Wind River Reservation in Wyoming, shot an eagle to obtain its tail fan for the ceremony. He was arrested for violating the Bald and Golden Eagle Protection Act, which prohibits killing these once endangered species. In defense, he cited the free exercise clause of the First Amendment.

The federal district court ruled for Friday, but the federal appellate court ruled for the government. The Supreme Court declined to hear the case.

In a diverse country, it's difficult to accommodate the needs and desires of all religious groups. And it's difficult to balance the needs and desires of any religious group with the commands of the secular laws. In the eagle, "You have a precious commodity," a federal official remarked. "It's precious to Native Americans, but it's also precious to the American people. How do you balance that?"

Members of Congress recognized the conflict when they passed the law, and they sought a balance. They created an exception for Native Americans who use the eagles in religious ceremonies. The law established the National Eagle Repository in Commerce City, Colorado, to collect dead eagles—usually struck by cars or electrocuted by utilities—and provide them to Indians. But some carcasses are poor specimens, and the repository, which collects about two thousand carcasses a year, has a waiting list of six thousand requests. Alternatively, the law established a permit process for Indians to kill eagles. But the process is obscure and unknown to most Indians, apparently by design. "We're not in the business of trying to generate interest in the taking of wildlife," another official said. So, some Indians, like Friday, shoot an eagle and risk an arrest.

After the Supreme Court declined to hear this case, federal prosecutors also sought a balance. They agreed to transfer the case from federal court, where the sentence could be harsher (a maximum fine of $100,000 and prison term of one year) to the reservation's tribal court, which sentenced Friday to a fine of $2,500 and a suspension of his hunting privilege on the reservation for one year.

SOURCES: DeeDee Correll, "Bald Eagle Case Raises Issue of Religious Liberty," Los Angeles Times, September 21, 2009, latimes.com/news/nationworld/nation/la-na-eagle-feather21-2009sep21,0,7225203.story; "Eagle-Killing Case Ends in Tribal–Court Guilty Plea," Billings Gazette, December 22, 2009, billingsgazette.com/news/state-and-regional/Wyoming/article-35cd45f2-6e5c-11df-001cc4c002e0.html. Quotes are from Correll article.

wanted the governments to reinforce their religion, yet the framers of the Constitution were products of the Enlightenment, which emphasized the importance of reason and deemphasized the role of religion. Many Founders, including the most important ones, were Deists rather than Christians, believing in a Supreme Being but rejecting much religious dogma.[119]

The two considered most responsible for the religious guarantees in the First Amendment, Thomas Jefferson and James Madison, especially feared the divisiveness of religion. They wanted separation of church and state, advocating not only freedom *of* religion for believers but freedom *from* religion for others.[120]

Even some religious groups wanted separation of church and state. The Baptists had been harassed and persecuted by the Anglicans (Episcopalians) and Congregationalists—for example, from 1760 to 1778, fifty-six Baptist preachers had been jailed in Anglican Virginia[121]—and they feared that these larger groups would use the power of the state to promote their views and practices.[122]

The Supreme Court initially reflected the first of these traditions. In 1892, Justice David Brewer proclaimed that "this is a Christian nation."[123] But as the country became more pluralistic, the Court moved toward the second of these traditions. Since the 1960s, the Court has *generally interpreted the establishment clause to forbid government not only from designating an official church,* like the Church of England, which receives tax money and special privileges, *but also from aiding one religion over another or even from aiding religion over nonreligion.*

School Prayers

Courts have used the establishment clause to resolve disputes about public school prayers. In 1962 and 1963, the Warren Court initiated its prayer rulings. At the start of each day, New York had students recite a nondenominational prayer, and Pennsylvania and Baltimore had students recite the Lord's Prayer or Bible verses. The Court, with only one justice dissenting, ruled that *these practices violated the establishment clause.*[124] Although the prayers officially were voluntary—students could leave the room—the Court doubted that the prayers really were voluntary. The justices noted that nonconforming students would face tremendous pressure from teachers and peers. The Court therefore concluded that the prayers fostered religion. According to Justice Black, "Government in this country should stay out of the business of writing and sanctioning official prayers and leave that purely religious function to the people themselves and to those the people . . . look to for religious guidance." Although schools could teach religion as a subject, they could not promote religion. For similar reasons, the Court ruled that Kentucky *could not require public schools to post the Ten Commandments* in classrooms.[125]

Many people sharply criticized the rulings. A representative from Alabama lamented, "They put the Negroes in

The country's religious diversity has led to demands for some exotic exemptions. Inspired by the Bible's statement that Jesus's followers "shall take up serpents" and "if they drink any deadly thing, it shall not hurt them," members of the Holiness Church of God in Jesus's Name handle snakes and drink strychnine. Some become enraptured and entranced to the point of hysteria, and occasionally some die. The Tennessee Supreme Court forbade such practices, saying that the state has "the right to guard against the unnecessary creation of widows and orphans." However, these practices continue in some places.

Courtesy of National Archives

the schools, and now they've driven God out."[126] Yet students, of course, can still pray on their own at any time.

Empirical studies in the years after the rulings found that prayers and Bible readings decreased but by no means disappeared, especially in the South.[127] A Tennessee school official asserted, "I am of the opinion that 99 percent of the people in the United States feel as I do about the Supreme Court's decision—that it was an outrage. . . . The remaining 1 percent do not belong in this free world."[128]

News reports in recent years indicate that some schools, especially in the rural South, still use prayers or Bible readings in violation of the Court's rulings. These practices are reinforced by social pressure. A woman whose family had moved to Pontotoc, Mississippi, discovered that Christian prayers were being broadcast on the intercom and the Bible was being taught in a class. When she objected, rumors circulated that she was an outside agitator paid by the ACLU to force the town to change. One of her children had a teacher who told the class that the child didn't believe in God, while another of her children kept "getting jumped" in the bathroom. Then the woman lost her job in a convenience store after customers threatened to boycott the store.[129] News reports also indicate that officials in Kentucky and Ohio allowed volunteers to put the Ten Commandments inside or outside public schools in violation of the Court's ruling.[130]

Although many people wanted a constitutional amendment to allow official prayers in public schools, Congress never passed one. Some people supported the rulings. Other people, who disagreed with the ruling but supported the authority of the Court, didn't want to challenge its authority and set a precedent for other groups on other matters. Some religious leaders doubted that the religious groups would ever agree on specific prayers. America's religious diversity means that any prayers would offend some students or parents. Prayers that suit Christians might offend Jews; those that suit Jews might offend adherents of other faiths. Recent immigrants from Asia and the Middle East, practicing Buddhism, Shintoism, Taoism, and Islam, have made the country even more pluralistic. Now, according to one researcher, America's religious diversity is greater than that of any country in recorded history.[131] Asking the students in this country to say a prayer would be like "asking the members of the United Nations to stand and sing the national anthem of one country."[132]

However, many small communities don't reflect this nationwide diversity, and their residents often assume that everyone, or at least "normal" people, share their views toward religion.

In lieu of an amendment, about half of the states have passed laws providing for a "moment of silence" to begin each school day. A majority of justices indicated that they *would approve a moment of silence if students were not urged to pray.*[133]

The Rehnquist Court reaffirmed and extended the prayer rulings of the Warren Court. It held that *clergy can't offer prayers at graduation ceremonies* for public elementary, middle, and high schools.[134] The prayers in question were brief and nonsectarian, but the majority concluded, "What to most believers may seem nothing more than a reasonable request that the nonbeliever respect their religious practices, in a school context may appear to the nonbeliever or dissenter to be an attempt to employ the machinery of the state to enforce a religious orthodoxy." Although attendance at the ceremony was voluntary, like participation in school prayers, the majority didn't consider it truly voluntary. Justice Kennedy wrote, "Everyone knows that in our society and in our culture high school graduation is one of life's most significant occasions. . . . Graduation is a time for family and those closest to the student to celebrate success and express mutual wishes of gratitude and respect."

Although the Court's language here was emphatic, its stance on student-led prayers has been ambiguous. In 1992, the Court refused to review a federal court of appeals ruling that allowed student-led prayers at graduation ceremonies.[135] A Texas school board permitted the senior class to decide whether to have a prayer and, if so, which student to give it. The appellate court held that this policy wasn't precluded by the Supreme Court's ruling because the decision wasn't made by officials and the prayer wasn't offered by a clergy member, so official coercion wasn't present. But in 1996, the Court also refused to review a federal court of appeals ruling from a different circuit that prohibited student-led prayers.[136] The Court's reluctance to resolve this controversy means that the ruling of each court of appeals remains but applies only to the schools in its circuit.

The first appellate court's holding encouraged opponents of the Supreme Court's rulings to use the same approach to circumvent these daily prayer rulings as well. Several southern states passed laws allowing student-led prayers to start each school day. Some school officials, who selected the students, let them give the prayers over the intercom. Federal courts in Alabama and Mississippi invalidated these laws because school officials were involved and because all students were required or at least pressured to listen to the prayers.

The Rehnquist Court did invalidate the use of schools' public address systems by clergy or students to give prayers at high school football games.[137] Although student attendance is voluntary, the games are official school events.

Muslim students in Dearborn, Michigan, reflect our religious pluralism. The Detroit area has the second-largest concentration of Arabs outside the Middle East.

The public desire for official school prayers is fueled by nostalgia for the less troubling times before the 1960s. As one writer perceived, the desire "doesn't have much to do with prayer anyway, but with a time, a place, an ethos that praying and pledging allegiance at the beginning of school each day represent."[138] For some people, buffeted by the upheavals and dislocations of our times, the reinstitutionalization of school prayers would symbolize that our society still stands for appropriate values.

The public desire for official school prayers is also fueled by occasional reports of school officials who mistakenly believe that court rulings require them to forbid all forms of religious expression. Some confused administrators have prohibited a few students from wearing religious jewelry, reading the Bible while riding the bus, and praying before eating their lunch.[139]

In another case, the Supreme Court held that the University of Missouri at Kansas City had to make its meeting rooms available to students' religious organizations on an equal basis with other organizations, even if the religious organizations use the rooms for prayer or worship.[140] Otherwise, the university would be discriminating against religion.

After this decision, Congress passed a law that *requires public high schools as well as colleges and universities to allow meetings of students' religious, philosophical, or political groups outside class hours.* The Court accepted this law.[141] Justice Sandra Day O'Connor said that high school students "are likely to understand that a school does not endorse or support student speech that it merely permits on a nondiscriminatory basis." Students have established Bible clubs in one-quarter of public high schools, according to one estimate.[142] (As a result of this act, students have also established gay-straight clubs—organizations of gay and straight students who support the rights of gays, lesbians, and bisexuals—in more than seven hundred high schools.)[143] The Rehnquist Court also held that the University of Virginia had to provide funding, from students' fees, to students' religious organizations on an equal basis with other campus organizations, even if a religious organization sought the money to print a religious newspaper.[144] Following this precedent, a federal court of appeals ruled that the University of South Alabama had to provide funding to a gay organization.

Religious Symbols

Despite its prayer rulings, the Court has been *reluctant to invalidate traditional religious symbols.* It has not questioned the motto "In God We Trust," on our coins since 1865 and paper money since 1955, or the phrase "one nation under God," in the Pledge of Allegiance since 1954.[145]

In 2002, a federal court of appeals held the phrase "under God" in the Pledge unconstitutional when recited in the public schools. The court said it promotes religion as much as if it professed that we are a nation "under Jesus" or "under Vishnu" or "under Zeus" or "under no god." It promotes Christianity and leaves out not only atheists and agnostics but also believers of other deities, such as Buddhists and many Native Americans. Although the ruling was a logical extension of the prayer rulings, it was a lightning rod for the public's anger, and the Supreme Court sidestepped the issue (deciding that the student's father, an atheist, lacked authority to bring suit on the student's behalf because the student's mother, a born-again Christian, had custody of the child after their divorce).[146]

The Burger Court upheld the display of a nativity scene on government property, at least when it's part of a broader display for the holiday season.[147] Pawtucket, Rhode Island, had a crèche, Christmas tree, Santa Claus, sleigh with reindeer, and talking wishing well. The Court said that Christmas had become a secular as well as a religious holiday and that the secular decorations diluted any religious impact the nativity scene would have. A crèche by itself, however, would be impermissible.[148]

The Rehnquist Court addressed Ten Commandments displays and ruled much like the Burger Court did for Christmas nativity scenes. A Ten Commandments monument on the Texas capitol grounds could remain because it was just one of sixteen other monuments and twenty-one historical markers, which were secular, and because it had been there for forty years.[149] But copies of the Ten Commandments in two Kentucky courthouses could not remain because they were not part of historical displays[150] and they were posted recently for religious purposes.[151]

Evolution

Courts have also used the establishment clause to resolve disputes about teaching evolution in schools. In 1968, the Supreme Court invalidated Arkansas' forty-year-old law forbidding schools from teaching evolution.[152] Arkansas and Louisiana then passed laws requiring schools that teach evolution to also teach "creationism"—the biblical version of creation.[153] In 1987, the Court *invalidated these laws because their purpose was to advance the fundamentalist Christian view.*[154]

Evolution remains controversial. In recent years, many states have considered antievolution proposals. In 2005, a suburban Atlanta school district pasted disclaimers onto ninth-grade biology textbooks stating, "Evolution is a theory, not a fact" and should be "critically considered." A federal court ordered the disclaimers removed because their denigration of evolution reflected a religious view.

Critics of evolution also promoted "intelligent design"— the notion that some life is so complex that it must have been designed by an intelligent creator rather than have evolved through natural selection and random chance, as the theory of evolution posits.[155] In 2005, the Dover, Pennsylvania, school district required teachers to discuss intelligent design. A federal court invalidated the policy because

A megachurch with twelve thousand members in Memphis, Tennessee, unveiled its "Statue of Liberation through Christ" in 2006. In contrast to the Statue of Liberty, this monument holds a cross rather than a torch and, with the other arm, the Ten Commandments. She also has a tear running down her cheek because of modern secularism, legal abortions, and the absence of school prayers. According to the pastor, the purpose of the monument is to let people know that "God is in the foundation of our nation." Hence the merger of church and state.

intelligent design isn't a science. Its proponents invoke a supernatural designer—that is, God[156]—whereas science deals with natural phenomena. Although intelligent design proponents make scientific critiques of evolution, intelligent design itself isn't based on empirical evidence and doesn't offer testable hypotheses.

Other Policies

Conservative Christians have pushed Republican officials to adopt policies and programs reflecting their beliefs. Despite the establishment clause, the Bush administration limited scientific research with stem cells, withheld federal money from family planning organizations and programs in the United States and abroad, gave federal money to abstinence education programs, and gave federal money to hundreds of church-run marriage, child care, and drug treatment programs. As a result, for example, the government gave federal money to Louisiana, which funneled it to Protestant groups to teach abstinence through Bible lessons and to Catholic groups to hold prayer sessions at abortion clinics.[157] So far, the courts haven't ruled that these policies and programs violate the establishment clause.

Despite ever-present tensions and very frequent conflicts, the effort to separate church and state has enabled the United States to manage, even nourish, its religious pluralism. The effort has kept potential religious fights out of the political arena. But today this practical arrangement is opposed by those religious conservatives who most fear the changes in modern society. They consider their religion

a shield protecting their family against these changes, and they want the authority of the government to reinforce their religion. In one of her last opinions, Justice O'Connor, a moderate conservative, addressed these religious conservatives: "At a time when we see around the world the violent consequences of the assumption of religious authority by the government, Americans may count themselves fortunate. . . . [Those] who would renegotiate the boundaries between church and state must therefore answer a difficult question: Why would we trade a system that has served us so well for one that has served others so poorly?"[158]

RIGHTS OF CRIMINAL DEFENDANTS

The Fourth, Fifth, Sixth, and Eighth Amendments provide numerous **due process** rights for criminal defendants. When the government prosecutes defendants, it must give them the process—that is, the procedures—they are due; it must be fair and "respect certain decencies of civilized conduct,"[159] even toward uncivilized people.

One defense attorney said that many of his clients "had been monsters—nothing less—who had done monstrous things. Although occasionally not guilty of the crime charged, nearly all my clients have been guilty of something."[160] Then why do we give them rights? We give criminal defendants rights because we give all individuals rights in court. As Justice Douglas observed, "respecting the

WHEN A COURT REVERSES A CONVICTION . . .

. . . the defendant does not necessarily go free. An appellate court only evaluates the legality of the procedures used by officials; it does not determine guilt or innocence. Therefore, when it reverses a conviction, it only indicates that officials used some illegal procedure in convicting the defendant—for example, evidence from an improper search and seizure. Then the prosecutor can retry the defendant, without this evidence, if the prosecutor thinks there is enough other evidence. Often prosecutors do retry the defendants, and frequently judges or juries reconvict them.

dignity even of the least worthy . . . citizen raises the stature of all of us."[161]

But why do we give all individuals rights in court? We do so because we have established the **presumption of innocence**. This presumption is "not . . . a naive belief that most or even many defendants are innocent, or a cavalier attitude toward crime." It reflects a mistrust of the state, as it recognizes the possibility of an overzealous prosecutor or an unfair judge. It requires the state to prove the defendant's guilt, essentially saying, "We won't take your word for it."[162] Of course, when the crime rate is high or a particular crime is heinous, many people fear the state less than the criminals. Then they want to give officials more authority and defendants fewer rights. But this is the way all people eventually lose their rights. (See box "When a Court Reverses a Conviction . . .")

Search and Seizure

England fostered the notion that a family's home is its castle, but Parliament made exceptions for the American colonies. It authorized writs of assistance, which allowed customs officials to conduct general searches for goods imported by the colonists without paying taxes to the crown. The English tradition of home privacy combined with the colonists' resentment of these writs led to adoption of the Fourth Amendment, which forbids **unreasonable searches and seizures**.

In these cases, the Supreme Court has tried to walk a fine line between acknowledging officials' need for evidence and individuals' desire for privacy. This judicial doctrine is so complex that we will note just its basic principles here.

One type of seizure is the arrest of a person. *Police must have evidence to believe that a person committed a crime.*

Another type of seizure is the confiscation of illegal contraband. *The general requirement is that police must get a search warrant from a judge by showing evidence that a particular thing is in a particular place.*

However, *the Court has made numerous exceptions to this requirement* that complicate the law. These exceptions account for most searches. If persons consent to a search, police can conduct a search without a warrant. If police see contraband in plain view, they can seize it; they don't have to close their eyes to it. If police have evidence to arrest

someone, they can search the person and the area within the person's control. If police have reason to suspect that someone is committing a crime but lack evidence to arrest the person, they can "stop and frisk" the person—conduct a pat-down search. If police have reason to believe that a person's life is in jeopardy, they can search for weapons. In some situations, if police want to search a motor vehicle, they can do so because vehicles are mobile and could be gone by the time police get a warrant.

Exclusionary Rule

To enforce search and seizure law, the Supreme Court has *established the* **exclusionary rule**, *which bars from the courts any evidence obtained in violation of the Fourth Amendment.* The purpose is to deter illegal conduct by police officers.

Although the Court created this rule for federal courts in 1914,[163] it didn't impose the rule on state courts until 1961 in *Mapp* v. *Ohio.*[164] Until this time, police in many states had ignored search and seizure law. *Mapp* was one of the Warren Court's most controversial rulings. Many people didn't think that evidence of guilt should be barred from court, even if search and seizure law had been violated by police.

The decision still hasn't been widely accepted, and the Burger Court created an exception to it. In a pair of cases, the justices allowed evidence obtained illegally to be used in court because the police had acted "in good faith."[165] The Roberts Court has also created an exception to it.[166] Nonetheless, the rule remains for most situations.

Electronic Surveillance of Suspected Criminals

The Fourth Amendment traditionally applied to searches involving a physical trespass and seizures producing a tangible object. Electronic surveillance, however, does not require a physical trespass or involve a tangible object.

This posed a problem for the Supreme Court when it heard its first wiretapping case in 1928. Federal prohibition agents tapped a bootlegger's telephone by installing equipment on wires in the basement of the bootlegger's apartment building. The Court's majority rigidly adhered to its traditional doctrine, saying that this was not a search and seizure, so the agents did not need a warrant.[167]

In a classic example of keeping the Constitution up-to-date with the times, the Warren Court overruled this precedent in 1967.[168] Because electronic eavesdropping might threaten privacy as much as traditional searching, *officials must get judicial authorization,* similar to a warrant, *to engage in such eavesdropping.*

Electronic Surveillance of Possible Terrorists

The law is quite different for surveillance of possible terrorists than for ordinary criminals. Soon after 9/11, the Bush administration encouraged the National Security Agency (NSA) to conduct an electronic "fishing expedition" to locate terrorists or people connected to terrorists in the United States and around the world. The NSA began to intercept international calls and e-mails *between people in the United States and people in foreign countries* (whether Americans or foreigners). It gained access through American telecommunications companies, which had created a robust network of fiber-optic cables that carry most worldwide communications that travel on wires. Then it used computer searches to look for telltale words and phrases that might be spoken or written by terrorists. Although the administration claimed that it was obtaining calls and e-mails "from very bad people to very bad people,"[169] the program was not restricted to suspected terrorists. It was far broader.

The NSA also began to analyze calls *between people within the United States* to uncover terrorists through social network analysis. By correlating callers' and receivers' numbers and the date, time, and duration of the calls,[170] computers can map patterns of interactions among people. If the government knows that one person is a member of al-Qaeda, this analysis might identify other members too.

The administration didn't seek judicial authorization for either of these programs. The interception of calls and e-mails between people in the United States and people in foreign countries was definitely a violation of the law.[171] (The analysis of calls between people within the United States may also have been a violation of the law.) After the programs were revealed by the press, the administration pressured Congress to amend the law to allow the programs to continue.[172] Now the law legalizes eavesdropping that had previously been illegal.

It's not known how extensive either the international surveillance or the domestic surveillance has been or is now, although both have examined the calls of many ordinary Americans—probably "tens of thousands."[173] The programs are sweeping dragnets, rather than targeted searches, with little or no oversight.[174] They show how a combination of technological advances and terrorist attacks can challenge our liberties.

Self-Incrimination

The Fifth Amendment stipulates that persons shall not be compelled to be witnesses against themselves—that is, to incriminate themselves. Because defendants are presumed innocent, the government must prove their guilt.

This right means that *defendants on trial don't have to take the witness stand and answer the prosecutor's questions,* and neither the prosecutor nor the judge can call attention to their decision to exercise this right. Neither can suggest or imply that the defendants must have something to hide and must therefore be guilty. (But if the defendants do take the stand, they thereby waive their right, so the prosecutor can cross-examine them and they must answer.)

This right also means that *prosecutors can't introduce into evidence statements or confessions from defendants that weren't voluntary.* The meaning of *voluntary* has evolved over time.

For years, police used physical brutality—"the third degree"—to get confessions. After 1936, when the Supreme Court ruled that confessions obtained in this manner were invalid,[175] police used psychological techniques. They held suspects incommunicado, preventing them from contacting relatives or lawyers and delaying them from going to court, to pressure them to confess.[176] They interrogated suspects for long periods of time without food or rest, in one case with alternating teams of interrogators for thirty-six hours straight,[177] to wear them down and break their will. The Court ruled that confessions obtained by these techniques were also invalid.

The Warren Court still worried that many confessions weren't truly voluntary, so it issued a landmark decision in 1966. Arizona police arrested a poor, mentally disturbed man, Ernesto Miranda, for kidnapping and raping a woman. After the woman identified him in a lineup, police interrogated him, prompting him to confess. He hadn't been told that he could remain silent or be represented by an attorney. In *Miranda* v. *Arizona,* the Court concluded that his confession wasn't truly voluntary.[178] Chief Justice Warren, as

"No, I'm not backing up our files—I'm just assuming that the F.B.I. is making copies."

© The New Yorker Collection 2003, Robert Mankoff from cartoonbank.com. All rights reserved.

a former district attorney, knew the advantage that police officers have in an interrogation and thought the suspects needed more protection. The Court ruled that *officials must advise suspects of their rights before their interrogation.* These came to be known as the **Miranda rights**:

> You have the right to remain silent.
> If you talk, anything you say can be used against you.
> You have the right to be represented by an attorney.
> If you can't afford an attorney, one will be appointed for you.

The Burger and Rehnquist Courts didn't require police and prosecutors to follow *Miranda* as strictly as the Warren Court did, but, contrary to expectations, they didn't abandon it. In 2000, the Rehnquist Court reaffirmed *Miranda* by a 7–2 vote.[179]

The Roberts Court addressed an ambiguity in *Miranda.* Although the Warren Court specified that suspects can invoke their rights to silence and an attorney any time during interrogation, what if the suspects neither clearly invoke their rights nor clearly waive them? In almost three hours of interrogation, a suspect didn't invoke or waive his rights, and he didn't answer any questions. Finally, he offered an incriminating answer to a single question. The federal appellate court concluded that he exercised his right to silence by not speaking for almost three hours, but the conservative majority on the Roberts Court concluded that he failed to exercise his right and, ultimately, waived his right by answering the one question.[180] Thus it appears that the Roberts Court will side with police and prosecutors in cases that could plausibly go either way.

Even with the warnings, most suspects talk anyway. Some don't understand the warnings. Others think the police, who may rattle off the warnings very fast or in a monotone, give them as a formality but won't follow them. Also, suspects being interrogated face a coercive atmosphere and law enforcement tactics designed to exploit their weaknesses. Detectives are trained to persuade suspects to talk despite the warnings. One said, "Before you ever get in there, the first thing an investigator usually thinks about is . . . how can I breeze through this *Miranda* thing so I don't set the guy off and tell him not to talk to me, song and dance it, sugarcoat it, whatever?"[181] So detectives frequently lie and trick suspects.

Counsel

The Sixth Amendment provides the **right to counsel** in criminal cases. Initially, this meant that defendants could hire an attorney to help them prepare a defense, and later it meant that defendants could also have the attorney represent them at the trial. But it was no help to most defendants because they were too poor to hire an attorney for either. Consequently, in 1938 the Supreme Court required federal trial courts to furnish an attorney to all indigent defendants.[182] But most criminal cases are state cases, and the Court was reluctant to require state trial courts also to furnish an attorney.[183]

However, the Warren Court was willing to do so in 1963. It heard the case of Clarence Earl Gideon, who was charged with breaking into a pool hall and stealing beer, wine, and change from a vending machine. At trial, Gideon asked the judge for a lawyer. The judge wouldn't appoint one, leaving Gideon to defend himself. The prosecution didn't have a strong case, but Gideon wasn't able to point out its weaknesses. He was convicted and sentenced to five years. On appeal, the Warren Court unanimously declared that Gideon was entitled to be represented by counsel.[184] Justice Black explained that "lawyers in criminal courts are necessities, not luxuries." The Court finally established a broad rule: state courts must provide an attorney to indigent defendants in felony cases.

When he was tried again, Gideon was given a lawyer, who proved the Court's point. The lawyer did an effective job defending him, which Gideon hadn't been able to do himself. This time Gideon wasn't convicted.

The Burger and Rehnquist Courts expanded the rule: state courts must provide an attorney to indigent defendants in misdemeanor cases, too, except those that result in no incarceration (or probation),[185] because misdemeanor cases as well as felony cases are too complex for the defendants to defend themselves. Thus *all courts must offer an attorney to indigent defendants in all cases except the most minor ones, such as traffic violations.* The Supreme Court also decided that, in addition to an attorney for the trial, *the courts must provide an attorney for one appeal.*[186]

Receiving counsel doesn't necessarily mean receiving effective counsel, however. Some assigned attorneys are inexperienced, some are incompetent, and most are overworked and have little time to prepare the best possible defense.

Some jurisdictions make little effort to provide effective counsel, even in murder cases where capital punishment looms. In Illinois, at least thirty-three convicts on death row had been represented at trial by attorneys who were later disbarred or suspended.[187] In Louisiana, a defendant was represented by an attorney who was living with the prosecutor in the case. In Florida, a defendant was represented by a part-time attorney who was a deputy sheriff. In Georgia, a black defendant was represented by a white attorney who had been the Imperial Wizard of the local Ku Klux Klan for fifty years.[188] Also in Georgia, an attorney was so unversed in criminal law that when he was asked to name criminal rulings he was familiar with, he could think of only one (*Miranda*).[189] In three murder cases in one recent year in Texas, defense attorneys slept through the trials. When one of these defendants appealed his conviction on the ground that he didn't receive his constitutional right to counsel, the appellate court announced that "the Constitution doesn't say the lawyer has to be awake."[190] (Stung by criticism, the appellate court sat *en banc*—that is, the

Clarence Earl Gideon, convinced that he was denied a fair trial because he was not given an attorney, read law books in prison so he could petition the Supreme Court for a writ of *certiorari*. He wrote his petition by hand. Although he had spent much of his life in prison, he was optimistic. "I believe that each era finds an improvement in law [and] each year brings something new for the benefit of mankind. Maybe this will be one of those small steps forward."

entire court, rather than a three-judge panel, reheard the case—and overruled itself.) At least these attorneys were present. In Alabama, a defendant was represented by an attorney who failed to appear when his case was argued before the state supreme court. The defendant lost and was executed.[191]

In recent years, the issue of legal counsel for the defendants subject to capital punishment has received more scrutiny because new investigations and technologies, involving DNA analysis, have demonstrated that dozens of inmates on death row didn't commit the murder they were convicted of and sentenced for (and hundreds of inmates didn't commit the lesser crimes they were convicted of and sentenced for).[192] Nonetheless, there is little effort to provide effective counsel for criminal defendants because few groups, other than lawyers' associations, urge adequate representation. Criminal defendants have no political power in our system, and the public has limited sympathy for their rights.[193]

Jury Trial

The Sixth Amendment also provides the **right to a jury trial** in "serious" criminal cases. The Supreme Court has defined "serious" cases as those that could result in more than six months' incarceration.[194]

The right was adopted to prevent oppression by a "corrupt or overzealous prosecutor" or a "biased . . . or eccentric judge."[195] It has also served to limit governmental use of unpopular laws or enforcement practices. Regardless of the evidence against a defendant, a jury can refuse to convict if it feels that the government overstepped its bounds.

The jury is supposed to be impartial, so persons who have made up their minds before trial should be dismissed. It is also supposed to be "a fair cross section" of the community, so no group should be systematically excluded.[196] But the jury need not be a perfect cross section and in fact need not have a single member of any particular group.[197] Most courts use voter registration lists to obtain the names of potential jurors. These lists aren't closely representative because poor people don't register at the same rate as others, but the courts have decided that the lists are sufficiently representative. And the "motor voter law," which requires drivers' license and welfare offices to offer voter registration forms, has prompted more people to register to vote and thus to make themselves available to serve on juries.

Cruel and Unusual Punishment

The Eighth Amendment forbids **cruel and unusual punishment** but doesn't define such punishment. The Supreme

Court had interpreted the phrase to mean torture or punishment grossly disproportionate to the offense. Thus the Roberts Court invalidated life terms for juvenile defendants who did not commit murder.[198]

The death penalty was used at the time the Eighth Amendment was adopted, so for many years it was assumed to be constitutional.[199] But in 1972 the Burger Court narrowly ruled that *the death penalty, as it was then being administered, was cruel and unusual punishment.*[200] The laws and procedures allowed too much discretion by those who administered the punishment and resulted in too much arbitrariness and discrimination for those who received it. The death penalty was imposed so seldom, according to Justice Potter Stewart, that it was "cruel and unusual in the same way that being struck by lightning is cruel and unusual." Yet when it was imposed, it was imposed on black defendants more often than on white defendants.

The decision invalidated the laws of forty states and commuted the death sentences of 629 inmates. But because the Court didn't hold capital punishment cruel and unusual in principle, about three-fourths of the states adopted revised laws that permitted less discretion in an attempt to achieve less arbitrariness and discrimination.

These changes satisfied a majority of the Burger Court, which ruled that *capital punishment isn't cruel and unusual for murder if administered fairly.*[201] But it can't be imposed automatically for everyone convicted of murder, because the judge or jury must consider any mitigating factors that would justify a lesser punishment.[202] Also, it can't be imposed for rape, as some states legislated, because it's disproportionate to that offense.[203]

The revised laws have reduced but not eliminated discrimination. Where past studies showed discrimination against black defendants, recent studies show discrimination against black or white defendants who murder white victims. People who affect the decision to impose the death penalty—prosecutors, defense attorneys, judges, and jurors—appear to value white lives more. Despite evidence from Georgia that those who killed whites were more than four times as likely to be given the death penalty as those who killed blacks, the Rehnquist Court, by a 5–4 vote, upheld capital punishment in the state.[204]

The revised laws have not addressed an equally serious problem—inadequate representation given to poor defendants who face the death penalty—which we discussed in conjunction with the right to counsel.

For years, most people dismissed any suggestions that innocent defendants might be put to death. They assumed that, at least in these cases, the criminal justice system used careful procedures and made no mistakes. However, since capital punishment was reinstated and stricter procedures were mandated in the 1970s, at least 124 inmates awaiting execution have been released because new evidence, including DNA tests, revealed their innocence.[205] This number represents one exoneration for every seven to eight executions—a disturbing frequency for the ultimate punishment.[206] And apparently at least one inmate who was innocent was executed (in Texas in 2004).[207] Some defendants were the victims of sloppy or biased police or overzealous prosecutors; some were the victims of mistaken witnesses; others were the victims of emotional or prejudiced jurors. Many were the victims of inadequate representation.

Because of the patterns of racial discrimination and inadequate representation, the American Bar Association and some state governors have called for a moratorium on the use of capital punishment.[208] Although a majority of the public still supports capital punishment, that support is declining as more inmates are being found innocent through new investigations and DNA analysis.[209] Consequently, more jurors are becoming reluctant to impose the death penalty, instead opting for life in prison.[210]

Even the Rehnquist Court, long a staunch supporter of the death penalty, reflected the public's mood. In 2002, it ruled that states cannot execute the mentally retarded.[211] Previously, it had allowed execution of the retarded, including a man who had the mental capacity of a seven-year-old and still believed in Santa Claus.[212] Now, the six-justice majority observed, there is a new "national consensus" against such executions. In 2005, it ruled that states cannot execute juveniles who were younger than eighteen when they killed.[213] Previously, it had allowed execution of juveniles as young as sixteen. Now, Justice Kennedy noted, there are "evolving standards of decency" in society. Nonetheless, most states retain the death penalty for adults even though nearly all other developed countries (except Japan) have abolished it.[214]

Rights in Theory and in Practice

Overall, the Supreme Court has interpreted the Bill of Rights to provide an impressive list of rights for criminal defendants (although a significant change from the Warren Court to the Burger and Rehnquist Courts was a narrowing of those rights). Yet not all rights are available for all defendants in all places. Some police, prosecutors, and judges don't comply with Supreme Court rulings.

When the rights are available, most defendants don't take advantage of them. About 90 percent of criminal defendants plead guilty, and many of them do so through a **plea bargain**. This is an agreement among the prosecutor, the defense attorney, and the defendant, with the explicit or implicit approval of the judge, to reduce the charge or the sentence in exchange for a guilty plea. A plea bargain is a compromise. For officials, it saves the time, trouble, and uncertainty of a trial. For defendants, it eliminates the fear of a harsher sentence. However, it also reduces due process rights. A guilty plea waives the defendants' right to a jury trial, at which the defendants can present their own witnesses and cross-examine the government's witnesses and at which they can't be forced to incriminate themselves. A guilty plea also reduces the defendants' right to counsel because it reduces their lawyers' need to prepare a defense. Most attorneys pressure their clients to forgo a trial so that the attorneys don't have to spend the time to investigate and try the case. Despite these drawbacks for due process rights, the Supreme Court allows plea bargaining, and the trial courts encourage the practice because it enables judges and attorneys to dispose of their cases quickly.[215]

RIGHT TO PRIVACY

Neither the Constitution nor the Bill of Rights mentions privacy. Nevertheless, the right to privacy, Justice Douglas noted, is "older than the Bill of Rights,"[216] and the framers undoubtedly assumed that the people would have such a right. In fact, the framers did include several amendments that reflect their concern for privacy: the First Amendment protects privacy of association; the Third, privacy of homes from quartering soldiers; the Fourth, privacy of persons and places where they live from searches and seizures; and the Fifth, privacy of knowledge and thoughts from compulsory self-incrimination. The Supreme Court would use these to establish an explicit **right to privacy**.

So far, the Court's right-to-privacy doctrine reflects a right to autonomy—what Justice Louis Brandeis called "the right to be left alone"—more than a right to keep things confidential. As noted earlier in the chapter, the Court has been reluctant to punish the press for invading people's privacy by publishing personal information.[217]

Birth Control

The Warren Court explicitly *established a right to privacy* in *Griswold* v. *Connecticut* in 1965. The case began when Planned Parenthood and a professor at Yale Medical School opened a birth control clinic in New Haven. This action violated an 1879 law in Connecticut that prohibited distributing or using contraceptives or even disseminating information about them. After the state shut down the clinic, its founders challenged the law and the justices invalidated it.[218] To enforce the law, the state would have to police people's bedrooms. The very idea of policing married couples' bedrooms, the Court said, was absurd. Then the Court struck down Massachusetts and New York laws that prohibited distributing contraceptives to unmarried persons.[219] "If the right of privacy means anything," Justice Brennan said, "it is the right of the individual, married or single, to be free from unwarranted governmental intrusion into matters so fundamentally affecting a person as the decision whether to bear or beget a child."[220]

Abortion

When twenty-two-year-old Norma McCorvey became pregnant in 1969, she was distraught. She had one young daughter, she had relinquished custody of two previous children,

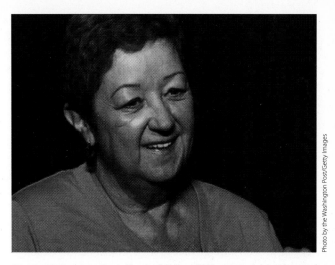

Norma McCorvey—"Jane Roe" of *Roe* v. *Wade*—switched sides and joined forces with Operation Rescue's Flip Benham in 1995.

and she was divorced. She sought an abortion, but Texas prohibited abortions unless the mother's life was in danger. "No legitimate doctor in Dallas would touch me," she discovered. "I found one doctor who offered to abort me for $500. Only he didn't have a license, and I was scared to turn my body over to him. So there I was—pregnant, unmarried, unemployed, alone, and stuck."[221] Unaware of states that permitted abortions, McCorvey put her baby up for adoption. But the state law rankled her. When she met two women attorneys who recently graduated from law school and also disliked the law, they offered to take her case to challenge the law. She adopted the name Jane Roe to conceal her identity.

In *Roe* v. *Wade* in 1973, the Burger Court *extended the right to privacy from birth control to abortion.*[222] Justice Harry Blackmun surveyed the writings of doctors, theologians, and philosophers over the years and found that these thinkers didn't agree when life begins. Therefore, the majority on the Court concluded that judges shouldn't assert that life begins at any particular time, whether at conception, which would make a fetus a person and abortion murder, or at birth. Without this factor in the equation, a woman's privacy, or control, of her body became paramount.

The Court ruled that *women have a **right to abortion** during the first six months of pregnancy.* States can prohibit an abortion during the last three months because the fetus becomes viable—it can live outside the womb—at this point. (However, states must allow an abortion during this time for a woman whose life is endangered by continuing her pregnancy.) Thus the right is broad but not absolute. The justices, as revealed in memos discovered years later, acknowledged that their division of the nine-month term was "legislative," but they saw this as a way to balance the rights of the mother in the early stages of pregnancy with the rights of the fetus in the later stage.[223]

Almost 90 percent of abortions are performed during the first trimester. Barely 1 percent are performed after

Photo by the Washington Post/Getty Images

twenty-one weeks, which is several weeks before the end of the second trimester.[224]

The *Roe* case has had an enormous impact on American politics. The Court's ruling invalidated the abortion laws of forty-nine states[225] and increased the number of abortions performed in the country (see Figure 1). It put abortion on the public agenda, galvanizing conservative groups who saw the decision as a symbol of loosening social restraints at a time of rampaging social problems. Disparate groups, such as Roman Catholics and evangelical Protestants (and some Orthodox Jews), rural residents and urban ethnics, who rarely saw eye to eye, coalesced around this issue and exercised leverage within the Republican Party.

In hindsight, some observers believe that the justices may have been imprudent or at least premature (even though majorities in both parties at the time supported leaving the decision to the woman and her doctor).[226] Before the ruling, some states began liberalizing their laws, but there wasn't time for others to follow or for citizens to ponder the issue. There was little public debate, let alone the extended debate necessary to develop a broad consensus. The Court's ruling short-circuited the normal political process and prompted opponents to mobilize and supporters to countermobilize. Both sides scorned the compromises that typify political solutions to most issues.[227]

The right-to-life movement pressured presidents and senators to appoint justices and lower court judges who opposed the ruling. The movement also lobbied members of Congress and state legislatures to overturn or circumvent the ruling. Although Congress refused to pass constitutional amendments banning abortions or allowing states to regulate them, Congress and state legislatures did pass statutes limiting abortions in various ways.

The Burger Court invalidated most of these statutes,[228] but it upheld a major limitation. The Medicaid program, financed jointly by the federal and state governments, began to pay for abortions for poor women. As a result, the program came to pay for a third of the abortions in the country each year.[229] But Congress eliminated federal funding (except when pregnancy threatens the life of the mother or is the result of rape or incest), and thirty-three state legislatures eliminated state funding. In these states, poor women need to pay the entire cost. The Court upheld these laws, ruling that *governments have no obligation to finance abortions,* even if this means that some women cannot take advantage of their right to have them.[230] For some women, these laws delay abortions while the women search for the money. For other women, these laws deny abortions because the women can't obtain the money.[231]

Many people, including pro-choice advocates, support these bans because they dislike welfare spending. Yet according to an analysis of the states that do provide abortion funding for poor women, the states save money. For every $1 they spend on abortions, they save $4 in welfare and medical expenses in what would have been the first two years of the child's life.[232] They save much more over a longer period. Ironically, public distaste for welfare spending actually leads to more welfare spending here.

Presidents Reagan and George H. W. Bush sought justices who opposed *Roe,* and after they filled their fifth vacancy on the Court, pro-life advocates expected the Court to overturn it. Yet the Rehnquist Court didn't overturn it.[233] In 1992, a bare majority reaffirmed the right to abortion.[234] At the same time, the majority *allowed more restrictions on the right—as long as the restrictions don't place an "undue burden" on the women seeking abortions.* In other words, states must permit abortions but can discourage them.[235]

Therefore, the majority upheld Pennsylvania's 24-hour waiting period between the time a woman indicates her desire to have an abortion and the time a doctor can perform one. Although a 24-hour waiting period is not a burden for many women, it can be for poor women who live in rural areas and must travel to cities for abortions. One Mississippi woman hitchhiked to the city and planned to sleep on outdoor furniture in the Kmart parking lot until the clinic offered to pay for her motel room.[236]

A waiting period can also affect teenagers. Some pro-life groups note the license numbers of cars driven to clinics

---

Figure 1 | **Abortion Rate since *Roe***

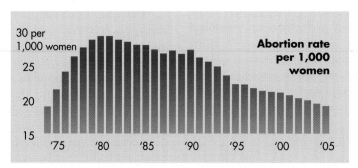

The abortion rate climbed after Roe *and peaked in the 1980s. Since then it has declined steadily.*
SOURCE: "The Right to Be a Father (Or Not)" from *The New York Times,* © November 6, 2005. All rights reserved. Used by permission and protected by the Copyright Laws of the United States. The printing, copying, redistribution, or retransmission of the Material without express written permission is prohibited.

by teenagers. After looking up the name and address of the family, they inform the parents in the hope that the parents will persuade or pressure their daughter to change her mind during the waiting period.

The majority also struck down Pennsylvania's requirement that a married woman notify her husband before having an abortion.[237] This was an undue burden because a woman who fears physical abuse from her husband would be deterred from seeking an abortion. Justice O'Connor wrote that a state "may not give to a man the kind of dominion over his wife that parents exercise over their children."

However, the Court upheld thirteen states' requirement that unmarried minors notify their parents and twenty-one states' requirement that unmarried minors obtain their parents' consent before having an abortion.[238] For either requirement, if a daughter doesn't want to tell her parents, she can seek permission from a judge. She must convince the judge that an abortion would be in her best interest or that she is mature enough to make the decision herself. If she's not mature enough, she's expected to become a mother.

Pro-life groups advocated these laws with the expectation that they would result in fewer abortions. They believed that many teenagers would go to their parents rather than face the forbidding atmosphere of a court hearing before an unknown judge and that their parents would persuade or pressure them not to have the abortion. Some evidence indicates that the laws have had this effect.[239]

When teenagers do go to court, they routinely get waivers in some states but not in others.

Many states adopted other restrictions designed to discourage abortions. Some require clinics to distribute a pamphlet about fetal development and a list of adoption agencies. Some require clinics to conduct an ultrasound of the fetus and offer to show the image to the patient.[240] Mississippi requires doctors to tell the patient that abortions increase the risks of breast cancer and infertility, although the scientific research shows no clear link.[241] South Dakota requires doctors to tell the patient that abortions "terminate the life of a whole, separate, unique living human being." When the requirement was challenged, the U.S. Court of Appeals for the Eighth Circuit upheld the language. The conservative majority asserted that life begins at conception, despite *Roe's* conclusion, and that the state can force doctors to say so, despite the First Amendment's guarantee of freedom of speech. (Six of the seven justices in the majority were appointed by President George W. Bush.)[242]

After the Rehnquist Court reaffirmed the right to abortion, pro-life groups tried to prohibit one abortion procedure known as "intact dilation and extraction" in medicine but referred to as "partial-birth abortion" in politics—a rhetorical success of antiabortion supporters. In this procedure, a doctor delivers the fetus except for the head, punctures the skull and drains the contents, and then removes the fetus from the woman.[243] Because the procedure seems gruesome,

pro-life groups used it to sway undecided people in the abortion debate. Numerous states passed laws banning the procedure. A bare majority of the Rehnquist Court struck down the laws in 2000.[244] But Justice Sandra Day O'Connor, who supported abortion rights, retired, and Justice Samuel Alito, who opposes abortion rights, was appointed by President Bush to replace her. The result was that Congress passed a similar law for the whole country,

Courtesy of Northern Sun, www.northernsun.com

The pro-choice movement uses this symbol, referring to the history of coathanger abortions in the back alleys before *Roe*. Sarah Weddington, an attorney who challenged Texas's law in *Roe*, often wears this pin while traveling. Not long ago a young flight attendant asked, "What do you have against coat hangers?"

and a bare majority of the Roberts Court upheld the law in 2007.[245] Writing for the majority, Justice Kennedy said the law protects women from themselves. "While we find no reliable data to measure the phenomenon," he concluded that some women "regret their choice to abort," so the law prevents other women from making that choice.

For the time being, a five-justice majority, including Kennedy, supports the basic right to abortion.

Nonetheless, in 2010 Nebraska banned abortions after twenty weeks based on the questionable conclusion that the fetus at that point feels pain from the procedure.[246] (As of fall 2010, the courts have not ruled on this direct challenge to the trimester foundation of the *Roe* ruling.)

The pro-life movement is divided over its current tactics. Some factions prefer an incremental strategy, passing numerous restrictions that might go unnoticed by most people, rather than a frontal attack that might prompt a backlash by the majority. When South Dakota, which had no doctors who performed abortions—Minnesota doctors flew in to the state's sole facility—banned all abortions in 2005, abortion supporters petitioned to put the issue on the ballot in 2006. Voters repealed the law.

In some states, pro-life groups have quietly pressed the legislatures to enact extrastringent building codes for abortion clinics. These codes specify such things as the heights of ceilings, widths of hallways and doorways, dimensions of counseling rooms and recovery rooms, rates of air circulation, and the types and angles of jets in drinking fountains. (Although all states have construction codes for their buildings, these new laws apply only to abortion clinics.) Some codes require equipment or levels of staffing, such as a registered nurse rather than a licensed practical nurse, beyond the norms for these clinics. Although the stated goal is health and safety, the real purpose is to drive up the clinics' expenses so they have to increase their patients' fees to the point where many women can no longer afford to have an abortion.[247] When South Carolina's law, which mandates twenty-seven pages of requirements just for abortion clinics, was challenged, a lower court upheld the law and the Supreme Court refused to hear the case, thus allowing the law to stand.

Despite dissatisfaction by activists on both sides of this controversy—pro-life groups are disappointed that the conservative Supreme Court has upheld the right to abortion, whereas pro-choice groups are critical that it has upheld some restrictions on abortion—it is worth noting that the nonelected, nonmajoritarian Supreme Court has come closer to forging a policy reflective of public opinion than most politicians have. Polls show that the public is ambivalent. A majority believes that abortion is murder, but a two-thirds majority opposes banning it. This two-thirds majority favors letting women choose. (The apparent contradiction occurs because over half of those who believe that abortion is murder nonetheless favor letting women choose.[248] See Figure 2.) Thus many people support the right to abortion but are uncomfortable with it and willing to allow restrictions on it. The Court's doctrine articulates this position.[249]

But the Court's rulings aren't necessarily the final word in this controversy, as they haven't been the final word in some other controversies. Frustrated by the Court's refusal to overturn *Roe,* activists in the pro-life movement (not most of the pro-life supporters) adopted more militant tactics. First they targeted abortion clinics. Organizations such as Operation Rescue engaged in civil disobedience, blockading clinics and harassing workers and patients as they came and went. Some activists sprayed chemicals inside clinics, ruining carpets and fabrics and leaving a stench that made the clinics unusable. Such incidents occurred fifty times in one year alone.[250]

Then activists targeted doctors, nurses, and other workers at the clinics. Operation Rescue ran a training camp in Florida that instructed members how to use public records to locate personal information about clinic employees, how to tail them to their homes, and how to organize demonstrations at their homes. Activists put up "Wanted" posters, with a doctor's picture, name, address, and phone number, and then encouraged people to harass the doctor, the doctor's spouse, and even their children. (One thirteen-year-old was confronted in a restaurant and told that he was going to burn in hell.)[251] Letters containing powder and threatening death by anthrax were sent to over one hundred doctors and clinics.[252] Some extremists even advocated killing the doctors. One minister wrote a book—*A Time to Kill*—and marketed a bumper sticker reading "execute abortionists–murderers."[253]

In this climate, four doctors, two clinic employees, and one clinic volunteer were killed, and seven other doctors, employees, and volunteers were wounded.[254] Numerous clinics were firebombed.

The tactics have had their intended effect on doctors.[255] Because they have made the practice of providing abortions seem dangerous and undesirable, fewer medical schools offer abortion classes, fewer hospitals provide abortion training, fewer doctors study abortion procedures, and fewer gynecologists and obstetricians, despite most being pro-choice, perform abortion operations.[256] As a result, the number of abortion providers has dropped significantly.[257]

One pro-life leader proclaimed, "We've found the weak link is the doctor."[258] Another observed, "When you get the doctors out, you can have all the laws on the books you want and it doesn't mean a thing."[259]

As a result of these actions, abortions remain available in most metropolitan centers but not in most rural areas. Eighty-seven percent of U.S. counties, containing 32 percent of the American women aged fifteen to forty-four, have no doctor who performs abortions. Some states have only one, and others have only two cities where women can obtain abortions.[260]

Nevertheless, an abortion is still one of the most common surgical procedures for American women. Moreover, the French abortion pill—RU-486, whose brand name is Mifeprex—offers a nonsurgical procedure (if used by the seventh week of pregnancy), allowing women to take one pill in the doctor's office and another at home. This procedure is increasingly being used.[261]

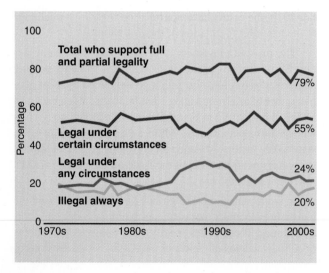

| Figure 2 | Opinion on the Legality of Abortions |

Total who support full and partial legality — 79%

Legal under certain circumstances — 55%

Legal under any circumstances — 24%

Illegal always — 20%

People were asked, "Do you think abortions should be legal under any circumstances, legal only under certain circumstances, or illegal in all circumstances?"

SOURCE: "The Right to Be a Father (Or Not)" from *The New York Times,* © November 6, 2005. All rights reserved. Used by permission and protected by the Copyright Laws of the United States. The printing, copying, redistribution, or retransmission of the Material without express written permission is prohibited.

Birth Control, Revisited

The pro-life movement, stimulated by the conservatism of the Bush administration, trained its sights on contraception in addition to abortion.[262] Initially the movement was dominated by Catholics, whose church opposes contraceptives, so the leaders muted their views to avoid scaring off potential supporters. (Ninety-three percent of all Americans, and 90 percent of Catholics, supported contraceptives in 2005.)[263] The movement was joined by conservative Protestants who didn't oppose birth control. In recent years, however, more movement leaders, Protestants as well as Catholics, have voiced opposition to contraception. The president of the American Life League declared, "We oppose all forms of contraception."[264] Now religious interest groups, such as the Christian Coalition and Focus on the Family, address birth control; increasing numbers of evangelical theologians oppose it and evangelical churches discuss it; and a cluster of representatives and senators spearheads congressional efforts against some forms of birth control.

Current opposition to contraception makes it difficult for the two sides in the abortion controversy to find common ground. Some on each side had called for greater availability of contraceptives so there would be less need for abortions. But this common ground is giving way as more who oppose abortion also oppose contraception.

What this indicates is that, for some in the pro-life movement, it's not so much about abortion as it is about sex. One leader said, "We see a direct connection between the practice of contraception and the practice of abortion." They both reflect "an anti-child mindset."[265] Both serve "the selfish demands of the individual."[266] The president of the Southern Baptist Theological Seminary stated, "The effective separation of sex from procreation may be one of the most important defining marks of our age—and one of the most ominous."[267] Their goal is to reverse the sexual revolution of the 1960s, when "the pill" became commonplace, and instead to confine sex to marriage.

This debate reflects sharp cultural differences between European countries and the United States. In those countries, contraceptives are readily available and unintended pregnancies and abortions are less frequent. There, "these things are in the open, and the only issue is to be careful. Here in the U.S., people are still arguing about whether it's O.K. to have sex."[268]

Homosexuality

Over the years, homosexuals have faced pervasive discrimination. In recent years, federal, state, and local governments have begun to address this discrimination, especially in the areas of sex, marriage, employment, and military service.

Although the language of the debates over these issues is dominated by the words *discrimination* and *equality,* the courts have considered homosexual rights to be a matter of civil liberties—encompassed within the right to privacy, like abortion rights—so the text will cover this topic in this chapter rather than in the civil rights chapter.

Running through the debates over these issues is a broader debate: Are homosexuals seeking equal rights or "special rights"? Homosexuals claim the former; opponents claim the latter. Homosexuals think it is self-evident that they want equal rights with heterosexuals. How, they ask, can

protection from discrimination be considered special treatment rather than equal treatment? Indeed, they want to end their special status as pariahs in law and society. Opponents, especially conservative Christians, insist that homosexuality is a lifestyle choice rather than an immutable characteristic like race or gender. (This conclusion is debatable and is rejected by most homosexuals, who claim to have been born as they are.) Therefore, according to opponents, homosexuals could renounce their homosexuality and alter their behavior. Then they would face no discrimination. Instead, they want governmental protection for a chosen lifestyle. Fundamentally, opponents find homosexuality abhorrent and contrary to biblical teachings, and they fear that equal rights will lead to full acceptance in society.[269]

Opponents also use the term *special rights* for political reasons. The phrase separates homosexuals' demands from previous demands by racial minorities and women for equal rights. To listeners, the phrase makes homosexuals' demands seem less defensible. To those who are leery about gay rights, the phrase provides an excuse for opposing such rights.

Sex

For years, states prohibited adultery, fornication, and sodomy. Reflecting Christian doctrine, the statutes targeted various forms of nonmarital sex and nonprocreative sex (including masturbation and withdrawal prior to ejaculation).[270] After the "sexual revolution" of the 1960s, many states repealed these statutes. However, most states retained their sodomy statutes, which prohibited oral or anal sex (performed by heterosexuals or homosexuals) because of legislators' disgust at homosexual practices and their opposition to the emerging gay rights movement.[271] Although these statutes were primarily symbolic, they were occasionally enforced against homosexuals.

John Lawrence *(left)* and Tyron Garner appealed their sodomy convictions to the Supreme Court, which invalidated state sodomy laws.

AP Photo/David J. Phillip

The Supreme Court refused to extend the right to privacy to protect homosexual practices in 1986,[272] but the Rehnquist Court reversed itself in 2003. When a neighbor phoned a false report of an armed intruder, police responded and discovered two men violating Texas's law. The men were arrested, jailed, and fined. The Texas courts affirmed their conviction, but in *Lawrence* v. *Texas,* the Supreme Court overturned it and *invalidated the sodomy laws* of the thirteen states that still had them.[273] In a broad opinion, Justice Kennedy wrote, "Liberty presumes an autonomy of self that includes freedom of thought, belief, expression, and certain intimate conduct." Therefore, homosexuals are entitled to "dignity" and "respect for their private lives."

A sizable shift in public opinion had occurred in the seventeen years between the two rulings.[274] As more homosexuals "came out," they gained greater acceptance from straights. Most Americans say they know someone who is gay or lesbian, and a majority say they are sympathetic to the gay and lesbian communities. Numerous states repealed their sodomy statutes after the 1986 ruling (even though the ruling at the time allowed the states to keep the statutes). Thus in the *Lawrence* case, according to one law professor, "The Court legitimized and endorsed a cultural consensus."[275]

Marriage

Although the majority in *Lawrence* said the ruling would not apply to same-sex marriages, the dissenters feared that establishing a right to privacy for homosexual practices would indeed lead to a right to marry for homosexual couples. Congress adopted the Defense of Marriage Act, which allows states to disregard same-sex marriages performed in other states. (About forty states have passed laws to do so.) The act also forbids federal recognition of same-sex marriages and thus denies federal benefits, such as Social Security, to same-sex couples.[276]

Although marriage was a fantasy for most homosexuals, their lack of legal rights was both a cause for concern and a source of anger. In the 1980s and 1990s, the AIDS epidemic swept gay communities across the United States. "Lovers, friends, and AIDS 'buddies' were spooning food, emptying bedpans, holding wracked bodies through the night. They were assuming the burdens of marriage at its hardest."[277] Yet gay partners had no legal rights. They encountered problems involving health insurance, hospital visitation, disability benefits, funeral planning, and estate settling. Gays were often unable to participate fully in these life-and-death matters because of legal impediments that didn't exist for married couples. In the same decades, lesbians gave birth with donated sperm, and gays got children through adoption and surrogate mothers, yet homosexual couples realized that they didn't have legal protections for their families. These developments increased the calls for legal rights commensurate with the rights of heterosexual couples.[278]

In 1999, the Vermont Supreme Court ruled that the state must either legalize same-sex marriages or equalize the rights and benefits received by same-sex couples and traditional married couples. The legislature decided to equalize the rights and benefits. To implement this policy, the legislature established "civil unions," with procedures for couples to become official partners (similar to marriage) and procedures for them to dissolve their relationship (similar to divorce).

Although these civil unions provide most of what regular marriages provide, the unions don't apply when couples move from Vermont to other states. And they don't apply to federal benefits. By one count, 1138 federal laws apply to married couples that don't apply to unmarried couples. Some impose responsibilities; most provide rights and benefits, such as tax breaks.[279] Also, of course, the unions don't provide the symbolism that regular marriages do. Instead, they imply that homosexuals are "subcitizens. . . . regarded as defective by the law," which especially stigmatizes homosexual parents in the eyes of their children.[280]

So the pressure for same-sex marriages continued. In 2004, the Massachusetts Supreme Judicial Court, hearing a suit brought by seven couples, ruled that same-sex marriages were allowed under the state's constitution. Otherwise, same-sex couples are relegated to "a different status. . . . The history of our nation has demonstrated that separate is seldom, if ever, equal."[281]

In quick succession, officials in San Francisco; Portland, Oregon; and smaller cities in New York, New Jersey, and New Mexico were inspired to issue marriage licenses to same-sex couples. State courts halted the licenses, but not until thousands of beaming couples had married and posed for news photos. Although the marriages were pronounced invalid, the head of the Lambda Legal Defense and Education Fund observed, "You can't put the toothpaste back in the tube."[282]

There was an immediate backlash. Polls showed that a majority of the public opposed same-sex marriages. President Bush proposed a constitutional amendment. One congressional sponsor claimed, "There is a master plan out there from those who want to destroy the institution of marriage." Another senator, comparing the threat of gay marriage to that

A couple in Connecticut celebrates their marriage.

© Mike Segar/Reuters/Corbis

By permission of Mike Luckovich and Creators Syndicate, Inc.

of terrorism, called the amendment "the ultimate homeland security." And an evangelist predicted that "the family as it has been known for five millennia will crumble, presaging the fall of Western civilization itself."[283] Yet there was more fire from the pulpits than there was in the pews. Evangelical leaders expressed puzzlement and frustration that there was no loud outcry from their faithful.[284] The fact was that many people who oppose gay marriage don't feel threatened by it. Consequently, the amendment failed to pass.

Nevertheless, voters in over thirty states adopted such amendments to their state constitution, most by a wide margin. Opponents to same-sex unions have found that the most effective tactic is to claim that same-sex marriages would lead to teaching homosexuality in school. A California commercial portrayed a field trip to a lesbian wedding.[285]

Despite many people's objections, gay rights leaders predicted that once homosexuals began to marry and straights saw that "the sky didn't fall," people would stop opposing their marriages.[286] They also noted that time is in their favor. Old people are the most opposed, and young people are the most supportive (see Figure 3).

Other states followed Massachusetts, with Connecticut, Iowa, New Hampshire, and Vermont (and the District of Columbia) also allowing same-sex marriage. In these states, the supreme court or legislature adopted the law; so far no referendum by voters has done so.

The California Supreme Court ruled that the state's domestic-partnership law wasn't sufficient and that same-sex marriages must be allowed in that state too. Yet this ruling was negated by voters.[287] After the ballot measure, the California court decided that the eighteen thousand couples who were married in the five months in which same-sex marriage was legal would remain married.

In addition to the five states that allow same-sex marriage, some other states allow civil unions or equivalent rights.[288]

Even states that don't allow same-sex marriage or civil unions find that a body of law indirectly supporting same-sex relationships is emerging, as couples who move from states that do allow these relationships are forcing courts to resolve legal issues such as divorce, custody, and inheritance. In New York, for instance, state courts have granted official divorces to same-sex couples even though state law doesn't recognize same-sex marriages. Judges must resolve cases before them, even if their state has no law on the books.

Through executive orders, President Obama has extended some benefits to the partners of federal workers, including access to medical treatment, long-term disability insurance (though not to full health care coverage), fitness centers, credit unions, and relocation assistance.

Employment

Some states and cities have passed laws barring discrimination against homosexuals in employment and also in housing, credit, insurance, and public accommodations. (And thirteen states have passed laws barring discrimination against transgendered persons—those who are born as one gender but live as the opposite gender.)[289]

In response, Colorado adopted a constitutional amendment that prohibited laws barring discrimination against homosexuals. But the Supreme Court rejected the claim that such laws amounted to "special rights." The majority struck down the amendment because it singled out homosexuals and denied them opportunity to seek protection from discrimination.[290] This ruling put the brakes on a drive to adopt similar provisions in other states.

Figure 3 | Opinion on Discrimination against Same-Sex Marriage

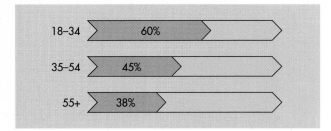

18–34   60%

35–54   45%

55+   38%

People were asked whether they agree that not allowing same-sex marriage is discrimination.
SOURCE: *Quinnipiac University.*

Yet homosexuals remain vulnerable at workplaces in states and cities without laws barring discrimination. Because Congress rejected a bill barring discrimination in employment at the same time it passed the Defense of Marriage Act, in most states employees can be fired for being homosexual.

Even so, homosexuals have gained equal benefits at more workplaces. Some state and city governments and many large corporations offer health care packages to same-sex couples as a way to attract and retain good workers.

Military Service

Since World War II, the military has rejected recruits who admit to being homosexual and discharged troops who are found to be homosexual, fearing that homosexuals would disrupt the morale and unit cohesion essential for fighting forces. When Bill Clinton, campaigning for president, pledged to end the ban, he ignited a firestorm that burned throughout his presidency. His proposal rallied evangelical groups, who launched an attack against the proposal and the president himself. They persuaded military officers, many of whom were evangelicals, to pressure Congress, and they got their followers to flood Congress with petitions and phone calls against the proposal. The volume of calls shut down phone lines on Capitol Hill. A public that had been divided, even apathetic, about the proposal now became opposed to it.

Although opponents claimed that military performance was their concern, the experiences of other countries belied this claim. European countries, Canada, Japan, and Israel, which has a battle-tested military, have all tolerated homosexuals in their services.[291] Rather than military performance, the opponents' motives were mostly cultural and religious. They wanted the military to remain "a bastion of traditional male values," and they wanted the military and the nation to retain its "Christian character."[292]

The opposition prompted Congress to block the proposal and forced Clinton to accept a compromise, called "don't ask, don't tell." The military (including the Reserves and National Guard) is not allowed to ask members about their sexual orientation but is allowed to discharge members for statements admitting homosexuality or conduct reflecting homosexuality (or bisexuality). Such conduct is defined to include not only sexual actions but also holding hands, dancing, or trying to marry someone of the same sex. The restrictions apply off base as well as on. They do not encompass reading gay publications, associating with gay people, frequenting gay bars or churches, or marching in gay rights parades, because these activities all reflect First Amendment rights.

The policy hasn't worked well. Some commanders have been confused, and others have been unwilling to follow the policy. They have continued to ask and discharge. The policy has also called attention to homosexuals and led to speculation among troops as to which ones might be homosexuals. One soldier's silence when fellow troops' talk turned to sex led to speculation that he was gay. Another soldier joined his colleagues on a trip to a brothel to avoid such speculation. (He sat with a prostitute in a room.)[293] As a result, more homosexuals have been discharged after the policy went into effect than before.[294] Over twelve thousand service members have been forced out, including almost sixty Arabic specialists who are in demand in Afghanistan and Iraq.[295] The military has had to spend money to recruit and train replacements.

As a candidate, Barack Obama opposed the policy, but as president he moved cautiously. Aware of Clinton's experience, he was leery about alienating the public and rallying conservative Christians while trying to assemble coalitions for his major initiatives. He did order the military to assess the policy, with an expectation that the brass would agree to repeal it.[296] Then congressional Democrats, fearful that they might lose their majority in the 2010 elections, passed a law to allow the Defense Department to repeal the policy when its study is completed. While waiting for the military to finish its assessment, a federal court in California ruled the "don't ask, don't tell" policy unconstitutional. As of fall 2010, the policy was in limbo.

Public opinion on this issue has reversed course since the 1990s. Now three-quarters of Americans support allowing homosexuals to serve openly.[297] Some officials still do not agree and try to exploit fear of homosexuals. One representative has warned that changing the policy will lead to "hermaphrodites" in the ranks.[298]

But animus toward gays and lesbians is far less than it used to be. Unlike public opinion toward abortion, which has remained relatively stable since *Roe*, public opinion toward homosexuality has changed dramatically. Until 1973, the American Psychiatric Association believed that homosexuality is a mental illness. In 1992, a gay leader said, "[W]hat we were begging Bill Clinton about—literally—[was] whether he was going to say the word *gay* in his convention speech. Even say it. We had to threaten a walk-out to get it in."[299] But now more than four hundred openly gay and lesbian officials hold elected office in the

United States.[300] And in 2010, for the first time, a majority of Americans, including men, who traditionally have been the most averse, consider "gay and lesbian relations" morally acceptable.[301]

Also in 2010, *Archie Comics* added its first openly gay character to the cast of teenagers in Archie's "Riverdale"—the quintessentially American town.

Right to Die

The Court has broadened the right to privacy to provide a limited right to die. When Nancy Cruzan's car skidded off an icy road and flipped into a ditch in 1983, doctors were able to save her life but not her brain, and she never regained consciousness. She lived in a vegetative state, similar to a coma, and was fed through a tube. Twenty-five at the time of the accident, she was expected to live another thirty years. When her parents asked the doctors to remove the tube, the hospital objected, and the state of Missouri, despite paying $130,000 a year to maintain her, also objected. This issue became entangled in other issues. Pro-life groups contended that denying life support was analogous to abortion; disability groups, claiming that her condition was merely a disability, argued that withholding food and water from her would lead to withholding treatment from others with disabilities.[302]

When Cruzan's parents filed suit, the Rehnquist Court established a limited **right to die**.[303] The justices ruled that *individuals can refuse medical treatment, including food and water, even if this means they will die.* But individuals must make their decision while competent and alert. They can also act in advance, preparing a "living will" or designating another person as a proxy to make the decision if they're unable to.

Cruzan's parents presented evidence to a Missouri court that their daughter would prefer death to being kept alive by machines. Three of Cruzan's coworkers testified that they recalled conversations in which she said she'd never want to live "like a vegetable." As a result, the Missouri court granted her parents' request to remove the feeding tube. She died twelve days later.

Although the legal doctrine is clear, various practical problems and emotional issues limit its use. For one thing, many people don't make their desires known in advance. Approximately ten thousand people in irreversible comas now didn't indicate their decision beforehand.[304] Then, some people who do indicate their decision beforehand waver when they face death. Finally, some doctors, who are in the habit of prolonging life even when their patients have no chance of enjoying life, resist their patients' decision.[305]

Although the Rehnquist Court established a right to die, it *refused* patients' pleas *to expand the limited right into a broader right to obtain assistance in committing suicide.*[306] The Court drew a distinction between stopping treatment and assisting suicide; individuals have a right to demand the former but not the latter. As is typical with an issue new to the courts, the justices seemed tentative. Chief Justice Rehnquist emphasized, "Our holding permits this debate to continue, as it should in a democratic society."

In Ashland, Oregon, Steve Mason suffered from terminal lung cancer and waited until he could no longer eat or sleep. Then he took the lethal drugs (on the table) prescribed by his doctor. He said, "I've lived my life with dignity. I want to go out the same way."

Oregon decided to allow assisted suicide, but its law provides some safeguards. The patient must submit written requests in the presence of two witnesses, get two doctors to concur that he or she has less than six months to live, and wait fifteen days. The Bush administration challenged Oregon's law, claiming that individual states can't allow assisted suicide. But the Supreme Court rebuffed the Bush administration and *allowed the state law to stand.*[307] So far, a modest number of terminally ill patients—about thirty a year—have taken advantage of the law.[308] (Washington and Montana also allow assisted suicide now.)

A majority of the public favors a right to assisted suicide,[309] but conservative religious groups oppose it, insisting that people, even when facing extreme pain and no hope of recovery, shouldn't take their own life. In addition, ethicists worry that patients will be pressured to give up their life because of the costs, to their family or health care provider, of continuing to live. They fear that a right will become a duty.

Meanwhile, the practice, even where officially illegal, is widely condoned, much as abortion was before *Roe.* Almost a fifth of the doctors who treat cancer patients in Michigan admitted in a survey that they have assisted suicide, and over half of two thousand doctors who treat AIDS patients in San Francisco also admitted that they have done so.[310]

Moreover, many doctors treat terminal patients with a strong sedative to relieve pain. The sedative, which can make it impossible to drink or eat, can hasten death. The treatment is called "palliative sedation," "terminal sedation" or, more provocatively, "slow euthanasia."[311]

CONCLUSION: Civil Liberties and the Role of Government

The Supreme Court has interpreted the Constitution to provide invaluable civil liberties. The Warren Court in the 1950s and 1960s, which included four of the most committed and forceful advocates of the Bill of Rights ever to sit on the High Court—Chief Justice Warren and Justices Black, Brennan, and Douglas—expanded civil liberties more than any other Court in history. It applied many provisions of the Bill of Rights to the states, and it greatly broadened First Amendment rights and criminal defendants' rights. It also established a right to privacy.

Observers predicted that the Burger Court would lead a constitutional counterrevolution. However, it didn't. The Burger Court in the 1970s and 1980s narrowed some rights, especially for criminal defendants, but it accepted the core of the Warren Court's doctrine and even extended the right to privacy to encompass abortions.

Nor did the Rehnquist Court in the 1980s, 1990s, and 2000s produce a constitutional counterrevolution. It, too, narrowed some rights, but it also accepted most of the Warren Court's doctrine and even extended the right to privacy to encompass homosexual practices. (It is too soon to draw conclusions about the Roberts Court now.)

When the Supreme Court has upheld civil liberties, it has fulfilled what many legal scholars consider the quintessential role of the highest court in a democracy—"to vindicate the constitutional rights of minorities, of dissidents, of the unrepresented, of the disenfranchised, of the unpopular." The other branches of government, whose officials are elected every two, four, or six years, are sensitive to the needs of "the majority, the politically powerful, the economically influential, and the socially popular."[312] According to this view, the judicial branch should be sensitive to the needs of the others.

In the process of upholding civil liberties, the Supreme Court has limited the power—in particular, the intrusiveness—of the government, whether federal, state, or local government. In Justice Black's words, the Bill of Rights is a list of "Thou shalt nots" directed at the government. In practice, it is a list of rights for the weak against the government. Thus civil liberties prevent the government from becoming as overbearing toward these people as it would otherwise.

Of course, the Court has substantial, though not absolute, independence from the other branches, and indirectly from public opinion, as Chapter 13 explained. Therefore, it doesn't have to mirror public opinion and follow the wishes of the majority, but it can't ignore this opinion either. The Warren Court went too far too fast for too many people, producing a backlash that led to the Burger and Rehnquist Courts. These courts then were somewhat more responsive to majority opinion—and somewhat less vigilant in protecting civil liberties.

KEY TERMS

Bill of Rights	420	exclusionary rule	440
Burger Court	428	First Amendment	421
civil liberties	420	free exercise clause	433
cruel and unusual punishment	443	freedom of association	429
due process	439	freedom of speech	421
establishment clause	435	freedom of the press	430
		hate speech	424

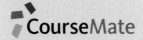

Access an interactive eBook, chapter-specific interactive learning tools (including flashcards, quizzes, videos), and more at CourseMate for *Understanding American Government*. Log in at CengageBrain.com.

Civil Rights

First Lady Michelle Obama

© Kevin J. Miyazaki 2008/Redux

Talking Points

When the elderly master of a South Carolina estate died in 1852, he left a will that divided his property—farm equipment, spinning wheels, tablecloths, and twenty-one slaves, including the "negro girl Melvinia."[1]

Shortly thereafter, the eight-year-old was valued at $475 and sold by the master's heirs to a Georgia farmer. At fifteen, and impregnated by a white man, she gave birth to her first child, whose skin was so light and hair was so straight that the child appeared almost white. Melvinia and the unknown white man—the farmer had four sons who ranged from nineteen to twenty-four at the time—would begin a family line that would stretch from rural Georgia to Birmingham, Alabama, to Chicago, and eventually to the White House. Melvinia and the unknown white man were the great-great-great grandparents of Michelle Obama, and their son, Dolphus Shields, her great-great grandfather.[2] (Melvinia gave her son the surname of her master, as many slaves did.)

Dolphus Shields learned to read and write, and he owned his own home and carpentry business. He cofounded two churches in Birmingham and supervised the Sunday schools at both.

Americans know that Barack Obama's father was a Kenyan and his mother was a Kansan, but Michelle was uncertain about her own ancestry. She had heard the rumors about a white forebear but didn't know the truth until her family line was traced by a genealogist in 2009.

Interracial liaisons, whether achieved by force, exploitation, or mutual consent, were common during slavery. A historian who discovered black relatives of his white slave-owning ancestors said that Michelle is "representative of how we have evolved and who we are. We are not separate tribes of Latinos and whites and blacks in America. We've all mingled, and we have done so for generations."[3]

The term *civil rights* means equal rights for persons regardless of their race, sex, or ethnic background. The **Declaration of Independence** proclaimed that "all men are created equal." The author, Thomas Jefferson, knew that all men were not created equal in many respects, but he meant that they should be considered equal in their rights and equal before the law. This notion represented a break with Great Britain, where rigid classes with unequal rights existed and nobles enjoyed more rights than commoners.

The Declaration's promise didn't include nonwhites or women, however. So although colonial Americans advocated equality, they envisioned it only for white men. Although other groups eventually gained more equality, for some the Declaration's promise remains unfulfilled.

RACE DISCRIMINATION

African Americans, Hispanics, and American Indians all have endured and continue to experience discrimination. This chapter recounts the struggle for equal rights by these groups.

This engraving depicts a woman who jumped from a window after being sold.

Discrimination against African Americans

Discrimination against African Americans occurred during the long and sordid history of slavery, neoslavery, segregation, and violence.

Slavery

The first Africans came to America in 1619, just twelve years after the first whites. Like many whites, the Africans initially came as indentured servants. In exchange for their passage across the ocean, they were bound to an employer, usually for four to seven years, and then freed.[4] Later in the century, however, the colonies passed laws making the Africans and their children slaves for life.

Once slavery was established, the slave trade flourished. In the South, slavery provided the foundation for an agricultural economy with huge and prosperous plantations. In the North, slavery also was common. Large plantations in Connecticut, Massachusetts, and Rhode Island shipped agricultural products to the West Indies in exchange for molasses used to make rum. Tradesmen and households in the cities also used slaves. In the mid-1700s, New York City had more slaves than any city in the colonies except Charleston (and in the early 1800s, it would have more slaves than any city in the country, including Charleston). About 40 percent of its households owned slaves—although, unlike in southern plantations, they had an average of two slaves per household.[5]

At the outbreak of the Revolutionary War in 1776, one-fifth of the American population was enslaved. The British, in an attempt to disrupt American society, promised freedom for the slaves. (The promise was a tactical maneuver rather than an ethical stand, as British generals themselves had slaves.) Perhaps as many as eighty thousand escaped and fought alongside the Redcoats.[6] After the war, some fled to Canada with the Loyalists, some sailed to Caribbean islands, where they would be enslaved again, and others shipped out to Sierra Leone. Most remained in America.

Before and after the war, abolitionist sentiment grew in the North. Most slaves were freed by the time of the war, although other slaves were kept for several decades. The 1820 census recorded thirty thousand slaves in northern states, and even as late as 1850, the census recorded some slaves in the North.[7] And these states, with their prominent merchants and bankers, served as the hub of the international trade in the commodities produced by slave labor—cotton, sugar, and tobacco.[8] Nevertheless, abolitionist sentiment among the populace in the North was strong enough that by the Constitutional Convention there were sharp differences between northern and southern attitudes toward slavery. In most parts of the North, slavery was condemned and abolished,[9] whereas in the South it was accepted and ingrained.

As a result of the compromises between northern and southern states, the Constitution protected slavery. It allowed

Library of Congress #LC-USZ62-30836

the importation of slaves until 1808, when Congress could bar further importation, and it required the return of escaped slaves to their owners.

In 1808, Congress did bar the importation of slaves but not the practice of slavery, which continued to flourish because there were so many slaves that their natural reproduction provided an ample number for the southern plantations. Yet Thomas Jefferson, a Virginia slave owner, foresaw its demise, "whether brought on by the generous energy of our own minds" or by a "bloody process."[10]

DEMOCRACY?

Ancient Greece developed democracy but also held prisoners of wars as slaves. We can ask the same question of the antebellum (pre-Civil War) United States as we ask of ancient Greece: Is slavery compatible with democracy?

Meanwhile, abolitionists called for an end to slavery. In response, southerners began to question the Declaration of Independence and to repudiate its notion of natural rights, attributing this idea to Jefferson's "radicalism."[11]

The Supreme Court tried to quell the antislavery sentiment in the **Dred Scott case** in 1857.[12] Dred Scott, a slave who lived in Missouri, was taken by his owner to the free state of Illinois and the free territory of Wisconsin and, after five years, was returned to Missouri. The owner died and passed title to his wife, who moved and left Scott in the care of people who opposed slavery. They arranged for Scott to sue his owner for his freedom, arguing that Scott's time in a free state and a free territory made him a free man even though he was returned to a slave state. Because his owner opposed slavery, she could have simply freed Scott, but they all sought a major court decision to keep slavery out of the territories.

In this infamous case, Chief Justice Roger Taney, from Tennessee, stated that blacks, whether slave or free, were not citizens and were, in fact, "so far inferior that they had no rights which the white man was bound to respect." Taney could have stopped here—if Scott wasn't a citizen, he couldn't sue in federal court at the time—but Taney went on to declare that Congress had no power to control slavery in the territories. This meant that slavery could extend into the territories that Congress had declared free. It also raised the possibility that slavery might extend into the states that had prohibited it.

By this time, slavery had become the hottest controversy in American politics, and this decision fanned the flames. It provoked vehement opposition in the North and produced bitter polarization in the country, leading to the Civil War. Today it is cited among the worst decisions ever made by the Supreme Court. (Yet three decades earlier, Taney had freed his own slaves, whom he had inherited from his parents, and he remained with the Union when the war broke out.)[13]

Although Scott received his freedom from his owner, most slaves weren't so lucky (see the box "Black Masters, Red Masters"). When the Civil War began, one of every nine black people in America was free; the rest were slaves.

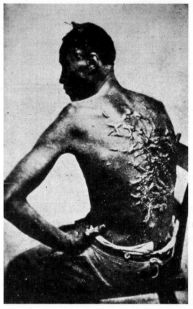

This photo, which shows a slave named Gordon who was whipped by his master in Mississippi, was taken after the slave escaped (by rubbing himself with onions to confuse the bloodhounds) and reached the Union Army. The photo was printed in a magazine and circulated as a postcard by abolitionists—an early example of photographs used as propaganda.

The slaves were so integral to the southern economy that the paper money of some Confederate states depicted slaves harvesting cotton.[14]

The North's victory in the Civil War gave force to President Lincoln's Emancipation Proclamation ending slavery.[15] But as the following sections show, blacks would find short-lived solace.

Reconstruction

After the war, Congress passed and the states ratified three constitutional amendments. The Thirteenth Amendment prohibited slavery. (In 1995, Mississippi became the last state to ratify the amendment, but of course the state's ratification was merely a symbolic act by then.) The Fourteenth Amendment granted citizenship to blacks, thus overruling the *Dred Scott* decision, and also granted "equal protection of the laws" and "due process of law." The **equal protection clause** would eventually become the primary guarantee that government would treat people equally. The Fifteenth Amendment gave black men the right to vote.

These amendments not only granted specific rights for African Americans but also transformed the relationship between the federal and state governments. Each amendment included the stipulation that "Congress shall have power to enforce" the provisions of the amendment. (In the wake of the war, Congress didn't trust the southern states to enforce the constitutional provisions.) This stipulation granted the federal government new power—whatever power was necessary to guarantee these rights—in marked

american diversity

Black Masters, Red Masters

Although most slave owners were white, some were black and some were red. In the South, as many as 3,700 were black.[1] William Ellison of South Carolina was one. Born a slave, he bought his freedom and then his family's by building and repairing cotton gins. Over time, he earned enough money to buy slaves himself and operate a plantation. With sixty-three slaves, Ellison ranked in the top 3 percent of all slaveholders, black or white. Ellison was unusual, but he was not unique. In Charleston, South Carolina, alone, more than one hundred African Americans owned slaves in 1860. Most black slave owners, however, owned fewer than four slaves.[2]

Some black slaveholders showed little sign that they shared the concerns of black slaves. Indeed, Ellison freed none of his slaves.

As a member of the slave-owning class, Ellison was allowed to sue a white man who didn't pay his bills (and even to win the case), and Ellison's family was granted a pew on the main floor of the Episcopal church. Yet in most respects the black owners weren't seen as equals by whites. They were expected to maintain the norms of black-white relations, especially to act deferentially toward whites.

As the Civil War approached, whites increasingly viewed free blacks, even slaveholders, as a threat to the established order, and state legislatures passed harsh legislation to regulate free blacks. For example, they had to have a white "guardian" to vouch for their moral character, and they had to carry special papers to prove their free status. Without these papers, they could be sold back into slavery.

The southeastern Indian tribes also adopted the practice of slavery. By 1820, they bought and sold slaves in the markets and stole slaves from other tribes. As a result, runaway slaves could no longer find refuge in Indian villages. By the time of the Civil War, the Cherokees, who were considered the "most civilized" of the southeastern Indians, owned four thousand black slaves and joined the Confederacy against the Union.

Several factors led to Indians' adoption of this practice. Outnumbered by both blacks and Indians, southern whites fostered hostility between the two groups to prevent them from joining forces. For example, white owners told their slaves hair-raising stories about Indian cruelty, and at times they armed their slaves to kill local Indians. Yet they also paid the Indians to capture escaped slaves. In addition, white missionaries who brought Christianity to the Indians were slaveholders themselves, and federal agents who implemented government policies toward the tribes encouraged the tribes to emulate white farmers to become "civilized." Of course, the most visible agriculture in the region (in other words, "civilization") was the plantation system with slave labor.

Dominated by whites, Indians saw slavery as an opportunity to rank higher than at least one group—black slaves—in the racial hierarchy. Indeed, although Indian masters initially weren't as brutal as white masters, they eventually treated their slaves as badly as whites did.[3]

[1] Loren Schweninger, *Black Property Owners in the South, 1790–1915* (Urbana: University of Illinois Press, 1990), cited in David Brion Davis, *Inhuman Bondage: The Rise and Fall of Slavery in the New World* (New York: Oxford University Press, 2006), 373, n. 17.
[2] For an acclaimed novel exploring the moral intricacies for black slave owners, read Edward P. Jones, *The Known World* (New York: Amistad, 2003).
[3] The Seminoles apparently were an exception. They required slaves to pay a nominal tribute but otherwise allowed them to run their own lives.
SOURCES: Michael Johnson and James L. Roark, *Black Masters* (New York: Norton, 1984); William McLoughlin, *The Cherokee Ghost Dance: Essays on the Southeastern Indians, 1789–1861* (Macon, Ga.: Mercer University Press, 1984), 261–283.

contrast to the Founders' original intention to limit federal power. The Civil War and these amendments together thus constituted a constitutional revolution, as explained in Chapter 2.[16]

Congress also passed a series of Civil Rights Acts that allowed blacks to buy, own, and sell property; to make contracts; to sue; and to serve as witnesses and jurors in court. The acts also allowed blacks to use public transportation, such as railroads and steamboats, and to patronize hotels and theaters.[17]

During Reconstruction, the Union Army, which occupied the South, enforced the new amendments and acts. Military commanders established procedures to register voters and hold elections. The commanders also started schools for the children of former slaves. But the army didn't have enough troops in the region to maintain Reconstruction policies. And in state after state, the South resisted.[18]

Eventually, the North capitulated. The 1876 presidential election between Republican Rutherford Hayes and Democrat Samuel Tilden was disputed in some states. To resolve the dispute, Republicans, most of whom were northerners, and Democrats, many of whom were southerners, agreed to a compromise: Hayes would be named president, and the remaining Union troops would be removed from the South. Without the Union troops, there was no way to enforce the Reconstruction policies.

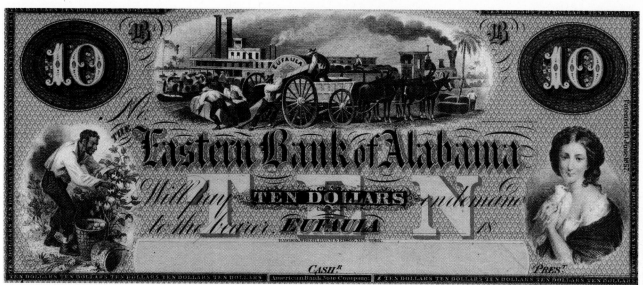

Slaves were so integral to the southern economy that some Confederate states printed money with pictures of slaves working.

The collapse of Reconstruction limited the impact of the Civil War. In effect, the South was allowed to nullify one result of the war—granting legal and political rights to blacks—in exchange for accepting two other results—preserving the Union and abolishing slavery.

In hindsight, it isn't surprising that Reconstruction didn't accomplish more. It was difficult, if not impossible, to integrate 4 million former slaves into a society that was bitter in its defeat and weak economically. Northerners who expected progress to come smoothly were naive. When it didn't come quickly, they grew weary. At the same time, there was a desire for healing between the regions and lingering feelings for continuity with the past.

Public attitudes during Reconstruction thus began a recurring cycle that continues to this day: Periodically the public gets upset about the treatment of African Americans and is determined to improve their conditions. But the public is naive and impatient, and when the efforts don't produce the results it expects as soon as it expects, the public becomes disillusioned with the efforts and dissatisfied with their costs. Then the public forces the government to put the race problem on the back burner until some future generation picks it up again.[19]

Neoslavery

Despite the outcome of the Civil War and the passage of the Thirteenth Amendment, many southern blacks were subjected to **neoslavery**, which entailed new forms of slavery or near slavery.

One type of neoslavery was **sharecropping**. After the war, Congress had rejected proposals to break up the plantations and give former slaves "forty acres and a mule" or to provide aid to establish schools. Without land or education, the former slaves had to work for their former masters as hired hands, or sharecroppers. They were dependent on the landowners, who had designed a system to bind the workers to the plantations. A landowner contracted with former slaves to work on his fields and live at his plantation. The sharecroppers were allowed to sell half of their crop to the landowner and keep the proceeds, but they were paid so little, regardless of how hard they worked, that they had to borrow to survive the winter. The next year, they had to work for the same landowner to pay off their debts. The cycle continued, year after year. And lacking education, most sharecroppers didn't keep any records, so they didn't know how much they were owed, and many were cheated.

Another type of neoslavery was even harsher. Landowners or factory owners who needed more workers conspired with local officials to charge black men with minor crimes, such as vagrancy, gambling, "selling cotton after sunset," or changing employers without permission.[20] The men would be tried, convicted, and fined more than they could afford, so they would be jailed. Then they would be leased to local plantations, mines, mills, lumber camps, turpentine camps, brick companies, or steel factories to work off their fines. The arrest rates seemed to fluctuate according to the labor needs of the local businesses. (Some factories owned by northern corporations also benefited from this scheme.)[21]

The prisoners were guarded—some were shackled to their bed at night—and many were worked to their death. One, convicted of "gaming" in 1903, was leased to a mine. His fine could be worked off in 10 days, but his "fees" to the sheriff, court clerk, and the witnesses at his trial required 104 more days. He didn't survive long enough to be released.

This industrial servitude was pervasive in rural Alabama and common in other southern states. It continued until the mid-1940s.

Segregation

In both the South and the North, blacks came to be segregated from whites.

AP Photo/US Civil War Center

Segregation in the South   As already mentioned, the reconciliation between Republicans and Democrats—northerners and southerners—was effected at the expense of blacks. Removing the troops enabled the South to govern itself again, and the former slave states used this power to establish segregation.

Before the Civil War, there was no segregation in rural areas, where slaves' shacks sat near plantation mansions, or in urban areas, where few blocks were solidly black. Segregation would have been inconvenient, with blacks and whites working in proximity, and it would have been unnecessary—slavery itself kept blacks at the bottom of society. But after slavery was abolished, southerners established segregation as a new way to keep blacks "in their place."

By the turn of the century the southern states had established a pervasive pattern of **Jim Crow laws** that segregated city blocks or whole neighborhoods.[22] Some small towns excluded blacks altogether, either by passing explicit laws or by adopting **sundown laws**, which required blacks to be off the streets by 10 p.m. Other Jim Crow laws segregated schools, which blacks had been allowed to attend during Reconstruction, and even textbooks: black schools' texts had to be stored separately from white schools' books. Many laws also segregated public accommodations, such as hotels, restaurants, bars, theaters, and streetcars. Others segregated sporting events, circuses, and parks. They separated black and white checkers players in Birmingham and districts for black and white prostitutes in New Orleans.

The laws were pervasive, segregating entrances, exits, ticket windows, waiting rooms, restrooms, and drinking fountains. They segregated the races in prisons, hospitals, and homes for the blind. They even segregated the races in death—in morgues, funeral homes, and cemeteries.

Although blacks were denied access to better locations or facilities, the greatest damage from segregation was that they were degraded. The system of Jim Crow laws was "an officially organized degradation ceremony, repeated day after day." Segregation told blacks that they were inferior and did not belong in the communities in which they lived.[23]

In addition to the laws, blacks were forced to defer to whites in informal settings as well—for instance, to move off the sidewalk when a white pedestrian approached. Failure to defer could bring punishment for being "uppity." Blacks were "humiliated by a thousand daily reminders of their subordination."[24]

Meanwhile, northern leaders, who had championed the cause of the slaves before and during the Civil War, abandoned African Americans a decade after the war. Congress

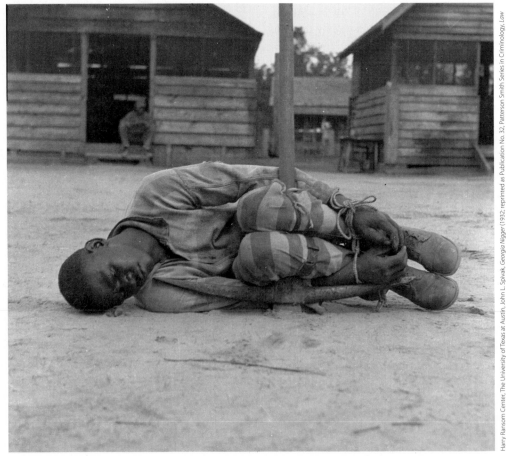

Harry Ransom Center, The University of Texas at Austin, John L. Spivak, *Georgia Nigger* (1932; reprinted as Publication No. 32, Patterson Smith Series in Criminology, *Law Enforcement and Social Problems*, Montclair, N.J. 1969).

Black men and boys were arrested and used like slave laborers for local landowners and factory owners. This boy is being punished in a forced labor camp in Georgia in the 1930s.

Some restaurants in the North, such as this one in Lancaster, Ohio, in the 1930s, maintained segregation by refusing to serve blacks.

declined to pass new laws, presidents refused to enforce existing laws, and the Supreme Court gutted the constitutional amendments and Civil Rights Acts.[25]

Then the Court upheld segregation itself. When Louisiana passed "an Act to promote the comfort of passengers," which mandated separate accommodations in trains, New Orleans black leaders sponsored a test case challenging the act's constitutionality. Homer Adolph Plessy, who was seventh-eighths white—an "octoroon" in the parlance of the time—nonetheless was considered black, and he sat in the white car. When the conductor ordered him to move to the black car, Plessy refused, maintaining that the act was unconstitutional under the Fourteenth Amendment. In *Plessy v. Ferguson* in 1896, the Court disagreed, claiming that the act was not a denial of equal protection because it provided equal accommodations.[26] The Court established the **separate-but-equal doctrine**, which allowed separate facilities if they were "equal." Of course, government required separate facilities only because people thought the races were not equal, but the Court brazenly commented that the act did not stamp "the colored race with a badge of inferiority" unless "the colored race chooses to put that construction on it." Only Justice John Harlan, a former Kentucky slaveholder, dissented: "Our Constitution is color-blind, and neither knows nor tolerates classes among citizens."

Three years later, the Court accepted segregation in schools.[27] A Georgia school board turned a black high school into a black elementary school without establishing a new high school for blacks or allowing them to attend the existing high schools for whites. Nevertheless, the Court said this action was not a denial of equal protection. Its ruling set a pattern in which "separate but equal" meant separation but not equality.

Segregation in the North   Although Jim Crow laws were not as pervasive in the North as in the South, they were quite common.[28] In fact, sundown laws were more prevalent in the North, especially in the Midwest. In the 1930s, Hawthorne, California, posted a sign at its city limits: "Nigger, Don't Let The Sun Set On YOU In Hawthorne."[29] Jim Crow laws in the northern states prompted one writer to proclaim, "The North has surrendered!"[30]

Yet job opportunities were better in the North. While southern blacks were sharecropping—as late as 1930, 80 percent of those who farmed were working somebody else's land[31]—northern factories were offering jobs. Between 1915 and 1940, more than a million southern blacks headed north in the **Great Migration**. Although they got decent jobs, they were forced to live in black ghettos because they couldn't afford better housing and they weren't allowed to live in some areas.

Denial of the Right to Vote

With the adoption of the Fifteenth Amendment, many African Americans voted and elected fellow African Americans to office during Reconstruction, but southern states began to disfranchise them in the 1890s (as explained in Chapter 8).

Violence

To solidify their control, whites engaged in violence against blacks. In the 1880s and 1890s, whites lynched about one hundred blacks a year, and vigilante "justice" continued in the 1900s (see Table 1). For example, a mob in Livermore, Kentucky, dragged a black man accused of murdering a white man into a theater. The ringleaders charged admission and hanged the man. Then they allowed the audience to shoot at the swinging body—those in the balcony could fire once; those in the better seats could empty their revolvers.[32]

Lynchings often began with a false report of a white woman being sexually assaulted by a black man. An irate mob would gather and, after locating the man, would subject him to an excruciating ordeal. Usually, they castrated him before they killed him. Frequently, they hacked off his fingers and ears as well.[33]

Lynchings were not the result of a few troublemakers; rather, they were a social institution in the South. The ritualized spectacles were a desperate attempt to cling to the antebellum order upset by the Civil War. At the same time, lynchings were related to the increase in white women who worked outside the home at the turn of the century. As these women experienced greater independence, insecure men feared that they would become too independent, perhaps even leave them for black men. Hence the ritual of castration.[34] Through lynchings, then, white men could remain in charge—at home and in the community—while appearing to defend women's honor.

Lynchings were considered entertaining as well as essential to maintain order. They would be photographed and, later, postcards would be sold (though after 1907, postal regulations banned them from the mail).

| Table 1 | Why Whites Lynched Blacks in 1907 |

Whites gave the following reasons for lynching blacks, who may or may not have committed the acts cited.

Reason	Number of Lynchings
Murder	5
Attempted murder	5
Manslaughter	10
Rape	9
Attempted rape	11
Burglary	3
Harboring a fugitive	1
Theft of 75 cents	1
Having a debt of $3	2
Winning a fight with a white man	1
Insulting a white man	1
Talking to white girls on the telephone	1
Being the wife or son of a rapist	2
Being the father of a boy who "jostled" white women	1
Expressing sympathy for the victim of mob violence	3

SOURCE: Adapted from Ray Stannard Baker, *Following the Color Line* (New York: Harper & Row, 1964), 176–177.

Whites engaged in other forms of violence as well. In 1919, twenty-five race riots erupted in six months. White mobs took over cities in the North and South, burning black neighborhoods and terrorizing black residents for days on end.[35] In 1921, ten thousand whites burned down thirty-five blocks of Tulsa's black neighborhood. The incident that precipitated the riot was typical—a report of an assault by a black man on a white woman. The report was false, fabricated by the woman (and later retracted), but residents were inflamed by a racist newspaper and encouraged by the city's officials. Almost three hundred people were shot, burned alive, or tied to cars and dragged to death. Survivors reported corpses stacked like firewood on street corners and piled high in dump trucks.[36]

The white-supremacist **Ku Klux Klan**, which began during Reconstruction and started up again in 1915, played a major role in inflaming prejudice and terrorizing blacks. It was strong enough to dominate many southern towns and even the state governments of Oklahoma and Texas. It also made inroads into some northern states, such as Indiana.

In addition, bands of white farmers known as "White-caps" nailed notes, with a drawing of a coffin and a warning to leave or die, on the doors of black farmers. Their goal was to drive black farmers off the land. Then the local governments put the land up for auction or simply gave it to the white families who owned the adjacent land.[37] The impact of this intimidation continued for many generations and, in fact, continues to this day. The black families lost wealth for themselves and their descendants, and the white families gained wealth that is appreciating in value for their descendants today, many of whom may be unaware of how "their" land changed hands.

Despite all this violence and injustice, federal officials contended that racial violence was a state problem. Presidents refused to speak out, and Congress refused to pass legislation making lynching a federal offense—yet state officials did nothing. For at least the first third of the twentieth century, white supremacy reigned, not just in the southern states but also in the border states and in many northern states. It also pervaded the nation's capital, where President Woodrow Wilson instituted segregation in the federal government.[38]

Overcoming Discrimination against African Americans

African Americans fought white supremacy primarily in three arenas: the courts, the streets, and Congress. In general, they fought in the courts first and Congress last, although as they gained momentum they increasingly fought in all three arenas at once.

The Movement in the Courts

The first goal was to convince the Supreme Court to overturn the separate-but-equal doctrine of *Plessy* v. *Ferguson*.

The NAACP In response to racial violence, a group of blacks and whites founded the National Association for the Advancement of Colored People, or **NAACP**, in 1909. In its first two decades, it was led by W. E. B. Du Bois, a black sociologist. In time, it became the major organization fighting for blacks' civil rights.

Frustrated by presidential and congressional inaction, the NAACP decided to appeal to the courts, which are less subject to political pressure from the majority. The association assembled a cadre of lawyers, mainly from Howard University Law School, a historically black school in Washington, D.C., to bring lawsuits attacking segregation and the denial of the right to vote. In 1915, they persuaded the Supreme Court to strike down the grandfather clause (which exempted persons whose ancestors could vote from the literacy test);[39] two years later, they convinced the Court to invalidate residential segregation laws.[40] But the Court continued to allow most devices to disfranchise blacks and most efforts to segregate.

Lynching occurred not only in the South but also in northern cities such as Marion, Indiana, in 1930. The girls on the left hold pieces of the victims' clothing, torn off as "souvenirs."

In 1938, the NAACP chose a thirty-year-old attorney, Thurgood Marshall, to head its litigation arm.[41] Marshall—whose mother had to pawn her engagement and wedding rings so he could go to an out-of-state law school because his in-state school, the University of Maryland, didn't admit blacks—would become a tireless and courageous advocate for equal rights. (In 1946, after defending four blacks charged with attempted murder during a riot in rural Tennessee, he would narrowly escape a lynch mob himself.)[42]

Desegregation of schools In the mid-twentieth century, seventeen states and the District of Columbia segregated their schools (and four other states allowed cities to segregate their schools). The states gave white students better facilities and white teachers larger salaries. Overall, they spent from two to ten times more on white schools than on black ones.[43] Few of these states had graduate schools for blacks: as late as 1950, they had fifteen engineering schools, fourteen medical schools, and five dental schools for whites and none for blacks; they had sixteen law schools for whites and five for blacks.

The NAACP's tactics were first to show that "separate but equal" actually resulted in unequal schools and then, attacking the concept head-on, to argue that "separate but equal" led to unequal status in general.

First the NAACP challenged segregation in graduate schools. For example, Missouri provided no black law school but offered to reimburse blacks who went to out-of-state law schools. Challenged by the NAACP, the Supreme Court ruled in 1938 that the state had to provide black

students a law school or admit them to the white school.[44] In Texas, where the black law school was clearly inferior to the white law school at the University of Texas, the Court ruled in 1950 that the black school had to be substantially equal to the white school.[45] And in Oklahoma, where a black student was allowed to attend the white graduate school at the University of Oklahoma but was designated a separate section of the classroom, library, and cafeteria, the Court said this, too, was inadequate because it deprived the student of the exchange of views with fellow students necessary for education.[46] In these decisions, the Court did not invalidate the separate-but-equal doctrine but made segregation almost impossible to implement in graduate schools.

The NAACP then turned its attention to the lower levels of the school system. Marshall filed suits in two southern states, one border state, one northern state, and the District of Columbia. The suit in the northern state was brought against Topeka, Kansas, where Linda Brown could not attend the school just four blocks from her home because it was a white school. Instead, she had to go to a school twenty-one blocks away.[47]

When these cases reached the Supreme Court, the justices were split. Although Chief Justice Fred Vinson might have had a majority to uphold the separate-but-equal doctrine, the Court put off a decision and rescheduled oral arguments for its next term. Between the Court's terms, Vinson suffered a heart attack, and President Dwight Eisenhower appointed Earl Warren to take his place. When the Court reheard the case, the president pressured his appointee to rule in favor of segregation. Eisenhower invited Warren and the attorney for the states to the White House for dinner.

Tulsa Historical Society

Tulsa's black neighborhood smolders after whites burned it down in 1921.

When the conversation turned to the segregationists, Eisenhower said, "These are not bad people. All they are concerned about is to see that their sweet little girls are not required to sit in schools alongside some big overgrown Negroes."[48] However, Warren not only voted against segregation but also used his considerable determination and charm to persuade the other justices, some of whom had supported segregation, to vote against it too. Justice Felix Frankfurter later said that Vinson's heart attack was "the first indication I have ever had that there is a God."[49]

In the landmark case of **Brown v. Board of Education** in 1954, the **Warren Court** ruled unanimously that school segregation violated the Fourteenth Amendment's equal protection clause.[50] In the opinion, Warren asserted that separate but equal not only resulted in unequal schools but also was inherently unequal because it made black children feel inferior. (See box "Passing the 'Brown Bag Test.'")

In overruling the *Plessy* doctrine, the Court showed how revolutionary the equal protection clause was—or could be interpreted to be. The Court required the segregated states to change their way of life to a degree unprecedented in American history. (See box "The Social Code.") After overturning laws requiring segregation in schools, the Court overruled laws mandating segregation in other places, such as public parks, golf courses, swimming pools, auditoriums, courtrooms, and jails.[51]

In *Brown,* the Court had ordered the schools to desegregate "with all deliberate speed."[52] This standard was a compromise between justices who thought schools should do so immediately and those who thought communities would need

to do so gradually.[53] The ambiguity of the phrase, however, allowed the communities to do so slowly, even imperceptibly. The ruling prompted much deliberation but little speed.

The South engaged in massive resistance. The Court needed help from the other branches, but Congress was controlled by southerners and President Eisenhower was reluctant to tell the states to change. In fact, the president criticized the decision. With his power and immense popularity, he could have speeded implementation by speaking out in support of the ruling, yet he offered no help for three years. When nine black students tried to attend a white high school under a desegregation plan in Little Rock, Arkansas, the governor's and state legislature's inflammatory rhetoric against desegregation encouraged local citizens to take the law into their own hands and stage a riot. Finally, Eisenhower acted, sending federal troops and federalizing the state's national guard to quell the violence.

President Kennedy also used federal marshals and paratroopers to stop the violence after the governor of Mississippi blocked the door to keep James Meredith from registering at the University of Mississippi. Kennedy again sent troops when the governor of Alabama, George Wallace, proclaiming "segregation now, segregation tomorrow, segregation forever," blocked the door to keep blacks from enrolling at the University of Alabama.

After trying outright defiance, some states attempted to circumvent the ruling by shutting down their public schools and providing tuition grants, textbooks, and recreation facilities for students to use at new private schools, which at the time could segregate. The states also tried less blatant

behind the scenes

Passing the "Brown Bag Test"

Whites' preoccupation with skin color affected blacks even in their relationships with other blacks. In the early twentieth century, African Americans who wanted to join some African American clubs and churches had to pass the **brown bag test**. They had to put their hand into a brown paper bag; if their skin was a lighter color than the bag, they were eligible for membership. A social club in Nashville had a similar test. Aspiring members had to demonstrate that their blue veins could be seen through their pale skin on the underside of their wrists.

This concern for lighter skin stemmed from the slavery era, when light-skinned blacks often brought higher prices and got better jobs as household workers and skilled craftsmen than as field hands. Light-skinned blacks also were more likely to be free. In 1860, the census classified fully 30 percent of free blacks as "mulatto" (having some white ancestry), compared with only 10 percent of the slaves.

After emancipation, lighter skin continued to be a social and economic advantage. Those who, as slaves, were able to learn crafts had a head start. Many blacks with darker skin used bleach, lye, or other products to lighten their color.

Although black colleges did not restrict admission to African Americans with lighter skin, in the 1930s most of their students did have lighter skin. They were the children of doctors, dentists, lawyers, and morticians, who themselves had lighter skin and were more successful in their communities. These professionals were predominant among African Americans who could afford to send their children to college in those years. At college, their children took up whites' pastimes, such as cotillions and tennis, in an attempt to distinguish themselves from poor blacks and to gain acceptance from whites. (But acceptance was not granted.) As late as the 1960s, when the slogan "Black is beautiful" became popular, the homecoming queen at Howard University usually had a light complexion.

This concern for lighter skin persists. Fashion models on *Ebony*'s covers often have pale skin, and the sales of bleaching products continue. Lighter-skinned African Americans have higher socioeconomic status, and many African Americans prefer lighter-skinned mates.

SOURCE: "For Black College Students in the 1930s, Respectability and Prestige Depended on Passing the Brown Bag Test," *Journal of Blacks in Higher Education*, January 31, 1999, 119–120; Louie E. Ross, "Mate Selection Preferences among African American College Students," *Journal of Black Studies* 27 (1997), 554–569; St. Clair Drake and Horace R. Clayton, *Black Metropolis* (New York: Harcourt, Brace, 1945); Mark Hill, "Color Differences in the Socioeconomic Statuses of African American Men," *Social Forces* 78 (2000), 1437–1460.

Sorority sisters at Fisk University, a historically black college, in 1936.

National Archives/Harmon Collection, 200(S)-HS-1-92

schemes, such as "freedom of choice" plans that allowed students to choose the school they wanted to attend. Of course, virtually no whites chose a black school, and due to social pressure very few blacks chose a white school. The idea was to achieve desegregation on paper, or token desegregation in practice, in order to avoid actual desegregation. But the Court rebuffed these schemes and even forbade private schools from discriminating.[54]

To black southerners, the Court's persistence raised hopes. Chief Justice Warren, according to Thurgood Marshall, "allowed the poor Negro sharecropper to say, 'Kick me around Mr. Sheriff, kick me around Mr. County Judge, kick me around Supreme Court of my state, but there's one person I can rely on.'"[55]

To white southerners, however, the Court's rulings reflected a federal government, a distant authority, that was exercising too much control over their traditional practices. The rulings engendered much bitterness. Justice Hugo Black, who was from Alabama, was shunned by former friends from the state, and his son was driven from his legal practice in the state. The justice wasn't even sent an invitation to his fiftieth reunion at his alma mater, the University of Alabama.[56]

Despite the Court's rulings, progress was excruciatingly slow. If a school district was segregated, a group like the NAACP had to run the risks and spend the money to bring a suit in a federal district court. Judges in these courts reflected the views of the state or local political establishment, so the suit might not be successful. If it was, the school board would prepare a desegregation plan. Members of the school board reflected the views of the community and the pressures from the segregationists, so the plan might not be adequate. If it was, the segregationists would challenge it in a federal district court. If the plan was upheld, the segregationists would appeal to a federal court of appeals. Judges in these courts, based in Richmond and New Orleans, came from the South, but they were not as tied to the state or local political establishment, and they usually ruled against the segregationists. But then the segregationists could appeal to the Supreme Court. Although they knew they would lose sooner or later, the process took several years, so they could delay the inevitable.

Thus the segregationists tried to resist, then to evade, and finally to delay. In this they succeeded. In 1964, a decade after *Brown,* 98 percent of all black children in the South still attended all-black schools.[57]

By this time, however, the mood in Congress had changed. Congress passed the Civil Rights Act of 1964, which, among other things, cut off federal aid to school districts that continued to segregate. The following year, it passed the first major program providing federal aid to education. This was the carrot at the end of the stick; school districts complied to get the money.

Finally, by 1970, only 14 percent of all black children in the South still attended all-black schools. Of course, many others went to mostly black schools. Even so, the change was dramatic.

DEMOCRACY?

Does the role of the Supreme Court in the civil rights era reflect or contradict the concept of democracy? That is, was it democratic for the nonelected justices to mandate equality to the elected officials of the southern states and cities? (Consider the tension between popular sovereignty and political equality and that between majority rule and minority rights.)

The first day for desegregated schools in Fort Myer, Virginia, brings apprehension and curiosity.

© Bettmann/Corbis

Busing *Brown* and related rulings addressed **de jure segregation**—segregation enforced by law—which can be attacked by striking down the law. *Brown* didn't address **de facto segregation**—segregation based on residential patterns. This segregation was typical of northern cities and large southern cities, where most blacks live in black neighborhoods and most whites live in white neighborhoods. Students attend their neighborhood schools, which are mostly black or mostly white. This segregation is more intractable because it doesn't stem primarily from a law and so can't be eliminated by striking down a law.

To address de facto segregation, civil rights groups proposed busing some black children to schools in white neighborhoods and some white children to schools in black neighborhoods. They hoped to improve black children's education, their self-confidence, and eventually, their college and career opportunities. They also hoped to improve black and white children's ability to get along together.

The **Burger Court**, which succeeded the Warren Court, authorized busing within school districts—ordinarily cities. These included southern cities where there was a history of de jure segregation and northern cities where there was a pattern of de facto segregation and evidence that school officials had located schools or assigned students in ways that perpetuated this segregation.[58] However, busing for desegregation was never extensive. In one typical year, only 4 percent of students were bused for desegregation. Far more students were bused, at public expense, to segregated public and private schools.[59]

Even so, court orders for mandatory busing ran into a wall of hostile public opinion. White parents criticized the courts sharply. Their reaction stemmed from a mixture of

behind the scenes

The Social Code

At the time the Supreme Court was deciding *Brown* v. *Board of Education,* a strict social code governed interactions between blacks and whites in the South. The code, which differed from place to place, was barely visible yet clearly understood by residents and very effective in keeping blacks "in their place."

The experience of one white woman who had moved from the North to Alabama in the 1950s illustrates how the code worked. The woman accidentally bumped into a black woman while shopping, causing the black woman to drop her packages. The white woman picked up the packages and handed them to her. After this courtesy, the store clerks, while making no comments, refused to wait on the white woman. In another store on another day, the white woman and her daughter were shopping when a black child offered her daughter a piece of candy. After her daughter accepted the candy, these clerks also refused to wait on the woman.

SOURCE: Tinsley E. Yarbrough, *Race and Redistricting: The Shaw-Cromartie Cases* (Lawrence: University Press of Kansas, 2003), 30.

---

prejudice against black people, bias against poor persons, fear of the crime in inner-city schools, worry about the quality of inner-city schools, and desire for the convenience of neighborhood schools.[60]

Because of the opposition of white parents, busing—and publicity about it—prompted an increase in "white flight" as white families moved from public schools to private schools and from the cities to the suburbs to avoid the busing in the cities.[61] This trend overlapped other trends that altered the racial and economic composition of our big cities, especially a reduction in the white birthrate and an increase in the nonwhite immigration rate. As a result, there were fewer white students to balance enrollments and fewer middle-class students to provide stability in the cities' schools.

Therefore, even extensive busing couldn't desegregate the school systems of most big cities, where blacks and other minorities together were more numerous than whites. Consequently, civil rights groups proposed busing some white children from the suburbs to the cities and some black children from the cities to the suburbs. This approach would provide enough of both races to achieve balance in both places.

The Burger Court rejected this proposal by a 5–4 vote in 1974.[62] It ruled that busing isn't appropriate between school districts unless there is evidence of intentional segregation in both the city and its suburbs. Otherwise, such extensive busing would require too long a ride for students and too much coordination by administrators. Although there was intentional segregation by many cities and their suburbs,[63] the evidence is not as clear-cut as that of the de jure segregation by the southern states, so it was difficult to satisfy the requirements laid down by the Court. The ruling made busing between the cities and their suburbs very rare.

Thurgood Marshall, by then a Supreme Court justice, dissented and predicted that the ruling would allow "our great metropolitan areas to be divided up each into two cities—one white, the other black." Indeed, the ruling was

the beginning of the end of the push to desegregate public schools in urban areas.

In 1991, the **Rehnquist Court**, which succeeded the Burger Court, ruled that school districts have no obligation to reduce de facto segregation, and the Court also diminished their obligation to reduce the vestiges of de jure segregation.[64] This ruling relieved the pressure on school districts, and most stopped busing.[65] The result was increasing resegregation.

Some districts tried other ways to balance enrollments. The county that includes Louisville, Kentucky, voluntarily adopted a "managed choice" program in which parents indicated their preference for the schools their children would attend, but the school district kept the black enrollment in each school between 15 and 50 percent through extensive busing. Yet the plan was popular with most parents, including white parents, almost all of whom got their first or second choice of schools.[66] Louisville became one of the most desegregated cities in the nation. In 2007, however, the **Roberts Court,** which succeeded the Rehnquist Court, invalidated the Louisville program and a limited program in Seattle.[67] The five-justice majority ruled that school districts can't use race as a basis for assigning students. The ruling jeopardized the programs in a thousand school districts across the country.[68]

The Court's decisions in the 1990s and 2000s reflect none of "the moral urgency of *Brown.*"[69] Instead, they reflect hostility toward government efforts, even school districts' voluntary efforts, to achieve desegregation. For most justices, desegregation is relatively unimportant, certainly less important than allowing white parents unfettered choice where they send their children. In this way, the Court's majority mirrors the views of the Republican presidents who appointed them.

Some districts have tried to integrate the races by integrating social classes. Because black students disproportionately come from the lower classes, assigning a percentage of poor students to middle-class schools would also integrate the races to some degree. This may require students to attend schools far from home and ride buses for long distances. But Raleigh, North Carolina, which used this approach, saw a dramatic improvement in poor students' performance (along with gains in other students' performance).[70] Such plans, based on class, aren't likely to be overruled by the courts because they aren't based, at least directly, on race. Yet these plans, too, have been opposed by white parents. In Raleigh, which was the model for other cities, a new school board halted its plan in 2010.

The Movement in the Streets

After the NAACP's early successes in the courts, other blacks, and some whites, took the fight to the streets. Their bold efforts gave birth to the modern civil rights movement.

The movement came to public attention in Montgomery, Alabama, in 1955, when Rosa Parks refused to move to the back of the bus. Her courage, and her arrest, roused others to boycott city buses. For their leader they chose a young Baptist minister, Dr. Martin Luther King Jr. The boycott catapulted the movement and King to national attention (as explained in Chapter 6).

As the first charismatic leader of the movement, King formed the Southern Christian Leadership Conference (SCLC) of black clergy and adopted the tactics of Mahatma Gandhi, who had led the movement to free India from Britain. The tactics included direct action, such as demonstrations and marches, and civil disobedience—intentional and public disobedience of unjust laws. The tactics were based

on nonviolence, even when confronted with violence. This strategy was designed to draw support from whites by contrasting the morality of the movement's position with the immorality of the opponents' discrimination and violence toward blacks.

For a long time, some southern whites, focusing on movement leaders and college students from other states, and fearing even infiltration by foreign communists, deluded themselves into thinking that "outside agitators" were responsible for the turmoil in their communities.[71] But the movement grew from the grass roots, and it eventually shattered this delusion.

The movement spread among black students. In 1960, four students of North Carolina A&T College sat at the lunch counter in Woolworth's, a chain of dime stores, and asked for a cup of coffee. The waitress refused to serve them, but they remained until they were arrested. On successive days, as whites waved the Confederate flag and jeered, more students sat at the lunch counter.[72] Within a year, such sit-ins occurred in more than one hundred cities.

When blacks asserted their rights, whites often reacted with violence. In 1963, King led demonstrators in Birmingham, Alabama, seeking desegregation of public facilities. Police unleashed dogs to attack the marchers. In 1964, King led demonstrators in Selma, Alabama, for voting rights. State troopers clubbed some marchers, and vigilantes beat and shot others.

In the summer of 1964, black and white college students mounted a voter registration drive in Mississippi. By the

Dorothy Counts, the first black student to attend one white high school in Charlotte, North Carolina, is escorted by her father in 1957.

Firefighters turn their hoses on demonstrators in Birmingham, Alabama, in 1963.

end of the summer, 1000 had been arrested, 80 beaten, 35 shot, and 6 killed.[73] When a black cotton farmer, who had tried to register to vote, was shot in the head in broad daylight by a white state legislator, the act wasn't even treated as a crime.[74]

Indeed, perpetrators of the violence usually were not apprehended or prosecuted. When they were, they usually were not convicted. Law enforcement was frequently in the hands of bigots, and juries were normally all white.[75]

During these years, whites told pollsters they disliked the civil rights movement's speed and tactics: "They're pushing too fast and too hard." At the same time, most said they favored integration more than ever. And they seemed repelled by the violence. The brutality against black demonstrators generated more support for black Americans and their cause.

The media, especially national organizations based in northern cities such as the *New York Times,* the Associated Press, and the major television networks, played a role simply by covering the conflict. The leaders of the civil rights movement staged events that captured attention, and violent racists played into their hands. As northern reporters and photographers relayed the events and violence to the nation, the movement gained public sympathy in the North. Yet the national press became as vilified as the federal government in the South. (This anger would fuel southerners' distrust of the media for many years.)[76]

Although the movement's tactics worked well against southern de jure segregation, they didn't work as well against northern de facto segregation or against job discrimination in either region. By the mid-1960s, progress had stalled and dissatisfaction had grown. Young blacks from the inner city, who hadn't been involved in the movement, questioned two of its principles: interracialism and nonviolence. As James Farmer, head of the Congress of Racial Equality (CORE), explained, they asked, "What is this we-shall-overcome, black-and-white-together stuff? I don't know of any white folks except the guy who runs that store on 125th Street in Harlem and garnishes wages and repossesses things you buy. I'd like to go upside his head. [Or] the rent collector, who bangs on the door demanding rent that we ain't got. I'd like to go upside his head."[77] These blacks criticized King and his tactics.

In place of the integration advocated by King, some leaders began to call for "black power." This phrase, which implied black pride and self-reliance, meant different things to different people. To some it meant political power through the ballot box, and to others it meant economic power through business ownership. To a few it meant violence in retaliation for violence by whites. The movement splintered further.

The Movement in Congress

As the civil rights movement expanded, it pressured presidents and members of Congress to act. President John Kennedy, who was most concerned about the Cold War, considered civil rights a distraction. President Lyndon Johnson, who was a champion of "the poor and the downtrodden and the oppressed"—a biographer calls him our second most compassionate president, after Abraham Lincoln[78]—supported civil rights but felt hamstrung by southerners in Congress who, through the seniority system, chaired key committees and dominated both houses. As a result, the presidents considered the civil rights leaders unreasonable, because their movement alienated the southerners on whom the presidents had to rely for other legislation.

However, once the movement demonstrated real strength, it convinced officials to act. After 200,000 blacks and whites marched in Washington in 1963, President Kennedy introduced civil rights legislation. His successor, President Johnson, with consummate legislative skill, forged a coalition of northern Democrats and northern Republicans to overcome southern Democrats and pass the Civil Rights Act of 1964. After 1000 blacks and whites had been attacked and arrested in Selma, Johnson introduced and Congress passed the Voting Rights Act of 1965. Three years later, Johnson introduced and Congress passed the Civil Rights Act of 1968. Within a span of four years, Congress passed legislation prohibiting discrimination in public accommodations, employment, housing, and voting. These would become the most significant civil rights acts in history.

It is impossible to exaggerate how controversial these laws were. In 1964, the Republican nominee for president, Sen. Barry Goldwater of Arizona, opposed the Civil Rights Act. He had been assured by two advisers—Phoenix attorney William Rehnquist and Yale professor Robert Bork—that it was unconstitutional.[79] The conservative Republican Ronald Reagan, preparing to run for California governor, also strongly opposed the act.[80] The opponents called the bill "a usurpation of states' rights" and claimed that it would create "a federal dictatorship." They also claimed that it would "destroy the free enterprise system."[81] (Years later, as president, Reagan would appoint Rehnquist as chief justice and nominate Bork to serve as an associate justice on the Supreme Court. Bork wasn't confirmed, in part because of his views toward civil rights laws and rulings.)

When three civil rights workers were murdered in Neshoba County, Mississippi, no one was indicted by the state. Later, eighteen persons, including the sheriff (left) and deputy sheriff (right), were indicted by the federal government for the lesser charge of conspiracy. (There was no applicable federal law for murder.) Ultimately, seven persons, including the deputy, were convicted by the federal court.

Although President Johnson believed he was doing the right thing, he realized the political ramifications. In pushing for civil rights, he said he was handing the South to the Republican Party "for the next fifty years."[82] And that's exactly what happened. In less than a decade, the South went from the most Democratic region to one of the most Republican regions in the country.[83]

After the 1966 congressional elections, when it was evident that the party was losing southern voters, Democratic governors in southern and border states demanded a meeting with Johnson. They criticized administration efforts to desegregate the schools and even suggested that the president was a traitor to his heritage. The next day Johnson was still fuming. To an aide he vented, "'Niggah! Niggah! Niggah!' That's all they said to me all day. Hell, there's one thing they'd better know. If I don't achieve anything else while I'm president, I intend to wipe that word out of the English language and make it impossible for people to come here and shout 'Niggah! Niggah! Niggah!' to me and the American people."[84]

Desegregation of public accommodations   The **Civil Rights Act of 1964** prohibits discrimination on the basis of race, color, religion, or national origin in public accommodations.[85] The act doesn't cover private clubs, such as country clubs, social clubs, or fraternities and sororities, on the principle that the government shouldn't tell people who they may or may not associate with in private. (The Court has made private schools an exception to this principle to help enforce *Brown,* so they can't discriminate.)

Desegregation of employment   The Civil Rights Act of 1964 also prohibits employment discrimination on the basis of race, color, religion, national origin, or sex and (as amended) physical disability, age, or Vietnam-era veteran status. The act covers employers with fifteen or more employees and unions.[86]

In addition to practicing blatant discrimination, some employers practiced more subtle discrimination by requiring applicants to meet standards unnecessary for the jobs, a practice that hindered blacks more than whites. A high school diploma for a manual job was a common example. The Supreme Court held that the standards must relate to the jobs.[87] (The Roberts Court, however, has signaled that it might not require that the standards *closely* relate to the jobs.)[88]

Desegregation of housing   Although the Supreme Court had struck down laws that prescribed segregation in residential areas, whites maintained segregation by making **restrictive covenants**—agreements among neighbors not to sell their houses to blacks. In 1948, the Court ruled that courts could not enforce these covenants because doing so would involve the government in discrimination.[89]

Real estate agents also played a role in segregation by practicing **steering**—showing blacks houses in black neighborhoods and whites houses in white neighborhoods.

President Lyndon Johnson and Martin Luther King Jr., compatriots with a tense relationship.

Unscrupulous real estate agents practiced **blockbusting**. After a black family bought a house in a white neighborhood, the agents would warn the white neighbors that more black families would move in. Because of prejudice and fear that their house values would decline, the whites would panic and sell to the agents at low prices. Then the agents would resell to black families at higher prices. In this way, neighborhoods that might have been desegregated were instead resegregated—from all white to all black.

Bank and savings and loan officers also played a role. For example, they were reluctant to lend money to blacks who wanted to buy houses in white neighborhoods. Some engaged in **redlining**—refusing to lend money to people who wanted to buy houses in racially changing neighborhoods. The lenders worried that if the buyers couldn't keep up with the payments, the lenders would be left with houses whose value had declined.

The government also played an important role. The Veterans Administration and the Federal Housing Authority, which guaranteed loans to some buyers, were reluctant to authorize loans to blacks who tried to buy houses in white neighborhoods (but they did provide loans to whites who fled from the cities to buy houses in all-white suburbs). And the federal government, which funded low-income housing, allowed local governments to locate such housing in ghettos. In these ways, the governments fostered and extended residential segregation (which is at the heart of the segregation of the schools and other activities such as neighborhood sports and businesses).[90]

The **Civil Rights Act of 1968** bans discrimination in the sale or rental of housing on the basis of race, color, religion, or national origin and (as amended) on the basis of sex, having children, or having a disability. The act covers 80 percent of the housing and prohibits steering, blockbusting, and redlining.

Restoration of the right to vote The Voting Rights Act of 1965, which implemented the Fifteenth Amendment, includes measures that enable blacks to vote (as explained in Chapter 8).

DEMOCRACY?

Consider the actions of the people who participated in the civil rights movement and the efforts by Congress during these years. In what ways do each of these reflect democracy?

Continuing Discrimination against African Americans

Although African Americans have overcome much discrimination, they still face lingering prejudice. Overt laws and blatant practices have been struck down, but subtle manifestations of old attitudes persist—and in ways far more numerous and with effects far more serious than this one chapter can convey.[91] Moreover, African Americans must cope with the legacy of generations of slavery, segregation, discrimination, and for many, the effects of poverty.

They also must cope with the attitudes of whites. Although few people say they want to return to the days of legal segregation, about half reject the dream of an integrated society.[92]

Discrimination in Education

Most black students attend segregated schools, and most schools for black students are unequal to the schools for white students.

Segregated schools Some black children, mostly those who have affluent parents who pay for private schools or live in well-off neighborhoods with good public schools, go to integrated schools. However, most black children, especially those who live in big cities or areas where private schools predominate, go to segregated schools.

Although de jure segregation of schools has been eliminated, de facto segregation remains. In fact, this segregation is getting worse. After progress in the 1960s, 1970s, and 1980s, the trend toward desegregation reversed itself in the 1990s. "For the first time since the *Brown* v. *Board* decision," one study concluded, "we are going backwards"[93] (see Figure 1). Smaller percentages of black students and Latino students attend schools that have a majority of white students than at any time since 1968.[94] Almost 40 percent of black students and fully 40 percent of Latino students attend schools that are 90 to 100 percent minority.[95]

The segregation is worse in the North, where it has been de facto, than in the South, where it had been de jure.[96] The

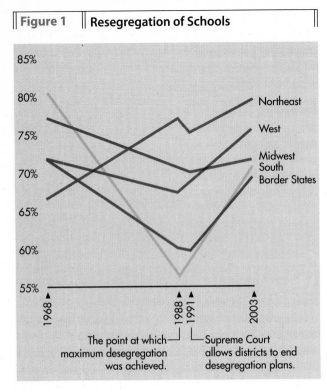

Figure 1 | **Resegregation of Schools**

- Northeast
- West
- Midwest
- South
- Border States

1968 ▲

1988 ▲ 1991 ▲   2003 ▲

The point at which maximum desegregation was achieved. ⌐ Supreme Court allows districts to end desegregation plans.

Percentage of students attending predominantly minority schools (schools in which 50–100% of students are nonwhite).
SOURCE: *Gary Orfield and Chungmei Lee, Racial Transformation and the Changing Nature of Segregation (Cambridge, Mass.: The Civil Rights Project, Harvard University, 2006), 10. This report is based on data through 2003, which are the most current data available. (The Civil Rights Project is now located at the University of California, Los Angeles.)*

segregation is worse in big cities, but it is spreading to their suburbs, especially to the inner-ring suburbs where numerous minorities live now.[97]

This **resegregation** is due to white flight to private schools and to the suburbs, leaving fewer white children, and also due to higher nonwhite birthrates and immigration rates, bringing more nonwhite children to the public schools. These changes affect the decisions of white parents who look for schools with low numbers of racial minorities.[98] Although many say they move for "better schools," few ever visit the schools or check the schools' test scores before moving. They use racial composition as a proxy for school quality. The more racial minorities, the poorer the quality, they assume.[99]

This resegregation is also due to a shift in government policies and court decisions resulting from conservative dominance of American politics from 1980 through 2008. Conservative presidents, beginning with Ronald Reagan and continuing through George W. Bush, and conservative justices on the Supreme Court, especially on the Rehnquist and Roberts Courts, based their social policy decisions on the assumptions that "race should be ignored, inequalities should be blamed on individuals and schools, and existing

civil rights remedies should be dismantled."[100] Their decisions sent a message to school districts that desegregation is no longer an important national goal.[101] Usually this message was implicit; for example, the Reagan administration ended the federal program that aided school districts in their efforts to desegregate. Occasionally the message was explicit; for example, the George W. Bush administration advised school districts to cut back on their efforts to desegregate.[102] In short, the three branches of the federal government have done "nothing significant" to foster school desegregation since 1981 (when the Reagan administration ended the federal program that aided school districts).[103]

The persistence of de facto segregation and the waning of society's commitment to integration have led national, state, and local officials to adopt a resigned attitude: "We still agree with the goal of school desegregation, but it's too hard, and we're tired of it, and we give up."[104]

Reforms proposed for urban schools rarely include desegregation. Officials speak of a ghetto school that is more "efficient" or one that gets more "input" from ghetto parents or offers more "choices" for ghetto children. But they seem to accept segregated education as "a permanent American reality."[105]

A writer who visited many central-city classrooms and talked with students, teachers, and administrators observed that Martin Luther King was treated as "an icon, but his vision of a nation in which black and white kids went to school together seemed to be effaced almost entirely. Dutiful references to 'The Dream' were often seen in school brochures and on wall posters in February, when 'Black History' was celebrated in the public schools, but the content of the dream was treated as a closed box that could not be opened without ruining the celebration."[106]

Indeed, many cities have a school named after King— a segregated school in a segregated neighborhood—"like a terrible joke on history," a fourteen-year-old, wise beyond her years, remarked.[107] In fact, if you want to find a school that's really segregated, look for schools named after champions of integration—Jackie Robinson, Rosa Parks, and Thurgood Marshall.[108]

Some minorities have gotten so frustrated that they themselves have questioned the goal of school desegregation. Instead, they have voiced greater concern about improving the quality and safety of their schools and neighborhoods.[109] However, one education analyst observes, "For African Americans to have equal opportunity, higher test scores will not suffice. It is foolhardy to think black children can be taught, no matter how well, in isolation and then have the skills and confidence as adults to succeed in a white world where they have no experience."[110]

Unequal schools   In areas where the schools are segregated, their quality varies enormously—from "the golden to the godawful," in the words of a Missouri judge.[111] And of course, blacks and Latinos are more likely to be in the "godawful" ones. By virtually every measure of school quality—school funding, class size, teacher credentials, teacher salaries, breadth of curriculum, number of computers, opportunities for gifted students—these black and Latino children attend worse schools.[112]

Public schools are financed largely by property taxes paid by homeowners and businesses. Wealthy cities, where property costs more to buy and is assessed more in taxes, collect more in taxes than poor ones. In modern America, this means that suburban school districts have more to spend per pupil than central-city school districts.[113]

In about three-fourths of the states, school districts with the highest percentages of black and Latino children receive less funding than the districts with the fewest.[114] Nationwide, the difference amounts to $25,000 less per *classroom* per year for school districts with the most black and Latino children. In Illinois, the difference totals $47,000 less per classroom, and in New York, it totals $50,000 less.[115] And these official figures don't count the extra money that affluent parents, on their own or through PTAs, contribute to hire additional teachers to reduce class sizes or to provide art and music instruction, or to buy books for the library or equipment for the gym and playground.

Spending-per-pupil figures also don't take into account the fact that the needs of poor children, after years of neglect and with scores of problems in their homes and neighborhoods, are greater than the needs of other children. Schools for poor children would require *more* funding to provide their students an *equal* education.[116]

So, many inner-city schools are bleak institutions, filthy and in disrepair. A thirty-year veteran of seven District of Columbia schools said all should be condemned. Of her current school, she said, "I have to cover books, computers, and student work stations with plastic to catch the falling plaster and water from the leaking roof. In the school cafeteria, 55-gallon garbage cans are strategically placed to catch the water from gaping holes in the ceiling."[117] Teachers in some Los Angeles schools said the children count the rats.[118]

Most inner-city schools are overcrowded. They lack up-to-date texts and paper and pencils. They lack books for literature classes, chemicals for chemistry classes, and computers for computer classes. (Teachers *talk* about using computers.)[119]

Most inner-city schools also can't attract enough good teachers. A New York City principal said he is forced to take the "tenth-best" teachers. "I thank God they're still breathing."[120] In Illinois, which measures the quality of its teachers, just 11 percent of the teachers in majority-white schools are in the lowest quartile of the teachers in the state, but 88 percent of the teachers in almost-all-minority schools are in the lowest quartile.[121] Yet the quality of its teachers might be the most important factor in the success of a school.[122]

Despite the pattern of unequal funding, cash alone wouldn't solve the problems of inner-city schools. Cultural and economic factors in these communities also limit the education provided. For example, black and Latino students say their school is a more rowdy, disrespectful, and dangerous place, with more drugs, weapons, and fights, than white students report in their school.[123] Nevertheless, cash would help, not only for the reasons cited so far, but also to fund intensive programs for lagging students, such as family counseling, language development, and longer school days and school years.[124]

Some states have equalized funding for public schools, but the attempts to do so in other states have encountered fierce opposition. As an alternative to equalized funding, some states have considered supplementary funding for inner-city schools, but people's priorities run in other directions.

A teacher tries to teach in the hallway of an overcrowded school in the underfunded system of Philadelphia.

In 1999, the Pennsylvania legislature approved $160 million of public financing for new stadiums for the Eagles and Phillies and another $160 million of public financing for new stadiums for the Steelers and Pirates, while the schools in Philadelphia and Pittsburgh languished.[125]

Charter schools are not a panacea for these problems. Numerous cities are experimenting with charter schools, which are operated by private companies or nonprofit organizations and are allowed to disregard some rules established by school districts and teachers' unions. With more leeway, they're expected to produce better results. Yet their results are mixed. Some charter schools are a real improvement over the public schools in their neighborhood; others, however, show a noticeable decline in test scores. Regardless, charter schools tend to reinforce existing segregation.[126]

Because of the persistence of segregated schools and unequal schools, one study concluded, "Millions of non-white students are locked into 'dropout factory' high schools, where huge percentages do not graduate, have little future in the American economy, and almost none are well prepared for college."[127]

Discrimination in Employment

Although the Civil Rights Act of 1964 and affirmative action (discussed later in the chapter) have prompted more employers to hire and promote African Americans, discrimination in employment remains.

Many blacks who are hired encounter negative stereotypes that question their competence on the job. These workers are passed over when they could be promoted.[128] Other blacks who are hired face racial slurs in comments, notes, and graffiti from coworkers. They endure an unfriendly or hostile environment.[129] Although most upper-level executives realize that it is economically advantageous to have a diverse workforce, some middle-level white managers and lower-level white workers interact poorly with the black employees.

Discrimination in Housing

The Civil Rights Act of 1968, which prohibits discrimination in housing, has fostered some desegregation of housing, but extensive segregation persists.

One reason is economic. Many blacks don't have enough money to buy homes in white neighborhoods. But another reason is discrimination. Social pressure and occasional violence discourage blacks who try to move into white neighborhoods. Continuing discrimination by homeowners, real estate agents, lenders, and insurers also stymies them. A study of twenty metropolitan areas, using white and minority testers responding to house and apartment ads, found that blacks who try to buy a house face discrimination 17 percent of the time, and those who try to rent an apartment do so 22 percent of the time.[130] If callers

sound black, landlords may claim that the apartment has already been rented.[131]

The federal government makes virtually no effort to enforce the Civil Rights Act of 1968.[132] The only attempts to enforce it occur when victims of discrimination file lawsuits.

Despite these facts, residential segregation is declining. The fast-growing suburban areas in the West and South are much more likely to have integrated neighborhoods than a decade earlier, and the stagnant "rust belt" cities in the East and Midwest are integrating too, but more slowly.[133] Middle-class blacks who escape the ghetto often end up in black neighborhoods in the suburbs of these cities.[134]

Segregation doesn't continue because black people "want to live among their own kind," as some whites insist. Surveys show that only about 15 percent want to live in segregated neighborhoods, and most of them cite their fear of white hostility as the reason. Eighty-five percent would prefer mixed neighborhoods. Many say the optimal level would be half black and half white. But whites tend to move out when the concentration of blacks reaches 8 to 10 percent.[135] These contrasting attitudes make integration an elusive goal. Blacks constitute 13 percent of the population in the country but a much larger percentage in some cities.

These patterns and attitudes are all the more troublesome because residential segregation, of course, is at the heart of school segregation.

Another form of housing discrimination emerged in the crisis over subprime mortgages in recent years. Major banks singled out minority neighborhoods for housing loans with inferior terms, such as high up-front fees, high interest rates, and lax underwriting practices. These terms made it more likely that minority homeowners would be unable to make their payments and unable to keep their home. When the crisis hit, these homeowners were among the first to lose their homes.[136]

Discrimination in Other Ways

African Americans encounter discrimination in other ways, especially as targets of law enforcement and insults.

Law enforcement African Americans face discrimination from police officers. The practice of **racial profiling**, which is based on the assumption that minorities, especially males, are more likely to commit crimes, especially those involving drugs, targets minorities for stops and searches. Without evidence, officers stop minority drivers and search them and their vehicles.[137] Sometimes officers stop minority pedestrians as well. Although police departments deny profiling, statistics show clear evidence of the practice.

Nationwide, black, Latino, and white drivers are equally likely to be stopped, though black and Latino drivers are twice as likely to be searched. Black and Latino drivers are also more likely to be given a ticket—and less likely to be given a warning—when stopped than white drivers.[138] In

African American communities often have tense relationships with local police departments. After Hurricane Katrina, Leonard Thomas's family were living in their flooded home when a SWAT team burst in, believing that they were squatting in another family's house.

some places, profiling is more pronounced. In Los Angeles, blacks are two times as likely to be stopped and four times as likely to be searched as other drivers. Yet they are less likely to be found with illegal substances.[139] Therefore, the higher rates of stops and searches aren't because police have more evidence, or better hunches, of illegal substances in the cars of black drivers.

African Americans speak of the moving violation "DWB"—*driving while black.* A school administrator has been stopped twenty times in the past decade.[140] Former Rep. J. C. Watts (R-Okla.) was pulled over six times in one day in his home state.[141]

A Chicago journalist who was stopped at least every other time he traveled through the Midwest learned not to rent flashy Mustangs or wear his beret. Others shun tinted windshields or expensive sunglasses—any flamboyance— to avoid the cops.[142]

Profiling might be justified if it led to the apprehension of dangerous criminals, but apparently it does not. Although African American young men evidently do commit a larger percentage of certain crimes,[143] profiling does not lead the police to many criminals. When police stop motorists, they find no greater evidence of crimes by blacks and Hispanics than by whites.[144] Meanwhile, the encounters often humiliate those who are stopped and spark animosity toward the police in these communities (as the movie *Crash* so clearly depicted).

Some states and many counties and cities have taken steps to reduce profiling, such as recording data on every stop to see whether the police, or individual officers, are prone to profile. Yet the cops on the beat, who feel that profiling is useful, are reluctant to change their habits.

Other discrimination from police officers is less common but more serious. Sometimes officers arrest black citizens without legal cause, and occasionally they use excessive force against them. Numerous examples attest to improper beatings.[145] Sometimes officers lie while testifying against black suspects in court. As a result, even prominent African Americans say their "worst fear" is to go before the criminal justice system.[146] It is little wonder that black jurors hearing the O. J. Simpson trial and black citizens following it put less faith in the police testimony than white observers did (even though legal experts believe Simpson was guilty).

Cautious parents teach their children how to avoid sending the wrong signals to police. Some parents urge their children not to wear street fashions and not to use cell phones, which from a distance might be mistaken as weapons. Some schools offer survival workshops for police encounters. Minority officers instruct the students what to do when they get stopped: don't reach for an ID unless the officer asks for one; don't mumble or talk loudly; don't antagonize by asking for a badge number or threatening to file a complaint.[147]

Insults   Most blacks, even professionals, face insults because of their race. Black women tell of being mistaken for hotel chambermaids by white guests at the hotels.[148] They also tell of being mistaken for prostitutes by white men and police officers while waiting in hotel lobbies. A distinguished black political scientist was mistaken for a butler in his own home. Black doctors tell of dressing up to go shopping to avoid being regarded as shoplifters. But dressing up is no guarantee. A black lawyer, a senior partner in a large law firm, arrived at work early one morning, before the doors were unlocked. As he reached for his key, a young white lawyer, a junior associate in the firm, arrived at the same time, blocked his entrance, and asked, repeatedly and demandingly, "May I help you?" The white associate had taken the black partner for an intruder.[149] Although in these encounters the insults were unintentional, the stings hurt just the same. The accumulation of such incidents, which more than eight in ten blacks say they occasionally experience, has created a "black middle-class rage" among many.[150]

Overall, discrimination against African Americans continues. Whites speak of "past discrimination"—sometimes referring to slavery, sometimes to official segregation—but this phrase is misleading. Of course, there is a lot less discrimination now because of the civil rights movement, Supreme Court decisions, and congressional acts. However, there is nothing "past" about much "past discrimination."[151] The effects linger, and the discrimination itself persists. As a black journalist observes, "Modern bigotry usually isn't some nitwit screaming the N-word. It is jobs you don't get and loans you don't get and health care you don't get and justice you don't get, for reasons you get all too clearly, even though no one ever quite speaks them."[152]

Even when blacks point out the discrimination, some whites insist that little discrimination is left. These whites apparently assume that they know more than blacks do about what it is like to be black. Indeed, the perceptual gap between blacks and whites about the existence of discrimination is a real barrier to improved race relations. Whites who believe nothing is wrong don't favor actions to fix what they see as a nonexistent problem.

Improving Conditions for African Americans?

Despite this continuing discrimination, however, the picture is not all bleak. In some respects African Americans have taken long strides toward achieving equal rights. These strides have led to much better living conditions for many and to a healthier racial climate in society. But, as pointed out in the previous section, serious problems remain.

Progress

As a result of the civil rights movement, Supreme Court decisions, and congressional laws, the United States has undergone a racial transformation in just one generation. As a black law professor observed, racism has become "unlawful, immoral, and, perhaps more important, déclassé" (out of style).[153] Antiracism has replaced racism as the dominant ideology toward race relations in our major institutions, such as the schools, the military, the media, big corporations, and labor unions. And the civil rights movement has become "as much a part of American nationalist lore as the Boston Tea Party or Paul Revere's midnight ride."[154]

Consequently, blacks' lives have improved in most ways that can be measured.[155] Blacks have a lower poverty rate and a longer life expectancy than before. They have completed more years of education, with larger numbers attending college and graduate school. They have also attained higher occupational levels—for example, tripling their proportion of the country's professionals[156]—and higher income levels. Many—well over half—have reached the middle class.[157] Almost half own their own homes,[158] and a third have moved to the suburbs.[159]

During the years that blacks' lives have improved, whites' racial attitudes have also improved. Numerous polls show that whites' views have changed significantly (even assuming that some whites gave socially acceptable answers rather than expressed their real feelings).

Since the 1960s, whites and blacks both report more social contact with members of the other race and more approval of interracial dating and marriage (see Figure 2), which is especially significant because these practices were the ultimate taboos. Interracial couples represented the clearest breach and their potential offspring the greatest threat to continued segregation.[160] According to one survey, four of every ten Americans say they have dated someone of another race, and almost three of every ten say it has been a "serious" relationship.[161] According to the 2000 census, 6.7 percent of all marriages—up from 4.4 percent in the 1990 census—are interracial. (And many cohabitations, which aren't included in the census, are interracial as well.) Thirteen percent of marriages involving blacks are interracial, and a third of marriages involving Hispanics and Asians are as well.[162]

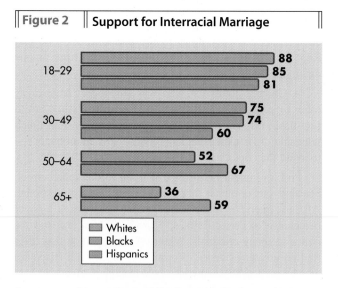

Figure 2 — **Support for Interracial Marriage**

18–29: 88 / 85 / 81
30–49: 75 / 74 / 60
50–64: 52 / 67
65+: 36 / 59

Whites
Blacks
Hispanics

Percentages of those who would be fine with a family member's marriage to someone of any other race/ethnicity. Whites include only non-Hispanic whites. Blacks include only non-Hispanic blacks. Hispanics are of any race. There were insufficient numbers of Hispanics ages 50–64 and 65+ for analysis.
SOURCE: *"Almost All Millennials Accept Interracial Dating and Marriage," Pew Research Center, February 1, 2010.*

Some whites, of course, remain blatant racists. Because of socioeconomic reasons, these whites are more likely to have contacts with blacks—to live near and work with them—than are tolerant whites, who are more educated and more prosperous. Even so, overt racist behavior occurs less frequently and is condemned more quickly than before. In some circles today, a blatant racist is considered not only a "fossil," but a "moral pervert" as well.[163] Yet covert racist attitudes persist in the minds of many whites, resulting in more subtle distrust and disapproval, rather than outright antipathy, toward blacks and toward policies that involve, or are perceived to involve, race, such as affirmative action and welfare spending.[164]

The election of Barack Obama shows how far we've come. In fact, his campaign appears to have decreased negative stereotypes about blacks held by many whites, especially older whites, who tend to be the most prejudiced.[165] But the reaction to Obama's campaign and presidency also shows how far we've got to go. During his campaign, numerous voters confided to reporters that they wouldn't vote for a black candidate. And during his presidency, many Americans have internalized the frantic attempts, not just by the loco fringe, to portray Obama as "the Other"—a foreigner, Muslim, fascist, socialist, communist—not a real American or a legitimate president. These attempts are fueled, at least in part, by his race. "Some people just can't believe a black man is president and will never accept it."[166] Of course, this does not mean that all or most of his opponents are motivated by racism, but it would be naïve to believe, as some pundits speculated after the election, that we're now living in a "post-racial society."[167] Most talk about a "post-racial society" comes from whites who want to congratulate themselves or those who want to pressure government to abandon efforts to promote equality.

Problems

Although the push for civil rights has opened many doors, some blacks aren't in a position to pass through. About a quarter of the black population live in poverty—two and one-half times the rate among the white population—and about a tenth, the poorest of the poor, exist in a state of economic and social "disintegration."[168] This "underclass" is trapped in a cycle of self-perpetuating problems from which it is extremely difficult to escape.

The problems of the lower class and the underclass have been exacerbated by economic changes that intensified in the 1970s and have continued since then. These changes hit the poor the hardest. Good-paying manufacturing jobs in the cities—the traditional path out of poverty for immigrant groups—disappeared. Chicago lost over 300,000 jobs, New York over 500,000.[169] Many jobs were eliminated by automation, while many others were moved to foreign countries or to the suburbs. Although service jobs increased, most were outside the cities and required more education or paid lower wages than the manufacturing jobs had.

As black men lost their jobs, they lost their ability to support a family. This led to a decrease in the number of "marriageable" black men and an increase in the number of households headed by black women.[170] The percentage of such households rose from 20 percent of all black families in 1960 to 45 percent in 2000.[171] And 60 percent of black children live in such households. These families are among the poorest in the country.

Meanwhile, the gains from civil rights enabled the black middle class to flee the inner cities for the suburbs. Their migration left the ghettos with fewer healthy businesses and strong schools to provide stability and fewer role models to portray mainstream behavior.[172] By the mid-1990s, one

Barack Obama's election shows how far we have come, but many Americans' reaction to his presidency shows how far we still have to go.

Black women are making great progress. They are more likely than black men to graduate from college and professional schools. At Tuskegee University, they dominate the veterinary school.

Chicago ghetto with 66,000 people had just one supermarket and one bank but forty-eight state-licensed lottery agents and ninety-nine state-licensed liquor stores and bars.[173]

Today many ghetto residents have "almost no contact with mainstream American society or the normal job market."[174] Too few jobs are available, and even fewer jobs pay a living wage. Debilitating drugs and serious crimes are ever present. As a result, too many residents have developed understandable but dysfunctional social norms, rejecting the work ethic, deferred gratification, and any investment in their future, all of which may seem pointless in their environment.[175]

Now, about 11 percent of black men between twenty and thirty-four are in jail or prison.[176] Consequently, about 41 percent of federal and state prisoners are black, although only 13 percent of the U.S. population is black. Three times as many black people live in prison cells as live in college dorms.[177]

It is commonly recognized that the plight of young black men is worse than that of any other group in society. More black men receive their GED (high school equivalence degree) in prison than graduate from college.[178] About half as many black men as black women attend college. A black man in Harlem has less chance of living past forty than a man in Bangladesh.[179]

These problems affect even middle-class blacks who have escaped to the suburbs. While returning to the city to see their relatives or old friends or to get a haircut, they may be in the wrong place at the wrong time. They may wear the wrong color shirt, wrong logo hat, or wrong brand of shoes and get caught up in gang violence. A father asks, "How many cultures can you say that when a guy turns twenty-five, he actually celebrates because he didn't think he would make it?"[180]

After widespread riots in the 1960s, the Kerner Commission, appointed by President Johnson to examine the cause of the riots, concluded, "What white Americans have never fully understood—but what the Negro can never forget—is that white society is deeply implicated in the ghetto. White institutions created it, white institutions maintain it, and white society condones it." After the riots, however, governments did little to improve the conditions that precipitated the riots.

After the riots in Los Angeles in 1992 following the trial of police officers who beat up Rodney King, there was more talk about improving the conditions in the ghetto. But a columnist who had heard such talk before commented, "My guess is that when all is said and done, a great deal more will be said than done. The truth is we don't know any quick fixes for our urban ills and we lack the patience and resources for slow fixes."[181]

And we lack the will to make the effort. A national focus on our big cities and their impoverished residents dissipated in the furious backlash against government and taxes that arose in the late 1970s and has continued for the three decades since then.[182] This backlash has starved governments of the revenue and sapped them of the desire necessary to act.

During these decades, the cities have lost political power as they have lost population due to white flight and black migration. Since 1992, more voters have lived in the suburbs than in the cities. (More than 40 percent of blacks live in the suburbs too.) Suburban voters don't urge action on urban problems, and sometimes they resist action if it means an increase in their taxes or a decrease in their services.

For the black lower class, and especially for the black underclass, it is apparent that civil rights aren't enough. As one black leader said, "What good is a seat in the front of the bus if you don't have the money for the fare?"[183]

But most blacks don't fall in the lower class or underclass, and most don't dwell in the inner cities. It would be a serious mistake to hold the stereotypical view that the majority reside in the inner cities and that most of them live in dysfunctional families that are filled with crackheads and prone to violence. Although black men lag behind, black women especially have vastly improved their lives—academically, professionally, and financially—over the span of one generation.[184]

Even so, many professional black women can relate to Michelle Obama's experience in the presidential campaign. An accomplished lawyer, she was quickly portrayed as someone who isn't "one of us"—not patriotic, because of an offhand remark she made; too radical, because of an article she wrote twenty years earlier; and, in general, an "angry black woman." Professional black women often face the same stereotypes at work.[185]

Discrimination against Hispanics

Hispanics, also called Latinos, are people in the United States who have a Spanish-speaking background. Although sometimes they are considered a separate race, in fact they can be of any race. Some are brown skinned, others black skinned, and still others white skinned. Many are an amalgam of European, African, and American Indian ancestry that makes it impossible to classify them by race. Thus Hispanics should be regarded as an ethnic group rather than a distinct race. (But Hispanics are so diverse, as we will see, that some scholars are reluctant to consider them even an ethnic group, preferring to consider them simply a statistical category for the convenience of government reports, academic research, and media coverage.)

About 60 percent of America's Hispanics trace their ancestry to Mexico.[186] They are heavily concentrated in the Southwest but are increasingly spreading throughout the United States, including the Midwest and the South. About 10 percent are from Puerto Rico, which is a commonwealth—a self-governing territory—of the United States. As members of the commonwealth, they are U.S. citizens. Most live in New York, Boston, Chicago, and other cities in the North. Another 4 percent are from Cuba. Following the establishment of a communist government in Cuba in 1959, many fled to the United States and settled in south Florida. A significant number are also from various islands in the Caribbean and countries in Central America, where emigrants have left turmoil and oppression. A smaller number are from countries in South America or from Spain.

Despite the diversity of their origins, Hispanics are especially concentrated in six states. More than half live in California and Texas, where they make up one-third of the population. Already they outnumber Anglos in Los Angeles and Houston.[187] Many of the rest live in Florida, New Jersey, New York, and Illinois, but there are growing pockets in the South, rural Midwest, and elsewhere.

Representing 15 percent of the population, Latinos have overtaken blacks as the largest minority in the United States. (This number includes legal and illegal residents.)

Cuban Americans are more likely than other Latinos to be middle class.

Fueled by high immigration rates and birthrates, this group is the fastest-growing minority (slightly faster growing than Asians) in the United States.

Hispanics never endured slavery in this country,[188] but some have faced severe discrimination. Although some Hispanics are Caucasian, many Puerto Ricans and Cubans have African ancestry, and many Mexicans have Indian ancestry, so they have darker skin than non-Hispanic whites.[189] Like blacks, Hispanics, especially Mexicans and Puerto Ricans,[190] have faced discrimination in education, employment, housing, and voting.[191]

Discrimination Due to Immigration

Latinos also endure discrimination because of immigration. The flood of illegal immigrants pouring in from Latin America, especially from Mexico, has produced a wave of anti-immigration sentiment throughout the United States, even in the states and cities with few immigrants.[192] This sentiment affects not only illegal immigrants but also the Latinos who are legal residents and U.S. citizens, including those who are native-born Americans, because the average person or law enforcement officer often can't tell, simply by watching or listening to them, which Latinos are legal and which ones are illegal.

Because illegal immigrants can't get driver's licenses and most don't get driver's insurance, police officers expect to identify illegal immigrants by demanding these documents. As a result, border patrol agents and local police officers often stop Latinos for questioning. Agents stopped the mayor of Pomona, California, a hundred miles from the Mexican border, and ordered him to produce papers proving that he's a legal resident. Local police officers also assume that many Latinos are involved in drug trafficking, so they practice profiling, as they do toward blacks.[193] Even when the officers are well intentioned, their conduct—the stopping and questioning and demanding of documents—seems like harassment to law-abiding residents and citizens.

This profiling was a problem even before 2010, when Arizona passed a law requiring state and local officers who stop a person for any infraction to determine the person's legal status if they have "reasonable suspicion" to think that the person is in the country illegally. This new law invites further profiling.[194] Whether Latinos will be detained will depend on how troopers and cops interpret the phrase "reasonable suspicion."[195] Other states considered similar laws in 2010.

The debate over Arizona's law unleashed strong emotions and nativist comments. At times the debate became irrational. Even Sen. John McCain (R-Ariz.), who previously cosponsored a bill that would reform immigration law and provide a path to citizenship for illegal immigrants, backtracked as he heard his constituents' views during his reelection bid. Defending Arizona's law, he said, "It's the . . . drivers of cars with illegals in it that are intentionally causing accidents on the freeway."[196]

Law enforcement officers in Arizona frisk a suspect before determining his legal status.

Fearing a wave of similar laws in other states, the federal government sued Arizona, claiming that the law is unconstitutional because the federal government is responsible for immigration. (The suit was still pending when this text was being printed.)

But more pervasive than the occasional stops by law enforcement officers is the hostility from ordinary Americans who are opposed to the influx of immigrants. In their looks and comments, some Americans send a message that immigrants, especially Latinos, aren't welcome here.

Actually, the controversy over illegal immigrants may be less about illegal immigration than about immigration in general—polls show that people who say they oppose illegal immigration tend to oppose legal immigration as well. The controversy may even be less about immigration in general than about assimilation into the American culture and adoption of the English language.[197] Among Anglos, there is widespread unease about the Latino culture and real anxiety about whether, and how fast, these recent arrivals will discard their culture in favor of Anglo culture. There are fears that immigrants will change white Americans more than white Americans will change them.

Figure 3 | Assimilation of Immigrants, by Country of Origin

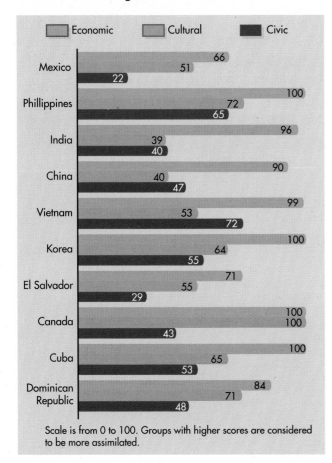

Researchers created indices reflecting the economic, cultural, and civic assimilation of immigrants, and they assessed immigrants from the ten countries that provide the most immigrants to the United States (listed in order). The figure shows the extent of each nationality's assimilation, based on data from 2006.

SOURCE: Manhattan Institute.

In fact, immigrants in the past quarter century have been assimilating at a faster rate than previous immigrants. They are assimilating economically, by holding jobs and earning money and by buying homes; culturally, by learning English and intermarrying with U.S. citizens; and politically, by becoming citizens, voting, and serving in the military. (See Figures 3 and 4. For further evidence of assimilation, see the box "Latinos Choose Anglo Names.") A study concluded that "the nation's capacity to assimilate new immigrants is strong."[201]

Immigrants in the past quarter century have also been learning English. Cuban Americans are learning English as fast or faster than any group in history.[202] Mexican Americans are learning English slower than other groups, but they are learning it as they reside longer in the United States. Although many who come for work and plan to return to Mexico don't speak English, most who remain in the United States learn to speak some English, and almost all of their children learn to speak fluent English.[203] Most of these second-generation Americans are bilingual, speaking Spanish at home with their parents and relatives and English outside of home. But many of *their* children—the third-generation Americans— are monolingual, speaking only English. The drive to learn English is so strong that just a third of Latinos born in the United States are bilingual. Most can't speak Spanish.[204]

It is true that some immigrant communities, especially Cubans in south Florida and Mexicans in some parts of the Southwest, are so large that residents can survive without learning English. But most feel pressure to learn English to function in society and for their children to succeed in school. Indeed, 89 percent of Latinos believe that those

These fears are aggravated by the fact that 40 percent of Latinos are first-generation immigrants, meaning that they themselves came from other countries.[198] In general, these immigrants haven't assimilated or learned English, just as the first generation of previous immigrant groups didn't assimilate or learn English.[199] With so many new immigrants in recent decades, Anglo Americans often encounter first-generation immigrants, and they draw conclusions about all Latinos from these immigrants.

Yet clear patterns of cultural assimilation and language acquisition are emerging. Many immigrants are illegal aliens who live in the shadows, in fear of deportation. They haven't been in a position to assimilate. Among legal residents, many immigrants came to the United States to work for a few years and then to return to their home country. They haven't wanted to assimilate. But most immigrants do remain here, and their children do assimilate.[200]

Figure 4 | Most Hispanics Accept Assimilation

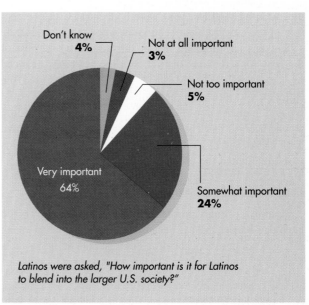

Latinos were asked, "How important is it for Latinos to blend into the larger U.S. society?"

SOURCE: Time, August 22, 2005, 56. Poll conducted by phone, with interviews in English and Spanish. N = 503.

who immigrate must learn English to succeed in the United States.[205] Children do learn English in schools, though it is harder for adults to find English classes that fit with their work schedules, especially given the long hours and multiple jobs that many immigrants have.[206]

While illegal immigration doesn't result in all of the harms that its opponents charge, it certainly leads to some problems. The communities and states near the Mexican border bear a disproportionate share of the burden from this immigration. Their education costs rise as children fill the schools; their health costs increase when immigrants without health insurance need health care; and their law enforcement costs rise too. Because the federal government has failed to act on the issue of illegal immigration, residents of these communities and states feel overwhelmed by problems largely not of their making (as explained in Chapter 3).

Discrimination in Education

As late as the mid-twentieth century, Hispanic children were not allowed to attend any schools in some places. In other places, they were segregated into "Mexican" schools that were inferior to Anglo schools.[207] When the Supreme Court declared segregation illegal, many school districts achieved "integration" by combining Hispanics with blacks, leaving non-Hispanic whites in their own schools.[208]

Although de jure segregation has been struck down,[209] de facto segregation exists in cities where Latinos are concentrated. Many Latinos attend schools with more than 90 percent minorities, and most attend schools with more than 50 percent minorities.[210]

Predominantly Latino schools, like predominantly black schools, aren't as well funded as other schools because they're located in poor communities that don't get as much revenue from property taxes. In San Antonio, wealthy families, who were concentrated in one section of the city, got their section incorporated as a separate school district, although it was surrounded by the rest of the city. As a separate district, its property taxes financed its schools only. When Mexican American parents sued, the Burger Court ruled that the Fourteenth Amendment's equal protection clause doesn't require states to equalize funding among school districts, even where artificial districts have been carved out of a city.[211] Despite the Court's ruling, this case highlighted the problem of unequal funding, prompting some states to equalize funding, though allowing other states to maintain the status quo.

Latinos' primary problem in education, however, is the language barrier. Many, because they are unable to speak English, fail in school and drop out of school at higher rates than other students, even African Americans. One-third of Latinos drop out before graduating from high school.[212]

Bilingual education was created in the 1970s to help such students. Bilingual classes used the students' native language to teach the students English and their other subjects. The goal was to transition them from their native

LATINOS CHOOSE ANGLO NAMES

Despite Anglos' concern that Latinos are not assimilating, Latinos are favoring Anglo names for their children.

For Boys	For Girls

For Hispanic children born in Texas in a recent year, the most popular names are:

For Boys	For Girls
Jose	Ashley
Daniel	Jennifer
Jonathan	Emily
David	Samantha
Christopher	Maria

For Hispanic children born in New York City, the most popular names are:

For Boys	For Girls
Justin	Ashley
Christopher	Jennifer
Kevin	Emily
Anthony	Brianna
Brandon	Samantha

SOURCE: Sam Roberts, "In a Changing Nation, Smith Is Still King." From *The New York Times*, © July 11, 2004 *The New York Times*. All rights reserved. Used by permission and protected by the Copyright Laws of the United States. The printing, copying, redistribution, or retransmission of the Material without express written permission is prohibited.

language to English rather than to immerse them in a foreign language—English—that they didn't understand.[213] Around the country, more than 150 languages were offered; Spanish was the most common.[214]

However, bilingual programs faced numerous problems. They were expensive because they required more teachers and smaller classes, and they were impractical because schools couldn't find enough teachers in various languages. Schools in California, where half of all students in bilingual programs lived, fell 21,000 teachers short in one year.[215] Thus the schools couldn't offer bilingual education to most students who were eligible for it.[216]

Bilingual programs were controversial as well. Although Latino groups advocated for these programs as a way to preserve Latino culture, many Latino parents worried that these programs would delay their children's mastery of English.[217] Many Anglos also opposed these programs for the same reason that Latino groups favored them. For all of these reasons, California citizens voted to abolish bilingual programs in 1998. Some states have followed California's lead, while other states have maintained bilingual programs.

Discrimination against Farmworkers

Latino farmworkers have encountered particular problems. Agribusinesses have long avoided regulations imposed on other businesses, and for decades, the minimum wage law didn't apply to farm workers. Even today, the laws providing overtime pay and the right to organize don't apply. In many states, laws establishing workers' compensation and unemployment benefits programs don't apply either. Farmworkers' lack of governmental protection, coupled with their economic desperation, makes them vulnerable to unscrupulous employers. The Department of Justice has investigated more than one hundred cases of involuntary servitude—slavery—and has prosecuted a half dozen from south Florida in recent years.[218]

Combating Discrimination against Hispanics

In the 1960s, Hispanic advocacy groups tried to imitate African American groups by using protests and other forms of direct action. The Chicano movement attempted to forge a powerful bloc from the diverse population of Hispanics. César Chávez successfully led a coalition of labor, civil rights, and religious groups to obtain better working conditions for migrant farm workers in California, but few other visible national leaders or organizations emerged.

Latinos remain more diverse and less cohesive than blacks. Most don't even consider themselves part of a common group.[219] They identify strongly with their national origin and have little contact with Latinos of other national origins. And they lack a shared, defining experience in their background, such as slavery for blacks, to unite them.

Where Latinos are highly concentrated, they are increasingly powerful at the local and state levels of government. Yet Latino politicians haven't shaped a common agenda, perhaps because Latino people don't share a common agenda.[220]

They are potentially powerful at the national level as well. When Congress considered harsh measures toward illegal immigrants in 2006, many Latinos were concerned because often their families include both legal and illegal residents—children who were born here living with parents who are illegal, or nuclear families who are legal residents living with grandparents or aunts and uncles who are illegal. They were also angered by politicians' comments that immigrants are taking jobs from citizens and not contributing anything to society. As a result, hundreds of thousands rallied against the measure. In their passion, some observers saw the stirrings of political activism, especially among young Latinos.

Yet many Latinos aren't citizens, and many of those who are citizens don't register and vote. Although the Latino population is slightly larger than the African American population, far fewer Latinos are registered to vote. Nonetheless, with their huge numbers, Latinos are a coveted bloc of voters, and in some states political candidates pay attention to them.

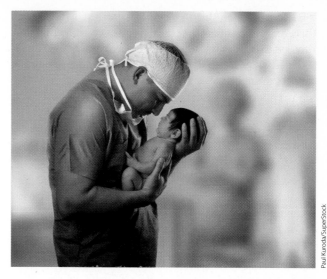

Latinos are gradually improving their status as more go to college and graduate school and become professionals, such as this doctor.

Meanwhile, Latino individuals are moving up society's ladder. More attend college and become managers and professionals. At least those who speak educated English appear to be following the pattern of earlier generations of immigrants from southern and eastern Europe—arriving poor, facing discrimination, but eventually working their way up. Along the way, they are also assimilating through high rates of marriage to non-Latinos.

Discrimination against American Indians

More than 2 million American Indians live in the United States. Most live in the West, and half live on reservations. Although some native Americans are Eskimos and Aleuts from Alaska, most are Indians, representing more than 550 tribes with different histories, customs, and languages. Proud of their tribal heritage, they prefer to be known by their tribal name, such as Cheyenne or Sioux, than by the collective terms *Indians* or *Native Americans*.[221] (Of the collective terms, they prefer to be called *Indians*, so our text will follow their preference.) American Indians have endured treatment quite different from what African Americans or Hispanics have experienced.

Government Policy toward American Indians

Government policy toward Indians has ranged from forced separation at one extreme to forced assimilation at the other.

Separation   The Constitution treats Indian tribes as separate entities. The commerce clause grants Congress authority to "regulate commerce with foreign nations, and among the several states, and with the Indian tribes." In early cases, Chief Justice John Marshall described the tribes as "dependent domestic nations."[222] They were within U.S. borders but outside its political process.

Reflecting this interpretation of the Constitution and this characterization of the tribes, early government policy promoted separation between Indians and non-Indians. Treaties established boundaries between Indians and non-Indians to minimize conflict, and white hunters or settlers who ventured across the boundaries could be punished by the Indians.

People believed that the North American continent was so vast that most of its interior would remain wilderness and would be populated by Indians who would have ample room to live and hunt. But as the country grew, it became increasingly difficult to contain the settlers within the boundaries. Mounting pressure to push the Indians farther west led to the Indian Removal Act of 1830, which mandated removal of tribes east of the Mississippi River and relocation on reservations west of the river. At the time, people considered the Great Plains as a great desert, unfit for habitation by whites but suitable for Indians.

Assimilation   As more settlers moved west, the vision of a separate Indian country far beyond white civilization faded. In the 1880s, the government switched its policy to assimilation. Prompted by Christian churches, government officials sought to "civilize" the Indians—to integrate them into American society, whether they wanted to be integrated or not. In place of their traditional means of subsistence, rendered useless once the tribes were removed from their historical homelands, the government subdivided reservation land into small tracts and allotted these tracts to tribe members in the hope that they would turn to farming as white and black settlers had. Bureau of Indian Affairs (BIA) agents, who supervised the reservations, tried to root out Indian ways and replace them with white dress and hairstyles, the English language, and the Christian religion. To instill these new practices, government boarding schools separated Indian children from their families.

As long as their tribes were considered separate nations, American Indians were not considered citizens.[223] In 1890, after government policy had switched to assimilation, Congress permitted Indians who remained on reservations to become citizens. In a formal ceremony marking his new citizenship, the Indian shot his last arrow and then took hold of the handles of a plow to demonstrate his assimilation.[224] After World War I, Congress granted citizenship to those who served in the military during the war, and finally, in 1924, Congress extended it to all who were born in the United States.

Citizenship enabled Indians to vote and hold office, although some states effectively barred them from the polls for decades. Arizona denied them the right to vote until 1948, Utah until 1956.[225]

Tribal restoration   By the 1930s, the government recognized the consequences of coerced assimilation. Most Indians, though able to speak English, were poorly educated. And with their traditional means of earning a living gone, most were poverty-stricken. The policy had led to the destruction of native culture without much assimilation into white society. Consequently, in 1934 Congress implemented a new policy of tribal restoration that recognized Indians as distinct persons and tribes as autonomous entities that were encouraged to govern themselves once again. Traditional cultural and religious practices were accepted, and Indian children, no longer forced to attend boarding schools, were taught some Indian languages.

Reflecting the policy of tribal restoration and the efforts of other minorities in the 1960s and 1970s, Indian interest groups became active. Indian law firms filed lawsuits, seeking to protect not only tribal independence and traditional ways but also land, mineral, and water resources.

The diversity and the dispersion of the tribes—they are divided by culture and by geography, often located in the remotest and poorest parts of the country—make it difficult for them to present a united front. Nevertheless, they have been able to wrest some autonomy from the government. In particular, they have gained more authority over the educational and social programs administered by the BIA for the tribes.[226]

In recent years, Indians have fought for the return of some tribal land and for an accounting of the money owed them for the use of their individual land held in trust by the government. In the early nineteenth century, the government took tribal land and put it in trust for the Indians. But then the government divided the land, classified large tracts as "surplus" land, and offered the tracts to white settlers. In return, it paid individual Indians a pittance. In this way, the Indians lost two-thirds of their territory. The government held the remaining land in trust for the Indians, leasing it to ranchers, loggers, and miners. Although the government collected the rents and royalties for the Indians, the BIA didn't bother to keep accurate records or even to preserve its records. A class-action lawsuit, dubbed "the Indian Enron

"I love the way you make those yams. You'll have to give me the recipe before your culture is obliterated from the face of the earth."

© The New Yorker Collection 1998. P. C. Vey from cartoonbank.com. All rights reserved.

Dilos Lonewolf became Tom Torlino during his transformation at a boarding school in Carlisle, Pennsylvania. Indians were shorn of their hair and clothes and trained to adopt white ways.

case," sought a reckoning of the accounts and a payment to the Indians who were owed money.[227] Ultimately, the Indians received a portion of the money they had lost.

After a Supreme Court ruling and a congressional law in the 1980s underscored tribal sovereignty on tribal land, tribes could establish gambling casinos on reservations, even if their state didn't allow any casinos.[228] Almost three hundred tribes have done so, although less than a dozen have found a bonanza—mostly small tribes in populous states where the casinos attract numerous customers.[229] And many of the casinos are bankrolled by unknown investors who keep most of the profits. A Malaysian businessman owns one, a South African developer another. From these casinos, little money trickles down to tribal members.[230]

Nevertheless, with their casino businesses, some tribes have begun to buy into the political process, as other groups have done. Threatened by gambling interests in Las Vegas and Atlantic City, which fear that tribal casinos will lure away their customers, the tribes have formed a lobby, the National Indian Gaming Association, and made political contributions. These contributions reportedly total more than the contributions by individual corporations such as AT&T, Boeing, or General Motors.[231]

DEMOCRACY?

Do you think that any one of the government's policies toward Indians—separation, assimilation, or tribal restoration—is more democratic than the others?

Now more Indians share the views of one activist who says, "You have a federal government, state governments, and tribal governments—three sovereigns in one country. This is the civil rights movement of Native Americans."[232] Indeed, enjoying renewed pride, tribes have established programs to preserve their language and culture.[233]

Nevertheless, Indians remain at the bottom of America's racial and ethnic ladder. They are the least educated and most unemployed group, and also the poorest and sickest group, of any people in the country, with the highest alcoholism rates and lowest life expectancy.

SEX DISCRIMINATION

Most sex discrimination has been directed at women, although some has been directed at men.

Discrimination against Women

The traditional view of gender roles fostered discrimination against women, but the vigorous efforts by the women's movement and by Congress and the Supreme Court have led to greater equality for women.

The Traditional View

People used to believe that natural differences between the sexes required men and women to occupy separate spheres of life. Men would dominate the public domain of work and government, and women would dominate the private domain of the home. Both domains were important, and men were considered superior in one and women were considered superior in the other.

Thomas Jefferson, the most egalitarian of the male Founders, reflected this view when he said, "Were our state a pure democracy there would still be excluded from our deliberations women, who, to prevent deprivation of morals and ambiguity of issues, should not mix promiscuously in gatherings of men."[234] That is, women are more moral than men, so they would be corrupted by politics, and they are more irrational, so they would confuse the issues. For both reasons, they should not participate in politics.

So, women were denied the right to vote, and married women were denied other rights—to manage property they acquired before marriage, to manage income they received from jobs, to enter into contracts, and to sue. Some states eventually granted these rights, but when disputes arose within families, male judges hesitated to tell other men how to treat their wives.

Even women's citizenship was tied to their husbands' citizenship. If a foreign woman married an American man, she automatically became a United States citizen. But if an American woman married a foreign man, she automatically lost her United States citizenship. (Women's citizenship wouldn't become independent of their husbands' citizenship until 1922.)

Women were barred from schools and jobs. Before the Civil War, they weren't admitted to public high schools. Because they were being prepared for motherhood, education was considered unnecessary, even dangerous. According to the *Encyclopaedia Britannica* in 1800, women had smaller brains than men.[235] Education would fatigue them and possibly ruin their reproductive organs. For the same reasons, women weren't encouraged to hold jobs. Those who did were shunted into jobs that were seen as extensions of the domestic domain, such as producing textiles, clothes, and shoes in sex-segregated factories.[236]

This traditional conception of gender roles created problems for women who didn't fit the standard mold. After the Civil War, Myra Bradwell ran a private school, founded a weekly newspaper, and worked for various civic organizations. She was active in the women's suffrage movement and instrumental in persuading the Illinois legislature to expand women's legal rights. After learning the law, however, she was denied a license to practice it solely because she was a woman. The Supreme Court upheld the Illinois policy in 1873.[237] Justice Joseph Bradley declared:

> Law, as well as nature itself, has always recognized a wide difference in the respective spheres and destinies of man and woman. Man is, or should be, the woman's protector and defender. The natural and proper timidity and delicacy which belongs to the female sex evidently unfits it for many of the occupations of civil life. . . . The constitution of the family organization . . . indicates the domestic sphere as that which properly belongs to the domain and functions of womanhood. The harmony . . . of interests and views which belong, or should belong, to the family institution is repugnant to the idea of a woman adopting a distinct and independent career from that of her husband. . . . The paramount destiny and mission of woman are to fulfill the noble and benign offices of wife and mother. This is the law of the Creator. And the rules of civil society must be adapted to the general constitution of things, and cannot be based upon exceptional cases.

Sometimes this separate-but-equal view gave way to even more clear-cut discrimination. In the 1860s and 1870s,

the doctors who practiced scientific medicine formed the American Medical Association (AMA) to drive out other people who offered medical services. These people included not only hucksters and quacks but also women who served as midwives or abortionists. Although abortions had been widely available, the AMA, drawing on popular fears about the women's suffrage movement, convinced state legislatures that abortions were "a threat to social order and to male authority." The woman who seeks an abortion, the AMA explained, is "unmindful of the course marked out for her by Providence, she overlooks the duties imposed on her by the marriage contract. She yields to the pleasure—but shrinks from the pains and responsibilities of maternity. . . . Let not the husband of such a wife flatter himself that he possesses her affection."[238]

Occasionally the discrimination even allowed physical brutality. The Mississippi Supreme Court acknowledged a husband's right to beat his wife.[239] Using the "rule of thumb," the court held that a husband could not beat his wife with a weapon thicker than his thumb.

The Women's Movement

Early feminists were determined to remedy these inequities. Many had gained political and organizational experience in the abolitionist movement. Because that movement was associated with religious groups, it wasn't considered "unladylike" for women to campaign for abolition of slavery. At the same time, the women weren't allowed to participate fully in antislavery societies. When Abigail Kelley was nominated as an official of the American Anti-Slavery Society, almost three hundred men left the meeting to form another antislavery society in which women couldn't vote or hold office. Later, when Kelley rose to speak at a meeting of the Connecticut Anti-Slavery Society, the chair insisted,

> No woman will speak or vote where I am moderator. It is enough for women to rule at home. It is woman's business to take care of the children in the nursery; she has no business to come into this meeting and by speaking and voting lord it over men. Where women's enticing eloquence is heard, men are incapable of right and efficient action. She beguiles and blinds men by her smiles and her bland winning voice. . . . I will not submit to PETTICOAT GOVERNMENT.[240]

Angry at such treatment, the women held a meeting to discuss the "social, civil, and religious rights of women." In 1848, this Women's Rights Convention adopted a declaration of rights based on the Declaration of Independence, proclaiming, "We hold these truths to be self-evident: that all men and women are created equal." The convention also passed a resolution calling for women's suffrage.

After the Civil War, the women who had worked in the abolitionist movement expected that women as well as blacks would get legal rights and voting rights. When the Fourteenth and Fifteenth Amendments did not include women, they felt betrayed, and disassociated themselves from the black movement, and formed their own organizations to campaign for women's suffrage. This movement, led by Susan B. Anthony and Elizabeth Cady Stanton, succeeded in 1920, when the Nineteenth Amendment gave women the right to vote.[241]

Then dissension developed within the movement. Many groups, feeling that the Nineteenth Amendment was just the first step in the struggle for equal rights, proposed the Equal Rights Amendment to remedy remaining inequities. Other groups felt that the battle had been won. They opposed the Equal Rights Amendment, arguing that it would overturn labor laws recently enacted to protect women. Because of this dissension and the conservatism in the country at the time, the movement became dormant.[242]

The movement reemerged in the 1960s when the civil rights movement led many women to recognize their own inferior status. Female writers sensitized other women. The most famous statement was Betty Friedan's book *The Feminine Mystique*, which grew out of a questionnaire she circulated at her fifteenth college reunion. The book addressed the malaise that afflicted college-educated women who were socialized into the feminine role but found it unsatisfying.[243] Friedan observed that women reared the children, shopped for groceries, cooked the meals, and cleaned the house, while secretly wondering, "Is this all?" Friedan's

manifesto became the best-selling nonfiction paperback in 1964. Its popularity spurred Friedan and other upper-middle-class, professional women to form the **National Organization for Women (NOW)** in 1966. They resolved "to bring women into full participation in the mainstream of American society *now.*"

Other women, also middle class but veterans of the civil rights and antiwar movements, had developed a taste for political action and formed other organizations. Whereas NOW fought primarily for women's political and economic rights, the other organizations fought broadly for women's liberation in all spheres of life. Together these organizations pushed the issue of women's rights back onto the public agenda.

Nevertheless, they weren't taken seriously for years. In 1970, *Time* magazine reported, "No one knows how many shirts lay wrinkling in laundry baskets last week as thousands of women across the country turned out for the first big demonstration of the women's liberation movement. They took over [New York City's Fifth Avenue], providing not only protest but some of the best sidewalk ogling in years."[244]

Although the movement tried to broaden its base beyond upper-middle-class and college-educated women, it was unable to do so. As a result, it fostered an image of privileged women who looked on other women with disdain.

During World War II, women were urged into the labor force to replace men called to war. "Rosie the Riveter" became the symbol of the women who were contributing to the war effort. Following the war, they were told that it was patriotic to give their jobs to returning veterans. The 1955 magazine cover depicts the stereotypical women's role in the postwar era before the modern women's movement. (But more women held jobs in the 1950s than is usually recognized.)

Printed by permission of the Norman Rockwell Family Trust. © 1943 The Norman Rockwell Trust.

© 1955 Saturday Evening Post: Licensed by The Curtis Publishing Company, Indianapolis, IN. All rights reserved.

Housewife became a derisive term, and traditional women viewed the movement as antimotherhood and antifamily and, when it became more radical in the 1970s, prolesbian. This image gave "women's liberation" a bad name, even though most women agreed with most goals of the movement.[245] This image persists. More Americans believe that extraterrestrials have visited the earth than think that the word *feminist* is a compliment.[246] (It is unclear, however, whether this says more about Americans' attitudes toward gender equality or their penchant for paranoid conspiracy theories.)

The Movement in Congress and the Courts

Congress initially didn't take the women's movement seriously either. When the House debated a bill forbidding racial discrimination in employment, eighty-one-year-old Rep. Howard Smith (D-Va.) proposed an amendment to add sex discrimination to the bill. A staunch foe of equal rights for blacks, Smith thought his proposal so ludicrous and so radical that it would help defeat the entire bill. Indeed, during their debate on the amendment, members of Congress laughed so hard that they could barely hear each other speak.[247] But the joke was on these members, because the amendment, and then the bill—the Civil Rights Act of 1964—passed. (For another reflection of officials' attitudes toward gender roles, see the box "The Mercury 13.")

Equal Rights Amendment   Congress also passed the **Equal Rights Amendment (ERA)**. The amendment simply declared, "Equality of rights under the law shall not be denied or abridged by the United States or by any state on account of sex." Introduced in 1923 and every year thereafter, the amendment was finally passed in 1972.

It looked like the amendment would zip through the states. Both parties endorsed it, and a majority of the public supported it. But the amendment stalled. Observers speculated that it could make women subject to the draft for the military (if there was another draft). Opponents charged, falsely, that it would result in unisex restrooms and homosexual rights.

The main problem, however, was the amendment's symbolism. For many women, the ERA represented an attack on the traditional values of motherhood, the family, and the home. Early feminists had emphasized equal employment so much that they gave some women the impression that they opposed these values. Traditional women sensed implicit criticism for becoming housewives.[248] To underscore the symbolism, the women in anti-ERA groups baked bread for state legislators scheduled to vote on ratification.

Consequently, numerous women, even some who favored equality, opposed the amendment. Although many young women supported it, fewer middle-age and elderly women did; and although many working women supported it, fewer housewives did. Women's organizations hadn't created an effective grassroots campaign to sway traditional women. Their disaffection allowed male legislators to vote according to their male attitudes. They didn't need to worry about a backlash from their female constituents.[249]

In 1980, the Republican Party became the first party not to endorse the ERA since 1940, and President Reagan became the first president not to support the amendment since Truman. When the deadline for ratification set by Congress expired in 1982, the ERA fell three states short of the three-fourths necessary. As with the Nineteenth Amendment, it was opposed primarily by the southern states.

Supreme Court rulings   Historically courts upheld laws that limited women's participation in the public domain and occasionally even laws that diminished their standing in the private domain. As late as 1970, the Ohio Supreme Court ruled that a wife is a husband's servant with "no legally recognized feelings or rights."[250]

The Burger Court finally reversed this pattern. In 1971, for the first time, the Court struck down a law that discriminated against women,[251] heralding a long series of rulings that invalidated a variety of such laws. 🔔 The Court used the congressional statutes and broadened the Fourteenth Amendment's equal protection clause to apply to women as well as to racial minorities.

The change was especially apparent in a pair of cases involving the selection of jurors. For the pool of potential jurors, some states drew the names of men, but not women, from voter registration or other lists. These states allowed women to serve only if they voluntarily signed up at the courthouse. Consequently, few women served. In 1961, the Court let Florida use these procedures because the "woman is still regarded as the center of home and family life."[252] In 1975, however, the Court forbade Louisiana from using similar procedures,[253] thus overturning a precedent only fourteen years old.

The Court's rulings rejected the traditional stereotypes that men are the breadwinners and women the child rearers in society. For example, the Court invalidated Utah's law that required divorced fathers to support their daughters until eighteen but their sons until twenty-one.[254] The state assumed that the daughters would get married and be supported by their husbands, whereas the sons would need to get educated for their careers. But the Court noted, "No longer is the female destined solely for the home."

Laws on discrimination in employment   The Civil Rights Act of 1964 forbids discrimination on the basis of both sex and race in hiring, promoting, and firing. It prohibits discrimination on the basis of sex, except where sex is a "bona fide occupational qualification" for the job. Sex is considered a legitimate qualification for very few jobs, such as restroom attendants, lingerie salesclerks, models, and actors. It is not considered a legitimate qualification for jobs men traditionally held, such as those that entail heavy physical labor, unpleasant working conditions, late-night hours, overtime, or travel. Employers can no longer reserve these jobs for male applicants.

behind the scenes

The Mercury 13

The Soviet Union shocked a complacent America in 1957 when it launched the first satellite into space. In the midst of the Cold War, Americans feared that this achievement would signal the superiority of the communist system over our capitalist system to other nations around the world. A year later, the National Aeronautics and Space Administration (NASA) was established to spearhead the U.S. program, and a year after that the first astronauts—the Mercury 7—were selected. In 1960, John F. Kennedy was elected president. Vowing to catch up with the Russians, he challenged NASA to put "a man on the moon" within the decade.

The promise of space exploration lured not only men who had been test pilots in the military, but also some women fliers. Although women weren't allowed to serve as pilots in the military and therefore weren't hired as pilots by passenger airlines, they were employed as pilots by charter airlines and flight schools. Some hauled cargo or ferried planes to South America, while others competed in the women's air-racing circuit.

Yet in the 1950s and early 1960s, the feminine ideal still prevailed—people "expected women pilots to look like fashion models when they stepped out of a cockpit, even if they had been up all night with their arms covered in grease"—so the pilots wore a dress under their flight suit and put on high heels and touched up their lipstick before emerging from the plane.

Two doctors who tested the men who applied to be astronauts wondered if any women might also qualify.

Aspiring astronaut Jerrie Cobb was an experienced pilot.

The doctors knew that NASA was encountering problems developing rockets with sufficient payload, and they realized that women astronauts, weighing less and consuming less oxygen and food, might alleviate these problems. But they didn't know whether women would be physically or psychologically capable. The assumption at the time, of course, was that women wouldn't be. Plus, officials said, when women menstruate, their brain changes, and they can't think clearly enough. NASA, reflecting the conventional wisdom, was leery of expanding its program to encompass women astronauts.

The doctors, however, weren't convinced. Without official approval, they began recruiting women pilots who were interested in space flight. Eventually, they winnowed their list from over a hundred to thirteen. All had logged many hours in the air, and one held world records for long-distance and high-altitude flights. In 1960 and 1961, the women were put through the same rigorous tests as the men had been subjected to.[1] The doctors found that the women performed as well as the men in all respects—physical capability, endurance, and resilience.

As word of potential women astronauts spread, the air force and the navy recoiled from the prospect of "girl astronauts"—or "astronettes," as they were dubbed by reporters. If women could become astronauts, they might also become test pilots and ultimately destroy the masculine culture in the air force and navy.

After two years of unofficial testing, Vice President Lyndon Johnson, who was the president's liaison with NASA and an enthusiast of space travel, met with two of the aspiring women astronauts. If women were allowed, he said, blacks, Mexicans, Chinese, and other minorities would also want a chance. Despite his sympathy for civil rights, after the meeting Johnson sent a message to his aides: "Lets [sic] Stop This Now!" Whether from NASA, the military, or the White House, officials weren't ready to foster this change in American culture.[2]

Barring women from the program became a Cold War blunder, as the Soviet Union put the first woman into space in 1963. The United States would not put a woman into space until Sally Ride two decades later.

[1] Ultimately, the doctors completed the first two batteries of tests; they weren't allowed to complete the final battery required of men.
[2] President Kennedy showed no interest in expanding the program either. There was some sentiment in Congress to do so, but that reflected a minority view.
SOURCE: Martha Ackmann, *The Mercury 13: The Untold Story of Thirteen American Women and the Dream of Space Flight* (New York: Random House, 2003). Quotations from pages 4 and 148.

However, discrimination in hiring, promoting, and firing persists, even forty years after the act. A major study examined the records in lawsuits alleging sex discrimination in one recent year. A surprising and staggering number, they required employers to pay $263 million to the female plaintiffs in that year alone.[255] Testimony by midlevel managers revealed that higher executives instructed them, "We do not employ women," or, "The day I hire a woman will be a cold day in hell." In dozens of cases, the managers were told to throw women's applications into the trash.[256]

The same result occurs when male managers decide according to their "gut instinct" that a man is more qualified. Their "gut instinct" may be biased without them realizing it.

The discrimination occurs up and down the ladder. Huge lawsuits have been brought against both Merrill Lynch and Wal-Mart in recent years. But the discrimination appears most prevalent for traditional male, blue-collar jobs. Some men don't want to work with women; they don't want to break up the "good-ol'-boys' clubhouse."[257] Mysteriously, a woman's application disappears; or the letter telling her when to come for the interview gets lost in the mail; or her examination is invalidated for some reason.[258]

Some companies that fill their positions through hiring agencies instruct the agencies to send them only men for traditional male jobs and only women for traditional female jobs.[259]

Discrimination in firing, especially for pregnancy, continues as well, despite the **Pregnancy Discrimination Act of 1978**, which forbids firing or demoting women when they become pregnant or after they return from maternity leave.[260] Some women have been fired as soon as they mentioned being pregnant; others as soon as their body showed it. Many have seen their performance evaluations drop as their bellies swelled, even though their actual performance did not decline.[261] Others have been demoted after giving birth. "When I returned from maternity leave," a lawyer recounted, "I was given the work of a paralegal and I wanted to say, 'Look, I had a baby, not a lobotomy.'"[262]

The cases examined in these studies probably represent the tip of the iceberg. To sue an employer for sex discrimination is to embark on an expensive and exhausting legal battle that will take several years of one's life. It requires a strong-willed woman who has experienced discriminatory behavior egregious enough for her to persuade a lawyer to take the case and then a company to settle or a judge or jury to find for her. Although there are some frivolous lawsuits in our legal system, there is more discriminatory behavior in our workplaces than is ever brought to court.

The **Equal Pay Act** of 1963 requires that women and men receive equal pay for equal work, with exceptions for merit, productivity, and seniority. As a result of the act, the gap between what women and men earn has slowly shrunk. In the 1960s, working women earned just 59 cents for every dollar men earned.[263] Today, working women earn 80 cents for every dollar men earn—an improvement but far short of real equality.[264]

However, a contrary trend is emerging for young women and young men. Women from 22-30 who are unmarried and childless are making 8 percent more than their male counterparts, because young women are more likely than young men to be college educated.[265] (This doesn't mean that young women are making more than young men who are college educated, and it doesn't mean that young women are making more than young men who have the same job. Young women who are college educated have better paying jobs than young men who aren't.) It's not clear whether this trend will continue after these women get married and have children.

One reason for the persistent gap among women and men overall is old-fashioned sex discrimination. Despite the Equal Pay Act, some male employers with ingrained attitudes are reluctant to pay women equally. The act allows exceptions for merit and productivity, which usually are determined subjectively. The employer may insist, whether sincerely or not, that the man is more meritorious or productive. Legions of women believe that they need to perform better to be paid equally.[266]

Although the Roberts Court made it more difficult for women to bring lawsuits for pay discrimination, Congress overrode the Court when it passed the Lilly Ledbetter Fair Pay Act (as explained in Chapter 13's "Talking Points").

Another reason for the gap between what women and men earn is that women and men have different jobs, whether due to discrimination or to choice. Despite the Civil Rights Act of 1964 and the societal changes—the blurring of lines between genders—many women have traditional women's jobs and most men have traditional men's jobs. And traditional women's jobs pay less.

Historically, women were shunted into a small number of jobs. Even by 2000, two-thirds of working women were crowded into just twenty-one of the occupations identified by the Department of Labor.[267] These "pink-collar" jobs include secretaries (98 percent are women), household workers (97 percent), child care workers (97 percent), nurses (93 percent), bank tellers (90 percent), librarians (83 percent), elementary school teachers (83 percent), and health technicians (81 percent). In contrast, few women are carpenters (1 percent), firefighters (2 percent), mechanics (4 percent), or truck drivers (5 percent).[268]

Although the Equal Pay Act mandates equal pay for equal work, it does not require equal pay for comparable work—usually called **comparable worth**. According to a study in Washington State, maintenance carpenters and secretaries performed comparable jobs in terms of the education, the skill, or other qualifications required, but the carpenters, mostly men, made about $600 a month more than the secretaries, mostly women. In general, "men's jobs" paid about 20 percent more than comparable "women's jobs." Yet courts rejected demands by public employees that

© The New Yorker Collection 2004, Matthew Diffee from cartoonbank.com. All rights reserved.

"I feel like a man trapped in a woman's salary."

thirty-five receive nearly equal pay. But when women get married and have children, their pay lags. Some interrupt their career until their children start school. Others continue to work but shift from the fast track to the so-called "mommy track," working fewer hours due to child care and household responsibilities.[271] Still others fall victim to stereotypes—that mothers aren't serious about their careers, that mothers aren't dependable because they won't show up when their children get sick, or that mothers will quit sooner or later anyway.[272] Through such stereotypes, managers move mothers to the "mommy track" in their own minds, whether the mothers want that track or not.

For whichever reasons, the difference in pay makes a difference in life. Early in her career, it means that a woman might not be able to pay off her credit card debts or college loans as quickly. She might not be able to have as nice a car or an apartment as her male counterpart. Later in her career, she might not be able to have as nice a house or as exotic vacations. Then, if her husband divorces her or dies before her, she might not be able to have as comfortable a retirement. The accumulated shortfall in her retirement savings means that she might struggle in her old age.[273]

Despite the barriers to equal pay, almost 40 percent of women in two-income households have become the primary breadwinner.[274]

Mothers with young children confront more obstacles than unequal pay. Male employers do little to accommodate the demands of child rearing. Most companies don't provide paid maternity leave, paid sick days, on-site day care, or flexible schedules. The United States lags far behind most other countries, including all wealthy countries, in creating family-friendly policies. Of 173 countries, all but the United States, Papua New Guinea, and three African countries guarantee paid maternity leaves. Sixty-five countries even provide paid paternity leaves. (In the United States, only California provides partly paid family leaves.) One hundred forty-five countries provide paid sick days.[275]

Congress passed and President Clinton signed a bill requiring employers to grant unpaid maternity and paternity leaves. Companies must allow unpaid leaves for up to three months for workers with newborn or recently adopted children or with seriously ill family members. The act applies to companies that have fifty employees and to workers who work twenty-five hours a week for a year.[276] This covers about half of American workers.

But relatively few workers take advantage of these leaves. Most workers can't afford to take unpaid leaves. Moreover, many managers don't support such measures, and some coworkers resent the additional burdens, so employees are reluctant to ask for leaves. When companies are laying off workers to cut costs, "If you look like you are not career oriented, you can lose your job."[277]

Because of the influx of women workers, the workforce has changed enormously since 1970 (then two-thirds of married couples had a stay-at-home spouse—normally

government employers boost the pay for "women's jobs." Nonetheless, some state and city governments implemented comparable worth for their employees after prodding by labor unions and women's groups. Private companies, however, did not, because doing so would require them to pay many female employees more.

Although the push for comparable worth has stalled, in recent years grassroots campaigns organized by labor unions and church groups have called for laws mandating a **living wage**.[269] These laws would require employers to pay more than the federal minimum wage, to pay whatever is necessary so a full-time worker doesn't fall below the poverty line.

Some proposals would apply only to government employees and to the employees of the companies that do business with the government. Other proposals would apply to all employees within a city or state. Still other proposals would apply just to the employees of "big-box stores," such as Wal-Mart and Home Depot, because these companies drive down the wages for workers throughout society. Most proposals would exempt small businesses with fewer than twenty-five workers.

So far, some cities (Baltimore, San Francisco, and Santa Fe) and one state (Nevada) have adopted such laws.[270] If many cities and states did, living wage laws would have a significant impact on women and minorities, because women and minorities hold a disproportionate number of the lowest-paying jobs. In addition, living wage laws would have a ripple effect, prompting employers to raise the wages of the workers just above the lowest level.

Another reason for the gap between what women and men earn is that women have children. The gap is mostly between married women and married men. Single women and single men between the ages of twenty-one and a wife; today just 40 percent do[278]). But the workplace is "stuck in a time warp, modeled for [*Leave It to Beaver's*] Ward and June Cleaver when the reality feels more like . . . 'Survivor.'"[279]

Workers in the United States put in longer hours than those in other industrialized countries, and these hours, for both sexes, have increased since the 1970s.[280] The result is that mothers and fathers with young children often face unreasonable demands on their time. Neither spouse has the time to do what the housewife once did. (It's not really a joke when someone quips, "Both spouses need a house-wife.") In many families, the woman tries to do these tasks at night and on weekends. Where both spouses work full-time, the woman does twice as much of the housework and four times as much of the child care as the man,[281] but both spouses frequently feel stretched thin and stressed out. Two-thirds of parents say they don't have enough time with their children, and nearly two-thirds of married workers say they don't have enough time with their spouse.[282]

So even though women have gained greater acceptance in the workplace, they—and their spouses—have not over-come the expectations that developed long before they were ever allowed in the workplace. And these expectations are exacerbated by Americans' glorification of work and, with new communications technology, a perverse celebration of a "24/7 workweek." "We glorify an all-work, all-the-time lifestyle," notes one commentator, "and then weep croco-dile tears for kids whose parents are never home."[283]

In addition to their difficulties in getting hired, pro-moted, and paid equally, some women also face sexual harassment. The Supreme Court has ruled that sexual harassment is a form of job discrimination prohibited by the Civil Rights Act of 1964,[284] and Congress has passed a law allowing victims to sue employers and collect money for distress, illness, or loss of their job due to such behavior. Although sexual harassment can be directed toward either sex,[285] it is usually directed toward women.

Courts recognize two types of **sexual harassment**. The most obvious is quid pro quo, in which a supervisor makes unwanted sexual advances and either promises good con-sequences (for example, a promotion or pay raise) if the employee goes along or threatens bad consequences (for example, an undesirable reassignment) if the employee refuses. The less obvious type is creating a hostile environ-ment that interferes with the employee's ability to perform the job. To prove that a hostile environment existed, the employee must demonstrate that the offensive conduct was severe or persistent.

As Arkansas' governor, Bill Clinton allegedly asked Paula Jones, a state employee, for oral sex. Her lawsuit was dismissed because his sexual advance was deemed neither severe enough nor, as a single incident, persistent enough to constitute a hostile environment. If it happened, the judge said, it was "boorish and offensive" but not technically harassment.

Despite some men's fears, occasional innocuous com-ments, jokes, or requests for dates would not be classified as harassment. Justice Antonin Scalia emphasized that the law did not create "a general civility code."[286]

Women in traditional female jobs, such as secretaries, are more likely to be subjected to quid pro quo harassment from supervisors, whereas women in traditional male jobs, especially blue-collar jobs, are more likely to be subjected to hostile-environment harassment from coworkers. Exam-ples abound of male laborers posting sexual pictures or writing sexual messages in women's lockers or restrooms or leaving plastic penises in their toolboxes; taunting the women with sexual questions and comments or addressing them as "Bitch," "Slut," or "Whore" instead of by name; and grabbing their breasts, buttocks, or genitals. Worse for new workers, however, is having supervisors or coworkers who refuse to train or help them, or who sabotage their work or equipment, making them appear slow and shoddy.

The dynamics of sexual harassment don't revolve around sex as much as they reflect abuse of power. (In fact, the law doesn't forbid sex between workers, even if one supervises another.) A supervisor or coworker who prac-tices harassment makes a woman feel vulnerable and thus exercises psychological dominance over her. He wants her to leave the workplace or, at least, to suffer inferior status if she remains there.

Laws on discrimination in education The Education Amendments of 1972 (to the Civil Rights Act of 1964) forbade discrimination on the basis of sex in schools and colleges that receive federal aid. The amendments were prompted by discrimination against women by undergradu-ate and graduate colleges, especially in admissions and financial aid.

The language of the amendments, often referred to as **Title IX**, is very broad, and the Department of Education, which administers the provisions, has established extensive rules that cover more aspects of education than Congress expected.[287] The department has used Title IX to prod insti-tutions into employing and promoting more female teach-ers and administrators, opening vocational training classes to girls and home economics classes to boys, and offering equal athletic programs to girls and women. If institutions don't comply, the government can cut off their federal aid. (See Table 2.)

Title IX has affected athletic programs especially. Before, schools provided far fewer sports for females than for males, and they spent far fewer dollars—for scholar-ships, coaches, and facilities—on women's sports. Now the department interprets Title IX to require a school either to have approximately the same percentage of female athletes as female undergraduates, to continually expand opportuni-ties for female athletes, or to fully accommodate the inter-ests and abilities of female students. (The latter would occur if female students at a school were satisfied that there were sufficient opportunities for them, given their interests and

| Table 2 | Women's Gains in Higher Education |

Percentage of Degrees Earned by Women		
	1971–72	2006–07
Bachelor's	43%	57%
Master's	41	61
Doctoral	16	50
Law	8	48
Medicine	9	49

Women's gains in education have been dramatic since the modern women's movement arose.
SOURCE: *National Center for Education Statistics, reported in Nancy Gibbs, "What Women Want Now," Time, October 26, 2009, 27.*

© Bettmann/Corbis

Men resisted the expansion of women's athletics. The Boston Marathon was traditionally for men only. When the first woman tried to participate in 1967, a marathon official assaulted her.

abilities, even if the opportunities were unequal to those for men.)

Very few colleges meet the first requirement. To comply, most are trying to meet the second requirement by expanding the number of women's sports. But they worry that they will have to fulfill the first requirement eventually, and they fear that they will have to cap the squad size of their football team, which has the most players and costs the most money, to do so. This would lessen the imbalance in the numbers of male and female athletes, and it would free more money for women's teams. Some colleges have resisted the enforcement of Title IX, partly because athletic departments are struggling to balance their budget and partly because the act threatens deeply ingrained cultural values reflected in men's athletics. Administrators and boosters fear that women's sports will take money from men's sports and thereby weaken the primacy of men's athletics.

However, Title IX has had a major impact. Colleges have increased their women's teams—more than three times as many as in the early 1970s—and their female athletes—more than ten times as many as before.[288] Women now make up 42 percent of all college athletes and receive 42 percent of the scholarship money, though their teams have lower coaches' salaries and operating expenses than men's teams, as well as a smaller proportion of women coaches than they used to.[289]

Colleges with successful football or basketball programs have increased their women's teams the most because these sports generate revenue that funds women's sports. Colleges with no football program have also increased their women's teams. Colleges with football programs that don't generate a profit (as most don't) lag behind. They pour money into football but lack revenue from television or bowl contracts to fund women's sports.[290]

To reduce the gender imbalance, many colleges have eliminated low-profile men's teams, especially wrestling, gymnastics, tennis, and track. Marquette University eliminated men's wrestling even though the team was financed mostly by private donations.[291]

Title IX has also had a major impact on high schools, which have increased their girls' teams. Before Title IX, 1 of every 27 girls played on a high school team; now 1 of every 2.5 girls does.[292]

But supporters have a broader goal in mind as well. "If girls are socialized the way boys are to take part in sports," the editor of a women's sports magazine says, and "if boys and girls grow up with the idea that girls are strong and capable, it will change the way girls and women are viewed—by themselves and by society."[293]

Overall, Congress and the courts have moved steadily toward legal equality for the sexes. Women have accomplished through congressional and judicial action much of what they would have accomplished with the ERA. It is an indication of the success of the movement that young women today take their equality for granted and focus on their personal lives rather than on the need for further progress.

However, challenges remain. Besides the noncompliance with congressional laws, as noted above, the demands on working parents are overwhelming. "The failure of the workplace to make accommodations for working parents is one of the biggest unmet demands of American voters."[294] Increasingly, the battle over "family values" is becoming a battle over workplace expectations that undermine family life.[295]

Discrimination against Men

The traditional conception of gender roles has also created problems for men who don't fit the standard mold.

When the Burger Court rejected stereotypes that led to discrimination against women, it also rejected some that led to discrimination against men. For example, it invalidated Mississippi's law barring men from a state university's nursing school.[296] It also invalidated Alabama's law allowing only women to seek alimony upon divorce.[297] Thus the Court rejected stereotypes that only women become nurses and only women are dependent on their spouses.

On the other hand, the Burger Court upheld some laws that were designed to protect women but that discriminate against men. It affirmed laws prohibiting statutory rape—intercourse with a minor, with consent—by males but not by females.[298] It also affirmed a law mandating draft registration for males but not for females.[299] The rationalization was that registration eventually could lead to the draft and the draft eventually could lead to combat, and it insisted that most women aren't capable of combat. Thus the Court accepted the stereotypes that only men initiate sex with underage partners and that only men can fight in a war.

In the absence of a draft, the most significant discrimination against men may occur in divorce cases, where the norm is to grant custody of children to mothers and require payment of support by fathers. Although courts give fathers visitation rights, they permit mothers to move miles away, making visitation difficult and sporadic. And although governments have taken steps to enforce support payments, they have done little to enforce visitation rights. This practice reflects the stereotype that fathers are capable of funding their children but not of raising them. The Supreme Court has ignored this problem.

Other discrimination against men may occur in cases of unintended pregnancy. Women may choose abortion, adoption, or raising the child. Men have no choice. The Supreme Court invalidated laws requiring a husband's consent before his wife's abortion, because the woman carries the fetus so she is most affected by the decision.[300] The Court's ruling affects unmarried couples as well. And if the woman decides to raise the child, the man must pay child support (probably for eighteen years).

AFFIRMATIVE ACTION

Assume that a black runner and a white runner compete at a track meet. But the officials force the black runner to carry heavy weights, and he falls behind. Eventually, the officials realize that this is unfair, and they take the weights off. Of course, the black runner is still behind. Would this be fair? Assume instead that the officials not only take the weights off but also allow him to catch up. Would this be fairer?

This scenario, sketched by President Johnson, captures the dilemma of civil rights policy today. Although most discrimination has been repudiated by the courts and legislatures, the effects of past discrimination persist. Now the question is whether civil rights policy should ignore race and sex or take race and sex into account to compensate for the effects of past discrimination. That is, should the policy require nondiscrimination only or **affirmative action** as well?

Affirmative action applies to employers when hiring and promoting minorities and women, colleges and universities

Although most single parents are women, an increasing number are men, such as this father of an eleven-year-old in Dallas.

when admitting minorities and women, and governments when reserving a portion of their contracts for businesses owned by minorities and women. We will examine affirmative action in employment and in education. We do not have sufficient space to discuss the pros and cons of affirmative action, but we will explain the policy, the law, and the primary consequences of affirmative action.

In Employment

The Civil Rights Act of 1964, which bars discrimination in employment, does not mention affirmative action, but it does authorize the bureaucracy to make rules to end discrimination. In 1969, the Department of Labor called for affirmative action by companies doing business with the federal government. Later, the Equal Employment Opportunity Commission called for affirmative action by governments themselves, and the Office of Education called for affirmative action by colleges as well. Presidents from Nixon through Carter supported it with executive orders, and the Supreme Court sanctioned it in a series of cases.[301]

Affirmative action requires positive steps to ensure that qualified minorities and women receive a fair share of the jobs at each level. What the positive steps and the fair share should be are the subjects of considerable controversy.

If the number of minorities or women who work in a government agency or in a private company that has government contracts is less than the number in the local labor force, the agency or company must agree to recruit more minorities or women or, in serious cases, draw up an affirmative-action plan that includes goals to hire or promote more minorities or women. If the agency or company does not reach the goals, it must show that it made an effort to do so. If the company does not satisfy the government, it can be denied future contracts (though in reality companies rarely are penalized).

Although affirmative-action plans speak of "goals," critics charge that they mandate quotas and that quotas amount to "reverse discrimination" and result in lower standards.[302] The terms do blur; if employers are pressured to meet goals, they might interpret *goals* to mean *quotas*. But only after a finding of deliberate and systematic discrimination does affirmative action entail actual quotas.[303]

The plans must allow white men, as well as minorities and women, to be hired and promoted, and the plans must be temporary (usually until the percentage of minority or female employees reaches the percentage of minority or female workers in the community).

Affirmative action applies to hiring and promoting but not to laying off workers. Because of a belief that affirmative action shouldn't impose much burden on innocent individuals, the Court has struck down the use of affirmative action—any protection for minorities and women—when employers pare their workforce for economic reasons. Instead, the Court has accepted the traditional practice, based on seniority, that the last hired can be the first fired, even if the last hired were minorities and women.[304]

In addition to these long-standing limits on affirmative action, the Rehnquist Court made it more difficult for the government to mandate affirmative action for government agencies or private companies.[305] The government must show clear evidence of particular past discrimination by a government agency or a private company (or by the entire industry in which the company is a part), rather than simply point to pervasive historical discrimination in society as the justification for affirmative action by the agency or company.

Affirmative action has helped minorities and women. White men dominate public and private institutions, and as the personnel director of a *Fortune* 500 company observed, "People tend to hire people like themselves."[306] Thus affirmative action has prodded employers to hire more minorities and women.[307] It has also prodded managers to promote more minorities and women who had been stuck in low-level positions.[308] In fact, a major consequence of affirmative action has been to pressure government agencies and private companies to hire and promote workers who should have been hired or promoted all along—that is, to pressure employers to stop discriminating. Contrary to one argument, it has not pressured employers to give "preferential treatment."

Although affirmative action is controversial among the public, it is routinely used and even championed, under the name of "diversity," by big businesses, which see it as a way to locate untapped talent in overlooked groups and to gain new insights for selling their products to minority and female consumers.[309] Corporations' use of "diversity" also provides a competitive advantage in the global economy.[310]

Whether affirmative action is mandated by the government or practiced by big businesses, it has helped some blacks move up a rung—from the lower middle class to the middle class or from the middle class to the upper middle class.[311] But affirmative action has not pulled many blacks out of the underclass. In families mired in poverty, these individuals often lack the education and skills necessary to compete for available jobs.[312] And, of course, affirmative action has not created new jobs or better jobs, so it has not helped minorities or women as much as a flourishing economy would.

In short, affirmative action should not be given more credit, or saddled with more blame, than it deserves. It has boosted some minorities and women but has not helped many others. It has displaced some white men but has not affected most others.

Yet 13 percent of white men think they have lost a job or promotion because of their race, and 10 percent think they have because of their sex.[313] Many others claim they have "heard about" another white man who did. However, affirmative action is not as pervasive as most people assume.[314] Many people view affirmative action as they do handicapped parking. When looking for a parking space in a crowded lot, many drivers see an empty handicapped space and think, "If it weren't for that, I could park here." Of course, if the space weren't reserved for handicapped drivers, only one other driver could park there.[315] So it is with affirmative action. Many white men think they would get a particular job if it weren't for affirmative action, but only one would. Meanwhile, the rest feel victimized by the policy.

In College Admissions

Colleges and universities began to use affirmative action in the 1970s. Some schools used limited programs that gave a boost to minority applicants, while other schools used extensive programs that reserved seats—essentially, set quotas—for minority applicants. The medical school of the University of California at Davis reserved sixteen seats in its class of one hundred students for minorities. In *University of California* v. *Bakke in 1978,* the Burger Court upheld the use of race as a factor in admissions, emphasizing the value of diversity, but struck down the use of quotas (unless the school has a history of intentional discrimination).

The Supreme Court would not rule on this issue again until 2003. In the meantime, voters in California and Washington, the governor of Florida, and federal courts in two circuits mandated an end to the use of race in admissions to public universities in those states. (The federal courts ignored the *Bakke* precedent of the Supreme Court.)

The moves against affirmative action prompted concerns that minority enrollments would plunge.[316] Some state legislatures and universities decided not to let this happen. The Texas legislature passed a law guaranteeing admission to its state universities for all high school graduates in the top 10 percent of their class, and the University of California Board of Regents guaranteed admission to at least one of the UC campuses for those in the top 4 percent.[317]

These programs use geography instead of race; in particular, they use residential segregation, which has stymied the efforts to desegregate grade schools through high schools, as a way to diversify the universities. Minority students who perform well in their schools can get admitted to the universities, even if their segregated schools provide a lower-quality education than the white schools offer.

Although the programs in both states have increased the numbers of minorities above the numbers there would be without the programs, the numbers are lower than they had been with affirmative action.[318] Asians—not whites—have been the prime beneficiaries of the demise of affirmative action in these states, as they would be with the end of affirmative action throughout the country.[319]

The Rehnquist Court revisited the *Bakke* ruling in 2003. In a pair of cases from the University of Michigan, one directed at undergraduate admissions and one directed at law school admissions, five justices upheld affirmative action, though only as part of a "holistic review" that gives "individualized consideration" to each application.

Rather than use formulas that add points for minority status, schools must use a more labor-intensive review.[320] The decision to uphold affirmative action came as a surprise, because the Rehnquist Court had limited affirmative action in employment cases. The majority's decision—or at least its fifth vote—evidently was influenced by friend-of-the-court briefs from *Fortune* 500 companies insisting that affirmative action is necessary to compete in the global marketplace, and from generals and admirals insisting that affirmative action is necessary to produce a diverse officer corps to lead a twenty-first-century military.[321]

The future of affirmative action is in doubt, however, because Justice O'Connor, the swing justice on affirmative action, retired and was replaced by the more conservative Justice Alito. Now at least four, if not five, justices on the Roberts Court are opposed to any use of race to ameliorate past discrimination.[322] And voters in more states (including Michigan) have adopted ballot measures outlawing the use of race or "preferential treatment" in education.

Just as some white men believe that affirmative action has cost them a job or promotion, some white students believe that it has cost them, or will cost them, a seat in the college or university of their choice. But 60 percent of colleges admit nearly all students who apply; only 20 percent are selective enough to use affirmative action.[323]

Students who apply to elite schools that do use affirmative action are more likely to be rejected because these schools give preferential treatment to their "legacies"— the sons and daughters of their alumni—than because these schools practice affirmative action. (Giving preferential treatment to their legacies encourages their alums to donate to the school.) Typically, a fifth of Harvard's students receive preferential treatment because their parents attended the school. Harvard's "legacies" are more than twice as likely to be admitted as blacks or Latinos. A similar advantage exists at other selective schools, including public schools such as the Universities of California and Virginia.[324]

Affirmative action may be more widespread in graduate and professional schools.[325] For some beneficiaries of affirmative action in law schools, recent social science research has found a mismatch between these students' abilities and the schools' demands. These students attended law schools that were too difficult for them, making it harder for them to graduate, pass the bar exam, and join the legal profession.[326] These findings are controversial, but, if confirmed, they suggest that some schools may need to adjust the scope of their affirmative-action programs.

For both sides in the controversy, affirmative action, whether in employment or education, has become a symbol. For civil rights leaders, it represents fairness and a step toward equality and progress. For critics, it represents unfairness and an attack on individuality and merit. It's important to debate these values, but it's also important to recognize that affirmative action is neither the key public policy for racial and sexual equality, as some supporters portray it, nor a big stumbling block for individual achievement, as some

WHERE HE'S FORCED TO WITNESS VIOLENCE

AVOID DRUGS

DANIEL LIVES ON DETROIT'S EAST SIDE

RESIST GANGS

WITHSTAND POVERTY

SUFFER RACISM

BUY

HOME

OVERCOME SUBSTANDARD SCHOOLS BY STUDYING HARD

TO GET INTO COLLEGE (WITH A LITTLE HELP FROM AFFIRMATIVE ACTION)

SUPREME COURT RULING

HEY, WHY DOES HE GET ALL THE BREAKS?!

FROM THE DETROIT FREE PRESS   MIKE THOMPSON, COPLEY NEWS SERVICE

© Mike Thompson, Detroit Free Press. Reprinted by permission of Copley News Service.

detractors characterize it. Indeed, affirmative action reaches so few individuals that in the eyes of some observers the policy is a "distraction,"[327] or even an attempt to achieve "racial justice on the cheap," without adopting the more extensive programs that would be necessary to address the much greater problem of the underclass.[328]

Eventually, when we achieve racial equality, affirmative action shouldn't be necessary and wouldn't be appropriate. As this chapter has made clear, however, we are still a long ways from a "post-racial society." Nonetheless, given the controversy that swirls around these programs, we might ask, How long should affirmative action continue? When will its gains be outweighed by its costs—the political costs to those who champion the programs or the psychological costs to those who feel victimized by the programs? And when will affirmative action be overtaken by the increasingly multiracial nature of the population, which makes it ever more difficult to define people by one race?

DEMOCRACY?

How do the existence and operation of affirmative action highlight the contradictions among the core values of democracy (discussed in Chapter 1)?

CONCLUSION: Civil Rights and the Role of Government

Blacks and women have taken long strides toward equality since the time when people would say, "A Negro's place is in the cotton field" or "A woman's place is in the home." The civil rights movement and the women's movement initiated the changes. They protested inequality, and they put that issue on the public agenda. As the movements grew and garnered support, they pressured the government. Eventually, the government acted—in the 1950s, 1960s, and 1970s for racial equality, and in the 1960s, 1970s, and 1980s for sexual equality.

The foundation for governmental action was laid during and after the Civil War. The constitutional amendments not only abolished slavery (Thirteenth) and allowed blacks to vote (Fifteenth), but they also guaranteed "equal protection" and "due process" (Fourteenth). These two clauses allowed an active role for the federal government in protecting civil rights, even though the government, following public opinion, wouldn't play this role for almost a century.

Eventually, the Supreme Court exercised decisive leadership. In the 1950s and 1960s, the Warren Court was activist in striking down racial segregation, and in the 1970s and 1980s, the Burger Court was activist in striking down sexual discrimination. These efforts may go down in history as the major achievements of these Courts. But the rulings themselves weren't sufficient. Because the Supreme Court lacks the means to enforce its decisions, the president and Congress had to help overcome public resistance. Several presidents, especially Lyndon Johnson, and Congress also exercised decisive leadership. The presidents proposed and pushed various bills, and Congress forged bipartisan coalitions and fostered public support for the bills. These measures reinforced and extended the Court's rulings.

The federal bureaucracy also reflected this active role. As the government took concerted actions to protect civil rights, it had to create new units, such as the Equal Employment Opportunity Commission, and new offices within existing departments, such as the Civil Rights Division in the Justice Department, to implement the laws and policies. This meant that the bureaucracy had to hire more workers and spend more money. In these ways, the government got bigger.

In pressuring the government to respond, African Americans have benefited from being numerous, visible, and—with their common legacy of slavery, segregation, and discrimination—cohesive. Their concentration in large northern cities and some southern states has helped them exercise political power. Their legacy, however, has fostered the ghetto, with its debilitating conditions, and denied them the resources to make faster progress. Thus there are two black Americas—a middle class that has benefited tremendously from the civil rights movement and the changes in our society, and a lower class, especially the underclass, that has been left behind to fend for itself.[329]

Latinos, whose movement is younger, have also taken strides toward equality. With increased immigration, they have become more numerous, and in coming years they will become even more numerous, giving them a large voting bloc. Their concentration in some states and cities has enabled them to influence these state and local governments. Their diversity and lack of cohesiveness, however, have hindered their ability to influence the national government.

American Indians are the smallest, most isolated, and least organized minority, so they have had the poorest success in pressuring the government.

As minority groups grow—they will constitute half of the U.S. population by 2050—they will be able to exert pressure on government more effectively. But they will increasingly come into conflict with each other, especially when economic conditions are stagnant and government jobs and services are scarce. Already there are tensions (as the Academy Award–winning movie *Crash* poignantly and powerfully depicts). For example, some blacks resent the faster progress of Latinos and Asians. Because African Americans were here before most Hispanics and all Asians and suffered more and struggled longer, these blacks feel they should reap rewards sooner. For their part, Latino leaders resent the reluctance of black groups to help them with their issues.[330] There have been conflicts, even riots. Blacks have rioted in Miami from frustration with the Cuban-dominated leadership, and Latinos have rioted in Washington, D.C., out of anger with the black power structure. Continuing illegal immigration could exacerbate the tensions by pitting new immigrants against poor blacks in competition for jobs.

Nonminority women were never subjugated as much as minority men and women, so they have had less to overcome. Moreover, women are a majority, they vote as frequently as men, and they have well-organized and well-funded interest groups. Consequently, they have made the greatest strides toward equality.

As American politics shifted from a liberal era during the 1960s and 1970s to a conservative era during the 1980s, 1990s, and early 2000s, the public reflected less willingness to address racial inequality or to expand government programs. Indeed, some groups have proposed shrinking the government's size and its role in protecting civil rights. Yet an unfinished agenda remains, despite the undeniable gains toward racial equality.

KEY TERMS

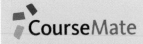

Access an interactive eBook, chapter-specific interactive learning tools (including flashcards, quizzes, videos), and more at CourseMate for *Understanding American Government*. Log in at CengageBrain.com.

The Declaration of Independence*

In Congress, July 4, 1776.

A Declaration by the Representatives of the United States of America, in General Congress assembled.

When in the Course of human Events, it becomes necessary for one People to dissolve the Political Bonds which have connected them with another, and to assume among the Powers of the Earth, the separate and equal Station to which the Laws of Nature and of Nature's God entitle them, a decent Respect to the Opinions of Mankind requires that they should declare the causes which impel them to the Separation.

We hold these Truths to be self-evident, that all Men are created equal, that they are endowed by their Creator with certain unalienable Rights, that among these are Life, Liberty, and the Pursuit of Happiness—That to secure these Rights, Governments are instituted among Men, deriving their just Powers from the Consent of the Governed, that whenever any Form of Government becomes destructive of these Ends, it is the Right of the People to alter or to abolish it, and to institute new Government, laying its Foundation on such Principles, and organizing its Powers in such Forms, as to them shall seem most likely to effect their Safety and Happiness. Prudence, indeed, will dictate that Governments long established should not be changed for light and transient Causes; and accordingly all Experience hath shewn, that Mankind are more disposed to suffer, while Evils are sufferable, than to right themselves by abolishing the Forms to which they are accustomed. But when a long Train of Abuses and Usurpations, pursuing invariably the same Object, evinces a Design to reduce them under absolute Despotism, it is their Right, it is their Duty, to throw off such Government, and to provide new Guards for their future Security. Such has been the patient Sufferance of these Colonies; and such is now the Necessity which constrains them to alter their former Systems of Government. The History of the present King of Great Britain is a History of repeated Injuries and Usurpations, all having in direct Object the Establishment of an absolute Tyranny over these States. To prove this, let facts be submitted to a candid World.

He has refused his Assent to Laws, the most wholesome and necessary for the public Good.

He has forbidden his Governors to pass Laws of immediate and pressing Importance, unless suspended in their Operation till his Assent should be obtained; and when so suspended, he has utterly neglected to attend to them.

He has refused to pass other Laws for the Accommodation of large Districts of People, unless those People would relinquish the Right of Representation in the Legislature, a Right inestimable to them, and formidable to Tyrants only.

He has called together Legislative Bodies at Places unusual, uncomfortable, and distant from the Depository of their Public Records, for the sole Purpose of fatiguing them into Compliance with his Measures.

He has dissolved Representative Houses repeatedly, for opposing with manly Firmness his Invasions on the Rights of the People.

He has refused for a long Time, after such Dissolutions, to cause others to be elected; whereby the Legislative Powers, incapable of Annihilation, have returned to the People at large for their exercise; the State remaining in the mean time exposed to all the Dangers of Invasion from without, and Convulsions within.

He has endeavoured to prevent the Population of these States; for that Purpose obstructing the Laws for Naturalization of Foreigners; refusing to pass others to encourage their Migration hither, and raising the Conditions of new Appropriations of Lands.

He has obstructed the Administration of Justice, by refusing his Assent to Laws for establishing Judiciary Powers.

He has made Judges dependent on his Will alone, for the Tenure of their offices, and the Amount and payments of their Salaries.

He has erected a Multitude of new Offices, and sent hither Swarms of Officers to harass our People, and eat out their Substance.

He has kept among us, in times of Peace, Standing Armies, without the consent of our Legislatures.

He has affected to render the Military independent of, and superior to the Civil Power.

He has combined with others to subject us to a Jurisdiction foreign to our Constitution, and unacknowledged

*The spelling, capitalization, and punctuation of the original have been retained here.

by our Laws; giving his Assent to their Acts of pretended Legislation:

For quartering large Bodies of Armed Troops among us:

For protecting them, by a mock Trial, from Punishment for any Murders which they should commit on the Inhabitants of these States:

For cutting off our Trade with all Parts of the World:

For imposing Taxes on us without our Consent:

For depriving us, in many cases, of the Benefits of Trial by Jury:

For transporting us beyond Seas to be tried for pretended Offences:

For abolishing the free System of English Laws in a neighbouring Province, establishing therein an arbitrary Government, and enlarging its Boundaries, so as to render it at once an Example and fit Instrument for introducing the same absolute Rule into these Colonies:

For taking away our Charters, abolishing our most valuable Laws, and altering fundamentally the Forms of our Governments:

For suspending our own Legislatures, and declaring themselves invested with Power to legislate for us in all Cases whatsoever.

He has abdicated Government here, by declaring us out of his Protection and waging War against us.

He has plundered our Seas, ravaged our Coasts, burnt our towns, and destroyed the Lives of our People.

He is, at this Time, transporting large Armies of foreign Mercenaries to compleat the works of Death, Desolation, and Tyranny, already begun with circumstances of Cruelty and Perfidy, scarcely paralleled in the most barbarous Ages, and totally unworthy the Head of a civilized Nation.

He has constrained our fellow Citizens taken Captive on the high Seas to bear Arms against their Country, to become the Executioners of their Friends and Brethren, or to fall themselves by their Hands.

He has excited domestic Insurrections amongst us, and has endeavoured to bring on the Inhabitants of our Frontiers, the merciless Indian Savages, whose known Rule of Warfare is an undistinguished Destruction, of all Ages, Sexes and Conditions.

In every state of these Oppressions we have Petitioned for Redress in the most humble Terms: Our repeated Petitions have been answered only by repeated Injury. A Prince, whose Character is thus marked by every act which may define a Tyrant, is unfit to be the Ruler of a free People.

Nor have we been wanting in Attentions to our British Brethren. We have warned them from Time to Time of Attempts by their Legislature to extend an unwarrantable Jurisdiction over us. We have reminded them of the Circumstances of our Emigration and Settlement here. We have appealed to their native Justice and Magnanimity, and we have conjured them by the Ties of our common Kindred to disavow these Usurpations, which would inevitably interrupt our Connections and Correspondence. They too have been deaf to the Voice of Justice and of Consanguinity. We must, therefore, acquiesce in the Necessity, which denounces our Separation, and hold them, as we hold the rest of Mankind, Enemies in War, in Peace Friends.

We, therefore, the Representatives of the UNITED STATES OF AMERICA, in General Congress Assembled, appealing to the Supreme Judge of the World for the Rectitude of our Intentions, do, in the Name, and by Authority of the good People of these Colonies, solemnly Publish and Declare, That these United Colonies are, and of Right ought to be, Free and Independent States; that they are absolved from all Allegiance to the British Crown, and that all political Connection between them and the State of Great Britain, is and ought to be totally dissolved; and that as Free and Independent States, they have full Power to levy War, conclude Peace, contract Alliances, establish Commerce, and to do all other Acts and Things which Independent States may of right do. And for the support of this declaration, with a firm Reliance on the Protection of divine Providence, we mutually pledge to each other our Lives, our Fortunes, and our sacred Honor.

Constitution of the United States of America*

We the people of the United States, in Order to form a more perfect Union, establish Justice, insure domestic Tranquility, provide for the common defence, promote the general Welfare, and secure the Blessings of Liberty to ourselves and our posterity, do ordain and establish this Constitution for the United States of America.

ARTICLE I

Section 1. All legislative Powers herein granted shall be vested in a Congress of the United States, which shall consist of a Senate and House of Representatives.

Section 2. The House of Representatives shall be composed of Members chosen every second Year by the People of the several States, and the Electors in each State shall have the Qualifications requisite for Electors of the most numerous Branch of the State Legislature.

No person shall be a Representative who shall not have attained to the Age of twenty-five Years, and been seven Years a Citizen of the United States, and who shall not, when elected, be an Inhabitant of that State in which he shall be chosen.

Representatives and direct [Taxes][1] shall be apportioned among the several States which may be included within this Union, according to their respective Numbers [which shall be determined by adding to the whole Number of free Persons, including those bound to Service for a Term of Years, and excluding Indians not taxed, three fifths of all other Persons].[2] The actual Enumeration shall be made within three Years after the first Meeting of the Congress of the United States, and within every subsequent Term of ten Years, in such Manner as they shall by Law direct. The Number of Representatives shall not exceed one for every thirty Thousand, but each State shall have at Least one Representative; and until such enumeration shall be made, the State of New Hampshire shall be entitled to chuse three, Massachusetts eight, Rhode Island and Providence Plantations one, Connecticut five, New-York six, New Jersy four, Pennsylvania eight, Delaware one, Maryland six, Virginia ten, North Carolina five, South Carolina five, and Georgia three.

When vacancies happen in the Representation from any State, the Executive Authority thereof shall issue Writs of Election to fill such Vacancies.

The House of Representatives shall chuse their Speaker and other Officers; and shall have the sole Power of Impeachment.

Section 3. The Senate of the United States shall be composed of two Senators from each State [chosen by the Legislature thereof],[3] for six Years; and each Senator shall have one Vote.

Immediately after they shall be assembled in Consequence of the first Election, they shall be divided as equally as may be into three Classes. The Seats of the Senators of the first Class shall be vacated at the Expiration of the second year, of the second Class at the Expiration of the fourth Year, and of the third Class at the Expiration of the sixth Year, so that one third may be chosen every second Year [and if Vacancies happen by Resignation, or otherwise, during the Recess of the Legislature of any State, the Executive thereof may make temporary Appointments until the next Meeting of the Legislature, which shall then fill such Vacancies.][4]

No Person shall be a Senator who shall not have attained to the Age of thirty Years, and been nine Years a Citizen of the United States, and who shall not, when elected, be an Inhabitant of that State for which he shall be chosen.

The Vice President of the United States shall be President of the Senate, but shall have no Vote, unless they be equally divided.

The Senate shall chuse their other Officers, and also a President pro tempore, in the Absence of the Vice President, or when he shall exercise the Office of President of the United States.

The Senate shall have the sole Power to try all Impeachments. When sitting for that Purpose, they shall be on Oath or Affirmation. When the President of the United States is tried, the Chief Justice shall preside: And no Person shall be convicted without the Concurrence of two thirds of the Members present.

Judgment in Cases of Impeachment shall not extend further than to removal from Office, and disqualification to

---

*The spelling, capitalization, and punctuation of the original have been retained here. Brackets indicate passages that have been altered by amendments to the Constitution.
1. Modified by the Sixteenth Amendment.

2. Modified by the Fourteenth Amendment.
3. Repealed by the Seventeenth Amendment.
4. Modified by the Seventeenth Amendment.

hold and enjoy any Office of honor, Trust or Profit under the United States; but the Party convicted shall nevertheless be liable and subject to Indictment, Trial, Judgment and Punishment, according to Law.

Section 4.
The Times, Places and Manner of holding Elections for Senators and Representatives, shall be prescribed in each State by the Legislature thereof; but the Congress may at any time by Law make or alter such Regulations, except as to the Places of chusing Senators.

[The Congress shall assemble at least once in every Year, and such Meeting shall be on the first Monday in December, unless they shall by Law appoint a different Day.][5]

Section 5.
Each House shall be the Judge of the Elections, Returns and Qualifications of its own Members, and a Majority of each shall constitute a Quorum to do Business; but a smaller Number may adjourn from day to day, and may be authorized to compel the Attendance of absent Members, in such Manner, and under such Penalties as each House may provide.

Each House may determine the Rules of its Proceedings, punish its Members for disorderly Behaviour, and, with the Concurrence of two thirds, expel a Member.

Each House shall keep a Journal of its Proceedings, and from time to time publish the same, excepting such Parts as may in their Judgment require Secrecy; and the Yeas and Nays of the Members of either House on any question shall, at the Desire of one fifth of those present, be entered on the Journal.

Neither House, during the Session of Congress, shall, without the Consent of the other, adjourn for more than three days, nor to any other Place than that in which the two Houses shall be sitting.

Section 6.
The Senators and Representatives shall receive a Compensation for their Services, to be ascertained by Law, and paid out of the Treasury of the United States. They shall in all Cases, except Treason, Felony and Breach of the Peace, be privileged from Arrest during their Attendance at the Session of their respective Houses, and in going to and returning from the same; and for any Speech or Debate in either House, they shall not be questioned in any other Place.

No Senator or Representative shall, during the Time for which he was elected, be appointed to any civil Office under the Authority of the United States, which shall have been created, or the Emoluments whereof shall have been encreased during such time; and no Person holding any Office under the United States, shall be a Member of either House during his Continuance in Office.

Section 7.
All Bills for raising Revenue shall originate in the House of Representatives; but the Senate may propose or concur with Amendments as on other Bills.

Every Bill which shall have passed the House of Representatives and the Senate, shall, before it become a Law, be presented to the President of the United States; If he approves he shall sign it, but if not he shall return it, with his objections to that House in which it shall have originated, who shall enter the Objections at large on their Journal, and proceed to reconsider it. If after such Reconsideration two thirds of that House shall agree to pass the Bill, it shall be sent, together with the Objections, to the other House, by which it shall likewise be reconsidered, and if approved by two thirds of that House, it shall become a Law. But in all such Cases the Votes of both Houses shall be determined by yeas and Nays, and the Names of the Persons voting for and against the Bill shall be entered on the Journal of each House respectively. If any Bill shall not be returned by the President within ten Days (Sundays excepted) after it shall have been presented to him, the Same shall be a Law, in like Manner as if he had signed it, unless the Congress by their Adjournment prevent its Return, in which Case it shall not be a Law.

Every Order, Resolution, or Vote to which the Concurrence of the Senate and House of Representatives may be necessary (except on a question of Adjournment) shall be presented to the President of the United States; and before the Same shall take Effect, shall be approved by him, or being disapproved by him, shall be repassed by two thirds of the Senate and House of Representatives, according to the Rules and Limitations prescribed in the Case of a Bill.

Section 8.
The Congress shall have Power To lay and collect Taxes, Duties, Imposts and Excises, to pay the Debts and provide for the common Defence and general Welfare of the United States; but all Duties, Imposts and Excises shall be uniform throughout the United States;

To borrow Money on the credit of the United States;

To regulate Commerce with foreign Nations, and among the several States, and with the Indian Tribes;

To establish a uniform Rule of Naturalization, and uniform Laws on the subject of Bankruptcies throughout the United States;

To coin Money, regulate the Value thereof, and of foreign Coin, and fix the Standard of Weights and Measures;

To provide for the Punishment of counterfeiting the Securities and current Coin of the United States;

To establish Post Offices and post Roads;

To promote the Progress of Science and useful Arts, by securing for limited Times to Authors and Inventors the exclusive Right to their respective Writings and Discoveries;

To constitute Tribunals inferior to the supreme Court;

To define and punish Piracies and Felonies committed on the high Seas, and Offences against the Law of Nations;

To declare War, grant Letters of Marque and Reprisal, and make Rules concerning Captures on Land and Water;

5. Changed by the Twentieth Amendment.

To raise and support Armies, but no Appropriation of Money to that Use shall be for a longer Term than two Years;

To provide and maintain a Navy;

To make Rules for the Government and Regulation of the land and naval Forces;

To provide for calling forth the Militia to execute the Laws of the Union, suppress Insurrections and repel Invasions;

To provide for organizing, arming, and disciplining the Militia, and for governing such Part of them as may be employed in the Service of the United States, reserving to the States respectively, the Appointment of the Officers, and the Authority of training the Militia according to the discipline prescribed by Congress;

To exercise exclusive Legislation in all Cases whatsoever, over such District (not exceeding ten Miles square) as may, by Cession of particular States, and the Acceptance of Congress, become the Seat of the Government of the United States, and to exercise like Authority over all Places purchased by the Consent of the Legislature of the State in which the Same shall be, for the Erection of forts, Magazines, Arsenals, dockYards, and other needful Buildings;—And

To make all Laws which shall be necessary and proper for carrying into Execution the foregoing Powers, and all other Powers vested by this Constitution in the Government of the United States, or in any Department or Officer thereof.

Section 9. The Migration or Importation of such Persons as any of the States now existing shall think proper to admit, shall not be prohibited by the Congress prior to the Year one thousand eight hundred and eight, but a Tax or duty may be imposed on such Importation, not exceeding ten dollars for each Person.

The Privilege of the Writ of Habeas Corpus shall not be suspended, unless when in Cases of Rebellion or Invasion the public Safety may require it.

No Bill of Attainder or ex post facto Law shall be passed.

[No Capitation, or other direct, Tax shall be laid, unless in Proportion to the Census or Enumeration herein before directed to be taken.][6]

No Tax or Duty shall be laid on Articles exported from any State.

No Preference shall be given by any Regulation of Commerce or Revenue to the Ports of one State over those of another; nor shall Vessels bound to, or from, one State, be obliged to enter, clear, or pay Duties in another.

No Money shall be drawn from the Treasury, but in Consequence of Appropriations made by Law; and a regular Statement and Account of the Receipts and Expenditures of all public Money shall be published from time to time.

No Title of Nobility shall be granted by the United States; and no Person holding any Office or Profit or Trust under them, shall, without the Consent of the Congress, accept of any present, Emolument, Office, or Title, of any kind whatever, from any King, Prince, or foreign State.

Section 10. No state shall enter into any Treaty, Alliance, or Confederation; grant Letters of Marque and Reprisal; coin Money; emit Bills of Credit; make any Thing but gold and silver Coin a Tender in Payment of Debts; pass any Bill of Attainder, ex post facto Law, or Law impairing the Obligation of Contracts, or grant any Title of Nobility.

No State shall, without the Consent of the Congress, lay any Imposts or Duties on Imports or Exports, except what may be absolutely necessary for executing its inspection Laws; and the net Produce of all Duties and Imposts, laid by any State on Imports or Exports, shall be for the Use of the Treasury of the United States; and all such Laws shall be subject to the Revision and Controul of the Congress.

No State shall, without the Consent of Congress, lay any duty of Tonnage, keep Troops, or Ships of War in time of Peace, enter into any Agreement or Compact with another State, or with a foreign Power or engage in War, unless actually invaded, or in such imminent Danger as will not admit of delay.

ARTICLE II

Section 1. The executive Power shall be vested in a President of the United States of America. He shall hold his Office during the Term of four Years, and, together with the Vice President, chosen for the Same Term, be elected, as follows.

Each State shall appoint, in such Manner as the Legislature thereof may direct, a Number of Electors, equal to the whole Number of Senators and Representatives to which the State may be entitled in the Congress; but no Senator or Representative, or Person holding an Office of Trust or Profit under the United States, shall be appointed an Elector.

[The Electors shall meet in their respective States, and vote by Ballot for two Persons of whom one at least shall not be an Inhabitant of the same State with themselves. And they shall make a List of all the Persons voted for, and of the Number of Votes for each; which List they shall sign and certify, and transmit sealed to the Seat of the Government of the United States, directed to the President of the Senate. The President of the Senate shall, in the Presence of the Senate and House of Representatives, open all the Certificates, and the Votes shall then be counted. The Person having the greatest Number of Votes shall be the President, if such Number be a Majority of the whole Number of Electors appointed; and if there be more than one who have such Majority, and have an equal Number of Votes, then the House of Representatives shall immediately chuse by Ballot one of them for President; and if no Person have a Majority, then from the five highest on

6. Modified by the Sixteenth Amendment.

the List the said House shall in like Manner chuse the President. But in chusing the President, the Votes shall be taken by States, the Representation from each State having one Vote; A quorum for this Purpose shall consist of a Member or Members from two thirds of the States, and a Majority of all the states shall be necessary to a Choice. In every Case, after the Choice of the President, the Person having the greatest Number of Votes of the Electors shall be the Vice President. But if there should remain two or more who have equal Votes, the Senate shall chuse from them by Ballot the Vice President.][7]

The Congress may determine the Time of chusing the Electors, and the Day on which they shall give their Votes; which Day shall be the same throughout the United States.

No person except a natural born Citizen, or a Citizen of the United States, at the time of the Adoption of this Constitution, shall be eligible to the Office of President; neither shall any Person be eligible to that Office who shall not have attained to the Age of thirty five Years, and been fourteen Years a Resident within the United States.

[In Case of the Removal of the President from Office, or of his Death, Resignation, or Inability to discharge the Powers and Duties of the said Office, the same shall devolve on the Vice President, and the Congress may by Law provide for the Case of Removal, Death, Resignation or Inability, both of the President and Vice President, declaring what Officer shall then act as President, and such Officer shall act accordingly, until the Disability be removed, or a President shall be elected.][8]

The President shall, at stated Times, receive for his Services, a Compensation, which shall neither be increased nor diminished during the Period for which he shall have been elected, and he shall not receive within that Period any other Emolument from the United States, or any of them.

Before he enter on the Execution of his Office, he shall take the following Oath or Affirmation:—"I do solemnly swear (or affirm) that I will faithfully execute the Office of President of the United States, and will to the best of my Ability, preserve, protect and defend the constitution of the United States."

Section 2. The President shall be Commander in Chief of the Army and Navy of the United States, and of the Militia of the several States, when called into the actual Service of the United States; he may require the Opinion, in writing, of the principal Officer in each of the executive Departments, upon any Subject relating to the Duties of their respective Offices, and he shall have Power to grant Reprieves and Pardons for Offences against the United States, except in Cases of Impeachment.

He shall have Power, by and with the Advice and Consent of the Senate, to make Treaties, provided two thirds of the Senators present concur; and he shall nominate, and by and with the Advice and Consent of the Senate, shall appoint Ambassadors, other public Ministers and Consuls, Judges of the supreme Court, and all other Officers of the United States, whose Appointments are not herein otherwise provided for, and which shall be established by Law; but the Congress may by Law vest the Appointment of such inferior Officers, as they think proper, in the President alone, in the Courts of Law, or in the Heads of Departments.

The President shall have Power to fill up all Vacancies that may happen during the Recess of the Senate, by granting Commissions which shall expire at the end of their next Session.

Section 3. He shall from time to time give to the Congress Information of the State of the Union, and recommend to their Consideration such Measures as he shall judge necessary and expedient; he may, on extraordinary Occasions, convene both Houses, or either of them, and in Case of Disagreement between them, with Respect to the Time of Adjournment, he may adjourn them to such Time as he shall think proper; he shall receive Ambassadors and other public Ministers; he shall take Care that the Laws be faithfully executed, and shall Commission all the Officers of the United States.

Section 4. The President, Vice President and all civil Officers of the United States, shall be removed from Office on Impeachment for, and Conviction of, Treason, Bribery, or other high Crimes and Misdemeanors.

ARTICLE III

Section 1. The judicial Power of the United States, shall be vested in one supreme Court, and in such inferior Courts as the Congress may from time to time ordain and establish. The Judges, both of the supreme and inferior Courts, shall hold their Offices during good Behaviour, and shall, at stated Times, receive for their Services, a Compensation, which shall not be diminished during their Continuance in Office.

Section 2. The judicial Power shall extend to all Cases, in Law and Equity, arising under this Constitution, the Laws of the United States, and Treaties made, or which shall be made, under their Authority;—to all Cases affecting Ambassadors, other public Ministers and Consuls;—to all Cases of admiralty and maritime Jurisdiction;—to Controversies to which the United States shall be a Party;—to Controversies between two or more States;—[between a State and Citizens of another State;][9]—between Citizens of different States,—between Citizens of the same State claiming Lands under Grants of different States, [and between a state, or the Citizens thereof, and foreign States, Citizens or Subjects.][10]

---

7. Changed by the Twelfth Amendment.
8. Modified by the Twenty-fifth Amendment.

9. Modified by the Eleventh Amendment.
10. Modified by the Eleventh Amendment.

In all cases affecting Ambassadors, other public Ministers and Consuls, and those in which a State shall be Party, the supreme Court shall have original Jurisdiction. In all the other Cases before mentioned, the supreme Court shall have appellate Jurisdiction, both as to Law and Fact, with such Exceptions, and under such Regulations as the Congress shall make.

The Trial of all Crimes, except in Cases of Impeachment, shall be by Jury; and such Trial shall be held in the State where the said Crimes shall have been committed; but when not committed within any State, the Trial shall be at such Place or Places as the Congress may by Law have directed.

Section 3. Treason against the United States, shall consist only in levying War against them, or in adhering to their Enemies, giving them Aid and Comfort. No Person shall be convicted of Treason unless on the Testimony of two Witnesses to the same overt Act, or on Confession in open Court.

The Congress shall have Power to declare the Punishment of Treason, but no Attainder of Treason shall work Corruption of Blood, or Forfeiture except during the Life of the Person attainted.

ARTICLE IV

Section 1. Full Faith and Credit shall be given in each State to the public Acts, Records, and judicial Proceedings of every other State. And the Congress may by general Laws prescribe the Manner in which such Acts, Records and Proceedings shall be proved, and the Effect thereof.

Section 2. The Citizens of each State shall be entitled to all Privileges and Immunities of Citizens in the several States.

A Person charged in any State with Treason, Felony, or other Crime, who shall flee from Justice, and be found in another State, shall on Demand of the executive Authority of the State from which he fled, be delivered up, to be removed to the State having Jurisdiction of the Crime.

[No Person held to Service or Labour in one State under the Laws thereof, escaping into another, shall, in Consequence of any Law or Regulation therein, be discharged from such Service or Labour, but shall be delivered up on Claim of the Party to whom such Service or Labour may be due.][11]

Section 3. New States may be admitted by the Congress into this Union; but no new State shall be formed or erected within the Jurisdiction of any other State; nor any State be formed by the Junction of two or more States, or Parts of States, without the Consent of the Legislatures of the States concerned as well as of the Congress.

The Congress shall have Power to dispose of and make all needful Rules and Regulations respecting the Territory or other Property belonging to the United States; and nothing in this Constitution shall be so construed as to Prejudice any Claims of the United States, or of any particular State.

Section 4. The United States shall guarantee to every State in this Union a Republican Form of Government, and shall protect each of them against Invasion, and on Application of the Legislature, or of the Executive (when the Legislature cannot be convened) against domestic Violence.

ARTICLE V

The Congress, whenever two thirds of both Houses shall deem it necessary, shall propose Amendments to this Constitution, or on the Application of the Legislatures of two thirds of the several States, shall call a Convention for proposing Amendments, which, in either Case, shall be valid to all Intents and Purposes, as Part of this Constitution, when ratified by the Legislatures of three fourths of the several States, or by Conventions in three fourths thereof, as the one or the other Mode of Ratification may be proposed by the Congress; Provided that no Amendment which may be made prior to the Year One thousand eight hundred and eight shall in any Manner affect the first and fourth Clauses in the Ninth Section of the first Article; and that no State, without its Consent, shall be deprived of its equal Suffrage in the Senate.

ARTICLE VI

All Debts contracted and Engagements entered into, before the Adoption of this Constitution, shall be as valid against the United States under this Constitution, as under the Confederation.

This Constitution, and the laws of the United States which shall be made in Pursuance thereof; and all Treaties made, or which shall be made, under the Authority of the United States, shall be the supreme Law of the Land; and the Judges in every State shall be bound thereby, any Thing in the Constitution or Laws of any State to the Contrary notwithstanding.

The Senators and Representatives before mentioned, and the Members of the several State Legislatures, and all executive and judicial Officers, both of the United States and of the several States, shall be bound by Oath or Affirmation, to support this Constitution; but no religious Test shall ever be required as a Qualification to any Office or public Trust under the United States.

ARTICLE VII

The Ratification of the Conventions of nine States, shall be sufficient for the Establishment of this constitution between the States so ratifying the Same.

Done in Convention by the Unanimous Consent of the States present the Seventeenth Day of September in the Year of our Lord one thousand seven hundred and Eighty

11. Repealed by the Thirteenth Amendment.

seven and of the Independence of the United States of America the Twelfth. In Witness whereof we have hereunto subscribed our Names.

Go. WASHINGTON

Presid't. and deputy from Virginia

Attest

William Jackson

Secretary

Delaware
Geo. Read
Gunning Bedford jun
John Dickinson
Richard Basset
Jaco. Broon

Massachusetts
Nathaniel Gorham
Rufus King

Connecticut
Wm. Saml. Johnson
Roger Sherman

New York
Alexander Hamilton

New Jersey
Wh. Livingston
David Brearley
Wm. Paterson
Jona. Dayton

Pennsylvania
B. Franklin
Thomas Mifflin
Robt. Morris
Geo. Clymer
Thos. FitzSimons
Jared Ingersoll

James Wilson
Gouv Morris

Virginia
John Blair
James Madison Jr.

North Carolina
Wm. Blount
Richd. Dobbs Spaight
Hu Williamson

South Carolina
J. Rutledge
Charles Cotesworth Pinckney
Charles Pinckney
Pierce Butler

Georgia
William Few
Abr. Baldwin

New Hampshire
John Langdon
Nicholas Gilman

Maryland
James McHenry
Dan of St Thos. Jenifer
Danl. Carroll

AMENDMENT I[12]

Congress shall make no law respecting an establishment of religion, or prohibiting the free exercise thereof; or abridging the freedom of speech, or of the press; or the right of the people peaceably to assemble, and to petition the Government for a redress of grievances.

12. The first ten amendments were passed by Congress on September 25, 1789, and were ratified on December 15, 1791.

AMENDMENT II

A well regulated militia, being necessary to the security of a free State, the right of the people to keep and bear arms, shall not be infringed.

AMENDMENT III

No Soldier shall, in time of peace be quartered in any house, without the consent of the owner, nor in time of war, but in a manner to be prescribed by law.

AMENDMENT IV

The right of the people to be secure in their persons, houses, papers, and effects, against unreasonable searches and seizures, shall not be violated, and no warrants shall issue, but upon probable cause, supported by oath or affirmation, and particularly describing the place to be searched, and the persons or things to be seized.

AMENDMENT V

No person shall be held to answer for a capital, or otherwise infamous crime, unless on a presentment or indictment of a Grand Jury, except in cases arising in the land or naval forces, or in the militia, when in actual service in time of war or public danger; nor shall any person be subject for the same offence to be twice put in jeopardy of life or limb; nor shall be compelled in any criminal case to be a witness against himself, nor be deprived of life, liberty, or property, without due process of law; nor shall private property be taken for public use, without just compensation.

AMENDMENT VI

In all criminal prosecutions, the accused shall enjoy the right to a speedy and public trial, by an impartial jury of the State and district wherein the crime shall have been committed, which district shall have been previously ascertained by law, and to be informed of the nature and cause of the accusation; to be confronted with the witnesses against him; to have compulsory process for obtaining witnesses in his favor, and to have the assistance of counsel for his defence.

AMENDMENT VII

In Suits at common law, where the value in controversy shall exceed twenty dollars, the right of trial by jury shall be preserved, and no fact tried by a jury, shall be otherwise reexamined in any Court of the United States, than according to the rules of the common law.

AMENDMENT VIII

Excessive bail shall not be required, nor excessive fines imposed, nor cruel and unusual punishments inflicted.

AMENDMENT IX

The enumeration in the Constitution, of certain rights, shall not be construed to deny or disparage others retained by the people.

AMENDMENT X

The powers not delegated to the United States by the Constitution, nor prohibited by it to the States, are reserved to the States respectively, or to the people.

AMENDMENT XI (RATIFIED FEBRUARY 7, 1795)

The Judicial power of the United States shall not be construed to extend to any suit in law or equity, commenced or prosecuted against one of the United States by Citizens of another State, or by Citizens or Subjects of any Foreign State.

AMENDMENT XII (RATIFIED JUNE 15, 1804)

The Electors shall meet in their respective states, and vote by ballot for President and Vice-President, one of whom, at least, shall not be an inhabitant of the same state with themselves; they shall name in their ballots the person voted for as President, and in distinct ballots the person voted for as Vice President, and they shall make distinct lists of all persons voted for as President, and of all persons voted for as Vice-President, and of the number of votes for each, which lists they shall sign and certify, and transmit sealed to the seat of the government of the United States, directed to the President of the Senate;—The President of the Senate shall, in the presence of the Senate and House of Representatives, open all the certificates and the votes shall then be counted;—The person having the greatest number of votes for President, shall be the President, if such number be a majority of the whole number of Electors appointed; and if no person have such majority, then from the persons having the highest numbers not exceeding three on the list of those voted for as President, the House of Representatives shall choose immediately, by ballot, the President. But in choosing the President, the votes shall be taken by states, the representation from each state having one vote; a quorum for this purpose shall consist of a member or members from two-thirds of the states, and a majority of all the states shall be necessary to a choice. [And if the House of Representatives shall not choose a President

whenever the right of choice shall devolve upon them, before the fourth day of March next following, then the Vice-President shall act as President, as in the case of the death or other constitutional disability of the President.][13]—The person having the greatest number of votes as Vice-President, shall be the Vice-President, if such number be a majority of the whole number of Electors appointed, and if no person have a majority, then from the two highest numbers on the list, the Senate shall choose the Vice-President; a quorum for the purpose shall consist of two-thirds of the whole number of Senators, and a majority of the whole number shall be necessary to a choice. But no person constitutionally ineligible to the office of President shall be eligible to that of Vice-President of the United States.

AMENDMENT XIII (RATIFIED ON DECEMBER 6, 1865)

Section 1. Neither slavery nor involuntary servitude, except as a punishment for crime whereof the party shall have been duly convicted, shall exist within the United States, or any place subject to their jurisdiction.

Section 2. Congress shall have power to enforce this article by appropriate legislation.

AMENDMENT XIV (RATIFIED ON JULY 9, 1868)

Section 1. All persons born or naturalized in the United States, and subject to the jurisdiction thereof, are citizens of the United States and of the State wherein they reside. No State shall make or enforce any law which shall abridge the privileges or immunities of citizens of the United States; nor shall any State deprive any person of life, liberty, or property, without due process of law; nor deny to any person within its jurisdiction the equal protection of the laws.

Section 2. Representatives shall be apportioned among the several States according to their respective numbers, counting the whole number of persons in each State, excluding Indians not taxed. But when the right to vote at any election for the choice of electors for President and Vice President of the United States, Representatives in Congress, the Executive and Judicial officers of a State, or the members of the Legislature thereof, is denied to any of the male inhabitants of such State, being [twenty-one][14] years of age, and citizens of the United States, or in any way abridged, except for participation in rebellion, or other crime, the basis of representation therein shall be reduced in the proportion which the number of such male citizens

13. Changed by the Twentieth Amendment.
14. Changed by the Twenty-sixth Amendment.

shall bear to the whole number of male citizens twenty-one years of age in such State.

Section 3.   No person shall be a Senator or Representative in Congress, or elector of President and Vice President, or hold any office, civil or military, under the United States, or under any State, who having previously taken an oath, as a member of Congress, or as an officer of the United States, or as a member of any State legislature, or as an executive or judicial officer of any State, to support the Constitution of the United States, shall have engaged in insurrection or rebellion against the same, or given aid or comfort to the enemies thereof. But Congress may by a vote of two-thirds of each House, remove such disability.

Section 4.   The validity of the public debt of the United States, authorized by law, including debts incurred for payment of pensions and bounties for services in suppressing insurrection or rebellion, shall not be questioned. But neither the United States nor any State shall assume or pay any debt or obligation incurred in aid of insurrection or rebellion against the United States, or any claim for the loss or emancipation of any slave, but all such debts, obligations and claims shall be held illegal and void.

Section 5.   The Congress shall have power to enforce, by appropriate legislation, the provisions of this article.

AMENDMENT XV (RATIFIED ON FEBRUARY 3, 1870)

Section 1.   The right of citizens of the United States to vote shall not be denied or abridged by the United States or by any State on account of race, color, or previous condition of servitude.

Section 2.   The Congress shall have power to enforce this article by appropriate legislation.

AMENDMENT XVI (RATIFIED ON FEBRUARY 3, 1913)

The Congress shall have power to lay and collect taxes on incomes, from whatever source derived, without apportionment among the several States, and without regard to any census or enumeration.

AMENDMENT XVII (RATIFIED ON APRIL 8, 1913)

The Senate of the United States shall be composed of two Senators from each State, elected by the people thereof, for six years; and each Senator shall have one vote. The electors in each State shall have the qualifications requisite for electors of the most numerous branch of the State legislatures.

When vacancies happen in the representation of any State in the Senate, the executive authority of such State shall issue writs of election to fill such vacancies: *Provided,* That the legislature of any State may empower the executive thereof to make temporary appointments until the people fill the vacancies by election as the legislature may direct.

This amendment shall not be so construed as to affect the election or term of any Senator chosen before it becomes valid as part of the Constitution.

AMENDMENT XVIII (RATIFIED ON JANUARY 16, 1919)

Section 1.   After one year from the ratification of this article the manufacture, sale, or transportation of intoxicating liquors within, the importation thereof into, or the exportation thereof from the United States and all territory subject to the jurisdiction thereof for beverage purposes is hereby prohibited.

Section 2.   The Congress and the several States shall have concurrent power to enforce this article by appropriate legislation.

Section 3.   This article shall be inoperative unless it shall have been ratified as an amendment to the Constitution by the legislatures of the several States, as provided in the Constitution, within seven years from the date of the submission hereof to the States by the Congress.[15]

AMENDMENT XIX (RATIFIED ON AUGUST 18, 1920)

The right of citizens of the United States to vote shall not be denied or abridged by the United States or by any State on account of sex.

Congress shall have power to enforce this article by appropriate legislation.

AMENDMENT XX (RATIFIED ON JANUARY 23, 1933)

Section 1.   The terms of the President and Vice President shall end at noon on the 20th day of January, and the terms of Senators and Representatives at noon on the 3rd day of January, of the years in which such terms would have ended if this article had not been ratified, and the terms of their successors shall then begin.

---

15. The Eighteenth Amendment was repealed by the Twenty-first Amendment.

Section 2. The Congress shall assemble at least once in every year, and such meeting shall begin at noon on the 3rd day of January, unless they shall by law appoint a different day.

Section 3. If, at the time fixed for the beginning of the term of the President, the President elect shall have died, the Vice President elect shall become President. If a President shall not have been chosen before the time fixed for the beginning of his term, or if the President elect shall have failed to qualify, then the Vice President elect shall act as President until a President shall have qualified; and the Congress may by law provide for the case wherein neither a President elect nor a Vice President elect shall have qualified, declaring who shall then act as President, or the manner in which one who is to act shall be selected, and such person shall act accordingly until a President or Vice President shall have qualified.

Section 4. The Congress may by law provide for the case of the death of any of the persons from whom the House of Representatives may choose a President whenever the rights of choice shall have devolved upon them, and for the case of the death of any of the persons from whom the Senate may choose a Vice President whenever the right of choice shall have devolved upon them.

Section 5. Sections 1 and 2 shall take effect on the 15th day of October following the ratification of this article.

Section 6. This article shall be inoperative unless it shall have been ratified as an amendment to the Constitution by the legislatures of three-fourths of the several States within seven years from the date of its submission.

AMENDMENT XXI (RATIFIED ON DECEMBER 5, 1933)

Section 1. The eighteenth article of amendment to the Constitution of the United States is hereby repealed.

Section 2. The transportation or importation into any State, Territory, or possession of the United States for delivery or use therein of intoxicating liquors, in violation of the laws thereof, is hereby prohibited.

Section 3. This article shall be inoperative unless it shall have been ratified as an amendment to the Constitution by conventions in the several States, as provided in the Constitution, within seven years from the date of the submission hereof to the States by the Congress.

AMENDMENT XXII (RATIFIED ON FEBRUARY 27, 1951)

No person shall be elected to the office of the President more than twice, and no person who has held the office of President, or acted as President, for more than two years of a term to which some other person was elected President shall be elected to the office of the President more than once. But this Article shall not apply to any person holding the office of President when this Article was proposed by the Congress, and shall not prevent any person who may be holding the office of President, or acting as President, during the term within which this Article becomes operative from holding the office of President or acting as President during the remainder of such term.

AMENDMENT XXIII (RATIFIED ON MARCH 29, 1961)

Section 1. The District constituting the seat of Government of the United States shall appoint in such manner as the Congress may direct:

A number of electors of President and Vice President equal to the whole number of Senators and Representatives in Congress to which the District would be entitled if it were a State, but in no event more than the least populous State; they shall be in addition to those appointed by the States, but they shall be considered, for the purposes of the election of President and Vice President, to be electors appointed by a State; and they shall meet in the District and perform such duties as provided by the twelfth article of amendment.

Section 2. The Congress shall have power to enforce this article by appropriate legislation.

AMENDMENT XXIV (RATIFIED ON JANUARY 23, 1964)

Section 1. The right of citizens of the United States to vote in any primary or other election for President or Vice President, for electors for President or Vice President, or for Senator or Representative in Congress, shall not be denied or abridged by the United States or any State by reason of failure to pay any poll tax or other tax.

Section 2. The Congress shall have power to enforce this article by appropriate legislation.

AMENDMENT XXV (RATIFIED ON FEBRUARY 10, 1967)

Section 1. In case of the removal of the President from office or of his death or resignation, the Vice President shall become President.

Section 2. Whenever there is a vacancy in the office of the Vice President, the President shall nominate a Vice

President who shall take office upon confirmation by a majority vote of both Houses of Congress.

Section 3. Whenever the President transmits to the President pro tempore of the Senate and the Speaker of the House of Representatives his written declaration that he is unable to discharge the powers and duties of his office, and until he transmits to them a written declaration to the contrary, such powers and duties shall be discharged by the Vice President as Acting President.

Section 4. Whenever the Vice President and a majority of either the principal officers of the executive departments or of such other body as Congress may by law provide, transmit to the President pro tempore of the Senate and the Speaker of the House of Representatives their written declaration that the President is unable to discharge the powers and duties of his office, the Vice President shall immediately assume the powers and duties of the offices as Acting President.

Thereafter, when the President transmits to the President pro tempore of the Senate and the Speaker of the House of Representatives his written declaration that no inability exists, he shall resume the powers and duties of his office unless the Vice President and a majority of either the principal officers of the executive department or of such other body as Congress may by law provide, transmit within four days to the President pro tempore of the Senate and the Speaker of the House of Representatives their written declaration that the President is unable to discharge the powers and duties of his office. Thereupon Congress shall decide the issue, assembling within forty-eight hours for that purpose if not in session. If the Congress, within twenty-one days after receipt of the latter written declaration, or, if Congress is not in session, within twenty-one days after Congress is required to assemble, determines by two-thirds vote of both Houses that the President is unable to discharge the powers and duties of his office, the Vice President shall continue to discharge the same as Acting President; otherwise; the President shall resume the powers and duties of his office.

AMENDMENT XXVI (RATIFIED ON JULY 1, 1971)

Section 1. The right of citizens of the United States, who are eighteen years of age or older, to vote shall not be denied or abridged by the United States or by any State on account of age.

Section 2. The Congress shall have the power to enforce this article by appropriate legislation.

AMENDMENT XXVII (RATIFIED ON MAY 7, 1992)

No law, varying the compensation for the services of the Senators and Representatives, shall take effect, until an election of Representatives shall have intervened.

Federalist Paper 10

Among the numerous advantages promised by a well-constructed Union, none deserves to be more accurately developed than its tendency to break and control the violence of faction. The friend of popular governments never finds himself so much alarmed for their character and fate as when he contemplates their propensity to this dangerous vice. He will not fail, therefore, to set a due value on any plan which, without violating the principles to which he is attached, provides a proper cure for it. The instability, injustice, and confusion introduced into the public councils have, in truth, been the mortal diseases under which popular governments have everywhere perished, as they continue to be the favorite and fruitful topics from which the adversaries to liberty derive their most specious declamations. The valuable improvements made by the American constitutions on the popular models, both ancient and modern, cannot certainly be too much admired; but it would be an unwarrantable partiality to contend that they have as effectually obviated the danger on this side, as was wished and expected. Complaints are everywhere heard from our most considerate and virtuous citizens, equally the friends of public and private faith and of public and personal liberty, that our governments are too unstable, that the public good is disregarded in the conflicts of rival parties, and that measures are too often decided, not according to the rules of justice and the rights of the minor party, but by the superior force of an interested and overbearing majority. However anxiously we may wish that these complaints had no foundation, the evidence of known facts will not permit us to deny that they are in some degree true. It will be found, indeed, on a candid review of our situation, that some of the distresses under which we labor have been erroneously charged on the operation of our governments; but it will be found, at the same time, that other causes will not alone account for many of our heaviest misfortunes; and, particularly, for that prevailing and increasing distrust of public engagements and alarm for private rights which are echoed from one end of the continent to the other. These must be chiefly, if not wholly, effects of the unsteadiness and injustice with which a factious spirit has tainted our public administration.

By a faction I understand a number of citizens, whether amounting to a majority or minority of the whole, who are united and actuated by some common impulse of passion, or of interest, adverse to the rights of other citizens, or the permanent and aggregate interests of the community.

There are two methods of curing the mischiefs of faction: the one, by removing its causes; the other, by controlling its effects.

There are again two methods of removing the causes of faction: the one, by destroying the liberty which is essential to its existence; the other, by giving to every citizen the same opinions, the same passions, and the same interests.

It could never be more truly said than of the first remedy that it was worse than the disease. Liberty is to faction what air is to fire, an aliment without which it instantly expires. But it could not be a less folly to abolish liberty, which is essential to political life, because it nourishes faction than it would be to wish the annihilation of air, which is essential to animal life, because it imparts to fire its destructive agency.

The second expedient is as impracticable as the first would be unwise. As long as the reason of man continues fallible, and his is at liberty to exercise it, different opinions will be formed. As long as the connection subsists between his reason and his self-love, his opinions and his passions will have a reciprocal influence on each other; and the former will be objects to which the latter will attach themselves. The diversity in the faculties of men, from which the rights of property originate, is not less an insuperable obstacle to a uniformity of interests. The protection of these faculties is the first object of government. From the protection of different and unequal faculties of acquiring property, the possession of different degrees and kinds of property immediately results; and from the influence of these on the sentiments and views of the respective proprietors ensues a division of the society into different interests and parties.

The latent causes of faction are thus sown in the nature of man; and we see them everywhere brought into different degrees of activity, according to the different circumstances of civil society. A zeal for different opinions concerning religion, concerning government, and many other points, as well of speculation as of practice; an attachment to different leaders ambitiously contending for pre-eminence and power; or to persons of other descriptions whose fortunes have been interesting to the human passions, have, in turn, divided mankind into parties, inflamed them with mutual animosity, and rendered them much more disposed to vex and oppress each other than to cooperate for their common good. So strong is this propensity of mankind to fall into mutual animosities that where no substantial occasion presents itself the most frivolous and fanciful distinctions have been sufficient to kindle their unfriendly passions and excite their most violent conflicts. But the most common and durable source of factions has been the various and unequal distribution of property. Those who hold and those who are without property have ever formed distinct interests in society. Those who are creditors, and those who are debtors, fall under a like discrimination. A landed interest, a manufacturing interest, a mercantile interest, a moneyed interest, with many lesser interests, grow up of necessity in civilized nations, and divide them into different classes, actuated by different sentiments and views. The regulation of these various and interfering interests forms the principal task of modern legislation and involves the spirit of party and faction in the necessary and ordinary operations of government.

No man is allowed to be a judge in his own cause, because his interest would certainly bias his judgment, and, not improbably, corrupt his integrity. With equal, nay with greater reason, a body of men are unfit to be both judges and parties at the same time; yet what are many of the most important acts of legislation but so many judicial determinations, not indeed concerning the rights of single persons, but concerning the rights of large bodies of citizens? And what are the different classes of legislators but advocates and parties to the causes which they determine? Is a law proposed concerning private debts? It is a question to which the creditors are parties on one side and the debtors on the other. Justice ought to hold the balance between them. Yet the parties are, and must be, themselves the judges; and the most numerous party, or in other words, the most powerful faction must be expected to prevail. Shall domestic manufacturers be encouraged, and in what degree, by restrictions on foreign manufacturers? are questions which would be differently decided by the landed and the manufacturing classes, and probably by neither with a sole regard to justice and the public good. The apportionment of taxes on the various descriptions of property is an act which seems to require the most exact impartiality; yet there is, perhaps, no legislative act in which greater opportunity and temptation are given to a predominant party to trample on the rules of justice. Every shilling with which they overburden the inferior number is a shilling saved to their own pockets. It is in vain to say that enlightened statesmen will be able to adjust these clashing interests and render them all subservient to the public good. Enlightened statesmen will not always be at the helm. Nor, in many cases, can such an adjustment be made at all without taking into view indirect and remote considerations, which will rarely prevail over the immediate interest which one party may find in disregarding the rights of another or the good of the whole.

The inference to which we are brought is that the *causes* of faction cannot be removed and that relief is only to be sought in the means of controlling its *effects.*

If a faction consists of less than a majority, relief is supplied by the republican principle, which enables the majority to defeat its sinister views by regular vote. It may clog the administration, it may convulse the society; but it will be unable to execute and mask its violence under the forms of the Constitution. When a majority is included in a faction, the form of popular government, on the other hand, enables it to sacrifice to its ruling passion or interest both the public good and the rights of other citizens. To secure the public good and private rights against the danger of such a faction, and at the same time to preserve the spirit and the form of popular government, is then the great object to which our inquiries are directed. Let me add that it is the great desideratum by which alone this form of government can be rescued from the opprobrium under which it has so long labored and be recommended to the esteem and adoption of mankind.

By what means is this object attainable? Evidently by one of two only. Either the existence of the same passion or interest in a majority at the same time must be prevented, or the majority, having such coexistent passion or interest, must be rendered, by their number and local situation, unable to concert and carry into effect schemes of oppression. If the impulse and the opportunity be suffered to coincide, we well know that neither moral nor religious motives can be relied on as an adequate control. They are not found to be such on the injustice and violence of individuals, and lose their efficacy in proportion to the number combined together, that is, in proportion as their efficacy becomes needful.

From this view of the subject it may be concluded that a pure democracy, by which I mean a society consisting of a small number of citizens, who assemble and administer the government in person, can admit of no cure for the mischiefs of faction. A common passion or interest will, in almost every case, be felt by a majority of the whole; a communication and concert results from the form of government itself; and there is nothing to check the inducements to sacrifice the weaker party or an obnoxious individual. Hence it is that such democracies have ever been spectacles of turbulence and contention; have ever been found incompatible with personal security or the rights of property; and have in general been as short in their lives as they have been violent in their deaths. Theoretic politicians, who have patronized this species of government, have erroneously supposed that by reducing mankind to a perfect equality in their political rights, they would at the same time be perfectly equalized and assimilated in their possessions, their opinions, and their passions.

A republic, by which I mean a government in which the scheme of representation takes place, opens a different prospect and promises the cure for which we are seeking. Let us examine the points in which it varies from pure democracy, and we shall comprehend both the nature of the cure and the efficacy which it must derive from the Union.

The two great points of difference between a democracy and a republic are: first, the delegation of the government, in the latter, to a small number of citizens elected by the rest; secondly, the greater number of citizens and greater sphere of country over which the latter may be extended.

The effect of the first difference is, on the one hand, to refine and enlarge the public views by passing them through the medium of a chosen body of citizens, whose wisdom may best discern the true interest of their country and whose patriotism and love of justice will be least likely to sacrifice it to temporary or partial considerations. Under such a regulation it may well happen that the public voice, pronounced by the representatives of the people, will be more consonant to the public good than if pronounced by the people themselves, convened for the purpose. On the other hand, the effect may be inverted. Men of factious tempers, of local prejudices, or of sinister designs, may, by intrigue, by corruption, or by other means, first obtain the suffrages, and then betray the interests of the people. The question resulting is, whether small or extensive republics are most favorable to the election of proper guardians of the public weal; and it is clearly decided in favor of the latter by two obvious considerations.

In the first place it is to be remarked that however small the republic may be the representatives must be raised to a certain number in order to guard against the cabals of a few; and that however large it may be they must be limited to a certain number in order to guard against the confusion of a multitude. Hence, the number of representatives in the two cases not being in proportion to that of the constituents, and being proportionally greatest in the small republic, it follows that if the proportion of fit characters be not less in the large than in the small republic, the former will present a greater option, and consequently a greater probability of a fit choice.

In the next place, as each representative will be chosen by a greater number of citizens in the large than in the small republic, it will be more difficult for unworthy candidates to practice with success the vicious arts by which elections are too often carried; and the suffrages of the people being more free, will be more likely to center on men who possess the most attractive merit and the most diffusive and established characters.

It must be confessed that in this, as in most other cases, there is a mean, on both sides of which inconveniencies will be found to lie. By enlarging too much the number of electors, you render the representative too little acquainted with all their local circumstances and lesser interests; as by reducing it too much, you render him unduly attached to these, and too little fit to comprehend and pursue great and national objects. The federal Constitution forms a happy combination in this respect; the great and aggregate interests being referred to the national, the local and particular to the State legislatures.

The other point of difference is the greater number of citizens and extent of territory which may be brought within the compass of republican than of democratic government; and it is this circumstance principally which renders factious combinations less to be dreaded in the former than in the latter. The smaller the society, the fewer probably will be the distinct parties and interests composing it; the fewer the distinct parties and interests, the more frequently will a majority be found of the same party; and the smaller the number of individuals composing a majority, and the smaller the compass within which they are placed, the more easily will they concert and execute their plans of oppression. Extend the sphere and you take in a greater variety of parties and interests; you make it less probable that a majority of the whole will have a common motive to invade the rights of other citizens; or if such a common motive exists, it will be more difficult for all who feel it to discover their own strength and to act in unison with each other. Besides other impediments, it may be remarked that, where there is a consciousness of unjust or dishonorable purposes, communication is always checked by distrust in proportion to the number whose concurrence is necessary.

Hence, it clearly appears that the same advantage which a republic has over a democracy in controlling the effects of faction is enjoyed by a large over a small republic—is enjoyed by the Union over the States composing it. Does this advantage consist in the substitution of representatives whose enlightened views and virtuous sentiments render them superior to local prejudices and to schemes of injustice? It will not be denied that the representation of the Union will be most likely to possess these requisite endowments. Does it consist in the greater security afforded by a greater variety of parties, against the event of any one party being able to outnumber and oppress the rest? In an equal degree does the increased variety of parties comprised within the Union increase this security. Does it, in fine, consist in the greater obstacles opposed to the concert and accomplishment of the secret wishes of an unjust and interested majority? Here again the extent of the Union gives it the most palpable advantage.

The influence of factious leaders may kindle a flame within their particular States but will be unable to spread a general conflagration through the other States. A religious sect may degenerate into a political faction in a part of the Confederacy; but the variety of sects dispersed over the entire face of it must secure the national councils against any danger from that source. A rage for paper money, for an abolition of debts, for an equal division of property, or for any other improper or wicked project, will be less apt to pervade the whole body of the Union than a particular member of it, in the same proportion as such a malady is more likely to taint a particular county or district than an entire State.

In the extent and proper structure of the Union, therefore, we behold a republican remedy for the diseases most incident to republican government. And according to the degree of pleasure and pride we feel in being republicans ought to be our zeal in cherishing the spirit and supporting the character of federalists.

Federalist Paper 51

To what expedient, then, shall we finally resort, for maintaining in practice the necessary partition of power among the several departments as laid down in the Constitution? The only answer that can be given is that as all these exterior provisions are found to be inadequate the defect must be supplied, by so contriving the interior structure of the government as that its several constituent parts may, by their mutual relations, be the means of keeping each other in their proper places. Without presuming to undertake a full development of this important idea I will hazard a few general observations which may perhaps place it in a clearer light, and enable us to form a more correct judgment of the principles and structure of the government planned by the convention.

In order to lay a due foundation for that separate and distinct exercise of the different powers of government, which to a certain extent is admitted on all hands to be essential to the preservation of liberty, it is evident that each department should have a will of its own; and consequently should be so constituted that the members of each should have as little agency as possible in the appointment of the members of the others. Were this principle rigorously adhered to, it would require that all the appointments for the supreme executive, legislative, and judiciary magistracies should be drawn from the same fountain of authority, the people, through channels having no communication whatever with one another. Perhaps such a plan of constructing the several departments would be less difficult in practice than it may in contemplation appear. Some difficulties, however, and some additional expense would attend the execution of it. Some deviations, therefore, from the principle must be admitted. In the constitution of the judiciary department in particular, it might be inexpedient to insist rigorously on the principle: first, because peculiar qualifications being essential in the members, the primary consideration ought to be to select that mode of choice which best secures these qualifications; second, because the permanent tenure by which the appointments are held in that department must soon destroy all sense of dependence on the authority conferring them.

It is equally evident that the members of each department should be as little dependent as possible on those of the others for the emoluments annexed to their offices. Were the executive magistrate, or the judges, not independent of the legislature in this particular, their independence in every other would be merely nominal.

But the great security against a gradual concentration of the several powers in the same department consists in giving to those who administer each department the necessary constitutional means and personal motives to resist encroachments of the others. The provision for defense must in this, as in all other cases, be made commensurate to the danger of attack. Ambition must be made to counteract ambition. The interest of the man must be connected with the constitutional rights of the place. It may be a reflection on human nature that such devices should be necessary to control the abuses of government. But what is government itself but the greatest of all reflections on human nature? If men were angels, no government would be necessary. If angels were to govern men, neither external nor internal controls on government would be necessary. In framing a government which is to be administered by men over men, the great difficulty lies in this: you must first enable the government to control the governed; and in the next place oblige it to control itself. A dependence on the people is, no doubt, the primary control on the government; but experience has taught mankind the necessity of auxiliary precautions.

This policy of supplying, by opposite and rival interests, the defect of better motives, might be traced through the whole system of human affairs, private as well as public. We see it particularly displayed in all the subordinate distributions of power, where the constant aim is to divide and arrange the several offices in such a manner as that each may be a check on the other—that the private interest of every individual may be a sentinel over the public rights. These inventions of prudence cannot be less requisite in the distribution of the supreme powers of the State.

But it is not possible to give to each department an equal power of self-defense. In republican government, the legislative authority necessarily predominates. The remedy for this inconveniency is to divide the legislature into different branches; and to render them, by different modes of election and different principles of action, as little connected with each other as the nature of their common functions and their common dependence on the society will admit. It may even be necessary to guard against dangerous encroachments by still further precautions. As the weight of the legislative authority requires that it should be thus divided, the weakness of the executive may require, on the other hand, that it should be fortified. An absolute negative on the legislature appears, at first view, to be the natural defense with which the executive magistrate should be armed. But perhaps it would be neither altogether safe nor alone sufficient. On ordinary occasions it might not be exerted with the requisite firmness, and on extraordinary occasions it might be perfidiously abused. May not this defect of an absolute negative be supplied by some qualified connection between this weaker department and the weaker branch of the stronger department, by which the latter may be led to support the constitutional rights of the former, without being too much detached from the rights of its own department?

If the principles on which these observations are found be just, as I persuade myself they are, and they be applied as a criterion to the several State constitutions, and the federal Constitution, it will be found that if the latter does not perfectly correspond with them, the former are infinitely less able to bear such a test.

There are, moreover, two considerations particularly applicable to the federal system of America, which place that system in a very interesting point of view.

First. In a single republic, all the power surrendered by the people is submitted to the administration of a single government; and the usurpations are guarded against by a division of the government into distinct and separate departments. In the compound republic of America, the power surrendered by the people is first divided between two distinct governments, and then the portion allotted to each subdivided among distinct and separate departments. Hence a double security arises to the rights of the people. The different governments will control each other, at the same time that each will be controlled by itself.

Second. It is of great importance in a republic not only to guard the society against the oppression of its rulers, but to guard one part of the society against the injustice of the other part. Different interests necessarily exist in different classes of citizens. If a majority be united by a common interest, the rights of the minority will be insecure. There are but two methods of providing against this evil: the one by creating a will in the community independent of the majority—that is, of the society itself; the other, by comprehending in the society so many separate descriptions of citizens as will render an unjust combination of a majority of the whole very improbable, if not impracticable. The first method prevails in all governments possessing an hereditary or self-appointed authority. This, at best, is but a precarious security; because a power independent of the society may as well espouse the unjust views of the major as the rightful interests of the minor party, and may possibly be turned against both parties. The second method will be exemplified in the federal republic of the United States. Whilst all authority in it will be derived from and dependent on the society, the society itself will be broken into so many parts, interests and classes of citizens, that the rights of individuals, or of the minority, will be in little danger from interested combinations of the majority. In a free government the security for civil rights must be the same as that for religious rights. It consists in the one case in the multiplicity of interests, and in the other in the multiplicity of sects. The degree of security in both cases will depend on the number of interests and sects; and this may be presumed to depend on the extent of country and number of people comprehended under the same government. This view of the subject must particularly recommend a proper federal system to all the sincere and considerate friends of republican government, since it shows that in exact proportion as the territory of the Union may be formed into more circumscribed Confederacies, or States, oppressive combinations of a majority will be facilitated; the best security, under the republican forms, for the rights of every class of citizen, will be diminished; and consequently the stability and independence of some member of the government, the only other security, must be proportionally increased. Justice is the end of government. It is the end of civil society. It ever has been and ever will be pursued until it be obtained, or until liberty be lost in the pursuit. In a society under the forms of which the stronger faction can readily unite and oppress the weaker, anarchy may as truly be said to reign as in a state of nature, where the weaker individual is not secured against the violence of the stronger; and as, in the latter state, even the stronger individuals are prompted, by the uncertainty of their condition, to submit to a government which may protect the weak as well as themselves; so, in the former state, will the more powerful factions or parties be gradually induced, by a like motive, to wish for a government which will protect all parties, the weaker as well as the more powerful. It can be little doubted that if the State of Rhode Island was separated from the Confederacy and left to itself, the insecurity of rights under the popular form of government within such narrow limits would be displayed by such reiterated oppressions of factious majorities that some power altogether independent of the people would soon be called for by the voice of the very factions whose misrule had proved the necessity of it. In the extended republic of the United States, and among the great variety of interests, parties, and sects which it embraces, a coalition of a majority of the whole society could seldom take place on any other principles than those of justice and the general good; whilst there being thus less danger to a minor from the will of a major party, there must be less pretext, also, to provide for the security of the former, by introducing into the government a will not dependent on the latter, or, in other words, a will independent of the society itself. It is no less certain than it is important, notwithstanding the contrary opinions which have been entertained, that the larger the society, provided it lie within a practicable sphere, the more duly capable it will be of self-government. And happily for the *republican cause,* the practicable sphere may be carried to a very great extent by a judicious modification and mixture of the *federal principle.*

Abraham Lincoln's Gettysburg Address

President Abraham Lincoln gave this speech on November 19, 1863 as he dedicated the Soldier's National Cemetary in Gettysburg, Pennsylvania. Earlier that year, in July, Union troops had defeated the Confederate Army at the Battle of Gettysburg, with a loss of 6000 lives and 38,000 wounded or missing of the estimated 160,000 troops fighting this three-day battle.

Four score and seven years ago our fathers brought forth on this continent a new nation, conceived in liberty and dedicated to the proposition that all men are created equal. Now we are engaged in a great Civil War, testing whether that nation or any nation so conceived and so dedicated can long endure. We are met on a great battlefield of that war. We have come to dedicate a portion of that field as a final resting place for those who here gave their lives that that nation might live.

It is altogether fitting and proper that we should do this. But in a larger sense, we cannot dedicate—we cannot consecrate—we cannot hallow this ground. The brave men, living and dead, who struggled here have consecrated it far above our poor power to add or detract. The world will little note nor long remember what we say here, but it can never forget what they did here. It is for us the living, rather, to be dedicated here to the unfinished work which they who fought here have thus far so nobly advanced. It is rather for us to be here dedicated to the great task remaining before us—that from these honored dead we take increased devotion to that cause for which they gave the last full measure of devotion—that we here highly resolve that these dead shall not have died in vain, that this nation, under God, shall have a new birth of freedom, and that government of the people, by the people, for the people shall not perish from the earth.

ENDNOTES ○

NOTE: *The page numbers and titles of articles cited from major newspapers vary depending on whether the citation is from an online or print edition or from a metropolitan or national edition.*

Introduction

[1] Garry Wills, *A Necessary Evil: A History of American Distrust of Government* (New York: Simon & Schuster, 1999), 320.

[2] Ibid.

[3] Thomas Hobbes (1588–1679), an English philosopher whose work was known and cited by the Founders.

[4] Margit Tavits, "The Size of Government in Majoritarian and Consensus Democracies," *Comparative Political Studies* 37 (2004), 340, / cps.sagepub.com/cgi/content/abstract/37/3/340 DOI: 10.1177/0010414003262068; Heinz Handler, Bertrand Koebel, Philipp Reiss, and Margit Schratzenstaller, "The Size and Performance of Public Sector Activities in Europe," *Public Economics,* No. 0507011, http://ideas.repec.org/p/wpa/wuwppe/0507011.html.

[5] There are some exceptions. The United States has a much larger military and defense establishment, a more extensive criminal justice system, a more extensive public education system, and more pervasive civil rights regulations. John W. Kingdon, *America the Unusual* (Boston: Bedford/St. Martin's, 1999).

[6] Although the Pilgrims had been persecuted in England, when they moved to Holland they were tolerated. In fact, they feared that their children would adopt Dutch ways and stray from their own religion, so they fled Holland for America. Richard Shenkman, *"I Love Paul Revere, Whether He Rode or Not"* (New York: HarperPerennial, 1991), 20–21.

[7] Seymour Martin Lipset, "Why No Socialism in the United States?" in *Sources of Contemporary Radicalism,* eds. Seweryn Bialer and Sophis Sluzar (Boulder, Colo.: Westview Press, 1977), 86.

[8] Robert Calhoon, *The Loyalists in Revolutionary America, 1766–1781* (New York: Harcourt Brace Javanovich, 1973).

[9] For elaboration of this process and an explanation of the theory of path dependence, see Kingdon, *America the Unusual.* There is also a hypothesis among scientists that the early settlers, as well as later immigrants, had a different genetic makeup than the people they left behind. That is, along with their views they brought their DNA, which predisposed them to restless curiosity, novelty seeking, and risk taking. The scientists are looking for genetic markers that would confirm this hypothesis. Thus immigrants may be a self-selected group in more than the obvious ways. Emily Bazelon, "The Hypomanic

American," *New York Times Magazine,* December 12, 2006, 76.

[10] Janes Madison, *Federalist Paper* 51.

[11] Richard Neustadt, *The American Presidency,* episode 5, PBS, April 2000.

[12] Adam Cohen, *Nothing to Fear: FDR's Inner Circle and the Hundred Days That Created Modern America* (New York: Penguin, 2009), 14–15.

[13] James L. Sundquist, *Dynamics of the Party System* (Washington, D.C.: Brookings Institution, 1973), 191.

[14] Cohen, *Nothing to Fear,* 16.

[15] The mother of a coauthor of this text has vivid memories of these requests night after night as a child in Davenport, Iowa.

[16] Cohen, *Nothing to Fear,* 1.

[17] Ibid., 15–16.

[18] *Time,* February 1, 1982, 25.

[19] Karl Vick, "A President Who Woke Up Washington," *Washington Post National Weekly Edition,* April 28, 1997, 8.

[20] Theodore J. Lowi, *The Personal President* (Ithaca, N.Y.: Cornell University Press, 1985), 44.

[21] Ibid., xi.

[22] Daniel J. Elazar, *The American Partnership* (Chicago: University of Chicago Press, 1962).

[23] For examination of this growth spurt, see Garry Wills, *Bomb Power: The Modern Presidency and the National Security State* (New York: Penguin, 2010).

[24] Timothy Conlan, *From Federalism to Devolution: Twenty-five Years of Intergovernmental Reform* (Washington, D.C.: Brookings Institution, 1998), 6.

[25] President Clinton and congressional Democrats were able to reduce military spending somewhat during the 1990s because the Cold War had ended and fears of terrorism had not yet taken hold among the public.

[26] Adam Sheingate, "Why Can't Americans See the State?" *The Forum* 7, no. 4 (2009), http://www.bepress.com/forum/vol7/iss4/art1.

[27] *Statistical Abstract of the United States, 2010,* tab. 449.

[28] The health spending data are from 2006, the most recent date that form of the question was asked on this national survey. An alternative question, asked most years since 1983, found that, over time, 54 percent thought government should help the sick and another 30 percent thought that both government and families

themselves should help the sick. The 2006 percentages were almost identical.

[29] Data from the American National Election Study of 2008. http://www.themonkeycage.org/2010/02/corrected_graph_for_conflicted.html.

[30] Frank Newport, "Americans Concerned about Government Spending, Expansion," http://www.gallup.com/poll/121829/americans-concerned-govt-spending-expansion.aspx.

[31] Frederick Rudolph, "The American Liberty League, 1934–1940," *American Historical Review* 56 (October 1950), 19–33.

[32] Frank Luntz, "What Americans Really Want," *Los Angeles Times,* September 27, 2009, latimes.com/news/opinion/la-oe-luntz27-2009sep27,0,4242608.story.

[33] Andy Serwer, "The Decade from Hell," *Time,* December 7, 2009, 30–38.

[34] Pollster Bill McInturff, quoted in Nina Easton, "The End of Audacity," *Time,* December 14, 2009, 33.

[35] Michael Hirsh and Daniel Gross, "The Wisdom of Crowds; When Populist Rage Leads to Smart Policy," *Newsweek,* February 8, 2010, 27.

[36] A reproduction of his birth certificate is found on line at http://latimesblogs.latimes.com/.shared/image.html?/photos/uncategorized/2008/06/13/bobirthcertificate.jp The Department of Health of the state of Hawaii has a website to deal with inquiries about the birth certificate, including a statement that both the Director of Health and the Registrar of Vital Statistics have personally seen and verified that the State Department of Health has Obama's original birth certificate on record. http://hawaii.gov/health/vital-records/obama.html; http://hawaii.gov/health/about/pr/2008/08-93.pdf.

[37] Joe Klein, "The Character Question," *Time,* September 21, 2009, 24.

[38] Sam Tanenhaus, "North Star: Populism, Politics, and the Power of Sarah Palin," *New Yorker,* December 7, 2009, 88.

[39] Robin Abcarian, Kate Linthicum, and Richard Fausett, "Conservatives Say It's Their Turn for Empowerment," *Los Angeles Times,* September 17, 2009, latimes.com/news/nationworld/nation/la-na-white-victimhood17-2009sep17,0,2618101.story.

[40] Tim Rutten, "America the Delusional."*Los Angeles Times, August 19, 2009.* http://articles.latimes.com/2009/aug/19/opinion/oe-rutten19.

[41] John Jeremiah Sullivan, "American Rage," *GQ*, January 2010, 69.

[42] After chastising the Republican representative who hosted the meeting for "ignoring" Obama's birth certificate. Jim Nelson, "What We Talk about When We Talk about Birth Certificates," *GQ*, September 2009, 108.

[43] See, in general, Ben McGrath, "The Movement," *New Yorker,* February 1, 2010, 40–49.

[44] Matt Bai, "The New Old Guard," *New York Times Magazine,* August 30, 2009, 11–12.

[45] http://www.nationaljournal.com/njonline/mp_20100219_9614.php.

[46] "Open-carry laws" allow people to carry loaded weapons in public places. At one appearance in Arizona, at least a dozen people displayed weapons, including assault rifles. Rutten, "America the Delusional."

[47] Robert Draper, "This Year's Maverick," *New York Times Magazine,* July 4, 2010, 24.

[48] Frank Rich, "The Obama Haters' Silent Enablers," *New York Times,* June 14, 2009, WK8.

[49] Kathleen Hennessey, "'Tea Party' Convention a Forum for Woes, Worries," *Los Angeles Times,* February 6, 2010, latimes.com/news/nationworld/nation/la-na-tea-party6-2010feb06,0,568141.story.

[50] Virginia A. Chanley, "Trust in Government in the Aftermath of 9/11," *Political Psychology* 23, no. 3, (December, 2002): 469–483; Timothy E. Cook and Paul Gronke, "The Skeptical American: Revisiting the Meanings of Trust in Government," *Journal of Politics* 67, no. 3 (August 2005), 784–803; Jack Citrin and Donald Philip Green, "Presidential Leadership and the Resurgence of Trust in Government," *British Journal of Political Science* 16, no. 4 (October 1986), 431–453.

[51] Elaine C. Karmack, "The Evolving American State: The Trust Challenge," *The Forum* 7, no. 4 (2009), 2, 10, http://www.bepress.com/forum/vol7/iss4/art9.

[52] CBS/New York Times poll, February 2010, http://document.nytimes.com/new-york-times-cbs-news-poll.

[53] In the Gallup poll. Christopher Hayes, "The Twilight of the Elites," *Time,* March 22, 2010, 56.

[54] http://www.gallup.com/poll/116599/Economy-Republicans-Trust-Business-Dems-Trust-Gov.aspx.

[55] Views on major institutions drawn from Harris poll, February 16–21, 2010, from a national survey of about 1000 adults. PollingReport.com.

[56] Wills, *A Necessary Evil*, 320 and 16.

[57] Karmack, "The Evolving American State," 1.

[58] The quote is from Harold Lasswell.

[59] Survey of Tea Party supporters and others, reported in http://www.nytimes.com/interactive/2010/04/14/us/politics/20100414-tea-party-poll-graphic.html?ref=politics#tab=0. This was a New York Times/CBS News poll done in April 2010 with 1580 adults, including an oversample of Tea Party supporters.

[60] John Hibbing and Elizabeth Theiss-Morse, *Congress as Public Enemy* (New York: Cambridge University Press, 1995).

Chapter 1

[1] In a copy of his 1915 book, *America and the World War,* presented to the great American novelist, Roosevelt wrote "To Edith Wharton from an American-American." Quoted in Alan Cowell, "After a Century, an American Writer's Library Will Go to America," *New York Times,* December 15, 2005, E1.

[2] Roosevelt quotations in this section are from Theodore Roosevelt, "True Americanism," in *American Ideals and Other Essays* (New York: Putnam's Knickerbocker Press, 1901), 15–34.

[3] Walt Whitman, Preface to *Leaves of Grass* (1855), in *Leaves of Grass and Selected Prose,* ed. Lawrence Buell (New York: Random House, 1981), 449.

[4] Edward Countryman, *Americans: A Collision of Histories* (New York: Hill & Wang, 1996).

[5] John Sugden, *Tecumseh: A Life* (New York: Holt, 1998).

[6] U.S. Immigration and Naturalization Service, *2000 Statistical Yearbook of the Immigration and Naturalization Service* (Washington, D.C.: Government Printing Office, 2000). These are estimates; the government collects detention and return figures but has not collected emigration data since 1957.

[7] James C. McKinley Jr. and Julia Preston, "U.S. Can't Trace Foreign Visitors on Expired Visas," *New York Times,* October 12, 2009.

[8] Jeffrey S. Passel and D'Vera Cohn, *A Portrait of Unauthorized Immigrants in the United States* Pew Hispanic Center, April 14, 2009), 2,pewhispanic.org/reports/report.php?ReportID=107.

[9] Randall Monger and Nancy Rytina, "U.S. Legal Permanent Residents: 2008," Department of Homeland Security: Office of Immigration Statistics, Annual Flow Report, March 2009, 1.

[10] Ibid., 3.

[11] Ibid., 2.

[12] *2008 Yearbook of Immigration Statistics,* tab. 2, 10, www.ins.gov.

[13] Pew Research Center, *U.S. Population Projections, 2005–2050* Pew Research Center, February 11, 2008, 9. (pewhispanic.org/files/reports/85.pdf)

[14] Kenneth C. Davis, "The Founding Immigrants," *New York Times,* July 3, 2007, A17.

[15] Rich Morin, "The Public Assesses Social Divisions," Pew Research Center, September 24, 2009, 1, pewsocialtrends.org.

[16] Patrick McGee, "They Don't Belong Here," *Champaign-Urbana News-Gazette,* October 28, 2007, B1.

[17] Jean Pfaelzer, *Driven Out: The Forgotten War against Chinese Americans* (Berkeley: University of California Press, 2008).

[18] Kenneth C. Davis, *America's Hidden History: Untold Tales of the First Pilgrims, Fighting Women and Forgotten Founders Who Shaped a Nation* (New York: Smithsonian Books/Collins, 2008).

[19] "Religion and the Founding of the American Republic. Part I: America as a Religious Refuge: The Seventeenth Century," Library of Congress exhibit, lcweb.loc.gov/exhibits/religion.

[20] Nicholas von Hoffman, "God Was Present at the Founding," *Civilization* (April–May 1998), 39.

[21] Michael J. Sandel, *Democracy's Discontent: America in Search of a Public Philosophy* (Cambridge, Mass.: Belknap Press, 1997), 56–57; Gordon S. Wood, *Empire of Liberty: A History of the Early Republic, 1789–1815* (New York: Oxford University Press, 2009), 582–583.

[22] Sarah Mondale and Sarah B. Patton, eds., *School: The Story of American Public Education* (Boston: Beacon Press, 2001), 36.

[23] Elizabeth Becker, "All White, All Christian, and Divided by Diversity," *New York Times*, June 10, 2001, sec. 4, 7. Becker was writing about her hometown.

[24] Anne Farris Rosen, "A Brief History of Religion and the U.S. Census," Pew Forum on Religion and Public Life, January 26, 2010, 1. (pewforum.org/Government/A-Brief-History-of-Religion-and-the-U-S-Census.aspx).

[25] "Summary of Key Findings: U.S. Religious Landscape Survey," Pew Forum on Religion and Public Life, February 26, 2008, 1. The findings are the results of two 2007 surveys for which more than 35,000 adults were interviewed. (religions.pewforum.org/affiliations)

[26] James Q. Wilson, "The History and Future of Democracy," lecture delivered at the Ronald Reagan Presidential Library, November 15, 1999.

[27] If you would like to check the religious affiliations of people in your community or state, the Association of Religion Data Archives contains a user-friendly set of data to allow you to do just that. http://www.thearda.com/.

[28] Morin, "The Public Assesses Social Divisions," 1.

[29] See, for example, the discussion in Larry M Bartels, *Unequal Democracy: The Political Economy of the New Gilded Age* (Princeton: N.J.: Princeton University Press, 2008).

[30] 2010 *Statistical Abstract of the United States,* tab. 690, 452.

[31] Ibid., tab. 8, 12.

[32] On identity politics, see Walter Benn Michaels, *Our America: Nativism, Modernism, and Pluralism* (Durham, N.C.: Duke University Press, 1997).

[33] U.S. Census Bureau, "We the People: American Indians and Alaska Natives in the United States," *Census 200 Special Reports,* February 2006, 2–4.

[34] Jack Hitt, "The Newest Indians," *New York Times Magazine,* August 21, 2005, 38.

[35] Rachel L. Swarns, "Hispanics Resist Racial Grouping by Census," *New York Times,* October 24, 2004, 1.

[36] ABC Evening News with Peter Jennings, February 21, 2005.

[37] Sam Roberts, "Census Shows Growing Diversity in New York City," *New York Times,* December 9, 2008.

[38] "Black Americans: One Race, or More?" *New York Times,* November, 18, 2007, Wk2. Based on survey data from the Pew Research Center.

[39] *Muslim Americans: Middle Class and Mostly Mainstream* (Washington, D.C.: Pew Research Center, November 28, 2007), 1. (pewforum.org/Muslim/Muslim-Americans-Middle-Class-And-Mostly-Mainstream.aspx))

[40] U.S. Census Bureau, *General Social and Economic Characteristics: U.S. Summary*

(Washington, D.C.: Government Printing Office, 1990), pt. 1, tab. 12.

41 *Guess Who's Coming to Dinner: 22% of Americans Have Relative in a Mixed-Race Marriage* (Washington, D.C.: Pew Research Center, May 14, 2008), 1. (pewsocialtrends.org/pubs/304/guess-whos-coming-to-dinner)

42 Estimate from Joshua R. Goldstein, the Max Planck Institute for Demographic Research, quoted in Jodi Kantor, "In First Family, a Nation's Many Faces," *New York Times*, January 21, 2009.

43 The origins of governmental systems are discussed by John Jay in *Federalist Paper 2*.

44 Garry Wills, *Lincoln at Gettysburg: The Words That Remade America* (New York: Simon & Schuster, 1992), 145.

45 Carl F. Kaestle, "Introduction," in *School*, ed. Mondale and Patton, 13.

46 Ibid., 16.

47 For many years, the flag was not flown in battle or over government buildings or public schools.

48 The Spanish-American War and World War I also gave a boost to efforts to use the flag as a symbol.

49 "The Educated Citizen," in *School*, ed. Mondale and Patton, 22.

50 Ibid.

51 Adam Cohen, "According to Webster: One Man's Attempt to Define 'America,'" *New York Times*, February 12, 2006, Sec. 4, 13.

52 Noah Webster quoted in Jack Lynch, "Dr. Johnson's Revolution," *New York Times*, July 2, 2005, sec. 4, A15.

53 Robert Reinhold, "Resentment against New Immigrants," *New York Times*, October 26, 1986, 6E.

54 Brian Friel, "Don't Know Much about History," *National Journal*, August 2, 2003, 2500–2501.

55 A number of polls survey civic literacy periodically, and most show high levels of civic illiteracy. See, for example, www.perforum.org, which regularly updates results from its civics knowledge quiz, and www.firstamendmentcenter.org.

56 For a discussion of the Declaration of Independence's origins in pragmatism versus the political philosophy of the Founders, see Pauline Maier, *American Scripture: Making the Declaration of Independence* (New York: Knopf, 1997).

57 Thomas Hobbes, *Leviathan*, any edition. Originally published London, 1651.

58 John Locke, *Two Treatises of Government* (New York: Hafner, 1947), 184ff. For a comparison of Hobbes's and Locke's influence on the Founders, see Donald S. Lutz and Jack Warren, *A Covenanted People* (Providence, R.I.: The John Carter Brown Library, 1987), 51–53.

59 The writings of Thomas Hobbes also shaped this belief. Hobbes wrote that individuals give up some rights they would have in "a state of nature" to government in exchange for government protection of their remaining rights.

60 For the parallels between a country's emphasis on individual liberty and its deemphasis on government help for less fortunate or successful citizens, see John W. Kingdon, *America the Unusual* (New York: St. Martin's/Worth, 1999).

61 Wilfred M. McClay, "Communitarianism and the Federal Idea," in *Community and Political Thought Today*, eds. Peter Augustine Lawler and Dale McConkey (Westport, Conn.: Praeger, 1998), 102.

62 Joyce Appleby, *Capitalism and a New Social Order: The Republican Vision of the 1790s* (New York: New York University Press, 1984), 50.

63 President Johnson quoted in Tim Funk, "Civil Rights Act of 1964 Paved Way for Prosperity," *Champaign-Urbana News Gazette*, July 11, 2004, B1.

64 Alexis de Tocqueville, *Democracy in America* (New York: Knopf, 1945; originally published 1835).

65 See Michael Parenti, *Democracy for the Few*, 7th ed. (Belmont, Calif.: Wadsworth, 2001), on "permanent losers."

66 For elaboration, see Thomas G. West, *Vindicating the Founders: Race, Sex, Class, and Justice in the Origins of America* (Lanham, Md.: Rowman & Littlefield, 1997), 43–54.

67 From the text of a Pinckney speech at the Constitutional Convention recorded in James Madison, *Notes on Debates in the Federal Convention of 1787* (Athens: Ohio University Press, 1966), 184.

68 Quoted in Anthony Lewis, "Hail and Farewell," *New York Times*, December 15, 2001, A31.

69 This discussion draws on Sidney Verba and Norman Nie, *Participation in America* (New York: Harper & Row, 1972), and Stephen Earl Bennett and Linda L. M. Bennett, "Political Participation," in *Annual Review of Political Science*, ed. Samuel Long (Norwood, N.J.: Ablex, 1986).

70 Alan Wolfe, "Couch Potato Politics," *New York Times*, March 15, 1998, sec. 4, 17.

71 League of Conservative Voters poll, March 2002.

72 John R. Hibbing and Beth Theiss-Morse, *Congress As Public Enemy: Public Attitude toward American Political Institutions* (Cambridge: Cambridge University Press, 1995); John R. Hibbing and Beth Theiss-Morse, "Civics is Not Enough: Teaching Barbarics in K–12," *PS*, March 1996, 57–62.

73 Quinnipiac University poll, March 24, 2010.

Chapter 2

1 Although the term "Tenther" originally was pejorative, lumping its advocates with the "birthers," the term has been embraced by its advocates. tenthamendmentcenter.com, qwertyaltofuori.blogspot.com.

2 For a discussion of the constitutional issues, see Akhil Reed Amar, "Constitutional Objections to Obamacare Don't Hold Up," *Los Angeles Times*, latimes.com/news/opinion/la-oe-amar20-2010jan20,0,4309186.story.

3 For an examination of the "Constitution in Exile" movement, which focuses primarily on regulation of business, see Jeffrey Rosen, "The Unregulated Offensive," *New York Times Magazine*, April 17, 2005, nytimes.com/2005/04/17/magazine/17CONSTITUTION.html?ei=5070&en8a.

4 Timothy Rutten, "Behind the Right's Attack on Obama," *Los Angeles Times*, latimes.com/news/opinion/la-oe-rutten16-2009sep16,0,4840714.story.

5 Or the ruling in *McCulloch* v. *Maryland* in 1819.

6 The Indians, of course, had their own governments, and the Spanish may have established Saint Augustine, Florida, and Santa Fe, New Mexico, before the English established Jamestown. The Spanish settlements were extensions of Spanish colonization of Mexico and were governed by Spanish officials in Mexico City.

7 This is not to suggest that the Pilgrims believed in democracy. Apparently, they were motivated to draft the compact by threats from some on the *Mayflower* that when the ship landed they would "use their owne libertie; for none had power to command them." Thus the compact was designed to bind them to the laws of the colony. Richard Shenkman, *"I Love Paul Revere, Whether He Rode or Not"* (New York: HarperCollins, 1991), 141–142.

8 David Hawke, *A Transaction of Free Men* (New York: Scribner, 1964), 209.

9 For an account of the foreign affairs problems under the Articles of Confederation, see Frederick W. Marks III, *Independence on Trial: Foreign Affairs and the Making of the Constitution* (Baton Rouge: Louisiana State University Press, 1973).

10 Louis Fisher, *President and Congress* (New York: Free Press, 1972), 14.

11 The government under the Articles, however, could boast one major accomplishment: the Northwest Ordinance, adopted in 1787, provided for the government and future statehood of the land west of Pennsylvania (land that would become most of the Great Lakes states). The law also banned slavery in this territory.

12 Gordon S. Wood, "The Origins of the Constitution," *This Constitution: A Bicentennial Chronicle* (Summer 1987), 10–11.

13 Eric Black, *Our Constitution* (Boulder, Colo.: Westview Press, 1988), 6.

14 For development of this idea, see Kenneth M. Dolbeare and Linda J. Medcalf, "The Political Economy of the Constitution," *This Constitution: A Bicentennial Chronicle* (Spring 1987), 4–10.

15 Black, *Our Constitution*, 59.

16 The Constitution would, however, retain numerous positive aspects of the Articles. See Donald S. Lutz, "The Articles of Confederation as the Background to the Federal Republic," *Publius* 20 (Winter 1990), 55–70.

17 Robert McCloskey, *The American Supreme Court* (Chicago: University of Chicago Press, 1960), 29.

18 Robert A. Dahl, *A Preface to Democratic Theory* (Chicago: University of Chicago Press, 1956), 5.

19 Yet according to a poll in 1987, the bicentennial of the Constitution, only 1 percent of the public identified Madison as the one who played the biggest role in creating the Constitution. Most—31 percent—said Thomas Jefferson, who was a diplomat in France during the convention. Black, *Our Constitution*, 15.

Some argue that Hamilton, rather than Madison, was the driving force behind the Constitution, especially if his efforts after ratification—as an influential member of Washington's cabinet and later—are taken into account. Kenneth M. Dolbeare and Linda Medcalf, "The Dark Side of the Constitution," in *The Case against the Constitution: From the Antifederalists to the Present,* eds. Kenneth M. Dolbeare and John F. Manley (Armonk, N.Y.: Sharpe, 1987), 120–141.

[20] Only Hamilton suggested a monarchy, and only one delegate—Gouverneur Morris of Pennsylvania—suggested an aristocracy.

[21] Robert A. Dahl, *How Democratic Is the American Constitution?* (New Haven, Conn.: Yale University Press, 2001), 11–12.

[22] Ibid., 14.

[23] The large states did extract a concession that all taxing and spending bills must originate in the house in which representation is based on population. This provision would allow the large states to take the initiative on these important measures.

[24] For further examination of the compromises at the convention, see Richard Beeman, *The Making of the American Constitution* (New York: Random House, 2009).

[25] Paul Finkelman, "Slavery at the Philadelphia Convention," *This Constitution: A Bicentennial Chronicle* (1987), 25–30.

[26] Ibid., 29.

[27] Ibid., 18.

[28] Quoted in Thomas G. West, *Vindicating the Founders: Race, Sex, Class, and Justice in the Origins of America* (Lanham, Md.: Rowman & Littlefield, 1997), 15.

[29] Theodore J. Lowi, *American Government* (Hinsdale, Ill.: Dryden, 1976), 97.

[30] William Gladstone, quoted in C. Herman Pritchett, *Constitutional Law of the Federal System* (Englewood Cliffs, N.J.: Prentice Hall, 1984), xi.

[31] Quoted in Richard Hofstadter, *The American Political Tradition* (New York: Vintage, 1948), 6–7.

[32] Under some state constitutions.

[33] Federalist Paper 51.

[34] Although we use this term today, neither it nor the word *federal* appears in the Constitution.

[35] In the United States, each state government is unitary with respect to its local governments. The state government can alter or eliminate cities, counties, townships, or school districts.

[36] James Madison, *Federalist Paper 10.*

[37] Madison also saw our vast territory as a way to limit factions, because it would be difficult for a group to extend its influence throughout the entire country.

[38] Creating a separate executive branch and making the selection of president independent of Congress also strengthened the national government, because it gave the president a political base from which to exercise national leadership.

[39] However, the amendment's checkered history indicates that it hasn't always played a significant role in limiting the national government.

[40] Max Farrand, *The Framing of the Constitution of the United States* (New Haven, Conn.: Yale University Press, 1913).

[41] Charles O. Jones, *The Presidency in a Separated System* (Washington, D.C.: Brookings Institution, 1994), 14.

[42] Charles O. Jones, *Separate but Equal Branches* (Chatham, N.J.: Chatham House, 1995), 12.

[43] Federalist Paper 51.

[44] Jones, *Presidency in a Separated System,* 16, thus modifying Neustadt's classic definition of "a government of separated institutions sharing powers." Richard E. Neustadt, *Presidential Power and the Modern Presidents* (New York: Macmillan, 1990), 29.

[45] For elaboration, see Dahl, *How Democratic Is the American Constitution?* 24–25.

[46] Ibid.

[47] Locke called for majority rule but never resolved the conflict between majority rule and natural rights—in particular, the rights of the minority.

[48] Donald S. Lutz, "The Relative Influence of European Writers on Later Eighteenth-Century American Political Thought," *American Political Science Review* 78 (1984), 139–197.

[49] Alpheus T. Mason and Richard H. Leach, *In Quest of Freedom: American Political Thought and Practice,* 2nd ed. (Englewood Cliffs, N.J.: Prentice Hall, 1973), 51.

[50] For development of this idea, see Martin Landau, "A Self-Correcting System: The Constitution of the United States," *This Constitution: A Bicentennial Chronicle* (Summer 1986), 4–10.

[51] John P. Roche, "The Founding Fathers: A Reform Caucus in Action," *American Political Science Review* 55 (1961), 799–816.

[52] Benjamin F. Wright Jr., "The Origins of the Separation of Powers in America," in *Origins of American Political Thought,* ed. John P. Roche (New York: Harper & Row, 1967), 139–162.

[53] Roche, "Founding Fathers," 805.

[54] James MacGregor Burns, *The Vineyard of Liberty* (New York: Knopf, 1982), 33.

[55] Bernard Bailyn, *Voyagers to the West* (New York: Knopf, 1982), 20.

[56] The Boston Tea Party, contrary to myth, was not prompted by higher taxes on British tea. Parliament lowered the taxes to give the British East India Company, facing bankruptcy, an advantage in the colonial market. This threatened American shippers who smuggled tea from Holland and controlled about three-fourths of the market. The shippers resented Parliament's attempt to manipulate the economy from thousands of miles away. Shenkman, *"I Love Paul Revere,"* 155.

[57] Federalist Paper 10.

[58] Of the fifty-five delegates, forty were owners of government bonds that had depreciated under the Articles, and twenty-four were moneylenders. Black, *Our Constitution,* 21.

[59] For elaboration, see Dolbeare and Medcalf, "Dark Side of the Constitution."

[60] Calvin C. Jillson and Cecil L. Eubanks, "The Political Structure of Constitution Making," *American Journal of Political Science* 29 (1984), 435–458.

[61] Jonathan Elliot, *The Debates in the Several State Conventions on the Adoption of the Federal Constitution as Recommended by the General Convention at Philadelphia, in 1787,* 2nd ed., 5 vols. (Philadelphia, 1896), 2: 102.

[62] On Anti-Federalist thinking, see William B. Allen and Gordon Lloyd, eds., *The Essential Antifederalist,* 2nd ed. (Lanham, Md.: University Press of America, 2002); John F. Manley and Kenneth M. Dolbeare, *The Case against the Constitution* (Armonk, N.Y.: Sharpe, 1987).

[63] Richard S. Randall, *American Constitutional Development,* vol. 1, *The Powers of Government* (New York: Longman, 2002), 54.

[64] "A Fundamental Contentment," *This Constitution: A Bicentennial Chronicle* (Fall 1984), 44.

[65] Quoted in Charles Warren, *The Making of the Constitution* (Boston: Little, Brown, 1928), xiv. Jefferson made this observation from afar, as he was serving as ambassador to France at the time of the Constitutional Convention.

[66] Keith Perine, "Congress Shows Little Enthusiasm for Bush's Marriage Amendment," *CQ Weekly* (February 28, 2004), 533.

[67] Alan P. Grimes, *Democracy and the Amendments to the Constitution* (Lexington, Mass.: Lexington Books, 1978). Grimes also shows how the adoption of new amendments reflects the rise of new power blocs in society.

[68] 4 Wheaton 316 (1819).

[69] Historian James McPherson, quoted in George P. Fletcher, *Our Secret Constitution: How Lincoln Redefined American Democracy* (New York: Oxford University Press, 2001), 57. For a similar view, see Bruce Ackerman, *We the People,* vol. 2, *Transformations* (Cambridge, Mass.: Belknap Press, 1998), 10. This discussion borrows heavily from Fletcher and Ackerman and also from Garry Wills, *Lincoln at Gettysburg* (New York: Simon & Schuster, 1992). For a complementary view, see Charles Black, *A New Birth of Freedom: Human Rights, Named and Unnamed* (New York: Grosset/Putnam, 1997).

[70] Many of Lincoln's prejudicial comments came in response to more blatant racist remarks by his opponents. Lincoln abandoned his support for black emigration before he was elected to a second term as president. For a critical perspective on Lincoln's racial views, see Lerone Bennett Jr., *Forced into Glory: Abraham Lincoln's White Dream* (Chicago: Johnson, 2000). For positive perspectives, see William Lee Miller, *Lincoln's Virtues: An Ethical Biography* (New York: Knopf, 2002); and Michael Burlingame, *Abraham Lincoln: A Life* (Baltimore: Johns Hopkins, 2008). Historian Henry Louis Gates aptly calls Lincoln "a recovering racist." "Ten Questions," *Time,* February 16, 2009, 6.

[71] Fletcher, *Our Secret Constitution,* 24.

[72] For examination of the role of abolitionist sentiment on Lincoln's decisions, see James Oakes, *The Radical and the Republican: Frederick Douglass, Abraham Lincoln, and the Triumph of Antislavery Politics* (New York: W. W. Norton, 2007).

[73] Thomas Mallon, "Set in Stone," *New Yorker,* October 13, 2008, 136.

[74] These paragraphs rely on the interpretations of Wills, *Lincoln at Gettysburg,* and Fletcher, *Our Secret Constitution.*

[75] Fletcher, *Our Secret Constitution,* 53.

[76] A precursor of this view was the era of Jacksonian democracy in the 1830s.

[77] A contemporary celebration of the nation as an entity can be seen in the poetry of Walt Whitman.

[78] Wills, *Lincoln at Gettysburg,* 38. Wills insists that this was not a coincidence, and he debunks the notion that Lincoln hastily dashed off his remarks while on his way to the town or to the speech itself (27–31).

[79] Fletcher, *Our Secret Constitution,* 35, 4. Others might nominate Lincoln's second inaugural address, in which he offered reconciliation to the South, or Martin Luther King Jr.'s "I Have a Dream" speech.

[80] The *Dred Scott* case is explained in Chapter 15.

[81] The equal protection clause is covered fully in Chapter 15, and the due process clause is covered fully in Chapter 14.

[82] Fletcher, *Our Secret Constitution,* 25.

[83] In this vein, Congress first experimented with an income tax during the war. It would return to this tax in the decades after the war.

[84] For example, the abolitionist movement and the Fifteenth Amendment would fuel the drive for women's suffrage, as explained in Chapter 15.

[85] E. J. Dionne Jr., "Culture Wars," *Washington Post National Weekly Edition,* March 17–23, 2008, 25.

[86] This section borrows heavily from Ackerman, *We the People,* and Theodore J. Lowi, *The Personal President* (Ithaca, N.Y.: Cornell University Press, 1985). For a different view about the impact of the New Deal, see G. Edward White, *The Constitution and the New Deal* (Cambridge, Mass.: Harvard University Press, 2001).

[87] We never had a pure laissez-faire approach—there always was some governmental regulation—but this is the term most associated with the attitudes of the time.

[88] At least one legal scholar dismisses the notion that the Court's "old men" were reactionaries or fools. Although today people consider them mistaken, at the time they were following established doctrine. Ackerman, *We the People.*

[89] Lowi, *Personal President,* 49. Writers during the Depression and in the decades after it also recognized this as a revolution. Ernest K. Lindley, *The Roosevelt Revolution, First Phase* (New York: Viking, 1933); Mario Einaudi, *The Roosevelt Revolution* (New York: Harcourt, Brace & World, 1959).

[90] Karl Vick, "A President Who Woke Up Washington," *Washington Post National Weekly Edition,* April 28, 1997, 8.

[91] Lowi, *Personal President,* 44.

[92] Ibid., xi; Ackerman, *We the People.*

[93] Of course, the process was evolutionary; the changes did not spring solely from these two crises. Moreover, some might maintain that the Supreme Court under the leadership of Chief Justice Earl Warren in the 1950s and 1960s also remade the Constitution because of its rulings expanding the Bill of Rights. Yet the changes brought about by the Warren Court probably had less impact overall than those wrought by Reconstruction or the New Deal.

[94] For a discussion of the role played by the philosophy of pragmatism in resolving these conflicts, see Fletcher, *Our Secret Constitution,* ch. 11.

[95] Thomas Friedman, "Where Did We Go?" *New York Times,* September 30, 2009, A31.

[96] Henry Steele Commager, *Living Ideas in America* (New York: Harper & Row, 1951), 109.

[97] West, *Vindicating the Founders,* xi.

[98] Parts of the Constitution have been copied by some Latin America countries, Liberia (founded by Americans), and the Philippines (formerly an American territory).

[99] "South Africa Looks at U.S. Constitution," *Lincoln Journal Star,* October 7, 1990; David Remnick, "'We, the People,' from the Russian," *Washington Post National Weekly Edition,* September 10, 1990, 11.

[100] European countries, Australia, Canada, Costa Rica, Israel, Japan, and New Zealand.

[101] Dahl, *How Democratic . . . ?* tabs. 1 and 2, 164–165. Dahl counts only countries that have "strong" federalism, bicameralism, and judicial review.

[102] Jones, *Presidency in a Separated System,* xiii.

[103] Dahl, *How Democratic . . . ?* 115.

[104] Jones, *Presidency in a Separated System,* 3.

[105] Richard Morin, "Happy Days Are Here Again," *Washington Post National Weekly Edition,* August 25, 1997, 35.

[106] About 25 percent split their ticket between candidates for president and representative. In addition, others split their vote between candidates for president and senator or between candidates for representative and senator. For an examination of the research about divided government, see Morris Fiorina, *Divided Government,* 2nd ed. (Boston: Allyn & Bacon, 1996), 153.

[107] John W. Kingdon, *America the Unusual* (Boston: Bedford/St. Martin's, 1999), 7–22. Exceptions include education and regulation of civil rights and the environment. They also include a massive national defense establishment and an extensive criminal justice system. In these aspects, our government is bigger than in many other advanced industrialized countries.

Chapter 3

[1] Kirk Johnson, "States' Rights Is Rallying Cry of Resistance for Lawmakers," *New York Times,* March 16, 2010, A1.

[2] Robert Draper, "It's Just a Texas-Governor Thing," *New York Times Magazine,* December 6, 2009, 34.

[3] Johnson, "States' Rights Is Rallying Cry."

[4] Quinnipiac University National Poll, March 24, 2010, questions 28 and 29, www.quinnipiac.edu/x1295.xml?ReleaseID=1436.

[5] The delegate was George Read of Delaware. See William H. Riker, *Democracy in America,* 2nd ed. (New York: Macmillan, 1965).

[6] William H. Riker, *The Development of American Federalism* (Boston: Kluwer Academic, 1987), 6.

[7] *Federalist Paper 39.*

[8] Riker, *Development of American Federalism,* 17.

[9] Bernard Bailyn, *The Federalist Papers* (Washington, D.C.: Library of Congress, 1998), 14. This is the text of a lecture Bailyn gave in the Bradley Lecture series.

[10] Part of this discussion is drawn from Richard Leach, *American Federalism* (New York: Norton, 1970), ch. 1. See also Christopher Hamilton and Donald Wells, *Federalism, Power and Political Economy: A New Theory of Federalism's Impact on American Life* (Englewood Cliffs, N.J.: Prentice Hall, 1990).

[11] See Madison's discussion of this in *Federalist Paper 39.*

[12] Vernon L. Parrington, *Main Currents in American Thought* (New York: Harcourt, Brace, 1927).

[13] David Truman, "Federalism and the Party System," in *Federalism: Mature and Emergent,* ed. Arthur W. MacMahon (New York: Russell & Russell, 1962), 123.

[14] Alfred Kelly and Winfred Harbeson, *The American Constitution: Its Origins and Development* (New York: Norton, 1976).

[15] Linda Greenhouse, "In Roberts Hearing, Specter Assails Court," *New York Times,* September 15, 2005, 1.

[16] Dan Carney, "Latest Supreme Court Rulings Reinforce the Federalist Trend," *Congressional Quarterly,* June 26, 1999, 1528; Linda Greenhouse, "High Court Faces Moment of Truth in Federalism Cases," *New York Times,* March 28, 1999, 20.

[17] On Nixon's managerial approach to federalism, see Lawrence D. Brown, *New Policies, New Politics: Government's Response to Government's Growth* (Washington, D.C.: Brookings Institution, 1983). The comparative discussion of Lyndon Johnson's, Richard Nixon's, and Ronald Reagan's federalism policies draws on Timothy Conlon, *From New Federalism to Devolution: Twenty-five Years of Intergovernmental Reform* (Washington, D.C.: Brookings Institution, 1998), chs. 1, 6, and 13.

[18] Conlon, *From New Federalism to Devolution,* 109.

[19] See, for example, William J. Clinton, "Federalism," Executive Order 13132, *Federal Register* 54, no. 163 (August 10, 1999), 43255–43259. Clinton discussed his views on state activism and federalism in general with the historian Gary Wills in "The War between the States and Washington," *New York Times Magazine,* July 5, 1998, 26.

[20] Grover Norquist, arguably the most powerful lobbyist in Washington, quoted in Philip Gourevitch, "Fight on the Right," *New Yorker,* April 12, 2004, 37.

[21] David Broder, "Take Back the Initiative," *Washington Post National Weekly Edition,* April 10, 2000, 6.

[22] James W. Brosnan, "Not Taxing Internet Sales Hurts," *Champaign-Urbana News-Gazette,* February 21, 2000, A6.

[23] Rep. Barney Frank (D-Mass.), quoted in Michael Grunwald, "Everybody Talks about States' Rights," *Washington Post National Weekly Edition,* November 1, 1999, 29. Frank was referring to Republicans only, but the quote fits Democrats as well.

[24] Alice Rivlin, *Reviving the American Dream: The Economy, the States, and the Federal Government* (Washington, D.C.: Brookings Institution, 1992).

[25] Jia Lynn Yang, "States: Battling Cleanup," *National Journal,* August 9, 2003, 2544.

[26] *U.S. Budget for Fiscal Year 2011, "Analytical Perspectives"* (Washington, D.C.: Government Printing Office, 2010), tab. 17-1, 254.

[27] For a review of the politics surrounding the law, its provisions, and limitations, see Conlon, *From New Federalism to Devolution,* ch. 13.

[28] National Council of State Legislatures, "Mandate Monitor Overview," 2010, ncls.org/default.aspx?tabid=15850.

[29] "2006 State Homeland Security Directors Survey," Issue Brief of the NGA Center for Best Practices, April 3, 2006, www.nga.org/center.

[30] Pam Belluck, "Mandate for ID Meets Resistance from States," *New York Times,* May 6, 2006, A1; "Real ID Law: States, Feds Working Out Issues," *Champaign-Urbana News-Gazette,* March 22, 2008, A4.

[31] David Dagan, "Personal Politics," Center for Public Integrity Special Report, September 24, 2004, www. publicintegrity.org, 1.

[32] Garry Wills, "War between the States and Washington."

[33] Stephen Labaton, "Washington's Deregulatory Mood Finds Its Opposite in Vexed States," *New York Times,* January 13, 2002, 1.

[34] Gar Alperovitz, "California Split," *New York Times,* February 10, 2007, A15. Alperovitz is a professor of political economy. For a related argument see Pietro S. Nivola, "Rediscovering Federalism," Issues on Governance Studies, Paper #8 (Brookings Institution, July 2007), 1–18.

[35] Quoted in Alperovitz, "California Split," A15.

[36] John Schwartz. "Obama Seems Open to a Broader Role for States," *New York Times,* January 30, 2009.

[37] Neela Banerjee, "Christian Conservatives Turn to Statehouses," *New York Times,* December 13, 2004, 1.

[38] John D. Donahue, "The Disunited States," *Atlantic Monthly,* May 1997, 20.

[39] "Lobbyists, Yes. The People, Maybe" (Editorial), *New York Times,* July 10, 2006, A16.

[40] Letter from the National Governors Association to President George W. Bush, February 3, 2006, www.nga.org.

[41] John M. Broder, "Geography Is Dividing Democrats over Energy," *New York Times,* January 27, 2009.

[42] John M. Broder, "Governors Join in Creating Regional Climate Pacts on Climate Change," *New York Times,* November 15, 2007, A20.

[43] Monica Davey, "States Barter Fish and Bullets to Save Money," *New York Times,* May 23, 2009.

[44] Broder, "Geography Is Dividing Democrats over Energy."

[45] Enid F. Beaumont and Harold Hovey, "State, Local, and Federal Development Policies: New Federalism Patterns, Chaos, or What?" *Public Administration Review* 45 (1985), 327–332; Barry Rubin and C. Kurt Zorn, "Sensible State and Local Development," *Public Administration Review* 45 (1985), 333–339.

[46] Shaila Dewan, "Cities Compete in Hipness Battle to Attract Young," *New York Times,* November 25, 2006, A1.

[47] Robert Pear, "U.S. Report Criticizes States' Use of Medicaid Consultants," *New York Times,* June 28, 2005, A20.

[48] John Tierney, "New York Wants Its Money Back, or at Least Some of It," *New York Times,* June 27, 2004, sect. 4, 4.

[49] A discussion of current issues in state-tribal relations can be found at the National Conference of State Legislatures' website, www.ncsl.org.

[50] Tom Brokaw, "Small-Town Big Spending," *New York Times,* April 20, 2009; Maura J. Casey, "When the Watchdogs Don't Bark," *New York Times,* December 31, 2008.

[51] Dagan, "Personal Politics," 1, www.publicintegrity.org.

[52] "Hot-Button Vox Pop" (Editorial), *New York Times,* November 10, 2006, A30.

[53] "That Flurry of Ballot Questions" (Editorial), *New York Times,* November 5, 2005, A16.

[54] Wills, "War between the States and Washington," 27.

[55] Jennifer Steinhauer, "In California, Coastal Commission Wields Vast Power," *New York Times,* February 23, 2008, A10.

[56] Jennifer Steinhauer, "Top Judge Calls Calif. Government 'Dysfunctional,'" *New York Times,* October 11, 2009, 23.

[57] Katherine Sullivan, "In Defense of Federal Power," *New York Times Magazine,* August 18, 1996, 36.

[58] NBC News/*Wall Street Journal* poll, December 2001; both CBS and Gallup polls in June 2002 showed declining approval levels for Congress and the Supreme Court. Data for 2006 from Pew Research Center survey cited by David Brooks, "The Age of Skepticism," *New York Times,* December 1, 2005, A33.

Chapter 4

[1] Scott Keeter, "Young Voters in the 2008 Presidential Primaries," Pew Research Center Publications, February 11, 2008, pewresearch.org/pubs/730/young-voters.

[2] Conducted by the National Constitution Center.

[3] The Center for Information & Research on Civic Learning and Engagement, Tufts University, Jonathan M. Tisch College of Citizenship and Public Service, Quick Facts, "Massachusetts Senate Election: Youth Turnout Was Just 15%, Compared to 57% for Older Citizens; Young Voters Favored Coakley," http://www.civicyouth.org/ (accessed February 4, 2010).

[4] Rasmussen Reports. *Obama Approval Index Month-by-Month.* June 2, 2010. http://www.rasmussenreports.com/public_content/politics/obama_administration/obama_approval_index_month_by_month. Accessed July 28, 2010.

[5] Timothy E. Cook, "The Bear Market in Political Socialization and the Costs of Misunderstood Psychological Theories," *American Political Science Review* 79 (1985), 1079–1093.

[6] S. W. Moore et al., "The Civic Awareness of Five- and Six-Year-Olds," *Western Political Quarterly* 29 (1976), 418.

[7] R. W. Connell, *The Child's Construction of Politics* (Carlton, Australia: Melbourne University Press, 1971).

[8] Fred I. Greenstein, *Children and Politics* (New Haven, Conn.: Yale University Press, 1965), 122; see also Fred I. Greenstein, "The Benevolent Leader Re-visited: Children's Images of Political Leaders in Three Democracies," *American Political Science Review* 69 (1975), 1317–1398; Robert D. Hess and Judith V. Torney, *The Development of Political Attitudes in Children* (Chicago: Aldine, 1967).

[9] Amy Carter and Ryan Teten, "Assessing Changing Views of the President: Ravishing Greenstein's Children and Politics," *Presidential Studies Quarterly* 32 (2002), 453–462.

[10] Greenstein, *Children and Politics.*

[11] Hess and Torney, *The Development of Political Attitudes in Children;* Connell, *The Child's Construction of Politics.*

[12] Greenstein, *Children and Politics;* Greenstein, "The Benevolent Leader Revisited"; and Hess and Torney, *The Development of Political Attitudes in Children.*

[13] Connell, *The Child's Construction of Politics.*

[14] Carter and Teten, "Assessing Changing Views."

[15] F. Christopher Arterton, "The Impact of Watergate on Children's Attitudes toward the President," *Political Science Quarterly* 89 (1974), 269–288; see also P. Frederick Hartwig and Charles Tidmarch, "Children and Political Reality: Changing Images of the President," paper presented at the 1974 Annual Meeting of the Southern Political Science Association; J. Dennis and C. Webster, "Children's Images of the President and Government in 1962 and 1974," *American Politics Quarterly* 4 (1975), 386–405; Robert Hawkins, Suzanne Pingree, and D. Roberts, "Watergate and Political Socialization," *American Politics Quarterly* 4 (1975), 406–436.

[16] Gallup Organization, "Public Trust in Federal Government Remains High," January 8, 1999.

[17] Michael Delli Carpini, *Stability and Change in American Politics: The Coming of Age of the Generation of the 1960s* (New York: New York University Press, 1986), 86–89.

[18] Richard M. Merelman, *Political Socialization and Educational Climates* (New York: Holt, Rinehart and Winston, 1971), 54; more recently, the percentage of liberals among college freshmen and the public is about the same.

[19] Roberta Sigel and Marilyn Hoskin, *The Political Involvement of Adolescents* (New Brunswick, N.J.: Rutgers University Press, 1981).

[20] John R. Hibbing and Elizabeth Theiss-Morse, *Congress as Public Enemy: Public Attitudes toward American Political Institutions* (Cambridge, England: Cambridge University Press, 1995). It is plausible to assume that the content of early political socialization influences what is learned later, but the assumption has not been adequately tested. Thus we might expect the positive opinions toward government and politics developed early in childhood to condition the impact of traumatic events later in life; David Easton and Jack Dennis, *Children in the Political System: Origins of*

Regime Legitimacy (New York: McGraw-Hill, 1969); Robert Weissberg, *Political Learning, Political Choice, and Democratic Citizenship* (Englewood Cliffs, N.J.: Prentice Hall, 1974). See also Donald Searing, Joel Schwartz, and Alden Line, "The Structuring Principle: Political Socialization and Belief System," *American Political Science Review* 67 (1973), 414–432.

[21] Jack Citrin, "Comment: The Political Relevance of Trust in Government," *Washington Post National Weekly Edition* 68, September 1974, 973–1001; Jack Citrin and Donald Green, "Presidential Leadership and the Resurgence of Trust in Government," *British Journal of Political Science* 16 (1986), 431–453.

[22] John Alford, Carolyn Funk, and John Hibbing, "Are Political Orientations Genetically Transmitted?" *American Political Science Review* 99 (May, 2005), 153–168. How do scientists determine hereditary traits from those environmentally determined? Much of this research looks at identical twins, who share the exact same genetic traits, and compares them with nonidentical twins, who do not.

[23] Christopher Achen, "Parental Socialization and Rational Party Identification," *Political Behavior* 24 (June, 2002), 151–170.

[24] Dean Jaros, Herbert Hirsch, and Frederic J. Fleron Jr., "The Malevolent Leader: Political Socialization in an American Subculture," *American Political Science Review* 62 (1968), 564–575.

[25] Kent Tedin, "The Influence of Parents on the Political Attitudes of Adolescents," *American Political Science Review* 68 (1974), 1579–1592.

[26] M. Kent Jennings, *Generations and Politics* (Princeton, N.J.: Princeton University Press, 1981).

[27] Kathleen Dolan, "Attitudes, Behaviors, and the Influence of the Family: A Re-examination of the Role of Family Structure," *Political Behavior* 17 (1995), 251–264.

[28] On the impact of the public schools and teachers on political socialization, particularly with respect to loyalty and patriotism, see Hess and Torney, *The Development of Political Attitudes in Children.*

[29] Gabriel A. Almond and Sidney Verba, *The Civic Culture: Political Attitudes and Democracy in Five Nations, an Analytic Study* (Boston: Little, Brown, 1965); John R. Hibbing and Elizabeth Theiss-Morse, "Civics Is Not Enough: Teaching Barbarics in K–12," *PS: Political Science and Politics* (1996), 12; Norman H. Nie, Jane Junn, and Kenneth Stehlik-Barry, *Education and Democratic Citizenship in America* (Chicago: University of Chicago Press, 1996).

[30] Nie et al., *Education and Democratic Citizenship in America.*

[31] Hibbing and Theiss-Morse, *Congress as Public Enemy.*

[32] Richard G. Niemi and Jane Junn, *Civic Education: What Makes Students Learn* (New Haven, Conn.: Yale University Press, 1998). See also Richard G. Niemi and Julia Smith, "Enrollments in High School Government Classes: Are We Shortchanging Both Citizenship and Political Science Training?" *PS: Political Science and Politics* 34 (2001), 281–288. Honors and advanced placement (AP) programs, along with active learning, can improve student understanding and achievement in American history.

[33] Stephen Bennett, Staci Rhine, and Richard Flickinger, "Reading's Impact on Democratic Citizenship in America," *Political Behavior* 22 (2000), 167–195.

[34] Nie et al., *Education and Democratic Citizenship in America.*

[35] Alfonso Damico, M. Margaret Conway, and Sandra Bowman Damico, "Patterns of Political Trust and Mistrust: Three Moments in the Lives of Democratic Citizens," *Polity* 32 (2000), 377–400.

[36] Joel Westheimer and Joseph Kahne, "Educating the 'Good' Citizen: Political Choices and Pedagogical Goals," *PS: Political Science and Politics* 2 (2004), 241–247.

[37] Material for this section is drawn from Everett C. Ladd and Seymour M. Lipset, *The Divided Academy: Professors and Politics* (New York: McGraw-Hill, 1975); Charles Kesler, "The Movement of Student Opinion," *National Review,* November 23, 1979, 29; Ernest L. Boyer, *College: The Undergraduate Experience in America* (New York: Harper & Row, 1987); "Fact File: Attitudes and Characteristics of This Year's Freshman," *Chronicle of Higher Education,* January 11, 1989, A33–A34; General Social Survey, *National Opinion Research Center,* 1984, 87. During the early 1970s, more college freshmen identified themselves as liberal compared with the public at large.

[38] David Horowitz, *The Professors: The 101 Most Dangerous Academics in America* (Washington, DC: Regnery Publishing, 2006).

[39] http://www.nytimes.com/2010/01/18/arts/18liberal.html.

[40] Ibid.

[41] Rebecca Trounson, "Poll Says College Freshmen Lean Left," www.commondreams.org/ headlines02/0128-01.htm.

[42] Ibid.

[43] Alexander W. Astin, William S. Korn, and Linda Sax, *The American Freshman: Thirty Year Trends* (Los Angeles: Higher Education Research Institute, Graduate School of Education and Information, 1997).

[44] "College Freshman More Politically Liberal Than in the Past, UCLA Survey Reveals," 2001 CIRP Press Release: CIRP Freshman Survey, January 28, 2001.

[45] J. H. Pryor, S. Hurtado, L. DeAngelo, L. Palucki Blake, and S. Tran, *The American Freshman: National Norms Fall 2009* (Los Angeles, Calif.: Higher Education Research Institute, UCLA, 2009).

[46] "Attitudes and Characteristics of Freshmen," *Chronicle of Higher Education,* August 27, 2004, 19; John H. Pryor, Sylvia Hurtado, Jessica Sharkness, and William Korn, *American Freshman: National Norms For Fall 2007* (Los Angeles, Calif.: Higher Education Research Institute, 2007), 37–38, February 3, 2006. See also http://www.heri.ucla.edu/PDFs/pubs/briefs/brief-pr012110-09FreshmanNorms.pdf.

[47] Maxwell McCombs and Donald Shaw, "The Agenda Setting Function of the Media," *Public Opinion Quarterly* 36 (1972), 176–187.

[48] Benjamin I. Page, Robert Y. Shapiro, and Glenn R. Dempsey, "What Moves Public Opinion?" *American Political Science Review* 81 (1987), 23–44.

[49] Herbert F. Weisberg, "Marital Differences in American Voting," *Public Opinion Quarterly* 51 (1987), 335–343.

[50] Michael A. Fletcher, "On Campus, a Patriotic Surge," *Washington Post National Weekly Edition,* December 10, 2001, 31.

[51] Philip E. Converse, Aage R. Clausen, and Warren E. Miller, "Electoral Myth and Reality: The 1964 Election," *American Political Science Review* 59 (1965), 321–326.

[52] John P. Robinson, "The Press as Kingmaker: What Surveys Show from the Last Five Campaigns," *Journalism Quarterly* 49 (1974), 592.

[53] See jacob@jacbian.org; also Nick Anderson, "Kerry Wins the Paper Endorsement Derby, for What It's Worth," *Los Angeles Times,* October 29, 2004, A5. A total of 212 newspapers endorsed Kerry; 199 recommended Bush. See also http://www.presidency.ucsb.edu/data/2008_newspaper_endorsements.php.

[54] For a review of the history of polling, see Bernard Hennessy, *Public Opinion,* 4th ed. (Monterey, Calif.: Brooks/Cole, 1983), 42–44, 46–50. See also Charles W. Roll and Albert H. Cantril, *Polls: Their Use and Misuse in Politics* (New York: Basic Books, 1972), 3–6.

[55] Peverill Squire, "Why the 1936 Literary Digest Poll Failed," *Public Opinion Quarterly* 52 (1988), 125–133; see also Don Cahalan, "The Digest Poll Rides Again," *Public Opinion Quarterly* 53 (1989), 107–113.

[56] Jack Rosenthal, "Precisely False vs. Approximately Right: A Reader's Guide to Polls," *New York Times,* August 27, 2006, Week in Review, p. 10.

[57] Hennessy, *Public Opinion,* 46.

[58] "Consulting the Oracle," *U.S. News and World Report,* December 4, 1995, 52–55; Joshua Green, "The Other War Room," *Washington Monthly,* April 2002, 11–16.

[59] Green, "The Other War Room."

[60] Joe Klein, *The Natural* (New York: Doubleday, 2002), 7.

[61] Green, "The Other War Room."

[62] Harris, "Presidency by Poll."

[63] Steven Mufson and John E. Harris, "Clinton's Global Growth," *Washington Post National Weekly Edition,* January 22, 2001, 8–9.

[64] Ibid., 11.

[65] Lawrence R. Jacobs and Robert Y. Shapiro, *Politicians Don't Pander: Political Manipulation and the Loss of Democratic Responsiveness* (Chicago: University of Chicago Press, 2000).

[66] Ibid., 12.

[67] Richard Morin, "Surveying the Surveyors," *Washington Post National Weekly Edition,* March 2, 1992, 37.

[68] David Broder, "Push Polls Plunge Politics to a New Low," *Lincoln Journal Star,* October 9, 1994, 5E.

[69] Jonathan Martin, "Apparent Pro-Huckabee Third Party Group Flooded Iowa with Negative Calls," *Politico.com,* December 3, 2007.

[70] Bill Kovack and Tom Rosensteil, "Campaign Lite," *Washington Monthly,* January–February 2001, 31–38.

[71] *All Things Considered,* National Public Radio, October 30, 1992.

[72] Richard Morin, "Voters Are Hung Up on Polling," *Washington Post National Weekly Edition,* November 1–7, 2004, 12.

[73] Ibid.

[74] Ibid.

[75] Claudia Deane, "And Why Haven't You Been Polled?" *Washington Post National Weekly Edition,* January 18, 1999, 34; Richard Morin, "The Election Post Mortem," *Washington Post National Weekly Edition,* September 30, 1996, 37.

[76] "Real Clear Politics," www.realclearpolitics.com/polls.html; see also "Pre-Election Polls Largely Accurate," *Pew Research Center for the People and the Press,* November 23, 2004, www.peoplepress.org/commentary/display.php3?AnalysisID5102.

[77] Larry Sabato, "The Lash of Unfair Criticism," *Crystalball '08* (Larry Sabato and the University of Virginia Center for Politics, 2008).

[78] http://www.cbsnews.com/stories/2008/11/07/politics/main4581355.shtml.

[79] Michael Lewis-Beck, Charles Tien, and Richard Nadeau, "Obama's Missed Landslide: A Racial Cost?" *PS: Political Science and Politics* 43, no. 1 (January 2010), 69–76.

[80] Richard Morin and Claudia Deane, "Why the Florida Exit Polls Were Wrong," *Washington Post,* November 8, 2000.

[81] Diana Owen, "Media Mayhem: Performance of the Press in Election 2000," in *Overtime! The Election 2000 Thriller,* ed. Larry J. Sabato (New York: Longman, 2002), 144.

[82] *New York Times Magazine,* December 31, 2006, p. 28.

[83] Steve Freeman, *Polling Bias or Corrupted Count* (Philadelphia: American Statistical Association, Philadelphia Chapter, October 14, 2005). (Freeman is a faculty member at the University of Pennsylvania.)

[84] *The New Yorker,* March 20, 1999, 18.

[85] A study by the Pew Foundation, http://people-press.org/reports/display.php3?ReportID5319.

[86] Richard Morin, "Tuned Out, Turned Off," *Washington Post National Weekly Edition,* February 5, 1996, 6–8.

[87] Ibid., 8.

[88] Pew Foundation study, 2007, people-press.org/reports/display.php3?ReportID5319.

[89] Ibid.

[90] Center for Political Studies, 1986 National Election Study, University of Michigan, "Wapner Top Judge in Recognition Poll," *Lincoln Journal Star,* June 23, 1989, 1.

[91] "Public Knowledge" and http://people-press.org/report/319/public-knowledge-of-current-affairs-little-changed-by-news-and-information-revolutions.

[92] Morin, "They Know Only What They Don't Like," 35.

[93] Ibid.

[94] Richard Morin, "Foreign Aid: Mired in Misunderstanding," *Washington Post National Weekly Edition,* March 20, 1995, 37.

[95] Richard Morin, "What Informed Public Opinion?" *Washington Post National Weekly Edition,* April 10, 1995, 36.

[96] Richard Morin, "We Love It—What We Know of It," *Washington Post National Weekly Edition,* September 22, 1997, 35.

[97] Michael Delli Carpini and Scott Keeter, "Stability and Change in the U.S. Public's Knowledge of Politics," *Public Opinion Quarterly* (1991), 583–612.

[98] Vladimer Orlando Key, *The Responsible Electorate* (Cambridge, Mass.: Harvard University Press, 1966); Norman H. Nie, Sidney Verba, and John R. Petrocik, *The Changing American Voter* (Cambridge, Mass.: Harvard University Press, 1976), ch. 18; Samuel L. Popkin, *The Reasoning Voter: Communication and Persuasion in Presidential Campaigns* (Chicago: University of Chicago Press, 1994).

[99] Gallup Organization, poll conducted April 6, 2004.

[100] Popkin, *The Reasoning Voter.*

[101] Morin, "Tuned Out, Turned Off," 8.

[102] Gallup Organization, poll conducted June 16, 2003.

[103] *Newsweek,* poll conducted September 2–3, 2004.

[104] Harold Meyerson, "Fact-Free News," *Washington Post National Weekly,* October 10–26, 2003, 26.

[105] Lloyd Free and Hadley Cantril, *The Political Beliefs of Americans* (New Brunswick, N.J.: Rutgers University Press, 1967).

[106] *General Social Survey, 2002* (Ns = 602 to 1301). NORC, University of Chicago: http://www.norc.org/GSS/GSS+Resources.htm.

[107] Jonathan Rauch, "Bipolar Disorder," *Atlantic Monthly,* January–February 2005, 102.

[108] Ibid., 165, 178, 192.

[109] http://www.washingtonpost.com/wp-dyn/content/article/2008/04/11/AR2008041103965_2.html?sid=ST2008041200232.

[110] E. J. Dionne Jr., "One Nation Deeply Divided," *Washington Post,* November 7, 2004, A31, quoted in Morris P. Fiorina with Samuel J. Abrams and Jeremy C. Pope, *Culture War? The Myth of a Polarized America* (New York: Pearson Longman, 2006), 6.

[111] Matthew Dowd, quoted in ibid.

[112] Fiorina, *Culture War?* 38–49.

[113] Conducted by the Gallup Organization for the online dating service Match.com during July 2004. Cited in Jonathan Rauch, "Bipolar Disorder," *Atlantic Monthly,* January–February 2005, 105.

[114] Various studies are summarized in Rauch, "Bipolar Disorder," 102–110.

[115] Editorial, "A Polarized Nation?" *Washington Post,* November 14, 2004, 6. Several of these ideas were summarized nicely in this article.

[116] This section draws heavily on Howard Schuman, Charlotte Steeh, and Lawrence Bobo, *Racial Attitudes in America* (Cambridge, Mass.: Harvard University Press, 1985); Howard Schuman, Charlotte Steeh, Lawrence Bobo, and Maria Krysan, *Racial Attitudes in America,* rev. ed. (1997); data summaries are drawn from the General Social Surveys of the National Opinion Research Center, University of Chicago, and National Elections Studies of CPS, University of Michigan; see also Lee Sigelman and Susan Welch, *Black Americans' Views of Racial Inequality* (Cambridge, Mass.: Cambridge University Press, 1991).

[117] General Social Survey, National Opinion Research Center, University of Chicago, 1996; Richard Morin, "Polling in Black and White: Sometimes the Answers Depend on Who's Asking the Questions," *Washington Post National Weekly Edition,* October 30, 1989, 37.

[118] General Social Survey, 1996; "Whites Retain Negative Views of Minorities, a Survey Finds," *New York Times,* January 10, 1991, C19; Mary R. Jackman, "General and Applied Tolerance: Does Education Increase Commitment to Racial Inequality?" *American Journal of Political Science* 25 (1981), 256–269; Donald Kinder and David Sears, "Prejudice and Politics: Symbolic Racism versus Racial Threats to the Good Life," *Journal of Personality and Social Psychology* 40 (1981), 414–431.

[119] Susan Welch and Lee Sigelman, "The 'Obama Effect' and White Racial Attitudes," forthcoming in *Annals of the Academy of Political and Social Science.*

[120] "Whites Retain Negative Views of Minorities, a Survey Finds," C19.

[121] General Social Survey, 1998; see also Donald Kinder and Lynn Saunders, *Divided by Color: Racial Politics and Democratic Ideals* (Chicago: University of Chicago Press, 1996); Howard Schuman and Lawrence Bobo, "Survey-Based Experiments on White Attitudes toward Residential Integration." *American Journal of Sociology* 94 (1988), 519–526; see also Schuman et al., *Racial Attitudes in America,* rev. ed.

[122] General Social Survey, 1998.

[123] Richard Morin, "It's Not as It Seems," *Washington Post National Weekly Edition,* July 16, 2001, 34.

[124] Ibid.

[125] Ibid.; ABC/*Washington Post* poll, 1981 and 1986.

[126] Steven A. Holmes and Richard Morin, "Poll Reveals Shades of Promise and Doubt," *Washington Post National Weekly Edition,* June 12–18, 2000, 9–11.

[127] http://people-press.org/report/576/.

[128] Jennifer Agiesta and Jon Cohen, "Fewer Americans Think Obama Has Advanced Race Relations, Poll Shows," *Washington Post,* January 18, 2010, A03.

[129] Benjamin I. Page and Robert Y. Shapiro, "Effects of Public Opinion on Policy," *American Political Science Review* 77 (1983), 175–190.

[130] Ibid.

[131] Morin, "Voters Are Hung Up on Polling."

[132] Lawrence Jacobs and Robert Y. Shapiro, *Politicians Don't Pander* (Chicago: University of Chicago Press, 2000).

Chapter 5

[1] Information for this vignette is drawn from Ashley Parker, "At Pundit School, Learning How to Smile and Interrupt," *New York Times,* October 26, 2008, ST1.

[2] James David Barber, *The Pulse of Politics* (New York: Norton, 1980), 9.

[3] Kevin Phillips, "A Matter of Privilege," *Harper's,* January 1977, 95.

[4] Media time overlaps with work time per day, because many people listen to music, watch TV, or surf the Web while working. Richard Harwood, "So Many Media, So Little Time," *Washington Post National Weekly Edition,* September 7, 1992, 28.

[5] Edwin Diamond, *The Tin Kazoo* (Cambridge, Mass.: MIT Press, 1975), 13.

[6] Study by Kaiser Family Foundation, cited in Lauran Neergaard, "Parents Encouraging TV Use among Young Kids, Study Says," *Lincoln Journal Star,* May 25, 2006, 4A, and in Ruth Marcus, "Is Decency Going Down the Tubes?" *Washington Post National Weekly Edition,* June 26–July 9, 2006, 26.

[7] Lindsey Tanner, "Studies Suggest Watching TV Harms Children Academically," *Lincoln Journal Star,* July 5, 2005, 6A.

[8] Doris A. Graber, *Mass Media and American Politics* (Washington, D.C.: Congressional Quarterly Press, 1980), 2.

[9] William Lutz, *Doublespeak* (New York: Harper & Row, 1989), 73–74.

[10] According to the Kaiser Family Foundation. Claudia Wallis, "The Multitasking Generation," *Time,* March 27, 2006, 50–51.

[11] Rob McGann, "Internet Edges Out Family Time More than TV Time," *ClickZ,* January 5, 2005, www.clickz.com/stats/sectors/demographics/article.php/3455061.

[12] Shanto Iyengar, *Is Anyone Responsible? How Television Frames Political Issues* (Chicago: University of Chicago Press, 1991), 1.

[13] Elizabeth Gleick, "Read All about It," *Time,* October 21, 1998, 66; Dana Millbank, "A Bias for Mainstream News," *Washington Post National Weekly Edition,* March 28–April 3, 2005, 23. See also Tom Rosenstiel, *The State of the News Media, 2004* (Washington, D.C.: Project for Excellence in Journalism, 2004).

[14] Eric Alterman, "Out of Print," *New Yorker,* March 31, 2008, 49.

[15] Since 1960. James Rainey, "More News Outlets, Fewer Stories: New Media 'Paradox,'" *Los Angeles Times,* March 13, 2006, www.latimes.com/news/ nationworld/nation/la-nanews13mar13,0,2018145.story?

[16] Belinda Luscombe, "Killing the News to Save It," *Time,* August 17, 2009, 49.

[17] Michael Sokolove, "What's a Big City without a Newspaper?" *New York Times Magazine,* August 9, 2009, 36.

[18] Project for Excellence in Journalism, "The Changing Newsroom," July 21, 2008, http://journalism.org/node/11963.

[19] Bill Keller, quoted in "Verbatim," *Time,* August 14, 2009, 14.

[20] Millbank, "A Bias for Mainstream News."

[21] "The New News Landscape: Rise of the Internet," Pew Research Center Publications, March 1, 2010, http://pewresearch.org/pubs/1508/internet-cell-phone-users-news-social-experience.

[22] Ibid.

[23] Brian Stelter, "Finding Political News Online, the Young Pass It On," *New York Times,* March 27, 2008, www.nytimes.com/2008/03/27/us/politics/27voters.html?ref5todayspaper&pagewant.

[24] Michael J. Wolf and Geoffrey Sands, "Fearless Predictions," *Brill's Content,* July–August 1999, 110. For a discussion of the future impact of the Internet on media concentration and diversity, see Robert W. McChesney, *The Problem of the Media* (New York: Monthly Review Press, 2004), 211–217.

[25] Pew Research Center Project for Excellence in Journalism, cited in Michael Liedtke, "Study: Newspapers Still a Step Ahead," *Lincoln Journal Star,* January 11, 2010, A7.

[26] Scarborough Research, cited in "Study: 74 Percent of U.S. Adults Read Papers at Least Weekly," *Lincoln Journal Star,* November 20, 2009, D1.

[27] Eve Gerber, "Divided We Watch," *Brill's Content,* February 2001, 110–111.

[28] Donald Kaul, "Effects of Merger between AOL, Time Warner Will Be Inescapable," *Lincoln Journal Star,* January 18, 2000; Ken Auletta, "Leviathan," *New Yorker,* October 29, 2001, 50.

[29] Cecilia Kang, "Stay Tuned for Details," *Washington Post National Weekly Edition,* December 14–20, 2009, 22; Joe Flint, "Comcast-NBC Deal Raises Concerns about Media Consolidation," *Los Angeles Times,* December 4, 2009, latimes.com/business/la-fi-ct-regulatory4-2009dec04,0,3334398.story.

[30] Robert W. McChesney and John Nichols, "It's the Media, Stupid," in *Voices of Dissent,* eds. William F. Grover and Joseph G. Peschek (New York: Longman, 2004), 120. Antitrust laws impose few restrictions on these activities. McChesney, *Problem of the Media,* 235–240.

[31] For examination of this development, see Lawrence Lessing, *The Future of Ideas* (New York: Random House, 2001). For an alternative view, see McChesney, *Problem of the Media,* 205–209.

[32] Benjamin M. Compaine, *Who Owns the Media?* (White Plains, N.Y.: Knowledge Industry Publications, 1979), 11, 76–77; Michael Parenti, *Inventing Reality* (New York: St. Martin's Press, 1986), 27; Paul Farhi, "You Can't Tell a Book by Its Cover," *Washington Post National Weekly Edition,* December 5, 1988, 21; Edmund L. Andrews, "A New Tune for Radio: Hard Times," *New York Times,* March 1992.

[33] Robert McChesney, "AOL–Time Warner Merger Is Dangerous and Undemocratic," *Lincoln Journal Star,* January 17, 2000.

[34] Rosenstiel, *State of the News Media,* 9.

[35] Daren Fonda, "National Prosperous Radio," *Time,* March 24, 2003, 50; Marc Fisher, "Sounds All Too Familiar," *Washington Post National Weekly Edition,* May 26, 2003, 23.

[36] McChesney, *Problem of the Media,* 178.

[37] Mary Lynn F. Jones, "No News Is Good News," *American Prospect,* May 2003, 39. For a history of the development of Clear Channel, see Alec Foege, *Right of the Dial: The Rise of Clear Channel and the Fall of Commercial Radio* (Faber & Faber, 2008).

[38] "Clear Channel Growth the Result of 1996 Deregulation," *Lincoln Journal Star,* October 5, 2003.

[39] David Gram, "Opponents of War Have Trouble Getting Message Out," *Lincoln Journal Star,* February 25, 2003.

[40] "Broadcaster: *Nightline* Won't Air on Its Stations," *Lincoln Journal Star,* April 30, 2004.

[41] Elizabeth Lesly Stevens, "Mouse.Ke.Fear," *Brill's Content,* December 1998–January 1999, 95. For other examples, see Jane Mayer, "Bad News," *New Yorker,* August 14, 2000, 30–36.

[42] Jim Hightower, *There's Nothing in the Middle of the Road but Yellow Stripes and Dead Armadillos* (New York: HarperCollins, 1997), 121.

[43] The Project for Excellence in Journalism, affiliated with Columbia University's Graduate School of Journalism, concluded after a five-year study that newscasts by stations owned by smaller companies were significantly higher in quality than newscasts by stations owned by larger companies. "Does Ownership Matter in Local Television News?" February 17, 2003, www.journalism.org.

[44] Neil Hickey, "Money Lust," *Columbia Journalism Review,* July–August 1998, 28.

[45] David Simon, "Does Anyone Care?" *Washington Post National Weekly Edition,* January 28–February 3, 2008, 27.

[46] *Now, with Bill Moyers,* PBS, April 11, 2003. Clear Channel uses "voice tracking" to give the illusion that the programming is originating locally. The company's disc jockey tapes short segments with local references and integrates these into the program feed to the local station.

[47] Ted Turner, "Break Up This Band!" *Washington Monthly,* July–August, 2004, 35.

[48] After an effort to lure conservatives from Fox by unleashing Lou Dobbs to bash immigrants and give the "birthers" a microphone.

[49] In response, ABC made all of its prime-time programming available in Spanish in 2005.

[50] Howard Kurtz, "Welcome to Spin City," *Washington Post National Weekly Edition,* March 16, 1998, 6. See also Roger Parloff, "If This Ain't Libel . . . ," *Brill's Content,* Fall 2001, 95–113.

[51] Virginia Heffernan, "Clicking and Choosing," *New York Times Magazine,* November 16, 2008, 22.

[52] Times Mirror Center for the People and the Press, *The Vocal Minority in American Politics* (Washington, D.C.: Times Mirror Center for the People and the Press, 1993).

[53] In addition, she received $50,000 for a book elaborating on her story, $250,000 for posing nude for *Penthouse* magazine, and about $20,000 for appearing on German and Spanish television shows. "Flowers Says She Made Half Million from Story," *Lincoln Journal Star,* March 21, 1998.

[54] Heffernan, "Clicking and Choosing."

[55] Ernest Tollerson, "Politicians Try to Balance Risk against Rewards of Reaching Talk-Radio Audiences," *New York Times,* March 31, 1996, 12.

[56] McChesney, *Problem of the Media,* 96; Paul Taylor, "The New Political Theater," *Mother Jones,* November–December 2000, 30–33.

[57] David Halberstam, "Preface," in Bill Kovach and Tom Rosenstiel, *Warp Speed: America in the Age of Mixed Media* (New York: Century Foundation Press, 1999), x.

[58] Louis Menand, "Comment: Chin Music," *New Yorker,* November 2, 2009, 40.

[59] Report by the Anti-Defamation League, cited in Tim Rutten, "In Beck, Fox Has a Familiar Demagogue," *Lincoln Journal Star,* November 11, 2009, B7.

[60] David Von Drehle, "The Agitator," *Time,* September 28, 2009, 33.

[61] *All Things Considered,* NPR, September 18, 2009.

[62] Leonard Pitts Jr., "The Other 'N' Word Roars Back in a Sick World," *Lincoln Journal Star,* August 20, 2009, B5.

[63] *Fresh Air,* NPR, September 10, 2009; Rick Perlstein, "Crazy Is a Preexisting Condition," *Washington Post National Weekly Edition,* August 24–30, 2009, 25.

[64] Quoted in Richard Corliss, "Look Who's Talking," *Time,* January 23, 1995, 25.

[65] Scott Shane, "For Liberal Bloggers, Libby Trial Is Fun and Fodder," *New York Times,* February 15, 2007, wwwnytimes. com/2007/02/15/washington/15bloggers.html?h p&ex=1171602000&en=5afe9e7498071C7f&ei =50948partner=homepage.

[66] Matt Bai, "Can Bloggers Get Real?" *New York Times Magazine,* May 28, 2006, 13.

[67] Daniel Lyons, "Arianna's Answer," *Newsweek,* August 2, 2010, 45.

[68] Ibid, 47.

[69] Elizabeth LeBel, "Life in This Girl's Army," www.sgtlizzie.blogspot.com, cited in Jonathan Finer, "The New Ernie Pyles: Sgtlizzie and 67cshdocs," www.washingtonpost.com/wp-dyn/content/article/2005/08/11/AR2005081102168.

[70] Jessica Ramirez, "Carnage.com," *Newsweek,* May 10, 2010, 38–39.

[71] Ibid.

[72] Garance Franke-Ruta, "Blog Rolled," *American Prospect,* April 2005, 40.

[73] Eli Saslow, "In Findlay, Ohio, False Rumors Fly," *Washington Post National Weekly Edition,* July 7–13, 2008, 16.

[74] Eugene Robinson, "The Berserk 'Birthers,'" *Washington Post National Weekly Edition,* August 10–16, 2009, 30.

[75] Mickey Kaus, quoted in James Poniewozik, "The 24-Minute News Cycle," *Time,* November 10, 2008, 50.

[76] The primary blogger was conservative Andrew Sullivan. Nick Gillespie, "A Politically Charged Lightning Rod," *Washington Post National Weekly Edition,* November 16–22, 2009, 39.

[77] Charles Peters, "Tilting at Windmills," *Washington Monthly,* September 2007, 8.

[78] Bill Keller, quoted in Eric Alterman, "Out of Print," *New Yorker,* March 31, 2008, 56.

[79] Richard A. Posner, "Bad News," *New York Times Book Review,* July 31, 2005, 10–11.

[80] Dom Bonafede, "Press Paying More Heed to Substance in Covering 1984 Presidential Election," *National Journal,* October 13, 1984, 19–23.

[81] Seth Mnookin, "Advice to Ari," *Brill's Content,* March 2001, 97.

[82] Ken Auletta, "Fortress Bush," *New Yorker,* January 19, 2004, 53.

[83] Charles Peters, *How Washington Really Works* (Reading, Mass.: Addison-Wesley, 1980), 18.

[84] Matthew Brzezinski, *Fortress America: On the Front Lines of Homeland Security—an Inside Look at the Coming Surveillance State* (New York: Bantam, 2004).

[85] William Greider, "Reporters and Their Sources," *Washington Monthly,* October 1982, 13–15.

[86] See, for example, Jeffrey Toobin, *A Vast Conspiracy: The Real Story of the Sex Scandal That Nearly Brought Down a President* (New York: Simon & Schuster, 1999), 310.

[87] Murray Waas, "Why Novak Called Rove," *National Journal,* December 17, 2005, 3874–3878.

[88] The initial leak came from the vice president's office. Barton Gellman, *Angler: The Cheney Vice Presidency* (New York: Penguin, 2008), 362–363. For another examination of this incident and the practice of leaking, see Max Frankel, "The Washington Back Channel," *New York Times Magazine,* March 25, 2007, 40.

[89] When a spy's identity becomes public, foreign governments try to retrace the spy's movements and determine his or her contacts to see how the CIA operated in their country.

[90] Howard Kurtz, "Lying Down on This Job Was Just Fine," *Washington Post National Weekly Edition,* April 19, 1999, 13.

[91] Ann Devroy, "The Republicans, It Turns Out, Are a Veritable Fount of Leaks," *Washington Post National Weekly Edition,* November 18, 1991, 23.

[92] Daniel Schorr, "A Fact of Political Life," *Washington Post National Weekly Edition,* October 28, 1991, 32.

[93] Howard Kurtz, "How Sources and Reporters Play the Game of Leaks," *Washington Post National Weekly Edition,* March 15, 1993, 25.

[94] And the Justice Department threatened media organizations with prosecution, under a 1917 statute, for revealing secret information. Dan Eggen, "Bush's Plumbers," *Washington Post National Weekly Edition,* March 13–19, 2006, 11.

[95] Andrew Rudalevige, The New Imperial Presidency (Ann Arbor, Mich.: University of Michigan Press, 2009), 104.

[96] Nancy Franklin, "Rather Knot," *New Yorker,* October 4, 2004, 108–109.

[97] Samuel Kernell, *Going Public: New Strategies of Presidential Leadership* (Washington, D.C.: Congressional Quarterly Press, 1986), 59. Woodrow Wilson also tried to cultivate correspondents and host frequent sessions, but he did not have the knack for this activity and so scaled back the sessions. Kernell, *Going Public,* 60–61. He did perceive that "some men of brilliant ability were in the group, but I soon discovered that the interest of the majority was in the personal and the trivial rather than in principles and policies." James Bennet, "The Flack Pack," *Washington Monthly,* November 1991, 27.

[98] Dwight Eisenhower was actually the first president to let the networks televise his press conferences, but he did not do so to reach the public. When he wanted to reach the public, he made a formal speech. The networks found his conferences so untelegenic that they stopped covering the entire session each time. Kernell, *Going Public,* 68.

[99] Bennet, "The Flack Pack," 19.

[100] Frank Rich, "The Armstrong Williams NewsHour," *New York Times,* June 26, 2005, WK13.

[101] Dom Bonafede, "'Mr. President,'" *National Journal,* October 29, 1988, 2756.

[102] Charles Hagen, "The Photo Op: Making Icons or Playing Politics?" *New York Times,* February 9, 1992, H28.

[103] "The Man behind the Curtain Award," *Mother Jones,* September–October 2002, 67.

[104] Molly Ivins, "It's Up to Us to Stop This War, and Now," *Lincoln Journal Star,* January 7, 2007, 8C. This incident is also shown and discussed in the documentary *Control Room.*

[105] Kiku Adatto, cited in Howard Kurtz, "Networks Adapt to Changed Campaign Role," *Washington Post,* June 21, 1992, A-19. See also Diana Owen, "Media Mayhem: Performance of the Press in Election 2000," in *Overtime! The Election 2000 Thriller,* ed. Larry J. Sabato (New York: Longman, 2002), 123–156.

[106] Lance Morrow, "The Decline and Fall of Oratory," *Time,* August 18, 1980, 78.

[107] Jill Lepore, "Back Issues," *New Yorker,* January 26, 2009, 73.

[108] George E. Reedy, *The Twilight of the Presidency* (New York: New American Library, 1970), 112.

[109] Auletta, "Fortress Bush," 61–62.

[110] Jim Rutenberg, "Behind the War between White House and Fox," *New York Times,* October 23, 2009, A16.

[111] W. Lance Bennett, *News: The Politics of Illusion,* 2nd ed. (White Plains, N.Y.: Longman, 1988).

[112] Larry J. Sabato, *Feeding Frenzy: How Attack Journalism Has Transformed American Politics* (New York: Free Press, 1991).

[113] Deborah Tannen, *The Argument Culture* (New York: Ballantine, 1998), 81.

[114] Ibid.

[115] Orville Schell, "Preface" to Michael Massing, *Now They Tell Us: The American Press and Iraq* (New York: New York Review of Books, 2004), xiv.

[116] James Fallows, *Breaking the News* (New York: Vintage, 1997), 62–63.

[117] Joan Konner, "Diane 'Got' Gore. But What Did We Get?" *Brill's Content,* September 1999, 59–60.

[118] See Sabato, *Feeding Frenzy,* for additional reasons for this increase.

[119] "Ticker," *Brill's Content,* July–August 1998, 152, citing the Project for Excellence in Journalism, "Changing Definitions of News: A Look at the Mainstream Press over 20 Years," March 6, 1998.

[120] Fallows, *Breaking the News,* 196.

[121] An examination of 224 incidents of criminal or unethical behavior by Reagan administration appointees found that only 13 percent were uncovered by reporters. Most were discovered through investigations by executive agencies or congressional committees, which then released the information to the press. Only incidents reflecting personal peccadilloes of government officials, such as sexual offenses, were exposed

first by reporters. John David Rausch Jr., "The Pathology of Politics: Government, Press, and Scandal," *Extensions* (University of Oklahoma), Fall 1990, 11–12. For the Whitewater scandal, reporters got most of their tips from a Republican Party operation run by officials from Republican presidential campaigns. Regarding sexual matters, reporters got most of their tips from prosecutors for the independent counsel, lawyers for Paula Jones, or a book agent for Linda Tripp. See Steven Brill, "Pressgate," *Brill's Content,* July–August 1998, 134.

[122] These are only a few of the key questions that have gone largely unexplored by the media. For an examination of these and others, see the documentary, *9/11: Press for Truth.*

[123] Except for a reporter at a small paper in North Carolina. Charles Peters, "Tilting at Windmills," *Washington Monthly,* October–November 2005, 15.

[124] Howard Kurtz, "Was the Watchdog Asleep?" *Washington Post National Weekly Edition,* October 13–19, 2008, 35.

[125] William Rivers, "The Correspondents after 25 Years," *Columbia Journalism Review* 1 (Spring 1962), 5. However, a 1939 poll found that 37 percent of the public hadn't listened to any fireside chats, and 39 percent listened to only some of them. According to presidential scholar George Edwards, cited in Sheryl Gay Stolberg, "A Rewired Bully Pulpit: Big, Bold and Unproven," *New York Times,* November 23, 2008, WK4.

[126] Coolidge, in his reelection campaign, was actually the first president to use radio as a means of addressing the public directly.

[127] James David Barber, *Presidential Character* (Englewood Cliffs, N.J.: Prentice Hall, 1992), 238.

[128] Reagan got his start in show business as a radio sportscaster in Des Moines, Iowa, announcing major league baseball games "live." Of course, he was not actually at the games: he got the barest details—who was at bat, whether the pitch was a strike or a ball or a hit—from the wireless and made up the rest to create a commentary that convinced listeners that he was watching in person.

[129] Timothy J. Russert, "For '92, the Networks Have to Do Better," *New York Times,* March 4, 1990, E23.

[130] Hedrick Smith, *The Power Game* (New York: Random House, 1988), 420.

[131] Steven K. Weisman, "The President and the Press," *New York Times Magazine,* October 14, 1984, 71–72; Dick Kirschten, "Communications Reshuffling Intended to Help Reagan Do What He Does Best," *National Journal,* January 28, 1984, 154.

[132] Auletta, "Fortress Bush," 60.

[133] Ibid., 54, 57, 64.

[134] *All Things Considered,* NPR, March 21, 2006.

[135] David Barstow and Robin Stein, "Is it News or Public Relations? Under Bush, Lines Are Blurry," *New York Times,* March 13, 2005, YT1. The Clinton administration also used these, though less extensively.

[136] In one 2 ½-year period, seven cabinet departments spent $1.6 billion on 343 public relations contracts for news releases and other services, according to a report by the Government Accountability Office (GAO).

Christopher Lee, "Report: White House Spent $1.6 Billion on PR," *Lincoln Journal Star,* February 19, 2006, 3A.

[137] John F. Harris, "On the World Stage, Bush Shuns the Spotlight," *Washington Post National Weekly Edition,* April 23, 2001, 11; Ronald Brownstein, "Bush Forced into Role He May Not Want: Communicator," *Lincoln Journal Star,* September 15, 2001.

[138] John F. Harris and Dan Balz, "A Well-Oiled Machine," *Washington Post National Weekly Edition,* May 14, 2001, 6.

[139] James Carville, quoted in John F. Harris, "Bush's Lucky Break," *Washington Post National Weekly Edition,* May 14, 2001, 23.

[140] Aides claimed that *Air Force One* was a target, but it was revealed that this claim was an exaggeration to parry the criticism that Bush received. Eric Pooley and Karen Tumulty, "Bush in the Crucible," *Time,* September 24, 2001, 49.

[141] Calvin Woodward, "Warrior Bush: It Doesn't Come Naturally," *Lincoln Journal Star,* October 6, 2002.

[142] Michael Duffy, "Marching Alone," *Time,* September 9, 2002, 42.

[143] Presidential historian Henry Graff, cited in Ron Fourier, "President Stumbles with Mideast Rhetoric," *Lincoln Journal Star,* April 20, 2002.

[144] Joe Klein, "Why the 'War President' Is under Fire," *Time,* February 23, 2004, 17.

[145] For an empirical examination, see David Domke, *God Willing? Political Fundamentalism in the White House, the War on Terror, and the Echoing Press* (Ann Arbor, Mich.: Pluto, 2004). Domke also examines the intolerance of dissent reflected in speeches and remarks issued by the administration.

[146] David Greenberg, "Fathers and Sons," *New Yorker,* July 12 and 19, 2004, 97.

[147] David L. Greene, "Bush Often Great Miscommunicator," *Lincoln Journal Star,* October 6, 2002.

[148] Philip Gourevitch, "Bushspeak," *New Yorker,* September 13, 2004, 38.

[149] Randy James, "Presidents and the Press," *Time,* September 28, 2009, 21.

[150] Virginia Heffernan, "The YouTube Presidency," *New York Times Magazine,* April 12, 2009, 15–16.

[151] Robert Draper, "Barack Obama's Work in Progress," *GQ,* November 2009, 156.

[152] Alec MacGillis, "Presidential Pragmatism," *Washington Post National Weekly Edition,* May 18–24, 2009, 26.

[153] Wayne Fields, quoted in Lolita C. Baldor, " 'War on Terror' Catchphrase Fading under President Obama," *Lincoln Journal Star,* February 1, 2009, A5.

[154] Jonathan Alter, *The Promise: President Obama, Year One* (New York: Simon & Schuster, 2010), 344.

[155] David Brooks, "The Oil Plume," *New York Times,* May 31, 2010, A27.

[156] Maureen Dowd, "Visceral Has Its Value," *New York Times,* November 22, 2009, WK11.

[157] Matt Bai, "No-Commoner Obama," *New York Times Magazine,* January 3, 2010, 13.

[158] For analysis, see Frank Rich, "Obama's Squandered Summer," *New York Times,* September 13, 2009, WK16.

[159] Stephen Hess, *Live from Capitol Hill!* (Washington, D.C.: Brookings Institution, 1991), 62; Timothy E. Cook, *Making Laws and Making News: Media Strategies in the U.S. House of Representatives* (Washington, D.C.: Brookings Institution, 1989), 2.

[160] Hess, *Live from Capitol Hill!* 102.

[161] Richard Simon, "Props Often Make Points in Congress," *Lincoln Journal Star,* December 21, 2008, A11.

[162] Joe Klein, *The Natural* (New York: Doubleday, 2002), 109.

[163] Robert Schmidt, "May It Please the Court," *Brill's Content,* October 1999, 74.

[164] For analysis, see Rorie L. Spill and Zoe M. Oxley, "Philosopher Kings or Political Actors? How the Media Portray the Supreme Court," *Judicature,* July–August 2003, 22–29.

[165] Ibid.

[166] During the invasion of Grenada in 1983, the military excluded all journalists, even turning away at gunpoint those who reached the island on their own. During the invasion of Panama in 1989 and the Persian Gulf War in 1990, the military created press pools with some journalists escorted to selective sites, who reported the news for news organizations in the pools.

[167] Auletta, "Fortress Bush," 62.

[168] Michael Kamber and Tim Arango, "4,000 U.S. Combat Deaths, and Just a Handful of Images," *New York Times,* July 26, 2008, nytimes. com/2008/07/26/world/middleeast/26censor. html?_r=1&oref=slogin&.

[169] Andrew M. Lindner, "Controlling the Media in Iraq," *Contexts* 7 (Spring 2008), 32–38.

[170] And President Bush tried to use Tillman for his reelection campaign, proposing to tape a memorial for a Cardinals game just before election day. (The family refused.) Frank Rich, "The Mysterious Death of Pat Tillman," *New York Times,* November 6, 2005, WK12. Tillman was killed in Afghanistan during the war in Iraq. For a full recap, see Jon Krakauer, *Where Men Win Glory: The Odyssey of Pat Tillman* (New York: Doubleday, 2009).

[171] Edward Jay Epstein, *News from Nowhere* (New York: Random House, 1973), 13.

[172] Graber, *Mass Media and American Politics,* 62.

[173] Milton Coleman, "When the Candidate Is Black like Me," *Washington Post National Weekly Edition,* April 23, 1984, 9.

[174] Roper Organization, "A Big Concern about the Media: Intruding on Grieving Families," *Washington Post National Weekly Edition,* June 6, 1984. See also Joseph N. Cappella and Kathleen Hall Jamieson, *Spiral of Cynicism* (New York: Oxford University Press, 1997), 210.

[175] Herbert J. Gans, *Democracy and the News* (New York: Oxford University, 2003), 87.

[176] For further examination of this phenomenon, see Neal Gabler, "Cannibal Liberals," *Los Angeles Times,* June 29, 2008, www.latimes. com/news/opinion/la-op-gabler29-2008jun29,0 ,2574530,print.story.

[177] In 1987 Reagan appointees to the Federal Communications Commission (FCC) abandoned the Fairness Doctrine, which had required broadcasters to maintain editorial balance. When Congress reinstated the doctrine, President Reagan vetoed the bill, thus allowing broadcasters to cater to any audience.

[178] McChesney, *Problem of the Media,* 116.

[179] Karen Tumulty, "I Want My Al TV," *Time,* June 30, 2003, 59. A new liberal network, Air America Radio, began in 2004 but went off the air five years later. Even the Sunday talk shows of the major television networks lean right. Significantly more guests are conservative or Republican than liberal or Democrat, and the journalists who question them are more conservative than liberal, according to a study of the shows from 1997 through 2005. Paul Waldman, "John Fund Again? It's Not Your Imagination—the Sunday Shows Really Do Lean Right," *Washington Monthly,* March 2006, 9–13.

[180] Liddy, who was convicted in the Watergate scandal, instructed listeners where to aim when shooting to kill agents of the Bureau of Alcohol, Tobacco, and Firearms.

[181] For examination, see Kathleen Hall Jamieson and Joseph N. Cappella, *Echo Chamber: Rush Limbaugh and the Conservative Media Establishment* (New York: Oxford University Press, 2010).

[182] McChesney, *Problem of the Media,* 117.

[183] "The Structural Imbalance of Political Talk Radio," Center for American Progress and Free Press, June 22, 2007. Report available from www.themonkeycage.org/2008/02/post_54.html.

[184] Julia Preston, "As Immigration Plan Folded, Grass Roots Roared," *New York Times,* June 10, 2007, YT1.

[185] For a history of the origins of Fox News, see David Carr, *Crazy like a Fox* (New York: Portfolio, 2004).

[186] For analysis, see Ken Auletta, "Vox Fox," *New Yorker,* May 26, 2003, 58.

[187] Geneva Overholser, "It's Time for News Networks to Take Sides," *Lincoln Journal Star,* August 26, 2001.

[188] Robert S. Boynton, "How to Make a Guerrilla Documentary," *New York Times Magazine,* July 11, 2004, 22. See also the documentary *Outfoxed* (2004) and Chandrasekaran, *Imperial Life in the Emerald City* (New York: Vintage, 2007), 147.

[189] According to the Project for Excellence in Journalism. David Bauder, "Study: Fox Spends Less Time on Iraq War than MSNBC, CNN," *Lincoln Journal Star,* June 14, 2007. In the first three months of 2007, Fox devoted half as much airtime to the war as MSNBC did and considerably less than CNN did.

[190] Joe Klein, "Above the Fray," *Time,* April 28, 2008, 27. For analysis of coverage by Fox News's "Special Report with Brit Hume," see "Election Watch: Campaign 2008 Final: How TV News Covered the General Election Campaign," *Media Monitor,* Winter 2009, cmpa.com. This analysis doesn't include the other newscasts and commentaries on Fox News.

[191] For a summary of its actions, see James Rainey, "Fox News, MSNBC Prejudge 'Tea Parties,'" *Los Angeles Times,* April 16, 2009, latimes.com/entertainment/news/la-et-onthemedia15-2009apr15,0,14235416.column.

[192] "Obama's Media Image—Compared to What?" Center for Media and Public Affairs, January 25, 2010, cmpa.com/media_room_press_1_25_10.html.

[193] Auletta, "Vox Fox," 63–64.

[194] Overholser, "It's Time"; David Plotz, "Fox News Channel," *Slate,* November 22, 2000, slate.msn.com. In sales pitches to potential advertisers, the network acknowledges its bias but claims that this bias makes its audience more faithful. The head of ad sales said that "people who watch Fox News believe it's the home team." Brian Stelter, "Fox's Volley with Obama Intensifying," *New York Times,* October 12, 2009, B1.

[195] Jeff Cohen and Jonah Goldberg, "Face-Off: Beyond Belief," *Brill's Content,* December 1999–January 2000, 54.

[196] For examination, see Tommy Nguyen, "The Reel Liberal Majority," *Washington Post National Weekly Edition,* August 2–8, 2004, 14.

[197] Edith Efron, *The News Twisters* (Los Angeles: Nash, 1971); L. B. Bozell and B. H. Baker, "And That's the Way It Isn't," *Journalism Quarterly* 67 (1990), 1139; Bernard Goldberg, *Bias* (New York: Regnery, 2002); Eric Alterman, *What Liberal Media?* (New York: Basic Books, 2003).

[198] S. Robert Lichter, Stanley Rothman, and Linda S. Lichter, *The Media Elite* (Bethesda, Md.: Adler & Adler, 1986), 21–25. See also Hess, *Live from Capitol Hill!* app. A, 110–130.

[199] John Johnstone, Edward Slawski, and William Bowman, *The Newspeople* (Urbana: University of Illinois Press, 1976), 225–226.

[200] Stanley Rothman and S. Robert Lichter, "Media and Business Elites: Two Classes in Conflict?" *Public Interest* 69 (1982), 111–125; S. Robert Lichter and Stanley Rothman, "Media and Business Elites," *Public Opinion,* October–November 1981, 44.

[201] Alterman, "Out of Print," 49.

[202] Stephen Hess, *The Washington Reporters* (Washington, D.C.: Brookings Institution, 1981), 89; see also Lichter et al., *Media Elite,* 127–128.

[203] James Fallows, "The Stoning of Donald Regan," *Washington Monthly,* June 1984, 57.

[204] Sometimes media executives or editors pressure reporters because they have contrary views. Kimberly Conniff, "All the Views Fit to Print," *Brill's Content,* March 2001, 105.

[205] Howard Kurtz, *Media Circus* (New York: Random House, 1994), 48.

[206] Russell J. Dalton, Paul A. Beck, and Robert Huckfeldt, "Partisan Cues and the Media Information Flows in the 1992 Presidential Election," *American Political Science Review* 92 (March 1998), 118.

[207] C. Richard Hofstetter, *Bias in the News* (Columbus: Ohio State University Press, 1976); Graber, *Mass Media and Politics,* 167–168; Michael J. Robinson, "Just How Liberal Is the News?" *Public Opinion,* February–March 1983, 55–60; Maura Clancy and Michael J. Robinson, "General Election Coverage: Part I," *Public Opinion,* December 1984–January 1985, 49–54, 59; Michael J. Robinson, "The Media Campaign, '84: Part II," *Public Opinion,* February–March 1985, 43–48.

[208] Dave D'Alessio and Mike Allen, "Media Bias in Presidential Elections: A Meta-Analysis," *Journal of Communication* 50 (2000), 133–156. Some studies did find some bias against incumbents, front-runners, and emerging challengers. For these candidates, the media apparently took their watchdog role seriously. Clancy and Robinson, "General Election Coverage"; Robinson, "Media Campaign, '84"; Michael J. Robinson, "Where's the Beef? Media and Media Elites in 1984," in *The American Elections of 1984,* ed. Austin Ranney (Durham, N.C.: Duke University Press, 1985), 184; Michael J. Robinson, "News Media Myths and Realities: What Network News Did and Didn't Do in the 1984 General Campaign," in *Elections in America,* ed. Kay Lehman Schlozman (Boston: Allen & Unwin, 1987), 143–170; Kim Fridkin Kahn and Patrick J. Kenney, *The Spectacle of U.S. Senate Campaigns* (Princeton, N.J.: Princeton University, 1999), 126–129.

[209] "Election Watch '08: The Primaries: How TV News Covered the GOP and Democratic Primaries," *Media Monitor,* March–April 2008, Center for the Media and Public Affairs, cmpa.com. According to an analysis by the "Public Editor" of the *New York Times,* however, coverage of Obama and Clinton was balanced in that paper. Clark Hoyt, "Playing Favorites? Don't Be So Sure," *New York Times,* March 9, 2008, WK12.

[210] "Election Watch: Campaign 2008 Final."

[211] Even so, this was more positive coverage than recent presidents received during their first year. "Obama's Media Image—Compared to What?"

[212] Robert Shogan, *Bad News: Where the Press Goes Wrong in the Making of the President* (Chicago: Dee, 2001), 231.

[213] It helped the Democrat Carter in 1976 but hurt him in 1980. It helped the Republican Bush in 1988 but hurt him in 1992. Thomas E. Patterson, *Out of Order* (New York: Vintage, 1994), 131. It helped the Democrat Clinton in 1996, and at different stages of the campaign, it helped the Republican Bush or the Democrat Gore in 2000.

[214] Shogan, *Bad News,* 204–245.

[215] Fewer than one in ten stories on the 2000 debates focused on policy differences; seven in ten focused on candidates' performance or strategy. Bill Kovach and Tom Rosenstiel, "Campaign Lite," *Washington Monthly,* January–February 2001, 31–32.

[216] The media, however, did pay a lot of attention to Ross Perot's presidential bid in 1992 because he said he would spend $100 million on his campaign and because polls showed he could compete with Bush and Clinton.

[217] For a recounting of his 2000 campaign, see Ralph Nader, "My Untold Story," *Brill's Content,* February 2001, 100.

[218] "Clinton Gains More Support from Big Papers," *Lincoln Journal Star,* October 25, 1992. Newspapers insist that there is little relationship between their editorial endorsements and their news coverage or even their political columns. An endorsement for one candidate does not mean more positive coverage or columns for

that candidate because American media have established a tradition of autonomy in the newsroom. Dalton et al., "Partisan Cues," 118. However, some research shows that when papers endorse candidates, the papers show a small bias toward the candidates in their news stories (if the candidates are incumbents). Kim Fridkin Kahn and Patrick J. Kenney, "The Slant of the News: How Editorial Endorsements Influence Campaign Coverage and Citizen's Views of Candidates," *American Political Science Review* 96 (June 2002), 381–394.

219 By Media Matters for America, cited in David Bauder, "Study Finds Conservatives Dominate Editorial Pages," *Lincoln Journal Star,* September 16, 2007, F5.

220 Hofstetter, *Bias in the News;* Hess, *Live from Capitol Hill!* 12–13.

221 Robinson, "Just How Liberal . . . ?" 58; Arthur H. Miller, Edie N. Goldenberg, and Lutz Erbring, "Type-Set Politics," *American Political Science Review* 73 (January 1979), 69; Patterson, *Out of Order,* 6; Charles M. Tidmarch and John J. Pitney Jr., "Covering Congress," *Polity* 17 (Spring 1985), 463–483.

222 Richard Morin, "The Big Picture Is out of Focus," *Washington Post National Weekly Edition,* March 6, 2000, 21.

223 Steven Brill, "Quality Control," *Brill's Content,* July–August 1998, 19–20.

224 Patterson, *Out of Order,* 25, 245.

225 Stanley Rothman and S. Robert Lichter, "The Nuclear Energy Debate," *Public Opinion,* August–September 1982, 47–48; Stanley Rothman and S. Robert Lichter, "Elite Ideology and Risk Perception in Nuclear Energy Policy," *American Political Science Review* 81 (June 1987), 383–404; Lichter et al., *Media Elite,* ch. 7; Sabato, *Feeding Frenzy,* 87, and sources cited therein. But a study examining twenty years' coverage of governors and their states' unemployment and murder rates shows no bias toward Democratic or Republican governors. David Niven, "Partisan Bias in the Media?" *Social Science Quarterly* 80 (December 1999), 847–857.

226 Goldberg, *Bias,* ch. 5; Alterman, *What Liberal Media?* ch. 7.

227 Alterman, *What Liberal Media?* 104–117.

228 For examination of "24," see Jane Mayer, "Whatever It Takes," *New Yorker,* February 19 and 26, 2007, 66.

229 Mireya Navarro, "On Abortion, Hollywood Is No Choice," *New York Times,* June 10, 2007, ST1.

230 Ibid., 118–138. For an analysis of the coverage of the economy in the booming 1990s, see John Cassidy, "Striking It Rich: The Rise and Fall of Popular Capitalism," *New Yorker,* January 14, 2002, 63–73.

231 Bruce Nussbaum, "The Myth of the Liberal Media," *Business Week,* November 11, 1996; Fallows, *Breaking the News,* 49.

232 Further, the media give scant attention to labor matters, except when strikes inconvenience commuters. Mark Crispin Miller, "The Media and the Bush Dyslexicon," in Grover and Peschek, *Voices of Dissent,* 137–146. In 2001, the three main television networks used representatives of corporations as sources thirty times more often than representatives of unions. McChesney, *Problem of the Media,* 70–71.

233 McChesney, *Problem of the Media,* 106.

234 Hightower, *There's Nothing in the Middle of the Road,* 137.

235 This tendency is reflected even in the nature of the reporters' questions at presidential press conferences. For foreign issues, their questions are less aggressive than for domestic issues. Steven E. Claymans, John Heritage, Marc N. Elliott, and Laurie L. McDonald, "When Does the Watchdog Bark? Conditions of Aggressive Questioning in Presidential Press Conferences," *American Sociological Review* 72 (February 2007), 23–41. The researchers examined the period from 1953 to 2000.

236 Robinson, "Just How Liberal . . . ?" 59.

237 Parenti, *Inventing Reality,* ch. 7–11; Charles E. Lindblom, *Politics and Markets* (New York: Basic Books, 1977); J. Fred MacDonald, *One Nation under Television: The Rise and Decline of Network TV* (New York: Pantheon Books, 1990); Dan Nimmo and James E. Combs, *Mediated Political Realities* (White Plains, N.Y.: Longman, 1983), 135; Benjamin I. Page and R. Y. Shapiro, *The Rational Public* (Chicago: University of Chicago Press, 1992); John R. Zaller and Dennis Chiu, "Government's Little Helper: U.S. Press Coverage of Foreign Policy Crises, 1945–1991," *Political Communication* 13 (1996), 385–405.

238 John R. MacArthur, *Second Front: Censorship and Propaganda in the Gulf War* (New York: Hill & Wang, 1992); James Bennet, "How They Missed That Story," *Washington Monthly,* December 1990, 8–16; Christopher Dickey, "Not Their Finest Hour," *Newsweek,* June 8, 1992, 66.

239 In the 1950s and early 1960s, newspapers, magazines, and television networks sent few correspondents to Vietnam, so most accepted the government's account of the conflict. Susan Welch, "The American Press and Indochina, 1950–1956," in *Communication in International Politics,* ed. Richard L. Merritt (Urbana: University of Illinois Press, 1972), 207–231; Edward J. Epstein, "The Selection of Reality," in *What's News?* ed. Elie Abel (San Francisco: Institute for Contemporary Studies, 1981), 124. When they did dispatch correspondents, many filed pessimistic reports, but their editors believed the government rather than the correspondents and refused to print these reports. Instead, they ran articles quoting optimistic statements by government officials. See David Halberstam, *The Powers That Be* (New York: Dell, 1980), 642–647. In 1968, the media did turn against the war, but rather than sharply criticize it, they conveyed the impression that it was futile. Daniel C. Hallin, *The "Uncensored War": The Media and Vietnam* (New York: Oxford University Press, 1986).

240 David Domke, *God Willing? Political Fundamentalism in the White House, the "War on Terror," and the Echoing Press* (London: Pluto, 2004).

241 "Return of Talk Show Is Healthy Sign," *Lincoln Journal Star,* October 6, 2001.

242 Alterman, *What Liberal Media?* 202.

243 Anthony Collings, "The BBC: How to Be Impartial in Wartime," *Chronicle of Higher Education,* December 21, 2001, B14.

244 *Weapons of Mass Deception,* a documentary film by Danny Schechter (Cinema Libre Distribution, 2005).

245 Alterman, *What Liberal Media?* 29; Todd Gitlin, "Showtime Iraq," *American Prospect,* November 4, 2002, 34–35.

246 *Weapons of Mass Deception.* And for good measure, MSNBC removed Phil Donohue from his afternoon show out of fear that his liberal sensibilities would offend conservative viewers during wartime.

247 James Poniewozik, "What You See vs. What They See," *Time,* April 7, 2003, 68–69. For example, that U.S. searches caused considerable damage to Iraqi homes and that these raids swept up many innocent family members, *Morning Edition,* National Public Radio, May 4, 2004. Also, that in the runup to the war, U.S. agents had bugged the homes and offices of United Nations Security Council members who had not proclaimed support for the war: Camille T. Taiara, "Spoon-Feeding the Press," *San Francisco Bay Guardian,* March 12, 2003, www .sfbg.com/37/24/x_mediabeat.html.

248 Frank Rich, "The Spoils of War," *New York Times,* April 13, 2003, AR1; Paul Janensch, "Whether to Show Images of War Dead Is Media Dilemma," *Lincoln Journal Star,* March 31, 2003.

249 Frank Rich, *The Greatest Story Ever Told* (New York: Penguin Press, 2006), 155.

250 Todd Gitlin, "Embed or in Bed?" *American Prospect,* June 2003, 43.

251 Schell, "Preface," vi.

252 Massing, *Now They Tell Us,* 7.

253 For an examination, see *ibid.*

254 For an example involving the *New York Times,* see Jane Mayer, *The Dark Side* (New York: Doubleday, 2008), 226.

255 "Buying the War," PBS, April 25, 2007.

256 Howard Kurtz, quoted in Todd Gitlin, "The Great Media Breakdown," *Mother Jones,* November–December, 2004, 58.

257 Rich, *The Greatest Story Ever Sold,* 87.

258 "The *Times* and Iraq," *New York Times,* May 26, 2004, A10; Daniel Okrent, "Weapons of Mass Destruction? Or Mass Distraction?" *New York Times,* May 30, 2004, WK1.

259 Jim Thompson, "Letters to the Public Editor," *New York Times,* June 6, 2004, WK2.

260 Reporters turn to officials because it is easy and because, ironically, they want to avoid charges of bias. They believe that their superiors and the public consider officials to be reliable, so ignoring or downplaying them might be construed as showing bias against them. Cook, *Making Laws and Making News,* 8. See also Leon V. Sigal, *Reporters and Officials* (Lexington, Mass.: Heath, 1973), 120–121; Lucy Howard, "Slanted 'Line'?" *Newsweek,* February 13, 1989, 6; Hess, *Live from Capitol Hill!* 50. Trivia buffs might wonder who has been the subject of the most cover articles in *Time* magazine—the answer is Richard Nixon (fifty-five). "Numbers," *Time,* March 9, 1998, 189.

261 W. Lance Bennett, "Toward a Theory of Press-State Relations in the United States," *Journal of Communication* 40 (1990), 103–125.

262 Three times as many people believe the media are "too liberal" than believe they are "too conservative" (45 percent to 15 percent). McChesney, *Problem of the Media,* 114.

263 M. D. Watts, D. Domke, D. V. Shah, and D. P. Fan, "Elite Cues and Media Bias in Presidential Campaigns: Explaining Public Perceptions of a Liberal Press," *Communication Research* 26 (1999), 144–175.

264 William Kristol, quoted in Alterman, *What Liberal Media?* 2–3.

265 Elizabeth Wilner, "On the Road Again," *Washington Post National Weekly Edition,* June 6–12, 2005, 22.

266 For further examination of this conclusion, see Alterman, "Out of Print," 55.

267 Robert Vallone, Lee Ross, and Mark R. Lepper, "The Hostile Media Phenomenon," *Journal of Personality and Social Psychology* 49 (1985), 577–585; Roger Giner-Sorolla and Shelly Chaiken, "The Causes of Hostile Media Judgments," *Journal of Experimental Social Psychology* 30 (1994), 165–180.

268 Dalton et al., "Partisan Cues."

269 And although these partisans say that biased coverage will not affect them, they fear it will affect others, who are less aware or astute. W. Phillips Davison, "The Third-Person Effect in Communication," *Public Opinion Quarterly* 47 (1983), 1–15.

270 Dave D'Alessio, "An Experimental Examination of Readers' Perceptions of Media Bias," unpublished manuscript, University of Connecticut, n.d.; Mark Peffley, James M. Avery, and Jason E. Glass, "Public Perceptions of Bias in the News Media," paper presented at the annual meeting of the Midwest Political Science Association, Chicago, April 19–22, 2001.

271 According to a statement by a CNN producer in the documentary *Outfoxed.*

272 Rather was anchor when the network displayed the letter about George W. Bush's National Guard service, but the producer of the piece was the one responsible.

273 Ted Koppel, "And Now, a Word for Our Demographic," *New York Times,* January 29, 2006, WK16.

274 Goldberg, *Bias,* 92.

275 Theodore H. White, *America in Search of Itself* (New York: Harper & Row, 1982), 186.

276 Goldberg, *Bias,* 92.

277 Kovach and Rosenstiel, *Warp Speed,* 64

278 Hess, *Live from Capitol Hill!* 34; Rosenstiel, *State of the News Media,* 21.

279 Molly Ivins, "Media Conglomerates Profit at Expense of News, Public," *Lincoln Journal Star,* October 26, 2001.

280 James Fallows, "On That Chart," *Nation,* June 3, 1996, 15.

281 Maureen Dowd, "Flintstone Futurama," *New York Times,* August 19, 2001, WK13.

282 A poll of reporters and executives found that a third admitted to avoiding stories that would embarrass an advertiser or harm the financial interests of their own organization. "Poll: Reporters Avoid, Soften Stories," *Lincoln Journal Star,* May 1, 2000; David Owen, "The Cigarette Companies: How They Get Away with Murder, Part II," *Washington Monthly,* March 1985, 48–54. See also Daniel Hellinger and Dennis R. Judd, *The Democratic Facade,* 2nd ed. (Belmont, Calif.: Wadsworth, 1994), 59.

Through the 1920s, newspapers refrained from pointing out that popular "patent medicines" were usually useless and occasionally dangerous because the purveyors bought more advertising than any other business. Mark Crispin Miller, "Free the Media," *Nation,* June 3, 1996, 10.

283 Roger Mudd, quoted in *Television and the Presidential Elections,* ed. Martin A. Linsky (Lexington, Mass.: Heath, 1983), 48.

284 "Q&A: Dan Rather on Fear, Money, and the News," *Brill's Content,* October 1998, 117.

285 Barry Sussman, "News on TV: Mixed Reviews," *Washington Post National Weekly Edition,* September 3, 1984, 37.

286 Bill Carter, "Networks Fight Public's Shrinking Attention Span," *Lincoln Journal Star,* September 30, 1990.

287 Epstein, *News from Nowhere,* 4.

288 William A. Henry III, "Requiem for TV's Gender Gap," *Time,* August 22, 1983, 57.

289 Richard Morin, "The Nation's Mood? Calm," *Washington Post National Weekly Edition,* November 5, 2001, 35.

290 According to the Tyndall Report, cited in Nicholas Kristof, "Please, Readers, Help Bill O'Reilly!" *New York Times,* February 7, 2006, A21.

291 Charles Peters, "Tilting at Windmills," *Washington Monthly,* September 2006, 7.

292 John Mecklin, "Over the Horizon," *Miller-McCune,* June–July 2008, 6.

293 For an examination of how the media exaggerated the Whitewater scandal, see Gene Lyons, *Fools for Scandal* (New York: Franklin Square Press, 1996).

294 The third and final special prosecutor concluded that there might be some evidence of wrongdoing in the law firm records of Hillary Clinton but that there was not enough evidence to justify prosecution.

295 The pope was making a historic visit to Cuba. The networks had considered this so important that they had sent their anchors to Havana. At the same time, renewed violence in Northern Ireland threatened to scuttle the peace talks between Catholics and Protestants, and continued refusal from Iraq to cooperate with United Nations biological and chemical weapons inspectors threatened to escalate to military conflict.

296 Eric Pooley, "Monica's World," *Time,* March 2, 1998, 40.

297 Quoted in Fallows, *Breaking the News,* 201.

298 Lawrie Mifflin, "Crime Falls, but Not on TV," *New York Times,* July 6, 1997, E3. According to one researcher, crime coverage is also "the easiest, cheapest, laziest news to cover" because stations just listen to the police radio and then send a camera crew to shoot the story.

299 Heather Maher, "Eleven O'Clock Blues," *Brill's Content,* February 2001, 99.

300 Molly Ivins, "Don't Moan about the Media, Do Something," *Lincoln Journal Star,* November 1999.

301 David S. Broder, "Can We Govern?" *Washington Post National Weekly Edition,* January 31, 1994, 23.

302 Newspaper ads were placed in college papers by Holocaust deniers, claiming that there is no proof that gas chambers actually existed. The editor of one paper justified accepting the ad by saying, "There are two sides to every issue and both have a place on the pages of any open-minded paper's editorial page." Tannen, *Argument Culture,* 38. For an examination of this phenomenon, see Deborah E. Lipstadt, *Denying the Holocaust: The Growing Assault on Truth and Memory* (New York: Plume, 1993).

303 For further analysis of the way this strategy takes advantage of the mainstream media's practice of objectivity, see Neal Gabler, "'Truth' Vs. 'Facts' from America's Media," *Los Angeles Times,* August 23, 2009, latimes.com/news/opinion/la-oe-gabler23-2009aug23,0,4834705.story.

304 Epstein, *News from Nowhere,* 179, 195.

305 Rosenstiel, *State of the News Media,* 18.

306 John Horn, "Campaign Coverage Avoids Issues," *Lincoln Journal Star,* September 25, 1988. Another survey found that 28 percent of women and 40 percent of men change channels every time during commercial breaks. "Ticker," *Brill's Content,* September 1999, 128.

307 John Eisendrath, "An Eyewitness Account of Local TV News," *Washington Monthly,* September 1986, 21.

308 Patterson, *Out of Order,* 53–59.

309 Lee Sigelman and David Bullock, "Candidates, Issues, Horse Races, and Hoopla: Presidential Campaign Coverage, 1888–1988," *American Politics Quarterly* 19 (January 1991), 5–32. So was emphasis on human interest. In 1846, the *New York Tribune* described the culinary habits of Rep. William "Sausage" Sawyer (D-Ohio), who ate a sausage on the floor of the House every afternoon: "What little grease is left on his hands he wipes on his almost bald head which saves any outlay for Pomatum. His mouth sometimes serves as a finger glass, his shirtsleeves and pantaloons being called into requisition as a napkin. He uses a jackknife for a toothpick, and then he goes on the floor again to abuse the Whigs as the British party." Cook, *Making Laws and Making News,* 18–19.

310 Patterson, *Out of Order,* 74; Marion R. Just, Ann N. Crigler, Dean E. Alger, Timothy E. Cook, Montague Kern, and Darrell M. West, *Crosstalk: Citizens, Candidates, and the Media in a Presidential Campaign* (Chicago: University of Chicago Press, 1996); Mathew Robert Kerbel, *Remote and Controlled* (Boulder, Colo.: Westview Press, 1995); Bruce Buchanan, *Electing a President* (Austin: University of Texas Press, 1991).

311 The remaining time was devoted to campaign conduct, vice presidential choices, presidential and vice presidential debates, and candidates' backgrounds and family and friends. Some of these stories also reflected the horse race and the candidates' strategy and tactics. "Election Watch: Campaign 2008 Final."

312 Richard Morin, "Toward the Millennium, by the Numbers," *Washington Post National Weekly Edition,* July 7, 1997, 35.

313 Patterson, *Out of Order,* 81–82.

314 Fallows, *Breaking the News,* 162, 27.

315 Thomas E. Patterson, *The Vanishing Voter* (New York: Knopf, 2002), 92.

316 Project for Excellence in Journalism, "Changing Newsroom."

317 Lara Logan, quoted in Brian Stelter, "Reporters Say Networks Put Wars on Back Burner," *New York Times,* June 23, 2008, nytimes.com/2008/06/23/business/media/23logan.html?dpc.

318 Peters, *How Washington Really Works,* 32.

319 Mark Bowden, "Mr. Murdoch Goes to War," *The Atlantic,* July–August 2008, 110.

320 Ibid.

321 Of course, long-term trends rarely "begin" at some specific time. Big-city newspapers began consolidating sooner than the 1980s, when the technology for cable TV and the growth of talk radio occurred.

322 Frank Rich, "The American Press on Suicide Watch," *New York Times,* May 10, 2009, WK8.

323 Clay Shirky, quoted in ibid.

324 Stephen Earl Bennett, "Trends in Americans' Political Information," *American Politics Quarterly* 17 (October 1989), 422–435; Richard Zoglin, "The Tuned-Out Generation," *Time,* July 9, 1990, 64.

325 Robert N. Entman, *Democracy without Citizens: Media and the Decay of American Politics* (New York: Oxford University Press, 1989), 17.

326 David Remnick, "Comment: Nattering Nabobs," *New Yorker,* July 10 and 17, 2006, 34.

Chapter 6

1 This total also includes a small amount of sugared iced tea, fruit punch, and other beverages with added sugar.

2 See Tom Hamburger and Kim Geiger, "Beverage Industry Douses Tax on Soft Drinks," *Los Angeles Times,* February 7, 2010, www.latimes.com/news/la-na-soda-tax7-2010feb07,0,3020424,print.story; Mark Bittman, "A Sin We Sip Instead of Smoke," *New York Times,* February 14, 2010. 1.

3 At some point, of course, a product could be taxed so heavily that its sales and the revenue from its tax would dry up, but as experience with cigarettes shows, the tax would have to be extremely high before it would be counterproductive economically.

4 http://www.mayoclinic.com/health/tanning/HQ01487.

5 Jeffrey H. Birnbaum, *The Lobbyists: How Influence Peddlers Get Their Way in Washington* (New York: Times Books, 1993), 32.

6 Mark A. Peterson and Jack L. Walker Jr., "Interest Group Responses to Partisan Change: The Impact of the Reagan Administration upon the National Interest Group System," in *Interest Group Politics,* 2nd ed., eds. Allan J. Cigler and Burdett A. Loomis (Washington, D.C.: CQ Press, 1987), 162.

7 Alexis de Tocqueville, *Democracy in America* (New York: Knopf, 1945), 191. (Originally published 1835.)

8 Gabriel Almond and Sidney Verba, *Civic Culture* (Boston: Little, Brown, 1965), 266–306.

9 David Truman, *The Governmental Process* (New York: Knopf, 1964), 25–26.

10 Ibid., 59.

11 James Q. Wilson, *Political Organizations* (New York: Basic Books, 1973), 198.

12 Graham K. Wilson, *Interest Groups in America* (Oxford: Oxford University Press, 1981), ch. 5; see also Graham K. Wilson, "American Business and Politics," in *Interest Group Politics,* 2nd ed., eds. Cigler and Loomis, 221–235.

13 Kay Lehman Schlozman and John T. Tierney, "More of the State: Washington Pressure Group Activity in a Decade of Change," *Journal of Politics* 45 (1983), 335–356.

14 Christopher H. Foreman Jr., "Grassroots Victim Organizations: Mobilizing for Personal and Public Health," in *Interest Group Politics,* 4th ed., eds. Allan J. Cigler and Burdett A. Loomis (Washington, D.C.: CQ Press, 1994), 33–53.

15 Beth Leech, Frank Baumgartner, Timothy LaPira, and Nicholas Semanko, "Drawing Lobbyists to Washington: Government Activity and the Demand for Advocacy," *Political Research Quarterly* 58 (March 2005), 19–30.

16 William Brown, "Exchange Theory and the Institutional Impetus for Interest Group Formation," in *Interest Group Politics,* 6th ed., eds. Allan J. Cigler and Burdett A. Loomis (Washington, D.C.: CQ Press, 2002), 313–329; William Brown, "Benefits and Membership: A Reappraisal of Interest Group Activity," *Western Political Quarterly* 29 (1976), 258–273; Terry M. Moe, *The Organization of Interests: Incentives and the Internal Dynamics of Political Interest Groups* (Chicago: University of Chicago Press, 1980).

17 This applies to public, or collective, goods rather than to private goods available only to the members.

18 Mancur Olson, *The Logic of Collective Action* (Cambridge, Mass.: Harvard University Press, 1971).

19 Nicholas Babchuk and Ralph V. Thompson, "The Voluntary Associations of Negroes," *American Sociological Review* 27 (1962), 662–665; see also Patricia Klobus-Edwards, John N. Edwards, and David L. Klemmack, "Differences in Social Participation of Blacks and Whites," *Social Forces* 56 (1978), 1035–1052.

20 Robert D. Putnam, *Bowling Alone* (New York: Simon & Schuster, 2000).

21 Richard Stengel, "Bowling Together," *Time,* July 22, 1996, 35.

22 Theda Skocpol, "Associations without Members," *American Prospect,* July–August 1999, 66–73.

23 Mark T. Hayes, "The New Group Universe," in *Interest Group Politics,* 2nd ed., eds. Cigler and Loomis, 133–145.

24 Jack L. Walker, "The Origins and Maintenance of Interest Groups," *American Political Science Review* 77 (June 1983), 390–406; E. E. Schattschneider, *Semi-Sovereign People* (New York: Holt, Rinehart and Winston, 1960), 118.

25 David S. Broder and Michael Weisskopf, "Finding New Friends on the Hill," *Washington Post National Weekly Edition,* October 3, 1994, 11.

26 Charles E. Lindblom, "The Market as Prison," *Journal of Politics* 44 (1982), 324–336; Michael Genovese, *The Presidential Dilemma: Leadership in the American System* (New York: HarperCollins, 1995).

27 Jeffrey H. Birhbaum, "Working Both Sides of the Aisle," *Washington Post National Weekly Edition,* March 17–23, 2008, 24.

28 Ibid.

29 "*Democracy on Drugs: The Medicare Prescription Drug Bill: A Study in How Government Shouldn't Work," Common Cause,* May 18, 2004, www.commoncause.org/atf/cf/%7BFB3C17E2 CDD1-4DF6-92BE-BD4429893665%7D/ democracy_on_drugs.pdf.

30 "Pharmaceutical Industry Ranks as Most Profitable Industry—Again," *Public Citizen,* April 18, 2002, www.citizen.org/pressroom/release.cfm?ID51088.

31 Unions contributed to their decline by becoming complacent toward the recruitment of new members. Instead, they focused on achieving greater gains for existing members. Harold Myerson, "Organize or Die," *American Prospect,* September 2003, 39–42.

32 Steven Greenhouse, "Union Membership Rose in '98, but Unions' Percentage of Workforce Fell," *New York Times,* January 20, 1999, A22; Paul E. Johnson, "Organized Labor in an Era of Blue-Collar Decline," in *Interest Group Politics,* 3rd ed., eds. Allan J. Cigler and Burdett A. Loomis (Washington, D.C.: CQ Press, 1991), 33–62.

33 Thomas B. Edsall, "Working with the Union You Have," *Washington Post National Weekly Edition,* March 14–20, 2005, 15.

34 Richard D. Kahlenberg, "Inequality and Solidarity," *Washington Monthly,* April 2008, 41.

35 Ibid.

36 Jeffrey Goldberg, "Selling Wal-Mart," *New Yorker,* April 2, 2007, 33.

37 Harold Meyerson, "Wal-Mart Comes North," *American Prospect,* April 2007, 28–29.

38 Kahlenberg, "Inequality and Solidarity," 41.

39 Ibid.; Paulo Frymer, "Labor and American Politics," *Perspectives on Politics* 8 (June 2010), 609–616.

40 Steven Brill, "The Teachers' Unions' Last Stand," *New York Times Magazine,* May 23, 2010, 35.

41 Steven Greenhouse, "The Most Innovative Figure in Silicon Valley? Maybe This Labor Organizer," *New York Times,* November 14, 1999, 26.

42 Steven Greenhouse, "Graduate Students Push for Union Membership," *New York Times,* May 15, 2001, A18.

43 Information on annual expenditures is found in U.S. Census Bureau, *Statistical Abstract of the United States, 2003* (Washington, D.C.: Government Printing Office, 2003), tab. 812.

44 Andrew S. McFarland, *Common Cause: Lobbying in the Public Interest* (Chatham, N.J.: Chatham House, 1984); see also Andrew S. McFarland, *Public Interest Lobbies: Decision Making on Energy* (Washington, D.C.: American Enterprise Institute, 1976).

45 Ronald G. Shaiko, "More Bang for the Buck: The New Era of Full-Service Public Interest Groups," in *Interest Group Politics,* 3rd ed., eds. Cigler and Loomis, 109.

46 For a discussion of the evolution of NOW and its success in lobbying Congress, see Anne N. Costain and W. Douglas Costain, "The Women's Lobby: Impact of a Movement on Congress," in *Interest Group Politics,* eds. Cigler and Loomis, 3rd edition.

47 Richard Morin and Claudia Deane, "The Administration's Right-Hand Women," *Washington Post National Weekly Edition,* May 7, 2001, 12.

48 Barbara Burrell, "Political Parties and Women's Organizations: Bringing Women into the Electoral Arena," in *Gender and Elections: Shaping the Future of American Politics,* eds. Susan J. Carroll and Richard Fox (Cambridge: Cambridge University Press, 2006, 143–168; Rebecca Hannagan, Jamie Pimlott, and Levente Littvay, "Does an EMILY's List Endorsement Predict Electoral Success, or Does EMILY Pick the Winners?" *PS* 43 (July 2010), 503–508.

49 Eric M. Uslaner, "A Tower of Babel on Foreign Policy," in *Interest Group Politics,* 3rd ed., eds. Cigler and Loomis, 309.

50 Kenneth D. Wald, *Religion and Politics* (New York: St. Martin's Press, 1985), 182–212.

51 Randall Balmer, *God and the White House* (New York: Harper One, 2008), 95–96.

52 Sidney Blumenthal, "Christian Soldiers," *New Yorker,* July 18, 1994, 36.

53 James L. Guth, John C. Green, Lyman A. Jellstedt, and Corwin E. Struck, "Onward Christian Soldiers: Religious Activist Groups in American Politics," in *Interest Group Politics,* 3rd ed., eds. Cigler and Loomis, 57; Charles Levendosky, "Alternative Religious Voice Finally Being Raised," *Lincoln Journal Star,* March 3, 1996, 7B.

54 Michael Lind, "The Right Still Has Religion," *New York Times,* December 9, 2001, sec. 4, 13; Blumenthal, "Christian Soldiers."

55 "Citing 'Moral Crisis,' a Call to Oust Clinton," *New York Times,* October 23, 1998, A1, A8.

56 Richard Parker, "On God and Democrats," *American Prospect,* March 2004, 40.

57 Frank Rich, "The Reverend Falwell's Heavenly Timing," *New York Times,* May 20, 2007, WK13.

58 Sam Tanenhaus, "Down, but Maybe Not Out," *New York Times,* May 20, 2007, WK14.

59 Harold Meyerson, "Target of Opportunism," *Washington Post National Weekly Edition,* March 28–April 3, 2005, 26.

60 David Kuo, *Tempting Faith: An Inside Story of Political Seduction* (New York: Free Press, 2006).

61 Ibid.

62 Levendosky, "Alternative Religious Voice."

63 Lynette Clemetson, "Clergy Group to Counter Conservatives," *New York Times,* November 17, 2003, A15.

64 Christopher J. Bosso, "Adaptation and Change in the Environmental Movement," in *Interest Group Politics,* 3rd ed., eds. Cigler and Loomis, 155–156.

65 Ibid., 162.

66 Katharine Q. Seelye, "Bush Team Still Reversing Environmental Policies," *New York Times,* November 18, 2001, A20.

67 Brent Kendall, "License to Kill," *Washington Monthly,* January–February 2003, 11–14.

68 John Mintz, "Would Bush Be the NRA's Point Man in the White House?" *Washington Post National Weekly Edition,* May 8, 2000, 14; Mike Doming, "NRA Promises an All-Out Assault on Al Gore's Presidential Campaign," *Lincoln Journal Star,* May 21, 2000, 2A; Thomas B. Edsall, "Targeting Al Gore with $10 Million," *Washington Post National Weekly Edition,* May 29, 2000, 11.

69 Linda Greenhouse, "U.S., in a Shift, Tells Justices Citizens Have a Right to Guns," *New York Times,* May 8, 2002, A1.

70 Linda Greenhouse, "Justices Rule for Individual Gun Rights," *New York Times,* June 27, 2008, http://www.nytimes.com/2008/06/27/washington/27scotuscnd.html?_r=1&scp=2&sq=supreme%20courts%20gun%20rights%20decision&st=cse&oref=slogin.

71 Blaine Harden, "The NRA Moves Away from Bush," *Washington Post National Weekly Edition,* January 15–21, 2007, 12.

72 Robin Toner, "Abortion's Opponents Claim the Middle Ground," *New York Times,* April 25, 2004, sec. 4, 1.

73 David S. Broder, "Let 100 Single-Issue Groups Bloom," *Washington Post,* January 7, 1979, C1–C2; see also David S. Broder, *The Party's Over: The Failure of Politics in America* (New York: Harper & Row, 1972).

74 Wilson, *Interest Groups in America,* ch. 4.

75 Robert Pear, "Lobbyists Seek Special Spin on Federal Bioterrorism Bill," *New York Times,* December 11, 2001, A1, A18.

76 The president usually has to get congressional approval for budgetary shifts and occasionally for bureaucratic reorganizations.

77 "On Finance Bill, Lobbying Switches to Regulations," *New York Times,* June 28, 2010, http://dealbook.blogs.nytimes.com/2010/06/28/on-finance-bill-lobbying-shifts-to-regulations/?scp=1&sq=finance%20bill%20lobbyists&st=cse.

78 Charles Peters, "Tilting at Windmills, " *Washington Monthly,* July–August 2004, 4.

79 "Obama Orders Tough Energy Efficiency Standards for Home Appliances," http://www.environmentalleader.com/2009/02/06/obama-orders-tough-energy-efficiency-standards-for-home-appliances/.

80 Daniel Berwick was the appointee. "Obama Outpaces Bush's Recess Appointments," http://www.heritage.org/Research/Commentary/2010/07/Obama-Outpaces-Bushs-Recess-Appointments.

81 "Some Funny Facts about D.C.," *Parade Magazine,* March 19, 2006, 25; an estimate of 90,000 lobbyists was made by political scientist James Thurbur on *Fresh Air,* National Public Radio, August 26, 2008.

82 And this was in 1986! This admission was reported only because it surfaced during a divorce. Charles Peters, "Tilting at Windmills," *Washington Monthly,* May 1986, 6, quoting *Washingtonian* magazine, April 1986.

83 As revealed in the documentary *Sicko.*

84 Todd S. Purdum, "Go Ahead, Try to Stop K Street," *New York Times,* January 8, 2006, WK4.

85 David Segal, "Bob Dole Leads the Cast of Rainmakers," *Washington Post National Weekly Edition,* September 27, 1997, 20.

86 For an examination of Enron's influence in this process, see Lowell Bergman and Jeff Gerth, "Power Trader Tied to Bush Finds Washington All Ears," *New York Times,* May 25, 2001, A1.

87 Quote attributed to Lord Acton, a nineteenth-century historian.

88 Jeffrey H. Birnbaum, "Seeking Influence," *Washington Post National Weekly Edition,* April 30–May 6, 2007, 17.

89 Diana M. Evans, "Lobbying the Committee: Interest Groups and the House Public Works and Transportation Committee in the Post-Webster Era," in *Interest Group Polities,* 3rd ed., eds. Cigler and Loomis, 257–276.

90 Birnbaum, *Lobbyists,* 40.

91 Elizabeth Drew, *Politics and Money: The New Road to Corruption* (New York: Macmillan, 1983), 78.

92 Ibid.

93 Tina Daunt, "Hollywood Leans Right, Too," *Los Angeles Times,* November 3, 2006, www.calendarlive.com/printedition/calendar/cl-et- cause3nov03,0,498316,print.story. However, individual contributions, rather than company contributions, went mostly to Democratic candidates.

94 Samuel Kernell, *Going Public: New Strategies of Presidential Leadership* (Washington, D.C.: CQ Press, 1986), 34.

95 William P. Browne, *Groups, Interests, and U.S. Public Policy* (Washington, D.C.: Georgetown University Press, 1998), 23.

96 Richard Harris, "If You Love Your Grass," *New Yorker,* April 20, 1968, 57.

97 Ibid.

98 "MoveOn's Big Moment," *Time,* November 24, 2003, 32.

99 Stephanie Mencimer, *Blocking the Courthouse Door* (New York: Free Press, 2007).

100 Birnbaum, *Lobbyists,* 40.

101 The Union of Concerned Scientists. Britain's leading scientific academy drew similar conclusions. "Scientists: ExxonMobil Misleads the Public," *Lincoln Journal Star,* January 4, 2007, 3A.

102 There have also been charges that ExxonMobil funded scientists who aren't experts in climatology and whose research wasn't reviewed by scholars in the field. Greenpeace, *Denial and Deception: A Chronicle of ExxonMobil's Efforts to Corrupt the Debate on Global Warming* (Washington, D.C.: Greenpeace, 2002).

103 The term was attributed to Paul Collier by Thomas Friedman, in *Hot, Flat, and Crowded.* (New York: Picador/Farrer, Strauss and Giroux, 2009), 292.

104 "Lobbyist Blitzkrieg Criticized," *Lincoln Journal Star,* September 23, 1994.

105 For many examples, see David Cay Johnston, *Perfectly Legal* (New York: Portfolio/Penguin, 2003).

106 Dan Clawson, Alan Neustadt, and Denise Scott, *Money Talks* (New York: Basic Books, 1992), 91.

107 John Christensen (R-Neb.), from Omaha. "It Takes Only One Cook to Spoil the Batter," *Time,* July 7, 1997, 18.

108 Dana Milbank, "Massey Energy's Blankenship: No Shame, but Plenty of Blame," *Washington Post,* July 25, 2010, www.washingtonpost.com/wp-dyn/content/article/2010/07/23/AR2010072303078.htm.

[109] E. E. Schattshneider, *Semi-Sovereign People* (New York: Holt, Rinehart and Winston, 1960), 35.

[110] Comment "Reckless Driver," *New Yorker Magazine,* March 8, 2004, 25. Nader was also one person uniquely responsible for the election of George W. Bush to the presidency, but that's another story.

Chapter 7

[1] Officially he was a Democrat, although he ran on the Republican ticket for Philadelphia district attorney in 1965. He switched his registration to the Republican Party after the election.

[2] Michael Grunwald, "Is the Party Over?" *Time,* May 18, 2009, 25.

[3] Ibid., 24.

[4] Mark Leibovich, "The Tea-Party Primary," *New York Times Magazine,* January 10, 2010, 30.

[5] E. E. Schattschneider, *Party Government* (New York: Holt, Rinehart and Winston, 1960), 1.

[6] Frank J. Sorauf, *Political Parties in the American System,* 4th ed. (Boston: Little, Brown, 1980).

[7] Maurice Duverger, *Political Parties* (New York: Wiley, 1963). See also Edward R. Tufte, "The Relationship between Seats and Votes in Two-Party Systems," *American Political Science Review* 67 (1973), 540–554.

[8] In a few PR systems, citizens vote for multiple candidates rather than for a party slate.

[9] Robert G. Kaiser, "Hindsight Is 20/20," *Washington Post National Weekly Edition,* February 19, 2001.

[10] Ralph Nader, "My Untold Story," *Brill's Content,* February 2001.

[11] In addition, some political scientists believe that American parties, compared with European parties, tend to be moderate because the United States lacks a history of feudalism with peasants and aristocrats pitted against each other. In Europe such a history seems to have produced more class-based divisions manifested in more ideologically based parties. For the classic explanations, see Louis Hartz, *The Liberal Tradition in America* (New York: Harcourt Brace, 1955); and Seymour Martin Lipset, "Radicalism or Reformism: The Sources of Working Class Politics," *American Political Science Review* 77 (1983), 1–18.

[12] *CQ Weekly,* January 12, 2002, 136; *CQ Weekly,* January 2, 2004, 53.

[13] Frank J. Sorauf, *Money in American Elections* (Glenview, Ill.: Scott, Foresman, 1988), 121–153; Paul Herrnson, *Party Campaigning in the 1980s* (Cambridge, Mass.: Harvard University Press, 1988).

[14] Janet Hook, "Meet the Powers behind the Democrats' Strategy," *Los Angeles Times,* July 5, 2006, www.latimes.com/news/nationworld/nation/la-na-dems5jul05,0,1314589,print.story?c.

[15] Ibid.

[16] Richard Hofstadter, *The Idea of the Party System: The Rise of Legitimate Opposition in the United States, 1780–1840* (Berkeley: University of California Press, 1969).

[17] Theodore Lowi, *The Personal President* (Ithaca, N.Y.: Cornell University Press, 1985), 35.

[18] James MacGregor Burns, *The Vineyard of Liberty* (New York: Knopf, 1982).

[19] Property requirements continued to exist in a few places until the 1850s.

[20] Instead of the party's members in Congress.

[21] In 1820, there had been about 1.2 million free white men over twenty-five years of age; by 1840, there were 3.2 million white men of over the age of twenty.

[22] When Harvard students established a charity for poor people in the city, they got few takers because the machine was already providing welfare for these people, so they shut down the charity.

[23] William L. Riordon, *Plunkitt of Tammany Hall* (New York: E. P. Dutton, 1963), 28.

[24] They also were allowed to dispense jobs with private companies, such as streetcar, gas, electric, and phone companies, that wanted to curry favor with local officials.

[25] Milton L. Rakove, *Don't Make No Waves, Don't Back No Losers* (Bloomington: Indiana University Press, 1975), 112.

[26] Benjamin Ginsberg and Martin Shefter, *Politics by Other Means* (New York: Viking, 1999), 19.

[27] When independent newspapers emerged as profit-making businesses, the party papers declined. But the independent papers tended to favor one side or the other for many years as a way to attract and retain readers used to the advocacy of party papers.

[28] Ibid.

[29] This was a gradual process, lasting about a century. First, independently owned newspapers replaced party-owned newspapers. Then more broad-based and objective-striving independently owned newspapers replaced narrower, biased, independently owned newspapers.

[30] Walter Dean Burnham, *Critical Elections and the Mainstream of American Politics* (New York: Norton, 1970); Helmut Norpoth and Jerrold Rusk, "Partisan Dealignment in the American Electorate," *American Political Science Review,* 76 (1982), 522–537; David W. Rhode, "The Fall Elections: Realignment and Dealignment," *Chronicle of Higher Education,* December 14, 1994, 131–132.

[31] National Election Studies, Center for Political Studies, University of Michigan, 1952–2004, www.umich.edu/nes.

[32] Larry Bartels, "Partisanship and Voting, 1952–1996," *American Journal of Political Science* 44 (January 2000), 35–50.

[33] According to Andrew Kohut of the Pew Research Center, cited in Doyle McManus, "Independents Are Calling the Electoral Shots," *Los Angeles Times,* January 24, 2010, www.latimes.com/news/opinion/la-oe-mcmanus24-2010jan24,0,6879014.column.

[34] Bartels, "Partisanship and Voting"; John Sides, "Three Myths about Independents," http://www.themonkeycage.org/2009/12/three_myths_about_political_in.html. The long-term survey data to this point can be found in http://www.electionstudies.org/nesguide/toptable/tab2a_1.html.

[35] John Sides, "Alan Brinkley Misunderstands Electoral Politics," www.themonkeycage.org,2008/09/alan_brinkley_misunderstands_e.html.

[36] A fuller discussion here would encompass the "culture wars"; cable television, talk radio, and narrowcasting; interest group pervasiveness and aggressiveness; Republican congressional efforts in the 1990s and Republican presidential and congressional efforts in the 2000s to create a disciplined and ideological party; Democratic responses to these efforts; and the decreasing number of competitive congressional races.

[37] For a discussion of party influence on voting in Congress, see William R. Shaffer, *Party and Ideology in the United States Congress* (Lanham, Md.: University Press of America, 1980).

[38] Bruce I. Oppenheimer, "The Importance of Elections in a Strong Congressional Era," in *Do Elections Matter?* eds. Benjamin Ginsberg and Alan Stone (Armonk, N.Y.: Sharpe, 1996), 120–138.

[39] Mary Lunn F. Jones, "Rock and a Hard Place," *American Prospect,* June 2003, 18–19.

[40] Dan Carney, "As Hostilities Rage on the Hill, Partisan-Vote Rate Soars," *Congressional Quarterly Weekly Report,* January 27, 1996, 199–200.

[41] John W. Kingdon, *America the Unusual* (Boston: Bedford/St. Martin's, 1999), 11.

[42] For examples, consider the pressure faced by conservative Republicans: Sen. Lindsey Graham (R-S.C.) over climate change, Sen. Charles Grassley (R-Ia.) over health care reform, and Sen. John McCain (R-Ariz.) over immigration reform.

[43] For years, discussion of party realignment and of realigning elections was standard in political science, but the concept of realigning elections has been challenged by David R. Mayhew, *Electoral Realignment: A Critique of an American Genre* (New Haven, Conn.: Yale University, 2002). In particular, Mayhew questions some specific criteria that previous researchers have put forth as markers for realigning elections. Mayhew also questions the overemphasis on realigning elections and the deemphasis on other significant elections that results from this focus. Mayhew's critique may be appropriate for the discipline's researchers, but general *party realignment,* as opposed to specific *realigning elections,* remains a useful concept, especially for introductory texts. And, as Mayhew notes, the realignment of the 1930s, which our chapter addresses, is the most clear-cut.

[44] In this realignment, the Republicans went from a bare majority to an overwhelming majority, so they remained the dominant party. However, this realignment is the least clear-cut. Mayhew asserts that it shouldn't be considered a realignment. *Electoral Realignments.*

[45] James L. Sundquist, *Dynamics of the Party System: Alignment and Realignment of Political Parties in the United States* (Washington, D.C.: Brookings Institution, 1973).

[46] Carter in 1976 and Clinton in 1992 and 1996. For a prediction and an analysis of this change, see Kevin Phillips, *The Emerging Republican Majority* (New York: Doubleday, 1969).

[47] If we take the 1960s, rather than 1948, as the starting point for southern whites, and the 1990s as the end point for white-collar professionals and regular churchgoers. If the movement of young voters to the Democratic Party, which

became pronounced in the 2000s, continues, or merely proves durable, this group and decade will also have to be featured.

48 Patrick Reddy, "Why It's Got to Be All or Nothing," *Washington Post National Weekly Edition,* October 18, 1999, 23.

49 Tali Mendelberg, *The Race Card* (Princeton, N.J.: Princeton University Press, 2001).

50 Ibid., 97.

51 Ibid., 3.

52 Despite its dubious political history, the phrase "states' rights" continues to elicit positive connotations among most Americans. In 2010, 77 percent of respondents considered it to be a positive rather than a negative phrase. (This was 1 percent more than said "civil liberties" is a positive phrase.) No doubt this positive connotation explains its frequent and enduring use. "'Socialism' Not So Negative, 'Capitalism' Not So Positive," Pew Research Center for the People and the Press, survey conducted April 21–26, 2010, http://pewresearch.org/pubs/1583/political-rhetoric-capitalism-socialism-militia-family-values-states-rights.

53 Thomas F. Shaller, "Forget the South," *Washington Post National Weekly Edition,* November 24, 2003, 21.

54 Thomas B. Edsall, "The Fissure Running through the Democratic Party," *Washington Post National Weekly Edition,* June 6, 1994, 11.

55 John R. Petrocik and Frederick T. Steeper, "The Political Landscape in 1988," *Public Opinion,* September–October 1987, 41–44; Helmut Norpoth, "Party Realignment in the 1980s," *Public Opinion Quarterly,* 51 (1987), 376–390.

56 Edsall, "Fissure," 11.

57 Thomas B. Edsall, "The Shifting Sands of America's Political Parties," *Washington Post National Weekly Edition,* April 9, 2001, 11.

58 Ibid.

59 According to Pew Research Center surveys. Ross Douthat, "Crises of Faith," *The Atlantic,* July–August 2007, 38.

60 Quoted in Robert B. Reich, "Deepening the Religious Divide," *American Prospect,* May 2005, 40.

61 Morley Winograd and Michael D. Hais, "'Millenial' Voters Avoid the Republican Party," *Lincoln Journal Star,* May 14, 2009, B7.

62 Kevin Phillips, "All Eyes on Dixie," *American Prospect,* February 2004, 24.

63 Ibid.

64 Gallup poll, reported in McManus, "Independents Are Calling the Electoral Shots."

65 Gebe Martinez and Mary Agnes Carey, "Erasing the Gender Gap Tops Republican Playbook," *CQ Weekly,* March 6, 2004, 565.

66 Mary Agnes Carey, "Democrats Want Women: Party Targets Single Female Voters," *CQ Weekly,* March 6, 2004, 567.

67 Mike Murphy, "The Ice Age Cometh," *Time,* June 22, 2009, 43.

68 In 2008, three in five Asian Americans backed Obama. Steven V. Roberts, "Lost in America, Found on a Field," *Washington Post National Weekly Edition,* May 4–10, 2009, 39.

69 Frank Rich, "The Rage Is Not about Health Care," *New York Times,* March 28, 2010, WK10.

70 Robert A. Dahl, *How Democratic Is the American Constitution?* (New Haven, Conn.: Yale University Press, 2003), 30.

71 To varying degrees. For health care reform, only one congressional Republican supported the bill. For financial industry reform, more Republicans supported the bill after initially opposing it but eventually acquiescing to public opinion in favor of it.

Chapter 8

1 Eileen Shields West, "Give 'Em Hell These Days Is a Figure of Speech," *Smithsonian,* October 1988, 149–151. The editorial was from the *Connecticut Courant.*

2 Larry Sabato, "Negative Campaigning—What's New?" *Los Angeles Times,* November 4, 2008, www.latimes.com/news/opinion/la-oe-sabato4-w008nov04,0,825765,print.story.

3 "Campaign Vitriol," http://main.gvsu.edu/hauenstein/?id=CC1039DF-07E1-A466-487D0921E38984B7.

4 Charles Paul Freund, "But Then, Truth Has Never Been Important," *Washington Post National Weekly Edition,* November 7, 1988, 29.

5 Robert McNamara, "The Election of 1828 Was Marked by Dirty Tactics," http://history1800s.about.com/od/leaders/a/electionof1828.htm.

6 Ibid., 29.

7 William H. Flanigan, *Political Behavior of the American Electorate,* 2nd ed. (Boston: Allyn & Bacon, 1972), 13. See also Chilton Williamson, *American Suffrage from Property to Democracy 1760–1860* (Princeton, N.J.: Princeton University Press, 1960).

8 Jill Lepore, "Rock, Paper, Scissors," *New Yorker,* October 13, 2008, 92.

9 James MacGregor Burns, *Vineyard of Liberty* (New York: Knopf, 1982), 363.

10 August Meier and Elliot M. Rudwick, *From Plantation to Ghetto: An Interpretive History of American Negroes* (New York: Hill & Wang, 1966), 69.

11 Robert Darcy, Susan Welch, and Janet Clark, *Women, Elections, and Representation* (Lincoln: University of Nebraska Press, 1994).

12 David S. Reynolds, "Sons of the South," *New York Times Book Review,* September 28, 2008, 20.

13 Ralph G. Neas, "The Long Shadow of Jim Crow: Voter Intimidation and Suppression in America Today," *People for the American Way Foundation,* August 2004, www.naacp.org/inc/pdf/jimcrow.pdf.

14 Grandfather clause: *Guinn* v. *United States,* 238 U.S. 347 (1915); white primary: *Smith* v. *Allwright,* 321 U.S. 649 (1944).

15 Data on black and white voter registration in the southern states are from the *Statistical Abstract of the United States* (Washington, D.C.: U.S. Bureau of the Census, various years).

16 California, Florida, Michigan, New Hampshire, New York, and South Dakota.

17 Richard J. Timpone, "Mass Mobilization or Government Intervention? The Growth of Black Registration in the South," *Journal of Politics* 57 (1995), 425–442.

18 *City of Mobile* v. *Bolden,* 446 U.S. 55 (1980).

19 *Thornburg* v. *Gingles,* 478 U.S. 301 (1986).

20 Bob Benenson, "Arduous Ritual of Redistricting Ensures More Racial Diversity," *Congressional Quarterly Weekly Report,* October 24, 1992, 3385. For a thorough review of the legal and behavioral impact of the Voting Rights Act, see Joseph Viteritti, "Unapportioned Justice: Local Elections, Social Science, and the Evolution of the Voting Rights Act," *Cornell Journal of Law and Public Policy* (1994), 210–270.

21 *Shaw* v. *Reno,* 125 L.Ed.2d 511, 113 S.Ct. 2816 (1993); *Miller* v. *Johnson,* 132 L.Ed.2d 762, 115 S.Ct. 2475 (1995); *Bush* v. *Vera,* 135 L.Ed.2d 248, 116 S.Ct. 1941 (1996).

22 Darcy et al., *Women, Elections, and Representation.*

23 Speech in 1867 by George Williams, cited in Peter Pappas's "Re-defining the Role of Women in Industrial America," www.peterpappas.com/journals/industry/women3.pdf.

24 The discussion in this paragraph is drawn largely from Lois W. Banner, *Women in Modern America: A Brief History* (New York: Harcourt Brace Jovanovich, 1974), 88–90; Glenn Firebaugh and Kevin Chen, "Vote Turnout of Nineteenth Amendment Women," *American Journal of Sociology* 100 (1995), 972–996.

25 See Pamela Paxton, *Women, Politics, and Power* (Los Angeles: Pine Forge Press, 2007), especially 38–43.

26 Alabama, Florida, Virginia, and Kentucky.

27 Nicholas Thompson, "Locking Up the Vote: Disenfranchisement of Former Felons Was the Real Crime in Florida," *Washington Monthly,* January–February 2001, 18.

28 "Groups Report Progress against Laws Banning Felons from Voting," *Lincoln Journal Star,* June 22, 2005, 4a.

29 Thompson, "Locking Up the Vote," 20.

30 Robert Pierre, "Botched Name Purge Denied Some the Right to Vote," *Washington Post,* May 31, 2001, A1, http://www.washingtonpost.com/ac2/wp-dyn/A99749-2001May30.

31 Tom Fiedler, "The Perfect Storm," in *Overtime! The Election 2000 Thriller,* ed. Larry J. Sabato (New York: Longman, 2002), 11.

32 Liz Krueger, "Budgeting for Another Florida," *New York Times,* February 8, 2004, 14.

33 Dale Keiger, "E-lective Alarm," *Johns Hopkins Magazine,* February 2004, 50.

34 See an up-to-date list of state laws on www.verifiedvotingfoundation.org/article.php?id=6430. The website www.votersunite.org/electionproblems.asp contains a tally of problems reported with electronic machines.

35 Sasha Abramsky, *Conned: How Millions Went to Prison, Lost the Vote, and Helped Send George W. Bush to the White House* (New York: New Press, 2006). This book is partly anecdotal but does point out the huge numbers of people disfranchised by both laws and intimidation.

36 See www.Tallahassee.com/mld/tallahassee/news/9202503.htm.

37 Richard Jensen, "American Election Campaigns: A Theoretical and Historical Typology," paper delivered at the 1968 Midwest Political Science Association Meeting, quoted in Walter Dean Burnham, *Critical Elections and the Mainsprings of American Politics* (New York: Norton, 1970), 73.

[38] Frances Fox Piven and Richard A. Cloward, *Why Americans Don't Vote* (New York: Pantheon Books, 1988), 30.

[39] These examples are from the editorial "Barriers to Student Voting," *New York Times,* September 28, 2004, 26.

[40] Part of the explanation for declining voting rates is that the number of citizens who are ineligible to vote has increased, which depresses voter turnout statistics. Immigrants, other noncitizens, and, in some states, convicted felons are not eligible to vote. When those individuals are removed from the calculation of proportion voting, the proportion voting is increased by about 5 points; and most of the turnout decline occurred in the 1960s. See Michael P. McDonald and Samuel Popkin, "The Myth of the Vanishing Voter," *American Political Science Review* 95 (2001), 963–974.

[41] Alan Wolfe, "The Race's Real Winner: Democracy," *Washington Post National Weekly Edition,* May 19–25, 2008, 25.

[42] Michael McDonald: http://elections.gmu.edu/voter_turnout.htm.

[43] Ibid.

[44] Daniel J. Elazar, *American Federalism: A View from the States* (New York: Crowell, 1972); *Statistical Abstract of the United States 2006,* tab. 406.

[45] Norman H. Nie, Sidney Verba, Henry Brady, Kay Lehman Schlozman, and Jane Junn, "Participation in America: Continuity and Change," paper presented at the Midwest Political Science Association, April 1988. The standard work on American political participation, though now dated, is Sidney Verba and Norman H. Nie, *Participation in America: Political Democracy and Social Equality* (New York: Harper & Row, 1972).

[46] Piven and Cloward, *Why Americans Don't Vote,* 162; *Statistical Abstract of the United States 2001,* tab. 401; Frances Fox Piven and Richard A. Cloward, *Why Americans Still Don't Vote: And Why Politicians Want It That Way* (Boston: Beacon Press, 2001).

[47] G. Bingham Powell, "American Voter Turnout in Comparative Perspective," *American Political Science Review* 80 (1986), 30; Piven and Cloward, *Why Americans Don't Vote,* 119; Arend Lijphart, "Unequal Participation: Democracy's Unresolved Dilemma," *American Political Science Review* 91 (1997), 1–14.

[48] Henry Brady, Sidney Verba, and Kay Lehman Schlozman, "Beyond SES: A Resource Model of Political Participation," *American Political Science Review* 89 (June 1995), 271–294.

[49] Nie et al., "Participation in America: Continuity and Change"; Verba and Nie, *Participation in America: Political Democracy and Social Equality.*

[50] Steven Hill and Rashad Robinson, "Demography vs. Democracy: Young People Feel Left Out of the Political Process," *Los Angeles Times,* November 5, 2002, 2. Posted by the Youth Vote Coalition, www.youthvote.org/news/newsdetail.cfm?newsid56. The survey cited was conducted by Harvard University.

[51] Eric Plutzer, "Becoming a Habitual Voter: Inertia, Resources, and Growth in Young Adulthood," *American Political Science Review* 96 (2002), 41–56.

[52] Anna Greenberg, "New Generation, New Politics," *American Prospect,* October 1, 2003, A3.

[53] *Time Magazine,* February 11, 2008, 36.

[54] Paul Allen Beck and M. Kent Jennings, "Political Periods and Political Participation," *American Political Science Review* 73 (1979), 737–750; Nie et al., "Participation in America: Continuity and Change."

[55] George F. Will, "In Defense of Nonvoting," *Newsweek,* October 10, 1983, 96.

[56] Richard Morin, "The Dog Ate My Forms, and, Well, I Couldn't Find a Pen," *Washington Post National Weekly Edition,* November 5, 1990, 38.

[57] Lawrence R. Jacobs and Robert Y. Shapiro, *Politicians Don't Pander: Political Manipulation and the Loss of Democratic Responsiveness* (Chicago: University of Chicago Press, 2000).

[58] Emmett H. Buell Jr. and Lee Sigelman, *Attack Politics: Negativity in Presidential Campaigns since 1960* (Lawrence: University of Kansas Press, 2008), especially 246ff. But see John Geer, *In Defense of Negativity: Attack Ads in Presidential Campaigns* (Chicago: University of Chicago Press, 2006), who found increased negativity in television ads.

[59] Richard Lau, Lee Sigelman, Caroline Heldman, and Paul Babbitt, "The Effects of Negative Political Advertisements," *American Political Science Review* 93 (1999), 851–875; Steven E. Finkel and John Geer, "A Spot Check: Casting Doubt on the Demobilizing Effect of Attack Advertising," *American Journal of Political Science* 42 (1998), 573–595. Research on turnout is found in Stephen Ansolabehere and Shanto Iyengar, *Going Negative* (New York: Free Press, 1996). In her book *Packaging the Presidency: A History and Criticism of Presidential Campaign Advertising* (New York: Oxford University Press, 1984), Kathleen Jamieson also argues that there are checks on misleading advertising, but later ("Is the Truth Now Irrelevant in Presidential Campaigns?"), she notes that these checks do not always work well. See Jamieson, *Dirty Politics: Deception, Distraction, and Democracy* (New York: Oxford University Press, 1992).

[60] Thomas E. Patterson, *The Vanishing Voter* (New York: Knopf, 2002); Curtis B. Gans, "The Empty Ballot Box," *Public Opinion* 1 (September–October 1978), 54–57; Curtis Gans, quoted in Jack Germond and Jules Witcover, "Listen to the Voters—and Nonvoters," *Minneapolis Star Tribune,* November 26, 1988. This effect was foreshadowed by Michael J. Robinson, "American Political Legitimacy in an Era of Electronic Journalism," in *Television as a Social Force: New Approaches to TV Criticism,* eds. Douglass Cater and Richard Adler (New York: Praeger, 1975). See also Austin Ranney, *Channels of Power: The Impact of Television on American Politics* (New York: Basic Books, 1983); and Richard Boyd, "The Effect of Election Calendars on Voter Turnout," paper presented at the annual meeting of the Midwest Political Science Association, April 1987, Chicago.

[61] Boyd, "The Effect of Election Calendars on Voter Turnout," 43. See Piven and Cloward, *Why Americans Don't Vote,* 196–197, for illustrations of these kinds of informal barriers, and Piven and Cloward, *Why Americans Still Don't Vote: And Why Politicians Want It That Way,* for further examples.

[62] Boyd, ibid.

[63] "Numbers," *Time,* May 15, 2006, 17.

[64] Anthony Downs, *An Economic Theory of Democracy* (New York: Harper, 1957).

[65] U.S. Census, reported at http://www.census.gov/population/socdemo/voting/p20-542/tab12.pdf.

[66] Kay Lehman Schlozman, Sidney Verba, and Henry Brady, "Participation's Not a Paradox: The View from American Activists," *British Journal of Political Science* 25 (1995), 1–36.

[67] Ruy Texeira, *Why Americans Don't Vote: Turnout Decline in the United States 1960–1984* (Boulder, Colo.: Greenwood, 1987); Ruy Texeira, *The Disappearing American Voter* (Washington, D.C.: Brookings Institution, 1992); and Peverill Squire, Raymond Wolfinger, and David Glass, "Residential Mobility and Voter Turnout," *American Political Science Review* 81 (1987), 45–66.

[68] Jennifer Joan Lee, "Pentagon Blocks Site for Voters outside U.S.," *International Herald Tribune,* September 20, 2004. The site was run by the Pentagon for both military and civilian overseas citizens.

[69] More recent studies of turnout include Richard J. Timpone, "Structure, Behavior and Voter Turnout in the United States," *American Political Science Review* 92 (1998), 145–158; Brady et al., "Beyond SES."

[70] Bill Winders, "The Roller Coaster of Class Conflict: Class Segments, Mass Mobilization, and Voter Turnout in the United States, 1840–1996," *Social Forces,* March 1999, 833–862. For a review of this literature, see John Petrocik, "Voter Turnout and Electoral Preference," in *Elections in America,* ed. Kay Lehman Schlozman (Boston: Allen & Unwin, 1987). See also Bernard Grofman, Guillermo Owen, and Christian Collet, "Rethinking the Partisan Effects of Higher Turnout," *Public Choice* 99 (1999), 357–376.

[71] Tom Hamburger and Peter Wallsten, "Parties Are Tracking Your Habits," *Los Angeles Times,* July 24, 2005, www.latimes.com/news/nationworld/nation/lanarncdnc24jul24,0,535024,full.story.

[72] Kim Quaile Hill, Jan Leighley, and Angela Hinton-Anderson, "Lower-Class Mobilization and Policy Linkage in the U.S. States," *American Journal of Political Science* 39 (1995), 75–86.

[73] Mark Gray and Miki Caul, "Declining Voter Turnout in Advanced Industrial Democracies, 1950 to 1997," *Comparative Political Studies* 33 (November 2000), 1091–1122.

[74] Piven and Cloward, *Why Americans Don't Vote,* 17.

[75] Ibid.

[76] Raymond E. Wolfinger and Steven J. Rosenstone, *Who Votes?* (New Haven, Conn.: Yale University Press, 1980), tab. 6-1.

[77] Steven J. Rosenstone and Raymond E. Wolfinger, "The Effect of Registration Laws on Voter Turnout," *American Political Science Review* 72 (1978), 22–45; Glenn Mitchell and

Christopher Wlezien, "Voter Registration Laws and Turnout, 1972–1982," paper presented at the annual meeting of the Midwest Political Science Association, April 1989, Chicago; Mark J. Fenster, "The Impact of Allowing Day of Registration Voting on Turnout in U.S. Elections from 1960 to 1992," *American Politics Quarterly* 22 (1994), 74–87.

[78] Kim Quaile Hill and Jan E. Leighley, "Racial Diversity, Voter Turnout, and Mobilizing Institutions in the United States," *American Politics Quarterly* 27 (1999), 275–295.

[79] "Block the Vote" (editorial), *New York Times,* May 30, 2006; *League of Women Voters of Florida* v. *Browning,* http://www.brennancenter. org/content/resource/league_of_women_voters_ of_florida_v_cobb.

[80] Piven and Cloward, *Why Americans Don't Vote,* 230–231.

[81] Stephen Knack, "Does 'Motor Voter' Work?" *Journal of Politics* 57 (1995), 796–811.

[82] Michael Martinez and David Hill, "Did Motor Voter Work?" *American Political Quarterly* 27 (1999), 296–315; Piven and Cloward, *Why Americans Still Don't Vote: And Why Politicians Want It That Way.*

[83] Jo Becker, "Voters May Have Their Say before Election Day," *Washington Post,* August 26, 2004, A01.

[84] Michael McDonald, "(Nearly) Final 2008 Early Voting Statistics," http://elections.gmu. edu/Early_Voting_2008_Final.html.

[85] Ibid.

[86] These examples are drawn from Raymond Wolfinger, Benjamin Highton, and Megan Mullin, "How Postregistration Laws Affect the Turnout of Blacks and Latinos," paper presented at the 2003 annual meeting of the American Political Science Association, Philadelphia, Pennsylvania, August 28–31.

[87] Diane Feldman and Cornell Belcher, "Democracy at Risk, the 2004 Election in Ohio," report for the Democratic National Committee, a9.g.akamai .net/7/9/8082/v001/ www.democrats.org/pdfs/ ohvrireport/fullreport.pdf.

[88] Miles Rapoport, "The Democracy We Deserve," *Prospect,* January 2005, A7.

[89] David S. Broder, "Voting's Neglected Scandal," *Washington Post,* June 26, 2008, A19.

[90] Jill Lepore, "Bound for Glory," *New Yorker,* October 20, 2008, 80.

[91] The following discussion draws heavily from John H. Aldrich, *Before the Convention: Strategies and Choices in Presidential Nomination Campaigns* (Chicago: University of Chicago Press, 1980).

[92] Ibid. See also David W. Rohde, "Risk Bearing and Progressive Ambition: The Case of Members of the United States House of Representatives," *American Journal of Political Science* 23 (1979), 1–26.

[93] Quoted in Audrey A. Haynes, Paul-Henri Gurian, and Stephen M. Nichols, "The Role of Candidate Spending in Presidential Nomination Campaigns," *Journal of Politics* 59 (February 1997), 213–225.

[94] "The Fall Campaign," *Newsweek Election Extra,* November–December 1984, 88.

[95] Hendrick Hertzberg, "This Must Be the Place," *New Yorker,* January 31, 2000, 36–39.

[96] B. Drummond Ayres Jr., "It's Taking Care of Political Business," *New York Times,* July 18, 1999, 22.

[97] Katharine Q. Seelye and Marjorie Connelly, "Republican Delegates Leaning to Right of G.O.P. and the Nation," *New York Times,* August 29, 2004, 13.

[98] Gerald M. Pomper and Susan S. Lederman, *Elections in America: Control and Influence in Democratic Politics* (New York: Longman, 1980), ch. 7.

[99] Quote from Gerald M. Pomper in Adam Nagourney, "What Boston Can Do for Kerry," *New York Times,* July 18, 2004, 5.

[100] David Carr, "Whose Convention Is It? Reporters Outnumber Delegates 6 to 1" *New York Times,* July 27, 2004, E1.

[101] As told by Gail Collins, "Vice Is Nice," *New York Times,* June 21, 2008.

[102] Lee Sigelman and Paul Wahlbeck, "The 'Veep-stakes': Strategic Choice in Presidential Running Mate Selection," *American Political Science Review* 94 (1997), 855–864.

[103] Ibid.

[104] Ibid.

[105] Robert L. Dudley and Ronald B. Rapaport, "Vice-Presidential Candidates and the Home State Advantage: Playing Second Banana at Home and on the Road," *American Journal of Political Science* 33 (1989), 537–540.

[106] *New York Times,* July 11, 2004, 16.

[107] Collins, "Vice Is Nice."

[108] Daron Shaw, "A Study of Presidential Campaign Event Effects from 1952 to 1992," *Journal of Politics* 61 (1999), 387–422.

[109] See *Congressional Quarterly,* July 23, 1988, 2015; Thomas M. Holbrook, "Campaigns, National Conditions and U.S. Presidential Elections," *American Journal of Political Science* 38 (1994), 973–998.

[110] "Election Tracker: Candidate Visits," www .cnn.com/ELECTION/2008/map/candidate. visits/.

[111] From a report by FairVote and quoted in Michael Waldman, "Majority Rule at Last," *Washington Monthly,* April 2008, 20.

[112] George F. Will, "Premature Triumphalism," *Time,* February 22, 2010, 24.

[113] See, for example, Adam Nagourney and Jeff Zeleny, "Already, Obama and McCain Map Fall Strategies," *New York Times,* May 11, 2008, 1ff.

[114] Benjamin I. Page and Richard A. Brody, "Policy Voting and the Electoral Process: The Vietnam War Issue," *American Political Science Review* 66 (1972), 979–995.

[115] The discussion of the functions of the media relies heavily on the excellent summary found in Stephen Ansolabehere, Roy Behr, and Shanto Iyengar, "Mass Media and Elections," *American Politics Quarterly* 19 (1991), 109–139.

[116] Kate Kenski, Bruce Hardy, and Kathleen Hall Jamieson, *The Obama Victory* (New York: Oxford University Press), 266.

[117] Kathleen Hall Jamieson, "Ad Wars," *Washington Post National Weekly Edition,* October 4, 2004, 22.

[118] Kenski et al., *The Obama Victory,* 309.

[119] Ibid.

[120] L. Marvin Overby and Jay Barth, "Radio Advertising in American Political Campaigns," *American Politics Research* 34 (July 2006), 451–478.

[121] Robert MacNeil, *People Machine: The Influence of Television on American Politics* (New York: Harper & Row, 1968), 182.

[122] Elisabeth Bumiller, "Selling Soup, Wine and Reagan," *Washington Post National Weekly Edition,* November 5, 1984, 6–8.

[123] Kenski et al., *The Obama Victory,* 284.

[124] Daron Shaw, "The Methods behind the Madness: Presidential Electoral College Strategies, 1988–1996," *Journal of Politics* 61 (1999), 893–913, shows the evolution of advertising focus during these three elections.

[125] Through early summer, about three-fourths of Bush's were negative, whereas only one-fourth of Kerry's were. As election day drew nearer, the proportion of negative ads increased. Dana Milbank and Jim VandeHei, "The Mean Season Is in Full Bloom," *Washington Post National Weekly Edition,* June 7, 2004, 13. Both campaigns agreed that the figures were accurate.

[126] John Theilmann and Allen Wilhite, "Campaign Tactics and the Decision to Attack," *Journal of Politics* 60 (1998), 1050–1062.

[127] Greg Sargent, "McCain's Campaign Spending Now Nearly 100 Percent Devoted to Negative Ads," tpmelectioncentral.talkingpointsmemo. com/2008/10/mccain_campaigns_ad_ spending_n.php.

[128] The study of negative advertising research was done by Richard Lau, Lee Sigelman, Caroline Heldman, and Paul Babbitt, "The Effects of Negative Political Advertisements," *American Political Science Review* 93 (1999), 851–875.

[129] Democratic consultants are more likely to find negative advertising distasteful than Republican consultants. However, this does not necessarily translate into partisan differences in use.

[130] Paul Taylor, "Pigsty Politics," *Washington Post National Weekly Edition,* February 13, 1989, 6.

[131] See Seth Borenstein, "Negative Political Ads Produce 'Shocking' Reactions on Brains," *Lincoln Journal Star,* November 4, 2006, 6a. The article reported research of Shanto Iyengar, *Going Negative: How Political Advertisements Shrink and Polarize the Electorate.*

[132] Ansolabehere and Iyengar, *Going Negative.*

[133] Jamieson, *Packaging the Presidency.*

[134] Kenski et al., *The Obama Victory,* 305.

[135] Ibid., 307.

[136] These data on Internet use are from the Pew Foundation's Internet and American Life Project, "The Internet and the 2008 Election," June 15, 2008, www.pewinternet.org.

[137] Kenski, *The Obama Victory,* ibid, 306.

[138] Adam Nagourney, "Internet Injects Sweeping Change into U.S. Politics," *New York Times,* April 2, 2006, 1ff.

[139] David Perlmutter, "Political Blogs: The New Iowa?" *Chronicle of Higher Education,* May 26, 2006, B6.

[140] Kenski et al., *The Obama Victory,* 307.

141 Thomas E. Patterson, *The Mass Media Election: How Americans Choose Their President* (New York: Praeger, 1980), 3.

142 Martin Schram, *The Great American Video Game: Presidential Politics in the Television Age* (New York: Morrow, 1987).

143 Daron Shaw, "A Study of Presidential Campaign Event Effects from 1952 to 1992," *Journal of Politics* 61 (May 1999), 387–422, reports on a systematic study of campaign events and their impact on the elections.

144 Kenski et al., *The Obama Victory*, 196–202.

145 John Heilemann and Mark Hallperin, *Game Change* (New York: Harper, 2010), 391.

146 Ibid., 392.

147 Ibid., 202–203.

148 Waldman, "Majority Rule at Last," 18.

149 Ibid.

150 Robert Dahl, *How Democratic Is the American Constitution?* (New Haven, Conn.: Yale University Press, 2001).

151 Waldman, "Majority Rule at Last."

152 Akhil Reed Amar, *America's Constitution: A Biography* (New York: Random House, 2005).

153 Ibid.

154 Quoted in Alan M. Dershowitz, *Supreme Injustice: How the High Court Hijacked Election 2000* (New York: Oxford University Press, 2001),25.

155 Hendrik Hertzberg, "Up for the Count," *New Yorker,* December 18, 2000, 41. At least 680 were flawed, including nearly 200 with U.S. postmarks, indicating that they had been mailed from within the country rather than from overseas; 344 were late, illegible, or missing postmarks; and even 38 reflected double voting by 19 voters.

156 Kosuke Imai and Gary King, "Did Illegally Counted Overseas Absentee Ballots Decide the 2000 U.S. Presidential Election?" gking.Harvard.edu.

157 David Barstow and Don Van Natta Jr., "How Bush Took Florida: Mining the Overseas Absentee Vote," *New York Times,* July 15, 2001, www.nytimes.com/2001/07/15/ www.national/15ball.

158 Ibid.

159 Jonathan Wand, Kenneth Shotts, Jasjeet Sekhon, Walter R. Mebane Jr., Michael Herron, and Henry Brady, "The Butterfly Did It: The Aberrant Vote for Buchanan in Palm Beach," *American Political Science Review* 95 (2001), 793–809. They examined the Palm Beach Buchanan vote in relation to all other counties in the United States compared to the absentee ballots (which did not use the butterfly format) in Palm Beach County, precinct-level data, and individual ballots.

160 Fiedler, "The Perfect Storm," 8.

161 Imai and King, "Did Illegally Counted Overseas Absentee Ballots Decide the 2000 U.S. Presidential Election?" 3.

162 Jimmy Carter, quoted from National Public Radio in Kéllia Ramares's special report "House Strikes Truth from the Record," *Online Journal,* July 23, 2004. The full Ramares article is at www. onlinejournal.com/Special_Reports/072304Ramares/072304ramares.html.

163 Paul Abramson, John H. Aldrich, and David Rohde, *Change and Continuity in the 2000 Elections* (Washington, D.C.: CQ Press, 2003); Paul Abramson, John H. Aldrich, and David Rohde, *Change and Continuity in the 2004 and 2006 Elections* (Washington, D.C.: CQ Press, 2007).

164 Ibid.

165 In recent elections, the percentages able to correctly identify general differences between the major party candidates varied between 26 and 55 percent.

166 Paul Abramson, John Aldrich, and David Rohde, *Change and Continuity in the 2008 Election* (Washington, D.C.: CQ Press, 2009), 157–159; Abramson, Aldrich, and Rodhe, *Change and Continuity in the 2004 and 2006 Elections.*

167 Abramson et al., *Change and Continuity in the 2008 Election,* 161.

168 Ibid.

169 Ibid., 166.

170 Morris Fiorina, *Retrospective Voting in American National Elections* (New Haven, Conn.: Yale University Press, 1981).

171 Edward R. Tufte, *Political Control of the Economy* (Princeton, N.J.: Princeton University Press, 1978); Douglas Hibbs, "The Mass Public and Macroeconomic Performance," *American Journal of Political Science* 23 (1979), 705–731; John Hibbing and John Alford, "The Electoral Impact of Economic Conditions: Who Is Held Responsible," *American Journal of Political Science* 25 (1981), 423–439.

172 Abramson et al., *Change and Continuity in the 2008 Election,* 182.

173 These election report data are from "Dissecting the Changing Electorate," *New York Times,* November 9, 2008, WK5.

174 www.fivethirtyeight.com/2008/11/obama-outperforms-kerry-among virtually.html; Charles Franklin, "White Vote for Obama in the States, Part 2," www.pollster.com/blogs/white_vote_for_o_in_the_st_1.php.

175 Morley Winograd and Michael D. Hais, "Millennial Voters Avoid the Republican Party," *Los Angeles Times,* May 14, 2009, B7.

176 For example, see Norman J. Ornstein and Thomas E. Mann, eds., *The Permanent Campaign and Its Future* (Washington, D.C.: American Enterprise Institute and the Brookings Institution, 2000).

177 Paul Abramson, John H. Aldrich, and David Rohde, *Change and Continuity in the 2010 Election* (Washington, D.C.: CQ Press, 2010), ch. 6.

178 http://www.cnn.com/2008/POLITICS/11/04/exit.polls/.

179 Benjamin I. Page and Robert Y. Shapiro, "Effects of Public Opinion on Policy," *American Political Science Review* 77 (1983), 175–190.

180 Arthur Schlesinger Jr., *Wall Street Journal,* December 5, 1986. But see also Jacobs and Shapiro, *Politicians Don't Pander.*

Chapter 9

1 Adam Nagourney and Jeff Zeleny, "Obama Foregoes Public Funds in a First for Major Candidate," *New York Times,* June 20, 2008, www.nytimes.com/2008/06/20/us/politics/20obamacnd.html?_r=1&hp&oref=slogin.

2 Matt Bai, "Promises to Keep," *New York Times Sunday Magazine,* July 13, 2008, 12.

3 Mark Halperin, "10 Things That Never Happened Before," *Time,* November 17, 2008, 53; Jim Kuhnhenn, "Money Makes Political World Turn 'Round," *Lincoln Journal Star,* November 3, 2008, 3a.

4 Jimmy Breslin, *How the Good Guys Finally Won: Notes from an Impeachment Summer* (New York: Ballantine, 1974), 14.

5 Federal Election Commission Report, www.fec.gov/press/press2005/20050203pressum/20050203pressum.html.

6 Robert E. Mutch, "Three Centuries of Campaign Finance Law," in *A User's Guide to Campaign Finance Reform,* ed. Gerald C. Lubenow (Lanham, Md.: Rowman & Littlefield, 2001).

7 Congressional Quarterly, *Dollar Politics,* 3rd ed. (Washington, D.C.: CQ Press, 1982), 3.

8 Haynes Johnson, "Turning Government Jobs into Gold," *Washington Post National Weekly Edition,* May 12, 1986, 6–7.

9 Richard Lacayo, "Fighting the Fat Cats," *Time,* July 3, 2006, 71.

10 Quoted in Richard Hofstadter, *The American Political Tradition* (New York: Vintage, 1958), 165.

11 Congressional Quarterly, *Dollar Politics,* 3.

12 Larry J. Sabato, *Feeding Frenzy* (New York: Free Press, 1991).

13 Kevin Phillips, "How Wealth Defines Power," *American Prospect,* Summer 2003, A9. The U.S. Constitution defines a quorum as a majority of senators currently in office.

14 Digital History, *Hypertext History,* "The Progressive Era," October 30, 2004, www.digitalhistory.uh.edu/database/hyper_titles.cfm. The history was made by steel baron Henry Frick.

15 Elizabeth Drew, *Politics and Money* (New York: Collier, 1983), 9.

16 *Citizens United* v. *FEC,* 175 L.Ed.2d 753 (2010). Jonathan Alter, "High Court Hypocrisy," *Newsweek,* February 1, 2010, 15.

17 Warren Richey, "Supreme Court: Campaign-Finance Limits Violate Free Speech," *CSMonitor,* January 21, 2010, www.csmonitor.com/USA/Justice/2010/0121/Supreme-Court-Campaign-finance-limits-violate-free-speech.

18 Ibid.

19 Ibid.

20 Dan Eggen, "Court Strikes Limits on Contributions to Independent Political Groups," *Washington Post,* March 26, 2010, www.washingtonpost.com/wp-dyn/content/article/2010/03/26/AR2010032602140.html?nav=hcmodule.

21 Quoted in Nancy Gibbs and Karen Tumulty, "A New Day Dawning," *Time,* April 9, 2001, 50.

22 Kuhnhenn, "Money Makes Political World Turn 'Round."

23 Matt Bai, "The Edge of the Mystery," *New York Times Magazine,* January 18, 2009, 48.

24 Glen Justice, "Kerry's Campaign Finances Soar," *International Herald Tribune,* June 28, 2004, 7.

25 *Buckley* v. *Valeo,* 424 U.S. 1 (1976); the Vermont case is *Randall* v. *Sorrell,* 548 U.S. (2006).

[26] See Larry J. Sabato and Glenn Simpson, *Dirty Little Secrets: The Persistence of Corruption in American Politics* (New York: Times Books, 1996); Marick Masters and Gerald Keim, "Determinants of PAC Participation among Large Corporations," *Journal of Politics* 47 (1985), 1158–1173; and J. David Gopoian, "What Makes PACs Tick?" *American Journal of Political Science* 28 (1984), 259–281.

[27] See Kevin Grier and Michael Mangy, "Comparing Interest Group PAC Contributions to House and Senate Incumbents," *Journal of Politics* 55 (1993), 615–643.

[28] J. David Gopoian, "Change and Continuity in Defense PAC Behavior," *American Politics Quarterly* 13 (1985), 297–322; Richard Morin and Charles Babcock, "Off Year, Schmoff Year," *Washington Post National Weekly Edition,* May 14, 1990, 15.

[29] *Federal Election Commission v. National Conservative PAC,* 470 U.S. 480 (1985).

[30] Pauol Farhi, "A Team Effort," *Washington Post National Weekly Edition,* March 29, 2004, 12.

[31] Recent legislation has attempted to close part of the soft money loophole by banning soft money contributions to national political parties. However, it left a huge loophole allowing soft money contributions to various independent groups and, to a lesser extent, to state and local parties.

[32] Walter Lippmann, "A Theory about Corruption," in *Political Corruption,* ed. Arnold J. Heidenheimer (New York: Holt, Rinehart and Winston, 1970), 294–297.

[33] Mike Allen, "Does an Embassy Trump the Lincoln Bedroom?" *Washington Post National Weekly Edition,* May 7, 2001, 14.

[34] Ibid.

[35] Mike Allen, "The Mother of All Fundraisers," *Washington Post National Weekly Edition,* May 20, 2002, 13.

[36] Allen, "Does an Embassy Trump the Lincoln Bedroom?"

[37] Thomas Edsall, Sarah Cohen, and James Grimaldi, "Pioneers Fill War Chest," *Washington Post* (May 16, 2004) A1.

[38] Ibid.

[39] Trudy Lieberman, "Obama's Lobbyist Line: A 'More Complicated Truth' on Campaign Contributions," *Columbia Journalism Review,* February 16, 2008, http://www.cjr.org/campaign_desk/obamas_lobbyist_line.php.

[40] "Money Wins Presidency and 9 out of 10 Congressional Races in Priciest Election Ever," *Open Secrets,* http://www.opensecrets.org/news/2008/11/money-wins-white-house-and.html.

[41] Larry Makinson and Joshua Goldstein, *Open Secrets: The Cash Constituents of Congress,* 2nd ed. (Washington, D.C.: CQ Press, 1994), 23.

[42] Amy Dockser, "Nice PAC You've Got There . . . A Pity If Anything Should Happen to It," *Washington Monthly,* January 1984, 21.

[43] Bradley Smith, *Free Speech: The Folly of Campaign Finance Reform* (Princeton, N.J.: Princeton University Press, 2001); Russ Lewis, "Foreign to the First Amendment," *Washington Post,* July 2, 2002, A15.

[44] George Will, "Corrupt Campaign 'Reform,'" *Washington Post,* June 29, 2006, A27.

[45] Thomas Byrne Edsall, "Campaign Reform Boomerang," *American Prospect,* September 2003, 61.

[46] Ibid.

[47] Most surveys on the topic are rather dated; see Ruth Marcus and Charles Babcock, "Feeding the Election Machine," *Washington Post National Weekly Edition,* February 17, 1997, 10.

[48] Paul Taylor, "TV's Political Profits," *Mother Jones,* May–June 2000, 32.

[49] Jeff Leeds, "TV Stations Balk at Free Air Time for Candidates," *Lincoln Journal Star,* May 14, 2000, 3A.

[50] Ibid.

[51] Robert Pastor, "America Observed," *Prospect,* January 2005, A3. An earlier study of 146 countries found that the United States was the only country without free media: *Washington Post,* February 24, 2002, B7.

[52] David S. Broder, "Where the Money Goes," *Washington Post National Weekly Edition,* March 26, 2001, 4.

[53] USA/Gallup poll, reported on October 28, 2008.

[54] "Public Order in the Courts," *American Prospect,* November 18, 2002, 8. See also Harold Stanley and Richard Niemi, *Vital Statistics on American Politics, 2001–02* (Washington, D.C.: CQ Press, 2002), tab. 2-3.

[55] Jack Levin in Michael Grunwald, "Neighborhood Watch," *Washington Post National Weekly Edition,* February 20–26, 2006, 22.

[56] Mark Twain, *Pudd'nhead Wilson's New Calendar.* http://etext.virginia.edu/railton/wilson/pwequat.html

[57] Quoted in *New York Times,* June 13, 1998, A7.

[58] Ibid.

[59] Quoted in Gary Jacobson, *Money in Congressional Elections* (New Haven, Conn.: Yale University Press, 1980), 61.

[60] Zell Miller, "A Sorry Way to 'Win,'" *Washington Post,* February 25, 2001, B7.

[61] Diana C. Mutz, "Effects of Horse-Race Coverage on Campaign Coffers: Strategic Contributing in Presidential Primaries," *Journal of Politics* 57 (1995), 1015–1042.

[62] Audrey Haynes, Paul-Henri Gurian, and Stephen Nichols, "Role of Candidate Spending in Presidential Nominating Campaigns,"*Journal of Politics* 57 (February, 1997): 223.

[63] Nelson Polsby and Aaron Wildavsky, *Presidential Elections* (New York: Scribner, 1984), 56.

[64] David Nice, "Campaign Spending and Presidential Election Results," *Polity* 19 (1987), 464–476, shows that presidential campaign spending is more productive for Republicans than for Democrats.

[65] John Alford and David Brady, "Person and Partisan Advantages in U.S. Congressional Elections, 1846–1990," in *Congress Reconsidered,* eds. Larry Dodd and Bruce Oppenheimer, 5th ed. (Washington, D.C.: CQ Press, 1993).

[66] David Epstein and Peter Zemsky, "Money Talks: Deterring Quality Challengers in Congressional Elections," *American Political Science Review* 89 (1995), 295–308.

[67] Robert S. Erickson and Thomas R. Palfrey, "Campaign Spending and Incumbency: An Alternative Simultaneous Equations Approach," *Journal of Politics* 60 (1998), 355–373; Alan Gerber, "Estimating the Effect of Campaign Spending on Senate Election Outcomes Using Instrumental Variables," *American Political Science Review* 92 (1998), 401–411.

[68] Jacobson, *Money in Congressional Elections;* Gary Jacobson, "The Effects of Campaign Spending in House Elections," *American Journal of Political Science* 34 (1990), 334–362; Christopher Kenny and Michael McBurnett, "A Dynamic Model of the Effect of Campaign Spending on Congressional Vote Choice," *American Journal of Political Science* 36 (1992), 923–937; Donald Green and Jonathan Krasno, "Salvation for the Spendthrift Incumbent," *American Journal of Political Science* 32 (1988), 884–907; Gary Jacobson, *The Politics of Congressional Elections,* 2nd ed. (Boston: Little, Brown, 1987), ch. 4; Stephen Ansolabehere and Alan Gerber, "The Mismeasure of Campaign Spending," *Journal of Politics* 56 (1994), 1106–1118; Gerber, "Estimating the Effect of Campaign Spending."

[69] /www.opensecrets.org/news/2008/11/money-wins-white-house-and.html.

[70] The other was Jeanne Shaheen, who defeated Republican incumbent John Sununu. Ibid.

[71] "Scandal Shocks Even Those Who Helped It Along," *New York Times,* February 3, 2002, 7.

[72] Richard Stevenson and Jeff Gerth, "Web of Safeguards Failed as Enron Fell," *New York Times,* January 20, 2002, 1; Dan Morgan, "Enron's Cash Was Good for Democrats, Too," *Washington Post National Weekly Edition,* January 21, 2002, 12.

[73] Paul Krugman, "A System Corrupted," *New York Times,* January 18, 2002, A25. "Political Giving Wins Firms a Hearing, Doesn't Assure Aid," *Wall Street Journal,* January 15, 2002, 1ff.

[74] See Woodrow Jones and K. Robert Keiser, "Issue Visibility and the Effects of PAC Money," *Social Science Quarterly* 68 (1987), 170–176. Janet Grenzke, "PACs and the Congressional Supermarket," *American Journal of Political Science* 33 (1989), 1–24, found little effect of PAC money on a series of votes that were not obscure. Laura Langbein, "Money and Access," *Journal of Politics* 48 (1986), 1052–1064, shows that those who receive more PAC money spend more time with interest group representatives.

[75] Jean Reith Schroedel, "Campaign Contributions and Legislative Outcomes," *Western Political Quarterly* 39 (1986), 371–389; Richard L. Hall and Frank Wayman, "Buying Time: Moneyed Interests and the Mobilization of Bias in Congressional Committees," *American Political Science Review* 84 (1990), 797–820.

[76] Thomas Downey (D-N.Y.), quoted in "Running with the PACs," *Time,* October 25, 1982, 20.

[77] "Congress Study Links Funds and Votes," *New York Times,* December 30, 1987, 7.

[78] John Frendreis and Richard Waterman, "PAC Contributions and Legislative Behavior: Senate Voting on Trucking Deregulation," *Social Science Quarterly* 66 (1985), 401–412. See

also W. P. Welch, "Campaign Contributions and Legislative Voting," *Western Political Quarterly* 25 (1982), 478–495.

[79] Diana Evans, "Policy and Pork: The Use of Pork Barrel Projects to Build Policy Coalitions in the House of Representatives," *American Journal of Political Science* 38 (1994), 894–917; Laura Langbein, "PACs, Lobbies, and Political Conflict: The Case of Gun Control," *Public Choice* 75 (1993), 254–271; Laura Langbein and Mark Lotwis, "The Political Efficacy of Lobbying and Money: Gun Control in the House, 1986," *Legislative Studies Quarterly* 15 (1990), 413–440; Schroedel, "Campaign Contributions and Legislative Outcomes."

[80] Adam Clymer, "84 PACs Gave More to Senate Winners," *New York Times,* January 6, 1985, 13.

[81] Quoted in Drew, *Politics and Money,* 79.

[82] See Grenzke, "PACs and the Congressional Supermarket"; also see Frank Sorauf, *Money in American Elections* (Glenview, Ill.: Scott, Foresman, 1988).

[83] Grenzke, "PACs and the Congressional Supermarket"; John Wright, "Contributions, Lobbying, and Committee Voting in the U.S. House of Representatives," *American Political Science Review* 84 (1990), 417–438; Henry Chappel Jr., "Campaign Contributions and Voting on the Cargo Preference Bill," *Public Choice* 36 (1981), 301–312.

[84] Jonathan Alter, "Which Boot Will Drop Next?" *Newsweek,* February 4, 2002, 25.

[85] Alford and Brady, "Person and Partisan Advantages in U.S. Congressional Elections"; Peter Slevin, "Postwar Contracting Called Uncoordinated," *Washington Post,* October 31, 2003, A23.

[86] "Study: Bush Donors Get Government Favors," *Lincoln Journal Star,* May 28, 1992.

[87] "Clinton Regrets Rich Pardon," March 31, 2002, CBSNEWS.com/stories/2002/03/31/politics/main505042.shtml; BBC News World Edition, "Rich's '$450,000' for Clinton Library," news.bbc.co.uk/hi/English/world/Americas /newid_1163000/1163917.stm. George H. W. Bush's last-minute pardon of a convicted $1.5 million heroin trafficker got much less publicity; John Monk and Gary Wright, "Why Did Bush Free Smuggler? Mystery Lingers in Charlotte Case," *Charlotte Observer,* March 27, 1993, 1A.

[88] Al Kamen, "Donors and Cronies Still Get Choice Postings," *Washington Post,* October 23, 2009, www.washingtonpost.com/wp-dyn/content/article/2009/10/22/AR2009102204547.html.

[89] Charles Lewis, quoted in "Book Details Candidates' Extensive Financial Alignments," *Lincoln Journal Star,* January 12, 1996, 5A.

[90] Tom Kenworthy, "The Color of Money," *Washington Post National Weekly Edition,* November 6, 1989, 13.

[91] Quoted in Daniel Franklin, "Heiristocracy," *Washington Monthly,* May 2005, 60.

[92] Kevin Phillips, "How Wealth Defines Power," *American Prospect,* Summer 2003, A9; U.S. Census Bureau, *Statistical Abstract of the United States, 2003* (Washington, D.C.: Government Printing Office, 2003), tab. 688.

[93] http://www.webcitation.org/query?url=http%3A%2F%2Fwww.census.gov%2Fhhes%2Fwww%2Fincome%2Fhistinc%2Ff01AR.html&date=2009-04-12.

[94] Aviva Aron-Dean and Isaac Shapiro, "New Data Show Extraordinary Jump in Income Concentration in 2004," Center on Budget and Policy Priorities, July 10, 2006, www.cbpp.org/7-10-06inc.htm.

[95] See Federal Reserve Bank of San Francisco's "Economic Research and Data: National Trends in Income Inequality," http://www.frbsf.org/publications/economics/letter/2007/el2007-28.html.

[96] Gary Wasserman, "The Uses of Influence," *Washington Post National Weekly Edition,* January 11, 1993, 35.

[97] Juliet Eilperin, "The 'Hammer' DeLay Whips Lobbyists into Shape," *Washington Post National Weekly Edition,* October 25, 1999, 8.

[98] Jeff Leeds, "TV Stations Balk at Free Air Time for Candidates," *Lincoln Journal Star,* May 14, 2000, 3A.

[99] Susan Welch and John Peters, "Private Interests in the U.S. Congress," *Legislative Studies Quarterly* 7 (1982), 547–555; see also John Peters and Susan Welch, "Private Interests and Public Interests," *Journal of Politics* 45 (1983), 378–396.

[100] Paul Kane, "Invested in the Health-Care Debate," *Washington Post National Weekly Edition,* June 22–28, 2009, 15.

[101] Ibid. Members only have to report a range of holdings, rather than the specific amount, though some report the specific amount.

[102] Robert O'Harrow Jr., Kimberly Kindy, and Dan Keating, "Policy, Portfolios and the Investor Lawmaker," *Washington Post National Weekly Edition,* November 30–December 6, 2009, 12–13.

[103] "Congress for Sale," *USA Today,* March 7, 2006, 17A.

[104] Jeffrey Birnbaum, "Privately Funded Trips Add Up on Capitol Hill," *Washington Post,* June 6, 2006, A1.

[105] Ibid.

[106] Many news media covered this scandal and the complicated interrelationships within it extensively. See, for example, Karen Tumulty, "The Man Who Bought Washington," *Time,* January 16, 2006, 31–39.

[107] Norman Ornstein, "The House That Jack Built," *New York Times Book Review,* January 14, 2007, 25. See also Peter H. Stone, *Heist* (New York: Farrar, Straus, and Giroux, 2007).

[108] Ibid. See also indianz.com/News/2006/014803.asp; Philip Shenon, "Senate Report Lists Lobbyists' Payments to Ex-Head of Christian Coalition," *New York Times,* June 23, 2006, 22.

[109] Norman Ornstein, a fellow at the American Enterprise Institution, as quoted in Lou DuBose, "Broken Hammer," *Salon,* http://dir.salon.com/story/news/feature/2005/04/08/scandals/ index1.html.

[110] R. Jeffrey Smith and Juliet Eilperin, "Caught in an Ethical Snare," *Washington Post National Weekly Edition,* January 16–22, 2006, 14.

[111] Lou DuBose, "K Street Croupiers," *Texas Observer,* observer.bryhost.com/article.php?aid52138.

[112] For a rundown of these confusing front organizations, see ibid. and Tumulty, "The Man Who Bought Washington."

[113] Eliza Newlin Carney, "Cleaning House (and Senate)," *National Journal,* January 28, 2006, 33.

[114] Ibid.; "Congress for Sale."

[115] "Congress for Sale."

[116] Birnbaum, "Privately Funded Trips."

[117] Jonathan Alter, *The Promise* (New York: Simon & Schuster, 2010), 84.

[118] Mike McIntire, "New House Majority Leader Keeps Old Ties to Lobbyists," *New York Times,* July 15, 2006.

[119] Elizabeth Drew, "Having It All, Then Throwing It Away," *Time,* May 25, 1987, 22.

[120] Frank Rich, "The Road from K Street to Yusafiya," *New York Times,* June 25, 2006, WK13.

[121] Elizabeth Drew, "Letter from Washington," *New Yorker,* May 1, 1989, 99–108; see also Dan Balz, "Tales of Power and Money," *Washington Post National Weekly Edition,* May 1, 1989, 11–12.

[122] George Will, "Conservatives Have Plenty of Reasons to Hold onto Hope," *Lincoln Journal-Star,* November 9, 2006, 7B.

[123] Keith Bradsher, "How to Pooh-Pooh $70 Million War Chests," *New York Times,* April 30, 2000, 6.

[124] Quoted in Drew, "Having It All," 22.

[125] Hank Paulson, CEO of Goldman Sachs, quoted in Joseph Nocera, "System Failure," *Fortune,* June 24, 2002, 62ff.

Chapter 10

[1] Matt Bai, "Voter Insurrection Turns Mainstream, Creating New Rules," *New York Times*, May 19, 2010, A13.

[2] Ibid.

[3] James R. Chiles, "Congress Couldn't Have Been This Bad, or Could It?" *Smithsonian,* November 1995, 70–80.

[4] Susan Webb Hammond, "Life and Work on the Hill: Careers, Norms, Staff, and Informal Caucuses," in *Congress Responds to the Twentieth Century,* eds. Sunil Ahuja and Robert Dewhirst (Columbus: Ohio State University Press, 2003), 74.

[5] David S. Broder, "Dumbing Down Democracy," *Lincoln Journal Star,* April 5, 1995, 18.

[6] Quoted in Kenneth J. Cooper and Helen Dewar, "No Limits on the Term Limits Crusade," *Washington Post National Weekly Edition,* May 29, 1995, 14.

[7] David Nather, "Term Limits Now Have Limited Interest," *CQ Weekly,* January 19, 2009, 102.

[8] A list of cities and states that have term limits can be found at www.termlimits.org.

[9] *Baker* v. *Carr,* 369 U.S. 186 (1962).

[10] *Wesberry* v. *Sanders,* 376 U.S. 1 (1964).

[11] Bob Benenson, "With Enemies like These," *CQ Weekly,* April 28, 2008, 1086–1097.

[12] "Congress of Relative Newcomers Poses Challenge to Bush, Leadership," *Congressional Quarterly Weekly Review,* January 20, 2001, 179–181.

[13] "Departing Members of the 110th Congress," *CQ Weekly,* November 10, 2008, 3056.

[14] Hanna F. Pitkin, *The Concept of Representation* (Berkeley: University of California Press, 1967), 60.

[15] Ibid., 60–61.

[16] Leslie Laurence, "Congress Makes Up for Neglect," *Lincoln Journal Star,* December 5, 1994, 8.

[17] "Fewer Voters Identify as Republicans," Pew Research Center Publications, March 20, 2008, 1.

[18] Roger H. Davidson, Walter J. Oleszek and Frances E. Lee, *Congress and Its Members,* 11th ed. (Washington, D.C.: CQ Press, 2008), 191–194; Richard Fenno, *Home Style: House Members in Their Districts,* 2nd ed. (New York: Longman, 2003), 232–247.

[19] "Senate Odd Couples," *National Journal,* March 3, 2007, 37.

[20] William A. Galston and Thomas E. Mann, "The GOP's Grass-Roots Obstructionists," *Washington Post,* May 16, 2010, A17.

[21] Lydia Saad, "Conservatives Finish 2009 as No. 1 Ideological Group," Gallop report, January 7, 2010, www.gallop.com/poll/124958.

[22] See Thomas E. Mann, "Elections and Change in Congress," in *The New Congress* eds. Thomas E. Mann and Norman J. Ornstein (Washington, D.C.: American Enterprise Institute for Public Policy Research, 1981; David R. Mayhew, *Congress: The Electoral Connection* (New Haven: Yale University Press, 1974).

[23] Edie N. Goldenberg and Michael W. Traugott, *Campaigning for Congress* (Washington, D.C.: CQ Press, 1984); Gary C. Jacobson and Samuel Kernell, *Strategy and Choice in Congressional Elections* (New Haven, Conn.: Yale University Press, 1981).

[24] Edward Walsh, "Wanted: Candidates for Congress," *Washington Post National Weekly Edition,* November 25, 1985, 9.

[25] See Paul Feldman and James Jondrow, "Congressional Elections and Local Federal Spending," *American Journal of Political Science* 28 (1984), 152; Glenn R. Parker and Suzanne Parker, "The Correlates and Effects of Attention to District by U.S. House Members," *Legislative Studies Quarterly* 10 (1985), 239.

[26] Christopher Buckley, "Hangin' with the Houseboyz," *Washington Monthly* (June 1992), 44.

[27] Linda L. Fowler and Robert D. McClure, *Political Ambition: Who Decides to Run for Congress?* (New Haven, Conn.: Yale University Press, 1989), 47; John Hibbing and Sara Brandes, "State Population and the Electoral Success of U.S. Senators," *American Journal of Political Science* 27 (1983), 808–819. See also Glenn R. Parker, "Stylistic Change in the U.S. Senate, 1959–1980," *Journal of Politics* 47 (1985), 1190–1202.

[28] Thomas E. Mann, *Unsafe at Any Margin: Interpreting Congressional Elections* (Washington, D.C.: American Enterprise Institute for Public Policy Research, 1978).

[29] Stephen Ansolabehere and Philip Edward Jones, "Constituents' Responses to Congressional Roll-Call Voting," *American Journal of Political Science* 54 (July 2010), 583–597.

[30] Roger H. Davidson and Walter J. Oleszek, *Congress and Its Members,* (Washington, D.C.: CQ Press, 2004), 9th ed., 114

[31] Fenno, *Home Style.*

[32] Ibid., 145.

[33] *Budget of the United States, Fiscal 2011: Appendix* (Washington, D.C.: Government Printing Office, 2010).

[34] Quoted in Kenneth Shepsle, "The Failures of Congressional Budgeting," *Social Science and Modern Society* 20 (1983), 4–10. See also Howard Kurtz, "Pork Barrel Politics," *Washington Post,* January 25, 1982.

[35] See Gerald C. Wright Jr. and Michael B. Berkman, "Candidates and Policy in United States Senate Elections," *American Political Science Review* 80 (1986), 567–588; Robert S. Erikson and Gerald C. Wright, "Voters, Candidates, and Issues in Congressional Elections," in *Congress Reconsidered,* 7th ed., eds. Lawrence C. Dodd and Bruce I. Oppenheimer (Washington, D.C.: CQ Press, 2001), 67–95.

[36] NBC/*Wall Street Journal* poll, May 2010.

[37] The official count of 541 members includes the nonvoting delegates from U.S. territories and the District of Columbia.

[38] Congressional Quarterly, *The Origins and Development of Congress* (Washington, D.C.: CQ Press, 1976).

[39] Historian David S. Reynolds, quoting a newspaper reporter of the time in Sheryl Gay Stolberg, "What Happened to Compromise," *New York Times,* May 29, 2005, sec. 4, 4.

[40] Neil McNeil, *Forge of Democracy* (New York: McKay, 1963), 306–309.

[41] Willie Brown, longtime speaker of the California state house, quoted in Edward Epstein, "Her Key to the House," *CQ Weekly,* October 29, 2007, 3161.

[42] Epstein, "Her Key to the House," quoting Rep. Alan Boyd (D-Fla.), 3159.

[43] Karen Tumulty, "#4Nancy Pelosi," *Time,* December 28, 2009, 112.

[44] Edward Epstein, "Struggle in the Best of Scenarios," *CQ Weekly,* January 4, 2010, 12. Ronald Peters, quoted in Edward Epstein, "A Place in the House Pantheon?" *CQ Weekly,* May 10, 2010, 1128.

[45] Michael Barone, Richard E. Cohen, and Charles E. Cook Jr., *Almanac of American Politics, 2002* (Washington, D.C.: National Journal, 2002), 46.

[46] Historian Robert Dallek, quoted in John M. Broder, "Let Them Persuade You," *New York Times,* November 19, 2006, WK2.

[47] Ibid.

[48] Mark Schmitt, "Our Senate Problem," *The American Prospect,* March 2008, 9.

[49] Quoted by Carl Hulse, "Breakdown in Relations in the Senate Hobbles Its Ability to Get Things Done," *New York Times,* July 20, 2007.

[50] Kathleen Hunter, "Safe Seat Is No Job Perk for Today's Senate Leaders," *CQ Weekly,* May 5, 2008, 1157–1158.

[51] For a review of all congressional committees and subcommittees in the 110th Congress, see the special report, "CQ Guide to the Committees," *CQ Weekly,* April 16, 2007, 1084–1117.

[52] Davidson and Oleszek, *Congress and Its Members,* 9th ed., 198.

[53] See Roger Davidson, "Subcommittee Government," in *The New Congress,* 110–111. Some of this occurs because members of Congress tend to be wealthy, and the wealthy make investments in corporations. It also occurs because members' financial interests are often similar to the interests in their districts (for example, representatives from farm districts are likely to be involved in farming or agribusiness).

[54] Ronald Utt, "Federal Farm Subsidy Programs," June 7, 2007, http://www.heritage.org/Research/Reports/2007/06/Federal-Farm-Subsidy-Programs-How-to-Discourage-Congressional-Conflicts-of-Interest.

[55] Robert O'Harrow Jr. and Dan Keating, "Lawmakers Committee Assignments and Industry Investments Overlap," *Washington Post,* June 14, 2010, http://www.washingtonpost.com/wp-dyn/content/article/2010/06/13/AR2010061304881_2.html?sid=ST2010061304930.

[56] Ibid.

[57] Rebecca Kimitch, "CQ Guide to the Committees: Democrats Opt to Spread the Power," *CQ Weekly,* April 16, 2007, 1080.

[58] Sara Brandes Crook and John Hibbing, "Congressional Reform and Party Discipline: The Effects of Changes in the Seniority System on Party Loyalty in the U.S. House of Representatives," *British Journal of Political Science* 15 (1985), 207–226.

[59] Richard E. Cohen, "Best Seats in the House," *National Journal,* March 4, 2000, 682; Karen Foerstel, "House Offers Mixed Reviews for Committee Term Limits," *Congressional Quarterly Weekly Review,* June 22, 2002, 1653–1655.

[60] "88, Count 'Em" (Editorial), *New York Times,* January 9, 2010, A18.

[61] For a review of how the task force has been used, see Walter J. Oleszek, "The Use of Task Forces in the House," Congressional Research Service, Report 96-8, 3-GOV, 1996, www.house.gov/rules/96-843.htm.

[62] Ida A. Brudnick, "The Congressional Research Service and the American Legislative Process," Congressional Research Service, Report RL33471, March 19, 2008, 2.

[63] *Budget of the United States, Fiscal 2011* (Washington, D.C.: Government Printing Office, 2010), 19–21.

[64] "111th Congress, First Session: By the Numbers," *CQ Weekly,* January 11, 2010, 144

[65] www.willrogerstoday.com/will_rogers_quotes/quotes.cfm?w_ID=4.

[66] Gail Collins, "The Age of Nancy," *New York Times,* June 26, 2010, A19.

[67] Kimitch, "CQ Guide to the Committees," 1080.

[68] Epstein, "Her Key to the House," 3164–3165.

[69] Sarah A. Binder, "The History of the Filibuster," testimony before the U.S. Senate Committee on Rules and Administration,

April 22, 2010, www.brookings.edu/testimony/2010/0422_filibuster_binder.aspx?p=1.

70 Ibid.

71 Joseph J. Schatz, "Looking for Room to Maneuver," *CQ Weekly*, April 19, 2010, 954.

72 Quoted in Carl Hulse, "In New Histories on Two Powerbrokers, Hints of the Future," *New York Times*, July 19, 2009, 22.

73 Thomas E. Mann, "The Negative Impact of the Use of Filibusters and Holds," testimony before the Senate Committee on Rules and Administration, June 23, 2010, www.brookings.edu/testimony/2010/0623_filibuster_mann.aspx?p=1.

74 George Packer, "The Empty Chamber," *The New Yorker*, August 8, 2010, 47.

75 Ibid., 49.

76 Ibid., 47.

77 Rep. George Miller, quoted in Schatz, "Looking for Room to Maneuver," 954.

78 Paul C. Light, "Filibusters Are Only Half the Problem," *New York Times,* June 3, 2005.

79 Clinton aide Chuck Brain, quoted in Richard E. Cohen, "The Third House Rises," *National Journal,* July 28, 2001, 2395.

80 David J. Vogler, *The Third House: Conference Committees in the United States Congress* (Evanston, Ill.: Northwestern University Press, 1971); see also Lawrence D. Longley and Walter J. Oleszek, *Bicameral Politics* (New Haven, Conn.: Yale University Press, 1989).

81 Edward Epstein, Dusting Off Deliberation," *CQ Weekly*, June 14, 2010, 1441.

82 "88, Count 'Em" (Editorial), A18.

83 Morris Ogul, "Congressional Oversight: Structures and Incentives," in *Congress Reconsidered,* eds. Dodd and Oppenheimer; see also Loch Johnson, "The U.S. Congress and the CIA: Monitoring the Dark Side of Government," *Legislative Studies Quarterly* 5 (1980), 477–501.

84 Joseph Califano, "Imperial Congress," *New York Times Magazine,* January 23, 1994, 41.

85 Richard E. Cohen, Kirk Victor, and David Bauman, "The State of Congress," *National Journal,* January 10, 2004, 104–105.

86 Quoted in ibid., 105.

87 Henry A. Waxman, "Free Pass from Congress," *Washington Post,* July 6, 2004, A19.

88 Cohen, Victor, and Bauman, "State of Congress," 96.

89 Jonathan Allen, "The Earmark Game: Manifest Disparity," *CQ Weekly*, October 1, 2007, 2836–2841.

90 David Baumann, "Tempest in a Barrel," *National Journal,* February 11, 2006, 58.

91 Sheryl Gay Stolberg, "What's Wrong with a Healthy Helping of Pork?" *New York Times,* May 28, 2006, WK4.

92 Rahm Emanuel, "Don't Get Rid of Earmarks," *New York Times*, August 24, 2007. Emanuel, later White House chief of staff, was a member of the House Democratic leadership when he wrote this.

93 Gail Collins, "George Speaks, Badly," *New York Times*, March 15, 2008, 19.

94 Kerry Young, "The Price of a Sluggish Purse," *CQ Weekly,* May 24, 2010,1262–1268.

95 Carl Hulse, "Spending Posts Now a Liability for Lawmakers," *New York Times*, August 12, 2010 A1.

96 Herbert Asher, "Learning of Legislative Norms," *American Political Science Review* 67 (1973), 499–513. Michael Berkman points out that freshmen who have had state legislative experience adapt to the job faster than other members. See "Former State Legislators in the U.S. House of Representatives: Institutional and Policy Mastery," *Legislative Studies Quarterly* 18 (1993), 77–104.

97 Richard Rubin, "Party Unity: An Ever Thicker Dividing Line," *CQ Weekly*, January 11, 2010, 122.

98 Thomas Mann of the Brookings Institution, quoted in Richard E Cohen, Kirk Victor and David Baumann, "The *State of Congress,*" *National Journal,* January 10, 2004, 85.

99 Citizens for Responsibility and Ethics in Washington, "Beyond Delay: The 22 Most Corrupt Members of Congress," www.beyonddelay.org/report.

100 Molly Hooper and Alan K. Ota, "House Votes for Outside Ethics Review," *CQ Weekly*, March 17, 2008, 726.

101 A list of members under investigation and of members who hire family members, have close relatives who lobby Congress, or have used their positions to financially benefit members of their families can be found at the website of Citizens for Responsibility and Ethics in Washington, www.citizensforethics.org.

102 Rep. Jim DeMint (R-S.C.), quoted in Davidson and Oleszek, *Congress and Its Members,* 9th ed., 264.

103 Gordon S. Wood, *Empire of Liberty: A History of the Early Republic, 1789–1815* (New York: Oxford University Press, 2009), 329–330.

104 *Minot* (N.D.) *Daily News,* June 17, 1976, quoted in Randall Ripley, *Congress: Process and Policy* (New York: Norton, 1983), 3rd ed.

105 Roger H. Davidson, Walter H. Oleszek, and Frances E. Lee, *Congress and Its Members,* 11th ed. (Washington, D.C.: CQ Press, 2008), 299.

106 Peter Baker, "100 Ways to Become a Senator," *New York Times*, January 4, 2009, WK1.

107 A complete listing of House and Senate caucuses can be found in the *Congressional Directory*, which is issued twice each year.

108 Baker, "100 Ways to Become a Senator," WK1.

109 Samuel Kernell, *Going Public* (Washington, D.C.: CQ Press, 1986).

110 Edward Epstein, "Weaving a Modern GOP Web," *CQ Weekly*, May 31, 2010, 1323; Faye Fiore, "Lawmakers Tweet Up a Storm," *Los Angeles Times*, February 22, 2010, 1.

111 Collen J. Shogan, "Blackberries, Tweets, and YouTube: Technology and the Future of Communicating with Congress," *PS*, April 2010, 232.

112 "C-Span Milestones," www.c-span.org,about/company/index.asp?code=MILESTONES.

113 Carl Hulse, "3 Right-Hand Men Take a Turn at Center Stage," *New York Times,* November 13, 2009.

114 Mildred Amer, "Membership of the 111th Congress: A Profile," Congressional Research Service, Report R40086, December 31, 2008, 2.

115 Michael Wines, "Washington Really Is in Touch. We're the Problem," *New York Times,* October 16, 1994, sec. 4, 2.

116 Davidson, Oleszek, and Lee, *Congress and Its Members,* 11th ed., 150.

117 *New York Times/*CBS poll, May 2006.

118 Schatz, "Looking for Room to Maneuver," 957; "Public Knowledge: State Legislative Process a Mystery to Many," PEW poll, January 2010, pewresearch.org/pubs/political-iq-quiz-knowledge-filibuster-debt-colbert-steel.

119 Richard Rubin, "Party Unity: An Ever Thicker Dividing Line," *CQ Weekly*, January 11, 2010, 122–126.

Chapter 11

1 Lyndon Johnson quoted by Bob Herbert, *New York Times*, March 3, 2009.

2 Doris Kearns Goodwin, *Lyndon Johnson and the American Dream* (New York: Harper and Row, 1976), 283.

3 On Johnson's realization that the Vietnam War was not winnable, see Michael Beschloss, *Reaching for Glory: Lyndon Johnson's Secret White House Tapes* (New York: Simon & Schuster, 2001), 166.

4 Presidential historian Alan Brinkley in "The Making of a War President," *New York Times Book Review,* August 20, 2006, 10.

5 Woodrow Wilson, *Congressional Government: A Study in American Politics* (New Brunswick, N.J.: Transaction, 2002). Originally published in 1885.

6 Theodore Lowi, *The Personal President: Power Invested, Promise Unfulfilled* (Ithaca, N.Y.: Cornell University Press, 1985).

7 Harold M. Barger, *The Impossible Presidency* (Glenview, Ill.: Scott, Foresman, 1984).

8 Carl M. Cannon, "Untruth and Consequences," *The Atlantic,* January–February, 2007, 59.

9 Bob Dole, a Republican who ran in 1996, was the exception. David Leonhardt, "Who's in the Corner Office?" *New York Times,* November 27, 2005, BU1.

10 Quoted in David von Drehle, "Does Experience Matter in a President?" *Time,* March 10, 2008, 30.

11 "George Mason: Forgotten Founder," *Smithsonian,* May 2000, 145.

12 Information on all three impeachment proceedings can be found at www.historyplace.com.

13 *Federalist Paper* 69, by Alexander Hamilton.

14 Thomas E. Mann, "The Negative Impact of the Use of Filibusters and Holds." Testimony before the Senate Committee on Rules and Administration, June 23, 2010, www.brookings.edu/testimony/2010/0623_filibuster_mann.aspx?p=1.

15 For discussion of the president's removal powers in light of a 1988 Supreme Court decision regarding independent counsels, see John A. Rohr, "Public Administration, Executive Power, and Constitutional Confusion," and Rosemary O'Leary, "Response to John Rohr," *Public Administrative Review* 49 (1989), 108–115.

[16] Jones, *The Presidency in a Separated System* (Washington, D.C.: Brookings Institution, 1994), 53.

[17] Dana Priest and William Arkin, "Top Secret America," *Washington Post.* The story ran on July 18, 19, 20, and 21, 2010. http://projects.washingtonpost.com/top-secret-america/.

[18] Michael Nelson, ed. *The Presidency A to Z* (Washington D.C.: CQ Press, 1998), 169.

[19] Ibid., 170.

[20] For elaboration, see Lee Epstein and Jeffrey A. Segal, *Advice and Consent* (New York: Oxford University Press, 2005), ch. 5.

[21] Jeb Stuart Magruder, "Ex-aide: Nixon Ordered Watergate Break-in," *Lincoln Journal Star,* July 27, 2003.

[22] Charlie Savage, "Bush, Out of Office, Could Oppose Inquiries," *New York Times,* November 13, 2008.

[23] Andrew Sullivan, "We Don't Need a New King George," *Time,* January 23, 2006, 74.

[24] Charlie Savage, "Obama Looks to Limit Impact of Tactic Bush Used to Sidestep New Laws," *New York Times,* March 10, 2009.

[25] Charlie Savage, "Bush Challenges Hundreds of Laws: President Cites Powers of his Office," *Boston Globe,* April 30, 2006, A1.

[26] Savage, "Obama Looks to Limit Impact."

[27] Francis Wilkinson, "Song of Myself," *New York Times,* January 31, 2006.

[28] Ted Widmer, "The State of the Union Is Unreal," *New York Times,* January 31, 2006.

[29] Quoted in George Lardner Jr., "A High Price for Freedom," *New York Times,* March 26, 2007.

[30] George Lardner Jr., "Begging Bush's Pardon," *New York Times,* February 4, 2008.

[31] A complete list of presidential pardons since 1790 can be found at www.infoplease.com.

[32] Rather than expressly authorizing the president to abrogate a treaty by himself, the majority ruled that the dispute was a "political question," which avoided a ruling on the merits of Carter's claim. Thus the Court allows, but doesn't authorize, the president to take this action. *Goldwater v. Carter,* 444 U.S. 996 (1979).

[33] He also refused to recognize the treaty creating the International Criminal Court, which Clinton had signed but never submitted for Senate approval. Because Clinton had signed it, the United States was a participant in discussions of rules for the court even while not being an official party to the treaty. Bush's "unsigning" pulled the United States from these talks.

[34] For some trade agreements, Congress delegates power to the president in advance; others require majority approval.

[35] John Marshall, as a member of the House of Representatives. Later, Marshall would become chief justice of the United States.

[36] *United States v. Curtiss-Wright Export Corporation,* 299 U.S. 304 (1936).

[37] See the discussion in *Federalist Paper* 69, written by Alexander Hamilton.

[38] Quoted in "Notes and Comment," *New Yorker,* June 1, 1987, 23.

[39] Ibid.

[40] *Youngstown Sheet and Tube Co. v. Sawyer,* 343 U.S. 579 (1952).

[41] Garry Wills, *Bomb Power: The Modern Presidency and the National Security State* (New York: Penguin Press, 2010), 1, 3.

[42] Ron Suskind, *The One Percent Doctrine: Deep Inside America's Pursuit of Its Enemies since 9/11* (New York: Simon & Schuster, 2006), 65.

[43] The two principal lawyers were longtime Cheney aide David Addington, who became Cheney's chief of staff when Lewis Libby was indicted on obstruction of justice charges in 2006, and Deputy Assistant Attorney General John Yoo, later a law professor at the University of California-Berkeley, who elaborated on his ideas in *The Powers of War and Peace: The Constitution and Foreign Affairs after 9/11* (Chicago: University of Chicago Press, 2005). For others involved, see Keith Perine, "Imbalance of Power," *CQ Weekly,* February 27, 2006, 545; and Charlie Savage, *Takeover: The Return of the Imperial Presidency and the Subversion of American Democracy* (New York: Little, Brown & Co., 2007). Savage's book won the Pulitzer Prize.

[44] Paul Starobin, "Long Live the King!" *National Journal,* February 18, 2006, 26.

[45] Jeffrey K. Tulis, *The Rhetorical Presidency* (Princeton, N.J.: Princeton University Press, 1987).

[46] Quoted in Garry Wills, *Lincoln at Gettysburg* (New York: Simon & Schuster, 1992), 31.

[47] Ibid., 8.

[48] Lowi, *The Personal President*, x.

[49] Richard E. Neustadt, *Presidential Power* (New York: Wiley, 1960), 5–6.

[50] Lowi, *The Personal President,* x.

[51] David Halberstam, *The Powers That Be* (New York: Dell, 1980), 30.

[52] Benjamin C. Bradlee, "When They Made George Washington, They Broke the Mold," *Washington Post National Weekly Edition,* November 25–December 1, 1991, 23.

[53] Thomas E. Patterson, *The Vanishing Voter* (New York: Knopf, 2002), 54.

[54] Samuel Kernell, *Going Public: New Strategies of Presidential Leadership* (Washington, D.C.: CQ Press, 1986), 15.

[55] Michael Waldman, Clinton's former chief speechwriter, interviewed on *Morning Edition,* National Public Radio, January 1, 2002.

[56] Ari Fleischer, quoted in *Congressional Quarterly Today News,* May 19, 2003, www.cq.com.

[57] Scott McClellan, *What Happened: Inside the Bush White House and Washington's Culture of Deception* (New York: Public Affairs, 2008).

[58] Nicholas Lemann, "Remember the Alamo," *New Yorker,* October 18, 2004, 153.

[59] James David Barber, *The Presidential Character,* 2nd ed. (Englewood Cliffs, N.J.: Prentice Hall, 1977), 157.

[60] Ibid.

[61] Bruce Miroff, "The Presidency and the Public: Leadership and Spectacle," in *The Presidency and the Political System,* 5th ed., ed. Michael Nelson (Washington: CQ Press, 1998), 320. This section draws heavily on Miroff's observations.

[62] Jones, *The Presidency in a Separated System,* ch. 4.

[63] Thomas F. Cronin, *The State of the Presidency* (Boston: Little, Brown, 1975), 118.

[64] Congress's anger at Roosevelt's court-packing scheme held up the reorganization for two years; see Chapter 13.

[65] Jones, *The Presidency in a Separated System,* 56–57.

[66] For more on Bush's White House staff and method of making appointments, see G. Calvin Mackenzie, "The Real Invisible Hand: Presidential Appointees in the Administration of George W. Bush," and Martha Joynt Kumar, "Recruiting and Organizing the White House Staff," *PS: Political Science and Politics* 1 (2002), 27–40.

[67] "Hell from the Chief: Hot Tempers and Presidential Timber," *New York Times,* November 7, 1999, sec. 4, 7.

[68] Quoted in Richard Pious, *The American Presidency* (New York: Basic Books, 1979), 244.

[69] Public Broadcasting System, *The American President,* episode 10.

[70] Ann Reilly Dowd, "What Managers Can Learn from Manager Reagan," *Fortune,* September 15, 1986, 32–41.

[71] See John H. Kessel, "The Structures of the Reagan White House," *American Journal of Political Science* 28 (1984), 231–258.

[72] Hillary Rodham Clinton, quoted in Carol Gelderman, *All the Presidents' Words: The Bully Pulpit and the Creation of the Virtual Presidency* (New York: Walker, 1997), 160.

[73] A good description of Clinton's relationship to his White House staff can be found in Joe Klein, *The Natural: The Misunderstood Presidency of Bill Clinton* (New York: Doubleday, 2002).

[74] For more on Bush's management style, see the several articles in the special section "C.E.O. U.S.A.," *New York Times Magazine,* January 14, 2001, 24–58.

[75] Mike Allen, "Living Too Much in the Bubble," *Time,* September 19, 2005, 44.

[76] Ron Suskind, *The Price of Loyalty: George W. Bush, the White House, and the Education of Paul O'Neill* (New York: Simon & Schuster, 2004).

[77] Edith P. Mayo, ed. *Smithsonian Book of First Ladies* (Washington, D.C.: Smithsonian Institution, 1996), 11.

[78] Gil Troy, *Affairs of State: The Rise and Rejection of the First Couple since World War II* (New York: Free Press, 1997), 250. Troy also discusses attempts at reorganizing the first lady's office. See especially 178–188 and 248–258.

[79] Nelson, *The Presidency A to Z,* 487–488.

[80] For a review of the backgrounds of men who have served in the vice presidency and the roles they have played, see L. Edward Purcell, *Vice Presidents* (New York: Facts on File, 2001); Michael Nelson, *A Heartbeat Away* (New York: Priority, 1988); Paul C. Light, *Vice-Presidential Power: Advice and Influence in the White House* (Baltimore: Johns Hopkins University Press, 1984); and George Sirgiovanni, "The 'Van Buren Jinx': Vice Presidents Need Not Beware," *Presidential Studies Quarterly* 18 (1988), 61–76.

[81] Karine Premont, "The Contemporary American Vice Presidency: A School for the

Presidency?" *World Political Science Review* 5, no. 1 (2009), 7–8, www.bepress.com/wpsr/vol5/iss1/art13.

[82] Jane Mayer, "The Hidden Power," *New Yorker,* July 3, 2006, 50.

[83] Nicholas Lemann, "The Quiet Man," *New Yorker,* May 7, 2001, 68.

[84] Paul Light, quoted in Daniel Radosh, "No. 1 Authority," *New Yorker,* July 26, 2004, 30.

[85] Former White House counsel Bradford A. Berenson, quoted in Jo Becker and Barton Gellman, "A Strong Push from Backstage," *Washington Post,* June 26, 2007, A01. This article is from a series by Becker and Gellman that ran in the *Post* June 24–27, 2007, under the title "Angler: The Cheney Vice Presidency."

[86] CBS News poll, March 2006.

[87] James Traub, "After Cheney," *New York Times Magazine,* November 29, 2009, 36.

[88] Goodwin, *Lyndon Johnson and the American Dream,* 226.

[89] Thomas P. O'Neill Jr., with William Novak, *Man of the House* (New York: Random House, 1987), 341–342.

[90] The representative wasn't identified. "Contra Proposal Heads for Showdown in House," *Lincoln Journal,* June 25, 1986, A1.

[91] Sen. Barry Goldwater (R-Ariz.), who was referring to Johnson's tenure as majority leader, although the same could have been said about his tenure as president. Burton Bernstein, "Profiles—AuH2O," *New Yorker,* April 28, 1988, 64.

[92] Goodwin, *Lyndon Johnson and the American Dream,* 122.

[93] Ibid., 140–141.

[94] Sheryl Gay Stolberg, "As Agenda Falters, Bush Tries a More Personal Approach in Dealing with Congress," *New York Times,* June 11, 2006, YT26.

[95] According to congressional scholar Thomas Mann, quoted in Janet Hook, "Bush Gets Personal on Social Security, *Los Angeles Times,* April 25, 2005, www.latimes.com/news/nationalworld/la=ha=bushlobby25apr25.story.

[96] Hook, "Bush Gets Personal on Social Security." However, when the president pushed his proposal for Social Security in 2006, he did make an effort to meet with and listen to lawmakers, once he realized that his proposal was in trouble.

[97] James A. Thurber, quoted in Stolberg, "As Agenda Falters."

[98] "Bush Starts a Strong Record of Success with the Hill," *Congressional Quarterly Weekly Review,* January 12, 2002, 112.

[99] Carl M. Cannon, "Veto This!" *National Journal,* October 13, 2007, 32.

[100] A complete list of vetoes cast since 1789 can be found at www.infoplease.com/ipa/A0801767.html.

[101] John M. Broder, "Report Urges Overhaul of War Powers Law," *New York Times,* July 9, 2008.

[102] A classic study on this topic is James David Barber, *Presidential Character: Predicting Performance in the White House* (Englewood Cliffs, N.J.: Prentice Hall, 1989), originally published in 1973.

[103] Quoted in Arthur M. Schlesinger Jr., "The Ultimate Approval Rating," *New York Times Magazine,* December 18, 1996, 50.

[104] Barger, *The Impossible Presidency.*

[105] Klein, *The Natural,* 208.

[106] See, for example, the comments of Arthur M. Schlesinger Jr. in Carl M. Cannon, "Judging Clinton," *National Journal,* January 1, 2000, 22; Steven A. Holmes, "Losers in Clinton-Starr Bouts May Be Future U.S. Presidents," *New York Times,* August 23, 1998, 18; and Adam Clymer, "The Presidency Is Still There, Not Quite the Same," *New York Times,* February 14, 1999, sec. 4, 1.

[107] Bruce Fein, former associate deputy attorney general in the Reagan administration, quoted in Mayer, "The Hidden Power," 46.

[108] Charles O. Jones and Kathryn Dunn, "Shaping the 44th Presidency," Issues in Governance Studies, Paper #9, Brookings Institution, August 2007, 5.

[109] Ibid.

[110] Jones found that evenly matched was more common in his study. Jones, *The Presidency in a Separated System,* 293.

[111] Ibid., 1.

[112] Charles O. Jones, *Separate but Equal Branches* (Chatham, N.J.: Chatham House, 1995), 107.

Chapter 12

[1] Andrew C. Revkin, "Climate Expert Says NASA Tried to Silence Him," *New York Times,* January 29, 2006, 1; Juliet Eilperin, "Censorship Is Alleged at NOAA: Scientists Afraid to Speak Out," *Washington Post,* February 11, 2006, A7. For an overview of findings on climate change, go to www.realclimate.org.

[2] Andrew Revkin, "Bush Aide Softened Greenhouse Gas Links to Global Warming," *New York Times,* June 8, 2005, 1.

[3] Gardiner Harris, "Surgeon General Sees Five Year Term as Compromised," *Washington Post,* July 11, 2006, www.nytimes.com/2007/07/11/washington/11surgeon.html?_r51&oref5slogin. For reports on these issues, go to the website of the Union of Concerned Scientists (www.ucsusa.org) and that of the Federation of American Scientists (www.usfas.org).

[4] Dennis Overbye, "Someday the Sun Will Go Out and the World Will End (but Don't Tell Anyone)," *New York Times,* February 14, 2006, F3.

[5] Revkin, "Climate Expert Says NASA Tried to Silence Him."

[6] Paul C. Light, quoted in Adam Sheingate, "Why Can't Americans See the State?" *The Forum* 7, no. 4 (2009), http://www.bepress.com/forum/vol7/iss4/art1.

[7] Bruce Adams, "The Frustrations of Government Service," *Public Administration Review* 44 (1984), 5. For more discussion of public attitudes about the civil service, see Herbert Kaufman, "Fear of Bureaucracy: A Raging Pandemic," *Public Administration Review* 41 (1981), 1.

[8] The classic early work on Western bureaucracy is Max Weber's. See H. H. Gerth and C. Wright Mills, trans., from Max Weber, *Essays on Sociology* (New York: Oxford University Press, 1946), 196–239.

[9] On distinctions between public and private bureaucracies, see Barry Bozeman, *All Organizations Are Public: Bridging Public and Private Organizational Theories* (San Francisco: Jossey-Bass, 1987).

[10] Bill Vlasic, "After Bankruptcy, G.M. Struggles to Shed a Legendary Bureaucracy," *New York Times,* November 13, 2009.

[11] Workplace death and accident statistics by year can be found at the Bureau of Labor Statistics, www.bls.gov.

[12] "Federal Executives' Bonuses Scrutinized," *Champaign-Urbana News-Gazette,* January 23, 2002, A4.

[13] From a letter to W. T. Barry, quoted in "A Citizen's Guide on Using the Freedom of Information Act and the Privacy Act of 1974 to Request Government Records," report to the U.S. House of Representatives 50 (1999), 2.

[14] Harold C. Relyea and Michael W. Kolakowski, "Access to Government Information in the United States," Congressional Research Service Report 97-71 GOV, December 5, 2007, 2–3.

[15] For a description of the nine exempt categories of information, see Harold C. Relyea, "Freedom of Information Act (FOIA) Amendments: 110th Congress," Congressional Research Service Report RL32780, January 7, 2008, 3. A link to CRS reports on openness in government can be found at www.fas.org.

[16] This information is posted by the Justice Department at www.usdoj.gov/04foia/04_6html.

[17] Reported in Sam Archibald, "The Early Years of the Freedom of Information Act, 1955–1974," *PS: Political Science and Politics,* December 1993, 730.

[18] Government Accounting Office, *Freedom of Information Act: State Department Request Processing* (Washington, D.C.: Government Printing Office, 1989).

[19] Clinton administration policy on compliance with FOIA can be found in Federation of American Scientists, Project on Government Secrecy, "Clinton Administration Documents on Classification Policy," 2003, www.fas.org/sgp/clinton/index.html.

[20] "President Declassifies Old Papers," *Omaha World-Herald,* April 18, 1995, 1.

[21] Linda Greenhouse, "A Penchant for Secrecy," *New York Times,* May 5, 2002, WK1.

[22] As a presidential aide in the Ford administration, Cheney encouraged President Ford to veto the 1974 bill that strengthened FOIA rights. Congress ultimately passed the bill over Ford's veto.

[23] "Sunshine on History" (editorial), *New York Times,* March 12, 2007, A22.

[24] Useful websites for tracking data removed from government websites include www.ombwatch.org; openthegovernment.org; and www.fas.org.

[25] Ellen Nakashima, "Frustration on the Left—and the Right," *Washington Post National Weekly Edition,* March 11, 2002, 29; Scott Shane, "Increase in the Number of Documents Classified by the Government," *New York Times,* July 3, 2005, 12.

[26] Shane, "Increase in the Number of Documents Classified by the Government," 12; David

Nather, "Classified: A Rise in State Secrets," *CQ Weekly*, July 18, 2005, 1960.

27 For a review of legislation introduced in the 110th Congress, see Relyea, CRS Report RL32780, 2–15.

28 Former OMB director Peter Orzag, quoted in "Data.gov" (editorial), *New York Times*, May 26, 2009.

29 "Obama Plan Takes Cautious Approach to Throwing Open Papers," *Champaign-Urbana News-Gazette,* December 21, 2009, A5.

30 Alan Feuer, "When Media Giants Face Off against Financial Heavyweights," *New York Times*, February 14, 2010, 27.

31 Noah Feldman, "In Defense of Secrecy," *New York Times Magazine*, February 15, 2009, 12. Feldman is a law professor at Harvard.

32 Evan Hendricks, *Former Secrets: Government Records Made Public through the Freedom of Information Act* (Washington, D.C.: Campaign for Political Rights, 1982); "Behind the Freedom of Information Act," *Now with Bill Moyers,* PBS, April 5, 2002.

33 Charlie Savage, "Loosening of F.B.I. Rules Stirs Privacy Concerns," *New York Times*, October 29, 2009.

34 Joyce Appleby, "That's General Washington to You," *New York Times Book Review*, February 14, 1993, 11, a review of Richard Norton Smith, *Patriarch* (Boston: Houghton Mifflin, 1993). See also James Q. Wilson, "The Rise of the Bureaucratic State," *Public Interest* 41 (1975), 77–103.

35 Wilson, "Rise of the Bureaucratic State."

36 Leonard D. White, *Introduction to the Study of Public Administration*, 4th ed. (New York: Macmillan, 1955), 4.

37 David H. Rosenbloom, "'Whose Bureaucracy Is This Anyway?' Congress's 1946 Answer," *PS: Political Science and Politics*, December 2001, 773.

38 Paul C. Light, *Thickening Government: Federal Hierarchy and the Diffusion of Accountability* (Washington, D.C.: Brookings Institution, 1995).

39 *Budget of the United States for Fiscal Year 2011, Analytical Perspectives* (Washington D.C.: Government Printing Office, 2010), 99.

40 Sheingate, "Why Can't Americans See the State?" 6.

41 Louis Uchitelle, "Uncle Sam Wants You . . . to Have a Job," *New York Times*, January 31, 2010, WK5.

42 Ibid.; "Federal Government Found to Have Gotten Bigger," *Champaign-Urbana News-Gazette*, January 23, 2004, A3.

43 Paul C. Light, "Fact Sheet on the Continued Thickening of Government," Brookings Institution, July 23, 2004, www.brookings.edu/views/papers/light/20040723.htm.

44 Ibid. Light does an "inventory" of senior positions in cabinet departments every six years.

45 Paul C. Light, "The Real Crisis in Government," *Washington Post*, January 12, 2010, A17.

46 Donald Moynihan, "The Politics Measurement Makes: Performance Management in the Obama Era," *The Forum* 7, no. 4 (2007), 4–5, www.bepress.com/forum/vol7/iss4/art 7.

47 Sheryl Gay Stolberg, "Obama Tells His Cabinet to Look for Efficiency, *New York Times*, April 21, 2009.

48 Uchitelle, "Uncle Sam Wants You," WK5.

49 Jim Hoagland, "Dissing Government," *Washington Post National Weekly Edition*, December 8, 2003, 5.

50 Paul C. Light, "What Federal Employees Want from Reform: Reform Watch Brief No. 5," Brookings Institution, March 2002, www.brookings.edu/comm/reformwatch/rw05.htm.

51 On the privatization of defense and foreign policy work, see Allison Stanger, *One Nation under Contract: The Outsourcing of American Power and the Future of Foreign Policy* (New Haven: Yale University Press, 2009).

52 Sheingate, "Why Can't Americans See the State?"

53 Michael D. Shear, "National Security, Inc.," *Washington Post*, July 20, 2010, A9.

54 Dana Priest and William M. Arkin, "A Modern World, Growing beyond Control," *Washington Post*, July 19, 2010, A7–8. This was the first in a three-part series reporting on the newspaper's two-year investigation into the growth of the intelligence bureaucracy.

55 Dana Priest and William M. Arkin, "The Secrets Next Door," *Washington Post*, July 21, 2010, A11.

56 Department of Defense, "Internal Controls over Payments in Iraq, Kuwait, and Egypt," May 2008. Auditing and oversight reports can be found at the website of the Department of Defense's Inspector General, www.dodig.osd.mil.

57 James Risen, "Electrical Risks at Iraqi Bases Are Worse than Said," *New York Times*, July 18, 2008.

58 John M. Broder and David Rohde, "Use of Contractors by State Department Has Soared," *New York Times*, October 24, 2007.

59 James Risen and Mark Mazzetti, "Blackwater Guards Tied to Secret Raids by the C.I.A.," *New York Times*, December 11, 2009, A1.

60 Stanger, One *Nation under Contract*.

61 Shear, "National Security, Inc.," A8.

62 For a discussion of these issues, see Peter T. Kilborn, "Big Change Likely as Law Bans Bias toward Disabled," *New York Times*, July 19, 1992, 1, 16.

63 Jill Smolows, "Noble Aims, Mixed Results," *Time*, July 31, 1995, 54.

64 Theodore Lowi, *The End of Liberalism* (New York: W. W. Norton, 1969).

65 George Packer, "The Empty Chamber," *New Yorker,* August 8, 2010, 51.

66 Stephen Lerner of the Service Employees International Union, quoted in Binyamin Appelbaum, "Warren's Candidacy Raises a Partisan Debate," *New York Times*, July 25, 2010, B1.

67 This quote from Roosevelt and others about the merit system can be found at www.opm.gov/about_opm/tr/quotes/asp.

68 Woodrow Wilson, "The Study of Administration," *Political Science Quarterly* 56 (1941), 481–506. Originally published in 1887.

69 See David H. Rosenbloom, "Have an Administrative Rx? Don't Forget the Politics!" *Public Administration Review* 53 (1993), 503–507.

70 The Hatch Act and subsequent revisions can be found at the Office of Personnel Management's website by linking to its Office of Special Counsel (www.opm.gov).

71 John Solomon, Alec MacGillis, and Sarah Cohen, "How Rove Harnessed Government for GOP Gains," *Washington Post*, August 19, 2007, 1, A6. The Hatch Act violation came in a briefing to the General Services Administration, where it was recommended that GSA contracts be awarded with an eye to helping Republican candidates. The head of the GAO was later forced to resign.

72 Charlie Savage, "For White House, Hiring Is Political," *New York Times*, July 31, 2008, 17.

73 The 146-page report is available at the Department of Justice website, www.justice.gov.

74 Claudia Dreifus, "A Conversation with Sherwood Boehlert: A Science Advocate and 'An Endangered Species,' He Bids Farewell," *New York Times*, May 9, 2006, F2.

75 Benjamin Wallace-Wells, "Cass Sunstein Wants to Nudge Us," *New York Times Magazine,* May 16, 2010, 38.

76 Charles Peters, *How Washington Really Works* (Reading, Mass.: Addison-Wesley, 1980), 46–47.

77 Nicolas Thompson, "Finding the Civil Service's Hidden Sex Appeal," *Washington Monthly*, November 2000, 31.

78 "Eight Years Is More than Enough" (editorial), *New York Times*, November 23, 2008.

79 Terry More, "Regulators' Performance and Presidential Administrations," *American Journal of Political Science* 26 (1982), 197–224; Terry More, "Control and Feedback in Economic Regulation," *American Political Science Review* 79 (1985), 1094–1116.

80 Ian Urbina, "U.S. Said to Allow Drilling without Needed Permits," *New York Times*, May 14, 2010, 1; Ian Urbina, "Inspector Generals' Inquiry Faults Regulators," *New York Times*, May 24, 2010, A16.

81 More, "Control and Feedback."

82 Use of the term *capture* by political scientists studying regulation seems to have originated with Samuel Huntington, "The Marasmus of the ICC," *Yale Law Journal* 61 (1952), 467–509; it was later popularized by Marver Bernstein, *Regulating Business by Independent Commission* (Princeton, N.J.: Princeton University Press, 1955).

83 W. John Moore, "Citizen Prosecutors," *National Journal,* August 18, 1990, 2006–2010.

84 Interview with David Brancaccio, *NOW* (PBS), October 14, 2005.

85 Robert Pear, "Congress Moves to Protect Federal Whistleblowers," *New York Times,* October 3, 2004, 21.

86 Philip Shenon, "F.B.I. Raids Office of Special Counsel," *New York Times*, May 7, 2008, 18.

87 Fred Alford, quoted in Barbara Ehrenreich, "All Together Now," *New York Times,* July 15, 2004, A23.

88 Schmitt, "Is This Any Way to Run a Nation?" *New York Times*, April 14, 2002, WK4.

Chapter 13

[1]This act is discussed in more detail in Chapter 15.

[2]The jury awarded her $3.8 million, to punish Goodyear as well as to compensate her, but the judge reduced the award to $300,000.

[3]167 L.Ed.2d 982 (2007).

[4]A bill was introduced in Congress to allow such suits, but it was blocked by a Republican filibuster in 2008. In some circumstances, the Equal Pay Act could be used instead, but Ledbetter's lawyers decided that it wouldn't work for her. This act is also discussed in Chapter 15.

[5]Lisa Takeuchi Cullen, "Show Us Our Money," *Time*, May 12, 2008, 137.

[6]Rickey Gard Diamond, "Lilly Ledbetter and Diana Levine: Living with the Heartbreak of SCOTUS," *Vermont Woman Newspaper*, April 2010, vermontwoman.com/articles/1009/ LillyLed.shtml.

[7]John Hibbing and Elizabeth Theiss-Morse, *Congress as Public Enemy: Public Attitudes toward American Political Institutions* (New York: Cambridge University Press, 1995), chs. 2 and 3.

[8]John R. Schmidhauser, *Justices and Judges* (Boston: Little, Brown, 1979), 11.

[9]However, federalism doesn't require this exact arrangement. Most federal countries have one national court over a system of regional courts.

[10]In addition, there is the Court of Appeals for the Federal Circuit, which handles customs and patents cases.

[11]Occasionally, for important cases, the entire group of judges in one circuit will sit together, "en banc." (In the large Ninth Circuit, eleven judges will sit.)

[12]If at least $75,000 is at stake, according to congressional law.

[13]Quoted in Henry J. Abraham, "A Bench Happily Filled," *Judicature* 66 (1983), 284.

[14]For elaboration on the Senate's role, see Stephen B. Burbank, "Politics, Privilege, and Power: The Senate's Role in the Appointment of Federal Judges," *Judicature* 86 (2002), 24.

[15]Victor Navasky, *Kennedy Justice* (New York: Atheneum, 1971), 245–246.

[16]Harry P. Stumpf, *American Judicial Politics*, 2nd ed. (Upper Saddle River, N.J.: Prentice Hall, 1998), 175. After Taft nominated a Catholic to be chief justice, the Speaker of the House cracked, "If Taft were Pope, he'd want to appoint some Protestants to the College of Cardinals." Henry J. Abraham, *Justices and Presidents: A Political History of Appointments to the Supreme Court*, 2nd ed. (New York: Oxford University Press, 1985), 168.

[17]The Nixon administration was the first to recognize that it could accomplish some policy goals by selecting lower court judges on the basis of ideology. Elliot E. Slotnick, "A Historical Perspective on Federal Judicial Selection," *Judicature* 86 (2002), 13.

[18]For an analysis of internal documents that established this process in the Reagan administration, see Dawn Johnsen, "Tipping the Scale," *Washington Monthly*, July–August 2002, 1–18.

[19]Jo Becker and Barton Gellman, "The Veep Steered While Vetting Conservatives for the Court," *Washington Post National Weekly Edition*, July 16–22, 2007, 9.

[20]Ibid.

[21]Ginsburg, Kagan, Scalia, and Sotomayor.

[22]The Jews are Breyer, Ginsburg, and Kagan.

[23]347 U.S. 483 (1954).

[24]Marilyn Nejelski, *Women in the Judiciary: A Status Report* (Washington, D.C.: National Women's Political Caucus, 1984).

[25]Sheldon Goldman, "Reagan's Second-Term Judicial Appointments," *Judicature* 70 (1987), 324–339.

[26]Sheldon Goldman, Elliott E. Slotnick, Gerard Gryski, Gary Zuk, and Sara Schiavoni, "W. Bush Remaking the Judiciary: Like Father like Son?" *Judicature* 86 (2003), 304, 308. For further examination, see Rorie L. Spill and Kathleen A. Bratton, "Clinton and Diversification of the Federal Judiciary," *Judicature*, March–April 2001, 256.

[27]Especially congressional power under the commerce clause.

[28]Lauren Collins, "Number Nine," *New Yorker*, January 11, 2010, 52.

[29]Tom Korologos, "Roberts Rx: Speak Up, but Shut Up," *New York Times*, September 4, 2005. www.nytimes.com/2005/09/04/ weekinreview/04stol.html.

[30]*Scott* v. *Sandford*, 60 U.S. 393 (1857).

[31]*Korematsu* v. *U.S.*,323 U.S. 214 (1944).

[32]"Judging Samuel Alito," *New York Times*, January 8, 2006, WK13.

[33]Janet Malcolm, "The Art of Testifying," *New Yorker*, March 13, 2006, 74.

[34]See, for example, Erwin Chemerinsky, "Conservative Justice," *Los Angeles Times*, June 29, 2007, www.latimes.com/news/opinion/la-oe-chemerinsky29jun29,0,504056,print.story?col.

[35]Arlen Specter (R-Pa.), quoted in Jeffrey Toobin, "Comment: Unanswered Questions," *New Yorker*, January 23 and 30, 2006, 30.

[36]David Greenberg, "Actually, It Is Political," *Washington Post National Weekly Edition*, July 26–August 1, 2004, 23.

[37]One of President Reagan's nominees, Douglas Ginsburg, withdrew his nomination due to widespread opposition in the Senate, so officially his nomination was not denied.

[38]Nixon's nomination of G. Harold Carswell was a notable exception. At his confirmation hearing, a parade of legal scholars called him undistinguished. Even his supporters acknowledged that he was mediocre. Nixon's floor manager for the nomination, Sen. Roman Hruska (R-Neb.), blurted out in exasperation, "Even if he is mediocre, there are a lot of mediocre judges and people and lawyers. They are entitled to a little representation, aren't they, and a little chance? We can't have all Brandeises, Cardozos, and Frankfurters, and stuff like that there." Abraham, *Justices and Presidents*, 6–7.

[39]For an examination of the relationship between ethical lapses and ideological reasons, see Charles M. Cameron, Albert D. Cover, and Jeffrey A. Segal, "Senate Voting on Supreme Court Nominees: A Neoinstitutional Model," *American Political Science Review* 84 (1990), 525–534.

[40]For some time, the Senate confirmed fewer nominees to the lower courts in the fourth year of a president's term when the Senate's majority was from the other party. The senators hoped their candidate would capture the White House in the next election. They delayed confirmation so there would be numerous vacancies for their president and, through senatorial courtesy, for themselves to fill as well. Jeffrey A. Segal and Harold Spaeth, "If a Supreme Court Vacancy Occurs, Will the Senate Confirm a Reagan Nominee?" *Judicature* 69 (1986), 188–189.

[41]Quoted in Savage, "Clinton Losing Fight for Black Judge," *Los Angeles Times*, July 7, 2000, A1.

[42]Scherer, "Judicial Confirmation Process," 240–250.

[43]Charlie Savage, "Conservatives Map Strategies on Court Fight," *New York Times*, May 17, 2009, Y1.

[44]Collins, "Number Nine," 52.

[45]By, among others, Rush Limbaugh, Newt Gingrich, and Rep. Tom Tancredo (R-Colo.), who accused her of being in the "Latino KKK."

[46]*Ricci* v. *DeStefano*, 174 L.Ed.2d 490 (2009).

[47]Robin Abcarian, Kate Linthicum, and Richard Fausset, "Conservatives Say It's Their Turn for Empowerment," *Los Angeles Times*, September 17, 2009, latimes.com/news/ nationworld/nation/la-na-white-victimhood17-2009sep17,0,2618101.story.

[48]Some other schools and groups of faculty filed lawsuits against the federal policy, seeking a ruling that would allow the schools to bar military recruiters from campus. Kagan followed the federal law until a federal court of appeals invalidated it; then she followed that court's ruling. When the Supreme Court reversed the court of appeals, Kagan followed the Supreme Court's ruling. For further explanation, see Amy Goldstein, "Foes May Target Kagan's Stance on Military Recruitment at Harvard," April 18, 2010, www.washingtonpost.com/wp-dyn/ content/article/2010/04/17/AR2010041701296. html?sid=ST20100417.

[49]James Oliphant, "GOP Looks beyond Court Pick," *Los Angeles Times*, April 13, 2010, latimes.com/news/nationworld/nation/la-na-gop-courts13-2010apr13,0,3941526.story. Savage, "Conservatives Map Strategies."

[50]Schmidhauser, *Justice and Judges*, 55–57.

[51]David Leonhardt, "Who Has a Corner Office?" *New York Times*, November 27, 2005, BU4.

[52]All except Kennedy, Sotomayor, and possibly Alito and Kagan.

[53]Bernie Becker, "Justices List Their Assets; Wide Range of Wealth," *New York Times*, June 7, 2008, query.nytimes.com/gst/fullpage.html? res=9B05E5DF1F3CF934A35755COA96E9C 8B63.

[54]Goldman et al., "W. Bush Remaking the Judiciary," 304, 308.

[55]As an alternative, Congress in 1980 established other procedures to discipline lower court judges. Councils made up of district and appellate court judges can ask their fellow judges to resign or can prevent them from hearing cases, but they cannot actually remove them. The procedures

have been used infrequently, although their existence has prompted some judges to resign before being disciplined.

[56]Merle Miller, *Plain Speaking* (New York: Berkeley Putnam, 1974), 121.

[57]Harold W. Chase, *Federal Judges* (Minneapolis: University of Minnesota Press, 1972), 189.

[58]John Gruhl, "The Impact of Term Limits for Supreme Court Justices," *Judicature* 81 (1997), 66–72.

[59]The fourth, Rehnquist, disqualified himself because he had worked on the administration's policy toward executive privilege.

[60]*Jones v. Clinton*, 137 L.Ed.2d 945, 117 S. Ct. 1636 (1997).

[61]Martin Shapiro, "The Supreme Court: From Warren to Burger," in *The New American Political System*, ed. Anthony King (Washington, D.C.: American Enterprise Institute, 1978), 180–181.

[62]Robert Scigliano, *The Supreme Court and the Presidency* (New York: Free Press, 1971), 147–148.

[63]Quoted in Abraham, *Justices and Presidents*, 62.

[64]Earl Warren, *The Memoirs of Earl Warren* (Garden City, N.Y.: Doubleday, 1977), 5.

[65]Quoted in Abraham, *Justices and Presidents*, 63.

[66]Linda Greenhouse, "In the Confirmation Dance, the Past but Rarely the Prologue," *New York Times*, July 24, 2005, WK5.

[67]For elaboration, see Lee Epstein and Jeffrey A. Segal, *Advice and Consent* (New York: Oxford University Press, 2005), ch. 5. Choosing judges with extensive records on lower courts especially limits surprises. Adam Liptak, "Why Newer Appointees Offer Fewer Surprises from Bench," *New York Times,* April 18, 2010, Y1.

[68]"How Much Do Lawyers Charge?" *Parade*, March 23, 1997, 14.

[69]Lois G. Forer, *Money and Justice* (New York: Norton, 1984), 9, 15, 102.

[70]Jonathan Casper, "Lawyers before the Supreme Court: Civil Liberties and Civil Rights, 1957–1966," *Stanford Law Review*, February 1970, 509.

[71]Peter Slevin, "Courting Christianity," *Washington Post National Weekly Edition*, July 17–23, 2006, 29.

[72]Karen O'Connor and Lee Epstein, "The Rise of Conservative Interest Group Litigation," *Journal of Politics* 45 (1983), 481. See also Richard C. Cortner, *The Supreme Court and the Second Bill of Rights* (Madison: University of Wisconsin Press, 1981), 282.

[73]Rick Perlstein, "Christian Empire," *New York Times Book Review*, January 7, 2007, 15.

[74]Jeffrey Rosen, "Supreme Court Inc.," *New York Times Magazine*, March 16, 2008, 44. The Court also takes about this many to decide summarily—without oral arguments and full written opinions. Dahlia Lithwick, "Realignment?" *Washington Post National Weekly Edition*, June 23–July 6, 2008, 25.

[75]The dentist agreed to fill the cavity only in a hospital, where the procedure would be far more expensive. *Bragdon v. Abbott*, 141 L.Ed.2d 540 (1998).

[76]*Toyota Motor Manufacturing v. Williams*, 151 L.Ed.2d 615 (2001).

[77]Henry J.Abraham, *The Judicial Process, 3rd ed.* (New York: Oxford University Press, 1975), 324.

[78]*United States v. Butler*, 297 U.S. 1, at 94.

[79]Walter F. Murphy and C. Herman Pritchett, *Courts, Judges, and Politics, 3rd ed.* (New York: Random House, 1979), 586.

[80]Anthony Peccarelli, "The Meaning of Justice?" *DCBA Brief Online* (Journal of the DuPage County Bar Association), no date, http://www. dcba.org/brief/marissue/2000/art10300.htm.

[81]*Furman v. Georgia*, 408 U.S. 238 (1972). Blackmun did vote against the death penalty later in his career.

[82]Quoted in Alexander Bickel, *The Morality of Consent* (New Haven, Conn.: Yale University Press, 1975), 120.

[83]"Judicial Authority Moves Growing Issue," *Lincoln Journal*, April 24, 1977.

[84]Jeffrey A. Segal and Albert D. Cover, "Ideological Values and the Votes of U.S. Supreme Court Justices," *American Political Science Review* 83 (1989), 557–564. For different findings for state supreme court justices, see John M. Scheb II, Terry Bowen, and Gary Anderson, "Ideology, Role Orientations, and Behavior in the State Courts of Last Resort," *American Politics Quarterly* 19 (1991), 324–335.

[85]Harold Spaeth and Stuart Teger, "Activism and Restraint: A Cloak for the Justices' Policy Preferences," in *Supreme Court Activism and Restraint*, eds. Stephen P. Halpern and Clark M. Lamb (Lexington, Mass.: Lexington Books, 1982), 277.

[86]*Burnet v. Coronado Oil and Gas*, 285 U.S. 293 (1932), at 406.

[87]*Engel v. Vitale*, 370 U.S. 421 (1962).

[88]*Abington School District v. Schempp*, 374 U.S. 203 (1963).

[89]*Stone v. Graham*, 449 U.S. 39 (1980).

[90]*Lee v. Weisman*, 120 L.Ed.2d 467 (1992).

[91]*Santa Fe Independent School District v. Doe*, 147 L.Ed.2d 295 (2000).

[92]*Roe v. Wade*, 410 U.S. 113 (1973).

[93]*Planned Parenthood of Southeastern Pennsylvania v. Casey*, 120 L.Ed.2d 674 (1992).

[94]*United States v. Butler*, 297 U.S. 1 (1936), at 79.

[95]Some might say that judges, rather than make law, mediate among various ideas that rise to the surface, killing off some and allowing others to survive. Robert Cover, "Nomos and Narrative," *Harvard Law Review* 97 (1983), 4.

[96]Quoted in Murphy and Pritchett, *Courts, Judges, and Politics*, 25.

[97]*Gratz v. Bollinger*, 156 L.Ed.2d 257 (2003); *Grutter v. Bollinger*, 156 L.Ed.2d 304 (2003).

[98]Quoted in David J. Garrow, "The Rehnquist Reins," *New York Times Magazine*, October 6, 1996, 70.

[99]Jeffrey Toobin, *The Nine: Inside the Secret World of the Supreme Court* (New York: Doubleday, 2007), 129, 195.

[100]Collins, "Number Nine," 44.

[101]Ibid., 263.

[102]Quoted in Robert Wernick, "Chief Justice Marshall Takes the Law in Hand," *Smithsonian*, November 1998, 162.

[103]Joan Biskupic, "Here Comes the Judge? Maybe Not," *Washington Post National Weekly Edition*, February 14, 2000, 30.

[104]Jeffrey A. Segal and Harold J. Spaeth, *The Supreme Court and the Attitudinal Model* (New York: Cambridge University Press, 1993), 262–264.

[105]Justice Breyer, quoted by Jeffrey Toobin, "Breyer's Big Idea," *New Yorker*, October 31, 2005, 43.

[106]*Morning Edition*, National Public Radio, March 5, 2004.

[107]Michael S. Serrill, "The Power of William Brennan," *Time*, July 22, 1985, 62.

[108]Ibid.

[109]David J. Garrow, "One Angry Man," *New York Times Magazine*, October 6, 1996, 68–69.

[110]*Webster v. Reproductive Health Services*, 492 U.S. 490 (1989).

[111]*United States v. Virginia*, 135 L.Ed.2d 735, 787–789 (1996).

[112]Charles Evans Hughes, *The Supreme Court of the United States* (New York: Columbia University Press, 1928), 68.

[113]Interview with Justice Ruth Bader Ginsburg, *Morning Edition*, National Public Radio, May 2, 2002. Ginsburg said that foreign jurists admit they disagree with each other but do not make it public.

[114]Craig R. Ducat, *2005 Supplement for Constitutional Interpretation*, 8th ed. (Belmont, Calif.: Wadsworth, 2006), 3.

[115]Linda Greenhouse, "The High Court and the Triumph of Discord," *New York Times*, July 15, 2001, sec. 4, 1. Perhaps this calls into question Rehnquist's reputation as an effective leader.

[116]*Federalist Paper* 78.

[117]Henry J. Abraham, *Justices and Presidents* (New York: Oxford University Press, 1974), 74.

[118]Henry J. Abraham, *The Judicial Process*, 3rd ed. (New York: Oxford University Press, 1975), 309.

[119]Drew Pearson and Robert S. Allen, *The Nine Old Men* (New York: Doubleday/Doren, 1937), 7; Barbara A. Perry, *The Priestly Tribe: The Supreme Court's Image in the American Mind* (Westport, Conn.: Praeger, 1999), 8–9.

[120]There's evidence that many Founders expected the federal courts to use judicial review eventually. Some state courts already used judicial review, and in *Federalist Paper* 78 Hamilton said that the federal courts would have authority to void laws contrary to the Constitution.

[121]5 U.S. 137 (1803). Technically, *Marbury* was not the first use of judicial review, but it was the first clear articulation of judicial review by the Court.

[122]Jefferson was also angry at the nature of the appointees. One had led troops loyal to England during the Revolutionary War. Eric Black, *Our Constitution: The Myth That Binds Us* (Boulder, Colo.: Westview Press, 1988), 66.

[123]Debate arose over whether the four should be considered appointed. Their commissions had been signed by the president, and the seal of

the United States had been affixed by Marshall, as secretary of state. Yet it was customary to require commissions to be delivered, perhaps because of less reliable record keeping by government or less reliable communications at the time.

[124]Marbury had petitioned the Court for a writ of *mandamus* under the authority of a provision of the Judiciary Act of 1789 that permitted the Court to issue such a writ. Marshall maintained that this provision broadened the Court's original jurisdiction and thus violated the Constitution. (The Constitution allows the Court to hear cases that have not been heard by any other court before—if they involve a state or a foreign ambassador. Marbury's involved neither.) Yet it was quite clear that the provision did not broaden the Court's original jurisdiction—so clear, in fact, that Marshall did not even quote the language he was declaring unconstitutional. Furthermore, even if the provision did broaden the Court's original jurisdiction, it is not certain that the provision would violate the Constitution. (The Constitution does not say that the Court shall have original jurisdiction only in cases involving a state or a foreign ambassador.) Many members of Congress who had drafted and voted for the Judiciary Act had been delegates to the Constitutional Convention, and it is unlikely that they would have initiated a law that contradicted the Constitution. And Oliver Ellsworth, who had been a coauthor of the bill, then served as chief justice of the Supreme Court before Marshall. But these interpretations allowed Marshall a way out of the dilemma.

[125]Quoted in Walter F. Murphy and C. Herman Pritchett, *Courts, Judges, and Politics,* 3rd ed. (New York: Random House, 1979), 4.

[126]John A. Garraty, "The Case of the Missing Commissions," in *Quarrels That Have Shaped the Constitution,* ed. John A. Garraty (New York: Harper & Row, 1962), 13.

[127]*Fletcher* v. *Peck,* 10 U.S. 87 (1810); *Martin* v. *Hunter's Lessee,* 14 U.S. 304 (1816); *Cohens* v. *Virginia,* 19 U.S. 264 (1821).

[128]In other cases, the Court narrowly construed state power, especially to regulate commerce. *Gibbons* v. *Ogden,* 22 U.S. 1 (1824).

[129]For a development of this idea, and a critique of judicial review, see James MacGregor Burns, *Packing the Court: The Rise of Judicial Power and the Coming Crisis of the Supreme Court* (New York: Penguin, 2009).

[130]However, the Warren Court may not have been as out of step with the political branches as is often believed. See Lucas A. Powe, *The Warren Court and American Politics* (Cambridge, Mass.: Harvard University Press, 2000), 160–178.

[131]Particularly regarding criminal defendants' rights.

[132]One legal scholar says the most striking feature about Supreme Court decision making in the 1990s was the effort by five justices to resolve most issues as narrowly as possible, shunning sweeping pronouncements for case-by-case examination. Cass R. Sunstein, *One Case at a Time: Judicial Minimalism on the Supreme Court* (Cambridge, Mass.: Harvard University Press, 2001).

[133]The Rehnquist Court reduced the scope of criminal defendants' rights, racial minorities' rights, and affirmative action. It also tightened access to the courts for individuals and groups trying to challenge government policies, and it limited efforts by Congress to impose new regulations on the states. However, the Court did take the first step toward homosexuals' legal rights.

[134]Thomas M. Keck, *The Most Activist Supreme Court in History* (Chicago: University of Chicago Press, 2004).

[135]531 U.S. 98 (2000).

[136]Scalia and Kennedy were appointed by Reagan; Thomas, Roberts, and Alito worked in the administration.

[137]The possible exception is Justice Ginsburg, who replaced Justice Byron White. Jeffrey Rosen, "The Dissenter," *New York Times Magazine,* September 23, 2007, 52.

[138]Thomas, Scalia, Roberts, and Alito. William M. Landes and Richard A. Posner, "Rational Judicial Behavior: A Statistical Analysis," *Journal of Legal Analysis* 1 (2009), 775–831.

[139]Lawrence Baum, *The Supreme Court* (Washington, D.C.: CQ Press, 2004),170, 173.

[140]Craig R. Ducat and Robert L. Dudley, "Federal Appellate Judges and Presidential Power," paper presented at the Midwest Political Science Association meeting, April 1987.

[141]Sheldon Goldman, "How Long the Legacy?" *Judicature* 76 (1993), 295.

[142]The Eleventh Amendment overturned *Chisholm* v. *Georgia* (1793), which had permitted the federal courts to hear suits against a state by citizens of another state. The Fourteenth overturned the Dred Scott case, *Scott* v. *Sandford* (1857), which had held that blacks were not citizens. The Sixteenth overturned *Pollock v. Farmers' Loan and Trust* (1895), which had negated a congressional law authorizing a federal income tax. The Twenty-sixth overturned *Oregon* v. *Mitchell* (1970), which had negated a congressional law allowing eighteen-year-olds to vote in state elections.

[143]William N. Eskridge Jr., "Overriding Supreme Court Statutory Interpretation Decisions," *Yale Law Journal* 101 (1991), 338.

[144]*Goldman* v. *Weinberger,* 475 U.S. 503 (1986).

[145]Detainee Treatment Act of 2005 and Military Commissions Act of 2006. *Hamdan* v. *Rumsfeld,* 548 U.S. 557 (2006); *Boumediene* v. *Bush, 553 U.S.* 723 (2008).

[146]Thomas R. Marshall, "Public Opinion and the Rehnquist Court," in *Readings in American Government and Politics,* 3rd ed. (Boston: Allyn & Bacon, 1999), 115–121. Also see Barry Friedman, *The Will of the People: How Public Opinion Has Influenced the Supreme Court and Shaped the Meaning of the Constitution* (New York: Farrar, Straus & Giroux, 2009).

[147]Richard Morin, "A Nation of Stooges," *Washington Post,* October 8, 1995, C5.

[148]Gregory A. Caldeira, "Neither the Purse nor the Sword," paper presented at the American Political Science Association meeting, August 1987.

[149]Quoted in Abraham, *Justices and Presidents,* 342–343.

[150]Robert G. McCloskey, *The American Supreme Court* (Chicago: University of Chicago Press, 1960), 225. Also see Friedman, *The Will of the People.*

[151]See, especially, Burns, *Packing the Court.*

Chapter 14

[1] In addition to the reference to a militia, the phrase "bear arms" at the time referred to military service, according to law professor Michael Dorf. Cited in Adam Liptak, "A Militia of One (Well Regulated)," *New York Times,* January 13, 2008, WK4.

[2] The Supreme Court had not ruled directly on this issue; the last Supreme Court decision, in *U.S.* v. *Miller,* 307 U.S. 174 (1939), held that there was no right to have sawed-off shotguns. Lower courts had ruled overwhelmingly that the Second Amendment was only a collective right. By 2007, nine U.S. courts of appeals had reached this conclusion. (Two had reached the opposite conclusion.) Adam Liptak, "A Liberal Case for Gun Rights Helps Sway Federal Judiciary," *New York Times,* May 6, 2007, YT1.

[3] Ibid., YT25.

[4] A few law professors may have contributed by concluding that the amendment provides an individual right, because the militias at the Founding included all individuals who had political rights, such as the rights to vote and to serve on juries—that is, all white males who owned property. Today the individuals who have political rights would encompass all adult citizens (except felons in most states). For examination of the conflicting views, see David C. Williams, *The Mythic Meanings of the Second Amendment* (New Haven, Conn.: Yale University Press, 2003).

[5] 171 L.Ed.2d 637 (2008).

[6] The majority cited these exceptions while acknowledging that future cases may test the limits.

[7] Richard Morin, "The High Price of Free Speech," *Washington Post National Weekly Edition,* January 8, 2001, 34.

[8] After 9/11, support for civil liberties dropped, reflecting people's fears. By 2005, however, support returned to pre–9/11 levels. First Amendment Center, in cooperation with the *American Journalism Review.* Survey conducted May 13–23, 2005 (N = 1003; sampling error = 3%).

[9] The states didn't ratify a proposed amendment that would have required at least one representative in Congress for every fifty thousand people. That amendment would have put about five thousand members in today's Congress. The states also didn't ratify, until 1992, another proposed amendment that would have prohibited a salary raise for members of Congress from taking effect until after the next election to Congress.

[10] *Reid* v. *Covert,* 354 U.S. 1 (1957).

[11] *Barron* v. *Baltimore,* 32 U.S. 243 (1833).

[12] Also, many states had their own bill of rights at the time, and other states were expected to follow.

[13] *Gitlow* v. *New York,* 268 U.S. 652 (1925). Gitlow is usually cited as the first because it initiated the twentieth-century trend. However, Chicago, *Burlington and Quincy R. Co.* v. *Chicago,* 166 U.S. 266 (1897), was actually the first. It applied the Fifth Amendment's just compensation clause, requiring government to pay owners "just compensation" for taking their property.

[14] *Argersinger* v. *Hamlin,* 407 U.S. 25 (1972).

[15] It hasn't applied the Fifth Amendment's guarantee of a grand jury in criminal cases or the Seventh Amendment's guarantee of a jury trial in civil cases. The grand jury no longer serves as a protective shield for potential criminal defendants; rather, it's become a prosecutorial tool. The Seventh Amendment guarantees a jury trial in civil cases when $20 or more is at stake, so that would require a commitment of scarce resources even for trivial cases.

[16] The amendment also includes a right "to petition the government for a redress of grievances," which is incorporated in freedom of speech and assembly. The language doesn't explicitly include freedom of association, but the Court has interpreted the amendment to encompass this right.

[17] Anna Johnson, "Know Your First Amendment Rights? Poll Shows Many Don't," *Lincoln Journal Star*, March 1, 2006, 10A.

[18] Even Justice Black, who claimed that he interpreted it literally. To do so, he had to define some speech as "action" so that it wouldn't be protected.

[19] *Milk Wagon Drivers Union* v. *Meadowmoor Dairies*, 312 U.S. 287 (1941).

[20] Thomas I. Emerson, *The System of Freedom of Expression* (New York: Random House/Vintage, 1971), 6–8.

[21] Quoted in Deborah Tannen, *The Argument Culture* (New York: Ballantine, 1998), 25.

[22] For a history of speech cases between the Civil War and World War I, see David M. Rabban, *Free Speech in Its Forgotten Years* (New York: Cambridge University Press, 1997).

[23] The Sedition Act of 1918. In addition, the Espionage Act of 1917 prohibited interfering with military recruitment, inciting insubordination in military forces, and mailing material advocating rebellion.

[24] Zechariah Chafee Jr., *Free Speech in the United States* (Cambridge, Mass.: Harvard University Press, 1941), 51–52.

[25] *Schenk* v. *United States*, 249 U.S. 47 (1919); *Frohwerk* v. *United States*, 249 U.S. 204 (1919); *Debs* v. *United States*, 249 U.S. 211 (1919); *Abrams* v. *United States*, 250 U.S. 616 (1919); *Gitlow* v. *New York*, 268 U.S. 652 (1925); *Whitney* v. *California*, 274 U.S. 357 (1927).

[26] *Gitlow* v. *New York*.

[27] David Cole, "The Course of Least Resistance: Repeating History in the War on Terrorism," in *Lost Liberties*, ed. Cynthia Brown (New York: New Press, 2003), 15.

[28] Novelist Philip Roth observes, "McCarthy understood better than any American politician before him that people whose job was to legislate could do far better for themselves by performing; McCarthy understood the entertainment value of disgrace and how to feed the pleasures of paranoia. He took us back to our origins, back to the seventeenth century and the stocks. That's how the country began: moral disgrace as public entertainment." *I Married a Communist* (New York: Vintage, 1999), 284.

[29] The Smith Act (1940). This act wasn't as broad as the World War I acts because it didn't forbid criticizing the government.

[30] *Dennis* v. *United States*, 341 U.S. 494 (1951).

[31] For the role of the Senate's Internal Security Committee, see Michael J. Ybarra, *Washington Gone Crazy: Senator Pat McCarran and the Great American Communist Hunt* (Hanover, N.H.: Steerforth, 2004).

[32] Charles Peters, "Tilting at Windmills," *Washington Monthly*, May 2006, 8. See also Ted Morgan, *Reds: McCarthyism in Twentieth-Century America* (New York: Random House, 2003). For a review of other books about Soviet spies in America, see Nicholas Lemann, "Spy Wars," *New Yorker*, June 27, 2009, 70.

[33] In the cases of *Yates* v. *United States*, 354 U.S. 298 (1957), and *Scales* v. *United States*, 367 U.S. 203 (1961), among others.

[34] The doctrine was created in a case in which a Ku Klux Klan leader said at a rally that the Klan might take "revengeance" against the president, Congress, and the Supreme Court if they continued "to suppress the white, Caucasian race." *Brandenburg* v. *Ohio*, 395 U.S. 444 (1969).

[35] *Brandenburg* v. *Ohio*.

[36] Attorney General Tom Clark quoted in *Esquire*, November 1974.

[37] Cole, "Course of Least Resistance," 1.

[38] Jean E. Jackson, "ACTA Report Criticizes Professors," *Anthropology News*, March 2002, 7.

[39] Gia Fenoglio, "Is It 'Blacklisting' or Mere Criticism?" *National Journal*, January 19, 2002, 188.

[40] For some examples, see Michael Tomasky, "Dissent in America," *American Prospect*, April 2003, 22. See also Ann Coulter, *Treason: Liberal Treachery from the Cold War to the War on Terrorism* (New York: Crown Forum, 2003), and Sean Hannity, *Deliver Us from Evil* (New York: Regan Books/HarperCollins, 2004).

[41] C. Herman Pritchett, *The American Constitution*, 2nd ed. (New York: McGraw-Hill, 1968), 476, n. 2. However, police in some places continue to arrest for swearing. Judy Lin, "ACLU Fights Police on Profanity Arrests in Pittsburgh Area," *Lincoln Journal Star*, July 11, 2002.

[42] *Gooding* v. *Wilson*, 405 U.S. 518 (1972); *Lewis* v. *New Orleans*, 408 U.S. 913 (1972).

[43] *Cohen* v. *California*, 403 U.S. 15 (1971).

[44] However, businesses can restrict the speech of their employees at work because they're private entities.

[45] *Collin* v. *Smith*, 447 F.Supp. 676 (N.D. Ill., 1978); *Collin* v. *Smith*, 578 F.2d 1197 (7th Cir, 1978).

[46] *United States* v. *Schwimmer*, 279 U.S. 644 (1929).

[47] *Virginia* v. *Black*, 155 L.Ed.2d 535 (2003). Previously, the Court invalidated a St. Paul, Minnesota, ordinance prohibiting the display of a Nazi swastika or a cross-burning on public or private land. *R.A.V.* v. *St. Paul*, 120 L.Ed.2d 305 (1992).

[48] For a legal analysis supporting these codes, see Richard Delgado and David H. Yun, "Pressure Valves and Bloodied Chickens: An Analysis of Paternalistic Objections to Hate Speech Regulation," *University of California Law Review* 82 (1994), 716.

[49] Mary Jordan, "Free Speech Starts to Have Its Say," *Washington Post National Weekly Edition*, September 21–27, 1992, 31.

[50] Michael D. Shear, "A Tangled World Wide Web," *Washington Post National Weekly Edition*, October 30–November 5, 1995, 36.

[51] Stephanie Simon, "Christians Sue for Right Not to Tolerate Policies," *Los Angeles Times*, April 10, 2006, www.latimes.com/news/nationworld/nation/la-nachristians10apr10,0,6204444.story?

[52] *All Things Considered*, National Public Radio, January 4, 2010.

[53] *Barnes* v. *Glenn Theater*, 501 U.S. 560 (1991).

[54] *Young* v. *American Mini Theatres*, 427 U.S. 50 (1976); *Renton* v. *Playtime Theatres*, 475 U.S. 41 (1986).

[55] *FCC* v. *Pacifica Foundation*, 438 U.S. 726 (1968).

[56] *FCC* v. *Fox Television Stations*, 173 L.Ed.2d 738 (2009), After the ruling, the FCC wrote a policy banning fleeting profanities, but in 2010 a federal appeals court decided that the policy was too vague. As this edition was going to press, it wasn't clear whether the FCC would appeal the ruling or re-write the policy.

[57] Jonathan D. Salant, "FCC Wants to Up Fine for Cursing," *Lincoln Journal Star*, January 15, 2004.

[58] *Wilkinson* v. *Jones*, 480 U.S. 926 (1987).

[59] *Southeastern Promotions* v. *Conrad*, 420 U.S. 546 (1975).

[60] *Jeannette Rankin Brigade* v. *Chief of Capital Police*, 409 U.S. 972 (1972); *Edwards* v. *South Carolina*, 372 U.S. 229 (1963); *United States* v. *Grace*, 75 L.Ed.2d 736 (1983). The grounds around jails and military bases are off-limits due to the need for security. *Adderley* v. *Florida*, 385 U.S. 39 (1966); *Greer* v. *Spock*, 424 U.S. 828 (1976).

[61] According to the Burger Court, which emphasized property rights over First Amendment rights. *Lloyd* v. *Tanner*, 407 U.S. 551 (1972); *Hudgens* v. *NLRB*, 424 U.S. 507 (1976).

[62] Leonard Pitts Jr., "Intolerance Meets Its Nemesis at an Albany Mall," *Lincoln Journal Star*, March 10, 2003.

[63] *Cox* v. *Louisiana*, 379 U.S. 536 (1965).

[64] *Schenk* v. *Pro-Choice Network*, 137 L.Ed.2d 1 (1997).

[65] *Frisby* v. *Schultz*, 101 L.Ed.2d 420 (1988).

[66] *United States* v. *O'Brien*, 391 U.S. 367 (1968).

[67] *Tinker* v. *Des Moines School District*, 393 U.S. 503 (1969).

[68] *Smith* v. *Goguen*, 415 U.S. 566 (1974); *Spence* v. *Washington*, 418 U.S. 405 (1974).

[69] *Texas* v. *Johnson*, 105 L.Ed.2d 342 (1989).

[70] *United States* v. *Eichman*, 110 L.Ed.2d 287 (1990).

[71] In some places, though not in Switzerland, Muslims are called to prayer from these minarets. The four existing minarets in Switzerland aren't affected by the provision.

[72] *Tinker* v. *Des Moines School District*, 393 U.S. 503 (1969).

[73] *Bethel School District* v. *Fraser*, 478 U.S. 675 (1986).

[74] School officials persuaded the justices that the students were watching as part of an official school event. Hence the officials had authority

over the students. If the students had been "out" of school and off of school property, the officials would have had no authority over them for this incident.

[75] *Morse* v. *Frederick*, 168 L.Ed.2d 290 (2007).

[76] *Hazelwood School District* v. *Kuhlmeier*, 98 L.Ed.2d 592 (1988).

[77] *Hurley* v. *Irish-American Gay, Lesbian and Bisexual Group of Boston*, 515 U.S. 557 (1995).

[78] *Boy Scouts of America* v. *Dale*, 147 L.Ed.2d 554 (2000).

[79] The Court invalidated racial discrimination in labor unions and private schools and sexual discrimination in law firms, despite claims of freedom of association. *Railway Mail Association* v. *Corsi*, 326 U.S. 88 (1945); *Runyon* v. *McCrary*, 427 U.S. 160 (1976); *Hison* v. *King & Spalding*, 467 U.S. 69 (1984) 6957.

[80] *Roberts* v. *U.S. Jaycees*, 468 U.S. 609 (1984); *Board of Directors of Rotary International* v. *Rotary Club of Duarte*, 481 U.S. 537 (1987).

[81] Quoted in David Halbertstam, *The Best and the Brightest* (Greenwich, Conn.: Fawcett, 1969), 769.

[82] Bill Moyers, "Our Democracy Is in Danger of Being Paralyzed," *Keynote Address to the National Conference on Media Reform*, November 8, 2003, www.truthout.org/docs_03/printer_ 111403E.shtml.

[83] *New York Times* v. *United States*, 403 U.S. 713 (1971). In addition to seeking injunctions, the Nixon administration sent a telegram to the *New York Times* demanding that it cease publication of the excerpts, but the FBI had the wrong telex number for the newspaper, so the telegram went first to a fish company in Brooklyn. R. W. Apple, "Lessons from the Pentagon Papers," *New York Times*, June 23, 1996, E5.

[84] Actually, the Pentagon Papers did include some current information regarding ongoing negotiations and the names of CIA agents in Vietnam, but Ellsberg had not passed this information to the newspapers. However, the government and the Court were unaware of this, so the government argued that publication could affect national security, and the Court decided the case with this prospect in mind. Thus the Court's ruling was stronger than legal analysts realized at the time. Erwin N. Griswold, "No Harm Was Done," *New York Times*, June 30, 1991, E15.

[85] *United States* v. *Progressive*, 467 F.Supp. 990 (W.D., Wisc., 1979).

[86] Then radio and television stations used actors with Irish accents to dub the comments made by IRA members. In 1994, the government lifted the ban.

[87] *Branzburg* v. *Hayes*, 408 U.S. 665 (1972).

[88] Jeffrey Toobin, "Name That Source," *New Yorker*, January 16, 2006, 30.

[89] *Cox Broadcasting* v. *Cohn*, 420 U.S. 469 (1975).

[90] This was not a Supreme Court case.

[91] *Time* v. *Hill*, 385 U.S. 374 (1967).

[92] *Wilson* v. *Layne*, 143 L.Ed.2d 818 (1999); *Hanlon* v. *Berger*, 143 L.Ed.2d 978 (1999).

[93] Adam Liptak, "When Free Worlds Collide," *New York Times*, February 28, 2010, WK1.

[94] *New York Times* v. *Sullivan*, 376 U.S. 254 (1964).

[95] Harry Kalven, "The New York Times Case: A Note on 'the Central Meaning of the First Amendment,'" *Supreme Court Review* (1964), 221.

[96] *Monitor Patriot* v. *Roy*, 401 U.S. 265 (1971).

[97] *Associated Press* v. *Walker*, 388 U.S. 130 (1967); *Greenbelt Cooperative* v. *Bresler*, 398 U.S. 6 (1970). This set of rulings began with *Curtis Publishing* v. *Butts*, 388 U.S. 130 (1967).

[98] *Gertz* v. *Robert Welch*, 418 U.S. 323 (1974), and *Time* v. *Firestone*, 424 U.S. 448 (1976).

[99] Eric Press, "Westmoreland Takes on CBS," *Newsweek*, October 22, 1984, 62.

[100] The Pilgrims, who had experienced religious toleration in Holland (after persecution in England), left because they wanted a place of their own, not because they could not worship as they pleased. The Dutch were so tolerant that the Pilgrims' children had begun to adopt Dutch manners and ideas. Richard Shenkman, *"I Love Paul Revere, Whether He Rode or Not"* (New York: HarperCollins, 1991), 20–21.

[101] The only religious reference in the Constitution occurs in the date when the document was written: "year of our Lord one thousand seven hundred and eighty-seven." And that may have been mere convention; "year of our Lord" is the English equivalent of A.D.

[102] Apparently Roger Williams, a clergyman and the founder of Rhode Island, was the first to use this metaphor. Lloyd Burton, "The Church in America," *New Yorker*, September 29, 2003, 10. James Madison was another of the Founders who pioneered our religious freedom. For an analysis of his views, see Vincent Phillip Munoz, "James Madison's Principle of Religious Liberty," *American Political Science Review*, 97 (2003), 17–32.

[103] Gary Wills, quoted on *Thomas Jefferson*, PBS, February 18, 1997.

[104] According to Mark Pachter, Curator of the National Portrait Gallery, *Morning Edition,* National Public Radio, June 25, 2006.

[105] See, for example, Forrest Church, *So Help Me God: The Founding Fathers and the First Great Battle over Church and State* (Orlando, Fla.: Harcourt, 2007); David L. Holmes, *The Faiths of the Founders* (New York: Oxford University Press, 2006); Martha Nussbaum, *Liberty of Conscience: In Defense of America's Tradition of Religious Equality* (New York: Basic Books, 2008); Steven Waldman, *Founding Faith: Providence, Politics, and the Birth of Religious Freedom in America* (New York: Random House, 2008); and Garry Wills, *Head and Heart: American Christianities* (New York: Penguin, 2007).

[106] *Torcaso* v. *Watkins*, 367 U.S. 488 (1961).

[107] *Pierce* v. *Society of Sisters*, 268 U.S. 510 (1925).

[108] *Cooper* v. *Pate*, 378 U.S. 546 (1963); *Cruz* v. *Beto*, 405 U.S. 319 (1972).

[109] *Church of the Lukumi Babalu Aye* v. *Hialeah*, 124 L.Ed.2d 472 (1993).

[110] *Reynolds* v. *United States*, 98 U.S. 145 (1879). Most Mormons, however, didn't approve of polygamy. Even when polygamy was most popular, perhaps only 10 percent of Mormons practiced it. Shenkman, *"I Love Paul Revere,"* 31. Yet today reports indicate that polygamy is still flourishing among Mormons, perhaps more than ever. Lawrence Wright, "Lives of the Saints," *New Yorker*, January 21, 2002, 43.

[111] *Sherbert* v. *Verner*, 374 U.S. 398 (1963).

[112] Although a congressional statute mandates "reasonable accommodation," the Court interpreted it so narrowly that it essentially requires only minimal accommodation. *Trans World Airlines* v. *Hardison*, 432 U.S. 63 (1977). For analysis, see Gloria T. Beckley and Paul Burstein, "Religious Pluralism, Equal Opportunity, and the State," *Western Political Quarterly* 44 (1991), 185–208. For a related case, see *Thornton* v. *Caldor*, 86 L.Ed.2d. 557 (1985).

[113] *United States* v. *Lee*, 455 U.S. 252 (1982).

[114] *United States* v. *American Friends Service Committee*, 419 U.S. 7 (1974).

[115] *Goldman* v. *Weinberger*, 475 U.S. 503 (1986); *O'Lone* v. *Shabazz*, 482 U.S. 342 (1986).

[116] *Employment Division* v. *Smith*, 108 L.Ed.2d 876 (1990).

[117] Congress did pass the American Indian Religious Freedom Act of 1994 to allow Indians to use peyote, but this law did not address the broader implications of the ruling. Ruth Marcus, "One Nation, under Court Rulings," *Washington Post National Weekly Edition*, March 18, 1991, 33.

[118] *Boerne* v. *Flores*, 138 L.Ed.2d 624 (1997). Congress then passed another law that addressed just two kinds of government action—zoning and the rights of inmates at public correctional and mental institutions. The law required state and local governments to consider exceptions for religious practices. Although this was another attempt to override the Court's ruling, the Court upheld the law. *Cutter* v. *Wilkinson*, 125 S.Ct. 2113 (2005).

[119] See page 21 of the twelfth edition of this text for a succinct summary and numerous sources.

[120] William Lee Miller, "The Ghost of Freedoms Past," *Washington Post National Weekly Edition*, October 13, 1986, 23–24.

[121] Richard Brookhiser, "Religious Intent," *New York Times Book Review,* April 13, 2008, 22.

[122] Steven Waldman, "The Framers and the Faithful," *Washington Monthly*, April 2006, 33–38.

[123] *Church of Holy Trinity* v. *United States*, 143 U.S. 457 (1892).

[124] *Engel* v. *Vitale*, 370 U.S. 421 (1962); *Abington School District* v. *Schempp*, 374 U.S. 203 (1963).

[125] *Stone* v. *Graham*, 449 U.S. 39 (1980). The Ten Commandments themselves have been divisive. In 1844, six people were killed in a riot in Philadelphia over which version of the Ten Commandments to post in the public schools. E. J. Dionne Jr., "Bridging the Church-State Divide," *Washington Post National Weekly Edition*, October 11, 1999, 21.

[126] George W. Andrews (D-Ala.), quoted in C. Herman Pritchett, *The American Constitution*, 3rd ed. (New York: McGraw-Hill, 1977), 406.

[127] Kenneth M. Dolbeare and Phillip E. Hammond, *The School Prayer Decisions* (Chicago: University of Chicago Press, 1971).

128 Robert H. Birkby, "The Supreme Court and the Bible Belt," *Midwest Journal of Political Science* 10 (1966), 304–315.

129 Julia Lieblich and Richard N. Ostling, "Despite Rulings, Prayer in School Still Sparks Debate, Still Practiced," *Lincoln Journal Star*, January 16, 2000.

130 "Five Schools Get Ten Commandments," *Lincoln Journal Star*, August 12, 1999.

131 J. Gordon Melton, quoted in Jon D. Hull, "The State of the Union," *Time*, January 30, 1995, 55.

132 Peter Cushnie, "Letters," *Time*, October 15, 1984, 21.

133 The Supreme Court invalidated Alabama's law that authorized a moment of silence "for meditation or voluntary prayer" because the wording of the law endorsed and promoted prayer. But most justices signaled approval of a moment of silence without such wording. *Wallace* v. *Jaffree*, 86 L.Ed.2d 29 (1985).

134 *Lee* v. *Weisman*, 120 L.Ed.2d 467 (1992).

135 *Jones* v. *Clear Creek*, 977 F.2d 965 (5th Cir., 1992).

136 *Moore* v. *Ingebretsen*, 88 F.3d 274 (1996).

137 *Santa Fe Independent School District* v. *Doe*, 530 U.S. 290 (2000).

138 Anna Quindlen, "School Prayer: Substitutes for Substance," *Lincoln Journal Star*, December 8, 1994.

139 A current guide for public school teachers, addressing practices that are permissible and those that are advisable in various situations, is Charles C. Haynes and Oliver Thomas, *Finding Common Ground* (Nashville, Tenn.: First Amendment Center, 2002).

140 *Widmar* v. *Vincent*, 454 U.S. 263 (1981). The law requires high schools that receive federal funds to allow meetings of students' religious, philosophical, or political groups if the schools permit meetings of any "noncurriculum" groups. Schools could prohibit meetings of all noncurriculum groups. A Salt Lake City high school banned all nonacademic clubs rather than let students form an organization for homosexuals in 1996. Interviews with teachers and students two years later indicated that, as a result of the ban on clubs, school spirit declined and class and racial rifts expanded. Clubs no longer brought students together, and clubs such as Polynesian Pride and the Aztec Club, for Latinos, no longer provided a link between these students and their school. "Club Ban Aimed at Gays Backfires," *Lincoln Journal Star*, December 6, 1998.

141 *Board of Education of the Westside Community Schools* v. *Mergens*, 496 U.S. 226 (1990).

142 David Van Biema, "Spiriting Prayer into School," *Time*, April 27, 1998, 28–31.

143 Harriet Barovick, "Fear of a Gay School," *Time*, February 21, 2000, 52.

144 *Rosenberger* v. *University of Virginia*, 132 L.Ed.2d 700 (1995). Yet the Rehnquist Court later ruled that states that provide scholarships for students at colleges and universities don't have to provide them for students preparing for the ministry. *Locke* v. *Davey*, 158 L.Ed.2d 21 (2004).

145 For the nation's first celebration of Columbus Day in 1892, Francis Bellamy wrote, "I pledge allegiance to my flag and the republic for which it stands, one nation indivisible, with liberty and justice for all." For Bellamy, the key words were "indivisible," which referred to the Civil War and emphasized the Union over the states, and "liberty and justice for all," which emphasized a balance between freedom for individuals and equality between them. During the Cold War in the 1950s, Americans feared "godless communism." Some objected to communism as much because of the Soviet Union's official policy of atheism as because of its totalitarianism. A religious revival swept the United States as preachers such as Billy Graham warned that Americans would perish in a nuclear holocaust unless they opened their arms to Jesus Christ. Congress replaced the traditional national motto—"E Pluribus Unum" ("Out of Many, One")—with "In God We Trust," and it added this new motto to our paper money. Fraternal organizations, especially the Catholic Knights of Columbus, and religious leaders campaigned to add "under God" to the Pledge of Allegiance. The Presbyterian pastor of President Eisenhower's church in Washington urged the addition in a sermon as the president sat in a pew. With little dissent, Congress passed and the president signed a bill to do so in 1954. The legislative history of the act stated that the intent was to "acknowledge the dependence of our people and our government upon . . . the Creator . . . [and] deny the atheistic and materialistic concept of communism." The president stated that "millions of our school children will daily proclaim in every city and town . . . the dedication of our nation and our people to the Almighty." Thus the phrase was adopted expressly to endorse religion. David Greenberg, "The Pledge of Allegiance: Why We're Not One Nation 'under God,'" *Slate*, June 28, 2002, slate.msn.com/?id_2067499 S.

146 *Elk Grove Unified School District* v. *Newdow*, 159 L.Ed.2d 98 (2004).

147 *Lynch* v. *Donnelly*, 79 L.Ed.2d 604 (1984).

148 *Allegheny County* v. *ACLU*, 106 L.Ed.2d 472 (1989). *Allegheny County* v. *ACLU*, 106 L.Ed.2d 472 (1989).

149 *Van Orden* v. *Perry*, 162 L.Ed. 2d 607 (2005).

150 Initially they stood alone. As the cases proceeded through the lower courts, officials added other historical documents but never made a sincere effort to integrate them.

151 *McCreary County* v. *ACLU*, 162 L.Ed.2d 729 (2005).

152 *Epperson* v. *Arkansas*, 393 U.S. 97 (1968).

153 Some groups use the more sophisticated-sounding term *creation science*. Although these groups do address the science of evolution, courts consider creationism and creation science as interchangeable.

154 *Edwards* v. *Aguillard*, 482 U.S. 578 (1987).

155 They do acknowledge that some, limited evolution has occurred.

156 However, to avoid court rulings similar to those against creationism—that it reflects a religious view—they try to avoid mention of God.

157 Wendy Kaminer, "The God Bullies," *American Prospect*, November 18, 2002, 9.

158 *McCreary County* v. *ACLU*, 162 L.Ed.2d 729 (2005).

159 *Rochin* v. *California*, 342 U.S. 165 (1952).

160 Seymour Wishman, *Confessions of a Criminal Lawyer* (New York: Penguin, 1981), 16.

161 *Stein* v. *New York*, 346 U.S. 156 (1953).

162 Wendy Kaminer, *It's All the Rage* (Reading, Mass.: Addison-Wesley, 1995), 78.

163 *Weeks* v. *United States*, 232 U.S. 383 (1914).

164 *Mapp* v. *Ohio*, 367 U.S. 643 (1961).

165 This exception applies when police use a search warrant that they did not know was invalid. *United States* v. *Leon*, 82 L.Ed.2d 677 (1984); *Massachusetts* v. *Sheppard*, 82 L.Ed.2d 737 (1984).

166 In situations in which police are required by law to knock and identify themselves before entering a residence, they can still use any evidence they find inside, even though the search is illegal because of their failure to knock and identify themselves. *Hudson* v. *Michigan*, 165 L.Ed.2d 56 (2006).

167 *Olmstead* v. *United States*, 277 U.S. 438 (1928).

168 *Katz* v. *United States*, 389 U.S. 347 (1967).

169 An administration official, quoted in Zev Borow, "Very Bad People," *New Yorker*, February 6, 2006, 44.

170 And perhaps the contents of the calls, too, though that is difficult to ascertain because the government has divulged little information about this program.

171 The Foreign Intelligence Surveillance Act required authorization for such eavesdropping from the Foreign Intelligence Surveillance Court.

172 The Protect America Act of 2007 amended the Foreign Intelligence Surveillance Act, which had required judicial authorization. Now, under the act, judicial authorization is required only if the government targets specific American citizens.

173 Seymour M. Hersh, "National Security Dept.: Listening In," *New Yorker*, May 29, 2006, 25.

174 The USA PATRIOT Act, which expanded surveillance within the United States since 9/11, also has numerous implications for civil liberties, but the act is quite technical and beyond the scope of this text.

175 *Brown* v. *Mississippi*, 297 U.S. 278 (1936).

176 *McNabb* v. *United States*, 318 U.S. 332 (1943); *Mallory* v. *United States*, 354 U.S. 449 (1957); *Spano* v. *New York*, 360 U.S. 315 (1959).

177 *Ashcraft* v. *Tennessee*, 322 U.S. 143 (1944).

178 *Miranda* v. *Arizona*, 384 U.S. 436 (1966).

179 *Dickerson* v. *United States*, 530 U.S. 428 (2000).

180 *Berghuis* v. *Thompkins*, 176 L.Ed.2d 1098 (2010).

181 Jan Hoffman, "Police Tactics Chipping Away at Suspects' Rights," *New York Times*, March 29, 1998, 35.

182 *Johnson* v. *Zerbst*, 304 U.S. 458 (1938).

183 The Court did require state courts to furnish an attorney when there were "special circumstances" involved. *Powell* v. *Alabama*, 287 U.S. 45 (1932).

[184] *Gideon* v. *Wainwright*, 372 U.S. 335 (1963).

[185] *Argersinger* v. *Hamlin*, 407 U.S. 25 (1972); *Scott* v. *Illinois*, 440 U.S. 367 (1974); *Alabama* v. *Shelton*, 152 L.Ed.2d 888(2002).

[186] *Douglas* v. *California*, 372 U.S. 353 (1953).

[187] Wendy Cole, "Death Takes a Holiday," *Time*, February 14, 2000, 68.

[188] Jill Smolowe, "Race and the Death Penalty," *Time*, April 29, 1991, 69.

[189] Peter Applebome, "Indigent Defendants, Overworked Lawyers," *New York Times*, May 17, 1992, E18.

[190] Alan Berlow, "Texas, Take Heed," *Washington Post National Weekly Edition*, February 21, 2000, 22.

[191] Richard Carelli, "Death Rows Grow, Legal Help Shrinks," *Lincoln Journal Star*, October 7, 1995.

[192] The Innocence Project alone freed 254 inmates through DNA evidence from 1992 through spring 2010. Nathan Thornburgh, "Resumed Innocent," *Time*, May 31, 2010, 26. Texas holds the dubious record for the most exonerated, with 38. "Lining Up for Justice in Texas," *Newsweek*, February 22, 2010, 8.

[193] The Burger Court did rule that the right to counsel entails the right to "effective" counsel, but the Court set such stringent standards for establishing the existence of ineffective counsel that few defendants can take advantage of this right. See *Strickland* v. *Washington*, 466 U.S. 668 (1984), and *United States* v. *Cronic*, 466 U.S. 640 (1984).

[194] *Baldwin* v. *New York*, 339 U.S. 66 (1970); *Blanton* v. *North Las Vegas*, 489 U.S. 538 (1989).

[195] *Duncan* v. *Louisiana*, 391 U.S. 145 (1968).

[196] *Taylor* v. *Louisiana*, 419 U.S. 522 (1975).

[197] *Swain* v. *Alabama*, 380 U.S. 202 (1965).

[198] *Graham* v. *Florida*, 176 L.Ed.2d 825 (2010).

[199] The Court implicitly upheld the death penalty in *Wilkerson* v. *Utah*, 99 U.S. 130 (1878), and *In re Kemmler*, 136 U.S. 436 (1890).

[200] *Furman* v. *Georgia*, 408 U.S. 238 (1972).

[201] *Gregg* v. *Georgia*, 428 U.S. 153 (1976).

[202] *Woodson* v. *North Carolina*, 428 U.S. 289 (1976).

[203] *Coker* v. *Georgia*, 433 U.S. 584 (1977); *Kennedy* v. *Louisiana*, 171 L.Ed.2d 525 (2008).

[204] *McCleskey* v. *Kemp*, 95 L.Ed.2d 262 (1987). Studies of Florida, Illinois, Mississippi, and North Carolina have found similar results. Fox Butterfield, "Blacks More Likely to Get Death Penalty, Study Says," *New York Times*, June 7, 1998, 16.

[205] Jeffrey Toobin, "Killer Instincts," *New Yorker*, January 17, 2005, 54.

[206] As of October 2007.

[207] David Grann, "Trial by Fire," *New Yorker*, September 7, 2009, 42–62.

[208] The American Law Institute, which numbers about four thousand judges, lawyers, and law professors, and which created the current framework for the death penalty, pronounced the framework and the penalty a failure in 2010. Adam Liptak, "Group Gives Up Death Penalty Work," *New York Times*, January 5, 2010, A11.

[209] Frank R. Baumgartner, Suzanna De Boef, and Amber E. Boydstun, *The Decline of the Death Penalty and the Discovery of Innocence* (Cambridge, England: Cambridge University Press, 2008).

[210] Adam Liptak, "Juries Reject Death Penalty in Nearly All Federal Trials," *New York Times*, June 15, 2003, 12; Alex Kotlowitz, "In the Face of Death," *New York Times Magazine*, June 6, 2003, 34.

[211] *Atkins* v. *Virginia*, 153 L.Ed. 2d 335 (2002).

[212] *Penry* v. *Lynaugh*, 106 L.Ed.2d 256 (1989).

[213] *Roper* v. *Simmons*, 161 L.Ed.2d 1 (2005).

[214] Some Asian countries (notably China) and many Middle Eastern countries also retain it.

[215] *Brady* v. *United States*, 397 U.S. 742 (1970).

[216] *Griswold* v. *Connecticut*, 38 U.S. 479 (1965).

[217] For a rare exception, see *Time* v. *Hill*, 385 U.S. 374 (1967).

[218] *Griswold* v. *Connecticut*.

[219] *Eisenstadt* v. *Baird*, 405 U.S. 438 (1972); *Carey* v. *Population Services International*, 431 U.S. 678 (1977).

[220] *Eisenstadt* v. *Baird*.

[221] Lloyd Shearer, "This Woman and This Man Made History," *Parade*, 1983.

[222] *Roe* v. *Wade*, 410 U.S. 113 (1973).

[223] Bob Woodward, "The Abortion Papers," *Washington Post National Weekly Edition*, January 30, 1989, 24–25.

[224] According to the Guttmacher Institute, cited in Rob Stein, "Another Look at Late-Term Abortions," *Washington Post National Weekly Edition*, June 15–21, 2009, 33.

[225] All but New York's. Three other states allowed abortion on demand, though not quite as extensively as *Roe*, so the ruling also invalidated their laws. Jeffrey A. Segal and Harold J. Spaeth, *The Supreme Court and the Attitudinal Model* (New York: Cambridge University Press, 1993), 333.

[226] Ironically, a Gallup poll a year before *Roe* found that more Republicans than Democrats were in favor of leaving the decision to the woman and her doctor. Linda Greenhouse, "One Man, Two Courts," *New York Times*, April 11, 2010, WK11.

[227] For example, Alan Dershowitz, *Supreme Injustice* (New York: Oxford University, 2001), 191–196. For a contrast with same-sex marriage, see Jonathan Rauch, "A Separate Peace," *Atlantic Monthly*, April 2007, 21.

[228] *Akron* v. *Akron Center for Reproductive Health*, 76 L.Ed.2d 687 (1983).

[229] "The Supreme Court Ignites a Fiery Abortion Debate," *Time*, July 4, 1977, 6–8.

[230] *Beal* v. *Doe*, 432 U.S. 438 (1977); *Maher* v. *Roe*, 432 U.S. 464 (1977); *Poelker* v. *Doe*, 432 U.S. 519 (1977); *Harris* v. *McRae* 448 U.S. 297 (1980).

[231] "The Abortion Dilemma Come to Life," *Washington Post National Weekly Edition*, December 25, 1989, 10–11.

[232] Alan Guttmacher Institute, *Facts in Brief: Abortion in the United States* (New York: Alan Guttmacher Institute, 1992); Stephanie Mencimer, "Ending Illegitimacy as We Know It," *Washington Post National Weekly Edition*, January 17, 1994, 24.

[233] *Webster* v. *Reproductive Health Services*, 106 L.Ed.2d 410 (1989).

[234] *Planned Parenthood of Southeastern Pennsylvania* v. *Casey*, 120 L.Ed.2d 674 (1992). Justice Anthony Kennedy changed his mind after the justices' conference, from essentially overturning *Roe* to reaffirming it. His was the fifth vote to reaffirm, as it would have been to overturn.

[235] Kathleen Sullivan, cited in Robin Toner and Adam Liptak, "In New Court, Roe May Stand, So Foes Look to Limit Its Scope," *New York Times*, July 10, 2005, YT16.

[236] William Booth, "The Difference a Day Makes," *Washington Post National Weekly Edition*, November 23, 1992, 31.

[237] *Planned Parenthood of Southeastern Pennsylvania* v. *Casey*, 120 L.Ed.2d 674 (1992).

[238] *Hodgson* v. *Minnesota*, 111 L.Ed.2d 344 (1990); *Ohio* v. *Akron Center for Reproductive Health*, 111 L.Ed.2d 405 (1990); *Planned Parenthood Association of Kansas City* v. *Ashcroft*, 462 U.S. 476 (1983). Number of states from Holly Ramer, "Never-Enforced Abortion Law to Go before Supreme Court," *Lincoln Journal Star*, November 27, 2005, A4.

[239] Margaret Carlson, "Abortion's Hardest Cases," *Time*, July 9, 1990, 24.

[240] Research shows that this procedure has not had the anticipated impact in British Columbia, and anecdotal evidence suggests that it has not in Alabama either. Kevin Sack, "In Ultrasound, Abortion Fight Has New Front," *New York Times*, May 27, 2010, A1.

[241] Peter Slevin, "Abortion in the States' Hands," *Washington Post National Weekly Edition*, June 15–21, 2009, 34. Although some pro-life groups insist that there is a link, the website operated by the U.S. National Library and the National Institutes of Health, with links to the American Cancer Society and the Mayo Clinic, concludes that there is no link. www.nlm.nih.gov/medlineplus/abortion.html.

[242] Charlie Savage, "Appeals Courts Pushed to Right by Bush Choices," *New York Times*, October 29, 2008, A1.

[243] Before this procedure was adopted for late-term abortions, doctors removed the fetus in pieces. Jeffrey Toobin, *The Nine: Inside the Secret World of the Supreme Court* (New York: Doubleday, 2007), 132.

[244] *Stenberg* v. *Carhart*, 530 U.S. 914 (2000).

[245] *Gonzales* v. *Carhart*, 167 L.Ed.2d 480 (2007). The Court didn't overrule the 2000 decision, because that Nebraska law, unlike this congressional law, was too broad.

[246] A review of the research concluded that it is "unlikely" that the fetus can feel pain before twenty-eight weeks. Sarah Kliff, "A New Way to Talk about Abortion in Nebraska," *Newsweek*, March 19, 2010, 3.

[247] Barry Yeoman, "The Quiet War on Abortion," *Mother Jones*, September–October 2001, 46–51.

[248] "Survey Reveals U.S. Views on Abortion to Be Contradictory," *Lincoln Journal Star*, June 19, 2000.

[249] For an analysis of the political dynamics that produced this moderate result, see William Saleton, *Bearing Right: How Conservatives Won the Abortion War* (Berkeley: University

of California Press, 2003). The title is an exaggeration.

250 Alissa Rubin, "The Abortion Wars Are Far from Over," *Washington Post National Weekly Edition*, December 21, 1992, 25.

251 Richard Lacayo, "One Doctor Down, How Many More?" *Time*, March 22, 1993, 47.

252 Rebecca Mead, "Return to Sender the Usual Hate Mail," *New Yorker*, October 29, 2001, 34.

253 Douglas Frantz, "The Rhetoric of Terror," *Time*, March 27, 1995, 48–51.

254 Dan Sewell, "Abortion War Requires Guns, Bulletproof Vests," *Lincoln Journal Star*, January 8, 1995. Plus Dr. George Tiller in 2009.

255 "Blasts Reawaken Fear of Domestic Terrorism," *Lincoln Journal Star*, January 17, 1997.

256 Richard Lacayo, "Abortion: The Future Is Already Here," *Time*, May 4, 1992, 29; Jack Hitt, "Who Will Do Abortions Here?" *New York Times Magazine*, January 18, 1998, 20.

257 Jodi Enda, "The Women's View," *American Prospect*, April 2005, 26. However, a counter-movement to train more doctors is emerging. Emily Bazelon, "The New Abortion Providers," *New York Times Magazine*, July 18, 2010, 30.

258 Randall Terry, quoted in Anthony Lewis, "Pro-Life Zealots 'Outside the Bargain,'" *Lincoln Journal Star*, March 14, 1993.

259 Joseph Scheidler, quoted in Sandra G. Boodman, "Bringing Abortion Home," *Washington Post National Weekly Edition*, April 15, 1993, 6.

260 Stanley K. Henshaw, "Abortion Incidence and Services in the United States, 1995–1996," *Family Planning Perspectives*, November–December 1998; Stephanie Simon, "Abortions Down 25% from Peak," *Los Angeles Times*, January 17, 2008, www.latimes.com/news/nationworld/nation/la-na-abort17jan17,0,1592814.

261 Rob Stein, "As Clinical Abortions Decline, an Alternative Rises," *Washington Post National Weekly Edition*, January 28–February 3, 2008, 33. However, this method is used less in the United States, where the first pill must be administered in the doctor's office, than in other countries, where the pill may be taken at home. Nicholas D. Kristof, "Another Pill that Could Cause a Revolution," *New York Times, August 1, 2010, WK 8.

262 Much of this section is taken from Russell Shorto, "Contra-Contraception," *New York Times Magazine*, May 7, 2006, 48–55, 68.

263 Harris poll, ibid., 54.

264 Judie Brown, quoted in ibid., 50.

265 Judie Brown, quoted in ibid.

266 As the author concludes from the leaders' statements. Ibid., 54.

267 R. Albert Mohler Jr., quoted in ibid., 50.

268 Sarah Brown of the National Campaign to Prevent Teen Pregnancy, quoted in ibid., 83.

269 For a representative explanation of this position, see Alysse Michelle Elhage, "Special Rights for Homosexuals," North Carolina Family Policy Council, ncfpc.org/PolicyPapers/Findings%209907%20Special%. For a critical analysis of this position, see Michael Nava and Robert Dawidoff, *Created Equal: Why Gay Rights Matter to America* (New York: St. Martin's, 1994).

270 For an elaboration of this history, see "In Changing the Law of the Land, Six Justices Turned to Its History," *New York Times*, July 20, 2003, WK7.

271 Four states at this time revised their statutes to bar sodomy only between homosexuals: Kansas, Missouri, Oklahoma, and Texas.

272 *Bowers* v. *Hardwick*, 92 L.Ed.2d 140 (1986); see also *Doe* v. *Commonwealth's Attorney*, 425 U.S. 901 (1976).

273 *Lawrence and Garner* v. *Texas*, 539 U.S. 558 (2003).

274 "Gays Getting More Acceptance as They're More Open, Poll Says," *Lincoln Journal Star*, April 11, 2004.

275 Paul Gewirtz, quoted in Joe Klein, "How the Supremes Redeemed Bush," *Time*, July 7, 2003, 27.

276 The House sponsor of the act, Robert Barr (R-Ga.), said the act was necessary because "the flames of hedonism, the flames of narcissism, the flames of self-centered morality are licking at the very foundation of our society, the family unit." At the time he was protecting the family unit, he was in his third marriage. Margaret Carlson, "The Marrying Kind," *Time*, September 16, 1996, 26.

277 Jonathan Rauch, "Families Forged by Illness," *New York Times*, June 11, 2006, WK15.

278 For elaboration, see David Von Drehle, "Same-Sex Unions Take Center Stage," *Washington Post National Weekly Edition*, December 1, 2003, 29.

279 John Cloud, "1,138 Reasons Marriage Is Cool," *Time*, March 8, 2004, 32. A few go in the opposite direction, such as eligibility for Medicaid, which takes into account a spouse's income.

280 Frank Rich, summarizing attorney David Boies's arguments, "Two Weddings, a Divorce, and 'Glee,'" *New York Times*, June 13, 2010, WK10.

281 Advisory Opinion on Senate No. 2175, Supreme Judicial Court of Massachusetts, February 3, 2004.

282 David J. Garrow, "Toward a More Perfect Union," *New York Times Magazine*, May 9, 2004, 54.

283 Senator Wayne Allard (R-Colo.); Senator Rick Santorum (R-Pa.); James Dobson. Andrew Sullivan, "If at First You Don't Succeed . . . ," *Time*, July 26, 2004, 78.

284 Alan Cooperman, "Anger without Action," *Washington Post National Weekly Edition*, June 28, 2004, 30.

285 Lisa Leff and David Sharp, "Gay Marriage Foes Use Winning Argument," *Lincoln Journal Star*, November 7, 2009, A9.

286 Garrow, "Toward a More Perfect Union," 57.

287 Especially by Republicans, conservatives, white evangelicals, weekly churchgoers, and African Americans, the last-mentioned of which had turned out in record numbers to vote for Obama for president. However, according to exit polls, the ballot measure would have passed (barely) even without African American opposition. Hendrik Hertzberg, "Comment: Eight Is Enough," *New Yorker,* December 1, 2008, 27.

288 California (which retains its civil union law after voters struck down its same-sex marriage law), Colorado, Maine, Maryland, Nevada, New Jersey, Oregon, Washington, and Wisconsin.

289 Geoff Mulvihill, "Transgender Protection Law Begins in New Jersey," *Lincoln Journal Star*, June 13, 2007, 7A.

290 *Roemer v. Evans,* 134 L.Ed.2d 855 (1996).

291 Israel does take homosexuality into account in the assignment of military jobs. Gays who admit their orientation to their superiors confidentially are restricted from security-sensitive jobs for fear that they could be subject to blackmail. But gays who acknowledge their orientation openly are treated the same as straights. Randy Shilts, "What's Fair in Love and War," *Newsweek,* February 1, 1993, 58–59. See also Randy Shilts, *Conduct Unbecoming: Gays and Lesbians in the U.S. Military* (New York: St. Martin's, 1993).

292 Nathaniel Frank, *Unfriendly Fire: How the Gay Ban Undermines the Military and Weakens America* (New York: St. Martin's, 2009), 35 and ch. 2 in general.

293 Joseph Rocha, "I Didn't Tell. It Didn't Matter," *Washington Post National Weekly Edition*, October 19–25, 2009, 27.

294 Dana Priest, "The Impact of the 'Don't Ask, Don't Tell' Policy," *Washington Post National Weekly Edition,* February 1, 1999, 35.

295 Michael O'Donnell, "Straight Away," *Washington Monthly,* March–April 2009, 45.

296 At least twenty-four countries have lifted their bans, and various assessments have found that gay troops have not undermined the recruitment, morale, cohesion, or effectiveness of their militaries. Ibid., 47.

297 *Washington Post*/ABC News poll, cited in "U.S. Majority Supports Open Gays in Military," *Lincoln Journal Star,* February 13, 2010, A3.

298 Representative Duncan Hunter (R-Calif.), in interview on National Public Radio, February 2, 2010.

299 David Mixner, quoted in Adam Nagourney, "Political Shifts in Gay Rights Are Lagging behind Culture," *New York Times,* June 28, 2009, Y18.

300 James C. McKinley Jr., "Gay Candidates Get Support That Causes May Not," *New York Times,* December 28, 2009, A17.

301 Charles M. Blow, "Gay? Whatever, Dude," *New York Times,* June 4, 2010, A25.

302 Al Kamen, "When Exactly Does Life End?" *Washington Post National Weekly Edition*, September 18, 1989, 31; Alain L. Sanders, "Whose Right to Die?" *Time*, December 11, 1989, 80.

303 *Cruzan* v. *Missouri Health Department*, 111 L.Ed.2d 224 (1990).

304 Otto Friedrich, "A Limited Right to Die," *Time*, July 9, 1990, 59.

305 Tamar Lewin, "Ignoring 'Right to Die' Directives, Medical Community Is Being Sued," *New York Times*, June 2, 1996, 1.

306 *Washington* v. *Glucksberg*, 138 L.Ed.2d 772 (1997); *Vacco* v. *Quill*, 138 L.Ed.2d 834 (1997).

Pennsylvania State University, Population Research Institute, 1997; Pew Hispanic Center, cited in Frank Greve, "English Grows Each Generation," *Lincoln Journal Star,* November 30, 2007, A1.

204 Ruben Navarrette Jr., "Hispanics See Themselves as Part of United States," *Lincoln Journal Star,* December 23, 2002.

205 Ibid.

206 National Public Radio, September 11, 2007.

207 Guadalupe San Miguel, "Mexican American Organizations and the Changing Politics of School Desegregation in Texas, 1945–1980," *Social Science Quarterly* 63 (1982), 701–715.

208 Ibid., 710.

209 Even children of illegal aliens have been given the right to attend public schools by the Supreme Court. The majority assumed that most of these children, although subject to deportation, would remain in the United States, given the large number of illegal aliens who do remain here. Denying them an education would deprive them of the opportunity to fulfill their potential and would deprive society of the benefit of their contribution. *Plyler* v. *Doe,* 457 U.S. 202 (1982).

210 Luis Ricardo Fraga, Kenneth J. Meier, and Robert E. England, "Hispanic Americans and Educational Policy: Structural Limits to Equal Access and Opportunities for Upward Mobility," unpublished paper, University of Oklahoma, 1985, 6.

211 *San Antonio Independent School District* v. *Rodriguez,* 411 U.S. 1 (1973).

212 Anjetta McQueen, "Dual-Language Schools Sought," *Lincoln Journal Star,* March 16, 2000.

213 In 1968 Congress encouraged bilingual education by providing funding, and in 1974 the Supreme Court, in a case brought by Chinese parents, held that schools must teach students in a language they can understand. *Lau* v. *Nichols,* 414 U.S. 563 (1974). This can be their native language, or it can be English if they have been taught English. These federal actions prompted states to establish bilingual education programs.

214 McQueen, "Dual-Language Schools Sought."

215 "Bilingualism's End Means a Different Kind of Change," *Champaign-Urbana News-Gazette,* June 7, 1998.

216 Margot Hornblower, "No Habla Español," *Time,* January 26, 1998, 63.

217 James Traub, "The Bilingual Barrier," *New York Times Magazine,* January 31, 1999, 34–35.

218 John Bowe, "Nobodies," *New Yorker,* April 21, 2003, 106.

219 "Survey: Hispanics Reject Cohesive Group Identity," *Lincoln Journal,* December 15, 1992.

220 Gregory Rodriguez, "Finding a Political Voice," *Washington Post National Weekly Edition,* February 1, 1999, 22–23.

221 A 1995 Census Bureau Survey indicated that 49 percent of native people preferred being called *American Indian,* 37 percent preferred *Native American,* 3.6 percent preferred "some other term," and 5 percent had no preference. Bureau of Labor Statistics, U.S. Census Bureau Survey, May 1995, www .census.gov/ prod/2/ gen/96arc/ivatuck.pdf.

222 *Cherokee Nation* v. *Georgia,* 30 U.S. 1 (1831); *Worcester* v. *Georgia,* 31 U.S. 515 (1832).

223 Treaties made exceptions for those who married whites and those who left their tribes and abandoned tribal customs.

224 Vine Deloria Jr. and Clifford M. Lytle, *American Indians, American Justice* (Austin: University of Texas Press, 1983), 221.

225 Ibid., 222–225.

226 Indian Self-Determination Act (1975).

227 Ellen Nakashima and Neely Tucker, "A Fight over Lost Lands, Money Owed," *Washington Post National Weekly Edition,* April 29, 2002, 30. The lawsuit was finally settled in 2009.

228 According to the Indian Gaming Regulatory Act (1988), tribes can establish casinos if their reservation lies in a state that allows virtually any gambling, including charitable "Las Vegas nights."

229 Kathleen Schmidt, "Gambling a Bonanza for Indians," *Lincoln Journal Star,* March 23, 1998.

230 Donald L. Bartlett and James B. Steele, "Wheel of Misfortune," *Time,* December 16, 2002, 44–48.

231 Ibid., 47.

232 W. John Moore, "Tribal Imperatives," *National Journal,* June 9, 1990, 1396.

233 Jack Hitt, "The Newest Indian," *New York Times Magazine,* August 21, 2005, 40–41.

234 Quoted in Ruth B. Ginsburg, *Constitutional Aspects of Sex-Based Discrimination* (Saint Paul, Minn.: West, 1974), 2.

235 Karen De Crow, *Sexist Justice* (New York: Vintage, 1975), 72.

236 Nadine Taub and Elizabeth M. Schneider, "Women's Subordination and the Role of Law," in *The Politics of Law: A Progressive Critique,* rev. ed., ed. David Kairys (New York: Pantheon, 1990), 160–162.

237 *Bradwell* v. *Illinois,* 83 U.S. 130 (1873).

238 From an *amicus curiae* ("friend of the court") brief by 281 historians filed in the Supreme Court case, *Webster* v. *Reproductive Health Services,* 106 L.Ed.2d 410 (1989).

239 Donna M. Moore, "Editor's Introduction" in *Battered Women,* ed. Donna M. Moore (Beverly Hills, Calif.: Sage, 1979), 8.

240 Jill Lepore, "Vast Designs," *New Yorker,* October 29, 2007, 92.

241 For a recent biography of Stanton, see Lori D. Ginzberg, *Elizabeth Cady Stanton* (New York: Hill & Wang, 2009). Ginzberg also explores Stanton's racism and elitism.

242 Barbara Sinclair Deckard, *The Women's Movement,* 2nd ed. (New York: Harper & Row, 1979), 303.

243 In the early 1960s, a board game for girls—*What Shall I Be?*—offered these options: teacher, nurse, stewardess, actress, ballerina, and beauty queen. David Owen, "The Sultan of Stuff," *New Yorker,* July 19, 1999, 60.

244 Reprinted in "Regrets, We Have a Few," *Time Special Issue: 75 Years of* Time, 1998, 192.

245 For an examination of Betty Friedan's role in the movement and the political dynamics among the various factions in the movement, see Judith Hennessee, *Betty Friedan: Her Life* (New York: Random House, 1999). For an examination of women's views toward feminism, see Elinor Burkett, *The Right Women* (New York: Scribner, 1998).

246 Robert Alan Goldberg, *Enemies Within* (New Haven, Conn.: Yale University Press, 2002).

247 De Crow, *Sexist Justice,* 119.

248 This is why Betty Friedan later felt compelled to write a book espousing the concept of motherhood: *The Second Stage* (New York: Summit, 1981).

249 For a discussion of these points, see Jane Mansbridge, *Why We Lost the ERA* (Chicago: University of Chicago Press, 1986); Mary Frances Berry, *Why ERA Failed* (Bloomington: Indiana University Press, 1986); Janet Boles, "Building Support for the ERA: A Case of 'Too Much, Too Late,'" *PS: Political Science and Politics* 15 (1982), 575–592.

250 Shenkman, *'I Love Paul Revere,'* 136–137.

251 *Reed* v. *Reed,* 404 U.S. 71 (1971).

252 *Hoyt* v. *Florida,* 368 U.S. 57 (1961).

253 *Taylor* v. *Louisiana,* 419 U.S. 522 (1975).

254 *Stanton* v. *Stanton,* 421 U.S. 7 (1975).

255 Cases were from 2002. They were compiled by the WAGE Project (www.wageproject. org) and examined and reported in Evelyn F. Murphy, with E. J. Graff, *Getting Even: Why Women Don't Get Paid like Men—and What to Do about It* (New York: Simon & Schuster, 2005), 40–48. This total also includes sexual harassment suits, which, of course, reflect a type of sexual discrimination.

256 Ibid., 56.

257 Ibid., 157.

258 Ibid., 153

259 Ibid., 60–61.

260 Ibid., 84–85.

261 Ibid., 200.

262 Ibid., 199.

263 Ibid., 4.

264 David Leonhardt, "Gender Pay Gap, Once Narrowing, Is Stuck in Place," *New York Times,* December 24, 2006, YT18.

265 "All Things Considered," National Public Radio, September 1, 2010.

266 Murphy, *Getting Even,* 185.

267 Ibid., 146.

268 U.S. Census Bureau, *Statistical Abstract of the United States, 1997* (Washington, D.C.: Government Printing Office, 1997), tab. 645.

269 The phrase itself is not new. It was used by workers in the nineteenth century and as the title of a book by a Catholic priest in 1906. Jon Gertner, "What Is a Living Wage?" *New York Times Magazine,* January 15, 2006, 42.

270 For discussion, see ibid., 38.

271 Lisa McLaughlin, "In Brief," *Time,* October 9, 2000, G12.

272 For discussion, see Murphy, *Getting Even,* 194–213.

273 See *ibid.* for numerous examples.

274 According to a *Time* poll. Nancy Gibbs, "What Women Want Now," *Time,* October 26, 2009, 30.

[275] David Crary, "U.S. among Worst in Family vs. Work Policies," *Lincoln Journal Star,* February 1, 2007, 5A. There's no federal law requiring employers to provide paid sick days. Most do provide them for salaried employees but not for hourly employees.

[276] The Family and Medical Leave Act. The act also requires employers to continue health insurance coverage during the leave and to give the employee the same job or a comparable one upon her or his return.

[277] Lisa Genasci, "Many Workers Resist Family Benefit Offers," *Lincoln Journal Star,* June 28, 1995.

[278] Tara Parker-Pope, "Now, Dad Feels as Stressed as Mom," *New York Times,* June 20, 2010, WK1.

[279] Jodie Levin-Epstein, "Responsive Workplaces," *American Prospect,* March 2007, A16.

[280] Joan C. Williams, "The Opt-Out Revolution Revisited," *American Prospect,* March 2007, A14.

[281] This pattern appears in all social classes. From the National Survey of Families and Households, University of Wisconsin, cited in Lisa Belkin, "When Mom and Dad Share It All," *New York Times Magazine,* June 15, 2008, 44.

[282] Heather Boushey, "Values Begin at Home, but Who's Home?" *American Prospect,* March 2007, A2.

[283] Ann Crittenden, "Parents Fighting Back," *American Prospect,* June, 2003, 22.

[284] *Mentor Savings Bank* v. *Vinson,* 91 L.Ed.2d 49 (1986).

[285] *Oncale* v. *Sundowner Offshore Services,* 140 L.Ed.2d 201 (1998).

[286] Ibid.

[287] Joyce Gelb and Marian Lief Palley, *Women and Public Policies* (Princeton, N.J.: Princeton University Press, 1982), 102. The author of Title IX, Rep. Patsy Mink (D.-Hawaii), had applied to medical schools but was not considered because she was a woman. Mink intended Title IX to open the doors. She said it was "never intended to mean equal numbers or equal money" in athletics. Susan Reimer, "Title IX Has Unintended Consequences," *Lincoln Journal Star,* April 9, 2000.

[288] R. Vivian Acosta and Linda Jean Carpenter, *Women in Intercollegiate Sport: A Longitudinal, National Study. A Thirty-Three-Year Update,* 2010; http://webpages.charter.net/womeninsport/, www.womenssportsfoundation.org/cgi-bin/iowa/issues/part/article.html?record=1107.

[289] Welch Suggs, "Uneven Progress for Women's Sports," *Chronicle of Higher Education,* April 7, 2000, A52–A56; Bill Pennington, "More Men's Teams Benched as Colleges Level the Field," *New York Times,* May 9, 2002, A1; Susan Welch and Lee Sigelman, "Who Calls the Shots: Women Coaches in Division I Women's Sports," forthcoming *Social Science Quarterly,* 2008.

[290] Suggs, "Uneven Progress for Women's Sports," A52.

[291] Michele Orecklin, "Now She's Got Game," *Time,* March 3, 2003, 57.

[292] "Title IX Facts Everyone Should Know," www.womensportsfoundation.org/cgibin/iowa/issues/geena/record,html?record=862.

[293] Mary Duffy, quoted in E. J. Dionne Jr., "Nothing Wacky about Title IX," *Washington Post National Weekly Edition,* May 19, 1997, 26.

[294] Karen Kornbluh, "The Joy of Flex," *Washington Monthly,* December 2005, 30.

[295] For elaboration, see Eyal Press, "Do Workers Have a Fundamental Right to Care for Their Families? The Latest Front in the Job-Discrimination Battle," *New York Times Magazine,* July 29, 2007, 37.

[296] *Mississippi University for Women* v. *Hogan,* 458 U.S. 718 (1982).

[297] *Orr* v. *Orr,* 440 U.S. 268 (1979).

[298] *Michael M.* v. *Sonoma County,* 450 U.S. 464 (1981).

[299] *Rostker* v. *Goldberg,* 453 U.S. 57 (1981).

[300] *Planned Parenthood of Southeastern Pennsylvania* v. *Casey,* 120 L.Ed.2d 674 (1992).

[301] Early decisions include *University of California Regents* v. *Bakke,* 438 U.S. 265 (1978); *United Steelworkers* v. *Weber,* 443 U.S. 193 (1979); and *Fullilove* v. *Klutznick,* 448 U.S. 448 (1980).

[302] Two critics include Thomas Sowell, *Preferential Policies: An International Perspective* (New York: Morrow, 1990), and Dinesh D'Souza, *Illiberal Education* (New York: Free Press, 1991).

[303] *United Steelworkers* v. *Weber; Sheet Metal Workers* v. *EEOC,* 92 L.Ed.2d 344 (1986); *Firefighters* v. *Cleveland,* 92 L.Ed.2d 405 (1986); *United States* v. *Paradise Local Union,* 94 L.Ed.2d 203 (1987).

[304] *Firefighters* v. *Stotts,* 467 U.S. 561 (1985); *Wygant* v. *Jackson Board of Education,* 90 L.Ed.2d 260 (1986).

[305] *Richmond* v. *Croson,* 102 L.Ed.2d 854 (1989); *Adarand Constructors* v. *Pena,* 132 L.Ed.2d 158 (1995).

[306] Quoted in Robert J. Samuelson, "End Affirmative Action," *Washington Post National Weekly Edition,* March 6, 1995, 5.

[307] Private companies that have government contracts, and therefore are subject to affirmative action, have shown more improvement in hiring minorities and women than other companies have. State and local governments, also subject to affirmative action, have shown more improvement in hiring than private companies have.

[308] James E. Jones, "The Genesis and Present Status of Affirmative Action in Employment," paper presented at the annual meeting of the American Political Science Association, Washington, D.C., September 1984; Nelson C. Dometrius and Lee Sigelman, "Assessing Progress toward Affirmative Action Goals in State and Local Government," *Public Administration Review* 44 (1984), 241–247; Peter Eisinger, *Black Employment in City Government* (Washington, D.C.: Joint Center for Political Studies, 1983); Milton Coleman, "Uncle Sam Has Stopped Running Interference for Blacks," *Washington Post National Weekly Edition,* December 19, 1983.

[309] This "is one of the better kept secrets of the debate." Alan Wolfe, "Affirmative Action, Inc.," *New Yorker,* November 25, 1996, 107. See also the numerous sources cited there.

[310] Joe Klein, "There's More than One Way to Diversity," *Time,* December 18, 2006, 29.

[311] Gertrude Ezorsky, *Racism and Justice: The Case for Affirmative Action* (Ithaca, N.Y.: Cornell University Press, 1991), 48–49, 63–65.

[312] Wilson, *The Truly Disadvantaged.*

[313] Donald Kaul, "Privilege in Workplace Invisible to White Men Who Enjoy It," *Lincoln Journal-Star,* April 9, 1995; Richard Morin and Lynne Duke, "A Look at the Bigger Picture," *Washington Post National Weekly Edition,* March 16, 1992, 9.

[314] Eisinger, *Black Employment in City Government.*

[315] Thomas J. Kane, "Racial and Ethnic Preference in College Admissions," paper presented at the Ohio State University College of Law Conference, "Twenty Years after *Bakke,*" Columbus, April 1998.

[316] This has happened in Florida. "Fewer Black Students Enrolled in Florida," *Lincoln Journal Star,* September 11, 2005, 3A.

[317] And the UC campuses at Berkeley and Los Angeles began to take into account "disadvantage" more than they used to. That is, they began to use "disadvantage" as a proxy for race. David Leonhardt, "The New Affirmative Action," *New York Times Magazine,* September 30, 2007, 76.

[318] Jeffrey Rosen, "How I Learned to Love Quotas," *New York Times Magazine,* June 1, 2003, 54; Lee Hockstader, "The Texas 10 Percent Solution," *Washington Post National Weekly Edition,* November 11, 2002, 30. A major effect on the University of California system has been "cascading," with minority enrollments dropping at the most competitive UC campuses but increasing at the less competitive ones. Minorities have been cascading from the top tier to the next tiers, where their academic records more closely match those of the other students. James Traub, "The Class of Prop. 209," *New York Times Magazine,* May 2, 1999, 51.

[319] Jacques Steinberg, "The New Calculus of Diversity on Campus," *New York Times,* February 2, 2003, WK3; Timothy Egan, "Little Asia on the Hill," *New York Times,* January 7, 2007, Education Life, 26.

[320] *Gratz* v. *Bollinger,* 156 L.Ed.2d 257; *Grutter* v. *Bollinger,* 156 L.Ed.2d 304.

[321] These manifestations of affirmative action weren't at issue in the case, but the companies and the officers assumed that they could be affected, at least indirectly, by the ruling. Jeffrey Toobin, *The Nine: Inside the Secret World of the Supreme Court* (New York: Doubleday, 2007), 212–214.

322 Chief Justice Roberts and Justices Alito, Scalia, and Thomas. The question mark is Justice Kennedy.

323 Traub, "Class of Prop. 209."

324 John Larew, "Why Are Droves of Unqualified, Unprepared Kids Getting into Our Top Colleges?" *Washington Monthly,* June 1991, 10–14; Theodore Cross, "Suppose There Was No Affirmative Action at the Most Prestigious Colleges and Graduate Schools," *Journal of Blacks in Higher Education,* March 31, 1994, 47, 50; Klein, "There's More than One Way to Diversify," 29.

325 For an examination of the *Bakke* ruling and its impact on graduate schools, see Susan Welch and John Gruhl, *Affirmative Action and Minority Enrollments in Medical and Law Schools* (Ann Arbor: University of Michigan Press, 1998).

326 Richard H. Sander, "House of Cards for Black Law Students," *Los Angeles Times,* December 20, 2004, www.latimes.com/news/ opinion/la-oe-sander20dec20,0,436015,print. story; Adam Liptak, "For Blacks in Law School, Can Less Be More?" *New York Times,* February 13, 2005, WK3.

327 Shelby Steele, "Affirmative Action Is Just a Distraction," W*ashington Post National Weekly Edition,* August 3–9, 2009, 27.

328 Stephen Carter, quoted in David Owen, "From Race to Chase," *New Yorker,* June 3, 2002, 54.

329 For further discussion, see David T. Canon, *Race, Redistricting, and Representation* (Chicago: University of Chicago Press, 1999), 23–25. Of course, there's also a small upper class of wealthy businesspeople, entertainers, and athletes.

330 Dick Kirschten, "Not Black-and-White," *National Journal,* March 2, 1991, 496–500.

⊙ GLOSSARY

Acid rain Emissions of sulfur, nitrogen, and other substances that are transformed by atmospheric chemical processes and returned to earth in either wet or dry forms. The wet form is called acid rain and can be in the form of rain, snow, or fog.

Activist judges Judges who are not reluctant to overrule the other branches of government by declaring laws or actions of government officials unconstitutional.

Administrative Procedure Act (APA) Legislation passed in 1946 that provides for public participation in the rule-making process. All federal agencies must disclose their rule-making procedures and publish all regulations at least thirty days in advance of their effective date to allow time for public comment.

Adversarial relationship A relationship in which two parties or groups are often in opposition, such as public officials and the media.

Affirmative action A policy in job hiring or university admissions that gives special consideration to members of historically disadvantaged groups.

Agents of political socialization Sources of information about politics; include parents, peers, schools, the media, political leaders, and the community.

American Civil Liberties Union (ACLU) A nonpartisan organization that seeks to protect the civil liberties of all Americans.

Americans with Disabilities Act Legislation passed to protect those with disabilities from discrimination in employment and public accommodations, such as stores, restaurants, hotels, and health care facilities.

Anti-Federalists Those who opposed the ratification of the U.S. Constitution.

Anti-Obesity Campaign A public education campaign waged by cities, states, and the federal government to address the health problems associated with the high incidence of obesity among Americans. The campaign's objectives are to make the public more aware of the fat and sugar and overall caloric content of foods they eat at home and in restaurants or purchase from vending machines, and the relationship of these foods to the onset of diabetes, high blood pressure, stroke, and cardiovascular disease. Obesity-related diseases, especially diabetes, are responsible for driving up health care spending by both government and private insurers.

Appropriations Budget legislation that specifies the amount of authorized funds that will actually be allocated for agencies and departments to spend.

Articles of Confederation The first constitution of the United States; in effect from 1781 to 1789.

Asymmetrical warfare Conflict between combatants of very unequal military strength.

Authorizations Budget legislation that provides agencies and departments with the legal authority to operate; may specify funding levels but does not actually provide the funding (the funding is provided by **appropriations**).

Ballot initiative A means for placing policy questions on state ballots and having them decided directly by voters.

Battleground states Also known as "swing states." During a presidential election, these are states whose Electoral College votes are not safely in one candidate's pocket; candidates will spend time and more money there to try to win the state.

Bible belt A term used to describe portions of the South and Midwest that were strongly influenced by Protestant fundamentalists.

Big Sort A term coined to describe how Americans tend to live among others of similar economic statuses and cultural beliefs.

Big tent The idea, usually accepted by the major political parties, that they should welcome diverse people holding diverse views as the way to gain supporters and win elections.

Bill of Rights The first ten amendments to the U.S. Constitution.

Biofuels Renewable resources produced from biomass, which is composed of recently living elements such as animals, plants, or wood. One popular biofuel is biodiesel, which is used to run automobiles.

Black budget The part of the U.S. budget, unknown to the public and to much of Congress, that funds certain intelligence activities.

Blockbusting The practice in which realtors would frighten whites in a neighborhood where a black family had moved by telling the whites that their houses would decline in value. The whites in panic would then sell their houses to the realtors at low prices, and the realtors would resell the houses to blacks, thereby resegregating the area from white to black.

Blog Common term for a web log, an independent website created by an individual or group to disseminate opinions or information.

Blue states The states that voted Democratic in 2000 and 2004 and are generally more liberal in outlook. They include New England, Middle Atlantic, Upper Midwest, and Pacific Coast states.

Bradley effect A discrepancy in polls and actual voting that overestimates the white vote for black candidates because some white voters might falsely report that they intend to vote for an African American candidate. Named after the 1982 California gubernatorial candidate Tom Bradley.

Broadcast An attempt by a network to appeal to most of the television or radio audience.

Brown bag test An informal requirement of some African American clubs and churches in the first half of the twentieth century that prospective members have enough "white blood" so that their skin color was lighter than the color of a brown paper bag.

Brown v. *Board of Education* The 1954 case in which the U.S. Supreme Court overturned the **separate-but-equal doctrine** and ruled unanimously that segregated schools violated the Fourteenth Amendment.

Bubble concept A pollution-control system that permits reductions in overall pollutants within a given area rather than requiring reductions for every individual point of pollution within that area.

Budget deficit Occurs when federal spending exceeds federal revenues.

Burger Court The U.S. Supreme Court under Chief Justice Warren Burger (1969–1986). Though not as activist as the **Warren Court**, the Burger Court maintained most of the rights expanded by its predecessor and issued important rulings on abortion and sexual discrimination.

Bush v. *Gore* U.S. Supreme Court case in 2000 where the Supreme Court set aside the Florida Supreme Court's order for a manual recount of the presidential votes cast in the state. The Court's decision meant that Bush got Florida's electoral votes, giving him a majority of all electoral votes and, thus, the election.

Cap-and-trade An approach to emissions trading used to control pollution by providing economic incentives to reduce emissions of pollutants. A governmental body usually sets a limit on permissible emissions levels in a geographical area. The limit (or cap) is allocated among entities, such as firms or industries, or other groupings as permits. Then entities within the geographical area that need to exceed their emissions can buy or "trade" permits from those who need fewer of them.

Capitalist economy An economic system in which the means of production are privately owned and prices, wages, working conditions, and profits are determined solely by the market.

Carbon dioxide (CO_2) One of the greenhouse gas chemical compounds. It is heavy, colorless, and formed by animal respiration and the decay or combustion of animal and vegetable matter. It is then absorbed by plants in photosynthesis.

Casework The assistance members of Congress provide to their constituents; includes answering questions and doing personal favors for those who ask for help. Also called **constituency service**.

Centers for Disease Control and Prevention (CDC) A federal agency founded in 1946 as the Communicable Disease Center, a successor to the agency that fought malaria in combat areas during World War II. The CDC was originally devoted to preventing the spread of mosquito-borne diseases but is now involved in all public health efforts directed at preventing and controlling infectious and chronic disease, injuries, workplace hazards, disabilities, and environmental health threats.

Central Intelligence Agency (CIA) Created after World War II, the CIA is a federal agency charged with coordinating overseas intelligence activities gathering and analysis.

Checkbook members People who "join" interest groups by donating money.

Checks and balances The principle of government that holds that the powers of the various branches should overlap to avoid power becoming overly concentrated in one branch.

Chernobyl The 1986 nuclear accident in the former Soviet Union that is considered to be the worst nuclear power plant disaster in history.

Chief executive The role the president serves as head and chief administrator of the federal bureaucracy.

Christian right Evangelical Protestant denominations that came together as a political movement to forward their conservative agenda, usually through the Republican Party.

Civil case A case in which individuals sue others for denying their rights and causing them harm.

Civil disobedience Peaceful but illegal protest activity in which those involved allow themselves to be arrested and charged.

Civil liberties Individual rights outlined in the Constitution and the Bill of Rights.

Civil rights The principle of equal rights for persons regardless of their race, sex, or ethnic background.

Civil Rights Act of 1964 Major civil rights legislation that prohibits discrimination on the basis of race, color, religion, or national origin in public accommodations.

Civil Rights Act of 1968 Civil rights legislation that prohibits discrimination in the sale or rental of housing on the basis of race, color, religion, or national origin; also prohibits **blockbusting**, **steering**, and **redlining**.

Civil Service Commission An agency established by the Pendleton Act of 1883 to curb **patronage** in the federal bureaucracy and replace it with a merit system.

Clean coal An umbrella term for technologies to reduce emissions of carbon dioxide and other greenhouse gases that come from burning coal for electrical power; often involves carbon capture and sequestration, which pumps and stores CO_2 emissions underground.

Climate change A change in global temperatures and precipitation due to natural variability or to human activity.

Climate skeptics Those who disagree with scientific conclusions about global warming.

Cloture A method of stopping a **filibuster** by limiting debate to only twenty more hours; requires a vote of three-fifths of the members of the Senate.

Coalition A network of **interest groups** with similar concerns that combine forces to pursue a common goal; may be short-lived or permanent.

Cold War The era of hostility between the United States and the Soviet Union that existed between the end of World War II and the collapse of the Soviet Union.

Commander in Chief The president's constitutional role as head of the armed forces with power to direct their use.

Commercial bias A slant in news coverage to please or avoid offending advertisers.

Comparable worth The principle that comparable jobs should pay comparable wages.

Concurring opinion The opinion by one or more judges in a court case who agree with the decision but not with the reasons given by the majority for it. The concurring opinion offers an alternate legal argument for the ruling.

Confederal system A system in which the central government has only the powers given to it by the subnational governments.

Conference committee A committee composed of members of both houses of Congress that is formed to try to resolve the differences when the two houses pass different versions of the same bill.

Conflict of interest The situation in which government officials make decisions that directly affect their own personal livelihoods or interests.

Conservative A person who believes that the domestic role of government should be minimized and that individuals are responsible for their own well-being.

Constituency Both the geographic area and the people a member of Congress represents: for a senator, the state and all its residents; for a member of the House, a congressional district and all its residents.

Constituency service The assistance members of Congress provide to residents in their districts (states, if senators); includes answering questions and doing personal favors for those who ask for help. Also called **casework**.

Constitutional Convention The gathering in Philadelphia in 1787 that wrote the U.S. Constitution; met initially to revise the **Articles of Confederation** but produced a new national constitution instead.

Containment A policy formulated by the Truman administration to limit the spread of communism by meeting any action taken by the Soviet Union with a countermove; led U.S. decision makers to see most conflicts in terms of U.S.-Soviet rivalry.

Contribution limits Ceilings set on the overall amount of money that individuals and groups give to candidates.

Cooperative federalism The day-to-day cooperation among federal, state, and local officials in carrying out the business of government.

Copenhagen Accord The nonbonding document agreed to by delegates at the 2009 Copenhagen Climate Conference. It includes timelines for nations to submit targets for the reduction of greenhouse gase emissions.

Cracking, stacking, and packing Methods of drawing district boundaries that minimize black representation. With cracking, a large concentrated black population is divided among two or more districts so that blacks will not have a majority anywhere; with stacking, a large black population is combined with an even larger white population; with packing, a large black population is put into one district rather than two so that blacks will have a majority in only one district.

Crafted talk A way of packaging policies that caters to a specific base while appearing to remain mainstream.

Creative destruction The economist Joseph Schumpeter's theory that American capitalism works because entrepreneurs and innovators are constantly introducing new products, forms of organization, marketing, and new technologies and thus destroying old and less efficient ways.

Criminal case A case in which a government (national or state) prosecutes a person for violating its laws.

Cruel and unusual punishment Torture or any punishment that is grossly disproportionate to the offense; prohibited by the Eighth Amendment.

Cyberterrorism A form of asymmetrical warfare that attempts to disrupt an economy, its communication system, or its military defenses by hacking into the computer systems that control them and immobilizing them. It is one of the most urgent threats to U.S. national security.

Dealignment Term used to refer to the diminished relevance of political parties.

Declaration of Independence A founding document that proclaimed "all men are created equal" and outlined the unalienable rights given to the American people.

Deepwater Horizon A deepwater offshore oil-drilling rig in the Gulf of Mexico that had drilled the deepest oil well in history. On April 20, 2010, it exploded and killed eleven crew members. On April 22, the rig sank, causing the largest offshore oil spill in U.S. history.

De facto segregation Segregation that is based on residential patterns and is not imposed by law; because it cannot be eliminated by striking down a law, it is more intractable than **de jure segregation**.

Deflation A condition in which prices fall so low that there is a disincentive to buy because consumers keep waiting for prices to fall lower; leads to sluggish economic growth and rising unemployment.

De jure segregation Segregation imposed by law; outlawed by *Brown* v. *Board of Education* and subsequent court cases.

Delegated legislative authority The power to draft, as well as execute, specific policies; granted by Congress to executive branch agencies when a problem requires technical expertise.

Democracy A system of government in which sovereignty resides in the people.

Democratic Party One of two major political parties in the United States; it grew out of the party established by Andrew Jackson in the early nineteenth century. In contrast to Republicans, Democrats are more likely to believe that government can help people improve their economic well-being and less likely to believe that government should regulate some forms of personal moral behavior, such as same-sex marriages and abortion.

Department of Health and Human Services (HHS) The cabinet department responsible for much of the government's work in health care. It administers the **Medicare** and **Medicaid** health insurance programs and is the parent agency of the **Food and Drug Administration (FDA)**, the **Public Health Service (PHS)**, the **National Institutes of Health (NIH)**, and the **Centers for Disease Control and Prevention (CDC)**.

Depression A period of prolonged high unemployment.

Deregulation The reduction or elimination of government **regulation** in a specific industry. The U.S. government began deregulating the utility industry in the late 1990s. The goal was to create more competition and, therefore, lower the costs to consumers.

Détente A policy designed to deescalate **Cold War** rhetoric and promote the notion that relations with the Soviet Union could be conducted in ways other than confrontation; developed by President Richard M. Nixon and Secretary of State Henry Kissinger.

Devolution The delegation of authority by the national government to lower units of government (such as at the state and local level) to make and implement policy.

Direct democracy A system of government in which citizens govern themselves directly and vote on most issues; e.g., a New England town meeting.

Discretionary spending Spending levels set by the federal government in annual **appropriations** bills passed by Congress; includes government operating expenses and the salaries of many federal employees.

Dissenting opinion The opinion by one or more judges in a court case who do not agree with the decision of the majority. The dissenting opinion urges a different outcome.

Divided government The situation in which one political party controls the presidency and the other party controls one or both houses of Congress.

Domino theory The idea that if one country fell under communist rule, its neighbors would also fall to communism; contributed to the U.S. decision to intervene in Vietnam.

Dred Scott case An 1857 case in which the U.S. Supreme Court held that blacks, whether slave or free, were not citizens and that Congress had no power to restrict slavery in the territories; contributed to the polarization between North and South and ultimately to the Civil War.

Dual federalism The idea that the Constitution created a system in which the national government and the states have separate grants of power with each supreme in its own sphere.

Due process The Fourteenth Amendment guarantees that the government will follow fair and just procedures when prosecuting a criminal defendant.

Earmark A specific amount of money designated—or set aside—at the request of a member of Congress for a favored project, usually in his or her district. The dollar amount may be included in one of the budget authorization bills, but more commonly it is in the committee report attached to the bill that instructs the relevant executive branch agency how to spend the money authorized for its operations.

Earth Summit A 1992 conference held in Rio de Janeiro to address environmental protection in the context of global economic development. It was also the largest group meeting of world leaders in history, with representatives from 178 countries. The topics were biodiversity, global warming, sustainable development, and preservation of tropical rain forests. Five international agreements were signed.

Electoral College A group of electors selected by the voters in each state and the District of Columbia; the electors officially elect the president and vice president.

Emancipation Proclamation Abraham Lincoln's 1863 proclamation that the slaves "shall be . . . forever free." At the time, it applied only to the Confederate states and so had little practical impact because the Union did not control them. However, it had an immense political impact, making clear that the Civil War was not just to preserve the Union but also to abolish slavery.

Environmental impact statement A report of the potential environmental effects of planned land use.

Environmental justice The U.S. **Environmental Protection Agency (EPA)** defines environmental justice as "the fair treatment and meaningful involvement of all people regardless of race, color, national origin, or income with respect to the development, implementation, and enforcement of environmental laws, regulations, and policies. . . . It will be achieved when everyone enjoys the same degree of protection from environmental and health hazards and equal access to the decision-making process to have a healthy environment in which to live, learn, and work" (http://www.epa.gov/compliance/ej/).

Environmental Protection Agency (EPA) The U.S. government agency that sets and enforces national pollution-control standards, established in 1970 by President Nixon. EPA action has led to substantial improvements in air-pollution emissions, water quality, and waste disposal in the United States. The EPA also oversees the cleanup of Superfund sites.

Equal Pay Act A statute enacted by Congress in 1963 that mandates that women and men should receive equal pay for equal work.

Equal protection clause The Fourteenth Amendment clause that is the Constitution's primary guarantee that everyone is equal before the law.

Equal Rights Amendment (ERA) A proposed amendment to the Constitution that would prohibit government from denying equal rights on the basis of sex; was passed by Congress in 1972 but failed to be ratified by a sufficient number of states.

Establishment clause The First Amendment clause that prohibits the establishment of a state religion.

European Union (EU) A union of European nations formed in 1957 to foster political and economic integration in Europe; formerly called the European Economic Community or Common Market.

Exclusionary rule A rule that prevents evidence obtained in violation of the Fourth Amendment from being used in court against the defendant.

Executive Office of the President (EOP) The president's personal bureaucracy that monitors the work done in cabinet departments and agencies.

Executive orders Rules or regulations issued by the president that have the force of law; issued to implement constitutional provisions or statutes.

Executive privilege The authority of the president to withhold specific types of information from the courts and Congress.

Exit polls Election-day polls of voters leaving the polling places, conducted mainly by television networks and major newspapers.

Externality An incidental condition that may affect a course of action or condition. In the case of the environment, environmental damage from the energy industry is treated as an externality, that is, something that is not factored into the costs of energy generation and consumption.

Faithless elector A member of the **Electoral College** who votes on the basis of personal preference rather than the way the majority of voters in his or her state voted.

Federal courts of appeals Intermediate appellate courts that hear appeals from cases that have been decided by the district courts. There are twelve, based on regions of the country.

Federal district courts The courts that try cases based on federal law. There are ninety-four in the United States.

Federal Election Commission Commission established by a 1974 statute that regulated campaign finance, provided for public financing of presidential campaigns, and limited contributions to campaigns for federal offices, among other things.

Federalism A system in which power is constitutionally divided between a central government and subnational or local governments.

Federalists Originally, those who supported the U.S. Constitution and favored its ratification; in the early years of the Republic, those who advocated a strong national government.

Filibuster A mechanism for delay in the Senate in which one or more members engage in a continuous speech to prevent the Senate from voting on a bill.

Fireside chats Short radio addresses given by President Franklin D. Roosevelt to win support for his policies and reassure the public during the Great Depression.

First Amendment The first amendment to the United States Constitution, guaranteeing freedom of expression, which includes freedom of speech, religion, assembly, and association, and freedom of the press.

Fiscal policy Government's actions to regulate the economy through taxing and spending policies.

527 organizations A 527 organization is designed to influence elections. These organizations are named this because of the U.S. tax code that authorizes them. They are of interest because they are unregulated by the Federal Election Commission, and thus they can receive money and spend it freely to influence elections.

Focus group A group of a dozen or so average men and women brought together by political consultants and pollsters to share their feelings and reactions to different things in an effort to develop a campaign strategy that will attract voters to or away from a particular candidate.

FOIA The Freedom of Information Act, passed in 1966 and amended in 1974, lets any member of the public apply to an agency for access to unclassified documents in its archives.

Food and Drug Administration (FDA) An agency within the Department of Health and Human Services responsible for protecting the public against unsafe food and drugs. It supervises testing of drugs for safety and effectiveness before pharmaceutical companies are allowed to market them. It also issues regulations for the sale and transport of food products and for labeling of food products to identify their ingredients and nutritional and caloric content. The FDA regulates about one-quarter of all consumer products and has been called the country's most important health agency.

Free exercise clause The First Amendment clause that guarantees individuals the right to practice their religion without government intervention.

free-rider problem The problem created when individuals benefit from actions of groups they are not a part of, such as workers whose raises are influenced by union pressure but who are not members of unions.

Free trade A policy of minimum intervention by government in trade relations.

Freedom of association The right of an individual to join with others to speak, assemble, and petition the government for a redress of grievances. This right allows a minority to pursue interests without being prevented from doing so by the majority.

Freedom of speech The First Amendment guarantee of a right of free expression.

Freedom of the press Freedom from censorship, so the press can disseminate the news, information, and opinion that it deems appropriate.

Friend of the court briefs Legal arguments filed in court cases by individuals or groups who aren't litigants in the cases. These briefs often provide new information to the court and usually urge the judges to rule one way.

Full faith and credit clause A clause in the U.S. Constitution that requires the states to recognize contracts that are valid in other states.

Gaining access The ability of lobbyists to reach policy makers to make their case.

Game orientation The assumption in political reporting that politics is a game and that politicians are the players; leads to an emphasis on strategy at the expense of substance in news stories.

Gender gap   An observable pattern of modest but consistent differences in opinion between men and women on various public policy issues.

Gerrymander   A congressional district whose boundaries are drawn so as to maximize the political advantage of a party or racial group; often such a district has a bizarre shape.

Gettysburg Address   Famous 1863 speech by President Lincoln to dedicate the battlefield where many had fallen during the Civil War. Lincoln used the occasion to advance his ideal of equality and to promote the Union.

Global warming   The term used to describe an increase in the temperature of the earth. Most often, it is used to refer to the warming predicted as a result of increased emissions of greenhouse gases.

Globalization   The international dispersion of economic activity through the networking of companies across national borders.

Going public   The process in which Congress or its members carry an issue debate to the public via the media, such as through televised floor debates or media appearances by individual members.

Government contracts   Agreements to provide goods or services to government.

Grandfather clause   A device used in the South to prevent blacks from voting; such clauses exempted those whose grandfathers had the right to vote before 1867 from having to fulfill various requirements that some people could not meet. Since no blacks could vote before 1867, they could not qualify for the exemption.

Grants-in-aid   Federal money provided to state and, occasionally, local governments for community development and to establish programs to help people such as the aged poor or the unemployed; began during the New Deal.

Grassroots lobbying   The mass mobilization of members of an **interest group** to apply pressure to public officials, usually in the form of a mass mailing.

Great Compromise   The decision of the **Constitutional Convention** to have a bicameral legislature in which representation in one house would be by population and in the other house, by states; also called the Connecticut Compromise.

Great Depression   The devastating economic depression beginning in 1929 and lasting until World War II. Many banks collapsed, ordinary people lost their savings, business activity declined, and from one-quarter to one-third of all workers were unemployed. As a response, government intervened to provide unemployment assistance, assistance to businesses and farmers, and social security.

Great Migration   The period during World War I and until World War II when more than a million southern blacks headed north to look for better jobs and housing.

Green economy   An economic model based on renewable energy such as solar energy that is predicted to create new green jobs, ensure sustainable economic development, and prevent increases in pollution, global warming, and resource depletion. The green economical model is contrasted to a "black" economic model based on fossil fuels (oil, coal, natural gas).

Greenhouse gases   Any of the atmospheric gases that contribute to the greenhouse effect, such as carbon dioxide, water vapor, and methane.

Habeas corpus   Latin for "have ye the body." A writ of *habeas corpus* is a means for criminal defendants who have exhausted appeals in state courts to appeal to a federal district court.

Hatch Act   A statute enacted in 1939 that limits the political activities of federal employees in partisan campaigns.

Hate speech   Racial, ethnic, sexual, or religious slurs that demean people for characteristics that are innate or beliefs that are deeply held.

Head of government   The president's partisan, policy-making role as head of his party in government, in contrast to his nonpartisan duties as head of state and representative of the country.

Head of state   The president's role as a symbolic leader of the nation and representative of all the people.

Health maintenance organization (HMO)   A group of doctors who agree to provide full health care for a fixed monthly charge.

Healthy Foods Initiative   A preventive health program organized and funded within the Department of Agriculture that encourages the consumption of healthier foods, especially fresh foods and vegetables, and makes more of these foods available to low-income people and in neighborhoods with no local supermarkets or vendors of fresh foods. Other branches of government, including the White House (through Michele Obama's childhood nutrition campaign), participate in the Healthy Foods public education campaign to promote dietary change as a means to prevent disease.

Home rule   The grant of considerable autonomy to a local government.

Horse race coverage   The way in which the media reports on the candidates' polling status and strategies, rather than covering their positions on relevant issues.

House of Representatives   The house of Congress all of whose members are elected directly by the people every two years on the principle of one person-one vote; House districts are apportioned to states proportional to population, as determined by the decennial census.

Identity politics   The practice of organizing on the basis of sex, ethnic or racial identity, or sexual orientation to compete for public resources and influence public policy.

Ideology   A highly organized and coherent set of opinions.

Impeachment   The process provided for in the Constitution by which the House of Representatives can indict (impeach) a president for "Treason, Bribery, or other High Crimes and Misdemeanors." If the House votes to lodge formal charges against the president, he is impeached. But a president cannot be removed from office unless two-thirds of the Senate finds him guilty of the charges.

Imperial presidency   A term that came into use at the end of the 1960s to describe the growing power of the presidency.

Implied powers clause   The clause in the U.S. Constitution that gives Congress the power to make all laws **"necessary and proper"** for carrying out its specific powers.

Independent   A voter who is not aligned with any political party.

Independent agencies   Government bureaus that are not parts of **departments**. Their heads are appointed by and responsible to the president.

Independent spending   Money spent on elections by groups that are not formally affiliated with the parties or candidates. Any interest group, business, or union can spend unlimited amounts, secretly, in this way.

Indirect democracy   A system of government in which citizens elect representatives to make decisions for them.

Inflation   The situation in which prices increase but wages and salaries fail to keep pace with the prices of goods.

Influence peddling   The use of one's access to powerful people to make money, as when former government officials use access to former colleagues to win high-paying jobs in the private sector.

Informal norms   Unwritten rules designed to help keep Congress running smoothly by attempting to diminish friction and competition among the members.

Infotainment   A word for television newscasts that attempt to entertain as they provide information.

Initiative   A process that allows citizens and interest groups to collect signatures on petitions and place a proposal on the ballot.

Interest groups   Organizations that try to achieve at least some of their goals with government assistance.

Intergovernmental Panel on Climate Change (IPCC) A scientific body set up by the United Nations in 1988 to evaluate the risks of climate change caused by human activity. It has over 2,500 scientists from more than 130 countries who are charged with determining how much the climate has changed over time and why. In response to its 2007 report on the climate, the IPCC shared the 2007 Nobel Peace Prize with former Vice President Al Gore.

Isolationism A policy of noninvolvement with other nations outside the Americas; generally followed by the United States during the nineteenth and early twentieth centuries.

Issue vote A vote for a candidate whose stands on specific issues are consistent with the voter's own.

Jacksonian democracy Democracy in which participation is open to common people. Named for Andrew Jackson, who first mobilized common people to participate in government.

Jeffersonians (Jeffersonian Republicans) Opponents of a strong national government. They challenged the **Federalists** in the early years of the Republic.

Jim Crow laws Laws enacted in southern states that segregated schools, public accommodations, and almost all other aspects of life.

Judicial review The authority of the courts to declare laws or actions of government officials unconstitutional.

Jurisdiction The authority of a court to hear and decide cases.

Keynesian economics The argument by John Maynard Keynes that government should stimulate the economy during periods of high unemployment by increasing spending even if it must run deficits to do so.

Ku Klux Klan A white supremacy group aimed at inflaming prejudice and terrorizing blacks during and after **Reconstruction**.

Kyoto Protocol A 1997 international agreement, initially among 137 developed countries, to reduce greenhouse gas emissions that cause global warming. It is set to expire in 2012. President Bill Clinton signed the Kyoto Protocol, but the Senate declined to ratify it; hence, it is nonbinding in the United States.

Labor unions Groups that seek agreements with business and policies from the government that protect workers' jobs, wages, and benefits and ensure the safety of workplaces.

Leaks Disclosures of information that some government officials want kept secret.

Libel Printed or broadcast statements that are false and meant to tarnish someone's reputation.

Liberal A person who believes in government activism to help individuals and communities in such areas as health, education, and welfare.

Limited government A government that is strong enough to protect the people's rights but not so strong as to threaten those rights; in the view of John Locke, such a government was established through a **social contract**.

Literacy tests Examinations ostensibly carried out to ensure that voters could read and write but actually a device used in the South to disqualify blacks from voting.

Living wage A wage that is high enough to allow full-time workers to meet the basic cost of living, something the minimum wage does not do.

Lobbying The efforts of **interest groups** to influence government.

Lobbyist A representative of a group or interest who attempts to influence government decisions, generally through personal contact.

Love Canal The neighborhood in Niagara Falls, New York, that is the site of the worst chemical waste disaster in U.S. history.

Love Canal became a dumping ground for chemical waste in the 1940s and 1950s. It was later filled in and housing was built on it. Leakage of toxic chemicals was detected in the 1970s, and residents were evacuated from their homes. Many received a monetary settlement from the chemical company responsible for the dumping, and the federal government worked to clean up the site. Later, the government declared parts of the neighborhood safe for residences.

Majority leader The title of both the leader of the Senate, who is chosen by the majority party, and the head of the majority party in the House of Representatives, who is second in command to the **Speaker of the House**.

Majority opinion The joint opinion by a majority of the judges in a federal court case that explains why the judges ruled as they did.

Majority-minority district A congressional district whose boundaries are drawn to give a minority group a majority in the district.

Mandate A term used in the media to refer to a president having clear directions from the voters to take a certain course of action; in practice, it is not always clear that a president, even one elected by a large majority, has a mandate or, if so, for what.

Mandatory spending Spending by the federal government that is required by permanent laws; e.g., payments for **Medicare**.

Marbury* v. *Madison The 1803 case in which the U.S. Supreme Court enunciated the doctrine of **judicial review**.

Markup The process in which a congressional subcommittee rewrites a bill after holding hearings on it.

Marshall Court Supreme Court under Chief Justice John Marshall (1801–1835). This Court was responsible for articulating judicial review and confirming the supremacy of federal law over state law.

Marshall Plan A plan that provided economic relief to the nations of western Europe in 1947, following World War II.

McCain-Feingold Act Also known as the Bipartisan Campaign Finance Reform Act of 2001, this legislation was created to regulate campaign financing. It limited the amount of gifts and banned soft money contributions to the national parties but not to certain types of private groups.

McCarthyism Methods of combating communism characterized by irresponsible accusations made on the basis of little or no evidence; named after Senator Joseph McCarthy of Wisconsin who used such tactics in the 1950s.

McCulloch* v. *Maryland An 1819 U.S. Supreme Court decision that broadly interpreted Congress's powers under the **implied powers clause**.

Medicaid A federal-state medical assistance program for the poor.

Medicare A public health insurance program that pays many medical expenses of the elderly and the disabled; funded through payroll taxes, general revenues, and premiums paid by recipients.

Merit system A system of filling bureaucratic jobs on the basis of competence instead of **patronage**.

Microtargeting Directing campaigns to specifically defined demographic groups.

Minority leader The leader of the minority party in either the House of Representatives or the Senate.

Minority rights The individual rights of those not in the political or religious majority.

***Miranda* rights** A means of protecting a criminal suspect's rights against self-incrimination during police interrogation. Before interrogation, suspects must be told that they have a right to remain silent; that anything they say can be used against them; that they have a right to an attorney; and that if they cannot afford an attorney, one will be provided for them. The rights are named after the case *Miranda* v. *Arizona*.

"Mischiefs of factions" A phrase used by James Madison in the *Federalist Papers* to refer to the threat to the nation's stability that factions could pose.

Mixed economies   Countries that incorporate elements of both capitalist and socialist practices in the workings of their economies.

Moderates   Also referred to as "middle of the roaders," these are persons with centrist positions on issues that distinguish them from liberals and conservatives.

Monetary policy   Actions taken by the Federal Reserve Board to regulate the economy through changes in short-term interest rates and the money supply.

Monroe Doctrine   A doctrine articulated by President James Monroe in 1823 that warned European powers not already involved in Latin America to stay out of that region.

Motor voter law   A statute that allows people to register to vote at public offices such as welfare offices and drivers' license bureaus.

Muckrakers   Reform-minded journalists in the early twentieth century who exposed corruption in politics and worked to break the financial link between business and politicians.

Multiparty system   A type of political party system where more than two groups have a chance at winning an election.

Mutual assured destruction (MAD)   The capability to absorb a nuclear attack and retaliate against the attacker with such force that it would also suffer enormous damage; believed to deter nuclear war during the **Cold War** because both sides would be so devastated that neither would risk striking first.

NAACP (National Association for the Advancement of Colored People)   An organization founded in 1909 to fight for black rights; its attorneys challenged segregation in the courts and won many important court cases, most notably *Brown* v. *Board of Education*.

Narrowcasting   An attempt by a network to appeal to a small segment of the television or radio audience rather than to most of the audience. The opposite of broadcasting, narrowcasting is targeted to specific groups, such as sports lovers and males.

National committee   The highest level of party organization; chooses the site of the national convention and the formula for determining the number of delegates from each state.

National debt   The total amount of money owed by the federal government; the sum of all **budget deficits** over the years.

National Institutes of Health (NIH)   The primary federal agency for conducting and supporting medical research. It is the parent organization for twenty-seven centers and institutes that do research on the causes and treatment of disease, from developing vaccines and drugs to mapping the human genome.

National Organization for Women (NOW)   A group formed in 1966 to fight primarily for political and economic rights for women.

National party chair   The party chair heads the national party organization. The president appoints the party chair in his party, while the national party committee of the opposition party chooses its chair. The chair raises money for party candidates and speaks on behalf of the party.

Nation-centered federalism   The view that the Constitution was written by representatives of the people and ratified by the people. Nation-centered Federalists believe that the national government is the supreme power in the federal relationship. (Hamilton articulated this view in the *Federalist Papers*.) Nation-centered federalism was the view used by northerners to justify a war to prevent the southern states from seceding in 1861. The alternative view, **state-centered federalism**, holds that the Constitution is a creation of the states.

Natural rights   Inalienable and inherent rights such as the right to own property (in the view of John Locke).

Necessary and proper clause   A phrase in the **implied powers clause** of the U.S. Constitution that gives Congress the power to make all laws needed to carry out its specific powers.

Negative externalities   The bad effects of an action taken by one set of actors on others who had no input or choice about the action.

In the case of the environment, a business may generate pollution or toxicity in a community that may cause its residents to suffer ill health.

Neoslavery   After slavery was declared unconstitutional, the practice of depriving southern blacks of their rights, casting them back to subordinate positions.

"Netroots"   Grassroots organizations mobilized by political websites.

Neutral competence   The concept that bureaucrats should make decisions in a politically neutral manner in policy making and should be chosen only for their expertise, not their political affiliation.

New Deal   A program of President Franklin D. Roosevelt's administration in the 1930s aimed at stimulating economic recovery and aiding victims of the Great Depression; led to expansion of the national government's role.

New Deal coalition   The broadly based coalition of southern conservatives, northern liberals, and ethnic and religious minorities that sustained the Democratic Party for some forty years.

North Atlantic Treaty Organization (NATO)   An alliance formed by treaty in 1949, joining the United States, Canada, and their western European World War II allies in a mutual defense pact against Soviet aggression in Europe. Since the end of the Cold War, the alliance has expanded to twenty-eight members, including most of the countries formerly aligned with the Soviet Union.

Outsourcing (offshoring)   Companies' transfer of jobs abroad in order to increase their profit (because they pay foreign workers less).

Oversight   Congress's responsibility to make sure the bureaucracy is administering federal programs in accordance with congressional intent.

Ozone hole   A hole or gap in the protective layer of ozone in the atmosphere of the earth that exposes people to increased levels of ultraviolet radiation. Chemical pollution from chlorofluorocarbons (CFCs), which are used as refrigerants, as propellants in aerosol cans, and in plastic foam products, can reduce this protective layer. An international protocol was signed in 1987 to phase out CFCs in order to protect the ozone layer.

Pardon power   Authority given to the president to erase the guilt and restore the rights of anyone convicted of a federal crime, except an impeached president.

Partisan   Affiliated with, believing in, or acting on behalf of a political party.

Party caucus   Meetings of members of political parties, often designed to select party nominees for office, or of all members of a party in the House or Senate to set policy and select their leaders.

Party government   A system in which the central party leaders recruit candidates for office, and when elected, the candidates vote with party leaders.

Party identification   A psychological link between individuals and a political party that leads those persons to regard themselves as members of that party.

Patronage system   A system in which elected officials appoint their supporters to administrative jobs; used by **political machines** to maintain themselves in power.

Pay-as-you-go (paygo)   Budgetary rules adopted by Congress that set caps on spending and bar legislation to increase spending without offsetting cuts in spending or increases in revenue.

Pentagon Papers   A top-secret study, eventually made public, of how and why the United States became embroiled in the Vietnam War; the study was commissioned by Secretary of Defense Robert McNamara during the Johnson administration.

Permanent campaign   The situation in which elected officials are constantly engaged in a campaign; fundraising for the next election begins as soon as one election is concluded.

Personal presidency A concept proposed by Theodore Lowi that holds that presidents since the 1930s have amassed tremendous personal power directly from the people and, in return, are expected to make sure the people get what they want from government.

Photo opportunity (photo op) A situation in which the politician is framed against a backdrop that symbolizes the points the politician is trying to make.

Plea bargain An agreement between the prosecutor, defense attorney, and defendant in which the prosecutor agrees to reduce the charge or sentence in exchange for the defendant's guilty plea.

Plessy v. *Ferguson* The 1896 case in which the U.S. Supreme Court upheld segregation by enunciating the **separate-but-equal doctrine**.

Pluralism The theory that American government is responsive to groups of citizens working together to promote their common interests and that enough people belong to **interest groups** to ensure that government ultimately hears everyone, even though most people do not participate actively in politics.

Pocket veto A legislative bill dies by pocket veto if a president refuses to sign it and Congress adjourns within ten working days.

Policy implementation The process by which bureaucrats convert laws into rules and activities that have an actual impact on people and things.

Political action committees (PACs) Groups that are developed to disperse money to political candidates and campaigns. PACs can be related to one business, to a group of businesses (e.g., poultry producers) or trades (e.g., chicken pluckers), or to interest groups of various sorts (e.g., civil liberties or right to life). Donations by PACs are regulated by federal law.

Political bias A preference for candidates of particular parties or for certain stands on issues that affects a journalist's reporting.

Political culture A shared body of values and beliefs that shapes perceptions and attitudes toward politics and government and, in turn, influences political behavior.

Political efficacy The belief that a person can make a difference in government.

Political equality The principle that every citizen of a democracy has an equal opportunity to try to influence government.

Political machines Political organizations based on **patronage** that flourished in big cities in the late nineteenth and early twentieth centuries. The machine relied on the votes of the lower classes and, in exchange, provided jobs and other services.

Political parties Groups that seek to gain and maintain political power though elections.

Political socialization The process of learning about politics by being exposed to information from parents, peers, schools, the media, political leaders, and the community.

Poll tax A tax that must be paid before a person can vote; used in the South to prevent blacks from voting. The Twenty-fourth Amendment prohibits poll taxes in federal elections.

Polychlorinated biphenyls (PCBs) A group of industrial compounds produced by chlorination of biphenyl, a pollutant that accumulates in animal tissue and has damaging effects on human health.

Popular sovereignty Rule by the people.

Pork barrel projects Special projects, buildings, and other public works in the district or state of a member of Congress that he or she supports because they provide jobs for constituents and enhance the member's reelection chances, rather than because the projects are necessarily wise.

Practice of objectivity The practice followed when newspapers and other mainstream media try to present the facts in their news stories, not opinions.

Preemptive war The strategy of striking a country before it has attacked, on the assumption that it might or that it could atttack.

Pregnancy Discrimination Act A congressional act from 1978 that forbids firing or demoting employees for becoming pregnant.

Presidential preference primary A direct primary in which voters select delegates to presidential nominating conventions; voters indicate a preference for a presidential candidate, delegates committed to a candidate, or both.

Presidential press conference A meeting at which the president answers questions from reporters.

Presumption of innocence A fundamental principle of the U.S. criminal justice system in which the government is required to prove the defendant's guilt. The defendant is not required to establish his innocence.

Primary elections Elections held several weeks or months before the general election that allow voters to select the nominees of their political party.

Private interest groups Interest groups that chiefly pursue economic interests that benefit their members; e.g., business organizations and labor unions.

Privatizing Outsourcing the work of government to private industry; these are jobs that would otherwise be done by civil servants or military personnel.

Pro-choice groups Groups that work to maintain women's right to choose abortion.

Productivity The ratio of total hours worked by the labor force to total goods and services produced.

Progressive movement Reform movement designed to wrest control from political machines and the lower-class immigrants they served. These reforms reduced corruption in politics, but they also seriously weakened the power of political parties.

Progressive reforms Election reforms introduced in the early twentieth century as part of the Progressive movement; included the secret ballot, primary elections, and voter registration laws.

Progressive tax A tax structured so that those with higher incomes pay a higher percentage of their income in taxes than do those with lower incomes.

Pro-life groups Groups that work to outlaw abortion.

Proportional representation An election system based on election from multimember districts. The number of seats awarded to each party in each district is equal to the percentage of the total the party receives in the district. Proportional representation favors the multiparty system.

Protectionism Government intervention to protect domestic producers from foreign competition; can take the form of tariffs, quotas on imports, or a ban on certain imports altogether.

Public disclosure The requirement that names of campaign donors be made public.

Public forum A public place such as a street, sidewalk, or park where people have a First Amendment right to express their views on public issues.

Public Health Service (PHS) An agency founded in the early nineteenth century as a quasi-military organization to diagnose and treat illnesses (such as venereal disease) in sailors and merchant marines returning from foreign ports. Its mission expanded into public health and sanitation and disease prevention for the population as whole, and today it provides rapid response to public health emergencies. Renamed the Public Health Service Commissioned Corps, its 6,000 uniformed members serve under the U.S. Surgeon General and HHS's Assistant Secretary of Health.

Public interest groups **Interest groups** that chiefly pursue benefits that cannot be limited or restricted to their members.

Public opinion The collection of individual opinions toward issues or objects of general interest.

Push poll A public opinion poll presenting the respondent with biased information favoring or opposing a particular candidate.

The idea is to see whether certain "information" can "push" voters away from a candidate or a neutral opinion toward the candidate favored by those doing the poll. Push polls seek to manipulate opinion.

Racial profiling   Practice that targets a particular group for attention from law enforcement based on racial stereotypes. A common occurrence is black drivers being stopped by police disproportionately.

Realignment   The transition from one stable party system to another, as occurred when the **New Deal coalition** was formed.

Reapportionment   The process of redistributing the 435 seats in the House of Representatives among the states based on population changes; occurs every ten years based on the most recent census.

Recall elections   A process that enables voters to remove officials from office before their terms expire.

Recession   Two or more consecutive three-month quarters of falling production.

Reconstruction   The period after the Civil War when black rights were ensured by a northern military presence in the South and by close monitoring of southern politics; ended in 1877.

Reconstruction Amendments   Three amendments (13th, 14th, and 15th), adopted after the Civil War from 1865 through 1870, that eliminated slavery (13), gave blacks the right to vote (15), and guaranteed due process rights for all (14).

Red Scare   Prompted by the Russian Revolution in 1917, this was a large-scale crackdown on so-called seditious activities in the United States.

Red states   The states that voted for George Bush in 2000 and 2004 and in general are more conservative in outlook. They include the states of the South, Great Plains, and Rocky Mountain West.

Redistricting   The process of redrawing the boundaries of congressional districts within a state after a census to take account of population shifts.

Redlining   The practice in which bankers and other lenders refused to lend money to persons who wanted to buy a house in a racially changing neighborhood.

Referendum   A process that allows the legislature to place a proposal on the ballot.

Re-Generation   A term coined by the journalist Thomas Friedman about college-age people, who he hopes will join with their parents and grandparents to ensure that sustainability is central to all activities.

Regressive tax   A tax structured so that those with lower incomes pay a larger percentage of their income in tax than do those with higher incomes.

Regulation   The actions of regulatory agencies in establishing standards or guidelines conferring benefits or imposing restrictions on business conduct.

Rehnquist Court   The U.S. Supreme Court under Chief Justice William Rehnquist (1986–2005); a conservative Court, but one that did not overturn most previous rulings.

Republic   A system of government in which citizens elect representatives to make decisions for them; an **indirect democracy**.

Republican Party   One of the major political parties in the United States since the era of the Civil War. Republicans tend to be more conservative than Democrats.

Resegregation   Increasing racial segregation in public schools since the 1980s, when desegregation efforts peaked.

Responsible party government   A governing system in which political parties have real issue differences, voters align according to those issue differences, and elected officials are expected to vote with their party leadership or lose their chance to run for office.

Restrained judges   Judges who are reluctant to overrule the other branches of government by declaring laws or actions of government officials unconstitutional.

Restrictive covenants   Agreements among neighbors in white residential areas not to sell their houses to blacks.

Retrospective voting   Voting for or against incumbents on the basis of their past performance.

Right to a jury trial   The Sixth Amendment's guarantee of a trial by jury in any criminal case that could result in more than six months' incarceration.

Right to abortion   U.S. Supreme Court ruling in *Roe* v. *Wade* (1973) establishing that women have a right to terminate a pregnancy during the first six months. States can prohibit an abortion during the last three months because at that time the fetus becomes viable—it can live outside the womb.

Right to counsel   The Sixth Amendment's guarantee of the right of a criminal defendant to have an attorney in any felony or misdemeanor case that might result in incarceration; if defendants are indigent, the court must appoint an attorney for them.

Right to die   The Rehnquist Court ruling that individuals can refuse medical treatment, including food and water, even if this means they will die. Individuals must make their decision while competent and alert. They can also act in advance, preparing a "living will" or designating another person as a proxy to make the decision if they are unable to do so.

Right to own property   The rights of individuals to own and work their private property.

Right to privacy   A right to autonomy—to be left alone; is not specifically mentioned in the U.S. Constitution but has been found by the U.S. Supreme Court to be implied through several amendments.

Roberts Court   The current Supreme Court under the leadership of Chief Justice John Roberts (2005–).

Rules Committee   The committee in the House of Representatives that sets the terms of debate on a bill.

Sample   A group of people who are surveyed. If the selection of the sample is random and large enough, their opinions should reflect those of the larger group from which they are drawn.

S-CHIP (State Children's Health Insurance Program)   A federal program, adopted in 1997 after the Clinton health reform failed to pass, that allocated money to the states to expand their existing programs of health coverage for children whose parents cannot afford to purchase health insurance but who earn too much to qualify for Medicaid.

Scoops   Leaks in information that enable reporters to break their stories before their competitors can report them.

Second Amendment   "The right of the people to keep and bear arms." Some interpret this as an absolute right to own and use guns, others as only an indication that guns can be owned if one is part of a state militia.

Secret ballot   A system of voting that protects the privacy of an individual's vote choice.

Seditious speech   Speech that encourages rebellion against the government.

Senate   One house of Congress, where each state is represented by two members.

Senate Judiciary Committee   A Senate committee charged, among other things, with recommending for or against presidential appointees to the federal courts.

Senatorial courtesy   The custom of giving senators of the president's party a virtual veto over appointments to jobs, including judicial appointments, in their states.

Seniority rule The custom that the member of the majority party with the longest service on a particular congressional committee becomes its chair; applies most of the time but is occasionally violated.

Separate-but-equal doctrine The principle, enunciated by the U.S. Supreme Court in *Plessy v. Ferguson* in 1896, that allowed separate facilities for blacks and whites as long as the facilities were equal.

Separation of church and state Constitutional principle that is supposed to keep church and state from interfering with each other. In practice it restricts government from major efforts either to inhibit or advance religion.

Separation of powers The principle of government under which the power to make, administer, and judge the laws is split among three branches—legislative, executive, and judicial.

Sexual harassment A form of job discrimination prohibited by the Civil Rights Act of 1964. Sexual harassment can consist of either (1) a supervisor's demands for sexual favors in exchange for a raise or promotion or in exchange for not imposing negative consequences; or (2) the creation of a hostile environment that prevents workers from doing their job.

Sharecroppers Tenant farmers who lease land and equipment from landowners, turning over a share of their crops in lieu of rent.

Shays's Rebellion A revolt of farmers in western Massachusetts in 1786 and 1787 to protest the state legislature's refusal to grant them relief from debt; helped lead to calls for a new national constitution.

Sierra Club An interest group whose goal is to protect the natural environment. It was created in 1890 to preserve the new Yosemite National Park from cattle ranchers who wanted the land.

Signing statements Written comments a president may attach to a law after signing it and sending it to the *Federal Register* for publication. Historically they have been used to indicate provisions in a law the president believes the federal courts may find unconstitutional. George W. Bush used them frequently to indicate sections of laws he would refuse to implement, thus setting up a conflict between the executive and legislative branches.

Single-issue groups **Interest groups** that pursue a single public interest goal and are characteristically reluctant to compromise.

Single-member districts Electoral districts in which only one individual is elected.

single-payer system A means for providing universal compulsory national health insurance coverage through a single plan funded and administered by the government. Canada and most western European countries have single-payer health care systems, but they do not prohibit private providers from offering health care to those who prefer to pay out of pocket rather than use the national health service.

Sixteenth Amendment A constitutional amendment giving Congress power to levy taxes on personal income.

Smart grid A system that delivers electricity from suppliers to consumers and uses technology to control appliances in order to save energy, reduce costs, and reduce dependence of fossil fuels.

SNAP (Supplemental Nutrition Assistance Program) A program founded during the Great Depression to make food available to malnourished Americans by giving those who qualified coupons (food stamps) that could be exchanged for basic foodstuffs. (Eligibility is determined by household income.) The program was expanded during the 1960s War on Poverty and in 2010 was serving 40 million Americans. The paper coupons have been replaced with electronic credits accessed with debit cards.

Social contract An implied agreement between the people and their government in which the people give up part of their liberty to the government in exchange for the government protecting the remainder of their liberty.

Social issue An important, noneconomic issue affecting significant numbers of the populace, such as crime, racial conflict, or changing values.

Social Security A social insurance program established by Congress during the Great Depression to reduce poverty among the elderly and to provide assistance to the disabled. It now functions as a retirement fund covering over ninety percent of all workers and is paid for largely with payroll taxes on workers and employers.

Soft money Donations to parties for "party-building" activities such as conventions, voter registration, polling, and related activities. It is exempt from regulations as long as it is not directly used for campaigning.

Soft power The ability of a country to get what it wants through the attractiveness of its culture, political ideals, and policies rather than military or economic coercion.

Sound bite A few key words or phrase included in a speech with the intent that television editors will use the phrase in a brief clip on the news.

Southern strategy The strategy followed by the Republicans in the latter part of the twentieth century to capture the votes of southern whites.

Speaker of the House The leader and presiding officer of the House of Representatives; chosen by the majority party.

Special interest caucuses Groups of members of the **House of Representatives** and **Senate** who are united by some personal interest or characteristic; e.g., the Black Caucus.

Spin What politicians do to portray themselves and their programs in the most favorable light, regardless of the facts, often shading the truth.

Split-ticket voting Voting for a member of one party for one office and for a member of another party for a different office, such as for a Republican presidential candidate but a Democratic House candidate.

Spoils system The practice of giving political supporters government jobs or other benefits.

Stagflation The combination of high inflation and economic stagnation with high unemployment that troubled the United States in the 1970s.

Standing committees Permanent congressional committees.

Stare decisis Latin for "stand by what has been decided." The rule that judges should follow precedents established in previous cases by their court or higher courts.

State-centered federalism The view that our constitutional system should give precedence to state sovereignty over that of the national government. State-centered Federalists argue that the states created the national government and the states are superior to the federal government.

States as laboratories The idea of states as places for policy experimentation.

States' rights The belief that the power of the federal government should not be increased at the expense of the states' power.

Statutes Laws passed by the legislative body of a representative government.

Steering The practice in which realtors promoted segregation by showing blacks houses in black neighborhoods and whites houses in white neighborhoods.

Straw polls Unscientific polls.

Suffrage The right to vote.

Sundown laws During the Jim Crow period in the South, laws adopted to require blacks to be off the streets by 10 P.M. as a way to maintain white supremacy.

Sunshine Act Adopted in 1976, this act requires that most government meetings be conducted in public and that notice of such meetings be posted in advance. Regulatory agencies, for example, must give notice of the date, time, place, and agenda of their meetings and follow certain rules to prevent unwarranted secrecy. Federal and state sunshine laws have made it difficult for any public body, such as a city council, to meet in secret to conduct official business.

Superfund The popular name of a governmental program established to clean up abandoned hazardous waste sites. The "Superfund" law passed by Congress is 1980 was enacted as a result of discovery of toxic waste dumps such as **Love Canal**. The law allows the EPA to either clean up these sites or to require responsible parties to clean them up.

Supermajority The 60-vote margin needed in the Senate to block a filibuster and bring a bill to the floor for an up or down vote.

Supply-side economics The argument that tax revenues will increase if tax rates are reduced; based on the assumption that more money would be available for business expansion and modernization, which in turn would stimulate employment and economic growth and result in higher tax revenues.

Supremacy clause A clause in the U.S. Constitution stating that treaties and laws made by the national government take precedence over state laws in cases of conflict.

Symbiotic relationship A relationship in which the parties use each other for mutual advantage.

Symbolic speech The use of symbols, rather than words, to convey ideas; e.g., wearing black armbands or burning the U.S. flag to protest government policy.

Tax neutrality A tax policy that does not favor certain kinds of economic activity over others.

Tea Party movement A movement originating in 2009 as a reaction to government spending for health care and to bail out the financial system and auto manufacturers. Consisting mostly of conservative Republicans, the group endorsed many candidates in the 2010 elections.

Teapot Dome scandal A 1921 scandal in which President Warren Harding's secretary of the interior received large contributions from corporations that were then allowed to lease oil reserves (called the Teapot Dome); led to the Federal Corrupt Practices Act of 1925, which required reporting of campaign contributions and expenditures.

Tenth Amendment Constitutional amendment stating that powers not delegated to the federal government or prohibited to the states are reserved to the states and to the people. This amendment has generally not had much impact, though a few recent Supreme Court cases have referred to it.

Tenthers People who assert a very broad interpretation of the Tenth Amendment to restrict federal authority on the grounds that it usurps states' authority.

The commons A term relating to communities as a whole; used to refer to the common good.

Three-fifths Compromise The decision of the **Constitutional Convention** that each slave would count as three-fifths of a person in apportioning seats in the House of Representatives.

Title IX Equal Opportunity in Education Act, which forbids discrimination on the basis of sex in schools and colleges that receive federal aid. The amendment was prompted by discrimination against women by colleges, especially in admissions, sports programs, and financial aid.

Tracking polls Polls in which a small number of people are polled on successive evenings throughout a campaign to assess changes in the level of voter support.

Tragedy of the commons The concept that although individuals benefit when they exploit goods that are common to all such as air and water, the community as a whole suffers from the resulting pollution and depletion of resources; a reason for **regulation**.

Two-party system A political system like that in the United States in which only two parties have a realistic chance of winning most government offices. This system is rare among the world's other democracies.

Undernews Political stories circulating in the fringe media, such as blogs or tabloids, but not covered by the mainstream media.

Unfunded mandates Federal laws that require the states to do something without providing full funding for the required activity.

Unified government The situation in which one party controls both the White House and Congress.

Unitary executive A minority interpretation of Article II of the Constitution made by lawyers in the Bush administration that claims the president has sole power to direct the work of executive branch agencies, without interference from Congress or the federal courts. This interpretation is considered at odds with the conventional understanding of the checks and balances built into our system of three branches of government.

Unitary system A system in which the national government is supreme; subnational governments are created by the national government and have only the power it allocates to them.

United States Census A census is a count, and a census of all U.S. inhabitants is done every ten years in years divisible by ten.

United States v. Nixon The landmark ruling that forced President Nixon to turn over tape recordings of Oval Office conversations to the Watergate special prosecutor. It established the principle that executive privilege cannot be used to withhold evidence of a crime.

Unreasonable searches and seizures Searches and arrests that are conducted without a warrant or that do not fall into one of the exceptions to the warrant requirement; prohibited by the Fourth Amendment.

Veto power The president's constitutional authority to refuse to sign a law passed by Congress. Vetoes may be overridden by a two-thirds vote in each house of Congress.

Vietnam syndrome An attitude of uncertainty about U.S. foreign policy goals and our ability to achieve them by military means; engendered among the public and officials as a result of the U.S. failure in Vietnam.

Voter registration A process that requires voters to register their name and address before an election.

Voting Rights Act (VRA) A law passed by Congress in 1965 that made it illegal to interfere with anyone's right to vote. The act and its subsequent amendments have been the main vehicles for expanding and protecting minority voting rights.

War Powers Resolution A 1973 statute enacted by Congress to limit the president's ability to commit troops to combat without congressional approval.

Warren Court The U.S. Supreme Court under Chief Justice Earl Warren (1953–1969); an activist Court that expanded the rights of criminal defendants and racial and religious minorities.

Whips Members of the House of Representatives who work to maintain party unity by keeping in contact with party members and trying to ensure they vote for party-backed bills. Both the majority and the minority party have a whip and several assistant whips.

Whistleblower An individual employee who exposes mismanagement and abuse of office by government officials.

White primary A device for preventing blacks from voting in the South. Under the pretense that political parties were private clubs, blacks were barred from voting in Democratic primaries, which were the real elections because Democrats always won the general elections.

WIC (Special Supplemental Nutritional Program for Women, Infants, and Children) A program administered by the Department of Agriculture to improve the nutrition of low-income pregnant women, their infants, and children ages one to four. It runs a pre-preschool program that offers family services and provides breakfasts for children until they are old enough to enroll in preschool.

Winner-take-all provision The rule that only one individual is elected from a district or state, the individual who receives the most votes. It contrasts with multimember systems in which more than one person wins seats in an election.

Wire services News-gathering organizations such as the Associated Press and United Press International that provide news stories and other editorial features to the media organizations that are their members.

World Trade Organization (WTO) Organization founded in 1995 to remove barriers to free trade and to mediate trade disputes between member countries. WTO policies are set primarily by consensus of its member countries, represented by their trade ministers. Its general council, to which all members belong, is empowered to resolve trade disputes.

Writ of _certiorari_ An order issued by a higher court to a lower court to send up the record of a case for review; granting the writ is the usual means by which the U.S. Supreme Court agrees to hear a case.

INDEX

Presidents, Elections, and Congresses, 1789–2008 (cont.)

Year	President	Vice President	Party of President	Election Year	Election Opponent with Most Votes*
1889–1893	Benjamin Harrison	Levi P. Morton	Rep	(1888)	Grover Cleveland
1893–1897	Grover Cleveland	Adlai E. Stevenson	Dem	(1892)	Benjamin Harrison
1897–1901	William McKinley	Garret A. Hobart (to 1901)	Rep	(1896)	William Jennings Bryan
		Theodore Roosevelt (1901)		(1900)	William Jennings Bryan
1901–1909	Theodore Roosevelt	(No VP, 1901–1905)	Rep		Took office upon death of McKinley
		Charles W. Fairbanks (1905–1909)		(1904)	Alton B. Parker
1909–1913	William Howard Taft	James S. Sherman	Rep	(1908)	William Jennings Bryan
1913–1921	Woodrow Wilson	Thomas R. Marshall	Dem	(1912)	Theodore Roosevelt
				(1916)	Charles Evans Hughes
1921–1923	Warren G. Harding	Calvin Coolidge	Rep	(1920)	James Cox
1923–1929	Calvin Coolidge	(No VP, 1923–1925)	Rep		Took office upon death of Harding
		Charles G. Dawes (1925–1929)		(1924)	John Davis
1929–1933	Herbert Hoover	Charles Curtis	Rep	(1928)	Alfred E. Smith
1933–1945	Franklin D. Roosevelt	John N. Garner (1933–1941)	Dem	(1932)	Herbert Hoover
		Henry A. Wallace (1941–1945)		(1936)	Alfred Landon
		Harry S. Truman (1945)		(1940)	Wendell Willkie
				(1944)	Thomas Dewey
1945–1953	Harry S. Truman	(No VP, 1945–1949) Alban W. Barkley	Dem		Took office upon death of Roosevelt
				(1948)	Thomas Dewey
1953–1961	Dwight D. Eisenhower	Richard M. Nixon	Rep	(1952)	Adlai Stevenson
				(1956)	Adlai Stevenson
1961–1963	John F. Kennedy	Lyndon B. Johnson	Dem	(1960)	Richard M. Nixon
1963–1969	Lyndon B. Johnson	(No VP, 1963–1965)	Dem		Took office upon death of Kennedy
		Hubert H. Humphrey (1965–1969)		(1964)	Barry Goldwater
1969–1974	Richard M. Nixon	Spiro T. Agnew	Rep	(1968)	Hubert H. Humphrey
		Gerald R. Ford (appointed)		(1972)	George McGovern
1974–1977	Gerald R. Ford	Nelson A. Rockefeller (appointed)	Rep		Took office upon Nixon's resignation
1977–1981	Jimmy Carter	Walter Mondale	Dem	(1976)	Gerald R. Ford
1981–1989	Ronald Reagan	George Bush	Rep	(1980)	Jimmy Carter
				(1984)	Walter F. Mondale
1989–1993	George Bush	J. Danforth Quayle	Rep	(1988)	Michael Dukakis
1993–2001	William J. Clinton	Albert Gore	Dem	(1992)	George Bush
				(1996)	Robert Dole
2001–2008	George W. Bush	Richard Cheney	Rep	(2000)	Albert Gore
				(2004)	John Kerry
2009–2011	Barack Obama	Joseph Biden	Dem	(2008)	John McCain